THE COMMON LAW LIBRARY

BOWSTEAD AND REYNOLDS

ON

AGENCY

VOLUMES IN THE COMMON LAW LIBRARY

BOWSTEAD AND REYNOLDS

ON

AGENCY

TWENTY-SECOND EDITION

BY

PETER WATTS QC, LLM (Cantab), FRSNZ
Senior Research Fellow, Harris Manchester College, Oxford
GENERAL EDITOR

AND

F.M.B. REYNOLDS QC (Hon), DCL, FBA
Honorary Bencher of the Inner Temple; Professor of Law Emeritus in the
University of Oxford and Emeritus Fellow of Worcester College, Oxford

SWEET & MAXWELL

 THOMSON REUTERS

Published in 2021 by Thomson Reuters, trading as Sweet & Maxwell.
Thomson Reuters is registered in England & Wales. Company number
1679046.
Registered Office and address for service: 5 Canada Square, Canary Wharf,
London, E14 5AQ.

For further information on our products and services, visit *http://
www.sweetandmaxwell.co.uk.*

Computerset by Sweet & Maxwell.
Printed and bound by CPI Group (UK) Ltd, Croydon, CR0 4YY.
A CIP catalogue record for this book is available from the British Library.

ISBN (print): 978-0-414-08045-4

ISBN (e-book): 978-0-414-08048-5

ISBN (print and e-book): 978-0-414-08047-8

Thomson Reuters, the Thomson Reuters Logo and Sweet & Maxwell ® are
trademarks of Thomson Reuters.

TITLE HISTORY

BOWSTEAD AND REYNOLDS ON AGENCY

First edition	(1896)	By William Bowstead
Second edition	(1898)	By William Bowstead
Third Edition	(1907)	By William Bowstead
Fourth Edition	(1909)	By William Bowstead
Fifth Edition	(1912)	By William Bowstead
Sixth Edition	(1919)	By William Bowstead
Seventh Edition	(1924)	By William Bowstead
Eighth Edition	(1932)	By William Bowstead
Ninth Edition	(1938)	By Arthur H. Forbes
Tenth Edition	(1944)	By Arthur H. Forbes
Eleventh Edition	(1951)	By Peter Allsop
Twelfth Edition	(1959)	By E.J. Griew
Thirteenth Edition	(1968)	By F.M.B. Reynolds and B.J. Davenport
Fouteenth Edition	(1976)	By F.M.B. Reynolds and B.J. Davenport
Fifteenth Edition	(1985)	By F.M.B. Reynolds
Sixteenth Edition	(1996)	By F.M.B. Reynolds
Seventeenth Edition	(2001)	By F.M.B. Reynolds
Eighteenth Edition	(2006)	By F.M.B. Reynolds
Nineteenth Edition	(2010)	By Peter Watts and F.M.B. Reynolds
Twentieth Edition	(2014)	By Peter Watts and F.M.B. Reynolds
Twenty-First Edition	(2018)	By Peter Watts and F.M.B. Reynolds
Twenty-Second Edition	(2021)	By Peter Watts and F.M.B. Reynolds

PREFACE

Issues of agency law continue to be frequently before the courts. A fairly comprehensive approach has been taken to integrating into this edition decisions from the courts of England and Wales and the United Kingdom since the previous edition. Significant and useful new cases from the Commonwealth have also been added to the work. In addition, some new subject matter has been introduced, and some topics revised. The chapter-by-chapter outline that follows refers to decisions only from the United Kingdom or the Privy Council.

In Chapter 1 (nature of agency), the text has been revised in a number of places to develop the argument that agency is not a status as such, unlike "employee" or "independent contractor", but a description given to a person while and only so long as that person is exercising authority voluntarily conferred on him or her by another. Just some of the many new cases that have addressed the question whether the full relation of principal and agent has arisen on the facts are: *Medsted Associates Ltd v Canaccord Genuity Wealth (International) Ltd* [2019] EWCA Civ 83; *Eze v Conway* [2019] EWCA Civ 88; *Dinglis Management Ltd v Dinglis Properties Ltd* [2019] EWCA Civ 127; *Marme Inversiones 2007 SL v Natwest Markets Plc* [2019] EWHC 366 (Comm); and *Pengelly v Business Mortgage Finance 4 Plc* [2020] EWHC 2002 (Ch). The section of the chapter addressing the significance of agency law for companies takes in *Singularis Holdings Ltd (in liq) v Daiwa Capital Markets Europe Ltd* [2019] UKSC 50, and *Ciban Management Corp v Citco (BVI) Ltd* [2020] UKPC 21.

Chapter 2 (creation of agency) has new material on corporations, public bodies and states as principals, taking into account *Ukraine v Law Debenture Trust Corp Plc* [2018] EWCA Civ 2026; *School Facility Management Ltd v Governing Body of Christ the King College* [2020] EWHC 1118 (Comm) and older case law. There is new content on co-principals, and on ratification (including, inter alios, *London Borough of Haringey v Ahmed* [2017] EWCA Civ 1861 and *Rolle Family & Co Ltd v Rolle* [2017] UKPC 35). New material on the status of agents appointed by insurers to represent insureds in litigation links to other new references to that topic in Chapters 3 and 5 (citing *Ramsook v Crossley* [2018] UKPC 9; *Travelers Insurance Co Ltd v XYZ* [2019] UKSC 48 and earlier case law).

Chapter 3 (authority) has new material on the point that a principal cannot rely on unauthorised acts without ratifying the acts (referring inter alia to *Aidiniantz v The Sherlock Holmes International Society Ltd* [2017] EWCA Civ 1875). It also has new material on the subject of usual authority (including *Ukraine v Law Debenture Trust Plc* [2018] EWCA Civ 2026; *Taylor v Rhino Overseas Inc* [2020] EWCA Civ 353, and *East Asia Co Ltd v PT Satria Tirtatama Energindo* [2019] UKPC 30). The paragraphs on the effect an agent's dishonesty has on the agent's authority have been further developed.

Chapter 4 (agency of necessity) takes account of *Tongue v Royal Society for the Prevention of Cruelty To Animals* [2017] EWHC 2508 (Ch) and *Glasgow v ELS Law Ltd* [2017] EWHC 3004 (Ch).

Chapter 5 (sub-agency) has a new paragraph on when a sub-agent or a junior agent should decline to follow the directions of the more senior agent (drawing on P Watts, "The *Quincecare* Duty: Misconceived and Misdelivered" [2020] J.B.L. 403, and referring to *Singularis Holdings Ltd v Daiwa Capital Markets Europe Ltd* [2019] UKSC 50; and *JP Morgan Chase Bank NA v Federal Republic of Nigeria* [2019] EWCA Civ 1641). The ability of a sub-agent to rely on the apparent authority of the agent gets further commentary (referring to *Ciban Management Corp v Citco (BVI) Ltd* [2020] UKPC 21).

There is considerable new material throughout Chapter 6 (duties of agents to their principals). The consequences of an agent's failing to adhere strictly to mandate continue to trouble the courts (see *Main v Giambrone & Law (a firm)* [2017] EWCA Civ 1193; *Stoffel & Co v Grondona* [2018] EWCA Civ 2031; *Interactive Technology Corp Ltd v Ferster* [2018] EWCA Civ 1594, and *Auden McKenzie (Pharma Division) Ltd v Patel* [2019] EWCA Civ 2291). The equitable duties of agents seem always to attract new case law (see, for instance: *Al Nehayan v Kent* [2018] EWHC 333 (Comm); *HPOR Servicos De Consultoria Ltd v Dryships Inc* [2018] EWHC 3451 (Comm); *Marino v FM Capital Partners Ltd* [2020] EWCA Civ 245; *De Sena v Notaro* [2020] EWHC 1031 (Ch); *Parr v Keystone Healthcare Ltd* [2019] EWCA Civ 1246; *Pengelly v Business Mortgage Finance 4 Plc* [2020] EWHC 2002 (Ch), and *Lehtimaki v Cooper* [2020] UKSC 33). In addition, there is expanded discussion of the position of agents when negotiating their appointment and otherwise dealing with their principal, and when holding assets as trustee for the principal.

Chapter 7 (rights of agents) opens by expanding the discussion of the scope for principals to owe agents duties of co-operation and of good faith (new case law includes *Bates v Post Office Ltd (No.3)* [2019] EWHC 606 (QB), and *Wales (t/a Selective Investment Services) v CBRE Managed Services Ltd* [2020] EWHC 16 (Comm)). There are new cases on rights to remuneration (*Wells v Devani* [2019] UKSC 4; *Gwinnutt v George* [2019] EWCA Civ 656, and *Travel (UK) Ltd v Pakistan International Airlines Corp* [2019] EWCA Civ 828), and on rights to a lien (*Gavin Edmondson Solicitors Ltd v Haven Insurance Co Ltd* [2018] UKSC 21, and *Bott & Co Solicitors Ltd v Ryanair DAC* [2019] EWCA Civ 143). Forfeiture of remuneration continues to be a problematic subject (see *Staechelin v ACLBDD Holdings Ltd* [2019] EWCA Civ 817).

Chapter 8 (relations between principals and third parties) covers many of the central problems of agency law. New commentary addresses a rash of recent cases where it has been contemplated that an agent might not have been intended to be liable on a contract despite being the named party to it (the cases include *Filatona Trading Ltd v Navigator Equities Ltd* [2020] EWCA Civ 109; *Aspen Underwriting Ltd v Kairos Shipping Co Ltd* [2018] EWCA Civ 2590; *Kaefer Aislamientos SA de CV v AMS Drilling Mexico SA de CV* [2019] EWCA Civ 10; *Turks Shipyard Ltd v Owners of the Vessel November* [2020] EWHC 661 (Admlty), and *Bell v Ivy Technology Ltd* [2020] EWCA Civ 1563). There are a number of new cases on apparent authority (*East Asia Co Ltd v PT Satria Tirtatama Energindo* [2019] UKPC 30; *Ciban Management Corp v Citco (BVI) Ltd* [2020] UKPC 21; *Winter v Hockley Mint Ltd* [2018] EWCA Civ 2480; *Anderson v Sense Network Ltd* [2019] EWCA Civ 1395; *Tinkler v Revenue & Customs* [2019] EWCA Civ 1392, and *High Commissioner for Pakistan in the United Kingdom v Prince Muffakham Jah* [2019] EWHC 2551 (Ch)). The treatment of ss.39 to 44 of the Companies Act 2006 has been revised. Some parts of the section on undisclosed principals have been modified, promoted in part by *Playboy Club London Ltd v Banca Nazionale del Lavoro SpA* [2018] UKSC 43. A new paragraph has been added on the role of agents in the law of rectification. The section on tort, the paragraphs on vicarious liability in particular, has had to take into account the important decisions of the Supreme Court in *Barclays Bank Plc v Various Claimants* [2020] UKSC 13, and *Wm Morrison Supermarkets Plc v Various Claimants* [2020] UKSC 12.

Chapter 9 (relations between agents and third parties) has new material on the action for breach of warranty of authority (taking into account *P&P Property Ltd v Owen White and Catlin LLP* [2018] EWCA Civ 1082; *Aidiniantz v The Sherlock Holmes International Society Ltd* [2016] EWHC 1392 (Ch), and *Zoya Ltd v Shaikh Nasir Ahmed* [2016] EWHC 2249 (Ch)). The sections on agents' liability in tort and for dishonest assistance in breach of fiduciary duty have been updated (the new cases include *Wingate v Solicitors Regulation Authority* [2018] EWCA Civ 366, and *Group Seven Ltd v Notable Services LLP* [2019] EWCA Civ 614).

Chapter 10 (termination of authority) has some new textual material on the revocation by an insured of the authority of lawyers appointed by an insurer on the insured's behalf, and on the topic of damages for wrongful termination. Otherwise, the new case law on termination includes: *W Nagel (A Firm) v Pluczenik Diamond Co NV* [2018] EWCA Civ 2640; *Jeddi v Sotheby's* [2018] EWHC 1491 (Comm); *Royal Petrol Trading Co UK v Total India Pvt Ltd* [2018] EWHC 1272 (Comm) at [40]; and *Bank of New York Mellon, London Branch v Essar Steel India Ltd* [2018] EWHC 3177 (Ch).

Chapter 11 (commercial agents) briefly addresses the possible effect of the United Kingdom leaving the EU on the material addressed in this chapter. It also incorporates the following new cases since the last edition: *Computer Associates UK Ltd v Software Incubator Ltd* [2018] EWCA Civ 518; *Ergo Poist'ovna a.s. v Barlikova (C-48/16)* [2018] Bus.L.R.41; *W Nagel (A Firm) v Pluczenik Diamond Co NV* [2018] EWCA Civ 2640; *Conseils et mise en relations (CMR) SARL v Demeures terre et tradition SARL (C-645/16)*; *Elsevier Masson v La Diffusion Sofradif* [2017] E.C.C. 30; *Zako SPRL v Sanidel SA (C-452/17)*; and *Green Deal Marketing Southern Ltd v Economy Energy Trading Ltd* [2019] EWHC 507 (Ch).

Chapter 12 (Conflict of laws) refers to the following new cases: *Law Debenture Trust Corp Plc v Ukraine* [2018] EWCA Civ 2026; *Canary Wharf (BP4) T1 Ltd v European Medicines Agency* [2019] EWHC 335 (Ch)); and *Kent v Paterson-Brown* [2018] EWHC 2008 (Ch).

Once again, I have relied on Francis Reynolds to revise and update Chapters 11 and 12. He has also made a number of useful suggestions for change in other chapters of the work (in particular on the *Filatona* case, above). I am most grateful for his continuing support.

The cut-off date for this edition was 31 July 2020, although one or two late entrants were admitted.

Peter Watts
Bankside Chambers, Auckland, and Fountain Court Chambers, London
20 November 2020

STANDARD ABBREVIATIONS

Books on the Law of Agency

As with previous editions, certain other works on the law of agency are referred to throughout this book without further description.

Bennett	H. Bennett, *Principles of the Law of Agency*, Hart Publishing, 2013.
Dal Pont	G.E. Dal Pont, *Law of Agency*, 4th edn, LexisNexis, 2020.
Fridman	G.H.L. Fridman, *Canadian Agency Law*, 3rd edn, LexisNexis, 2017.
Macgregor	L. Macgregor, *The Law of Agency in Scotland*, W. Green, 2013.
Munday	R. Munday, *Agency—Law and Principles*, 3rd edn, OUP, 2016.
Powell	Raphael Powell, *The Law of Agency*, 2nd edn, Pitman, 1961.
Restatement	*Restatement of the Law 3rd, Agency*, American Law Institute, 2007.
Stoljar	S.J. Stoljar, *The Law of Agency*, Sweet & Maxwell, 1961.
Tan	Tan Cheng Han, *The Law of Agency*, 2nd edn, Academy Publishing, 2017.

Modern European "Codes"

There have been produced in Europe in the last decade or so a number of sets of non-statutory "codes". The first two listed below were produced for the purposes of a putative European law, and the third as a guiding law for international arbitration.

PECL	*The Principles of European Contract Law* (ed. Lando and Beale, Kluwer, 2000).
DCFR	Draft Common Frame of Reference. The Outline version of the text of this can be downloaded free from *http://www.storme.be/2009_02_DCFR_OutlineEdition.pdf*. The six volume commentary that accompanies the code is published as *Principles, Definitions and Model Rules of European Private Law* (ed. Von Bar and Clive, OUP, 2010).
Unidroit Principles	UNIDROIT Principles of International Commercial Contracts (UNIDROIT, 2004).

Commonwealth Case Law Abbreviations

The citations to cases from the United Kingdom use standard abbreviations, which it is not necessary to set out herein. However, it may be useful for the reader to have an explanation of some of those used for Commonwealth cases. All recent Australian and New Zealand cases that are cited are available free at *http://www.austlii.edu.au*. Many Singapore cases are available free at *http://*

www.commonlii.org/ and Hong Kong cases at *http://legalref.judiciary.gov.hk/lrs/common/ju/judgment.jsp.* Abbreviations with points refer to report series; those without are neutral citations.

A.C.L.C.	Australian Company Law Cases
A.C.S.R.	Australian Company and Securities Reports
ACTCA	Australian Capital Territory Court of Appeal
A.L.R.	Australian Law Reports
A.T.R.	Australian Tax Reports
A.N.Z. Conv.R.	Australian and New Zealand Conveyancing Reports
BCCA	British Columbia Court of Appeal
B.P.R.	Butterworths Property Reports
C.L.R.	Commonwealth Law Reports
D.L.R.	Dominion Law Reports
FCAFC	Federal Court of Australia Full Court
F.C.R.	Federal Court Reports
F.L.R.	Federal Law Reports
G.L.R.	Gazette Law Reports (New Zealand)
HCA	High Court of Australia
HKCA	Hong Kong Court of Appeal
H.K.C.F.A.R.	Hong Kong Court of Final Appeal Reports
HKCFI	Hong Kong Court of First Instance
HKCU	Hong Kong Cases Unreported
H.K.L.R.	Hong Kong Law Reports
H.K.L.R.D.	Hong Kong Law Reports & Digest
NSCA	Nova Scotia Court of Appeal
NSWCA	New South Wales Court of Appeal
NSWSC	New South Wales Supreme Court
N.Z.C.L.C.	New Zealand Company Law Cases
N.Z.C.P.R.	New Zealand Conveyancing and Property Reports
NZHC	New Zealand High Court
NZCA	New Zealand Court of Appeal
N.Z.L.R.	New Zealand Law Reports
NZSC	New Zealand Supreme Court
P.R.N.Z.	Procedure Reports of New Zealand
QCA	Queensland Court of Appeal
QSC	Queensland Supreme Court
SCC	Supreme Court of Canada
SGCA	Singapore Court of Appeal
SGHC	Singapore High Court

S.L.R.	Singapore Law Reports
V.R.	Victorian Reports
VSC	Supreme Court of Victoria
VSCA	Court of Appeal of Victoria
W.A.R.	Western Australia Reports

TABLE OF CONTENTS

CONTENTS

TABLE OF CASES

Paragraph references in bold indicate that the case is referred to in an illustration.

UNITED KINGDOM

INTERNATIONAL CASES

AFRICA

AUSTRALIA

CANADA

EUROPE

HONG KONG

INDIA

IRELAND

MALAYSIA

NEW ZEALAND

SINGAPORE

SOUTH AFRICA

UNITED STATES OF AMERICA

TABLE OF STATUTES

TABLE OF STATUTORY INSTRUMENTS

CHAPTER 1

NATURE OF THE SUBJECT

Article 1

AGENCY AND AUTHORITY

(1) Agency is the fiduciary relationship which exists between two persons, one of   **1-001**
whom expressly or impliedly manifests assent that the other should act on his
behalf so as to affect his legal relations with third parties, and the other of
whom similarly manifests assent so to act or so acts pursuant to the
manifestation. The one on whose behalf the act or acts are to be done is called
the principal. The one who is to act is called the agent. Any person other than
the principal and the agent may be referred to as a third party.[1]

(2) In respect of the acts to which the principal so assents, the agent is said to have
authority to act; and this authority constitutes a power to affect the principal's
legal relations with third parties.[2]

(3) Where such authority results from a manifestation of assent that the agent
should represent or act for the principal expressly or impliedly made by the
principal to the agent personally, the authority is called actual authority,
express or implied. But the agent may also have authority resulting from such
a manifestation made by the principal to a third party; such authority is called
apparent authority.[3]

(4) A person may have the same fiduciary relationship with a principal where that
person acts on behalf of that principal but has no authority to affect the
principal's relations with third parties. Because of the fiduciary relationship
such a person may also be called an agent.[4]

Comment

1. Theoretical basis of agency in the common law

Purpose of definition   It is customary to begin a systematic treatise with some sort   **1-002**
of definition of its subject-matter. The definition given here is partly based on that
in the American *Restatement*, and it is hoped that it may provide a useful starting
point to an area of law where concepts have been "peculiarly troublesome".[5]

---

[1]   *Restatement, Third*, § 1.01. See too *London Borough of Haringey v Ahmed* [2017] EWCA Civ 1861
at [27].

[2]   *Restatement, Third*, §§ 2.01, 2.03 and Comment c to § 1.01.

[3]   *Restatement, Third*, § 2.01 and 2.03. And see in general Conant, "Proposed Code of Agency
Contracts" (1971) 13 Mal. L.R. 98.

[4]   See below, para.1-020.

[5]   W. Müller-Freienfels, "The Law of Agency" in A. Yiannopoulos (ed.), *Civil Law in the Modern
World* (1965), p.79. See also F.M.B. Reynolds and Tan Cheng Han, "Agency Reasoning—a Formula

Definitions such as that above serve two purposes. They may, first, simply form an introduction to the subject-matter following. But recourse may also be had to such a definition when general words such as (in this context) "agent" and "agency" appear in propositions of law, particularly in statutes and other formal documents. What meaning should be attributed to these terms in such contexts is discussed later.[6] A major problem in the application of the law in this area is that questions are frequently asked of lawyers in forms such as "Is A an agent?", "Is A B's agent or C's agent?", as if a clear all-purpose answer could be given for the purposes of resolving a dispute. Any useful response must be couched in a much more restricted form, for agency is a relative notion and there are many acceptable uses of the term which do not always coincide with each other.

It must be stressed at the outset therefore that the definition given above is intended to be read as a whole. No single sentence should be treated as encapsulating the whole notion of agency. The first of the above propositions, (1), is no more than the first of four. Taken by itself it is very wide, as Woolf J noted in a case involving the distinction between sale and agency for the purpose of a taxing statute.[7] For the purposes of most legal usage, (2) and (3) provide an essential restriction, in limiting the central use of the term to cases where the agent has authority to affect the principal's legal position. The proposition in (4) adds for completeness another situation (referred to below as that of the "canvassing" or "introducing" agent[8]) where the terms "agent" and "agency" may be not inappropriately used.

1-003   **Limits on definition**   But in any case definitions are, however commonplace, of limited utility in law as elsewhere; in particular, reasoning based on presupposed definitions is often suspect. A longer explanation is usually required than can be encapsulated in the definitional form. No one has the monopoly of the "correct" use of this or any other term. The word "agency", to a common lawyer, refers in general to a branch of the law under which one person, the agent, may directly affect the legal relations of another person, the principal, as regards yet other persons, called third parties, by acts which the agent is said to have the principal's authority to perform on the principal's behalf and which when done are in some respects treated as the principal's acts. These acts are probably thought of as most likely to occur in connection with the formation and discharge of contracts and in the disposition of property, but the same idea appears, sometimes in modified form, in many other parts of the law. Even in this context, the term "agency" may be used to refer to: the relationship between the principal and the agent; to the function of the agent with respect to the outside world; or to the sum total of all legal relations involving principal, agent and third parties arising in such situations.[9] But these are only some possibilities: even in legal terminology the term may be used in other senses, and lay usage of the words "agency" and "agent" provides further variations. The definition given in (1) above selects as the initial referent of the term "agency" the

---

or a Tool" [2018] Sing J.L.S. 43; R. Leow, "Understanding Agency: a Proxy Power Definition" [2019] C.L.J. 99.

6   See below, para.1-023.
7   *Customs and Excise Commissioners v Johnson* [1980] S.T.C. 624 at 629 (though the formulation there referred to is that of the 15th edition of this work: the present formulation is narrower). The definition in the *Restatement, Third* is much wider: see below, para.1-004.
8   See below, para.1-020.
9   Powell, pp.31–32.

internal relationship between principal and agent which, since it involves the reposing of special trust and confidence, is a fiduciary one. In view of the other relationships which are also involved this selection may appear somewhat arbitrary. But in what follows it will be argued that that relationship is fundamental to this whole branch of the law, since it provides the paradigm situation and justification for the application of the typical rules regarding the agent's power to affect the principal's legal position vis-à-vis third parties, which in fact then dominate the subject.

Affecting principal's relations with third parties   This definition not only   **1-004**
requires that the agent act on the principal's behalf; it also requires that the acting be "so as to affect [the principal's] relations with third parties". This is a narrowing of the definition, and necessitates another provision, Rule (4), which then extends the term to the position of certain persons who act for others but do not necessarily act in such a way. The *Restatement*, on the other hand, simply refers to a person who acts "on the principal's behalf",[10] which is very much wider and can be taken to include agents of the sort just referred to without a special exception, and also can more easily encompass other phenomena of agency reasoning such as its application in tort, or as regards the acquisition of notice—though of course it encounters reciprocal difficulties as to how to limit the phrase "on behalf of".[11]

The choice of the principal definition selected here is largely a matter of exposition: it has then to be supplemented by exceptions. But the special features of an agent, in particular the fiduciary duties, derive from the power that some agents have to affect their principal's legal position. It seems best, therefore, to stress these aspects of agency, that is to say, both its fiduciary nature and its application to the process of contracting, transfers of property, and other alterations of the principal's legal position. The absence of both these features would make a finding of agency unlikely.[12] As to the presence of authority, it has been said that: "The term 'agency' is best used ... 'to connote an authority or capacity in one person to create legal relations between a person occupying the position of principal and third parties.' Usually the legal relations so created will be contractual in nature".[13]

Conversely, where there is no conferral of authority to alter legal relations, but merely a chain of contracts, the intermediate contracting parties will not normally be agents and will not routinely owe fiduciary duties up the chain.[14] Equally, the mere fact that one person does something in order to benefit another, and the latter is relying on the former to do so or may have requested or even contracted for performance of the action, does not make the former the agent of the latter.[15] So too a non-owner of property, with or without the owner's consent, can contract to sell

---

[10]   § 1.01.
[11]   See, e.g. *Emerald Meat Ltd v Minister of Agriculture (No.2)* [1997] 1 I.R. 1 (person obtaining import licence "on behalf of" may be the importer); *Plevin v Paragon Personal Finance Ltd* [2014] UKSC 61; [2014] 1 W.L.R. 4222 at [30], where Lord Sumption says that the ordinary and natural meaning of the term "on behalf of" imports agency.
[12]   See *UBS AG (London Branch) v Kommunale Wasserwerke Peipkiz GmbH* [2017] EWCA Civ 1567 at [91]; *Marme Inversiones 2007 SL v Natwest Markets Plc* [2019] EWHC 366 (Comm) at [416].
[13]   *Scott v Davis* (2000) 204 C.L.R. 333 at [227], per Gummow J, citing the judgment of the High Court of Australia delivered by Dixon J in *International Harvester Co of Australia Pty Ltd v Carrigan's Hazeldene Pastoral Co* (1958) 100 C.L.R. 644 at 652. See also *UBS AG (London Branch) v Kommunale Wasserwerke Peipkiz GmbH* [2017] EWCA Civ 1567 at [97].
[14]   See *Garnac Grain Co Inc v HMF Faure & Fairclough Ltd* [1968] A.C. 1130; and *Dinglis Management Ltd v Dinglis Properties Ltd* [2019] EWCA Civ 127.
[15]   *Tonto Home Loans Australia Pty Ltd v Tavares* [2011] NSWCA 389 at [175]: "it is to be borne in mind that the concept of agency is not merely functional, whereby something that is necessary to

it or to have it repaired or improved without necessarily being the agent of the owner.[16] Nor does the fact that a third party, X, pays the remuneration of Y make Y the agent of X if Y is properly the agent of Z.[17] It is quite common (and not improper if assented to by the principal) for an agent's remuneration to be paid by the third party or some other person. More generally, mere economic interdependence between two parties does not create one the agent of the other.[18]

A focus on the conferral of authority to alter legal relations is also important in determining when one person with two potential principals is agent for one or the other. So an estate agent might be an agent for the vendor in marketing the property but, in receiving a deposit from the purchaser in advance of a binding contract, an agent for the purchaser, or just a stakeholder.[19]

The centrality to agency of the conferral of authority to alter legal relations suggests that at common law being an agent is not a status, but a description of a person while and only so long as the person is exercising such authority. As to status, an agent's status will usually be that of employee or independent contractor (but sometimes a gratuitous actor), and agency is not a separate category. Equally, employees and contractors often have no authority to alter their appointer's legal relations, and if not exercising any authority are not properly described as an agent. Thus, a solicitor is usually a type of independent contractor, and when merely giving advice to a client is not an agent, but while acting for the client in communicating with outside parties would be an agent. An employee while formally on sick leave remains an employee but would not have actual authority as agent during the leave.[20] One of the implications of this is that agency is of limited utility in the application of vicarious liability in tort, which usually operates on the basis of a party's status.[21]

1-005   **Fundamental role of agency**   The basic notion behind the common law of agency can be explained along the following lines. The mature law recognises that people need not always personally do things that change their legal relations: they may

---

be done for P and that could be done by P itself is done by A under some arrangement; rather it is a consensual arrangement, a relationship, whereby A is to be taken as, or as representing, P"; *London Borough of Haringey v Ahmed* [2017] EWCA Civ 1861 at [36]–[38] (husband not agent in procuring rented accommodation for wife and family); *Marme Inversiones 2007 SL v Natwest Markets Plc* [2019] EWHC 366 (Comm) at [444] (lead arranging bank not acting as agent for other banks in putting together syndicated financing); *Ventra Investments Ltd v Bank of Scotland Plc* [2019] EWHC 2058 (Comm) at [88]–[89] (bank-appointed adviser to receivers not agent of bank); *Zedra Trust Co (Jersey) Ltd v The Hut Group Ltd* [2019] EWHC 2191 (Comm) at [37] (contractual requirement that, if requested by X, Y commission independent report at expense of X does not make Y the agent of X); *Barness v Ingenious Media Ltd* [2019] EWHC 3299 (Ch) at [83] (banks as lenders into tax-driven scheme not principals of promoters of the scheme).

[16] See *Foster v Action Aviation Ltd* [2014] EWCA Civ 1368 at [38]. cf. *The Swan* [1968] 1 Lloyd's Rep. 5; Article 98, Illustration 6.

[17] See *Plevin v Paragon Personal Finance Ltd* [2014] UKSC 61; [2014] 1 W.L.R. 4222 at [33]. A solicitor paid for by an insurer to represent the insured in litigation is usually the agent of the insured, not the insurer: see *Groom v Crocker* [1939] 1 K.B. 194 at 227–228; *Travelers Insurance Co Ltd v XYZ* [2019] UKSC 48 at [114].

[18] See *Tonto Home Loans Australia Pty Ltd v Tavares* [2011] NSWCA 389 at [194]–[196]; *UBS AG (London Branch) v Kommunale Wasserwerke Leipzig GmbH* [2017] EWCA Civ 1567 at [100] (noted P. Kelshiker (2018) 134 L.Q.R. 363); *London Borough of Haringey v Ahmed* [2017] EWCA Civ 1861 at [38].

[19] See *Sorrell v Finch* [1977] A.C. 728 at 750.

[20] See *Harrisons & Crosfield Ltd v L & NW Ry Co Ltd* [1917] 2 K.B. 755.

[21] See below, paras 8-177 and 8-182.

utilise the services of another to change them, or to do something during the course of which their relations may be changed. Thus, where one person, the principal, requests or authorises another, the agent, to act on his behalf, and the other agrees or does so, the law recognises that the agent has power to affect the principal's legal position by acts which, though performed by the agent, are to be treated in certain respects as if they were acts of the principal. This result is not confined to cases where the agent simply has specific instructions to do one thing, e.g. to hand over, or perhaps sign, a document. A person who acts in such a way (sometimes called a *nuntius* or messenger) performs no more than a ministerial function, which is attributable to the person for whom he acts without much stretching of elemental notions.[22] Any developed system must also recognise the more advanced notion of permitting a person to give to another a general authority to act according to his own discretion within certain limits.

Basis in unilateral manifestation of will The basic justification for the agent's   **1-006**
power as so far explained seems to be the idea of a unilateral manifestation by the principal of willingness to have his legal position changed by the agent.[23] The conferral of authority is voluntary or consensual. To this conferral any contract between principal and agent is secondary,[24] though there will usually be one, which often provides the reason for the conferral and indeed may contain it. The phrase "consensual agency" used here and below,[25] and "agency by agreement" used later in this book,[26] are to be understood in this sense and not as relating to any supporting contract. There is certainly no conceptual reason which requires a contract between principal and agent to achieve this creation of power, and it is indeed clear that no contract is necessary, for a person without juristic capacity may be an agent.[27] Nor need the agent undertake to act as such. It is sufficient if the principal manifests to the agent that the principal is willing for the agent to act, and the agent does so in circumstances indicating that the agent's acts arise from the principal's manifestation.[28] This is not dissimilar from the formation of a contract, but is notionally separate, as the example of a power of attorney shows. In common with other situations where in the civil law it is important to derive a party's intention, the principal's manifestation of will is generally determined on an objective basis, whether or not the conferral of power meets the requirements of the law of contract.[29]

The phrase "manifestation of assent" is selected by *Restatement, Third* instead

---

[22] See further below, para.1-047.
[23] Montrose (1938) 16 Can.B.R. 757 at 779; Müller-Freienfels (1964) 13 Am.J.Comp.L. 193 at 203. See also *Sinfra A-G. v Sinfra Ltd* [1939] 2 All E.R. 675 at 682 (power of attorney a "one-sided instrument").
[24] See *HKSAR v Luk Kin* [2016] HKCFA 81 at [29], per Lord Hoffmann; and para.2-003. This point is most obviously exposed in the context of the conflict of laws: see below, para.12-009. It is also noticeable in connection with revocation of authority, which is effective even if it constitutes a breach of any attendant contract: see below, para.10-004.
[25] See below, paras 1-012 and 1-025.
[26] See Ch.2, Section 2.
[27] See Article 5; *Yasuda Fire and Marine Ins. Co v Orion Marine Ins. Underwriting Agency Ltd* [1995] Q.B. 174; *Medsted Associates Ltd v Canaccord Genuity Wealth (International) Ltd* [2019] EWCA Civ 83 at [29].
[28] See Comment to Article 8 for discussion of the specific question whether the *agent* needs to know of the principal's manifestation or whether the manifestation, assuming that it can be proved, is sufficient.
[29] See *Freeman & Lockyer v Buckhurst Park Properties (Mangal) Ltd* [1964] 2 Q.B. 480 at 502.

of "manifestation of consent" in *Restatement, Second*, seemingly to stress the objective nature of the inquiry.

> "A manifestation is conduct by a person, observable by others, that expresses meaning. It is a broader concept than communication. The relevant state of mind is that of the person who observes or otherwise learns of the manifestation."[30]

1-007 **Not an imposed relationship** It follows from agency's being founded on the principal's consent that agency is paradigmatically not a relationship imposed by law. In 1863, Lord Cranworth said: "No one can become the agent of another person except by the will of that other person".[31] One hundred years later the same starting point was selected by Lord Pearson when he said: "The relationship of principal and agent can only be established by the consent of the principal and the agent".[32] Although the notions of "will" and "consent" are objectively determined, they clearly remain fundamental.

Notwithstanding its voluntary nature, where there is evidence of a conferral of authority to alter a principal's legal relations, the normal incidents of agency are, prima facie, likely to apply even if the parties' contract expressly disavows one being the "agent" of the other.[33] It is one thing, however, to find that a disavowal is not conclusive, it is another for a court to find an agency for purely instrumental reasons without regard to the fact that the relationship of agency is fundamentally an intentional and voluntary one.[34] So, where no authority to alter legal relations is conferred, an express denial of an agency relationship is likely to be effective.[35] Equally, the mere use of a label such as agent or "manager" may not attract the incidents of agency, if there is no authority to alter the other's legal position conferred: "The court should not impose an agency analysis upon a relationship which may better be analysed in other terms".[36] It does not detract from the forego-

---

[30] *Restatement, Third*, § 1.031 Comment b.
[31] *Pole v Leask* (1863) 33 L.J. Ch. 155 at 161 (a dissenting speech).
[32] *Garnac Grain Co Inc v H.M.F. Faure & Fairclough Ltd* [1968] A.C. 1130 fn. at 1137; see also *Atlas Maritime Co SA v Avalon Maritime Ltd (The Coral Rose) (No.1)* [1991] 4 All E.R. 769 at 774–775, 779; *ACN 007528207 Pty Ltd v Bird Cameron* (2005) 54 A.C.S.R. 505 at [96] (accountancy firm creates company, using a variant of the firm name, and hives off to it some of its accounting services—company found not to be agent of firm, there being no intention to create an agency); *Fortis Bank SA NV v Indian Overseas Bank* [2011] EWHC 538 (Comm); [2012] 1 All E.R. (Comm) 41 (consignee not principal of shipper though named in bill of lading); *The Lorenz Consultancy Ltd v Fox-Davies Capital Ltd* [2011] EWHC 574 (Ch) (leasing agent could not look to nominee tenant for commission when contract was only with nominator).
[33] *Garnac Grain Co Inc v HMF Faure & Fairclough Ltd* [1968] A.C. 1130 at 1137; *South Sydney District Rugby League Football Club Ltd v News Ltd* (2000) 177 A.L.R. 611 at [131] onwards; affirmed (2003) 215 C.L.R. 563; cf. *UBS AG (London Branch) v Kommunale Wasserwerke Peipkiz GmbH* [2017] EWCA Civ 1567 at [82]. For a useful consideration of indicia of agency, see *Serventy v Commonwealth Bank of Australia (No.2)* [2016] WASCA 223 at [29]–[37]. For the converse situation (parties use word "agent" but no agency found), see below, para.1-035.
[34] For further discussion, see above, para.1-004, and para.1-026, below.
[35] It is on this basis that the common law has routinely upheld provisions that make bank-appointed receivers of companies agents of the company not the bank: for discussion, see Lightman and Moss, *Law of Administrators and Receivers of Companies* (6th edn); and *Ventra Investments Ltd v Bank of Scotland Plc* [2019] EWHC 2058 (Comm) at [73] et seq; *Menon v Pask* [2019] EWHC 2611 (Ch).
[36] *UBS AG (London Branch) v Kommunale Wasserwerke Leipzig GmbH* [2017] EWCA Civ 1567 at [88] and [91]. See too *Alliance Craton Explorer Pty Ltd v Quasar Resources Pty Ltd* [2013] FCAFC 29 (no entitlement of one party to a joint venture to demand access to business papers of the other).

ing propositions to conclude by noting that the words used between the parties will often be important in determining whether there is an agency relationship.[37]

Extensions of reasoning   The basic idea of agency is extended to cases where the words and conduct of one person towards another are such that the law treats that other as entitled to assume that authorisation has occurred even though the first person cannot be shown to have had, and may indeed not have had, a specific intention of conferring authority (conferral of authority is to be judged objectively); and to cases where a person subsequently approves an act done by another on the former's behalf without prior authority. The paradigm situation, in which the principal intends to confer authority, is in this work referred to as agency by express agreement.[38] The first extension set out above is called agency by implied agreement[39]; and the second is dealt with under the heading of ratification.[40]   **1-008**

No requirement that agent purport to act for principal   In some legal systems such reasoning would normally only be accepted in the case of an agent who when acting purported, or at least was understood, to do so on behalf of, or "in the name of", a principal, though usually the principal need not actually be named.[41] The common law, however, has no such requirement: if there is preceding authority to act for the principal, the rules so far set out, other than those as to ratification, will apply despite the fact that the existence of the principal, or his connection with the transaction, is unknown to the third party. Where his existence or connection with the transaction is not known, the principal is referred to as undisclosed,[42] and the rules then applicable are referred to as the doctrine of the undisclosed principal, which can be regarded as a unique feature of common law (though some civil law systems now approach some of its results, and such results were earlier known to the *ius commune*). In addition to the exclusion of ratification, however, the doctrine is limited by other safeguards appropriate to the fact that it in substance involves intervention on a contract by one not contemplated as a party to it.   **1-009**

No requirement that agent pursue recognised commercial function   Although the main operation of agency principles is in the commercial sphere, they are in fact absolutely general and may apply to domestic and other non-commercial situations. There is no requirement that the agent pursue a commercial function at all, and certainly none that an agent pursue a commercial function of a recognised type.   **1-010**

Apparent authority   By a further extension, the law may treat a third party dealing with a person who appears to have authority from a principal as entitled, by virtue of the principal's manifestations to that party by words or conduct, to assume that the person in question has such authority, regardless of whether anything has occurred from which the law would draw that conclusion if the matter were in issue only between the supposed agent and the supposed principal. This reasoning   **1-011**

---

[37]   See *Good v Bruce* [1917] N.Z.L.R. 514 (CA) at 536 (agency not sale): "No doubt acts are sometimes more potent than words, but if the acts are dubious then the words are the more important"; *Pengelly v Business Mortgage Finance 4 Plc* [2020] EWHC 2002 (Ch) at [68].
[38]   Articles 7 and 24–26.
[39]   Articles 8 and Articles 27–32.
[40]   Articles 13–20.
[41]   See, e.g. French CC, Articles 1119 and 1984. There may be exceptions in some systems for situations where the agent is a "man of straw".
[42]   See Article 76.

takes effect in the doctrine of apparent authority. This applies both where the supposed agent is not authorised to act at all, and also where the agent appears to have a greater authority than was actually conferred. It is said in the English cases that this reasoning depends on estoppel. But it is suggested below that it is a very weak form of estoppel, and to be distinguished from other agency-related situations where the principles of estoppel as normally stated more obviously apply.[43] The doctrine operates regardless of whether the agent personally believed that the principal had conferred authority, provided that the agent reasonably appeared to the third party to be authorised. But the basis of the doctrine makes it essential that the agent has purported to act on the principal's behalf. Because the full consequences of the basic agency relationship are not applicable, the general doctrine of apparent authority is not fully discussed until the section dealing with the relations between the principal and third parties,[44] though certain problems of estoppel are briefly treated at an earlier stage[45] in Chapter 2.

1-012   **Consensual agency as paradigm case**   Under the above explanation, the basic situation of agency is treated as being that in which the principal agrees that the agent should act for the principal and the agent expressly or impliedly agrees to do so. This is the paradigm, and it is from their similarity in various respects to this situation that the others derive their legal force. It is for this reason that the term "agency" is assigned to this relationship in the wording of Article 1(1). The other cases may fairly be regarded as derivatives. Ratification cases can, but only with difficulty, be assimilated into the paradigm situation; and in English law at any rate apparent authority cases only affect third parties in the first instance, so do not give rise to the full range of results flowing from the paradigm situation.

1-013   **Authority as the basis of power**   The technical description of the results which the law puts on the agency situations described is, however, to say that in all of them the agent has a power to affect the principal's legal relations[46]: and this terminology has already been used above. It is nevertheless more commonly said that the agent has authority. When examined, this authority amounts to no more than a power of a special sort, a power by doing an act to affect the principal's legal relations as if the principal had done the act personally. But the notions of authority and power are different.[47] Where such a power is voluntarily conferred by one person on another (the paradigm case), the person on whom it is conferred is said to "be authorised" by the other, or to "have authority". But, as can be seen from what is said above, the power may exist in a person upon whom it cannot be said to have been voluntarily conferred. In the common law, such cases seem exceptional, and it is said that there is only "agency by estoppel" or "apparent authority". Yet the power is the same: there is no temptation to talk of "apparent power". "Authority", like "possession", carries the image of a paradigm case justifying a legal result: "power" is neutral and simply states the result regardless of the justifications for it.

1-014   **Actual and apparent authority**   The placing of actual and apparent authority

---

[43] See below, para.8-029.
[44] Articles 72 and 83.
[45] Article 21.
[46] Hohfeld, *Fundamental Legal Conceptions as Applied in Judicial Reasoning* (4th printing, 1966), p.52; Montrose (1938) 16 Can.B.R. 757.
[47] Powell, p.6; Corbin (1925) 34 Yale L.J. 788 at 794; Montrose (1938) 16 Can.B.R. 757 at 763; Falconbridge (1939) 17 Can.B.R. 248 at 251–252; Dowrick (1954) 17 M.L.R. 24 at 37; McMeel (2000) 116 L.Q.R. 387; Tiberg, in *Lex Mercatoria* (Rose ed., 2000), Ch.4.

together in the definition in Article 1(3) can therefore be criticised, for actual authority arises where the principal agrees that the agent shall act for the principal (the paradigm case), whereas apparent authority can be said to be no authority at all, in that the principal has not authorised the agent to act, even if a third party is entitled to assume that the principal has. But the two types of authority are frequently spoken of together, and both create a power in the agent: it seems important, therefore, to reflect this usage at the outset. This scheme can also be justified on the basis that in both cases the authority stems from the principal's objectively determined assent, the difference being that in one case the assent is manifested to the agent and in the other to the third party. The wording of Article 1(3) reflects this reasoning,[48] though the notion of manifestation to the third party is frequently an artificial one and involves considerable difficulties.[49]

Fiduciary relationship between agent and principal Since the paradigm agent **1-015** has received special powers which enable the agent to change the legal position of another, the law also imposes special duties of a fiduciary nature towards that other.[50] These duties are not necessarily contractual (though of course they may be) for it is not necessary that there be any contract between principal and agent. Rather, they originate from equity, and are connected with the duties imposed by equity on express trustees. Consequently, their application is not confined to agents.[51] It has been said in the Privy Council that:

> "agency is a contract made between principal and agent ... like every other contract, the rights and duties of the principal and agent are dependent upon the terms of the contract between them, whether express or implied".[52]

This approach is discussed later,[53] where it is submitted that the statement should be treated with reserve, not least because agency need not be contractual. For the present it is sufficient to say that while the presence of fiduciary duties may not be a sine qua non of an agency relationship, and though such duties can be modified by contract, they are nevertheless a sufficiently prominent part of the agent's position to be incorporated within the original definition and noted at the outset.[54]

Other features: remuneration but not independent profit The fiduciary du- **1-016** ties lead to another feature of agency. It is inconsistent with those duties that an agent should act in respect of the relationship with the principal for the agent's own profit (unless any profit is disclosed to the principal and the principal consents). The agent's relationship with the principal may be commercially related but not commercially adverse. This does not entail that the agent should not be remunerated, whether on the basis of commission or otherwise. A commission need not be related

---

[48] cf. *Restatement, Second*, §§ 26 and 27; Abbott (1896) 9 Harvard L.R. 507; Montrose (1938) 16 Can.B.R. 757.

[49] See below, para.8-029.

[50] Articles 43–53; Dowrick (1954) 17 M.L.R. 24; *Guerin v R.* [1984] 2 S.C.R. 335 at 383–385, 394; (1984) 13 D.L.R. (4th) 321 at 339–341, 348–349; *Amaltal Corp Ltd v Maruha Corp* [2007] 3 N.Z.L.R. 192 at [22]; Illustration 14 to Article 43.

[51] See *Guerin v R.* [1984] 2 S.C.R. 335.

[52] *Kelly v Cooper* [1993] A.C. 205 at 213–214, per Lord Browne-Wilkinson.

[53] See below, para.6-034.

[54] See *McWilliam v Norton Finance (UK) Ltd* [2015] EWCA Civ 186; [2015] 1 All E.R. (Comm) 1026 at [40];*UBS AG (London Branch) v Kommunale Wasserwerke Peipkiz GmbH* [2017] EWCA Civ 1567 at [98] (right fully to pursue self-interest an indicator against agency).

to the value of the transaction: it can be by a mark-up. But the essence of the payment received by the agent is that it is not an independent profit taken by the agent, but rather a fee paid by the principal in return for the agent's acting on the principal's behalf.[55]

1-017   **Duty only one of due diligence**   There is a further feature of the relationship between principal and agent which may be taken as typical. It is that the agent owes to the principal, unless there are other indications, only a duty to use due diligence, or, if appropriate, best endeavours to achieve the result required. An agent does not owe the strict duties customarily imposed on, for instance, a seller, who has an adverse commercial relationship with the buyer.[56] To some extent this is of course a feature of contracts for services, as opposed to contracts for the transfer of property, in general; but though no doubt an agent *can* undertake strict liability in some respect,[57] the duty of due diligence is, when combined with the features already referred to, also a typical indication of agency.

1-018   **Control**   It is common to regard control by the principal as a defining characteristic of agency. Thus, *Restatement, Third*, defines agency in terms of acting "on the principal's behalf and subject to the principal's control".[58] This notion has obvious relevance in employment law, where it can be treated as an identifying characteristic of the employment relationship, and hence to the vicarious liability of an employer for an employee. In agency in general however it plays a more limited role.[59] A distinction between agent and trustee, and between agent and some bailees, is that control cannot in general be exercised by beneficiaries over trustees, nor by many bailors over their bailees.[60] The same is true of lenders who take powers to act in their own interests in ways which affect the borrower's position.[61] But agents will often not accept control by their principals as to the manner in which they act, and some will only accept instructions to act in accordance with usages of their own market. Others may be authorised only to do specific things. In many such situations the principal's only control lies in his power to revoke the authority, a power which agency law assumes that he has at all times.[62] It might seem therefore that control is not a significant feature of the internal relationship, except in so far as the relationship by definition posits a person, the principal, giving authority, and the agent's duty to obey instructions if the latter wishes to continue as agent. Nevertheless, if the principal gives up all control of his supposed agent the relationship is only doubtfully one of agency.[63] The idea of control may also be relevant where it is contended that a company is an agent of its parent.[64] For this reason the idea requires mention; but if the central notion of agency is not required, as it is not on

---

[55]   Articles 45 and 46.
[56]   See below, para.1-035.
[57]   e.g. a *del credere* agent: see below, para.1-042.
[58]   This feature is, contrary to the approach here adopted, made much of in *Restatement, Third*: see § 1.01, Comments f, g and corresponding reporter's notes.
[59]   See *South Sydney District Rugby League Football Club Ltd v News Ltd* (2000) 177 A.L.R. 611, at [131] onwards, actual decision affirmed (2003) 215 C.L.R. 563.
[60]   See below, paras 1-032 and 1-033.
[61]   See Article 118.
[62]   See Article 120. This point is further developed in the Comment to Article 37.
[63]   This makes some of the usages of Lloyd's difficult to account for. See *CFTO-TV Ltd v Mr Submarine Ltd* (1994) 108 D.L.R. (4th) 517; affirmed (1997) 151 D.L.R. (4th) 382; *Alliance Craton Explorer Pty Ltd v Quasar Resources Pty Ltd* [2013] FCAFC 29 at [74].
[64]   See the *South Sydney* case, (2000) 177 A.L.R. 611 at [137].

the explanation given in this book, to extend to tort, the idea of control does not seem sufficiently important to be inserted into the formal definition. Control remains an important aspect of vicarious liability in tort (even if recent authority suggests that absence of control does not provide immunity from such liability)[65] and in liability for procuring wrongs.[66]

Internal and external aspects of agency   The full reasoning above has been developed to meet the case of a person who may be called an agent in a strict sense, who has the power to affect the principal's legal relations. To such an agent legal rules attach which require the drawing of a distinction between what may be called the internal and external aspects of agency. The *external* aspect is that under which the agent has powers to affect the principal's legal position in relation to third parties. The *internal* aspect is the relationship between principal and agent, which imposes on the agent special duties vis-à-vis the principal, appropriate to the powers which the agent can exercise on the principal's behalf. These may arise in connection with an accompanying contract, but may arise only from the agent's fiduciary liability. They follow from the need to control agents' opportunities to exploit their position. To an agent in the fullest sense, both aspects are relevant. Some persons may, however, be described as agents by virtue of the internal relationship but have no external powers, as appears below.   **1-019**

Incomplete agency: internal relationship only—the "canvassing" or "introducing" agent   Article 1(4) seeks to achieve completeness by taking in a well-established type of intermediary who makes no contracts and disposes of no property, but is hired, whether as an employee or independent contractor, to introduce parties desirous of contracting and leaves them to contract between themselves, or otherwise performs some function relevant to a proposed transaction but does not effect a contract between the parties. In effecting and performing such introductions or limited functions the intermediary is often remunerated by commission, which may sometimes be taken from both parties.[67] Such a person is a common figure in most western legal systems and may well be referred to as an agent. The most obvious example of such an intermediary in the English cases is the estate agent, who introduces purchasers to vendors and tenants to lessors of houses, and vice versa.[68] Such persons are sometimes also referred to as brokers, and indeed in some English-speaking countries the estate agent is referred to as a "real estate broker": but this may be misleading since the current practice, at any rate in England, is to use the term "broker" for persons who go beyond introductions and certainly do make contracts for their principals, e.g. commodity brokers, insurance brokers and stockbrokers. Other examples include people whose approval of aspects of the subject-matter of a contract is stipulated for as a condition of the principal committing to the contract.[69] These people may owe the principal fiduciary duties in giving such approval, and hence may attract the law on bribes   **1-020**

---

[65] For discussion see below, para.8-178.
[66] For discussion in the context of banks giving directions to receivers, see *Ventra Investments Ltd v Bank of Scotland Plc* [2019] EWHC 2058 (Comm) at [75]–[77].
[67] As has been pointed out (see para.1-004), a wider definition of agency such as that adopted in *Restatement, Third*, does not require an exception for this type of agent: but it creates its own difficulties.
[68] There is an elaborate discussion of a statutory definition of a "real estate agent" in *Freehold Land Investments Ltd v Queensland Estates Pty Ltd* (1970) 123 C.L.R. 418.
[69] See *Shipway v Broadwood* [1899] 1 Q.B. 369 (veterinarian to certify as to soundness of horses);

and secret commissions if payments or other inducements are given by the third party. But their role is internal only.

Canvassing agents, as they are often called, are a difficult category about which to generalise.[70] Some do little or nothing more than effect an introduction. They have no express authority to alter their principals' legal relations, and advice and loyalty are not things they offer, nor are those things expected of them. Hence, where acting for purchasers, the introducer may be showing other purchasers the same property, hoping in order to maximise commission that the others will pay a higher price. In such circumstances, fiduciary duties are likely to be very limited (but the taking of commission from the vendor could well involve a breach of duty unless consented to).[71] Much turns on the degree of trust that the parties understand and accept is being placed in the intermediary by the principal.[72]

Others, though, may be the main go-between in negotiations on behalf of one of the parties, and certainly trusted by that party to pursue that party's interests. They will usually in so doing have authority to receive and communicate information on their principals' behalf, and thereby have the capacity to alter their principals' legal position. In that respect, such persons fit within the core definition of agency, since without that authority to make and receive communications, the principal may not secure a deal.[73] It is not necessary that an agent have authority to make a contract for the principal. Yet others may be authorised to negotiate and settle all the terms of a contract but do not have authority to complete the formalities. The evidenced intentions of such persons may, for instance, be relevant to the rectification of a written contract should it not accord with the informal consensus that had been reached.[74] Because they act in a capacity which involves the repose of trust and confidence, people in the latter two examples are likely to be fiduciaries.[75] They are also subject of typical rules, largely developed in estate agent cases, as to entitlement to commission, which are normally regarded as part of agency law.[76] They may sometimes hold money (e.g. deposits) for their principals.[77] The rules applicable to the internal relationship between principal and agent will therefore ap-

---

Alexander v Webber [1922] 1 K.B. 642 (chauffeur to approve of car to be bought); *Taylor v Walker* [1958] 1 Lloyd's Rep. 490 (accident assessor).

[70] See Article 30, Illustration 7, for a range of examples.

[71] See *Eze v Conway* [2019] EWCA Civ 88; *Marme Inversiones 2007 SL v Natwest Markets Plc* [2019] EWHC 366 (Comm) at [444] (lead arranging bank had no fiduciary relationship with other finance providers); *CH Offshore Ltd v Internaves Consorcio Naviero SA* [2020] EWHC 1710 (Comm) at [86] (shipping broker acting only as conduit between parties).

[72] Compare *Medsted Associates Ltd v Canaccord Genuity Wealth (International) Ltd* [2019] EWCA Civ 83; [2019] 1 W.L.R. 4481 at [32] (introducer to main agent had fiduciary relationship with client, albeit limited); with *Commercial First Business Ltd v Pickup* [2017] CTLC 1 (Ch). See too *Rowland v Chapman* (1901) 17 TLR 669 (agent who was also co-principal had no real conflict of interest).

[73] See *Pengelly v Business Mortgage Finance 4 Plc* [2020] EWHC 2002 (Ch) at [68].

[74] See, e.g. *Hawksford Trustees Jersey Ltd v Stella Global UK Ltd* [2012] EWCA Civ 55; [2012] 2 All E.R. 748 at [41]; *Murray Holdings Ltd v Oscatello Investments Ltd* [2018] EWHC 162 (Ch) at [198]; *FSHC Group Holdings Ltd v Barclays Bank Plc* [2018] EWHC 1558 (Ch) at [51].

[75] See *McWilliam v Norton Finance (UK) Ltd* [2015] EWCA Civ 186; [2015] 1 All E.R. (Comm) 1026 at [44] (mortgage broker); and Article 45, Illustrations 16 and 17. But cf. *Northeast General Corp v Wellington Advertising Inc*, 604 N.Y.S. (2d) 1 (Ct.App.1993) ("Non-exclusive independent investment broker and business consultant for the purposes of finding and presenting candidates for purchase, sale, merger or other business combination" held not to owe fiduciary duty to disclose information regarding persons introduced).

[76] Articles 56–58.

[77] See Comment to Article 52.

ply as appropriate, and for this reason such persons should certainly be treated in a work on agency even though they lack most of the external powers of the agent. It is an advantage of the formulation of basic agency principle in Article 1, which selects the internal relationship between principal and agent as a distinguishing feature of agency, that it can be taken to cover such persons.[78]

Indirect representation[79]   There is another situation that can be said to amount   **1-021**
to "incomplete agency": that which may be called indirect representation. In commercial spheres a method of dealing can be adopted whereby a principal appoints a person, who may be called an agent, to deal (especially to buy[80]) on the principal's behalf, on the understanding that when dealing with any third party the agent will deal in the agent's own name as principal. As between principal and agent, however, the relationship is one of agency[81]; viz. the agent: does not promise to achieve a result but only to use best endeavours, so does not answer to the principal on the strict basis appropriate to seller or buyer[82] (though the agent may have some of the rights of a seller, e.g. a lien[83]); is normally remunerated by commission; owes fiduciary duties and thus may not without disclosure take commission from the other party; and is in the above sense under the principal's control. Here, again, the internal aspect of agency is found but not the external. This arrangement is sometimes referred to in civil law countries as indirect representation, and intermediaries operating on such a basis, often by virtue of their professions (such as freight forwarders), may be referred to as operating under a contract of *commission* or the equivalent in other languages (the title referring to the task entrusted to

---

[78]   For a useful general survey see Yiannopoulos (1959) 19 La.L.Rev. 777 especially at p.799 onwards. In *Vogel v R. & A. Kohnstamm Ltd* [1973] Q.B. 133 an introducer of business was held not to be an agent for the purposes of enforcement of a foreign judgment: see pp.136–137 and 147; and in *Rakusens Ltd v Baser Ambalaj Plastik Sanayi Ticaret AS* [2001] EWCA Civ 1820; [2002] 1 B.C.L.C. 104 the office of such a representative was held not to be the company's "place of business" for the purposes of s.695(2) of the Companies Act 1985 (now Companies Act 2006 s.1139). See also *Okura & Co Ltd v Forsbacka Jernverks A/B* [1914] 1 K.B. 715.

[79]   See Busch, *Indirect Representation in European Contract Law* (The Hague: Kluwer Law International, 2005); Kortmann and Kortmann, in *Agency Law in Commercial Practice* (Busch, Macgregor and Watts eds, 2016), Ch.6.

[80]   For analogous arrangements regarding selling, see *Kirkham v Peel* (1880) 44 L.T. 195; *New Zealand and Australian Land Co v Watson* (1881) 7 Q.B.D. 374; and cases on factors generally (below, para.1-046); *Bosanquet v Mofflin* (1906) S.R. (N.S.W.) 617; *Benmag Ltd v Barda* [1955] 2 Lloyd's Rep. 354; *Fleming v London Produce Co Ltd* [1968] 1 W.L.R. 1013.

[81]   See *Ireland v Livingston* (1872) L.R. 5 H.L. 395 at 407–409; *Armstrong v Stokes* (1872) L.R. 7 Q.B. 598; *Robinson v Mollett* (1875) L.R. 7 H.L. 802 at 809–810; *Cassaboglou v Gibb* (1883) 11 Q.B.D. 797 at 803–804; *Montgomerie v UK Mutual SS Assn* [1891] 1 Q.B. 370 at 372; *Butlers (London) Ltd v Roope* [1922] N.Z.L.R. 549; *Downie Bros v Henry Oakley & Sons* [1923] N.Z.L.R. 734; *Bolus & Co Ltd v Inglis Bros Ltd* [1924] N.Z.L.R. 164 at 175; *Sopwith Aviation & Engineering Co Ltd v Magnus Motors Ltd* [1928] G.L.R. (N.Z.) 380; *Isaac Gundle v Mohanlal Sunderji* (1939) 18 Kenya L.R. 137; *Witt & Scott Ltd v Blumenreich* [1949] N.Z.L.R. 806; *Rusholme & Bolton & Roberts Hadfield Ltd v S.G. Read & Co* [1955] 1 W.L.R. 146 at 152; *J.S. Robertson (Australia) Pty Ltd v Martin* (1956) 94 C.L.R. 30; *Teheran-Europe Co Ltd v ST Belton (Tractors) Ltd* [1968] 2 Q.B. 53 at 59–60; affirmed [1968] 2 Q.B. 545; Hill [1964] J.B.L. 304; [1967] J.B.L. 122; (1968) 31 M.L.R. 623; (1972) 3 J. Maritime Law & Commerce 307; Schmitthoff, 1970 I *Hague Recueil des Cours* 115 at 151–154; Lando [1965] J.B.L. 179 at 374; [1966] J.B.L. 82. For a more modern example, see *Triffit Nurseries v Salads Etcetera Ltd* [1999] 1 All E.R. (Comm) 110 at 115; affirmed [2000] 1 All E.R. (Comm) 737, where such reasoning seems essential and below, para.10-010; and *OMV Petrom SA v Glencore International AG* [2015] EWHC 666 (Comm) at [138] (indirect principal able to plead deceit made to agent).

[82]   See below, para.1-036.

[83]   See the important material collected in Article 69.

[13]

the agent rather than, as might seem more natural to a common lawyer, the method of remuneration).[84] In many such situations the third party may infer, often from the nature of the agent's profession, or may even know that a principal is involved: the principal's name may even be known. Its recognition can lead to a method of expounding agency law on the basis that a person wishing to appoint a representative has the choice of two methods, direct or indirect representation: such an approach is in fact adopted in the PECL and indeed the DCFR, for which a measure of universality is claimed, though the UNIDROIT Principles have abandoned it as a classification.[85] The notion of authority can also be employed in both contexts, in the sense that the indirect agent can be said to be "authorised" to deal in the agent's own name, but for the account and at the risk of the principal.[86] This can be pressed so as to consider other doctrines of direct agency, especially apparent authority and ratification, in the context of indirect representation.[87]

On some views the idea of indirect representation is also applicable where the agent has authority to create direct representation, but for some reason (whether the principal's or his own) does not indicate that that is the case.[88] This is nearer to the common law doctrine of the undisclosed principal, a much narrower doctrine which common lawyers treat as an unusual form of *direct* representation.[89] In civil law countries the "principal" of the indirect agent (or *commissionnaire*) is not usually liable to the third party, though may be so in special situations, and the principal may rather more easily be able to sue.[90] Where that is so, the case for applying doctrines by analogy applicable to direct agency obviously becomes stronger.

1-022 **Is indirect representation accepted at common law?** This dichotomy between direct and indirect representation is unlikely to be attractive to common law systems, which tend to reach the result of direct representation with more facility than the civil law. But this apart, it is difficult to see any doctrinal objection at common law to the setting-up of a situation of indirect representation. Indeed, something like this seems to have been the mode of operation of the nineteenth-century factor,[91] who received goods on consignment and sold them without always making clear whether they were the factor's own goods or those of another. A commercial intermediary operating on this basis is sometimes even referred to in nineteenth-century cases as a "commission agent" or "commission merchant"[92]; and the cases

---

[84] See, e.g. Hamel, *Le Contrat de Commission* (Paris, 1949); Cohn, *Manual of German Law* (2nd edn), Vol.2, p.40 onwards; Horn, Kötz and Leser, *German Private and Commercial Law* (1982), pp.232–234; Schmitthoff, 1970 I *Hague Recueil des Cours* 115, 122–125; *Müller-Freienfels* (1955) 18 M.L.R. 33 at 36–38; Busch, fn.79 above.

[85] See above, p.xvii.

[86] See Busch, fn.79 above, pp.11 and 14.

[87] See Busch, passim.

[88] See Busch, fn.79 above, pp.13, 23–26, 231 and 234.

[89] See below, Article 76.

[90] In Dutch law the principal is in certain cases liable and entitled: see Busch, pp.44–48; as to German law, see Busch, p.93 onwards.

[91] See below, para.1-046.

[92] As to commission agents, see the leading case of *Ireland v Livingston* (1872) L.R. 5 H.L. 395 at 408; *Armstrong v Stokes* (1872) L.R. 7 Q.B. 598; Story, *Agency* (1839), § 33. The term "commission agent" or "commission merchant" appears in *Taylor v Kymer* (1832) 3 B. & Ad. 320; *Armstrong v Stokes* (1872) L.R. 7 Q.B. 598, Illustration 7 to Article 80; *Elbinger Actien-Gesellschaft v Claye* (1873) L.R. 8 Q.B. 313; *Hutton v Bulloch* (1874) L.R. 9 Q.B. 572; *Maspons y Hermano v Mildred, Goyeneche & Co* (1882) 9 Q.B.D. 530; affirmed (1883) 8 App.Cas. 874; *Cassaboglou v Gibb* (1883)

on the old "foreign principal" rule[93] refer to this method of operation. It was most clearly enunciated by Blackburn J when he said:

"Any person, if he chooses, may give an order to an agent to buy as his agent, not only with an express dispensation from any obligation to establish privity of contract between him and the person from whom the agent buys, but even expressly refusing authority to the agent to establish such privity.

This is the ordinary authority given to a foreign commission merchant who (on account of the great inconvenience which would result from establishing privity of contract between the foreign producer and the home merchant) is not allowed (far less required) to establish privity of contract between them. This, however, in no way interferes with the existence of a fiduciary relation."[94]

But by a unique development of the common law, the factor's principal was held entitled to intervene not only to sue, but also to be liable on the factor's contracts. This is said to be the origin of the common law doctrine of the undisclosed principal, though the case law on that doctrine appears to confine it to situations where the agent has authority to create privity of contract without disclosing that fact.[95] Such an intermediary may therefore sometimes in English law be regarded as creating *direct* representation, at least where no indication is given that the intermediary is acting for a principal and perhaps on occasion even where such indication is given.[96] This seems to have led to an assimilation of this special arrangement with normal agency. Several cases seem therefore to assume, without the point being properly argued, one of two possible interpretations to such a situation. The first is that the intermediary is a normal agent of an undisclosed principal, and that the undisclosed principal rules therefore apply with the result that the principal is liable and entitled whatever the intentions of the parties.[97] The second is that because the agent in such a situation has no external authority to create privity of contract between the principal and the third party, the undisclosed principal rules do not apply at all and the agent must alone be a party to the contract of sale, carriage, or whatever transaction has been performed for the principal, the resulting dealing being principal to principal.[98] If the approach to be derived from such cases is correct, however, this is an area where the breadth of common law agency

---

11 Q.B.D. 797 at 804; *J. N. Lyon & Co Ltd v N. Fuchs* (1920) 2 Lloyd's Rep. 333. See also *Fleming v London Produce Co Ltd* [1968] 1 W.L.R. 1013 as to the term "general commission agent" in connection with tax legislation. See in general Munday (1977) 6 Anglo-Am. L.Rev. 221, esp. at p.232 onwards.

[93] See below, para.8-071; Busch, *Indirect Representation in European Contract Law* (2005), pp.168–173.

[94] *Robinson v Mollett* (1875) L.R. 7 H.L. 802 at 809–810 (a dissenting speech). See also his famous speech in *Ireland v Livingston* (1872) L.R. 5 H.L. 395.

[95] See Comment to Article 76.

[96] See, e.g. *Maspons y Hermano v Mildred, Goyeneche & Co* (1882) 9 Q.B.D. 530 (holding the foreign principal rule inapplicable); affirmed on other grounds (1883) 8 App.Cas. 874.

[97] See, e.g. the *Maspons* case, above; and see *Brown & Gracie Ltd v F.W. Green & Co Pty Ltd* [1960] 1 Lloyd's Rep. 289; Reynolds [1983] *Current Legal Problems* 119. It could be said that *Scrimshire v Alderton* (1743) 2 Strange 1182 is an early example of such judicial analysis; see Stoljar, pp.207–208; Chorley (1929) 45 L.Q.R. 221 at 224–225.

[98] See, e.g. the dissenting judgment of Diplock LJ in *Anglo-African Shipping Co of New York Inc v J. Mortner Ltd* [1962] 1 Lloyd's Rep. 610 (which, it is respectfully submitted, presents an analysis which does not accord with commercial reality). See also the same judge in *Garnac Grain Co Inc v H.M.F. Faure & Fairclough Ltd* [1966] 1 Q.B. 650 at 684; affirmed [1968] A.C. 1130; *Limako BV v Hentz & Co Inc* [1979] 2 Lloyd's Rep. 23; *B. & M. Readers' Service Ltd v Anglo Canadian Publishers Ltd* [1950] O.R. 159 (subscription to magazine). But cf. *L/M International Construction Inc (now*

principles, which normally produce a more flexible result, act as a limiting factor and exclude the recognition of such an arrangement.[99] There seems no obvious reason why this should be so, unless it be thought undesirable that a principal should be able, by agreement with the agent, to determine the principal's liability to third parties. Indeed, such a situation may arise even now where, under the undisclosed principal doctrine, the intervention of a third party is excluded.[100]

1-023 **Meaning of term "agent", where a question of construction** When it is necessary, as in statutory interpretation or in the construction of an agreement, to attribute a meaning to the word "agent", it may be said that the central significance of the term agent refers to a person who attracts both the external and internal aspects of agency, for it is here that the complete complex of rules is most fully worked out, and it is because of the external powers that the internal duties are imposed. And where the term agent is used in a statute or formal document, it has been said that it may be presumed that the word is used in this, its proper legal connotation, unless there are strong contrary indications.[101] But there is certainly no rule to that effect, and the term is often used of any form of intermediary, or of persons who simply perform functions for others.[102] Conversely, the context may suggest that the word encompasses only professional agents who are independent contractors.[103] Similarly, the word "authority" in a statute may not require actual authorisation by the principal, but extend to acts, authorised or not, occurring in the performance of authorised tasks.[104] Another common form of words comes from the context of injunctions, which are often issued against "the defendant, its servant and

---

Bovis International Inc) v The Circle Ltd Partnership (1995) 49 Con.L.R. 12; and *Triffit Nurseries v Salads Etcetera Ltd* [2000] 1 All E.R. (Comm) 737, in both of which the "indirect representation" reasoning may assist the analysis.

[99] It is possible to identify situations of a different type where a person who may be called a representative acts as principal but accounts on an agency basis: e.g. the position of an issuing and correspondent bank in documentary credits (as to which see, e.g. *Benjamin's Sale of Goods* (10th edn), para.23-029 onwards). But this does not involve an act which the principal could do personally, and hence is not easily regarded as agency.

[100] See below, para.8-079.

[101] *Shell Co of Australia Ltd v Nat Shipping and Bagging Services Ltd (The Kilmun)* [1988] 2 Lloyd's Rep. 1 at 16, per Sir Denys Buckley (in a dissenting judgment); *Canada v Merchant Law Group* 2010 FCA 206 (Can. Fed. CA) at [17] (incidence of goods and services tax); *Plevin v Paragon Personal Finance Ltd* [2014] UKSC 61; [2014] 1 W.L.R. 4222 at [30].

[102] See, e.g. *Laemthong International Lines Co Ltd v Artis (The Laemthong Glory)* [2005] EWCA Civ 519; [2005] 1 Lloyd's Rep. 688 (promise to indemnify "you, your servants or agents" considered in the context of the Contracts (Rights of Third Parties) Act 1999: shipowner held "agent" of charterer for delivering cargo and so able to sue). Another example is the reference to "servants or agents" in Art.IV bis 2 of the Hague-Visby Rules scheduled to the Carriage of Goods by Sea Act 1971: see *Carver on Bills of Lading* (4th edn), para.9-303. See further *The Happy Day* [2002] EWCA Civ 1068; [2002] 2 Lloyd's Rep. 487 (agency of receiver for charterer); *Commerce Commission v Vero Insurance New Zealand Ltd* (2006) 8 N.Z.C.L.C. 101, 871 (possession of apparent authority enough to meet the operative provision of a statute that a person be an agent); *Commissioners for Revenue and Customs v Insurancewide.Com Services Ltd* [2010] EWCA Civ 422; [2010] S.T.C. 1572 at [87] (exemption from VAT for insurance brokers and agents); *Revenue and Customs v Secret Hotels2 Ltd* [2014] UKSC 16; [2014] S.T.C. 937 (VAT intermediaries); *Actavis Group hf v Eli Lilly & Co* [2013] EWCA Civ 517; [2013] R.P.C. 37 at [57] (business carried on through an agent); *NYK Bulkship (Atlantic) NV v Cargill International SA* [2016] UKSC 20; [2016] 1 W.L.R. 1853, discussed in F.M.B. Reynolds and C.H. Tan [2018] Sing J.L.S. 43, 54 (only irrelevant functions of sub-charterers were those of "agent" and otherwise they were independent parties).

[103] See, e.g. *Public Prosecutor v Lam Leng Hung* [2018] SGCA 7 at [125].

[104] See *Kemeh v Ministry of Defence* [2014] EWCA Civ 91; [2014] I.C.R. 625 at [11] (racial discrimination). See too *Unite the Union v Nailard* [2018] EWCA Civ 1203; [2019] I.C.R. 28..

agents". The only direct party will be the defendant, but the wording signals that the defendant needs to control those whom it has engaged to do the enjoined activity, who might be independent contractors that are not exercising any agency functions in the common law sense.[105]

Essence of agency   Should the essence of agency then be regarded as the internal   **1-024**
or external aspect of the concept, or as both? In the fullest sense it requires both; and the internal aspect follows the external, i.e. as stated above, it is because the agent has the power to alter the principal's position that the fiduciary duties are imposed on the agent. In another sense, however, it is the internal conferring of the power that justifies that power, and such reasoning would make the internal aspect primary. However this question is viewed, it is useful to note the typical features of the internal position which distinguish agency from other relationships. So, the agent: undertakes to use due diligence on behalf of another, rather than undertake strict duties to another in a situation commercially adverse to that other; is subject to fiduciary duties; and is remunerated by commission or an equivalent rather than by controlling the agent's own profit. Though any of these three features can be modified in an appropriate case, they nevertheless remain typical.[106]

"Externalised" theories   The explanation of the common law of agency offered   **1-025**
above can, however, be subjected to fundamental criticisms. A simple version of such criticisms is to say that it is the law that imposes certain consequences on the facts in all these cases; thus all agency arises by operation of law, and the insistence on consent in the internal relationship as the ground base of agency is misplaced.[107] This view can fairly easily be said to fail to attach sufficient importance to the paradigm case, the degree of similarity to which renders appropriate or inappropriate the use of the sort of reasoning to which that situation gives rise. The controversy is similar to that as to whether there is a distinction between "possession in fact" and "possession in law", or whether all possession, being attributed by the law, should be treated as possession in law.[108] Admittedly there are few limits on the situations where the law can regard someone as possessing: but the paradigm case where there is physical control or something very near to it nevertheless regulates to some extent what are thought to be acceptable uses of the term "possession", in whatever context. Hence the notion of "possession in fact" is contrasted with "possession in law". The same is true of the notion of authority as opposed to that of power.

More elaborately, but to similar effect, it may be argued that cases of genuine express conferring of authority are in fact the exception rather than the rule, at least where disputes arise, and that the external power conferred by the law on the agent, which applies also in situations of apparent authority, is so clearly predominant that it, and not subjective consent, should be emphasised and analysed as the connect-

---

[105] There is a useful discussion in *Kirkpatrick v Kotis* (2004) 62 N.S.W.L.R. 567 at [81]–[100].

[106] As to the significance of the right of control, see above, para.1-018.

[107] See, e.g. Salmond and Winfield, *Law of Contracts* (1927), p.340: "An agent may be defined as a person who is authorised by law to exercise on behalf of another person … any power possessed by that other person of entering into a contract or other agreement, or of doing any other act in law"; Dowrick (1954) 17 M.L.R. 24 at 35–38.

[108] This is rather a dated controversy. See Salmond, *Jurisprudence* (12th edn), Ch.9.

ing link between cases of agency.[109] Agency situations should therefore be viewed in the first place from the point of view of the third party, and apparent authority should, again, be an application of the normal rules rather than an exception accommodated by elaborate explanations. In some continental European legal systems a distinction sharper than would be appropriate to common law authority is made between the internal relationship of principal and agent and the general external power of the agent. This seems to be particularly so in German law, and systems influenced by it, where the distinction achieved prominence following a famous article by Paul Laband published in 1866.[110] It leads to greater emphasis on the external aspect of agency situations than the approach set out in Article 1: the conferring of power may in all cases be regarded as a unilateral act in the law directed from the principal not to the agent, but rather to the third party.[111]

The contrast between such an approach and that of the common law as here explained can be likened to the conflict of principle frequently recognised in the law of property between security of title and security of transactions. In some jurisdictions the approach that prefers the value of protecting apparently valid transactions predominates. At common law, or at any rate in the English common law, the predominant principle is, however, that a person does not lose ownership except by that person's own voluntary act. Significant exceptions are created only by statute (principally the Factors Act 1889[112]) and under the doctrine of estoppel.[113] The same is true of contractual obligations: a person cannot be subjected to a contractual obligation through another except by that person's volition. Exceptions can in general only be created by statute (the most obvious being the Partnership Act 1890[114]) and under the doctrine of apparent authority, which can be said to be based on estoppel, though there are difficulties with this view.[115]

It seems that common law unaided is almost bound to arrive at the particular balance, which it does, since it must proceed by the use of commonly accepted lines of reasoning. The principles concerning loss of property or imposition of obligations seem an inevitable starting point, even if their results are later to be modified by secondary doctrines. With one possible exception, to be discussed below, no other reasoning seems readily available for initial use. Therefore agency depends on the assent of the principal except where corrective (apparent authority) reasoning can be found or the result is modified by statute, as in the Factors Act. To achieve a completely different emphasis would require a general statute, or at least

---

[109] Seavey (1920) 29 Yale L.J. 859 at 872 onwards; Fridman (1968) 84 L.Q.R. 224 at 228–231.

[110] Die Stellvertretung bei dem Abschluss von Rechtsgeschäften nach dem Allgemeinen Deutschen Handelsgesetzbuch (1866) 10 *Zeitschrift für Handelsrecht* 183. See Müller-Freienfels (1964) 13 Am.J.Comp.L. 193 at 197–202; Schmitthoff 1970 I *Hague Recueil des Cours* 115 at 120 onwards; Schlesinger, *Comparative Law* (7th edn); Tiberg, in *Lex Mercatoria* (Rose ed., 2000), Ch.4. It appears that the approach of French law is somewhat nearer the English approach. For a recent comparative study of the question in various European jurisdictions, see Busch and Macgregor (eds), *The Unauthorised Agent* (2009). See too Macgregor, Ch.2.

[111] It has some similarity with the reasoning used of general agents, and agents of specific types (e.g. factors) in England in the nineteenth century. See Brown [2004] J.B.L. 391.

[112] Article 87; see also Sale of Goods Act 1979 ss.24 and 25 (derived from the Factors Act).

[113] Articles 83 and 85; see also Sale of Goods Act 1979 s.21.

[114] ss.5 and 10.

[115] Articles 21 and 72. The requirements for an estoppel are less stringent in the area of obligations than in that of property to such an extent that it can be doubted whether estoppel is in truth the basis of the results reached in the law of obligations. This is not surprising, for it has long been established that obligations can be imposed on the basis of objective appearances: but it perhaps indicates that the rules protecting against loss of ownership are too severe. See below, para.8-028.

the acceptance of a technique of judicial reasoning which can derive general policies from particular statutes.[116] The German doctrinal separation referred to above was in fact derived from the *Prokura*, a general authority in commercial matters created by the Commercial Code of 1861.[117] Reasoning by analogy from statutes has not been a feature of the English common law.[118]

But even the most extreme externalised theories are in fact likely to derive the agent's power ultimately from such an internal starting point, for example, creation of *Prokura*, or appointment to a specific position, which the principal need not have made, and may, with appropriate publicity, cancel.[119] Indeed, on one view the principal's main protection lies in this possibility of cancelling the agent's authority.

When this is borne in mind, common law is not so different as may appear. It has been said that its approach to agency, as outlined above, fails to make the proper distinction between the internal relation between principal and agent and the external relation between the agent and third parties, but simply derives the one from the other.[120] But although there are certainly dicta which can be taken to support such a view, it has been submitted above that there is an essential difference between the conferring of authority, which is a unilateral act of will even if like a contract it is to be justified by the consent of the parties, and an accompanying contract, if there is one. In so far as there is a genuine difference of approach, each generates its own difficulties. The common law approach has some difficulty in completely explaining the basis of apparent authority[121]: but its concentration on the conferring of authority enables it (for better or worse) to accommodate the rights and liabilities of the undisclosed principal.[122] The "external" approach certainly protects innocent third parties dealing with the agent, and no doubt many more claims are in practice based on apparent than on actual authority. But the protection can perhaps be excessive: for it can (unless other, corrective doctrines can be invoked) lead to the conclusion that third parties are entitled to rely on the appearance of agency even though they have reason to know that the agent was not in fact authorised.[123] It appears also to be associated with a tendency to isolate numerous

---

[116] See Tiberg, in *Lex Mercatoria* (Rose ed., 2000), Ch.4, esp. at p.61. ("Thus, the 'dependent' or 'mandate' power which is the exception in Nordic and Continental law is 'actual authority' and the rule in English law, while the independent powers that are the rule in Continental law are the exceptions ('apparent authority') in English law").

[117] HGB, para.49; see Müller-Freienfels (1964) 13 Am.J.Comp.L. 193 at 207 onwards and 341–346.

[118] But see *Beverley Acceptances Ltd v Oakley* [1982] R.T.R. 417 at 426, per Lord Denning MR (dissenting); "This means that we need no longer interpret the Factors Acts by the letter. We can go by spirit which lies behind them. Modern law has made them a particular application of general principle". See also Beatson (2001) 117 L.Q.R. 247.

[119] See Grönfors (1962) 6 *Scandinavian Studies in Law* 95 (in English), referring to s.10(2) of the Uniform Scandinavian Contracts Act of 1915. The same writer's *Ställningsfullmakt och Bulvanskap* (Stockholm, 1961) contains an exhaustive international bibliography to that date. It was reviewed by Müller-Freienfels (1963) 12 Am.J.Comp.L. 272 (together with Stoljar's *Law of Agency* (1961)). See further Tiberg, in *Lex Mercatoria* (Rose ed., 2000), Ch.4.

[120] See Müller-Freienfels (1957) 6 Am.J.Comp.L. 165 at 170–173; cf. the same writer in *Civil Law in the Modern World*, (Yiannopoulos ed., 1965), 77 at 86–89. A similar point can be made of French law: see Müller-Freienfels (1964) 13 Am.J.Comp.L. 341 at 346–349; Graziadei, Mattei and Smith, *Commercial Trusts in European Private Law* (Cambridge: Cambridge University Press, 2015) pp.48–52.

[121] See Comment to Article 72.

[122] See above, para.1-009; Article 76.

[123] Müller-Freienfels (1964) 13 Am.J.Comp.L. 193 at 211 onwards.

different types of agent, each with its own special rules; though this is more probably a legacy of the Romanistic notion of nominate contracts.[124]

1-026 **The tort approach** From time to time a different approach to agency problems has been urged by common law writers, an approach quite separate from the "externalised" theories referred to above. It has been argued that traditional agency reasoning, which requires authority or its appearance for one person to alter the legal position of another, is inadequate, and that recourse should be had to a line of reasoning which seeks more generally to place responsibility on the instigator or beneficiary of the enterprise in relation to which a person acts.[125] Sometimes it has been suggested that a principle similar to that of vicarious liability in the law of torts should be adopted in place of normal agency reasoning.[126] A suggestion for the adoption of such an approach was put forward by Lord Wilberforce:

> "It may be that some wider conception of vicarious responsibility other than that of agency, as normally understood, may have to be recognised in order to accommodate some of the more elaborate cases which now arise when there are two persons who become mutually involved or associated in one side of a transaction."[127]

The case itself involved the potential liability of a finance company for the representations of a car dealer who assisted buyers in obtaining finance from the company for their purchases from the dealer—a common enough situation. If it was sought to generalise on this situation alone, it might perhaps be possible to develop a doctrine that where two parties are in a business association of some sort, the nature of which is unclear to the outside world, the burden should rather be on the party who appears to be the instigator of, or possibly even merely a participator in, the combined business to show that there was not and would not reasonably be expected to have been authority in the other party, rather than the reverse. Lord Wilberforce had said earlier in his speech:

> "Thus there are two rival views as to the manner in which a typical hire purchase transaction should be regarded. That expressed by Holroyd Pearce L.J. and by Pearson L.J. involves an analysis without any initial presumption of each individual transaction, on the available documents and evidence, in order to see whether, in any respect, the finance company (or, if that is relevant, the hirer) should be held to have conferred authority (actual or apparent) upon the dealer to act as his agent. That of Lord Denning M.R. and Donovan L.J. takes as a starting point the established mercantile background of hire-purchase transactions, as known to and accepted by all three parties, takes that as establishing in general the basis for an agency relationship, and finally considers, against that background, any individual features of the particular case to see whether they confirm or weaken the agency inference. My Lords, for my part I think that the latter approach is now to be preferred."[128]

This was however a dissenting speech; the majority of the House of Lords decided the question in issue against liability by the application of normal agency principles,

---

[124] See Schmitthoff, 1970 I *Hague Recueil des Cours* 115 at 123–124 (listing 13 types of intermediary known to German law); Bonell [1984] Uniform L.Rev. 52.

[125] Seavey (1920) 29 Yale L.J. 859, esp. at pp.883–885.

[126] See, e.g. Wright (1936) 1 U. Toronto L.J. 17 at 40 onwards; Mearns (1962) 48 Va.L.Rev. 50; Brown [2004] J.B.L. 391.

[127] *Branwhite v Worcester Works Finance Ltd* [1969] 1 A.C. 552 at 587. See also *First Energy (UK) Ltd v Hungarian International Bank Ltd* [1993] 2 Lloyd's Rep. 194 at 196, 204, per Steyn LJ.

[128] *Branwhite v Worcester Works Finance Ltd* [1969] 1 A.C. 552 at 585–586.

and Lord Wilberforce himself was able also to justify the (minority) result which he reached in favour of liability on the basis of orthodox doctrine. Subsequently it was held that a person employing the services of an estate agent to sell his house was not liable when the agent without authority took deposits from a number of people, who were thereby defrauded[129]; that a finance company was not bound by the representations of a hire-purchase information service, set up by finance companies as an independent, non-profit-making organisation, as to whether a particular vehicle was the subject of a hire-purchase agreement[130]; that an insurance company was not liable for representations made by a branch manager (an employee who was more or less a canvassing agent or a controller of canvassing agents[131]) which were neither actually nor apparently authorised[132]; and that a company was not liable in tort for fraudulent misrepresentations by a manager not within the scope of the manager's apparent authority.[133] Such decisions tend against any generalised approach of the sort mentioned,[134] which is in any case directed towards the principal's *duties*. Orthodox agency law gives the principal rights also.

A more drastic use of such reasoning might seek to make the principal liable regardless even of whether the principal was known by the third parties to be connected with the transaction. This, which is again a liability doctrine only, might for agency law be justified as an extension of the undisclosed principal doctrine[135]; but it would more probably require to be based on reasoning similar to that now used in tort cases, where the recent tendency has been to invoke principles for vicarious liability much broader than those formerly employed.[136] In the speech of Lord Wilberforce quoted above he later suggested[137] that this was the true matter in issue in *Garnac Grain Co Inc v HMF Faure & Fairclough Ltd*,[138] where it was sought to say that a commercial concern which sold goods and at the same time secretly contracted to repurchase them from a sub-sub-buyer was liable to the sub-buyer as an undisclosed principal of the sub-sub-buyer. The argument in that case was unsuccessful, however; and subsequently a company was held not liable for the act of an employee (a true agent) who caused the loss to third parties by a negligent valuation set out on the principal's notepaper, effected contrary to his instructions and in such a way that the third parties did not know who had prepared the valuation.[139] The trend of decisions again suggests, therefore, that the orthodox basis of agency law, which requires some indication of authority or of the appearance of it, will still

---

[129] *Sorrell v Finch* [1977] A.C. 728, Illustration 4 to Article 92: see Articles 92 and 111.
[130] *Moorgate Mercantile Co v Twitchings* [1977] A.C. 890, Illustration 7 to Article 84. Both the above two cases are criticised by Fridman (1982) 20 U. of W.Ont.L.Rev. 23.
[131] As to canvassing agents see above, para.1-020.
[132] *British Bank of the Middle East v Sun Life Assurance Co of Canada (UK) Ltd* [1983] 2 Lloyd's Rep. 9, Illustration 10 to Article 77 (noted [1982] J.B.L. 496; [1983] J.B.L. 409).
[133] *Armagas Ltd v Mundogas SA (The Ocean Frost)* [1986] A.C. 717. But as to vicarious liability for the negligent misstatements of employees, see now *So v HSBC Bank Plc* [2009] EWCA Civ 296; and below, para.8-180.
[134] See Fridman (1983) 13 Manitoba L.J. 1. But see the observations in the difficult and specialised case of *Heatons Transport (St Helens) Ltd v Transport and General Workers' Union* [1973] A.C. 15 at 99–100, which suggests a similarity between authority and scope of employment; *Re Supply of Ready Mixed Concrete* [1992] Q.B. 213; *First Energy (UK) Ltd v Hungarian International Bank Ltd* [1993] 2 Lloyd's Rep. 194, Illustration 12 to Article 72.
[135] See Comment to Article 22; Montrose (1937) 17 Can.B.R. 224.
[136] See Article 90.
[137] *Branwhite v Worcester Works Finance Ltd* [1969] 1 A.C. 552 at 587.
[138] *Garnac Grain Co Inc v HMF Faure & Fairclough Ltd* [1968] A.C. 1130n.
[139] *Kooragang Investments Pty Ltd v Richardson & Wrench Ltd* [1982] A.C. 462.

be followed.[140] The doctrine of apparent authority is in some ways similar to vicarious liability in tort, since (in English law) it involves liability only. In the US it was at one time fashionable to seek to link agency reasoning in contract and property with vicarious liability in tort with a view to the development of more general principles.[141] But it seems that such schemes are now less in fashion, and if this is so it can be justified.[142] For a tort situation is in general not one voluntarily entered into by the aggrieved party, whereas an agency situation is. This means that the duty to compensate in tort may be more readily imposed than a similar duty in contractual situations. Although it is now recognised that the boundary between contract and tort is more fluid than may sometimes have been thought in the past, the distinction between the two types of obligation still seems a valid one and no satisfactory organising technique based on different notions has yet been propounded. Furthermore, a major reason for the imposition of liability on one person for the torts of another is the degree of control exercised over him: the main instance of vicarious liability is that of an employee (formerly "master") for the torts of an employee ("servant"). But, although an agent may be an employee, the typical agent is not, and acts in an independent manner. Finally, in agency disputes the question is not, as it is usually in tort, merely one of liability of the instigator of an enterprise: a person designated as principal to a transaction will also be able to sue, except in situations of pure apparent authority—and even here there may be ratification. Agency is therefore more instructively viewed as a notion facilitating commerce rather than as part of a generalised area of law providing compensation for the acts of others; and for these reasons it is submitted that the approach adopted and developed over the past century remains correct.

In short, orthodox agency principles, and the requirement for actual or apparent authority, are a reflection of a balance the law has long drawn between not subjecting parties to the potentially draconian law of contract without at least an adequate appearance of consent and upholding an expectation that rights have been obtained when it is not easy to check that the principal is consenting.[143] Mere expectations, however reasonable, are not enough; the principal must have done enough to warrant the reliance.[144]

If the contractual context is important in understanding standard agency principles, one question that has not so far been fully addressed in the case law is whether restitutionary liability of a principal for the statements and other acts of agents turns on the authority, actual or apparent, of the agent: see the discussion in Article 79.

1-027   **Diverse use of agency reasoning**   The ruling notion of agency law may be said to be that the acts of a person (the agent) authorised, or to be treated as authorised,

---

[140] But see below, para.8-180 for consideration of *So v HSBC Bank Plc* [2009] EWCA Civ 296; [2009] 1 C.L.C. 503.

[141] See Conard (1949) 1 J. Legal Ed. 540; Mechem (1949) 2 J. Legal Ed. 203; Street, *Foundations of Legal Liability* (1906), Vol. 2, Pt. IV; and *Restatement, Second.* (*Restatement, Third* is more limited.) See also Wyse (1979) 40 Mont. L.Rev. 31.

[142] See Ferson (1951) 4 Vand.L.Rev. 260; Müller-Freienfels in *Civil Law in the Modern World* (Yiannopoulos ed., 1965), 77 at 107–108, 117–120.

[143] For recognition of this, see *Smith v Henniker-Major & Co* [2002] EWCA Civ 762; [2003] Ch. 182 at [120]. More generally, see P. Watts, "Some Wear and Tear on *Armagas v Mundogas*—the Tension Between Having and Wanting in the Law of Agency" [2015] L.M.C.L.Q. 36.

[144] See *Lavarack v Woods of Colchester Ltd* [1967] 1 Q.B. 278 (CA) at 294; *PEC Ltd v Asia Golden Rice Co Ltd* [2014] EWHC 1583 (Comm) at [69].

by another are in certain circumstances to be treated as having the same legal effect as if they had been done by that other (the principal).[145] This is sometimes expressed by the idea that the agent's acts *are* those of the principal—*qui facit per alium facit per se*, though such a complete identification is usually regarded as inappropriate. Reasoning along these lines may be found in the spheres of contract, property, tort, restitution, criminal law, evidence, administrative law, taxation,[146] labour law and elsewhere. But though this approach has value in imposing some unity on the law applicable to situations where one party represents or acts for another, it should not be taken too literally. It is misleading to assume that a single set of principles, valid for the whole law, relating to the representation of one person by another can be evolved under the title of agency.[147] The main application of such reasoning is in the law of contract, where it is obviously desirable for rules to exist under which a person may make a contract for another, and such reasoning was necessary to render the principal liable in *assumpsit*. Different policies may regulate the considerations applicable in the law of property, of restitution, of tort and elsewhere. Nor is it possible exhaustively to analyse agency principles separately in each branch of the law, since the boundaries between the branches are too fluid. Finally, agency principles in English law evolve from disparate sources: from common law as to master and servant, from Admiralty cases concerned with shipmasters, from equity and the law of trusts, from cases on deeds, and from the action of account.[148] Agency reasoning needs to take account of context and is fact sensitive.[149] The study and separate treatment of agency as a subject is valuable, but no hidden key is to be found thereby.

That does not mean, however, that all applications of agency reasoning are acceptable. The basic notion is that the agent acts on behalf of another. This makes the use of agency terminology in creating irrevocable authority[150] and assignment inappropriate (though use of representation in the latter context goes back to Roman law). Its use (as "agency of necessity") in the context of conferring of benefits now appears inappropriate also,[151] and to be the result of the lack of any concept of *negotiorum gestio* in common law. Agency reasoning is rarely an appropriate solution to problems of subsidiary companies[152]; or of undue influence exercised over the guarantor or mortgagor by a third party to a guarantee or mortgage.[153] Its use in creating or protecting security over chattels also causes unintended repercussions.[154] The use of the concept of agency as a device to impose vicarious

---

[145] See further below, Article 6.
[146] Some interesting reasoning can be found in *Conservative and Unionist Central Office v Burrell* [1982] 1 W.L.R. 522; see Emery (1983) 133 N.L.J. 87.
[147] See the first *Restatement* criticised on these grounds by Miller (1936) 20 Marquette L.Rev. 141.
[148] Holdsworth, *H.E.L.* VIII, pp.222–229 and 248–254; Pollock and Maitland, *H.E.L.*, Vol. 2, p.225 onwards; Holmes, 3 *Select Essays in Anglo-American Legal History* (1909), p.368; Stoljar, pp.14–17; Simpson, *History of the Common Law of Contract* (1975), pp.552–557.
[149] cf. the difficulties put forward by Fridman (1968) 84 L.Q.R. 224; (1982) 20 U.W.Ont. L.Rev. 23.
[150] See Article 118 and Comment.
[151] See Article 33 and Comment.
[152] See above, para.1-028.
[153] See, e.g. *Coldunell Ltd v Gallon* [1986] Q.B. 1184; *Kings North Trust Ltd v Bell* [1986] 1 W.L.R. 119. A different approach to such questions was established (though not without difficulty) in *Barclays Bank Plc v O'Brien* [1994] 1 A.C. 180; and *Royal Bank of Scotland Plc v Etridge (No.2)* [2001] UKHL 44; [2002] 2 A.C. 773. But cf. *Dollars & Sense Finance Ltd v Nathan* [2008] 2 N.Z.L.R. 557 at [25].
[154] The "Romalpa" clause (below, para.8-165) often seeks to use agency terminology. For a striking

liability where the relevant actor is plainly not an employee (or in a relationship akin to employment) is also unsatisfactory.[155]

2. Agency law and companies[156]

1-028   **Attributing acts, omissions and states of mind to companies**   A company (as with other corporations) can operate only through individuals, but in relation to the rules of the common law (including equity) the rules of agency and vicarious liability suffice to enable a company to be held liable and entitled in respect of acts performed, and the states of mind held, by its agents and employees in the same way as a human principal. No special rules are needed. The position was well stated by Lord Diplock in *Tesco Supermarkets Ltd v Nattrass*[157]:

> "A corporation is an abstraction. It is incapable itself of doing any physical act or being in any state of mind. Yet in law it is a person capable of exercising legal rights and of being subject to legal liabilities which may involve ascribing to it not only physical acts which are in reality done by a natural person on its behalf but also the mental state in which that person did them. In civil law, apart from certain statutory duties, this presents no conceptual difficulties. Under the law of agency the physical acts and state of mind of the agent are in law ascribed to the principal, and if the agent is a natural person it matters not whether the principal is also a natural person or a mere legal abstraction. Qui facit per alium facit per se: qui cogitat per alium cogitat per se."

However, in relation to duties that result from drafting (such as those created by statutes or a contract) that are directed at owners of businesses, including companies, it is always a question of construction as to whose acts, omissions and states of mind the drafter intended be attributed to the owner.[158] Sometimes the drafter may have intended to draw on the common law concepts of attribution, but in others special rules may be required to give effect to the relevant provision. This point is elaborated upon in the next paragraph. Even at common law, the rules by which the acts and states of mind of agents are attributed to their principals must remain sensitive to the legal question that is engaged by the facts.[159] In particular, a principal will not usually be precluded from suing an agent for a breach of duty owed the principal, including as a result of the agent having exposed the principal

---

nineteenth-century example of such misclassification, see the "attornment of money" cases discussed under Article 112.

[155] See para.8-178. Compare *S. v Att.-Gen.* [2003] 3 N.Z.L.R. 450 with *Lowe v Director General of Health* [2017] NZSC 115.

[156] See Müller-Freienfels in *Civil Law in the Modern World* (Yiannopoulos edn, 1965), 77 at 90–92; *Gower's Principles of Modern Company Law* (10th edn), Ch.7; Watts (2000) 116 L.Q.R. 525; Worthington (2017) 133 L.Q.R. 118.

[157] *Tesco Supermarkets Ltd v Nattrass* [1972] A.C. 153 at 198–199; *Bilta (UK) Ltd v Nazir (No.2)* [2015] UKSC 23; [2016] A.C. 1 at [181] and [205], per Lords Toulson and Hodge.

[158] *Meridian Global Funds Management Asia Ltd v Securities Commission* [1995] 2 A.C. 500 at 507 and 511–512. See too *Julien v Evolving Technologies and Enterprise Development Co Ltd* [2018] UKPC 2 (noted P. Watts, "Attribution and limitation" (2018) 134 L.Q.R. 350); *Singularis Holdings Ltd (in liq) v Daiwa Capital Markets Europe Ltd* [2019] UKSC 50; [2019] 3 W.L.R. 997; *Royal Mail Group Ltd v Jhuti* [2019] UKSC 55 (imputing motivation for dismissal of employee, a problem not confined to incorporated employers).

[159] *Bilta (UK) Ltd v Nazir (No.2)* [2015] UKSC 23; [2016] A.C. 1 at [9], [41], [181], [191] and [202]; *Cool Seas (Seafoods) Ltd v Interfish Ltd* [2018] EWHC 2038 (Ch) at [159] (attribution of director's conduct to appointing shareholder for purpose of unfair prejudice claim under Companies Act 2006 s.994); *Singularis Holdings Ltd (in liq) v Daiwa Capital Markets Europe Ltd* [2019] UKSC 50; [2019] 3 W.L.R. 997 at [34]. See below, para.8-208.

to liability to a third party, on the basis of an agent's argument that his actions or knowledge are attributed to the principal.[160] Similarly, the agent may not be able to initiate action against the principal in respect of conduct for which the agent is factually responsible simply on the basis that for other purposes the principal is prima facie answerable for it.[161] Again, these principles are as applicable to companies as any other principal, and do not cease to apply merely because the agents in question are directors or otherwise have control of the company's affairs. In general, it is useful to conceive of the company as in exactly the same position as an absentee human owner of a business who has no direct knowledge of its affairs and whose participation is otherwise always remote.[162]

In *Meridian Global Funds Management Asia Ltd v Securities Commission*,[163] Lord Hoffmann drew a distinction between the primary rules for attributing the acts of humans to a company, such as the rule that decisions of the board bind the company, and the general rules for attributing conduct to another that apply both to corporations and individuals, namely the principles of the law of agency. However, Lord Hoffmann did not go so far as to state that the bodies of persons who engage the primary rules are not agents, and Lord Diplock's dictum, above, together with the weight of authority, clearly takes the view that they are.[164] The primary rules of attribution are best seen, it is suggested, as simple sources of actual authority vested usually in the board of directors, but sometimes in shareholders. The point was put in the following way by Diplock LJ in *Freeman & Lockyer v Buckhurst Park Properties (Mangal) Ltd*[165]:

"Such 'actual' authority may be conferred by the constitution of the corporation itself, as, for example, in the case of a company, upon its board of directors."

On this basis, the board of directors when acting to bind the company, or to authorise others to bind the company, operates as a body of co-agents.[166] Equally, to the extent that some of the functions of shareholders in general meeting, or in

---

[160] *Bilta (UK) Ltd v Nazir (No.2)* [2015] UKSC 23; [2016] A.C. 1 at [42]–[45], [129], and [208]; *HKSAR v Luk Kin* [2016] HKCFA 81 at [41].

[161] See *Brumder v Motornet Service and Repairs Ltd* [2013] EWCA Civ 195; [2013] 1 W.L.R. 2783.

[162] See, e.g. *Williams v Natural Life Health Foods Ltd* [1998] 1 W.L.R. 830 at 835; *Standard Chartered Bank v Pakistan National Shipping Corp (Nos 2 and 4)* [2003] 1 A.C. 959 at [23]; *Prest v Petrodel Resources Ltd* [2013] UKSC 34; [2013] 2 A.C. 415 at [31]; *Bilta (UK) Ltd v Nazir (No.2)* [2015] UKSC 23; [2016] A.C. 1 at [205]; *Financial Conduct Authority v Da Vinci Invest Ltd* [2015] EWHC 2401 (Ch); [2016] Bus L.R. 274. See too *Moulin Global Eyecare Trading Ltd v CIR* [2014] HKCFA 22 at [106].

[163] *Meridian Global Funds Management Asia Ltd v Securities Commission* [1995] 2 A.C. 500 at 506.

[164] Recognition that bodies corporate primarily operate through the concept of agency dates back at least as far as *Yarborough v Governor and Company of The Bank of England* (1812) 16 East 6 at 7, per Lord Ellenborough. See also *Ranger v Great Western Ry Co* (1854) 5 H.L. Cas. 73; *Ferguson v Wilson* (1866) L.R. 2 Ch.App. 77 at 89, per Cairns LJ; and *Citizen's Life Assurance Co Ltd v Brown* [1904] A.C. 423 (PC) at 426, per Lord Lindley; *Cargill v Bower* (1878) 10 Ch.D. 502 at 513; *Rolled Steel (Holdings) Ltd v British Steel Corp* [1986] Ch. 246 at 304; *Charles Terence Estates Ltd v Cornwall Council* [2012] EWCA Civ 1439; [2013] 1 W.L.R. 466 at [46]; *Ranson v Customer Systems Plc* [2012] EWCA Civ 841 at [20]; *VTB Capital Plc v Nutritek International Corp* [2013] UKSC 5; [2013] 2 A.C. 337 at [138]; *Petrodel Resources Ltd v Prest* [2012] EWCA Civ 1395; [2013] Fam Law 150 at [105] (reversed on other grounds [2013] UKSC 34; [2013] 2 A.C. 415); *Bilta (UK) Ltd v Nazir (No.2)* [2015] UKSC 23; [2016] A.C. 1 at [183].

[165] *Freeman & Lockyer v Buckhurst Park Properties (Mangal) Ltd* [1964] 2 Q.B. 480 at 505.

[166] See *Aberdeen Railway Co v Blaikie Bros* (1854) 1 Macq. 461 at 471, per Lord Cranworth LC: "The directors are a body to whom is delegated the duty of managing the general affairs of the company. A corporate body can only act by agents". See Watts, in *Agency Law in Commercial Practice* (Busch,

giving informal unanimous assent, involve participating in decision-making on the company's behalf with a view to alteration in the company's legal position, they act as co-agents.[167] The source of their authority is the incorporation statute and the company's constitutional documents.[168] It would not follow, however, that everything shareholders or directors do is as agent for the company; sometimes, for instance, directors may act on behalf of shareholders rather than the company (such as when acting for shareholders who have received a takeover offer), and it is also the case that in exercising some functions shareholders act solely in their own interests as principals (for example, in changing the constitution).

Normally, directors and shareholders will have actual authority, as opposed to apparent authority, only when they make their decisions in accordance with the procedures established by the statute and constitution.[169] However, both in relation to directors and shareholders the courts recognised early on that these groups could also bind their company informally, so long as it could be established that all directors,[170] or all shareholders,[171] as the case may be, assented unanimously to the decision being made on the company's behalf.[172] In respect of shareholders, Lord Hoffmann in the *Meridian* case approved the formulation of the concept of informal unanimous assent as follows[173]:

Macgregor and Watts eds, 2016), Ch.7. As to co-agency in general, see Article 11.

[167] See *Ciban Management Corp v Citco (BVI) Ltd* [2020] UKPC 21; [2020] 3 W.L.R. 705 at [37]–[38] (noted P. Watts, "Acting on the Apparent Authority of Shareholders" (2021) 137 L.Q.R. 20).

[168] In some circumstances, it may be necessary for both the board and the general meeting to resolve upon a matter before actual authority exists. In the Companies Act 2006, see, e.g. Pt 10, Ch.4 (transactions with directors requiring approval of members); s.601 (agreement to transfer of non-cash assets made by public company with subscriber to the memorandum of association); s.694 (approval of off-market purchases by company of its own shares). In many such cases, informal but unanimous action by directors and shareholders would be adequate.

[169] *Rolled Steel Products (Holdings) Ltd v British Steel Corp* [1986] 1 Ch. 246 at 304. For the usual authority of individual directors, see below, para.3-029.

[170] *Reuter v Electric Telegraph Co* (1856) 6 E. & B. 341; *Re Portuguese Consolidated Copper Mines Ltd Ex p. Badman* (1890) 45 Ch.D. 16; *TCB Ltd v Gray* [1986] Ch. 621 at 637, affirmed [1987] Ch. 458; *Haddow Nominees Ltd v Rarawa Farm Ltd* [1981] 2 N.Z.L.R. 16; *Base Metal Trading Ltd v Shamurin* [2004] EWCA Civ 1316; [2005] 1 All E.R. (Comm) 17.

[171] The concept of informal unanimous assent seems to have its origins in an implication into the deeds of partnerships: see *Const v Harris* (1824) T. & R. 496 at 522, per Lord Eldon LC; and *Re Vale of Neath and South Wales Brewery Co, Morgan's Case* (1849) 1 De G. & S. 750 at 776 (joint stock company). The assent need be only of voting shareholders: *Jackson v Dear* [2012] EWHC 2060 (Ch) at [68]; reversed on other issues [2013] EWCA Civ 89; [2014] 1 B.C.L.C. 186. Difficult issues arise, however, where the assent is only of the beneficial owner of shares. If the legal owner has delegated particular, or all, decision-making to the beneficial owner, then the latter is likely to have authority to bind the former: see Watts (2006) 122 L.Q.R. 15; and *Ciban Management Corp v Citco (BVI) Ltd* [2020] UKPC 21; [2020] 3 W.L.R. 705 at [47].

[172] *Meridian Global Funds Management Asia Ltd v Securities Commission* [1995] 2 A.C. 500 at 506; approving *Multinational Gas and Petrochemical Co v Multinational Gas and Petrochemical Services Ltd* [1983] Ch. 258. Other leading cases include *Salomon v Salomon & Co Ltd* [1897] A.C. 22 at 57; *Ho Tung v Man On Insurance Co Ltd* [1902] A.C. 232; *Re Duomatic Ltd* [1969] Ch. 975; *Cane v Jones* [1981] 1 All E.R. 533; and *Atlas Wright (Europe) Ltd v Wright* [1999] 2 B.C.L.C. 30; *Randhawa v Turpin* [2017] EWCA Civ 1201. For further discussion, see *Gower's Principles of Modern Company Law* (10th edn), at paras 15-15–15-21; Watts, *Directors' Powers and Duties*, (2nd edn, 2015), p.42 onwards.

[173] *Meridian Global Funds Management Asia Ltd v Securities Commission* [1995] 2 A.C. 500 at 506. See also *Bilta (UK) Ltd v Nazir (No.2)* [2015] UKSC 23; [2016] A.C. 1 at [187]. It may be more difficult to find that a company has omitted to take some step as a result of a failure of all its shareholders: see *Julien v Evolving Technologies and Enterprise Development Co Ltd* [2018] UKPC 2.

"... the unanimous decision of all the shareholders in a solvent company about anything which the company under its memorandum of association has power to do shall be the decision of the company".

Assent must be proven, but may be tacit and need not be manifested in concert,[174] and may occur before or after the events in question have taken place.[175] Informal unanimous assent cannot, however, be used to do anything that could not be achieved by formal resolution.[176]

Liquidators, administrators and receivers of companies can also be regarded as agents of the affected company for many, if not all, purposes,[177] although special rules apply to them, including as to the revocability of their authority. Reference should be made to specialist works on these topics.[178]

Directing mind and will—a tool of construction   In construing statutes,   **1-029** contracts, or other documents intended to have legal effect, it will frequently be necessary to consider how the text applies to the owners of businesses who rely on agents to run the business, as all companies must. Usually, there will be little difficulty in assuming that the drafter intended the acts, omissions, and states of mind of appropriate agents to be attributed to the owner. Occasionally, however, commonly as a result of the drafter's oversight, a rule may be drafted on the basis that an act or state of mind must be that of the principal personally. Such drafting is problematic for companies (and often absentee human owners of businesses as well). A court may have to conclude that the relevant rule does not apply to companies at all.[179] But it may also be necessary, in order to make the provision work with companies, to make a distinction between "mere" agents, and a person who is so centrally concerned with the company's operations, its "directing mind and will",[180] that that person's acts may be regarded as those of the company itself. Artifice is involved. Thus, it may be necessary by the use of such reasoning to determine whether there is "actual fault or privity" in the company itself[181]; and in criminal law it may be necessary to attribute mens rea to the company itself.[182] In *Meridian* it was held, again in a statutory context, that the person concerned need

---

[174] See *Evans v Smallcombe* (1868) L.R. 3 H.L. 249; *The Phosphate of Lime Co Ltd v Green* (1871) L.R. C.P. 43; *Re Bailey, Hay & Co Ltd* [1971] 1 W.L.R. 1357; *Pascoe Ltd v Lucas* (2000) 33 A.C.S.R. 357 at [264]; *Parker & Cooper Ltd v Reading* [1926] 1 Ch. 975; *Brick & Pipe Industries Ltd v Occidental Life Nominees Pty Ltd* (1990) 3 A.C.S.R. 649 at 684–689; affirmed (1991) 6 A.C.S.R. 464.

[175] *Bowthorpe Holdings Ltd v Hills* [2002] EWHC 2331 (Ch); [2003] 1 B.C.L.C. 226 at [54]. See further below, para.2-067.

[176] *Re New Cedos Engineering Co Ltd* [1994] 1 B.C.L.C. 797 at 814; *Madoff Securities International Ltd v Raven* [2011] EWHC 3102 (Comm) at [111] (no shareholder ratification of fraud).

[177] See, e.g. *Re Southern Pacific Personal Loans Ltd* [2013] EWHC 2485 (Ch); [2014] 1 Ch. 246 at [24] (liability under Data Protection Act 1998); *Dunphy v Sleepyhead Manufacturing Co Ltd* [2007] 3 N.Z.L.R. 602 (NZCA) at [22]. See also Wee and Tan, in *Agency Law in Commercial Practice* (Busch, Macgregor and Watts eds), Ch.8.

[178] See *Palmer's Corporate Insolvency* (looseleaf); Goode, *Principles of Corporate Insolvency* (5th edn); Lightman and Moss, *Law of Administrators and Receivers of Companies* (6th edn).

[179] See, for example, *Motel Marine Pty Ltd v IAC Finance Pty Ltd* (1964) 110 C.L.R. 9.

[180] *Lennard's Carrying Co v Asiatic Petroleum Co Ltd* [1915] A.C. 705 at 713–714, per Viscount Haldane LC; *Bilta (UK) Ltd v Nazir (No.2)* [2015] UKSC 23; [2016] A.C. 1 at [40]. Ideally, the statute itself will advert to how it is to apply to companies.

[181] *Lennard's Carrying Co v Asiatic Petroleum Co Ltd* [1915] A.C. 705 (on Merchant Shipping Act 1894 s.502).

[182] See, e.g. *DPP v Kent & Sussex Contractors Ltd* [1944] K.B. 146; *R. v ICR Haulage Ltd* [1944] K.B. 551; *Moore v Bresler Ltd* [1944] 2 All E.R. 515; *Tesco Supermarkets Ltd v Nattrass* [1972] A.C. 153; *Seaboard Offshore Ltd v Secretary of State for Transport* [1994] 1 W.L.R. 541 (HL).

not be the central directing mind and will, but may instead be the person whose functions within the company lead to the conclusion that his or her act must be regarded as that of the company for the purposes of the relevant provision.[183] This development in "identifying" certain conduct as the company's has been referred to in the context of perjury by a company as a "liberating principle",[184] but others have expressed caution in broadening the classes of person whose conduct is directly attributed to the company, at least in the context of criminal law.[185] Most of the cases that have required resort to direct attribution have concerned statutes, but there are also examples involving contracts.[186]

The distinction between direct corporate action and that via agents has also manifested itself in other ways. So, some statutes require personal signature, rather than that of an agent. To apply such a provision to a company, the signature must purport to be that of the company itself[187]; this is essentially a conceit.

The directing-mind-and-will concept has on occasion been extended beyond the resolution of problems in the construction of text, into the ordinary civil law,[188] usually on the basis of some perceived difficulty in using the general principles of the law of agency. However, these extensions are open to criticism on the basis that, in some instances, the rule that was said to preclude the use of agency law was misunderstood,[189] and, in others, the relevant rule of the law of agency was misstated.[190] The result, it has been argued, has been unhelpful distinctions in the common law between incorporated and unincorporated businesses, and the introduction of unnecessary complexity.[191] In one case, the Court of Appeal found itself having to disapply the notion of the "directing-mind-and-will" when, as the

---

[183] *Meridian Global Funds Management Asia Ltd v Securities Commission* [1995] 2 A.C. 500. See also *Sudarshan Chemical Industries Ltd v Clariant Produkte (Deutschland) GmbH* [2013] EWCA Civ 919; [2014] R.P.C. 6 at [132].

[184] *Odyssey Re (London) Ltd v OIC Run-Off Ltd* [2001] L.R.L.R. 1 at 64, per Brooke LJ.

[185] *Odyssey Re (London) Ltd v OIC Run-Off Ltd* [2001] L.R.L.R. 1 at 64, per Buxton LJ. See also *Attorney-General's Reference (No.2 of 1999)* [2000] Q.B. 796; *Cullen v R* [2015] NZSC 73; [2015] 1 N.Z.L.R. 715.

[186] See, e.g. *Americano's Ltd v State Insurance Ltd* (1999) 6 N.Z. Business L.C. 102, 892; *Bilta (UK) Ltd v Nazir (No.2)* [2015] UKSC 23; [2016] A.C. 1 at [198]. *Group Josi Re v Walbrook Insurance Co Ltd* [1996] 1 W.L.R. 1152 can be viewed as another instance: see Watts (2001) 117 L.Q.R. 300 at 326–328.

[187] *Newborne v Sensolid (Great Britain) Ltd* [1954] 1 Q.B. 45; *Hilmi & Associates Ltd v 20 Pembridge Villas Freehold Ltd* [2010] EWCA Civ 314; [2010] 1 W.L.R. 2750 (Leasehold Reform Housing and Urban Development Act 1993); *Williams v Redcard Ltd* [2011] EWCA Civ 466; [2011] 2 B.C.L.C. 350 (execution in two capacities under Companies Act 2006 s.44). But this distinction has no significance in connection with Companies Act 2006 s.51 (see below, paras 9-085 and 9-086): *Phonogram Ltd v Lane* [1982] Q.B. 938, a case under the original provision, s.9(2) of the European Communities Act 1972, which casts some doubt on the distinction in general); *UBAF Ltd v European American Banking Corp* [1984] Q.B. 713. See further below, para.8-197.

[188] See *El Ajou v Dollar Land Holdings Ltd* [1994] 2 All E.R. 685; *Odyssey Re (London) Ltd v OIC Run-Off Ltd* [2001] L.R.L.R. 1; and *Stone & Rolls Ltd v Moore Stephens Ltd* [2009] UKHL 39; [2009] 1 A.C. 1391.

[189] *Odyssey Re (London) Ltd v OIC Run-Off Ltd* [2001] L.R.L.R. 1 (rescission of judgment on the basis of perjury); and *Stone & Rolls Ltd v Moore Stephens Ltd* [2009] UKHL 39; [2009] 1 A.C. 1391 (application of maxim ex turpi causa non oritur actio).

[190] *El Ajou v Dollar Land Holdings Ltd* [1994] 2 All E.R. 685; *Lebon v Aqua Salt Co Ltd* [2009] UKPC 2; [2009] 1 B.C.L.C. 549 (imputation of agent's knowledge acquired before appointment); cf. *Bilta (UK) Ltd v Nazir (No.2)* [2015] UKSC 23; [2016] A.C. 1 at [197], per Lords Toulson and Hodge. See further below, paras 8-180 and 8-188.

[191] See Watts (2000) 116 L.Q.R. 525; Campbell and Armour [2003] C.L.J. 290; and Watts (2010) 126 L.Q.R. 14; see now *Bilta (UK) Ltd v Nazir (No.2)* [2015] UKSC 23; [2016] A.C. 1 at [41].

Supreme Court subsequently found, it was not necessary in the first place to impute the conduct to the company for the purposes of an action by the company against its controllers.[192] It is indeed arguable that no rule of the common law or equity requires the deployment of special rules for companies. One possible candidate is the rule that a deed must be signed personally or by power of attorney (itself signed personally).[193] Corporations cannot sign anything personally. Either the designated signatories for a corporation must be directly identified with the company or they remain agents and provide an exception to the general rule that deeds must be signed personally. The latter view has some very old support, see *Yarborough v Governor and Company of The Bank of England*, per Lord Ellenborough[194]:

> "As a corporation, they can do no act, not even affix their corporate seal to a deed, but through the instrumentality and agency of others."

Agency of companies for each other or for shareholders   It may appear tempt-   **1-030**
ing to regard a subsidiary company as agent for the principal company; or even the principal as agent for the subsidiary. This would have the effect of circumventing (rather than piercing) the corporate veil. English courts have not looked favourably on such arguments, and situations where there is such agency would be required to be proved by normal criteria,[195] as where a trader converted his or her business into a limited company and it was specifically provided that the new company would perform sale contracts entered into by the previous company as agent for the vendor.[196] Similarly, courts will not lightly find that companies, or their directors, are agents for their human shareholders, but cases will arise where this is the correct conclusion.[197] Sometimes too the facts may support a conclusion that a director or employee of a parent company has authority, actual or apparent, to bind

---

[192] See *Jetivia SA v Bilta (UK) Ltd* [2013] EWCA Civ 968; [2014] Ch. 52; discussed in Watts [2014] J.B.L. 162, upheld on different grounds in [2015] UKSC 23; [2016] A.C. 1.

[193] See below, para.2-040.

[194] *Yarborough v The Governor and Company of the Bank of England* (1812) 16 East 6 at 7.

[195] See *Savill v Chase Holdings (Wellington) Ltd* [1989] 1 N.Z.L.R. 257 (CA, affirmed PC); *Adams v Cape Industries Plc* [1990] Ch. 439 (doing business for purpose of jurisdiction as relevant to enforcement of foreign judgment); *Scriven v Scriven* [2015] EWHC 1690 (Ch) at [269]; *Dinglis Management Ltd v Dinglis Properties Ltd* [2019] EWCA Civ 127. See too *Telewest Communications Plc v Customs and Excise Commissioners* [2005] EWCA Civ 102; [2005] S.T.C. 481; *Premier Building and Consulting Pty Ltd v Spotless Group* (2008) 64 A.C.S.R. 114 at [339]. cf. *Globex Foreign Exchange Corp v Launt* 2011 NSCA 67.

[196] *Southern v Watson* [1940] 3 All E.R. 439. See also *Rainham Chemical Works Ltd v Belvedere Fish Guano Co Ltd* [1921] 2 A.C. 465 (newly formed company in possession of land as agent of the vendor); *Chief Executive of the New Zealand Customs Service v Nike New Zealand Ltd* [2004] 1 N.Z.L.R. 238 (parent company held buying agent of subsidiary); *Chandler v Cape Plc* [2011] EWHC 951 (QB) at [75]; affirmed [2012] EWCA Civ 525; [2012] 1 W.L.R. 3111 (parent company undertaking responsibility for health and safety issues for subsidiaries in the group); *Strategic Formwork Pty Ltd v Hitchen* [2018] NSWCA 54; *Vedanta Resources Plc v Lungowe* [2019] UKSC 20 (noted W. Day (2019) 135 L.Q.R. 551). cf. *Thompson v Renwick Group Plc* [2014] EWCA Civ 635 (noted W. Day [2014] L.M.C.L.Q. 454); *Okpabi v Royal Dutch Shell Plc* [2018] EWCA Civ 191; *AAA v Unilever Plc* [2018] EWCA Civ 1532.

[197] See *Prest v Petrodel Resources Ltd* [2013] UKSC 34; [2013] 2 A.C. 415 at [32]–[33]; explaining *Trustor AB v Smallbone (No.2)* [2001] 1 W.L.R. 1177; *Park's of Hamilton's (Holdings) Ltd v Campbell* [2014] CSIH 36; 2014 S.C. 726 (directors as negotiating agent for shareholders in takeover); *Wise v Jimenez* [2014] 1 P. & C.R. DG9 (company mere conduit for money provided by shareholder).

or otherwise act on behalf of a subsidiary, or vice versa.[198] Otherwise, it is recognised that:

"In commercial terms the creation of a corporate structure is by definition designed to create separate legal entities for entirely legitimate purposes which would often if not usually be defeated by any general agency relationship between them."[199]

It remains possible that a shareholder, including a parent company, may have done things in its own right that are sufficient to create a direct tortious liability.[200] Otherwise, the question of when the corporate veil may be pierced is a matter for company law.[201]

3. Agency distinguished from other relationships

1-031   The nature of agency is sometimes further elucidated by comparing it with other legal relationships. It is common, for instance, for someone to contract, or otherwise act, as principal, and not as an agent, even though he manifests an intention that another will benefit from the contract or other action. This is true even where, under modern law, that other party may sue on the contract pursuant to the Contracts (Rights of Third Parties) Act 1999.[202]

1-032   **Agent and trustee**[203]   Agents and trustees have many similarities, for both are persons who act on behalf of others and, though agency is essentially a common law notion, much of the law of agency is derived from, or is connected with, the law of trusts, which is of course equitable.[204] But the two roles, though they have considerable overlap, are conceptually different. An agent acts for another; a trustee

---

[198] See, e.g. *Enron (Thrace) Exploration and Production BV v Clapp* [2005] EWHC 401 (Comm) at [92]; *Cromwell Corp Ltd v Sofrana Immobilier (NZ) Ltd* (1992) 6 N.Z.C.L.C. 67, 997; *HKSAR v Luk Kin* [2016] HKCFA 81 at [33]. A director who ceases to be an executive director of the parent company and moves to become an executive director of a subsidiary normally ceases to have actual authority to bind the parent, though apparent authority may linger: see *Benourad v Compass Group Plc* [2010] EWHC 1882 (QB) at [113]. See too *Hudson Bay Apparel Brands LLC v Umbro International Ltd* [2010] EWCA Civ 949; [2011] 1 B.C.L.C. 259 (managing director of subsidiary with authority to administer US licences had no authority on behalf of parent company to vary those licences); *London Executive Aviation Ltd v The Royal Bank of Scotland Plc* [2018] EWHC 74 (Ch) at [295] (employee of parent company, and possibly parent company itself, acting as agent of subsidiary).
[199] *Peterson Farms Inc v C&M Farming Ltd* [2004] EWHC 21 (Comm); [2004] 1 Lloyd's Rep. 603 at [62], per Langley J (arbitrators had awarded damages for "parent losses"). See also *The Coral Rose* [1991] 1 Lloyd's Rep. 563 (borrower not agent); *Yukong Lines v Rendsburg Investment Corp (The Rialto) (No.2)* [1998] 1 Lloyd's Rep. 322 ("owners" of company not undisclosed principals of company as named charterer); *IBM United Kingdom Holdings Ltd v Dalgleish* [2017] EWCA Civ 1212 at [372] (motives of senior employee of parent company not attributed to subsidiary). See also Harris (2005) 23 Coy & Securities, L.J. 7.
[200] See *Vedanta Resources Plc v Lungowe* [2019] UKSC 20 at [49].
[201] As to which see *Gower's Principles of Modern Company Law* (10th edn), p.197 onwards; and *Prest v Petrodel Resources Ltd* [2013] UKSC 34; [2013] 2 A.C. 415. Fiduciary duties, or duties in negligence, can sometimes be owed to the company or person "behind" a company: see *Johnson v Gore Wood & Co* [2002] 2 A.C. 1; *Ratiu v Conway* [2005] EWCA Civ 1302; cf. *Diamantis v JP Morgan Chase Bank* [2005] EWCA Civ 1612.
[202] *Fortis Bank SA NV v Stemcor UK Ltd* [2011] EWHC 538; [2012] 1 All E.R. (Comm) 41 at [65].
[203] Street (1892) 8 L.Q.R. 220; *Restatement, Third*, § 8 and comment; *Restatement, Third, Trusts*, § 6 and comment; *Scott on Trusts* (5th edn), § 2.3.4.
[204] See Dowrick (1954) 17 M.L.R. 24 at 28–32.

holds property for another as principal, not as agent, but subject to equitable obligations.[205]

Thus a *trustee* holds money or property for another, to which the trustee has the legal title, but which belongs in equity to the beneficiary and to whom, accordingly, the trustee owes a number of obligations. The property may well be vested in the trustee by a person who is not the beneficiary. As such, a trustee may have no agency functions at all. Furthermore, a trustee's duty is to carry out the terms of the trust; the trustee is not (unless there is express provision to that effect) subject to control by the beneficiary, nor to revocation by the beneficiary of the trust. Lastly, the position of express trustee is a well-recognised and specialised one to which various forms of statutory regulation apply.[206]

An *agent*, on the other hand, may often hold no money or property for the principal at all; if the agent does receive money from or for the principal, the agent may merely be in the position of debtor to the principal in respect of it,[207] and if the agent receives goods they may be held as bailee only.[208] As such, therefore, an agent may have no trustee functions or liabilities at all. The agent may well be subject to some degree of control by the principal, and an agent's authority can normally be revoked.[209] The agent's function is too varied in the many spheres in which it may operate to be the subject of general statutory regulation, though statutes may affect particular types of agent or agency situation.[210]

But of course a trustee *may* also in appropriate circumstances have agency powers. This may particularly be so when there are two or more trustees, and the issue arises whether one trustee becomes an agent for the others. Although the starting assumption of equity is that trustees are expected to act unanimously, in relation to any legal property (or rights recognised at law) that the trustees may hold together, each trustee would have the powers at law of any other co-owner, and co-owners may generally confer agency powers on others, including their colleagues.[211] This is so even if the delegation were to involve a breach of trust. Equally, where the express or implied terms of the trust permit delegation of one or more tasks involving alteration of the trustees' legal relations, then the delegate, even if one of the trustees, would be an agent. By the same token, an agent *may* hold money or property as trustee, whether express or constructive[212]: the principal may well seek to secure this in order to achieve protection should the agent become insolvent.[213] Sometimes agents hold as bare trustees: in such cases the agency function predominates.[214] And agents are subject to fiduciary duties which usually lead also to money which they receive improperly being regarded as money of the

---

[205] See, e.g. *Hunt v Hosking* [2013] EWCA Civ 1408 at [37].
[206] Trustee Act 1925; Trustee Delegation Act 1999; Trustee Act 2000.
[207] e.g. *Neste Oy v Lloyd's Bank Plc* [1983] 2 Lloyd's Rep. 658, below, para.6-041.
[208] e.g. a factor: below, para.1-046.
[209] See Article 120.
[210] e.g. Powers of Attorney Act 1971; Estate Agents Act 1979 (as amended by Enterprise Act 2002); Commercial Agents (Council Directive) Regulations 1993.
[211] See further below, para.2-022. See, Watts, in *Equity, Trusts and Commerce* (Davies and Penner eds, 2017), Ch.2. Note that co-owners are not automatically agents of one another: see *Kennedy v De Trafford* [1897] A.C. 180 at 188.
[212] Or he may hold under a *Quistclose* trust: see *Lewin on Trusts* (20th edn), para.9-040 onwards.
[213] See Comment to Article 43; Articles 49 and 51.
[214] e.g. *Trident Holdings Ltd v Danand Investments Ltd* (1988) 49 D.L.R. (4th) 1, where it was held that a bare trustee subject to the control of beneficiaries was their agent and could bind them by contract.

principal held upon constructive trust, and hence subject to a proprietary claim.[215] But, it does not follow that all bare trustees are agents. A bare trustee would usually contract as principal only, if directed to sell the trust property by the beneficiary, and similarly would receive moneys on a disposition as principal.[216]

Thus the two functions, though conceptually distinct, may be difficult to differentiate: one person may have both capacities in relation to another.[217]

1-033   **Agent and bailee**[218]   Like a trustee, a bailee holds for another, but only holds as possessor, and ownership remains in the bailor. The notion of bailment is moreover restricted to chattels, and does not of itself involve control by the bailor. An agent may hold no property for the principal at all; or may hold property as trustee. Equally, a bailee as such may have no agency powers.[219] However, an agent *may* hold the principal's chattels as bailee: this was the practice, for example, of the nineteenth-century factor.[220] And a bailee *may* sometimes be regarded as having agency powers to do such things as are reasonably incidental to the use of the goods which the bailee holds, e.g. have them repaired, in which connection an artificer's lien created by the agent may be valid against the principal.[221] The authority may, in accordance with normal principles, be actual, express or implied,[222] or apparent[223]: in the latter case limitations on authority may be ineffective against a third party who did not know of them.[224] Again, the categories are not mutually exclusive: one person may have both capacities in relation to another, and indeed that of trustee also. Thus a commercial intermediary may be a bailee of goods, an agent to sell them and a trustee of the proceeds of sale.

1-034   **Agent and employee; agent and independent contractor**   The dichotomy of employee (or servant) and independent contractor stems from the law of tort. Although something turns on the nature of the tort, a principal is generally vicariously liable for torts committed by employees that have a close connection with their employment, but is not generally liable for torts committed by independent

---

[215] Articles 43–53.

[216] See *Ingram v IRC* [2000] 1 A.C. 293 at 305; *Skandinaviska Enskilda Banken AB (Publ) v Conway* [2019] UKPC 36 at [88]–[89]; and *AWH Fund Ltd v ZCM Asset Holding Co (Bermuda) Ltd* [2019] UKPC 37 at [84].

[217] See also *Pople v Evans* [1969] 2 Ch. 255, where it was held that an agent who sued on behalf of an undisclosed principal was not a trustee for the purposes of estoppel *per rem judicatam*. The beneficiary of a bare trust is not an agent of the trustee: *Stait v Femner* [1912] 2 Ch. 504 at 511. See *British Energy Power & Trading Ltd v Credit Suisse* [2008] EWCA Civ 53; [2008] 2 All E.R. (Comm) 524; [2008] 1 Lloyd's Rep. 413 ("as agent and security trustee" in context of syndicated loan agreement); cf. *Granada Group Ltd v Law Debenture Pension Trust Corp Plc* [2016] EWCA Civ 1289; [2017] Bus. L.R. 870 at [45].

[218] Fridman (1964) 114 L.J. 265.

[219] See *Buxton v Baughan* (1834) 6 C. & P. 674; *Cassils & Co v Holden Wood Bleaching Co* (1914) 112 L.T. 373; *Pennington v Reliance Motor Works Ltd* [1923] 1 K.B. 127; cf. *Smith v General Motor Cab Co Ltd* [1911] A.C. 188. See also *Bart v British West Indian Airways Ltd* [1967] 1 Lloyd's Rep. 239 (person collecting and forwarding football pool coupons not agent of investors to make contract with carrier).

[220] See below, para.1-046. Another example is an auctioneer.

[221] *Tappenden v Artus* [1964] 2 Q.B. 185. See also *Coldman v Hill* [1919] 1 K.B. 443 at 456. cf. *Gallimore v Moore* (1867) 6 S.C.R. (N.S.W.) 388.

[222] *Singer Mfg. Co v L. & S.W. Ry Co* [1894] 1 Q.B. 833; *Keene v Thomas* [1905] 1 K.B. 136; *Greene v All Motors Ltd* [1917] 1 K.B. 625. See Articles 24 onwards.

[223] *Albemarle Supply Co Ltd v Hind & Co* [1928] 1 K.B. 307; *Bowmaker Ltd v Wycombe Motors Ltd* [1946] 1 K.B. 505 at 509.

[224] See cases cited above, fn.221; Articles 72 and 83.

contractors. The difference traditionally turned on the degree of control exercised. A servant has been defined as a:

"person employed by another to do work for him on terms that he, the servant, is to be under the control and directions of his employer in respect of the manner in which his work is to be done."[225]

An independent contractor has been defined as:

"one who undertakes to produce a given result, but so that in the actual execution of the work he is not under the orders or control of the person for whom he does it, and may use his discretion in things not specified beforehand."[226]

Much space has been devoted in books to considering the relationship between these figures and the agent.[227] It is submitted that the controversy is somewhat beside the point. Some employees have agency powers, and these may be (as in the case of a manager) very wide; in other cases (e.g. a domestic employee) they may be very limited. Others have no agency powers. Many agents (e.g. brokers) could be called independent contractors; other independent contractors (e.g. repairers) are unlikely to have agency powers. An independent contractor who has authority to alter another's legal relations is likely to be an agent, and one who does not is unlikely to be treated as an agent.[228] Persons may exercise agency powers who fall into neither category: an obvious example is a gratuitous agent.

Distributors, concessionnaires and franchisees[229] Suppliers of the goods of a   **1-035**
manufacturer, whether on a retail or wholesale basis, who have some form of concession as a regular stockist, distributor or franchisee are often described as "agent", "selling agent", "main agent" and the like, for the manufacturer of the goods which they supply. Although it is possible that a distributor is an agent in the common law sense,[230] it is nowadays much more likely that the distributor actu-

---

[225] *Salmond and Heuston on the Law of Torts* (21st edn), p.434; wording approved in *Hewitt v Bonvin* [1940] 1 K.B. 188 at 191. See also *Ready Mixed Concrete (South East) Ltd v Minister of Pensions and National Insurance* [1968] 2 Q.B. 497. The substance overrides the form: a person who purports to be, or to be employed as, "labour only subcontractor" may be a servant or employee: see *Ferguson v John Dawson & Partners (Construction) Ltd* [1976] 1 W.L.R. 1213; *O'Kelly v Trusthouse Forte Plc* [1984] Q.B. 90. See also *Australian Mutual Provident Society v Chaplin* (1978) 18 A.L.R. 385; *Chadwick v Lypiatt Studio Ltd* [2018] EWHC 1986 (Ch) at [89]. As to vicarious liability, see Article 90.

[226] Pollock, *Torts* (15th edn), p.63. See also *Honeywill & Stein Ltd v Larkin Bros Ltd* [1934] 1 K.B. 191 at 196.

[227] Powell, pp.7–24; Fridman, para.1.28–1.30; Stoljar, pp.3–5; *Restatement, Third*, Reporter's Notes to § 1.01. See also *Lower Hutt City v Att.-Gen.* [1965] N.Z.L.R. 65. An agent can still be an employee though he is rewarded principally by commissions: *Hanna v Imperial Life Assurance Co of Canada* [2007] UKPC 29 (insurance agent required to work full-time for principal, eligible for company's pension plan, all equipment provided by principal, seconded to a management role for a period). Similarly, the fact that a contractor is described as such and is paid by an employment agency does not preclude his being an employee of the party for whom he performs services: *Cable & Wireless Plc v Muscat* [2006] EWCA Civ 220; [2006] I.C.R. 975.

[228] See *Alliance Craton Explorer Pty Ltd v Quasar Resources Pty Ltd* [2013] FCAFC 29 at [72]–[74].

[229] The topic of franchising is a specialised one. See, e.g. Pratt, *Franchising: Law and Practice* (looseleaf); Mendelsohn, *Guide to Franchising* (7th edn); Adams, Hickey and Prichard-Jones, *Franchising* (5th edn). For a case where a franchising company was held to have ordered goods as agent for its franchisee, see *Toycorp Ltd v Milton Bradley Australia Pty Ltd* [1992] 2 V.R. 572.

[230] This seems to have been a practice more favoured some time ago. See *Williamson v Rover Cycle*

ally buys from the manufacturer and resells to its own customer. In one case the typical position was made very clear by a clause reading:

> "The term 'agent' is used in a complimentary sense only, and those firms whom we style our agents are not authorised to advertise, incur any debts, or transact any business whatever on our account, other than the sale of goods which they may purchase from us; nor are they authorised to give any warranty or make any representation on our behalf other than those contained in the above guarantee."[231]

Such a person or concern may have limited agency functions such as those of guarantee referred to, or as to transmission of complaints and rectification of faults. But in general the relationship is an adverse commercial relationship quite different from agency and is therefore not treated in this book except for the purpose of distinguishing it from agency. In continental European countries and elsewhere, the protection given to commercial agents[232] may sometimes be extended to distributors and the like. The EC Directive on this subject is, however, confined to commercial agents, and in the UK there has therefore been no reason to extend it further. The analogy of agency is not normally followed where a purchase for resale is identified: the contract is one of sale. Any additional relationship between the parties to a distributorship agreement turns on the terms of the particular contract and such contracts therefore require careful drafting.

There is however overlap between such distributors and true agents in that the contracts under which both act may be affected by mandatory general rules such as those of EC competition law[233] and those relating to restraint of trade.[234] Indeed, the restrictions contractually imposed on distributors, such as requirements not to compete, sometimes place them under the manufacturer's control in a way that makes the analogy of agency not inappropriate. Thus in an important case the High Court of Australia were split by three to two on the question whether a particular distributorship contract gave rise to fiduciary duties.[235] Such distributors may also hold goods as bailees only, and in general their contracts may contain reservation of title clauses, so-called "*Romalpa*" clauses,[236] which in authorising the distributor to resell goods on which the seller has reserved title may use expressly or by

---

Co Ltd [1901] 2 I.R. 189 at 615; *Sproule v Triumph Cycle Co Ltd* [1927] N.I. 83.

[231] *Sproule v Triumph Cycle* [1927] N.I. 83 (where the distributor was nevertheless held an agent). Such clauses are not uncommon. In *Vogel v R. & A. Kohnstamm Ltd* [1973] Q.B. 133 at 136 such a concern was said (in the context of enforcement of a foreign judgment) to be "in no legal sense of the word an agent at all". See also *The Kronprinzessin Cecilie* (1917) 33 T.L.R. 292; *W.T. Lamb & Son v Goring Brick Co Ltd* [1932] 1 K.B. 710; *B. Davis Ltd v Tooth & Co Ltd* [1937] 4 All E.R. 118; *Martin-Baker Aircraft Co Ltd v Canadian Flight Equipment Ltd* [1955] 2 Q.B. 556 ("selling agents").

[232] See Ch.11.

[233] See, e.g. Bellamy and Child, *European Union Law of Competition* (8th edn), especially Ch.7; Whish, *Competition Law* (9th edn).

[234] See, e.g. *Chitty on Contracts* (33rd edn), Vol. 1, para.16-106 onwards.

[235] *Hospital Products Ltd v US Surgical Corp* (1984) 156 C.L.R. 41. See also *Cadbury Schweppes Inc v FBI Foods Ltd* [1999] 1 S.C.R. 142; (1999) 167 D.L.R. (4th) 577 (product licensing agreement); *BB Australia Pty Ltd v Danset Pty Ltd* [2018] NSWCA 101.

[236] See *Aluminium Industrie Vaassen BV v Romalpa Aluminium Ltd* [1976] 1 W.L.R. 676; *Re Bond Worth Ltd* [1980] Ch. 228; *Borden (UK) Ltd v Scottish Timber Products Ltd* [1981] Ch. 25; *Re Peachdart Ltd* [1984] Ch. 131; *Clough Mill Ltd v Martin* [1985] 1 W.L.R. 111; *Fairfax Gerrard Holdings Ltd v Capital Bank Plc* [2007] EWCA Civ 1226; [2008] 1 Lloyd's Rep. 297 (party had actual authority to pass title to goods, which was effective even though acquirer could not establish apparent authority or one of the exceptions to the *nemo dat* principle); *FG Wilson (Engineering) Ltd v John Holt & Co (Liverpool) Ltd* [2013] EWCA Civ 1232; [2014] 1 W.L.R. 2365, discussed Gullifer [2014] L.M.C.L.Q. 564; *Unitherm Heating Systems Ltd v Wallace* [2015] IECA 191. See below,

implication the terminology of agency. The question whether a power of resale is exercised as agent would affect the liability and rights on that sale of the original seller and/or its right to the proceeds of sale.[237] Comparable principles for determining whether a trader operates independently or as an agent apply to franchisees of services as to franchisees of goods.[238]

It is always a question of fact whether someone is a franchisee or an agent. The mere use of the language of "licensee" will not preclude there being an agency, if in fact the licensee is intended to find customers who will have direct links with the "licensor".[239]

Agent and seller; agent and buyer   The above discussion raises the distinction   **1-036** between agency and sale. These relationships, unlike the others dealt with above, are mutually exclusive: in respect of a particular transaction a person cannot be acting as agent if a buyer from or seller to his principal and vice versa.[240] Sale is a commercially adverse relationship; agency involves a fiduciary relationship of trust and confidence. The solution to commercial disputes may frequently turn on whether the parties are to be regarded as parties to one or the other relationship. Thus a manufacturer may contract not to market its goods through anyone but a particular supplier, who is said to be "sole" or "exclusive agent". If the supplier is on the true construction of the agreement a buyer from the manufacturer, the manufacturer may be in breach of contract if it sells the goods personally[241]; but if the supplier is a true agent the manufacturer will usually be entitled to sell personally as well.[242] If the supplier buys from the manufacturer and resells, it is the supplier who answers to the ultimate buyer for the quality of the goods, and the manufacturer is liable, in the absence of other indications, in tort or by statute only.[243] If the supplier is the manufacturer's agent, the supplier's liability to the ultimate buyer may turn on

---

para.8-165; and *Chitty on Contracts* (33rd edn), Vol.2, para.44-173 onwards.

[237] Reynolds (1978) 94 L.Q.R. 224 at 235–238; Watts (1986) 6 O.J.L.S. 456.

[238] *ACN 007528207 Pty Ltd v Bird Cameron* (2005) 54 A.C.S.R. 505 (see above,fn.32).

[239] *Heperu Pty Ltd v Morgan Brooks Pty Ltd (No.2)* [2007] NSWSC 1438; reversed on other points [2009] NSWCA 84 (mortgage broker operated offices using independent agents, called licensees; the licensees were held to be agents).

[240] The question has arisen in the specialised context of value added tax. See *Customs and Excise Commissioners v Johnson* [1980] S.T.C. 624 (provision of educational courses); *Potter v Customs and Excise Commissioners* [1985] S.T.C. 45 ("Tupperware" sold at specially convened functions); *Hill v Customs and Excise Commissioners* [1989] S.T.C. 424 (craft pottery); *Customs and Excise Commissioners v Paget* [1989] S.T.C. 773 (school photographs sold to parents); *Cornhill Management Ltd v Commissioners of Customs and Excise* [1991] 1 VAT.T.R. 1 (fund managers); *Customs and Excise Commissioners v Music and Video Exchange Ltd* [1992] S.T.C. 220 (profit on resale as commission); *Umbro International Ltd v Revenue and Customs Commissioners* [2009] EWHC 438 (Ch); [2009] S.T.C. 1345; *Kingston-upon-Thames RLBC v Moss* [2019] EWHC 3261 (Ch) (role of local authority in supply of water). See also *AMB Imballaggi v Pacflex Ltd* [1999] 2 All E.R. (Comm) 249; *Mercantile International Group Plc v Chuan Soon Huai Industrial Group Plc* [2002] EWCA Civ 288; [2002] 1 All E.R. (Comm) 788 (Commercial Agents Regulations); *R. (Jet Services Ltd) v Civil Aviation Authority* [2001] EWCA Civ 610; [2001] 2 All E.R. (Comm) 769.

[241] *W.T. Lamb & Sons v Goring Brick Co* [1932] 1 K.B. 710. It may, however, be that today the question might turn on whether the word "exclusive" had been used rather than "sole". See below, para.7-036.

[242] See *Bentall, Horsley & Baldry v Vicary* [1931] 1 K.B. 253 (an estate agent case); Article 58.

[243] *Sproule v Triumph Motor Cycle Co* [1927] N.I. 83; *International Harvester Co of Australia Pty Ltd v Carrigan's Hazeldene Pastoral Co* (1958) 100 C.L.R. 644; and see *Wheeler & Wilson Mfg. Co v Shakespear* (1869) 39 L.J.Ch. 36; *Pearlson Enterprises Ltd v Hong Leong Co Ltd* [1968] 1 Malaya L.J. 24 (where agent buys for resale, price increase imposed by manufacturer subsequent to resale contract may not be passed on). The statutory liability could be under the Consumer Protection Act

whether or not the supplier is what is above described as a commission agent.[244] If the supplier is, he or she may likewise answer as seller for quality, but will have the agent's rights of reimbursement and indemnity against the principal.[245] If not a commission agent, it is the manufacturer who is the seller and it, and not (normally[246]) the agent, must answer for quality of the goods.[247] If the supplier buys from the manufacturer and resells, money paid or due to the supplier from the ultimate buyer may be part of the supplier's assets in bankruptcy: if the supplier is an agent, it may not.[248] Similar issues arise in determining whether a party has assigned a debt or has simply given a mandate to collect payment of the debt as the party's agent.[249]

The distinction between agent and buyer for resale normally turns on whether the person concerned acts personally to make such profit as can be made, or is remunerated by pre-arranged commission.[250] A supplier who fixes the resale price is likely to be a buyer for resale[251]: but the fact that the resale price is fixed by the manufacturer does not necessarily make the supplier an agent,[252] for resale prices are frequently fixed by manufacturers. Exceptionally a buyer for resale may also be paid commission,[253] or an agent remunerated by being allowed to keep the excess over and above a stipulated price.[254] But the making of such a profit by an agent would normally be improper.[255]

Conversely, there may be difficulty in deciding whether a person who has agreed to procure goods for another is acting as that other's agent or seller. Again, the first question is to ask whether the party takes a profit on the resale which will make him or her a seller, or a commission, in which case the party is likely to be an agent and indeed the making of any further profit would usually be improper. But here another criterion also is relevant. If a person is selling, a seller normally undertakes absolutely to supply the goods on the terms agreed: but agents prima facie only binds themselves to use their best endeavours to make a contract or procure the goods, depending on whether they are a genuine agent or what is above described as a commission agent.[256] Thus a seller answers for defects in description and quality: an agent may not do so at all, because the agent is not a party to the

---

1987.

[244] See above, para.1-021.

[245] See, e.g. *Liu Wing Ngai v Lui Kok Wai* [1996] 3 Singapore L.R. 508.

[246] But see Article 98: the agent may sometimes be liable in addition.

[247] e.g. *Parkar's Music & Sports House v Motorex Ltd* [1959] E. Africa L.Rep. 534.

[248] *Ex p. White, re Neville* (1871) L.R. 6 Ch.App. 397; affirmed sub. nom. *John Towle & Co v White* (1873) 29 L.T. 78 (a case on *del credere* agency: below, para.1-042).

[249] See *Burridge v MPH Soccer Management Ltd* [2011] EWCA Civ 835.

[250] See *Weiner v Harris* [1910] 1 K.B. 285; *Restatement*, § 14 J (listing relevant factors); *Bosanquet v Mofflin* (1906) 6 S.R. (N.S.W.) 617; *AMB Imballaggi v Pacflex Ltd* [1999] 2 All E.R. (Comm) 249; *Jackson v Royal Bank of Scotland* [2000] C.L.C. 1457; *Hannaford v Australian Farmlink Pty Ltd* [2008] FCA 1591; cf. above, para.1-016.

[251] *Ex p. White, re Neville* (1871) L.R. 6 Ch.App. 397; *Jones v Southwark LBC* [2016] EWHC 457 (Ch) at [52].

[252] *Michelin Tyre Co Ltd v McFarlane (Glasgow) Ltd* (1917) 55 Sc.L.Rep. 35 (a House of Lords case containing a full review of the authorities, and again on *del credere* agency: below, para.1-042).

[253] *Kelly v Enderton* [1913] A.C. 191; *Gannow Engineering Co Ltd v Richardson* [1930] N.Z.L.R. 361. cf. *Kitson v P.S. King & Son Ltd* (1919) 36 T.L.R. 162 (publishing).

[254] *Ex p. Bright, re Smith* (1879) 10 Ch.D. 566 at 570; *Western Digital Corp v British Airways Plc* [2000] 2 Lloyd's Rep. 142 at 148; *Mercantile International Group Plc v Chuan Soon Huat Industrial Group Plc* [2002] EWCA Civ 288; [2002] 1 All E.R. (Comm) 788.

[255] Articles 45–48.

[256] See *Anglo-African Shipping Co of New York Inc v J. Mortner Ltd* [1962] 1 Lloyd's Rep. 610; above,

contract,[257] or if is a commission agent may only answer for failure to carry out instructions as closely as is practicable.[258]

There may also in either situation be repercussions as regards the damages obtainable: the measure of damages appropriate to a breach of a contract of sale may not be applicable to breach of the agent's duty.[259] Questions of the passing of property also may depend on how the case is analysed.[260]

Each transaction must be examined on its facts, considering the extent to which an agent's duties are appropriate. Much turns on the extent to which the principal can call for an account, for the duty to account is a typical feature of the agent's position.[261] The ways in which the parties describe themselves are not conclusive. "There is no magic in the word 'agency.' It is often used in commercial matters where the real relationship is that of vendor and purchaser."[262] There may indeed be reasons for principal and agent adopting the relationship of vendor and purchaser, for example, to avoid tax, exchange control rules or trade embargoes. It is also the case that the trading functions of intermediaries may imperceptibly alter over a period.[263]

Agent and borrower　A person may act as agent and as such use money stem-　**1-037**
ming from the principal: this money the agent may hold on trust for the principal, or receive it as the agent's own subject to a duty to return or account for it.[264] Alternatively, the agent may borrow from another on a commercial basis and hence receive money not as agent at all, even though he may appearing to conduct business for that other. This distinction may be important in the case of subsidiary companies.[265] Sometimes however there may be provisions in contracts which protect creditors' interests. They will not usually make the debtor the creditor's agent.[266] Questions can also arise as to whether a person providing finance for another has a charge over that other's property or whether the creditor buys it from that other, who then resells as the creditor's agent.[267]

Agent and person supplying services　An agent obviously supplies services.　**1-038**
Most persons supplying services, however, do so on a commercially adverse basis: that is to say, as in the case of sellers, they supply their services for the best price

---

para.1-021.

[257] See *Ireland v Livingston* (1872) L.R. 5 H.L. 395; *Brown & Gracie v F.W. Greene & Co Pty Ltd* [1960] 1 Lloyd's Rep. 289.

[258] See *Johnston v Kershaw* (1867) L.R. 2 Ex. 82; *Butlers (London) Ltd v Roope* [1922] N.Z.L.R. 549; *Downie Bros v Henry Oakley & Sons* [1923] N.Z.L.R. 734.

[259] *Cassaboglou v Gibb* (1883) 1 Q.B.D. 797, Illustration 4 to Article 69.

[260] See Article 69.

[261] *Michelin Tyre Co Ltd v McFarlane (Glasgow) Ltd* (1917) 55 Sc.L.Rep. 35; Article 52.

[262] *Ex p. White, re Neville* (1871) L.R. 6 Ch.App. 397 at 399. cf. *Weiner v Harris* [1910] 1 K.B. 285, where a person buying on sale or return was held an agent. See also *Livingstone v Ross* [1901] A.C. 327; *Garnac Grain Co Inc v H.M.F. Faure & Fairclough Ltd* [1968] A.C. 1130n.

[263] See Hill, "The Broker and the Commodity Markets" in *New Directions in International Trade Law* (UNIDROIT, 1977), Vol.2, p.523 onwards.

[264] See below, para.6-041.

[265] For an example of the second situation, see *Atlas Maritime Corp v Avalon Maritime Ltd (The Coral Rose) (No.1)* [1991] 4 All E.R. 796. Related problems occur in connection with receivers appointed by debenture holders: e.g. *Gosling v Gaskell* [1897] A.C. 575; see Goode, *Principles of Corporate Insolvency Law* (5th edn), paras 10-01 and 10-41 onwards.

[266] But see *A. Gay Jenson Farms Co v Cargill Inc* 309 N.W. 2d 285 (Minn. 1981); see further Hynes (1991) 58 Tenn.L.Rev. 635.

[267] See *Welsh Development Agency v Export Finance Co Ltd* [1992] B.C.L.C. 148.

that they can obtain. This is true of, for example, a repairer or a portrait painter. The mere fact, therefore, that one person undertakes work at the other's request and for the other's benefit is insufficient to establish agency.[268] Such a person normally owes a duty of best endeavours only, but is not usually remunerated on commission and owes no fiduciary duties. An agent offers services of a personal and confidential type: as such the agent is subject to fiduciary duties also. There is, however, an intermediate category. Some persons offering personal services, such as solicitors, charge fees rather than commission (though their fees may in some way be controlled); but in so far as they give advice and may have agency powers they are under fiduciary duties not as regards profits made from the exercise of their profession, but in respect of information held and profits made from their special positions vis-à-vis their clients.[269] This is true also of others, who if their work is directed towards a fixed target which may be valued may actually be remunerated by commission also, such as patent agents,[270] travel agents,[271] or even persons assisting in the preparation of a contractual offer or bid.[272] All these, other than those who render commercial services on a purely commercial basis, may attract some, but not all, of the features of agency law.

Article 2

FURTHER DEFINITIONS

1-039   (1)   A disclosed principal, for the purposes of this book, is a principal, whether identified or unidentified, whose interest in the transaction as principal is known to the third party at the time of the transaction in question.[273]

(2)   An identified principal, for the purposes of this book, is a disclosed principal whose name is known to the third party at that time.[274]

(3)   An unidentified principal, for the purposes of this book, is a disclosed principal whose name is not known, but who could if necessary be identified, at that time.[275]

(4)   An undisclosed principal, for the purposes of this book, is a principal whose

---

[268] See *Colonial Mutual Life Assurance Society Ltd v Producers and Citizens Co-operative Assurance Co of Australia Ltd* (1931) 46 C.L.R. 41 at 48–49; *Alliance Craton Explorer Pty Ltd v Quasar Resources Pty Ltd* [2013] FCAFC 29 at [72]; *Janus Capital Management LLC v Safeguard World International Ltd* [2016] EWHC 1355 (Ch) at [245].

[269] Articles 44–48.

[270] See *Re Frazer's Patent* [1981] R.P.C. 53, where a solicitor failed to pay the renewal fee for a patent, with the result that it lapsed. The solicitor may have been negligent, but it was held that the proprietor of the patent was not: the solicitor was merely the system set up by him for renewal, which was reasonable even though it had failed on the particular occasion.

[271] Nelson-Jones and Stewart, *A Practical Guide to Package Holiday Law and Contracts* (3rd edn). However, some travel agents and tour operators may in effect supply services as principal and not merely as an agent: see *Wong Mee Wan v Kwan Kin Travel Services Ltd* [1996] 1 W.L.R. 38; *Moore v Hotelplan Ltd (t/a Inghams Travel)* [2010] EWHC 276 (QB). See Package Travel and Linked Travel Arrangements Regulations 2018 (SI 2018/634).

[272] For an example of a claim on such a contract, see *Sharab v HRH Prince Al-Waleed bin Talal* [2008] EWHC 1893 (Ch); affirmed [2009] EWCA Civ 353.

[273] See Comment.

[274] See Comment.

[275] See Comment.

existence as such is not known to the third party at the time of the transaction in question.[276]

(5) A *del credere* agent is an agent who, in consideration of extra remuneration, which may be called a *del credere* commission, guarantees to the principal that third parties with whom the agent enters into contracts on behalf of the principal will duly pay any sums becoming due under those contracts.[277]

(6) A commercial agent is a self-employed intermediary who has continuing authority to negotiate the sale or purchase of goods on behalf of another person (the "principal"), or to negotiate and conclude the sale or purchase of goods on behalf of and in the name of that principal.[278]

(7) A general agent is an agent who has authority to act for the principal in all matters concerning a particular trade or business, or of a particular nature; or to do some act in the ordinary course of his trade, profession or business as an agent, on behalf of the principal.[279]

(8) A special agent is an agent who has only authority to do some particular act, or to represent the principal in some particular transaction, such act or transaction not being in the ordinary course of the agent's trade, profession or business.[280]

(9) A factor is an agent whose ordinary course of business is to sell or dispose of goods, of which the agent is entrusted with the possession or control by the principal.[281]

(10) A broker is an agent whose ordinary course of business is to negotiate and make contracts for the sale and purchase of goods and other property, of which the broker is not entrusted with the possession or control.[282]

(11) A nuntius, or other ministerial agent, is a person who alters a principal's legal position as a result of undertaking a specific task for the principal under close direction of the principal and sometimes in the principal's presence. Other labels are also sometimes applied, such as amanuensis, or conduit, depending on the task involved.

Comment

1-040 Many of the terms here defined are terms of art and are found in legal sources. Some are of limited contemporary significance, but their appearance in some of the leading cases warrants brief explanation here.

Disclosed principal (identified or unidentified); undisclosed principal **1-041** A principal is referred to in this work as disclosed in all situations where the third party knows that there is a principal involved, and it does not matter whether the principal is named to, or even identifiable by, the third party so long as the third party realises that there is a principal involved and does not at the time of the transaction in question think that he is dealing with the agent alone. The term "disclosed principal"

---

[276] See Comment.
[277] *Morris v Cleasby* (1816) 4 M. & S. 566; *Hornby v Lacy* (1817) 6 M. & S. 166: see Comment.
[278] Commercial Agents (Council Directive) Regulations 1993 reg.2(1): see Comment and Ch.11.
[279] See Comment; Articles 29 and 30.
[280] See Comment.
[281] *Baring v Corrie* (1818) 2 B. & A. 137 at 143; *Stevens v Biller* (1883) 25 Ch.D. 31 at 37; *Rolls Razor Ltd v Cox* [1967] 1 Q.B. 552 at 568. See Comment.
[282] *Baring v Corrie* (1818) 2 B. & A. 137 at 143; *Fowler v Hollins* (1872) L.R. 7 Q.B. 616. See Comment.

therefore includes both identified and unidentified[283] principals.[284] There might be a group or class of unidentified principals, amongst whom an agent allocates a contract.[285] The term "undisclosed principal" is reserved for cases where the third party does not intend to deal with a principal at all and intends to deal with the agent personally: these cases are regulated by special rules, and raise different equities. There are however difficult marginal cases where the existence of a principal was suspected or even known, but because the third party intended to deal with the agent, the undisclosed principal rules have been applied; and there are also cases which clearly involve unnamed but disclosed principals, where the term "undisclosed" has been used.[286] The matter is discussed under the heading of undisclosed principal,[287] where it will be seen that it is in fact not clear in exactly what circumstances a person may rank as an "undisclosed principal".

1-042 **Del credere agent**[288]   A *del credere* agent is an agent who for a special commission undertakes in effect the liability of a surety to the principal for the due performance, by the persons with whom the agent deals, of contracts made with them on the principal's behalf.[289] Such an agent's obligation is generally confined to answering for the failure of the other contracting parties, owing to insolvency or the like, to pay any ascertained sums which may become due from them as debts (largely in respect of the price of goods bought).[290] The principal is therefore not entitled to litigate with a *del credere* agent any disputes arising out of contracts made by the agent, nor is such an agent responsible to the third party for the due performance of the principal's contract.[291] In this respect the *del credere* agent is the antithesis of the commission agent, whose function is effectively the reverse.[292] A *del credere* agency may in principle be inferred from the course of conduct between the parties,[293] though such inference would nowadays be rare.[294] An agreement by an agent to act on a *del credere* commission is not a promise to answer for the debt,

---

[283] i.e. principals whose identity is known to the third party at the time of the transaction, and principals whose identities are not known, though it is known that there is a principal involved.

[284] See *Restatement, Third*, § 1.04. In earlier editions of this book the words "named" and "unnamed" were used, but these have been altered to conform with the *Restatement*. The change reflects the fact that an unnamed principal may nevertheless be identified.

[285] See below, para.2-067.

[286] See, e.g. *Benton v Campbell, Parker & Co* [1925] 2 K.B. 410 at 414; *Thornton v Fehr & Co* (1935) 51 Ll.Rep. 330; *Hersom v Bernett* [1955] 1 Q.B. 98; *Teheran-Europe Co Ltd v S.T. Belton (Tractors) Ltd* [1968] 2 Q.B. 545; *Marsh & McLennan Pty Ltd v Stanyers Transport Pty Ltd* [1994] 2 V.R. 232.

[287] See Article 76.

[288] Chorley (1929) 45 L.Q.R. 221; (1930) 46 L.Q.R. 11. See also Schmitthoff, 1970 I *Hague Recueil des Cours* 115 at 162–165; Hill (1968) 31 M.L.R. 623 at 639; Derham, *Law of Set-Off* (4th edn), paras 13-112–13-114; below, para.9-022.

[289] i.e. the person remains an agent and not a principal: see cases cited at fn.277 above. Such an agent cannot sue for advances made to the principal which are covered by sums due to the principal the payment of which the agent has guaranteed: *Graham v Ackroyd* (1853) 10 Hare 192. See also *Bramwell v Spiller* (1870) 21 L.T. 672.

[290] *Thomas Gabriel & Sons v Churchill & Sim* [1914] 3 K.B. 1272; *Rusholme & Bolton & Roberts Hadfield v S.G. Read & Co* [1955] 1 W.L.R. 146. Indeed, the principal would have to sue the third party to quantify the damages arising from the third party's insolvency: see at p.151. The execution of a deed of assignment does not establish a loss: *Montague Stanley & Co v J.C. Solomon Ltd* [1932] 2 K.B. 287.

[291] *Churchill & Sim v Goddard* [1937] 1 K.B. 92.

[292] See above, para.1-021.

[293] *Shaw v Woodcock* (1827) 7 B. & C. 73.

[294] *Nouvelles Huileries Anversoises SA v H.C. Mann & Co* (1924) 40 T.L.R. 804 (mere description in

default or miscarriage of another person within the meaning of s.4 of the Statute of Frauds but a contract of indemnity, and it is therefore not necessary that such an agreement should be evidenced in writing.[295]

A *del credere* agency would often in modern conditions involve liabilities which an ordinary commercial agent acting for commission would be reluctant to undertake, and has been largely superseded by documentary credits, credit guarantees, confirmations and similar methods of securing payment from overseas buyers undertaken by institutions with special expertise.[296] But it seems that such arrangements are still made in certain contexts, for example dealings with numerous and unknown buyers, or with parties in undeveloped countries.

Distinction between del credere agent and buyer Problems as to the distinction between agent and buyer arise conspicuously in the case of *del credere* agents. The general topic is discussed above,[297] but it should be noted that some of the leading cases have involved this type of agent.[298]   **1-043**

Commercial agent The term "commercial agent" stems from continental European legal systems and is not known to the common law. It is significant in English law now because of the EC Directive on Self-Employed Commercial Agents,[299] which regulates the relations between commercial agents and their principals, and in particular gives them special rights on termination of their agency. Such rights have long been known to continental legal systems, but were unknown to the common law. The Directive was implemented in Great Britain[300] by the Commercial Agents (Council Directive) Regulations 1993,[301] made under s.2(2) of the European Communities Act 1972 and effective on January 1, 1994. The rules for commercial agents as defined are therefore somewhat different from the general rules of agency law described in this bookwork. They are dealt with together as a unit in Chapter 11, where the definition given above is further expanded. They are also referred to at the relevant points in the description of the general rules of English law.   **1-044**

The remaining distinctions are mainly significant in the understanding of old cases.

General agent, special agent This distinction, an obvious and common sense one, is relevant to the question of the nature and extent of the authority conferred on the agent, and was principally significant in the early development of the doctrine of apparent authority. It was a general agent who had such authority and might bind   **1-045**

---

contract of agents as *del credere* agents did not constitute them such): *J.M. Wotherspoon & Co Ltd v Henry Agency House* (1961) 28 M.L.J. 86 (no *del credere* agency where no special commission paid).

[295] *Couturier v Hastie* (1852) 8 Exch. 40; *Wickham v Wickham* (1855) 2 K. & J. 478; *Sutton & Co v Grey* [1894] 1 Q.B. 285; *Walker Crips Stockbrokers Ltd v Savill* [2007] EWHC 2598 (QB).

[296] See further below, para.9-022.

[297] See above, para.1-035 onwards.

[298] *Ex p. White, re Neville* (1871) L.R. 6 Ch.App. 397; affirmed sub nom. *John Towle & Co v White* (1873) 29 L.T. 78; *Michelin Tyre Co Ltd v Macfarlane (Glasgow) Ltd* (1917) 55 Sc.L.Rep. 35.

[299] Directive 86/653 [1986] OJ L382/17.

[300] As to Northern Ireland, see Commercial Agents (Council Directive) Regulations (Northern Ireland) (SR 1993 No.483).

[301] SI 1993/3053, as amended by SI 1993/3173 and SI 1998/2868.

the principal by an act which the agent had been forbidden to do.[302] Similar reasoning appears to have been used in the civil law to fix the principal with liability for the agent's unauthorised acts.[303] But the doctrine of apparent authority is nowadays in England normally explained without reference to the distinction, but rather by invocation of the notion of estoppel or similar reasoning.[304] Therefore, though the distinction between general and special agents is a well-established one, it is doubtful whether it is of much utility in English law at the present day.[305]

1-046   **Factor, broker**[306]   The distinction between these was again of great importance in the nineteenth century, when many of the cases from which our present rules are derived were decided.[307] Some knowledge of the commercial practices of that time helps in understanding those cases. The distinction concerned commercial sales, but within that area of activity was general and not confined to particular trades. A factor was an agent for sale, often of goods sent from another country which the agent held on consignment: the agent had possession or control of the goods to be sold and usually sold in the agent's own name without disclosing the name of the principal.[308] Indeed, factors might not indicate whether they were dealing on behalf of a principal or on their own account. Such a person would readily be held to have apparent authority to sell the goods, or even to have apparent ownership of them, so that dispositions might be valid even if unauthorised. Payment to a factor was a good discharge even to a buyer who knew of the agency, and where the factor sold personally the factor had the right to sue for the price.[309] The broker is a figure who emerges later than the factor, a person who negotiates and makes contracts between buyers and sellers of goods whom the broker may never see: of such a person the above propositions are not therefore necessarily true. The broker should not sell in

---

[302]   See *Smith v M'Guire* (1858) 3 H. & N. 554; *Brady v Todd* (1861) 9 C.B. (N.S.) 592; *Butler v Maples* 76 U.S. 822 (1869). A dramatic example is *Hatch v Taylor* 10 N.H. 538 (1840) (complicated instructions regarding sale of a team of horses). See also Stoljar, pp.77–80. The meaning of "general agent" in the context of an insurance policy is considered in *Excess Life Assurance Co Ltd v Fireman's Insurance Co Ltd* [1982] 2 Lloyd's Rep. 599. In *Barrett v Irvine* [1907] 2 I.R. 462 it was held that a multiplicity of separately authorised transactions does not constitute a general agency (as to which also see *Pole v Leask* (1863) 33 L.J. Ch. 155 at 162).

[303]   Müller-Freienfels (1964) 13 Am.J.Comp.L. 193 at 341; Schmitthoff, 1970 I *Hague Recueil des Cours* 115.

[304]   See Comment to Article 72. The notion of usual authority can however be related to the concept of the general agent.

[305]   See also Müller-Freienfels (1964) 13 Am.J.Comp.L. 193 at 341; Seavey (1955) 1 Howard L.J. 79, where he approves the distinction on the ground that it facilitates the wider liability of an undisclosed principal; he had expressed a similar view in (1920) 29 Yale L.J. 859 at 882; Comment to Article 29. Contrast "The most useful thing that can be said about a special agent is that he is one who falls outside the ambit of any useful generalisation": Mechem, *Outlines of Agency* (4th edn), p.46. The notion of general agent is however utilised in the context of landlord and tenant in *Dun & Bradstreet Software Services Ltd v Provident Mutual Life Assurance Assn* [1998] 2 E.G.L.R. 175; cf. *Hexstone Holdings Ltd v AHC Westlink Ltd* [2010] EWHC 1280 (Ch); [2010] 32 E.G. 62; [2010] 2 E.G.L.R. 13 at [37]. But for a view that it provides a better route to liability for agents than the uncertainties of apparent authority see Brown [2004] J.B.L. 391.

[306]   See in general Munday (1977) 6 Anglo-Am.L.Rev. 221 (a valuable survey).

[307]   See Stoljar, pp.242–247.

[308]   *Baring v Corrie* (1818) 2 B. & A. 137 at 143; *Rolls Razor Ltd v Cox* [1967] 1 Q.B. 552 at 568. But he may do: cf. *Stevens v Biller* (1883) 25 Ch.D. 31. An interesting explanation is given in The Matchless (1822) 1 Hagg. 97. As to his discretion, see *Smart v Sandars* (1846) 3 C.B. 380 (see also (1848) 5 C.B. 895). See as to the general trade background Miller (1957) 24 U.Chi.L.Rev. 256.

[309]   *Drinkwater v Goodwin* (1775) 1 Cowp 251 at 255–256. As to the ways in which this could be explained in modern terminology see below, para.9-009.

the broker's own name[310] and payment to such a person would not be a good discharge,[311] though these were only prima facie rules. The distinction was far from clear. Thus a factor might act also as an independent merchant; and one person might act as both factor and broker. An understanding of the distinction is however essential for the reading of many nineteenth century cases: for example, several decisions are based on the notion that a person dealing with a broker must have known that the agent had a principal whether that was revealed or not, but would not necessarily know this of a factor.[312] Indeed, there was at that time the beginnings of an approach to agency which addressed nominate types of agent. But the term "factor" is little used in the above sense today (indeed it is used in other senses, e.g. that of credit factoring[313]); and the term "broker" has been applied to many more types of activity than the commodity broker referred to above, and is often applied to intermediaries whom the definition given does not fit at all, e.g. insurance brokers, mortgage brokers, shipbrokers. Further, the Factors Act 1889, the culmination of legislation formulating and extending the special rules applicable to unauthorised dispositions by factors and protecting those who dealt with them, introduced a new term for its purposes, that of "mercantile agent": this is discussed elsewhere.[314] The general distinction is therefore out of date, but important for the comprehension of early case law.

Nuntius and other ministerial agents   Sometimes a person may be asked to   **1-047**
undertake a specific task on behalf of a principal under close direction of the principal and sometimes in the principal's presence. The task may be no more than to deliver a document, or orally communicate the principal's decision, when delivery or communication, as the case may be, is likely to change the principal's legal position. Such a person may be called a nuntius, or messenger. The term is not, however, one of art, and there are various other cognates, such as amanuensis, functionary, ministerial agent, and conduit,[315] depending on the task. So, an amanuensis may be asked to sign a document for the principal, who perhaps because of physical disability may not be able to sign personally.[316] Another context is the courtroom, where a barrister in some circumstances may be no more than the mouthpiece of the client, having taken specific instructions from the client, perhaps at the request of the tribunal in order immediately to convey the answer to the tribunal.[317] It may be argued that a person while performing such tasks is not an agent at all, not least because in the absence of discretion there will be limited place for the application of fiduciary duties.[318] Nonetheless, the participation of the nuntius or other ministerial agent may have been critical in effecting a change in

---

[310] *Baring v Corrie* (1818) 2 B. & A. 137.
[311] *Linck, Moeller & Co v Jameson & Co* (1885) 2 T.L.R. 206.
[312] e.g. *Baring v Corrie* (1818) 2 B. & A. 137; *Armstrong v Stokes* (1872) L.R. 7 Q.B. 598 at 610. For a modern example see *N. & J. Vlassopulos Ltd v Ney Shipping Ltd (The Santa Carina)* [1977] 1 Lloyd's Rep. 478.
[313] See Ruddy, Mills and Davidson, *Salinger on Factoring* (5th edn). See also Steffen and Danziger, "The Rebirth of the Commercial Factor" (1936) 36 Col.L.Rev. 745.
[314] Article 87.
[315] See below, para.9-129 (ministerial agents not liable for conversion).
[316] See, e.g. *Barrett v Bem* [2012] EWCA Civ 52; [2012] Ch. 573 (signing will by direction of testator); *Ramsay v Love* [2015] EWHC 65 (Ch) at [7] (operation of signature machine by another).
[317] See the oblique reference to this idea in *Dunhill v Burgin* [2014] UKSC 18; [2014] 1 W.L.R. 933 at [31].
[318] See, e.g. *Torre Asset Funding Ltd v The Royal Bank of Scotland Plc* [2013] EWHC 2670 (Ch) at [30] (limited agency of lead bank for syndicated lenders, but more than mere postal service); *Marme*

the principal's legal position, one of the key features of agency. The issue whether or not a nuntius is an agent is likely to be significant only for a rule of law that requires personal action; the conclusion being that the proscription of delegation does not necessarily prohibit the use of a nuntius. In such cases, the relevant act is treated as effected by, as opposed to on behalf of, the principal. Such a rule is more likely to be statutory,[319] or created by a contract, since the normal position of the common law is that whatever can be done personally can be done by an agent.[320] But the rule, for example, that requires a deed to be executed by the party making the deed (unless an attorney is authorised by a separate deed to do so) can be met by the use of an amanuensis, with the principal present.[321]

Inversiones 2007 SL v Natwest Markets Plc [2019] EWHC 366 (Comm) at [444] (lead arranging bank not acting as agent in setting terms of financing). See further below, para.6-037.

[319] See, e.g. *Hilmi & Associates Ltd v 20 Pembridge Villas Freehold Ltd* [2010] EWCA Civ 314; [2010] 1 W.L.R. 2750 (Leasehold Reform Housing and Urban Development Act 1993), and fn.187, above.

[320] See below, para.2-017. See too para.2-023.

[321] See below, Article 10.

CHAPTER 2

CREATION OF AGENCY

1. GENERAL

Article 3

HOW AGENCY ARISES

(1) The relationship of principal and agent may be constituted—   **2-001**
   (a) by the conferring of authority by the principal on the agent, which may be express, or implied from the conduct or situation of the parties, and may or may not involve a contract between them;
   (b) retrospectively, by subsequent ratification by the principal of acts done on the principal's behalf.[1]
(2) A person may be liable under the doctrine of apparent authority in respect of another who is not that person's agent at all[2]; or may be estopped as against a third party from denying the existence of an agency relationship.[3]

Comment

This general statement seeks only to give an indication of the ways in which the   **2-002**
relationship of principal and agent can arise in the full sense, creating internal rights and duties between principal and agent and giving the agent external authority to affect the principal's legal relations with third parties.

Relevance of contract It has been explained in Chapter 1 that the essence of   **2-003**
agency must lie in a unilateral manifestation of will, but that very often arises from, or is accompanied by, a contract between principal and agent.[4] If there is no such contract there is still an internal relationship, though a non-contractual one. These features make it appropriate to attribute in exposition a fundamental role to consensual agency. One example where there is often but may not always be a contractual relationship between principal and agent is where an insurer appoints and pays for a solicitor to represent the insured in litigation by an outside party. In the leading case,[5] it was assumed that there was a contract between the solicitor and insured even though the solicitor was appointed and paid for by the insurer, but this

---

[1] Section 3.
[2] See Article 72.
[3] Article 21.
[4] See above, paras 1-005 and 1-006.
[5] *Groom v Crocker* [1939] 1 K.B. 194. See also *Re Crocker* [1936] Ch. 696 at 700–701; *Travelers Insurance Co Ltd v XYZ* [2019] UKSC 48 at [114]. cf. *Re Enterprise Insurance Co Plc, White v Ozon*

may not always be the case. But on any analysis the solicitor will act as fiduciary agent for the insured when representing the insured in claims brought by an outside party.[6]

2-004 **Ratification** A principal may ratify the unauthorised acts of a person who purported to act for the principal while having no actual authority. This in general retrospectively creates the relationship of principal and agent, and the full consequences of such relationship, but although the analogy of authority having been initially conferred is in many respects followed, the relationship cannot easily be said to arise by agreement. Further, certain special rules are found in this area to prevent the retroactivity from operating unfairly.[7] This, therefore, must be treated as a separate type of case. The doctrine of ratification applies also, and perhaps more commonly, to situations where the person who acts is already an agent, but exceeds the agent's authority. Since however it can also create agency it is most conveniently taken in this chapter.

2-005 **Apparent authority and estoppel** There is also a way in which some of the consequences of agency can arise, under the doctrine of apparent authority. Under this, principals may as against a third party be unable to deny that a person is or was their agent. The principal is here bound by the acts of the apparent agent: but the full relationship of principal and agent does not arise between them, the legal position being governed by rules which start from the assumption that there is no agreement between them, at least in respect of the transaction in question. Apparent authority is therefore referred to above as a way in which a person not already an agent can bind a principal.[8] But since its main application is to persons already agents, and only operates between principal and third party, discussion is deferred till Chapter 8, which deals with that relationship.[9] Reference is also made in Article 21 below to cases where a person is estopped by conduct, prior or subsequent, from disputing the validity of an unauthorised transaction entered into on the person's behalf. An agent may also be found to have sufficient apparent authority to bind the purported principal to a collateral contract of arbitration, or to a collateral contract designating a jurisdiction for determining disputes, without necessarily having such authority to conclude the main contract.[10]

Solicitors [2017] EWHC 1595 (Ch).

[6] *Groom v Crocker* [1939] 1 K.B. 194 at 226–227.

[7] Articles 16–19.

[8] See Article 3(2).

[9] See Article 72.

[10] See *Premium Nafta Products Ltd v Fili Shipping Co Ltd* [2007] UKHL 40; [2008] 1 Lloyd's Rep. 254 (arbitration clause); and *Deutsche Bank AG v Asia Pacific Broadband Wireless Communications Inc* [2008] EWCA Civ 1091; [2008] 2 Lloyd's Rep. 619 at [25] (jurisdiction clause). See further below, para.3-012.

Article 4

CAPACITY TO ACT AS PRINCIPAL

Capacity to contract or do any other act by means of an agent is co-extensive with the capacity of the principal alone to make the contract or do the act which the agent is authorised to make or do.[11]

2-006

Comment

"It would seem that the proper view should be that anyone may be a principal who has the mental power to act at all, and that if he is a person of no, or limited, contractual power, his incapacity should be reflected solely in the contract made for him by his agent, which contract would stand on the same footing as if he had made it in person."[12]

2-007

Such a simple approach, which is also formulated in this Article, cannot however be left without further comment, for where, as often, incapacity leads to voidable transactions, a more complex analysis may be necessary. As with most principles, there are likely also to be some exceptional cases.[13] It seems right to confirm, however, a general principle that if the would-be principal cannot bring about a legal result personally, it cannot be effected by an agent.[14]

Minors In old cases it is suggested that minors cannot appoint agents at all.[15] The dicta were wider than was necessary for the decisions in connection with which they were uttered,[16] and are nowadays interpreted restrictively. The following judicial statement may provide a better guide: "Whenever a minor can lawfully do an act on his own behalf, so as to bind himself, he can instead appoint an agent to do it for him".[17] This to some extent follows from the general principle that whatever a person may do personally can be done through an agent.[18] Thus a minor may by an agent enter into a contract that binds the minor in accordance with the general law[19]; and it has been held that a minor may authorise another to make admissions, even contrary to the minor's interest.[20] On the other hand, contracts which would not otherwise bind a minor will not do so merely because made through an adult agent; and a minor cannot by an agent, any more than is possible personally, make an irrevocable disposition taking effect by deed, for such a disposition is avoidable by the minor within a reasonable time of coming of age,[21] and the interposition of an agent should make no difference. This latter proposition probably does not,

2-008

---

[11] See further Article 6, below.
[12] Mechem, *Outlines of Agency* (4th edn), p.9. See also *Restatement, Third*, § 3.04.
[13] See Article 6.
[14] So, for example, if a partner cannot sue his or her partners in relation to moneys lent to or invested in the partnership except as part of an equitable accounting, neither can a receiver appointed to the affairs of the partner: see *Re Pinata Pty Ltd* [2012] NSWSC 162 at [52].
[15] *Zouch d. Abbot and Hallett v Parsons* (1765) 3 Burr. 1794 at 1804; *Doe d. Thomas v Robert* (1847) 16 M. & W. 778.
[16] See *Chaplin v Leslie Frewin (Publishers) Ltd* [1966] Ch. 71 at 96–97.
[17] *G. (A.) v G. (T.)* [1970] 2 Q.B. 643 at 652, per Lord Denning MR, limiting earlier dicta of his own in *Shephard v Cartwright* [1953] Ch. 728 at 735; affirmed on another point [1955] A.C. 431.
[18] Article 6.
[19] See *R. v Longnor (Inhabitants)* (1833) 4 B. & Ad. 647; *Doyle v White City Stadium Ltd* [1935] 1 K.B. 110.
[20] *G. (A.) v G. (T.)* [1970] 2 Q.B. 643, (where it was held that in the event there had been no authority).
[21] *Edwards v Carter* [1893] A.C. 360; *Paget v Paget* (1882) 11 L.R.Ir. 26; *Burnaby v Equitable*

however, extend to dispositions of property taking effect otherwise than by deed, e.g. by writing or delivery, though the matter is not clear.[22]

It is frequently said that a minor cannot execute a power of attorney appointing an agent. The cases cited, however, mostly concern warranty of attorney in litigation,[23] where minors are only permitted to act by their next friend or guardian ad litem. The true proposition may rather be that any deed disposing of a minor's property executed by an agent appointed by means of such a power would be voidable by the minor as if the minor had executed it personally: "an infant cannot appoint an agent to make a disposition of his property so as to bind him irrevocably".[24] But where the power of attorney is executed in deed form, which is now requisite,[25] it may be possible to argue that the deed itself is caught by this rule: that not only is the power revocable for the future, but the deed itself is also voidable. It seems that the contract (if there is a contract) with the agent is to be treated like a contract of service, and binding on the minor if it is for the minor's benefit[26]: the effect of this contract is of course a separate question from that of the validity of the agent's acts.[27]

2-009   **Mentally incapacitated persons**[28]   The general principle of the common law is that transactions entered into by a mentally incapacitated person are prima facie effective, and, in relation to transactions other than gifts, cannot be set aside unless the person with whom the transaction was entered into knew, or ought to have known, of the incapacity.[29] This principle is consistent with the higher level general principle that intention in the formation of contracts and other transactions is judged objectively. However, in cases of extreme incapacity, or where it can be established that for other reasons an actor had no appreciation whatsoever of the document to which he is said to have given consent, the transaction may be a nullity under the non est factum doctrine.[30] The incapacity in such a case will usually be apparent to the world, and the beneficiary of the document will often be aware of it too.

Although the case law on the topic is surprisingly thin, it is suggested that these

---

Reversionary Interest Society (1885) 28 Ch.D. 416 at 424; unless, presumably, the disposition is in pursuance of a contract which is in law binding on the minor. See also *Carnell v Harrison* [1916] 1 Ch. 328; *Chitty on Contracts* (33rd edn), para.9-036 onwards.

[22]   See *Chaplin v Leslie Frewin (Publishers) Ltd* [1966] 1 Ch. 71 at 90, 93, 94, 97. Sometimes of course the disposition may be in pursuance of a contract which is itself voidable: *Chaplin* [1966] Ch. 71.

[23]   e.g. *Oliver v Woodroffe* (1839) 4 M. & W. 650. See also *Zouch d. Abbot and Hallett v Parsons* (1765) 3 Burr. 1794; *Gibbons v Wright* (1904) 91 C.L.R. 423 at 447; Alcock, *Powers of Attorney* (1935), pp.63–64; Aldridge, *Powers of Attorney* (11th edn).

[24]   *G. (A.) v G. (T.)* [1970] 2 Q.B. 643, at 652, per Lord Denning MR. See *Megarry and Wade: Law of Real Property* (9th edn), Ch. 34.

[25]   Powers of Attorney Act 1971 s.1.

[26]   *Chaplin v Leslie Frewin (Publishers) Ltd* [1966] 1 Ch. 71. See further Webb (1955) 18 M.L.R. 461; *McLaughlin v Darcy* (1918) 18 S.R.(N.S.W.) 585.

[27]   See O'Hare (1970) 3 U.Tas.L.Rev. 312.

[28]   This paragraph replaced the text on this subject that appeared from the 13th edn (1968) to the 19th edn (2010), but is consistent with such material as there was on the subject in all editions before the 13th. For elaboration of the points made in this paragraph, see Watts [2015] C.L.J. 140. cf. Varney (2017) 37 Leg. Stud. 493; E. Varney, "Agency Contracts and the Scope of the Incapacity Defence in English Contract Law" [2020] J.B.L. 382.

[29]   *Molton v Camroux* (1849) 4 Exch. 17 at 19–20; *Imperial Loan Co v Stone* [1892] 1 Q.B. 599; *Daily Telegraph Newspaper Co Ltd v McLaughlin* (1904) 1 C.L.R. 243 at 272–273; affirmed [1904] A.C. 776 (PC); *Hart v O'Connor* [1985] A.C. 1000. As to gifts, see *Day v Day* [2013] EWCA Civ 280; [2014] Ch. 114 (principal sane, but mistaken gift made through innocent attorney was subject to rectification).

[30]   See *Saunders v Anglia Building Society* [1971] A.C. 1004.

principles apply to the creation of authority, actual or apparent, in an agent.[31] Hence, mental incapacity in a principal will not preclude the principal's conferring actual authority on an agent when the agent had no reason to know of the incapacity, and such authority will endure until the agent becomes aware of the incapacity (or the agency otherwise terminates under general principles).[32] There would, however, be no need for the principal, or someone on the principal's behalf, to take steps to terminate the mandate once the agent becomes aware of the incapacity. It ought not to matter whether or not the agent is appointed under a contract.[33] The same principles should apply to the existence of apparent authority, the incapacity of the principal not preventing any representation made by the principal to the third party as to the agent's authority from being effective, unless the third party is aware of the incapacity.[34] There is insufficient reason for treating representations of authority made to the third party by the principal differently from communications which would be sufficient to create a contract directly between those parties. Where mental incapacity occurs after the grant of authority, or the holding out of authority, the relevant authority will terminate only once known (or it ought to have been known) to the agent or third party, as the case may be.[35]

The fullest judicial discussion is in *Daily Telegraph Newspaper Co Ltd v McLaughlin*,[36] where, however, the High Court of Australia was relieved from ruling on the principles by its conclusion that the relevant power of attorney was caught by the non est factum doctrine and void on that ground. The court otherwise appeared to favour the view that the general principles, above, apply to the creation of actual authority in an agent.[37] Older cases sometimes cited for automatic voidness of an appointment of an agent by an incapax principal do not on analysis support that conclusion.[38] There are, in addition, some obiter dicta that suggest that

---

[31] That the conferral of actual authority is judged objectively is confirmed by *Freeman & Lockyer v Buckhurst Park Properties Ltd* [1964] 2 Q.B. 480 at 502–503.

[32] See too *Restatement, Third*, § 3.08 and § 3.11. In the absence of apparent authority, the third party's position in relation to the principal is dependent on the agent's actual authority, again in accordance with general principle. See too *Sandman v McKay* [2019] NZSC 41 at [81] (validity of solicitor's instructions where doubt as to client's capacity).

[33] In *Blankley v Central Manchester and Manchester Children's University Hospitals NHS Trust* [2015] EWCA Civ 18; [2015] 1 W.L.R. 4307 at [36], a case concerned with supervening incapacity (as to which, see below, para.10-020) the Court of Appeal favoured a review of the case law that suggests that incapacity automatically terminates an agent's actual authority, and indicated support for a view that the agent's state of knowledge of the incapacity ought to be relevant to the issue.

[34] *Drew v Nunn* (1879) 4 Q.B.D. 661. Brett LJ in this case appears to have thought that it was significant that the incapacity was supervening, but Bramwell LJ, and possibly Cotton LJ, took a broader view.

[35] *Drew v Nunn* (1879) 4 Q.B.D. 661. See further below, paras 10-020 and 10-032. The position may be different if the terms of appointment expressly provide for automatic termination of the agency upon the principal's becoming mentally incapable. For the position where the agent is unaware of the incapacity, but the third party is aware, see below, para.8-008.

[36] *Daily Telegraph Newspaper Co Ltd v McLaughlin* (1904) 1 C.L.R. 243; affirmed [1904] A.C. 776. See also *Taylor v Walker* [1958] 1 Lloyd's Rep. 490 at 514 where, however, the principal signed the relevant compromise.

[37] *Daily Telegraph Newspaper Co Ltd v McLaughlin* (1904) 1 C.L.R. 243 at 272 and 276. But cf. at 275.

[38] *Stead v Thornton* (1832) 3 B. & Ad. 357; and *Tarbuck v Bispham* (1836) 2 M. & W. 2 are both cases where the insanity was known to the agent; *Elliot v Ince* (1857) 7 De G.M. & G. 475 was decided on the basis that the disposition under the power of attorney was voluntary. In *Yonge v Toynbee* [1910] 1 K.B. 215 it was assumed, without argument, that incapacity automatically terminated the authority of a solicitor to continue to defend court proceedings; the question of liability for costs plainly raised no issue of the validity of a contract or other transaction. See too *Evans v James* [2000]

a power of attorney granted by an incapax person is automatically void.[39] This view is also hard to justify, except perhaps on an argument that the open-ended nature of the mandate often granted by such documents exposes the donor to too much risk. The better view, apparently favoured in *Daily Telegraph*,[40] is that there is no such exception.

Statutory provisions now add an overlay to the common law on powers of attorney. These provisions may have been drafted on an assumption of automatic voidness, but such an assumption could not be determinative of the relevant common law. So, where an instrument is registered as a lasting power of attorney under the Mental Capacity Act 2005 but was not in fact validly created, the Act gives protection to the donee of the power and to third parties who deal with the donee, so long as, in each case, they did not know of the invalidity at the time of the dealing.[41] Similarly, the Powers of Attorney Act 1971 gives protection against later revocation of a power of attorney, including on the grounds of incapacity, again so long as the donee or third party, as the case may be, did not know of the revocation at the time of the relevant transaction.[42] Other provisions permit, in certain circumstances, a power of attorney to continue in operation where supervening incapacity occurs even where the agent knows of the incapacity.[43]

There are other legislative provisions that may bear on the application of the common law, including those that result in an incapax person being the subject of formal orders under the Mental Capacity Act 2005,[44] and the Civil Procedure Rules that apply to compromises of court proceedings.[45] In respect of the latter, it has been held that the failure to appoint a litigation friend where one is required by the CPR and then to obtain the court's approval of any compromise invalidates the compromise even if the incapax person was legally represented and the third party was unaware of the mental incapacity.[46]

2-010   **Alien enemies**   An alien enemy probably cannot appoint an agent, at any rate if the transaction involved would be of benefit to the enemy country.[47]

2-011   **Corporations, public bodies, and states**   Corporations can act only through

---

3 E.G.L.R. 1 (stroke victim, but illness known to agent). The issues arising were expressly left open by the Supreme Court in *Dunhill v Burgin* [2014] UKSC 18; [2014] 1 W.L.R. 933 at [31].

[39]   *Gibbons v Wright* (1954) 91 C.L.R. 423 at 444–445 and 448. This was not a case involving agents, and the court seems to have misread its earlier decision in the *Daily Telegraph* case.

[40]   *Daily Telegraph Newspaper Co Ltd v McLaughlin* (1904) 1 C.L.R. 243 at 276. See too V. St Clair Mackenzie, *The Law of Powers of Attorney and Proxies* (2nd edn, 1913), pp.4–5, 92–94.

[41]   Mental Capacity Act 2005 s.14.

[42]   Powers of Attorney Act 1971 s.5(1) and (2). See below, para.10-034.

[43]   Mental Capacity Act 2005 s.9 (see below, para.10-009) and Powers of Attorney Act 1971 s.5 (see below, para.10-008).

[44]   The contracts of a person found to be of unsound mind by inquisition were void even if made during a lucid interval: *Re Walker* [1905] 1 Ch. 160. The same rule presumably applies where a person's property is under present legislation under the control of the court (see Mental Capacity Act 2005 ss.15–21; and see Mental Health Act 1983 as amended). But it is not clear whether the principle applies only to contracts relating to property. See Treitel, *Law of Contract* (15th edn), paras 12-057–12-058.

[45]   See CPR rr.21.2, 21.10.

[46]   *Dunhill v Burgin* [2014] UKSC 18; [2014] 1 W.L.R. 933.

[47]   *Stevenson & Sons Ltd v Aktiengesellschaft für Cartonnagen-Industrie* [1918] A.C. 239; *Ottoman Bank v Jebara* [1928] A.C. 269; *Sovfracht, etc. v Van Udens* [1943] A.C. 203; *Nordisk Insulinlaboratorium v Gorgate Products Ltd* [1953] Ch. 430 (on termination of agency); *Boston Deep Sea Fishing & Ice Co v Farnham* [1957] 1 W.L.R. 1051 (on ratification). cf. *Lepage v San Paulo Copper Estates Ltd* (1917) 33 T.L.R. 457 (administrator-sequestrator appointed by French court to act for

agents,[48] so there can be no question of the capacity of a corporation to appoint agents. There will need to be rules providing for how appointment occurs. But what the corporation itself has the capacity to do turns at common law on the source of its incorporation. This is a complex topic beyond the scope of this work,[49] but in general it can be noted that a corporation the existence of which turns on a statute has only such capacity as the statute expressly or impliedly permits. A charter corporation, on the other hand, has unlimited capacity.[50] No agent can have actual authority to do what the corporation does not have capacity to do. It is frequently suggested that an act that is ultra vires is a nullity whatever the state of innocence of the outside party.[51] However, it is arguable that this overstates the general position. The cases point in different directions. What is clear is that all persons are deemed to know the statutory or constitutional limits of the powers of the corporation (unless the statute otherwise provides). But where the lack of capacity turns on facts which were not apparent on the face of the transaction, the act may still be valid unless the outside party knows or ought to have known of those facts.[52] In this regard, there are compelling reasons for thinking that corporations are in no more secure position than a human who lacks capacity.[53] In relation to companies incorporated under general companies legislation, the foregoing position has been much modified, and is discussed below.[54]

The position with public bodies is even more complicated. Such bodies may not only have limited capacity to contract, but their decision-making may be subject to judicial review. The former question is largely governed by the same principles as corporations that have limited vires, and indeed the public body may in fact be a body corporate.[55] Whether a failure to meet the standards of conduct that public law requires of a public body affects the validity of a contract that results from the flawed decision-making is much less clear. Ultimately, it is a question of the construction of the relevant statutory power, but often there will be little guidance on the issue in the statute. The cases do not yet establish clear default rules. It is beyond the scope of this book to address the issue in detail, but it is suggested that

---

enemy alien may claim dividends due to alien); *Hangkam Kwingtong Woo v Liu Lan Fong* [1951] A.C. 707 (application of rule when territory occupied by enemy). See also Article 119.
48   See above, para.1-028.
49   See *Halsbury's Laws of England*, Vol.9(2), paras 1230 and 1231.
50   See *Ukraine v Law Debenture Trust Corp Plc* [2018] EWCA Civ 2026; [2019] Q.B. 1121 at [67] (under appeal to the UK Supreme Court).
51   See, e.g. *Law Debenture Trust Corp Plc v Ukraine* [2017] EWHC 655 (Comm) at [108], a point not discussed on appeal, [2018] EWCA Civ 2026.
52   See *Re Marseilles Extension Railway Co, Ex p. Credit Foncier and Mobilier of England* (1871) L.R. 7 Ch. App. 161, where the borrowing was for a purpose that was not only ultra vires but illegal, yet held valid when lender did not know of the purpose; *Re David Payne & Co Ltd* [1904] 2 Ch. 608. The latter case was analysed as involving directors' authority rather than corporate capacity in *Rolled Steel Products (Holdings) Ltd v British Steel Corp* [1986] Ch. 246; but this is not consistent with the reasoning in *David Payne* nor *Sinclair v Brougham* [1914] A.C. 398 and cannot provide the explanation of the *Marseilles* case (see Watts [1986] N.Z.L.J. 270). See also the need for knowledge before shareholders can be required to return ultra vires dividends: *Re Denham & Co* (1883) 25 Ch.D. 752; *Moxham v Grant* [1900] 1 Q.B. 88. cf. *Fountaine v Carmarthen Railway Co* (1868) L.R. 5 Eq. 316; *Chapleo v Brunswick Permanent Building Society* (1881) 6 Q.B.D. 696 (where, however, it was suggested there was a duty of inquiry that had not been met by the outside party).
53   See above, para.2-009. See also *Mason v Clarke* [1955] A.C. 778 at 794 (voidness for illegality).
54   See below, para.8-031.
55   See, e.g. *School Facility Management Ltd v Governing Body of Christ the King College* [2020] EWHC 1118 (Comm).

a blanket rule that any public law breach makes a resulting contract a nullity is unlikely to provide a satisfactory solution.[56]

Recognised foreign states have unlimited capacity to contract and dispose of their assets notwithstanding any restrictions there might be in their constitutions.[57] Such restrictions might, however, affect the actual authority of state agents whose actions are inconsistent with them.[58]

Article 5

CAPACITY TO ACT AS AGENT

2-012
(1) All persons including minors and other persons with limited or no capacity to contract on their own behalf, but excluding the profoundly insane, are competent to act or contract as agents.

(2) But the personal liability of the agent upon any contract of agency, and upon any contract entered into with a third party, is dependent on the agent's capacity to contract personally.[59]

(3) An agent can have authority to act concurrently for both parties to a transaction, and one party to a transaction is not incapable of acting as agent for the other.

Comment

2-013 **Rule (1) No need for capacity to contract** The rationale for Rule (1) seems to be that the agent is a mere instrument and that it is the principal who bears the risk of inadequate representation.[60] An early example was the married woman, who could act as agent, though she had no contractual capacity till 1882: indeed it was her lack of capacity that led to her being held to be an agent for her husband.[61] Thus a minor may act as agent provided that the minor has sufficient understanding to consent to the agency and to do the act required.[62] A person who cannot read may be an agent to sign a written contract.[63] Persons lacking all understanding of what they are doing cannot act as agent, but a lesser degree of mental incapacity would not preclude the conferral of actual authority, even if the principal were unaware

---

56 See the difference of views expressed in *Crédit Suisse v Allerdale BC* [1997] Q.B. 306 CA at 343 (per Neill LJ) and 350 (per Hobhouse LJ); *Charles Terence Estates Ltd v Cornwall Council* [2012] EWCA Civ 1439; [2013] 1 W.L.R. 466; and *School Facility Management Ltd v Governing Body of Christ the King College* [2020] EWHC 1118 (Comm) at [159].

57 *Ukraine v Law Debenture Trust Corp Plc* [2018] EWCA Civ 2026; [2019] Q.B. 1121 at [71].

58 *Ukraine v Law Debenture Trust Corp Plc* [2018] EWCA Civ 2026; [2019] Q.B. 1121 at [81], but point conceded. As to apparent authority, see below, para.8-042.

59 *Smally v Smally* (1700) 1 Eq.Ca.Abr. 6. See *Restatement, Third*, § 3.05.

60 Müller-Freienfels (1957) 6 Am.J.Comp.L. 165 at 180–181; (1964) 13 Am.J.Comp.L. 193 at 204; *Norwich and Peterborough B.S. v Steed* [1993] Ch. 116 at 128. As to the bankruptcy of an agent, see para.10-021.

61 See below, para.3-044.

62 *Smally v Smally* (1700) 1 Eq.Ca.Abr. 6; *Watkins v Vince* (1818) 2 Starke 368; *Re D'Angibau* (1880) 15 Ch.D. 228 at 246; *Travelers Guarantee Co of Canada v Farajollahi* [2012] B.C.S.C. 1283 (son signs indemnity for father). See *Restatement, Third*, Comment to § 3.05, giving the example of a child ordering books for a parent through the internet.

63 Illustration 1.

of the incapacity.[64] Agency by an alien enemy would often be void on grounds of public policy.[65]

Statutes sometimes require certain qualifications in persons who act as agents, e.g. solicitors, and company directors.[66] When this is so, persons who act without such qualifications may commit offences by doing so, and may not be entitled to remuneration, reimbursement or indemnity; the matter is discussed under Articles 61 and 63. But they will nevertheless bind their principals unless the statute also expressly or impliedly invalidates their acts.[67]

Rule (2) Agent's own liability regulated by capacity to contract   A minor's li-   **2-014**
ability to a principal, or on the contract which the minor has made with a third party (where this involves personal liability[68]) is regulated by the minor's capacity to contract. Where the agency is not contractual, the minor may nevertheless be subject to the non-contractual rights and duties of an agent.[69] The extent to which an agent who is a minor would be subject to fiduciary duties is beyond the scope of this work. A minor cannot be an express trustee[70]: but it has been held that a minor can be a resulting trustee of personalty,[71] and there seems no reason why a minor should not be a constructive trustee. It has been held that a restitutionary claim against a minor is controlled by the minor's contractual capacity.[72] Whether this is good law or not, an equitable claim, whether in rem or in personam, may not be so controlled,[73] and there is also a statutory jurisdiction to order the minor to transfer property where it is just and equitable to do so.[74] A minor is liable in tort provided that the tortious action is not merely a way of evading a contractual immunity.[75]

Rule (3) Agent acting for both parties to a transaction   The agent of one party   **2-015**
is not incompetent to act as agent of the other. Thus solicitors frequently act for both the buyer and the seller of a house, though there are many judicial warnings as to the dangers of this practice.[76] It is perhaps more likely that an agent can accept

---

[64] See *Norwich and Peterborough B.S. v Steed* [1993] Ch. 116 at 128 (but dictum addressed only to situation where the principal was aware of the agent's incapacity).

[65] See Articles 4 and 117; *Kuenigl v Donnersmarck* [1955] 1 Q.B. 515; *Rayner v Sturges* (1916) 33 T.L.R. 87; *Schostall v Johnson* (1919) 36 T.L.R. 75 (friendly enemy aliens resident in England).

[66] See Companies Act 2006 s.157 (minimum age of 16).

[67] In respect of directors, see the express preservation of authority in Companies Act 2006 s.161. See further below, para.8-037. For general illustration, see *Re Euromaster Ltd* [2012] EWHC 2356 (Ch); [2013] Bus. L.R. 466 (appointment of administrator outside statutory period not invalid).

[68] See Article 98.

[69] Article 42.

[70] Law of Property Act 1925 s.20.

[71] *Re Vinogradoff* [1935] W.N. 68.

[72] *Cowern v Nield* [1912] 2 K.B. 419; criticised, Goff and Jones, *Law of Unjust Enrichment* (9th edn), paras 24-13–24-27 and 34-13–34-17.

[73] But see *R. Leslie Ltd v Sheill* [1914] 3 K.B. 607; criticised, Goff and Jones, above.

[74] Minors' Contracts Act 1987 s.3(1).

[75] See Treitel, *Law of Contract* (15th edn), paras 12-034–12-036. For discussion of the possibility of a minor's tortious liability to a principal where as agent the minor exceeds the mandate conferred, see Watts (2009) 17 Torts L.J. 100 at 103.

[76] See *Moody v Cox and Hatt* [1917] 2 Ch. 71 at 91; *Spector v Ageda* [1973] Ch. 30 at 47; below, para.6-048. For other examples of agents acting for both parties see *Emmerson v Heelis* (1809) 2 Taunt. 38 (auctioneer); *Newsholme v Road Transport Insurance Co*, Illustration 2 to Article 95 (insurance agent); *Briess v Woolley* [1954] A.C. 333 (director); *The Giancarlo Zeta* [1966] 2 Lloyd's Rep. 317 (freight broker) (Can.); *BS Developments No.12 Ltd v PB & SF Properties Ltd* (2006) 7 N.Z. Conveyancing and Property R. 603 (real estate agent found to act for both sides); *Halloran v Minister*

ably acquire the second capacity after the relevant contract has been made.[77] Although there may not be an implied term of the traditional sort in the contract of agency that would preclude the agent's acting for the other party,[78] the rules of equity will apply to the situation, and equity presumes that a person in a fiduciary position must avoid conflicts of interest unless the parties assent to the conflict.[79] Equity may intervene with an injunction in appropriate cases.[80] Otherwise, agents who act for both parties run grave risks of finding themselves in a position in which their duty to one party is inconsistent with their duty to the other, for example as regards information coming into their possession. In such a case the agent will be in breach of the agent's duty to the first principal, and liable accordingly, unless that principal has given informed consent to the transaction with the other principal.[81] Where the agent's acts result in a transaction with a third party who knew of the agent's dual capacity, that transaction may be voidable.[82] But in other cases an action taken by the agent on behalf of the other principal may be valid in itself, though wrongful.[83] In a slightly different context, the employee of one party can in principle be agent for another.[84]

2-016   **One party to a transaction as agent of the other**   Similarly, one party is not in principle incompetent to act as agent for the other party to a transaction. This can occur not merely where the third party performs only some functions as agent for the principal, but also where the agent actually makes a contract with himself on behalf of the principal.[85] An agent cannot, however, contract with his principal only as agent for the principal so as to make the principal not personally liable to sue and be sued on the contract; there must be two parties to a contract.[86]

Administering National Parks and Wildlife Act 1974 [2006] HCA 3; (2006) 229 C.L.R. 545 at [56] (director acts for two companies simultaneously); *Newcastle United Plc v Revenue and Customs Commissioners* [2007] EWHC 612 (Ch); [2007] S.T.C. 1330 (sports agent acting for two parties). For further discussion, see below, para.2-033.

[77]   See Story, *Agency* (1839), § 31; and *Royal Securities Corp Ltd v Montreal Trust Co* (1966) 59 D.L.R. (2d) 666; affirmed (1967) 63 D.L.R. (2d) 15; *P&P Property Ltd v Owen White and Catlin LLP* [2018] EWCA Civ 1082 (solicitor for vendor limited agent for solicitor for purchaser under Law Society's Code for Completion by Post).

[78]   *Newcastle United Plc v Revenue and Customs Commissioners* [2007] EWHC 612 (Ch); [2007] S.T.C. 1330 at [29].

[79]   See below, Article 44, and in particular para.6-048. See too *UBS AG (London Branch) v Kommunale Wasserwerke Peipkiz GmbH* [2017] EWCA Civ 1567 at [95] (conflict of interest a pointer away from dual agency).

[80]   See below, para.6-044.

[81]   *Fullwood v Hurley* [1928] 1 K.B. 498 at 502; *Anglo-African Merchants Ltd v Bayley* [1970] 1 Q.B. 311 (insurance broker); *Eagle Star Insurance Co Ltd v Spratt* [1971] 2 Lloyd's Rep. 116 at 133; *Richard Ellis Ltd v Van Hong-tuan* [1988] 1 H.K.L.R. 169; *Hilton v Barker Booth and Eastwood* [2005] UKHL 8; [2005] 1 W.L.R. 567. See further below, para.6-039.

[82]   *Re a Debtor* [1927] 2 Ch. 367; *Taylor v Walker* [1958] 1 Lloyd's Rep. 490; *North and South Trust Co v Berkeley* [1971] 1 W.L.R. 470 at 485. See further Article 96.

[83]   See Illustration 3.

[84]   *Man Nutzfahrzeuge AG v Ernst & Young* [2005] EWHC (Comm) 2347 at [99], per Moore-Bick J; though in general not at the same time and in relation to the same transaction; affirmed on other points [2007] EWCA Civ 910.

[85]   See *Rowley Homes & Co v Barber* [1977] 1 W.L.R. 371; *Lee v Lee's Air Farming Ltd* [1961] A.C. 12. For a comparative study of the power of an agent to contract on behalf of his principal with himself, see Badr (1982) 30 Am.J.Comp.L. 255.

[86]   *Ingram v Inland Revenue Commissioners* [1997] 4 All E.R. 395 at 423, per Millett LJ (dissenting, but approved on appeal: [2000] 1 A.C. 293 at 305).

Capacity is one thing, authority is another.[87] The common law has not produced much modern case law on the circumstances in which there might be implied limitations on an agent's authority to self-contract. It has largely been left to equity to address self-dealing, which rules make a transaction prima facie voidable whatever authority the agent might have. Protections of "fair dealing" also apply even where the agent deals with the principal in person. For example, agents will be in breach of duty if while agent they fail to disclose their interest on the other side of the contract (e.g. as undisclosed principal of the third party),[88] and the transaction is in such a case likely to be voidable.[89] But there will be cases where a finding of lack of authority is appropriate, and in which case there would be no contract at all. There are older cases involving self-dealing where the court concluded that the transaction was void for want of authority.[90] And in the case of the Statute of Frauds, there is a rule of actual competence: it has long been established that a party to a contract is not competent to sign a contract or a note or memorandum thereof, as agent of the other party.[91] The reasoning is based on the purpose of the statute, and it is submitted that it should also be applied to s.2 of the Law of Property (Miscellaneous Provisions) Act 1989, which now requires the actual contract to be in writing. However, one party can authorise the agent of the other party to sign, though it may be difficult to establish that such authority has in fact been given[92]: thus the signature of an auctioneer to a contemporary memorandum or contract of sale operated as the signature of both parties within s.40 of the Law of Property Act 1925,[93] provided that the auctioneer was not personally the claimant.[94] If the auctioneer was the claimant, however, the auctioneer was self-contracting and could not claim to have signed as agent for the other party. But the signature of a clerk (if authorised) might suffice[95]; or even in one case the signature of the employee, also a licensed auctioneer, who conducted the auction (and who had prima facie authority to sign).[96] Contracts made in the course of public auctions are exempted from s.2 of the 1989 Act referred to above, with the result that these cases may on their facts be no longer relevant. They are, however, retained as examples of general principle, and as being still relevant to contracts of guarantee, the only type of contract still covered by the Statute of Frauds. It is also at least arguable that the requirements of the 1989 Act can be met where a person makes a contract with a company, and signs personally and for the company.

Other examples can be found of situations where the third party performs only some functions as agent for the counter-party. These include where one party signs

---

87 See *Tang Ying Ip v Tang Ying Loi* [2017] HKCFA 3 at [19].
88 See Articles 45 and 96.
89 e.g. *Moody v Cox and Hatt* [1917] 2 Ch. 71; *Spector v Ageda* [1973] Ch. 30 (solicitors).
90 See, e.g. *Salomons v Pender* (1865) 3 H. & C. 639 at 642. See further below, Article 45.
91 *Wright v Dannah* (1809) 2 Camp. 203; *Farebrother v Simmons* (1882) 5 B. & A. 333; *Sharman v Brandt* (1870–71) L.R. 6 Q.B. 720.
92 *Bird v Boulter* (1833) 4 B. & Ad. 443; *Durrell v Evans* (1862) 1 Hurl. & C. 174; cf. *Murphy v Boese* (1874–75) L.R. 10 Ex. 126.
93 *Emmerson v Heelis* (1809) 2 Taunt. 38; *White v Proctor* (1811) 4 Taunt. 209; *Chaney v Maclow* [1929] 1 Ch. 461.
94 *Farebrother v Simmons* (1882) 5 B. & A. 333.
95 *Bird v Boulter* (1833) 4 B. & Ad. 443; *Sims v Landray* [1894] 2 Ch. 318. But an auctioneer's clerk had no prima facie authority to sign; *Bell v Balls* [1897] 1 Ch. 663. And see Article 8, Illustration 1.
96 *Wilson & Sons v Pike* [1949] 1 K.B. 176.

a bill of exchange in blank,[97] or signs a contract leaving the other party to complete gaps in it; in completing the document on behalf of the former, the latter acts as agent to the extent that the latter thereby alters the legal position of the former.[98] It was also at one time assumed that a party purchasing land from a solicitor engaged the solicitor as the party's agent for the purposes of performing the standard duty to make inquiries as to title if there was no other solicitor acting for the party, an assumption no longer made.[99]

Illustrations

2-017 (1) A farmer sends cattle by rail: his drover, who cannot read, signs a consignment note containing contractual terms. The farmer is bound.[100]

(2) The buyer and seller of a house sign a printed form of contract which covers all details except date of completion. The seller's solicitor is instructed to act for the buyer. The seller tells the solicitor the date subsequently agreed for completion, and being asked by the solicitor to confirm this, the buyer does so. The solicitor is authorised to create an additional memorandum binding the buyer.[101]

(3) Lloyd's brokers, who act as agents for the assured,[102] are instructed by the underwriters to obtain an assessor's report in connection with a claim made by the brokers' principals. The brokers obtain such a report and in the course of litigation refuse to show it to their principals. Any custom of Lloyd's by which brokers act also for the underwriters is unreasonable[103] and the brokers are in breach of duty to their principals: but their principals are nevertheless not entitled to see the report, which the brokers obtained while acting for the underwriters.[104]

---

[97] See Bills of Exchange Act 1882 s.20(1); and commentary in *Chalmers and Guest on Bills of Exchange* (18th edn), para.2-131. See also *Colonial Bank v Hepworth* (1884) 36 Ch.D. 36 (share certificates in blank with authority to complete).

[98] See *Wright v Gasweld Pty Ltd* (1991) 22 N.S.W.L.R. 317 at 323; *Madden v UDC Finance Ltd* [1996] 1 N.Z.L.R. 542 CA (affirmed PC 71/1996, 30 October 1997). See also the controversial case, *Newsholme Bros v Road Transport & General Insurance Co Ltd* [1929] 2 K.B. 356, Illustration 2 to Article 95 and note thereto. See too the discussion of *Milroy v Lord* (1862) 4 De G.F. & J. 264, below, para.10-010; and *Barrett v Bem* [2011] EWHC 1247 (Ch); [2011] 3 W.L.R. 1193; reversed on facts [2012] EWCA Civ 52; [2012] Ch. 573 (beneficiary under will was not incompetent to sign will by direction of testator present at the time); *P v Bridgecorp Ltd* [2013] NZSC 152; [2014] 1 N.Z.L.R. 195 at [104] (debtor authorises creditor to file admission of liability).

[99] See, e.g. *Dryden v Frost* (1838) 3 My. & Cr. 670 from where earlier cases can be traced. The change of approach commenced with *Espin v Pemberton* (1859) 3 De G. & J. 547. See also *Barclays Bank Plc v O'Brien* [1994] 1 A.C. 180 at 195.

[100] *Foreman v G.W. Ry Co* (1878) 38 L.T. 851.

[101] *Gavaghan v Edwards* [1961] 2 Q.B. 220. The analysis of this situation would now be different by virtue of s.2 of the Law of Property (Miscellaneous Provisions) Act 1989, but the reasoning still seems valid.

[102] This is the standard position: see *HIH Casualty & General Insurance Ltd v JLT Risk Solutions Ltd* [2007] EWCA Civ 710; [2007] 2 Lloyd's Rep. 278; [2007] 2 All E.R. (Comm) 1106 at [60]; *Flexirent Capital Pty Ltd v EBS Consulting Pty Ltd* [2007] VSC 158 at [211].

[103] See Article 31.

[104] *North and South Trust Co v Berkeley* [1971] 1 W.L.R. 470. See (1972) 35 M.L.R. 78 and the explanation of this case in *Callaghan and Hedges v Thompson* [2000] Lloyd's Rep. I.R. 125 at 132. cf. *Goshawk Dedicated Ltd v Tyser & Co Ltd* [2006] EWCA Civ 54; [2007] Lloyd's Rep. I.R. 224. In *Stockton v Mason* [1978] 2 Lloyd's Rep. 430 a broker was held to have authority to issue temporary cover. It is also arguable that a broker in many cases has authority to receive premiums on behalf

Article 6

ACTS WHICH MAY BE DONE BY MEANS OF AN AGENT

An agent may execute a deed, or do any other act on behalf of the principal,   **2-018**
which the principal might personally execute, make or do; except for the purpose
of executing a right, privilege or power conferred, or of performing a duty imposed,
on the principal personally, the exercise or performance of which requires discretion or special personal skill, or for the purpose of doing an act which the principal
is required, by or pursuant to any statute or other relevant rule, to do in person.[105]

Comment

The authorities cited for the proposition contained in this Article indicate that it   **2-019**
is a general rule of common law which will apply unless displaced. The idea behind
the proposition can be traced back as least as far as *Coke on Littleton*:

> "Here it appeareth that where the servant doth all that which he is commanded, and which
> his master ought to doe, there it is as sufficient as if his master did it himselfe: for the rule
> is, *Qui per alium facit, per se ipsum facere videtur.*"[106]

Similar considerations operate in the reverse situation, viz. where it is sought to use
the rule against a principal. Thus it has been held that a notice to quit may be served
on an agent.[107] In contrast, a memorandum under the Moneylenders Act may not
be furnished to an agent,[108] and it was held at common law that a member of a
corporation could not vote at meetings by proxy or other agent unless the
incorporating statute or the constitution of the organisation provided for that.[109]
Court proceedings cannot usually be commenced in the name of an agent, including under a power of attorney; the principal must be the party named.[110]

Contracts and deeds   In general a person may make any contract through an   **2-020**
agent. Anyone can also perform a contract through an agent unless it is a contract
that involves the promisor's personal attributes or otherwise expressly or impliedly

---

of the underwriter.

[105] *R. v Kent JJ* (1872–73) L.R. 8 Q.B. 305; *Re Whitley Partners Ltd* (1886) 32 Ch.D. 337; *Jackson & Co v Napper* (1886) 35 Ch.D. 162 at 172; *R. v Assessment Committee of St Mary Abbotts, Kensington* [1891] 1 Q.B. 378; *Bevan v Webb* [1901] 2 Ch. 59 at 77; *Christie v Perhewan, Wright & Co Ltd* (1904) 1 C.L.R. 693 at 700; *McRae v Coulton* (1986) 7 N.S.W.L.R. 644 at 663–664; *Bega v Lauvan Pty Ltd* [2019] NSWCA 36 at [43] (authority to give drawdown notice under loan); *Causwell v General Legal Council* [2019] UKPC 9 at [19] (commencement of disciplinary proceedings). See too Powers of Attorney Act 1971 s.10(1).

[106] *Coke on Littleton* (1628), Section 434. See also Story, *Agency* (1839), § 2; *Newbold v Coal Author-ity* [2013] EWCA Civ 584; [2014] 1 W.L.R. 1288 at [58].

[107] *Doe d. Prior v Ongley* (1850) 10 C.B. 25 at 34; and statutes frequently provide for service on agents, e.g. Rent Act 1977 ss.41(2) and 151(1).

[108] *John W. Grahame (English Financiers) Ltd v Ingram* [1955] 1 W.L.R. 563. The Moneylenders Act 1927 was repealed by the Consumer Credit Act 1974.

[109] *Harben v Phillips* (1883) 23 Ch.D. 14. A right to appoint one or more proxies in relation to companies is now provided for by the Companies Act 2006 s.324. See further, Ahern and Maher [2011] J.B.L. 125.

[110] *Davis v Anthony* (Unreported 5 July 1995, English Court of Appeal); *Yu Hing Tong Ltd v Fung Hing Chiu* [2016] HKCFI 1798.

excludes vicarious performance.[111] But this is not an assignment of the burden of
the contract and the principal remains liable personally.[112] An agent may sign in the
agent's own name a memorandum of a guarantee within the requirements of the
Statute of Frauds s.4,[113] since it refers to a person "thereunto lawfully authorised"[114]:
there is no requirement that agents state for whom they act, and agents need not be
specifically authorised, nor (necessarily) intend to bind their principal by contract,[115]
or memorandum of contract.[116] An agent may likewise sign a contract for the sale
or other disposition of an interest in land for the purposes of the Law of Property
(Miscellaneous Provisions) Act 1989; but here, since the document constitutes the
contract, an intention to bind by contract is required.[117]

A deed may be executed through an agent provided that the agent is duly
authorised by deed.[118] An individual authorised to act by power of attorney may
execute an instrument in the attorney's own name.[119]

2-021 **Delegation: sub-agency, and delegations by trustees and other holders of
discretionary powers** A person who is given a power of a discretionary nature
must as a rule exercise it in person. However, the power to delegate is very context-
specific and turns on the consent of the principal rather than issues of capacity. It
will frequently be implicit that an agent will be able to employ other persons to help
perform the tasks undertaken for the principal. The question of sub-agency is dealt
with in Chapter 5. For some officeholders the question of delegation turns on the
express or implied terms of their appointment. Thus where the consent of a
particular person was required for the execution of a power of appointment, it was
held that that person had no power to appoint an agent to consent on that person's
behalf.[120] Trustees are in general in the same position and cannot delegate their
duties: *delegatus non potest delegare*. But there were exceptions to this[121] and they
have been extended and modified by statute.[122] Moreover, the mere fact that a trustee
wrongly delegates powers to a colleague or to another agent will not entail that at

---

[111] See *Davies v Collins* [1945] 1 All E.R. 247; *Chitty on Contracts* (33rd edn), para.19-082 onwards.
[112] *Stewart v Reavell's Garage* [1952] 2 Q.B. 545. Nor can the agent be sued in contract by the other
party to the contract, unless, of course, the principal has acted as agent for the purpose of setting up
contractual relations between the agent and the other party.
[113] As amended by the Law Reform (Enforcement of Contracts) Act 1954.
[114] It seems that the agent can sign his own name or the principal's name: *Graham v Musson* (1839) 5
Bing.N.C. 603. But as to forms of signature see below, para.2-023.
[115] *Griffiths Cycle Corp Ltd v Humber & Co Ltd* [1899] 2 Q.B. 414; *Daniels v Trefusis* [1914] 1 Ch.
788; *North v Loomes* [1919] 1 Ch. 378; *Grindell v Bass* [1920] 2 Ch. 487; *Wright v Pepin* [1954] 1
W.L.R. 635. Liability for representations as to credit under s.6 of the Statute of Frauds Amendment
Act 1828 (Lord Tenterden's Act) does not arise if the representation is merely signed by an agent,
except in the case of a limited company: see Article 91.
[116] *Golden Ocean Group Ltd v Salgaocar Mining Industries PVT Ltd* [2011] EWHC 56 (Comm); [2011]
1 W.L.R. 2575 at [94]; affirmed [2012] EWCA Civ 265; [2012] 1 W.L.R. 3674 at [35]. The agent
who signs a memorandum, so long as authorised to do so, need not be the agent who made the
contract: [2011] EWHC 56 (Comm) at [85].
[117] See below, para.2-037.
[118] See Article 10.
[119] Powers of Attorney Act 1971 s.7(1); below, para.2-039.
[120] *Hawkins v Kemp* (1803) 3 East 410. See also *Ingram v Ingram* (1740) 2 Atk. 88 (special power of
appointment). Aliter, if the duty is merely ministerial: *LCC v Hobbis* (1897) 75 L.T. 688.
[121] *Speight v Gaunt* (1883–84) 9 App.Cas. 1; *Fry v Tapson* (1885) 28 Ch.D. 268; *Learoyd v Whiteley*
(1887) 12 App.Cas. 727. cf. the position of executors, any one of whom can generally bind the others in relation to the affairs of an estate: *Birdseye v Roythorne & Co* [2015] EWHC 1003 (Ch).
[122] Trustee Delegation Act 1999; Trustee Act 2000 ss.11–23; *Snell's Equity* (34th edn), paras 28-01
onwards; *Lewin on Trusts* (20th edn), para.28-110 onwards.

law the agent has no authority, including, for instance, the power to pass title to property owned at law by the trustee.[123] The third party in such a case would get good title, but would take subject to the trust if possessed of notice of the trust and the identity of its trustees. Some trust documents expressly give protection to third parties dealing with a trustee against the trustee's failure to get approval from colleagues.[124]

Historically, individual executors (and it appears administrators), in contrast to trustees, can act alone without the consent of their colleagues in the disposition of personalty, and can also delegate their powers to one of their number.[125] This power of delegation has been extended by statute.[126]

It has been held that an affidavit verifying documents cannot be sworn by the holder of a power of attorney,[127] and where Chitty J delegated the appointment of the official liquidator of a company to his chief clerk, the appointment was held invalid.[128]

Signature by proxy As a general rule, "at common law a person sufficiently **2-022** 'signs' a document if it is signed in his name and with his authority by somebody else".[129] An indication that the signature is *per procurationem* is desirable but not essential.[130] Thus it was held that an agent might subscribe the name of the principal to the memorandum of association of a company,[131] or the instrument of dissolution of a building society,[132] and such a signature still seems sufficient compliance with the similar wording of the present Companies Act 2006 s.8, and the Building Societies Act 1986 s.87(1), respectively. But there may be cases where a statute requires personal signature: thus it was held that an agent could not sign a proposal for a scheme of composition under the Bankruptcy Act 1914 s.16(1).[133] There is conflicting authority as to whether a statute requiring signature "under the hand of"

---

[123] See *McLellan Properties Ltd v Roberge* [1947] S.C.R. 561 (ratification by trustee); *Fielden v Christie-Miller* [2015] EWHC 87 (Ch); *Preedy v Dunne* [2015] EWHC 2713 (Ch). For discussion, see P. Watts, "Intersection of Law of Agency with the Law of Trusts" in *Equity, Trusts and Commerce* (P.S. Davies and J. Penner eds, 2017), Ch.2.

[124] See *Staechelin v ACLBDD Holdings Ltd* [2019] EWCA Civ 817 at [106].

[125] See *Fountain Forestry Ltd v Edwards* [1975] Ch. 1; *Birdseye v Roythorne & Co* [2015] EWHC 1003 (Ch); [2015] W.T.L.R. 961.

[126] Administration of Estates Act 1925 s.2(2).

[127] *Clauss v Pir* [1988] Ch. 267. *Clauss v Pir* was distinguished in *General Legal Council Ex p. Whitter v Frankson* [2006] UKPC 42; [2006] 1 W.L.R. 2803 at [10] where the affidavit was designed to function as a statement of complaint rather than as evidence (son held entitled to make affidavit on behalf of mother).

[128] *Re Great Southern Mysore Gold Mining Co* (1882) 48 L.T. 11.

[129] *LCC v Agricultural Foods Products Ltd* [1955] 2 Q.B. 218 at 223–224, per Romer LJ. See also *R. v Kent JJ* (1872–73) L.R. 8 Q.B. 305 (notice of appeal); *France v Dutton* [1891] 2 Q.B. 208 (solicitor's claim for costs); Bills of Exchange Act 1882 s.91(1); *Tennant v LCC* (1957) 121 J.P. 428 (notice to terminate tenancy); *Barrett v Bem* [2012] EWCA Civ 52; [2012] Ch. 573 (signing of will on behalf of testator under Wills Act 1837 s.9, not established on facts); *Newbold v Coal Authority* [2013] EWCA Civ 584; [2014] 1 W.L.R. 1288 at [58]; *Ramsay v Love* [2015] EWHC 65 (Ch) at [7]; *Elim Court RTM Co Ltd v Avon Freeholds Ltd* [2017] EWCA Civ 89; [2017] H.L.R. 18 at [48] (not fatal that authorised signatory purported to sign in another capacity); *Prempeh v Lakhany* [2020] EWCA Civ 1422.

[130] *LCC v Agricultural Food Products Ltd* [1955] 2 Q.B. 218, at 223. cf. *Nielsen v Capital Finance Australia Ltd* [2014] QCA 139; [2014] 2 Qd R. 459 (execution by attorney in own name using power of attorney acceptable where not a deed).

[131] *Re Whitley Partners Ltd* (1886) 32 Ch.D. 337.

[132] *Dennison v Jeffs* [1896] 1 Ch. 611.

[133] *Re Prince Blücher Ex p. Debtor* [1931] 2 Ch. 70. This case has now been disapproved in *General*

a person permits signature by an agent.[134] The better view seems to be that it does not. In relation to companies, where a statute requires signature in person, it is likely that compliance with the execution provisions of s.44(2) of the Companies Act 2006 will be required.[135]

2-023   **Form of signature**   The reference above to signature "in his name" can be taken to suggest that the agent should write the principal's name first, adding, optionally, the agent's own signature below, and there is further support for such a requirement in the case cited:

> "On this view if Richard Roe wished to sign as agent for John Doe he can sign John Doe by his agent Richard Roe, but he cannot sign Richard Roe as agent for John Doe."[136]

This would be the rule unless there was an indication in the relevant wording that the agent could sign in the agent's name first, indicating if desired the person for whom the agent had signed. The latter procedure is justified, for example, in the case of the Statute of Frauds, which contemplated signature by an agent "thereunto lawfully authorised"[137] and by the Powers of Attorney Act 1971,[138] which refers in s.7 to signature and other acts by the agent "in his own name". However, despite the above dicta, the inflexibility of such reasoning (the burden of which would be quite unknown to most signers who had not taken legal advice and to many who had) may be doubted: it has been said in the Australian decisions[139] that such requisites for ordinary signature by an agent should not be rigidly insisted on, at least unless the wording of the enabling provision appears to require it.[140] The crucial question must surely be whether signature by an agent is permissible: so long as the purport of such a signature is clear, it is difficult to see that the form should be of particular consequence. It seems also that an electronic signature may suffice for the purposes of the Statute of Frauds and its amending Acts.[141] It is not yet clear whether a footer with the sender's name and contact details automatically generated at the end of an email would be sufficient, particularly where it was evident from previous correspondence that the sender normally typed his or her name above the footer; it is well known that accidents can happen in the use of

---

Legal Council, Ex p. Whitter v Frankson [2006] UKPC 42; [2006] 1 W.L.R. 2803 at [7]. For examples where it was concluded that the drafting required personal signature, see, *Cascades and Quayside Ltd v Cascades Freehold Ltd* [2007] EWCA Civ 1555; [2008] L. & T.R. 23; *Hilmi & Associates Ltd v 20 Pembridge Villas Freehold Ltd* [2010] EWCA Civ 314; [2010] 1 W.L.R. 2750 (Leasehold Reform Housing and Urban Development Act 1993).

[134] *Wilson v Wallani* (1880) 5 Ex.D. 155; but cf. *Re Diptford Parish Lands* [1934] Ch. 151. See also *Hyde v Johnson* (1836) 2 Bing. N.C. 776 ("signed by the party chargeable thereby").

[135] See *Hilmi & Associates Ltd v 20 Pembridge Villas Freehold Ltd* [2010] EWCA Civ 314; [2010] 1 W.L.R. 2750 at [31]. As to the requirements of the Companies Act 2006 s.44, and the application of that section where there is a lack of actual authority, see below, para.8-039.

[136] *McRae v Coulton* (1989) 7 N.S.W.L.R. 644 at 664, per Hope JA. See also *UBAF Ltd v European American Banking Corp* [1982] Q.B. 713; Article 91.

[137] *Graham v Musson* (1839) 5 Bing. N.C. 603.

[138] As amended by Law of Property (Miscellaneous Provisions) Act 1989 Schs 1 and 2.

[139] See *McRae v Coulton* (1989) 7 N.S.W.L.R. 644, at 666; *Nielsen v Capital Finance Australia Ltd* [2014] QCA 139.

[140] See 664. An example is s.91 of the Bills of Exchange Act 1882, which provides that it is "sufficient if his signature is written thereon by some other person or under his authority".

[141] *Lindsay v O'Loughnane* [2010] EWHC 529 (QB); [2012] B.C.C. 153 at [95]; *Golden Ocean Group Ltd v Salgaocar Mining Industries PVT Ltd* [2012] EWCA Civ 265; [2012] 1 W.L.R. 3674 at [32]; affg [2011] EWHC 56 (Comm); [2011] 1 W.L.R. 2575 at [95]; *WS Tankship II BV v The Kwangju Bank Ltd* [2011] EWHC 3103 (Comm) at [155]; *Ramsay v Love* [2015] EWHC 65 (Ch) at [7].

computerised communications.[142]

Right to be represented before courts and tribunals The right to be represented **2-024** in court, and restrictions on the use of agents to carry out "restricted legal activities", is settled by statute.[143] Converse difficulties can arise where a person seeks to be legally (or otherwise) represented before a domestic or statutory tribunal before which that person is entitled or bound to appear, but which by its rules, or in the exercise of its discretion to control its own proceedings, does not wish to permit legal (or any) representation. There is some authority for applying the general private law principles of agency to such cases.[144] Viewed from the standpoint of public law, on the other hand, it may be said that the requirements of natural justice do not often demand professional representation or even representation at all[145] and that a tribunal may have perfectly good reasons for seeking to exclude such representation (though exclusion of professional representation is easier to justify than exclusion of all representation). It may be suggested that agency reasoning is not really relevant: the matter is one of contract and natural justice.[146] In the case of a domestic tribunal, although contractual terms contrary to the requirements of natural justice are probably unenforceable,[147] a clear contractual provision or rule excluding representation would normally not contravene those requirements and so would be valid[148]: but in the control of its own proceedings the tribunal may not adopt an absolute rule of no representation[149] and should retain a discretion to allow or disallow representation for good reason.[150] In the case of a statutory tribunal the matter is frequently settled by statute or delegated legislation.[151] In the absence of such guidance, it seems again that general agency reasoning is not relevant, and that there is no right to representation even where the facts under investigation may constitute a crime.[152]

Authority to act illegally An issue that has not received much attention is **2-025**

---

[142] cf. *Neocleous v Rees* [2019] EWHC 2462 (Ch) (where the words "many thanks" had been typed above the footer).

[143] Legal Services Act 2007: see *Gregory v Turner* [2003] EWCA Civ 183; [2003] 1 W.L.R. 1149; and *Avinue Ltd v Sunrule Ltd* [2003] EWCA Civ 1942; [2004] 1 W.L.R. 634; *Ndole Assets Ltd v Designer M&E Services UK Ltd* [2017] EWHC 1148 (TCC). As to making an affidavit by an agent, see above, para.2-021.

[144] *R. v Assessment Committee of St Mary Abbotts, Kensington* [1891] 1 Q.B. 378; *R. v Board of Appeal Ex p. Kay* (1916) 22 C.L.R. 183; *Pett v Greyhound Racing Association Ltd* [1969] 1 Q.B. 125.

[145] *Pett v Greyhound Racing Association Ltd (No.2)* [1970] 1 Q.B. 46; *Enderby Town Football Club Ltd v Football Association Ltd* [1971] Ch. 591.

[146] *Kok Seng Chong v Bukit Turf Club* [1993] 2 Singapore L.R. 388.

[147] See *Faramus v Film Artistes Association* [1964] A.C. 925 at 941; *Edwards v SOGAT* [1971] Ch. 354 at 376, 381; *Enderby Town Football Club Ltd v Football Association Ltd* [1971] Ch. 591 at 606.

[148] *Enderby Town Football Club Ltd v Football Association* [1971] Ch. 591. But Lord Denning MR thought that an absolute exclusion without the possibility of exceptions might be invalid: at 607.

[149] Save for obvious cases such as representation by a "manifestly improper person": see *R. v Assessment Committee of St Mary Abbotts, Kensington* [1891] 1 Q.B. 378.

[150] See *Enderby Town Football Club Ltd v Football Association Ltd* [1971] Ch. 591 at 605–606, suggesting that where serious consequences are in issue, representation may be more appropriate; *R. v Visiting Justice at H.M. Prison, Pentridge* [1975] V.R. 883.

[151] e.g. the Police (Conduct) Regulations 2012 (SI 2012/2632) reg.7.

[152] *R. v Board of Visitors of H.M. Prison, The Maze* [1988] A.C. 379; following *Fraser v Mudge* [1975] 1 W.L.R. 1132; and *R. v Secretary of State for the Home Department Ex p. Tarrant* [1985] Q.B. 251. See also *R. v Visiting Justice of H.M. Prison, Pentridge* [1975] V.R. 883; *Kok Seng Chong v Bukit Turf Club* [1993] 2 Singapore L.R. 388; Craig, *Administrative Law* (8th edn), Ch.12.

whether a principal can expressly authorise an agent to act illegally.[153] In principle, there is no reason why such authority cannot be given as a matter of law, and in practice it must be a common occurrence.[154] Actual authority to act illegally will not usually be implied.[155] However, the authority of a board of directors of a company to act illegally on its behalf and to authorise delegates to act illegally can probably be taken to be implied. At least before the judgments of the Supreme Court in *Patel v Mirza*,[156] the issue of actual authority or lack of it in relation to a principal's rights and duties under a contract affected by illegality would be of little relevance; where the illegality was known to the third party,[157] no rights or duties would generally arise under an illegal contract, whether that contract was between the principal and agent,[158] or one between principal and third party.[159] On the other hand, authorisation of fraud would not preclude a contract arising between the principal and third party; the contract might be voidable at the option of the defrauded party.[160] The majority judgments in *Patel* now support a more flexible approach to the enforceability of contracts affected by illegality. In these circumstances, it may become important for a principal faced with a claim to enforce a contract that might formerly have been treated as illegal to take the point that there was no contract, not because of illegality, but because the relevant agents had no authority to make it. Arguments of this sort have always had potential relevance where what is being sought is recovery of money or other property transferred under a contract affected by illegality. If the principal did not authorise the actual or proposed illegal action, in principle his rights to recover property (purportedly) transferred by the agent should not be affected by the maxim *ex turpi causa non oritur actio*.[161] In relation to restitutionary claims, *Patel* has now adopted an approach which presumptively gives a party to an illegal transaction (at least where

---

[153] See the more detailed treatment of the issues in Watts [2011] J.B.L. 213.

[154] It seems that, at least under companies statutes which confer unlimited capacity on companies, it would be intra vires the board of directors to commit the company to illegal action: see *Morgan v Babcock & Wilcox Ltd* (1929) 43 C.L.R. 163 at 173–174; *Australian Agricultural Co v Oatmont Pty Ltd* (1992) 8 A.C.S.R. 255 at 265; *Sabaf SpA v MFI Furniture Centres Ltd* [2002] EWCA Civ 976; [2003] R.P.C. 264. The Companies Act 2006 s.39 does not go as far as other jurisdictions in expressly conferring capacity on companies (see, e.g. Corporations Act 2001 (Aust.) s.124; Companies Act 1993 (NZ) s.16). See too *Bowman v Secular Society* [1917] A.C. 406 at 438–439 (but cf. Lord Sumner at 454); *Campbell v Paddington Corp* [1911] 1 K.B. 869 at 878. As to the possibility of a company's engaging in a conspiracy to act illegally with its officers and employees, see *Barclay Pharmaceuticals Ltd v Waypharm LP* [2012] EWHC 306 (Comm) at [229] (for criticism, see Watts, in *Agency Law in Commercial Practice* (Busch, Macgregor and Watts eds, 2016), Ch.5).

[155] *Mackay v Commercial Bank of New Brunswick* (1874) L.R. 5 P.C. 394 at 411]; *Glenn v Watson* [2018] EWHC 2016 (Ch) at [491] (no implied authority to act in breach of injunction by which principal bound). As to unlawful customs, see below, para.3-038. The payment of bribes is normally outside the actual or apparent authority of an agent: see *E. Hannibal & Co Ltd v Frost* (1988) 4 B.C.C. 3, Illustration 4 to Article 29.

[156] *Patel v Mirza* [2016] UKSC 42; [2017] A.C. 467.

[157] Where the illegality was unknown to the third party, the agent may have apparent authority to make the contract: see *Gurtner v Beaton* [1993] 2 Lloyd's Rep. 369.

[158] See, e.g. *RTA (Business Consultants) Ltd v Bracewell* [2015] EWHC 630 (QB); [2015] Bus. L.R. 800. As to an agent's duty to account to the principal for money received in relation to illegal activity, see below, para.6-099, and as to the effect of illegality on rights to commission, para.7-051.

[159] See in general, *Chitty on Contracts* (33rd edn), Ch.16. See also *Safeway Stores Ltd v Twigger* [2010] EWHC 11 (Comm); [2010] 2 Lloyd's Rep. 39 at [71]–[72]; reversed on other issues [2010] EWCA Civ 1472; [2011] 1 Lloyd's Rep. 462 (discussed Watts [2011] J.B.L. 214).

[160] *Shalson v Russo* [2005] Ch. 281 at 316.

[161] See, e.g. *Belmont Finance Corp Ltd v Williams Furniture Ltd* [1979] Ch. 250 at 261; and *Belmont Finance Corp v Williams (No.2)* [1980] 1 All E.R. 393 (also explicable as a case where the relevant

the transaction has not been executed) a right to recover money or other property. Even so, to the extent that this regime does give an automatic right of recovery, it may remain important for a principal to take the point that the activity was not in any event authorised if in fact that was true. Equally, a principal who did authorise illegal action will not be able straightforwardly to disown it.[162]

A principal's liability in tort does not usually turn on whether or not the agent's conduct was expressly authorised (apart perhaps from those torts requiring an assumption of responsibility). Hence the question whether the principal authorised illegal activity which causes damage to the claimant may be sufficient for liability but will not usually be necessary, at least where the agent is an employee and vicarious liability is in play.[163] Where it is a question whether a principal is liable to some criminal or civil penalty for illegal conduct committed by an agent, the liability of the principal will usually turn on the construction of the relevant statute.[164]

Illustrations

(1)   A bill of sale may be executed by an attorney on behalf of the grantor, and the grantee of the bill of sale is not necessarily incapable of acting as such attorney.[165]   **2-026**

(2)   An agent may be appointed to execute a deed of arrangement.[166]

(3)   A partner may exercise a right to inspect and take copies from partnership books under s.24(9) of the Partnership Act 1890 by means of an agent to whom no reasonable objection could be taken by the co-partners.[167]

(4)   Where the rules of a trade union provided that its books should be open to the inspection of all the members, the members might inspect the books by means of an accountant, the accountant undertaking to use the information obtained only to inform the clients of the results of the inspection.[168] Similarly, a "person interested" under the Public Health Act 1875 s.247(4), was entitled to inspect the books and accounts of a local authority by means of an accountant.[169]

(5)   A tenancy agreement provided that if the landlords, the LCC, wished to determine the tenancy, it must be by "a written notice signed by the valuer to the council". The name of the valuer to the council appeared as signatory to a notice to quit, but the valuer's name had been written on the document by an assistant valuer, and there was no indication that the signature was by

---

statutory provision was designed to protect the company from the conduct in question). As to rights to recover property wrongly disposed of by an agent, see below, Articles 88 and 96.

[162]   *Bilta (UK) Ltd v Nazir (No.2)* [2015] UKSC 23; [2016] A.C. 1 at [29], [48]–[49]; disapproving dicta to the opposite effect in *Stone & Rolls Ltd v Moore Stephens* [2009] UKHL 39; [2009] 1 A.C. 1391 at [8], [27]–[28].

[163]   See para.2-056 and Article 90.

[164]   See, e.g. *Director General of Fair Trading v Pioneer Concrete (UK) Ltd* [1995] 1 A.C. 456; *Giltrap City Ltd v The Commerce Commission* [2004] 1 N.Z.L.R. 608; *Kemeh v Ministry of Defence* [2014] EWCA Civ 91; [2014] I.C.R. 625. Some statutory regimes expressly define whose acts count as the principal's, see Financial Services and Markets Act 2000 s.90A; Corporate Manslaughter and Corporate Homicide Act 2007 s.1; and Bribery Act 2010 s.7.

[165]   *Furnivall v Hudson* [1893] 1 Ch. 335.

[166]   *Re Wilson* [1916] 1 K.B. 382.

[167]   *Bevan v Webb* [1901] 2 Ch. 59; *Dodd v Amalgamated Marine Workers' Union* [1923] 2 Ch. 236; affirmed [1924] 1 Ch. 116.

[168]   *Norey v Keep* [1909] 1 Ch. 561; *Dodd v Amalgamated Marine Workers' Union* [1923] 2 Ch. 236.

[169]   *R. v Bedwelty UDC Ex p. Price* [1934] 1 K.B. 333.

proxy. Held, the signature was valid provided the valuer had authorised the signature.[170]

(6) A "sampling officer" under food and drugs legislation may purchase or take a sample by means of an agent, and lay an information in the officer's own name in respect of an analysis of the sample so procured.[171]

(7) An acknowledgment or part payment under the Limitation Act may be made by or to an agent duly authorised[172]; a right of action may be concealed by fraud for the purposes of the same Act where the fraud is that of an agent[173]; and land may be adversely possessed through an agent.[174]

(8) A notice to quit may be given by and served on an agent.[175]

(9) A declaration under the Law of Distress (Amendment) Act 1908 (repealed as of April 6, 2014[176]) may be signed by an agent.[177]

(10) An option may take effect by an agent giving notice of its exercise.[178]

2. AGENCY ARISING BY CONFERRAL OF AUTHORITY

Article 7

EXPRESS AGREEMENT TO CONFER AUTHORITY

2-027   Where there is an express agreement between principal and agent for the conferral of authority, this will constitute the relationship of principal and agent, and the assent of both parties will be contained in it.

Comment

2-028   This Article commences the working out of the notion of assent stated in Article 1. The simplest way in which agency arises, both between principal and agent and as regards third parties, is by an express appointment whether written or oral, by

---

[170] *LCC v Agricultural Food Products Ltd* [1955] 2 Q.B. 218.

[171] See *Tyler v Dairy Supply Co* (1908) 98 L.T. 867; *Garforth v Esam* (1892) 56 J.P. 521; *Horder v Scott* (1880) 5 Q.B.D. 552. The relevant provision is now the Food Safety Act 1990. And see *Foster v Fyfe* [1896] 2 Q.B. 104, a case on the Metalliferous Mines Regulation Act 1872.

[172] Limitation Act 1980 s.30(2); see *Wright v Pepin* [1954] 1 W.L.R. 635 (solicitor: authorised); *Re Transplanters (Holding Co) Ltd* [1958] 1 W.L.R. 822 (auditor: not authorised); *Bradford & Bingley Plc v Cutler* [2008] EWCA Civ 74 (Government Benefits Agency pays interest on outstanding mortgage).

[173] Limitation Act 1980 s.32(1); see *Applegate v Moss* [1971] 1 Q.B. 406 (concealment by builder acting as independent contractor to developer); *King v Victor Parsons & Co* [1973] 1 W.L.R. 29; *Lewisham LBC v Leslie & Co Ltd* (1978) 250 E.G. 1289; cf. *Thorne v Heard* [1895] A.C. 495.

[174] *Lyell v Kennedy* (1889) L.R. 14 App.Cas. 437. See in general A. McGee, *Limitation Periods* (8th edn); Prime and Scanlan, *Modern Law of Limitation* (2nd edn), Ch.3; Oughton, Lowry and Merkin, *Limitation of Actions* (1998).

[175] *Jones v Phipps* (1867–68) L.R. 3 Q.B. 567; *Harmond Properties Ltd v Gajdzis* [1968] 1 W.L.R. 1858; *Townsends Carriers Ltd v Pfizer Ltd* (1977) 33 P. & C.R. 361; *Tanham v Nicholson* (1871–72) L.R. 5 H.L. 561; *Galinski v McHugh* [1989] 1 E.G.L.R. 109; *Dun & Bradstreet Software Services (England) Ltd v Provident Mutual Life Assurance Assn* [1998] 2 E.G.L.R. 175; *Yenula Properties Ltd v Naidu* [2002] EWCA Civ 719; [2002] 3 E.G.L.R. 28; *Papantoniou v Stonewall Hotel Pty Ltd* [2018] NSWCA 85.

[176] See Tribunals, Courts and Enforcement Act 2007 Sch.23.

[177] *Lawrence Chemical Co. Ltd v Rubinstein* [1982] 1 W.L.R. 284.

[178] *Mineaplenty Pty Ltd v Trek 31 Pty Ltd* (2007) A.N.Z. Conveyancing R. 123 at [38].

the principal,[179] and acquiescence by the agent, or person similarly empowered to act for the agent:

"An 'actual' authority is a legal relationship between principal and agent created by a consensual agreement to which they alone are parties. Its scope is to be ascertained by applying ordinary principles of construction of contracts, including any proper implications from the express words used, the usages of the trade, or the course of business between the parties."[180]

The agreement may be accompanied by or even contained in a contract, to which the normal rules as to offer and acceptance, consideration, mistake, misrepresentation,[181] duress,[182] undue influence,[183] illegality, etc. apply, and the relations between principal and agent are regulated by the normal law of contract. But the conferral of authority is not itself contractual, and it will not be where there is no consideration, or the agent lacks contractual capacity.[184] Sometimes there will be neither conferral nor contract, e.g. where so much coercion is applied to the principal that there is no real consent to the agency.[185]

Many illustrations will be found in Chapter 3, which deals with the agent's authority, for, as throughout the law of agency, there is a tie between the question whether a person is agent of another, and whether the agent has the authority of that other.

Article 8

IMPLIED AGREEMENT

Agreement between principal and agent for the conferral of authority may be implied in a case where one party has acted towards another in such a way that it is reasonable for that other to infer from that conduct assent to an agency relationship.

2-029

Comment

No special rules of law peculiar to agency are involved here: this Article simply represents, in the sphere of agency, the obvious proposition that contracts are not always expressly made, but often inferred by the court from the circumstances.[186] The same principle applies to non-contractual liability:

2-030

---

[179] See Article 9 as to formalities.

[180] *Freeman & Lockyer v Buckhurst Park Properties (Mangal) Ltd* [1964] 2 Q.B. 480 at 502, per Diplock LJ. For informal extension of initial authority, see *Aviva Life & Pensions UK Ltd v Strand Street Properties Ltd* [2010] EWCA Civ 444.

[181] See *Bristol and West Building Society v Mothew* [1998] Ch. 1 at 22.

[182] See *Haines Bros Earthmoving Pty Ltd v Rosecell Pty Ltd* [2016] NSWCA 112 (no authority where de facto controller of company had taken over its affairs as a result of physical duress applied to its shareholder and director).

[183] See *Antov v Bokan* [2018] NSWSC 1474 at [553] (power of attorney).

[184] See Articles 4 and 5 as to capacity; Article 42 as to gratuitous agents.

[185] See *Haines Bros Earthmoving Pty Ltd v Rosecell Pty Ltd* [2016] NSWCA 112, above.

[186] See *Garnac Grain Co Inc v HMF Faure and Fairclough Ltd* [1968] A.C. 1130n at 1137; *Ashford Shire Council v Dependable Motors Pty Ltd* [1961] A.C. 336 at 349–350; *Reynell v Lewis* (1846) 15 M. & W. 517. The distinction between express contract and implied contract is of doubtful utility. "A contract implied in fact is like any other contract in legal effect: it differs from an express contract only in that the promise is expressed, wholly or in part, by conduct rather than by words": Mechem,

"While agency must ultimately derive from consent, the consent need not necessarily be to the relationship of principal and agent itself (indeed the existence of it may be denied) but it may be to a state of fact upon which the law imposes the consequences which result from agency."[187]

In accordance with the usage in *Restatement, Third*, "consent" is replaced by "assent".[188]

The principle stated in this Article must not be confused with the notions of apparent authority and applications of estoppel, whereby a third party is in certain cases entitled to assume, from the conduct of the principal, that the agent has authority, even where this is not so.[189] The reasonable interpretation must in the present case be applied to determine whether it is reasonable for the agent to think that the agent has been appointed or authorised, and likewise as regards the principal in respect of the agent: not, as in the case mentioned above, whether the third party is entitled to assume that the agent has authority. In some cases, of course, the court is not considering whether relations exist between principal and agent, nor even whether relations exist between principal and third party, but merely whether a person is an "agent" for the purpose of some statute: in this inquiry the two considerations mentioned may, but need not, be determinative.

2-031 **Assent of the principal** Assent of the principal may be implied when the principal places another in such a situation that, according to ordinary usage, that person would understand themselves to have the principal's authority to act on the principal's behalf[190]: or where the principal's words or conduct, coming to the knowledge of the agent, are such as to lead to the reasonable inference that the principal is authorising the agent to act for the principal.[191] But where one person purports to act on behalf of another, the assent of that other will not be presumed merely from silence, unless there is further indication that the latter acquiesces in the agency.[192] The substance of the matter is more important than the form: a contract describing the parties as principal and agent is not conclusive that they are such,[193] and conversely there may be an agency relationship though the agreement

---

Outlines of Agency (4th edn), p.28. In *Targe Towing Ltd v Marine Blast Ltd* [2004] EWCA Civ 346; [2004] 1 Lloyd's Rep. 721 the Court of Appeal disapproved a formulation that for implied agreement the relevant act must be necessarily incident to the commercial venture upon which the parties were to engage.

[187] *Branwhite v Worcester Works Finance Ltd* [1969] 1 A.C. 552 at 587, per Lord Wilberforce (dissenting). See further Fridman (1968) 84 L.Q.R. 224.

[188] See above, para.1-006.

[189] Articles 21 and 72.

[190] See, more generally, para.1-012, above. See also *Pole v Leask* (1863) 33 L.J.Ch. 155 at 161–162; and *Technology Leasing Ltd v Lennmar Pty Ltd* [2012] FCA 709 at [158].

[191] *Little v Spreadbury* [1910] 2 K.B. 658; *Ashford Shire Council v Dependable Motors Pty Ltd* [1961] A.C. 336, at 349; *Restatement, Third*, § 3.01 ("manifestation").

[192] *Dixon v Broomfield* (1814) 2 Chit. 205; *Burnside v Dayrell* (1849) 3 Exch. 224; *London Borough of Haringey v Ahmed* [2017] EWCA Civ 1861 at [40]; *Jiangsu Shagang Group Co Ltd v Loki Owning Co Ltd* [2018] EWHC 330 (Comm); [2018] 2 Lloyd's Rep. 359 at [57]; *MVV Environment Devonport Ltd v NTO Shipping GmbH & Co KG* [2020] EWHC 1371 (Comm) at [33]. As to ratification by silence, see below, para.2-079.

[193] *Nouvelles Huileries Anversoises SA v HC Mann & Co* (1924) 40 T.L.R. 804; *Motor Union Insurance Co Ltd v Mannheimer Versicherungs Gesellschaft* [1933] 1 K.B. 812; *Kennedy v De Trafford* [1897] A.C. 180 at 188. See also above, paras 1-004 and 1-036.

creating it purports to exclude the possibility.[194] It will be rare, however, that it would be appropriate to ignore an express denial of agency, at least outside a statutory or regulatory context, since agency is in general a voluntary relationship.

Assent of the agent   It is traditional to state that the agent's assent (or consent)   **2-032**
is required,[195] and to discuss the ways in which this can be implied from acts or waived by the principal. Consent is certainly relevant to the relationship between principal and agent: only mutual consent will give rise to a contract, rendering the agent liable for non-performance of what he has undertaken; and the duties arising in non-contractual agency would normally only do so if there was consent to the relationship. But as regards the position between principal and third party, the relevant act is the conferring of authority.[196] It is suggested above that the basis of agency is a unilateral manifestation of will: a power of attorney, for instance, does not require acceptance by the donee of the power.[197] When all that is in issue is whether the supposed agent's act was authorised, it may not be necessary that the agent's assent should have been manifested at all, provided the authority has clearly been conferred. Thus when the principal confers authority on the agent, and the agent purports to act on the principal's behalf, he is not permitted to deny that it was on the principal's behalf that he acted.[198] On the other hand the agent must have purported to act for the principal: he will not be regarded as doing so merely because he does what was authorised or requested without other indications.[199] The idea that the conferring of authority is a unilateral act could be argued to have the further consequence that provided it is proved that the principal has conferred authority (as for example where he tells someone else that he is doing or has done so) the agent is authorised though there is no manifestation to him at all. For example, the principal may grant authority by renewing or extending an existing authority, and the agent may act on the principal's behalf without knowing of this, perhaps because the communication has not reached him,[200] because he has forgotten that his authority has lapsed,[201] because he wrongly thinks that his existing authority covers the matter in question,[202] or simply because he decides to take a risk. It is arguable that in such situations the agent should be regarded as authorised. Such reasoning is certainly accepted where what the principal does is ratify the

---

[194] *Re Megevand Ex p. Delhasse* (1878) 7 Ch.D. 511; *Garnac Grain Co Inc v H.M.F. Faure and Fairclough Ltd* [1968] A.C. 1130n at 1137; *South Sydney DRLFC v News Ltd* (2000) 177 A.L.R. 611 at 645 onwards (a useful discussion of the general principles by Finn J).

[195] See, e.g. *Garnac Grain Co Inc v HMF Faure and Fairclough Ltd* [1968] A.C. 1130n at 1137; *Freeman & Lockyer v Buckhurst Park Properties (Mangal) Ltd* [1964] 2 Q.B. 480 at 501.

[196] cf. Müller-Freienfels (1964) 13 Am.J.Comp.L. 193 at 203.

[197] See above, para.1-006. This is not, however, true of a lasting power of attorney under the Mental Capacity Act 2005, which requires execution by donor and attorney (Sch.1, replacing Enduring Powers of Attorney Act 1985 s.2(1)). See further below, para.10-009.

[198] See *Roberts v Ogilby* (1821) 9 Price 269; *Moore v Peachey* (1891) 7 T.L.R. 748 (receipt of money by agent).

[199] See *Kennedy v De Trafford* [1897] A.C. 180; Powell, p.297. See too *Cromwell Corp Ltd v Sofrana Immobilier (NZ) Ltd* (1992) 6 N.Z. Company L.C. 67,997 (company director of parent company not intending to bind wholly-owned subsidiary).

[200] As in *Ruggles v American Central Insurance Co of St Louis*, 114 N.Y. 415, 76 N.Y. Supp.787 (1889).

[201] See *Restatement, Third*, Illustration 3 to § 2–01.

[202] See *Opp v Wheaton Van Lines*, 231 F.3d 1060 (10th Cir. 2000); *Chilsan Merchant Marine Co Ltd v M/V K.Fortune*, 110 F.Supp.2d 492 at 497 (E.D.La. 2000).

agent's act: there is no need that the ratification be communicated to the agent.[203] Both *Restatement, Second* and *Restatement, Third* are clear however that in such circumstances the agent is not to be regarded as authorised by virtue of such facts alone: a manifestation by the principal to the agent is required for actual authority, and one by the principal to the third party for apparent authority.[204] It may then be asked why this is not so for ratification, which in many respects is likened to a conferring of prior authority. The answer may be that a consent to future acts is a serious enough matter to require communication, because *ex hypothesi* the exact nature of the future acts may not be known, and also because the agent may need to act on the communication in the future; whereas an adoption of something known already to have been done only requires proof that the principal "has exercised choice and has consented" to what is *ex hypothesi* known about, and, further, has no significance as to the future.[205] The view that if it can be established that an act was authorised even though neither the agent nor the relevant third party was told, this is enough to hold the principal, is not however without merit. It would of course frequently be possible in such a case to prove ratification, or sufficient manifestation to a third party to create apparent authority.

2-033   **Dual agency**   It has already been seen (above, para.2-013) that there is no outright bar on an agent acting for more than one party to a contract or other transaction, including where the parties have opposing interests. Usually, a dual appointment will be manifested by express agreement. However, dual agency can arise by implied agreement. While industry practice and previous judicial decisions may create something like a presumption that a person is the agent of one side to a common commercial relationship rather than the other, or agent for both, each case must ultimately be decided on its facts.[206] A statement in a contract negotiated by an agent between one party and another that the agent acts for one of the parties is not conclusive that he only does so, if in some respects he in fact acts for the other.[207] The fact that commission is paid by one party is not necessarily inconsistent with the agent's acting for the other party: the source of commission or payments is relevant but not conclusive in determining an agency relationship.[208] The presence of a detailed contract between the third party and the agent of the other party may indicate a dual agency, but is again unlikely to be decisive unless the contract provides for the third party to be able to direct the agent how to act.[209]

Issues of dual agency can arise in a number of settings. Dual agency is likely to

---

[203] See below, para.2-076.

[204] See *Restatement, Second*, § 26, Comment a; *Restatement, Third*, §§ 2.01 and 3.01 (note the discussion of the *Ruggles* case, above, in reporter's note b).

[205] See *Restatement, Third*, § 4.01, Comment d.

[206] *Branwhite v Worcester Works Finance Ltd* [1969] 1 A.C. 552 at 573 and 586–587. See further, the useful discussion in Dal Pont, paras 1.31 and 1.51.

[207] *Commissioners of Customs & Excise v Pools Finance Ltd* [1952] 1 All E.R. 775; *Newcastle United Plc v Revenue and Customs Commissioners* [2007] EWHC 612 (Ch); [2007] S.T.C. 1330. See also above, para.2-013.

[208] *Royal Securities Corp v Montreal Trust Co* (1967) 59 D.L.R. (2d) 666; affirmed (1967) 63 D.L.R. (2d) 15; cf. *Les Affréteurs, etc. v Leopold Walford (London) Ltd* [1919] A.C. 801; *BS Developments No.12 Ltd v PB & SF Properties Ltd*, (2006) 7 N.Z. Conveyancing and Property R. 603; and *Custom Credit Corp v Lynch* [1993] 2 V.R. 469 (mortgage broker agent for borrower not lender notwithstanding lender pays commission to broker); *Plevin v Paragon Personal Finance Ltd* [2014] UKSC 61; [2014] 1 W.L.R. 4222 at [33].

[209] See *Tonto Home Loans Australia Pty Ltd v Tavares* [2011] NSWCA 389; *UBS AG (London Branch) v Kommunale Wasserwerke Leipzig GmbH* [2017] EWCA Civ 1567 at [100]. cf. *South Sydney*

be particularly relevant when questions of a party's knowledge of potential defects in the other party's coming to contract are at issue.[210] The fact that an agent is acting in a dual capacity can also be of importance in determining when acceptance of an offer has been communicated to the offeror, or when an offer has been revoked.[211] Otherwise, nice questions can arise as to on whose behalf an agent with multiple principals acts when performing certain acts under the relevant transaction.[212] So, where an agent dishonestly runs off with the funds intended for the transaction, it can become important to know in what capacity the dual agent had possession of the funds.[213] Difficulties in determining the capacity in which an agent acts can also arise where an agent shares dual roles within a group of companies. An employee of a parent company, for instance, who is appointed a director of a subsidiary is not normally assumed to be acting as agent of the parent when making decisions in his capacity as a director,[214] but regard must always be had to the particular circumstances.[215] Equally, the fact that one of the directors of a debtor is also a director of the creditor would not automatically confer authority on the director to communicate acknowledgement of the debt by the debtor.[216]

Illustrations

(1)   A called at B's office and orally agreed to be responsible for the price of certain goods to be supplied by B to a third person. B's clerk, in A's presence, made and signed a memorandum of the agreement. Held, that the clerk had no implied authority to sign as A's agent, and that there was not a sufficient memorandum in writing of the agreement to satisfy s.4 of the Statute of Frauds.[217]

2-034

(2)   Property is sold under a decree. The solicitor having the management of the

---

DRLFC v News Ltd (2000) 177 A.L.R. 611 at [155]–[156].

[210] See below, para.8-209.

[211] *Powierza v Daley* [1985] 1 N.Z.L.R. 558, Illustration 10; *BS Developments No.12 Ltd v PB & SF Properties Ltd* (2006) 7 N.Z. Conveyancing and Property R. 603 (vendor's estate agent held agent for purchaser also, and had authority from purchaser to give written notice to solicitor for vendor of purchaser's decision to terminate agreement). See too Dal Pont, at paras 1.51 to 1.55.

[212] See, e.g. *Oldendorff GmbH & Co KG v Sea Powerful Ii Special Maritime Enterprises (The Zagora)* [2016] EWHC 3212 (Comm); [2017] 1 Lloyd's Rep. 194 at [23] (delivery of cargo to shipping agent which held appointments from both the shipowner and the buyer). For an untested argument on fraud on a dual agent, see M. McGhee, "Dual capacity brokers, seen through the prism of man-in-the-middle frauds" [2017] L.M.C.L.Q. 435.

[213] See *Aldermore Bank Plc v Rana* [2015] EWCA Civ 1210; [2016] 1 W.L.R. 2209.

[214] See *Kuwait Asia Bank EC v National Mutual Life Nominees Ltd* [1991] 1 A.C. 187 (PC); *LMI Australasia Pty Ltd v Baulderstone Hornibrook Pty Ltd* [2003] NSWCA 74; *Hawkes v Cuddy* [2009] EWCA Civ 291; [2009] 2 B.C.L.C. 427; *F&C Alternative Investments (Holdings) Ltd v Barthelemy* [2011] EWHC 1731 (Ch); [2012] Ch. 613 (directors of limited liability partnership); *Thompson v Renwick Group Plc* [2014] EWCA Civ 635; *Bumi Armada Offshore Holdings Ltd v Tozzi Srl* [2018] SGCA(I) 05.

[215] *Cromwell Corp Ltd v Sofrana Immobilier (NZ) Ltd* (1992) 6 N.Z. Company L.C. 67,997; *London Executive Aviation Ltd v The Royal Bank of Scotland Plc* [2018] EWHC 74 (Ch) at [295] (employee of parent company, and possibly parent company itself, acting as agent of subsidiary); *Cool Seas (Seafoods) Ltd v Interfish Ltd* [2018] EWHC 2038 (Ch) at [159] (director's misconduct attributed to shareholder for purpose of unfair prejudice claim under 2006 s.994).

[216] *Emile Elias and Co Ltd v Attorney General of Trinidad and Tobago* [2011] UKPC 19.

[217] *Dixon v Broomfield* (1814) 2 Chit 205.

sale is, in the conduct of it, deemed to be the agent of all the parties to the suit, as between them and the purchaser.[218]

(3)   Where a letter of credit is opened, the issuing bank and the confirming bank are in the positions, at any rate in some respects, of principal and agent respectively.[219]

(4)   Auditors are not agents of the company whose accounts they audit for the purposes of making an acknowledgment under the Limitation Act.[220]

(5)   A dealer selling goods on credit may by statute act in the capacity of agent of the finance company which finances the arrangement, as regards antecedent negotiations[221] and for the purpose of receiving notice of withdrawal, cancellation and rescission.[222] He may sometimes be its agent in other respects at common law, e.g. to deliver the goods,[223] and to receive notice of revocation of an offer in circumstances where the statutory regulation does not apply.[224] To some extent the question may turn on whether the payments are to be collected directly by the company, or whether the dealer is to collect them. But while he may be agent for certain purposes, there is no general agency relationship and he acts primarily on his own behalf.[225]

(6)   Agents of insurance companies frequently act as agents for persons making insurance proposals to such companies by filling in the forms for them.[226]

(7)   A car is damaged in an accident. The insurers instruct a garage to effect repairs. It is a question of fact whether they do so on their own account or as agent of the assured. Similar rules apply where the assured orders the repairs. The normal interpretation of such a situation seems to be that the repairers contract with the insurers.[227]

(8)   Shop stewards may act as agents for a trade union in negotiation, and in taking industrial action, even contrary to the advice of union officials, provided that they act within union rules or policy.[228] This authority derives from all the members: thus the union also may sometimes act as agent for the

[218] *Dalby v Pullen* (1830) 1 Russ. & M. 296.
[219] *Bank Melli Iran v Barclays Bank* [1951] 2 T.L.R. 1057; *European Asian Bank AG v Punjab and Sind Bank (No.2)* [1983] 1 W.L.R. 642; *Credit Agricole Indosuez v Muslim Commercial Bank Ltd* [2000] 1 Lloyd's Rep. 275. See further *Benjamin's Sale of Goods* (10th edn), para.23–029 onwards.
[220] *Re Transplanters (Holding Co) Ltd* [1958] 1 W.L.R. 822.
[221] Consumer Credit Act 1974 s.56. See *Scotland v British Credit Trust Ltd* [2014] EWCA Civ 790; [2014] Bus. L.R. 1079 at [65].
[222] Consumer Credit Act 1974 ss.57, 69 and 102.
[223] *Branwhite v Worcester Works Finance Ltd* [1969] 1 A.C. 552 at 573; *Shogun Finance Ltd v Hudson* [2003] UKHL 62; [2004] 1 A.C. 919 at [52].
[224] *Financings Ltd v Stimson* [1962] 1 W.L.R. 1184; *CF Asset Finance Ltd v Okonji* [2014] EWCA Civ 870 at [22].
[225] *Branwhite v Worcester Works Finance Ltd* [1969] 1 A.C. 552; but the dissenting opinion (on this point) of Lord Wilberforce repays study. See also *Powell v Lloyds Bowmaker Ltd* 1996 S.L.T. (Sh. Ct.) 117; *Quikfund (Australia) Pty Ltd v Prosperity Group International Pty Ltd (In Liquidation)* [2013] FCAFC 5 at [86].
[226] See Article 95, Illustration 2. But insurance brokers act for the assured in placing insurance: see above, para.2-016.
[227] See *Bowers (Maghull) Ltd v Morton* (1940) 67 Lloyd's Rep. 1; *Godfrey Davis Ltd v Culling & Hecht* [1962] 2 Lloyd's Rep. 349; *Cooter & Green Ltd v Tyrrell* [1962] 2 Lloyd's Rep. 377. But cf. *Gebhard Hoelzler Construction Ltd v Seidler* [2008] B.C.C.A. 77.
[228] *Heaton's Transport (St Helens) Ltd v Transport and General Workers' Union* [1973] A.C. 15; *Howitt Transport Ltd v TGWU* [1973] I.C.R. 1; cf. *General Aviation Service (UK) Ltd v TGWU* [1976] I.R.L.R. 224.

members in doing the same.[229] But an official of a trade union who expels a member does not act as that member's agent so as to prevent the member suing for wrongful expulsion.[230]

(9)   A mortgage broker normally acts as agent for borrowers in procuring loans.[231]

(10)   A purchaser's agent who has been instructed to find a suitable commercial property approaches a vendor who also appoints him agent by written mandate. The purchaser makes an offer which is followed by a counter-offer by the vendor, the documents being carried between the parties by the agent. This counter-offer is initially rejected by the purchaser but is then accepted, initialled and given to the agent. Before the vendor is made aware of this outcome, the vendor agrees to sell the property to a third party at a higher price and tells the agent he has done so before the agent is able to inform him of the purchaser's acceptance. The vendor is held liable to the purchaser. It was too late for the vendor to revoke the counter-offer, acceptance of the counter-offer having been communicated to the vendor's agent who had authority to receive it.[232]

Article 9

FORMALITIES FOR APPOINTMENT

Subject to the provisions of Article 10, and except where otherwise expressly provided by or pursuant to any statute, or by the terms of the power or authority (if any) under which the agent is appointed, an agent may be appointed and authority conferred by deed, by writing, or by word of mouth.   **2-035**

Comment

In general no formalities are required for the creation of agency and the conferral of authority. This is normally so even where the agent is authorised to enter into a contract that is required to be in writing or evidenced in writing, or to sign a memorandum of such a contract.[233] The approach of English law contrasts with that of some other countries, which may require the same form for authorisation as that   **2-036**

---

[229] See *Chappell v Times Newspapers Ltd* [1975] 1 W.L.R. 482 at 500; *Harris v Richard Lawson Autologistics Ltd* [2002] EWCA Civ 442; [2002] I.C.R. 765.

[230] *Bonsor v Musicians' Union* [1956] A.C. 104. These cases, which were famous when decided, are retained as illustrations of ways in which agency reasoning can be deployed in the area of labour law, and because the general dicta in some of them might on occasion be of use. They should not, however, be regarded as significant authorities on general agency principle; and as to the law now governing the contexts in which they were decided, reference should be made to up-to-date works on labour law.

[231] *Morlend Finance Corp (Vic.) Pty Ltd v Westendorp* [1993] 2 V.R. 284 at 308; *Custom Credit Corp v Lynch* [1993] 2 V.R. 469; *NMFM Property Pty Ltd v Citibank* (2000) 107 F.C.R. 270; *Tonto Home Loans Australia Pty Ltd v Tavares* [2011] NSWCA 389.

[232] *Powierza v Daley* [1985] 1 N.Z.L.R. 558; *Intergulf Investment Corp v 0954704 BC Ltd* 2018 BCCA 337.

[233] *Coles v Trecothick* (1804) 9 Ves. 234 at 250; *Deverell v Lord Bolton* (1812) 18 Ves. 505 at 509; *Heard v Pilley* (1868–69) L.R. 4 Ch. App.548. Assuming that the writing can be executed through an agent: see Article 6. For "equal dignity" requirements in the US see *Restatement, Third*, § 2.02, Comment b.

necessary for the act authorised, or special forms for powers of a general nature.[234] Thus it has been held that authority to subscribe the name of the principal to the memorandum of association of a company, or to the instrument of dissolution of a building society, may be given orally.[235] But some appointments are required by statute to be in writing,[236] and some must be by deed.[237] The most conspicuous example of the latter requirement is a power of attorney.[238]

2-037   **Agent for the purchase of land**   A contract for the purchase of land made by an agent as such (whether his principal is disclosed or undisclosed) vests the equitable estate in the principal, and the contract may be enforced by the principal against both the vendor and the agent, even if the agent was appointed orally, provided that the legal estate has not been conveyed to the agent.[239] When the land has actually been conveyed to the agent so as to vest the legal estate in him, he is trustee for the principal and is not entitled to take advantage of the Law of Property Act 1925 s.53, which provides that a declaration of trust respecting land or any interest therein must be evidenced by writing, because to allow this would be to permit the statute to be used as an instrument of fraud.[240]

2-038   **Exercise of authority on behalf of corporations**   Until 1960 the basic rule was that a corporation must contract under seal[241]: thus a corporation could only contract using agents who had themselves been appointed under seal. But the rule had many exceptions and was abolished completely by the Corporate Bodies Contracts Act 1960, whereby a corporation can make contracts by means of any person acting under its authority, express or implied, in the same manner as a private person.[242] Thus a corporation can appoint an agent by parol where a private person could do so, by means of any person acting under its authority, express or implied.[243] Companies formed under the relevant companies legislation had long been subject to much more informal requirements, and that generally remains the case under the

---

[234] See Müller-Freienfels, in *Civil Law in the Modern World* (Yiannopoulos edn, 1965), 77 at 108–111 (citing comparative material). See also below, para.11-013 as to commercial agents.

[235] *Re Whitley Partners Ltd* (1886) 32 Ch.D. 337; *Dennison v Jeffs* [1896] 1 Ch. 611; above, para.2-022.

[236] e.g. Law of Property Act 1925 ss.53 and 54, which require an agent signing certain types of instrument relating to land to be "lawfully authorised in writing", with certain alternatives. See *Richardson v Landecker* (1950) 50 S.R. (N.S.W.) 250, where it was held in connection with a section similar to s.53 that a company manager had signed as the company, not as its agent, and did not therefore require written authorisation.

[237] e.g. Trustee Act 1925 s.25, as substituted by Trustee Delegation Act 1999 s.5.

[238] See below, para.2-039.

[239] *Heard v Pilley* (1868–69) L.R. 4 Ch.App. 548; *Cave v Mackenzie* (1877) 46 L.J.Ch. 564; *Lowther v Kim* [2003] 1 N.Z.L.R. 327; *Jiao v Barge* (2006) 18 Procedure R.N.Z. 396 (NZSC). See further para.8-004.

[240] *Rochefoucauld v Boustead* [1897] 1 Ch. 196; disapproving the earlier view shown in *Bartlett v Pickersgill* (1785) 4 East 577n.; and *James v Smith* [1891] 1 Ch. 384; *Heard v Pilley* (1868–69) L.R. 4 Ch.App. 548 at 553; *Du Boulay v Raggett* (1989) 58 P. & C.R. 138. The trust is said to be constructive in *Paragon Finance Plc v DB Thackerar & Co* [1999] 1 All E.R. 399 at 408. See *Megarry and Wade: Law of Real Property* (9th edn), para.10-045. See also Article 53.

[241] *Kidderminster Corp v Hardwicke* (1873–74) L.R. 9 Ex. 13; *Cape v Thames Haven Dock, etc., Co* (1849) 3 Exch. 841; *A.R. Wright & Son Ltd v Romford BC* [1957] 1 Q.B. 431.

[242] See s.1(1).

[243] The statute itself should be regarded as the source of the authority of the person appointing the agent.

Companies Act 2006.[244] Where writing or other formalities are required by a statute, those requirements will generally be tracked where the party is a company.[245] In circumstances, where authority must be exercised by a board or other committee, normally the board will have actual authority only where the decision results from a properly called and held meeting.[246] Similarly, if the matter requires prior approval by shareholders, normally a resolution will have validity only where the relevant meeting was properly called and held.[247]

Powers of attorney   A power of attorney is "a formal instrument by which one person empowers another to represent him, or act in his stead for certain purposes".[248] It may confer general or particular powers. Before 1971 it was not necessary that such an instrument be a deed, though an unsealed document might not often be called a power of attorney[249] and if the authority to execute deeds was to be conferred it would require to be conferred by deed under the rule stated in the next Article. Now, however, the Powers of Attorney Act 1971 s.1(1), as amended by the Law of Property (Miscellaneous Provisions) Act 1989, requires that instruments creating powers of attorney be executed as deeds: the requirements are given in the next Article. The Act does not define the term "power of attorney": presumably what is referred to is a formal grant of power, especially of general power to represent a person in all matters. It is difficult to believe that it is intended to affect any conferring of authority which could previously have been effected without a deed. Nor does the Act state what is to happen if a power of attorney is executed other than by deed. But where an appointment purports to be by deed, and the document is for some reason ineffective as a deed, the appointment may sometimes be valid as an appointment in writing.[250]

2-039

Article 10

AUTHORITY TO EXECUTE A DEED

Where an agent is authorised to execute a deed on behalf of his principal, his authority must be given in a deed,[251] except where the deed is signed at the direction and in the presence of the principal and of two witnesses who each attest the signature.[252]

2-040

Comment

Certain acts must by law be performed by deed, notably conveyances and many leases. In these cases authority to an agent to execute such a deed must itself be

2-041

---

[244] See s.43; and *Signature Living Hotel Ltd v Sulyok* [2020] EWHC 257 (Ch) at [18].
[245] See s.43(2).
[246] See *Re Portuguese Consolidated Copper Mines Ltd* (1889) 42 Ch.D. 160; *Young v Ladies' Imperial Club Ltd* [1920] 2 K.B. 525; *Smith v Henniker-Major & Co* [2002] EWCA Civ 762; [2003] Ch. 182 at [110].
[247] *Garden Gully United Quartz Mining Co v McLister* (1875) 1 App.Cas. 39 (PC); *Pacific Coast Coal Mines Ltd v Arbuthnot* [1917] A.C. 607 (PC); *Rose v McGivern* [1998] 2 B.C.L.C. 593.
[248] Jowitt, *Dictionary of English Law* (5th ed). See also below, para.3-011.
[249] See Alcock, *Powers of Attorney* (1935), pp.1–2.
[250] See cases cited at fn.262 below.
[251] *Steiglitz v Egginton* (1815) Holt N.P. 141; *Berkeley v Hardy* (1826) 5 B. & C. 355; Powers of Attorney Act 1971 ss.1 and 7. See also *Vella v Permanent Mortgages Pty Ltd* [2008] NSWSC 505 at [206].
[252] Law of Property (Miscellaneous Provisions) Act 1989 s.1(3).

given by deed, usually called a power of attorney. This formerly applied not only to authority to execute a deed, but also to authority to fill up a deed partly executed,[253] or to deliver a deed already sealed,[254] for it was "well-known law that an agent cannot execute a deed, or do any part of the execution which makes it a deed, unless he is appointed under seal".[255] It is not, however, now necessary that deeds be sealed at all; and authority (given, e.g. to a solicitor) to deliver a deed need no longer be given by deed.[256] It has long been established also that a deed may be executed for another in his presence by an amanuensis[257]; and this practice now has statutory authority, requiring the attestation of two witnesses instead of the one normally required.[258]

2-042 **Powers of attorney** By virtue of the Powers of Attorney Act 1971, as amended,[259] s.1, an instrument creating a power of attorney[260] must be executed as a deed by, or by direction and in the presence of, the donor of the power; in the first case one and in the latter two witnesses are required to attest the instrument. Under s.25 of the Trustee Act 1925 (as substituted by s.5 of the Trustee Delegation Act 1999) a trustee may under certain conditions delegate his powers by power of attorney.[261]

Where an agent not appointed by deed purports to execute a deed, the document may be taken to have a lesser effect if the intended result could in fact be achieved without a deed: thus an invalid appointment by deed may take effect as an appointment in writing.[262] It was held that a party might be estopped from denying that a document was sealed[263]; but now that sealing is no longer required a similar estoppel would be more difficult to establish, except perhaps as to delivery. A purported exercise of power under an invalid power of attorney may not preclude a contract arising between the agent and the third party.[264]

---

[253] *Hibblewhite v M'Morine* (1840) 6 M. & W. 200.

[254] *Windsor Refrigerator Co v Branch Nominees Ltd* [1961] Ch. 88.

[255] *Powell v London and Provincial Bank* [1893] 2 Ch. 555 at 563, per Bowen LJ. See also *Phoenix Properties Ltd v Wimpole Street Nominees Ltd* [1992] B.C.L.C. 737; *Lift Capital Partners Pty Ltd v Merrill Lynch International* (2009) 73 N.S.W.L.R. 404 at [37].

[256] Law of Property (Miscellaneous Provisions) Act 1989 s.1(1).

[257] *R. v Longnor (Inhabitants)* (1833) 4 B. & Ad. 647; *Ball v Dunsterville* (1791) 4 T.R. 313.

[258] Law of Property (Miscellaneous Provisions) Act 1989 s.1(3).

[259] By Law of Property (Miscellaneous Provisions) Act 1989 Sch.1.

[260] As to the meaning of this term, see Comment to Article 9. For a strict approach to proof that a power of attorney was in deed form, see *Katara Hospitality v Guez* [2018] EWHC 3063 (Comm).

[261] The Act also makes provision for proof of powers of attorney (s.3), and provides a form of general power of attorney (s.10 and Sch.1). Depositing or filing of instruments creating powers of attorney is not necessary: s.2. The donee may normally execute any instrument, sign or do any act in his own name; s.7. See in general *Law Com. No.30*, Cmnd. 4473 (1970); (1971) New L.J. 746 at 751, 764, 771, 795; (1971) 115 S.J. 596; (1971) 35 Conv (N.S.) 310; (1971) 68 L.S.Gaz. 434 at 437; Land Registration (Powers of Attorney) Rules 1986 (SI 1986/1537); Aldridge, *Powers of Attorney* (10th edn); Thurston, *Powers of Attorney: a Practical Guide* (8th edn).

[262] *Windsor Refrigerator Co Ltd v Branch Nominees Ltd* [1961] Ch. 375; *Hunter v Parker* (1840) 7 M. & W. 322 at 343–344 (sale of ship); *Marchant v Morton, Down & Co* [1901] 2 K.B. 829 (assignment); *Butler v Duckett* (1891) 17 V.L.R. 439. See also *Haddow Nominees Ltd v Rarawa Farms Ltd* [1981] 2 N.Z.L.R. 16; *MYT Engineering Pty Ltd v Mulcon Pty Ltd* (1999) 195 C.L.R. 636; *Jiao v Barge* (2006) 18 Procedure R.N.Z. 396 (NZSC) (power of attorney alleged to be invalid, but Court finding appointment of agent can be oral for the purposes of signature to contract for the sale of land).

[263] *TCB Ltd v Gray* [1986] Ch. 821 (and see [1987] Ch. 458n).

[264] See *Lundie v Rowena Nominees Pty Ltd* (2007) 32 W.A.R. 404 at [53] (see further below, para.9-016).

Article 11

CO-AGENTS

(1) Where an authority is given to two or more persons, it is presumed to be given   **2-043**
to them jointly,[265] unless a contrary intention appears from the nature or terms
of the authority, or from the circumstances of the particular case.[266]
(2) Where an authority is given to two or more persons severally, or jointly and
severally, any one or more of them may execute it without the concurrence of
the others.[267]
(3) All the co-agents must concur in the execution of a joint authority in order to
bind the principal, unless there is a provision that a certain number shall form
a quorum,[268] or there is provision for majority decision-making. But where the
authority is of a public nature, and the matter to be determined is of public
concern, and the persons in whom it is invested meet for the purpose of executing it, the act of the majority is for this purpose deemed to be the act of the
whole body, unless a contrary intention is to be collected from the nature of
the power and the duty to be performed under it.[269]

Illustrations

(1) A provisional committee appointed eight specified persons to act as a manag-   **2-044**
ing committee on their behalf. Six of such persons gave an order within the
scope of the authority conferred. Held, that the provisional committee were not
bound by the order.[270]
(2) Two persons filled the office of clerk to the trustees of a road. Held, that they
must contract jointly in order to bind the trustees.[271]
(3) The directors of a company, being duly authorised in that behalf, resolved that
all their powers, except their power to make calls, should be delegated to three
of their number as a committee. Held, that at a meeting of the committee for
the purpose of exercising such powers, all the members of the committee must
be present.[272]
(4) A power of attorney was given to 15 persons, "jointly or severally to execute
such policies as they or any of them should jointly or severally think proper."

---

[265] Illustrations 1 to 3.
[266] See *Moore v Ullcoats Mining Co Ltd* (1907) 97 L.T. 845 (power to inspect a mine). For the statutory form of power of attorney conferring joint and several authority see Powers of Attorney Act
1971 s.10(1), Sch.1. As to joint and joint and several authority under the Mental Capacity Act 2005,
see s.10 and Sch.4. See further below, para.10-009.
[267] Illustration 4.
[268] *Brown v Andrew* (1849) 18 L.J.Q.B. 153, Illustration 1. This is commonly provided for in the case
of companies, in relation both to the board of directors and the shareholders in general meeting (see,
e.g. Companies (Model Articles) Regulations 2008 (SI 2008/3229).
[269] *Grindley v Barker* (1798) 1 B. & P. 229; *Cortis v Kent Waterworks Co* (1827) 7 B. & C. 314; Judicial
Committee of the Privy Council's Report on the Irish Boundary Commission (1924) 59 L.J. 517;
Atkinson v Brown [1963] N.Z.L.R. 755; *Picea Holdings Ltd v London Rent Assessment Panel* [1971]
2 Q.B. 216. This is really a matter of public law.
[270] *Brown v Andrew* (1849) 18 L.J.Q.B. 153.
[271] *Bell and Head v Nixon and Davison* (1832) 9 Bing. 393.
[272] *Re Liverpool Household Stores* (1890) 59 L.J.Ch. 616. But the articles will usually deal with this
problem.

Held, that a policy executed by four of such persons was binding on the principal.[273]

Article 12

CO-PRINCIPALS AND MULTIPLE PRINCIPALS

2-045   Where two or more persons give authority to an agent to do the same thing, it is presumed that the authority is to act for their joint account only, unless a contrary intention appears from the nature of the terms of the authority, or from the circumstances of the particular case.[274] There is no presumption, outside partnership, that one co-principal is authorised to bind the others.[275]

Comment

2-046   The prima facie rule is that the obligation arising from a contract made by two or more persons on one side is joint.[276] Thus where two or more persons give authority to an agent, the presumption is that they are authorising him to act only in such matters as concern them jointly, e.g. their joint property, and not in matters concerning one or the other alone.[277] But there may be indications to the contrary: and of course the contractual liability (if there is a contract) of the co-principals may be held to be joint and several rather than joint, in appropriate cases.[278] An agent acting for joint principals is not bound to account to one alone.[279] Payment to or release by one of joint creditors may however discharge a debt under the rules for joint obligations, even where the person concerned is not authorised to receive payment or release the debt[280]: but these rules have exceptions.[281] Where one co-principal dies, if the authority is joint it is not terminated by the death.[282]

The principals may be members of a class,[283] and may not be identified, or even disclosed.[284] However, the general rule is that any principal who wishes to take advantage of the agent's conduct must have been in existence at the date of the making of the contract (or other conduct) and have either authorised the action or rati-

---

[273] *Guthrie v Armstrong* (1822) 5 B. & A. 628.
[274] cf. *Restatement, Third*, § 3.16; Partnership Act 1890 s.9; Glanville Williams, *Joint Obligations* (1949), pp.35–37; *Cox v Goldcrest Developments (NSW) Pty Ltd* (2000) 50 N.S.W.L.R. 76 (evidence of subsequent conduct admitted); see also Treitel, *Law of Contract* (15th edn), Ch.13.
[275] See *Farrer v Copley Singletons (a firm)* [1997] EWCA Civ 2127; (1998) 76 P.&C.R. 169. As to partnership, see Partnership Act 1890 s.6.
[276] See above.
[277] e.g. *Keay v Fenwick* (1876) 1 C.P.D. 745; *Constitution Road Pty Ltd v Downey* (2008) 68 A.C.S.R. 118 (statutory demand on joint debt must be authorised by both creditors).
[278] Glanville Williams, *Joint Obligations* (1949), at pp.38–39.
[279] *Hatsall v Griffith* (1834) 2 Cr. & M. 679; *Trajkovski v Simpson* [2019] NSWCA 52. See also below, para.6-100.
[280] *Wallace v Kelsall* (1840) 7 M. & W. 264 at 274; *Husband v Davis* (1851) 10 C.B. 645; *Powell v Brodhurst* [1901] 2 Ch. 160 at 164.
[281] e.g. joint banking accounts: *Husband v Davis* (1851) 10 C.B. 645 at 650. See also *Lee v Sankey* (1872–73) L.R. 15 Eq. 204 (trustees).
[282] See *Cox v Goldcrest Developments (NSW) Pty Ltd* (2000) 50 N.S.W.L.R. 76.
[283] For example, a director or other agent may have authority to bind more than one company at once: see *Halloran v Minister Administering National Parks and Wildlife Act 1974* [2006] HCA 3; (2006) 229 C.L.R. 545 at [56].
[284] As to unidentified and undisclosed principals, see para.1-041, above.

fied it.[285] A contract for multiple principals may confer rights of action on the principals, such as rights to claim on an insurance policy obtained for them by the agent,[286] or it may confer immunities.[287]

Independently of whether two or more principals are intending to act together as co-principals, it is possible for an agent to act in two or more capacities at once for independent principals.[288]

3.   RATIFICATION

Article 13

GENERAL PRINCIPLE

Where an act is done purportedly in the name or on behalf of another by a person who has no actual authority to do that act, the person in whose name or on whose behalf the act is done may, if the third party had believed the act to be authorised, by ratifying the act, make it as valid and effectual, subject to the provisions of Articles 14 to 20, as if it had been originally done by his authority, whether the person doing the act was an agent exceeding his authority, or was a person having no authority to act for him at all.[289]

2-047

Comment

This Article sets out by way of introduction the general principle of ratification, which is that it is "equivalent to an antecedent authority".[290] The whole notion is much criticised and is often treated as exceptional,[291] mainly in the context of contract because of the lack of reciprocity: the third party may be in the power of the principal while the latter decides whether or not to ratify. It is submitted, however, that in typical contract situations ratification is not anomalous. The primary application of the doctrine is indeed in the law of contract, where it fills a practical need in validating the acts of agents who act outside their authority in circumstances where it appears advisable to do so. As the comment to *Restatement, Second* says, "It operates normally to cure minor defects in an agent's authority, minimising technical defences and preventing unnecessary lawsuits".[292] In such a case, as between principal and third party, where the principal seeks to intervene

2-048

---

[285] See further below, paras 2-064 and 2-067.

[286] *National Oilwell (UK) Ltd v Davy Offshore Ltd* [1993] 2 Lloyd's Rep. 582 cf. *Haberdashers' Aske's Federation Trust Ltd v Lakehouse Contracts Ltd* [2018] EWHC 558 (TCC) at [55].

[287] As to "vicarious immunity", see para.9-122, below.

[288] For dual agency, see para.2-033, above.

[289] *Wilson v Tunman and Fretson* (1843) 6 M. & G. 236 at 242; *Bird v Brown* (1850) 4 Exch. 786 at 798; *Firth v Staines* [1897] 2 Q.B. 70; *Causwell v General Legal Council* [2019] UKPC 9 at [16]. *Restatement, Third*, Ch.4; and see below, para.2-050. As to the distinction between agency doctrine and use of the term "ratification" in connection with the release of directors from liability in company law, see *Gower and Davies' Principles of Modern Company Law* (7th edn), pp.437–442 (not carried forward in subsequent editions).

[290] *Koenigsblatt v Sweet* [1923] 2 Ch. 314 at 325, per Lord Sterndale MR.

[291] Powell, pp.121–122 and 138–139; Seavey (1920) 29 Yale L.J. 859, especially at 891; (1954) 21 U.Chi.L.Rev. 248. cf. Krebs, in *Contract Formation and Parties* (Burrows and Peel eds, 2010), Ch.10; Munday, Ch.6; Krebs, in, *Agency Law in Commercial Practice* (Busch, Macgregor and Watts eds, 2016), Ch.2; Schultz (2014) 20 Auckland Univ. L.R. 20.

[292] § 82, comment d. Lord Macnaghten called the doctrine "a wholesome and convenient fiction":

and enforce the contract, the third party is getting exactly what he bargained for. Where the third party seeks to enforce the contract against a ratifying principal he cannot possibly be prejudiced, and the principal is simply held to the transaction which he chose to adopt. Since a master can be liable even for forbidden acts done by an employee in the scope of his employment, it is not surprising that a principal can sometimes be liable for what he has actually ratified.[293] It would seem that ratification should be regarded as providing a normal case of agency, but one where the intention of the parties is given effect to retrospectively.

The position between principal and agent requires slightly more careful formulation. In many cases it is possible to say that the agent, by purporting to act on the principal's behalf, makes an offer to the principal to act as his agent (though not necessarily as his contractual agent), or (where he is already an agent) as his agent in respect of the act concerned, which the principal accepts by ratifying. But the acting outside authority may be a breach of contract; and it seems that there may be cases where the principal ratifies but nevertheless reserves his right to treat the agent as liable to him for the cost of so doing.[294]

Overall it is also true that the potentially retrospective nature of the doctrine of ratification requires special rules to prevent its application having oppressive results, and this makes it a topic requiring special treatment. It does not follow that it is anomalous; and it is certainly convenient:

"The various requirements of ratification, as given in the books, sound largely in terms of a principal who wishes in cold blood to become bound on a contract made in his name but by a purported agent who lacked authority. This is quite unrealistic. Rarely indeed is the principal trying to ratify: he is trying to escape from ratification."[295]

As stated above, the doctrine is primarily applicable to contract, and the tendency is largely to think of it in this connection. However, the term, and the general notion, are used in other parts of the law also. Different considerations arise in different cases, and it is misleading to think that there is any set of rules for ratification applicable to all parts of the law.[296] Many of the cases where the general notion of ratification is invoked are properly to be classified as involving questions of restitution, conversion, formation or performance of contract, novation, waiver, estoppel, notification or notice. Indeed, it may be that such cases form the majority, and that situations of deliberate ratification of unauthorised acts are rare.[297] Cases where the general notion of ratification is employed should therefore be examined carefully in order to ascertain exactly what is in issue.[298]

Ratification of itself only creates agency in respect of the transaction ratified, though a ratification may sometimes be used as evidence of already existing author-

Keighley, Maxsted & Co v Durant [1901] A.C. 240 at 247. A simple example is that if there is no actual authority, and there is uncertainty as to whether apparent authority can be established, a valid ratification puts the matter beyond doubt.

[293] See Stoljar, pp.177–178; Twerski (1968) 42 Temple L.Q. 1.
[294] See below, para.2-096.
[295] Mechem, *Outlines of Agency* (4th edn), § 197.
[296] *Bird v Brown* (1850) 4 Exch. 786 at 799; cf. Stoljar, p.178.
[297] Mechem, *Outlines of Agency* (4th edn), § 198.
[298] See, e.g. *Imperial Bank of Canada Ltd v Begley* [1936] 2 All E.R. 367 at 374–375, (misappropriation of proceeds of cheque); *Banque Jacques Cartier v Banque d'Epargne de Montreal* (1888) 13 App.Cas. 111 (liquidator acquiescences in false accounts); *De Bussche v Alt* (1878) 8 Ch.D. 286 at 312–315 (sub-delegation by agent); *Royal Albert Hall Corp v Winchilsea* (1891) 7 T.L.R. 362 (use of hall justified quantum meruit). See also Procaccia (1978) 4 Tel Aviv U. Studies in Law 9.

ity,[299] and a series of ratifications may on the facts be held to confer authority for the future, or to generate apparent authority.[300] For this reason it is to be distinguished from the other examples of creation of agency contained in this chapter. Like apparent authority it can apply where the person whose act is ratified is already an agent, and where he is not an agent at all, though cases of the second type are rarer.[301]

Ratification in advance of act ratified   Powers of attorney and other docu-   2-049
ments frequently contain clauses whereby the principal purports to ratify in advance acts which the attorney may do. Such a clause cannot constitute ratification. It operates, if anything, as a grant of authority; as creating apparent authority; possibly as a contractual offer, whether to agent or third party, which may be accepted by some form of action in reliance; if consideration can be found, as part of a contract; or as evidence supporting an alleged subsequent ratification.[302]

Juristic nature of ratification[303]   Ratification seems to be a notion sui generis. It   2-050
involves the idea that in certain circumstances a person can by expression of will adopt a transaction entered into by another on his behalf on which he is not liable or entitled so as to become liable and/or entitled as if he had made it at the time. It requires no consideration; and a novation would be juristically different.[304] In so far as it depends on the choice of the person concerned, it can be said to be an application of the doctrine of election. But in the case of election to treat a contract as discharged, there is a choice of remedies in respect of a legal relationship already existing: the innocent party to a breach of contract can choose to treat it as discharged, but if he does not do so the contract continues.[305] The other form of election normally cited is that between inconsistent existing rights.[306] In both these cases it is usually said that the election must be communicated to the other party involved, and that it is irrevocable once made.[307] It would appear, however, that ratification need not be communicated to anyone if it can be established by probative material[308]; that a party who initially refused to ratify may in some circumstances later do so[309]; and that the doctrine overlaps with estoppel and restitutionary doctrine, which is manifested especially in the case of ratification by acquiescence or inactivity.[310]

Ratification in the Restatements   In *Restatements, Second* and *Third* it appears   2-051
that the role left for ratification is rather different from its function in English law.

---

[299] See *Hutchings v Nunes* (1863) 1 Moo.P.C.(N.S.) 243.
[300] cf. *Restatement*, § 43(2). As to apparent authority, see Article 72.
[301] But see *Bird v Brown*, above; also the dissenting judgment of Atkin J in *R. v Chapman Ex p. Arlidge* [1918] 2 K.B. 298.
[302] See *Midland Bank Ltd v Reckitt* [1933] A.C. 1, Illustration 7 to Article 24.
[303] See the valuable discussion by Seavey in *Restatement, Second*, Appendix, reporter's notes to § 94 (also printed in (1954) 103 U.Pa. L.Rev. 30).
[304] *Re Portuguese Consolidated Copper Mines Ltd* (1890) 45 Ch.D. 16 at 34.
[305] *Photo Production Ltd v Securicor Transport Ltd* [1980] A.C. 827 at 849.
[306] *Scarf v Jardine* (1882) 7 App.Cas. 345; *United Australia Ltd v Barclays Bank Ltd* [1941] A.C. 1.
[307] *The Kanchenjunga* [1990] 1 Lloyd's Rep. 391 at 397–399; see also *Kammins Ballroom Co Ltd v Zenith Investment (Torquay) Ltd* [1971] A.C. 850 at 883.
[308] See below, para.2-078.
[309] Article 18.
[310] Article 18. This paragraph is considered by the Court of Appeal in *AMB Generali Holdings AG v SEB Trygg, etc.* [2005] EWCA Civ 1237; [2006] 1 Lloyd's Rep. 318 at [46].

First, *Restatement, Third* gives as its sphere of application "acts done without actual or apparent authority".[311] In this it follows *Restatement, Second*, which refers to ratification as "affirmance by a person of an act which did not bind him",[312] and clearly proceeds on the basis of the view of Professor Seavey, the Reporter, that where there is apparent authority the principal is not only bound but also entitled.[313] This leaves a very limited role for ratification. In particular, it appears to mean that the safeguards against unfair ratification do not apply against a principal who seeks to enforce a contract under which he would be liable under the doctrine of apparent authority only, for he is not ratifying but enforcing an existing contract. Thus it would appear to mean that a third party who discovers that the agent had no actual authority could not on that ground alone withdraw from the contract, despite the uncertainties of establishing apparent authority. This is an unattractive proposition. Ratification in the *Restatements* therefore appears to be confined to situations where there is no apparent authority because the third party's belief in the agent's authority was unreasonable, or where the third party actually knew or had reason to know that the agent had no authority or that the agent was genuinely uncertain as to the extent of his authority, yet in either case did not expressly contract subject to ratification.[314] It is indeed expressly stated in the Comment to *Restatement, Third*, that "Ratification is effective even when the third party knew that the agent lacked authority to bind the principal but nonetheless dealt with the agent".[315]

This leads to a second point, under which ratification in the *Restatements* appears by contrast to have a wider operation than it would in English common law. In English law it is submitted that a transaction with an agent known to have no authority would be a complete nullity, a contract with the agent himself, or what might be called a transaction "subject to ratification". The last mentioned would actually be no more than an offer by or to the third party to be bound on certain terms.[316] The third party might be regarded as promising the agent to keep an offer open or to accept an offer made to him. Consideration might be found in some promise by the agent to seek his principal's adoption of the transaction. But the result of such reasoning is that if the third party withdraws before the principal has adopted the contract, his liability if any is to the agent only and recourse to ratification doctrine is unnecessary and inappropriate.[317]

2-052   **European sources**[318]   Since quite an important point of principle is involved, it seems appropriate to go further. The UNIDROIT *Principles of International Com-*

---

[311] § 4.01.

[312] *Restatement, Second*, § 82.

[313] See *Restatement, Second*, § 8, Comment d, and below, para.8-029.

[314] See *Restatement, Second*, § 85, Comment e, 92(f) and Comment.

[315] See *Restatement, Third*, § 4.01, Comment b. The case given as example, however, simply concerns a contract made for a company not yet formed, and holds the transaction adopted.

[316] See the firm statement in *Watson v Davies* [1931] 1 Ch. 455 at 468–469; *Warehousing and Forwarding Co of East Africa Ltd v Jafferali & Sons* [1964] A.C. 1, where a distinction is taken between contracting subject to ratification and negotiating subject to approval. The point seems to be that in the latter case the agent may not have enough authority even to formulate an offer which the third party might make. There are more uncertainties, opportunities for misunderstanding, and possible differences of analysis in this area than may initially appear. An example is *First Energy (UK) Ltd v Hungarian International Bank Ltd* [1993] 2 Lloyd's Rep. 194, below, para.8-021, where considerations such as those above were raised by the facts but did not need to be considered.

[317] See also below, para.2-087.

[318] For identificatory details, see the Standard Abbreviations, above, p.xi. For commentary, see Busch and Macgregor (eds), *The Unauthorised Agent* (2009), Chs 11 and 12; Vogenauer and Kleinhes-

mercial Contracts appear to apply ratification to cases of lack of actual authority[319]; but they seem also to contemplate it where the third party knows that the agent is unauthorised, for they give such a third party the right to specify a reasonable time for ratification; though if he did not know of the lack of authority, they also allow him to withdraw from the transaction when he discovers the fact. The *Principles of European Contract Law* and the *Draft Common Frame of Reference* appear to take the same approach.[320] Of course, the problem of the revocability of an offer is a common law one and not necessarily to be taken account of in such international codifications. However, the approach taken in this work is to confine the special ratification rules, with their retroactivity and consequent protective features, to situations where the third party believed the agent to have authority: it is only to such situations that the rather rough and ready rationale of ratification, that the third party gets what he expected,[321] applies. The text of Article 13 has been modified to make this clear.[322]

Illustrations

(1) A entered into and signed a written contract on behalf of B, without authority. A memorandum of the contract was required by statute to be in writing. B subsequently ratified the contract. Not only was the contract itself effective, but A was also deemed to have been B's duly authorised agent to sign the memorandum.[323]   **2-053**

(2) An agent, without authority, insures goods on behalf of his principal. The principal ratifies the policy. The policy is as valid as if the agent had been expressly authorised to insure the goods.[324]

(3) An agent of the Crown does an act, which would normally be a tort, outside the realm and in excess of his authority. The Crown ratifies the act. The act is deemed to be an act of state and the agent is not liable for it.[325]

---

terkamp (eds), *Commentary on the UNIDROIT PICC* (2009), Ch.2, Section 2; and DeMott (2009) 6 *European Review of Private Law* 987; Reynolds, *ICC International Court of Arbitration Bulletin* (2005) at 9.

[319] They apply ratification to acts of an agent who acts without authority or exceeds his authority (§ 2.2.9), and the wording of § 2.2.5 and other wording suggests that what is referred to is actual authority, since apparent authority is presented merely as a case where the principal may not invoke the lack of authority of the agent.

[320] See PECL arts 3:201(1) and (3), 3:204(1) and 3:207: but their interrelationship is not entirely clear; and DCFR, II, 6:111.

[321] See above, para.2-048. *Restatement, Third*, however, also allows ratification by an undisclosed principal: see below, para.2-063: the justification would not apply to that either.

[322] By the insertion of the words "if the third party had believed the act to be authorised". Contra, Seavey in *Restatement, Second, Appendix*, pp.148–149.

[323] *Maclean v Dunn* (1828) 4 Bing. 722; *Soames v Spencer* (1822) 1 D. & R. 32; *Koenigsblatt v Sweet* [1923] 2 Ch. 314; *Sheridan v Higgins* [1971] I.R. 291. There seems no reason why the same reasoning should not apply where the contract is required to be in writing, as now under the Law of Property (Miscellaneous Provisions) Act 1989 s.2.

[324] *Wolff v Horncastle* (1798) 1 B. & P. 316; *Williams v North China Insurance Co* (1876) 1 C.P.D. 757; *Bedford Insurance Co Ltd v Instituto de Resseguros do Brasil* [1985] Q.B. 966, Illustration 6 to Article 14. See further Article 18.

[325] *Burton v Denman* (1848) 2 Exch. 167; *Secretary of State for India v Kamachee Boye Sahaba* (1859) 7 Moo.Ind.App. 476. See further Article 113. In such cases, it may well be said that the doctrine is oppressive to third parties despite the principle of Article 19.

Article 14

WHAT ACTS MAY BE RATIFIED

2-054 Every unauthorised act, whether lawful or unlawful,[326] which is capable of being done by means of an agent (except an act which is in its inception void[327]) is capable of ratification by the person in whose name or on whose behalf it was purportedly done.[328]

Comment

2-055 **Lawful or unlawful: contracts** As indicated in the Comment to Article 13, the doctrine, and therefore this Article, applies primarily to transactions, normally contracts. The making of a contract on behalf of another without authority could perhaps be described as unlawful, but such a contract can certainly be ratified. Even a contract induced by a fraudulent, and therefore tortious, profession of agency can be ratified, though the agent might be liable to the principal. The right to rescind for misrepresentation, whether fraudulent or innocent, is clearly extinguished.[329]

2-056 **Torts** The words "lawful or unlawful" are included primarily to indicate that the doctrine can apply to torts. From them it would follow that a principal by ratification may retrospectively turn what was previously an act wrongful against the principal, e.g. an unauthorised sale by the agent, or against a third party, e.g. a wrongful distress, into a legitimate one; or become liable for the tort of another by ratifying. The first proposition is clearly valid: ratification can make an unlawful act lawful ex post facto.[330] But as regards liability, the importance of ratification in the law of torts generally is nowadays, except as regards conversion and trespass to goods, open to question.[331] For the cases giving the widest operation to the doctrine of ratification in tort represent an attempt to extend the notion of command to commit a tort, and originate before the establishment of a general doctrine of vicarious liability.[332] Since the acceptance of a general doctrine, these cases will not usually be relevant, save possibly where the act ratified is not within the course of the servant's employment, or where the tortfeasor is not a servant: and even here the doctrine of casual delegation may cover the situation.[333] It may obviously, furthermore, be extremely difficult to determine what constitutes ratification in non-proprietary torts.[334] It may therefore be suggested that the doctrine of ratification, in so far as it makes one person liable for the torts of another (as opposed to provid-

---

[326] See below, para.2-053; Illustrations 1 to 3; *Wilson v Tunman and Fretson* (1843) 6 M. & G. 236 at 242; *Bird v Brown* (1850) 4 Exch. 786 at 799.

[327] See below, para.2-058.

[328] See Article 15.

[329] See, e.g. *Bolton Partners v Lambert* (1889) 41 Ch.D. 295, Illustration 1 to Article 18.

[330] Illustration 3; *Hull v Pickersgill* (1819) 1 B. & B. 282.

[331] See the valuable discussion in Stoljar, pp.179–182; Tedeschi (1969) 4 Israel L.Rev. 1.

[332] See 4 Co. Inst 317, referred to in *Eastern Counties Ry Co v Broom* (1851) 6 Exch. 314, Illustration 2.

[333] See below, para.8-187. If the tortfeasor is not a servant, it may in any case be held that his act cannot be ratified: see *Wilson v Tunman and Fretson* (1843) 6 M. & G. 236, Illustration 1 to Article 15. See too *Powercor Australia Ltd v Pacific Power Ltd* [1999] VSC 110 at [1274].

[334] See *Moon v Towers* (1860) 8 C.B.(N.S.) 611 at 614 (a case of trespass and false imprisonment): Stoljar, pp.179–180. A case often cited in the books is *Novick v Gouldsberry* 173 F. 2d 496 (1949) ("If I had been there I would have broke your God damn neck" held ratification of assault). See also

[82]

ing a defence to an action in tort), normally applies only to conversion, and possibly also to trespass to goods, where the fields of contract, tort and property overlap[335] and liability is strict; and that in torts requiring personal fault it should not be regarded as significant.

Even in the restricted field suggested it will rarely be crucial to the result, since many of the cases can be explained alternatively on the basis of contract, in that they deal with principals who by accepting goods ratify unauthorised contracts[336]; and further, an act said to be a ratification of a conversion may itself be regarded as a conversion.[337] The cases that depend most obviously on the doctrine of ratification are those envisaging ratification of unlawful distress levied by a bailiff[338]; but most are cases of trespass or conversion, and in many of them liability was denied on the grounds that there was no acting for the supposed principal, or that the supposedly ratifying principal did not know the facts. In some cases the possibility of ratifying other torts has been considered,[339] but the decision has usually been that there was no ratification.

However, other situations can be envisaged where the doctrine of ratification could arise incidentally in a tort case. Thus a coach proprietor might ratify an unauthorised hiring of one of his coaches in order to demand payment for the hire, thereby rendering himself liable for negligence causing damage during the journey: and the owner of a car might ratify unauthorised use of it in order to take advantage of the insurance policy.[340]

Notices and court filings   The notion of ratification arises also in other contexts,   **2-057** such as that of the unauthorised commencement of court proceedings,[341] and the validity of a notice issued by a person who was at the time of issue unauthorised, but whose act was subsequently ratified.[342] Where the notice affects property rights, as in the case of a notice to quit, ratification may not be permitted.[343] Other cases

---

Manduoit v Ross (1884) 10 V.L.R. 264; and *Barns v Guardians of St Mary, Islington* (1911) 76 J.P. 11.

[335] See, e.g. Illustration 1.

[336] i.e. the tort ceases to exist. See *United Australia Ltd v Barclays Bank Ltd* [1941] A.C. 1 at 28; *Verschures Creameries Ltd v Hull & Netherlands SS Co Ltd* [1921] 2 K.B. 608, Illustration 6 to Article 20.

[337] See the explanation of *Hilberry v Hatton* (1864) 2 H. & C. 822, Illustration 1, given in Powell, p.122; Stoljar, p.179.

[338] See Powell, p.122; Article 16, Illustrations 1, 2 and 3; *Haseler v Lemoyne* (1858) 5 C.B.(N.S.) 530; *Green v Wroe* [1877] W.N. 130; *Carter v St Mary Abbotts, Kensington, Vestry* (1900) 64 J.P. 548, Illustration 5 to Article 17; *Becker v Riebold* (1913) 30 T.L.R. 142, Illustration 3; *Clerk and Lindsell on Torts* (22nd edn), paras 6-86–6-88; Atiyah, *Vicarious Liability in the Law of Torts* (1967), Chs 14, 28.

[339] e.g. Illustration 2; *Roe v Birkenhead, etc., Ry* (1851) 7 Exch. 36; *Moon v Towers* (1860) 8 C.B.(N.S.) 611 (trespass and false imprisonment); *Marsh v Joseph* [1897] 1 Ch. 213; *Briess v Woolley* [1954] A.C. 333 (fraud); *Edwards v L & NW Ry* (1869–70) L.R. 5 C.P. 445; *Walker v South Eastern Ry* (1869–70) L.R. 5 C.P. 640 at 643; *Rowe v London Pianoforte Co Ltd* (1876) 34 L.T. 450 (false imprisonment). As to trespass to goods, see *Eastern Construction Co v National Trust Co* [1914] A.C. 197; *Manduoit v Ross* (1884) 10 V.L.R. 264.

[340] cf. *Dempsey v Chambers*, 154 Mass. 330, 28 N.E. 279 (1891), cited by Stoljar, pp.181–182.

[341] See the cases discussed in para.2-091, below; and *McHugh v Eastern Star Gas Ltd* [2012] NSWCA 169; *Causwell v General Legal Council* [2019] UKPC 9.

[342] See Illustration 4.

[343] See below, para.2-091; Article 19, Illustration 1.

arise in a public law context and may turn on the interpretation of statutes or otherwise raise special considerations.[344]

2-058 **Void acts: companies** The proposition that a nullity cannot be ratified is in principle uncontroversial. However, much turns on what is meant by "nullity" or "void act". An unauthorised act could in some contexts be regarded as void, but the starting point of ratification is that such an act can be ratified. There are in fact few situations where such a principle is significant. The main context for its application was formerly that of ultra vires acts of companies. But even if the notion of ratification was relevant in this context, the changes to the ultra vires rule made by the companies legislation[345] actually permit ratification,[346] so that the point ceases to require discussion in this context.

2-059 **Forgeries** It has been held that a forgery cannot be ratified, and the reason given that a forgery is a nullity. The leading case[347] seeks to make a distinction between voidable acts, which can be ratified, and void acts, such as forgery, which cannot. As a general criterion, however, this is unsatisfactory. It is certainly true that in the case of some voidable acts, e.g. the contract of a mentally incapable person, the terminology of ratification has been used.[348] But acts done without authority, e.g. the unauthorised issue of a writ, are not appropriately called voidable. If anything, they could be called void; but they can often be regarded as simply suffering from a defect that can be cured.[349] As regards forgery, it is submitted that the true reason why there can normally be no ratification is that the forger who counterfeits a signature or seal makes no profession of being an agent, so that agency doctrines do not apply to him.[350] An unauthorised signature or affixing of a seal for another may also, however, constitute a forgery[351]; and in such a case it seems that there can be ratification.[352]

[344] *St Leonard's Vestry v Holmes* (1885) 50 J.P. 132; *Firth v Staines* [1897] 2 Q.B. 70; *R. v Chapman, Ex p. Arlidge* [1918] 2 K.B. 298; *Blackpool Corp v Locker* [1948] 1 K.B. 349 (requisitioning); *Warwick RDC v Miller-Mead* [1962] Ch. 441 (statutory notices to abate nuisances); *Bowyer, Philpott & Payne Ltd v Mather* [1919] 1 K.B. 419 (institution of proceedings under Public Health Act); *Ainsworth v Creeke* (1868–69) L.R. 4 C.P. 476 (insertion on list of ratepayers); *Re Gloucester Municipal Election Petition, Ford v Newth* [1901] 1 Q.B. 683 (disqualification of councillor); Lanham (1981) 5 Otago L.Rev. 35.
[345] See now Companies Act 2006 ss.39 and 40; see below, para.8-030 onwards.
[346] Companies Act 2006 s.35(3). As to ratification of pre-incorporation contracts see below, para.2-062.
[347] *Brook v Hook* (1870–71) L.R. 6 Ex. 89, Illustration 5.
[348] See below, para.2-065.
[349] See the judgments in *Danish Mercantile Co v Beaumont* [1951] Ch. 680, Illustration 4; *Pontin v Wood* [1962] 1 Q.B. 737; *Spackman v Evans* (1868) L.R. 3 H.L. 171 at 244; *Re Portuguese Consolidated Copper Mines Ltd* (1890) 45 Ch.D. 16 at 30; below, para.2-091.
[350] Treitel, *Law of Contract* (15th edn), paras 16–052–16–057; *Brook v Hook* (1870–71) L.R. 6 Ex. 89, at 100; *Greenwood v Martins Bank Ltd* [1932] 1 K.B. 371 at 378–379; affirmed [1933] A.C. 51; *Algemeene Bankvereeniging v Langton* (1935) 40 Com.Cas. 247; 51 Ll. List Rep. 275; *Imperial Bank of Canada v Begley* [1936] 2 All E.R. 367 at 374–375; *Rowe v B. & R. Nominees Pty Ltd* [1964] V.R. 477; *Demco Investment & Commercial SA v Interamerican Life Assurance (International) Ltd* [2012] EWHC 2053 (Comm) at [122]; *Commonwealth Bank of Australia v Perrin* [2011] QSC 274 at [144]; *Williams Group Australia Pty Ltd v Crocker* [2016] NSWCA 265 at [137] (unauthorised use of electronic signature but issue left undetermined). But cf. *English v English* [2010] EWHC 2058 (Ch) (where the rule appears to have been overlooked).
[351] Forgery and Counterfeiting Act 1981 s.9(1).
[352] See Campbell (1960) 76 L.Q.R. at p.130 onwards; *Bank of Ireland v Evans' Trustees* (1855) 5 H.L.

This proposition is sometimes criticised as being over-technical.[353] It is submitted, however, that it is correct: a forger who counterfeits a signature or seal no more professes agency than does a person who disguises himself as another. The reason why the notion of ratification is invoked in these cases is that an adoption of a forgery would often be treated as a promise requiring consideration.[354] Nevertheless, the proper solution to the problem of the adoption of forgeries must, as in many other cases where ideas of ratification, adoption and acquiescence are invoked, lie within the areas of formation of contract, waiver, estoppel, and perhaps the rules as to gifts. Thus it has been held that an estoppel can be raised against a person who induces a third party to believe that a signature is his, if the third party acts on the representation.[355]

Illegality   It has been said that "life cannot be given by ratification to prohibited transactions"[356]; and in that case ratification of a prohibited insurance contract was refused validity. The extent to which it is correct to regard a transaction affected by illegality as actually void will, however, turn on the nature of the illegality, the wording of any relevant statute, and the extent of the illegality. The law is far from clear. A detailed treatment is beyond the scope of this work.[357]   **2-060**

Illustrations

(1) A, on B's behalf but without his authority, purchases from C a chattel which   **2-061**
     C has no right to sell, under such circumstances that the purchase of the chattel is a conversion. B ratifies the purchase. B is guilty of converting the chattel.[358]
(2) A, an agent of a corporation, assaults B on its behalf. The corporation ratifies the assault. The corporation is civilly liable to B for the assault. Sed quaere.[359]
(3) A distrains B's goods in the name of B's landlord, but without the landlord's

---

Cas. 389 at 414; *M'Kenzie v British Linen Co* (1881) 6 App.Cas. 82 at 99–100; *Rowe v B. & R. Nominees Pty Ltd* [1964] V.R. 477; *Northside Development Pty Ltd v Registrar-General* (1990) 170 C.L.R. 146 at 184–185, 200, 207–208; *Demco Investment & Commercial SA v Interamerican Life Assurance (International) Ltd* [2012] EWHC 2053 (Comm) at [123].

[353] Stoljar, pp.185–186; Atiyah, *Vicarious Liability in the Law of Torts* (1967), p.315. In the US ratification is made effective by UCC s.3–403(a).

[354] In *Brook v Hook* (1870–71) L.R. 6 Ex. 89 itself, the consideration was the suppression of a prosecution and so illegal.

[355] *Greenwood v Martins Bank Ltd* [1933] A.C. 51, Illustration 5 (criticised by Stoljar, pp.185–186, on the basis that there was no detriment: sed quaere); *M'Kenzie v British Linen Co* (1881) 6 App.Cas. 82; *Fung Kai Sun v Chan Fui Hing* [1951] A.C. 489 (setting rather strict limits); *Rowe v B. & R. Nominees Pty Ltd* [1964] V.R. 477; *English v English* [2010] EWHC 2058 (Ch) at [59]. See also *Welch v Bank of England* [1955] Ch. 508; *Spiro v Lintern* [1973] 1 W.L.R. 1002; *Amalgamated Investment & Property Co. Ltd v Texas Commerce International Bank Ltd* [1982] Q.B. 84; below, para.8-040. A different view is taken in *Restatement, Third*, § 4.03, Comment c.

[356] *Bedford Insurance Co. Ltd v Instituto de Resseguros do Brasil* [1985] Q.B. 966 at 986, per Parker J (Illustration 6).

[357] See the brief treatment in para.2-025; and *Chitty on Contracts* (33rd edn), Ch.16.

[358] *Hilberry v Hatton* (1864) 2 H. & C. 822. And see *Irvings v Motly* (1831) 7 Bing. 543.

[359] *Eastern Counties Ry v Broom* (1851) 6 Exch. 314. This proposition might be correct if based on the general rules of vicarious liability, but it seems out of date on the point of ratification, and rests on obiter dicta only, since it was held that there was no ratification. See *Clerk and Lindsell on Torts* (22nd edn), para.6-87.

authority. The landlord may ratify the distress, and it is then deemed to have been levied by his authority.[360]

(4) The managing director of a company, without having authority to do so, instructed solicitors to commence an action in the name of the company. An order for the winding-up of the company having been made, the liquidator adopted the action. A motion to strike out the name of the plaintiff company failed; for, although not properly constituted when commenced (so that the defendant acting promptly could have obtained a stay), the action was not a nullity, and the subsequent ratification cured the defect in the proceedings as originally constituted.[361]

(5) A signs an instrument in B's name without his authority and with intent to defraud. B cannot ratify the signature.[362] But if B, knowing of the forgery, by his conduct induces a third person to believe that the signature is his, and if such third person acts on that belief to his detriment, B will be estopped from denying that it is his signature in any action between him and such third person[363]; as he will be if, knowing of the forgery, he delays in repudiating the signature, so that the third person's chance of recovering from the forger is materially prejudiced.[364]

(6) B in Hong Kong authorises A in London to write marine insurance risks on his behalf, subject to financial limitations as to the size of the risk. He also has an open cover reinsurance policy. A exceeds the limits in writing risks on B's behalf and declares the risks to the reinsurers. The insurances are void and unenforceable by statute because B is not authorised to carry on insurance business in Great Britain. Claims are made under the insurances. B ratifies the insurances and claims on the reinsurance policy. The original insurances are void whether made with B's authority or not and so cannot be ratified. There is thus no claim on the reinsurance policy.[365]

---

[360] *Whitehead v Taylor* (1839) 10 A. & E. 210. The common law of distraint in relation to commercial tenancies has been abolished and replaced as from April 6, 2014 pursuant to Tribunals, Courts and Enforcement Act 2007 s.71. See also *Hull v Pickersgill* (1819) 1 B. & B. 282 (seizure of bankrupt's property ratified by assignee). For consideration of this problem in connection with liability in tort, see Atiyah, *Vicarious Liability in the Law of Torts* (1967), pp.314–316.

[361] *Danish Mercantile Co Ltd v Beaumont* [1951] Ch. 680. See also *Ancona v Marks* (1862) 7 H. & N. 686; *Hooper v Kerr, Stuart & Co Ltd* (1901) 83 L.T. 729, Illustration 2 to Article 20; *Presentaciones Musicales SA v Secunda* [1994] Ch. 271 at 280, Illustration 6 to Article 19. cf. *Re State of Wyoming Syndicate* [1901] 2 Ch. 431. And see *Re Portuguese Consolidated Copper Mines* (1890) 45 Ch.D. 16 (allotment of shares by irregular meeting); *Warwick RDC v Miller-Mead* [1962] Ch. 441 (local authority); *Bamford v Bamford* [1970] Ch. 12 (but may not be on ratification); *Alexander Ward & Co Ltd v Samyang Navigation Co Ltd* [1975] 1 W.L.R. 673 (arrest of ship in Scotland *ad fundandam jurisdictionem*: see (1976) 39 M.L.R. 327); Article 20, Illustration 10.

[362] *Brook v Hook* (1870–71) L.R. 6 Ex. 89; but see Comment, above.

[363] *M'Kenzie v British Linen Co* (1881) 6 App.Cas. 82; *English v English* [2010] EWHC 2058 (Ch).

[364] *Greenwood v Martins Bank Ltd* [1933] A.C. 51; *Brown v Westminster Bank Ltd* [1964] 2 Lloyd's Rep. 187; *Tina Motors Pty Ltd v ANZ Banking Group Ltd* [1977] V.R. 205.

[365] *Bedford Insurance Co Ltd v Instituto de Resseguros do Brasil* [1985] Q.B. 966, approved on the illegality issue in *Phoenix General Ins Co of Greece SA v Halvanon Ins. Co Ltd* [1988] Q.B. 216 (effect reversed by Financial Services Act 1986 s.132, now repealed).

Article 15

WHO MAY RATIFY

The only person who has power to ratify an act is the person in whose name or on whose behalf the act was purported to be done,[366] and it is necessary that he should have been in existence at the time when the act was done,[367] and competent at that time and at the time of ratification to be the principal of the person doing the act[368]; but it is not necessary that at the time the act was done he was known, either personally or by name, to the third party.[369] Ratification can be effected on the principal's behalf by an agent who has authority to ratify; usually such agent will have authority to do an act of the type in question.[370]

2-062

Comment

Person acted for: agent must purport to have authority to bind principal It is clear that ratification only applies where the person whose act is in question professed or purported at the time of acting to do so as agent and to have authority to bind the principal.[371] Although if the agent had authority at that time, an undisclosed principal could take the benefit of the contract and likewise would be liable to be sued,[372] it has been held that an undisclosed principal cannot ratify. The reason given in the leading case of *Keighley, Maxsted & Co v Durant*[373] is that "civil obligations are not to be created by, or founded upon, undisclosed intentions".[374] It is however difficult to see that this is not exactly what happens under the doctrine of the undisclosed principal. A more general reason sometimes given is that to allow ratification in such a case would be to allow too easy intervention upon a contract by a person not in truth connected with it. In one sense this is obvious: the doctrine of ratification would not be appropriately invoked to allow intervention by a person, uncontemplated by the purported agent, who simply found it convenient to ratify the transaction. This would, indeed, not be ratification by an undisclosed principal. But *Keighley Maxsted*'s case did not involve such a situation. The person whose acts were purportedly ratified was already an agent, and had merely exceeded his authority in respect of the price at which he agreed to buy. Furthermore, the principal chose to ratify and it was the third party who, in suing the principal, sought to rely on the ratification. He was not permitted to do so. It is arguable therefore that at the very least a principal who ratifies should be held liable in the situation

2-063

---

[366] Illustrations 1–4; *Watson v Swann* (1862) 11 C.B.(N.S.) 756; *Smith v Cox* [1940] 2 K.B. 558 (payment of rent by stranger); *Att.-Gen. v Wylde* (1946) 47 S.R.(N.S.W.) 99 (ratification of act of Crown agent by another officer of the Crown); *Howard Smith & Co Ltd v Varawa* (1907) 5 C.L.R. 68 at 82; *Crampsey v Deveney* [1968] S.C.R. 267, (1968) 2 D.L.R. (3d) 161; *Restatement, Second*, §§ 85 and 87 (not followed by *Restatement, Third*, which allows ratification by an undisclosed principal: see § 4.03).

[367] *Kelner v Baxter* (1866–67) L.R. 2 C.P. 174, Illustration 6; *Restatement, Third*, § 4.04(1).

[368] *Firth v Staines* [1897] 2 Q.B. 70 at 75; and see Illustrations.

[369] See Comment.

[370] See below, paras 2-068 and 2-069.

[371] See, e.g. *Secured Residential Funding Plc v Douglas Goldberg Hendeles and Co (a Firm)* [2000] EWCA Civ 144; *Bennett v Strauss* [2016] NSWCA 324, Illustration 10.

[372] Article 76.

[373] *Keighley, Maxsted & Co v Durant* [1901] A.C. 240, Illustration 3. See Rochvarg (1989) 34 McGill L.J. 286.

[374] per Lord Macnaghten at 247.

where a person who is already an agent exceeds his authority; and possibly should be able to sue in such a case, the third party being adequately protected by the normal restrictions against unfair results of ratification.[375] The decision is however clear that ratification in such a case is ineffective, and is one of the House of Lords.[376]

Conversely, however, where the agent purports to act for a principal but actually intends to act for himself the principal can ratify.[377] And where the agent purports to act for one person, no other person can ratify[378]:

"If there is one legal principle better established than another it is this, that nobody can ratify a contract purporting to be made by an agent except the party on whose behalf the agent purported to act."[379]

It is under this principle that some forgeries cannot be ratified, for a forger does not usually purport to act for someone else but as someone else.[380] In tort cases, it is clear that in principle there can be no ratification of a tort unless the tortfeasor has in some way purported to act for the party who subsequently ratifies[381] but exactly what interpretation is to be given to the idea of "purporting to act" in this context is a difficult matter.[382]

2-064　**In existence when act done**　The requirement that the principal exist at the time of the alleged contract arises most commonly in relation to contracts made on behalf of companies not yet registered.[383] Where the promoters of a prospective company enter into a contract on its behalf before its incorporation, the company cannot after incorporation ratify the contract, because it was not in existence at the time when the contract was made and so could not have made the contract at that time.[384] The company may make a new contract on the same terms as the old,[385] and this may be proved by part performance,[386] but it cannot ratify the contract with retrospective effect. Other remedies have sometimes been found in respect of pre-incorporation contracts[387]; but it has also been held that a company is not bound in equity to pay for work done before its formation, even though it has taken the

---

[375] Article 19.
[376] *Restatement, Third*, abandons the rule altogether: see § 4.03 and Comment *b*. But see the defence of the rule by Krebs, in *Agency Law in Commercial Practice* (Busch, Macgregor and Watts eds, 2016) Ch.2.
[377] *Re Tiedemann and Ledermann Frères* [1899] 2 Q.B. 66, Illustration 4.
[378] Illustrations 1 and 2.
[379] *Jones v Hope* (1880) 3 T.L.R. 247n. at 251, per Brett LJ (Illustration 5).
[380] See above, para.2-059.
[381] See, e.g. *Wilson v Barker* (1833) 4 B. & Ad. 614; *Eastern Construction Co Ltd v National Trust Co Ltd* [1914] A.C. 197 at 213. See Atiyah, *Vicarious Liability in the Law of Torts* (1967), pp.314–316.
[382] See Seavey, 21 U.Chi.L.Rev. 248 (1954); cf. Twerski, 42 Temple L.Q. 1 (1968).
[383] See Companies Act 2006 s.16.
[384] *Kelner v Baxter* (1866–67) L.R. 2 C.P. 174, Illustration 6; *Re Empress Engineering Co* (1880–81) 16 Ch.D. 125; *Re Northumberland Avenue Hotel Co* (1886) 33 Ch.D. 16; *Melhado v Porto Alegre, etc., Ry Co* (1873–74) L.R. 9 C.P. 503; *Natal Land, etc., Co v Pauline, etc., Syndicate* [1904] A.C. 120. But the person acting for the company may be personally liable: see Article 107.
[385] *Howard v Patent Ivory Co* (1888) 38 Ch.D. 156; cf. *Touche v Metropolitan Ry Warehousing Co* (1870–71) L.R. 6 Ch.App. 671.
[386] *Howard v Patent Ivory Co* (1888) 38 Ch.D. 156; cf. *Touche v Metropolitan Ry Warehousing Co* (1870–71) L.R. 6 Ch.App. 671.
[387] See *Re Empress Engineering Co* (1880–81) 16 Ch.D. 125; *Re Dale & Plant* (1889) 61 L.T. 206; *Rover International Ltd v Cannon Film Sales Ltd (No.3)* [1989] 1 W.L.R. 912; *Gower's Principles*

benefit of the work.[388] Such results have proved inconvenient in practice and in some jurisdictions are changed by statute.[389] Issues relating to the existence of the principal also arise with unidentified principals and are discussed below.[390]

Competent at the time when the act was done Again, a person cannot ratify an act which he was not competent to do at the time it was done: an example appears in Illustration 9. Apart from alien enemies, with whom Illustration 9 is concerned,[391] the main case for considering this requirement is that of minors. Where a contract made for a minor would, if made by the minor himself, be valid,[392] it can presumably be ratified in the normal way. Other contracts are void against the minor but bind the other party: they can be "ratified" by the minor after reaching full age. If entered into through an agent, they can likewise presumably be ratified by the minor personally or through an agent: except that it was long ago held that a penal bond could not be ratified.[393] The distinction between void and voidable acts may regulate the ratification by mentally incapable persons of contracts made on their behalf: they can ratify, when of sound mind, acts which if effected by themselves would have been voidable.[394] **2-065**

Competent at the time of ratification A minor clearly cannot ratify a contract that would not bind him, while still under age, nor a mentally incapable person while still incapable (at least unless he appeared to be sane to the party to whom the ratification was communicated), nor a person who is an alien enemy, even if he was not such when the act was done.[395] **2-066**

Unidentified principal In general, as will be seen from the above rules regarding the existence and competence of the principal, the rules for ratification follow those for initial authority: the test is to inquire whether the principal could have entered into such a transaction at the time when the agent originally acted. If this analogy is followed, since an agent need not always name his principal but may and often does act for a completely unidentified principal (e.g. "bought for our principals"), ratification should be possible in such a case also. If the third party is willing to deal on this basis, he should arguably be bound under the doctrine of ratification just as under the normal principles of authority. A number of dicta however suggest that the principal must be known or ascertainable by the third party at the time of contracting. Thus in one case it was said that: **2-067**

> "The law obviously requires that the person for whom the agent professes to act must be a person capable of being ascertained at the time. It is not necessary that he should be

---

of Modern Company Law (10th edn), paras 5-24–5-28.
[388] *Re English & Colonial Produce Co* [1906] 2 Ch. 435.
[389] Companies Act (Singapore) cap.50 s.41; Companies Ordinance (Hong Kong) s.32A; Corporations Act 2001 (Cth) ss.131–132; Companies Act 1993 (NZ) ss.182–185. See too *Rolle Family & Co Ltd v Rolle* [2017] UKPC 35; [2018] A.C. 205.
[390] See below, para.2-067.
[391] And see *Kuenigl v Donnersmarck* [1955] 1 Q.B. 515 at 539.
[392] e.g. a contract for necessaries, or a beneficial contract of service.
[393] *Baylis v Dineley* (1815) 3 M. & S. 477. It may be regarded as a nullity.
[394] *City Bank of Sydney v McLaughlin* (1909) 9 C.L.R. 615. See Comment to Article 4. In *Dibbins v Dibbins* [1896] 2 Ch. 348, Illustration 3 to Article 19, it was assumed that the ratification would have been valid had it been effected in time.
[395] See Comment to Article 117.

named; but there must be such a description of him as shall amount to a reasonable designation of the person intended to be bound by the contract."[396]

An example of the latter category is that of an agent who acts for the heirs of property, whoever they are.[397] Such dicta would, if applied as a rule, restrict the scope of ratification. If there is any policy reason for doing this, it is that the ability to ratify where the principal was completely unidentified and undescribed will depend on the agent having had a particular person in mind; and this may effectively permit him at a later stage to choose the person who is to ratify by declaring that this was the person whom he had originally had in mind. This is not, at least in theory, true in ordinary dealings on behalf of unidentified principals, where actual authority would in the event of dispute need to be proved. Even in such cases however there may be an element of choice, for agents may have identical instructions from several principals and thus be free in practice to choose to which principal a particular contract should be allocated. There is also some possibility of such choice where the question of the intervention or liability of an undisclosed principal arises.[398] Such uncertainties are not therefore unknown to agency law. The dicta quoted come from a nineteenth-century case on insurance, where the difficulty of distinguishing between identifying the person who can sue on the policy as principal and identifying the interests covered by the policy is notorious.[399]

A carefully reasoned judgment of Colman J confirms the above view.[400] It also states (in wording appropriate to its context, that of insurance) that:

> "Evidence as to whether in any particular case the principal assured or other contracting party did have the relevant intention may be provided by the terms of the policy itself, by the terms of any contract between the principal assured or other contracting party and the alleged co-assured or by any other admissible material showing what was subjectively intended by the principal assured."[401]

Although this decision and these dicta seem, with respect, correct, they do raise considerable problems of evidence, whether within or outside the context of insurance. Where an agent has no principal in mind at the time of the act, but proposes to "allocate" the contract, there can in principle be no ratification. Where he has a principal in mind, there can. The two situations may be difficult to distinguish.

A related point arises from the fact that policies of marine insurance on goods

---

[396] *Watson v Swann* (1862) 11 C.B.(N.S.) 756 at 771, per Willes J. See also *Kelner v Baxter* (1866–67) L.R. 2 C.P. 174 at 184; *Eastern Construction Co Ltd v National Trust Co Ltd* [1914] A.C. 197 at 213.

[397] *Lyell v Kennedy* (1889) 14 App.Cas. 437, Illustration 7.

[398] See below, para.8-072.

[399] See below; Arnould, *Marine Insurance* (18th edn) (9 and 10 British Shipping Laws), paras 8-26–8-27 and 8-29–8-32. See also *The Albazero* [1977] A.C. 774.

[400] *National Oilwell (UK) Ltd v Davy Offshore Ltd* [1993] 2 Lloyd's Rep. 582; Powell, pp.125–126; Reynolds, in *Consensus ad Idem* (Rose ed., 1997), pp.80–83; Reynolds, "Unidentified Principals in Common Law", in *Agency Law in Commercial Practice* (Busch, Macgregor and Watts eds, 2016), Ch.4.

[401] *National Oilwell (UK) Ltd v Davy Offshore Ltd* [1993] 2 Lloyd's Rep. 582 at 597, per Colman J. The judgment contains authority for this proposition and consideration of such evidence. See too *Lai Wo Heung v Cheung Kong Fur Pty Co Ltd* [2004] 1 H.K.L.R.D. 959 (subjective intention of agent important). In *Magellan Spirit ApS v Vitol SA* [2016] EWHC 454 (Comm) at [19] Leggatt J said that he had "serious doubts as to whether this proposition is correct": but gave no specific reasons.

have long been taken out for the benefit of "all those to whom they do, may or shall appertain", or similar wording; and it has often been assumed that beneficiaries of such policies may sue on them. It seems that in such a case the understanding is that the agent who procures the insurance need not at the moment have in mind any particular person or persons as the intended principal or principals, provided that there is some general contemplation as to the person or persons intended to benefit.[402] Although there are dicta to the contrary it is submitted that, as regards agency reasoning, a person who had no interest at the time of the insurance should not in principle be able to ratify, and therefore should not be able to sue on such a policy as principal.[403] The analogy of authorised contracts should again be followed, and a contract could not be validly made on behalf of a person who might at a future time acquire a particular qualification.[404] Trust reasoning is not so limited. It is possible for a policy on goods to be taken out which covers the interests of such persons; and the person who takes it out may have an insurable interest to do so and be able to recover an indemnity in respect of loss incurred by such persons, which he would hold in trust.[405] Equally such a policy may be assigned; and in an appropriate case such a policy might be held to convey a contractual offer to persons later acquiring the qualification mentioned. It is submitted that it is on this basis that such provisions should be explained, and that their efficacy in favour of future beneficiaries cannot satisfactorily be based on reasoning that there is agency for a person not at the time ascertainable.[406]

Ratification by agents   Ratification can clearly be effected by an agent, subject to the normal principles of authority.[407] The agent who ratifies requires only authority to ratify, not authority to have performed the act ratified.[408] Conversely, the mere fact that an agent has authority to perform an act of the type purportedly being ratified does not entail that that agent has authority to retrospectively approve the transaction of another agent. The authority may in appropriate cases be apparent.   **2-068**

Ratification by companies   An act or transaction done or entered into on behalf of a company may be ratified by the directors, if they have power to do or enter into such an act or transaction on behalf of the company[409]: and a ratification by the directors may be implied from part performance made or permitted by the   **2-069**

---

[402] See *Boston Fruit Co v British & Foreign Marine Insurance Co* [1906] A.C. 336 at 389 (insurance by shipowner could not benefit charterer); *P. Samuel & Co Ltd v Dumas* [1923] 1 K.B. 592; [1924] A.C. 431; *Routh v Thompson* (1811) 13 East 274; *Robinson v Gleadow* (1835) 2 Bing. N.C. 156; cf. *Watson v Swann* (1862) 11 C.B.(N.S.) 756; *Byas v Miller* (1897) 3 Com.Cas. 39. See also *Alfred McAlpine Construction Ltd v Panatown Ltd* [2001] 1 A.C. 518 at 582.

[403] See *Haberdashers' Aske's Federation Trust Ltd v Lakehouse Contracts Ltd* [2018] EWHC 558 (TCC) at [46].

[404] See *Kelner v Baxter* (1866–67) L.R. 2 C.P. 174 at 184.

[405] *A. Tomlinson (Hauliers) Ltd v Hepburn* [1966] A.C. 451. See also *Petrofina (UK) Ltd v Magnaload Ltd* [1983] 2 Lloyd's Rep. 91.

[406] This reasoning was accepted in the Court of Appeal of New South Wales in *Trident General Ins. Co Ltd v McNiece Bros Pty Ltd* (1987) 8 N.S.W.L.R. 270 at 276–277, Illustration 8 (affirmed on other grounds (1988) 165 C.L.R. 107: but see p.113).

[407] *Suncorp Insurance and Finance v Milano Assecurazioni SpA* [1993] 2 Lloyd's Rep. 225 at 235; *Yona International Ltd v La Réunion Française SA d'Assurances* [1996] 2 Lloyd's Rep. 84 at 103; *Lawson v Hosemaster Co Ltd* [1966] 1 W.L.R. 1300; see also *Restatement, Third*, § 4.01, Comment *e*.

[408] *Re Portuguese Consolidated Copper Mines Ltd* (1890) 45 Ch.D. 16.

[409] *Reuter v Electric Telegraph Co* (1856) 6 E. & B. 341; *Wilson v West Hartlepool Ry & Harbour Co* (1865) 2 De G.J. & S. 475; *Hooper v Kerr, Stuart & Co Ltd* (1901) 83 L.T. 729; *New Falmouth Resorts Ltd v International Hotels Jamaica Ltd* [2013] UKPC 11.

company.[410] Where an act or transaction is beyond the powers of the directors, it can only be effectively ratified by the shareholders.[411] An act done by the directors in excess of their powers, but within the scope of the articles of association, may be ratified by ordinary resolution of the shareholders,[412] or by an informal meeting of all the shareholders.[413] A number of cases go further and indicate that a ratification by the shareholders may be implied if they can be regarded as having acquiesced in such an act with knowledge of the circumstances, even in the absence of a formal meeting.[414] In some circumstances, the third party will be protected by statute against unauthorised acts of directors.[415]

Illustrations

2-070   (1)   A sheriff, acting under a valid writ of execution, wrongfully seizes goods which are not the property of the debtor. The execution creditor does not, by becoming a party to an interpleader issue or otherwise, ratify the act of the sheriff so as to render himself liable for the wrongful seizure, because the act was not done by the sheriff on his behalf, but in performance of a public duty.[416]

(2)   A enters into an agreement professedly on behalf of B's wife and C. B cannot ratify the agreement so as to give himself a right to sue upon it jointly with his wife and C.[417]

(3)   A is authorised to buy wheat on the joint account of himself and B, with a certain limit as to price. A, intending to buy on the joint account of himself and B, and expecting that B will ratify the contract, but not disclosing such intention to the seller, enters into a contract in his own name to buy at a price which is above the limit. B ratifies, but later refuses to take the wheat. He cannot be sued by the seller.[418]

(4)   A sells wheat to X on P's behalf, and repurchases it himself. He then purports to sell it to Q, R and S on P's behalf, knowing that Q, R and S would not deal with him personally. He really intends to carry through the whole transaction on his own behalf. Q, R and S repudiate the transaction. P may ratify.[419]

(5)   A contracts on behalf of a volunteer corps with B, both parties thinking that the corps as an entity may be bound. The corps as an entity cannot be bound. The contract cannot be ratified by individual members of the corps, because it was not made on their behalf as individuals.[420]

(6)   A contract for the supply of goods is made by "A, B and C on behalf of" a

---

[410]   *Reuter v Electric Telegraph Co* (1856) 6 E. & B. 341; *Wilson v West Hartlepool Ry & Harbour Co* (1865) 2 De G.J. & S. 475; Illustration 7 to Article 17.

[411]   *Spackman v Evans* (1868) L.R. 3 H.L. 171.

[412]   *Grant v UK Switchback Ry Co* (1888) 40 Ch.D. 135. cf. *Boschoek Pty Co Ltd, etc. v Fuke* [1906] 1 Ch. 148.

[413]   *Re Express Engineering Works Ltd* [1920] 1 Ch. 466; *Re Oxted Motor Co* [1921] 3 K.B. 32.

[414]   See para.1-028; and *Gower's Principles of Modern Company Law* (10th edn), paras 14-11–14-14 and 15-15–15-21.

[415]   Companies Act 2006 ss.39 and 40: below, para.8-033 onwards.

[416]   *Wilson v Tunman and Fretson* (1843) 6 M. & G. 236; *Woollen v Wright* (1862) 1 H. & C. 554; *Williams v Williams and Nathan* [1937] 2 All E.R. 559; *Barclays Bank v Roberts* [1954] 1 W.L.R. 1212. cf. *Morris v Salberg* (1889) 22 Q.B.D. 614.

[417]   *Saunderson v Griffiths* (1826) 5 B. & C. 909; *Heath v Chilton* (1844) 12 M. & W. 632.

[418]   *Keighley, Maxsted & Co v Durant* [1901] A.C. 240.

[419]   *Re Tiedemann & Ledermann Frères* [1899] 2 Q.B. 66.

[420]   *Jones v Hope* (1880) 3 T.L.R. 247n.

company not yet formed. This company cannot when formed render itself liable by ratification for the price of the goods.[421]

(7) A person may act on behalf of an heir, or an administrator, or the owner of particular property, whoever he may be, though unascertained and unknown to him, and the person on whose behalf the act was done may ratify it.[422]

(8) A policy of insurance is taken out describing the assured as "X, all its subsidiary associated and related companies, all contractors and subcontractors and/or suppliers". A subcontractor appointed in the following year cannot ratify the contract so as to sue on it as a party to it by virtue of the law of agency.[423]

(9) A trawler owned by a French company is at an English port when, as a result of enemy occupation of France, the company becomes an alien enemy. While this state of affairs continues, A, without the company's authority, acts as manager of the trawler. A's conduct cannot subsequently be ratified by the company, which was not at the time of A's acts competent to be A's principal.[424]

(10) A daughter purporting to act on behalf of her mother in respect of the prospective sale of the latter's interest in land orally indicates she will need to get her mother's consent to proposed terms but indicates that her mother would be likely to accept her recommendation. Mother later signs a receipt for part-payment of the purchase price. Ratification was not available because the daughter did not purport to have present authority to bind her mother, and the receipt was not unequivocal evidence that her mother understood what was alleged to have been agreed.[425]

Article 16

KNOWLEDGE NECESSARY FOR RATIFICATION

In order that a person may be held to have ratified an act done without his authority, it is necessary that, at the time of the ratification, he should have full knowledge of all the material circumstances in which the act was done,[426] unless he intended to ratify the act and take the risk whatever the circumstances may have been.[427] But

2-071

---

[421] *Kelner v Baxter* (1866–67) L.R. 2 C.P. 174. See also Article 107.

[422] *Lyell v Kennedy* (1889) 14 App.Cas. 437; *Foster v Bates* (1843) 1 D. & L. 400. See also *Hull v Pickersgill* (1819) 1 B. & B. 282.

[423] *Trident General Ins. Co Ltd v McNiece Bros Pty Ltd* (1987) 8 N.S.W.L.R. 270 at 276–277 (affirmed on other grounds (1988) 165 C.L.R. 107, but see p.113).

[424] *Boston Deep Sea Fishing & Ice Co v Farnham* [1957] 1 W.L.R. 1051.

[425] *Bennett v Strauss* [2016] NSWCA 324.

[426] *Suncorp Insurance and Finance v Milano Assecurazioni SpA* [1983] 2 Lloyd's Rep. 225; see Illustrations 1, 2 and 6. It seems clear that the knowledge of the agent should not in such a case be imputed to him; see Corbin (1906) 15 Yale L.J. 331. See also *Royal Albert Hall Corp v Winchilsea* (1891) 7 T.L.R. 362; *Eastern Construction Co Ltd v National Trust Co Ltd* [1914] A.C. 197 at 213; *McLean Bros & Rigg Ltd v Grice* (1906) 4 C.L.R. 835; *Taylor v Smith* (1926) 38 C.L.R. 48, Illustration 8; *Bedford Insurance Co Ltd v Instituto de Resseguros do Brasil* [1985] Q.B. 966 at 987; *Aotearoa International Ltd v Westpac Banking Corp* [1984] 2 N.Z.L.R. 34; *National Union of Mineworkers v Scargill* [2012] EWHC 3750 (Ch) at [159]; *Restatement, Third*, § 4.06.

[427] Illustrations 3 and 5; *Marsh v Joseph* [1897] 1 Ch. 213; *Restatement, Third*, § 4.06. See also *Donegal International Ltd v Republic of Zambia* [2007] EWHC 197 (Comm); [2007] 1 Lloyd's Rep. 397 at [454].

knowledge of the legal effect of the act may be imputed to him,[428] and it is not necessary that he should have notice of collateral circumstances affecting the nature of the act.[429]

Comment

2-072   This proposition has appeared in all editions of this work, and it is therefore preserved as a general guide. It is a rule protecting the principal against being found to have ratified sooner than is appropriate. It is obvious that some sort of rule to this effect is appropriate, both for ratification and for situations where similar reasoning is employed.[430] Although most rules relating to ratification are directed towards protecting the third party against unfair results, this rule protects the principal against being too easily treated as having ratified. But it is in fact doubtful whether any satisfactory formulation can in fact be found for all the different circumstances in which such reasoning is encountered.

Many of the clearest cases from which this rule is to be derived concern unlawful distress, and conclude that there was no ratification. It has already been argued that the doctrine of ratification has only limited application to torts.[431] In so far as ratification is applicable to make a person liable in tort, it would seem that the requirement of knowledge should be more strictly interpreted in that branch of the law,[432] whereas in a contractual situation a "blanket ratification" (as by receipt of goods) should be more easily able to be established. The objective interpretation of contractual situations, and the related notion that a person may be taken to know matters of which he might be expected to be aware,[433] may obviously allow the inference of ratification where this would not be permissible in a tort case, and it is right that it should.[434] Thus where a person ratified a lease negotiated by an agent under a misapprehension as to its provisions which would not have affected the validity of the contract had the parties made it without an intermediary, he was held bound by it.[435] But where a person to whom a duty of disclosure was owed purported to ratify a transaction (not effected through an agent) which was to his prejudice and voidable as such, this was held inoperative since he did not know that the transaction was voidable.[436] The burden of proof is on the person alleging

---

[428] *Powell v Smith* (1872) L.R. 14 Eq. 85; *Brown v Innovatorone Plc* [2012] EWHC 1321 (Comm) at [858]: see Comment. See also *Restatement, Third*, § 4.06 Comment *d*: "A factfinder may conclude that the principal has made such a choice when the principal is shown to have knowledge of facts that would lead a reasonable person to investigate, but the principal ratified without further investigation"; Corbin (1906) 15 Yale L.J. 331.

[429] Illustration 4.

[430] See above, para.2-048.

[431] See Comment to Article 14; Atiyah, *Vicarious Liability in the Law of Torts* (1967), pp.316–318.

[432] cf. *Marsh v Joseph* [1897] 1 Ch. 213, at 246–247; see also *Edwards v L & NW Ry Co* (1869–70) L.R. 5 C.P. 445; *Briess v Woolley* [1954] A.C. 333 at 344. But a general ratification of an employer-employee relationship may perhaps involve implied ratification of torts committed by the employee: Atiyah, *Vicarious Liability in the Law of Torts* (1967), pp.316–318.

[433] See Comment to Article 73.

[434] Mechem, *Outlines of Agency* (4th edn), pp.206–211.

[435] *Powell v Smith* (1872) L.R. 14 Eq. 85; but this is not in fact an agency case: see *AMB Generali Holdings AG v SEB Trygg, etc.* [2005] EWCA Civ 1237; [2006] 1 Lloyd's Rep. 318 at [42]. See also *Hunter v Parker* (1840) 7 M. & W. 322, Illustration 6.

[436] *Savery v King* (1856) 5 H.L. Cas. 627. See also *Spackman v Evans* (1868) L.R. 3 H.L. 171.

ratification.[437] Where the principal is aware of the agent's acts and the terms of the purported contract, it appears not to be necessary that the principal had realised, perhaps because of lack of internal records, that the agent had exceeded his authority.[438] Assent may otherwise be manifested by the principal's commencing to perform the contract, and where, to the principal's knowledge, the third party commences to act on it, the principal may become estopped from disowning it.[439] Much may turn on whether the retrospective effect of ratification is important. A principal who, for instance, is simply confirming a sale of a chattel or accepting a payment in respect of a sale, may be able to do so without knowing or caring that an agent had ineffectively purported to sell it the week before. But if much turns on the transaction being backdated, it is likely to be more important that the principal is aware that its decision will have retrospective effect. There is some authority that the knowledge of a director of the relevant facts may be sufficient to bind the director's company,[440] though quaere whether the knowledge does not have to be held by all persons whose assent is necessary to constitute ratification.[441] This is a situation where the claimant is seeking to enforce a contract, and not merely seeking restitution.

Illustrations

(1) An agent wrongfully distrains goods which were neither on the debtor's land **2-073** nor his property, without the authority of the principal, and pays over the proceeds to the principal. The principal is not deemed to have ratified the wrongful distress by receiving the proceeds, unless he received them with knowledge of the irregularity, or intended without inquiry to take the risk upon himself.[442]

(2) An agent, with authority to distrain for rent, wrongfully seized and sold a fixture, and paid the proceeds to the principal, who received them without notice that it was a fixture which had been sold. Held, that the principal had not ratified the trespass.[443]

(3) An agent, without authority, signed a distress warrant and, after the distress, informed his principal, who said that he should leave the matter in the agent's hands. Held, that this was a ratification of the whole transaction, though there had been irregularities in levying the distress of which the principal had no knowledge.[444]

(4) An agent purchased a chattel on his principal's behalf from a person who had no right to sell it, and the principal ratified the purchase. Held, that the principal was guilty of a conversion of the chattel, though he had no knowledge at the time of the ratification that the sale was unlawful. Here, the circumstances rendering the transaction a conversion were collateral to, and

---

[437] *Gunn v Roberts* (1874) L.R. 9 C.P. 331 at 335; *Marsh v Joseph* [1897] 1 Ch. 213 at 246–247.
[438] *Ing Re (UK) Ltd v R & V Versicherung AG* [2006] EWHC 1544 (Comm); [2006] Lloyd's Rep. I.R. 653 at [155]; *Brown v Innovatorone Plc* [2012] EWHC 1321 (Comm) at [858].
[439] See *Geniki Investments International Ltd v Ellis Stockbrokers Ltd* [2008] EWHC 549 (QB); [2008] 1 B.C.L.C. 662 at [46]. See further below, para.2-103.
[440] *Norwich Union Life & Pensions Ltd v Strand Street Properties Ltd* [2009] EWHC 1109 (Ch) at [243].
[441] See *PEC Ltd v Asia Golden Rice Co Ltd* [2014] EWHC 1583 (Comm) at [58]. See further below, para.8-214.
[442] *Lewis v Read* (1845) 13 M. & W. 834.
[443] *Freeman v Rosher* (1849) 13 Q.B. 780.
[444] *Haseler v Lemoyne* (1858) 5 C.B.(N.S.) 530. See also *Becker v Riebold* (1913) 30 T.L.R. 142.

did not form part of, the contract ratified. The ratification of the purchase as such was however sufficient to make the principal liable for conversion, liability for which is strict.[445]

(5) An agent entered into an unauthorised contract for the purchase of land on behalf of his principal. A letter from the principal, saying that he did not know what the agent had agreed to, but that he must support him in all he had done, was held to be sufficient ratification of the agreement, whatever it might be.[446]

(6) The master of a ship sells it in circumstances where no agency of necessity arises. The owner receives the proceeds of the sale by bills of exchange, believing that a situation of necessity had in fact arisen. On hearing the true facts he arrests the ship, presents the bills for payment and pays the money into court. He has not ratified the sale.[447] But he may be held to have done so if in similar circumstances the only irregularity unknown to him was as to the procedure by which the sale was effected.[448]

(7) An estate agent makes a contract to sell his principal's land. The principal ratifies, not knowing that the estate agent has subsequently received an inquiry about the land from someone else. The ratification is effective.[449]

(8) An estate agent thinking he is entitled to commission lodges a claim with the vendor's solicitor who simply pays the sum. This is not an act of ratification, since the vendor was unaware of the facts.[450]

Article 17

WHAT CONSTITUTES RATIFICATION

2-074 (1) Ratification may be express or by conduct.

(2) An express ratification is a manifestation by one on whose behalf an unauthorised act has been done that he treats the act as authorised and becomes a party to the transaction in question.[451] It need not be communicated to the third party.[452]

(3) Ratification will be implied whenever the conduct of the person in whose name or on whose behalf the act or transaction is done or entered into is such as to amount to clear evidence that he adopts or recognises such act or transaction[453]:

---

[445] *Hilberry v Hatton* (1864) 2 H. & C. 822. See Powell, p.122; Stoljar, p.179. The distinction between these cases and Illustrations 1 and 2 is perhaps that in those Illustrations the principal did not know of the act constituting the conversion at all.
[446] *Fitzmaurice v Bayley* (1856) 6 E. & B. 868 (see also (1860) 9 H.L. Cas. 78).
[447] *The Bonita, The Charlotte* (1861) Lush. 252.
[448] *Hunter v Parker* (1840) 7 M. & W. 322.
[449] *Brennan v O'Connell* [1980] I.R. 13.
[450] *Taylor v Smith* (1926) 38 C.L.R. 48.
[451] See *Restatement, Third*, § 4.01(2): "A person ratifies an act by (a) manifesting assent that the act shall affect the person's legal relations; or (b) conduct that is justifiable only on the assumption that the person so consents".
[452] See below, para.2-078.
[453] Illustrations 1–7; Illustration 12; *Waiwera Co-operative Dairy Co Ltd v Wright, Stephenson & Co Ltd* [1917] N.Z.L.R. 178 (ratification of contract by sending goods forward); *Akel v Turner* [1926] G.L.R. 574 (NZ) (ratification of sale of partnership business to company by acting as manager of company); Atiyah, *Vicarious Liability in the Law of Torts* (1967), p.318 onwards.

and may be implied from the mere acquiescence or inactivity of the principal.[454]

(4) The adoption of part of a transaction operates as a ratification of the whole.[455]

(5) It is not necessary that the ratification of a written contract should be in writing,[456] but the execution of a deed can only be ratified by deed.[457]

Comment

Rule (1) Just as a grant of authority may be express or implied, so may   2-075
ratification. Thus suing on a transaction, or basing a defence on it, will (subject to any rules as to ratifications which come too late[458]) often amount to an implied ratification of it.[459] So also receipt or retention of money with knowledge of the circumstances of a contract under which it is paid will normally constitute ratification of that contract,[460] as will use or disposal of goods received under it,[461] unless the supposed principal did not assent to the transaction and had no alternative but to receive them and use them as they were, e.g. where they were already his own.[462] It is clear therefore that ratification of an executed contract will be easier to establish than ratification of an executory contract, for there are few cases where a person can keep another's property, or benefit otherwise at the expense of another, without paying, unless he is unaware of the circumstances.[463] However, where the principal was unaware of the circumstances of receipt of property, liability, if any, may more appropriately be founded in conversion or in the law of restitution, than in contract. Such cases are different from those in which inactivity is no more than evidence of a voluntary ratification.[464]

---

[454] *Suncorp Insurance and Finance v Milano Assecurazioni SpA* [1993] 2 Lloyd's Rep. 225 at 234; *Yona International Ltd v La Réunion Française SA d'Assurances* [1996] 2 Lloyd's Rep. 84 at 103, 106; Illustration 9; and see Comment.

[455] Illustrations 2, 3, 10 and 11; see also *Bristow v Whitimore* (1861) 9 H.L. Cas. 391; *Republic of Peru v Peruvian Guano Co* (1887) 36 Ch.D. 489; *Re Mawcon Ltd* [1969] 1 W.L.R. 78; *Restatement, Third*, § 4.07 (ratification not effective unless it encompasses "the entirety of an act, contract or other single transaction"); *Sahota v Prior* [2019] EWHC 1418 (Ch) at [18].

[456] *Maclean v Dunn* (1828) 4 Bing. 722; *Soames v Spencer* (1822) 1 D. & R. 32; *Koenigsblatt v Sweet* [1923] 2 Ch. 314; *Sheridan v Higgins* [1971] I.R. 291.

[457] See *Hunter v Parker* (1840) 7 M. & W. 322; *Kidderminster Corp v Hardwicke* (1873) L.R. 9 Ex. 13; *Oxford Corp v Crow* [1893] 3 Ch. 535; *Athy Guardians v Murphy* [1986] 1 I.R. 65. But see Comment.

[458] Article 19.

[459] e.g. Illustration 6; *Verschures Creameries Ltd v Hull & Netherlands SS Co Ltd* [1921] 2 K.B. 608, Illustration 6 to Article 20; *Celthene Pty Ltd v WJK Hauliers Pty Ltd* [1981] 1 N.S.W.L.R. 606 at 615; *Life Savers (Aust.) Pty Ltd v Frigmobile Pty Ltd* [1983] 1 N.S.W.L.R. 431 at 438; *Trident General Ins. Co Ltd v McNiece Bros Pty Ltd* (1987) 8 N.S.W.L.R. 270 at 280, Illustration 8 to Article 15; affirmed on other grounds (1988) 165 C.L.R. 107.

[460] Illustrations 1 and 3; *Restatement, Third*, § 4.01 Comment *g*.

[461] Illustrations 2, 4 and 7.

[462] Illustration 8. See also *The Martin P* [2003] EWHC 3470; [2004] 1 Lloyd's Rep. 389 at [129] (approving cancellation of unauthorised contract not a ratification).

[463] See, e.g. *Royal Albert Hall Corp v Winchilsea* (1891) 7 T.L.R. 362. But the situation may be otherwise where the principal does not use the goods personally, e.g. in a husband and wife case like *Morel Bros & Co Ltd v Earl of Westmorland* [1904] A.C. 11.

[464] *Restatement, Second*, Appendix, reporter's note to § 94 at pp.178–180 (also printed in (1954) 103 U. Pa. L.Rev. 30).

The same factors as can vitiate the granting of authority, such as duress and undue influence, can also affect ratification.[465]

2-076   **Rule (2): Express ratification**   This needs no explanation: it is obvious that if the principle of ratification is accepted at all, an express statement will constitute its prime example. It would seem that a conditional ratification would, if the condition was as to a future event, take effect only as a promise to ratify, and only bind if supported by consideration or the requirements of estoppel.

2-077   **Rule (3): Implied ratification**   Express ratification will however be comparatively rare, and a ratification will more often be implied from words or conduct.[466] Such words or conduct must be unequivocal: they must not be such that they could be accounted for by other interpretations,[467] e.g. that the principal is simply resuming possession of his own property.[468] It is possible too that a principal may have made a book entry by accident or tentatively; a principal "may have dipped its toe in the Rubicon but had not crossed it".[469] Such reasoning is necessary to protect the principal against too easily being held liable as having ratified. Ratification can, however, be implied from a position taken in litigation.[470]

2-078   **Ratification need not be communicated, so long as manifested**   There is in principle no necessity for the ratification to be communicated to the other party: it seems long established that it operates, if proved, as a unilateral manifestation of will.[471] It will normally be communicated, or at least manifested, to the agent, or sometimes to the third party only. It is sometimes said that ratification need not be communicated at all.[472] But it is not clear that a principal could not have a change of mind if ratification had not yet been communicated to either agent or third party,

---

[465]   See *Ukraine v Law Debenture Trust Corp Plc* [2018] EWCA Civ 2026; [2019] 2 W.L.R. 655 at [149]. See further para.2-028.

[466]   See, e.g. *Crest Nicholson (Londinium) Ltd v Akaria Investments Ltd* [2010] EWHC 243 (Ch) at [72]; *Aviva Life & Pensions UK Ltd v Strand Street Properties Ltd* [2010] EWCA Civ 444; *Brown v Innovatorone Plc* [2012] EWHC 1321 (Comm) at [863] (submitting tax return and claiming tax relief on basis that had joined partnership was ratification of partnership).

[467]   *Petersen v Moloney* (1951) 84 C.L.R. 91 at 101; *McLauchlan-Troup v Peters* [1983] V.R. 53 (receipt of rent through agent whose authority was withdrawn, explicable on basis that he acted as agent for payer); *Swotbooks.com Ltd v Royal Bank of Scotland Plc* [2011] EWHC 2025 (QB) at [46] (inconsistent entries in principal's own records); *National Union of Mineworkers v Scargill* [2012] EWHC 3750 (Ch) at [160].

[468]   *Forman & Co Pty Ltd v The Liddesdale* [1900] A.C. 190, Illustration 8.

[469]   *Limpgrange Ltd v Bank of Credit and Commerce International SA* [1986] F.L.R. 36 at 55; cited with approval in *Swotbooks.com Ltd v Royal Bank of Scotland Plc* [2011] EWHC 2025 (QB) at [46].

[470]   e.g. Illustrations 6 and 7. See also *Scott v Bagshaw* (1999) 92 F.C.R. 424; *The Borvigilant* [2003] EWCA Civ 935; [2003] 2 Lloyd's Rep. 520 at [59]–[61] (letter before action); *Australian Workers' Union v Leighton Contractors Pty Ltd* [2013] FCAFC 4 at [96].

[471]   See *Harrisons & Crosfield Ltd v L & NW Ry Co Ltd* [1917] 2 K.B. 755 at 758; *Pagnan SpA v Feed Products Ltd* [1987] 2 Lloyd's Rep. 601 at 613; *Shell Co of Australia Ltd v Nat Shipping and Bagging Services Ltd (The Kilmun)* [1988] 2 Lloyd's Rep. 1 at 11, 14; *AMB Generali Holdings AG v SEB Trygg, etc.* [2005] EWCA Civ 1237; [2006] 1 Lloyd's Rep. 318 at [37] onwards; *Brown v Innovatorone Plc* [2012] EWHC 1321 (Comm) at [861]; *McHugh v Eastern Star Gas Ltd* [2012] NSWCA 169 at [58] (signing of board minutes ratifies court proceedings). In the case of a contract made "subject to ratification", however, the situation is different, for what is in issue is formation of the contract, not ratification of it. Hence notice would normally be required unless the offeror had waived notice of acceptance. See *Warehousing and Forwarding Co of East Africa Ltd v Jafferali & Sons* [1964] A.C. 1 at 9–10; above, para.2-050, below, para.2-087.

[472]   Mechem, *Principles of Agency* (4th edn), § 216; *Restatement, Second*, §§ 92(g), 93(1) and 95;

such as by tearing up a letter of ratification before sending it, or, in the case of a company, revoking a board resolution[473] Where the manifestation is to the third party it can operate as a form of estoppel, should, for instance, there have been an inconsistent communication to the agent. Equally, a court may conclude that there has been a novation of a transaction rather than a ratification.

In accordance with general principles, it is objective appearances that matter not the internal intentions of the principal:

"It seems to me that it should not be open to a principal, who to the outside world by his conduct, or that of his duly authorised agents, appears to have adopted a transaction to be able to prove subjectively that in fact he had not."[474]

Ratification by inactivity and acquiescence[475]   The issue whether ratification can   **2-079** be inferred from inactivity or acquiescence is more likely to arise with executory contracts, since in the cases of executed contracts it will be difficult to remain totally inactive, except in the case of unasked-for improvements to one's own property[476] (though, as seen, the possibility of an analysis based on conversion or the law of restitution may also be preferable in some such cases[477]). If inactivity of the principal can be taken as manifesting assent, it may constitute ratification.[478] Several cases involving executory contracts have been explained in this way.[479] However, it is also true that "silence or inaction may simply reflect an unwillingness or in-ability on the part of the principal to commit himself",[480] and there can be a range of other explanations for inactivity that make a finding of an intention to ratify unproven.[481] It has been held that to the extent that silence can amount to ratifica-

---

Restatement, Third, § 4.01 Comment d; UNIDROIT Principles art.2.2.9, Comment 1. In the context of a statutory provision extending the concept of ratification to pre-incorporation contracts, it has been held that ratification by the company post-incorporation need not be communicated to the other party to be effective, even though the parties must have been aware that there would be no contract with the company until ratification: Aztech Science Pty Ltd v Atlanta Aerospace (Woy Woy) Pty Ltd (2005) 55 A.C.S.R. 1 (NSWCA).
[473] See in relation to actual authority, para.3-003, below.
[474] Suncorp Insurance and Finance v Milano Assecurazioni SpA [1993] 2 Lloyd's Rep. 225 at 235.
[475] See Restatement, Second, Appendix, reporter's note to § 94 (also printed in (1954) 103 U.Pa.L.Rev. 30).
[476] Forman & Co Pty v The Liddesdale [1900] A.C. 190, Illustration 8; Prince v Clark (1823) 1 B. & C. 186, Illustration 9; Rodmell v Eden (1859) 1 F. & F. 542; The Australia (1859) 13 Moo.P.C. 132; City Bank of Sydney v McLaughlin (1909) 9 C.L.R. 615; Bank Melli Iran v Barclays Bank Ltd [1951] 2 T.L.R. 1057; cf. Taylor v Smith (1926) 38 C.L.R. 48.
[477] See above, para.2-075.
[478] City Bank of Sydney v McLaughlin (1909) 9 C.L.R. 615; Bank Melli Iran v Barclays Bank Ltd [1951] 2 T.L.R. 1057 at 1063; Yona International Ltd v La Réunion Française SA d'Assurances [1996] 2 Lloyd's Rep. 84 at 106: ratification can be inferred from silence where the principal "allows a state of affairs to come about which is inconsistent with treating the transaction as unauthorised", per Moore-Bick J; National Australia Bank Ltd v Dionys [2016] NSWCA 242 at [127]; Narandas-Girdhar v Bradstock [2016] EWCA Civ 88 at [31].
[479] Robinson v Gleadow (1835) 2 Bing. N.C. 156; Bigg v Strong (1858) 4 Jur.(N.S.) 983; Phillips v Homfray (1871) L.R. 6 Ch.App.770; Scots Church Adelaide Inc v Fead [1951] S.A.S.R. 41.
[480] Yona International Ltd v La Réunion Française S.A. d'Assurances [1996] 2 Lloyd's Rep. 84, at 106; Ing Re (UK) Ltd v R & V Versicherung AG [2006] EWHC 1544 (Comm); [2006] Lloyd's Rep. I.R. 653 at [162]; Sea Emerald SA v Prominvestbank-Joint Stockpoint Commercial Industrial and Investment Bank [2008] EWHC 1979 (Comm) at [105]. See above, para.2-072.
[481] See Commonwealth Bank of Australia v Perrin [2011] QSC 274 at [146]; Perpetual Trustees Victoria Ltd v Cox [2014] NSWCA 328 (no ratification by borrower of broker's dishonest drawdown purport-edly on borrower's behalf merely by borrower receiving notice from lender); Sino Channel Asia Ltd

tion, the third party cannot assume assent without allowing at least a reasonable period for (assumed) deliberation to pass.[482]

Past inactivity in respect of what was done by agents may also be held to confer actual or apparent authority[483]: a person who acts by representatives runs risks in doing so, and may owe a duty to make his position clear where a person acting alone would not. In all these cases, the principal is more likely to be bound where the person concerned is already an agent than when he is not.[484]

2-080 **Estoppel**   Ratification merges almost imperceptibly into estoppel.[485] When the silence or inactivity is known to and relied on by the third party, an estoppel may in appropriate cases arise against the principal, who may be estopped from saying that he has not ratified.[486] This will be different from an implied ratification if it comes as later and unrelated conduct, or if there is some difficulty as to the ratification, e.g. in respect of form or capacity.[487] Conversely, an estoppel may arise if the principal leads the third party to believe that he will not ratify, or does not do so within a reasonable time.[488]

2-081 **Rule (4)**   The principal cannot adopt the favourable parts of a transaction and disaffirm the rest: he cannot approbate and reprobate, for this would enable him to effect a transaction into which the third party had never intended to enter.[489] He must therefore adopt or reject the transaction in toto, and where it can be said that this has not been done, the conclusion may be drawn that there was no ratification[490] (though where an agent has effected several separate transactions, the principal may ratify certain transactions individually and refuse to ratify others[491]). This does not, however, mean that there are no circumstances whatever where he may ratify a transaction for one purpose while rejecting it for another. Thus in *Harrisons & Crossfield Ltd v London and North Western Ry Co*[492] a principal whose servant had, while on sick leave, stolen, before the commencement of transit, consignments which the principal had been employed to carry, ratified the transaction to the extent of laying the possession in himself for the purpose of the law of larceny. It was held

---

[   ] *v Dana Shipping and Trading PTE Singapore* [2016] EWHC 1118 (Comm); [2016] 2 Lloyd's Rep. 97 at [60] (no duty actively to repudiate being made party to arbitration proceedings).

[482] *Ing Re (UK) Ltd v R & V Versicherung AG* [2006] EWHC 1544 (Comm); [2006] Lloyd's Rep. I.R. 653 at [155]. It was for this reason that the plea of ratification failed on the facts.

[483] *City Bank of Sydney v McLaughlin* (1909) 9 C.L.R. 615 at 625. This could also be relevant if other requirements for ratification were not present, e.g. capacity or form. See below, paras 8-043 and 8-045.

[484] As with apparent authority: see Comment to Article 21.

[485] See the discussion by Waller J in *Suncorp Insurance and Finance v Milano Assecurazioni SpA* [1993] 2 Lloyd's Rep. 225 at 234–235; and also *West v Dillicar* [1920] N.Z.L.R. 139; *Geniki Investments International Ltd v Ellis Stockbrokers Ltd* [2008] EWHC 549 (QB); [2008] 1 B.C.L.C. 662 at [46]. cf. *The Bunga Melati 5* [2016] SGCA 20 at [12].

[486] cf. *Spiro v Lintern* [1973] 1 W.L.R. 1002, Illustration 3 to Article 21; *Worboys v Carter* [1987] 2 E.G.L.R. 1.

[487] See *Restatement, Third*, § 4.08.

[488] Article 19.

[489] See Illustration 11; cases cited at fn.455 above. But cf. *Langlands Foundry Co Ltd v Worthington Pumping Engine Co* (1896) 22 V.L.R. 144.

[490] *Smith v Henniker-Major & Co* [2002] EWCA Civ 762; [2003] Ch. 182 at [56].

[491] See *Fitzmaurice v Bayley* (1860) 9 H.L. Cas. 78 at 112; Illustration 10.

[492] *Harrisons & Crossfield Ltd v London and North Western Ry Co* [1917] 2 K.B. 755. See also *Kinsella v Hamilton* (1890) 26 L.R.Ir. 671 (ratification of distress does not ratify homicide committed in course of it).

that he had not ratified so as to vest possession in himself under the contract of carriage, so as to make him liable as a common carrier for non-delivery.

Rule (5) Since authority to execute a contract required to be in writing, or to be **2-082** evidenced in writing, need not be in writing,[493] it follows that ratification need not be in writing either.[494] But authority to execute a deed must be conferred by deed,[495] and hence ratification of such an action must equally be by deed.[496] But what appears to be a parol ratification may in fact amount to a second delivery[497]; and if a deed was not necessary for the transaction, the document executed may be treated as a written instrument so that a parol ratification of it is valid.[498]

Illustrations

(1) A shipmaster without authority of the owner sells his ship. The owners receive **2-083** the purchase money with full knowledge of the circumstances in which the ship was sold. The receipt of the purchase money is a ratification of the sale.[499]
(2) A is a bankrupt. B, at the request of A's wife, purchases certain bonds with A's money, and hands them to her. The trustee in bankruptcy seizes some of the bonds as part of A's estate. The trustee in bankruptcy has ratified the act of B, and thereby discharged him from liability in respect of money used for purchasing the other bonds.[500]
(3) A is a bankrupt. B wrongfully sells part of A's property. The trustee in bankruptcy accepts the proceeds or part of them, or otherwise recognises B as his agent in the transaction. B is deemed to have been duly authorised by the trustee to sell the property.[501]
(4) An agent purchases goods on behalf of his principal at a price exceeding his limit. The principal objects to the contract, but disposes of some of the goods as his own. He is deemed to have ratified the contract, and is bound by it.[502]
(5) A employs a broker to execute a distress warrant. The broker, in executing the warrant, illegally seizes goods belonging to B. In answer to a letter from B demanding compensation, A writes that he is at a loss to understand the threat of proceedings, but that his solicitor will accept service of any process

---

[493] Article 9.
[494] *Soames v Spencer* (1822) 1 D. & R. 32; *Maclean v Dunn* (1828) 4 Bing. 722; *Sheridan v Higgins* [1971] I.R. 291.
[495] Article 10. But authority to deliver a deed need no longer be given by deed: Law of Property (Miscellaneous Provisions) Act 1989 s.1(3)(c).
[496] See cases cited at fn.455 above. They are not conclusive, but the proposition seems correct in principle.
[497] *Tupper v Foulkes* (1861) 9 C.B.(N.S.) 797.
[498] *Hunter v Parker* (1840) 7 M. & W. 322; cf. above, para.2-042.
[499] *Hunter v Parker* (1840) 7 M. & W. 322; cf. *The Bonita, The Charlotte* (1861) Lush. 252; Illustration 6 to Article 16. See also *Simpole v Chee* [2013] EWHC 4444 (Ch) at [29].
[500] *Wilson v Poulter* (1724) 2 Str. 859.
[501] *Brewer v Sparrow* (1827) 7 B. & C. 310; *Smith v Baker* (1872-73) L.R. 8 C.P. 350; cf. *Valpy v Sanders* (1848) 5 C.B. 887. See also *Gardiner v Grigg* (1938) 38 S.R.(N.S.W.) 524 (adoption of sale by auctioneer with unauthorised warranty renders principal liable on warranty unless it was collateral); *Clark v Libra Developments Ltd* [2007] 2 N.Z.L.R. 709 (NZCA) at [166] (company which rendered invoices was held thereby to have ratified contract made by purporting agent); *Simpole v Chee* [2013] EWHC 4444 (Ch).
[502] *Cornwal v Wilson* (1750) 1 Ves. 510.

B thinks proper to issue. This reply is evidence of a ratification by A of the wrongful seizure.[503]

(6)   A receives the rents of certain property for many years without the authority of the owner (who is unknown, it not being clear who inherited the land on the death of the previous owners). The owner sues A for possession, and for an account of the rents and profits. The action is a sufficient ratification to render A the agent of the owner from the commencement.[504]

(7)   The chairman and deputy-chairman of directors, and the secretary, of a manufacturing company, respectively, ordered goods which were necessary for the purposes of the business of the company, and the goods were supplied and used therein. Held, that though the goods were ordered without authority, the directors must be taken to have known that they had been supplied and used in the business, and that therefore the company was liable for the price.[505]

(8)   A contracts to do certain specified repairs to a ship. An agent of the shipowner, whose authority is to the knowledge of A limited to the repairs so specified, sanctions certain variations in the work, and the repairs are executed according to the contract as varied. The shipowner sells the ship as repaired. The sale is not a ratification of the unauthorised variations.[506]

(9)   A ships goods to Calcutta and entrusts them to the captain of the ship to dispose of them as best he can in the interest of A, and to invest the proceeds in certain specified articles, or in bills at the exchange of the day. The captain sells the goods and invests the proceeds in unauthorised goods. A, on hearing of this, does nothing for ten weeks, after which he attempts to repudiate the captain's act. A is bound by the sale.[507]

(10)   D, the managing owner of a ship, sells it, through a broker, without authority. The other owners formally ratify the sale and receive their shares of the purchase money. They are liable to the selling agent for commission, the employment of a broker being an essential part of the whole transaction.[508] But ratification by a joint owner of the sale of a house may not constitute ratification of the contract with the estate agent who effects the sale, for the house need not have been sold through such an agent and there is therefore no need to regard the acquiescence in one contract as covering the other.[509]

(11)   A, who was B's manager, fraudulently and without authority obtained from B's bankers, in exchange for cheques drawn by B upon the bankers, drafts drawn by the bankers upon themselves, payable to bearer and crossed "not negotiable". A paid these drafts into an account which he had with the C Bank, and the C Bank collected the amounts. In an action by B against the C Bank for conversion of the drafts it was held that B must, in order to have a title to sue, ratify A's act in obtaining the drafts; but that B could not ratify this act without also ratifying A's payment of the drafts into his account with

---

[503] *Carter v St Mary Abbotts, Kensington, Vestry* (1900) 64 J.P. 548. cf. *Barrett v Irvine* [1907] 2 I.R. 462 (negotiation for a compromise does not amount to ratification).

[504] *Lyell v Kennedy* (1889) 14 App.Cas. 437.

[505] *Smith v Hull Glass Co* (1852) 11 C.B. 897; *Allard v Bowne* (1863) 15 C.B.(N.S.) 468.

[506] *Forman & Co Pty Ltd v The Liddesdale* [1900] A.C. 190.

[507] *Prince v Clark* (1823) 1 B. & C. 186.

[508] *Keay v Fenwick* (1876) 1 C.P.D. 745.

[509] *Hughes v Hughes* (1971) 115 S.J. 911.

the C Bank, for the form of the drafts necessitated payment into some bank for collection; and that the action therefore failed.[510]

(12) D instructs an estate agent to act in the sale of a house, no.17. No.7 is also on the agent's books. A purchaser wishing to acquire no.7 is persuaded to sign a contract relating to no.17 and to pay a deposit, on the agent's representation that the properties are the same. D objects to some of the terms of the contract and refuses to sign it. The agent refuses to return the deposit without an order from D. D by letter requests the agent to return the deposit but the agent again refuses. There is evidence from which it could be determined that D has ratified the agent's receipt of it and may be liable to repay it.[511]

Article 18

EVENTS NOT PREVENTING RATIFICATION

Ratification is effective—   2-084

(1) although the person ratifying had refused at first to recognise the act,[512] unless to allow ratification would unfairly prejudice the third party[513];

(2) although proceedings have been commenced against the person purporting to act as agent[514];

(3) of a contract, notwithstanding that the third party has given notice to the principal of his withdrawal from it,[515] unless the contract was made by the agent expressly or impliedly subject to ratification, in which case the offer or purported acceptance may be withdrawn at any time before ratification.[516]

Comment

Rule (1)   It has been held that where the principal refused to ratify but, being   2-085
nevertheless urged to do so, eventually did, he could sue the third party[517]: but that where he indicated that he would not do so, and the third party acted to his prejudice on that basis, the principal could not subsequently ratify.[518] It has also been held that an *uncommunicated* refusal to ratify can be reversed, so that the principal can take advantage of the act ratified.[519] In general it seems, therefore, that the rule is correctly expressed as above: a ratification may be effective against the principal though originally he refused to ratify, and also in his favour unless the third party has relied on a previous refusal in a way that would make a subsequent ratification

---

[510] *Union Bank of Australia v McClintock* [1922] 1 A.C. 240; *Commercial Banking Co of Sydney v Mann* [1961] A.C. 1. But see Hornby (1961) 24 M.L.R. 271; Megrah [1961] J.B.L. 35; *Canadian Laboratory Supplies Ltd v Engelhard Industries of Canada Ltd* (1977) 78 D.L.R. (3d) 232, 236–237, 247; [1979] 2 S.C.R. 787 at 801–804; (1979) 97 D.L.R. (3d) 1 at 11–14.

[511] *Benham v Batty* (1865) 12 L.T. 266.

[512] *Soames v Spencer* (1822) 1 D. & R. 32; *Simpson v Eggington* (1855) 10 Exch. 845; see Comment.

[513] See Comment.

[514] Illustration 4.

[515] *Bolton Partners v Lambert* (1889) 41 Ch.D. 295, Illustration 1; *Re Tiedemann & Ledermann Frères* [1899] 2 Q.B. 66, Illustration 4 to Article 15.

[516] *Watson v Davies* [1931] 1 Ch. 455, Illustration 3; *Warehousing & Forwarding Co of East Africa v Jafferali & Sons* [1964] A.C. 1: see Comment.

[517] *Soames v Spencer* (1822) 1 D. & R. 32. See also *Akel v Turner* [1926] G.L.R. 574 (NZ).

[518] See *McEvoy v Belfast Banking Co Ltd* [1935] A.C. 24 at 45.

[519] *Simpson v Eggington* (1855) 10 Exch. 845.

unfairly prejudicial. These conclusions seem better based on the rules as to limits on ratification than an estoppel, since there may be difficulties concerning representations of intention as founding estoppel. The reasoning seems best based on an analogy with the grant of preceding authority, which cannot be withdrawn as regards the transaction authorised once acted on: since the agent's action has already taken place, a ratification cannot without the consent of the other party be withdrawn. A refusal to ratify, on the other hand, is merely equivalent to a refusal to grant authority: this does not prevent a subsequent grant of authority, subject to the doctrine of estoppel. The other limitations on the power to ratify are of course also applicable.[520]

2-086 **Rule (2)** This proposition covers cases where ratification renders lawful an act which was initially a tort, notwithstanding that proceedings have been instituted against the agent prior to ratification: an example appears in Illustration 4. In the case of contract, there is authority that where proceedings have been commenced against a *principal*, he may ratify thereafter and so render himself liable.[521] But a purported ratification by the principal after the commencement of proceedings against the agent would sometimes not be within a reasonable time[522] and so inoperative against a third party who did not wish to take advantage of it.[523]

2-087 **Rule (3)** This proposition is a conspicuous and controversial application of the technical notion that ratification creates authority which relates back to the time of the act ratified. It is often referred to as the rule in *Bolton Partners v Lambert*,[524] a leading case which appears as Illustration 1. Such a rule is rejected in *Restatement, Third*,[525] and the case has been criticised by distinguished writers as giving an inappropriately full effect to the doctrine of relation back.[526] The third party, though he may not know it, is in the power of the principal, not merely as to whether he has made a contract, but also as to whether he must already answer for breach of it. Furthermore, when the third party discovers before any ratification that the agent is unauthorised (which was not the case in *Bolton Partners v Lambert*), it may well be argued that he should be able to escape from the transaction rather than have to wait, if only for a reasonable time, to see if he has a contract. In *Fleming v Bank of New Zealand*[527] the Privy Council reserved the right to reconsider the case. It is certainly true that the judgments in *Bolton Partners v Lambert* itself consist largely of assertion. It is also true that the rule can only work fairly if it is made the subject of exceptions, discussed in the next Article, which are extremely difficult to

---

[520] e.g. that the ratification must be within a reasonable time: though this may also be based in estoppel. See in general Comment to Article 19.

[521] *Richardson v Oxford* (1861) 2 F. & F. 449.

[522] See Article 19.

[523] Except as regards the rules relating to mitigation of damages.

[524] *Bolton Partners v Lambert* (1889) 41 Ch.D. 295, Illustration 1. See also *Re Portuguese Consolidated Copper Mines Ltd* (1890) 45 Ch.D. 16, Illustration 4 to Article 19; *Hooper v Kerr, Stuart & Co Ltd* (1901) 83 L.T. 729, Illustration 2 to Article 20; *Koenigsblatt v Sweet* [1923] 2 Ch. 314.

[525] § 4.05.

[526] Wambaugh (1895) 9 Harvard L.Rev. 60; Fry, *Specific Performance* (6th edn), Additional Note A; Seavey (1920) 29 Yale L.J. 859 at 890–891; Tamaki (1941) 19 Can.B.R. 733; Pappas (1948) 2 Vand.L.Rev. 100; Hambrook (1982) 8 Adelaide L.Rev. 119 at 134–140; *Restatement, Third*, § 4.05(1) and Comment *c*; Dal Pont, para.5-40 onwards; Krebs, in *Agency Law in Commercial Practice* (Busch, Macgregor and Watts eds), pp.28–32; L. Macgregor (2019) 23 Edin. L.R. 94.

[527] *Fleming v Bank of New Zealand* [1900] A.C. 577 at 587. See the elaborate dissenting judgment of Isaacs J in *Davison v Vickery's Motors Ltd* (1925) 37 C.L.R. 1 and cases and dicta there cited.

formulate. This difficulty casts some doubt on the initial rule. The rule has however been assumed to be binding on the Court of Appeal.[528] Perhaps the rule's strongest rationale is that the third party's inability to withdraw is the consideration for the agent's warranty of authority; "I will warrant my authority so long as you permit the principal to ratify if I am wrong". If this is right, it ought to follow that if the agent consents to the third party's withdrawal from the contract, the principal ceases to be able to ratify.[529]

If the English courts had a free hand, however, it is unlikely that many would disagree with the proposition that if a third party at the time of contracting believes an agent to be authorised, and subsequently finds that this was not so, he should, if he wishes, be able to withdraw from the transaction on that ground alone, and should not remain potentially bound until the principal decides whether or not to ratify. But the matter is less clear if the third party, not knowing of the lack of authority and believing himself to be bound, simply repudiates the contract, i.e. refuses or can be shown to be unable to perform, even if he uses the word "withdraw" to refer to his conduct—and it is this which appears to have been *Bolton Partners v Lambert* itself (with the added feature that the third party there apparently "withdrew" because he believed that the negotiations had not reached the stage at which he was bound at all). If one assumes that such a third party would normally have believed on reasonable grounds that the agent had authority, he can rely on the doctrine of apparent authority (or even ratification) and sue the principal for non-performance. In such a situation it is therefore the supposed principal, if he cannot ratify, who is potentially bound until the third party decides whether or not to proceed against him. *Restatement, Third* rejects the reasoning behind *Bolton Partners v Lambert* completely and treats the third party as being able to "withdraw" in this second situation also[530]; but the scope of ratification in the Restatements is in some respects different from that under English common law.[531] It is not clear that a party, X, who believed themselves bound (and perhaps anticipating being in breach) and is able to sue even only if apparent authority (or ratification) is established, is fairly released by the fact that unknown to X the person with whom X had dealt had no actual authority. Perhaps X's release could be based for English law on the known rule that a party who gives one reason justifying what appears to be a repudiation of contract may subsequently give another if it was in existence at the time of the original repudiation.[532] But as stated above, the *Bolton Partners* case, whatever it stands for, is binding on any court in England and Wales other than the Supreme Court.

It is in any case clear that where a contract is made expressly or impliedly subject to ratification, it is not binding at all and there is nothing to ratify.[533] Such an interpretation can be put on most cases where the third party is aware of the lack

---

[528] *Presentaciones Musicales S.A. v Secunda* [1994] Ch. 271 at 280 (Illustration 6 to Article 19).
[529] See *Walter v James* (1870–1871) L.R. 6 Ex. 124; *London Borough of Haringey v Ahmed* [2017] EWCA Civ 1861 at [54].
[530] See *Restatement, Third*, § 4-05(1).
[531] See above, para.2-050.
[532] *Boston Deep Sea Fishing and Ice Co v Ansell* (1888) 39 Ch.D. 339.
[533] *Watson v Davies* [1931] 1 Ch. 455, Illustration 3; *Warehousing and Forwarding Co of East Africa v Jafferali & Sons* [1964] A.C. 1; *Rothmans Industries Ltd v Floral Holdings Ltd* [1986] 2 N.Z.L.R. 480 (contract "subject to approval of shareholders", a nullity). See also above, para.2-050. The judgment in *Jafferali*'s case is not easy to follow. It distinguishes between negotiating subject to approval and contracting subject to ratification. Obviously in the first case the details of the proposed agreement may be vaguer, but in neither case is there any transaction binding the third party.

of authority, whatever the reasons for it. The purported ratification, would in fact simply create the contract, unless the other party had previously withdrawn. The case is the same as that where the agent does not purport to have authority.[534] The third party's promise is at best one made to the agent, not to withdraw from the transaction, and unless there is independent consideration does not bind him. Although it is possible to enter into a contract which binds in the sense that neither party may withdraw from the moment of agreement, but the main obligation does not come into operation unless certain events occur,[535] it is difficult to see that such a contract can be found to exist where the condition relates to the question whether one purported party is bound at all.

It seems also that the rule in *Bolton Partners v Lambert* is one of agency law only and to be restricted to cases of lack of authority. If the original agreement is ineffective for any other reason (e.g. lack of a deed) there is no contract to withdraw from and the doctrine of relation back does not apply.[536]

It has further been held that where the act the subject of purported ratification ceases to be operative before ratification, there is nothing to ratify.[537] The case in question involved unauthorised payment of a debt, and it was said that in such a case the party to whom the debt was paid was entitled to return the money on discovering that the payment had been unauthorised, and apply to his debtor for payment.[538]

Illustrations

2-088   (1)   A made an offer to B, the managing director of a company, and it was accepted by him on the company's behalf. B had no authority to accept the offer. Not knowing of the lack of authority, but on the basis of disagreement in subsequent negotiations, which appear to have led him to assume that he was not yet bound, A gave the company notice that he withdrew his offer. The company subsequently ratified B's unauthorised acceptance. Held, that the ratification dated back to the time of the acceptance, rendering the purported withdrawal of the offer a breach. Specific performance was decreed against A.[539]

(2)   A, without B's authority, pays a debt owed by B. The creditor, upon discovering that A was not authorised to pay the debt, returns the money to him. B cannot subsequently ratify or take advantage of the payment.[540]

(3)   A offers land to a charity at a certain price. The chairman and 14 of the 18 members of the board of the charity visit the property. They tell A that they

---

[534] Contra, Seavey (1954) 21 U.Chi.L.Rev. 248; cf. Twerski (1948) 42 Temple L.Q. 1. See *Goodison Thresher Co v Doyle* (1925) 57 O.L.R. 300.

[535] See Treitel, *Law of Contract* (15th edn), para.2-100 onwards.

[536] *Kidderminster Corp v Hardwick* (1873) L.R. 9 Ex. 13 at 22 (followed in *Oxford v Crow* [1893] 3 Ch. 535) as explained in *Athy Guardians v Murphy* [1896] 1 I.R. 65. However, *Kidderminster Corp v Hardwick* was not referred to in *Bolton Partners v Lambert* and the approaches of the two cases are not easily reconciled. If the reasoning in *Athy Guardians v Murphy* is correct, it could also be used to explain *Metropolitan Asylums Board v Kingham & Sons*, below, Illustration 5 to Article 19.

[537] *Walter v James* (1870–71) L.R. 6 Ex. 124, Illustration 2; see *Birks and Beatson* (1976) 92 L.Q.R. 188 esp. at p.190 onwards.

[538] *Walter v James* (1870–71) L.R. 6 Ex. 124 at 127.

[539] *Bolton Partners v Lambert* (1889) 41 Ch.D. 295. A had also later claimed misrepresentation.

[540] *Walter v James* (1870–71) L.R. 6 Ex. 124. But see as to this case Birks and Beatson (1976) 92 L.Q.R. 188, especially at 190 onwards; Watts [1993] N.Z. Recent L.R. 248. As to the position in Scotland, see Macgregor and Whitty (2010) 15 Edin. L.R. 57.

have all made up their minds to purchase it and that a board meeting to be summoned to approve the purchase will be a mere formality. A may withdraw before the meeting, and a purported ratification by the meeting is ineffective, there being no initial agreement which can be ratified.[541]

(4) An agent, after the death of his principal, distrained in the principal's name for rent due. Held, that the executor might ratify the distress, and so justify the agent, although an action was at the time of the ratification pending against the agent for the trespass, and although the distress was levied before probate.[542]

Article 19

LIMITS ON RATIFICATION

Ratification is not effective where to permit it would unfairly prejudice a third party, and in particular: **2-089**

(1) where it is essential to the validity of an act that it should be done within a certain time, the act cannot be ratified after the expiration of that time, to the prejudice of any third party[543];

(2) ratification may not be recognised if it will affect proprietary rights in either real or personal property, including intellectual property rights, which have arisen in favour of the third party or others claiming through him since the act of the unauthorised agent[544];

(3) the ratification of a contract can only be relied on by the principal if effected within a time after the act ratified was done which is reasonable in all the circumstances.[545]

Comment

It is clear that although the principle of ratification is convenient it could operate unfairly on the third party, particularly if it is given full retroactive effect, as in *Bolton Partners v Lambert*.[546] This Article seeks to formulate limits on the efficacy, and in particular on the retroactivity, of ratification. However, the basic rule is that first stated, that the ratification must not cause unfair prejudice: this has been accepted twice recently in the Court of Appeal.[547] The more detailed formulations which follow are therefore to be read subject to this. **2-090**

---

[541] *Watson v Davies* [1931] 1 Ch. 455.

[542] *Whitehead v Taylor* (1839) 10 A. & E. 210; see also *Foster v Bates* (1843) 12 M. & W. 226; *Hull v Pickersgill* (1819) 1 B. & B. 282; and *Sunde v Sunde* [2019] NZHC 3056.

[543] Illustrations 1–3; *Audley (Lord) v Pollard* (1596) Cro.Eliz. 561; 78 E.R. 806; *Restatement, Third*, § 4.05(2).

[544] See Comment.

[545] *Re Portuguese Consolidated Copper Mines Ltd* (1890) 45 Ch.D. 16, Illustration 4; *Celthene Pty Ltd v WKJ Hauliers Pty Ltd* [1981] 1 N.S.W.L.R. 606 at 615; *Life Savers (Australasia) Ltd v Frigmobile Pty Ltd* [1983] 1 N.S.W.L.R. 431 at 438; *Trident General Insurance Co v McNiece Bros Pty Ltd* (1987) 8 N.S.W.L.R. 270 at 282; affirmed on other grounds (1988) 165 C.L.R. 107.

[546] *Bolton Partners v Lambert* (1889) 41 Ch.D. 295, Illustration 1 to Article 18; see Comment to Article 18.

[547] *Smith v Henniker-Major & Co* [2003] EWCA Civ 762; [2003] Ch. 182 (see Robert Walker LJ at [71]); and *The Borvigilant* [2003] EWCA Civ 935; [2003] 2 Lloyd's Rep. 520, Illustration 7 (see Clarke LJ at [70]). See also *Restatement, Third*, § 4.05(3).

2-091   **Rules (1) and (2)**   The strongest examples of this exception concern property rights. In what is often treated as the leading case, *Bird v Brown*,[548] goods were stopped in transit by an agent who had no authority to do so. They were formally demanded on behalf of the consignee, whose property they were and who tendered the freight. The consignor later ratified the stoppage. It was held that this was ineffective to affect the proprietary right which had vested in the consignee, and the agent was liable in conversion. It was said in *Bolton Partners v Lambert* itself that "an estate once vested cannot be divested by the doctrine of ratification".[549] A similar interpretation could be given to *Dibbins v Dibbins*,[550] in which it was held that where an option was exercised within its time limit by an agent who had no authority, its exercise could not be ratified outside that time. There are also cases holding ineffective ratification of unauthorised notices to quit after their operative date[551] which should perhaps be brought within this reasoning, in that the leasehold interest terminates on the expiry of the period set by a valid notice.[552] It cannot in fact be doubted that the doctrine cannot change property rights.

Bird v Brown is also frequently cited outside the context of property reasoning, but it does not of itself solve the contractual issues. In the case of an option, even though the ratification might not alter the equitable property rights involved, if property is the only exception it could be that ratification would render the holder of the property concerned nevertheless liable in contract to the person ratifying.[553] The reasoning of *Dibbins v Dibbins* nevertheless indicates that ratification is not possible even as regards the contractual liability. There are other cases where ratification is not permitted outside a time limit for the doing of the act: in particular, service of a notice to quit, already referred to in connection with pure property reasoning, could be brought within this wider rubric. Some rule regarding time limits is therefore needed. It may therefore be that outside property reasoning the cases should be approached on the basis that there is a simple rule preventing ratification outside time limits set for the doing of an act. This is supported by *Bird v Brown* also, where it was said that the right of stoppage can only be exercised during the transit. In *Presentaciones Musicales SA v Secunda*,[554] dealing with ratification of an unauthorised writ outside the limitation period, such a view was taken by two members of the Court of Appeal,[555] though the third[556] restricted the limit on ratification to situations involving property rights in a broad sense. The major-

---

[548] *Bird v Brown* (1850) 4 Exch. 786, Illustration 2; cf. *Hutchings v Nunes* (1863) 1 Moo.P.C.(N.S.) 243, where the court apparently held that an agent already had general authority, despite a purported ratification after the end of the transit. There are animadversions on some of the reasoning in *Bird v Brown* in *Keighley, Maxsted & Co v Durant* [1901] A.C. 240 at 247–248.

[549] *Bolton Partners v Lambert* (1889) 41 Ch.D. at 307.

[550] *Dibbins v Dibbins* [1896] 2 Ch. 348, Illustration 3.

[551] e.g. *Right d. Fisher, Nash and Hyrons v Cuthell* (1804) 5 East 491; and the argument of Coleridge J in *Doe d. Mann v Walters* (1830) 10 B. & C. 626 at 627–631; *Doe d. Lyster v Goldwin* (1841) 2 Q.B. 143; *Aldford House Freehold Ltd v Grosvenor (Mayfair) Estate* [2018] EWHC 3430 (Ch); [2019] 1 W.L.R. 1489 at [98]; reversed on other points [2019] EWCA Civ 1848; [2020] 2 W.L.R. 116. See Illustration 1.

[552] *Ancona v Marks* (1862) 7 H.& N. 686 at 697.

[553] See Tan Cheng-Han (2001) 117 L.Q.R. 626 at 630–634.

[554] [1994] Ch. 271, Illustration 6. See Brown (1994) 111 L.Q.R. 531. In addition to the cases there cited see *Shaw Savill & Albion Co v Timaru Harbour Board* (1888) 6 N.Z.L.R. 456; affirmed on other grounds (1890) 15 App.Cas. 429 (see argument).

[555] Dillon and Nolan LJJ; particular reliance was placed on *Ainsworth v Creeke* (1868–69) L.R. 4 C.P. 476, a case on a borough poor-rate.

[556] Roch LJ. But see Robert Walker LJ in *Smith v Henniker-Major & Co* [2003] EWCA Civ 762; [2003] Ch. 182.

ity view has been justified by an assertion that the principal can only ratify where he could have performed the act at the time of ratification.[557] This however does not square with the rule that a principal can ratify an insurance contract after loss,[558] which would require to be explained as an exception. It is also difficult to reconcile with *Bolton Partners v Lambert*[559] itself, where no such rule was referred to.

A viable "time limits" rule would however require some reference to the purpose of the limit in question. In this context reference to the notion of validity is sometimes suggested. It can be said that where it is essential to the validity of an act that it should be done within a certain time, it cannot be ratified after that time to the prejudice of the third party (though the third party can always accept the ratification). In *Presentaciones Musicales SA v Secunda* it was in fact held that since a writ issued without authority was not a complete nullity[560] it could be ratified after the expiry of the limitation period.

But the workability of a rule that void acts cannot be ratified has already been doubted,[561] and it may be better simply to proceed on the basis that certain acts are by their context required to be valid and effective when done,[562] lest a time limit be extended or the party affected be in a state of uncertainty. Such a rule would require discrimination between situations. Thus although the unauthorised issue of a writ can apparently be ratified[563] (at least before entry of judgment in favour of the defendant[564]), an assignment probably cannot after action on the right assigned has been commenced by the purported assignee,[565] nor a demand for payment or delivery,[566] a notice of abandonment in marine insurance,[567] a notice of dishonour of a negotiable instrument[568] or a notice to quit.[569] It may be possible to say that a ratification will be given retrospective effect unless there are cogent reasons why to give it such effect would contravene the purpose of any time element involved or otherwise be unfair to the third party. The third party can always however accept the ratification if he pleases.

Rule (2) is taken from the judgment of Roch LJ in the *Presentaciones Musicales* case, and represents a passage favourably referred to in the other two principal

---

[557] *Bird v Brown* (1850) 4 Exch. 786 at 799; *Ainsworth v Creeke* (1868–69) L.R. 4 C.P. 476, at 486 and 487; *Williams v North China Insurance Co* (1875–76) 1 C.P.D. 757 at 764 (arguendo), 766. But the argument was rejected in *Hooper v Kerr, Stuart & Co Ltd* (1900) 83 L.T. 729, Illustration 2 to Article 20.
[558] See below, para.2-093.
[559] Illustration 1 to Article 18; see Comment to Article 18.
[560] On the ground that adoption or ratification does not require any application to the court: [1994] Ch. 271 at 279–280.
[561] See Article 14 and Comment.
[562] See *Re Construction Forestry Mining and Energy Union* (1994) 181 C.L.R. 539 at 545.
[563] *Presentaciones Musicales SA v Secunda*, Illustration 6; *Nottinghamshire NHS Trust v Prison Officers Assn* [2003] I.C.R. 1192 (complaint of unfair dismissal after expiry of time limit: useful discussion). *Danish Mercantile Co Ltd v Beaumont* [1951] Ch. 680, Illustration 4 to Article 14; *Alexander Ward & Co Ltd v Samyang Navigation Co Ltd* [1975] 1 W.L.R. 673; and see *Pontin v Wood* [1962] 1 Q.B. 594; *Matthews v SPI Electricity Pty Ltd* [2011] VSC 167; (2011) 34 V.R. 560 at [65] (nominal plaintiff able to ratify representative proceedings).
[564] See *Gelley v Shepherd* [2013] EWCA Civ 1172 at [73].
[565] See Mechem, *Law of Agency* (2nd edn), § 530 (deprivation of defence).
[566] See *Solomons v Dawes* (1794) 1 Esp. 83; *Coore v Callaway* (1794) 1 Esp. 115; *Coles v Bell* (1808) 1 Camp. 478n.
[567] See *Jardine v Leathley* (1863) 3 B. & S. 700 at 708.
[568] *East v Smith* (1847) 16 L.J.Q.B. 292.
[569] See cases cited at fn.551 above.

recent decisions by Robert Walker LJ in *Smith v Henniker-Major & Co*[570] and by Clarke LJ in *The Borvigilant*.[571] In particular, Robert Walker LJ said that the "deprivation of an accrued right" was "an important example of the general rationale identified in ... Article 19, that is, unfair prejudice".[572] It may be assumed that interests in real and personal property cannot, at any rate normally, and certainly not against a third party, be divested by ratification.[573] The words used in Rule (2) however permit the extension of such reasoning to other occurrences which could be regarded as analogous, such as an accrued right of action: but, it would appear, not in all cases. For the *Presentaciones Musicales* case holds that immunity from suit by reason of limitation is not automatically barred and can, at least sometimes, be extinguished by ratification, and *The Borvigilant* that a right of action in tort can be extinguished or limited by ratification of a contract containing an applicable exclusion of liability clause (which it must always have been assumed would be operative). It seems therefore that the rule is being clarified as a flexible one; but it is also a "judgmental application of principle ... not ... an exercise of judicial discretion, though for practical purposes the two are closely akin".[574]

2-092   **Rule (3): reasonable time**   There is a dictum by Fry LJ that "if the ratification is to bind it must be made within a reasonable time after acceptance by an authorised person".[575] Fry LJ went on, however, to say that "such a reasonable time can never extend after the time at which the contract is to commence". This part of the dictum has been disapproved[576] and cannot now be regarded as valid.[577] The first part of the dictum seems, however, an appropriate restriction on ratification; but that not all delay makes ratification too late is shown by the fact that a letter before action may amount to ratification.[578] It is probably best based on a wider principle, such as that suggested in *Restatement, Third*,[579] that:

> "A ratification of a transaction is not effective unless it precedes the occurrence of circumstances that would cause the ratification to have adverse and inequitable effects on the rights of third parties".[580]

In different words, the rule is one for the protection of the third party against whom

---

[570] *Smith v Henniker-Major & Co* [2002] EWCA Civ 762; [2003] Ch. 182.

[571] *The Borvigilant* [2003] EWCA Civ 935; [2003] 2 Lloyd's Rep. 520, Illustration 7. See also *Challinor v Juliet Bellis & Co* [2013] EWHC 347 (Ch) at [643]; reversed on other points, sub nom. *Bellis v Challinor* [2015] EWCA Civ 59.

[572] *The Borvigilant* [2003] EWCA Civ 935; [2003] 2 Lloyd's Rep. 520 at [71].

[573] See Clarke LJ in *The Borvigilant* [2003] EWCA Civ 935; [2003] 2 Lloyd's Rep. 520 at [84]–[86].

[574] *Smith v Henniker-Major & Co* [2002] EWCA Civ 762; [2003] Ch. 182 at [82], per Robert Walker LJ.

[575] *Metropolitan Asylums Board v Kingham & Sons* (1890) 6 T.L.R. 217 at 218 (Illustration 5).

[576] *Celthene Pty Ltd v WKJ Hauliers Pty Ltd* [1981] 1 N.S.W.L.R. 606 at 615; *Life Savers (Aust.) Pty Ltd v Frigmobile Pty Ltd* [1983] 1 N.S.W.L.R. 431 at 438; *Bedford Insurance Co Ltd v Instituto de Resseguros do Brasil* [1983] Q.B. 966 at 987. See also *Morrell v Studd and Millington* [1913] 2 Ch. 648.

[577] It is extremely difficult to reconcile with *Bolton Partners v Lambert* itself. Fry LJ was a declared opponent of the rule in any case: see Fry, *Specific Performance* (6th edn), Additional Note A.

[578] As in *The Borvigilant* [2003] EWCA Civ 935: [2003] 2 Lloyd's Rep. 520, Illustration 7.

[579] § 4.05.

[580] Tan Cheng-Han (2001) 117 L.Q.R. 626, suggests that this rule can solve the retroactivity problems discussed above, para.2-091. It seems doubtful however whether the rule can bear such a weight of specific criteria as are needed.

the ratification might be invoked. If the principal ratifies and the third party actually wishes to rely on this, he should be entitled to do so. Where the third party wishes to resist ratification, the mere lapse of time may often make it inequitable,[581] particularly when "a modest degree of prejudice is magnified by delay".[582] But there may be other circumstances which do so. For a start, the third party who discovers that the agent was unauthorised may be put in a state of uncertainty in which a rapid indication by the principal of his position is required: it would then behove the principal to ratify quickly or not at all. And it is sometimes said that if an agent contracts without authority to sell property to another, and the property is then destroyed without anyone's fault, the principal can no longer ratify.[583]

Ratification of policies of insurance after loss   It has, however, long been established that a policy of marine insurance may be ratified after loss[584]: this was justified on the basis that: **2-093**

> "where an agent effects an insurance subject to ratification, the loss insured against is very likely to happen before ratification, and it must be taken that the insurance so effected involves that possibility as the basis of the contract."[585]

It had been controversial whether this principle applies to other insurances also, but it now seems clear that it does,[586] and this seems correct. If the commercial background dictates that policies are entered into on this basis, it is not inequitable to hold the insurer liable.[587]

Illustrations

(1)   A, without the authority of the landlord, gives a tenant notice to quit. The notice cannot be made binding on the tenant by the landlord's ratification after the time for giving notice has expired.[588]   **2-094**
(2)   The agent of a consignor of goods, without the authority of his principal, gave notice of stoppage in transit on the principal's behalf. The goods afterwards arrived at their destination, and were formally demanded by the trustee in bankruptcy of the consignee. It was held that the consignor could not subsequently ratify the stoppage in transit and so divest the property in the

---

[581]   In *Trident General Insurance Co Ltd v McNiece Bros Pty Ltd* (1987) 8 N.S.W.L.R. 270 at 282–283 it was held that ratification against an insurer was not valid seven years after the making of the policy. The case was affirmed on other grounds, (1988) 165 C.L.R. 107. See too *Rolle Family & Co Ltd v Rolle* [2017] UKPC 35; [2018] A.C. 205 (purported ratification of pre-incorporation contract using statute); *London Borough of Haringey v Ahmed* [2017] EWCA Civ 1861 at [57] (delay of 26 years).
[582]   See *Smith v Henniker-Major & Co* [2002] EWCA Civ 762; [2003] Ch. 162 at [73].
[583]   See *Williams v North China Insurance Co* (1876) 1 C.P.D. 757 at 770; but cf. Stoljar, p.196.
[584]   *Routh v Thompson* (1811) 13 East 275; *Hagedorn v Oliverson* (1814) 2 M. & S. 485; *Jardine v Leathley* (1863) 3 B. & S. 700.
[585]   *Williams v North China Insurance Co* (1876) 1 C.P.D. 757 at 764–765; see also 770.
[586]   *Trident General Insurance Co v McNiece Bros Pty Ltd* (1987) 8 N.S.W.L.R. 270 at 280–281; (decision affirmed on other grounds (1988) 165 C.L.R. 107); and see *National Oilwell (UK) Ltd v Davy Offshore Ltd* [1993] 2 Lloyd's Rep. 582; *The Borvigilant* [2003] EWCA Civ 935; [2003] 2 Lloyd's Rep. 520; *MacGillivray on Insurance Law* (14th edn), para.1-198.
[587]   cf. *Restatement, Second*, § 89, Comment c.
[588]   *Doe d. Mann v Walters* (1830) 10 B. & C. 626; *Doe d. Lyster v Goldwin* (1841) 2 Q.B. 143; *Right d. Fisher, Nash and Hyrons v Cuthell* (1804) 5 East 491; *Hexstone Holdings Ltd v AHC Westlink Ltd* [2010] EWHC 1280 (Ch); [2010] 32 E.G. 62; [2010] 2 E.G.L.R. 13 at [32]; *Aldford House Freehold Ltd v Grosvenor (Mayfair) Estate* [2018] EWHC 3430 (Ch); [2019] 1 W.L.R. 1489 at [98]; reversed on other points [2019] EWCA Civ 1848; [2020] 2 W.L.R. 116.

goods, which had in the meantime vested in the consignee's trustee in bankruptcy.[589]

(3) It is agreed between A and B, who are partners, that on the death of either of them the survivor shall have the option of purchasing the share of the deceased upon giving notice to the executors within three months after the death. A dies, and within three months after his death, C, on B's behalf, but without his authority, gives notice to the executors of B's intention to exercise the option. Such notice cannot be ratified after the expiration of the three months so as to bind the executors.[590]

(4) Directors of a company purport to allot shares by procedures which are not valid. The allottees complain but do not repudiate the allotments. In the circumstances, ratification of the allotments by the company several months later may be valid.[591]

(5) A corporation advertises for tenders for the supply of eggs for six months from September 30. K puts in a tender, and on September 22 the board of the corporation resolves to accept it and notifies K. On September 24 K writes that he had made a mistake in drawing up his tender and inserted the wrong price. On October 6 the corporation ratifies the acceptance by affixing its common seal. The ratification is ineffective.[592]

(6) A solicitor issues a writ without authority, within the period of limitation applicable for the proceedings in question. The person on whose behalf the writ was issued ratifies the issue of the writ after the period of limitation has expired. The ratification is effective.[593]

(7) A shipowner entering port is required to sign a contract for tug service which provides that the port operator is not liable in respect of the service and that this immunity is extended to the tug owner. The tug collides with the ship. Tug and ship sue each other. The port operator had implied authority to sign a contract on behalf of the tug owner containing the exemption from liability; but if this is not so, a letter before action sent by the tug owner ranks as ratification and is not unfair, even though there was by that time an accrued cause of action.[594]

Article 20

EFFECT OF RATIFICATION

2-095 (1) The effect of ratification is to invest the person on whose behalf the act ratified was done, the person who did the act, and third parties, with the same rights, duties, immunities and liabilities in all respects as if the act had been done with the previous authority of the person on whose behalf it was done[595];

---

[589] *Bird v Brown* (1850) 4 Exch. 786; see Comment.
[590] *Dibbins v Dibbins* [1896] 2 Ch. 348; *Hughes v NM Superannuation Pty Ltd* (1993) 29 N.S.W.L.R. 653. See also *Holland v King* (1848) 6 C.B. 727.
[591] *Re Portuguese Consolidated Copper Mines* (1890) 45 Ch.D. 16.
[592] *Metropolitan Asylums Board v Kingham & Sons* (1890) 6 T.L.R. 217; see Comment.
[593] *Presentaciones Musicales SA v Secunda* [1994] Ch. 271; *Adams v Ford* [2012] EWCA Civ 544; [2012] 1 W.L.R. 3211; see Comment.
[594] *The Borvigilant* [2003] EWCA Civ 935; [2003] 2 Lloyd's Rep. 520.
[595] See *Wilson v Tunman and Fretson* (1843) 6 M. & G. 236; *Bird v Brown* (1850) 4 Exch. 786; Illustrations 1–5; *Restatement, Third*, § 4.02.

subject to the agent's liability to the third party for any loss caused by his breach of the warranty of authority, and to his principal for loss caused by his breach of duty except in so far as this has been waived as between them.[596]

(2) But the doctrine of ratification may not be invoked to divest or affect prejudicially any proprietary or possessory right vested in any third party at the time of the ratification.[597]

(3) Ratification does not of itself give any new authority to the person whose act is ratified.[598]

(4) A ratification once effected cannot be withdrawn without the consent of the third party.[599]

Comment

Rule (1) Rule (1) is a general statement of the effect of a valid ratification and to a certain extent overlaps with the introductory Article 13. Thus where A, on behalf of P, but without authority, makes a contract with T, and P ratifies the contract, the normal effects of such ratification will be as follows: **2-096**

(i) P and T can enforce the contract against each other as though it had been originally authorised, even though T has meanwhile purported to withdraw from the contract.[600]

(ii) Although in general A remains liable to T for any breach of warranty of authority, it will not normally be possible for T to prove damages[601]: A is thus no longer liable to T unless he contracted personally.[602] If, however, he has caused loss to the third party, e.g. because the third party has taken advice as to, or even instituted proceedings against him, A might be liable to that extent, subject to the possible duty of the third party to mitigate his damages on ratification, if the ratification was not too late.[603]

(iii) In general it may be said that A is not liable to P for exceeding his authority,[604] for the doctrine of ratification normally contemplates a principal who is glad to waive the technical irregularity and adopt the transaction. This may however not always be so; a principal may ratify a transaction for convenience, or to preserve his commercial reputation, or even from commercial necessity. It is necessary therefore:

> "to consider the matter in two stages. First, is there ratification of the contract which the agent purported to make. Secondly, has the principal waived the breach of duty if any vis-à-vis the agent. Often the facts will lead to ratification and exoneration, but not always."[605]

---

[596] See Comment.

[597] See above, para.2-091; Illustration 9; *Re Gloucester Municipal Election Petition, 1900, Ford v Newth* [1901] 1 K.B. 683.

[598] Illustration 10.

[599] See Comment.

[600] See above, para.2-087.

[601] Article 106.

[602] See Article 98.

[603] Article 98.

[604] *Smith v Cologan* (1788) 2 T.R. 188n.; Illustrations 6 and 7; *Union Bank of Australia Ltd v Rudder* (1911) 13 C.L.R. 152, below, para.6-005.

[605] *Suncorp Insurance and Finance v Milano Assicurazioni SpA* [1993] 2 Lloyd's Rep. 225 at 234–235, per Waller J. See also *Restatement*, § 416; Mechem, *Treatise on the Law of Agency* (2nd edn),

(iv)   Equally, in many cases, by ratifying, P may be regarded as accepting an offer by the agent to act as his agent in a manner not previously authorised, on the normal basis as to remuneration, reimbursement and indemnity. Hence P may be liable to pay A such sum in respect of remuneration as A would have been entitled to had the contract been authorised[606] and must reimburse and indemnify A in respect of the transaction.[607] Conversely, A also becomes a fiduciary retrospectively if he was not previously so. But again, where P's ratification is not voluntary, it is submitted that he may ratify but not waive the agent's breach or accept any offer by the agent. In such a case the agent may by virtue of the terms of his contract or because of the gravity of his breach be entitled to no payments at all, and the principal may have a valid claim in damages.

(v)   Any title acquired by P relates back to the moment of ratification.[608]

2-097 **Rule (2)**   Rule (2) has already been considered in connection with time limits. Where an act to be effective must be done within a certain time (e.g. the exercise of an option, or of the right of stoppage in transit), to allow a ratification to operate after that time would be to prejudice rights vested in the other party, or in third parties. But the principle as stated here is wider and can apply to proprietary rights vested in persons not connected with the instant transaction at all,[609] or cases where the right is hardly of a proprietary nature, such as the interests of electors or candidates in avoiding corruption in local elections.[610] Such cases will, however, be rare.

2-098 **Rule (3)**   Rule (3) may seem obvious: it confines ratification to the act done, though doubtless ratification may be evidence of some other authority.[611] It is this rule which makes it difficult to say loosely that ratification creates agency, for it is clear that if it did, an authority would be set up that might thereafter need revocation.

2-099 **Rule (4)**   Once a contract is validly ratified, it is binding. The third party may agree to rescind it, but the ratifying principal has no unilateral power to dissolve the contract once he has affirmed it. There is no analogy with the withdrawal of authority, for that relates to the future. But it may be that where the ratification has been induced by a misrepresentation by the third party, the contract may be rescinded.[612] Similar reasoning will apply in other situations of ratification.

---

§§ 492-493; *Mineworkers' Union v Brodrick* 1948 (2) S.A.L.R. 959, 979; *Delco Australia Pty Ltd v Darlington Futures Ltd* (1986) 43 S.A.S.R. 519; reversed on other grounds (1986) 161 C.L.R. 500; *Ing Re (UK) Ltd v R & V Versicherung AG* [2006] EWHC 1544 (Comm); [2006] 2 All E.R. (Comm) 870; [2006] Lloyd's Rep. I.R. 653; [2007] 1 B.C.L.C. 108 at [152] (suggesting that a more complete knowledge of the facts may be required before exoneration is found).

[606] *Keay v Fenwick* (1876) 1 C.P.D. 745, Illustration 10 to Article 17; *Mason v Clifton* (1863) 3 F. & F. 899.

[607] Illustrations 3, 7 and 8; *Hartas v Ribbons* (1889) 22 Q.B.D. 254; Article 62.

[608] *Lawson v Hosemaster Co Ltd* [1966] 1 W.L.R. 1300 at 1314 (shares and dividends).

[609] Illustration 9.

[610] *Re Gloucester Municipal Election Petition, 1900, Ford v Newth* [1901] 1 K.B. 683; this is perhaps a doubtful case.

[611] See above, para.2-049.

[612] See *Restatement, Third*, § 4.02(2)(a) (any situation that would make a contract voidable).

Illustrations

(1) A, on B's behalf, but without his authority, distrains goods belonging to C. **2-100**
B ratifies the distress. If B had a right to distrain, A is discharged from liability, then the ratification having a retroactive effect, and rendering the distress lawful ab initio[613] if B had no right to distrain, A and B are jointly and severally liable as trespassers.[614]

(2) The secretary of a company, without the authority of the directors, sends out a notice purporting to have been issued by order of the board, convening an extraordinary general meeting, a requisition for such meeting having been duly served on the company in accordance with the articles of association. At a board meeting held two days before the date for which the general meeting is called, the directors resolve to ratify and confirm the issuing of the notice by the secretary. The notice is thereby rendered valid, and the meeting is duly summoned.[615]

(3) A insures goods, in which he has no insurable interest, on behalf of B. B, who has an insurable interest in goods, ratifies the insurance. The insurable interest of B is sufficient to support an action by A on the policy,[616] and B is liable for the premium.[617]

(4) A factor contracts to purchase goods on his principal's behalf at a price exceeding his limit. The principal ratifies the contract by disposing of the goods. He must pay the factor the full price.[618]

(5) A buys goods from T on behalf of P without authority. P pays A and ratifies the transaction. It turns out that the goods had been fraudulently disposed of prior to the transaction by the captain of the ship on which they had been. P may not sue A.[619]

(6) A firm of carriers, employed to deliver goods to A, delivers them to B. The senders invoice the goods to B, sue him for the price, recover judgment and take bankruptcy proceedings against him. They may not subsequently sue the carriers for misdelivery.[620]

(7) A shipmaster entered into contracts with the Admiralty for the transport of troops, and paid and incurred various sums and liabilities to enable him to perform the contracts, the shipowner being bankrupt and having mortgaged the vessel. Held, that the master had a right to be repaid the expenses and indemnified against the liabilities, out of the freight due from the Admiralty, the assignees in bankruptcy and mortgagees not being entitled to take the

---

[613] *Whitehead v Taylor* (1839) 10 A. & E. 210; *Hull v Pickersgill* (1819) 1 B. & B. 282.
[614] See *Bird v Brown* (1850) 4 Exch. 786 at 799. The common law of distraint in relation to commercial tenancies has been abolished and replaced as from April 6, 2014 pursuant to Tribunals, Courts and Enforcement Act 2007 s.71.
[615] *Hooper v Kerr, Stuart & Co Ltd* (1901) 83 L.T. 729.
[616] *Wolff v Horncastle* (1798) 1 B. & P. 316.
[617] *New Zealand Insurance Co Ltd v Tyneside Pty Ltd* [1917] N.Z.L.R. 569.
[618] *Cornwal v Wilson* (1750) 1 Ves. Sen. 510. And see *Brice v Wilson* (1834) 8 A. & E. 349 (relatives of deceased order extravagant funeral: ratifying executor personally liable); cf. *Lucy v Walrond* (1837) 3 Bing. N.C. 841.
[619] *Risbourg v Bruckner* (1858) 3 C.B.(N.S.) 812. The case is complicated by the foreign principal rule (below, para.9-020); and there may have been prior authority.
[620] *Verschures Creameries Ltd v Hull & Netherlands SS Co* [1921] 2 K.B. 608; see explanation in *United Australia Ltd v Barclays Bank Ltd* [1941] A.C. 1 at 31 and criticism in Goff and Jones, *Law of Restitution* (4th edn) p.733 (not in later editions).

benefit of the contract, unless they also adopted the burdens connected therewith.[621]

(8) An agent who is personally liable unsuccessfully defends an action brought against him for breach of an unauthorised contract entered into by him on behalf of his principal. The principal ratifies what he has done. The principal must indemnify the agent against the damages and costs recovered by the plaintiff in the action.[622] So, where a person is made a party to an action without his authority, he cannot avail himself of the benefit of the action, unless he pays the costs of conducting it.[623]

(9) A commodore in the navy, without authority to do so, appointed a captain. Held, that even if the Crown ratified the appointment, that would not give the commodore the right to share as a commodore with a captain under him, in prizes taken before the date of the ratification, because the rights to the various shares in those prizes would then be already vested.[624]

(10) The directors of a company borrow money in excess of the amount which they have power to borrow. This may be ratified by a simple majority of the shareholders at an extraordinary meeting. But such a ratification confers no further power to borrow in excess of the directors' powers: such power would require a vote of more than one half of the shareholders in accordance with the terms of the articles.[625]

4. ESTOPPEL FROM DENYING EXISTENCE OF AGENCY RELATIONSHIP

Article 21

ESTOPPEL FROM DENYING EXISTENCE OF AGENCY RELATIONSHIP

2-101   A person may be held liable as principal where it cannot be said that he has made a manifestation or representation as to the authority of another to that other or to a third party as required in Articles 7, 8, 72 or 83, but he is affected in an agency context by the operation of the doctrine of estoppel.[626]

Comment

2-102   **Estoppel as creating agency**   In most situations where the question of estoppel arises in respect of an agent's authority, the relevant agent will have possessed some actual authority but has proceeded to exceed it. This topic is considered in detail in Chapter 8, under the heading of "Apparent Authority".[627] But some reference to the establishment of a relationship of agency ab initio is appropriate in a chapter

---

[621] *Bristow v Whitmore* (1861) 9 H.L. Cas. 391.
[622] *Frixione v Tagliaferro & Sons* (1856) 10 Moo.P.C. 175. But in this case there may have been prior authority. Quaere as to the extent to which this result would apply where the principal ratified a contract in respect of which the agent had already incurred expenditure in defending an action for breach of warranty of authority. There seems no reason why it should unless the principal was in some way in breach of his duty to the agent in not ratifying earlier.
[623] *Hall v Laver* (1842) 1 Hare 571.
[624] *Donelly v Popham* (1807) 1 Taunt. 1.
[625] *Irvine v Union Bank of Australia* (1877) 2 App.Cas. 366. Though the third party lender would normally be protected by s.40 of the Companies Act 2006. See below, para.8-036.
[626] See Comment; and the Comments to the related Articles 72 and 83.
[627] Article 72. See also Tan Cheng Han, "Estoppel in the Law of Agency" (2020) 136 L.Q.R. 315.

on "Creation of Agency" even if most of the law concerned is to be found in cases on apparent authority (and even though the full relationship of agency, including the principal's right to sue, and that between principal and agent, was not created in such situations). Any difference of terminology could be given some slight justification on the basis that stronger evidence would usually be required to support the authority of one who had not previously been in an agency relationship with the principal than would be required where the person concerned already had agency powers; but this was misleading.[628]

This arrangement of the work could have been, and was,[629] taken to mean that in situations of the first type referred to above (no initial authority at all) the operative reasoning was based on estoppel; but that this was not or might not be so of cases of the second type (some but insufficient authority). A highly relevant question is therefore whether the operative reasoning for both situations is indeed based on estoppel. Although a judicial statement by Slade J that all apparent authority is based on estoppel,[630] though often cited, was perhaps not strong authority, the same attribution was made by Diplock LJ in the leading case of *Freeman & Lockyer v Buckhurst Park Properties (Mangal) Ltd*.[631] However, it is pointed out in the discussion of apparent authority in Article 72 that in many or even most cases of such authority the full requirements of estoppel as normally explained are not really satisfied, and it is there suggested that it is probably appropriate to regard the estoppel as a special one with weak requirements, special to agency. This explanation must apply to cases of both types.

Restatement, Third, however, takes a different approach and bases all apparent authority, of both types, on the objective interpretation normally applied to contractual situations.[632] (This technique of interpretation was indeed also at one time attributed, at any rate in England, to estoppel,[633] but such an explanation would not now be thought appropriate.) This enables the *Restatement* to mark off what may be called "true" estoppel cases from cases of apparent authority.[634]

The *Restatement*'s explanation of apparent authority is not accepted in this book.[635] But there is no doubt that agency situations can give rise to estoppel under the general law, in situations where the full, normally stated requirements of clear manifestation, causal connection and detrimental reliance are in fact satisfied. The present function of this Article is therefore a different one: leaving apparent authority and its basis completely aside, to draw attention to the possibility of the application of orthodox estoppel doctrines in the agency context where it may be difficult to say that the normal principles of apparent authority, whether by way of extending authority or of creating it in a person who never had authority, apply.

Estoppel in agency situations   *Restatement, Third* (from which the title, though   **2-103**
not the wording, of this Article is taken) gives two types of such situation where a third party is induced to make a detrimental change in position because a transac-

---

[628] See DeMott, in *Agency Law in Commercial Practice* (Busch, Macgregor and Watts eds, 2016), Ch.3.
[629] See *Spencer Bower: Reliance-Based Estoppel* (5th edn), para.9.3.
[630] *Rama Corp v Proved Tin and General Investments* [1952] 2 Q.B. 147 at 149–150. See also *Lloyd's Bank Plc v Independent Insurance Co Ltd* [2000] Q.B. 110 at 122.
[631] *Freeman & Lockyer v Buckhurst Park Properties (Mangal) Ltd* [1964] 2 Q.B. 480, 503. See below, para.8-011.
[632] See § 2.03, Comment c and below, para.8-028 onwards.
[633] See Hughes (1930) 54 L.Q.R. 370.
[634] § 2.05.
[635] See below, para.8-029.

tion into which he has entered is believed to be on account of another, but no manifestation by the principal can be detected under ordinary principles. The first is that in which the "principal", while making no manifestation of authority, by conduct (usually before the operative transaction) intentionally or carelessly caused belief that the agent was authorised. The second is that where, having notice of such a belief and that it might induce others to change their position, the "principal" did not take (often after the operative transaction) easily taken steps to notify those others of the facts.[636] So, an estoppel by acquiescence will arise where the putative principal is aware that an agent is purporting to act as such or to have certain authority but fails to take steps to intervene when those could readily have been taken.[637] In each case it must be assumed that there is no possibility of explaining the case on the basis that a representation was made by a person authorised by the principal.[638] As noted already in relation to ratification,[639] it can sometimes be difficult to assess whether the principal's conduct evidences a true conferral of actual authority, or merely a failure to voice opposition to the purported agent's unauthorised activity. Where the evidence permits it, a court is likely to favour a finding of actual authority.[640]

2-104   **First category**   In some cases of the first category mentioned above such an estoppel can be regarded as an example of estoppel by representation.[641] When the representation was negligent it may raise questions not only of causation and detrimental reliance, but also the initial question whether a duty of care is owed to the particular claimant: in this context it seems that the duty can be owed to quite a wide class of persons.[642] The courts have also, however, sometimes been willing to see an estoppel based merely on the breach of duty of care by the negligence of a person in facilitating, or failing to take reasonable steps to prevent, situations in which a third party might be led to assume that a person was authorised, even though there was no manifestation that this was so. An Australian decision in a contract context which may be explicable on this basis appears in Illustration 2

---

[636] See § 2.05. A fairly clear case is *Spiro v Lintern* [1973] 1 W.L.R. 1002, Illustration 3. See too *Ramsden v Dyson* (1866) L.R. 1 H.L. 129 at 158; *Grand Trunk Railway Co of Canada v Robinson* [1915] A.C. 740 at 747–748; *Geniki Investments International Ltd v Ellis Stockbrokers Ltd* [2008] EWHC 549 (QB); [2008] 1 B.C.L.C. 662 at [46], and above, para.2-077; *Ted Baker Plc v Axa Insurance UK Plc* [2017] EWCA Civ 4097 at [88]. cf. *English v English* [2010] EWHC 2058 (Ch) (mother failing to reveal son's forgery of her signature, and herself making payments referable to purported contract).

[637] *City Bank of Sydney v McLaughlin* (1909) 9 C.L.R. 615 at 625; *Clayton Robard Management Ltd v Siu* (1988) 6 A.C.L.C. 57 at 60; *AJU Remicon Co Ltd v Alida Shipping Co Ltd* [2007] EWHC 2246 (Comm) at [15]; *VLM Holdings Ltd v Ravensworth Digital Services Ltd* [2013] EWHC 228 (Ch) at [70]. In some markets, it may not be reasonable to require putative principals to prevent persons from purporting to act as their agents (but the position will be different if they adopt the benefit of the intervenor's actions): *Montrio Ltd v Tse Ping Shun David* [2012] HKEC 1781.

[638] This possibility was rejected in the leading property case of *Moorgate Mercantile Co Ltd v Twitchings* [1977] A.C. 890, Illustration 7 to Article 84. See also *Crabtree-Vickers Pty Ltd v Australian Direct Mail Advertising Co Pty Ltd* (1975) 133 C.L.R. 72.

[639] See above, para.2-080.

[640] See *Suncorp Insurance and Finance v Milano Assecurazioni SpA* [1993] 2 Lloyd's Rep. 225 at 234–235.

[641] See a useful discussion in Spencer Bower, *Reliance-Based Estoppel* (5th edn), para.3.27 onwards.

[642] See *Swan v North British Australasian Co Ltd* (1863) 2 Hurl. & C. 175 at 182; *RE Jones Ltd v Waring & Gillow Ltd* [1926] A.C. 670 at 693; *Mercantile Bank of India v Central Bank of India Ltd* [1938] A.C. 287 at 298–299; *Wilson & Meeson v Pickering* [1946] K.B. 422 at 425; *Mercantile Credit Co Ltd v Hamblin* [1965] 2 Q.B. 242 at 271; *Moorgate Mercantile Co Ltd v Twitchings* [1977] A.C. 890. See also Comment to Article 84.

below. There is however very little other authority applying such reasoning in contract situations. There is slightly more in connection with property, largely in connection with the doctrine of apparent ownership; but there are also many authoritative dicta that persons owe no general duty to look after their own property,[643] and it is fairly clear that (for example) giving another a blank signed document is not necessarily a breach of duty owed to third parties.[644] In general it seems doubtful whether such an estoppel construction should often be put on facts which create no right of action under any other head.[645] There is no general obligation in the common law not to cause another's economic loss, and the starting point is that individuals should protect themselves in attempting to contract with others. To impose liability would further require the making of what may be rather an arbitrary choice between the negligence of the plaintiff and that of the defendant, without any possibility of apportioning blame as might be possible in a negligence claim in tort. The general argument for a contract analysis would sometimes have to be the rather dubious one, by no means always accepted by the law, that a person whose chooses to act through others must take the risk of the ways in which those others act.[646]

Second category   Cases in the second category are easier to explain. They are **2-105** generally cases where there is no manifestation of authority, but the principal is in full possession of the facts and has stood by allowing the agent to overstate his authority; an example appears in Illustration 3 below. The law must, however, be careful not to impose an onerous duty on the principal to intervene to correct the false impression gained by the third party. The position was persuasively stated in *City Bank of Sydney v McLaughlin*[647]:

> "In general a man is not bound actively to repudiate or disaffirm an act done in his name but without his authority. But this is not the universal rule. The circumstances may be such that a man is bound by all rules of honesty not to be quiescent, but actively to dissent, when he knows that others have for his benefit put themselves in the position of disadvantage, from which, if he speaks or acts at once, they can extricate themselves, but from which, after a lapse of time, they can no longer escape."

The inactivity must be of the principal or of persons who would have had authority to do what the more junior agent is purporting to have done. Where there is co-agency, and there has been no holding out, it is possible that even the inactivity of a majority of their number cannot create the estoppel if their actual authority turns on compliance with rules for group decision-making.[648] Other cases of this type of estoppel can arise where a principal, perhaps by contractual term, has in defined circumstances bound itself not to disown transactions purportedly made on its

---

[643] e.g. *Farquharson Brothers & Co v King & Co* [1902] A.C. 325 at 332; see Comment to Article 84.

[644] See Comment to Article 84.

[645] See *Spencer Bower: Reliance-Based Estoppel* (5th edn), paras 3-50–3.51.

[646] An example where the court falls back on this is the American case of *MacAndrews & Forbes Co v United States*, 23 F. 2d 667 (1928) (where a delivery order was left in a drawer). See *Reliance-Based Estoppel*, above, paras 5.23–5.24; cf. *Essington Investments Pty Ltd v Regency Property Pty Ltd* [2004] NSWCA 375. See too Watts (2005) 26 Aust. Bar Rev. 185.

[647] *City Bank of Sydney v McLaughlin* (1909) 9 C.L.R. 615 at 625.

[648] See *PEC Ltd v Asia Golden Rice Co Ltd* [2014] EWHC 1583 (Comm) at [58] (majority of board knew junior agent had been purporting to exercise unusual powers only open to the board, but minority did not).

behalf with the relevant third party.[649]

2-106   **Contractual operation of estoppel**   Although this can be said to be a straightforward example of estoppel, the way in which it operates in this context is to ground contract liability. The prevailing view in the US seems to be that estoppel reasoning is related to tort,[650] and it is certainly true that the requirements for negligence liability (in particular a duty of care to the person or persons affected) apply in some degree. But in the context of contract it seems that damages are to be calculated on the basis that the contract had been authorised, and need not be based on the reliance interest appropriate to tort claims.[651] The use of such reasoning seems historically to have gone some distance towards filling the gap in misrepresentation liability caused by the narrow view taken of the scope of the tort of deceit in *Derry v Peek*.[652] It seems possible that the second category of estoppel could also be used to justify a rescission of any relevant contract on the basis of misrepresentation.[653]

2-107   **Possibility of tort action**   Where the negligence has arisen in an estoppel context, the courts have, as stated above, looked for a duty of care towards the third party. It is not clear whether the criteria applied are the same as those required for a tort action for pure economic loss, which is what is normally caused in such cases. The better view seems to be that they are[654]; and that the other requirements of estoppel (clarity of representation (where relevant), causation and reliance) will also be required.[655] Hence it may be asked whether an action in tort based only on the duty of care (and matters of causation) would sometimes be an alternative way of proceeding.[656] Even if it were available, the contract action, supported by an estoppel, will usually be better because it will attract the contract rules for assessment of damages on the basis that the transaction was authorised, and hence loss of profit, where the tort rules would only give loss caused.

2-108   **Ratification**   The conduct of the supposed principal may often instead be interpreted as a ratification.[657] This does not require that the third party acted on the ratification, nor even (probably) that it be communicated to the third party at all.[658]

---

[649] See e.g. *Major Shipping & Trading Inc v Standard Chartered Bank (Singapore) Ltd* [2018] SGHC 4.

[650] See *Restatement, Third*, § 2-05, Comment d.

[651] e.g. *Pacific Carriers Ltd v BNP Paribas* (2004) 218 C.L.R. 451, Illustration 2 below. But cf. *ACN074971109 v National Mutual Life Association of Australasia Ltd* (2008) 69 A.C.S.R. 118 at [171] (estoppel as to authority only justified a remedy less than full expectation damages).

[652] See the leading estoppel case of *Low v Bouverie* [1891] 3 Ch. 82. (The other route was by the notion of warranty.) See also a valuable exposition of when estoppel operates by Dixon J in *Thompson v Palmer* (1933) 49 C.L.R. 507 at 547.

[653] See further para.8-065 below.

[654] See Hobhouse J at first instance in *Bank of Nova Scotia v Hellenic Mutual War Risks Assn (Bermuda) Ltd (The Good Luck)* [1988] 1 Lloyd's Rep. 514 at 547–548, basing himself on *Moorgate Mercantile Co Ltd v Twitchings* [1977] A.C. 890 (not raised in the appeals culminating in [1992] 1 A.C. 233). See also *The Odenfeld* [1978] 1 Lloyd's Rep. 357 at 375–378 per Kerr J. But cf. *Saunders v Anglia BS* [1971] A.C. 1004 at 1038.

[655] See Spencer Bower, *Reliance-Based Estoppel* (5th edn), para.3.32 onwards.

[656] See *So v HSBC Bank Plc* [2009] EWCA Civ 296; and below, para.8-180.

[657] For a case where it was not, with the results that estoppel as to past events had to be relied on, see *Worboys v Carter* [1987] 2 E.G.L.R. 1.

[658] See Article 17.

But it requires that the principal has been known at the time of the act ratified: an undisclosed principal cannot ratify.[659]

Illustrations

(1) A goes into a spacious furniture shop and is approached by a person with grey-   **2-109**
ing hair whose dress and manner suggest that he is a senior salesman. A selects
a mirror and bedroom furniture. The supposed salesman calculates the total
price on a notepad which he produces. A is told that the goods will be delivered
in two weeks. She pays cash but is not given a receipt. The supposed salesman was an impostor who keeps the money and is not seen again. There is
nothing indicating a manifestation by the owner of the shop, but if the facts
permit, it may perhaps be held that he has been negligent towards the customer
in having arrangements in place which permit such activity of an impostor on
the shop floor, and hence is estopped from saying that it is not bound by the
purported sale and the payment made under it.[660]

(2) The Documentary Credit Manager of a bank has actual authority to sign letters of credit and authentications of signature, but not to sign guarantees of letters of indemnity against delivery of goods without a bill of lading. She signs
such a guarantee (in fact on an inappropriate form) illegibly, not making clear
what her status is, and stamps it with the bank's rubber stamp which she is allowed to use for purposes within her authority. In reliance on the document the
carrier delivers without bill of lading, is thereby landed with liability to the true
receiver and sues the bank on the guarantee. In view of the illegibility of the
signature and lack of indication of the signer's identity or status it cannot be
said that there was any manifestation of authority by the bank conferring apparent authority, and the carrier relying on the document (as faxed to it) had
no other contact with the bank at all, as its issue had been procured by the shipper of the goods. The question of the usual authority of such an official is not
considered. There are no or inadequate procedures laid down by the bank for
control of signatures or use of the stamp. The bank had been held in a lower
court not liable in negligence, but was nevertheless held liable in contract on
the guarantee.[661]

(3) A husband who owns a house asks his wife to put it into the hands of estate

---

[659] See above, para.2-063. This was the first point considered in *Spiro v Lintern and West v Dillicar*
[1920] N.Z.L.R. 139, Illustration 3 below.

[660] *Hoddesdon v Koos Bros* 135 A.2d 702 (1957), where a new trial was ordered on just this issue.
Similar situations can arise in connection with supposed car salesman: see *Luken v Buckeye Parking Corp* 68 N.E.2d 217 (1945); or supposed car park attendants or "parking jockeys": see *Mendelssohn v Normand Ltd* [1970] 1 Q.B. 177; or persons allowed the use of offices: *Howard v Carline*
(1956) 7 D.L.R.(2d) 324. See also *Raclaw v Fay, Conmy & Co* 668 N.E.2d 114 at 118 (1996).

[661] *Pacific Carriers Ltd v BNP Paribas* (2004) 218 C.L.R. 451. In view of the lack of contact between
the parties, and the obscurity of the signature, this decision of the High Court of Australia goes further
than might be expected and should be received with caution. See Reynolds (2004) 121 L.Q.R. 55;
Watts (2005) 26 Aust. Bar Rev. 185; Peden and Carter (2005) 21 J.C.L. 172 (considering the application of the principles of contractual construction to the decision). For similar reasoning, see *Essington Investments Pty Ltd v Regency Property Pty Ltd* [2004] NSWCA 375, also considered by
Watts, above. See also the criticism of the *Pacific Carriers* decision by Fridman (2006) 22
J.Contract.L. 105. For judicial recognition that Australian courts seem to be adopting a broader ap-
proach to the concept of a holding out of authority than in the United Kingdom, see *Flexirent Capital
Pty Ltd v EBS Consulting Pty Ltd* [2007] VSC 158 at [221]. cf. *Sea Emerald SA v Prominvestbank-
Joint Stockpoint Commercial Industrial and Investment Bank* [2008] EWHC 1979 (Comm) at [109].

agents, and this she does. An offer is made to the agents, who telephone the wife. She instructs them to accept it, and authorises them over the telephone to sign a contract, which they do. She has no authority on her husband's behalf to contract to sell, nor purports to act for him. Later the purchasers become aware that the house belongs to the husband. However, the husband subsequently behaves as if he had authorised the transaction, as by receiving visits from the purchasers and allowing repairs. He gives his wife a power of attorney to transfer the house and goes abroad. She subsequently conveys the house to another purchaser. The husband is estopped from saying that she had had no authority, and the first contract is binding on him.[662]

(4) The solicitors of a claimant pursuing a claim on a bill of lading seek from the agents of the P&I insurers an extension of time in respect of the time bar of Article III.6 of the Hague Rules. They ask for this extension from the "owners". The ship is under demise charter and the appropriate defendants, from whom extension should have been sought via the same agents, are the demise charterers. The agents grant an extension on behalf of the "owners", who would not be liable. The demise charterers, who are the appropriate defendants, later allege that this was not granted on their behalf and that the claim against them is therefore time-barred. They are estopped from doing so, as if the extension was really to be interpreted as granted on their behalf, the agents must have been aware of the mistake and it was unconscionable to take advantage of it.[663]

---

[662] *Spiro v Lintern* [1973] 1 W.L.R. 1002; see also *West v Dillicar* [1920] N.Z.L.R. 139, Illustration 3 to Article 83; *Worboys v Carter* [1987] 2 E.G.L.R. 1; *Pascoe Properties Ltd v Att.-Gen.* [2014] NZCA 616 at [54] (Crown estopped by conduct of ministry official).

[663] *The Stolt Loyalty* [1993] 2 Lloyd's Rep. 281 (affirmed without reference to this point [1995] 1 Lloyd's Rep. 598), doubting dicta in *Shearson Lehman Hutton Inc v Maclaine Watson & Co* [1989] 2 Lloyd's Rep. 570 at 596.

CHAPTER 3

AUTHORITY OF AGENTS

1. ACTUAL AND APPARENT AUTHORITY

Article 22

GENERAL PRINCIPLES

(1) The authority of an agent may be— **3-001**
    (a) actual (express or implied) where it results from a manifestation of assent that the agent should represent or act for the principal expressly or impliedly made by the principal to the agent; or
    (b) apparent, where it results from such a manifestation made by the principal to third parties.[1]
(2) The burden of establishing a conferral of authority rests on the party asserting its existence.
(3) A conferral of authority does not remove the principal's privilege to perform the same tasks personally.
(4) A principal cannot rely on the unauthorised acts of an agent unless the principal ratifies those acts.

The propositions contained in Articles 23 to 32 relate directly to actual authority only; but they may also be relevant to the ascertainment of apparent authority.

Comment

The notion of authority is explained in Article 1 and this Article broadly fol- **3-002**
lows the scheme there adopted. It has already been pointed out that the placing together of the concepts of actual and apparent authority can easily be criticised,[2] and this point is now due for further discussion. This chapter deals primarily with actual authority, and the rules for determining what is and what is not to be regarded as actually authorised. The scope of an agent's authority may require to be investigated from the point of view of any of three relationships: (i) that of principal and third party dealing with the agent; (ii) that of principal and agent; and (iii) that of agent and third party. Thus where there is actual authority, the principal will prima facie be liable to, and entitled to sue, the third party on the agent's transactions; the principal may be liable to indemnify and reimburse the agent and/or

---

[1] See Comment and Article 1. As to apparent authority, see especially Articles 72 and 83.
[2] See above, para.1-014. See Falconbridge (1939) 17 Can. B.R. 248 at 251–252; Seavey (1920) 29 Yale L.J. 859; Corbin (1934) 34 Yale L.J. 788.

entitled to proceeds received by the agent; and the agent will be free from liability for breach of warranty of authority to the third party. In this chapter no distinction is expressly made between these three relationships, to all of which the agent's actual authority may be relevant. Other general aspects of authority, including the fact that a conferral of authority is not usually to the exclusion of the principal's own powers, and the issue of the onus of proving a conferral of authority, are dealt with in the following paragraphs.

3-003　**Actual authority**　Actual authority is the authority which the principal has given the agent wholly or in part by means of words or writing (called here express authority) or is regarded by the law as having given the agent because of the interpretation put by the law on the relationship and dealings of the two parties. Although founded in the principal's assent, the conferral of authority is judged objectively:

> "An 'actual' authority is a legal relationship between principal and agent created by a consensual agreement to which they alone are parties. Its scope is to be ascertained by applying ordinary principles of construction of contracts, including any proper implications from the express words used, the usages of the trade, or the course of business between the parties. To this agreement the contractor is a stranger: he may be totally ignorant of the existence of any authority on the part of the agent. Nevertheless, if the agent does enter into a contract pursuant to the 'actual' authority, it does create contractual rights and liabilities between the principal and the contractor."[3]

Note that it is implicit in the foregoing quotation that actual authority is effective only once acted upon by the agent in relation to a third party. It follows that a principal can withdraw actual authority before the third party has obtained any rights.[4] In the context of companies, a board may by resolution confer actual authority for a transaction, but then cancel that resolution which would terminate any actual authority in a delegate if the resolution had not already been acted upon.[5] It is common to distinguish express actual authority from implied actual authority. The most obvious case of express authority is a power of attorney. In a commercial setting, express authority can also arise when the principal authorises the agent to do something "by express words, such as when a board of directors pass a resolution which authorises two of their members to sign cheques".[6] Letters conferring authority are also common. The most obvious cases of implied authority arise in the forms of incidental authority (implied authority to do whatever is necessarily or normally incidental to the activity expressly authorised[7]), usual authority (implied authority to do whatever an agent of the type concerned would usually have authority to do[8]) and customary authority (implied authority to act in accordance with such applicable business customs as are reasonable[9]); there is a further general category of implied authority arising from the course of dealing between the parties and the

---

3　*Freeman & Lockyer v Buckhurst Park Properties (Mangal) Ltd* [1964] 2 Q.B. 480 at 502, per Diplock LJ. See further Article 8, above; and *Suncorp Insurance & Finance v Milano Assicuranzioni SpA* [1993] 2 Lloyd's Rep. 225 at 234–235.
4　See further below, Article 120.
5　*Brookton Co-operative Society Ltd v FCT* (1979) 24 A.L.R. 547; *Dixon v Blindley Heath Investments Ltd* [2015] EWCA Civ 1023 at [110].
6　*Hely-Hutchinson v Brayhead Ltd* [1968] 1 Q.B. 549 at 583.
7　Article 27.
8　Articles 29 and 30.
9　Article 31.

circumstances of the case.[10] But where the express authority is not clear the court will interpret it, and in this and other situations, whether the authority is to be regarded as express or implied is obviously a question susceptible of argument.

Apparent authority   The placing of apparent authority beside actual authority in this rule can easily be criticised, for the reasoning behind the doctrine of apparent authority involves the assumption that there is in fact no authority at all. Under this doctrine, where a principal represents, or is regarded by the law as manifesting, that another has authority, the principal may be bound as against a third party by the acts of that other person within the authority which that person appears to have, though the principal had not in fact given that person such authority or had limited the authority by instructions not made known to the third party.[11] "Ostensible or apparent authority is the authority of an agent as it *appears* to others."[12]

3-004

   On the other hand, the term "apparent authority" is very frequently used, and a chapter on authority that did not mention it alongside actual authority would be misleading. It should, however, be remembered that, at any rate on the approach taken in the English cases,[13] the idea is significantly different from that of actual authority. The notion of apparent authority is essentially confined to the relationship between principal and third party: the principal may under it be bound by unauthorised acts of the agent. The principal cannot sue without ratifying; and consideration of the other two relationships in cases where there is apparent authority proceeds from the starting-point that there is no actual authority. Therefore apparent authority is primarily dealt with in Chapter 8 on the relationship between principal and third party. The cases cited in this chapter are nevertheless relevant, as the authority which the third party is entitled to assume the agent has is in most situations the authority which would normally be implied between principal and agent in the circumstances. The actual and apparent authority will therefore normally coincide,[14] and it will often not matter which of the two notions is relied on: indeed, some of the cases cited in this chapter are decisions on apparent authority. In many nineteenth century cases, it is not possible to tell upon which doctrine the court bases its decision, and even in the cases that are clearly based on what is now called apparent authority, the authority is sometimes referred to as implied.[15] The isolation of the doctrine of apparent authority is not of long standing: it is only comparatively recently that a sharp distinction has been made in the English cases.[16]

   The difference between them occurs in two main situations. First, there may be

---

[10] Article 32.

[11] Article 72; *Freeman & Lockyer v Buckhurst Park Properties (Mangal) Ltd* [1964] 2 Q.B. 480 at 503.

[12] *Hely-Hutchinson v Brayhead Ltd* [1968] 1 Q.B. 549 at 583, per Lord Denning MR. "Apparent authority, which negatives the existence of actual authority" (*Rama Corp v Proved Tin & General Investments* [1952] 2 Q.B. 147 at 149, per Slade J) is, however, too extreme a statement. So, but in the other direction, at any rate if taken out of context, is "The apparent authority is the real authority" (*Pickering v Busk* (1812) 15 East 38 at 43, per Lord Ellenborough CJ; it appears that what he meant was that the authority actually conferred in the case was that which the agent would normally have conferred).

[13] See below, para.8-029.

[14] *Freeman & Lockyer v Buckhurst Park Properties (Mangal) Ltd* [1964] 2 Q.B. 480 at 502.

[15] e.g. *Brooks v Hassall* (1883) 49 L.T. 569.

[16] See, e.g. *Ryan v Pilkington* [1959] 1 W.L.R. 403, criticised by Powell, pp.51–52 and finally disapproved by the House of Lords in *Sorrell v Finch* [1977] A.C. 728. Clear examples of the two being by modern standards run together are to be found in the Partnership Act 1890: see esp. ss.5, 8 and 14.

cases where there is an actual manifestation by the principal to the third party upon which the apparent authority is based, which may indicate something different from the authority which the agent would on general criteria impliedly have. Secondly, there may be apparent authority even though in fact as between principal and agent the agent does not have the implied authority which would be normal in the circumstances, either because the principal has, unknown to the third party, forbidden the act in question, or because of facts known to the agent which negate such authority. Thus it is said that a solicitor normally has implied authority to compromise a suit, and hence apparent authority to do so.[17] It could be offensive on the part of the other party's solicitor to demand evidence of authority: yet the first solicitor may have been told specifically not to act in this way, or may have knowledge of the client's finances which would negate any possibility of the solicitor's having implied authority to act in this way.[18]

3-005 **Usual authority** A case has been made for adding a third type of authority, usual authority.[19] This has been defined by one writer as "the authority which a person normally possesses in certain circumstances to act on behalf of another person, whether or not he is actually authorised so to act".[20]

The expression "usual authority" is referred to in three contexts,[21] the first two of which are uncontroversial. In those cases, usual authority is simply a sub-category of each of actual and apparent authority[22]:

(i) *As a type of implied authority* Many cases show that where an agent is put in a position which normally carries with it certain authority, the agent impliedly has such authority unless it is withdrawn by the principal.[23] Examples appear below. A person can in such circumstances be said to have "usual authority". Where an agent has express authority to do the act in question, usual authority will be superfluous.[24]

(ii) *As a type of apparent authority* Apparent authority seems to involve two types of case[25]: cases where there can be said to be something like a specific representation by the principal of the agent's authority, on which the third party relied, which could be called cases of "genuine apparent authority"; and cases where the only representation made by the principal lies in putting the agent in a position carrying with it a usual authority as

---

[17] *Waugh v H.B. Clifford & Sons Ltd* [1982] Ch. 374; and see Article 30, Illustration 5.

[18] *Waugh v H.B. Clifford & Sons Ltd* [1982] Ch. 374 at 387. This is a well-reasoned modern case; but cf. *Nandrame v Ramsaran* [2015] UKPC 20, and para.3-032 below. But it was decided before the days of most recent communications technology, and it is doubtful whether a solicitor would be regarded as so authorised today, and whether it would be "officious", as suggested in the case, to inquire further. See Foskett, *Law and Practice of Compromise* (9th edn), Ch. 21. This would affect his apparent authority also. The court may sometimes in such cases refuse to give effect to the compromise: *Harvey v Phillips* (1956) 95 C.L.R. 235; *Wandel and Goltermann GmbH v Wandel Global Services Pty Ltd* [2002] FCA 1609.

[19] See especially Powell, Ch.II; Treitel, *Law of Contract* (15th edn), paras 16-034–16-036.

[20] Powell, p.37.

[21] For its recognition in the first two categories, see *Hely-Hutchinson v Brayhead Ltd* [1968] 1 Q.B. 549 at 583; *ING Re (UK) Ltd v R&V Versicherung AG* [2006] EWHC 1544 (Comm); [2006] 2 All E.R. (Comm) 870 at [125].

[22] See *Ukraine v Law Debenture Trust Plc* [2018] EWCA Civ 2026; [2019] 2 W.L.R. 655 at [90].

[23] Articles 29 and 30.

[24] *Ukraine v Law Debenture Trust Plc* [2018] EWCA Civ 2026; [2019] Q.B. 1121 at [92].

[25] See Comment to Article 72.

described above.[26] In both cases the principal is liable despite reservations in the authority uncommunicated to the third party: but the two could be differentiated as "apparent" and "usual" authority respectively. In this sense usual authority would have affinities with the "externalised" theories of civil law discussed earlier, under which the principal may be liable simply by permitting another to assume a recognised type of position.[27] The common law approach remains one based on a representation of assent by the principal to the agent's action.

(iii) *As an independent type of authority* There is a small number of cases in which an *undisclosed* principal has been held liable on a contract made by his agent within such powers as would usually be possessed by a person in such a position, where that authority had in fact been withdrawn. The leading case is *Watteau v Fenwick*,[28] where Wills J said:

> "The principal is liable for all the acts of his agent which are within the authority usually confided to an agent of that character, notwithstanding limitations, as between the principal and the agent, put upon such authority. It is said that this is only so where there has been a holding out of authority ... But I do not think so."

In view of the fact that the agent's authority was limited, these cases cannot be treated as based on actual authority: but since the principal was undisclosed, no representation can have been made by the principal to the third party, therefore the authority could not have been apparent. The cases can simply be criticised as incorrect,[29]. If however, they are to be supported on agency grounds they must either be treated as exceptional or as indicating an independent notion which could be called "usual authority". It might then be possible to build on these cases to erect such a third type of authority, and to say that a principal is bound by the acts of the agent when that agent acts, not only within actual or apparent authority, but also when acting within usual authority.[30] This would provide perhaps the readiest framework for seeking to emancipate the principal's liability from notions of authorisation and reliance, a matter discussed earlier.[31] It is far from obvious, however, that justice calls for these extensions of liability. Such extensions would largely be in the area of undisclosed principals, but it is said that cases where the liability of a disclosed principal could be extended can be envisaged:

> "P appoints A as his general manager for the purchase of houses in Leeds, instructing A, however, not to disclose the existence of the agency and not to purchase except on a surveyor's report. A discloses his position to T, withholding, however, the requirement of a surveyor's report, and purchases houses in Leeds from T as agent for P without a surveyor's report."

---

[26] The difference is accepted by Buxton LJ in *AMB Generali Holding AG v SEB Trygg Liv, etc.* [2005] EWCA Civ 1237; [2006] 1 Lloyd's Rep. 318 at [32]; see also *Marubeni Hong Kong and South China Ltd v Mongolian Government* [2002] 2 All E.R. (Comm) 873 at [46]. It is however rejected by Dal Pont, p.524. For an example, see *Lexi Holdings Plc v Pannone & Partners* [2009] EWHC 2590 (Ch).

[27] See above, para.1-025.

[28] *Watteau v Fenwick* [1893] 1 Q.B. 346, discussed below, para.8-077.

[29] See below, para.8-077.

[30] cf. Powell, p.73 onwards; Montrose (1939) 17 Can. B.R. 693; Treitel, *Law of Contract* (15th edn).

[31] See above, para.1-025.

The writer's assumption seems to be that only an independent doctrine of usual authority would sustain liability.[32]

Restatement, Second, the Reporter for which was Professor Seavey, provided in a somewhat vaguer way for the liability of a principal beyond the actual and apparent authority:

> "The liability of a principal to a third person upon a transaction conducted by an agent, or the transfer of his interests by an agent, may be based upon the fact that: (a) the agent was authorised; (b) the agent was apparently authorised; or (c) the agent had a power arising from the agency relation and not dependent upon authority or apparent authority."[33]

The notion referred to under (c) is elsewhere described as "inherent agency power" and explained as follows[34]:

> "Inherent agency power is a term used in the restatement of this subject to indicate the power of an agent which is derived not from authority, apparent authority or estoppel, but solely from the agency relation and exists for the protection of persons harmed by or dealing with a servant or other agent."[35]

This approach would accommodate not only the supposed doctrine of *Watteau v Fenwick*[36] but also other intractable cases which a doctrine of usual authority would not, viz. cases where an agent has actual authority to effect a disposition of property but does so in a manner different from that authorised,[37] cases where the agent acts within authority but for personal ends,[38] and cases of apparent ownership.[39] It can be likened to the "external" view of civil law,[40] but occurring as an exception rather than as a rule.[41] But though this approach was welcomed and approved by some writers[42] and may have provided a convenient receptacle into which to consign difficult decisions and fact situations, it is submitted that the cases it covers are too disparate, and it is too vague to serve as a systematic basis for the formation and prediction of legal decisions.[43] Not only are some of the existing exceptional cases difficult to justify, including *Watteau v Fenwick*, but others are

---

[32]   Montrose (1939) 17 Can. B.R. 693 at 711.

[33]   § 140.

[34]   § 8A.

[35]   See comments to these sections and reporter's notes to § 161; Seavey (1948) 1 U.Okla.L. Rev. 1; *Studies in Agency* (1949), p.181.

[36]   *Watteau v Fenwick* [1893] 1 Q.B. 346. Seavey said that the case was "based upon the theory that the principal is the principal and that because the agent is doing his work the principal ought to be liable": (1933) 13 Nebraska L. Bull. 55 at 63.

[37]   The supposed doctrine of *Brocklesby v Temperance Building Society* [1895] A.C. 173: see Article 85 and Comment.

[38]   See *Hambro v Burnand* [1904] 2 K.B. 10, Illustration 1 to Article 74.

[39]   See Article 86. Also the old cases on agency of necessity: see Article 33.

[40]   See above, para.1-025.

[41]   See Tiberg, in *Lex Mercatoria* (Rose ed., 2000), Ch.4.

[42]   *Wright* (1936) 1 U. Toronto L.J. 17 at 40 onwards; Falconbridge (1939) 17 Can.B.R. 248 at 252 onwards (more equivocal); Montrose (1939) 17 Can. B.R. 693 at 693; Munro (1958) 20 U. Pittsburgh L. Rev. 33; Mearns (1962) 48 Va.L.Rev. 50; Bester (1972) 89 S.A.L.J. 49.

[43]   cf. Conant (1968) 47 Neb.L.Rev. 678 at 686: "so vague it can cause more analytical problems that it can solve".

better supported on more specific rationales than by a concept of usual authority.[44] The Reporter for *Restatement, Third*, Professor DeMott, makes no use of it.[45]

On the current trend of English case law,[46] it is clear that there is little support for any generalised form of liability of the principal beyond the agent's actual or apparent authority. Not much weight can be put on the dictum of Lord Wilberforce referred to in Chapter 1[47] and the dubious decision in *Watteau v Fenwick*.[48] Recent judicial statements of the basic principles of agency are clearly based on the assumption that the principal is only bound where the agent had actual or apparent authority.[49] References to any notion of usual authority should therefore be made and interpreted with caution. As regards usual authority as a form of implied authority, it covers two different types of situation which, it is submitted, should be distinguished.[50] As to apparent authority, the two types referred to above, of specific and general representations,[51] are in the cases both subsumed under the same heading and treated together,[52] sometimes being connected with estoppel: the "usual authority" cases are not separated off.[53] Further, to treat a type of actual authority and a type of apparent authority together may cause confusion.[54]

The notion of usual authority is nevertheless one that should be borne in mind; for the distinction between the two types of apparent authority is a significant one which illuminates various points of difficulty in the cases.

Authority of necessity   Emergencies may sometimes enlarge the implied author-   **3-006** ity of an agent. To some extent cases of such extended authority can be subsumed under the accepted heads of implied authority. But many old cases relating to the authority of an agent to act in an emergency contain highly specific requirements linking them with a special but limited doctrine of agency of necessity, whereby a person not previously an agent is by an emergency constituted an agent. The cases are dealt with together under that head in Chapter 4, where it is submitted that the category should now be assimilated into normal principles of implied authority.

Onus of proof and evidence of authority   The onus of proving authority, actual   **3-007** or apparent, lies on the party asserting it against the principal, whether the third party or the agent.[55] The principal may, however, be obliged to plead lack of

---

[44]   Watts (2002) 2 O.U. Commonwealth L.J. 93, discusses a number of the exceptional cases, but does not argue for any overarching concept of inherent agency power.

[45]   See *Restatement, Third*, Comment to § 2.01; DeMott (2014) U. Illinois L.R. 1813.

[46]   See above, para.1-026; and *Ukraine v Law Debenture Trust Plc* [2018] EWCA Civ 2026 at [90]. Dicta from older cases to a different effect can of course be found, for as in other areas, nineteenth-century cases contain many lines of reasoning, not all of which were eventually settled on as being acceptable.

[47]   See above, para.1-026.

[48]   See above.

[49]   See above, para.1-026.

[50]   See Article 29, 30.

[51]   And see below, para.8-015.

[52]   *Freeman & Lockyer v Buckhurst Park Properties (Mangal) Ltd* [1964] 2 Q.B. 480 at 502–504; *Hely-Hutchinson v Brayhead Ltd* [1968] 1 Q.B. 549. The same assumption is made in *Miles v McIlwraith* (1833) 8 App.Cas. 120; *Att.-Gen. for Ceylon v Silva* [1953] A.C. 461; and in *Eagle Star Insurance Co Ltd v Spratt* [1971] 1 Lloyd's Rep. 295; [1971] 2 Lloyd's Rep. 116.

[53]   See below, para.8-028.

[54]   See *Freeman & Lockyer v Buckhurst Park Properties (Mangal) Ltd* [1964] 2 Q.B. 480 at 503.

[55]   Third party: *Reynell v Lewis* (1846) 15 M. & W. 517 at 526; *Pole v Leask* (1863) L.J. 33 Ch. 155 at 162; *Lysaght Bros v Falk* (1905) 2 C.L.R. 421; *Hoare v McCarthy* (1916) 22 C.L.R. 296 at 303; *Pol-*

authority.[56] If a principal makes a written statement as to the putative agent's lack of authority but then declines to be available for cross-examination, adverse inferences may be drawn.[57] As will be seen below (para.3-009), it is relatively rare for a third party to wish to deny a putative agent's authority to act (as opposed to be asserting that there is authority) and if the third party does so it may find in any event that the principal ratifies the agent's actions. There is little case law authority on where the burden of proof lies where it is the third party who is asserting that there is no authority. It seems that where the third party is challenging an agent's authority to commence litigation in the principal's name and the principal is represented by a solicitor, the onus does lie on the third party to establish that the solicitor was improperly instructed.[58] In other circumstances, once the defendant puts in issue the agent's authority to act, it is at least arguable that the burden lies on the agent to show that the principal gave authority. Principals who assert that they were undisclosed principals would have the onus of proving the conferral of actual authority on the agent. The standard principles of evidence apply to the proof of authority. In relation to actual authority, evidence of a principal's conduct subsequent to the alleged commencement of authority will usually be admissible, although it is likely to be given less weight than contemporaneous evidence.[59] The difficult evidential issues that can arise where it is not clear for whom amongst an agent's many unidentified or undisclosed principals the agent may have been acting are dealt with elsewhere.[60]

3-008   **Principal retains right to act personally**   A principal's conferral of authority on an agent will not usually be to the exclusion of the principal's own powers to act. Much will turn on the context, but one would normally expect clear agreement before it would be concluded that a principal had surrendered the privilege to act personally. Many of the leading cases involve commission agencies, and are directed to claims by agents for lost commission when the principal acts

---

ish SS Co v A.J. Williams Fuels (Overseas Sales) Ltd, The Suwalki [1981] 1 Lloyd's Rep. 511 at 514; Suncorp Insurance & Finance v Milano Assecurazioni SpA [1993] 2 Lloyd's Rep. 225 at 233; Gurtner v Beaton [1993] 2 Lloyd's Rep. 369 (CA) at 380; Hudson Bay Apparel Brands LLC v Umbro International Ltd [2010] EWCA Civ 949; [2011] 1 B.C.L.C. 259 at [48]; Seiwa Australia Pty Ltd v Beard (2010) 75 N.S.W.L.R. 74 at [248] (onus of proving apparent authority of a partner); Pavlovic v Universal Music Australia Pty Ltd [2015] NSWCA 313; (2015) 90 N.S.W.L.R. 605 at [8]; Boyle v Maritime Travel Inc 2014 NSCA 44 at [14]; Business Mortgage Finance 6 Plc v Roundstone Technologies Ltd [2019] EWHC 2917 (Ch) at [57]. Agent: McKittrick v Jordan Sandman Smythe Ltd [1991] NZCA 16. As to allegations by a principal that the agent has exceeded mandate, or that the agent's authority has been terminated, see below, para.6-004, and para.10-027. As to assertions of lack of authority by a third party in an action for breach of warranty of authority, see below, para.9-066. As to admissibility of evidence from unrelated proceedings of appointment by the principal of same agent, see Mitsui OSK Lines Ltd v Salgaocar Mining Private Ltd [2015] EWHC 565 (Comm); [2015] 2 Lloyd's Rep. 518 at [31].

56   See Wisecal Ltd v Conwell International Ltd [2011] H.K.L.R.D. 27.
57   Spar Shipping AS v Grand China Logistics Holding (Group) Co Ltd [2015] EWHC 718 (Comm) at [81].
58   See Hawksford v Hawksford (2005) 191 F.L.R. 173 at [55]; and Zoha Ltd v Ahmed [2016] EWHC 1981 (Ch); [2017] Ch. 127. See also Sherlock Holmes International Society Ltd v Aidiniantz [2016] EWHC 1076 (Ch) at [113]; affirmed [2017] EWCA Civ 1875; [2018] 1 B.C.L.C. 188 (proceedings struck out for lack of authority to bring them).
59   See Hutchings v Nunes (1863) 1 Moo.P.C.(N.S.) 243; Garnac Grain Co Inc v HMF Faure & Fairclough Ltd [1968] A.C. 1130n at 1137; Cox v Goldcrest Developments (NSW) Pty Ltd (2000) 50 N.S.W.L.R. 76; Tuke v JD Classics Ltd [2018] EWHC 755 (QB) at [76].
60   See paras 2-067 and 8-072.

personally.[61] However, the issue of retention by a principal of the freedom to act personally (and in priority to the agent) is a more general one, and arises in many contexts.[62] Hence, a third party which has a contract with the principal cannot assert that it will have regard only to decisions by and communications from the nominated agent, without clear provision supporting such a stance.[63] Lord Wright put the point clearly when he said that it is difficult to imply a term "restricting in the interests of an agent the freedom of a principal to deal with his own property or business according to his own judgment".[64] The position is different in those limited situations where a grant of authority is irrevocable.[65] There, it is usually implicit in the grant of authority that the right to exercise the powers conferred is exclusive. In such cases, the donee of the power frequently has a proprietary interest in particular assets that inhibits the principal's ability to deal with them, in any event.

Rule (4): Principal cannot rely on unauthorised acts, unless ratifies Although   **3-009**
the issue rarely arises in the courts, it seems clear enough that a principal cannot assert legal rights as a result of action by an agent that the principal has not authorised unless the principal ratifies the actions of the agent. This principle was a step in the reasoning in *Keighley, Maxsted & Co v Durant*,[66] discussed above, even if the facts of the case concerned a suit *against* the would-be principal. The principle seems to operate even where the agent had apparent authority to bind the principal.[67] The principle is not limited to cases where a contractual claim is at issue, and extends, for instance, to cases where a defendant alleges that court proceedings in the principal's name were not authorised.[68]

Illustrations

(1) The dean and canons of a Cathedral each have power to appoint one of their   **3-010**
    number as proxy and a canon does so. The fact that the canon then attends in
    person does not revoke the proxy for later occasions.[69]
(2) A shareholder of a company who grants a proxy attends a company meeting
    and asserts the right to vote in person. The power of the proxy in such

---

[61] See *Brinson v Davies* (1911) 105 L.T. 134 at 135; *Luxor (Eastbourne) Ltd v Cooper* [1941] A.C. 108 at 143–145.

[62] See Illustrations. See also *Molthes Rederi Akt v Ellerman's Wilson Line Ltd* [1927] 1 K.B. 710 at 715; *Dry Bulk Handy Holding Inc v Fayette International Holdings Ltd* [2013] EWCA Civ 184; [2013] 1 W.L.R. 3440 at [25]; *Angove's Pty Ltd v Bailey* [2016] UKSC 47; [2016] 1 W.L.R. 3179 at [16] (agent's right to collect in price did not exclude principal's right to collect price directly); and *ACCC v Flight Centre Travel Group Ltd* [2016] HCA 49; (2016) 261 C.L.R. 203 (travel agents in competition with airlines for the sale of air tickets).

[63] See *Duffy Kennedy Pty Ltd v Galileo Miranda Nominee Pty Ltd* [2020] NSWCA 25 at [100].

[64] *Luxor (Eastbourne) Ltd v Cooper* [1941] A.C. 108 at 145. As to the principal's right to give further instructions, see below, para.6-009. As to termination of an exclusive agency, see below, Article 120.

[65] As to which, see below, Article 118.

[66] *Keighley, Maxsted & Co v Durant* [1901] A.C. 240 at 246, Article 15 Illustration 3. In *Australian Workers' Union v Leighton Contractors Pty Ltd* [2013] FCAFC 4; (2013) 209 F.C.R. 191, a majority of the Full Federal Court considered that an outside party could not take the point that a transaction was not properly authorised by a company, but see Kratzmann J (dissenting) at [80].

[67] See below, para.8-030.

[68] See *Aidiniantz v The Sherlock Holmes International Society Ltd* [2017] EWCA Civ 1875.

[69] *Eyre v Lovell* (1782) 3 Doug. 66; 99 E.R. 541.

circumstances is superseded, or suspended if not confined to the particular meeting.[70]

(3) A bank's written mandate is to make payments on behalf of a company on the direction of certain named persons. It is protected if the company's sole director, not a notified signatory, authorises payment.[71]

Article 23

NO AUTHORITY TO ACT OTHER THAN FOR PRINCIPAL'S BENEFIT

3-011   Authority to act as agent includes only authority to act honestly in pursuit of the interests of the principal.[72]

Comment

3-012   It is implicit in a conferral of authority that the principal intends the agent to exercise the relevant powers in the interests of the principal. An agent who deliberately or recklessly exercises powers against the interests of the principal must know that the agent acts without the principal's consent, and therefore acts without authority. A clear statement of the principle can be found in *Lysaght & Co Ltd v Falk*[73]:

> "Every authority conferred upon an agent, whether express or implied, must be taken to be subject to a condition that the authority is to be exercised honestly and on behalf of the principal. That is a condition precedent to the right of exercising it, and, if that condition is not fulfilled, then there is no authority, and any act purporting to have been done under it, unless in dealing with innocent parties, is void."

It might be noted that the passage contains the qualification "unless in dealing with innocent parties", but this is, it is suggested, an allusion to the concept of apparent authority rather than a true rider to the concept of actual authority. If actual authority all turned on the state of innocence or otherwise of the third party it would not be accurate to say that honesty is a condition precedent to the exercise of actual authority. But it would be odd to have the conferral of authority turn on the state

---

[70]   *Cousins v International Brick Co* [1931] 2 Ch. 90.

[71]   *Hill Street Services Co Ltd v National Westminster Bank Plc* [2007] EWHC 2379 (Ch) at [17]. See too *London International Trust Ltd v Barclays Bank Ltd* [1980] 1 Lloyd's Rep. 241 at 248–249; *Morrell v Workers Savings & Loan Bank* [2007] UKPC 3 at [10] (dictum that conferral on party holding power of attorney or other agent of power to operate bank account did not preclude bank acting directly on instructions from the account holder).

[72]   See Comment. The approach taken here was approved in *Hopkins v T.L. Dallas Group Ltd* [2004] EWHC 1379; [2005] 1 B.C.L.C. 543 at [89]; and *Sweeney v Howard* [2007] NSWSC 852 at [56] (power of attorney did not extend to borrowing on mortgage for the purpose of on-lending the funds for the attorney's own ends). See too *Relfo Ltd v Varsani* [2012] EWHC 2168 (Ch) at [86]; affirmed [2014] EWCA Civ 360.

[73]   *Lysaght & Co Ltd v Falk* (1905) 2 C.L.R. 421 at 439, per O'Connor J (see too at 430, per Griffith CJ). The reference to innocent parties should be taken as a reference to there being apparent authority. See also *Architects of Wine Ltd v Barclays Bank Plc* [2006] EWHC 1648 (QB); [2007] 1 Lloyd's Rep. 55; reversed on other grounds [2007] EWCA Civ 239; [2007] 2 All E.R. (Comm) 285 (quaere whether mere fraud on a company's creditors ought to deprive directors of authority); *Parti v Al Sabah* [2007] EWHC 1869 (Ch) at [50]; *Flexirent Capital Pty Ltd v EBS Consulting Pty Ltd* [2007] VSC 158 at [166]; *Thanakharn Kasikorn Thai Chamchat v Akai Holdings Ltd (In Liquidation)* (2010) 13 H.K.C.F.A.R. 479 at [77], per Lord Neuberger NPJ.

of knowledge of the third party, and it is well established that the third party's state of knowledge is irrelevant to the concept of actual authority. The concept is solely focused on the relationship between principal and agent, to which the third party "is a stranger".[74]

The *Restatement, Third* contains a comparable principle, as follows:

> "An agent acts with actual authority when, at the time of taking action that has legal consequences for the principal, the agent reasonably believes, in accordance with the principal's manifestations to the agent, that the principal wishes the agent so to act."[75]

This is reinforced by other provisions.[76] This formulation may go too far, insofar as it requires the agent's belief to be reasonable. In this context, however, it may be that what is intended is "rationally believes" rather than "competently believes". A rule that an agent lacks authority merely because the agent incompetently thought a decision was in his principal's interests would prove problematic for the principal, let alone the agent and third parties.[77] For one thing, a forensic decision as to "reasonableness" would be needed before it were known whether it were necessary for a principal who had not disowned the decision to have ratified it. The agent's liability to the principal for unreasonable action would, of course, remain.

An agent who is acting dishonestly in relation to the principal may still, of course, have apparent authority.[78] But where a transaction is transparently not in the principal's interests, the agent is also unlikely to have apparent authority. The body of case law that affirms that there is no apparent authority where the third party ought to have realised that the agent was acting purely for personal benefit[79] inferentially also affirms the general principle that an agent who acts dishonestly lacks actual authority. If an agent has no apparent authority where dishonesty is reasonably patent, then it is clear that the agent cannot have actual authority.

The substance of Article 23 did not appear before the 17th edition of this work, and earlier editions contained a general statement in the chapter on relations between principal and third parties that:

> "An act of an agent within the scope of his actual or apparent authority does not cease to bind the principal merely because the agent was acting fraudulently and in furtherance of his own interests."[80]

That earlier proposition, obscure in itself, was probably based on a case at the

---

[74] See *Freeman and Lockyer v Buckhurst Park Properties (Mangal) Ltd* [1964] 2 Q.B. 480 at 502.

[75] *Restatement, Third*, § 2.01.

[76] § 2.02, Comment *h:* "acts that create no prospect of economic advantage for a principal ... require specific authorisation"; § 8.10: "An agent has a duty "to refrain from conduct that is likely to damage the principal's enterprise".

[77] *Bieber v Teathers Ltd* [2012] EWHC 190 (Ch) at [86]; affirmed [2012] EWCA Civ 1466; [2012] 2 B.C.L.C. 585 ("an investor cannot say that the stockbroker is authorised only to make successful investments"). See further below, para.3-016.

[78] See below, Article 74.

[79] See, e.g. *Reckitt v Barnett, Pembroke and Slater Ltd* [1929] A.C. 176 at 190, Illustration 6 to Article 24; and the other cases below, para.8-048; *Rolled Steel (Holdings) Ltd v British Steel Corp* [1986] Ch. 246 at 306–307, per Browne-Wilkinson LJ; *Heinl v Jyske Bank (Gibraltar) Ltd* [1999] Lloyd's Rep. Bank. 511 at 521; per Nourse LJ; *Wrexham Ass. Football Club Ltd v Crucialmove Ltd* [2006] EWCA Civ 237; [2008] 1 B.C.L.C. 508.

[80] Article 76 in the 16th edition. For a defence of this approach, see Worthington (2017) 133 L.Q.R. 118. But cf. Watts [2017] J.B.L. 269.

turn of the twentieth century, *Hambro v Burnand*.[81] In *Macmillan Inc v Bishopsgate Investment Trust Plc (No.3)* at first instance,[82] Millett J cited the statement with approval, saying also that English law distinguishes between the act and the motive with which it was done; and that English law recognises the distinction between want of authority and abuse of authority.

There is no reason to doubt that English law recognises that distinction. But it is a non sequitur to argue that motive, and in particular fraud, is altogether foreign to the concept of authority. Indeed, basic honesty in an agent is arguably a more fundamental implied requirement of a conferral of authority than any other. So long as the concept of *actual* authority turns on consent, as it does, it is not possible, in determining the scope of the mandate intended to be conferred, to exclude the purpose for which a power is given, whether express[83] or implied, such as the purpose of promoting the interests of the principal is. The weight of authority also supports that position.[84]

As to *Hambro v Burnand*, the case concerned a member of Lloyd's authorised to write insurance for others who did so in the ordinary course of business, but for improper motives. It was held that his principals were bound. The judgments were plainly concerned to protect the innocent third party, and the case was decided at a time before the distinction between actual and apparent authority was perceived as clearly as it is now. There seems little doubt that his principals did not *actually* authorise him to act in the way he did; indeed, no premiums were paid and he did not enter the policies in his books nor introduce them into the accounts rendered to his principals, and he intercepted letters addressed to his principals.[85] To modern eyes the case might have been founded on *apparent* authority: to the third party, he was acting in the ordinary course of business, it would have been odd to ask for evidence of his authority and even had he shown it he would still have appeared authorised.[86] But in fact, it appears from the report of the case at first instance, that the claimants had not only not seen the document of appointment but they had had no direct dealings with the principals, and their counsel, Scrutton KC, is reported to have expressly disowned any reliance on apparent authority.[87] Nonetheless, in *AL*

---

[81]   *Hambro v Burnand* [1904] 2 K.B. 10, Illustration 1 to Article 74 (where more literature is cited). But cf. *Heilbut v Nevill* (1869–1870) L.R. 5 C.P. 478 at 482 and 484.

[82]   *Macmillan Inc v Bishopsgate Investment Trust Plc (No.3)* [1995] 1 W.L.R. 978 at 984; affirmed without reference to this point [1996] 1 W.L.R. 387.

[83]   An exemplar of express purposes are those formerly found in memoranda of association of companies: see, for example, *Sinclair v Brougham* [1914] A.C. 398 (building society had power to borrow but only in the pursuit of the business of a building society).

[84]   See *Official Manager of the Athenaeum Life Insurance Co v Pooley* (1858) 28 L.J. (N.S.) Ch. 119 at 129–130 (contract void for agent's fraud on principal, and innocent assignee could not sue on it); *Reckitt v Barnett, Pembroke and Slater Ltd* [1929] A.C. 176 (agent authorised to draw cheques "without restriction": no authority to do so for paying private debts); *A.L. Underwood Ltd v Bank of Liverpool* [1924] 1 K.B. 775; *EBM Co Ltd v Dominion Bank* [1937] 3 All E.R. 555 (PC) at 568–569; *Hopkins v T.L. Dallas Group Ltd* [2004] EWHC 1379; [2005] 1 B.C.L.C. 543; *Parti v Al Sabah* [2007] EWHC 1869 (Ch) at [49]; *Saad v Doumeny Holdings Pty Ltd* [2005] NSWSC 893 at [24] (holder of power of attorney purports to allot shares for the purpose of diluting principal's shareholding); *Despot v Registrar-General of NSW* [2013] NSWCA 313 at [55] (power of attorney used to pay debts owed to donee's companies)); *Vernon v Public Trustee* [2016] NZCA 388 at [37] (fiduciary duties of attorney).

[85]   See [1904] 2 K.B. 10 at 15.

[86]   See para.8-020, below, and Article 74. Alternatively, the case can be viewed as exceptional: see Watts (2002) 2 O.U. Commonwealth L.J. 93 at 96–98.

[87]   *Hambro v Burnand* [1903] 2 K.B. 399 at 413–414.

Underwood Ltd v Bank of Liverpool,[88] Scrutton LJ, as that counsel had by then become, seems to have treated the case as involving apparent authority. The breadth of the concept of apparent authority makes it doubtful that any other analysis is necessary.[89]

Even in its own terms, *Hambro* does not decide that purpose is irrelevant to the scope of authority since it appears that if the third party had known of the agent's mismotivation the transaction would have been treated as unauthorised, rather than simply affected by breach of fiduciary duty.[90] The case seems to turn on the proposition that where what the agent is doing is so routinely attached to the agent's usual instructions that had the third party inquired of the principal the latter would have confirmed the agent's mandate, there is no need to inquire. It is not clear, however, that this notion can be squared with older authority.[91] Further, the third party in *Hambro* was aware that the agent had a conflict of interest, and both the result and reasoning in the case remain problematic.[92]

Consideration should also be given to the situation where an agent is directed to do exactly what is done, rather than given a discretion. In such cases, it may not matter that the agent realises that the instructions are contrary to the principal's interests and proceeds anyway. This may have been the case in *Macmillan v Bishopsgate* itself, where the person concerned (Mr Robert Maxwell) was authorised as a result of a specific resolution of the executive committee to effect a transfer of shares to a nominee company (Bishopsgate) and did so, though intending subsequently to use them for personal benefit.[93] On the other hand, if the very acting is contrary to the principal's interests, it cannot be regarded as authorised unless expressly.[94] An example where the agent does exactly what is authorised could be where an agent for sale becomes aware of poor quality in the principal's goods the significance of which the principal may not realise, but continues with sales because the agent is at that time on bad terms with and wishes the principal harm—or indeed simply to increase the agent's commission. It would be otherwise if the agent had actively concealed defects. This should also be so of an agent in the insurance market knowingly accepting losing risks.[95]

It is important to note that the result of the foregoing reasoning is that the transaction is, as regards the principal, void as being unauthorised. This is quite independent of the possibility of setting the transaction aside, or giving other relief, in equity. This may also exist.[96] Equity too may recognise a broader range of improper

---

[88] *AL Underwood Ltd v Bank of Liverpool* [1924] 1 K.B. 775 at 791–792.

[89] See Article 72, below, and para.8-020 in particular.

[90] See too *Reckitt v Barnett, Pembroke and Slater Ltd* [1929] A.C. 176; *Tobin v Broadbent* (1947) 75 C.L.R. 378.

[91] *Jones v Williams* (1857) 24 Beav. 47 at 62. See too *A.L. Underwood Ltd v Bank of Liverpool* [1924] 1 K.B. 775 at 789; and *Crédit Agricole Corp and Investment Bank v Papadimitriou* [2015] UKPC 13; [2015] 1 W.L.R. 4265.

[92] See further, Watts [2017] J.B.L. 269 at 277–278.

[93] cf. *Bank of Bengal v Fagan* (1849) 7 Moo.P.C. 61 at 74, per Lord Brougham: "[indorser's purpose] only refers to the use of the funds to be made from the indorsement, not to the power".

[94] This point appears to have been misunderstood in *Dollars & Sense Ltd v Nathan* [2008] 2 N.Z.L.R. 557 (NZSC) at [42]. For an example of express instructions contrary to the principal's interest see Article 39, Illustration 4; cf. Article 39, Illustration 9.

[95] See *Sphere Drake Insurance Ltd v Euro International Underwriting* [2003] EWHC 2376 (Comm); [2003] Lloyd's Rep. I.R. 525 at [49].

[96] See commentary to Article 96; and *Criterion Properties Plc v Stratford UK Properties LLC* [2004] UKHL 28; [2004] 1 W.L.R. 1846 (Illustration 10 to Article 96). *Heinl v Jyske Bank (Gibraltar) Ltd*

purposes than the common law.[97] In such cases, the agent's honesty will mean that the agent still has actual authority at common law, even if a challenge to the resulting transaction might be mounted in equity against a third party with knowledge of the breach of equitable duty.[98] A conflict of interest may also help to establish the agent's liability to the principal for breach of the former's duties of care and skill.[99]

3-013 **Arbitration clauses and jurisdiction clauses** Contracts containing arbitration and jurisdiction clauses raise particular issues where the defendant asserts that its agent, purporting to make the contract, was not acting in the defendant's interests, and that the contract was on that basis unauthorised. In *Premium Nafta Products Ltd v Fili Shipping Co Ltd*,[100] the House of Lords held that the fact that a contract had been procured by bribing the promisor's agents would not entail that an arbitration clause in the contract was ineffective. This conclusion is unproblematic where all that is at issue is bribe-taking. An agent who takes a bribe may nonetheless believe that the relevant contract is still in the principal's interests, and thereby act within authority. There, the resulting contract will be voidable only. Where, however, the bribe-taker both makes the contract and knows that the contract is contrary to the principal's interests, the agent is, under the above Article, likely to be acting beyond authority, and any purported contract will be void.[101] *Premium Nafta* was decided on procedural issues and it is not clear that the bribe-taker actually made the contracts, though it does appear that the relevant contracts were very unfavourable to the principal. It is a fair inference that the House considered that an arbitration clause would remain effective even where the agent had exceeded authority. So long as the relevant agent would have had authority to enter into an arbitration contract, independent of the particular contract in respect of which there is a dispute, the arbitration clause would be effective.[102] Lord Hoffmann, who gave the leading judgment, did accept that if the agent had no authority whatever to enter into arbitration agreements then the clause would be ineffective.[103] The reasoning is said to be based on the intention of the parties, but given that the principal will not usually have anticipated the wrong and the agent has acted without authority,

---

[1999] Lloyd's Rep. Bank. 511 at 521. For full discussion see Stevens [2004] L.M.C.L.Q. 421; Prentice and Payne [2005] L.M.C.L.Q. 447; Watts (2005) 121 L.Q.R. 4, arguing that some dicta in *Criterion Properties* too readily assimilated equitable grounds of intervention within that of lack of authority.

[97] See commentary to Article 96; Watts (2005) 121 L.Q.R. 4. See too, *Hurstanger Ltd v Wilson* [2007] EWCA Civ 299; [2007] 1 W.L.R. 2351; [2007] 4 All E.R. 1118, note to para.8-219 below.

[98] See, e.g. *Senex Holdings Ltd v National Westminster Bank Plc* [2012] EWHC 131 (Comm); [2012] 1 All E.R. (Comm) 1130. See too *Ramsook v Crossley* [2018] UKPC 9 (conflict of interest not removing attorney's actual authority in relation to innocent third party).

[99] See, e.g. *Groom v Crocker* [1939] 1 K.B. 194; *Hilton v Barker Booth & Eastwood* [2005] UKHL 8; [2005] 1 W.L.R. 567. See further, para.6-021, below.

[100] *Premium Nafta Products Ltd v Fili Shipping Co Ltd* [2007] UKHL 40; [2007] 4 All E.R. 951; [2007] 2 All E.R. (Comm) 1053 (affirming the Court of Appeal, sub nom. *Fiona Trust and Holding Corp v Privalov* [2007] EWCA Civ 20; [2007] 2 Lloyd's Rep. 267; [2007] 1 All E.R. (Comm) 891); *Interprods Ltd v De La Rue International Ltd* [2014] EWHC 68 (Comm) at [7].

[101] A point apparently accepted by Longmore LJ in the Court of Appeal in *Fiona Trust and Holding Corp v Privalov* [2007] EWCA Civ 20; [2007] 2 Lloyd's Rep. 267; [2007] 1 All E.R. (Comm) 891 at [26].

[102] *Fiona Trust and Holding Corp v Privalov* [2007] EWCA Civ 20; [2007] 2 Lloyd's Rep. 267; [2007] 1 All E.R. (Comm) 891 at [18].

[103] *Fiona Trust and Holding Corp v Privalov* [2007] EWCA Civ 20; [2007] 2 Lloyd's Rep. 267; [2007] 1 All E.R. (Comm) 891 at [17].

a strong element of pragmatism seems to be involved. Nonetheless, similar reasoning has since been applied in testing the validity of jurisdiction clauses.[104]

2. EXPRESS ACTUAL AUTHORITY

Article 24

CONSTRUCTION OF POWERS OF ATTORNEY

Powers of attorney are strictly construed and are interpreted as giving only such **3-014** authority as they confer expressly or by necessary implication.[105] The following are the most important rules of construction:

(1) The operative part of a deed is controlled by the recitals where there is ambiguity.[106]
(2) Where authority is given to do particular acts, followed by general words, the general words are restricted to what is necessary for the proper performance of the particular acts.[107]
(3) General words do not confer general powers, but are limited to the purpose for which the authority is given, and are construed as enlarging the special powers only when necessary for that purpose.[108]
(4) A deed must be construed so as to include all incidental powers necessary for the effective execution of the power it confers.[109]

Comment

The term "power of attorney" is usually applied to a formal grant of power to act **3-015** made by deed or contained in a deed relating also to other matters. There was in fact no rule that agency must be created by deed, except where the agent is to be empowered personally to execute a deed, and it seems that a power of attorney could at common law be granted by simple writing.[110] However the Powers of Attorney Act 1971 s.1 requires that powers of attorney be executed by deed. The term "power of attorney" is not defined, but presumably means a formal grant of agency

---

[104] See *Deutsche Bank AG v Asia Pacific Broadband Wireless Communications Inc* [2008] EWCA Civ 1091; [2008] 2 Lloyd's Rep. 619 at [25].
[105] *Bryant, Powis & Bryant v La Banque du Peuple* [1893] A.C. 170 at 177; *Withington v Herring* (1829) 5 Bing. 442 at 458; *Sweeney v Howard* [2007] NSWSC 852 at [54] (power to grant mortgage not conferring power to on-lend proceeds for purposes unrelated to donor of power of attorney); *Great Investments Ltd v Warner* [2016] FCAFC 85 at [92]. See also Dal Pont, in *Agency Law in Commercial Practice* (Busch, Macgregor and Watts eds, 2016), Ch.12. As to execution of deeds under powers of attorney, see Article 77. The Trustee Delegation Act 1999 s.10, somewhat enlarges the scope of powers concerning land unless a contrary intention appears. See also s.1, which authorises an attorney to exercise trustee functions of the donor in certain circumstances.
[106] Illustration 1.
[107] *Perry v Holl* (1860) 2 De G.F. &J. 38 at 48; *Katara Hospitality v Guez* [2018] EWHC 3063 (Comm) at [86]; Illustrations 2 and 3.
[108] *Attwood v Munnings* (1827) 7 B. & C. 278 at 284; Illustrations 4, 5 and 7. But cf. *Brown v Innovatorone Plc* [2012] EWHC 1321 (Comm) at [809] (context remains important in construing power of attorney).
[109] *Howard v Baillie* (1726) 2 H.Bl. 618 at 619; Illustrations 6 and 8. See in general Aldridge, *Powers of Attorney* (10th edn), para.2-16 onwards; Thurston, *Powers of Attorney* (8th edn), Ch.7; Dal Pont, *Powers of Attorney* (2nd edn).
[110] See Articles 9 and 10. See also the definition above, para.2-039.

powers, often of a general nature. To such deeds the strict rules stated above apply: but to other conferring of authority, even where written, the laxer rules given in the following Articles apply.

It is worth noting that the basic rule here given for powers of attorney is even contrary to the normal rule for deeds, which is that they are construed against the grantor.[111] A reason given is "because the rights of other persons may be affected",[112] though this does not seem very convincing since the rule will usually operate to the prejudice of those other persons. However, the normal rule favouring the grantee has behind it the idea of non-derogation from grant, a principle of the law of property which is not necessarily appropriate in situations of representation. As such the above rule has parallels with the specific requirements which exist in some countries that there be an express authorising clause for certain acts such as alienation of land, mortgage, etc.[113] The comparison should not however be pressed too far, for these rules may operate on agency powers of potentially greater generality than may be required in common law systems, which can make use of the trust to transfer powers. In any case, the rule here seems well established in nineteenth-century cases, though the notion of protecting the principal as opposed to the third party, which seems to lie behind it, may be regarded now as being somewhat unfashionable, especially in the commercial sphere. The whole idea of strict construction is, indeed, inconsistent with the doctrine of apparent authority, which is now so prominent in the law of agency.[114] Many powers of attorney are however used in non-commercial situations such as absence abroad, illness or debility of the principal. It may be right in such circumstances to place a duty of inquiry on the third party.[115] And in the commercial sphere, powers of attorney tend to be drawn by lawyers and use technical wording which may be assumed to have been carefully chosen. Where an absolutely general power is required, doubts can be avoided by using the form provided by s.10 of the Powers of Attorney Act 1971 (as amended), which confers authority to do on behalf of a donor anything which the donor can lawfully do by attorney.[116]

Extrinsic evidence that the agent was not intended to have these powers, or to have additional powers, will not normally be accepted. This is the more so since powers of attorney are required to be conferred by deed. Such evidence may however be admissible where the wording is ambiguous, or to prove custom.[117] It is also possible that an attorney may have authority conferred by the principal independently of the power of attorney, which the agent can rely upon without calling in aid the power of attorney.[118]

---

[111] See Stoljar, pp.91–92.
[112] *Re Dowson and Jenkins' Contract* [1904] 2 Ch. 219 at 223.
[113] e.g. French CC, art.1988. See Müller-Freienfels in *Civil Law in the Modern World* (Yiannopoulos ed., 1965), 77 at 100–102.
[114] See Stoljar, pp.92–95.
[115] For a survey of the use of powers of attorney in international practice see Eder (1950) 98 U.Pa.L.Rev. 840, who puts forward the view that "the burden of a badly drafted power of attorney should be cast on the principal, not on the third party" (p.857).
[116] *Spina v Permanent Custodians Ltd* [2008] NSWSC 561 (power of attorney permitting self-benefit is effective for the purpose of determining scope of authority, whether or not self-benefit would put the attorney in breach of fiduciary duty); *Taheri v Vitek* [2014] NSWCA 209; (2014) 320 A.L.R. 555. For the construction of lasting powers of attorney granted under the Mental Capacity Act 2005, see *Re Various Lasting Powers of Attorney* [2019] EWCOP 40.
[117] See Article 31.
[118] See *Day v Harris* [2013] EWCA Civ 191; [2014] Ch. 211. See also below, paras 6-009 and 10-009.

Illustrations

Rule (1)

(1) A power of attorney recited that the principal was going abroad, and the opera-   **3-016**
tive part gave authority in general terms. Held, that the authority subsisted only
during the principal's absence abroad.[119] But where the operative words are
clear, they will prevail over a recital.[120]

Rule (2)

(2) Power was given:

> "to demand and receive all moneys due to the principal on any account whatsoever
> and to use all means for the recovery thereof, to appoint attorneys to bring actions,
> and to revoke such appointments, and to do all other business."

> Held, that "all other business" must be construed to mean all other busi-
> ness necessary for the recovery of the moneys, or in connection with it; and
> that the power of attorney gave the agent no authority to indorse a bill of
> exchange received by him under it.[121]

(3) X, who carried on business in Australia, gave an agent in England a power of
attorney to purchase goods in connection with the business, either for cash or
on credit, and where necessary in connection with any such purchases, or in
connection with the business, to make, draw, sign, accept or indorse for him
and on his behalf any bills of exchange or promissory notes which should be
requisite or proper. It was held that the power of attorney gave no power to
borrow money, and the agent, purporting to act in pursuance of the power, having given bills of exchange in respect of a loan, and misapplied the money, that
X was not liable on the bills.[122]

Rule (3)

(4) A power of attorney:

> "to recover and receive all sums of money owing ... by virtue of any security ... and
> to give, sign, and execute receipts, releases, or other discharges for the same, ... and
> to sell any real or personal property ... belonging" to the principal, does not
> authorise the agent to exercise the statutory power of sale of real property vested in
> the principal as a mortgagee."[123]

(5) A power of attorney "from time to time to negotiate, make sale, dispose of,

---

[119] *Danby v Coutts & Co* (1885) 29 Ch.D. 500.

[120] *Rooke v Lord Kensington* (1856) 2 K. & J. 753 at 769.

[121] *Hogg v Snaith* (1808) 1 Taunt. 347. See also *Esdaile v La Nauze* (1835) 1 Y. & C.Ex. 394; *Murray
v East India Co* (1821) 5 B. & A. 204; *Harper v Godsell* (1870) L.R. 5 Q.B. 422; *Totara Investments Ltd v Crismac Ltd* [2010] NZSC 36; [2010] 3 N.Z.L.R. 285.

[122] *Jacobs v Morris* [1902] 1 Ch. 816. See also *Esmail v Bank of Scotland* (1999) S.L.T. 1289 (power
referring to "his" accounts did not refer to joint accounts).

[123] *Re Dowson and Jenkins' Contract* [1904] 2 Ch. 219. See also *Re Bowles' Mortgage Trust* (1874) 31
L.T. 365; *Lewis v Ramsdale* (1886) 55 L.T. 179; *Hawkesley v Outram* [1892] 3 Ch. 359; *Bryant,
Powis & Bryant v La Banque du Peuple* [1893] A.C. 170; *Xie v Huang* [2012] NZHC 960; (2012)
N.Z. Conveyancing P.R. 239 at [28] (power to manage properties did not extend to a power of sale).

assign and transfer" gives no authority to pledge.[124] But a power "to sell, indorse and assign" authorises an indorsement to a bank as security for a loan to the agent; such a power being construed as giving (i) authority to sell, (ii) authority to indorse and (iii) authority to assign.[125]

(6)   A power of attorney to manage the principal's affairs while he is abroad, amplified by a letter from the principal to his bankers stating that he wished the power to cover the drawing of cheques upon the bank without restriction, does not authorise the attorney to draw cheques in payment of his own private debts.[126]

(7)   A clause in a power of attorney, whereby the principal agrees to ratify and confirm whatsoever the attorney shall do or purport to do by virtue of the power, does not extend the authority given by the power.[127]

(7a)   A power of attorney given over the whole of the donor's property did not entitle the attorney to exercise donor's powers as director of a company.[128]

Rule (4)

(8)   A partner gave his son a power of attorney "to act on his behalf in dissolving the partnership, with authority to appoint any other person as he might see fit". Held, this gave the son power to submit the partnership accounts to arbitration.[129]

(9)   A power of attorney:

> "to commence and carry on, or to defend at law or in equity, all actions, suits, or other proceedings touching anything in which the principal or his ships or other personal estate may be in anywise concerned"

---

[124] *Jonmenjoy Coondoo v Watson* (1884) 9 App.Cas. 561; *Tobin v Broadbent* (1947) 75 C.L.R. 378.

[125] *Bank of Bengal v Macleod* (1849) 5 Moo.Ind.App.1; *Bank of Bengal v Fagan* (1849) 5 Moo.Ind.App. 27.

[126] *Reckitt v Barnett, Pembroke & Slater Ltd* [1929] A.C. 176 (a famous case which is noted at (1929) 45 L.Q.R. 6; (1929) 3 C.L.J. 445; (1929) 17 Calif.L.Rev. 258; (1929) 77 U.Pa.L.Rev. 271); *Midland Bank Ltd v Reckitt* [1933] A.C. 1. See also *Morison v Kemp* (1912) 29 T.L.R. 70; *Hayes v Standard Bank of Canada* [1928] 2 D.L.R. 898. cf. *Australia and New Zealand Bank Ltd v Ateliers de Constructions Electriques de Charleroi* [1967] 1 A.C. 86 (authority to indorse principal's cheque and pay into own bank account necessary to give business effect to transactions authorised); distinguished in *Day v Bank of New South Wales* (1978) 19 A.L.R. 32. Wide wording would not normally authorise an agent to make gifts to or transfer to himself. See *King v Bankerd* 492 A 2d 608 (Ct.App.Md., 1985); *Lamb v Scott* 643 So.2d 972 (S.C.Ala 1994); cited in Hynes and Loewenstein, *Agency, Partnership and the LLC* (7th edn, 2007) pp.276–277; *Sweeney v Howard* [2007] NSWSC 852 at [56]; *Siahos v JP Morgan Trust Australia Ltd* [2009] NSWCA 20; *Despot v Registrar-General of NSW* [2013] NSWCA 313; *Great Investments Ltd v Warner* [2016] FCAFC 85 at [84] (authorisation of conflict of interest does not license appropriation by donee of donor's property); *Vernon v Public Trustee* [2016] NZCA 388 at [37]; *Katara Hospitality v Guez* [2018] EWHC 3063 (Comm) at [128].

[127] *Midland Bank Ltd v Reckitt* [1933] A.C. 1. Nor can it amount to ratification, since it comes before the act. See above, para.2-049.

[128] *Levin v Rastkar* [2011] NZCA 210 at [46]; *Godfrey v Marshall* [2017] NZHC 420 (powers of donor not extending to power as trustee); *Mohd Afrizan Bin Hussain v Thein Hong Teck* (Malaysian CA, www.kehakiman.gov.my/en/node/187 (power attached to assignment of interest in partnership not make attorney a partner) [Accessed 3 September 2018]. cf. *Maharaj v Johnson* [2015] UKPC 28; [2015] P.N.L.R. 553 at [13] (in obiter, power of attorney by necessary implication extending to powers of donor in capacity as executor).

[129] *Henley v Soper* (1928) 8 B. & C. 16. See also *Withington v Herring* (1829) 5 Bing. 442; *Willis v Palmer* (1859) 7 C.B.(N.S.) 340.

authorises the attorney to sign on behalf of the principal a bankruptcy petition against a debtor of the principal.[130]

Article 25

CONSTRUCTION OF AUTHORITY NOT GIVEN BY DEED

Where the authority of an agent is given by an instrument not under seal, or is given orally, it is construed liberally, with regard to the object of the authority and to the usages of trade or business.[131] Courts will assume that a principal has not made the existence of an agent's authority turn on impractical or impossible conditions. Hence, an agent may warrant success to the principal, but the agent's possession of authority could not be made to turn on committing the principal only to profitable transactions.[132]

3-017

Comment

The rules for the construction of documents other than deeds are clearly very much laxer, and it was said at first instance in the leading case of *Pole v Leask*[133] that where authority is general it will be construed liberally. It is presumably often, though not necessarily, true that a deed is more carefully drawn than a less formal document, and so should be more strictly construed: and powers of attorney may often be executed to establish an agency against a non-commercial background, which would also make strict interpretation appropriate.[134] Be that as it may, in the commercial sphere the interpretation of documents and correspondence concerning the agency relationship is plainly far more liberal where no formal power of attorney by deed has been executed, as can be seen from the cases cited. Reference should also be made to subsequent Articles, for most of the cases there cited concern instructions given in writing.[135] The rule applies a fortiori to authority given orally, and indeed *Pole v Leask*[136] itself was a case of oral authority. The interpretation of both written and oral authority is a matter of law: but in the latter case questions of fact as to what was said and done may make law and fact difficult to distinguish. Furthermore, in both cases questions of the normal course of business, and of trade

3-018

---

[130] *Re Wallace Ex p. Wallace* (1884) 14 Q.B.D. 22.

[131] *Pole v Leask* (1860) 28 Beav. 562 at 574; affirmed (1863) 33 L.J.Ch. 155; *Ireland v Livingston* (1872) L.R. 5 H.L. 395; *Freeman and Lockyer v Buckhurst Park Properties (Mangal) Ltd* [1964] 2 Q.B. 480 at 502; *Unaoil Ltd v Amona Ranhill Consortium Sdn Bhd* [2012] EWHC 1595 (Comm) at [58] (usual approaches to contract construction applied).

[132] *Whitehead v Tuckett* (1812) 15 East 400; *Bieber v Teathers Ltd* [2012] EWHC 190 (Ch) at [86]; affirmed [2012] EWCA Civ 1466; [2012] 2 B.C.L.C. 585; *Forsta AP-Fonden v Bank of New York Mellon SA/NV* [2013] EWHC 3127 (Comm) at [105]; *LNOC Ltd v Watford Association Football Club Ltd* [2013] EWHC 3615 (Comm) at [64] (negligence does not remove actual authority); *Gabriel v Little* [2013] EWCA Civ 1513 at [57] (affirmed on different points sub nom. *BPE Solicitors v Hughes-Holland* [2017] UKSC 21; [2018] A.C. 599).

[133] *Pole v Leask* (1860) 28 Beav. 562 at 574; affirmed (1863) 33 L.J.Ch. 155. The judgment of Lord Romilly MR should, however, be read with caution, as it does not clearly distinguish between (what would now be called) actual and apparent authority: see the case on appeal (1863) 33 L.J.Ch. 155, especially the speech of Lord Cranworth.

[134] Stoljar, pp.91–92.

[135] See especially Article 26.

[136] Above.

customs, may arise, which are questions of fact.[137] Where it is clear that the principal and agent were not ad idem, no actual authority will exist.[138]

The principle that courts will assume that a principal has not made the existence of an agent's authority turn on vague or impossible conditions goes back a long way, reflected in the following dictum of Lord Ellenborough CJ, albeit not drawing a clear distinction between what would now be termed actual and apparent authority[139]:

> "If these expressions are to be construed into so many restrictions of the power of the brokers, it will follow that they were not only limited as to price, but also as to the terms of sale, which according to the latter were to be the best, and as to the purchasers who were to be safe men: and if in either of these respects the contract made by them should fail, their principal would have a right to reject it. But if this could be done, in what a perilous predicament would the world stand in respect of their dealings with persons who may have secret communications with their principal. Such communications therefore must not be taken as limitations of their power, however wise they may be as suggestions on the part of the principal."

Illustrations

3-019   (1)   An agent was instructed to sell goods at such a price as would realise 15s. per ton, net cash. He sold them at 15s. 6d. per ton, subject to two months' credit. Held, that the instructions might fairly be construed as meaning *15s. net* cash, or such a price as would eventually realise 15s. after allowing for interest, or a *del credere* commission; that the contract might be presumed to have reference to some well-known usage of the coal trade; and that the sale was within his authority.[140]

(2)   100 bales of cotton are ordered by a Liverpool merchant from a merchant at Pernambuco. The Pernambuco merchant buys 94 bales. There is evidence to show that it is not normally possible to purchase 100 bales at Pernambuco. The purchase is authorised.[141]

(3)   A is authorised to sell and warrant certain goods. He cannot bind his principal by a warranty given at any other time than at the sale of his goods.[142]

(4)   On the dissolution of a partnership, authority is given to one of the partners by his co-partners (i) to settle the partnership affairs,[143] or (ii) to receive all debts owing to, and to pay all debts owing by, the firm.[144] In neither case has the authority to draw, accept or indorse bills of exchange in the name of the firm.

(5)   A land agent of a property authorised to be sold for £900 sends a telegram to the owner intended to inform him that the agent has an offer for £825. By a

---

[137]   See Articles 27–32; though what constitutes a custom is a question of law: see Article 31. See *Globex Foreign Exchange Corp v Launt* 2011 NSCA 67 at [19].

[138]   See *Shortal v Buchanan* [1920] N.Z.L.R. 103, Illustration 5.

[139]   *Whitehead v Tuckett* (1812) 15 East 400 at 408–409 (albeit in reasoning directed to the older concept of a general authority).

[140]   *Boden v French* (1851) 10 C.B. 886.

[141]   *Johnston v Kershaw* (1867) L.R. 2 Ex. 82; *Ireland v Livingston* (1872) L.R. 5 H.L. 395, Illustration 1 to Article 26.

[142]   *Helyear v Hawke* (1803) 5 Esp. 72.

[143]   *Abel v Sutton* (1800) 3 Esp. 108. See also *Odell v Cormack Brothers* (1887) 19 Q.B.D. 223; cf. *Smith v Winter* (1838) 4 M. & W. 454.

[144]   *Kilgour v Finlyson* (1789) 1 H.Bl. 155.

transcription error the telegram puts the offer at £925. The owner telegrams his approval not mentioning price. Held that there was no binding contract, because the principal and agent were not ad idem as to authority, and the agent had no apparent authority to represent the principal's acceptance of the price.[145]

Article 26

AUTHORITY GIVEN IN AMBIGUOUS TERMS

Where the authority of an agent is conferred in such ambiguous terms, or the instructions given the agent are so uncertain, as to be fairly capable of more than one construction, an act reasonably done by the agent in good faith which is justified by any of those constructions is deemed to have been duly authorised, though the construction adopted and acted upon by the agent was not that intended by the principal.[146] But with modern communications it may be possible to obtain clarification, and an agent may not act reasonably unless there has been an attempt to contact the principal.[147] Where a principal makes a mistake in giving instructions to an agent, including one acting under a power of attorney, and the agent in response conveys an interest in property by way of gift to a third party, the principal may still be able to have the conveyance rectified if it was not the principal's intention to make a gift.[148]

3-020

Illustrations

(1) A commission agent in Mauritius was authorised to buy and ship 500 tons of sugar (subject to a certain limit in price, to cover cost, freight and insurance), 50 tons more or less of no moment, if it enabled him to secure a suitable vessel. The principal stated that he would prefer the option of sending the vessel to London, Liverpool or the Clyde, but that if that was not possible the goods might be shipped to Liverpool or London. Held that a shipment of 400 tons in a vessel carrying other cargo direct to London and thus not amenable to orders was a good execution of the authority, it being doubtful what the instructions meant.[149]

3-021

(2) An agent undertook to sell and transfer certain stock when funds should be at 85 or over. Held, that he was bound to sell when the funds reached 85, and had no discretion to wait until they went higher than that price.[150]

(3) A shipowner by telegram requests shipbrokers to "fix steamer" on certain

---

[145] *Shortal v Buchanan* [1920] N.Z.L.R. 103.

[146] *Ireland v Livingston* (1872) L.R. 5 H.L. 395, Illustration 1. See above, para.1-021.

[147] See *Woodhouse AC Israel Cocoa Ltd SA v Nigerian Produce Marketing Co Ltd* [1972] A.C. 741 at 772; *European Asian Bank AG v Punjab and Sind Bank (No.2)* [1983] 1 W.L.R. 642 at 655, saying that the principle is "only available in very limited circumstances"; *Veljkovic v Vrybergen* [1985] V.R. 419. See also cases cited under Article 25; Article 38; *Moore v Mourgue* (1776) 2 Cowp. 479; *Comber v Anderson* (1808) 1 Camp. 523; *Pariente v Lubbock* (1856) 8 De G.M. & G. 5; *Miles v Haslehurst* (1906) 23 T.L.R. 142.

[148] *Day v Day* [2013] EWCA Civ 280; [2014] Ch. 114 (noted Dawson (2014) 130 L.Q.R. 356).

[149] *Ireland v Livingston* (1872) L.R. 5 H.L. 395. See also *Loring v Davis* (1886) 32 Ch.D. 625; *International Paper Co v Spicer* (1906) 4 C.L.R. 739; *Gould v South Eastern and Chatham Ry* [1920] 2 K.B. 186; *J. Vale & Co v Van Oppen & Co Ltd* (1921) 37 T.L.R. 367; *Brown and Gracie v F.W. Green & Co Pty Ltd* [1960] 1 Lloyd's Rep. 289; and see a useful discussion in *Veljkovic v Vrybergen* [1985] V.R. 419.

[150] *Bertram, Armstrong & Co v Godfray* (1830) 1 Knapp. 381. See also *Tallentire v Ayre* (1884) 1 T.L.R.

terms. The brokers take this as an instruction to let out one of the shipowner's vessels, to be named subsequently, on such terms. The owner intended them to obtain a ship on charter. The brokers' interpretation is justified.[151]

3. IMPLIED ACTUAL AUTHORITY

Article 27

TO DO WHAT IS NECESSARY FOR, OR INCIDENTAL TO, EFFECTIVE EXECUTION OF EXPRESS AUTHORITY (INCIDENTAL AUTHORITY)

3-022   An agent has implied authority to do whatever is necessary for, or ordinarily incidental to, the effective execution of the agent's express authority in the usual way.[152]

Comment

3-023   This Article only refers to actual authority. A good statement of the notion behind it is that:

"an authority of this nature necessarily includes medium powers, which are not expressed. By medium powers I mean all the means necessary to be used in order to obtain the accomplishment of the object of the principal power ...".[153]

But a similar notion is relevant to apparent authority, and statements of the rule appear in this context[154]: indeed in many cases it is unnecessary and even impossible to decide whether the decision rests on implied or on apparent authority.[155] By way of example, it is said that an agent has authority, unless there are special circumstances, to disclose the existence of the agency, the identity of the principal, the agent's relationship with the principal,[156] and documents evidencing the authority which the principal might reasonably expect that third parties would wish to see for their own protection.[157] On the other hand, a recurring theme is that authority to do an act does not necessarily involve authority to receive payment in relation to it.[158] Some cases usually associated with the notion of agency of necessity could also be regarded as examples of incidental authority.[159]

143.

[151] *Weigall & Co v Runciman & Co* (1916) 85 L.J.K.B. 1187. As to the legal position of shipbrokers in general, see *H. Edwin Anderson III* (2000) 31 J.M.L.C. 89.

[152] *Pole v Leask* (1860) 28 Beav. 562 at 574–575 (affirmed (1863) 33 L.J.Ch. 155); *SMC Electronics v Akhter Computers Ltd* [2001] 1 B.C.L.C. 433; *Bayley v Wilkins* (1849) 7 C.B. 886; *Collen v Gardner* (1856) 21 Beav. 540; *Nayyar v Sapte* [2009] EWHC 3218 (QB); [2010] P.N.L.R. 15 at [132]; and see Illustrations.

[153] *Howard v Baillie* (1796) 2 H.Bl. 618 at 619, per Eyre CJ. See too *The West of England Ship Owners Mutual P. & I. Assoc. v Hellenic Industrial Development Bank SA* [1999] 1 Lloyd's Rep. 93.

[154] e.g. *Beaufort v Neeld* (1845) 12 C. & F. 248; *Dingle v Hare* (1859) 7 C.B.(N.S.) 145; *Wiltshire v Sims* (1808) 1 Camp. 258.

[155] cf. above, para.3-005. See *Ryan v Pilkington* [1959] 1 W.L.R. 403; criticised by Powell, pp.51–52 and finally disapproved by the House of Lords in *Sorrell v Finch* [1977] A.C. 728.

[156] *United Bank of Kuwait Ltd v Hammoud* [1988] 1 W.L.R. 1051 at 1066–1067.

[157] Powell, p.46.

[158] See Illustrations 2 and 10; and *Smith v Peter & Diana Hubbard Pty Ltd* [2006] NSWCA 109.

[159] e.g. *Gokal Chand-Jagan Nath v Nand Ram Das-Atma Ram* [1939] A.C. 106; see below, para.4-

Illustrations

(1)   A is authorised to enter into a binding contract relating to land. He has implied **3-024** authority to sign a memorandum thereof to satisfy the Law of Property Act 1925 s.40.[160] But it must relate to the contract authorised; and where solicitors, acting upon instructions, bid for three separate lots of property at an auction and the property was knocked down to them, it was held that they had no authority to sign one indivisible agreement to purchase all the lots.[161]

(2)   An assistant in a shop normally has authority to receive payment for goods sold in the shop, but not necessarily to receive it elsewhere[162] or in other circumstances outside the ordinary course of business.[163] A person delivering goods may have no such authority,[164] and a traveller taking orders for the purchase of goods may have no authority to receive the price,[165] though there may be a course of dealing or of business whereby payment to such a traveller is normal.[166]

(3)   A is authorised to buy certain shares. He has implied authority to do everything in the usual course of business necessary to complete the bargain, e.g. reimburse the seller for payment on a call.[167]

(4)   An agent is authorised to institute proceedings for liquidation of a company. He has authority to give a notice of demand on behalf of the creditor.[168]

(5)   An agent is employed to obtain payment of a bill of exchange from the acceptor. He has no implied authority to receive payment subject to a condition that the acceptor shall not be liable for the expenses of protesting the bill for nonpayment.[169]

(6)   An agent is employed to sell a consignment of goods by description while afloat. He has no implied authority to warrant them to be of any particular condition or quality.[170]

(7)   An agent authorised to deliver a horse has no authority to give a warranty,[171] and an agent authorised to deliver milk has no authority to sell it to someone

---

007.

[160]   *Rosenbaum v Belson* [1900] 2 Ch. 267; the relevant provision is now s.2 of the Law of Property (Miscellaneous Provisions) Act 1989. And see *Gavaghan v Edwards* [1961] 2 Q.B. 220; Article 6.

[161]   *Smith v MacGowan* [1938] 3 All E.R. 447. See also *Smith v Webster* (1876) 3 Ch.D. 49; *Van Praagh v Everidge* [1902] 2 Ch. 266, reversed on other grounds [1903] 1 Ch. 434. But sales by auction no longer require a memorandum, nor to be in writing: Law of Property (Miscellaneous Provisions) Act 1989 s.2.

[162]   *Kaye v Brett* (1850) 5 Exch. 269 at 274.

[163]   See *Sanderson v Bell* (1833) 2 C. & M. 304.

[164]   *Lettice v Judkins* (1840) 9 L.J.Ex. 142.

[165]   *Butwick v Grant* [1924] 2 K.B. 483, Illustration 1 to Article 81. See also *Drakeford v Piercy* (1866) 7 B. & S. 515.

[166]   *International Sponge Importers Ltd v Andrew Watt & Sons* [1911] A.C. 279, Illustration 2 to Article 81; *Capel v Thornton* (1828) 3 C. & P. 352. See further Articles 28 and 81.

[167]   *Bayley v Wilkins* (1849) 7 C.B. 886.

[168]   *Metropolitan Waste Disposal Authority v Willoughby Waste Disposals Ltd* (1987) 9 N.S.W.L.R. 7. See also *Paget v Pearson* (1949) 49 S.R. (N.S.W.) 235 (authority to obtain possession of premises included authority to sign notice to quit).

[169]   *Bank of Scotland v Dominion Bank (Toronto)* [1891] A.C. 592.

[170]   *Benmag Ltd v Barda* [1955] 2 Lloyd's Rep. 354 at 357 (but on the facts of the case such authority could be inferred from the conduct of the parties); cf. *Abrahams v Spitz* (1963) 107 S.J. 113 (agent to sell car had authority to warrant that it was insured).

[171]   *Woodin v Burford* (1834) 2 Cr. & M. 391.

other than the person to whom it is being sent.[172] A furniture salesman may have authority to cancel the sale.[173]

(8)   A bailee for use may have authority to part with possession of the goods when it is reasonably incidental to the reasonable use of them to do so. Thus if he delivers goods for repair, the repairer may acquire a valid lien over them.[174]

(9)   A solicitor handling a conveyancing transaction after "subject to contract" agreement has authority to receive all relevant information from the other party.[175]

(10)   A person engaged in freight forwarding, and in particular in preparing documents for presentation under a letter of credit, has no authority to receive the payment under the credit.[176]

(11)   An agent appointed as project manager for a land development is given authority to appoint planning professionals and consultants for the project. It has implied authority to agree the fees that should be paid to those persons.[177]

(12)   A solicitor engaged in litigation is impliedly authorised to take all steps necessary to conduct the litigation to its conclusion.[178] Such a solicitor can continue to act even though the client is a company the only director of which has died.[179]

Article 28

AUTHORITY TO RECEIVE PAYMENT OF MONEY

3-025   An agent who is authorised to receive payment of money has prima facie no authority to receive payment otherwise than in cash, unless it is in the normal course of business to do so, or it is usual or customary in the particular business to receive payment in some other form, and such usage or custom is reasonable or known to the principal at the time when conferring the authority.[180]

Comment

3-026   Many agents have no authority to receive payment at all.[181] For others, receipt of payments may be their only agency function.[182] Where they have authority, nineteenth-century cases reiterate a basic rule that there is normally no authority to

---

[172] *Whittaker v Forshaw* [1919] 2 K.B. 419.

[173] *Leckenby v Wolman* [1921] W.N. 100.

[174] *Tappenden v Artus* [1964] 2 Q.B. 185. See further cases cited above, para.1-033.

[175] *Strover v Harrington* [1988] Ch. 390 at 409–410.

[176] *Cleveland Mfg. Co Ltd v Muslim Commercial Bank Ltd* [1981] 1 Lloyd's Rep. 646.

[177] *Norwich Union Life & Pensions Ltd v Strand Street Properties Ltd* [2009] EWHC 1109 (Ch) at [231].

[178] *Underwood, Son & Piper v Lewis* [1894] 2 Q.B. 306 at 310. Lodging a notice of appeal in time may also be within the solicitor's incidental authority, but proceeding to hearing without fresh authorisation is unlikely to be incidental to the original retainer: see *Donsland Ltd v van Hoogstraten* [2002] EWCA Civ 253; [2002] P.N.L.R. 26 at [26].

[179] *Donsland Ltd v van Hoogstraten* [2002] EWCA Civ 253; [2002] P.N.L.R. 26 at [26].

[180] See Comment and Illustrations. See also Comment to Article 81; Article 27, Illustration 2; Article 30, Illustrations 6 and 7.

[181] See further above, para.3-022.

[182] Apart from banks as receiving agents, see *Cheng Yuen v Royal Hong Kong Golf Club* [1998] I.C.R. 131 at 138 (PC) (golf club as collecting agent for caddies).

accept payment except in cash.[183] Under this rule an agent has prima facie no authority to give credit,[184] nor to accept a cheque. Although business practices have changed, it seems worth retaining the collection of cases and the statement of the rule, for care over payment is plainly to be required of any agent. But the rule is conditioned by the general principles as to the authority of agents, under which agents are normally authorised to do whatever is usual in the course of business.[185] It is thus not necessary to establish an actual custom that the agent need not receive cash, though it is obviously permissible to do so[186]: and this is important because customs are difficult to prove.[187] Therefore it has long been fairly easy to establish implied authority to sell on credit.[188] As to cheques, a cheque is usually regarded not as a separate form of payment but as conditional payment,[189] and no problem arises when it is duly met on presentation, for it is then equivalent to payment in cash even where it is in the agent's favour.[190] Disputes can however arise as to whether a cheque is a valid tender,[191] whether an agent is in breach of duty in accepting a cheque,[192] and whether an agent has actual or apparent authority to transfer property or release goods (which may, for instance, be subject to a lien) against a cheque rather than cash. Though the basic rule doubtless remains, it seems likely that a practice of accepting payment by cheque (especially if supported by some form of bank card), whether in favour of agent or principal, will fairly readily be recognised nowadays as being in the normal course of business, and hence within the scope of an agent's authority without proof of special usage.[193] The same is true (probably even more so as usage of cheques declines) of payment by credit card,

---

[183] *Sweeting v Pearce* (1859) 7 C.B.(N.S.) 449 at 480, 484; affirmed (1861) 9 C.B.(N.S.) 534, Illustration 4; *Farrer v Lacy, Hartland & Co* (1885) 31 Ch.D. 42; *Papé v Westacott* [1894] 1 Q.B. 272; *Blumberg v Life Interests and Reversionary Securities Corp Ltd* [1897] 1 Ch. 171; [1898] 1 Ch. 27; *Studholme v Government Advances to Settlers Office Superintendent* (1899) 18 N.Z.L.R. 257; *Southbourne Investments Ltd v Greenmount Manufacturing Ltd* [2008] 1 N.Z.L.R. 30 (NZSC) at [19] (solicitor has no implied authority to accept payment of deposit by cheque in relation to land transaction).

[184] Though if he does he may be estopped against the principal from saying that he has not received the money: *Gillard v Wise* (1826) 5 B. & C. 134.

[185] See Articles 25, 27, 29 and 30.

[186] See Article 31.

[187] See Comment to Article 31.

[188] See *Houghton v Matthews* (1803) 3 B. & P. 485 at 489; *Pelham v Hilder* (1841) 1 Y. & C.C.C. 3; *Boden v French* (1851) 10 C.B. 886; *Papé v Westacott* [1894] 1 Q.B. 272 at 278; *R. & E. Tingey & Co Ltd v John Chambers & Co Ltd* [1967] N.Z.L.R. 785.

[189] *D. & C. Builders Ltd v Rees* [1966] 2 Q.B. 617.

[190] *Bridges v Garrett* (1870) L.R. 5 C.P. 451; *International Sponge Importers Ltd v Andrew Watt & Sons* [1911] A.C. 279; *Papé v Westacott* [1894] 1 Q.B. 272; *Bradford & Sons v Price Brothers* (1923) 92 L.J.K.B. 871 (authorities reviewed); *Clay Hill Brick & Tile Co Ltd v Rawlings* [1938] 4 All E.R. 100.

[191] *Blumberg v Life Interests and Reversionary Securities Corp Ltd* [1897] 1 Ch. 171.

[192] *Farrer v Lacy, Hartland & Co* (1885) 31 Ch.D. 42; *Papé v Westacott* [1894] 1 Q.B. 272; *Kearney v Cullen* [1955] I.R. 18 (solicitor).

[193] See *Underwood v Nicholls* (1855) 17 C.B. 239 at 244; *Papé v Westacott* [1894] 1 Q.B. 272 at 278, 283 (estate agent); *Farrer v Lacy, Hartland & Co* (1885) 31 Ch.D. 42 (auctioneer). In many transactions the supporting of a cheque by a cheque card or credit card may be normal. As to notification that only certain forms of cheque are acceptable, see *International Sponge Importers Ltd v Andrew Watt & Sons* [1911] A.C. 279; *Bradford & Sons v Price Brothers* (1923) 92 L.J.K.B. 871. As to payment by cheque under a stipulation for payment in cash, see *Tankexpress A/S v Cie. Financière Belge des Petroles SA* [1949] A.C. 76. Where the delivery of goods has the effect of releasing a lien, it may be held that a mere driver, for instance, is not authorised to deliver against a cheque, which may not be met: see *Esterhuyse v Selection Cartage (Pty) Ltd* (1965) 1 S.A. 360; *McGraw-Edison (Canada) Ltd v Direct-Winters Tpt. Ltd* [1969] 1 O.R. 663. See further van Zyl (1974) 91 S.A.L.J. 337 (on South African cases).

which may rank as absolute payment.[194] It will not however prima facie be within the agent's authority to accept abnormal forms of payment, such as an adjustment of the account between agent and third party. "The payer who knows he is paying an agent must pay in such a manner as to facilitate and encourage the agent to pay it to his principal."[195] Here it may be necessary to prove an actual custom permitting such payment, and, if the custom is held unreasonable, knowledge of it.[196] But where the debtor to the principal is financially embarrassed, an agent's duty may be to do the agent's best to collect all that can be collected in the circumstances, and "the onus is on the [principal] in such a case to prove that the [agent] has failed in that duty".[197] In such a case the agent may have discharged any duty by getting what cash the agent can and giving credit for the rest.[198]

Illustrations

3-027   (1)   It is provided by the conditions of a sale by auction that the purchase-money shall be paid to the auctioneer. The auctioneer has no authority to receive a bill of exchange in payment, and if his authority to receive payment is revoked during the currency of the bill, such a payment does not discharge the purchaser.[199] So, an insurance broker has no authority to take a bill of exchange in payment of a claim in respect of which he is authorised to receive payment.[200]

(2)   An agent is authorised to receive payment of an account, and to retain part of the amount in discharge of a debt due to him from the principal. He has authority, to the extent of his debt, to settle in his own way with the debtor of his principal.[201]

(3)   A authorises B, a country stockbroker, to receive money due from C, a London stockbroker. B has no authority to settle with C by way of set-off, and a custom permitting such settlement is unreasonable.[202]

(4)   A authorises B, an insurance broker, to receive the amount due from the underwriters under a policy of insurance. The underwriters in good faith settle with B by setting off a debt due to them from him, and their names are struck out of the policy. By a custom at Lloyd's, a set-off is considered equivalent to payment as between broker and underwriter. If A is aware of the custom when he authorises B to receive payment, he is bound by the settlement. Otherwise he is not bound, because the custom is unreasonable.[203]

(5)   An agent authorised to receive money has prima facie no authority to receive

---

[194] *Re Charge Card Services Ltd* [1989] Ch. 497.

[195] *Pearson v Scott* (1878) 9 Ch.D. 198 at 205, per Fry J; and see in general Illustrations.

[196] See Article 31; *Sweeting v Pearce* (1859) 7 C.B.(N.S.) 449; affirmed (1861) 9 C.B.(N.S.) 534, Illustration 4.

[197] *Gokal Chand-jagan Nath v Nand Ram Das-Atma Ram* [1939] A.C. 106 at 113, per Lord Wright.

[198] *Gokal Chand-jagan Nath v Nand Ram Das-Atma Ram* [1939] A.C. 106 at 113, per Lord Wright.

[199] *Williams v Evans* (1866) L.R. 1 Q.B. 352; *Sykes v Giles* (1839) 5 M. & W. 645. See also *Hogarth v Wherley* (1875) L.R. 10 C.P. 630; *Howard v Chapman* (1831) 4 C. & P. 508 (no authority to accept payment in goods). cf. *Farrer v Lacy, Hartland & Co* (1888) 31 Ch.D. 42 (cheque).

[200] *Hine Brothers v Steamship Insurance Syndicate Ltd (The Netherholme)* (1895) 72 L.T. 79 (but facts rather special).

[201] *Barker v Greenwood* (1837) 2 Y. & C. Ex. 414.

[202] *Pearson v Scott* (1878) 9 Ch.D. 198; *Blackburn v Mason* (1893) 68 L.T. 510; *Crossley v Magniac* [1893] 1 Ch. 594; *Anderson v Sutherland* (1897) 13 T.L.R. 163 (all stockbroker cases). As to custom, see Article 31. See also *Underwood v Nicholls* (1855) 17 C.B. 239; *Wrout v Dawes* (1858) 25 Beav. 369; *Coupe v Collyer* (1890) 62 L.T. 927 (solicitors).

[203] *Sweeting v Pearce* (1859) 7 C.B.(N.S.) 449; affirmed (1861) 9 C.B.(N.S.) 534; *Stewart v Aberdein*

payment before it is due, and if his authority is revoked before that time, the debtor is not discharged by such payment[204]; he may have no authority to receive payment after it is due,[205] nor to accept it on terms different in some other respect from those prescribed by the contract.[206]

Article 29

MANAGERIAL AGENTS: IMPLIED AUTHORITY WHERE EMPLOYED TO CONDUCT TRADE OR BUSINESS OR ACT GENERALLY IN CERTAIN MATTERS (USUAL AUTHORITY)

An agent who is authorised to conduct a particular trade or business or gener-   **3-028**
ally to act for the principal in matters of a particular nature, or to do a particular class of acts, has implied authority to do whatever is incidental to the ordinary conduct of such trade or business,[207] or of matters of that nature, or is within the scope of that class of acts,[208] and whatever is necessary for the proper and effective performance of the duties undertaken[209]: but not to do anything that is outside the ordinary scope of the agent's employment and duties.[210] Even in relation to express powers of a certain type, there may be an implied limitation that they are to be deployed only for transactions on usual terms and conditions.[211]

Comment

The authority referred to here is that which arises from appointment to a   **3-029**
particular managerial post. When the board of directors appoint one of their number to be managing director, for example, "they thereby impliedly authorise him to do all such things as fall within the usual scope of that office".[212]
Many of the cases refer to an agent of this type as a general agent, as distinguished from a special agent. Much use is made of the distinction in nineteenth-century English cases, mainly in the context of what is now called apparent authority[213]: and it has sometimes been referred to in more recent times.[214] But it is submitted that the distinction should now be regarded in England as no

---

(1838) 4 M. & W. 211; *Legge v Byas, Mosley & Co* (1901) 7 Com.Cas. 16; *Matveieff & Co v Crosfield* (1903) 51 W.R. 365; *McCowin Lumber and Export Co v Pacific Marine Insurance Co* (1922) 38 T.L.R. 901; *Stolos Cia. SA v Ajax Insurance Co Ltd (The Admiral C)* [1981] 1 Lloyd's Rep. 9. But see *Trading & General Investment Co v Gault Armstrong & Kemble Ltd (The Okeanis)* [1986] 1 Lloyd's Rep. 196 at 200 where reference is made to evidence given that certain accounts of the customs of insurance companies were "completely out of date". See in general Hodgin, *Insurance Intermediaries: Law and Practice* (1992).

[204] *Breming v Mackie* (1862) 3 F. & F. 197. But there may be a custom permitting this: *Catterall v Hindle* (1867) L.R. 2 C.P. 368; *Heisch v Carrington* (1833) 5 C. & P. 471; see Article 31.
[205] See Article 29, Illustration 7 (insurance agent); *New Zealand Tenancy Bonds Ltd v Mooney* [1986] 1 N.Z.L.R. 280 (estate agent); cf. *Jawara v Gambian Airways* [1992] E.G.C.S. 54 (PC) (lawyer).
[206] *Campbell v Hassel* (1816) 1 Stark. 233. But a contract can be varied by custom: see Article 31.
[207] Illustrations 1 and 4.
[208] Illustrations 2, 4, 5 and 9.
[209] Illustrations 3, 6, 10 and 11.
[210] Illustrations 2, 3, 7 and 10. See too *Taylor v Van Dutch Marine Holding Ltd* [2019] EWHC 1951 (Ch); [2019] Bus. L.R. 2610 at [270] (limited power to borrow on principal's behalf).
[211] See *Taylor v Rhino Overseas Inc* [2020] EWCA Civ 353; [2020] Bus. L.R. 1486 at [34]–[36].
[212] *Hely-Hutchinson v Brayhead Ltd* [1968] 1 Q.B. 549 at 583, per Lord Denning MR. See further Illustration 4.
[213] See, e.g. *Smith v M'Guire* (1858) 3 H. & N. 554; see Article 72.
[214] e.g. *Barrett v Irvine* [1907] 2 I.R. 462.

more than a rather specific example of the obvious fact that, from the point of view of implied authority, a person made agent with general authority to do acts of various types or to negotiate a number of transactions of the same type is likely to have a wider authority than one appointed with limited authority to do acts of a particular class or to negotiate a particular transaction. The borderline between general and special agents is so indistinct that it is unwise to regard the test as a definitive one.[215]

The authority here discussed is an example of what can be called usual authority.[216] It should be noted, as with other Articles in this chapter, that the principle here cited is relevant not only to actual authority but also to apparent authority, in that in many cases the normal implied authority was negatived as between the parties by the circumstances, yet the third party was held entitled to assume that it existed, since the authority concerned would regularly be implied. The "general agent" cases are in fact, as stated above, in the main relevant to the development of the doctrine of apparent authority. However, they can, of course, support the proposition that implied authority will normally extend thus far.[217] It would be unusual for a general manager to have greater implied authority to make contracts with foreign parties than with domestic ones.[218]

Many of the examples relate to ways of living and trading which no longer exist; their value is simply as providing examples of the typical reasoning used, and analogies.

Illustrations

3-030   (1)   A is the manager of an estate. He has implied authority to contract for the usual and customary leases,[219] and to give and receive notice to quit to and from tenants[220] and to enter into agreements with tenants authorising them to change the mode of cultivation, and providing for the basis on which compensation for improvements shall be payable on the determination of the tenancy.[221]

(2)   A rent collector has no implied authority, as such, to receive a notice to quit from a tenant.[222] A steward has such implied authority,[223] but not to grant leases for terms of years.[224]

(3)   A is the managing owner of a ship. He has implied authority to pledge the credit of his co-owners for all such things, including repairs, as are neces-

---

[215] See above, para.1-045.

[216] As to this term see above, para.3-005.

[217] e.g. *Collen v Gardner* (1856) 21 Beav. 540, Illustration 2; *Wright v Glyn* [1902] 1 K.B. 745 (coachman); *Hely-Hutchinson v Brayhead Ltd* [1968] 1 Q.B. 549 at 583. See also *Brady v Todd* (1861) 9 C.B.(N.S.) 592; *Howard v Sheward* (1866) L.R. 2 C.P. 148; *Brooks v Hassall* (1883) 49 L.T. 560; *Baldry v Bates* (1885) 52 L.T. 620. These are cases where the usual authority of the agent is relied on, and therefore the representation giving rise to apparent authority would be very general indeed: see Comment to Article 72.

[218] *Sea Emerald SA v Prominvestbank-Joint Stockpoint Commercial Industrial and Investment Bank* [2008] EWHC 1979 (Comm) at [70].

[219] *Peers v Sneyd* (1853) 17 Beav. 151.

[220] *Papillon v Brunton* (1860) 5 H. & N. 518; *Jones v Phipps* (1868) L.R. 3 Q.B. 567; *Townsends Carriers Ltd v Pfizer Ltd* (1977) 33 P. & C.R. 361; *Peel Developments (South) Ltd v Siemens Plc* [1992] 2 E.G.L.R. 85.

[221] *Re Pearson and I'Anson* [1899] 2 Q.B. 618.

[222] *Pearse v Boulter* (1860) 2 F. & F. 133.

[223] *Roe d. Rochester (Dean & Chapter) v Pierce* (1809) 2 Camp. 96.

[224] *Collen v Gardner* (1856) 21 Beav. 540.

sary for the usual or suitable employment of the ship.[225] But he has no authority as such to insure the vessel on behalf of his co-owners,[226] or to agree to pay a sum of money for the cancellation of a charter party made by him on their behalf.[227]

(4)   Individual directors of companies, at least those without an executive role, have little usual authority to bind the company.[228] However, s.44 of the Companies Act 2006 provides that a document is validly executed if signed by a director whose signature is witnessed.[229] The managing director of a company has a broad authority (subject to the company's constitution) to make decisions for the company in the ordinary course of business,[230] including to sign cheques and bills of exchange,[231] borrow money and give security over the company's property,[232] guarantee loans made by a subsidiary of the company and agree to indemnify other guarantors,[233] and authorise the commencement of legal proceedings.[234] He may reimburse himself for expenses on the company's behalf,[235] but should do so by payment through a bank account and not by using company money to pay for private items of consumption.[236] He may direct the method of discharge of debts owed to the company, but not by directing payment to a family member.[237] A managing director may have usual authority to instruct solicitors as to the drafting of his own remuneration contract.[238] A managing director would not have usual authority to make extraordinary decisions (those would normally need to be taken by the board of directors),[239] such as the sale or termination of the

---

[225] *The Huntsman* [1894] P. 214; *Barker v Highley* (1863) 15 C.B.(N.S.) 27.

[226] *Robinson v Gleadow* (1835) 2 Bing. N.C. 156.

[227] *Thomas v Lewis* (1878) 4 Ex.D. 18. See *Scrutton on Charterparties* (17th edn), Article 16 (omitted in later eds). Quaere as to the present day.

[228] *Re Haycraft Gold Reduction and Mining Co Ltd* [1900] 2 Ch. 230; *Houghton & Co v Nothard Lowe & Wills Ltd* [1927] 1 K.B. 246 at 267; *Northside Developments Pty Ltd v Registrar-General* (1990) 170 C.L.R. 146 at 205; *Hughes v NM Superannuation Pty Ltd* (1993) 29 N.S.W.L.R. 653 (chairperson of directors); *Colin R Price & Associates Pty Ltd v Four Oaks Pty Ltd* [2017] FCAFC 75 at [150]; *Neale v Ku De Ta SG Pte Ltd* [2015] SGCA 28; *Bishop Warden Property Holdings Ltd v Autumn Tree Ltd* [2018] NZCA 285; [2018] 3 N.Z.L.R. 809 at [27]; *East Asia Co Ltd v PT Satria Tirtatama Energindo* [2019] UKPC 30 at [58].

[229] See further, para.8-040 below.

[230] *Hely-Hutchinson v Brayhead Ltd* [1968] 1 Q.B. 549; *Rimpacific Navigation Inc v Daehan Shipbuilding Co Ltd* [2009] EWHC 2941 (Comm); [2010] 2 Lloyd's Rep. 236.

[231] *Dey v Pullinger Engineering Co* [1921] 1 K.B. 77.

[232] *Biggerstaff v Rowatt's Wharf Ltd* [1896] 2 Ch. 93.

[233] *Hely-Hutchinson v Brayhead Ltd* [1968] 1 Q.B. 549.

[234] *AMB Generali Holding AG v SEB Trygg Liv, etc.* [2005] EWCA Civ 1237; [2006] 1 Lloyd's Rep. 318 at [32]; *Hawksford v Hawksford* (2005) 191 F.L.R. 173.

[235] *Bank of New South Wales v Goulburn Valley Butter Co Pty Ltd* [1902] A.C. 543 (PC); *Corporation Agencies v Home Bank of Canada* [1927] A.C. 318 (PC).

[236] See *Midland Bank Ltd v Reckitt* [1933] A.C. 1.

[237] *Acute Property Developments Ltd v Apostolou* [2013] EWHC 200 (Ch) at [40].

[238] *Newcastle International Airport Ltd v Eversheds LLP* [2012] EWHC 2648 (Ch); [2013] P.N.L.R. 5 at [111]; affirmed on this point [2013] EWCA Civ 1514; [2014] 1 W.L.R. 3073 at [76] (but finding of express authority).

[239] See *Freeman & Lockyer v Buckhurst Park Properties (Mangal) Ltd* [1964] 2 Q.B. 480 at 509; *Smith v Butler* [2012] EWCA Civ 314; [2012] Bus. L.R. 1836 at [30]; *Spedley Securities Ltd v Greater Pacific Investments Pty Ltd* (1992) 7 A.C.S.R. 155 at 16; *Thanakharn Kasikorn Thai Chamchat v Akai Holdings Ltd (In Liquidation)* (2010) 13 HKCFAR 479 at [110]. It is doubtful whether a board of directors would any longer be expected to delegate total management power to a managing director: the broad dicta in *Biggerstaff v Rowatt's Wharf Ltd* [1896] 2 Ch. 93 at 102, 106, should be

company's business.[240] He has no authority to bribe representatives of other companies,[241] but would have authority to cause the company to breach a contract.[242] A managing director has no authority to use his powers to suspend employees in order to suspend the chairman of directors in that role, even though the latter is an employee.[243] It can be assumed that a chief executive officer who is not a director would have less usual authority than a managing director.[244]

(5)   A company secretary has authority to order cars to meet visitors at airports, and in general to make contracts in connection with the administration of the company's affairs.[245] Similarly, a corporate "general counsel" might be expected to have authority to instruct solicitors to oppose an application to wind up the company.[246] A company secretary would normally also have usual authority to communicate the decisions of the board of the company, and to authenticate documents which record what the board has decided.[247]

(6)   The general manager of a railway company has implied authority to order medical attendance for an employee of the company.[248] But a station-master has no implied authority to pledge the credit of the railway company for medical attendance to an injured passenger.[249]

(7)   A is the agent of an insurance company, and has authority to receive the payment of premiums within 15 days of their becoming due. He has no implied authority to accept payment after the expiration of that time.[250] So, a local agent of an insurance company, employed to introduce business, has as a rule no implied authority to grant, or contract to grant, policies on behalf of the company, that being outside the ordinary scope of his employment and duties,[251] though he may be authorised to grant temporary cover.[252]

(8)   The master of a stranded ship has in the absence of express instructions authority to bind his owners or demise charterers by entering into a reasonable salvage contract.[253]

---

viewed in the light of later authorities.
[240] *Interactive Technology Corp Ltd v Ferster* [2016] EWHC 2896 (Ch) at [188]; *East Asia Co Ltd v PT Satria Tirtatama Energindo* [2019] UKPC 30 at [58].
[241] *E. Hannibal & Co Ltd v Frost* (1988) 4 B.C.C. 3. But cf. *Morgan v Babcock & Wilcox Ltd* (1929) 43 C.L.R. 163. See further Watts [2011] J.B.L. 214 at 215.
[242] *Lexi Holdings Plc v Pannone & Partners* [2009] EWHC 2590 (Ch).
[243] *Smith v Butler* [2012] EWCA Civ 314; [2012] Bus. L.R. 1836 at [31].
[244] See *Left Bank Investments Pty Ltd v Ngunya Jarjum Aboriginal Corp* [2020] NSWCA 144.
[245] *Panorama Developments (Guildford) Ltd v Fidelis Furnishing Fabrics Ltd* [1971] 2 Q.B. 711, recognising the change in the function of company secretaries since the early years of that century. As to a secretary's usual authority to communicate board decisions, see *Mahony v East Holyford Mining Co* (1875) L.R. 7 H.L. 869 at 887 and 902; *Montreal and St Lawrence Light and Power Co v Robert* [1906] A.C. 196 at 203 (joint representation of president and secretary). See too *Daimler Co Ltd v Continental Tyre & Rubber Co* [1916] 2 A.C. 307 at 323 (but cf. 326).
[246] *Telstra Corp Ltd v Ivory* [2008] QSC 123 at [89].
[247] *Kelly v Fraser* [2012] UKPC 25; [2013] 1 A.C. 450 at [13].
[248] *Walker v Great Western Ry Co* (1867) L.R. 2 Ex. 228.
[249] *Cox v Midland Ry Co* (1849) 3 Exch. 268. See also *Houghton v Pilkington* [1912] 3 K.B. 308; cf. *Langan v Great Western Ry Co* (1873) 30 L.T. 173. See also Article 33.
[250] *Acey v Fernie* (1840) 7 M. & W. 151. See *MacGillivray on Insurance Law* (14th edn), para.7-068 onwards.
[251] *Linford v Provincial, etc., Ins Co* (1864) 34 Beav. 291. See Article 77, Illustrations 8, 9 and 10.
[252] *Wilkinson v General Accident Fire and Life Insurance Co Ltd* [1967] 2 Lloyd's Rep. 182.
[253] *The Unique Mariner* [1978] 1 Lloyd's Rep. 438; but see below, para.4-008.

(9)   The engineer of a local authority has authority to specify the purpose for which goods are required by the authority, for the purposes of the Sale of Goods Act 1893 s.14.[254]

(10) Authority to arrest or give persons into custody is normally implied when the duties of the agent could not efficiently be performed without such authority. A bank manager has no implied authority to arrest or prosecute supposed offenders on behalf of the bank.[255] The manager of a restaurant has implied authority to give into custody persons behaving in a riotous manner,[256] but not persons who refuse to pay a disputed bill.[257]

(11) A manager of a building project, even where the husband of the owner, has no usual authority to grant an easement to a neighbour in return for the latter's co-operation with the project.[258]

(12) An importer engages an agent to arrange for the receipt, storage and subsequent carriage of its products. The agent signs a standard-form carriage contract without reading its terms which include a broad exclusion clause. The agent's actions held to be within the scope of its actual authority.[259]

Article 30

IMPLIED AUTHORITY WHERE EMPLOYED IN THE COURSE OF BUSINESS AS AGENT (USUAL AUTHORITY)

An agent who is authorised to do any act in the course of the agent's employ-   **3-031**
ment, trade, profession or business has implied authority to do whatever is normally incidental, in the ordinary course of such employment, trade, profession or business, to the execution of the express authority,[260] but not to do anything which is unusual in such employment, trade, profession or business, or which is neither necessary for nor incidental to the execution of the express authority.[261] Again, even with express powers there may be an implied limitation that they are to be exercised only for transactions on usual terms and conditions.[262]

Comment

In this case the implied authority arises, not from the managerial nature of the   **3-032**
post to which the agent has been appointed, as in the previous Article, but from the

---

[254] *Ashford Shire Council v Dependable Motors Pty Ltd* [1961] A.C. 336.
[255] *Bank of New South Wales v Owston* (1879) 4 App.Cas. 270, where there is a full review of the authorities; *Abrahams v Deakin* [1891] 1 Q.B. 516. But many of the old cases on false imprisonment may be out of date in England at least. Whereas in former times a person was "given in charge", the increased speed of communications today means that police officers are normally able to arrive soon enough to effect arrests on their own responsibility. See Atiyah, *Vicarious Liability in the Law of Torts* (1967), pp.266–267.
[256] *Ashton v Spiers & Pond* (1893) 9 T.L.R. 606.
[257] *Stedman v Baker & Co* (1896) 12 T.L.R. 451.
[258] *McKeand v Thomas* (2006) 12 B.P.R. 23, 593 at [74] (NSWSC).
[259] *Toll (FGCT) Pty Ltd v Alphapharm Pty Ltd* (2004) 219 C.L.R. 165.
[260] Illustrations 1, 2 and 7. See too *AIB Group (UK) Plc v Mark Redler & Co (A Firm)* [2012] EWHC 35 (Ch) at [21]–[22]; affirmed on different grounds [2014] UKSC 58; [2015] A.C. 1503 (solicitor's usual authority in disbursing client moneys).
[261] Illustrations 3–6.
[262] See *Taylor v Rhino Overseas Inc* [2020] EWCA Civ 353; [2020] Bus. L.R. 1486 at [34]–[36].

nature of the general occupation which the agent carries on apart from this particular agency. Agents of this type also are sometimes referred to as general agents, though as has already been stated, the utility of this term is doubtful.[263] The examples given here are for illustrative purposes, but more specific information should be sought in specialist works dealing with the authorities of those practising the various types of trade and profession. Expert evidence as to current practice is more likely to be relevant than old illustrations: as Staughton LJ said in connection with the authority of a solicitor, "I prefer to have regard to the expert evidence of today in deciding what is the ordinary authority".[264]

This proposition is again an example of what may be called usual authority.[265] As in the previous Articles, the primary reference is to actual authority, but the reasoning will apply also to apparent authority: indeed many of the cases relate to apparent authority, since the notion of general agency was primarily relevant to what is now called apparent authority.[266]

Illustrations

3-033 (1) A bailiff is authorised to distrain for rent. He has implied authority to receive the rent and expenses due, and a tender thereof to him operates as a tender to the landlord.[267]

(2) A horse-dealer is authorised to sell a horse. He has implied authority to warrant it.[268] So also has his employee. But the employee of a private seller has not[269] unless he sells in circumstances where custom requires a warranty.[270]

(3) An architect was employed to make plans for building certain houses. He instructed a quantity surveyor to take out quantities, and then invited tenders, all of which exceeded the limits of the building-owner's proposed expenditure. The quantity surveyor sued the building-owner for his fees, relying on an alleged custom in the building trade, by which the liability for such fees was thrown on the building-owner where no tender was accepted. The jury having found that there was no custom by which an architect was authorised to employ a surveyor without the sanction of the building-owner, and the owner not having expressly authorised the employment, it was held that the defendant was not liable.[271]

(4) A ship's agent has implied authority to arrange and pay for the stowage of

---

[263] See above, para.3-028.

[264] *United Bank of Kuwait Ltd v Hammoud* [1988] 1 W.L.R. 1051 at 1063; *Sea Emerald SA v Prominvestbank-Joint Stockpoint Commercial Industrial and Investment Bank* [2008] EWHC 1979 (Comm) at [108] (experts should give evidence of their experience not just opinion); *Seiwa Australia Pty Ltd v Beard* (2010) 75 N.S.W.L.R. 74 at [269] onwards (deprecating use of judicial notice in this context). See also Illustration 5.

[265] See above, para.3-005.

[266] See above, para.3-028.

[267] *Hatch v Hale* (1850) 15 Q.B. 10. Tender to a man left in possession by the bailiff is ineffective: *Boulton v Reynolds* (1859) 2 E. & E. 369.

[268] *Howard v Sheward* (1866) L.R. 2 C.P. 148; *Baldry v Bates* (1885) 52 L.T. 620. See also *Bank of Scotland v Watson* (1813) 1 Dow. 40 at 45. But this question is now of less importance in view of warranties implied by statute.

[269] *Brady v Todd* (1861) 9 C.B.(N.S.) 592.

[270] *Brooks v Hassall* (1883) 49 L.T. 569; see Article 31.

[271] *Antisell v Doyle* [1899] 2 I.R. 275.

cargo.[272] A loading superintendent employed by a f.o.b. buyer has no authority to waive a term of the contract as to description: but failure by him to object to goods which do not conform with the contract description may be attributed to the buyer for the purpose of the buyer's duty to mitigate damages.[273]

(5) A solicitor or barrister entrusted with the conduct of litigation has authority to agree to a settlement of it or to make admissions of liability provided that the settlement or admissions do not concern matters collateral to the action.[274] He has in general no implied authority to accept notices on behalf of his clients.[275] Agents, including employees and solicitors, have no implied authority to receive service of court proceedings in circumstances where personal service on a party is required. Subsequent delivery of the documents by the agent to the principal will not in itself be service.[276]

(6) A solicitor negotiating the sale of land on a "subject to contract" basis has no usual authority to sign the contract, nor otherwise to make a contract,[277] but

---

[272] *Blandy Bros & Co Ltd v Nello Simoni Ltd* [1963] 2 Lloyd's Rep. 393. cf. *Sickens v Irving* (1858) 29 L.J.C.P. 25 (no authority to make substantially new contract); *Lindsay & Son v Scholefield* (1897) 24 R. (Ct. of Sess.) 530. See in general as to ship's agents Trappe [1978] L.M.C.L.Q. 595; Morris [1982] L.M.C.L.Q. 218; also *Intermediaries in Shipping* (Grönfors ed., Gothenburg Maritime Law Association, 1990). As to agency in chartering, see Anderson (2000) 31 J.M.L.C. 89.

[273] *Toepfer v Warinco AG* [1978] 2 Lloyd's Rep. 569. See further as to authority to waive contract terms *Dawson Line Ltd v Aktiengesellschaft für Chemische Industrie* [1932] 1 K.B. 433; *Ismail v Polish Ocean Lines* [1976] Q.B. 893; *Mardorf Peach & Co Ltd v Attica Sea Carriers Corp (The Laconia)* [1977] A.C. 850 (authority of bank to accept late payment); *Surrey Shipping Co Ltd v Cie. Continentale (France) SA (The Shackleford)* [1978] 1 W.L.R. 1080 (receiver of goods had authority to waive defects in notice of readiness); *The Happy Day* [2002] EWCA Civ 1068; [2002] 2 Lloyd's Rep. 487 (receivers' agents); *The Northgate* [2007] EWHC 2796; [2008] All E.R. (Comm) 330 at [108] (implied power to waive in relation to notice of readiness); *State Rail Authority of NSW v Heath Outdoor Pty Ltd* (1986) 7 N.S.W.L.R. 170 at 194 (advertising manager had authority to indicate circumstances in which employer would terminate advertising contract, but not to vary contract); *Nowrani Pty Ltd v Brown* [1989] 2 Qd.R. 582 (solicitor had no authority to insert term into sale of land). See further *Restatement, Third*, § 6.08 and Comment.

[274] *Waugh v H.B. Clifford & Sons Ltd* [1982] Ch. 374 (authorities reviewed); *Lucke v Cleary* (2011) 111 S.A.S.R. 134; *Nandrame v Ramsaran* [2015] UKPC 20; *Pavlovic v Universal Music Australia Pty Ltd* [2015] NSWCA 313; (2015) 90 N.S.W.L.R. 605 at [7]; *Owners of Strata Plan No 57164 v Yau* [2017] NSWCA 341 at [177]; *Ramsook v Crossley* [2018] UKPC 9 (admissions of liability by attorney). But cf. *Re Newen* [1903] 1 Ch. 812; *Little v Spreadbury* [1910] 2 K.B. 658; *Thompson v Howley* [1977] 1 N.Z.L.R. 16; *Holmes v Kennard & Son* (1984) 44 P. & C.R. 202 (solicitor for purchaser had no authority to cancel notice on land register); *Donnellan v Watson* (1990) 21 N.S.W.L.R. 335 (no authority to agree to different compromise from that authorised); Cordery, *Solicitors* (8th edn), p.80 (not reproduced in later editions); Fridman (1987) 36 U. New Brunswick L.J. 9. cf. above, para.3-005. It has been held that a Citizens' Advice Bureau worker had a somewhat wider authority: *Freeman v Sovereign Chicken Ltd* [1991] I.C.R. 853.

[275] *Re Munro Ex p. Singer* [1981] 1 W.L.R. 1358; *IVI Pty Ltd v Baycrown Pty Ltd* [2005] QCA 205 at [33] (notice of revocation of offer given to purchaser's solicitor held ineffective where negotiations had principally been face-to-face). cf. *Von Essen Hotels 5 Ltd v Vaughan* [2007] EWCA Civ 1349 at [36] (see below, para.8-206). See further Article 94.

[276] *Cherney v Deripaska* [2007] EWHC 965 (Comm); [2007] 2 All E.R. (Comm) 785; *Lantic Sugar Ltd v Baffin Investments Ltd* [2009] EWHC 3325 (Comm); [2010] 2 Lloyd's Rep. 141 at [44]; *Glencore Agriculture BV v Conqueror Holdings Ltd* [2017] EWHC 2893 (Comm); [2017] Bus. L.R. 2090. cf. *Sino Channel Asia Ltd v Dana Shipping and Trading PTE Singapore* [2017] EWCA Civ 1703.

[277] *Lockett v Norman-Wright* [1925] Ch. 56; *James v Evans* [2000] 3 E.G.L.R. 1; *Vella v Permanent Mortgages Pty Ltd* [2008] NSWSC 505 at [207]; *Pavlovic v Universal Music Australia Pty Ltd* [2015] NSWCA 313; (2015) 90 N.S.W.L.R. 605 at [6].

would have usual authority to deliver and receive signed counterparts to a contract.[278]

(7) An estate agent in England has normally no authority to sell land: even though he is instructed as to the price at which the vendor will sell, his function is to solicit offers and transmit them to his principal.[279] But he may be authorised expressly or impliedly to sell[280] though in such circumstances he normally has no authority to sign anything but an open contract.[281] In any case he is prima facie authorised to describe the property and state to an intending purchaser circumstances which may affect its value[282]; but not to accept a deposit on such terms as will make the prospective vendor liable in respect of it[283]; to receive payment[284]; to warrant that the property may legally be used for a particular purpose[285]; it seems, to receive notice of cancellation of the contract under a statutory cooling-off provision.[286]

(8) An auctioneer has authority not only to sell but also at the time of the sale to sign a contract or memorandum of the sale for both vendor and purchaser.[287] In general there is no authority to receive payment,[288] but authority to describe the property[289] and receive a post-contract deposit may be usual,[290] and, except in the case of land, authority to receive the whole price may likewise be

---

[278] *Domb v Isoz* [1980] 1 Ch. 548. See also *Wise Think Global Ltd v Finance Worldwide Ltd* [2013] H.K.E.C. 1790 (authority to receive deposit). cf. *Southbourne Investments Ltd v Greenmount Manufacturing Ltd* [2008] 1 N.Z.L.R. 30 (NZSC) at [19] (no authority to receive deposit in form of cheque).

[279] *Hamer v Sharp* (1874) L.R. 19 Eq. 108; *Prior v Moore* (1887) 3 T.L.R. 624; *Chadburn v Moore* (1892) 61 L.J.Ch. 674; *Thurman v Best* (1907) 97 L.T. 239; *Lewcock v Bromley* (1920) 37 T.L.R. 48; *Keen v Mear* [1920] 2 Ch. 574; *Wragg v Lovett* [1948] 2 All E.R. 968; (but cf. *Jawara v Gambian Airways* [1992] E.G.C.S. 54, PC); *Law v Robert Roberts & Co* [1964] I.R. 292 (authorities reviewed). He is a "canvassing" or "introducing" agent: above, para.1-020. This does not exclude the possibility of other usages in other countries, e.g. *Powierza v Daley* [1985] 1 N.Z.L.R. 558; *Ngoi v Wen* [2017] NZCA 519 (receipt of acceptance of counter-offer by vendor's agent).

[280] *Rosenbaum v Belson* [1900] 2 Ch. 267; *Allen & Co v Whiteman* (1920) 89 L.J.Ch. 534; *Wragg v Lovett* [1948] 2 All E.R. 968; *Spiro v Lintern* [1973] 1 W.L.R. 1002.

[281] *Keen v Mear* [1920] 2 Ch. 574; *Wragg v Lovett* [1948] 2 All E.R. 968. cf. *Wisecal Ltd v Conwell International Ltd* [2011] 4 H.K.L.R.D. 275 at [22].

[282] *Mullens v Miller* (1882) 22 Ch.D. 194. But cf. *Overbrooke Estates Ltd v Glencombe Properties Ltd* [1974] 1 W.L.R. 1335; *Presser v Caldwell Estates Pty Ltd* [1971] 2 N.S.W.L.R. 471.

[283] *Sorrell v Finch* [1977] A.C. 728. See Articles 92 and 111. See also *New Zealand Tenancy Bonds Ltd v Mooney* [1986] 1 N.Z.L.R. 280 (no authority to accept late payment of deposit); cf. *Kohn v Devon Mortgage Ltd* (1985) 20 D.L.R. (4th) 480 (mortgage broker had authority to receive capital).

[284] See *Mynn v Joliffe* (1834) 1 Moo. & Rob. 326; *Petersen v Moloney* (1951) 84 C.L.R. 91; *Smith v Peter & Diana Hubbard Pty Ltd* [2006] NSWCA 109; cf. *Butwick v Grant* [1924] 2 K.B. 483.

[285] *Hill v Harris* [1965] 2 Q.B. 601.

[286] *Lo v Russell* [2016] VSCA 323 at [37].

[287] *Emmerson v Heelis* (1809) 2 Taunt. 38; *White v Proctor* (1811) 4 Taunt. 209; *Kenneys v Proctor* (1820) 1 Jac. & W. 350; *Earl of Glengal v Barton* (1836) 1 Keen 769 at 788; *Bell v Balls* [1897] 1 Ch. 663; *Chaney v Maclow* [1929] 1 Ch. 461. cf. *Van Praagh v Everidge* [1903] 1 Ch. 434. By virtue of s.2 of the Law of Property (Miscellaneous Provisions) Act 1989 the contract must now be in writing; but this does not apply in public auctions, which now require neither writing nor memorandum. Quaere whether an auctioneer has authority to sign a written contract. See Murdoch, *Law of Estate Agency* (5th edn), p.174 onwards.

[288] See *Mynn v Joliffe* (1834) 1 Moo. & Rob. 326; cf. *Butwick v Grant* [1924] 2 K.B. 483.

[289] See, e.g. *Smith v Land and House Property Corp* (1884) 28 Ch.D. 7. But cf. *Overbrooke Estates Ltd v Glencombe Properties Ltd* [1974] 1 W.L.R. 1335; and *Collins v Howell-Jones* (1980) 259 E.G. 331, where this authority was excluded.

[290] See *Sykes v Giles* (1830) 5 M. & W. 645; Murdoch, *Law of Estate Agency* (5th edn), p.229 onwards.

usual.[291] An auctioneer has normally no authority to rescind a sale,[292] to warrant,[293] to negotiate terms[294] or to sell by private contract after the auction, even where the public sale proves abortive and he is offered more than the reserve price.[295]

(9) Evidence of industry practice would be needed to show that it was within the usual authority of a firm of accountants to be holding and operating custodial (non-trust) accounts in off-shore tax havens on behalf of clients.[296]

Article 31

AUTHORITY IMPLIED FROM SPECIAL USAGES (CUSTOMARY AUTHORITY)

(1) An agent has implied authority to act, in the execution of the express authority conferred, according to the usages and customs of the particular place, market or business in which the agent is employed.[297]   **3-034**

(2) But an agent has no implied authority to act in accordance with any usage or custom which is unreasonable, unless the principal had actual notice of such usage or custom at the time when the authority was conferred[298]; or to act in accordance with any usage or custom which is unlawful.[299]

(3) The question whether any usage or custom is unreasonable or unlawful is a question of law. In particular, a usage or custom inconsistent with the intrinsic character of the contract of agency,[300] or a usage or custom whereby an agent who is authorised to receive payment of money may require payment by way of set-off, or by way of settlement of accounts between the agent and the person from whom the agent is authorised to receive payment,[301] is unreasonable.

Comment

General rule This Article embodies the general rule that an agent is authorised   **3-035**
to act in accordance with the commercial customs in the sphere in which he operates, e.g. a stock or commodity exchange. The rule is, however, of limited

---

[291] cf. Factors Act 1889 s.12(3); *Chelmsford Auctions Ltd v Poole* [1973] Q.B. 542.

[292] *Nelson v Aldridge* (1818) 2 Stark. 435.

[293] *Payne v Lord Leconfield* (1882) 51 L.J.Q.B. 642; *Gardiner v Grigg* (1938) 38 S.R.(N.S.W.) 524.

[294] *Seton v Slade* (1802) 7 Ves. 265 at 276.

[295] *Daniel v Adams* (1764) Ambl. 495; *Marsh v Jelf* (1862) 3 F. & F. 234. cf. *Else v Barnard* (1860) 28 Beav. 228; *Bousfield v Hodges* (1863) 33 Beav. 90. See in general Murdoch, *Law of Estate Agency* (5th edn), Ch.3.

[296] *Seiwa Australia Pty Ltd v Beard* (2010) 75 N.S.W.L.R. 74 at [310] (general discussion of usual authority of accountants).

[297] Illustrations 1–7; *Sutton v Tatham* (1839) 10 A. & E. 27; *Ex p. Howell, re Williams* (1865) 12 L.T. 785. There is a useful discussion of the requirement and effects of custom in Law Com. C.P. No. 124, *Fiduciary Duties and Regulatory Rules* (1992), pp.63–76.

[298] *Robinson v Mollett* (1874) L.R. 7 H.L. 802, Illustration 8.

[299] *Harker v Edwards* (1887) 57 L.J.Q.B. 147; and see Comment. Rules (1) and (2) were cited with approval in *Anglo Overseas Transport (United Kingdom) Ltd v Titan Industrial Corp (United Kingdom) Ltd* [1959] 2 Lloyd's Rep. 152 at 160.

[300] Illustrations 8 and 9. See also *Accidia Foundation v Simon C. Dickinson Ltd* [2010] EWHC 3058 (Ch) at [75] (appointment of art sales sub-agent on terms that contemplated suppression of terms of remuneration).

[301] Illustration 10.

application. The rules concerning proof of custom are strict, for their effect in the general law is to imply terms into contracts, which is not normally permitted unless they are to be derived from the nature of the transaction or essential to give it business efficacy.

Accordingly, proof of custom is notoriously difficult:

"In the mind of a layman there is often a confusion between custom and that which is customarily done, and he wrongly imagines that the latter amounts to a legal custom."[302]

The latter would of course be evidence of what authority is reasonably to be implied, or, in other contexts, of what is reasonably to be expected of principal or agent in the circumstances.[303] This Article therefore only applies to generally recognised and established customs in markets or the like, and not to mere customary courses of dealing between agent and third party, or between agents of the particular type and third parties.[304] Evidence of such courses of dealing may be well relevant to establish some other form of implied authority.

3-036   **Custom**   The burden of proving the existence of a custom or usage is a heavy one. It is not normally one that can be discharged by evidence given on affidavit if that evidence is challenged.[305] In order to establish the existence of a custom or usage the plaintiff must show that the alleged custom is (i) reasonable[306]; (ii) universally accepted by the particular trade or profession or at the particular place; (iii) certain; (iv) not unlawful; and (v) not inconsistent with the express or implied terms of the contract.[307] Therefore, even if a custom is proved to exist, the court will ignore it if it is expressly or impliedly excluded. But where the custom does exist and is not excluded, it is:

---

[302] *Re North Western Rubber Co Ltd and Hüttenbach & Co* [1908] 2 K.B. 907 at 919, per Fletcher Moulton LJ. The case itself was overruled in *Produce Brokers Co Ltd v Olympia Oil & Cake Co Ltd* [1916] 1 A.C. 314, which contains a detailed consideration of much of this topic. See also *Drexel Burnham Lambert International NV v El Nasr* [1986] 1 Lloyd's Rep. 356 at 365, per Staughton LJ: "What has to be shown by evidence is that the custom is recognised as imposing a binding obligation".

[303] See Articles 27–30.

[304] See *Hamilton v Young* (1881) 7 L.R.Ir. 289; *Ex p. Howell, Re Williams* (1865) 12 L.T. 785; *Cunliffe-Owen v Teather & Greenwood* [1967] 1 W.L.R. 1421 at 1438; *General Reinsurance Corp v Forsakringsaktiebolaget Fenna Patria* [1983] Q.B. 856.

[305] *Stag Line Ltd v Board of Trade* (1950) 83 Lloyd's Rep. 356 at 360. See also *Blandy Bros v Nello Simoni* [1963] 2 Lloyd's Rep. 24 at 29; [1963] 2 Lloyd's Rep. 393 at 400, 404.

[306] Thus in *Anglo-African Merchants Ltd v Bayley* [1970] 1 Q.B. 311 at 323 Megaw J said that the court would not uphold a custom which contradicted the principle that an agent might not serve both parties simultaneously. This was followed in *North and South Trust Co v Berkeley* [1971] 1 W.L.R. 470, Illustration 3 to Article 5; but cf. *Goshawk Dedicated Ltd v Tyse & Co Ltd* [2006] EWCA Civ 54. And see Article 44, Illustration 5.

[307] These well-known principles were accepted in *Oricon Waren-Handels GmbH v Intergraan NV* [1967] 2 Lloyd's Rep. 82 at 96 and in *Cunliffe-Owen v Teather & Greenwood* [1967] 1 W.L.R. 1421 at 1439. See also *Con-Stan Industry of Australia Pty Ltd v Norwich Winterthur Insurance (Australia) Ltd* (1986) 160 C.L.R. 226. As to (v) see further *Palgrave, Brown & Son Ltd v SS Turid* [1922] 1 A.C. 397 at 406; *London Export Corp v Jubilee Coffee Roasting Co* [1958] 1 W.L.R. 661 at 675; *Kum v Wah Tat Bank* [1971] 1 Lloyd's Rep. 437; *Accidia Foundation v Simon C. Dickinson Ltd* [2010] EWHC 3058 (Ch) at [69] and [71] (art agent not authorised to appoint sub-agent on terms that the latter could keep as commission any sums in excess of floor price).

"to be considered as part of the agreement: and if the agreement be in writing, though the custom is not written it is to be treated exactly as if that unwritten clause had been written out at length."[308]

Rules The position as regards rules, e.g. of a market or organisation, as opposed to customs, seems, despite suggestions to the contrary,[309] to be the same.[310] It is however obvious that special problems may arise when rules are changed. It has been held that a resolution of a regulatory body passed after a transaction cannot bind the principal or alter the contract between the parties,[311] though it may validly decide a dispute between the parties.[312]

3-037

Unreasonable customs There was much authority for applying the criterion of reasonableness to usages and customs, and especially to the rules of the Stock Exchange,[313] though the law does not normally protect contracting parties from unreasonable terms with much tenderness. But the situations referred to in Rule (3) of this Article are better regarded as sui generis rather than examples of unreasonable arrangements[314]: they were held to be actually inconsistent with the nature of the contract of agency, and were in the first edition of this work treated as in themselves a ground for the non-operation of custom. In all these cases the agent has no authority unless the principal knew of the custom when giving or confirming the authority for the particular transaction.

3-038

Unlawful customs Knowledge of an unreasonable custom may import assent to it. But it is difficult to see how the law can permit a principal to assent to a custom which is actually unlawful.[315] Nevertheless, a different conclusion could be derived from a group of cases relating to the former custom of the Stock Exchange to disregard Leeman's Act,[316] under which contracts for the sale of shares in banking companies were void if they did not contain certain information. In *Perry v Barnett*[317] it was held that this custom did not bind persons without notice,[318] but it was implied that it might, like an unreasonable custom, bind someone who had notice.[319] In *Seymour v Bridge*[320] it had been held that this custom could bind a plaintiff who was at the time unaware of the existence of the Act: the case was

3-039

---

[308] *Tucker v Linger* (1883) 8 App.Cas. 508 at 511, per Lord Blackburn.
[309] *Benjamin v Barnett* (1903) 19 T.L.R. 564.
[310] *Harker v Edwards* (1887) 57 L.J.Q.B. 147; *Cunliffe-Owen v Teather & Greenwood* [1967] 1 W.L.R. 1421. But see *Anderson v Sutherland* (1897) 13 T.L.R. 163.
[311] *Union Corp Ltd v Charrington & Brodrick* (1902) 19 T.L.R. 129; *Benjamin v Barnett* (1903) 19 T.L.R. 564. And see, on the changing of rules, *Doyle v White City Stadium Ltd* [1935] 1 K.B. 110.
[312] *Harker v Edwards* (1887) 57 L.J.Q.B. 147; *Reynolds v Smith* (1893) 9 T.L.R. 474; *Bell Group Ltd v Herald and Weekly Times* [1985] V.R. 613.
[313] e.g. *Pearson v Scott* (1878) 9 Ch.D. 198, Illustration 3 to Article 28; *Blackburn v Mason* (1893) 9 T.L.R. 286; *Anderson v Sutherland* (1897) 13 T.L.R. 163; *Sweeting v Pearce* (1861) 9 C.B.(N.S.) 534; *Hamilton v Young* (1881) 7 L.R.Ir. 289; *Harker v Edwards* (1887) 57 L.J.Q.B. 147; *Benjamin v Barnett* (1903) 19 T.L.R. 564; *Reynolds v Smith* (1893) 9 T.L.R. 474.
[314] The matter is exhaustively discussed in *Robinson v Mollett* (1874) L.R. 7 H.L. 802. But in *Perry v Barnett* (1885) 15 Q.B.D. 388 the two grounds are treated as the same: see 393–394.
[315] See *Bailey v Rawlins* (1829) 7 L.J.(O.S.) K.B. 208; *Josephs v Pebrer* (1825) 3 B. & C. 639, Illustration 3 to Article 61, where it was held that an agent was not entitled to reimbursement for illegal transactions.
[316] Banking Companies (Shares) Act 1867; repealed by Statute Law Revision Act 1966.
[317] *Perry v Barnett* (1885) 15 Q.B.D. 388.
[318] Following *Neilson v James* (1882) 9 Q.B.D. 546. And see *Coates v Pacey* (1892) 8 T.L.R. 351.
[319] *Perry v Barnett* (1885) 15 Q.B.D. 388 at 394, 395 and 397–398.

explained in *Perry v Barnett* as referring to a situation where there was notice of the usage, even if not of the Act. *Seymour v Bridge* followed *Read v Anderson*,[321] where it was held that a principal might come under an obligation to indemnify an agent for paying lost bets, and could not revoke the authority to do so, though the bets were themselves void.[322] However, the payment of a lost bet is in the nature of a gift, and while there is no reason why an agent should not be employed to make gratuitous payments (though revocation of authority would normally be a simple matter[323]), whether an agent can validly be employed to act in such a way as to contravene a statute is more doubtful. The purpose of the Gaming Act 1845 s.18, was simply to render void and unenforceable wagering transactions: but that of Leeman's Act was:

"to make Provision for the Prevention of Contracts for the Sale and Purchase of Shares and Stock in Joint Stock Banking Companies of which the Sellers are not possessed or over which they have no Control."[324]

The particular problem is now obsolete, not least because of the repeal of Leeman's Act,[325] but it is submitted that much will turn on the nature of the illegality when it is sought to determine whether a principal can assent to an unlawful custom.

3-040 **Burden of proof** Although the question is one of fact, it seems that the person alleging that there was knowledge of the custom must establish that fact.[326] There may, however, be occasions when judicial notice is taken of a custom that is very well known.

Illustrations

3-041 (1) A was authorised to sell manure. The jury found that it was customary to sell manure with a warranty. Held, that A had implied authority to give a warranty on a sale of the manure.[327]

(2) An agent buys tallow for a foreign principal, undertaking, in accordance with custom, personal liability. The principal becomes insolvent without having paid the agent, who is liable for the price. The agent sells the tallow. If this is the customary procedure in such a situation, the agent is not liable for doing so.[328]

(3) A stockbroker, employed to transact business at a particular place, has implied authority to act in accordance with the reasonable usages of that place, and

---

[320] *Seymour v Bridge* (1885) 14 Q.B.D. 460.
[321] *Read v Anderson* (1884) 13 Q.B.D. 779.
[322] This result was reversed by the Gaming Act 1892; and the whole problem has been removed by the Gambling Act 2005.
[323] See *Read v Anderson* (1884) 13 Q.B.D. 779 at 783.
[324] Preamble (though this was deleted by the Statute Law Revision Act 1893).
[325] Above.
[326] See *Sweeting v Pearce* (1859) 7 C.B.(N.S.) 449 at 481–482, 484 and 486; affirmed (1861) 9 C.B.(N.S.) 534.
[327] *Dingle v Hare* (1859) 7 C.B.(N.S.) 145. Most of the following Illustrations are out of date; but they represent useful examples of principle.
[328] *Lienard v Dresslar* (1862) 3 F. & F. 212.

if he incurs liability when his principal defaults and the vendor, in accordance with local custom, resells the shares, he can recover from his principal.[329]

(4) A broker, a member of the Stock Exchange, when authorised to sell certain bonds, had implied authority, if it was discovered that the bonds were not genuine, to rescind the sale and repay the purchaser the price, in accordance with the usage of the Stock Exchange.[330]

(5) A stockbroker, authorised to buy or sell or carry over shares or stock, had implied authority, according to usage, to execute the order by means of several contracts, or to execute any portion or portions of it.[331]

(6) A bill-broker in London was entrusted with bills for discounting. The jury found that it was usual for bill-brokers in London to raise money by depositing their customers' bills en bloc, the brokers alone being looked to by the customers, and that the parties contracted in reference to such usage. Held, that the broker had implied authority to pledge their bills together with bills of his own and those of other customers.[332]

(7) A broker is authorised to buy wool in the Liverpool market. By a custom of that market, a broker so authorised may buy either in his own name or in the name of his principal, without giving the principal notice whether or not he has bought in his own name. Such a custom is not unreasonable, and the principal is bound by a contract made in the name of the broker, though he had no notice of the custom or of the fact that the contract was made by the broker in his own name.[333]

(8) A broker is authorised to buy 50 tons of tallow. It is customary in the tallow trade for a broker to make a single contract in his own name for the purchase of a sufficiently large quantity of tallow to supply the orders of several principals, and to parcel it out amongst them. The broker has no implied authority to purchase a larger quantity than 50 tons and allocate 50 tons of it to the principal, unless the principal was aware of the usage at the time when he gave the authority, because the effect of such a usage is to change the intrinsic character of the contract of agency by turning the agent into a principal, and thus giving him an interest at variance with his duty.[334]

(9) A broker is authorised to sell stock. All alleged custom of the Stock Exchange, whereby he is himself permitted to take over the stock at the price of the day, if he is unable to find a purchaser, is unreasonable, and such a transaction is not binding on the principal unless he had notice of the custom.[335]

(10) An insurance broker is authorised to receive from the underwriters payment

---

[329] *Pollock v Stables* (1848) 12 Q.B. 765; *Hodgkinson v Kelly* (1868) L.R. 6 Eq. 496.

[330] *Young v Cole* (1837) 3 Bing.N.C. 724.

[331] *Benjamin v Barnett* (1903) 19 T.L.R. 564.

[332] *Foster v Pearson* (1835) 1 C.M. & R. 849.

[333] *Cropper v Cook* (1868) L.R. 3 C.P. 194.

[334] *Robinson v Mollett* (1874) L.R. 7 H.L. 802 (but the dissenting opinion of Blackburn J has much force: cf. above, para.1-022). For a case where the principal was held to have accepted a usage of similar effect see *Limako BV v Hentz & Co Inc* [1978] 1 Lloyd's Rep. 400. *Robinson v Mollett* was distinguished in cases concerning the right of stockbrokers to buy quantities of shares in a single contract and allocate quantities to particular clients: e.g. *Scott & Horton v Godfrey* [1901] 2 K.B. 76; *Consolidated Gold Fields of South Africa v E. Spiegel & Co* (1909) 100 L.T. 351. As to "marrying" of buying and selling transactions by a broker, see *Jones v Canavan* [1972] 2 N.S.W.L.R. 236 (custom to do so in Sydney and Brisbane held reasonable).

[335] *Hamilton v Young* (1881) 7 L.R.Ir. 289. See also *Thornley v Tilley* (1925) 36 C.L.R. 1 (custom that broker can deal on his own behalf with shares bought for principal unreasonable).

of money due under a policy. A custom at Lloyd's whereby the broker may settle with the underwriters by way of set-off is unreasonable, and the principal is not bound by such a settlement unless he was aware of the custom when he authorised the broker to receive payment.[336] The same rule has been applied to stockbrokers settling with country brokers, solicitors or other agents.[337]

(11) A shipping broker has not customary authority to conclude a charterparty.[338]

Article 32

AUTHORITY IMPLIED FROM COURSE OF DEALING AND CIRCUMSTANCES OF CASE

3-042   An agent has, in addition to the forms of authority indicated in Articles 27 to 31, such authority as is to be inferred from the conduct of the parties and the circumstances of the case.[339]

Comment

3-043   The types of authority indicated in Articles 27 to 31 do not exhaust the notion of implied authority, for it is clear that over and above authority to do incidental acts, the acts usually performed by a person holding the position in question, the acts usually performed by a person following the agent's particular profession or occupation, and authority to follow usages customary in the place, market or business concerned, an agent may have an authority peculiar to the circumstances of the particular case where such authority can be inferred. The question as to implication does not stop at the matters previously mentioned, but goes on to involve consideration of the whole circumstances of the agent's position. This may lead to an agent's having a wider authority initially, or to the agent's authority being enlarged by the principal's acquiescence in the assumption of further powers.[340] Thus in *Hely-Hutchinson v Brayhead Ltd*[341] the chairman of a company acted as de facto managing director and chief executive of it, and entered into larger transactions on its behalf which he would sometimes merely report to the board without seeking prior authority or subsequent ratification. The Board acquiesced in this course of dealing. The chairman was held to have had actual authority equivalent to that of a managing director, though he was acting beyond the normal powers of a chairman.

This type of implied authority corresponds to the implied appointment of an agent

---

[336] See Article 28, Illustration 4.

[337] See Article 28, Illustration 3.

[338] *AJU Remicon Co Ltd v Alida Shipping Co Ltd* [2007] EWHC 2246 (Comm) at [11]; following *Polish SS Co v A.J. Williams Fuels (Overseas Sales) Ltd, The Suwalki* [1981] 1 Lloyd's Rep. 511. But cf. *Woodstock Shipping Co v Kyma Compania Naviera SA (The "Wave")* [1981] 1 Lloyd's Rep. 521; *BP Oil International Ltd v Target Shipping Ltd* [2012] EWHC 1590 (Comm) at [221].

[339] *Hely-Hutchinson v Brayhead Ltd* [1968] 1 Q.B. 549 at 583; *Freeman & Lockyer v Buckhurst Park Properties (Mangal) Ltd* [1964] 2 Q.B. 480 at 502; *Brick and Pipe Industries Ltd v Occidental Life Nominees Pty Ltd* [1992] 2 V.R. 279 at 362; *Equiticorp Finance Ltd v Bank of New Zealand* (1993) 32 N.S.W.L.R. 50.

[340] *Hely-Hutchinson v Brayhead Ltd* [1968] 1 Q.B. 549 at 583; *Pole v Leask* (1860) 28 Beav. 560; affirmed (1864) 33 L.J.Ch. 155.

[341] *Hely-Hutchinson v Brayhead Ltd* [1968] 1 Q.B. 549. Perhaps the court in *Freeman & Lockyer v Buckhurst Park Properties (Mangal) Ltd* [1964] 2 Q.B. 480 was too cautious in rejecting on the facts a finding of actual authority by acquiescence.

dealt with in Article 8. It results from the application of the general rules as to interpretation and construction of contracts and agreements. There may of course also be cases where such facts may merely be taken, as a matter of evidence, to point to the fact that express authority was actually conferred.[342] For the relevance of a course of dealing to the concept of apparent authority, see below, para.8-014.

4. PRESUMED AUTHORITY

Position of husband and wife   In the 13th edition of this book it was stated that: **3-044**

> "what is sometimes called presumed authority is not a type of authority at all: the phrase simply refers to the fact that the existence of actual authority may sometimes be presumed subject to rebuttal."[343]

The main case of presumed authority is that arising, usually in a wife, from cohabitation, which was in the first 13 editions of this book treated in a special chapter on the agency of married women. Such a chapter was appropriate because the position of married women for long provided the focus for the intersection of a number of agency rules of different kinds of which a presumed authority arising from cohabitation was only one. Her special position was caused by two factors: her husband's obligation to support her, and her inability until the late nineteenth century to own separate property and thus to be liable on contracts.[344]

The latter inability has been long removed[345]; and the most specialised set of rules involved, those as to the powers of a deserted wife to pledge her husband's credit for necessaries, was abolished by statute in 1970.[346] The law as to the agency of a deserted wife, a full account of which was given in the 13th edition,[347] is no longer treated here; and consequently the position of a wife in the law of agency no longer requires a separate chapter. On the other hand the rules as to presumed authority in the case of cohabitation had a status of their own which could conceivably still be relevant, and it seemed proper to consider them in the chapter on authority. Therefore, though it is true that the phrase "presumed authority" does not refer so much to a type of authority as to a situation where authority may be presumed, the cases can be isolated as a category.

It is however obvious that social habits have changed since the various times at which these cases were decided, and will continue to do so. In most consumer

---

[342] Mechem, *Outlines of Agency* (4th edn), pp.30–31. See, e.g. *A/S Dan Bunkering Ltd v F.G. Hawkes (Western) Ltd* [2009] EWHC 3141 (Comm) (evidence on discovery that agent had been undertaking similar transactions without objection from principal for some time); *Aviva Life & Pensions UK Ltd v Strand Street Properties Ltd* [2010] EWCA Civ 444.

[343] At p.65.

[344] See the leading case of *Manby v Scott* (1660) 1 Lev. 4; 2 Sm.L.C. 417.

[345] The last main statute on this topic was the Law Reform (Married Women and Tortfeasors) Act 1935.

[346] Matrimonial Proceedings and Property Act 1970 s.41(1). Section 41 of the 1970 Act was repealed by the Matrimonial Causes Act 1973 s.54 and Sch.3, but not so as to revive the doctrine: Interpretation Act 1889 s.38(2). cf. (1973) 36 M.L.R. at 642. Powers were conferred by the 1970 Act on the court to make orders in cases of divorce, nullity and judicial separation with respect to financial provision for the wife and children of the marriage, and in cases of wilful neglect to maintain: these could be made for the purpose of covering liabilities or expenses reasonably incurred before the making of the application. These powers now derive from Pt II of the Matrimonial Causes Act 1973 (a consolidation) as amended principally by Matrimonial and Family Proceedings Act 1984, and the Family Law Act 1996. The powers are extended by the Welfare Reform and Pensions Act 1999.

[347] Articles 37–41. For a somewhat more recent account see Hardingham (1980) 54 A.L.J. 661 (discussing also Commonwealth authorities).

transactions today, the supplier will look to the person placing the order rather than to another person with whom that person is living; and the use of credit cards makes supply of goods on ordinary retailer's credit less common, though services are not infrequently supplied in this way. Discussion of this curious and intriguing group of cases, many of which concern clothing charged to a husband,[348] is therefore omitted from this edition despite its interest as social history. A full account appears in the 17th edition of 2001. In general, one spouse has no usual authority to bind the other in contract,[349] or to receive notices,[350] although, of course, it is common for one spouse to have actual authority to act for the other, and a person who receives money or other value through the agency of a spouse may be burdened with the latter's knowledge.[351]

3-045   **Classification of presumed authority**   This type of authority could be said to be an example of implied authority: indeed it was sometimes so described in nineteenth-century cases, which contain many attempts to set the doctrines in order in different ways. But the most authoritative statement of the applicable rule suggests that there is or was a rebuttable presumption of fact,[352] viz. that from the mere fact of cohabitation and the absence of contrary indications, the finders of fact may, but need not, draw the inference that authority had actually been granted.[353] This differs from implied authority in four ways. First, the accepted categories of implied authority do not cover this case.[354] Secondly, implied authority affects apparent authority: a third party is normally entitled to assume that a person has such authority as would normally be implied.[355] But it is clear that the presumed agency from cohabitation was quite separate from apparent authority.[356] Thirdly, the presumed authority was confined to necessaries. Fourthly, it is possible to say that *implication* of authority is a question of law.[357] But the difference in practice, after such cases ceased to be tried by jury, was likely to be slight.

---

[348] Three that may be mentioned are *Miss Gray Ltd v Earl Cathcart* (1922) 38 T.L.R. 562; *Seymour v Kingscote* (1922) 38 T.L.R. 586; and *Callot v Nash* (1923) 39 T.L.R. 291 ("the dress of women has been ever the mystery and sometimes the calamity of the ages").

[349] See *Farrer v Copley Singletons (a firm)* [1997] EWCA Civ 2127; *London Borough of Haringey v Ahmed* [2017] EWCA Civ 1861 at [36]; *Temarama 2004 Ltd (In Liquidation) v McRobie* [2011] NZHC 1456 (husband no actual or apparent authority to bind wife to joint borrowing); *Trajkovski v Simpson* [2019] NSWCA 52.

[350] See *Ng Hock Kon v Sambawang Capital Pte Ltd* [2010] 1 S.L.R. 307.

[351] See, e.g. *Barclays Bank Plc v Kalamohan* [2010] EWHC 1383 (Ch) at [82].

[352] *Debenham v Mellon* (1880) 6 App.Cas. 24 (the leading case).

[353] See in general *Phipson on Evidence* (19th edn), para.6-25 onwards.

[354] See Articles 27–32.

[355] See above, para.3-005.

[356] See *Debenham v Mellon* (1880) 6 App.Cas. 24, at 32.

[357] See *Phipson on Evidence* (18th edn), para.6-25 onwards.

Chapter 4

AGENCY OF NECESSITY

Article 33

DOCTRINE OF AGENCY OF NECESSITY

(1) A person may have authority to act on behalf of another in certain cases where   **4-001**
that person is faced with an emergency in which the property or interests of
that other are in imminent jeopardy and it becomes necessary, in order to
preserve the property or interests, so to act.
(2) In some cases this authority may entitle the agent to affect the principal's legal
position by making contracts or disposing of property. In others it may merely
entitle the agent to reimbursement of expenses or indemnity against liabilities incurred in so acting, or to a defence against a claim that what the
agent did was wrongful as against the person for whose benefit the action was
taken.[1]

Comment

Introduction   The term "agency of necessity" is used to indicate a general no-   **4-002**
tion derived from a group of cases in which a person is regarded as justified in taking action for the benefit of another in an emergency. They are said to create a
special category of agency which arises by operation of law in such situations. In
earlier editions these cases were treated in Chapter 2 under the heading of "Creation of Agency". They cannot, however, be classified entirely as creating agency,
for although some can be regarded as recognising agency powers in persons who
had none before the event concerned, the majority refer to a person who is already
an agent, but is by this doctrine given greater powers. This, together with the fact
that it is highly doubtful whether any coherent doctrine is to be derived from them
for the modern law, makes it appropriate now to place the topic apart in its own
chapter.

The cases from which the doctrine stems seem to be analytical of two quite different types, and treating these two groups of cases as components of a single
doctrine has caused confusion. The two types of cases have been treated together
because it is said that similar specific rules regarding the emergency requisite to trigger off certain legal results apply to both; and that these are rules which create a

---

[1]   See Comment. See also Powell, Ch.IX; Treitel (1954) 3 U. Western Australia L.Rev. 1; W.B. Williston (1944) 22 Can. Bar Rev. 492; Wade (1966) 19 Vanderbilt L.Rev. 1183; Birks [1971] *Current
Legal Problems* 110; Hunter (1974) 23 U.New Brunswick L.J. 5; Marasinghe (1976) 8 Ottawa L.Rev.
573; McCamus (1979) 11 Ottawa L.Rev. 297; Matthews [1981] C.L.J. 340; Rose (1989) 9 O.J.L.S.
167; Brown (1992) 55 M.L.R. 414; McMeel (2000) 116 L.Q.R. 387 at 408–410; Goff and Jones,
Law of Unjust Enrichment (9th edn), Ch.18; Burrows, *Law of Restitution* (3rd edn), Ch.18; Virgo,
Principles of the Law of Restitution (3rd edn, 2015), Ch.11. But the relevance of discussion in books
and articles on the law of restitution to pure agency issues is doubtful: see Comment.

special form of agency or authority by operation of law. It is suggested below that the first proposition does not now appear to be true: that the emergency rules do not apply to all the cases. It is also suggested that even if the second proposition was formerly regarded as true, the notion of a special type of authority by operation of law is in this context at the present time no longer necessary or appropriate.

4-003   **The traditional cases: the shipmaster and the acceptor for honour**   The two traditional cases from which the concept of agency of necessity derives are those of the shipmaster, who has wide powers to bind by contract the owner, and also sometimes the cargo owners, in situations of emergency[2]; and the person who accepts a bill of exchange for honour and succeeds to the rights of the holder against the person for whom the acceptor accepts.[3] The second case appears to originate from the law merchant[4] and is now statutory[5]: it may in effect confer a right to reimbursement on the acceptor but its relation to agency is tenuous from the start. The dissimilarity between these two cases is enough to indicate immediately that a category comprising them both is unlikely to be a satisfactory one.

4-004   **First category: the shipmaster**   The first category, based on the case of the shipmaster, creates full agency in that it involves both the external and the internal aspects of the agency relationship. As to the external aspect, the master can create contracts binding and conferring rights on the principal (usually the shipowner or demise charterer), make dispositions of the principal's property and receive money and property for the principal also. The agent has also the internal entitlement to reimbursement and indemnity against the principal in respect of what the agent has done[6]; even if that is not needed, the agent has a defence to any action brought by the principal in respect of the acts done. And the act will be valid where validity is in issue. Thus there is old authority that the master can sell[7] or hypothecate[8] the ship, enter into a salvage agreement regarding it[9] and contract for the cargo to be transhipped and carried forward.[10] The master can also sell or hypothecate the cargo, whether together with or separately from the ship,[11] and enter into a salvage agreement regarding it.[12] There are a few cases suggesting that these powers may apply also to land carriers.[13] The actual decisions concerning the latter type of carrier involve only claims to reimbursement and indemnity between principal and agent

2   See below, para.4-004.
3   Bills of Exchange Act 1882 ss.65–68; and see *Hawtayne v Bourne* (1841) 7 M. & W. 595 at 599.
4   See *Hawtayne v Bourne* (1841) 7 M. & W. 595 at 599 at 599.
5   See fn.3 above.
6   See Article 62.
7   *The Glasgow* (1856) Swab. 145; *The Australia* (1859) Swab. 480; *Atlantic Mutual Insurance Co v Huth* (1880) 16 Ch.D. 474.
8   *The Gratitudine* (1801) 3 Ch. Rob. 240; *The Bonaparte* (1853) 8 Moo.P.C. 459; *The Hamburg* (1864) 2 Moo.P.C.(N.S.) 289; *The Onward* (1873) L.R. 4 A. & E. 38; *Gunn v Roberts* (1874) L.R. 9 C.P. 331 at 337; *Kleinwort, Cohen & Co v Cassa Maritima of Genoa* (1877) 2 App.Cas. 156 (cases of bottomry, viz. hypothecating the cargo also).
9   *The Renpor* (1883) 8 P.D. 115; *The Unique Mariner* [1978] 1 Lloyd's Rep. 438, Illustration 3, discussed also below.
10   See *The Soblomsten* (1866) L.R. 1 A. & E. 293; *Scrutton on Charterparties* (24th edn), Arts 140–141.
11   As to sale, see *Tronson v Dent* (1853) 8 Moo.P.C. 419; *Australasian S.N. Co v Morse* (1872) L.R. 4 P.C. 222; *Acatos v Burns* (1878) 3 Ex. D. 282; *Atlantic Mutual Insurance Co v Huth* (1880) 16 Ch.D. 474. As to hypothecation, see cases cited in fn.8 above.
12   *The Winson* [1982] A.C. 939, Illustration 1. See below, para.4-008.
13   *Great Northern Ry Co v Swaffield* (1874) L.R. 9 Ex. 132 (stabling uncollected horse); *Sims & Co v*

and so may only be examples of the second category: they are further referred below in that connection. It is there submitted, however, that they should in fact be attributed to the first category if that category can be enlarged and re-explained on a broader basis than that of agency by operation of law.

In respect of the shipmaster selling, hypothecating or contracting for salvage of the ship, this can be treated as involving no more than the extension of the authority of one who is already an agent in the full sense, for the master obviously has already in many situations actual authority, express or implied, from the shipowner (or demise charterer) to make normal trading contracts. However, where the action taken relates to the *cargo*, the master as such has no legal relationship with the cargo owner; and it can therefore be said that the master is by the emergency created an agent where there was no agency before, and that this requires special rules. Yet the master is still agent for the shipowner, who is bailee of the cargo: and although the shipowner may well have had no agency powers prior to the emergency, the shipowner's position as bailee means that it has a legal relationship with the cargo owner which is in principle capable of giving rise to such powers, which can be exercised through the master, who is its agent. So the significance of the distinction between ship and cargo is doubtful.

Rules determining necessity   The traditional rules applicable to the exercise of   **4-005**
this authority may be stated as follows. They derive largely from the shipmaster case, and it will be obvious later that they are in large measure inapplicable to the second category. Indeed in *The Winson*,[14] discussed below, Lord Diplock said that they should be confined to cases of the first category[15]:

(a)   It must be impossible, or at any rate impracticable, for the agent to communicate with the principal. Some cases imply that communication must be impossible,[16] but this seems too strict: as long ago as 1851 Parke B spoke of the principal's being unable to be "conveniently communicated with",[17] and in 1895 Lord Esher MR of an "opportunity to consult".[18] In *Springer v Great Western Railway Co* Bankes LJ approved the phrase "practically impossible"[19] and Scrutton LJ spoke of communication as being "commercially impossible".[20] This would include situations where there are too many principals to consult (e.g. owners of cargo shipped under bills of lading on liner terms[21]).

(b)   The action taken must be necessary[22] for the benefit of the principal.[23] The agent's opinion as to the necessity is irrelevant. It is, however, sufficient if

---

Midland Ry Co [1913] 1 K.B. 103 (sale of uncollected goods); cf. *Springer v Great Western Ry Co* [1921] 1 K.B. 257.

[14]   *China Pacific SA v Food Corp of India (The Winson)* [1982] A.C. 939, Illustration 1, also discussed below.

[15]   *China Pacific SA v Food Corp of India (The Winson)* [1982] A.C. 939 at 958.

[16]   e.g. *Prager v Blatspiel, Stamp & Heacock Ltd* [1924] 1 K.B. 566 at 571.

[17]   *Beldon v Campbell* (1851) 6 Exch. 886 at 890. See also *Australasian S.N. Co v Morse* (1872) L.R. 4 P.C. 222.

[18]   *Gwilliam v Twist* [1895] 2 Q.B. 84 at 87.

[19]   *Springer v Great Western Railway Co* [1921] 1 K.B. 257 at 265.

[20]   *Springer v Great Western Railway Co* [1921] 1 K.B. 257 at 268. And see *Barker v Burns, Philp & Co Ltd* (1944) 45 S.R. (N.S.W.) 1 (communication possible despite wartime conditions); *Sachs v Miklos* [1948] 2 K.B. 23.

[21]   See *The Choko Star* [1990] 1 Lloyd's Rep. 516, Illustration 2, also discussed below.

[22]   For the meaning of "necessary", see *Prager v Blatspiel, Stamp & Heacock Ltd* [1924] 1 K.B. 566

a reasonable person would think there was a necessity.[24] Mere inconvenience does not create necessity.[25] The necessity must of course be for the protection of the interests of the principal, not of the agent.

(c)   The agent must have acted bona fide in the interests of the principal.[26]

(d)   The person in whose interest the agent is acting must be competent: for example, a dissolved corporation,[27] or an alien enemy,[28] cannot be a principal under these rules. This limitation is inevitable if the doctrine is one of agency, but its results can be criticised.[29]

(e)   It would also seem that in both types of situation the authority could not prevail against express instructions to the contrary: this follows from the fact that it does not operate where the principal can be consulted.[30] The inference is that the principal could forbid the action at the time: if so, the principal can do so in advance.[31]

4-006   **Second category: the acceptor for honour**   The second type of case involves situations where a person who acts for another in an emergency seeks only reimbursement or indemnity from the person benefited, or to raise a defence in respect of what that person has done in an action for breach of contract (if there is a contract) or in tort (usually conversion, which might otherwise have been committed by the dealing with property of the principal). No issue arises as regards third parties: if this is an example of agency reasoning, it involves only the internal relationship between principal and agent. Although in 1841 Parke B said that the acceptor for honour was, after the shipmaster, the only other example of agency of necessity,[32] it is clear that the second category is not in fact confined to the acceptor for honour. Thus it has been held that a carrier may make a contract for the stabling of an uncollected horse and recover the charges from the consignor[33]; that the carrier is justified in selling perishable goods which remain uncollected and are deteriorating[34]; and that a salvor may warehouse goods on behalf of their owner at

---

at 571–572; *The Australia* (1859) Swab. 480; *Australasian S.N. Co v Morse* (1872) L.R. 4 P.C. 222; *Atlantic Mutual Ins. Co v Huth* (1879) 16 Ch.D. 474. And see *Phelps, James & Co v Hill* [1891] 1 Q.B. 605.

[23] See *Burns, Philp & Co Ltd v Gillespie Bros Pty Ltd* (1947) 74 C.L.R. 148 (doctrine inapplicable where measures undertaken (in wartime) for security of ship and cargo considered as one adventure).

[24] *Tetley & Co v British Trade Corp* (1922) 10 Ll. Rep. 678.

[25] *Sachs v Miklos* [1948] 2 K.B. 23.

[26] *Prager v Blatspiel, Stamp & Heacock Ltd* [1924] 1 K.B. 566 at 570; *Tronson v Dent* (1853) 8 Moo.P.C. 419 at 449–452; *The Winson* [1982] A.C. 959, Illustration 1, discussed also below; *Re F (Mental Patient: Sterilisation)* [1990] 2 A.C. 1 at 75, per Lord Goff of Chieveley.

[27] *Re Banque des Marchands de Moscou* [1952] 1 T.L.R. 739.

[28] *Jebara v Ottoman Bank* [1927] 2 K.B. 254; reversed [1928] A.C. 269.

[29] See Goff and Jones, *Law of Restitution* (7th edn), para.17-006 (not carried forward in subsequent editions).

[30] See Illustrations 1 and 2. See also Goddard [1984] L.M.C.L.Q. 255; but cf. *Great Northern Ry Co v Swaffield* (1874) L.R. 9 Ex. 132.

[31] But in *Graanhandel T. Vink BV v European Grain & Shipping Ltd* [1989] 2 Lloyd's Rep. 531 at 533, Evans J said that there could be circumstances where "it might well be argued that the seller's refusal to acknowledge these facts would not prevent the buyer from alleging that the agency did exist". The deserted wife's agency of necessity, now obsolete, applied even though the husband had forbidden the act: see below, para.4-011.

[32] *Hawtayne v Bourne* (1841) 7 M. & W. 595 at 597.

[33] *Great Northern Ry Co v Swaffield* (1874) L.R. 9 Ex. 132.

[34] *Sims & Co v Midland Ry Co* [1913] 1 K.B. 103; cf. *Springer v Great Western Ry Co* [1921] 1 K.B.

the termination of the salvage service and recover the cost of doing so.[35] These cases may in fact be examples of the first category: it may be that these carriers made or could have made contracts binding the goods owners to third parties. The actual decisions, however, relate only to the internal relationship between principal and agent. It has also been held that an agent for sale was justified in shipping the goods elsewhere, even contrary to instructions, where they were in danger because of potentially hostile conditions.[36] On the other hand it has been held that a bailee of furniture was liable in conversion when the bailee sold it after fruitless attempts to contact the owner: though in this case it appears that necessity, as opposed to inconvenience, had not arisen.[37] It should be noted that in these cases the supposed agent may have no prior relationship with the principal, as in the leading case of the acceptor for honour: but equally the actor may already be an agent, and is at any rate likely to have some relationship with the person for whom he or she acts, such as that of bailee.

Since cases in the second category only give rise to internal rights, duties and defences between the person acting and the person benefited, they are not dissimilar to the *negotiorum gestio* of Roman law, which is a quasi-contractual institution entitling the *gestor*, a person intervening in situations of necessity, to reimbursement and also making the intervenor liable for acting inappropriately.[38] As such they seem in the modern law more appropriately dealt with as part of the law of restitution. The second category in fact contains a limited number of rather miscellaneous situations where the law of agency was pressed into service long ago to provide a way of dealing with problems which probably ought nowadays to be approached differently. The cases usually involve an inappropriate use of agency reasoning, as in another context does the use of a notion of irrevocable agency to create what are really property or security interests.[39] The problems of this category should nowadays, therefore, be considered against the background not of agency but of a possible general principle of necessitous intervention within the law of restitution.[40]

Only first category a true example of agency   Thus only the first category is a **4-007** true example of agency reasoning, and only that category is therefore really relevant for discussion in this book. It is also much less significant than it was, for modern communications will normally make dramatic actions by shipmasters, or indeed others, unnecessary even in remote places: even in maritime salvage situations a

---

257.

[35] *The Winson* [1982] A.C. 939, Illustration 1: see below.

[36] *Tetley & Co v British Trade Corp* (1922) 10 Ll. Rep. 678. See too *Liu Wing Ngai v Lui Kok Wai* [1996] 3 Singapore L.R. 508.

[37] *Sachs v Miklos* [1948] 2 K.B. 23; followed in *Anderson v Erlanger* [1980] C.L.Y. 133. See also *Munro v Wilmott* [1949] 1 K.B. 295 (similar facts). In *Ridyard v Roberts* Unreported May 16, 1980, CA a bailee of ponies was held justified in selling them when the owner in breach of contract failed to remove them. In *Coldman v Hill* [1919] 1 K.B. 443 at 456 Scrutton LJ suggested that a bailee of cattle from whom they are stolen ought, if he cannot contact the owner, to "act as agent of necessity on behalf of and at the expense of the owner". Sometimes statute gives a power of sale: e.g. unpaid seller's right to resell: Sale of Goods Act 1979 s.48(3); Protection of Animals Act 1911 s.7; Unsolicited Goods and Services Act 1971 as amended; Torts (Interference with Goods) Act 1977 ss.12 and 13.

[38] See Buckland, *Textbook of Roman Law* (3rd edn), pp.537–538.

[39] See Article 118.

[40] See Goff and Jones, fn.1 above; *Tongue v Royal Society for the Prevention of Cruelty To Animals* [2017] EWHC 2508 (Ch) at [68].

master may often be in touch by radio. Situations can obviously still arise, however, where communication is impossible or impracticable; and as regards cargo, where the ship contains goods covered by many bills of lading it may be impracticable to trace and/or communicate with all the cargo owners.[41] Cases may also arise where the cargo owner does not answer, or does not answer clearly, requests for instructions.[42]

This type of agency of necessity seems in origin to be a primitive example of what would now be regarded as vicarious liability reasoning. To impose liability on the principal in such cases was more important than to think of any correlative rights for the principal. A justification given in 1808 was that the master "is seldom of ability to make good a loss of any considerable amount"[43]: hence the owner should be liable. The idea of authority arising in specified circumstances by operation of law is not, however, so satisfactory as the combination of the more general rules of implied and apparent authority, which (particularly the latter) have been developed subsequently to the old cases. For the old rules require that the third party dealing with the agent take the risk as to whether the circumstances creating authority by operation of law have arisen—whether there really is an emergency and whether it really is impracticable for the agent to communicate with the principal. Furthermore, if it is correct, as is suggested above, that there is no possibility of authority if the principal has been communicated with and has forbidden the act in question, this also is not easy to reconcile with the idea of authority by operation of law. Yet as the law at present stands, if the full requirements are not complied with, the agency power does not exist, whatever the appearance to the third party. Such an approach is much less sensitive to the merits of the cases than the normal rules of implied and apparent authority.[44] It is true that under the doctrine of apparent authority the third party cannot rely merely on the statement of an agent that the agent has authority, so that if the requirements for operation of the doctrine have not arisen but the master says that they have, the third party will not on that ground alone be protected.[45] But if there was an appearance of authority, modern doctrine would make the shipowner liable in some cases where old cases would not—for example, where it appeared that the act was justified; where the act had been forbidden by the principal but this was not known to the third party; and perhaps where the agent gave the impression that the principal could not be consulted.[46]

The old English rules were much more elaborately worked out than the corresponding law in the US, which has been content with the idea of implied (incidental) authority to act in emergency.[47] There is, however, some other English case law which approaches the question of emergency powers simply on the basis of implied (and hence in appropriate cases apparent) authority, suggesting that the

---

[41] See *The Choko Star* [1990] 1 Lloyd's Rep. 516, Illustration 2, also discussed below.
[42] As in *The Winson* [1982] A.C. 939, Illustration 1, also discussed below.
[43] Abbott, *Merchant Ships and Seaman* (3rd edn), cited in Holdsworth, H.E.L. VIII, p.250.
[44] See in general below, para.4-008. The same can in fact be said of the Factors Acts: see Article 89.
[45] *Armagas Ltd v Mundogas SA (The Ocean Frost)* [1986] A.C. 717.
[46] cf. *United Bank of Kuwait Ltd v Hammoud* [1988] 1 W.L.R. 1051, where a solicitor was held liable on an unauthorised and fraudulent transaction by an assistant where the transaction could have been authorised had a certain background of facts existed: the third party was entitled to assume from the conduct of the agent that it did. "The bank, knowing that [X] was a practising solicitor with established firms, were entitled to assume the truth of what he said unless alerted to the fact that the contrary might be the case"—per Lord Donaldson of Lymington MR at 1066. But cf. *Hirst v Etherington* [1999] Lloyd's Rep. P.N. 938 and below, para.8-021.
[47] See *Restatement, Third*, § 2.02, Comments e, f.

authority of an agent may be enlarged in situations of emergency. This reasoning has been used to justify delegation by an agent of the agent's powers,[48] lending on unusual terms[49] and giving credit in circumstances where this would not be normal.[50] It is submitted that this is the correct approach. If it is correct, it entails that the person acting already has a legal relationship with the principal. It is necessary, however, to add to it the proposition, to be derived from *Tappenden v Artus* and *The Winson*, discussed below, that a person already in some other legal relationship with the principal which is not one of agency (such as a bailee) may likewise have agency powers in certain situations, some of which may involve emergencies. If such an approach is followed, the supposedly separate notion of agency of necessity, or at any rate much of it, could, and, it is submitted, should be absorbed into the general law relating to implied and apparent authority.

Salvage contracts: an opportunity for improved analysis   In the case of salvage   **4-008**
agreements, where rapid decisions may be required, the advantages of detaching from the ancient, strict rules and subsuming the problem under the general rules of authority can readily be seen. The first step in doing so was taken by Brandon J in *The Unique Mariner*,[51] where in a salvage situation he held owners bound by the master's signature on Lloyd's Open Form on the basis of apparent authority, without reference to the old rules (which probably were not satisfied, because the master had already been in touch with the owners at the time). The case only concerned salvage in respect of the *ship*, for whose owner the master is certainly agent. Subsequently however in *The Choko Star*[52] the Court of Appeal applied the ancient case law to hold that the master's signature to a Lloyd's Open Form did not bind *cargo* unless it had been impracticable to consult cargo (which was not so).

The main reason given was that though a master is agent of the *owner*, the master is not an agent for *cargo*, and so cannot act for it except when the special rules of agency of necessity are complied with. There are certainly abundant old dicta to that effect against the background of shipping operations in the nineteenth century. Against this it may be said, as has been suggested above, that the master acts for the shipowner, and the shipowner as bailee may be regarded as having implied and therefore normally also apparent authority to do what is necessary to preserve the cargo during the voyage. This argument was rejected on the basis that there were no grounds for implying such a power (beyond what the agency of necessity doctrine permits) into the contract of carriage between cargo owner and shipowner. The rules regarding the implication of terms into contracts are of course strict[53]: perhaps too much so. But even if those rules are accepted, despite suggestions that "[a]gency of necessity is traditionally regarded as part of the law of contract",[54] it is not clear that questions of authority are always to be determined by reference to

---

[48] *De Bussche v Alt* (1878) 8 Ch.D. 286, Illustration 7 to Article 34. See also *Walker v G.W. Ry Co* (1867) L.R. 2 Ex. 228; *Langan v G.W. Ry Co* (1873) 30 L.T. 173 (railway officials ordering medical attention for passengers: company liable: but here the emergency is not that of the principal, the company).

[49] *Montaignac v Shitta* (1890) 15 App.Cas. 357, Illustration 15 to Article 72.

[50] *Gokal Chand-Jagan Nath v Nand Ram Das-Atma Ram* [1939] A.C. 106.

[51] *The Unique Mariner* [1978] 1 Lloyd's Rep. 438, Illustration 3.

[52] *The Choko Star* [1990] 1 Lloyd's Rep. 516, Illustration 2; noted [1991] L.M.C.L.Q. 1; (1992) 55 M.L.R. 414; followed in *The Pa Mar* [1999] 1 Lloyd's Rep. 338.

[53] See *Liverpool City Council v Irwin* [1977] A.C. 239.

[54] Goff and Jones, *Law of Restitution* (7th edn), para.17-006 (not carried forward in subsequent editions); citing *Notara v Henderson* (1872) L.R. 7 Q.B. 225; and *Cargo ex Argos* (1873) L.R. 5 P.C.

implied terms of the contract between the supposed principal and the supposed agent. Particular relationships, such as that of bailor and bailee, may carry their own implications of implied, and hence apparent, authority. Implied *authority* is inferred "from the conduct of the parties and the circumstances of the case",[55] which is quite different reasoning from that relating to implied *terms of contracts*.

In the third of the three principal recent cases on the doctrine, *The Winson*,[56] a salvor procured the warehousing of the goods salved, after completion of the salvage service, and claimed reimbursement of the cost of so doing. This was therefore a case in the second, not the first, category. The full requirements for the operation of traditional agency of necessity were not operative, for the salvor was able to communicate with the cargo owners (who did not give a clear answer) and was in any case acting partly for personal benefit (to preserve a lien). But the salvor was held able to recover, Lord Diplock saying that the strict requirements were inapplicable to the second (*negotiorum gestio*) category.[57] It was said that the salvor was under a duty to the goods owner to care for the goods, and that the salvor had "a correlative right to charge the owner of the goods with the expenses reasonably incurred".[58] But with subsequent development of principle, it may be argued that the strict rules are not needed in the first category either. It can then be argued that the bailment relationship is sufficient to give the bailee authority not only to do things entitling the bailee to reimbursement but also to make contracts binding on the principal. On this basis the principal might in an appropriate case have been liable directly to the warehouse proprietor. (Though in this particular situation, if the salvor warehoused to protect his lien, the salvor would be unlikely to do so on behalf of another.) Thus in *Tappenden v Artus*[59] it was held that the bailee of a car could leave it for repair in circumstances creating a lien against the owner. The case is not directly in point, because the decision was based on the bailee's right to use the goods, and hence to keep them in a usable state: but the reasoning is relevant.

The statement by Lord Diplock in *The Winson* that the strict rules should be eliminated from the assessment of cases of the second category is therefore to be welcomed in so far as it provides support for the detachment of the second category from the first. But it does not follow that all the cases where the only questions that have arisen were as to the internal relationship between principal and agent, and in particular the case of the bailee who makes a contract in respect of the goods bailed, are really no more than examples of the second category. Some may in fact be real agency cases, attributable to the first category, and now to be explained on the basis of implied or apparent authority. It has already been suggested that this is true of the land carrier decisions. It is submitted therefore that the old strict rules should no longer have any part to play in cases of the first category any more than in the second; and that the substance of all cases in the first category should be assimilated to the general rules as to implied and apparent authority. On this basis a master may be held to have a general implied authority (under the category of incidental authority) to sign a salvage agreement for ship and (because of the bail-

---

134. It is not clear exactly what this means. If it indicates that it stems from an extension of authority granted by contract, this may be so in most cases, but agency can be gratuitous (as indeed the text goes on to point out).

55 *Hely-Hutchinson v Brayhead Ltd* [1968] 1 Q.B. 549 at 583.

56 *The Winson* [1982] A.C. 939, Illustration 1. See too *Brasileiro SA (Petrobas)* [2012] UKSC 17; [2012] 2 A.C. 164.

57 *The Winson* [1982] A.C. 939 at 958.

58 *The Winson* [1982] A.C. 939 at 960.

59 *Tappenden v Artus* [1964] 2 Q.B. 185.

ment reasoning above) cargo, except perhaps where consultation is practicable and expected; and hence apparent authority even in some circumstances where the implied authority is not applicable (e.g. because the owner has forbidden the contract, or could easily have been consulted). As for the more drastic acts of selling or hypothecating ship or cargo, this would normally require consultation, and it may well be that the third party's belief that the master's act is justified is less likely to appear reasonable under the doctrine of apparent authority.

The present law as to the first category   As regards salvage contracts, the matter is now settled by statute. Article 6 of the International Convention on Salvage of 1989, now law under the Merchant Shipping Act 1995,[60] gives the master or owner the power to sign a salvage contract for cargo. But although the Court of Appeal in *The Choko Star*[61] had thought this topic an unsuitable one for judicial development, it is submitted that the Supreme Court should, if the opportunity arises, take the opportunity to bring the case law on situations of necessity into line so far as possible with present-day thinking on agency authority, which no longer needs a special and rather rigid notion of agency by operation of law, a notion which antedates the development of the doctrine of apparent authority, and even the full development of that of implied authority, and depends on the existence of facts which may not be known or even knowable to the third party.   **4-009**

Development of the second category: restitutionary doctrine   In this area, the analogy of agency is a mistaken one, perhaps caused by the lack of the civil law concept of *negotiorum gestio*. If any wider principle in respect of necessitous intervention is to emerge from the cases in the second category, however, creative development of a different order within the principles of restitution would be required. In 1924 McCardie J, in a case of the first category, spoke strongly in favour of enlarging the whole doctrine of agency of necessity, and was prepared in principle to apply it to an agent for purchase who was unable because of wartime conditions to forward goods purchased to his principal in Romania and resold them in England.[62] The dicta were, however, doubted by Scrutton LJ three years later in a case of the second category,[63] and other dicta against extension of the reasoning can be cited.[64] Proper analysis has been hampered by the running together of the two categories. Any attempt at development within the second category has to contend initially with the dictum of Bowen LJ in 1886 that "work or labour done or money expended by one man to preserve or benefit the property of another do not according to English law create any lien upon the property saved, nor even, if standing alone, create any obligation to repay the expenditure".[65] Nevertheless, though they were said by Bowen LJ to be a special exception, the rules of maritime   **4-010**

---

[60]   Merchant Shipping Act 1995 s.224(1) and Sch.11. See this provision applied in *The Altair* [2008] EWHC 612 (Comm); [2008] 2 All E.R. (Comm) 805.

[61]   *The Choko Star* [1990] 1 Lloyd's Rep. 516, Illustration 2. The judgment of Sheen J at first instance repays study.

[62]   *Prager v Blatspiel, Stamp & Heacock Ltd* [1924] 1 K.B. 566. In this category, extension in cases where the principal has forbidden the act might be easier: cf. *Tetley & Co v British Trade Corp* (1922) 10 Lloyd's Rep. 678; above, para.4-006.

[63]   *Jebara v Ottoman Bank* [1927] 2 K.B. 254 at 270–271; reversed [1928] A.C. 269 (selling goods overseas after outbreak of war).

[64]   *Gwilliam v Twist* [1895] 2 Q.B. 84 at 87, per Lord Esher MR (substitute driver where official driver drunk); *Sachs v Miklos* [1948] 2 K.B. 23 at 35–36, per Lord Goddard CJ.

[65]   *Falcke v Scottish Imperial Insurance Co* (1886) 34 Ch.D. 234 at 248; *Glasgow v ELS Law Ltd* [2017]

salvage,[66] including the decision in *The Winson*, can be used to justify movement towards generalisation; as can certain cases concerning the payment of funeral expenses of a deceased person[67]; and an established line of cases remunerating liquidators and other insolvency practitioners for work done in preserving and realising property belonging to others but in the possession of the company or other insolvent person.[68] On the other hand it has been held that no lien arises in favour of a person who succours a stray animal,[69] or conveys timber on the bank of a river to a place of safety.[70] Though writers strongly advocate the development of generalised principle, the picture remains unclear and the case law very limited indeed.[71] Other doctrines may sometimes secure a similar result by different means. Thus where there is an established cause of action, the damages awarded may cover expenses incurred in emergencies[72]; and a person who seeks to recover property may sometimes be able to do so only if payment is made for work done on it.[73] But the appropriate reasoning for cases of necessitous intervention in general must be found outside the law of agency, and further discussion is beyond the scope of this work.[74]

4-011   **Agency of deserted wives**   Until comparatively recently a line of cases whereby a deserted wife was regarded as having, even if forbidden to do so, authority to pledge her husband's credit for necessaries was said to be a further instance of agency of necessity, and of agency by operation of law. These cases made any general principle behind the notion even more difficult to extract, for the necessity

---

EWHC 3004 (Ch); [2018] 1 W.L.R. 1564 at [42]. See Birks, *Introduction to the Law of Restitution* (1989), p.194 onwards.

[66] See Goff and Jones, *Law of Unjust Enrichment* (9th edn), Ch.18.

[67] *Jenkins v Tucker* (1788) 1 H.Bl. 90; *Tugwell v Heyman* (1812) 3 Camp. 298; *Rogers v Price* (1829) 3 Y. & J. 28; *Ambrose v Kerrison* (1851) 10 C.B. 776; *Shallcross v Wright* (1850) 12 Beav. 558; *Bradshaw v Beard* (1862) 12 C.B.(N.S.) 344; *Rees v Hughes* [1946] K.B. 517; *Croskery v Gee* [1957] N.Z.L.R. 586. See also *Matheson v Smiley* [1932] 2 D.L.R. 787 (medical expenses).

[68] See *Re Berkeley Applegate (Investment Consultants) Ltd* [1989] Ch. 32; *Green v Bramston* [2010] EWHC 3106 (Ch). See too *MF (Australia) Ltd v Meadow Springs Fairway Resort Ltd* [2009] FCAFC 9.

[69] *Binstead v Buck* (1776) 2 Wm. Bl. 1117. But there may in appropriate cases be distress damage feasant. See *Sorrell v Paget* [1950] 1 K.B. 252, where both matters are discussed. See also Protection of Animals Act 1911 s.7.

[70] *Nicholson v Chapman* (1793) 2 H.Bl. 254. See also *J. Gadsden Pty Ltd v Strider 1 Ltd (The AES Express)* (1990) 20 N.S.W.L.R. 57 (carriage of goods after termination of time charter).

[71] For example, as to the relevance of the fault of the person concerned in getting into the situation of emergency, it has been held that a car recovery company instructed by the police to remove an abandoned stolen car did not act as agent of necessity for the owner: *Surrey Breakdown Ltd v Knight* [1999] R.T.R. 84 CA; and see *Lambert v Fry* [2000] C.L.Y. 113. The *Surrey Breakdown* case is doubtful authority, as it appears to proceed on the basis that the company was agent for the owner (with whom it had no prior connection), and was claiming reimbursement of expenses under the second category of agency of necessity. The argument had been however that the *police* were agent for the owner to make a contract with the company, which sued for its normal charges: i.e. a first category situation. In this category the police, having no prior relationship with the owner, have by private law at least no authority to make such a contract for another. See Kortmann, *Altruism in Private Law* (2005), pp.167–169.

[72] *Schneider v Eisovitch* [1960] 2 Q.B. 430 (tort); *Kolfor Plant Ltd v Tilbury Plant Ltd* (1977) 121 S.J. 390 (sale of rejected goods).

[73] *Munro v Wilmott* [1949] 1 K.B. 295; *Greenwood v Bennett* [1973] 1 Q.B. 195.

[74] See Goff and Jones, *Law of Restitution* (7th edn, not carried forward in subsequent editions), para.17-009 onwards (which, since it approaches the law from a different angle, should be taken into account by any reader of this chapter); Birks, *Introduction to the Law of Restitution* (1989), p.193 onwards.

in such cases was that of the agent and not of the principal. This seems another example of agency law being deployed to achieve a desired result which did not at the time seem attainable by other means. This method of protecting deserted wives has, however, been superseded by other institutions for that purpose, and the doctrine inherent in the cases has in consequence been abolished in England by statute.[75] Discussion of these cases is therefore omitted: a full account appeared in the thirteenth edition of this work.

Mentally incapacitated persons The Mental Capacity Act 2005 creates what **4-012** may be called a statutory form of agency of necessity. It permits a person intervening on behalf of a mentally incapacitated person to pledge that person's credit and use that person's money for acts in connection with his or her care or treatment: the person intervening may also be entitled to indemnity for expenditure incurred.[76] This does not affect any power or any other power which a person may have who has lawful control of the mentally incapacitated person's property or power to spend money for his or her benefit.[77]

Illustrations

(1) A salvor, after the completion of the salvage operation, warehouses salved **4-013** goods at a nearby port, principally to preserve them but partly with a view to preserving his lien. He asks the cargo owner to make arrangements to accept the goods at that port. The cargo owner does not respond. The salvor was bailee of the cargo owner from the time the goods were put into the vessels which he provided, and even if the salvage service was finished when the vessels arrived at the port, he remained bailee of the cargo owner thereafter. As such he had a duty to the cargo owner to take reasonable measures to preserve the cargo, and a correlative right to charge its owner with the warehousing expenses, which had been reasonably incurred in fulfilling that duty.[78]
(2) A ship strands in the River Paraná in Argentina. The master signs a salvage agreement on Lloyd's Open Form with Greek salvors, though local salvors are available. There is only one cargo owner, who could have been consulted but was not. The master has no authority to sign for cargo (as opposed to the ship itself) except under the agency of necessity rules, which are not satisfied because of the lack of consultation, quite apart from the question whether the act of the master was reasonable or the third party was aware of the lack of consultation.[79]
(3) A ship strands. The master contacts his owners, who notify him that a tug will be sent. By chance the captain of another tug with different owners is completing a salvage service nearby. He notices the stranded ship, goes to it and offers his services. The master takes this to be the tug sent by his owners and signs a salvage agreement. As his owners are already sending another tug, he

---

[75] See above, para.3-041.
[76] See Mental Capacity Act 2005 ss.5, 6 and 8. The Act also provides for the appointment of a "deputy" who may have more extensive powers.
[77] As under a lasting power of attorney, created by the 2005 Act.
[78] *China Pacific SA v Food Corp of India (The Winson)* [1982] A.C. 939. Quaere, however, whether the salvage service was really terminated: if it had not been, the case would have been more easily solved.
[79] *Industrie Chimiche Italia v Alexander G. Tsavliris & Sons Maritime Co (The Choko Star)* [1990] 1 Lloyd's Rep. 516. But see Comment above.

is not authorised to do so, and the agency of necessity rules do not apply: but his owners are nevertheless liable under the doctrine of apparent authority.[80]

---

[80]   *The Unique Mariner* [1978] 1 Lloyd's Rep. 438.

CHAPTER 5

SUB-AGENCY

Article 34

WHEN AGENT MAY DELEGATE AUTHORITY

(1) Agents may not delegate their authority in whole or in part except with the **5-001** express or implied authority of the principal, but a delegation may be ratified by the principal.[1]
(2) The authority of the principal is implied in the following cases:
   (a) Where the principal knows and accepts, at the time of the agent's appointment, that the agent intends to delegate the authority.[2]
   (b) Where the authority conferred is of such a nature as to necessitate its execution wholly or in part by means of a sub-agent.[3]
   (c) Where the employment of a sub-agent is justified by the usage of the particular trade or business in which the agent is employed, provided that such usage is not unreasonable, and not inconsistent with the express terms of the agent's authority.[4]
   (d) Where in the course of the agent's employment unforeseen circumstances arise which render it necessary for the agent to employ a sub-agent.[5]
   (e) Where, from the conduct of the principal or of the principal and the agent, it may reasonably be presumed to have been intended that the agent should have power to employ a sub-agent.[6]
(3) The above principles are inapplicable where the act done or to be done is purely ministerial and does not involve confidence or discretion.[7]

---

[1] *De Bussche v Alt* (1878) 8 Ch.D. 286 at 310–311 (Illustration 5). It seems that the converse position is taken by French CC, art.1994. As to apparent authority see Comment; as to ratification, see Articles 13–20. See in general *Restatement, Third*, § 3.15, especially Comment *c*.

[2] *Quebec & Richmond Railway Co v Quinn* (1858) 12 Moo.P.C. 232 at 265 (English contractor employed to construct railroad in Canada); *Jacques Lichtenstein v Clube Atletico Mineiro* [2005] EWHC 1300 (QB) (football agent sues "football consultant"). *Norwich Union Life & Pensions Ltd v Strand Street Properties Ltd* [2009] EWHC 1109 (Ch) at [223]; *Ramsook v Crossley* [2018] UKPC 9; [2018] Lloyd's Rep. I.R. 471 (insurer authorised to employ lawyers for insured).

[3] *Quebec & Richmond Railroad Co v Quinn* (1858) 12 Moo.P.C. 232.

[4] *De Bussche v Alt* (1878) 8 Ch.D. 286. See also Article 31.

[5] *De Bussche v Alt* (1878) 8 Ch.D. 286; cf. *Gwilliam v Twist* [1895] 2 Q.B. 84; *Harris v Fiat Motors Ltd* (1906) 22 T.L.R. 556; reversed on other grounds (1907) 23 T.L.R. 504). See also Ch.4.

[6] *De Bussche v Alt* (1878) 8 Ch.D. 286. See also *Re Deutsch* (1976) 82 D.L.R. (3d) 567 (consul as administrator of estate had power to delegate); *Dollars & Sense Finance Ltd v Nathan* [2008] 2 N.Z.L.R. 557 at [28].

[7] See Illustration 5; *Rossiter v Trafalgar Life Ass. Assn* (1859) 27 Beav. 377 (insurance proposal); *Hemming v Hale* (1859) 7 C.B. (N.S.) 487 (attorney's clerk); *Allam & Co Ltd v Europa Poster Services Ltd* [1968] 1 W.L.R. 638 (solicitor acting for agent gave notice to terminate licence agreement); *The Berkshire* [1974] 1 Lloyd's Rep. 185 at 188; *Lep International Pty Ltd v Atlanttrafic*

Comment

5-002 General rule of no delegation The general rule is that an agent may not delegate the discretions to act for another which are reposed in the agent: *delegatus non potest delegare*. This maxim is founded on the confidential nature of the contract of agency: whenever authority is coupled with a discretion or confidence it must, as a rule, be exercised by the agent in person[8]:

> "The reason is fairly obvious: the risks of agency are substantial, and a person has a right not to be represented, save at his own election and by an agent of his own choice."[9]

Thus auctioneers,[10] factors,[11] directors,[12] liquidators,[13] brokers,[14] estate agents,[15] solicitors,[16] etc. have normally no implied authority to employ deputies or subagents to exercise their agency powers.[17] But this is no more than a general starting-point and its significance should not be overstated.[18] Plainly, where a principal appoints a company as agent, it must be envisaged that at least the company's directors, and probably its employees, will carry out the tasks requested. A principal's appointment as agent of other corporations or even of unincorporated employers known to have large numbers of employees will often also carry an implication that employee sub-agents may be used.

5-003 Ministerial acts On the other hand an agent may delegate the performance of purely ministerial or ancillary acts, unless there are statutory or other provisions to the contrary or evidence of usage not permitting this[19]; and in general other, non-fiduciary functions of persons who have agency powers may be performed vicariously in accordance with normal contractual principles. This is not delegation.

5-004 Effect of unauthorised delegation Where the agent is not authorised to delegate and does so, acts performed by a purported sub-agent will not be valid, where validity is in question, nor bind or entitle the principal[20]; payment to such sub-agent will not rank as payment to the principal[21]; the principal is not, of course, liable to the

---

    Express Service Inc (1987) 10 N.S.W.L.R. 614 (signature of bill of lading); *Parkin v Williams* [1986] 1 N.Z.L.R. 294, Illustration 4 (Statute of Frauds); *Amoutzas v Tattersalls Ltd* [2010] EWHC 1696 (QB) at [128].

[8] *De Bussche v Alt* (1878) 8 Ch.D. 286.

[9] Mechem, *Outlines of Agency* (4th edn), p.50.

[10] *Coles v Trecothick* (1804) 9 Ves.Jun. 234.

[11] *Solly v Rathbone* (1814) 2 M. & S. 298.

[12] *Saad v Doumeny Holdings Pty Ltd* [2005] NSWSC 893 at [17] (holder of power of attorney could not act as director); *Re Ledir Enterprises Pty Ltd* [2013] NSWSC 1332; (2013) 96 A.C.S.R. 1.

[13] Illustration 5.

[14] *Cockran v Irlam* (1813) 2 M. & S. 301; *Henderson v Barnewall* (1827) 1 Y. & J. 387.

[15] *John McCann & Co v Pow* [1974] 1 W.L.R. 1643. See also *Benjamin v Clothier* (1969) 210 E.G. 29; *Maloney v Hardy and Moorsehead* (1970) 216 E.G. 1582.

[16] *Re Becket, Purnell v Paine* [1918] 2 Ch. 72. But see Illustration 6 as to London agents.

[17] Delegation by trustees is a specialised topic. See Trustee Delegation Act 1999; Trustee Act 2000 ss.11–23.

[18] See fn.2 above.

[19] See Illustrations 4 and 5, and other authorities cited in fn.7 above.

[20] Illustrations 3 and 5.

[21] *Dunlop & Sons v De Murrieta & Co* (1886) 3 T.L.R. 166 (shipping agent acting for shipbrokers); *Maloney v Hardy and Moorsehead* (1970) 216 E.G. 1582; *John McCann & Co v Pow* [1974] 1 W.L.R. 1643.

sub-agent for commission[22]; the sub-agent has no lien against the principal[23]; and the agent may be liable in respect of money received by such a person[24] and in general for wrongful execution of the agent's authority.[25] In the case of companies, the issue of unauthorised delegation can take the form of purported appointments made by a board of directors that was itself not properly constituted.[26] But an agent may be expressly authorised to delegate or may have implied authority to do so in the situations specified in this Article; or the agent's act in doing so may be ratified.[27]

Apparent authority   The principle here stated is one of actual authority, but the rules of apparent authority may also apply where third parties are involved, and to these the Article is also relevant. There may be a specific representation or conduct by the principal from which the third party will be entitled to assume that the agent had the authority to delegate where such authority to do so would normally be implied. In such a case the third party will be entitled to make that assumption even though the authority to delegate had actually been negatived between principal and agent, provided that the party did not know of this.[28]   **5-005**

Administrative law   The same maxim *delegatus non potest delegare* is often invoked in administrative law to declare invalid the exercise of powers by persons other than those to whom they have been entrusted. Some cases purport to distinguish between delegation and appointment of an agent, on the basis that the second is permitted but the first is not; other cases treat the two notions as the same. It is doubtful whether private law agency terminology assists in clarifying or solving these problems of public law, which is itself moving towards considering such issues under the heading of "legitimate expectation". An account of the topic is beyond the scope of this work and should be sought in specialised books.[29] One point may however be noted: that a Government Minister may normally act through departmental officials without infringing the maxim.[30]   **5-006**

Illustrations

(1)   A shipmaster was authorised to sell certain goods. He was held to have no implied authority to send them on to another person for sale when he could not himself find a purchaser, and hence was liable in respect of them.[31]   **5-007**

(2)   A notice to quit given by the agent of an agent is not sufficient without further evidence of authority or ratification.[32]

(3)   An agent buys property at a sale by auction, and the auctioneer enters his name

---

[22]   *Schmaling v Tomlinson* (1815) 6 Taunt. 147; *Mason v Clifton* (1863) 3 F. & F. 899.
[23]   *Solly v Rathbone* (1814) 2 M. & S. 298; see Article 70.
[24]   *Mackersy v Ramsay, Bonars & Co* (1843) 9 C. & F. 818; *Re Mutual Aid Permanent Benefit B.S.* (1883) 49 L.T. 530; *National Employers Mutual General Insurance Assn Ltd v Elphinstone* [1929] W.N. 135; *Balsamo v Medici* [1984] 1 W.L.R. 951; *Trading and General Investment Corp v Gault, Armstrong & Kemble Ltd (The Okeanis)* [1986] 1 Lloyd's Rep. 195.
[25]   e.g. Illustration 1.
[26]   See, e.g. *Morris v Kanssen* [1946] A.C. 459 HL.
[27]   e.g. *Keay v Fenwick* (1876) 1 C.P.D. 745. See Articles 13–20.
[28]   See Article 72.
[29]   e.g. Wade and Forsyth, *Administrative Law* (11th edn), p.281 onwards; Craig, *Administrative Law* (8th edn), Ch.22.
[30]   *Carltona Ltd v Commissioner of Works* [1943] 2 All E.R. 560 at 563.
[31]   *Catlin v Bell* (1815) 4 Camp. 183.
[32]   *Doe d. Rhodes v Robinson* (1837) 3 Bing.N.C. 677. But cf. *Allam & Co v Europa Poster Services*

as buyer without objection by the principal, who is present at the sale. The entry is sufficient memorandum of the contract as against the principal.[33] But entry by the auctioneer's clerk would not suffice unless there was other evidence of authority.[34] And where a tenant for life had power to lease, and a memorandum of the contract for a lease was signed by his agent's clerk with the approval of the agent and in the ordinary course of business it was held that the memorandum was not sufficient to satisfy the Statute of Frauds, not having been proved to have been signed by a duly authorised agent within the meaning of that statute.[35]

(4)   Attorneys under a power of attorney may delegate the signature of an agreement for sale to the auctioneer.[36]

(5)   An agent has authority to draw bills of exchange in the principal's name. Signature by the agent's clerk is sufficient if it is in accordance with the usual practice.[37] So, an authority given to an agent to indorse a particular bill in the principal's name may be delegated, because such acts are purely ministerial and involve no discretion. Where four liquidators had no power to authorise one of their number to accept bills of exchange on behalf of them all, it was held that they might authorise him to accept a particular bill on their behalf, because the execution of the former authority would involve discretion, whereas the latter was an authority to do a purely ministerial act.[38]

(6)   A country solicitor has implied authority to act through his London agent when necessary or usual in the ordinary course of business: thus the issue of proceedings by his London agent acting as such is valid.[39] Where a London agent has the general conduct of an action, he has the same general authority in conducting it, including authority to compromise, as the country solicitor employing him, in the absence of any express limits on such general authority.[40] But a solicitor cannot delegate his entire employment to his London agent so as to make the agent his client's solicitor: a retainer to a country solicitor does not justify an action in which the London agents are the solicitors on the record.[41]

(7)   A shipowner employed merchants carrying on business at Hong Kong, Shanghai and Yokohama to sell a ship at any port where the ship might happen to be from time to time in the course of employment under charter. The merchants had authority to appoint a sub-agent with branches at Nagasaki and other Japanese ports.[42]

Ltd [1968] 1 W.L.R. 638 (notice given by solicitor of company).

33   *White v Proctor* (1811) 4 Taunt. 209; *Emmerson v Heelis* (1809) 2 Taunt. 38.

34   *Bell v Balls* [1897] 1 Ch. 663; *Bird v Boulter* (1833) 4 B. & Ad. 443.

35   *Blore v Sutton* (1817) 3 Mer. 237. These questions would not now arise in the same form because of the different requirements of the Law of Property (Miscellaneous Provisions) Act 1989 s.2. The cases are retained as illustrations of principle.

36   *Parkin v Williams* [1986] 1 N.Z.L.R. 294.

37   *Re Marshall Ex p. Sutton* (1788) 2 Cox 84. See also *Lord v Hall* (1848) 2 C. & K. 698; *Brown v Tombs* [1891] 1 Q.B. 253.

38   *Re London and Mediterranean Bank Ex p. Birmingham Banking Co* (1868) L.R. 3 Ch.App. 651 at 653–654.

39   *Solley v Wood* (1852) 16 Beav. 370. See Article 35, Illustrations 3 and 4.

40   *Re Newen, Carruthers v Newen* [1903] 1 Ch. 812.

41   *Wray v Kemp* (1884) 26 Ch.D. 169; *Re Scholes & Sons* (1886) 32 Ch.D. 245; see also *Re Beckett, Purnell v Paine* [1918] 2 Ch. 72. These cases also are largely out of date but are retained as good examples of principle.

42   *De Bussche v Alt* (1878) 8 Ch.D. 286. But see further discussion of this case below.

Article 35

Relation Between Principal and Sub-agent

(1) Acts done on the principal's behalf by a sub-agent whose appointment was authorised or ratified by the principal bind the principal as if they had been performed by the agent personally.[43]

(2) The relation of principal and agent may be established by an agent between the principal and a sub-agent if the agent is expressly or impliedly authorised to constitute such relation, or if the agent's act is ratified, and it is the intention of the agent and of such sub-agent that such relation should be constituted.[44]

(3) But there is no privity of contract between a principal and a sub-agent as such merely because the delegation was effected with the authority of the principal; and in the absence of such privity the rights and duties arising out of any contracts between the principal and the agent, and between the agent and the sub-agent, respectively, are only enforceable by and against the immediate parties to those contracts.[45] However, the sub-agent in the latter case may in some circumstances be liable to the principal as a fiduciary, in tort, and possibly to account generally.[46] A sub-agent may also become implicated in a breach of duty by the agent, and be liable for dishonest assistance in a breach of the former's duty.[47]

(4) A sub-agent must not follow the directions of a more senior agent if the sub-agent knows, and in some circumstances ought to know, that the senior agent is acting dishonestly.

5-008

Comment

Rule (1) The acts of an authorised sub-agent bind the principal. This is not because the sub-agent is the principal's agent:

5-009

> "it is rather that he is bound by the act of his own agent, who, in this instance, is (properly) doing the act through the sub-agent."[48]

Thus the principal may receive notification or be held to have acquired knowledge

---

[43] See Comment. As to apparent authority, see below, para.5-015.

[44] *De Bussche v Alt* (1878) 8 Ch.D. 286, Illustration 5. Alternatively, it may be found that, properly construed, there was no intermediate agency but a direct agency made through one of the principal's agents: *Homecare Direct Shopping Pty Ltd v Gray* [2008] VSCA 111.

[45] *New Zealand & Australian Land Co v Watson* (1881) 7 Q.B.D. 374, Illustration 1; *Calico Printers Assn. Ltd v Barclays Bank Ltd* (1931) 145 L.T. 51; *Schwensen v Ellinger, Heath, Western & Co* (1949) 83 Ll. L.Rep. at 81; *Kahler v Midland Bank Ltd* [1950] A.C. 24; *Grosvenor Casinos Ltd v National Bank of Abu Dhabi* [2008] EWHC 511 (Comm); [2008] 2 Lloyd's Rep. 1; [2008] 2 All E.R. (Comm) 112 at [157]; noted by Bennett (2008) 124 L.Q.R. 532. This statement was approved in *Henderson v Merrett Syndicates Ltd* [1995] 2 A.C. 145 at 202.

[46] *Powell & Thomas v Evan Jones & Co* [1905] 1 K.B. 11; *Henderson v Merrett Syndicates Ltd* [1995] 2 A.C. 145; *Markel International Insurance Co Ltd v Surety Guarantee Consultants Ltd* [2008] EWHC 1135 (Comm) at [225], Illustration 11; affirmed [2009] EWCA Civ 790. See Comment.

[47] *Markel International Insurance Co Ltd v Surety Guarantee Consultants Ltd* [2008] EWHC 1135 (Comm) at [237]; *Indutech Canada Ltd v Gibbs Pipe Sales Ltd* [2011] 8 W.W.R. 60 at [411]; *Fiona Trust & Holding Corp v Privalov* [2010] EWHC 3199 (Comm) at [66]. See further below, para.9-135.

[48] Mechem, *Outlines of Agency* (4th edn), p.51.

through a sub-agent[49]; signature by a sub-agent may bind the principal[50]; issue of process by a sub-agent may be valid[51]; the principal may be bound by a contract made by a sub-agent[52]; and payment to a sub-agent may rank as payment to the principal.[53] These propositions are obvious where the sub-agent is in privity of contract with the principal, but it is clear that the same results obtain where the sub-agent is not; for example, an insurance policy obtained through a sub-agent, giving the insured rights against the insurer.[54]

The consequences of authorised sub-delegation between principal and sub-agent depend on the way in which this was effected. There are two possibilities.

5-010 **Rule (2): Privity of contract** The agent, A, may appoint another agent for the principal, whether in substitution for,[55] or in addition to,[56] A. Complete handing-over of functions is obviously unlikely to be authorised, except as regards particular geographical locations,[57] a specific time or in abnormal circumstances.[58] This may create privity of contract between the principal and the new agent, and the full consequences of agency ensue, including a duty in the sub-agent to exercise care and skill. Since this all may occur where the new agent is to perform different functions from those performed by the appointing agent (e.g. where a manager hires staff), and where the appointing agent has no agency relationship with the person appointed, there will be many cases where the terms "sub-agency" and "delegate" will be inappropriate, and it has been suggested that such a person should not be called a sub-agent at all.[59] The agent is in fact a co-agent. But usage in the cases is indiscriminate. Whether privity of contract arises is always a question of intention of the parties. The standard position in England, for example, where an insurer appoints a solicitor for an insured as a result of a claim under a liability policy seems to be that the solicitor is in direct privity with the insured, even if there is no direct contact between them.[60]

There may be express authority to delegate by this means, or there may be ratification.[61] But it seems that such authority will not readily be implied.[62] Indeed, it has been said that the influence of the leading authority where direct privity was

---

[49] See Article 95, Illustration 16; cf. Article 95, Illustration 10. The position is otherwise, it seems, where the sub-agency was unauthorised, at least where the principal cannot be said to be approbating and reprobating the actions of the sub-agent: *O'Keefe v London and Edinburgh Insurance Co Ltd* [1927] N.I. 85; *Perpetual Trustee Co Ltd v Burniston (No.2)* [2012] WASC 383 at [241].
[50] See Article 34, Illustrations 3 and 5.
[51] See Article 34, Illustration 6.
[52] Illustration 5.
[53] *Hemming v Hale* (1859) 7 C.B.(N.S.) 487; *Maloney v Hardy and Moorsehead* (1970) 216 E.G. 1582 at 1586; but cf. p.1583.
[54] *Chua Yew Phong v A.S.Yeo* [1966] 2 M.L.J. 257.
[55] e.g. *Schwensen v Ellinger, Heath, Western & Co* (1949) 83 Ll. L.Rep. 79 (wartime conditions): but in this case it seems that the principal himself appointed the new agent.
[56] See Illustration 5; *Ecossaise SS Co Ltd v Lloyd, Low & Co* (1890) 7 T.L.R. 76.
[57] e.g. *De Bussche v Alt* (1878) 8 Ch.D. 286, Illustration 5.
[58] e.g. *Schwensen v Ellinger, Heath, Western & Co* (1949) 83 Ll. L.Rep. 79.
[59] *Restatement, Second*, Appendix, reporter's note to § 5.
[60] See *Re Crocker* [1936] Ch. 696 at 700–701, Illustration 12; *Groom v Crocker* [1939] 1 K.B. 194 CA at 205 and 229; *Ramsook v Crossley* [2018] UKPC 9 at [27]; *Travelers Insurance Co Ltd v XYZ* [2019] UKSC 48 at [114]. cf. *Re Enterprise Insurance Co Plc, White v Ozon Solicitors* [2017] EWHC 1595 (Ch).
[61] e.g. *Keay v Fenwick* (1876) 1 C.P.D. 745.
[62] See *Calico Printers Assn Ltd v Barclays Bank Ltd* (1931) 145 L.T. 51. But cf. *De Bussche v Alt* (1878) 8 Ch.D. 286, Illustration 5; *Keay v Fenwick* (1876) 1 C.P.D. 745; *Ecossaise SS Co Ltd v Lloyd,*

found, *De Bussche v Alt*,[63] "seems to have waned".[64] However, where it does exist, the duty of the appointing agent to the principal is normally no more than to exercise due care in making the appointment,[65] and the agent does not, without further circumstances (e.g. if a *del credere* agent or the agent undertakes a duty of supervision), undertake that the appointed agent will perform the work adequately.[66]

Rule (3): No privity of contract   Agents may equally appoint their own agent to   **5-011**
do the requisite work; again, authority may be express or implied or there may be ratification. The prima facie rule seems to be that a delegation has been effected by this means[67]: this is not surprising as it retains the responsibility of the person in whom trust is reposed by the principal. Thus, for the default of such a sub-agent the agent is normally responsible[68]; and if such person receives money for the principal, that is sufficient to charge the agent with its receipt.[69]

The full position of such a person, who may genuinely be called a sub-agent, is not, however, fully worked out in English law. The tacit assumption in case law seems to be that if the sub-agent is not appointed to be in privity with the principal, the sub-agent is only in privity with the agent and owes common law (and less decisively, equitable duties) only to the agent. It is arguable that the very fact that such a sub-agent binds the principal when acting in connection with the principal's affairs shows that the sub-agent is at least in some respects to be regarded as an agent of the principal, and that there will be circumstances when that person should be also directly liable to the principal. In a sense, this is a contract for the benefit of a third party, and in the US[70] reasoning along such lines made it possible for Seavey to write in 1955 that a:

"sub-agent is liable to the principal for negligence in performing or failing to perform du-

---

Low & Co (1890) 7 T.L.R. 76. Country solicitors did not normally have the power to create such privity between their clients and their London agents: see Article 34, Illustration 6. But compare the position of solicitors or stockbrokers employing stockbrokers; *Blackburn v Mason* (1893) 68 L.T. 510. See Article 28, Illustration 3.

63   *De Bussche v Alt* (1878) 8 Ch.D. 286, Illustration 5.

64   *Prentis Donegan & Partners Ltd v Leeds & Leeds Co Inc* [1998] 2 Lloyd's Rep. 326 at 331, per Rix J (Illustration 9).

65   See *Thomas Cheshire & Co v Vaughan Bros & Co* [1920] 3 K.B. 240 at 259; *Ecossaise SS Co Ltd v Lloyd Low & Co* (1890) 7 T.L.R. 76; *Fry v Tapson* (1884) 28 Ch.D. 268; *Re Weall* (1889) 42 Ch.D. 674.

66   *Sampson v Wilson* [1996] Ch. 39; *Aiken v Stewart Wrightson Members Agency Ltd* [1995] 1 W.L.R. 1281. There are also cases on the liability of directors for acts of co-directors. And see Article 115.

67   *Calico Printers Assn Ltd v Barclays Bank Ltd* (1931) 145 L.T. 51; *Royal Products Ltd v Midland Bank Ltd* [1981] 2 Lloyd's Rep. 194; *Prentis Donegan & Partners Ltd v Leeds & Leeds Co Inc* [1998] 2 Lloyd's Rep. 326. See also *Trengrouse & Co v Official Assignee of Steeds* (1896) 14 N.Z.L.R. 636.

68   *Re Mitchell* (1884) L.J.Ch. 342; *Meyerstein v Eastern Agency Co Ltd* (1885) 1 T.L.R. 595; *Ecossaise SS Co Ltd v Lloyd, Low & Co* (1890) 7 T.L.R. 76; *Stewart v Reavell's Garage* [1952] 2 Q.B. 545; *Swire v Francis* (1877) 3 App.Cas. 106. But cf. *Thomas Cheshire & Co v Vaughan Bros & Co* [1920] 3 K.B. 240. This would apply even where the delegation was unauthorised.

69   *Matthews v Haydon* (1786) 2 Esp. 509; *Mackersy v Ramsays, Bonars & Co* (1843) 9 C. & F. 818; *Skinner & Co v Weguelin, Eddowes & Co* (1882) C. & E. 12; *National Employers' Mutual General Insurance Assn Ltd v Elphinstone* [1929] W.N. 135; *Trading and General Investment Corp v Gault, Armstrong & Kemble Ltd (The Okeanis)* [1986] 1 Lloyd's Rep. 195. This would apply even where the delegation was unauthorised: see above, para.5-004.

70   Seavey (1955) 68 HarvL.Rev. 658 at 666–667; also printed as *Restatement, Second*, Appendix, reporter's note to § 5 (a valuable article). The provision in *Restatement, Third*, is more general: see § 3.15, especially Comment *d*.

ties undertaken for the principal. He is also under a duty to account for anything received for the principal, and is liable as a fiduciary for any breach of a fiduciary duty."[71]

Under this approach the principal may also be liable to indemnify the subagent.[72] These propositions do not rest on contract: indeed the sub-agent is not liable to the principal for breach of contract, for there is normally no contract with the principal, nor is the principal liable to the sub-agent for remuneration.[73]

The position in England, where the authorities are, as always, more limited, cannot be stated so clearly because of the existence of old case law which has not been reconsidered.[74] There can however be said to be some movement in the same direction. Although it was held in 1931 that the sub-agent could not be liable to the principal in tort for negligently performing the work,[75] this is not an absolute rule. Where it can be shown that the sub-agent has assumed a legal responsibility to the principal (usually in addition to the contractual duties owed the agent) a duty in tort may arise, as was affirmed in 1995 in *Henderson v Merrett Syndicates Ltd*.[76] The facts of the case indicated quite close relations between principal and sub-agent which will not be found in all other situations of sub-agency: it was stressed that the persons concerned:

"hold themselves out as possessing a special expertise ... the Names ... placed implicit reliance on that expertise."[77]

It was said that in other cases an action in tort might be:

"short circuiting the contractual structure ... put in place by the parties. It cannot therefore be inferred from the present case that other sub-agents will be held directly liable to the agent's principal in tort."[78]

As mentioned earlier, it may also be possible in some cases to regard the contract between agent and sub-agent as one for the benefit of a third party, the principal. Where it is possible to say that a term in the contract purports to confer a benefit on the principal and envisages the principal's being able to enforce that term, the principal might have a right of action under the Contracts (Rights of Third Par-

---

[71] Seavey (1955) 68 HarvL.Rev. at 666–667.

[72] Seavey (1955) 68 HarvL.Rev. at 669.

[73] Seavey (1955) 68 HarvL.Rev. at 667.

[74] *Donoghue v Stevenson* [1932] A.C. 562.

[75] *Calico Printers Assn Ltd v Barclays Bank Ltd* (1931) 145 L.T. 51, still however a significant case because of its analysis of the legal position in such situations. See also *Involnert Management Inc v Aprilgrange Ltd* [2015] EWHC 2225 (Comm); [2016] 1 All E.R. (Comm) 913 at [291].

[76] *Henderson v Merrett Syndicates Ltd* [1995] 2 A.C. 145. See also *Riyad Bank v Ahli United Bank* [2005] EWHC 279; [2005] 2 Lloyd's Rep. 409 at [64], per Moore-Bick J. See also *Dunlop Haywards Ltd v Erinaceous Insurance Services Ltd* [2008] EWHC 520 (Comm) at [66]; reversed on other points [2009] EWCA Civ 354.

[77] *Henderson v Merrett Syndicates Ltd* [1995] 2 A.C. 145 at 182, per Lord Goff of Chieveley.

[78] *Henderson v Merrett Syndicates Ltd* [1995] 2 A.C. 145 at 195; citing as an example *Simaan Contracting Co v Pilkington Safety Glass Ltd (No.2)* [1988] Q.B. 758 (a case on construction subcontracts). A case where a sub-agent had earlier been held not liable in tort is *Balsamo v Medici* [1984] 1 W.L.R. 951, Illustration 7. It is submitted that the decision in that case was correct but much of the reasoning extremely doubtful even at the time, and certainly in the light of subsequent developments. See Whittaker (1985) 48 M.L.R. 86. A sub-agent (a Lloyd's broker) was held not liable in *Pangood Ltd v Barclay Brown & Co Ltd* [1999] P.N.L.R. 678.

ties) Act 1999.[79] This would be subject to defences, in particular in this context set-offs, available against the agent.[80]

When one turns to consider the rights of sub-agent against principal, while no one suggests that the principal should be liable to the sub-agent for remuneration in the absence of a contract,[81] restitutionary reasoning can sometimes also be used to justify a right of reimbursement for expenses and liabilities incurred: although these can usually be justified on the basis of contract,[82] the restitutionary explanation now available outside contract gives a scope which is not so limited, though narrower in that it is confined to the extent of any benefit conferred on the principal.[83] Otherwise, it is always possible for a principal to undertake contractual obligations in favour of the sub-agent, in addition to or in substitution for the agent.[84]

Equitable liability   The position in English law of the sub-agent in respect of the   **5-012** various forms of equitable liability is not much clearer. A sub-agent who knowingly misapplies the property of the principal will undoubtedly be liable in equity to the principal for such actions, but so too would most third parties who implicate themselves in such events.[85] On the other hand, an innocent, even negligent, misapplication of funds or other failure by the subagent to comply with the principal's instructions, at least where the sub-agent did not benefit therefrom, would not necessarily expose the sub-agent to liability to the principal in equity.[86] This would be so even where the sub-agent's actions caused the agent to be liable to the principal, including for breach of trust.[87]

The legal position where the sub-agent makes profits which could not have been made but for the agent's position as such, or where the sub-agent engages in a

---

[79] Contracts (Rights of Third Parties) Act 1999 s.1(1),(2); subject to the requirement of identification in s.1(3). A rights-of-third-parties clause is not conclusive against there being a contractual relationship between principal and sub-agent: *Temple Legal Protection Ltd v QBE Insurance (Europe) Ltd* [2008] EWHC 843 (Comm); [2008] Lloyd's Rep. I.R. 643 at [110]; affirmed on other grounds [2009] EWCA Civ 453; [2009] 1 All E.R. (Comm) 703.

[80] Contracts (Rights of Third Parties) Act 1999 s.3.

[81] See *Schmaling v Tomlinson* (1815) 6 Taunt: 147; *Mason v Clifton* (1863) 3 F.&F. 899 (subject to the Contracts (Rights of Third Parties) Act 1999); *Berezovsky v Edmiston & Co Ltd* [2010] EWHC 1883 (Comm) at [69] (reversed on one issue [2011] EWCA Civ 431). But cf. *Accidia Foundation v Simon C. Dickinson Ltd* [2010] EWHC 3058 (Ch) at [94] (remuneration of sub-agent by equitable allowance in an account by that sub-agent, but to be met out of commission that might otherwise have gone to the head agent).

[82] See Comment to Article 62.

[83] See Comment to Article 62; *Goff and Jones, Law of Unjust Enrichment* (9th edn), Chs 19–20.

[84] See, e.g. *Prentis Donegan & Partners Ltd v Leeds & Leeds Co Inc* [1998] 2 Lloyd's Rep. 326, Illustration 9: see 334; *Fitzpatrick v Allan Associates Architects Ltd* [2015] NIQB 41 (solicitors seeking fees from ultimate principal). But cf. *Temple Legal Protection Ltd v QBE Insurance (Europe) Ltd* [2009] EWCA Civ 453 at [26].

[85] See *Bath v Standard Land Co Ltd* [1911] 1 Ch. 618 at 626, Illustration 10; *Ross River Ltd v Waveley Commercial Ltd* [2013] EWCA Civ 910 at [59]. See further below, Articles 96 and 116.

[86] *Gregson v HAE Trustees Ltd* [2008] EWHC 1006 (Ch); *Revenue and Customs Commissioners v Holland* [2010] UKSC 51; [2010] 1 W.L.R. 2793, noted Watts (2011) 127 L.Q.R. 162; Ferran [2011] C.L.J. 321; Ji Lian Yap [2012] J.B.L. 57 (director of incorporated director not a de facto director of head company and hence not liable for honest misapplication of company property). Not all breaches of trust involve breaches of fiduciary duty: see Rt Hon. Lord Millett (1998) 114 L.Q.R. 399 at 405 and 417. cf. *P&P Property Ltd v Owen White and Catlin LLP* [2018] EWCA Civ 1082 at [98] (solicitor a sub-agent but also a direct trustee for principal).

[87] See *Bath v Standard Land* [1911] 1 Ch. 618 at 627 and 637; *Revenue and Customs Commissioners v Holland* [2010] UKSC 51; [2010] 1 W.L.R. 2793.

transaction where the sub-agent can be said to have interests conflicting with those of the principal, is unsettled. It was held in 1905 that the sub-agent might be liable to the principal in respect of a secret profit[88]: the view was expressed that there was a contract between principal and sub-agent, but that ground was not the basis of the decision. Such reasoning would in fact have solved the earlier case of *De Bussche v Alt*,[89] where the issue was again one of a (considerable) secret profit, but the problem was solved by finding privity of contract between principal and sub-agent. The sub-agent would be liable to the agent for such profits, and the latter, at least once the sub-agent had accounted to the agent, would usually be liable to the principal, but direct liability to the principal seems also tenable.[90]

In *Bath v Standard Land Co Ltd*[91] a majority of the Court of Appeal took the view that the directors of a company that was itself an agent of the claimant did not owe fiduciary duties to the claimant. However, that was a case where the claimant, on the basis of conflict of interest, was attempting to deny the relevant directors any remuneration at all for valuable services they had performed in an external capacity for the company, and thereby the claimant. The decision may have been different if the relevant contracts had been unexecuted and the claimant had been simply seeking to have them rescinded, or, if executed, the claimant had been willing to seek rescission on terms that the directors were to receive reasonable remuneration. Buckley LJ, one of the majority judges, indicated that a sub-agent who buys from or sells to a trustee or principal would be subject to the same constraints in respect of conflict of interest as the agent.[92] It has since been held that a sub-agent may undertake fiduciary duties to the principal, and can therefore be directly liable for diverting business opportunities to a competitor of the principal.[93] But the mere existence of a conflict of interest, or simple profiting from position, where there is no suggestion that the principal was harmed by the sub-agent's actions, may be capable of being excused by the agent, properly informed of the circumstances.[94]

Whether there can be said to be a general duty in a sub-agent to account to the principal, as was argued by Seavey in 1955[95] and more recently again suggested,[96] remains uncertain, though it seems desirable. It may first be noted that there are undoubtedly cases where the sub-agent may hold property on trust for the principal, including the fruits of bribes and secret commissions received by the sub-agent.[97]

---

[88] *Powell & Thomas v Evan Jones & Co* [1905] 1 K.B. 11, Illustration 6; *Markel International Insurance Co Ltd v Surety Guarantee Consultants Ltd* [2008] EWHC 1135 (Comm), Illustration 11; but cf. *New Zealand & Australian Land Co v Watson* (1881) 7 Q.B.D. 374; *Royal Products Ltd v Midland Bank Ltd* [1981] 2 Lloyd's Rep. 194. See further Finn, *Fiduciary Obligations* (1977), pp.177–178 and 202–203.

[89] *De Bussche v Alt* (1878) 8 Ch.D. 286, Illustration 5.

[90] See *FM Capital Partners Ltd v Marino* [2018] EWHC 2905 (Comm) at [106].

[91] *Bath v Standard Land Co Ltd* [1911] 1 Ch. 618.

[92] *Bath v Standard Land Co Ltd* [1911] 1 Ch. 618 at 644. In some jurisdictions, statutory provisions may expressly regulate the conflicts of interest of sub-agents: see, e.g. *Dyas v Diel* [2013] NZHC 2645 (employees of real estate agent).

[93] *JD Wetherspoon Plc v Van De Berg & Co Ltd* [2009] EWHC 639 (Ch) at [77].

[94] In *Regal (Hastings) Ltd v Gulliver* [1967] 2 A.C. 134n the directors of the claimant company were held capable of condoning a profit made by the company's solicitor, even though they could not retain their own profits.

[95] See Seavey (1955) 68 Harv.L.Rev. 658.

[96] Tettenborn (1999) 115 L.Q.R. 655. It is however not easy to accept all the explanations of the cases discussed in this article.

[97] *Att.-Gen. for Hong Kong v Reid* [1994] 1 A.C. 324. *FHR European Ventures LLP v Cedar Capital*

But there can also be other situations.[98] Any further argument for such a right would need to overcome the nineteenth-century cases, mostly but not all on solicitors, relying on the lack of privity of contract between sub-agent and principal.[99] It is true that other cases might appear to take a different line[100]; but where a duty to account has been found it is usually not clear whether or not the court has proceeded on the basis that there is a contract between principal and sub-agent. If there is, the problem of course vanishes; and some cases may have taken this approach in order to secure an appropriate result. This is arguably what happened in the leading case of *De Bussche v Alt*.[101]

Set-off, etc.   Failure of the intermediary agent features in many of the cases.[102] A **5-013** major reason for argument by sub-contractors that their contract is with the agent rather than the principal is that a sub-contractor may have paid, or have a set-off against, or otherwise be able to adjust accounts with the agent, and this has been relevant in several cases.[103] Even where there is actual privity of contract with the principal, however, the sub-agent, who cannot of course in such a case set off in the strict sense a debt owed by the agent,[104] may seek to argue that there has in effect been an accounting between sub-agent and agent, hoping thereby to retain money in adjustment of the financial position between them. This last argument can sometimes be met by saying that unless there are other indications the agent normally has no authority to accept payment other than in cash.[105]

Lien   The question of the sub-agent's lien involves special considerations, since **5-014** a lien is a property interest. It is therefore dealt with elsewhere.[106]

Apparent authority   This Article again deals with actual authority. But it should **5-015** be remembered that the principles of apparent authority still apply where third parties are involved. Thus a person appointed as sub-agent to the principal by another agent may be able to rely on the apparent authority of the appointing agent if there was some specific representation by the principal, or if the case is one where authority to delegate would normally be implied, despite instructions not to delegate given by the principal to the agent but unknown to the appointed agent. And a person dealing with an agent so appointed may be able to rely on the principal's holding out such person as an agent, or on the apparent authority of the appointing agent to

---

Partners LLC [2014] UKSC 45; [2014] 3 W.L.R. 535. See further below, para.6-042.

[98] Money received was held not impressed with a trust in *New Zealand & Australian Land Co v Watson* (1881) 7 Q.B.D. 374; but this can be true of property held by an agent: see, e.g. *Neste Oy v Lloyd's Bank Plc* [1983] 2 Lloyd's Rep. 658; see below, para.6-042; also Tettenborn (1999) 115 L.Q.R. 655 at 657–658.

[99] *Robbins v Fennell* (1847) 11 Q.B. 248, Illustration 3; *Cobb v Becke* (1845) 6 Q.B. 930, Illustration 4; *Stephens v Badcock* (1832) 3 B. & Ad. 354; *Sims v Brittain* (1832) 4 B. & Ad. 375; but cf. *Robbins v Heath* (1848) 11 Q.B. 257n; *Collins v Brook* (1860) 5 H. & N. 700.

[100] See *Pearson v Scott* (1878) 9 Ch.D. 198, Illustration 3 to Article 28; *Harsant v Blaine McDonald & Co* (1887) 56 L.J.Q.B. 511, cited by Tettenborn (1999) 115 L.Q.R. 655.

[101] *De Bussche v Alt* (1878) 8 Ch.D. 286, Illustration 5. The case could also be explained on the basis of secret profit, whether there was privity or not.

[102] See Article 98.

[103] A leading example is *New Zealand & Australian Land Co v Watson* (1881) 7 Q.B.D. 374, Illustration 1.

[104] See Article 81.

[105] See, e.g. *Pearson v Scott* (1878) 9 Ch.D. 198; Article 28, Illustrations 3 and 4.

[106] See Article 68.

make the appointment. So also a person may be able to rely on apparent authority to be appointed as a sub-agent, e.g. where the sub-agent wishes to exercise a lien. It seems that where the agent who appoints the sub-agent has only apparent authority to make the appointment, third parties who deal with the sub-agent (whether disclosed or not) need not establish that they knew of the original holding out. The principal is precluded from denying the sub-agent's actual authority to bind, so long at least as there has been no communication otherwise.[107] The basis for this result seems to be the justice of the sub-agent's position. The sub-agent should be able to rely on the head-agent's apparent authority, lest the sub-agent become liable to the third party in breach of warranty of authority. The position will be different where the sub-agent exceeds the scope of the expressly delegated authority; there it may be necessary for the third party to show that it relied on the chain of representations.[108] Where the appointment of the sub-agent is without actual authority, and there is no apparent authority, the principal will not in general be bound by the acts of such a sub-agent.[109]

5-016 **Rule (4): Duty not to follow dishonest agent's instructions** The circumstances in which a sub-agent ought not, in the interests of the principal, to follow the directions of an agent cannot readily be reduced to fixed principles. This is an issue that affects not just sub-agents in the strict sense but also agents who are in privity of contract with the principal but generally answerable to a more senior agent of the principal. The position will obviously turn on the express and implied terms of the agent's undertaking, the content of which may vary with the type of agent and with the particular agency created. It can, however, be assumed as a general rule that a junior agent (including in that expression a sub-agent) should not follow the directions of a senior agent when the junior agent knows that the senior agent is acting dishonestly vis-à-vis the principal. In some circumstances, it may be appropriate to conclude that the duty is more onerous, such that the agent should not follow the senior agent's instructions where there are merely strong grounds for thinking that the senior agent is acting dishonestly.

There is not much case law on this topic, although some of the cases on dishonest assistance in a breach of fiduciary duty have concerned defendants who are agents of the claimant where those agents have assisted trustees or other agents who are committing a breach of fiduciary duty.[110] Another line of cases, more problematic, involves the circumstances in which a bank should decline to follow instructions to make payments given by signatories on bank accounts where the signatory is acting dishonestly. Here, the current position in England and Wales seems to be that[111]:

"[a] bank should refrain from executing an order if and for so long as it was put on inquiry

---

[107] *AJU Remicon Co Ltd v Alida Shipping Co Ltd* [2007] EWHC 2246 (Comm) at [18]. See too *Ciban Management Corp v Citco (BVI) Ltd* [2020] UKPC 21; [2020] 3 W.L.R. 705.

[108] See *Ing Re (UK) Ltd v R & V Versicherung AG* [2006] EWHC 1544 (Comm); [2006] 2 All E.R. (Comm) 870; [2006] Lloyd's Rep. I.R. 653; [2007] 1 B.C.L.C. 108 at [100]; *Flexirent Capital Pty Ltd v EBS Consulting Pty Ltd* [2007] VSC 158 at [213].

[109] See *Schmaling v Tomlinson* (1815) 6 Taunt. 147; *Mason v Clifton* (1863) 3 F. & F. 899.

[110] See below, paras 8-221 and 9-135. In *Singularis Holdings Ltd v Daiwa Capital Markets Europe Ltd* [2019] UKSC 50; [2019] 3 W.L.R. 997 at [6], the claimant relied both upon dishonest assistance, and a duty of care.

[111] *Singularis Holdings Ltd v Daiwa Capital Markets Europe Ltd* [2019] UKSC 50; [2019] 3 W.L.R. 997 at [1].

by having reasonable grounds for believing that the order was an attempt to misappropriate funds."

The source of this test is a dictum of Steyn J in *Barclays Bank Plc v Quincecare Ltd*,[112] purporting to rely on this work.[113] On the facts of the case no breach of duty was found, but the test has been assumed to be correct in subsequent cases.[114] It is clear, however, that this work did not in fact provide support for Steyn J's test, and it remains arguable that, of all agents, a bank should decline to follow a mandatary's instructions only where it has actual knowledge that the mandatary is acting dishonestly.[115] It is probable, however, that only the Supreme Court can now restore a test that requires dishonesty in the bank.

Illustrations

(1) A factor was employed to sell goods on a *del credere* commission. The fac-   **5-017**
tor, with the principal's authority, employed a broker on an ordinary commission to sell the goods. The broker sold the goods and received the proceeds, and made payments on account to the factor from time to time. While the balance of the proceeds was still in the hands of the broker, the factor, being then indebted to the broker in respect of other independent transactions, became bankrupt. Held, (i) that there was no privity of contract between the principal and the broker; (ii) that the broker was not liable to account to the principal for the proceeds of the goods sold; and (iii) that the principal was not entitled to recover the balance of the proceeds from the broker in the factor's name without allowing the amount due from the factor to the broker in respect of other transactions to be set off, though the broker had reason to believe that the factor was acting as an agent.[116]

(2) An agent, being expressly authorised to do so, appointed a solicitor as subagent to manage the principal's affairs. The sub-agent took over their entire management, and communicated with the principal direct. Held, that the subagent was not liable to render an account of his agency to the principal.[117]

(3) The London agent of a country solicitor, in the ordinary course of business, receives, as such, the proceeds of a cause in which he is engaged. There is no privity of contract between the client and the London agent, and the client cannot recover the proceeds from him as money received to the client's use.[118] So, a London agent, in the ordinary course of business, gives credit to the country solicitor and not to the client, and has no remedy, except his lien, against the client for costs, and such lien, as against the client, is limited to

---

[112] *Barclays Bank Plc v Quincecare Ltd* [1992] 4 All E.R. 363 (Comm).
[113] In particular, para.6-017, below.
[114] *Singularis Holdings Ltd v Daiwa Capital Markets Europe Ltd* [2019] UKSC 50 and *JP Morgan Chase Bank NA v Federal Republic of Nigeria* [2019] EWCA Civ 1641. But cf. *Westpac New Zealand Ltd v MAP & Associates Ltd* [2011] NZSC 89; [2011] 3 N.Z.L.R. 751 and *Lexi Holdings v Pannone and Partners* [2009] EWHC 2590 (Ch) (solicitor in relation to company director).
[115] See P. Watts, "The *Quincecare* Duty: Misconceived and Misdelivered" [2020] J.B.L. 403.
[116] *New Zealand & Australian Land Co v Watson* (1881) 7 Q.B.D. 374.
[117] *Lockwood v Abdy* (1845) 14 Sim. 437. And see *Att.-Gen. v Earl of Chesterfield* (1854) 18 Beav. 596; *Re Spencer* (1881) 51 L.J.Ch. 271.
[118] *Robbins v Fennell* (1847) 11 Q.B. 248. And see *Hannaford v Syms* (1898) 79 L.T. 30; cf. *Collins v Brook* (1860) 5 H. & N. 700. See in general Cordery, *Solicitors* (8th edn), p.279–281 onwards (not reproduced in the current (looseleaf) edition). These cases are largely out of date, but are retained as relevant examples of principle.

the amount due from the client to the country solicitor.[119] The court may, however, in exercise of its summary jurisdiction over its own officers, order a London agent to pay over to the client money received, the agent claiming to retain the amount in satisfaction of a debt due to him from the country solicitor,[120] or having received it without the authority of either the country solicitor or the client.[121]

(4) A client gives money to his solicitor to pay a debt and costs. The solicitor remits the amount, by means of his own cheque, to his London agent for the purpose of paying such debt and costs. The agent retains the amount in satisfaction of a debt due to him from the solicitor. The agent is not liable to the client in an action for money had and received to the client's use.[122] So, if a London agent receives money improperly, the remedy of the client is against his own solicitor, not against the agent.[123]

(5) A ship was consigned to A, an agent in China, for sale, a minimum price being fixed. A employed B to sell the ship in circumstances in which he had authority to do so.[124] B, being unable to find a purchaser, bought the ship himself at the minimum price, and subsequently resold it at a large profit. It was held that privity of contract existed between the principal and B, and that B was liable to account to the principal for the profit made on the resale.[125]

(6) Shipowners employ agents to obtain for them a loan secured by means of debentures on their ships. The agents, with the shipowners' consent, employ a sub-agent, who negotiates such a loan but accepts a commission from the lender. The shipowners can recover this sum from the sub-agent, whether or not they are in privity of contract with him.[126] The sub-agent cannot, however, be compelled to enforce the contract for the commission for the benefit of the principal.

(7) The Italian owner of a vintage car asks a friend to sell it for him in England and remit the proceeds to the owner's mother-in-law in England. The friend sells the car but has to return to Italy before the proceeds have been received. Without the owner's knowledge he asks an English associate to receive and transmit the money. By his own negligence the associate is tricked out of the money. The associate is not liable in tort to the owner.[127]

(8) "Names" investing in the Lloyd's market entrust their business to "members' agents". These agents further entrust the business to "managing agents". The managing agents handle the investors' funds negligently. They have no priv-

---

[119] *Ex p. Edwards* (1881) 8 Q.B.D. 262; affirming 7 Q.B.D. 155. See further Article 70, Illustration 3.

[120] *Ex p. Edwards* (1881) 8 Q.B.D. 262; *Hanley v Cassam* (1847) 11 Jur. 1088.

[121] *Robbins v Fennell* (1847) 11 Q.B. 248; but cf. *Robbins v Heath* (1848) 11 Q.B. 257n.

[122] *Cobb v Becke* (1845) 6 Q.B. 930. See, however, *Ex p. Edwards* (1881) 8 Q.B.D. 262.

[123] *Gray v Kirby* (1834) 2 Dowl. 601. See, however, *Robbins v Fennell* (1847) 11 Q.B. 248; *Robbins v Heath* (1848) 11 Q.B. 257n.

[124] See Article 34, Illustration 7.

[125] *De Bussche v Alt.* (1878) 8 Ch.D. 286; see also *Tarn v Scanlan* [1928] A.C. 34. But see above, text to fn.83.

[126] *Powell & Thomas v Evan Jones & Co* [1905] 1 K.B. 11. See further below, para.6-042.

[127] *Balsamo v Medici* [1984] 1 W.L.R. 951. But see fn.78 above. A similar decision was reached in a more substantial banking case, *Calico Printers Assn v Barclays Bank Ltd* (1931) 145 L.T. 51. See above, para.5-012.

ity of contract with the names, only with the managing agents. They are liable in tort directly to the names.[128]

(9) American insurance brokers approach Lloyd's brokers for marine insurance. The slip is written "Account: Offshore Service (U.K.) Ltd" (a managing company for the owners of the ship insured). The insurance is effected and the Lloyd's brokers pay premiums. Being not reimbursed by the American brokers they sue the brokers, who argue that the only contract is between the assured (as principal) and the Lloyd's brokers. The Lloyd's brokers have a contract with the American brokers, who are liable.[129]

(10) A landowner in financial difficulties agrees to the appointment of a company as managing agent. The company's articles of association permit its directors to provide services to the company in their professional capacities for reward. Four directors (a solicitor, an auctioneer, an accountant, and a pit manager) provide services under contract in the operation of the landowner's estate. The landowner unsuccessfully seeks to deny the directors any remuneration for their services.[130]

(11) The claimant insurance company appoints a corporate underwriting agent to write surety bonds on its behalf. The appointment designates the defendants (officers and employees of the agent) as approved personnel to conduct the business. The defendants dishonestly write bonds that do not conform to the instructions, thereby exposing the claimant to losses, and also obtain for the agent secret commissions on the unauthorised business. The defendants are held to be sub-agents, and liable directly for breach of fiduciary duty. Alternatively, they are liable for dishonestly procuring breaches of duty by their company.[131]

(12) An insurer, pursuant to a liability insurance policy, appointed a solicitor to act for the insured in a suit by a passenger injured in an accident while in the insured's vehicle. Under the policy, the insurer was to have "control and conduct" of any court proceedings. Without the insured's consent, the solicitor admitted partial responsibility on the insured's part for the accident. The insured, offended by the admission since he was confident of his lack of fault, demanded access to all the relevant papers from the solicitor, who demurred, arguing that he owed no duties as agent to the insured. Held, the solicitor had acted in the litigation as agent of the insured and was obliged to let him have access to the papers.[132] Even in cases where a solicitor's contract is with the insurer rather than the insured, the solicitor acts as agent for the insured in the litigation.[133]

---

[128] *Henderson v Merrett Syndicates Ltd* [1995] 2 A.C. 145. See also *Aiken v Stewart Wrightson Agency* [1995] 1 W.L.R. 1281.

[129] *Prentis Donegan & Partners Ltd v Leeds & Leeds Co Inc* [1998] 2 Lloyd's Rep. 326; distinguishing *Velos Group Ltd v Harbour Insurance Services Ltd* [1977] 2 Lloyd's Rep. 461. See also *Heath Lambert Ltd v Sociedad de Corretaje de Seguros* [2003] EWHC 2269 (Comm); [2004] 1 Lloyd's Rep. 495.

[130] *Bath v Standard Land Co Ltd* [1911] 1 Ch. 618.

[131] *Markel International Insurance Co Ltd v Surety Guarantee Consultants Ltd* [2008] EWHC 1135 (Comm); affirmed [2009] EWCA Civ 790.

[132] *Re Crocker* [1936] 1 Ch. 696.

[133] *Nicholson v Icepak Coolstores Ltd* [1999] 3 N.Z.L.R. 475 (HC) at 492–493.

CHAPTER 6

DUTIES OF AGENTS TOWARDS THEIR PRINCIPALS

INTRODUCTORY NOTE

In legal systems where agency is fragmented into certain typical sorts of activ-   **6-001**
ity, it may be possible to lay down fairly detailed rules as to the duties of agents
towards their principals. The immense breadth of the agency concept at common
law means that it is not easy to do so in a general work on agency.[1] Many agents
work under written contracts which contain detailed provisions as to the agent's duties, and perhaps specify the circumstances in which the principal can terminate the
contract for breach by the agent. They may contain provisions which require to be
measured against the rules relating to contracts in restraint of trade, and also
considered in the light of EC law.[2] The same is true of distributorship contracts.[3]
Some agents, such as estate agents, are subject to a degree of statutory regulation.[4]
Other persons exercising agency powers may be parties to contracts of employment and entitled to the protections of employment law.[5] Beyond this, the question is one of interpretation. Where the contract is silent, the court may be willing
to find implied terms: although the English courts are traditionally reluctant to do
this, there are circumstances where they will do so.[6] But often the question is one
of interpretation of an oral transaction. And some agents, e.g. canvassing agents,
undertake no duties. They are simply entitled to certain contractual rights if they
do certain things, though they may be liable for various forms of misconduct.[7]
Again, some persons to whom the term "agent" may be applied act gratuitously:
there may be difficulties in ascribing a liability to them for acting in a way which
is unsatisfactory to the principal, and even more in holding them liable when they
have undertaken to act but have not done so.

All this means that the common law duties of an agent can only be referred to
in very general terms, which indicate the sorts of way in which an agent may be

---

[1]   *Torre Asset Funding Ltd v The Royal Bank of Scotland Plc* [2013] EWHC 2670 (Ch) at [147].
[2]   For international agents, see R. Christou, *International Agency, Distribution and Licensing Agreements* (6th edn, 2011).
[3]   See, e.g. *Decro-Wall International SA v Practitioners in Marketing Ltd* [1971] 1 W.L.R. 361; *Wickman Machine Tool Sales Ltd v L. Schuler A.G.* [1974] A.C. 235; *Proactive Sports Management Ltd
v Rooney* [2011] EWCA Civ 1444 (exclusive image-marketing agency of eight years' duration at 20
per cent commission found void on grounds of restraint of trade).
[4]   See the Estate Agents Act 1979 (as amended by Enterprise Act 2002); and the Consumers, Estate
Agents and Redress Act 2007 Sch.6. See too the Unfair Terms in Consumer Contracts Regulations
1999, as applied in *Office of Fair Trading v Foxtons Ltd* [2009] EWCA Civ 288; [2010] 1 W.L.R.
663.
[5]   See Freedland (ed), *The Contract of Employment* (2016).
[6]   See *Liverpool City Council v Irwin* [1977] A.C. 239; *J. & H. Ritchie Ltd v Lloyd Ltd* [2007] UKHL
9; [2007] 1 Lloyd's Rep. 544; *Att.-Gen. of Belize v Belize Telecom Ltd* [2009] UKPC 10; [2009] 1
W.L.R. 1988; and *Mediterranean Salvage & Towage Ltd v Seamar Trading & Commerce Inc* [2009]
EWCA Civ 531; *Chitty on Contracts* (33rd edn), Ch.14; below, para.7-001.
[7]   See above, para.1-020 onwards; below, para.7-016.

held in breach of duty. An obvious example is the duty not to exceed authority, where the agent is under a duty to make good to the principal loss caused by so doing. Generally speaking, an agent is expected to know the scope of the mandate conferred and adhere to it. Otherwise, however, the agent does not normally warrant success in what the agent does, but only to use reasonable endeavours; but there can be cases where strict liability is undertaken.[8] In one area a specialised body of law has developed, and is still developing. This is the law relating to the fiduciary obligations of agents, which connects with the rules of equity applicable to express trustees. The principles of fiduciary obligation are not confined to agents, but apply to agents among others, because of the special trust which is reposed in them. It is only in this area that it can be said that special rules on the duties of agents towards their principals can be identified. Sometimes the fiduciary obligations give rise to implied terms in the contract. But often they are to be regarded as operating independently of contract.

1. Duties of Performance

Article 36

Agent's Duty to Perform Undertaking

6-002   An agent is bound to act in accordance with the terms of the authority conferred, and to perform what the agent has legally undertaken to do.[9]

Comment

6-003   This rule is certainly fundamental to every contractual agency. Subject as always to the express provisions of the contract, an agent appointed under contract must comply with the terms of what has been agreed, and is in breach of contract if the agent's authority is exceeded on the one hand, or there is a failure to act on directions on the other.[10] But even agents who act gratuitously are expected to adhere to their instructions, and may be found to have assumed a legal responsibility to their principal to do so. So, they may be liable for money had and received if they disperse the principal's money without mandate,[11] or otherwise liable in tort, as discussed below. Where the agent has been entrusted with the principal's money and holds it as trustee then any disbursement that is inconsistent with the mandate will

---

[8]   e.g. *Harlow & Jones Ltd v P.J. Walker Shipping and Transport Ltd* [1986] 2 Lloyd's Rep. 141 (freight forwarder warrants freight rate). cf. *Martin v JRC Commercial Mortgages Plc* [2012] EWCA Civ 63 (fixed-fee mortgage broker undertook duty of care but did not warrant success in obtaining a mortgage for client).

[9]   cf. *Restatement, Third*, §§ 8.07 and 8.09; see too DeMott, in *Philosophical Foundations of Fiduciary Law* (Gold and Miller eds, 2014), Ch.16. As to a company director's duty to act in accordance with a company's constitution, see Companies Act 2006 s.171.

[10]   See Illustrations; *Smith v Lascelles* (1788) 2 T.R. 187; *Comber v Anderson* (1808) 1 Camp. 523; *Barber v Taylor* (1839) 5 M. & W. 527; *L.S. Harris Trustees Ltd v Power Packing Services (Hermit Road) Ltd* [1970] 2 Lloyd's Rep. 65; *Restatement, Third*, § 8.07. As to commercial agents in the technical sense, see Commercial Agents (Council Directive) Regulations 1993 reg.3(1); and para.11-024, below.

[11]   *Martin v Pont* [1993] 3 N.Z.L.R. 25.

normally also involve a breach of trust.[12] Equity provides its own remedies for breach of trust, but these in many respects parallel those of contract.

Failure to adhere to instructions is by definition a breach of duty and in principle results in strict liability for resulting loss. How such liability is worked out in terms of remedy is somewhat controversial. Recent case law at equity has concluded that if the principal would have suffered the same or other loss had the instructions been correctly carried out, this may result in no recovery.[13] It remains arguable that these cases are explicable on their facts, and in a clear case of deviation involving the expenditure of the principal's money, a principal may simply be able to call for the return of the money, in an action for money had and received or for an account at equity.[14] Were, for instance, an agent to send the principal's money to the wrong person, it would ordinarily be inappropriate to permit the agent to attempt to show that the money would have been lost even had it been sent to the correct person. Where the agent uses personal money in misconceived pursuit of the principal's affairs, the principal may simply be able to disown the agent's action.[15] A principal who finds that the agent has deviated from instructions may nonetheless have to take the point early and not wait to see how things turn out—such a failure occurred in what is now the leading case in this area, *AIB Group (UK) Plc v Mark Redler & Co Solicitors*.[16] A failure to adhere to instructions may also be capable of being cured if the agent can rescue the situation before the principal terminates the agent's mandate and calls for return of any money provided the agent.[17] It is further possible that upon construction of the agency contract an apparently absolute obliga-

---

[12] See *Re Collie, Ex p. Adamson* (1878) 8 Ch.D. 807 at 819; *British America Elevator Co Ltd v Bank of British North America* [1919] A.C. 658 (PC); *Anguilla v Estate and Trust Agencies Ltd* [1938] A.C. 624 (PC) at 637; *Re Dawson (dec'd)* [1966] 2 N.S.W.R. 211 at 244; *Alexander v Perpetual Trustees WA Ltd* (2003) 216 C.L.R. 109 at [44], [47] and [59]; *Madoff Securities International Ltd v Raven* [2013] EWHC 3147 (Comm) at [291]; *Libertarian Investments Ltd v Hall* [2013] HKCFA 94; 16 H.K.C.F.A.R. 681 at [168]; *Allied Irish Bank v Maguire & Co* [2016] IESC 57; *P&P Property Ltd v Owen White and Catlin LLP* [2018] EWCA Civ 1082; ; [2019] Ch. 273. See also Rt Hon. Lord Millett (1998) 114 L.Q.R. 214 at 226–227; Watts [2016] L.M.C.L.Q. 118; Penner (2014) 8 J. Eq. 202; Conaglen (2016) 40 Melb. U.L.R. 126. For further discussion of the position in equity see below, para.6-043.

[13] *Target Holdings Ltd v Redferns* [1996] A.C. 421; *AIB Group (UK) Plc v Mark Redler & Co Solicitors* [2014] UKSC 58; [2015] A.C. 1503.

[14] See, in addition to the cases in fn.12 above, *Re Lands Allotment Co* [1894] 1 Ch. 616 at 638 (director who innocently pay dividends in breach of dividend rules strictly liable); *H.M. Revenue and Customs v Holland* [2010] UKSC 51; [2010] 1 W.L.R. 2793 at [45]; *Lloyds Tsb Bank Plc v Markandan & Uddin (A Firm)* [2012] EWCA Civ 65; [2012] 2 All E.R. 884 (solicitor, victim of fraud, commits breach of trust in releasing funds in breach of mandate); *Main v Giambrone & Law (a firm)* [2017] EWCA Civ 1193 (noted P. Davies, "Equitable compensation and the SAAMCO principle" (2018) 134 L.Q.R. 165); *Interactive Technology Corp Ltd v Ferster* [2018] EWCA Civ 1594 at [16]. cf. *Auden McKenzie (Pharma Division) Ltd v Patel* [2019] EWCA Civ 2291 (noted S. Worthington, "More Disquiet with Equitable Compensation" [2020] C.L.J. 220; P. Turner and L. Ho, "Misapplication of Company Assets: a Moving Target" [2020] L.M.C.L.Q. 354).

[15] *Barclays Bank Ltd v WJ Simms Son & Cooke (Southern) Ltd* [1980] Q.B. 677; *Agip (Africa) Ltd v Jackson* [1990] Ch. 265 at 283–294, per Millett J; [1991] Ch. 547 (CA) at 561–562.

[16] *AIB Group (UK) Plc v Mark Redler & Co Solicitors* [2014] UKSC 58; [2015] A.C. 1503, Illustration 5.

[17] See *Target Holdings Ltd v Redferns* [1996] A.C. 421.

tion may be found to be one only to exercise reasonable care and skill.[18] In some circumstances too, relief from liability may be available under statute.[19]

Consistently with the principles of this Article, a solicitor who is retained to conduct an action and instructed not to compromise it will be in breach of contract if the solicitor does compromise it without the client's instructions, although both solicitor and counsel may consider that a settlement is in the client's best interests and strongly advise in favour of such a course.[20] Barristers are in a similar position.[21] On the other hand, even if the principal's instructions are foolhardy, the agent must carry out what has been instructed.[22] Agents may sometimes be under a duty to warn and advise,[23] but if such advice is ignored, they are bound to carry out the terms of the agency contract and may be liable to their principal for breach of contract if they do not do so.[24]

In some circumstances at least, an agent may also be liable to the principal in tort if the agent commits the principal to a contract or other obligation without, or in excess of, authority. In *OBG Ltd v Allan*,[25] Lord Hoffmann in dicta was of the opinion that liability could arise only in contract in such circumstances. However, it seems likely that those who assume the role of agent without having a contract with the principal (such as minors, gratuitous agents (dealt with below), and dismissed former agents) could be liable to their principals in tort for acting without or beyond mandate.[26] Contractual agents may not automatically be immune from the same liability. Many of the details of such liability remain to be worked out.

---

[18] *Bristol and West Building Society v Mothew* [1998] Ch. 1 at 24; *Davisons Solicitors (a firm) v Nationwide Building Society* [2012] EWCA Civ 1626 at [57].

[19] See s.61 of the Trustee Act 1925: *Davisons Solicitors (a firm) v Nationwide Building Society* [2012] EWCA Civ 1626; *Santander UK Plc v R.A. Legal Solicitors* [2014] EWCA Civ 183; *Purrunsing v A'Court & Co (a firm)* [2016] EWHC 789 (Ch); [2016] 4 W.L.R. 81. cf. *P&P Property Ltd v Owen White and Catlin LLP* [2018] EWCA Civ 1082; [2019] Ch. 273; and in relation to directors, the Companies Act 2006 s.1157.

[20] *Fray v Voules* (1859) 1 E. & E. 839; *Butler v Knight* (1867) L.R. 2 Ex. 109; *The Hermione* [1922] P. 162; *Apatu v Peach Prescott & Jamieson* [1985] 1 N.Z.L.R. 50 at 64; *Amalgamated Metal Corp Plc v Wragge & Co (A Firm)* [2011] EWHC 887 (Comm); [2011] P.N.L.R. 24 (damages awarded on loss of chance of better settlement). As to a solicitor's apparent authority to compromise a suit, see Article 30, Illustration 5.

[21] *Swinfen v Lord Chelmsford* (1860) 5 H. & N. 890; *Neale v Gordon Lennox* [1902] A.C. 465; cf. *Harvey v Phillips* (1956) 95 C.L.R. 235. See too *Kendirjian v Lepore* [2017] HCA 13 at [15].

[22] See *R.H. Deacon & Co Ltd v Varga* (1972) 30 D.L.R. (3d) 653; affirmed 41 D.L.R. (3d) 767n (stockbroker); Illustration 4; *Volkers v Midland Doherty* (1985) 17 D.L.R. (4th) 343, Illustration 4 to Article 39.

[23] Especially where there is a fiduciary obligation (see Article 43): *Clark Boyce v Mouat* [1994] 1 A.C. 428 at 437; *Haira v Burbery Mortgage Finance and Savings Ltd* [1995] 3 N.Z.L.R. 396 at 406. Frequently, however, it will be concluded that giving advice is not part of the agent's undertaking: see e.g. *Eric Preston Pty Ltd v Euroz Securities Ltd* [2011] FCAFC 11 at [160] (stockbroker no duty to advise); *Cherney v Neuman* [2011] EWHC 2156 (Ch) at [108] (solicitor no duty to advise on commercial merits of transaction, but duty to reveal known facts relevant to transaction that client had entered into).

[24] See *Boyce v Rendells* [1983] E.G.D. 26 at 37.

[25] *OBG Ltd v Allan* [2007] UKHL 21; [2008] 1 A.C. 1 at [93] (noted Watts (2007) 123 L.Q.R. 519). cf. *Brown v Boorman* (1844) 11 Cl. & Fin. 1 (broker handing over goods without securing payment, in breach of instructions, is held liable in tort)); *Kendirjian v Lepore* [2017] HCA 13; (2017) 259 C.L.R. 275 at [15].

[26] For the range of torts potentially applicable in this context, see Watts (2009) 17 Torts L.J. 100 at 120. See too *Markel International Insurance Co Ltd v Surety Guarantee Consultants Ltd* [2008] EWHC 1135 (Comm); affirmed [2009] EWCA Civ 790 (liability of sub-agents for conspiracy to defraud in writing contracts in excess of authority). As to the possibility of tortious liability for lack of care and skill in the exercise of due authority, see below, para.6-018.

Where, for example, an ex-agent deliberately exploits lingering apparent authority it seems likely that any carelessness on the principal's part in allowing an appearance of authority could not reduce the extent of the agent's liability.[27] Where the agent purports to pass title to the principal's property in breach of instructions, even if only by mistake, the agent and the recipient may be liable in conversion,[28] and, in the case of money, in breach of trust, as seen above.

Onus of proof The question as to who as between principal and (putative) agent   **6-004**
bears the onus of proving absence, or breach, of mandate is unclear. The general
principle is that the party asserting a proposition bears the onus of proof,[29] but it is
arguable that proof that one's legal position has been changed coupled with an allegation that the defendant effected the change without authority is sufficient to shift
the burden to the defendant to prove authority to do so. Where the agent has paid
out the principal's money, again the onus is on the agent properly to account for
such dispositions.[30]

Exceeding authority: apparent authority and ratification Sometimes an   **6-005**
unauthorised act of the agent may bind the principal. This occurs where the agent
has apparent, though no actual, authority, viz. the agent appears to a reasonable third
party to have authority[31]; and when the principal chose to ratify an act done on the
principal's behalf without authority.[32] In such cases the question may arise as to
whether the agent is liable to the principal for exceeding authority. In the case of
apparent authority the matter seems fairly clear in relation to contractual agencies;
on principle, if the agent has caused loss to the principal by exceeding authority,
the agent must answer for it.[33] As seen above, liability may also arise in tort and
equity.

The second case, that of ratification, is perhaps more arguable, inasmuch as the
principal has chosen to ratify when it need not have done so, and there is authority
by way of general dicta that ratification validates an unauthorised act for all
purposes.[34] There can however obviously be circumstances where a principal ratifies, not because it wishes to do so but because it finds it commercially expedient
or even essential. In such a case it must be asked whether, while ratifying the

---

[27] See *Standard Chartered Bank v Pakistan National Shipping Corp (No.2)* [2002] UKHL 43; [2003]
1 A.C. 959.
[28] *Bishop v Shillito* (1819) note to 2 Barn. & Ald. 327; *Solloway v McLaughlin* [1938] A.C. 247; *Bennett v Goodwin* (2005) 62 A.T.R. 515; *J.S. Brooksbank & Co (Australasia) Ltd v EXFTX Ltd* (2009)
10 N.Z.C.L.C. 264,520 (goods mistakenly released by agent in breach of instructions).
[29] *Joseph Constantine Steamship Line Ltd v Imperial Smelting Corp Ltd* [1942] A.C. 154 at 174; and
see *Amalgamated Metal Corp Plc v Wragge & Co (A Firm)* [2011] EWHC 887 (Comm) at [90]
where it was assumed that the principal bore the burden of proving lack of mandate in a solicitor.
[30] *GHLM Trading Ltd v Maroo* [2012] EWHC 61 (Ch). See further, Article 51. In relation to the onus
of proof of loss following a breach of trust or breach of fiduciary obligation, see below, para.6-043.
[31] See Article 72.
[32] See Articles 13–20.
[33] cf. *Papé v Westacott* [1894] 1 Q.B. 272; *Thompson v Howley* [1977] 1 N.Z.L.R. 16; *Restatement,
Third*, § 8.09. He may also sometimes commit a crime by so doing: see *R. v Charles* [1977] A.C.
177. The view to the contrary expressed in *Great Atlantic Insurance Co v Home Insurance Co* [1981]
2 Lloyd's Rep. 219 at 222 (noted [1982] J.B.L. 39), was strongly criticised by Mance LJ, dissenting, in *OBG Ltd v Allan* [2005] EWCA Civ 106; [2005] Q.B. 762 at [88].
[34] e.g. *Wilson v Tunman and Fretson* (1843) 6 M. & G. 236 at 242.

contract, the principal has waived the agent's breach of duty. "Often the facts will lead to both ratification and exoneration, but not always."[35]

6-006 **Wrongful resignation or refusal to carry out instructions** A principal cannot force an agent to continue to act, if the agent resigns or otherwise refuses to carry out instructions. This reflects the general position that the law will not force parties to maintain a personal relationship.[36] However, an agent who resigns or declines to carry out instructions may well be in breach of contract. Some agents in resigning may also be found to have acted in breach of professional obligations.[37]

Illustrations

6-007 (1) A was instructed by P to sell certain shares when the funds reached 85 or more. It was held that he was bound to sell when the funds reached 85, and had no discretion to wait until they went higher.[38]

(2) A, an auctioneer, was instructed by P to sell some furniture for ready money only. A sold the furniture to X, taking a bill of exchange from him. A was liable to P for the proceeds of sale on X's default.[39]

(3) A foreign merchant (P) sent a bill of lading to his English correspondent (A) with instructions to insure the goods and sell them for P's account. A did not wish to accept P's instructions, but, with the intention of safeguarding P's interests by getting the goods insured, indorsed the bill of lading over to X, who insured the goods. A was held liable to P, because, having accepted the bill of lading by indorsing it, he was bound to carry out P's instructions in full.[40]

(4) A company was formed for the purpose of purchasing the goodwill and assets of a partnership. At the time the partnership was deeply in debt, and shortly after the purchase the whole business failed. The company brought proceedings against one of its directors for negligence in purchasing the partnership when he knew it was in difficulties. Held, an agent who was expressly authorised to do an act which was itself imprudent, and one which the principal ought not, as a matter of prudence, to have authorised, was not liable for the consequences of doing it. The director, as an agent of the

---

[35] *Suncorp Insurance and Finance v Milano Assacurazioni SpA* [1993] 2 Lloyd's Rep. 225 at 235, per Waller J; *Ing Re (UK) Ltd v R & V Versicherung AG* [2006] EWHC 1544 (Comm); [2006] 2 All E.R. (Comm) 870 at [152]. See above, para.2-094. See also Mechem, *Treatise on the Law of Agency* (2nd edn), §§ 492–493; *Mineworkers' Union v Brodrick* 1948 (2) S.A.L.R. 959 at 979. See also Comment to Article 20. Sometimes the agent may be protected by an exclusion clause. In *Darlington Futures Ltd v Delco Australia Pty Ltd* (1986) 161 C.L.R. 500 an agent who by unauthorised commodity transactions caused loss to the client was not protected by one form of words in the contract but under another could limit his liability to $100. The general statements in the case merit approval, but the final result seems surprising.

[36] The position is the same where a principal wrongly terminates an agent's position and with it the agent's authority: see below, Article 59. See also paras 10-004 and 10-023, below.

[37] See, for example, former Solicitors' Code of Conduct 2007 r.2.01(2). The current rules are less prescriptive: see *Solicitors Regulation Authority Standards and Regulations* 2019.

[38] *Bertram, Armstrong & Co v Godfray* (1830) 1 Knapp 381. See also *Dufresne v Hutchinson* (1810) 3 Taunt. 117.

[39] *Ferrers v Robins* (1835) 2 C.M. & R. 152. See also *Brown v Boorman* (1844) 11 Cl. & Fin. 1; *Williams v Evans* (1866) L.R. 1 Q.B. 352; and *Westerman Realty Ltd v McKinstry* (2007) 8 N.Z.C.P.R. 553 (auctioneer sells on a tax-inclusive basis when instructions were tax-exclusive).

[40] *Corlett v Gordon* (1813) 3 Camp. 472. See also *Smith v Lascelles* (1788) 2 T.R. 187.

company, had been expressly authorised to buy the partnership, and was not liable for having done so.[41]

(5) Solicitors acting for a lender are instructed to pay off an existing mortgage before releasing the balance of the £3.3 million loan to the borrower. They overlook a debt of £300,000 secured by the existing mortgage, and thereby fail to obtain a first mortgage for the lender. The lender is made aware of the error. The borrower subsequently defaults on the whole loan and the security proves very inadequate. The solicitors are not liable for all the lender's loss even though none of the funds should have been released without a first mortgage being in place. They are liable for approximately £300,000.[42]

Article 37

CONTRACTUAL AGENT'S DUTY TO OBEY FURTHER INSTRUCTIONS GIVEN BY PRINCIPAL

In the title delete the word "Further".

(1) Subject to any special circumstances indicating the contrary, the agent is bound to obey all lawful and reasonable instructions of the principal in relation to the manner in which the agent carries out the mandate conferred.   **6-008**

(2) In determining what is reasonable the court will have regard to all the circumstances of the case, including the nature of the agency and the customs, practices and ethics of the business to be undertaken by the agent.[43]

Comment

Wording to similar effect as the above has appeared in all previous editions of this work, and from the time of the introduction of Comments to the Articles it has been said that although there is little authority for the proposition contained in the Article, it is almost self-evident.[44] In some ways it must be; but the lack of illustrative case law perhaps derives from the limited ways in which issues are likely to arise. The internal agency relationship, usually but not always a contract, is based on the grant of authority to the agent, accompanied by a duty to indemnify and reimburse the agent against the consequences of so doing (as explained in Article 62, though not necessarily based on a contractual implication). This is the only implication in an arrangement for representation that has no further features. The principal's control over the agent is based on the principal's powers not to grant authority, to limit the authority and to withdraw or revoke authority (as explained in Article 118). In general there is no other implication as regards authority in such a bare agency arrangement, and this right is reciprocal to the agent's duty not to exceed the authority conferred, which (subject to any contract term) can be translated into a duty to compensate the principal for loss caused if the agent does (as explained in Article 36).   **6-009**

It has been held that a principal can give directions to an agent in relation to a

---

[41] *Overend, Gurney & Co v Gibb* (1872) L.R. 5 H.L. 480; and see *Commerce Realty Ltd v Olenyk* (1957) 8 D.L.R. (2d) 60.

[42] *AIB Group (UK) Plc v Mark Redler & Co Solicitors* [2014] UKSC 58; [2015] A.C. 1503.

[43] cf. *Restatement, Third*, § 8.09.

[44] DeMott, in *Philosophical Foundations of Fiduciary Law* (Gold and Miller eds, 2014).

specific matter, even where the agent holds a broad power of attorney.[45] Similarly, it has been held that the sole director of a company can orally override general instructions to a bank that it is to act only on written instructions.[46]

Whether or not an agent must obey new instructions in other respects, for example as regards the method by which the agent carries out the mandate, cannot always be determined by considering whether the agent's authority has been modified or withdrawn.[47] Any further duty to accept instructions outside the sphere of existing authority must be based on the interpretation of some other relationship that may exist between agent and principal, for example a contract of employment, or, to take a random example in the sphere of independent contractors, a contract made by a shipper with a freight forwarder.[48] Even in that context, instructions which involve the performance of an illegal or void act normally need not be obeyed.[49] However, an agent would not normally be excused from carrying out the principal's directions on the basis of a mere suspicion that the principal is engaged in furthering an illegal object; some agents, such as banks in relation to the operation of their customers' accounts, may have even less discretion to decline to follow instructions.[50] In the case of a professional person the agent will be bound to a considerable extent by the rules and ethical standards of the profession and could not be required to perform an act which was contrary to those rules or standards.[51]

For discussion of when a junior agent should decline to follow the instructions of a senior agent, see above, para.5-016.

Article 38

AMBIGUOUS INSTRUCTIONS

6-010   Where the principal's instructions are ambiguous (viz. capable of bearing two or more interpretations), if the agent fairly and honestly assumes them to bear one of

---

[45] *Morrell v Workers Savings & Loan Bank* [2007] UKPC 3 at [10]; *Day v Day* [2013] EWCA Civ 280; [2014] Ch. 114 at [26]. See too *Duffy Kennedy Pty Ltd v Galileo Miranda Nominee Pty Ltd* [2020] NSWCA 25 at [100]; and more generally, para.3-009, above.

[46] *Hill Street Services Co Ltd v National Westminster Bank Plc* [2007] EWHC 2379 (Ch) at [17].

[47] For the general significance of control, see above, para.1-018. As to the difference between agents and trustees on this issue, see above, para.1-029.

[48] See cases on serious breach by an agent, below, para.7-050, and in general above, para.1-018.

[49] See e.g. *Cohen v Kittell* (1889) 22 Q.B.D. 680 (failure to make bets): *Donovan v Invicta Airways Ltd* [1970] 1 Lloyd's Rep. 486; *Association of British Travel Agents Ltd v British Airways Plc* [2000] 1 Lloyd's Rep. 169. If the instructions involve performing an illegal act, the agent may not be liable if he carries them out negligently: *T. Cheshire v Vaughan Bros & Co* [1920] 3 K.B. 240, where an agent instructed to effect a ppi policy failed to disclose a material fact. But see *Fraser v B.N. Furman (Productions) Ltd* [1967] 1 W.L.R. 898; *Everett v Hogg, Robinson & Gardner Mountain (Insurance) Ltd* [1973] 2 Lloyd's Rep. 217; *L.B. Martin Construction Ltd v Gagliardi* (1978) 91 D.L.R. (3d) 393. See further below, para.6-023.

[50] *Westpac New Zealand Ltd v Map & Associates Ltd* [2011] 3 N.Z.L.R. 751 (NZSC) (bank wrongly declining to transfer funds to customer's order); *Stoffel & Co v Grondona* [2018] EWCA Civ 2031.

[51] Thus a stockbroker was only required to carry out a sale of shares in accordance with the rules of the Stock Exchange and could not be required to act other than in accordance with those rules: *Hawkins v Pearse* (1903) 9 Com.Cas. 87; *Cunliffe-Owen v Teather & Greenwood* [1967] 1 W.L.R. 1421. A company liquidator is similarly an agent subject to external duties: *Dunphy v Sleepyhead Manufacturing Co Ltd* [2007] 3 N.Z.L.R. 602 at [22].

those interpretations and acts accordingly, the agent will not be in breach of contract by so acting.[52]

Comment

This is certainly a general principle of the law of agency, and can be applied **6-011** elsewhere.[53] But it must necessarily have limits. If the agent realised or ought to have realised that the instructions were ambiguous, the agent ought, if the circumstances so permit, to seek clarification from the principal before starting to act.[54]

Article 39

CONTRACTUAL AGENT'S DUTIES OF DILIGENCE

(1) Subject to circumstances indicating the contrary, a term will normally be **6-012** implied into a contract of agency that the agent should carry out the mandate with reasonable dispatch. What is reasonable will depend on all the circumstances of the case.[55] In relation to agents who are not employees, a similar implied term may arise under the Supply of Goods and Services Act 1982 s.14.[56]

(2) If an agent appointed by a contract cannot, or will not, carry out the mandate when instructed or within a reasonable time the agent must inform the principal of that fact.[57]

---

[52] *Ireland v Livingston* (1872) L.R. 5 H.L. 395, Illustration 1 to Article 24; *Comber v Anderson* (1808) 1 Camp. 523; *Bertram, Armstrong & Co v Godfrey* (1830) 1 Knapp. 381, Illustration 1 to Article 36; *Boden v French* (1851) 10 C.B. 886; *Cobridge SS Co Ltd v Bucknall SS Lines Ltd* (1910) 15 Com.Cas. 138; *Weigall & Co v Runciman & Co* (1916) 85 L.J.K.B. 1187, Illustration 3 to Article 26; *Pariente v Lubbock* (1856) 8 De G.M. & G. 5; *Lindsay, Gracie & Co v Barter & Co* (1885) 2 T.L.R. 4; *Loring v Davis* (1886) 32 Ch.D. 5; *Miles v Haslehurst & Co* (1906) 12 Com.Cas. 83; *International Paper Co v Spicer* (1906) 4 C.L.R. 739 at 751; *Larsen v Anglo-American Oil Co Ltd* (1924) 20 Lloyd's Rep. 40 at 67; *Brown & Gracie Ltd v F.W. Green & Co Pty Ltd* [1960] 1 Lloyd's Rep. 289. And see in general Article 26.

[53] See *Woodhouse A.C. Israel Cocoa Ltd SA v Nigerian Produce Marketing Co* [1972] A.C. 741; *Miles v Haslehurst & Co* (1906) 12 Com.Cas. 83; *Veljkovic v Vrybergen* [1985] V.R. 419 at 424.

[54] See the *Woodhouse A.C. Israel Cocoa Ltd SA v Nigerian Produce Marketing Co* [1972] A.C. 741 at 772; *European Asian Bank AG v Punjab and Sind Bank* [1983] 1 W.L.R. 652 at 656; *Veljkovic v Vrybergen* [1985] V.R. 419 at 424 (request to "get insurance"); *Horsell International Pty Ltd v Divetwo Pty Ltd* [2013] NSWCA 368 at [238].

[55] *Varden v Parker* (1798) 2 Esp. 710; *Barber v Taylor* (1839) 5 M. & W. 527, Illustration 1; *Turpin v Bilton* (1843) 5 M. & G. 455; *Potter v Equitable Bank* (1921) 8 Ll. L.Rep. 291 at 332; *World Transport Agency Ltd v Royte (England) Ltd* [1957] 1 Lloyd's Rep. 381; *Tom Hoskins Plc v EMW Law (A Firm)* [2010] EWHC 479 (Ch) (liability for consequential business losses as well as losses on transaction); *Equitas Ltd v Walsham Brothers & Co Ltd* [2013] EWHC 3264 (Comm) at [47] (duty to account timeously for moneys received).

[56] *Equitas Ltd v Walsham Brothers & Co Ltd* [2013] EWHC 3264 (Comm) at [51].

[57] *Smith v Lascelles* (1788) 2 T.R. 187; *Prince v Clark* (1823) 1 B. & C. 186; *Callander v Oelrichs* (1838) 5 Bing.N.C. 58, Illustration 2; *Smith v Price* (1862) 2 F. & F. 748; *Cassaboglou v Gibb* (1883) 11 Q.B.D. 797; *Tallerman v Rose* (1886) 15 L.T. 450; *Salvesen & Co v Rederi A/B Nordstjernan* [1905] A.C. 302; *Mark Lever & Co Ltd v W. Wingate & Johnson Ltd* (1950) 84 Lloyd's Rep. 156; *John Koch Ltd v C. & H. Products Ltd* [1956] 1 Lloyd's Rep. 59; *Havas v Carter*, 515 P. 2d 397 (1975); *Fine's Flowers Ltd v General Accident Ass. Co of Canada* (1977) 81 D.L.R. (3d) 139 at 149 (Illustration 3); *Volkers v Midland Doherty* (1985) 17 D.L.R. (4th) 393, Illustration 4; *Youell v Bland*

Comment

6-013   The principle expressed in this Article is part of the agent's duty to exercise the required degree of care in and about the performance of the mandate. It is also a general rule of contract that where no time for performance is stated, the contract must be performed within a reasonable time having regard to all the circumstances of the case.[58] It has been said that a stipulation as to the time of performance will prima facie not be held to be of the essence of a contract.[59] These and similar expressions do not mean that a time stipulation is merely a target date: if it is appropriately expressed, failure to comply would give rise to an action in damages.[60] The expression simply means that the contract cannot be treated as discharged for breach of that term as such. And the contract may expressly state[61] or be interpreted on the basis[62] that time is of the essence. Finally, in the case of the obligation to complete in transactions regarding land, and perhaps other obligations, and possibly outside land transactions also, one party can give notice requiring performance within a reasonable time, and failure to comply with this may entitle that party to treat the contract as discharged.[63]

6-014   **Estate and other canvassing agents**   On the traditional analysis, the normal contract of an estate agent is unilateral, i.e. the agent only earns commission by performing the act entitling the agent to it. Until then the agent is under no duty to act. An agent is only under such a duty if a bilateral contract can be inferred, which will normally be so if the agent is a "sole" or "exclusive" agent.[64] The same reasoning may be applied to other canvassing agents acting on commission. If this analysis is correct, the estate agent acting, or failing to act, in respect of such a contract cannot be liable under the reasoning given in this and the Article immediately following. An assertion of this sort was described in one case as "startling",[65] but no other reasoning was offered and the proposition is consistent with the assumptions behind this type of contract. But such an agent may be liable if a collateral contract can be inferred and the omission or conduct in question is a breach of it;

Welch & Co Ltd (the Superhulls Cover case) (No.2) [1990] 2 Lloyd's Rep. 431 at 446–447.

[58]   See, e.g. *Pantland Hick v Raymond & Reid* [1893] A.C. 22; *Sims & Co v Midland Ry Co* [1913] 1 K.B. 103; *Hartwells of Oxford Ltd v BMTA* [1951] Ch. 50; *Monkland v Jack Barclay Ltd* [1951] 2 K.B. 252.

[59]   *United Scientific Holdings Ltd v Burnley BC* [1978] A.C. 904 at 940; Law of Property Act 1925 s.41. See *Chitty on Contracts* (33rd edn), para.21-011 onwards; Treitel, *Law of Contract* (15th edn), paras 18-111 onwards..

[60]   *Raineri v Miles* [1981] A.C. 1050.

[61]   *Steedman v Drinkle* [1916] 1 A.C. 275; *Brickles v Snell* [1916] 2 A.C. 599; *Harold Wood Brick Co v Ferris* [1935] 2 K.B. 198; *Mussen v Van Diemen's Land Co* [1938] Ch. 253.

[62]   See, e.g. *Tilley v Thomas* (1867) L.R. 3 Ch.App. 61; *Tadcaster Tower Brewery v Wilson* [1897] 1 Ch. 705 at 710; *Lock v Bell* [1931] 1 Ch. 35; *Hare v Nicoll* [1966] 2 Q.B. 130. Stipulations as to time in mercantile contracts may well be of the essence: *Bunge Corp v Tradax Export SA* [1981] 1 W.L.R. 711 at 725; but stipulations as to the time of payment are not of the essence in a contract for the sale of goods unless a contrary intention appears from the contract: Sale of Goods Act 1979 s.10.

[63]   See, e.g. *Stickney v Keeble* [1915] A.C. 386; *Finkielkraut v Monohan* [1949] 2 All E.R. 234; *Behzadi v Shaftesbury Hotels Ltd* [1992] Ch. 1; but cf. *Re Olympia & York Canary Wharf Ltd (No.2)* [1993] B.C.C. 159. As to other contracts see *Charles Rickards Ltd v Oppenhaim* [1950] 1 K.B. 616; Treitel, *Law of Contract* (14th edn), para.18-127.

[64]   See Comment to Article 56.

[65]   *Prebble & Co v West* (1969) 211 E.G. 831 at 832, per Edmund Davies LJ.

or in tort, as where the agent gives negligent advice or a negligent valuation,[66] or if the agent can be regarded as having assumed responsibility and not carried through what was assumed[67] (as is also true in the case of gratuitous agents[68]); or sometimes for breach of fiduciary duty.[69]

Dealing for competitors   Whether an agent has undertaken to work full time and solely for the principal plainly turns on the terms of appointment. More difficulty arises as to whether an agent can work for a competitor of the principal. This question also turns on the terms, express or implied, of the contract of appointment. There may be room too for the operation of equitable principles in this context[70]; including the issuing of an injunction prohibiting an employee from working for a competitor.[71] The issues that arise are not peculiar to agents. So, it frequently arises in connection with distributorship contracts whether the distributor is entitled to deal on behalf of the supplier's competitors, and this field is the source of considerable case law. Usually, the matter turns on an express contractual provision, or the inference to be drawn from other contractual provisions. Thus a promise to "push the sale" of a brand of whisky was not complied with by inaction and merely not preferring other brands, and was also broken in the circumstances by soliciting orders for other brands.[72] Where there were no clear terms, the Court of Session held that there is no principle that the agent will not "even in an outside matter" act in such a way as to bring the agent's interests in conflict with the principal's: thus an agent (perhaps a distributor) was entitled to deal also in competing products.[73] But an exclusive licensing and distributorship agreement requiring the agent to "make every endeavour" has been held terminable on the grounds that the agent sold similar products of competitors.[74] In a leading Australian case it was held that there was no term to be implied that a distributor would not do anything "inimical" to the market for the manufacturer's products, since a "best efforts" obligation to distribute them made this unnecessary. But it was also held that it was a breach of contract to defer fulfilling orders for the manufacturer's products in anticipation of fulfilling them personally.[75]

In relation to agents, it has recently been held that the starting point is that agents appointed to sell a type of product are not expected to be acting for competing principals in the same market.[76] On the other hand, in the case of estate agents[77] and

6-015

---

[66] *Kenney v Hall, Pain & Foster* [1976] E.G.D. 629, Illustration 6 to Article 40.
[67] See *Henderson v Merrett Syndicates Ltd* [1995] 2 A.C. 145, per Lord Goff of Chieveley. But this reasoning may not easily extend to pure nonfeasance: below, para.6-029.
[68] Article 42.
[69] See Articles 44–49.
[70] See *Hospital Products Ltd v United States Surgical Corp* (1984) 156 C.L.R. 41, per Mason J; cf. *Cadbury Schweppes Inc v FBI Foods Ltd* [1999] 1 S.C.R. 142; (1999) 167 D.L.R. (4th) 577; and see Article 43 onwards.
[71] See *Sunrise Brokers LLP v Rodgers* [2014] EWCA Civ 1373; [2015] I.C.R. 272.
[72] *B. Davis Ltd v Tooth & Co Ltd* [1937] 4 All E.R. 118. And see *James Shaffer Ltd v Findlay Durham & Brodie* [1953] 1 W.L.R. 106.
[73] *Lothian v Jenolite Ltd*, 1969 S.C. 111.
[74] *Re Arbitration between Deb Chemical Proprietaries Ltd and Dreumex Chemie BV*, QBD, November 2, 1979; European Law Letter, Feb. 1980, p.4.
[75] *Hospital Products Ltd v United States Surgical Corp* (1984) 156 C.L.R. 41; but cf. *Artifakts Design Group Ltd v N.P. Rigg Ltd* [1993] 1 N.Z.L.R. 196.
[76] See *Rossetti Marketing Ltd v Diamond Sofa Co Ltd* [2012] EWCA Civ 1021; [2013] 1 All E.R. (Comm) 308 at [20]; *The Northampton Regional Livestock Centre Co Ltd v Cowling* [2014] EWHC

travel agents,[78] it may be expected that they will be acting for competing principals in the same market. However, a principal should not have to anticipate that an agent might wish to act for parties with opposed interests in the same transaction, and the agent's consequent failure to do the agent's best for a principal is likely to lead to liability in contract, negligence and, at least where disloyalty is present, in equity.[79] It is an unsettled issue whether non-executive company directors may, in the absence of express prohibition, hold office with competing businesses.[80] Executive directors would normally be expected to devote all their time to the one company, and certainly not work for competitors.[81] The duties of disclosure that can arise when certain types of agent are planning to resign and compete with their principal are dealt with elsewhere.[82]

Illustrations

6-016 (1) P instructed A to purchase 150 bales of cotton for P's account and to send him the bill of lading. A failed to release the bill of lading to P for some days after the arrival of the goods in the UK. He was held to have been in breach of contract in failing to send the bill to P within a reasonable time, which was within 24 hours of the arrival of the goods.[83]

(2) P, a merchant in England, instructed A, his correspondent in America, to effect an insurance on certain special terms upon a cargo of wheat to be shipped by P from London to Baltimore. A tried in vain to effect an insurance on the special terms requested and eventually, without informing P, insured on the usual terms. Held that A was in breach of duty in failing to tell P that he could not carry out P's instructions relating to special insurance.[84]

(3) An insurance broker is instructed to obtain "full coverage". He obtains cover

---

30 (QB) at [178], varied on other points [2015] EWCA Civ 651. cf. *One Mail Money Ltd v RIA Financial Services* [2015] EWCA Civ 1084 at [5] (restraint of trade doctrine can in rare circumstances protect liberty of someone still employed by the promisee).

[77] *Kelly v Cooper* [1993] A.C. 205 (PC), Illustration 9 to Article 43; *Colyer Fehr Tallow Pty Ltd v KNZ Australia Pty Ltd* [2011] NSWSC 457 (purchasing agent). See further below, para.6-048. But cf. *JD Wetherspoon Plc v Van De Berg & Co Ltd* [2009] EWHC 639 (Ch) (purchaser's agent found to be precluded from acting for competitors).

[78] See *ACCC v Flight Centre Travel Group Ltd* [2016] HCA 49 (in fact concerned with the principal's rights to compete with its agents in the sale of tickets).

[79] *Hilton v Barker, Booth & Eastwood (a firm)* [2005] 1 W.L.R. 567; *HIH Casualty & General Insurance Ltd v JLT Risk Solutions Ltd* [2007] EWCA Civ 710; [2007] 2 Lloyd's Rep. 278; [2007] 2 All E.R. (Comm) 1106; and *Premium Real Estate Ltd v Stevens* [2009] 2 N.Z.L.R. 384; *The Northampton Regional Livestock Centre Co Ltd v Cowling* [2015] EWCA Civ 651; [2016] 1 B.C.L.C. 431. See further below, para.6-048.

[80] Compare *Mashonaland Exploration Co Ltd v New Mashonaland Exploration Co Ltd* [1891] W.N. 165 with *In Plus Group Ltd v Pyke* [2002] EWCA Civ 370; [2002] 2 B.C.L.C. 201. See too *Links Golf Tasmania Pty Ltd v Sattler* [2012] FCA 634; (2012) 292 A.L.R. 382 at [575] (potential breach recognised but director had resigned before competing business commenced earning revenue); and *Poon Ka Man v Cheng Wai Tao* [2016] HKCFA 23 at [104].

[81] *Hivac v Park Royal Scientific Instruments Ltd* [1946] Ch. 169; *Breitenfeld UK Ltd v Harrison* [2015] EWHC 399 (Ch); [2015] 2 B.C.L.C. 275 at [90] (employees diverting work to their own new business). As to what is a competitor in this context, see *Plumbly v Beatthatquote.com Ltd* [2009] EWHC 321 (QB) at [118]; *Gamatronic (UK) Ltd v Hamilton* [2016] EWHC 2225 (QB) at [95].

[82] See below, para.6-054.

[83] *Barber v Taylor* (1839) 5 M. & W. 527.

[84] *Callander v Oelrichs* (1838) 5 Bing.N.C. 58 (but see the criticism of the case on the question of damages in Duer, *Law and Practice of Marine Insurance* (1845), Vol. 2, pp.222–225). See also *Hood v West End Motor Car Parking Co* [1917] 2 K.B. 38 at 47: "When a person is instructed to procure

for a number of risks but not for those which in fact occurred. He is liable for failure to obtain the cover promised; or alternatively, for failure to warn that he had not obtained it.[85]

(4) A representative of a firm of stockbrokers is instructed at 4.30 p.m. to buy a quantity of designated stock "at the market price first thing in the morning". He accepts the instructions but does not carry them out when he arrives at 7 a.m. because he thinks it more prudent to wait for the arrival of the representative who usually deals with that customer. That representative arrives between 8.30 and 9 a.m., at which time the order is referred to him. But at 8.45 a.m. dealings in the shares are suspended, and when they are resumed the shares have doubled in price. The firm is liable to the client for loss of profits.[86]

Article 40

Contractual Agent's Duty to Exercise Skill and Care

Every agent acting for reward is bound to exercise such skill, care and diligence in the performance of the mandate as is usual or necessary in or for the ordinary or proper conduct of the profession or business in which the agent is employed, or is reasonably necessary for the proper performance of the duties undertaken by the agent.[87] This is subject to the agent's overriding duty to comply strictly with instructions (see Article 37).   **6-017**

Comment

Contract, tort or both?   A gratuitous agent's liability, if any, cannot lie in contract and must clearly lie in tort.[88] Where the agency is contractual, however, it is obvious that the primary action is one for breach of contract. Where what is alleged is negligence, as it often is, the question then arises whether it is possible to sue in tort instead of contract. There may be advantages in doing so, particularly in connection with the running of limitation periods. For in contract time runs from the moment of the breach (but the position is different if there is an ongoing duty of performance); in tort, since the gist of the action is damage, it runs from when damage is suffered.[89] The matter has been one of dispute for a considerable time in common law jurisdictions. For England, it is clear that an action in tort may concurrently lie in some circumstances,[90] with the incidental advantages that this may bring.[91]   **6-018**

---

an insurance he is bound to use reasonable care and skill to effect the policy. If he is unable to procure the policy, he must at once inform his principal of his inability to do so".

[85] *Fine's Flowers v General Accident Co of Canada* (1977) 81 D.L.R. (3d) 139; see also *Youell v Bland Welch & Co Ltd (the Superhulls Cover case) (No.2)* [1990] 2 Lloyd's Rep. 431 (failure to inform assured that reinsurance subject to 48-month cut-off); *Standard Life Assurance Ltd v Oak Dedicated Ltd* [2008] EWHC 222 (Comm); [2008] 2 All E.R. (Comm) 916 at [102] (proffering inadequate wording to underwriter); *Marchand v Jackson* [2012] NZHC 2893.
[86] *Volkers v Midland Doherty* (1985) 17 D.L.R. (4th) 343. See also *R.H. Deacon & Co v Varga* (1972) 30 D.L.R. (3d) 653; affirmed (1973) 41 D.L.R. (4th) 767n.
[87] cf. *Restatement, Third,* § 8.08.
[88] See Article 42.
[89] Some relief is provided by Limitation Act 1980 s.2.
[90] *Henderson v Merrett Syndicates Ltd* [1995] 2 A.C. 145. See also *Midland Bank Trust Co Ltd v Hett,*

6-019   **Degree of skill and care**   The degree of skill and care which may be expected of an agent acting for reward has been stated many times.[92] It is objective but its content and scope are governed by the particular responsibility assumed by the agent.[93] An agent employed for the purpose of effecting a contract between the principal and a third party must use due skill and care in making that contract. Thus, a broker is under a duty not to sell goods at less than the best obtainable price[94] and an estate agent must use reasonable care to ascertain the general solvency of tenants.[95] Agents must use proper care to ensure that contracts they make are binding in law.[96] An agent does not, however, guarantee the contract; the agent's duty is to exercise reasonable care in making it.

Many agents for reward will be professional agents. They must show the skill and care to be expected of those engaged in such a profession.[97] Not only must they be adequately qualified; they must take reasonable care to keep themselves up to date with current developments in their profession.[98] Their duty is not, however, to make no mistakes; it is only to use the required degree of care. In the case of agents other

---

> *Stubbs & Kemp* [1979] Ch. 384, holding a solicitor liable in contract and tort, the reasoning of which was approved in the *Henderson* case; *Equitas Ltd v Walsham Brothers & Co Ltd* [2013] EWHC 3264 (Comm) at [57]; *Berney v Saul (t/a Thomas Saul & Co)* [2013] EWCA Civ 640 (limitation issues); *Maharaj v Johnson* [2015] UKPC 28 (solicitors' negligence); *Central Trust Co v Rafuse* [1986] 2 S.C.R. 147; (1986) 31 D.L.R. (4th) 481 (Canada); *Hill v van Erp* (1997) 188 C.L.R. 159 (Australia); *R.M. Turton & Co v Kerslake & Partners* [2000] 3 N.Z.L.R. 406 (New Zealand); *Wellesley Partners LLP v Withers LLP* [2015] EWCA Civ 1146; *Caliendo v Mishcon De Reya (a firm)* [2016] EWHC 150 (Ch) (solicitor assumed limited duties of care to shareholder of client company); *Golden Belt 1 Sukuk Co BSC(c) v BNP Paribas* [2017] EWHC 3182 (Comm); [2018] Bus. L.R. 816 (duty of care owed by bank intermediary to holders of promissory notes to obtain debtor's signature). See too *Arthur JS Hall & Co v Simons* [2002] 1 A.C. 615 at 688. As to tortious liability for exceeding mandate, see above, para.6-005.

[91] As to the pleading of contributory negligence in contract cases see Treitel, *Law of Contract* (15th edn), para.20-112 onwards; *Chitty on Contracts* (33rd edn), para.26-085; *Forsikringsaktieselskapet Vesta v Butcher* [1986] 2 All E.R. 488; affirmed on other grounds [1989] A.C. 852; *Youell v Bland Welch & Co Ltd (the Superhulls Cover case) (No.2)* [1990] 2 Lloyd's Rep. 431; and *Dunlop Haywards (DHL) Ltd v Barbon Insurance Group Ltd* [2009] EWHC 2900 (Comm); [2010] Lloyd's Rep I.R. 149 (not established against principal, but established by sub-agent against agent).

[92] See, e.g. *Beal v South Devon Ry Co* (1864) 3 H. & C. 337 at 341 for the classical statement which forms the basis of this Article. See also *Boorman v Brown* (1842) 3 Q.B. 511; *Price v Metropolitan House Investment and Agency Co Ltd* (1907) 23 T.L.R. 630; *Commonwealth Portland Cement Co Ltd v Weber, Lohmann & Co Ltd* [1905] A.C. 66, Illustration 8; *Weld-Blundell v Stevens* [1920] A.C. 956; *Whitehouse v Jordan* [1981] 1 W.L.R. 246; *Maynard v West Midlands RHA* [1984] 1 W.L.R. 632.

[93] See *Hughes-Holland v BPE Solicitors* [2017] UKSC 21; [2017] 2 W.L.R. 1029 at [20].

[94] *Solomon v Barker* (1862) 2 F. & F. 726. For other cases see Stoljar, p.274.

[95] *Heys v Tindall* (1861) 1 B. & S. 296, Illustration 5. See also *Carlile Steamship Co v Simpson, Spence & Young* (1926) 25 Lloyd's Rep. 278; *Dampskibsselskab Halla v Catsell & Co* (1928) 30 Lloyd's Rep. 284.

[96] *Grant v Fletcher* (1826) 5 B. & C. 436; *Neilson v James* (1882) 9 Q.B.D. 546; *Scott and Horton v Godfrey* [1901] 2 K.B. 726; *Rainbow v Howkins & Sons* [1904] 2 K.B. 322; *McManus v Fortescue* [1907] 2 K.B. 1.

[97] *Lanphier v Phipos* (1838) 8 C. & P. 475; *Hart and Hodge v Frame, Son & Co* (1839) 6 C. & F. 193; *Lee v Walker* (1872) L.R. 7 C.P. 121; *New Zealand Farmers Cooperative Ltd v National Mortgage and Agency Co of New Zealand Ltd* [1961] N.Z.L.R. 969; *Duchess of Argyll v Beuselinck* [1972] 2 Lloyd's Rep. 172; *Wimpey Construction UK Ltd v Poole* [1984] 2 Lloyd's Rep. 499. See further Article 30.

[98] See *Park v Hammond* (1816) 6 Taunt. 495, Illustration 2; a fortiori a solicitor must take reasonable care to keep himself abreast with changes in the law; *Hurlingham Estates Ltd v Wilde & Partners* [1997] 1 Lloyd's Rep. 525; *Dean v Allin & Watts* [2001] 2 Lloyd's Rep. 249.

than employees, an implied obligation of care and skill may arise under the Supply of Goods and Services Act 1982 s.13.[99]

Where an agent has a conflict of interest in a matter, this will often assist in a finding of a failure to exercise due care.[100] It is obvious enough that agents cannot be responsible for failing to do things that are outside the tasks for which they were retained.[101]

Discretion   Where the agent has a discretion it must be exercised with proper care **6-020** and skill. Thus a solicitor may compromise a case in the absence of instructions to the contrary from the principal, but proper care and skill must be exercised in arranging the compromise.[102] A similar situation may arise where an agent cannot obtain instructions from the principal but some action is required. If the agent acts in a way which the agent reasonably considers to be in the principal's best interests and exercises the proper degree of care no liability should ensue.[103] Where the terms of appointment expressly confer on an agent a "complete discretion" in making decisions as to when and how powers are to be exercised, the terms are generally construed as leading to liability only where the agent has acted with "arbitrariness, capriciousness, perversity [or] irrationality".[104] Similarly, a company's constitution may provide that any validly appointed proxy is entitled to vote on resolutions at the relevant meeting as the proxy thinks fit unless the appointing shareholder expressly directs how the vote should be exercised.[105] Where the relevant powers of action of the agent arise upon default by the principal in its obligations to the agent, again it may be inappropriate to imply duties of care and skill in the exercise of those powers.[106]

Information[107]   An agent is, in general,[108] under a duty to keep the principal ap- **6-021** propriately informed.[109] Thus, a solicitor must inform the client of any overtures of settlement[110] and a broker must inform the principal of any contracts made on the

---

[99]   *Equitas Ltd v Walsham Brothers & Co Ltd* [2013] EWHC 3264 (Comm) at [51].

[100]   See para.6-043. See too *Groom v Crocker* [1939] 1 K.B. 194.

[101]   See, e.g. *Lyons v Fox Williams LLP* [2018] EWCA Civ 2347.

[102]   *Chown v Parrott* (1863) 14 C.B.(N.S.) 74; *Langsam v Beachcroft LLP* [2012] EWCA Civ 1230 at [84]. See above, para.6-003; Article 30, Illustration 5.

[103]   *Moore v Mourgue* (1776) 2 Cowp. 479; *Smith v Cologan* (1786) 2 T.R. 188n.; *East India Co v Henchman* (1791) 1 Ves.Jun. 287; *Gwatkin v Campbell* (1854) 1 Jur.(N.S.) 131; *Lagunas Nitrate v Lagunas Syndicate* [1899] 2 Ch. 392; *Morten v Hilton, Gibbes & Smith* (1908), reported in [1937] 2 K.B. 176n. (HL), Illustration 9; *Re Cobridge and Bucknall SS Lines Ltd* (1910) 15 Com.Cas. 138; *Gokal Chand-Jagan Nath v Nand Ram Das-Atma Ram* [1939] A.C. 106.

[104]   See *Elidor Investments SA v Christie's, Mansons Woods Ltd* [2009] EWHC 3600 (QB) citing *Socimer International Bank Ltd v Standard Bank London Ltd* [2008] EWCA Civ 116; [2008] 1 Lloyd's Rep. 558 at [66] (advertising for auction); *Torre Asset Funding Ltd v The Royal Bank of Scotland Plc* [2013] EWHC 2670 (Ch) at [37].

[105]   *Horler v Rubin* [2012] EWCA Civ 4 at [21].

[106]   *Euroption Strategic Fund Ltd v Skandinaviska Enskilda Banken AB* [2012] EWHC 584 (Comm) at [129].

[107]   cf. *Restatement, Third,* § 8.11.

[108]   For one potential exception, see the Proceeds of Crimes Act 2002 s.333, in relation to moneylaundering, briefly discussed in *Shah v HSBC Private Bank (UK) Ltd* [2010] EWCA Civ 31 at [37]–[39]; *Shah v HSBC Bank (UK) Ltd* [2012] EWHC 1283 (QB); [2012] 1 All E.R. (Comm) 72 at [172].

[109]   See *Ocean City Realty Ltd v A & M Holdings Ltd* (1987) 36 D.L.R. (4th) 94 at 98; *John D Wood & Co (Residential & Agricultural) Ltd v Knatchbull* [2002] EWHC 2822; [2003] 1 E.G.L.R. 33 (Illustration 6); *Premium Real Estate Ltd v Stevens* [2009] 2 N.Z.L.R. 384.

[110]   *Sill v Thomas* (1839) 8 C. & P. 762. For more recent examples see *McKaskell v Benseman* [1989] 1

principal's behalf.[111] An estate agent must notify the principal of offers received up to the time of exchange of contracts.[112] A ship's agent must likewise inform the principal of any facts which the principal ought to know in order to make full disclosure to underwriters.[113] Moreover, an insurance broker owes a special duty of disclosure, not only to the principal but to the underwriters. This duty, for breach of which the agent may be liable to the principal, arises from the nature of the insurance contract, which is uberrimae fidei.[114] A solicitor or other agent in a position of conflict of interest cannot normally use the conflict as an excuse for not passing on information relevant to the retainer to a principal.[115] As always, the scope of an agent's duties is governed by the terms and context of any contract between the principal and agent, and there will be cases where mere neglect to pass on information will not create liability.[116] As to duties to keep records of transactions, see below, para.6-093, and as to equitable duties of disclosure, see para.6-054.

6-022 **Special skill** Some agents may be regarded as holding themselves out as possessed of special skills. In such cases it would seem that the standard of care which they owe should be higher. Thus in one case where a provincial auctioneer was held not liable for failure to recognise pictures possibly by Stubbs, the decision was affected by the fact that they were described as "general practitioners"[117]: it would seem that a person offering more specialised skills should be liable if they are not exercised.[118]

6-023 **Illegal conduct** Difficult issues arise where an agent has acted illegally. It will be rare that an agent will have implied authority to act illegally,[119] and without authority the agent may be liable to compensate the principal where the principal is not directly complicit in the illegality but suffers loss as a result of the conduct.[120] The mere fact that the principal is attributed with responsibility for the agent's illegality for some purposes ought not to preclude the principal's suing the agent for

---

N.Z.L.R. 75 (offensive letter from solicitors acting for other side); *Waimond Pty Ltd v Byrne* (1989) 18 N.S.W.L.R. 642 (failure to guard interests of client when they were prejudiced by another client).

[111] *Johnson v Kearley* [1908] 2 K.B. 514. See also *Dampskibsselskab Halla v Catsell & Co* (1928) 30 Lloyd's Rep. 284; *Dunton Properties Ltd v Coles, Knapp & Kennedy* (1959) 174 E.G. 723.

[112] *Keppel v Wheeler* [1927] 1 K.B. 577, Illustration 6 to Article 60; see also Estate Agents (Undesirable Practices) (No.2) Order 1991 (SI 1991/1032) Sch.3 para.2.

[113] *Proudfoot v Montefiore* (1867) L.R. 2 Q.B. 511.

[114] See Marine Insurance Act 1906 s.19; and *Blackburn Low & Co v Vigors* (1887) 12 App.Cas. 531 at 537, 541. A broker may also owe a duty to its client to inform the client of its duties of disclosure to the insurer: *Involnert Management Inc v Aprilgrange Ltd* [2015] EWHC 2225 (Comm) at [318].

[115] *Hilton v Barker Booth & Eastwood* [2005] UKHL 8; [2005] 1 W.L.R. 567; *Mortgage Express Ltd v Bowerman & Partners* [1996] 2 All E.R. 836; *Goldsmith Williams Solicitors v E.Surv Ltd* [2015] EWCA Civ 1147; [2016] 4 W.L.R. 44. See further below, para.6-048.

[116] See, e.g. *National Home Loans Corp Plc v Giffen Couch & Archer* [1998] 1 W.L.R. 207 (default on existing mortgage not reported to client lender but existing credit performance of debtor not within instructions); *Torre Asset Funding Ltd v The Royal Bank of Scotland Plc* [2013] EWHC 2670 (Ch) at [156] (agent in syndicated lending had assumed limited duties, and was not required to assess whether an event of default by a borrower had occurred in order to inform principals).

[117] *Luxmoore-May v Messenger May Baverstock* [1990] 1 W.L.R. 1009 at 1020.

[118] See *Duchess of Argyll v Beuselinck* [1972] 2 Lloyd's Rep. 172 at 183–184; but cf. *Wimpey Construction UK Ltd v Poole* [1984] 2 Lloyd's Rep. 499 at 506.

[119] See further above, para.2-026.

[120] See *Bilta (UK) Ltd v Nazir* [2015] UKSC 23; [2016] A.C. 1 at [42]–[43], [130], [160] and [191]. See too *Safeway Stores Ltd v Twigger* [2010] EWHC 11 (Comm) (action against directors and employees for causing company to engage in unlawful competitive action), reversed on point of statutory construction: [2010] EWCA Civ 1472; [2011] 1 Lloyd's Rep. 462.

breach of mandate or other breach of contract. Even where there is evidence that a principal has in fact given some discretion to act illegally, the exercise of the discretion without due cause may not preclude an action by the principal against the agent. In cases, however, where there was some colour of right to the action taken by the agent, there may not be the want of due care necessary for liability.[121] Principals may also be taken to have warranted that their instructions are lawful.[122] Further, where the principal or a duly authorised senior agent expressly authorised, or acquiesced in, the agent's illegal conduct then it is unlikely that the agent will be liable for breach of contract because there will not have been a breach. It is possible too that any action brought by the principal against the agent could be barred by the ex turpi maxim.[123] In some circumstances it may be contrary to the policy of the particular rule infringed for the principal to be compensated for loss.[124] Authority, however, holds that an agent who is given money by a principal for the purpose of illegal gaming remains accountable for any winnings.[125] The fact that the principal has engaged in, or former agents of the principal have caused it to engage in and be responsible for, unlawful activity cannot excuse a later agent's unconnected acts of negligence or other breaches of duty.[126]

Where the principal is a company, the company will not automatically be treated as knowing and condoning illegal conduct even where its senior management is apprised of it, especially where the question is the liability to the company of that senior management for engaging in the conduct.[127]

Illustrations

(1) "[A solicitor's liability] is the same as anybody else's liability; having regard to the degree of skill held out to the public by solicitors, does the conduct of the solicitor fall short of the standard which the public had been led to expect of the solicitor?"[120] A solicitor "is bound to bring a fair and reasonable amount of skill to the performance of his professional duty".[129] A solicitor who is being instructed to draft a contract by an agent of the client should bring to the

6-024

---

[121] cf. *Re Vining Sparks Ltd* [2019] EWHC 2885 (Ch); [2020] S.T.C. 410 (tax avoidance by director on legal advice).

[122] See *Strongman v Sincock* [1955] 2 Q.B. 525. See also above, para.6-009.

[123] See, e.g. *Nayyar v Sapte* [2009] EWHC 3218 (QB) (principal authorises and funds agent to pay bribe). Older case law needs to be reconsidered in the light of *Patel v Mirza* [2016] UKSC 42; [2017] A.C. 467. As to the agent's rights against the principal, see Article 61.

[124] See *Safeway Stores Ltd v Twigger* [2010] EWCA Civ 1472; [2011] 1 Lloyd's Rep. 462 (this surprising result is discussed in Watts [2011] J.B.L. 213). cf. *Griffin v Uhy Hacker Young & Partners (a firm)* [2010] EWHC 146 (Ch) (accountants). See further, paras 3-035 and 6-009.

[125] *De Mattos v Benjamin* (1894) 63 L.J.Q.B. 248; *Cheshire (Thomas) & Co v Vaughan Bros & Co* [1920] 3 K.B. 240; *Jeffrey v Bamford* [1921] 2 K.B. 351; *Close v Wilson* [2011] EWCA Civ 5. The position may be otherwise where the claimant needs to rely on a contractual claim, the contract being illegal: *Close v Wilson* [2011] EWCA Civ 5.

[126] *Sharma v Top Brands Ltd* [2015] EWCA Civ 1140; [2016] P.N.L.R. 12 (liquidator of company the business of which largely involved VAT fraud not excused for negligence in paying away remaining funds); *Stoffel & Co v Grondona* [2018] EWCA Civ 2031. See further, para.6-009.

[127] *Bilta (UK) Ltd v Nazir* [2015] UKSC 23; [2016] A.C. 1 at [42]–[43], [130], [160] and [191]; *Crown Prosecution Service v Aquila Advisory Ltd* [2019] EWCA Civ 588 at [25].

[128] *Simmons v Pennington* [1955] 1 W.L.R. 183 at 188, per Hodson LJ, citing with approval this dictum from a judgment of Harman J (unreported). See too *Tom Hoskins Plc v EMW Law (a firm)* [2010] EWHC 479 (Ch).

[129] *Parker v Rolls* (1854) 14 C.B. 691 at 695, per Talfourd J. See in general Cordery, *Solicitors*, Ch.6. A solicitor may be liable to others than his client: *White v Jones* [1995] 2 A.C. 207 (prospective

client's notice provisions in respect of which the agent has a conflict of interest.[130]

(2)   An insurance broker is bound to exercise reasonable and proper care, skill and judgment in obtaining a policy to cover the principal's interests and protecting the principal generally in relation to the underwriters.[131] The expert evidence of other brokers may be called to prove what is the requisite standard of care. A broker is bound to keep up to date on the current developments of the law relating at least to that part of the business of insurance with which the broker is concerned.[132] If a broker does give advice on points of insurance law generally reasonable care must be taken to ensure that such advice is correct.[133] The broker must act with due speed in obtaining insurance cover[134] and if such cover cannot be obtained the broker must at once inform the principal.[135] Liability may arise if the broker erroneously and negligently informs the principal that cover is unobtainable, with the result that the principal does not make further attempts to obtain it.[136] A broker may also be liable in tort to others than the client.[137] A broker may be found to have undertaken ongoing duties to advise as to the suitability of cover earlier obtained if relevant facts come to light.[138] Similar duties are owed by invest-

---

beneficiary); and if he acts for those on both sides of a transaction (e.g. a conveyance) he may owe duties to both: *Mortgage Express Ltd v Bowerman & Partners* [1996] 2 All E.R. 836.

[130] *Newcastle International Airport Ltd v Eversheds LLP* [2013] EWCA Civ 1514 at [80].

[131] *Chapman v Walton* (1833) 10 Bing. 57; *Osman v J. Ralph Moss Ltd* [1970] 1 Lloyd's Rep. 313; *Claude R. Ogden & Co Pty Ltd v Reliance Fire Sprinkler Co Pty Ltd* [1975] 1 Lloyd's Rep. 52; *Fine's Flowers v General Accident Assurance Co of Canada* (1977) 81 D.L.R. (3d) 139; *Warren v Henry Sutton & Co* [1976] 2 Lloyd's Rep. 276; *Cherry v Allied Insurance Brokers Ltd* [1978] 1 Lloyd's Rep. 274; *McNealy v Pennine Insurance Co Ltd* [1978] 2 Lloyd's Rep. 18; cf. *O'Connor v B.D. Kirby & Co* [1972] 1 Q.B. 90; *Provincial Insurance Australia Pty Ltd v Wood Products Pty Ltd* (1991) 25 N.S.W.L.R. 541 at 556 ("go through with the insured the list of exceptions in the policy secured"); *FNCB Ltd v Barnet Devanney & Co Ltd* [1999] 2 All E.R. (Comm) 233; *Ground Gilbey Ltd v Jardine Lloyd Thompson UK Ltd* [2011] EWHC 124 (Comm); [2011] P.N.L.R. 15; [2012] Lloyd's Rep. I.R. 12 at [73]; *Synergy Health (UK) Ltd v CGU Insurance Plc (t/a Norwich Union)* [2010] EWHC 2583 (Comm); [2011] Lloyd's Rep I.R. 500 at [204] (duty to advise principal as to what types of information must be disclosed to insurer to avoid rescission for non-disclosure); *Horsell International Pty Ltd v Divetwo Pty Ltd* [2013] NSWCA 368 at [235]. A broker cannot be excused from his duty to advise by reason of a conflict of interest: *HIH Casualty & General Insurance Ltd v JLT Risk Solutions Ltd* [2007] EWCA Civ 710; [2007] 2 Lloyd's Rep. 278; [2007] 2 All E.R. (Comm) 1106 (see below, para.6-048).

[132] *Park v Hammond* (1816) 6 Taunt. 495; *The Ultra Processor* (1983) Lloyd's Maritime Law Newsletter, September 15, 1983 (SC, BC); *Provincial Insurance Australia Pty Ltd v Consolidated Wood Products Pty Ltd* (1991) 25 N.S.W.L.R. 541 at 556 ("pointing out legal pitfalls").

[133] *Sarginson Bros v Keith Moulton & Co* (1942) 73 Ll.Rep. 104. See too *Horsell International Pty Ltd v Divetwo Pty Ltd* [2013] NSWCA 368 at [238].

[134] *Turpin v Bilton* (1843) 5 M. & G. 455. See further above, para.6-014.

[135] See Article 61. See also *Youell v Bland Welch & Co Ltd (the Superhulls Cover case) (No.2)* [1990] 2 Lloyd's Rep. 431 at 445. As to insurance brokers generally see *MacGillivray on Insurance Law* (14th edn), Chs 36 and 37; Clarke, *Law of Insurance Contracts* (6th edn), Ch.9; Hodgin, *Insurance Intermediaries: Law and Regulation* (1992).

[136] *Sarginson Bros v Keith Moulton & Co* (1942) 73 Ll.Rep. 104; *Markal Investments Ltd v Morley Shafron Agencies Ltd* (1987) 44 D.L.R. (4th) 745.

[137] *Punjab National Bank v de Boinville* [1992] 1 W.L.R. 1138 (to assignee of policy).

[138] *Ground Gilbey Ltd v Jardine Lloyd Thompson UK Ltd* [2011] EWHC 124 (Comm); [2011] P.N.L.R. 15; [2012] Lloyd's Rep. I.R. 12 at [73].

ment brokers who advise and act for clients in the acquisition of investments.[139]

(3) A patent agent is "bound to bring reasonable and ordinary care and knowledge to the performance of his duty as such skilled agent".[140] Such agent is bound to know and keep abreast of the most recent decisions of the courts relating to the business of obtaining patents.[141]

(4) Brokers who are employed to sell goods are bound to employ due care and diligence in obtaining the best available price.[142]

(5) An estate agent was employed to let houses and was paid a commission of 5 per cent for doing so. It was held that the agent was bound to use reasonable care to ascertain the solvency of the tenants[143]:

> "The house agent must use reasonable care and diligence in ascertaining the condition of a person before he introduces him to the landlord as a tenant. It cannot be supposed that the commission of 5 per cent is to be paid for only putting the name of the owner and the particulars of the premises upon the house agent's books for the information of those who may come to make inquiries at his office."[144]

(6) An estate agent suggests a "reasonable asking price" of £100,000 to a prospective seller of land. He is then asked to act for the seller and does not suggest any change to the asking price. The advice was negligent. He is liable for negligent valuation when the seller buys another property at a price which proves ruinous when the original land can only be sold for £36,000.[145]

(7) In the case of an ordinary commercial transaction a freight forwarder will not be negligent by omitting to insure the goods.[146] But in the case of a transaction involving a private individual where the goods are known to be valuable the agent may be negligent if the goods are neither insured nor instructions obtained from the principal.[147] In the former instance the agent may

---

[139] *Wingecarribee Shire Council v Lehman Brothers Australia Ltd* [2012] FCA 1028; (2013) 301 A.L.R. 1 at [787]–[789].

[140] *Lee v Walker* (1872) L.R. 7 C.P. 121 at 125, per Brett J. See *Arbiter Group Plc v Gill Jennings & Every* [2001] R.P.C. 67.

[141] *Lee v Walker* (1872) L.R. 7 C.P. 121.

[142] *Solomon v Barker* (1862) 2 F. & F. 726. See also *Grant v Fletcher* (1826) 5 B. & C. 436; *Sievwright v Richardson* (1852) 19 L.T.(O.S.) 10; *Alexander & Co v Wilson Holgate & Co* (1923) 14 Ll.Rep. 538.

[143] *Heys v Tindall* (1861) 1 B. & S. 296; and see *P.G. Prebble & Co v West* (1969) 211 E.G. 831; *Brutton v Alfred Savill, Curtis & Henson* [1971] E.G.D. 497; *Faruk v Wyse* [1988] 2 E.G.L.R. 26; *Messenger v Stanaway Real Estate Ltd* [2015] NZHC 1795; (2015) 16 N.Z. Conv. P.R. 335 (failure to draft for security on sale of land with deferred payment).

[144] *Heys v Tindall* (1861) 1 B. & S. 296 at 298, per Cockburn CJ arguendo. As to the liability of an exclusive agent for not trying hard enough, see *Styles v Rogers Realty Ltd* (1987) 43 D.L.R. (4th) 629; *Commissioner of Taxation v Byrne Hotels Queensland Pty Ltd* [2011] FCAFC 127 at [113]. See further as to estate agents Murdoch, *Law of Estate Agency* (5th edn), p.52 onwards.

[145] *Kenney v Hall, Pain & Foster* [1976] E.G.D. 629; see Brazier (1977) 41 Conv. 233. The "asking price" may also be too low: *John D. Wood & Co v Knatchbull* [2002] EWHC 2822; [2003] 1 E.G.L.R. 33 (reasonable when set, but agent should have advised of subsequent change in market).

[146] *W.L.R. Traders (London) Ltd v British & Northern Shipping Agency and Leftley Ltd* [1955] 1 Lloyd's Rep. 554; *Club Speciality (Overseas) Inc v United Marine (1939) Ltd* [1971] 1 Lloyd's Rep. 482. See also Hill, *Freight Forwarders* (1974); *British Shipping Laws*, Vol.13, 635–656; *Scrutton on Charterparties* (24th edn) at para.4-053 onwards; *Contracts for Carriage of Goods* (Yates ed., 1993), Ch.7, "Freight Forwarders"; Bugden, *Goods in Transit* (4th edn).

[147] *Von Traubenberg v Davies, Turner & Co Ltd* [1951] 2 Lloyd's Rep. 462.

expect the principals to have made their own arrangements for insurance. In the latter case the principal may well not have made any such arrangements. The agent may well also be liable if no appropriate claims are lodged by the agent against the carrier.[148]

(8)   A contracted to lighter and load certain machinery, and pass it through the customhouse. It was common knowledge that import duties were about to be imposed on machinery, and A might have cleared it in time to escape the taxation, but did not do so, though he cleared it within the time prescribed by the customs regulations. In an action against A for the amount of the duty paid, it was held that there was no evidence to go to the jury of any negligence or breach of duty for which he would be liable.[149]

(9)   Stockbrokers who were speculating on P's instructions had to know from P before the end of the accounting period which of P's accounts to close and which to leave open. They were unable to obtain instructions from P and so they closed some and left others open, exercising their discretion in what they considered to be in P's interests. In fact it would have been better to have closed all the accounts, and P sued them for negligence. Held, that they had acted reasonably and in P's best interests[150]:

> "I think brokers so situated were not only entitled but bound to carry through the transaction in the reasonable way they honestly thought most to the advantage of their principal and themselves, and that they did so. These considerations dispose of the case."[151]

(10)   Auctioneers who sell goods have no duty to get in the price, even though they have the right to sue for it.[152] An auctioneer asked to express a view on the sale of pictures is liable for the negligence of a valuer whose advice the auctioneer simply transmitted to the client; but the formation of a wrong view may not be negligent.[153]

Article 41

NOT LIABLE TO PRINCIPAL IN RESPECT OF CONTRACTS ENTERED INTO ON PRINCIPAL'S BEHALF

6-025   An agent is in general not liable to the principal on contracts made by the agent between the principal and third parties.[154]

---

[148] *Marbrook Freight Ltd v K.M.I. (London) Ltd* [1979] 2 Lloyd's Rep. 341.
[149] *Commonwealth Portland Cement Co v Weber, Lohmann & Co Ltd* [1905] A.C. 66. See also *World Transport Agency Ltd v Royte (England) Ltd* [1957] 1 Lloyd's Rep. 381.
[150] *Morten v Hilton, Gibbes & Smith (1908)* [1937] 2 K.B. 176n. HL. See also *Samson v Frazier Jelke & Co* [1937] 2 K.B. 170; *Stafford v Conti Commodity Services Ltd* [1981] 1 All E.R. 691; *Merrill Lynch Futures Inc v York House Trading Ltd, The Times,* May 24, 1984 (losses on commodity market are not of themselves evidence of negligence by broker); *Drexel Burnham Lambert Ltd NV v El Nasr* [1986] 1 Lloyds Rep. 356 at 366–367 (commodity broker).
[151] *Morten v Hilson, Gibbes & Smith (1908)* [1937] 2 K.B. 176n. HL at 178, per Lord Loreburn LC.
[152] *Fordham v Christie, Manson & Woods* [1977] E.G.D. 94. cf. *Brown v Staton* (1816) 2 Chit. 353.
[153] *Luxmoore-May v Messenger May Baverstock* [1990] 1 W.L.R. 1009. As to the duties of auctioneers see further *Alchemy (International) Ltd v Tattersalls Ltd* [1985] 2 E.G.L.R. 17; Murdoch, *Law of Estate Agency and Auctions* (4th edn), Ch.2 (see also more specifically on auctioneers 3rd edn, Ch.9).
[154] *Varden v Parker* (1798) 2 Esp. 710; *Alsop v Sylvester* (1823) 1 C. & P. 107; *Risbourg v Bruckner*

Comment

This is the general rule for contracts: an authorised contract is that of the **6-026** principal. But just as the agent may in some case be liable to, and entitled to sue, the third party,[155] so also the agent may be liable to the principal, by express or implied agreement or by usage. This may occur, for example, when the agent is a *del credere* agent,[156] or where in some other way the agent agrees to answer to the principal in respect of transactions which the agent negotiates; where the agent in some respects deals as principal with a person for whom the agent is in other respects an agent (e.g. an insurance broker[157]); or where the person acts also as agent for the third party and undertakes liability to the first principal as such agent.[158] And of course the entering into of the transaction may be a breach of duty under the principles stated in the previous Articles.

Article 42

LIABILITY OF GRATUITOUS AGENTS

A gratuitous agent will be liable to the principal if in carrying out the work the **6-027** agent fails to exercise the degree of care which may reasonably be expected of the agent in all the circumstances.[159]

Comment

Liability in tort There is no general requirement in the law of agency that an **6-028** agent has a contract with the principal, and the external position between principal and third party can certainly be changed by a gratuitous agent.[160] The internal position between principal and agent however, is, in such a case only imperfectly enforceable. Where there is no contract between principal and agent, it would seem that the alleged agent cannot be liable for pure failure to do what was undertaken without consideration. However, where he assumed responsibility to exercise care and skill, the agent can be liable in tort for negligently failing to complete, or to complete with due care, work that was undertaken and upon which the agent has embarked. The agent must also take care to adhere to the mandate conferred.[161] Thus a person who gratuitously agrees to procure insurance for another may owe a duty of care in respect of the manner in which the policy is obtained.[162] Not all the cases which can be cited as instances of such a duty are necessarily to be regarded as true

---

(1858) 3 C.B.(N.S.) 812.
[155] See Articles 98–103 and 107–109.
[156] See above, para.1-040.
[157] *Universo Insurance Co of Milan v Merchants Marine Insurance Co* [1897] 2 Q.B. 93; *MacGillivray on Insurance Law* (14th edn), para.37-009 onwards; and see *Wilson v Avec Audio-Visual Equipment Ltd* [1974] 1 Lloyd's Rep. 81. See also Hon. Mrs Justice Gloster [2007] L.M.C.L.Q. 302.
[158] e.g. *Queensland Investment Co v O'Connell* (1896) 12 T.L.R. 502 (stockbroker).
[159] See Comment. For the position of minors as agents, see above, para.2-015.
[160] See Article 3.
[161] See further above, para.6-003.
[162] *Wilkinson v Coverdale* (1793) 1 Esp. 74; *Norwest Refrigeration Services Pty Ltd v Bain Dawes (W.A.) Pty Ltd* (1984) 157 C.L.R. 149 at 168–170 (Illustration 6); *Veljkovic v Vrybergen* [1985] VR. 419; *Youell v Bland Welch & Co Ltd (the Superhulls Cover case) (No.2)* [1990] 2 Lloyd's Rep. 431. But when his principal is a company, he does not necessarily owe a duty to its directors personally: *Verderame v Commercial Union Ass. Co, The Times,* April 2, 1992.

cases of gratuitous agency—some involve at the very least a strongly commercial background, in that the agent is a professional person who anticipates being remunerated or has already earned commission (as where the agent obtains insurance and subsequently undertakes gratuitously to change it).[163] In some the agent is already agent for the other side to the transaction.[164] However, the proposition itself seems clearly established.[165]

6-029 **Non-feasance** The dividing line between not carrying out the work at all and carrying it out negligently, or negligently failing to carry out part of it, whether as a gratuitous agent or not, can be fine in some instances. Some time ago it was suggested that where a gratuitous agent has undertaken to do a particular task, a duty of care is owed to the principal if the agent knows that, in reliance on the undertaking, the principal has refrained from instructing anyone else to do the work or otherwise acted in reliance. At least, it was suggested, the agent must inform the principal if the agent is not going to perform the task undertaken, and must do so in time to enable the principal not to suffer damage by having insufficient time to instruct anyone else.[166] However, authority justifying liability in tort for pure failure to act is difficult to find. Thus in one case an insurance broker acting who, having placed all risks insurance with underwriters, gratuitously undertook to a reinsurance underwriter in respect of the same risks to obtain further signatures on a slip and failed to do so, causing loss to the reinsurer, was held at first instance liable in tort[167]; but the Court of Appeal was able to detect an implied contractual promise to justify the liability, and doubt was expressed as to the appropriateness of a tort action.[168] Although the House of Lords formerly cast doubt on the significance of the notion of assumption of responsibility as a basis of negligence liability,[169] there has been a strong movement back towards such reasoning,[170] which indeed stems

[163] See *General Accident Fire & Life Assurance Corp Ltd v Tanter (The Zephyr)* [1985] 2 Lloyd's Rep. 529 at 537, per Mustill LJ. This could be true of *Gomer v Pitt & Scott* (1922) 12 Ll. L.Rep. 115, Illustration 5, and many insurance broker cases. As to barristers, see *Arthur JS Hall & Co v Simons* [2002] 1 A.C. 615 (as to the ability of barristers now to sue for fees, see below, para.7-006); *Chamberlains v Lai* [2006] NZSC 70; [2007] 2 N.Z.L.R. 7.
[164] As in *Donaldson v Haldane* (1840) 7 C. & F. 762, Illustration 4; *Al-Kandari v J.R. Brown & Co* [1987] Q.B. 514, Illustration 13 to Article 113; and in various other cases where the agent of one party is held to owe a duty to the other, as to which see *Avery v Salie* (1972) 25 D.L.R. (3d) 495 and Article 113.
[165] It is clearly accepted in *Chaudhry v Prabakhar* [1989] 1 W.L.R. 29, though see discussion of this case below. See also *Wallace v Tellfair* (1786) 2 T.R. 188n.; *Smith v Lascelles* (1788) 2 T.R. 187; *Seller v Work* (1801) Marsh. Ins. 305; *Thorne v Deas* (1809) 4 Johns N.Y.R. 84; *Massey v Banner* (1820) 1 Jac. & W. 241; *Balfe v West* (1853) 13 C.B. 466; *Turnbull v Garden* (1869) 38 L.J. Ch. 331.
[166] See Powell, p.303; Seavey, *Studies in Agency* (1949), pp.395–400; (1951) 64 HarvL.R. 913; Prosser, *Selected Topics on the Law of Torts* (1953), p.380; *Wallace v Tellfair* (1786) 2 T.R. 188n.
[167] *General Accident Fire and Life Assurance Corp Ltd v Tanter (The Zephyr)* [1984] 1 Lloyd's Rep. 58.
[168] *General Accident Fire & Life Assurance Corp Ltd v Tanter (The Zephyr)* [1985] 2 Lloyd's Rep. 529: see at 538, where Mustill LJ refers to negligence liability as applicable to an "obligation to avoid doing something, or to avoid doing something badly". He also says that "doing something badly may often involve a neglect to carry out an act which would turn bad performance into adequate performance".
[169] *Smith v Eric S. Bush* [1990] 1 A.C. 831; *Caparo Industries Plc v Dickman* [1990] 2 A.C. 605.
[170] *Spring v Guardian Assurance Plc* [1995] 2 A.C. 296 (negligent letter of reference); *Henderson v Merrett Syndicates Ltd* [1995] 2 A.C. 145 (negligent management by sub-agent); *Williams v Natural Life Health Foods Ltd* [1998] 1 W.L.R. 830; *Steel v NRAM Ltd* [2018] UKSC 13; [2018] 1 W.L.R. 1190; *Poole Borough Council v GN* [2019] UKSC 25; [2019] 2 W.L.R. 1478. cf. *Customs and Excise*

directly from *Hedley Byrne & Co Ltd v Heller & Partners Ltd*[171] itself. Many of these cases involve misfeasance, and it will be rare to find a tort liability on facts indicating no more than a failure to do an act promised.[172] However, the line between this and failure to go through with a responsibility undertaken is a fine one.

In jurisdictions willing to recognise an estoppel liability based on reliance only, it might be possible to hold the gratuitous agent who completely fails to act liable on this basis to a person who acted or refrained from acting on the basis of the agent's undertaking.[173]

Exclusions of liability   A person may in principle limit what is undertaken by some form of disclaimer or exclusion clause.[174] Although it is arguable that such reservations are not exclusions of liability at all, but rather determine the scope and degree of the tortious duty undertaken, they have often been treated as exclusions, and hence subject to s.2(2) of the Unfair Contract Terms Act 1977, which imposes a requirement of reasonableness on exclusions of liability for loss caused by negligence.[175]   **6-030**

Standard of care   It was formerly customary to state, and old editions of this work did state, that the duty of care owed by a gratuitous agent was one of such skill and care as persons ordinarily exercise in their own affairs. This idea, which is similar to the *diligentia quam suis rebus* of Roman law (where different contracts had different prescribed levels of care), was derived in English law from old cases on bailment, which suggested (in like manner) that whereas a contractual bailee was liable for negligence, a gratuitous bailee was only liable for gross negligence.[176] But as Rolfe B remarked in 1843,[177] gross negligence can be said to be no more than negligence with a vituperative epithet; and the determination of fixed standards for different types of case is not a technique now used by English law. Ormerod LJ said in 1962[178]:   **6-031**

> "It seems to me that to try and put a bailment, for instance, into a watertight compartment—such a gratuitous bailment on the one hand, and bailment for reward on the other—is to overlook the fact that there might well be an infinite variety of cases, which

---

Commissioners v Barclays Bank Plc [2006] UKHL 28; [2007] 1 A.C. 181 (no liability on bank for negligently breaching freezing order over customer's funds); and *CGL Group Ltd v The Royal Bank of Scotland Plc* [2017] EWCA Civ 1073.

[171] *Hedley Byrne & Co Ltd v Heller & Partners Ltd* [1964] A.C. 435.

[172] See *Restatement, Third*, § 378: "When the gratuitous agent has not entered upon performance, it is not clear that liability will be imposed". A solicitor was held liable to the intended beneficiary under a will when he took no steps to carry out instructions from the testator, who died, in *White v Jones* [1995] 2 A.C. 207; but the "disappointed beneficiary" cases are probably sui generis. cf. *Hill v van Erp* (1997) 188 C.L.R. 159; *Badenach v Calvert* [2016] HCA 18; (2016) 257 C.L.R. 440. See *Clerk and Lindsell on Torts* (22nd edn), para.10-109 onwards; and Gordley (1995) 83 Calif L Rev. 547 at 582–584.

[173] See *Waltons Stores (Interstate) Ltd v Maher* (1988) 164 C.L.R. 387; *Amalgamated Investment and Property Co Ltd v Texas Commerce International Bank Ltd* [1982] Q.B. 84.

[174] As in the leading case of *Hedley Byrne & Co Ltd v Heller & Partners Ltd* [1964] A.C. 465 itself.

[175] See, e.g. *Smith v Eric S. Bush* [1990] 1 A.C. 831.

[176] See *Coggs v Bernard* (1703) 2 Ld.Raym. 909; see also *Wilson v Brett* (1843) 11 M.&W. 113; *Giblin v McMullen* (1869) L.R. 2 P.C. 317; *Moffat v Bateman* (1869) L.R. 3 P.C. 115. But cf. *Port Swettenham Authority v T.W.Wu & Co* [1979] A.C. 580.

[177] *Wilson v Brett* (1843) 11 M.&W. 113 at 115.

[178] *Houghland v R.R. Low (Luxury Coaches) Ltd* [1962] 1 Q.B. 694 at 698; see also *Grill v General Iron Screw Collier Co* (1866) L.R. 1 C.P. 694 at 698.

might come into one or the other category. The question that we have to consider in a case of this kind, if it is necessary to consider negligence, is whether in the circumstances of this particular case a sufficient standard of care has been observed by the defendants or their servants."

This view was subsequently specifically accepted for gratuitous agency. In *Chaudhry v Prabakhar*[179] a person undertook to find a suitable second-hand car for a friend to buy, and negligently recommended a car which had been in an accident. He was held liable in tort. The case was argued as turning on the duty owed by a gratuitous agent, though it is not clear that the defendant was in inspecting the car appropriately described as an agent[180]; indeed it is not clear that he should have been regarded as undertaking any duty at all, though this was expressly conceded and the case decided on the basis of the concession.[181] In substance accepting the view put forward[182] in the Comment (but not the Article itself) in a previous edition of this work, the Court of Appeal can be said to have taken the overall view that the agent's duty is "that which may be reasonably expected of him in all the circumstances".[183] Factors relevant to the determination of the standard owed are whether the agent is paid, and if so whether the agent exercises any trade, profession or calling; and where the agent is unpaid, any skill and experience the agent has represented himself as having.[184]

Illustrations

6-032   (1)   A gratuitously undertakes to arrange an insurance policy on P's cargo. He then changes his mind and decides not to do so. P's cargo is lost, but it has been said that P has no claim against A.[185] Sed quaere. If A started to make the necessary arrangements but negligently failed to answer letters from the underwriters so that no policy was effected, or if A obtained a policy but negligently failed to obtain cover against the usual risks, semble, P would have a claim against A for the loss he suffered.

(2)   E purchased a motor car from X. It was agreed that X's insurance would be transferred to E. E then arranged with X's insurance brokers for them to arrange the transfer. The insurers were not satisfied with the information given them by the brokers relating to E and in default of any answer to their questions cancelled the temporary insurance which they had granted. The brokers failed to inform E, who later had an accident. Held, the brokers were liable to indemnify E against the sums he had to pay in consequence of the accident. They were liable for their negligence notwithstanding that they were acting gratuitously.[186]

(3)   A general merchant undertakes, without reward, to enter a parcel of P's goods at the custom-house together with a parcel of his own. By mistake he enters

---

[179] *Chaudhry v Prabakhar* [1989] 1 W.L.R. 29.
[180] He subsequently took a cheque for part of the purchase price and passed it to the seller, so could perhaps be regarded as having negotiated, or at least introduced, the sale.
[181] A concession doubted by May LJ at 38–39.
[182] In a passage originally written by Mr Brian Davenport QC.
[183] See Stuart-Smith LJ at 34; see also Stocker LJ at 37.
[184] See at 34.
[185] See Duer, *Law and Practice of Marine Insurance* (1845), Vol. 2, pp.128–130, who comments unfavourably on the hardship inflicted on P, who has trusted A to carry out his promise.
[186] *London Borough of Bromley v Ellis* [1971] 1 Lloyd's Rep. 97.

both parcels under the wrong denomination of goods, and both parcels are, in consequence, seized. He has not held himself out as having any special skill in this respect (i.e. he is not a broker or customs clerk) and is therefore not liable to P, because he has taken as much care with P's goods as with his own.[187]

(4) A writer to the signet was employed to invest money for a client and did so without obtaining adequate security. He charged no fee for his services but was held liable to the lenders for his negligence.[188]

(5) P asked A, a shipping agent, to check with P's bank to ensure that the marine insurance policy on certain of P's goods covered a voyage to Lisbon. A acted gratuitously in accepting this request. He obtained an oral assurance from the bank but did not look at the terms of the policy itself (although he had been requested by P to "see the policy"). A was liable, since he had not shown that care which a reasonably careful man of business would have exercised in his own affairs.[189]

(6) The owner of a fishing vessel is required by his banker to get it insured. He contacts the manager of a fisherman's co-operative which he has recently joined, and which has said that it can obtain insurance for members at a reduced rate. The vessel is added to the co-operative's fleet policy, but the manager fails to tell the owner that the insurance is inoperative if the vessel does not have a certificate of survey. A loss occurs and the insurers repudiate liability because of the absence of such a certificate. The co-operative is liable.[190]

(7) Solicitors make a will for a testatrix and retain it. On her death they make no effort to locate the executor and notify him of the will for six years, during which time the main asset, a house, lies vacant and falls into decay. The solicitors are liable to the executor.[191]

(8) An accountant volunteers to be appointed joint signatory on a bank account operated by an attorney for the claimants. The attorney fraudulently procures the accountant's signature in blank on cheques and proceeds to misappropriate funds from the account. The accountant is liable to the claimants.[192]

2. FIDUCIARY AND OTHER EQUITABLE DUTIES

Article 43 provides an overview of the subject matter of an agent's fiduciary and other equitable duties. Succeeding Articles provide a more detailed treatment of various aspects of those duties.

---

[187] *Shiells v Blackburne* (1789) 1 Hy.Bl. 158.
[188] *Donaldson v Haldane* (1840) 7 C. & F. 762. See also *Dartnall v Howard & Gibbs* (1825) 4 B. & C. 345; *Whitehead v Greetham* (1825) 2 Bing. 464.
[189] *Gomer v Pitt & Scott* (1922) 12 Ll. L.Rep. 115.
[190] *Norwest Refrigeration Services Pty Ltd v Bain Dawes (W.A.) Pty Ltd* (1984) 157 C.L.R. 149.
[191] *Hawkins v Clayton* (1988) 164 C.L.R. 539.
[192] *Nicholls v Peers* (1993) 4 N.Z.B.L.C. 103,313.

Article 43

AGENTS' EQUITABLE DUTIES—GENERAL MATTERS

6-033   An agent owes to the principal a duty of loyalty, a duty that attracts fiduciary obligations.[193]

Comment

6-034   **The duties of a fiduciary**   Most of the material in this Article, and those that immediately follow it, is concerned with fiduciary duties. It should be noted, however, that the meaning of the expression "fiduciary duties" and its connections to other concepts remain contentious in many respects. It is common, for instance, for courts to refer to the duty of loyalty owed by trustees, agents and other "fiduciaries" as a fiduciary duty, whereas some commentators argue that only those sub-duties which reinforce the duty of loyalty should be termed fiduciary.[194] Others draw a distinction between a simple breach of trust and a breach of fiduciary duty, the former, but not the latter, extending to entirely innocent misapplications of the principal's property in breach of instructions.[195] A third troublesome issue is the relationship between fiduciary duties and duties not to disclose confidential information, now, in England anyway, treated as discrete sets of obligation.[196] A fourth area of difficulty is the relationship between fiduciary duties and the duty of fidelity said to be owed by all employees to their employers.[197] Finally, there is the relationship between fiduciary duties and the concept of undue influence, the latter concept particularly affecting some types of agent, such as solicitors, and possibly having operation before the contract of retainer is entered into, and extending after the retainer has ceased.[198]

The essence of the duties owed by a fiduciary has been expressed in the following statement:

"[A] person will be in a fiduciary relationship with another when and in so far as that person has undertaken to perform such a function for, or has assumed such a responsibil-

---

[193] The literature on this topic is enormous and constantly increasing. See, Conaglen, *Fiduciary Loyalty* (2010); *Meagher, Gummow and Lehane's Equity Doctrines and Remedies* (5th edn), Ch.5; Finn, *Fiduciary Obligations* (1977), Pt II; *Equity and Commercial Relationships* (Finn ed., 1987), Chs 6, 7; Glover, *Commercial Equity: Fiduciary Relationships* (1995); *Snell's Equity* (34th edn), Ch.7; Worthington, *Equity* (2nd edn), p.127 onwards; *Equity in Commercial Law* (Degeling and Edelman eds, 2005); *Contract, Status, and Fiduciary Law* (Miller and Gold eds, 2016); and other material cited in the following pages.

[194] See Flannigan (2004) 83 Can. Bar Rev. 35; Conaglen (2005) 121 L.Q.R. 452; Flannigan (2008) 124 L.Q.R. 274 cf. *Lehtimaki v Cooper* [2020] UKSC 33 at [46].

[195] See the Rt Hon. Lord Millett (1998) 114 L.Q.R. 399 at 403–406.

[196] See *Prince Jefri Bolkiah v KPMG* [1999] 2 A.C. 222 at 235; *Arklow Investments Ltd v Maclean* [2000] 1 W.L.R. 594 PC. cf. *Att.-Gen. v Blake* [1998] Ch. 439 at 454; *University of Nottingham v Fishel* [2000] EWHC 2221 (QB); [2000] I.C.R. 1462; *Generics (UK) Ltd v Yeda Research & Development Co Ltd* [2012] EWCA Civ 726; [2013] F.S.R. 13 at [48]. cf. Rt Hon. Lord Millett (1998) 114 L.Q.R. 214. See further below, paras 6-051 and 6-077.

[197] See *University of Nottingham v Fishel* [2000] EWHC 2221 (QB); [2000] I.C.R. 1462; *Helmet Integrated Systems Ltd v Tunnard* [2006] EWCA Civ 1735; [2007] F.S.R. 16 at [26]–[27] and [37]; *Ranson v Customer Systems Plc* [2012] EWCA Civ 841; [2012] I.R.L.R. 769; *Generics (UK) Ltd v Yeda Research & Development Co Ltd* [2012] EWCA Civ 726; [2013] F.S.R. 13 at [79] onwards; *Re-use Collections Ltd v Sendall* [2014] EWHC 3852 (QB); [2015] I.R.L.R. 226 at [153] (employee recruiting colleagues to leave). cf. Flannigan [2015] J.B.L. 189; Frazer (2015) 131 L.Q.R. 53.

[198] See para.6-038 and Article 45.

ity to, another as would thereby reasonably entitle that other to expect that he or she will act in that other's interest to the exclusion of his or her own or a third party's interest."[199]

In a leading case, *Bristol and West Building Society v Mothew*,[200] Millett LJ stated:

"A fiduciary is someone who has undertaken to act for or on behalf of another in a particular matter or circumstances which give rise to a relationship of trust and confidence."

Millett LJ went on to say:

"The distinguishing obligation of a fiduciary is the obligation of loyalty. The principal is entitled to the single-minded loyalty of his fiduciary. This core liability has several facets. A fiduciary must act in good faith; he must not make a profit out of his trust; he may not act for his own benefit or the benefit of a third person without the informed consent of his principal".[201]

The dictum opens by referring to a general obligation of loyalty, in respect of which the particular fiduciary duties not to profit from position and not to place oneself in a position of conflict of interest are manifestations. Those duties, including an agent's liability for self-dealing, are dealt with in detail in Articles 44–48. They are designed to remove any temptation in the fiduciary to act disloyally, and hence operate whether or not the fiduciary is in fact disloyal.[202] Actual disloyalty, on the other hand, can take a myriad of forms, from deliberately misapplying the principal's funds, accepting bribes, soliciting (before termination of the agency) colleagues and customers to cease to work for and do business with the principal,[203] to conduct that is malicious or spiteful,[204] and to a bad faith omission to act.[205] It is

---

[199] *Grimaldi v Chameleon Mining NL (No.2)* (2012) 287 A.L.R. 22 at [177]; *Lehtimaki v Cooper* [2020] UKSC 33 at [47]. See too *Arklow Investments Ltd v Maclean* [2000] 1 W.L.R. 594 PC at 598: "In the present context, the concept encaptures a situation where one person is in a relationship with another which gives rise to a legitimate expectation, which equity will recognise, that the fiduciary will not utilise his or her position in such a way which is adverse to the interests of the principal".

[200] *Bristol and West Building Society v Mothew* [1998] Ch. 1 at 18. See *Restatement, Third*, § 8.01: "An agent has a fiduciary duty to act loyally for his principal's benefit in all matters connected with the agency relationship". See also *Al Nehayan v Kent* [2018] EWHC 333 (Comm) at [159].

[201] *Bristol and West BS v Mothew* [1998] 1 Ch. 1 at 18, per Millett LJ. As to duties of a manager towards a music group see: *Martin-Smith v Williams* [1999] E.M.L.R. 571.

[202] *Hamilton v Wright* (1842) 9 Cl. & Fin. 111 at 123–124 HL.

[203] *Wessex Dairies Ltd v Smith* [1935] 2 K.B. 80; *Aubanel & Alabaster Ltd v Aubanel* (1949) 66 R.P.C. 343 at 347; *Sybron Corp v Rochem Ltd* [1984] Ch. 112; *Balston Ltd v Headline Filters Ltd* [1990] F.S.R. 385 at 417; *Coleman Taymar Ltd v Oakes* [2001] 2 B.C.L.C. 749; *Také Ltd v BSM Marketing Ltd* [2006] EWHC 1085 (QB); and subsequent damages appeal at [2009] EWCA Civ 45; *Willis Ltd v Jardine Lloyd Thompson Group Plc* [2015] EWCA Civ 450 (interim injunction against manager on "gardening leave" soliciting employees to leave and compete); *Breitenfeld UK Ltd v Harrison* [2015] EWHC 399 (Ch); [2015] 2 B.C.L.C. 275 at [77] (assisting competitor to be ready for business). See too *Warman International Ltd v Dwyer* (1995) 182 C.L.R. 544; *RBC Dominion Securities Inc v Merrill Lynch Canada Inc* [2008] 3 S.C.R. 79.

[204] See *Mordecai v Mordecai* (1988) 12 N.S.W.L.R. 58 (company directors running down company business to leave nothing for estranged wife and child of deceased shareholder). cf. *Bishopsgate Investment Management Ltd v Maxwell (No.2)* [1994] 1 All E.R. 261 at 264.

[205] *British Midland Tool Ltd v Midland International Tooling Ltd* [2003] EWHC 466 (Ch); [2003] 2 B.C.L.C. 523 (company director fails to reveal that former colleague is recruiting key company staff because he too is planning to leave and join colleague); *Chan v Zacharia* (1984) 154 C.L.R. 178 (partner's refusal to renew lease so that available for self). See further below, para.6-080.

also disloyal for an agent consciously to mislead the principal.[206] Breach of fiduciary duty can, it seems, also found the illegality necessary for liability in conspiracy.[207]

Whether or not one regards the paradigm fiduciary as the express trustee, with the duties of agents and others as an extension of the trustee's duties,[208] or whether one says that a trustee is a special sort of fiduciary holding property,[209] is probably no longer of relevance. The attribution of such duties forms a significant area where the common law techniques of strict interpretation of contract, and reluctance to imply terms which the parties did not choose to make express, are modified by different techniques.[210] These fiduciary duties apply whether or not the agency is gratuitous: they do not depend on the fact that the principal is paying for the agent's services.

The fiduciary, and other, duties of directors of companies are now governed by statute, in the form of the Companies Act 2006 Pt 10 Ch.2. These provisions have replaced their common law and equitable equivalents.[211]

6-035   **Agent as fiduciary**   An agent in the strict sense of the word holds a power to affect the legal relations of the principal.[212] This power is conferred by the law in the implementation of the supposed intentions of the parties; but it is not surprising that the law also imposes controls on the way in which the holder of such a strong power may behave towards the person who conferred it. This is not a situation like the more usual one regulated by the law in which the parties are in an adverse commercial relationship, for example a simple hire of services. Agency services are services of a special kind. Even when no such power to affect legal relations was conferred, as in the "incomplete agency" case of the canvassing agent,[213] the relationship of the parties can still, depending on the facts, import an undertaking by one to act in the interests of the other rather than the agent's own, and this likewise, though to a lesser extent, justifies the law's intervention.

It has however been said in the context of an agent's fiduciary obligations that:

> "Agency is a contract made between principal and agent ... like every other contract, the rights and duties of the principal and agent are dependent upon the terms of the contract between them, whether express or implied."[214]

---

[206] *Murad v Al-Saraj* [2005] EWCA Civ 959; 1 W.T.L.R. 1573; *Daly v Sydney Stock Exchange Ltd* (1986) 160 C.L.R. 371; *Amaltal Corp Ltd v Maruha Corp* [2007] 3 N.Z.L.R. 192 (NZSC), Illustration 14 to Article 43; and *Premium Real Estate Ltd v Stevens* [2009] 2 N.Z.L.R. 384 (estate agent misleads vendor principal as to intentions of purchaser). See too *Odyssey Entertainment Ltd v Kamp* [2012] EWHC 2316 (Ch) at [234] (director intentionally misleads colleagues with unduly pessimistic advice on profitability of projects).
[207] See *First Subsea Ltd v Balltec Ltd* [2014] EWHC 866 (Ch).
[208] See Maitland, *Equity* (1936 edn), pp.81–82 and 230–232; Worthington, *Equity* (2nd edn), pp.129–130.
[209] See *Restatement, Third, Trusts*, T.D.No.1, § 2.
[210] See Goodhart and Jones (1980) 43 M.L.R. 489.
[211] Companies Act 2006 s.170(3). See *Palmer's Company Law* (2007); *Company Directors: Duties, Liabilities and Remedies* (Mortimore, ed., 3rd edn); Keay, *Directors' Duties* (2nd edn); Watts, *Directors' Powers and Duties* (2nd edn, 2015). As to the application of fiduciary principles between members of limited liability partnerships, see *F&C Alternative Investments (Holdings) Ltd v Barthelemy* [2011] EWHC 1731 (Ch).
[212] See Article 1.
[213] See above, para.1-020.
[214] *Kelly v Cooper* [1993] A.C. 205 at 213–214 PC, per Lord Browne-Wilkinson (Illustration 9). See

Although older dicta of a similar nature can be cited,[215] not everyone may agree with the emphasis inherent in this statement. Agency need not be contractual; and although there is much overlap with common law duties[216] the notion of fiduciary obligation is independent of contract. It is submitted that the law's control over the agents' exercise of their powers of intervention is not to be derived from contract terms alone. As was said in a subsequent case: "The essence of a fiduciary obligation is that it creates obligations of a different character from those deriving from the contract itself".[217] The role itself will, however, usually be one that is voluntarily assumed by the fiduciary.[218]

Even where the relationship is contractual (as it normally will be), the matter is too important to be left entirely to the agreement of the parties and the interpretation of that agreement. This is an area where the vulnerability of the principal has for more than two centuries[219] been recognised as requiring a degree of supervision. The relief is principally given by the application of fiduciary duties, though other equitable (or partly equitable) doctrines such as duress or undue influence and the special rules for confidential information may on occasion be relevant. The agreement of the parties or the background of the case may however establish that the relationship is not one of agency[220] or that a fiduciary relationship either did not exist or had been modified from the normal standards[221]; but equally a fiduciary relationship may, while consistent with them, increase the contract duties.[222] The long-standing application of fiduciary duties to company promoters, who may have

---

also *Clark Boyce v Mouat* [1994] 1 A.C. 428 at 437; *Henderson v Merrett Syndicates Ltd* [1995] 2 A.C. 145 at 206; *Global Container Lines Ltd v Bonyad Shipping Co* [1998] 1 Lloyd's Rep. 528 (joint venture); *F&C Alternative Investments (Holdings) Ltd v Barthelemy* [2011] EWHC 1731 (Ch) at [223].

[215] e.g. *Lamb v Evans* [1893] 1 Ch. 218 at 228, per Bowen LJ.

[216] See below, para.6-043.

[217] *Re Goldcorp Exchange Ltd* [1995] 1 A.C. 74 at 98, per Lord Mustill; *Lehtimaki v Cooper* [2020] UKSC 33 at [46]. See also *Casson Beckman & Partners v Papi* [1991] B.C.L.C. 299 at 313, per Sir Denys Buckley: "The existence of a fiduciary duty to account would eliminate or negative any need to imply anything". See also *Yasuda Fire and Marine Ins. Co of Europe Ltd v Orion Marine Ins. Underwriting Agency Ltd* [1995] Q.B. 174 at 186, per Colman J: "The rights and obligations arising as a matter of law from the existence of duty creating relationships, such as bailment, are not in principle displaced by contractual rights and obligations unless the contract provides that such rights and obligations are to be excluded or includes remedies which are inconsistent with the duties attributable as a matter of law to the relationship"; *Wingecarribee Shire Council v Lehman Bros Australia Ltd* (2013) 301 A.L.R. 1 at [731]. See too DeMott, (2007) 58 Alabama L.R. 1049; Conaglen (2013) 7 J.Eq. 105; L. Smith in *Contract, Status, and Fiduciary Law* (Miller and Gold, eds, 2016) Ch.5. cf. Edelman (2010) 126 L.Q.R. 302; and (2013) 7 J.Eq. 128.

[218] *Alberta v Elder Advocates of Alberta Society* 2011 SCC 24 at [30] (noted Flannigan (2011) 127 L.Q.R. 505); *Dubai Aluminium Co Ltd v Salaam* [2002] UKHL 48; [2003] 2 A.C. 366 at [128]; *Ross River Ltd v Waveley Commercial Ltd* [2012] EWHC 81 (Ch) at [256]; affirmed on these issues in [2013] EWCA Civ 910. See too Rt Hon. Lord Millett (1998) 114 L.Q.R. 399 at 404–405.

[219] See *York Buildings v MacKenzie* (1795) 8 Bro. P.C. 42. See further, Getzler, in *Philosophical Foundations of Fiduciary Law* (Gold and Miller eds, 2014), Ch.2.

[220] See *Coachcraft Ltd v SVP Fruit Co Ltd* (1980) 28 A.L.R. 319 at 328–329 (PC) (proxy with no obligations to vote as shareholder directed).

[221] See *Hospital Products Ltd v US Surgical Corp* (1984) 156 C.L.R. 41 at 96–97, per Mason J. See para.1-020, and para.6-056.

[222] See Mason J in the *Hospital Products* (1984) 156 C.L.R. 41 case, at 99; *Conway v Ratiu* [2005] EWCA Civ 1302; [2006] 1 All E.R. 571 at [74]; *Cia. Fianciera "Soleada" SA v Hamoor Tanker Corp Inc (The Borag)* [1980] 1 Lloyd's Rep. 111 (reversed on a different point [1981] 1 W.L.R. 274) (unusual terms imposed higher duty of loyalty); *John Youngs Insurance Services Ltd v Aviva Insurance Service UK Ltd* [2011] EWHC 1515 (TCC) at [120] (duty to account survives termination of contract).

had no appointment, contractual or otherwise, with the claimant company, and who sometimes show little conscious regard for the interests of investors, is an example of the reach of equitable doctrine.[223] Similar considerations apply to those, admittedly circumscribed, cases where company directors have been found to have assumed a responsibility to advise shareholders.[224]

6-036   **Development of doctrine**   The duties of fiduciaries such as agents have been developed over the last two centuries to accommodate the difference between express trustees and others who hold special powers similar in varying degrees to those of the trustee. In particular, the position of company promoters and directors was at one time a focal point of such development; hence cases on promoters and directors figure prominently in the older illustrations to this part of the book. The full trust analogy has however long appeared less cogent, and a whole separate area of the law has been developed (or perhaps rediscovered) with broader usage and less stringent controls. The immediate origins in nineteenth century trust law must nevertheless be borne in mind when old cases are read, which apply harsher rules to trustees than those appropriate to agents as a class,[225] and abound in cautionary statements[226]; and they often have fairly easy recourse to notions such as that of trust property when speaking of property in the hands of agents, and of "breach of trust" when referring to even innocent deviation from instructions.

Fiduciary reasoning has been much developed in other common law jurisdictions, perhaps most conspicuously in Canada[227]; but is under discussion

---

[223] See *Erlanger v New Sombrero Phosphate Co* (1878) 3 App.Cas. 1218; *Gluckstein v Barnes* [1900] A.C. 240. See also *Bagnall v Carlton* (1877) 6 Ch.D. 371; *Emma Silver Mining Co v Lewis & Sons* (1879) 4 C.P.D. 396; *Emma Silver Mining Co v Grant* (1879) 11 Ch.D. 918; *Whaley Bridge Calico Printing Co v Green* (1879) 5 Q.B.D. 109; *Lydney and Wigpool Ore Co v Bird* (1886) 33 Ch.D. 85; *Re Cape Breton Co* (1885) 29 Ch.D. 795; affirmed sub nom. *Cavendish-Bentinck v Fenn* (1887) 12 App.Cas. 652; *Lagunas Nitrate Co v Lagunas Syndicate* [1899] 2 Ch. 392; *Re Lady Forrest (Murchison) Gold Mine* [1901] 1 Ch. 582; *Re Leeds & Hanley Theatres of Varieties* [1902] 2 Ch. 809; *Omnium Electric Palaces Ltd v Baines* [1914] 1 Ch. 332; *Jacobus Marler Estates Ltd v Marler* (1916) 85 L.J.P.C. 167n.; *Jubilee Cotton Mills v Lewis* [1924] A.C. 958; *Tracy v Mandelay Pty Ltd* (1953) 88 C.L.R. 215.

[224] *Briess v Woolley* [1954] A.C. 333; *Coleman v Myers* [1977] 2 N.Z.L.R. 225; *Brunninghausen v Glavanics* (1999) 46 N.S.W.L.R. 538 (noted by Goddard (2000) 116 L.Q.R. 197); *Park's of Hamilton (Holdings) Ltd v Campbell* [2014] CSIH 36; 2014 SC 726 at [27]; *Kiriwai Consultants Ltd v Holmes* [2015] NZCA 149. cf. *Percival v Wright* [1902] 2 Ch. 421.

[225] e.g. as to purchase of the trust property: *Lewin on Trusts* (20th edn), Ch.46 and as to rights to remuneration, see below, Article 55. As to the earlier history of fiduciary obligations, see Getzler, in *Mapping the Law* (Burrows and Lord Rodger of Earlsferry eds, 2006), Ch.31.

[226] e.g. *Aberdeen Ry Co v Blaikie Bros* (1854) 1 Macq. 461 at 471, per Lord Cranworth LC. It has been said that such statements "are to be explained by judicial acceptance of the inability of the courts 'in much the greater number of cases' to ascertain the precise effect which the existence of a conflict with personal interest has had upon the performance of fiduciary duty": *Chan v Zacharia* (1984) 154 C.L.R. 178 at 204, per Deane J.

[227] e.g. *Canson Enterprises Ltd v Boughton & Co* [1991] 3 S.C.R. 534; (1991) 85 D.L.R. (4th) 129, Illustration 8 (solicitor); *Strother v 3464920 Canada Inc* [2007] 2 S.C.R. 177; (2007) 281 D.L.R. (4th) 640 (solicitor); *Hodgkinson v Simms* [1994] 3 S.C.R. 377; (1995) 117 D.L.R. (4th) 161 (accountant); *Soulos v Korkontzilas* [1977] 2 S.C.R. 217; (1997) 146 D.L.R. (4th) 214 (real estate broker) (noted L.D. Smith (1998) 114 L.Q.R. 14); *Cadbury Schweppes Inc v FBI Foods Ltd* [1999] 1 S.C.R. 142; (1999) 167 D.L.R. (4th) 577 (no fiduciary relationship in product licensing agreement). See also *Guerin v R.* [1984] 2 S.C.R. 335; (1984) 13 D.L.R. (4th) 321; *Blueberry River Indian Band v R.* [1995] 2 S.C.R. 344; (1996) 130 D.L.R. (4th) 193 (public law); *Frame v Smith* [1987] 3 S.C.R. 99; (1987) 42 D.L.R. (4th) 81, per Wilson J (refusal of access to children); *Norberg v Wynrib* [1992] 2 S.C.R. 226; (1992) 92 D.L.R. (4th) 449 (doctor and patient); *M. (K.) v M. (H.)* [1992] 3 S.C.R. 6;

everywhere.[228] It should not however be taken too far; and it may be that the dictum of Lord Browne-Wilkinson quoted above is best interpreted as a warning against excessive use of such reasoning.[229] It is sometimes imprecisely and mistakenly invoked to justify results which would be more appropriately attributed to express or implied contract terms, or to breach of the common law duty of care in tort; and there have been warnings against invoking such reasoning simply to justify particular remedies, especially the constructive trust.[230] But other available doctrines are duress, undue influence, unconscionability or even, if such could be developed, a requirement of good faith in commercial transactions.[231] Also of potential importance is the equitable concept of "fraud on a power". This concept has had particular application to trustees and company directors, and has not so far been a prominent feature of the general law of agency. Where it applies, it does not require disloyalty in the actor, and it operates independently of the strictly fiduciary duties. An outline of its operation is given in Chapter 8.[232]

Are all agents always fiduciaries?[233]   Turning first to the question of how the incidence of the duties should be explained, it will be noted that the formulations in Article 1 and in the present Article treat the relationship of principal and agent as by definition a fiduciary one, and therefore in effect say that every agent is a fiduciary and hence owes fiduciary duties. This can be criticised on the basis that not every person who can be described by the word "agent" is subject to fiduciary duties; and that a person who certainly is so to be described may owe such duties in some respects and not in others.[234] Hence it is said that there may be a "non-fiduciary agent", and that in some functions an acknowledged agent may not act as

6-037

(1992) 96 D.L.R. (4th) 289 (parent and child); Shepherd, *Law of Fiduciaries* (1981); Rotman, *Fiduciary Law* (2005); *Waters on Trusts* (4th edn), Ch.19.

[228] As to Australia see *Hospital Products Ltd v US Surgical Corp* (1984) 156 C.L.R. 41 (distributor: no fiduciary relationship); *Breen v Williams* (1996) 186 C.L.R. 71 (doctor and patient: no fiduciary relationship) (noted Nolan (1997) 113 L.Q.R. 220); *Maguire v Makaronis* (1997) 188 C.L.R. 449 (solicitor: fiduciary relationship: rescission); *Pilmer v Duke Group Ltd* (2001) 207 C.L.R. 165; *Youyang Pty. Ltd v Minter Ellison Morris Fletcher* (2003) 212 C.L.R. 484; *Harris v Digital Pulse Pty. Ltd* (2003) 56 N.S.W.L.R. 298 (no exemplary damages). As to New Zealand see *Bank of New Zealand v New Zealand Guardian Trust Co Ltd* [1999] 1 N.Z.L.R. 213; affirmed [1999] 1 N.Z.L.R. 664 (bank and trust company: no breach of fiduciary duty); *L. v Robinson* [2000] 3 N.Z.L.R. 499 (doctor and patient: not fiduciary relationship); cf. *S. v Att.-Gen.* [2003] 3 N.Z.L.R. 450 (foster parents agents of Crown). There are also significant cases in the area of remedies, e.g. *Day v Mead* [1987] 2 N.Z.L.R. 443 (contributory negligence); *Aquaculture Corp v New Zealand Green Mussel Co Ltd* [1990] 3 N.Z.L.R. 299; *Cook v Evatt (No.2)* [1992] 1 N.Z.L.R. 676 (see Watts [1992] L.M.C.L.Q. 439) (exemplary damages); *Chirnside v Fay* [2007] 1 N.Z.L.R. 433.

[229] See below, at the end of para.6-043. See also the Rt Hon. Lord Millett (1998) 114 L.Q.R. 214; Davies, in *Consensus ad Idem* (Rose ed., 1996), pp.170–174.

[230] See *Breen v Williams* (1996) 186 C.L.R. 71 at 110.

[231] See Finn in *Equity, Fiduciaries and Trusts* (Youdan ed., 1989), Ch.1; cf. Conaglen (2005) 121 L.Q.R. 452 at 456.

[232] See below, para.8-219.

[233] See *Meagher, Gummow and Lehane's Equity Doctrines and Remedies* (5th edn), para.5-210 onwards.

[234] *John Youngs Insurance Services Ltd v Aviva Insurance Service UK Ltd* [2011] EWHC 1515 (TCC) at [98] (defendant was agent in placing repair work on behalf of insurer, but not in so far as defendant also undertook repair work itself for the insurer under detailed contractual provisions). See too *UBS AG (London Branch) v Kommunale Wasserwerke Peipkiz GmbH* [2017] EWCA Civ 1567 at [92] (noted P. Kelshiker, "Rescission and attribution of knowledge in multi-party cases of dishonest assistance" (2018) 134 L.Q.R. 363).

fiduciary at all.[235] Rather than talk of a "non-fiduciary agent" it seems better to say that where an agent does not act in a fiduciary capacity (e.g. because simply carrying out specific instructions), this is a reflection of the scope of the agent's duties and the boundaries of the equitable rules.

Another view is that the approach should rather be to identify the general circumstances in which a fiduciary duty may arise of itself and note these as situations in which agents may sometimes, but do not always, find themselves. Thus in *Boardman v Phipps*,[236] Lord Upjohn said:

"The facts and circumstances must be carefully examined to see whether in fact a purported agent and even a confidential agent is in a fiduciary relationship to his principal. It does not necessarily follow that he is in such a position (see *In Re Coomber*)."

And in the case referred to, *Re Coomber*,[237] Fletcher Moulton LJ said, in a much quoted passage[238]:

"It is said that the son was the manager of the stores and therefore was in a fiduciary relationship to his mother. This illustrates in a most striking form the danger of trusting to verbal formulae. Fiduciary relations are of many different types; they extend from the relation of myself to an errand boy who is bound to bring me back my change up to the most intimate and confidential relations which can possibly exist between one party and another where the one is wholly in the hands of the other because of his infinite trust in him. All these are cases of fiduciary relations, and the Courts have again and again, in cases where there has been a fiduciary relation, interfered and set aside acts which, between persons in a wholly independent position, would have been perfectly valid. Thereupon in some minds there arises the idea that if there is any fiduciary relation whatever any of these types of interference is warranted by it. They conclude that every kind of fiduciary relation justifies every kind of interference. Of course that is absurd. The nature of the fiduciary relation must be such that it justifies the interference. There is no class of case in which one ought more carefully to bear in mind the facts of the case, when one reads the judgment of the Court on those facts, than cases which relate to fiduciary and confidential relations and the action of the Court with regard to them. In my opinion there was absolutely nothing in the fiduciary relations of the mother and the son with regard to this house which in any way affected this transaction."

It is certainly true that fiduciary relationships arise in situations other than those of agency. Nevertheless, it is submitted that the fact that an agent in the strictest sense of the word has a power to alter the principal's legal position makes it appropriate and salutary to regard the fiduciary duty as a typical feature of the paradigm agency relationship. To do so will not mislead so long as two things are borne in mind.

The first is that the word "agent" can be used in varying senses, and not all persons to whom the word is applied are agents in the full (or sometimes, any) legal sense. A canvassing, or introducing agent,[239] for instance, may do no more than bring two parties together and thus may in many situations do little involving the

---

[235] *Coachcraft Ltd v SVP Fruit Co Ltd* (1980) 28 A.L.R. 319 at 328–329 (PC) (proxy but with no obligations to vote as shareholder directed). See too *UBS AG (London Branch) v Kommunale Wasserwerke Peipkiz GmbH* [2017] EWCA Civ 1567 at [92].

[236] *Boardman v Phipps* [1967] 2 A.C. 46 at 127; followed in *Hendy Lennox (Industrial Engines) Ltd v Grahame Puttick Ltd* [1984] 1 W.L.R. 485. See also Article 48.

[237] *Re Coomber* [1911] 1 Ch. 723.

[238] *Re Coomber* [1911] 1 Ch. 723 at 728–729.

[239] See above, para.1-020.

incidence of fiduciary responsibilities at all.[240] But not infrequently the correct conclusion will be that an introducing agent did assume a responsibility to promote the principal's interests, and thereby, in some circumstances become liable for breach of such duties, as when concealing from the principal the existence of further offers.[241] Further, even canvassing agents usually have authority to make and receive communications on behalf of their principals, and can be expected to act loyally in exercising those powers. A distributor or franchisee, though sometimes called an agent, is in most respects in a position commercially adverse, rather than fiduciary, to the person whose goods he distributes: he buys and resells.[242] But again it is conceivable that circumstances might give him knowledge of and power over his principal's affairs which could justify the imposition of some fiduciary duties[243]; and this is quite apart from the possibility that he may also in some circumstances exercise true agency functions, for example as regards complaints concerning the goods, and be subject to fiduciary duties in that respect. There will be other commercial relationships that in general are arm's-length but where in some aspect there is an agency function; to that aspect fiduciary duties can apply.[244]

The second matter which should be borne in mind is that the extent of an agent's equitable duties (a phrase that embraces more than the strictly fiduciary duties to avoid conflicts of interest and not to profit) and also common law duties may vary from situation to situation. For example, a person who is certainly an agent in general, but who is authorised on a particular occasion to carry out an exactly specified act, may on the occasion act in no more than a ministerial capacity, even if in so doing the principal's legal position is altered.[245] Nevertheless, even a messenger may have to decide what to do if the person to whom the message is to be delivered is not there. To take another example, a person otherwise at arm's length with a claimant with whom the person is proposing to contract may have a limited authority to act for the claimant, for example in filling out the blanks in the document recording the contract.[246] In so doing the person may be required both to adhere to the mandate given and to exercise it in good faith. In many situations the

---

[240] See, e.g. *Eze v Conway* [2019] EWCA Civ 88.
[241] *Keppel v Wheeler* [1927] 1 K.B. 577, Illustration 6 to Article 60; *Jackson v Packham Real Estate Ltd* (1980) 109 D.L.R. (3d) 277; and see *Regier v Campbell-Stuart* [1939] Ch. 766, Illustration 16 to Article 45; *Premium Real Estate Ltd v Stevens* [2009] N.Z.L.R. 384. Or if he gives information to third parties about those he has introduced. But cf. *Knoch Estate v John Picken Ltd* (1991) 83 D.L.R. (4th) 447.
[242] See *Jirna Ltd v Mister Donut of Canada Ltd* (1971) 22 D.L.R. (3d) 639; affirmed (1973) 40 D.L.R. (3d) 303; see also *Keith Henry & Co Pty Ltd v Stuart Walker & Co Pty Ltd* (1958) 100 C.L.R. 342; *Lothian v Jenolite Ltd* 1969 S.C. 11; *Hospital Products Ltd v US Surgical Corp* (1984) 156 C.L.R. 41 (a leading case on this point, where the court was divided)—see in this context the judgment of Mason J; cf. *Watson v Dolmark Industries Ltd* [1992] 3 N.Z.L.R. 311. See also *Cadbury Schweppes Inc v FBI Foods Ltd* [1999] 1 S.C.R. 142; (1999) 167 D.L.R. (4th) 577; above, paras 1-032 and 6-015.
[243] This might even be so of the franchisor's position vis-à-vis the franchisee: cf. *Jirna Ltd v Mister Donut of Canada Ltd* (1971) 22 D.L.R. (3d) 639.
[244] See *New Zealand Netherlands Society "Oranje" Inc v Kuys* [1973] 1 W.L.R. 1126 PC at 1130; *Hospital Products Ltd v US Surgical Corp* (1984) 156 C.L.R. 41 at 98; *Amaltal Corp v Maruha Corp* [2007] 3 N.Z.L.R. 192 at [21].
[245] See, e.g. *Volkers v Midland Doherty* (1985) 17 D.L.R. (4th) 343, Illustration 4 to Article 39; see also *R.H. Deacon & Co v Varga* (1972) 30 D.L.R. (3d) 653; affirmed (1973) 41 D.L.R. (4th) 767n.
[246] For the engagement of agency law in such circumstances, see *Colonial Bank v Hepworth* (1884) 36 Ch.D. 36; *Koch v Dicks* [1933] 1 K.B. 307; *Armor Coatings (Marketing) Pty Ltd v General Credits (Finance) Pty Ltd* (1978) 17 S.A.S.R. 259; and *Wright v Gasweld Pty Ltd* (1991) 22 N.S.W.L.R. 317. See too *Barrett v Bem* [2012] EWCA Civ 52; [2012] Ch. 573 (signature of will on behalf of testator).

duty may be, by virtue of the circumstances, limited; or restricted or even excluded by contract. "The precise scope of [the obligation] must be moulded according to the nature of the relationship."[247]

The converse problem to that of conceiving of an agent who has no fiduciary duties is one that attempts to find fiduciary aspects to all of an agent's duties. Many of the duties that an honest agent might breach, including those that have already been addressed such as the duties to comply with mandate and with due care and skill, do not turn on fiduciary obligations (though they may involve a breach of trust). There are many clear warnings about the unwarranted attachment of the label "fiduciary" to obligations that are not in fact fiduciary. One of the best known is that of Millett LJ in *Bristol and West BS v Mothew*[248]:

> "The expression 'fiduciary duty' is properly confined to those duties which are peculiar to fiduciaries and the breach of which attracts legal consequences differing from those consequent upon the breach of other duties. Unless the expression is so limited it is lacking in practical utility. In this sense it is obvious that not every breach of duty by a fiduciary is a breach of fiduciary duty."

6-038 **When do fiduciary duties start and end?** A subject not without difficulty is when, in relation to an agent, fiduciary duties (and the underlying duty of loyalty) begin and cease to operate? The issues are, in part at least, a reflection of the difficulties that have already been noted in differentiating fiduciary duties from other equitable controls on conduct, in particular the principles of undue influence. Sharp lines are often not drawn between the two.[249]

The basic principle, at least in English law, seems to be that fiduciary duties commence[250] and end[251] with the relationship of agency, which may or may not coincide with any contract between the parties.

The issue most likely to arise in relation to the period before the commencement of the agency is whether a person who is about to undertake fiduciary responsibility is obliged to reveal facts about the fiduciary's past that may be relevant to the duties to be performed, including such things as past wrongs,[252] and whether the terms on which it is offering to provide services (including as to

---

[247] *New Zealand Netherlands Society "Oranje" Inc v Kuys* [1973] 1 W.L.R. 1126 at 1130, per Lord Wilberforce. See also *Birtchnell v Equity Trustee, Executor and Agency Co Ltd* (1929) 42 C.L.R. 384 at 408; and *Medsted Associates Ltd v Canaccord Genuity Wealth (International) Ltd* [2019] EWCA Civ 83; [2019] 1 W.L.R. 4481 at [45].

[248] *Bristol and West BS v Mothew* [1998] Ch. 1 at 16. See also *De Sena v Notaro* [2020] EWHC 1031 (Ch) at [191]: "[I]t is unwise to refer to a *person* as 'fiduciary' rather than to an *obligation*. This is because, if a person is labelled a 'fiduciary', there is a temptation to regard *every* obligation owed by that person as fiduciary, which is not necessarily correct. It is surely better to reserve the word 'fiduciary' to describe the content of particular *obligations*, so as to distinguish those owed by a particular person which *are* fiduciary from those owed by the same person which are not". But cf. D. Heydon, in *Equity in Commercial Law* (Degeling and Edelman eds, 2005), Ch.9. See further, para.6-043, below.

[249] See R. Flannigan, "Presumed Undue Influence: the False Partition from Fiduciary Accountability" (2016) 34 U. of Queensland L.J. 171.

[250] See *Arklow Investments Ltd v Maclean* [2000] 1 W.L.R. 594 at 599–600 PC. See too *Sharbern Holding Inc v Vancouver Airport Centre Ltd* [2011] 2 S.C.R. 175; (2011) 331 D.L.R. (4th) 1 at [144].

[251] See *Twigg Farnell (a firm) v Wildblood* [1998] P.M.L.R. 211 CA at 214; *Prince Jefri Bolkiah v KPMG* [1999] 2 A.C. 222 at 235–236; *Walsh v Shanahan* [2013] EWCA Civ 411 at [38]. But cf. *Ratiu v Conway* [2005] EWCA Civ 1302; [2006] 1 All E.R. 571 at [72].

[252] See *HPOR Servicos De Consultoria Ltd v Dryships Inc* [2018] EWHC 3451 (Comm); [2019] 1 Lloyd's Rep. 260 (failure to reveal giving of bribes on behalf of a different client in relation to same third party but some time before current transaction). See further, para.6-047.

remuneration) are consistent with the fiduciary's normal terms.[253] There is little authority in England and Wales on whether the relationship is one uberrimae fidei so that fiduciary duties apply to the appointment process, and mixed views in other jurisdictions.[254] Statutory regulation may also impose pre-contractual duties on some types of agent.[255]

It will be rare that fiduciary duties cease to operate before any contractual relationship or officeholding terminates. It has been held that in a case of total exclusion from participation as a director, some aspects at least of the director's fiduciary duties can cease to operate.[256] Once an agent's appointment has ceased, the agent is in general free to compete with, or work for a competitor of, the former principal.[257] A useful modern statement of the position, addressed to the case of directors, is that of Lawrence Collins J in *CMS Dolphin Ltd v Simonet*[258]:

> "In English law a director's power to resign from office is not a fiduciary power. A director is entitled to resign even if his resignation might have a disastrous effect on the business and reputation of the company. So also in English law, at least in general, a fiduciary obligation does not continue after the determination of the relationship which gives rise to it."

In *Longstaff v Birtles*,[259] on the other hand, it was held that a solicitor continued to owe the duties of trust and confidence of a fiduciary even though the particular matter for which he had been engaged had come to an end. In the case, the solicitor, immediately after his client had told him in his offices that the client was not proceeding with the relevant transaction, raised with the client the possibility of the client's investing in a similar business in which the solicitor had a personal interest. The solicitor was found to have had a conflict of interest, which ultimately led to a liability in damages (a remedy which may not have been available if only undue influence were the basis of the complaint).

Other controls on conduct may commence to operate before, and continue to operate after, the end of the agent's retainer. Hence, duties to uphold confidences (including trade secrets) will usually start with the imparting of the confidential information, which may be before any agency arises, and will continue until the

[253] See *Medsted Associates Ltd v Canaccord Genuity Wealth (International) Ltd* [2019] EWCA Civ 83; [2019] 1 W.L.R. 4481 at [32] and [44]; *Rahme v Benjamin & Khoury Pty Ltd* [2019] NWSCA 211.

[254] Against, Canada: *Sharbern Holding Inc v Vancouver Airport Centre Ltd* [2011] 2 S.C.R. 175; (2011) 331 D.L.R. (4th) 1 at [144] (no pre-appointment duty, but duty to disclose pre-appointment facts arose anyway after appointed); in favour, Australia: *Law Society of New South Wales v Foreman* (1994) 34 N.S.W.L.R. 408 at 435–436; *Szmulewicz v Recht* [2011] VSC 368; *Rahme v Benjamin & Khoury Pty Ltd* [2019] NSWCA 211 at [86].

[255] See, for instance, Consumer Rights Act 2015 s.62; and in relation to directors, Companies Act 2006 Ch.4 (transactions with directors requiring approval of members).

[256] See *In Plus Group Ltd v Pyke* [2002] EWCA Civ 370; [2002] 2 B.C.L.C. 210. cf. *First Subsea Ltd v Balltec Ltd* [2017] EWCA Civ 186 at [23]; *Re Systems Building Services Group Ltd* [2020] EWHC 54 (Ch) (director's fiduciary duties continue when company in administration).

[257] *Wessex Dairies Ltd v Smith* [1935] 2 K.B. 80; *FSS Travel and Leisure Systems Ltd v Johnson* [1997] EWCA Civ 2759; [1998] I.R.L.R. 382 at 385; *Ultraframe (UK) Ltd v Fielding* [2005] EWHC 1638 (Ch) at [1309]; *Helmet Integrated Systems Ltd v Tunnard* [2006] EWCA Civ 1735; [2007] I.R.L.R. 126; *Vestergaard Frandsen A/S v Bestnet Europe Ltd* [2013] UKSC 31; [2013] 1 W.L.R. 1556 at [44] (employees).

[258] *CMS Dolphin Ltd v Simonet* [2001] 2 B.C.L.C. 704 at 733.

[259] *Longstaff v Birtles* [2001] EWCA Civ 1219; [2002] 1 W.L.R. 470; criticised Conaglen, *Fiduciary Loyalty* at 192–193. See also *Ratiu v Conway* [2005] EWCA Civ 1302; [2006] 1 All E.R. 571; *Richards v Law Society* [2009] EWHC 2087 (Admin); *Rahme v Benjamin & Khoury Pty Ltd* [2019] NSWCA 211. cf. *Swycher v Vakil* [2002] EWCA Civ 1668.

information ceases to be confidential or the party receiving the information is released from the obligation. Some types of agent, most conspicuously solicitors, may be subject to particularly exacting duties in relation to confidential information that endure after the retainer,[260] and can also be subject to a presumption of influence in relation to transactions (both gifts and contracts), taking place both during and after the retainer (quaere in relation to the terms of the retainer itself, where professional regulation may also operate).[261] As will be seen below, agents who attempt to profit from position or who are under a duty to pursue for their principal relevant business opportunities, cannot free themselves from those duties by simply resigning.[262]

6-039 **Disclosure and consent**[263] The fiduciary duties not to profit and to avoid conflicts have been said to be purely negative duties.[264] They forbid the agent from having a conflict and from profiting from position, but impose no positive obligations. However, as a matter of practicalities, it will often be in the principal's interests as much as the agent's that the conflict exists or the profiting takes place. In such circumstances, it becomes essential that the agent fully informs the principal of all relevant facts and then obtains consent to the conflict or profiting. Those duties of disclosure and obtaining consent, albeit arising only secondarily, are positive duties. In other words, the fiduciary duties are not outright prohibitions, but merely proscribe profiting and conflicts that have not been consented to by the principal.[265] What constitutes a fully informed consent is a question of fact and "there is no precise formula which will determine all cases".[266] Consent must be positively shown, but it can be inferred if the principal is plainly fully aware of all the facts and raises no objection.[267] The burden of proving full disclosure of a conflict of interest and of obtaining consent lies on the agent.[268] It is not sufficient for the agent merely to disclose the existence of an interest[269] or to make such statements as

---

[260] See below, para.6-051.

[261] See below, paras 6-067 and 6-069.

[262] See paras 6-067, 6-077 and 6-081. See also *Tigris International NV v China Southern Airlines Co Ltd* [2014] EWCA Civ 1649 at [163].

[263] See *Restatement, Third*, § 8.06(1); *Meagher, Gummow and Lehane's Equity Doctrines and Remedies* (5th edn), paras 5-130 and 5-135; Payne, "Consent" in *Breach of Trust* (Birks and Pretto eds, 2002), Ch.10.

[264] See, e.g. *Breen v Williams* (1996) 186 C.L.R. 71 at 95 and 113 (noted Nolan (1997) 113 L.Q.R. 220); *Att. Gen. v Blake* [1998] Ch. 439 at 455; *P & V Industries Pty Ltd v Porto* (2006) 14 V.R. 1 at [24].

[265] *New Zealand Netherlands Society "Oranje" Inc v Kuys* [1973] 1 W.L.R. 1126.

[266] *Maguire v Makaronis* (1997) 188 C.L.R. 449 at 466; *Farah Constructions Pty Ltd v Say-Dee Pty Ltd* (2007) 230 C.L.R. 89; *Beach Petroleum NL v Kennedy* (1999) 48 N.S.W.L.R. 1; *Sharbern Holding Inc v Vancouver Airport Centre Ltd* [2009] BCCA 224; affirmed [2011] 2 S.C.R. 175; (2011) 331 D.L.R. (4th) 1. As to the possibility of an estoppel against a principal who is aware of all the facts, see *Rossetti Marketing Ltd v Diamond Sofa Co Ltd* [2012] EWCA Civ 1021; [2013] 1 All ER (Comm) 308 at [41]; *Northampton Regional Livestock Centre Co Ltd v Cowling* [2015] EWCA Civ 651 at [77]; [2016] 1 B.C.L.C. 431. As to the stricter approach applicable to trustees, see *Lewin on Trusts* (20th edn), para.41-106 onwards; *Spellson v George* (1992) 26 N.S.W.L.R. 666.

[267] *Paton v Rosesilver Group Corp* [2017] EWCA Civ 158 at [34].

[268] *Dunne v English* (1874) L.R. 18 Eq. 524; *Hurstanger v Wilson* [2007] 1 W.L.R. 2351 at [36]; *JD Wetherspoon Plc v Van De Berg & Co Ltd* [2009] EWHC 639 (Ch) at [68]; *Cobbetts LLP v Hodge* [2009] EWHC 786 (Ch) at [108]. On the analogy of concurrence with breach of trust, it should not be necessary to show that the principal knew that what he was consenting to was a breach of duty, so long as he knew clearly what the facts were: *Re Pauling's Settlement Trusts* [1962] 1 W.L.R. 86 at 108.

[269] *Imperial Mercantile Credit Association Co v Coleman* (1873) L.R. 6 H.L. 189; *Alexander v*

would put the principal on inquiry[270] nor is it a defence to assert that had the agent asked for permission it would have been given.[271] In that regard, it is no answer for an agent who has not obtained consent to a conflict or undisclosed profit to show that the principal was content with the deal the agent had obtained.[272] It is possible that the consent itself may be recalled if obtained by undue influence,[273] duress or misrepresentation. Consent may be given in advance or retrospectively. In some circumstances it may not be necessary for the agent to give details of the amount of a commission being paid by a third party where the principal knows that the remuneration will be received and the commission is at a rate standard in the industry.[274] It is not always necessary that the principal understand that without consent there would be a breach of fiduciary duty, but usually the principal should be aware that its consent is being sought.[275] Where the consent is asserted to have been given by another agent, that other agent has to have authority to give it, and disclosure of the conflict will usually be effective only when given to such a person.[276]

In the case of company directors, equity took the stance that in relation to conflicts of interest, disclosure to the principal, the company, could not be effected by a director simply disclosing to colleagues on the board,[277] but rather required disclosure to shareholders. Further, in relation to at least some cases of interception by a director of corporate opportunities (as to which, see below, para.6-081), consent even of a majority of shareholders may be insufficient; only unanimity will suffice.[278] These rules, however, have been modified by the Companies Act 2006. Authorisation may now be given by directors so long as the affected director is not counted as part of the quorum and does not vote, and in the case of public companies, the constitution provides for directors to give the relevant dispensation.[279]

Automatic Telephone Co [1900] 2 Ch. 56; *Gluckstein v Barnes* [1900] A.C. 240; *Gray v New Augarita Porcupine Mines* [1952] 3 D.L.R. 1 PC; *Cobbetts LLP v Hodge* [2009] EWHC 786 (Ch) at [110]; *FHR European Ventures LLP v Mankarious* [2011] EWHC 2308 (Ch) at [78]; reversed on other points at [2014] UKSC 45; [2015] A.C. 250.

[270] *Dunne v English* (1874) L.R. 18 Eq. 524; *Novoship (UK) Ltd v Mikhaylyuk* [2012] EWHC 3586 (Comm) at [83]; affirmed on this point [2014] EWCA Civ 908. cf. *Swale v Ipswich Tannery Co Ltd* (1906) 11 Com.Cas. 88 at 86–97. The mere fact that a solicitor acting for both agent and principal in a transaction is aware of an agent's undisclosed personal benefit, is not disclosure to the principal by the agent: *Park's of Hamilton (Holdings) Ltd v Campbell* [2014] CSIH 36; 2014 SC 726 at [28].

[271] *Murad v Al-Saraj* [2005] EWCA Civ 959; 1 W.T.L.R. 1573, Illustration 12 to Article 48; *Gidman v Barron* [2003] EWHC 153 (Ch) at [126]; *FHR European Ventures LLP v Mankarious* [2011] EWHC 2308 (Ch) at [79]; reversed on other points at [2014] UKSC 45; [2015] A.C. 250.

[272] See *Keppel v Wheeler* [1927] 1 K.B. 577, Illustration 6 to Article 60; and *Pengelly v Business Mortgage Finance 4 Plc* [2020] EWHC 2002 (Ch) at [68].

[273] *Curtis v Pulbrook* [2009] EWHC 782 (Ch) (donee of power of attorney in respect of donor, his father).

[274] See below, para.6-086.

[275] *Knight v Frost* [1999] B.C.C. 819 at 828; *EIC Services Ltd v Phipps* [2003] EWHC 1507 (Ch); [2003] B.C.C. 931 at [133]; *Sharma v Sharma* [2013] EWCA Civ 1287; [2014] B.C.C. 73 at [47].

[276] *Ross River Ltd v Cambridge City Football Club Ltd* [2007] EWHC 2115 (Ch); [2008] 1 All E.R. 1004 at [215]. See further below, para.6-086.

[277] *Benson v Heathorn* (1842) 1 Y. & C. Ch. Cas. 326; *Woolworths Ltd v Kelly* (1991) 22 N.S.W.L.R. 189 at 207. But cf. *Queensland Mines Ltd v Hudson* (1978) 18 A.L.R. 1 PC; and *New Zealand Netherlands Society "Oranje" Inc v Kuys* [1973] 1 W.L.R. 1126; *GHLM Trading Ltd v Maroo* [2012] EWHC 61 (Ch) at [200].

[278] *Cook v Deeks* [1916] 1 A.C. 554.

[279] See Companies Act 2006 s.175. See too ss.177 and 182. As to the possibility of ratification after the

Similar issues could arise where an agent has joint principals, where disclosure to one principal may not be sufficient.[280]

As for modification by consent of the fiduciary duties themselves, see below, para.6-056. As for positive duties of disclosure that may be imposed on at least some types of agent, see below, para.6-054. As for disclosure in the context of secret commissions, see para.6-086.

6-040 **Remedies: proprietary or personal?** Turning to the question of remedies, an important question to ask is when the principal's remedies against the agent are proprietary and when they are personal. A proprietary remedy for breach of fiduciary duty is an application of a main technique of equity, of requiring the legal owner of money or other property to hold it as trustee; it involves the notion that the agent holds such money or property on constructive trust. The money or property belongs in equity to the principal. A personal remedy on the other hand holds the agent liable to pay money to the principal as upon an obligation. As has been stated above, such obligations can often in agency situations be derived from common law independently of the fiduciary duties, being formulated by way of breach of implied terms of a contract, or a claim in restitution or tort.

The main advantages of a proprietary remedy from the point of view of the principal are that (i) the principal is generally entitled to any profits made with its money or property[281]; (ii) if the agent mixes the money with personal funds, the principal will be entitled to the contents of the mixture, or anything acquired by expenditure from the mixture, up to the value of its input[282]; (iii) the property will not in general be available to the agent's creditors in the event of a bankruptcy[283]; (iv) the principal may be able to trace the money, not only against the agent but also into the hands of third parties other than bona fide purchasers for value[284]; (v) there may be no limitation period applicable in relation to recovery of the property as a result of relevant provisions of the Limitation Act[285]; (vi) the principal may be able

---

event, see s.239. However, s.239(7) provides that the statutory procedure for ratification does not affect any rule of law imposing additional requirements for ratification. See *Sharma v Sharma* [2013] EWCA Civ 1287.

[280] See *FHR European Ventures LLP v Mankarious* [2011] EWHC 2308 (Ch) at [84] (disclosure to one co-principal only would turn on actual or apparent authority to do so); reversed on other grounds at [2014] UKSC 45; [2015] A.C. 250.

[281] *Docker v Somes* (1834) 2 My. & K. 655; *Foskett v McKeown* [2000] 1 A.C. 102; Goff and Jones, *Law of Unjust Enrichment* (9th edn), para.37-02 onwards. See Finn, *Fiduciary Obligations* (1977), Ch.18. This may include interest (see Article 52); an account attributing the profits in a mixed fund to the constituent elements of it: see *Scott v Scott* (1963) 109 C.L.R. 649; *Re Tilley's Will Trusts* [1967] Ch. 1179; Article 51; and sometimes an award in respect of savings effected for the trustee by the use of the property: see Finn, op cit., pp.127–129.

[282] *Lupton v White* (1808) 15 Ves. 432; *Cook v Addison* (1868) L.R. 7 Eq. 466; *Re Oatway* [1903] 2 Ch. 356; *James Roscoe (Bolton) Ltd v Winder* [1915] 1 Ch. 62; *Indian Oil Corp Ltd v Greenstone Shipping SA* [1988] Q.B. 345; *Ryde Holdings Ltd v Rainbow Corp Ltd* [1993] UKPC 40; *Bishopsgate Investment Management Ltd v Homan* [1995] Ch. 211: see also *Re Tilley's Will Trusts* [1967] Ch. 1179. But the matter is sometimes put on the basis that the defendant can prove that something is his: see *Van Rassel v Kroon* (1953) 87 C.L.R. 298 (lottery ticket); *Warman International Ltd v Dwyer* (1995) 182 C.L.R. 544 at 561–562.

[283] *Barclays Bank Ltd v Quistclose Investments* [1970] A.C. 567.

[284] See Article 91.

[285] Limitation Act 1980 s.21(1)(b); older cases, of course, related to earlier legislation. See e.g. Illustrations 1 and 3. See now *Williams v Central Bank of Nigeria* [2014] UKSC 10; [2014] A.C. 1189; *Burnden Holdings (UK) Ltd v Fielding* [2018] UKSC 14; [2018] 2 W.L.R. 885; *First Subsea Ltd v Balltec Ltd* [2017] EWCA Civ 186 and the discussion of trusteeship in this context by Millett LJ in

to obtain an order for the return of specific property and an interim order for its preservation pending trial.[286] It seems that the claimant may elect whether to take the asset in specie or to seek merely an order for the payment of its value.[287] The claimant will also be able to elect whether to claim the asset or its value (whether or not the defaulting party can show that the asset could, if desired, have been acquired using personal funds) or to reject the expenditure and claim the original sum taken plus interest.[288]

It is generally accepted, however, that it would be inappropriate for a breach of fiduciary duty to create proprietary rights in assets that have not been derived from the breach.[289]

Remedies: agent holding money for principal[290] It is convenient first to consider **6-041** situations where the agent simply holds for the principal without any issue of breach of fiduciary obligation. The analogy with trust might be taken to suggest first, that when agents hold title to money or other property for their principal, they always do so (in situations where the principal does not itself own it) as trustee. This would often be impractical and has never been the rule. It is perfectly possible for property so held, especially money, to be the agent's own, and mixed with personal assets subject only to a duty to transfer or account for it to the principal. Equally however the agent may certainly hold as trustee.

Often the answer turns on the contract between principal and agent. It is clear in this context and in general that the existence of a contractual relationship of debtor and creditor between the parties does not prevent the existence of a simultaneous trust relationship, or a fiduciary relationship of a less onerous nature, involving nevertheless that certain money or property is held on trust.[291] Thus it may be provided expressly between principal and agent that money received is so held. At

---

Paragon Finance Plc v D.B. Thakerar & Co [1999] 1 All E.R. 400; *J.J. Harrison (Properties) Ltd v Harrison* [2001] EWCA Civ 1467; [2002] 1 B.C.L.C. 162; *Yong Kheng Leong v Panweld Trading Pte Ltd* [2012] SGCA 59 at [42] onwards. See further *Lewin on Trusts* (20th edn), Ch.50.

[286] Now fused into "Interim Remedies" (together with freezing injunctions) in CPR 25.1.

[287] See *FHR European Ventures LLP v Cedar Capital Partners LLC* [2014] UKSC 45; [2015] A.C. 250 at [7]; *Global Energy Horizons Corp v Gray* [2015] EWHC 2232 (Ch) at [139]–[143].

[288] See *Scott v Scott* (1963) 109 C.L.R. 649 at 660 and 662; *Tang Ying Ip v Tang Ying Loi* [2017] HKCFA 3 at [27], per Lord Millett.

[289] See *Daly v Sydney Stock Exchange Ltd* (1986) 160 C.L.R. 371; *Hancock Family Memorial Foundation Ltd v Porteous* (2000) 22 W.A.R. 198; *Fortex Group Ltd v Macintosh* [1998] 3 N.Z.L.R. 471 (Illustration 6). Dicta to the contrary in *Space Investments Ltd v Canadian Imperial Bank of Commerce Trust Co (Bahamas) Ltd* [1988] 1 W.L.R. 1072 have not been followed: see *Re Goldcorp Exchange Ltd* [1995] 1 A.C. 74; *Serious Fraud Office v Lexi Holdings Plc* [2008] EWCA Crim 1443; [2009] Q.B. 376; *Lehman Brothers International (Europe) v CRC Credit Fund Ltd* [2009] EWHC 3228 (Ch) at [192] (ultimately reversed on basis of statutory provisions: [2012] UKSC 6; [2012] 3 All E.R. 1). See also the Rt Hon. Lord Millett [1993] Restitution L.Rev. 7; (1998) 114 L.Q.R. 214 at 225–227.

[290] The text of this paragraph received general approval in *Pearson v Lehman Brothers Finance SA* [2010] EWHC 2914 (Ch) at [253]; affirmed [2011] EWCA Civ 1544.

[291] See *Barclays Bank Ltd v Quistclose Investments Ltd* [1970] A.C. 567 (giving rise to the so-called "Quistclose trust": see *Lewin on Trusts* (20th edn), para.9-040 onwards); *Re Kayford* [1975] 1 W.L.R. 279; *Carreras Rothmans Ltd v Freeman Matthews Treasure Ltd* [1985] Ch. 207; *General Communications Ltd v Development Finance Corp of New Zealand* [1990] 3 N.Z.L.R. 406; *Pearson v Lehman Brothers Finance SA* [2011] EWCA Civ 1544 at [68] (trust sustained even though identification of varying beneficial ownership of assets would be complex); *Hughmans Solicitors v Central Stream Services Ltd* [2012] EWCA Civ 1720 at [21]; *Bambury v Jensen* [2015] NZHC 2384; *Lehman Bros International (Europe) v CRC Credit Fund Ltd* [2012] UKSC 6; [2012] 3 All E.R. 1 at [194]; *Bellis v Challinor* [2015] EWCA Civ 59 (solicitor's client account held on trust even though

other times the intention to create a trust may be inferred; the matter turns on the objective interpretation, according to general principles, of the intentions of the parties.[292] Equally, it is possible that a person may be appointed agent to collect moneys owed a principal, such as rent, but then have the express right to have recourse to those funds for discharge of obligations owed by the principal to the agent (whether or not those obligations relate to the agency relationship).[293]

It is sometimes said that there is a prima facie duty on an agent to keep the principal's money and property separate[294]; but it seems likely that this is overstated.[295] Earlier editions of this work suggested that the situations where a trust has been held to exist largely fall into two broad categories: (i) where money or property has been specifically entrusted to the agent by the principal to hold for the principal's benefit or to use for a specific purpose[296]; and (ii) where money or property has been handed to the agent by a third party to hold or convert into a specific property for the benefit of the principal.[297] Another relevant consideration is whether money or property was received in pursuance of a single transaction for which the agent was appointed, or as part of a group of transactions in respect of which a general account was to be rendered later or periodically. No implication of a personal right to use agency moneys would normally be appropriate where the agent was of a type who is not expected to handle money for the principal at all. These are all useful indications, though the cases are not all easily reduced to such form.[298]

The present trend seems to be to approach the matter more functionally and to ask whether the trust relationship is appropriate to the commercial relationship in which the parties find themselves[299]; whether it was appropriate that money or property should be, and whether it was, held separately, or whether it was

---

no certainty as to who was beneficiary of the funds).

[292] A trust so inferred is still a type of express trust: see *Bahr v Nicolay (No.2)* (1987) 164 C.L.R. 604 at 618–619; *Re Lehman Brothers International (Europe)* [2010] EWHC 2914 (Ch) at [225], [245] and [250] (affirmed on appeal on other grounds [2011] EWCA Civ 1544; [2012] 2 B.C.L.C. 151).

[293] See *Clarence House Ltd v National Westminster Bank Plc* [2009] EWCA Civ 1311 at [35]. cf. *Ferrera v Hardy* [2013] EWHC 4164 (Ch) at [18].

[294] See Article 50; *Palette Shoes Pty Ltd v Krohn* (1937) 58 C.L.R. 1 at 30; *Westpac Banking Corp v Savin* [1985] 2 N.Z.L.R. 41 at 49. See also *Cohen v Cohen* (1929) 42 C.L.R. 91 at 101–102.

[295] See the valuable discussion by the Court of Appeal of New South Wales in *Walker v Corboy* (1990) 19 N.S.W.L.R. 382; Article 50.

[296] e.g. *Burdick v Garrick* (1870) L.R. 5 Ch.App. 233, Illustration 1; *Flitcroft's case* (1882) 21 Ch.D. 519; *Dooby v Watson* (1888) 39 Ch.D. 178; *North American Land and Timber Co Ltd v Watkins* [1904] 2 Ch. 233, Illustration 3; *Royal Norwegian Government v Calcutta Marine Engineering Co Ltd* [1960] 2 Lloyd's Rep. 431 (but compare this case with *Potters (A Firm) v Loppert* [1973] Ch. 399; and see Article 53); *Cooper v PRG Powerhouse Ltd* [2008] EWHC 498 (Ch); [2008] B.P.I.R. 492; [2008] 2 All E.R. (Comm) 964.

[297] e.g. *Littlewood v Williams* (1815) 6 Taunt. 277; *Mathew v Brise* (1851) 14 Beav. 341; *Seagram v Tuck* (1881) 18 Ch.D. 296; *Brown v IRC* [1965] A.C. 244, Illustration 1 to Article 53; *Zumax Nigeria Ltd v First City Monument Bank Plc* [2017] EWHC 2804 (Ch) at [80]. cf. *Ex p. Dale & Co* (1879) 11 Ch.D. 772.

[298] e.g. as to stockbrokers: *Hancock v Smith* (1889) 41 Ch.D. 456; *Re Wreford* (1897) 13 T.L.R. 153 (trustee of client account); see also *Re Fleet Disposal Services Ltd* [1995] 1 B.C.L.C. 345 (selling agent a trustee); *Re Ararimu Holdings Ltd* [1989] 3 N.Z.L.R. 487; cf. *King v Hutton* (1860) 83 L.T. 68 (not a trustee); and auctioneers: *Re Cotton Ex p. Cooke* (1913) 103 L.T. 310 (trustee); cf. *Murphy v Howlett* [1960] E.G.D. 231 (not a trustee).

[299] See *New Zealand and Australian Land Co v Watson* (1881) 7 Q.B.D. 374 at 382; *Templeton Insurance Ltd v Motorcare Warranties Ltd* [2010] EWHC 3113 (Comm) at [194]; *Bieber v Teathers Ltd* [2012] EWHC 190 (Ch) at [25]; affirmed [2012] EWCA Civ 1466; [2012] 2 B.C.L.C. 585 (no trust where impossible to carry out instructions if keep moneys separate).

contemplated that the agent should use the money, property or proceeds of the property as part of the agent's normal cash flow in such a way that the relationship of debtor and creditor is more appropriate.[300] There are a great number of cases.[301] At the same time, there is no absolute rule that the absence of a duty to keep the principal's property separate is fatal to there being a trust. Such a trust would have to be over a mixed fund,[302] and there would also have to be a personal duty on the agent to maintain the balance of the fund at or above the amounts owed the principal. Where this occurs, the appropriate analysis is likely to be that the agent is simply one of the beneficiaries of the trust along with the principal or principals, something perfectly possible in equity. It is also certainly possible, and in some contexts routine (as with solicitors), for an agent to keep the funds of multiple clients in the same trust account.[303]

Further, even where an agent does not hold money provided by the principal for specific purposes, there may be a duty to use it only for purposes relevant to the agency, with the consequence that if the money is used for non-agency purposes, any asset acquired with it is held on trust.[304] Sometimes the position is secured by statute or regulation providing that particular types of functionary (e.g. estate agents and solicitors) hold clients' money on trust, pay into client accounts and keep trust accounts.[305]

Many disputes over an agent's obligations in relation to moneys or other property in the agent's hands do not surface until the agent has become insolvent. There had

---

[300] This passage as it appeared in the 15th edition of this book was approved by Lord Goff of Chieveley in the context of equitable lien in *Lord Napier and Ettrick v Hunter* [1993] A.C. 713 at 744. As to such liens, see Phillips, in *Interests in Goods* (Palmer and McKendrick, eds, 2nd edn), Ch.39.

[301] See *King v Hutton* (1860) 83 L.T. 68; *Henry v Hammond* [1913] 2 K.B. 515, Illustration 4; *Neste Oy v Lloyd's Bank Plc* [1983] 2 Lloyd's Rep. 658, Illustration 5; *Stephens Travel Service Inc Pty Ltd v Qantas Airways Ltd* (1988) 13 N.S.W.L.R. 331 (distinguished in *Canadian Pacific Airlines Ltd v Canadian Imperial Bank of Commerce* (1987) 42 D.L.R. (4th) 375; affirmed (1990) 71 Q.R. (2d) 63); *Walker v Corboy* (1990) 19 N.S.W.L.R. 382; *Kingscroft Insurance Co Ltd v H.S. Weavers (Underwriting Agencies) Ltd* [1993] 1 Lloyd's Rep. 187; *Style Financial Services Ltd v Bank of Scotland (No.2)* 1998 S.L.T. 851; *Paragon Finance Plc v D.B. Thackerar & Co* [1999] 1 All E.R. 400 at 415; *Hinckley Singapore Trading Pte Ltd v Sogo Department Stores (S) Pte Ltd* [2001] 4 Singapore L.R. 154 (concessionaire agreement); *Duggan v Governor of Full Sutton Prison* [2004] EWCA Civ 78; [2004] 1 W.L.R. 1010 (prisoners depositing cash); *Pearson v Lehman Bros Finance SA* [2011] EWCA Civ 1544; *Bellis v Challinor* [2015] EWCA Civ 59; *Korda v Australian Executor Trustees (SA) Ltd* [2015] HCA 6; (2015) 255 C.L.R. 62 at [111]. See too *Re Farepak Food & Gifts Ltd* [2006] EWHC 3272 (Ch); [2007] 2 B.C.L.C. 1 (alleged agent held agent only for seller and not buyer, and no duty to keep proceeds separate). For the position in relation to travel agents and air tickets, see Smith, in *Commercial Trusts in European Private Law* (Graziadei, Mattei and Smith eds, 2005), p.294.

[302] See *Lehman Brothers International (Europe) Ltd v CRC Credit Fund Ltd* [2012] UKSC 6; [2012] 3 All E.R. 1 at [194]; *Bambury v Jensen* [2015] NZHC 2384 at [119].

[303] See *Lomas v RAB Market Cycles (Master) Fund Ltd* [2009] EWHC 2545 (Ch) at [54] and [56]; *Re Lehman Brothers International (Europe)* [2010] EWHC 2914 (Ch) at [225] and [233].

[304] *Zhong v Wang* (2007) N.Z.C.P.R. 488. See too *Lehman Bros International (Europe) v CRC Credit Fund Ltd* [2009] EWHC 3228 (Ch) at [151] (power to maintain mixed fund of client and personal moneys, but duty to maintain buffer to cover amount owed clients), ultimately reversed on some issues [2012] UKSC 6; [2012] 3 All E.R. 1.

[305] Estate Agents Act 1979 ss.13–16 (in fact, persons engaged in "estate agency work") (see Murdoch, *Law of Estate Agency* (5th edn), p.233 onwards; Murdoch, *The Estate Agents and Property Misdescriptions Acts* (3rd edn), Ch.3D); see also Solicitors Act 1974 s.32 as amended; Financial Services and Markets Act 2000 s.139 and regulations thereunder, as construed in *Re Lehman Bros International (Europe) (In Administration)* [2012] UKSC 6; [2012] 3 All E.R. 1 (subsequently amended by Financial Services Act 2012 s.24). See further *Walker v Corboy* (1990) 19 N.S.W.L.R. 382. As to interest, see Article 53.

been longstanding authority, albeit at first instance, that where money received from, or due to, the principal came into the agent's hands only after the agent had become insolvent, such that the agent was never going to be in a position to execute the agent's undertakings to the principal, equity could impose a constructive trust over the money in the principal's favour, independently of any express or implied agreement for this result.[306] The approach taken in these cases has now been disapproved of by the Supreme Court, albeit in what strictly were obiter dicta.[307] On this approach, any trust must arise by express or implied agreement, and not be constructed by the court.

6-042   **Remedies: profits made in breach of duty to principal**   Turning now to breach of duty, perhaps the most specific of the agent's fiduciary duties is that not to make a profit at the principal's expense.[308] There is no doubt that a fiduciary is not permitted to profit from use of position, without the fully-informed consent of the principal. There is also no doubt that the remedy of account of profits is available to remove those profits.[309] Although that remedy is discretionary, it would be rare for a court to withhold the remedy where breach of fiduciary duty is established.[310] There has until relatively recently been much less certainty about whether the agent holds any specific assets obtained from a breach of duty on trust for the principal. Assets derived from the misapplication of money or other property belonging legally or beneficially to the principal have consistently been found to be held on constructive trust for the principal (it is irrelevant that the agent could have used personal moneys to acquire the asset). Where an asset was not so derived but is of a type the acquisition of which would be beneficial to the principal's business, and the agent's tasks include obtaining such assets, or assisting in obtaining such assets, for the principal, then the asset will also be held on constructive trust for the principal.[311] This is so even if, had the agent not acquired the asset at all, there would not have been any breach of duty on the part of the agent. But the position where an agent obtains money or other property from the simple use of position, such as by taking a secret commission or bribe, which should never have been obtained at all, has been much less clear. However, the longstanding uncertainty has been settled by the Supreme Court in *FHR European Ventures LLP v Cedar Capital Partners LLC*.[312] In this important decision the Court held that all money and other property constituting a bribe or secret commission, and any fruits derived therefrom, will be held on constructive trust for the principal. It seems, in fact, that any identifiable property derived by an agent from a breach of fiduciary duty, innocent or not, will be held on constructive trust.[313] In so ruling, the Court disapproved the contrary

---

[306] *Neste Oy v Lloyd's Bank Plc* [1983] 2 Lloyd's Rep. 658; *Re Japan Leasing (Europe) Plc* [1999] B.P.I.R. 911.

[307] See *Angove's Pty Ltd v Bailey* [2016] UKSC 47; [2016] 1 W.L.R. 3179 at [31] (noted Watts (2017) 133 L.Q.R. 11).

[308] As to the detail of when the liability to account can arise, see Articles 46–49.

[309] The detail as to how an account of profits is measured is beyond the scope of this book. For discussion, see P. Devonshire, *Account of Profits* (2013); M. Conaglen, "Identifying the Profits for which a Fiduciary Must Account" [2020] C.L.J. 38.

[310] See *Goyal v Florence Care Ltd* [2020] EWHC 659 (Ch) at [33]–[37].

[311] See below, Article 48.

[312] *FHR European Ventures LLP v Cedar Capital Partners LLC* [2014] UKSC 45; [2015] A.C. 250 (noted Gummow (2015) 131 L.Q.R. 21; Conaglen [2014] C.L.J. 490; Campbell (2015) 39 Aust. Bar Rev. 320).

[313] *FHR European Ventures LLP v Cedar Capital Partners LLC* [2014] UKSC 45 at [35]; *Akita Hold-*

ruling of the House of Lords in *Tyrrell v Bank of London*,[314] and overruled several decisions of the Court of Appeal.[315] The Court saw itself as bringing the law of England and Wales into line with leading Commonwealth authorities.[316] It is clear that the trust remedy will apply even where the principal has rescinded any contract with a third party infected by the agent's breach of duty, and has hence avoided any loss. Nor will the fact that the principal has not suffered any loss prevent the principal's prevailing over a party who has innocently taken an equitable security over the trust property, or over the agent's general creditors in an insolvency.[317] Where any gain has ceased to be identifiable, the principal will retain a personal claim against the agent, including in any insolvency of the agent, again without regard to whether any loss has been suffered or to the innocence of the breach. Once the claimant has established relevant breaches of fiduciary duty and a plausible connection to a profit made by the agent (including a particular asset if a constructive trust is being sought), the agent will bear the burden of proving that there was no causative connection between the breach and the profit (or acquisition of the asset).[318] Similar principles apply where a fiduciary has mixed the principal's property with the fiduciary's own in determining the extent of the principal's proprietary claim on the mixture.[319]

There remains some uncertainty whether an agent can be made accountable for profits not derived personally, but diverted by the agent to a third party.[320] Where the third party is a company wholly owned by the agent, it may be possible to treat the company as identified with the agent,[321] although that will not normally be necessary.

---

ings Ltd v Attorney General of Turks and Caicos Islands [2017] UKPC 7; [2017] A.C. 590 at [16]. Sinclair Investments Ltd v Versailles Trade Finance Ltd [2012] Ch. 453, which involved only indirect profiting from position, was expressly overruled in *FHR European*, above at [50], although only on the issue of remedy.

[314] *Tyrrell v Bank of London* (1862) 10 H.L. Cas. 26. *Tyrrell*, however, remains a sound authority as to the general fiduciary duties of solicitors and in its affirmation of a constructive trust over business opportunities: see the full discussion of the case in Watts, (2013) 129 L.Q.R. 526.

[315] Including *Metropolitan Bank v Heiron* (1880) 5 Ex.D. 319; *Lister & Co v Stubbs* (1890) 45 Ch.D. 1; and *Sinclair Investments Ltd v Versailles Trade Finance Ltd* [2012] Ch. 453.

[316] In particular, *Att.-Gen. for Hong Kong v Reid* [1994] 1 A.C. 324; and *Grimaldi v Chameleon Mining NL (No.2)* (2012) 287 A.L.R. 22 at [576].

[317] See *FHR European Ventures LLP v Cedar Capital Partners LLC* [2014] UKSC 45 at [43].

[318] *Ryde Holdings Ltd v Rainbow Corp Ltd* [1993] UKPC 40; *United Pan-Europe Communications NV v Deutsche Bank AG* [2000] 2 B.C.L.C. 461 at [34]; *Murad v Al-Saraj* [2005] EWCA Civ 959 at [77]. cf. *Global Energy Horizons Corp v Gray* [2015] EWHC 2232 (Ch) at [135] (burden of proof often not determinative). See also below, para.6-077.

[319] *Lupton v White* (1808) 15 Ves. Jun. 432; *Sze Tu v Lowe* [2014] NSWCA 462. See further, para.8-162.

[320] Support for the view that a company director can be accountable for gains made by third parties as a result of the director's breach of duty can be found in *CMS Dolphin Ltd v Simonet* [2001] 2 B.C.L.C. 704. See too *Walsham v Stainton* (1863) 1 De G.J. & S. 678. But cf. *Ultraframe (UK) Ltd v Fielding* [2005] EWHC 1638 (Ch) at [1575]–[1576]; *Fiona Trust Holding Corp v Privalov* [2007] EWHC 1217 (Comm) at [29]; *National Grid Electricity Transmission Plc v McKenzie Harbour Management Resources Ltd* [2009] EWHC 1817 (Ch) at [118] (indicating special rules where the defaulting agent is a member of a partnership which derives the resulting gains); *Aerostar Maintenance International Ltd v Wilson* [2010] EWHC 2032 (Ch) at [204]; *Novoship (UK) Ltd v Mikhaylyuk* [2012] EWHC 3586 (Comm) at [99] (issue not addressed on appeal: [2014] EWCA Civ 908; [2015] Q.B. 499). See too *Northampton Regional Livestock Centre Co Ltd v Cowling* [2015] EWCA Civ 651; [2016] 1 B.C.L.C. 431 at [96] (partner liable for improper profit derived by colleague in the course of partnership).

[321] See *Trustor AB v Smallbone (No.2)* [2001] 1 W.L.R. 1177; and *Quarter Master UK Ltd v Pyke* [2005] 1 B.C.L.C. 245. See too *Antonio Gramsci Shipping Corp v Stepanovs* [2011] EWHC 333 (Comm);

6-043   **Losses caused: equitable restitution and compensation**[322]   The prophylactic nature of the fiduciary duties, operating whether or not any harm has been done to the beneficiary of the duties, has encouraged a focus on remedies such as rescission of transactions where the fiduciary has a conflict of interest and on the account of profits where the fiduciary has profited from position. However, there has always been a range of situations where restorative (restitutionary) and compensatory remedies (comparable to damages for loss caused) have been available at equity. Hence, trustees (and other fiduciaries) can be liable for misapplying trust property, failing to invest, and exercising a discretion negligently.[323] Many of the trustee cases relate to application of the trust property inconsistently with the trust deed (honesty not being a defence).[324] The principles of these cases have also been applied to agents, but, as has been seen above, spending a principal's money in breach of mandate is likely also to lead to liability at common law, in particular to an order for money had and received, or for damages for breach of contract.[325] Equity has also long awarded compensation for loss resulting from a trustee's or agent's active disloyalty. For example, an agent who disloyally encourages the principal's suppliers to supply other traders, and who secretly encourages the principal's customers to cease to deal with it will be liable for ensuing loss to the principal, which can include compensation for loss of a chance of continuing business with the customers.[326]

It has been less clear whether the mere failure to disclose a conflict of interest (having not avoided the conflict in the first place) can support a duty on an honest fiduciary to pay compensation at equity,[327] as opposed to merely assisting to evidence a breach of a duty of care, which duty might for an agent arise in equity, contract or tort.[328] In relation to liability for negligence, a fiduciary cannot use a

---

[2011] C.L.C. 396 at [21] and [26] (both puppet company and puppeteer might be liable); *Akita Holdings Ltd v Attorney General of Turks and Caicos Islands* [2017] UKPC 7; [2017] A.C. 590 at [16]. But cf. *VTB Capital Plc v Nutritek International Corp* [2013] UKSC 5; [2013] 2 A.C. 337 at [147]; and *Prest v Petrodel Resources Ltd* [2013] UKSC 34; [2013] 2 A.C. 415. For discussion, see Glister, in Davis and Penner (eds) *Equity, Trusts and Commerce* (2017), Ch.12.

[322] See Snell's *Equity* (34th edn), Ch.20; *Meagher, Gummow and Lehane's Equity Doctrines and Remedies* (5th edn), Ch.24; Conaglen (2003) 119 L.Q.R. 246; Conaglen (2010) 126 L.Q.R. 72; Conaglen, *Fiduciary Loyalty* (2010), Ch.6; *Equitable Compensation and Disgorgement of Profit* (Degeling and Varuhas eds, 2017).

[323] See *Lewin on Trusts* (20th edn), Ch.35.

[324] See, e.g. *Re Dawson* [1966] 2 N.S.W.R. 211; *AIB Group (UK) Plc v Mark Redler & Co (A Firm)* [2014] UKSC 58; [2015] A.C. 1503 at [19] (solicitor disbursing client funds without authority). For further authority see above, para.6-003.

[325] See above, Article 36.

[326] See e.g. *Také Ltd v BSM Marketing Ltd* [2006] EWHC 1085 (QB), and subsequent damages appeal at [2009] EWCA Civ 45; *Premium Real Estate Ltd v Stevens* [2009] 2 N.Z.L.R. 384; *Hydrocool Pty Ltd v Hepburn (No.4)* [2011] FCA 495; (2011) 83 A.C.S.R. 652 (director puts own job protection ahead of company's interest in negotiating sale of business); *Lloyd v Pangani Properties Ltd* [2019] NZCA 314 (estate agent suppresses alternative transaction from principal). cf. *Rama v Millar* [1996] 1 N.Z.L.R. 257 (PC) where no disloyalty was found. See too Glister (2014) 8 J.Eq. 235.

[327] For argument, and supporting authorities, that mere breach of fiduciary duty can sustain damages where causation is established, see Conaglen (2003) 119 L.Q.R. 246; and (2010) 126 L.Q.R. 72. See too *Hodgkinson v Simms* [1994] 3 S.C.R. 377; (1994) 117 D.L.R. (4th) 161; *Gwembe Valley Development Co Ltd v Koshy (No.3)* [2003] EWCA Civ 1048; [2004] 1 B.C.L.C. 131 at [159] (but causation not established); *PNC Telecom Plc v Thomas* [2007] EWHC 2157 (Ch); [2008] 2 B.C.L.C. 95; *Glenn v Watson* [2018] EWHC 2016 (Ch) at [542] (findings of dishonesty).

[328] See e.g. *Hilton v Barker Booth & Eastwood* [2005] UKHL 8; [2005] 1 W.L.R. 567 (claim pleaded and decided on the basis of negligence in performance of duties).

conflict of interest as an excuse for standing back when the fiduciary possesses information that is adverse to a proposed transaction for the principal.[329]

Traditionally, equity distinguished between actions seeking to have lost trust capital restored and claims for consequential losses.[330] So, where the complaint was that the trustee had wrongly disbursed trust capital, whether through stepping outside the terms of the trust or by the careless exercise of discretion, equity responded through the beneficiaries bringing an action for an account in common form (different from an account of profits).[331] The trustee was required "to effect a restitution to the estate".[332] This did not entail that liability was in all cases strict. Strict liability did apply to failure to comply with the terms of the trust (the parallel position to the common law where an agent fails to adhere to instructions), but usually carelessness would be needed where it was a discretionary decision relating to the management of the trust property that was being challenged. However, in all cases the restitutionary action was not generally governed by the common law principles of damages regarding time of assessment, causation, remoteness, contributory negligence and so forth.[333] In such proceedings, defaults in the disposition of trust property have simply not been recognised as having any validity as far as the trustee is concerned[334]; the transactions are said to be "falsified" and the trustee left to ensure that the trust assets that were formerly there are made available when called for. The trustee has not been permitted to argue that had there been no breach, loss would have occurred anyway. If, however, the beneficiaries' claim was for more than reconstitution of lost capital, such as for consequential losses as a result of a "wilful default", then principles of causation did become applicable.[335] Reconstitution of capital is one thing, assessing what the claimant's financial position might have been had the trustee performed its duties is another. Neither type of claim was conceived of as a damages claim in the common law sense.

---

[329] In addition to *Hilton* [2005] UKHL 8; [2005] 1 W.L.R. 567, see *Permanent Building Society v Wheeler* (1994) 14 A.C.S.R. 109 at 160; and *Burns v Financial Conduct Authority* [2017] EWCA Civ 2140; [2018] 1 W.L.R. 4161 at [78].

[330] For an enlightening discussion, see Conaglen (2016) 40 Melb.U.L.R. 126. Cases include *Cocker v Quayle* (1830) 1 Russ. & M. 535; *Re Collie, Ex p. Adamson* (1878) 8 Ch.D. 807 at 819; *Magnus v Queensland National Bank* (1888) 37 Ch.D. 466; *British America Elevator Co Ltd v Bank of British North America* [1919] A.C. 658 (PC) at 666; *Re Dawson* [1966] 2 N.S.W.R. 211; *Main v Giambrone & Law (a firm)* [2017] EWCA Civ 1193 at [62]; *Interactive Technology Corp Ltd v Ferster* [2018] EWCA Civ 1594 at [16].

[331] See below, Article 51.

[332] *Re Dawson* [1966] 2 N.S.W.R. 211 at 214–216, per Street J; *Bristol and West BS v Mothew* [1998] Ch. 1 at 18; *Lloyds TSB Bank Plc v Markandan & Uddin (A Firm)* [2012] EWCA Civ 65 at [54]; *Re Ruscoe Ltd* Unreported August 7, 2012 Ch.D.; *Libertarian Investments Ltd v Hall* [2013] HKCFA 93 at [168]; *Creggy v Barnett* [2016] EWCA Civ 1004; [2017] Ch. 273 at [45] (where, however, the particular claimant was not a beneficiary and had only a damages claim). See *Heydon* (1997) 113 L.Q.R. 8.

[333] See the Hon. Justice Gummow in *Equity, Fiduciaries and Trusts* (Youdan ed., 1989), Ch.2; *Meagher, Gummow and Lehane's Equity Doctrines and Remedies* (5th edn), Ch.24; Davidson (1982) Melb.U.L. Rev. 349; Davies, in *Equity, Fiduciaries and Trusts* (Waters ed., 1993), Ch.14; Edelman and Elliott (2003) 119 L.Q.R. 545; (2004) Trusts Law Int. 116; the Rt Hon. Lord Millett, in *Commercial Law: Principles and Practice* (2006), para.1.44 onwards; McDermott, *Equitable Damages* (1994); Penner (2014) 8 J.Eq. 202; Shaw-Mellors [2015] J.B.L. 165; Watts [2016] L.M.C.L.Q. 118; Conaglen (2016) 40 Melb.U.L.R. 126.

[334] *Knott v Cottee* (1852) 16 Beav. 77 at 79–80; *Ultraframe (UK) Ltd v Fielding* [2005] EWHC 1638(4) (Ch) at [1513]; *Libertarian Investments Ltd v Hall* [2013] HKCFA 93 at [169].

[335] See *Re Brogden* (1886) 38 Ch.D. 546; *Bartlett v Barclays Bank Trust Co Ltd (No.2)* [1980] Ch. 515 at 545.

Much of this learning, in England, seems to be in the process of being swept away, and replaced by a general concept of equitable compensation.

The modern origin of a compensation remedy is usually supported by reference to the speech of Lord Haldane in *Nocton v Ashburton*,[336] though what is said in that case is not easy to follow.[337] However, since the decision of the House of Lords in *Target Holdings Ltd v Redferns*,[338] the concept of damages in equity has become generalised, almost to the point where the stricter approach taken in the accounting process, just described, has been supplanted. The court there favoured an approach analogous to that taken to damages in tort, looking to see what position the beneficiary would have been in had no breach of trust occurred.[339] If the beneficiary would have suffered the same loss even had there been no breach there would be no liability. Lord Browne-Wilkinson stated:

"Equitable compensation for breach of trust is designed to achieve exactly what the word compensation suggests: to make good a loss in fact suffered by the beneficiaries and which, using hindsight and common sense, can be seen to have been caused by the breach."[340]

In fact, Lord Browne-Wilkinson did not altogether rule out the older restitutionary approach.[341] The facts of the case, a case of a bare trust of intended loan moneys where the moneys had been released by the trustee (the lender's solicitor) without the required mortgage being in place, fitted with the older remedy of the common account. But, that remedy ceased to be applicable, his Lordship said, when the trustee had got in the required mortgage after the event. That may have been all that was needed for deciding the case.[342] However, the broader approach, based on analogies with common law damages, which formed the heart of his judgment, has now been taken up and affirmed by the Supreme Court in *AIB Group (UK) Plc v Mark Redler*,[343] a case on similar facts to *Target Holdings*. Lord Toulson, who gave the lead judgment, favoured a broad remedy of equitable compensation being available for all honest breaches of trust, one that mimicked the expectation remedy in contract.[344] Lord Reed's judgment was more cautious about assimilating remedies for breach of trust with tort or contract damages, but accepted much of the reasoning of *Target Holdings*, including the notion that equitable remedies are designed to put the beneficiaries in the position they would have been in had the trustee cor-

---

[336] *Nocton v Ashburton* [1914] A.C. 398, Illustration 7. For cases before *Nocton*, see Conaglen (2016) 40 Melb. U.L.R. 126 at 146–150. cf. *Henderson v Merrett Syndicates Ltd* [1995] 2 A.C. 145 at 204–205, per Lord Browne-Wilkinson. See Meagher, *Gummow and Lehane's Equity Doctrines and Remedies* (5th edn); cf. Getzler, in *Restitution and Equity* (Birks and Rose eds, 2000), Vol.1, p.251.

[337] See *Hedley Byrne & Co Ltd v Heller & Partners Ltd* [1964] A.C. 465 at 530.

[338] *Target Holdings Ltd v Redferns* [1996] A.C. 421.

[339] *Target Holdings Ltd v Redferns* [1996] A.C. 421 at 432.

[340] *Target Holdings Ltd v Redferns* [1996] A.C. 421 at 439, per Lord Browne-Wilkinson, following dicta of McLachlin J in *Canson Enterprises Ltd v Boughton & Co* [1991] 3 S.C.R. 335. See also *Beach Petroleum NV v Kennedy* (1999) 48 N.S.W.L.R. 1 at 91–94.

[341] *Target Holdings Ltd v Redferns* [1996] A.C. 421 at 436.

[342] See the Rt Hon. Lord Millett (1998) 114 L.Q.R. 214; Conaglen (2010) 4 J.Eq. 288 (trustee's continuing authority to act as such is key to ability to rectify earlier wrongful disbursement).

[343] *AIB Group (UK) Plc v Mark Redler* [2014] UKSC 58; [2015] A.C. 1503 (noted Hon. W. Gummow (2015) 41 Aust. Bar Rev. 5; Rt Hon. Lord Millett (2015) UK Supreme Ct Yearbook 193; (2018) 32 T.L.I. 44; Turner [2015] C.L.J. 188; Davies (2015) 78 M.L.R. 681).

[344] *AIB Group (UK) Plc v Mark Redler* [2014] UKSC 58; [2015] A.C. 1503 at [71].

rectly performed his duties.[345] As with *Target Holdings*, it is probable that the same result could have been reached in *AIB Group* using the older learning. While this was not a case where the solicitors' breach of instructions was cured, it was arguable that the client had ratified what had happened (without prejudice to a claim for damages) and therefore could not falsify the disbursal of the loan.[346]

It appears that some other jurisdictions, most notably Australia and Hong Kong, are not yet willing to abandon the older, stricter, approach where what is in question is the disbursal by a trustee of trust funds in breach of instructions or in the exercise of a discretion incautiously exercised.[347] Even in England and Wales there are signs that the older view may yet survive.[348] The older view is most compelling in cases where the conditions for releasing funds were simply not met at the time of the release. It has been noted earlier (above, para.6-003) that even at common law it is not usually a defence for an agent to say that had the conditions been met the money would still have been lost. Within the general law of contract, a promisee is not confined to expectation damages but can call for restitution when there has been a total failure of consideration. It might be thought remarkable, for instance, if a solicitor holding trust moneys earmarked for a loan accidentally released them to a complete stranger and was then permitted to set up an argument that even had they been sent to the correct borrower they would not have been recoverable. Such a solicitor may have been authorised to send the funds to the insolvent borrower but could not vis-à-vis the client claim a *right* to do so.

Where what is at issue is loss caused by breach of fiduciary duty unrelated to misapplication of the principal's moneys, issues of causation do become relevant, as they do with the account on the basis of wilful default.[349] Further restraints on recovery may result if the loss was not within the risk created by the default, or was caused by the claimant personally.[350] But where actual disloyalty has been proven, the fiduciary can be liable for resulting loss even if a careful and loyal agent might have made the same choice of action,[351] and the onus of proving that loss would

---

[345] *AIB Group (UK) Plc v Mark Redler* [2014] UKSC 58; [2015] A.C. 1503 at [134].

[346] For elaboration, see Watts [2016] L.M.C.L.Q. 118.

[347] See *Youyang Pty Ltd v Minter Ellison Morris Fletcher* (2003) 212 C.L.R. 484 at [39] and [42]; *Alexander v Perpetual Trustees WA Ltd* [2004] HCA 7; (2004) 216 C.L.R. 109 at [46] and [59]; *Agricultural Land Management Ltd v Jackson (No.2)* [2014] WASC 102; (2014) 285 F.L.R. 121 at [344] and [368]; *Libertarian Investments Ltd v Hall* [2013] HKCFA 93 at [90] and [168].

[348] See *Main v Giambrone & Law (a firm)* [2017] EWCA Civ 1193; and *Interactive Technology Corp Ltd v Ferster* [2018] EWCA Civ 1594 at [16]. Cf. *Auden McKenzie (Pharma Division) Ltd v Patel* [2019] EWCA Civ 2291.

[349] See *Swindle v Harrison* [1997] 4 All E.R. 705, Illustration 12; *Nationwide BS v Balmer Radmore* [1999] Lloyd's Rep. P.N. 241; *Collins v Brebner* [2000] Lloyd's Rep. P.N. 587. But cf. *Bristol & West BS v May, May & Merrimans* [1996] 2 All E.R. 801, where there were positive misrepresentations by the fiduciary. See also *Gilbert v Shanahan* [1998] 3 N.Z.L.R. 528; *Mantonella Pty Ltd v Thompson* (2009) 255 A.L.R. 367; *Rawleigh v Tait* [2008] NZCA 525; [2009] N.Z. Family L.R. 802. For discussion of *Swindle* and later cases, see Conaglen (2010) 126 L.Q.R. 72 at 81–86.

[350] See, e.g. *BPE Solicitors v Hughes-Holland* [2017] UKSC 21; [2018] A.C. 599 (contractual negligence). In so far as a breach of duty is deliberate, it does not seem appropriate to permit a contributory negligence argument: see *Nationwide BS v Balmer Radmore* [1999] Lloyd's Rep. P.N. 241 at 281, per Blackburne J. See too Conaglen (2010) 126 L.Q.R. 72 at 96–100. Contributory negligence cannot be pleaded against fraud: *Standard Chartered Bank v Pakistan National Shipping Corp (No.4)* [2002] UKHL 43; [2003] 1 A.C. 959.

[351] See *Bishopsgate Investment Management Ltd v Maxwell (No.2)* [1994] 1 All E.R. 261; *Permanent Building Society v Wheeler* (1994) 14 A.C.S.R. 109 (Illustration 13); *Bairstow v Queens Moat Houses Plc* [2001] EWCA Civ 712; [2001] 2 B.C.L.C. 531 (recovery from directors of amount of

have resulted irrespective of the agent's action is likely to lie on the agent.[352] The general position has been stated as follows:

"the Court should assess the compensation in a robust manner, relying on the presumption against wrongdoers, the onus of proof, and resolving doubtful questions against the party whose actions have made an accurate determination so problematic."[353]

Nothing in the foregoing addresses the situation where an agent acts carelessly in a way which does not involve the handling of trust moneys. In such case the duties of care may arise only at common law, or if they arise in equity they are governed by similar principles.[354] Attempts to label a breach of a duty of care as a breach of fiduciary duty in order to argue for the special equitable rules, whatever they may be, whether as to damages, or limitation of actions (where the Limitation Act does not apply to claims for money held on trust[355]) have generally met with little sympathy from English courts,[356] and the common law rules have been applied where they would justify the claim. In the area of confidential information considerable flexibility has been employed in the award of remedies, and there seems to be some tendency to extend this to the area of breach of fiduciary duty generally.[357]

6-044 **Other remedies: rescission, injunction, and declaration**   The principal other remedy is rescission of the transaction with the agent (as where the agent deals with the principal without disclosing the fact[358]); or, where a third party is involved in the transaction, against the third party, as in the case of transactions obtained by

---

improper dividend dishonestly made, whether or not a lawful dividend could have been properly authorised at the time). But cf. *Murray Vernon Holdings Ltd v Hassall* [2010] EWHC 7 (Ch) at [65] (director acted honestly and dividend could lawfully have been made, hence no causation). See too *Auden McKenzie (Pharma Division) Ltd v Patel* [2019] EWCA Civ 2291.

[352] *Bank of New Zealand v New Zealand Guardian Trust Co Ltd* [1999] 1 N.Z.L.R. 664 at 687. See too *Condliffe v Sheingold* [2007] EWCA Civ 1043 at [23] (measure of value of mis-sold goodwill belonging to claimant company); *Ross River Ltd v Waveley Commercial Ltd* [2013] EWCA Civ 910 at [94]; *Libertarian Investments Ltd v Hall* [2013] HKCFA 93; (2013) 16 H.K.C.F.A.R. 681 at [93] (noted Turner [2014] C.L.J. 257) (agent who misspends funds given him for the purpose of buying shares bears onus of proving that it was not possible to acquire the shares).

[353] *Houghton v Immer* (1997) 44 N.S.W.L.R. 46, per Handley JA. See too *Libertarian Investments Ltd v Hall* [2013] HKCFA 93 at [139].

[354] See, e.g. *Lagunas Nitrate Co v Lagunas Syndicate* [1899] 2 Ch. 392 at 435–437; *The Borag* [1980] 1 Lloyd's Rep. 111 at 125; *Bristol and West BS v Mothew* [1998] Ch. 1, Illustration 11; *Nationwide BS v Balmer Radmore* [1999] Lloyd's Rep. P.N. 241; *Bank of New Zealand v New Zealand Guardian Trust Co Ltd* [1999] 1 N.Z.L.R. 213; *Forsta AP-Fonden v Bank of New York Mellon SA/NV* [2013] EWHC 3127 (Comm) at [185]. For a contrary view, see Heydon, in *Equity in Commercial Law* (Degeling and Edelman eds, 2005), Ch.9; and *Youyang Pty Ltd v Minter Ellison Morris Fletcher* (2003) 212 C.L.R. 484 at [39].

[355] Limitation Act s.21(1). The doctrine of laches would still apply. But the Act may in any case apply by analogy to certain types of constructive trustee: see s.35(1) and *Cia de Seguros Imperio v Heath (REBX) Ltd* [2001] 1 W.L.R. 113, where the equitable claims were identical with common law claims in tort or contract: following *Coulthard v Disco Mix Club Ltd* [2000] 1 W.L.R. 707. See also *Clarke v Marlborough Fine Art (London) Ltd, The Times,* July 5, 2001; and in general *Lewin on Trusts* (20th edn), Ch.5.

[356] See the cases cited above and *Paragon Finance Plc v D.B. Thakerar & Co* [1999] 1 All E.R. 400 (amendment of pleadings); *Williams v Central Bank of Nigeria* [2014] UKSC 10; [2014] A.C. 1189. See too *Halton International Inc v Guernroy Ltd* [2006] EWCA Civ 801.

[357] See below, para.6-077; Abdullah and Tey (1999) 115 L.Q.R. 376; *Corp Nacional del Cobre de Chile v Sogemin Metals Ltd* [1997] 1 W.L.R. 1396.

[358] e.g. *Maguire v Makaronis* (1997) 188 C.L.R. 449. For more detailed discussion, see Article 45 and

bribery or other conflict of interest on the part of the agent.[359] But other remedies such as declaration and injunction are possible.[360] The injunction is often used to prevent agents, particularly solicitors, from continuing to act where there is a conflict of interest or risk of disclosure of confidential information.[361]

Illustrations

(1) An agent in London had a power of attorney from his principal in America **6-045** to sell his English property and invest the proceeds as he thought fit. The agent, who was a solicitor, paid the interest received from the investments into the account of his firm. Held, he was a trustee of the profits and must account for them. Accordingly the Statute of Limitations did not run against the principal.[362]

(2) A selling agent agrees to sell goods in India against an advance. He pays 85 per cent of the price to the principal and then sells the goods. He uses the balance of the price to buy goods in India and sell them in England, which is very profitable to him. Held, the agent does not have to account to the principal for the profit but only for the balance of the price, since he is not in a fiduciary position in relation to the money.[363]

(3) An agent was employed to buy timber lands for a company. All these had already been bought up and he recommended the company to buy prairie land instead. The company agreed and sent the agent money for that specific purpose. It was later discovered that the agent had charged the company more than he had himself paid for the land. Held, as the money had been sent to the agent for investment in a specified manner, he was a trustee of the improper profit and so could not plead the Statute of Limitations.[364]

(4) An agent is employed to sell cargo from a wrecked ship for average adjusters. After deducting claims for salvage and other expenses, £96 remains in his hands. He is not bound to keep the proceeds of sale of the cargo in a separate fund, and he is not a trustee of the £96 but only a debtor to his principal.[365]

(5) Shipping agents are placed in funds by shipowners from time to time to enable them to discharge jetty and river dues, pilotage and towage, berth fees and similar expenses on ships which visit the local port, and for their agency fee. They do not hold the money in trust, but in their insolvency and in respect

---

para.6-068 in particular.

[359] See Articles 49.

[360] In *Yasuda Fire and Marine Insurance Ltd v Orion Marine Insurance Underwriting Ltd* [1995] Q.B. 174 declarations and an order of specific performance were granted to permit the principal to inspect the agent's records. As to the injunction, see *QBE Management Services (UK) Ltd v Dymoke* [2012] EWHC 80 (QB) (injunction to prevent competition by former management employees who, amongst other breaches of duty, solicited colleagues to join them in leaving to compete with their employer); *Forse v Secarma Ltd* [2019] EWCA Civ 215.

[361] *Prince Jefri Bolkiah v KPMG* [1999] 2 A.C. 222 at 235–236 (the case itself is concerned with confidential information). See too *PCCW-HKT Telephone Ltd v Aitken* [2009] HKCFA 11.

[362] *Burdick v Garrick* (1870) L.R. 5 Ch. App. 233.

[363] *Kirkham v Peel* (1880) 43 L.T. 171; affirmed (1880) 44 L.T. 195.

[364] *North American Land and Timber Co v Watkins* [1904] 1 Ch. 242; [1904] 2 Ch. 233.

[365] *Henry v Hammond* [1913] 2 K.B. 515. See also *Wilsons and Furness-Leyland Line v British and Continental Shipping Co* (1907) 23 T.L.R. 397.

of claims by their bank to set off other debts they are simply debtors to the shipowners in respect of money received and not disbursed.[366]

(6) A company had authority to make deductions from its employees' wages to be paid to a trustee of the staff superannuation fund. It made the deductions but used the credit to reduce its own bank account which at all times was in overdraft. The company was in breach of its duties as agent but the employees were not entitled to any proprietary interest in the company's other assets.[367]

(7) A solicitor is associated with a client in transactions relating to the development of land. He persuades the client to release part of a mortgage over land on which he (the solicitor) has a second mortgage; this advances the solicitor's security and leaves the client with insufficient security. The solicitor does not explain to the client the advantage which the solicitor gains from this, nor fully explains other matters relating to the release. The solicitor is liable for the loss caused to the client.[368]

(8) A solicitor acts for the purchaser of land. He does not disclose that between the apparent vendor of the land and the purchaser there is an intermediate vendor, for whom he has acted, who bought from the original vendor and resold at a profit; and he conveys the property direct from the original vendor to the ultimate purchaser and bills the entire cost of the transaction to the purchaser. Subsequently a warehouse is built on the acquired land, but because of the negligence of the engineer and the pile-driving contractor the purchaser suffers loss, not all of which he recovers from the contractors concerned. The solicitor is liable for the profit made by the intermediate purchaser, but not for the subsequent losses.[369]

(9) An estate agent acts for the vendor of land and negotiates a sale of it "subject to contract". She is subsequently asked by the prospective purchaser if she can assist in obtaining a sale to him of the adjacent land, for the owner of which she has previously acted unsuccessfully. She approaches that second owner and gives minimal advice in respect of the price; she does not disclose that the offeror has just entered into a "subject to contract" arrangement in relation to the adjacent land. The information would have been of consequence to the second vendor, as the purchaser desired to secure a "family compound" of the two properties. The second vendor sells the property. The estate agent is not liable for loss (in so far as provable) suffered by the second vendor, and is not disentitled to commission, for there is:

> "an implied term of the contract with such an agent that he is entitled to act for other principals selling competing properties and to keep confidential the information obtained from each of his principals".[370]

---

[366] *Neste Oy v Lloyd's Bank Plc* [1983] 2 Lloyd's Rep. 658; following *Henry v Hammond* [1913] 2 K.B. 515; one particular payment was held on trust, but this holding has in effect been overruled in *Angove's Pty Ltd v Bailey* [2016] UKSC 47; [2016] 1 W.L.R. 3179.

[367] *Fortex Group Ltd v MacIntosh* [1998] 3 N.Z.L.R. 471.

[368] *Nocton v Ashburton* [1914] A.C. 398.

[369] *Canson Enterprises Ltd v Boughton & Co* [1991] 3 S.C.R. 534; (1991) 85 D.L.R. (4th) 129; cf. *Hodgkinson v Simms* [1994] 3 S.C.R. 377; (1994) 117 D.L.R. (4th) 161 (accountant).

[370] *Kelly v Cooper* [1993] A.C. 205 PC: as to the implied term see at 214, per Lord Browne-Wilkinson. Sed quaere in view of the fact that advice was given and because the reasoning relies on the proposition that all agency is contractual. The decision may be correct for estate agents, who are only imperfectly agents (above, para.1-020) and are known to act for many principals. It is doubtful whether its reasoning should be generalised. Both parties would have benefited from disclosure

(10) Solicitors acting for purchasers of land receive money lent by mortgagees, for whom they are also acting, and release it to the purchaser without authority before the mortgage security is executed. The security is later executed. The borrower defaults and the property is repossessed and sold for less than the mortgage debt. The solicitors are liable, not to replace the trust estate, but to compensate the mortgagee for loss which he would not have suffered but for the breach of duty.[371]

(11) A solicitor acts for a husband and wife in the purchase of a house, and also for the mortgage lender. The lender offers to lend on the express basis that the rest of the price is provided by the purchasers without resort to further borrowing. The solicitor knows that the purchasers are arranging for an existing loan to be secured by a second mortgage on the property, but by an oversight tells the lenders that their requirements are complied with. The purchase is completed but the purchasers default and the house is sold by the lenders on a fallen market. The solicitor's negligence is unconnected with the fact that he is acting for both parties to the transaction. He is liable on a common law basis for loss attributable to his negligence, but not for the whole sum lost by the lender on the transaction.[372]

(12) A solicitor acts for a purchaser of a restaurant, who already has a loan on the security of her own house for the purchase, but needs further money which is not forthcoming. He makes to the purchaser a bridging loan secured by a first charge, without disclosing that he is making a small profit on it and that he had been aware that other finance would not be available. The purchaser defaults on the mortgage of her own house and the lender takes possession of it. Later the solicitor sues for possession of the restaurant. The non-disclosure was a breach of fiduciary duty to her, but the circumstances were such that she would have had to accept the loan anyway. The loss which she suffered was not caused by the non-disclosure, but by the risk taken by her in mortgaging her home.[373]

(13) Directors of the claimant building society commit it to a purchase of commercial land, a transaction outside its normal business, at a price found to be reasonable. A number of the defendant directors who had promoted the transaction did so for improper reasons (there was an undisclosed side deal between them and the vendor). Another director was aware of this improper motivation but kept silent about it. A yet further director was innocent of the impropriety. There is a downturn in the property market and the claimant loses money on the land. The improperly motivated directors are liable for the loss on the basis of breach of fiduciary duty, as is the director who condoned their actions. The innocent director is not liable because he committed no breach of fiduciary duty and the transaction was one which a

---

by the agent. The fiduciary duties were treated as affected, not by the express terms of any contract, but by an implied term that they did not apply. See [1994] J.B.L. 147; and further as to estate agents in this context Murdoch, *Law of Estate Agency* (5th edn), p.62 onwards. See now *Rossetti Marketing Ltd v Diamond Sofa Co Ltd* [2012] EWCA Civ 1021 at [27].

[371] *Target Holdings Ltd v Redferns* [1996] A.C. 421.

[372] *Bristol & West BS v Mothew* [1998] Ch. 1.

[373] *Swindle v Harrison* [1997] 4 All E.R. 705 (see Tjio and Yeo (1998) 114 L.Q.R.181); cf. *Maguire v Makaronis* (1997) 188 C.L.R. 449.

reasonable director might have supported not knowing of the corruption of his colleagues.[374]

(14) An agreement between the two shareholders in a company, X and Y, provided for X to undertake the necessary accounting and tax functions for the company and the shareholders, which task was contemplated as possibly requiring the parties to make capital payments to keep the company in sufficient funds. X in keeping the accounts misled Y into making larger capital contributions than were necessary, and later siphoned off the excess. X was held to be the agent of Y and in breach of fiduciary duty, and accountable to Y for the excess payments.[375]

(15) Company A is established to receive investments from the public to be on-lent to company B for its business, ostensibly a type of factoring business. Company B is the wholly owned subsidiary of company C which is listed on the stock exchange. D is a director of company A, and a major shareholder in company C. In fact, company B has no legitimate business, but is engaged, in D's hands, in an elaborate "ponzi scheme", involving massive movements of money between parties but no genuine trading transactions. The appearance of a successful business leads to the shares in company C trading very well, and D makes a £28 million profit by selling his shares. Once the scheme collapses, company A brings proceedings alleging that the profits made by D resulted from his breaches of his director's duties to company A, and that the land and other assets acquired by D from those profits are held on trust for company A. Held, D is accountable for his gains.[376]

(16) A company, D, is appointed agent to the claimant consortium (of which it is also potentially a member) to assist in the purchase of a Monaco hotel for the best price obtainable. D also enters into a sole-agency agreement with the owner of the shares in the hotel under which it is to receive a â10 million commission if a sale occurs within the period of the agency. D reveals some but insufficient details of this arrangement to the claimants. When the purchase goes through D receives its commission. It is held that the commission contract and the resulting payment were held on constructive trust for the claimants.[377]

Article 44

DUTY TO AVOID CONFLICTS OF INTEREST, UNLESS WITH CONSENT[378]

6-046   Agents may not put themselves in a position or enter into transactions in which their personal interest, or their duty to another principal, may conflict with their duty

---

[374] *Permanent Building Society v Wheeler* (1994) 14 A.C.S.R. 109.
[375] *Amaltal Corp v Maruha Corp* [2007] 3 N.Z.L.R. 192.
[376] *Sinclair Investments (UK) Ltd v Versailles Trade Finance Group Plc* [2011] EWCA Civ 347; [2012] Ch. 453. This case is assumed to be overruled in *FHR European Ventures LLP v Cedar Capital Partners LLC* [2014] UKSC 45; [2015] A.C. 250, on the issue of the form of remedy.
[377] *FHR European Ventures LLP v Cedar Capital Partners LLC* [2014] UKSC 45; [2015] A.C. 250.
[378] See, in general, Hollander and Salzedo, *Conflicts of Interest* (5th edn); Conaglen, *Fiduciary Loyalty* (2010), Chs 5 and 6.

to their principal, unless the principal, with full knowledge of all the material circumstances and of the nature and extent of the agents' interest, consents.[379]

Comment

The foregoing statement is derived from Lord Herschell's judgment in *Bray v Ford*. Equally well known is Lord Cranworth LC's dictum in *Aberdeen Railway Co v Blaikie Bros*[380]:

> "No one having [fiduciary] duties to discharge, shall be allowed to enter into engagements in which he has, or can have, a personal interest conflicting, or which may possibly conflict, with the interests of those whom he is bound to protect."

6-047

While it is clear from this that potential conflicts of interest are within the proscription, there must be "a real sensible possibility of conflict" before equity's rules commence to operate.[381]

Whether there is a material conflict of interest will always be fact sensitive and a matter of judgement. So, the fact that an agent is owed a debt in the agent's personal capacity by the third party would not automatically entail that the agent had a conflict in dealing on the principal's behalf with the third party, but it might do if it was known that the transaction was likely materially to assist the third party to discharge its debts.[382]

Most commonly, a conflict of interest will involve financial considerations, either relating to the agent's own position (or that of relatives)[383] or to that of another party for whom the agent is also acting. It is possible, however, that a conflict might arise on other grounds. To take a hypothetical example, an agent might commit the principal to a transaction as part of an understanding, or even a hope, that the third party will not as a result commence a prosecution against the agent. Although not an obvious conclusion, the fact that an agent has been involved in bribing employees of the third party while acting for a different principal in unrelated earlier transactions has been held to place the agent in a position of conflicting interests even though there has been no corruption in the instant transaction.[384]

Again, in the usual case the conflicts principle will be concerned with some aspect of the exercise by the agent of the powers conferred by the principal. It is possible, however, that a conflict, actual or potential, might also affect a personal undertaking, whether or not legally binding, given by the agent *not* to exercise his powers.

---

[379] See *Bray v Ford* [1896] A.C. 44 at 51. See the very much simpler provisions in Article 3:205 of PECL and Article 2.2.7 of the UNIDROIT Principles. The attention paid to the origins of doctrine in (some) common law countries creates more complexity, but also greater sensitivity to fact situations. The operation of the above provisions would require considerable working out.

[380] *Aberdeen Railway Co v Blaikie Bros* (1854) 1 Macq. 461 at 471, Illustration 2.

[381] *Boardman v Phipps* [1967] 2 A.C. 46 at 124, per Lord Upjohn; *Paton v Rosesilver Group Corp* [2017] EWCA Civ 158 at [33]. See too *Sharbern Holding Inc v Vancouver Airport Centre Ltd* [2011] 2 S.C.R. 175; (2011) 331 D.L.R. (4th) 1 at [151] and [160], suggesting that the principal must establish the materiality of an alleged conflict (unless, presumably, it is self-evident).

[382] *Cowan de Groot Properties Ltd v Eagle Trust Plc* [1991] B.C.L.C. 1045. See now Companies Act 2006 s.177(6)(a).

[383] As to which, see *Newgate Stud Co v Penfold* [2004] EWHC 2993; [2008] 1 B.C.L.C. 46, the holding in which is noted below, para.6-065; *Breitenfeld UK Ltd v Harrison* [2015] EWHC 399 (Ch); [2015] 2 B.C.L.C. 275.

[384] See *HPOR Servicos De Consultoria Ltda v Dryships Inc* [2018] EWHC 3451 (Comm); [2019] 1 Lloyd's Rep. 260 at [110].

The liability of an agent to account for profits made as a result of holding conflicting interests is treated in Article 48.

There has been little judicial discussion of what equitable controls may be necessary to govern what might loosely be called "future client" conflicts. It seems that, ordinarily, an agent will not be taken to have a conflict of interest merely because there is evidence that the agent entertains hopes of obtaining business in the future from a current counterparty of the principal; doing a good job for the existing principal may be the best way of obtaining that business.[385] However, if the agent has begun to take steps to procure a position with, or work from, the third party a conflict would arise.[386] And disloyalty would be established if there were evidence that the prospect of such business actually motivated the agent in the steps taken on the principal's behalf.[387] The prospect of such future business may also have some evidential role to play in an allegation of negligence against the agent.

A director's duty to avoid conflicts of interest is now the subject of statutory provision: see Companies Act 2006 s.175.

6-048 **Conflict of duty and duty[388]** One manifestation of the agent's fiduciary duty to avoid conflicts is that the agent must not serve two principals whose interests may conflict. So agents may not act for both parties to a transaction unless they ensure that they fully disclose all the material facts to each party and obtain their informed consent to their so acting.[389] In this situation there is not preferment of the agent's own interest, but equally the agent may not act entirely in the interests of either single principal. There may also be breach of the duty of loyalty in the sense that the loyalty must be undivided.[390] In such cases the agent may cause loss to one by failure to disclose information acquired in connection with the other—information, indeed, the disclosure of which would be a breach of duty to the first.[391]

Thus, a solicitor who is a trustee of trust property which is for sale should not act also for the purchaser and if that happens the solicitor may be liable in respect of non-disclosure of information known to the solicitor as trustee[392]; an agent who is employed by a borrower to negotiate a loan may not receive a commission from the lender[393]; a hotel broker who is acting for the vendor of a hotel may not also claim commission from the purchaser[394]; a sports agent who represents a player should not, without consent, also act for the sports club in obtaining a work permit

---

[385] See *Dennard v PricewaterhouseCoopers LLP* [2010] EWHC 812 (Ch) at [218]; affirmed [2010] EWCA Civ 1437.

[386] *Burns v Financial Conduct Authority* [2017] EWCA Civ 2140; [2018] 1 W.L.R. 4161.

[387] See *Premium Real Estate Ltd v Stevens* [2009] 2 N.Z.L.R. 384 (see below, fn.405).

[388] See Conaglen (2009) 125 L.Q.R. 111. See also *Restatement, Third*, § 8.06(2); *Snell's Equity* (34th edn), para.7-036 onwards.

[389] This passage was cited with approval by Megaw J in *Anglo-African Merchants Ltd v Bayley* [1970] 1 Q.B. 311 at 323; and by Douglas J in *Dargusch v Sherley Investments Pty Ltd* [1970] Qd.R. 338 at 347; see also *Eagle Star Insurance Co Ltd v Spratt* [1971] 2 Lloyd's Rep. 116 at 133; *McDonnell v Barton Realty Ltd* [1992] 3 N.Z.L.R. 418. cf. *Swain v Law Society* [1983] 1 A.C. 598 (statutory scheme for solicitors' insurance).

[390] *Beach Petroleum NL v Kennedy* (1999) 48 N.S.W.L.R. 1. See *Snell's Equity* (34th edn), para.7-036.

[391] See also *Bristol and West BS v Mothew* [1998] Ch. 1 at 18–20.

[392] *Moody v Cox and Hatt* [1917] 2 Ch. 71; cf. *Clark Boyce v Mouat* [1994] 1 A.C. 428. For a recent reconsideration of the problem see *Hilton v Barker Booth and Eastwood* [2005] UKHL 8; [2005] 1 W.L.R. 567: the breach does not lie in failing to terminate the retainer, but in not informing the client of the relevant facts (even though to do so would have been a breach to the other client).

[393] *Re a Debtor* [1927] 2 Ch. 367; *Advanced Realty Funding Corp v Bannink* (1979) 106 D.L.R. (3d) 137. cf. *Turner v Laurentide Financial Realty Corp (Western) Ltd* (1979) 97 D.L.R. (3d) 429.

[394] *Fullwood v Hurley* [1928] 1 K.B. 498; *FHR European Ventures LLP v Cedar Capital Partners LLC*

for the player[395]; and an insurance broker (who is the assured's agent) may not act as agent for underwriters in obtaining an assessor's report, because such report may be adverse to the assured's claim against the underwriters.[396] In general, a custom to the contrary will not be upheld.[397] It is not material that the agent is acting gratuitously for one or both parties; the mere fact of being agent for two or more parties who may have adverse interests is improper unless all principals have given their informed consent.

The foregoing states the general position. Perhaps where it is notorious that agents do act for both sides to a transaction, and where the agent explains all the circumstances fully to the principal and the principal consents to the agent receiving two commissions, the principal cannot subsequently call the agent to account for the commission paid by the other party,[398] nor can the principal refuse to pay its own commission.[399] Even if the agent is improperly acting for two opposing principals, the court will not normally make an order on the application of one of the principals which will result in the agent breaking the agent's confidence towards the other principal, at least where that other principal has acted in good faith.[400]

In the best-known case, *Kelly v Cooper*, where an estate agent acted for the vendors of adjacent or nearby properties she was held entitled to do so on the basis that the normal fiduciary duty was impliedly excluded in the circumstances.[401] But this was a case not of an agent acting for both sides, but for competing principals,[402] and a more recent decision regarding a solicitor handling business between two clients, who did not disclose to one that the other had criminal convictions, while in a different context, prompts caution about reading too much into the first decision.[403] So, while acting for competing sellers in the same market might be an

---

[2014] UKSC 45; [2015] A.C. 250. cf. *Foster v Reaume* [1924] 2 D.L.R. 951.

[395] *Imageview Management Ltd v Jack* [2009] EWCA Civ 63; [2009] 2 All E.R. 666 (see further below, para.7-050).

[396] *Anglo-African Merchants Ltd v Bayley* [1970] 1 Q.B. 311; *North and South Trust Co v Berkeley* [1971] 1 W.L.R. 470, Illustration 3 to Article 5: cf. *Goshawk Dedicated Ltd v Tyser & Co Ltd* [2006] EWCA Civ 54 (insurance broker must reveal documents relating to placing, claims and premium accounting).

[397] *Bartram & Sons v Lloyd* (1903) 88 L.T. 286; reversed on other grounds (1904) 90 L.T. 357; *Fullwood v Hurley* [1928] 1 K.B. 498; *Cec. McManus Realty Ltd v Bray* (1970) 14 D.L.R. (3d) 564 at 568; and compare *Jones v Canavan* [1971] 2 N.S.W.L.R. 243. See also *Knoch Estate v Jon Picken Ltd* (1991) 83 D.L.R. (4th) 447.

[398] *Re Haslam and Hier-Evans* [1902] 1 Ch. 765, Illustration 7 to Article 49. This reasoning would presumably cover the "buyer's premium" charged by some auctioneers. As to auctioneers bidding for third parties, see Murdoch, *Law of Estate Agency and Auctions* (4th edn), pp.66–70.

[399] *Harrods Ltd v Lemon* [1931] 2 K.B. 157, Illustration 8 to Article 60; cf. *Owen v Trickett* (1908) 27 N.Z.L.R. 950.

[400] *North and South Trust Co v Berkeley* [1971] 1 W.L.R. 470, Illustration 3 to Article 5; but see (1972) 35 M.L.R. 78; Rider (1978) 42 Conv. 114. See also *Vehicle and General Insurance Co Ltd v Elmbridge Insurances* [1973] 1 Lloyd's Rep. 325, where effect was (surprisingly) given to a clause by which an insurance broker agreed to hold money received from clients in trust for the insurance company.

[401] *Kelly v Cooper* [1993] A.C. 205, Illustration 9 to Article 43. This case, which was welcomed among legal advisers in the financial markets, is the source of Lord Browne-Wilkinson's dictum on the primacy of contract considered above, para.6-034.

[402] See further on this topic above, para.6-015.

[403] *Hilton v Barker Booth & Eastwood* [2005] UKHL 8; [2005] 1 W.L.R. 567 (noted Getzler (2006) 122 L.Q.R. 1). See also *Nationwide BS v Radmore* [1999] Lloyd's Rep. P.N. 237; and *HIH Casualty & General Insurance Ltd v JLT Risk Solutions Ltd* [2007] EWCA Civ 710; [2007] 2 Lloyd's Rep. 278; [2007] 2 All E.R. (Comm) 1106, Illustration 9.

acceptable implication,[404] it is unlikely that an entitlement to act for both buyer and seller (with or without a formal appointment), or indeed any two parties with opposed interests, would be acceptable.[405] In general, the implication of a term excluding fiduciary duties, or particular fiduciary duties, is not easy to justify.

Where there is a duty, its breach may be remediable by way of an action for breach of contract, and in some cases in tort by way of negligence, or deceit. But the duty may also derive from equity:

> "Fully informed consent apart, an agent cannot lawfully place himself in a position in which he owes a duty of care to another which is inconsistent with his duty to his principal."[406]

In particular, any affected transaction is likely to be rescindable at the principal's behest.

6-049 **Application of conflict of interest rules, including to companies and partnerships** The principles stated above were developed largely in the context of individual agents and individual principals, though there were some cases involving partnerships. Their application to companies, and even to large partnerships, has yet to be fully worked out. Thus an individual agent is not permitted to act on both sides of the same transaction without disclosure; but different parts of a company, or of solicitors' or accountants' firms, may do so at the same time in absolute good faith, without the company or firm necessarily being even aware that this is happening. This has been called a "same matter" conflict.[407] A company or firm may act for a client in respect of a particular matter, and subsequently act for another client who is on the other side of the dispute: this may be called a "former client" conflict. A company or firm may acquire knowledge from a client in respect of one matter, and an employee or partner may then move employment and subsequently act for another client in another matter to which information gained in connection with the first matter may be relevant: this may be called a "separate matter" conflict. Finally, part of a company or firm may appear to act in an agency or at least advisory capacity for a client while another part is acting in a different capacity in respect of the same client, for example as a seller or market-maker. This may be called a "fair dealing" conflict; such conflicts are not confined to conglomerates, though in modern conditions are more likely to arise in that context. It may be

---

[404] In *Kelly v Cooper* the claimant, surprisingly, conceded that the agent owed a duty to the other vendor-principal to keep confidential the fact of his treating with the purchaser. Arguably, the two vendors had a common interest which the agent failed to pursue, to the benefit of the purchaser to whom the agent owed no duties. On the topic of acting for competing principals, see further above, para.6-015.

[405] See *Premium Real Estate Ltd v Stevens* [2009] 2 N.Z.L.R. 384 (estate agent failing to reveal to its vendor principal its connections to buyer and misleading the vendor as to the buyer's intentions in relation to the house); *The Northampton Regional Livestock Centre Co Ltd v Cowling* [2015] EWCA Civ 651; [2016] 1 B.C.L.C. 431. As to the appointment of administrators to related companies that may have conflicting interests on certain matters, see *Tailby v Hutchinson Telecom FZCO* [2018] EWHC 360 (Ch), where earlier cases are discussed.

[406] *North & South Trust Co v Berkeley* [1971] 1 W.L.R. 470 at 484–485, per Donaldson J.

[407] Much of what follows draws heavily on the essay by Finn, "Fiduciary Law and the Modern Commercial World", in *Commercial Aspects of Trusts and Fiduciary Obligations* (McKendrick ed., 1992), Ch.1, pp.19–36. See also Finn, "Conflicts of Interest and Professionals" in *Professional Responsibility* (Legal Research Foundation, 1987), Ch.1; Law Com.C.P. No.124, *Fiduciary Duties and Regulatory Rules* (1992); and Hollander and Salzedo, *Conflicts of Interest* (5th edn). See too the Solicitors' Code of Conduct 2007, Rule 3.

sought to address these conflicts by the creation of so-called "Chinese (or Ethical) Walls", that is, by arrangements which seek to isolate the business activities of different parts of firms from each other.

Of these conflicts the first three raise general questions of agency law, and stem from the agent's duty of loyalty. There is likely to be a conflict between the right of one client (principal) that information regarding its business is not disclosed to anyone else, and the right of another that the agent, as fiduciary, make available all knowledge that the agent has and does not conceal relevant information. On the other hand, the case law, which has become very complex and even contradictory, does suggest that much may turn on the nature of the duties particular classes of agent (and indeed individual agents) have undertaken. Many of the cases involve solicitors where particularly high standards of conduct may be expected, for example in the maintenance of confidentiality, and managerial agents, such as company directors, may be subject to similar standards. There has also, as already noted, been a movement to separate the obligation not to disclose confidential information from general fiduciary doctrine,[408] the implications of which are not yet fully worked out.

Situation 1: "same matter" conflicts   This situation concerns companies and firms which, for example through different departments or partners, are simultaneously involved as agents on the two sides of a transaction or dispute. Against the background of the situation of the single agent, it is clear that this would, if not disclosed, involve a breach of duty to each party.[409] The agent must therefore in such a situation disclose to each party the extent of the double employment,[410] so that that party can decide for itself whether to continue using the services of the agent. Furthermore, the agent must make further disclosure if an actual conflict of interests between clients arises[411]; and if at that point the agent has information acquired on behalf of one party which would be relevant to the other, the agent's position is extremely difficult, for an unauthorised disclosure would be a breach of duty to the first party, and a concealment of the information a breach towards the second. In the corporate context it seems unlikely that, absent statutory provision, the law will accept either ignorance of the conflict or Chinese Walls as a defence to proceedings for breach of duty in such cases.[412] The agent should avoid the conflict arising in the first place, but if it arises the agent has little option but to cease to act for one party and sometimes for both.[413] An injunction would normally follow if the fiduciary persisted in acting while conflicted.[414]

Sometimes confidential or privileged information relevant to litigation is ac-

6-050

---

[408] See above, para.6-034.
[409] See *North & South Trust Co v Berkeley* [1971] 1 W.L.R. 470, Illustration 3 to Article 5. See also above, para.2-013; below, para.6-060; *Restatement, Third*, § 8.03.
[410] *Moody v Cox and Hatt* [1917] 2 Ch. 71 (solicitor). See too *Hesse v Briant* (1856) 6 G.M. & G. 623 (solicitor); *Harrods Ltd v Lemon* [1931] 2 K.B. 157 (estate agent).
[411] See *Hilton v Barker Booth and Eastwood* [2005] UKHL 8; [2005] 1 W.L.R. 567; *Farrington v Rowe McBride & Partners* [1985] 1 N.Z.L.R. 83; *Day v Mead* [1987] 2 N.Z.L.R. 443; *Stewart v Layton* (1992) 111 A.L.R. 687.
[412] See *Harrods Ltd v Lemon* [1931] 2 K.B. 157, Illustration 8 to Article 60; *Standard Investments Ltd v Canadian Imperial Bank of Commerce* (1985) 22 D.L.R. (4th) 410. But cf. *In re a Firm of Solicitors* [2000] 1 Lloyd's Rep. 31.
[413] *Bristol & West Building Society v Mothew* [1998] Ch. 1 at 19.
[414] See *A Company v XYZ* [2020] EWHC 809 (TCC) (expert in litigation placing itself in position of conflict).

cidentally disclosed to an opposing party's solicitor. Where this happens, the court must decide whether justice requires an order that the latter cease to act, rather than merely not make use of the confidential information.[415]

6-051   **Situation 2: "former client" conflicts**[416]   The problems here have usually arisen in connection with solicitors, and have mostly focused on issues of confidential information. In general, the equitable restrictions on solicitors and other litigation advisers are more extensive than those that apply to former employees and other agents who have not been involved in providing litigation support to a former employer or client.[417] The position of in-house solicitors and patent attorneys in relation to their former employer is uncertain, and has been the subject of divided judgments in the Court of Appeal.[418] In many cases there will be no doubt that in-house counsel are in possession of confidential information about relevant litigation, and subject to injunctive relief if they commence working for a party with adverse interests.

In the standard fact pattern, a partner or employee of one law firm who has knowledge of or access to a client's affairs moves to another firm which is acting against, or more generally, in a manner adverse to that client; or it is simply sought to employ another part of the same firm against the client after the firm's retainer with the client has been terminated. This has been authoritatively held to be a problem of confidential information, not of fiduciary duty,[419] on the basis that the fiduciary relationship ends with the retainer; a client cannot be taken to have purchased the solicitor's loyalty forever. It can be noted, however, that some cases, particularly in Australia and New Zealand, manifest a reluctance to confine the former solicitor's duties only to maintaining confidential information, or at least take a stricter view of what is confidential as between solicitor and client than might be taken with other parties.[420] The solicitor's knowledge of the client's business habits and disposition is said to make it inappropriate for the solicitor to be acting adversely to the client. On the other hand, where a solicitor has acted for two parties in an earlier matter with their consent, a restraint against later acting for only one of them would not normally succeed.[421] Nor are heightened duties of confidentiality applicable where the only basis for a claimant's objection to a

---

[415] *Stiedl v Enyo Law LLP* [2011] EWHC 2649 (Comm); [2012] P.N.L.R. 4 at [42]; *Avonwick Holdings Ltd v Shlosberg* [2016] EWCA Civ 1138 at [92].

[416] See McVea [2000] C.L.J. 370.

[417] See *PCCW-HKT Telephone Ltd v Aitken* (2009) 12 H.K.C.F.A.R. 114 (noted Nolan (2009) 125 L.Q.R. 374); *Caterpillar Logistics Services (UK) Ltd v de Crean* [2012] EWCA Civ 156; [2012] F.S.R. 33 at [60].

[418] *Generics (UK) Ltd v Yeda Research & Development Co Ltd* [2012] EWCA Civ 726; [2013] F.S.R. 13 (the court's decision was, however, unanimous).

[419] *Prince Jefri Bolkiah v KPMG* [1999] 2 A.C. 222 (litigation accountant conceded to be in similar position to solicitor); *PCCW-HKT Telephone Ltd v Aitken* [2009] HKCFA 11; *Western Avenue Properties Ltd v Soni* [2017] EWHC 2650 (QB). cf. *The Baby Hammock Co Ltd v AJ Park Law* [2011] NZHC 686 (patent attorneys able to act successively for clients with potentially competing products but no clash of patents). cf. *McMaster v Byrne* [1952] 1 All E.R. 1362, Illustration 8 to Article 45. See too Flannigan (2014) 130 L.Q.R. 498.

[420] See *Black v Taylor* [1993] 3 N.Z.L.R. 403 at 406; *Wagdy Hanna and Associates Pty Ltd v National Library of Australia* (2004) 185 F.L.R. 367 at [55]. This broader view of "former client" conflicts was adverted to in *Winters v Mishcon De Reya* [2008] EWHC 2419 (Ch) at [93]. For the mass of case law on this issue in Australia, see Conaglen, *Fiduciary Loyalty* (2010), p.194. See too para.6-067.

[421] See *Singla v Stockler* [2012] EWHC 1176 (Ch) at [10]; *Marshall v Prescott* [2015] NSWCA 110 (information acquired while acting for two parties available to both even after they fall into dispute).

defendant retaining a solicitor (or firm) is that while acting for a different defendant the solicitor became engaged in a mediation with the claimant.[422]

The first question that arises is the extent to which knowledge from previous employment is to be inferred. Should knowledge of relevant information be presumed? And should it be imputed to all partners or employees involved in the first firm or department?[423] The second is the extent to which the relevant person or firm is to be restrained from acting in the matter: for if strict controls are imposed, the choice of the second client of legal representation may become much restricted, especially in communities where there are not many lawyers, or law firms with suitable resources, available. The case law so far suggests that once the former client convinces the court that its former solicitor or firm of solicitors possesses relevant confidential information the interest of the first client in confidence will normally prevail over those of the second in being able to choose a lawyer; and that the relevant party will be restrained from acting unless the court is satisfied that there is no risk of disclosure.[424] The value of a Chinese Wall, i.e. an administrative arrangement which should exclude the person concerned from either receiving or imparting the relevant information, has been viewed with some scepticism by the courts, albeit in the context of solicitors, to whom special considerations concerned with the administration of justice apply.[425]

Situation 3: "separate matter" conflicts   These raise straight conflicts between the duty of a firm to provide skill and knowledge to a client on one matter and to do so for another client in another matter. There is a danger that the loyalties may clash. As Megarry VC said in connection with a solicitor: **6-052**

> "A solicitor must put at his client's disposal not only his skill but also his knowledge, so far as it is relevant; and if he is unwilling to reveal his knowledge to his client, he should not act for him. What he cannot do is to act for the client and at the same time withhold from him any relevant knowledge that he has."[426]

Similar reasoning can be applied to other professionals.

There can be no doubt that the disclosure of the first client's information will (un-

---

[422] See *Glencairn IP Holdings Ltd v Product Specialities Inc* [2020] EWCA Civ 609; [2020] 3 W.L.R. 810.

[423] See *Mallesons Stephen Jaques v KPMG Peat Marwick* (1990) 4 W.A.R. 357; but the same judge modified his view in *Unioil International Pty Ltd v Deloitte Touche Tohmatsu* (1997) 17 W.A.R. 98.

[424] *Prince Jefri Bolkiah v KPMG* [1999] 2 A.C. 222, per Lord Millett; approving *McDonald Estate v Martin* [1990] 3 S.C.R. 1235, sub nom. *Martin v Gray* (1990) 77 D.L.R. (4th) 249, where the Supreme Court of Canada by a majority preferred a rebuttable presumption that information would be imparted and required that all reasonable measures had been taken to ensure that no disclosure would occur (Lord Millett preferred "effective" to "reasonable"); *Georgian American Alloys Inc v White & Case LLP* [2014] EWHC 94 (Comm).This approach was regarded as too strict in Singapore: *Alrich Development Pte Ltd v Rafiq Jumabhoy* [1994] 3 Singapore L.R. 1, and a less restrictive approach has been taken in New Zealand: see *Russell McVeagh McKenzie Bartleet & Co v Tower Corp* [1998] 3 N.Z.L.R. 641 (expressly disapproved in *Bolkiah*). cf. *Torchlight Fund No.1 LP v NZ Credit Fund (GP) 1 Ltd* [2014] NZHC 2552. See also *National Mutual Holdings Pty v Sentry Corp* (1987) 87 A.L.R. 539.

[425] *David Lee (Lincoln) Ltd v Coward Chance* [1991] Ch. 259; *Re a Firm of Solicitors* [1997] Ch. 1; *Prince Jefri Bolkiah v KPMG* [1999] 2 A.C. 222; *Newman v Phillips Fox* (1999) 21 W.A.R. 309; cf. *Young v Robson Rhodes* [1999] 3 All E.R. 524; and *Halewood International Ltd v Addleshaw Booth & Co* [2000] Lloyd's Rep. P.N. 298, where precautions and undertakings were accepted; *Bloomsbury International Ltd v Holyoake* [2010] EWHC 1150 (Ch) at [55] (accounting firm with sufficiently discrete departments). See also Law Com. C.P. No.124, pp.144–149.

[426] *Spector v Ageda* [1973] Ch. 30 at 48.

less specifically authorised) be a breach of contract towards that client; no development of rules to cover such situations is likely to change this. It can be argued that the information which the second client "buys" is limited to that held by the fiduciary independently of that acquired through the client or clients, with the result that there need be no breach of duty at all. It has been so held, in effect, in the case of an estate agent who did not disclose information coming to her when acting for an adjacent proprietor.[427] But failure to disclose known facts to the second client may make other statements fraudulent; or it may falsify advice given and so cause avoidable and foreseeable loss to the second client.[428] The grant of relief requires a "reasonable apprehension of potential conflict (not a mere theoretical possibility)".[429] This postulates "some reasonable relation between the two matters".[430] In this situation it may be that a Chinese Wall defence would be more acceptable, if it indicated that the precautions taken were such as effectively to prevent the knowledge from the first transaction being available to those handling the second.[431] However, there may be problems when a person with oversight of two departments is aware of the conflict or its possibility; or if one department is aware that information may be available elsewhere in the firm. If the problem has been foreseen and provided for, the terms on which the agent accepts engagement from the second client may afford protection, subject to the difficulties discussed below.

Separate matter conflicts could concern matters other than knowledge. To take a hypothetical example, a firm could find itself compromised by acting for an employee in an employment dispute if at the same time it were tendering for business work for the employer.[432]

6-053   **Situation 4: "fair dealing" conflicts**   The fourth situation raises the problems created by the abolition of "single capacity" rules in some stock and other markets, including the securities markets of the UK. The functions previously performed by persons and organisations which were certainly agents (e.g. stockbrokers) may now be performed by parts of multi-function companies which advise clients, undertake execution of orders and may then sell securities which they themselves hold, or have purchased for the purpose, or in which they have an interest.[433] Chinese Walls have no relevance here; indeed the problem could arise with a sole trader. In view of the stringency of the duties which can be imposed by fiduciary law, organisations which act in such markets in a potentially fiduciary capacity must seek to define the scope of their duties by way of contract terms, quite regardless of the requirements of specific forms of regulation. The most obvious example is that of providers of financial services, who may well appear to act as (what would previously have been called) agents, or at least advisers, but also may now act, sometimes by way of a different part of the organisation, in ways which are potentially adverse to any fiduciary responsibilities which they may have: examples have already been given.

---

[427] *Kelly v Cooper* [1993] A.C. 205, Illustration 9 to Article 43.

[428] "We have been given no sufficient reason for permitting a person to avoid one fiduciary obligation by accepting another which conflicts with it": *Black v Shearson, Hammill & Co* 72 Cal.Rptr. 157 at 161 (1968); and see *Moody v Cox and Hatt* [1917] 2 Ch. 71.

[429] *Re Baron Investment (Holdings) Ltd* [2000] 1 B.C.L.C. 272.

[430] *Marks & Spencer Plc v Freshfields Bruckhaus Deringer* [2004] EWHC 1337; [2004] 1 W.L.R. 2331 (conflict of interest and confidential information).

[431] They were held insufficient in *Marks & Spencer Plc v Freshfields Bruckhaus Deringer* [2004] EWHC 1337; [2004] 1 W.L.R. 2331.

[432] See, e.g. *Mike Pero Mortgages Ltd v Pero* [2015] 3 N.Z.L.R. 246 (solicitor attempting to act both for and against client in separate matters).

[433] As to the general principles concerning agents dealing with their principals, see Article 45.

Such changes in the patterns of dealing have been followed by the making, by delegated legislation, of principles, rules and codes for the proper conduct of business, of which the most relevant in the UK are those made under the Financial Services and Markets Act 2000. There have been iterations of regulation under this Act.[434] It is important here for the law to maintain the strength of fiduciary duties and to recognise that a person engaged to act on another's behalf is undertaking thereby to prefer that other's interests and must be held to that undertaking. At the same time it must be recognised that commercial patterns change, and that as in other areas of activity some of those who were formerly intermediaries may adopt a new role as independent traders. Further, it is important not to set requirements such that financial services become impossible to carry out to the standards set by the law, for this would be subverting the mechanisms established under the aegis of statute by those authorised to establish them. These mechanisms may sometimes indeed be stronger and more effective than the rules of the general law, because they cover situations to which fiduciary duties might not apply, and also because they may be more specific and addressed to identified forms of dealing. For example, so-called "riskless principals" who buy on specific instructions and immediately sell to their client is not unlike an agent in doing so and may be required to disclose his mark-up.

Positive obligation to inform—duties of fidelity?   It has been seen that fiduci-   **6-054** ary duties are frequently said to be proscriptive not prescriptive; they do not impose positive obligations but rather state what must *not* be done.[435] This view may be true of fiduciary duties in the narrow or strict sense (the duties to avoid conflicts of interest and not to profit from position), but it does not follow that positive obligations on an agent to communicate information to a principal cannot otherwise exist. Plainly, a duty of disclosure arises if an agent wishes safely to continue to act notwithstanding the conflict of interest. But other positive duties can arise. One source of such obligations would be the contract of agency.[436] Equitable obligations of good faith may also impose positive obligations. However, it seems unlikely that, in contrast to the position with the core fiduciary duties, uniform rules of disclosure applicable to all agents can be arrived at.[437]

Hence, until recently the leading case of *Bell v Lever Bros Ltd*[438] was taken to establish that an employee, and on that account other agents, were under no duty to disclose their own past breaches of duty. This seems to be true as regards disclosure by an employee negotiating a severance payment, which is what the case concerns.[439] But it has now been held that, at least where a breach has ongoing implications for the principal's business, an employee is normally required to disclose breaches of duty by other employees even if this involves disclosing the

---

[434] Further change, including some directed to conflicts of interest, will occur when the Markets in Financial Instruments Directive II (MiFID II) comes into force, projected to be January 3, 2018. The impact of "Brexit" on this is unknown at the time of writing. For an analysis of the conflict of interest provisions of MiFID II, see Busch, in *Agency Law in Commercial Practice* (Busch, Macgregor and Watts eds, 2016), Ch.9.

[435] See above, para.6-039.

[436] See above, para.6-019.

[437] cf. *Restatement, Third*, § 8.11. See too R Lee [2009] Conv. 236.

[438] *Bell v Lever Bros Ltd* [1932] A.C. 161. The case was of course finally decided on grounds of mistake. See a valuable historical account of the case by MacMillan in (2003) 119 L.Q.R. 625.

[439] See further *Horcal Ltd v Gatland* [1984] B.C.L.C. 549.

employee's own,[440] and in general there may be a duty on the employee, under the general obligation of fidelity and care, to disclose other wrongdoing at the time (as opposed to on severance negotiations) if it concerns some matter which the employer should know about in order to take appropriate action.[441] It is possible that this duty even extends to past wrongdoing in relation to the third party with whom the principal now has a contract.[442]

Bell v Lever did not involve directors: the persons concerned were employees of Lever Bros appointed to act as directors of a subsidiary, and the non-disclosure was also at the time of severance negotiations. It was recognised in the case that the position might be different for directors, and it has indeed been held by the Court of Appeal in *Item Software (UK) Ltd v Fassihi*[443] that a director is liable for not disclosing breaches of duty that have ongoing relevance, as well as any such breaches by colleagues and employees.[444]

Another issue that has received consideration is the circumstances in which an agent might come under a positive obligation to reveal to the principal an intention to terminate the agency in order to compete with the principal. Again, authority now supports the view that company directors owe such a duty—for a director in such circumstances there is a conflict of interest between one's duty to do one's best for the company and one's interest in promoting the interests of the prospective employer.[445] Note that there is no duty not to resign, but rather a positive duty to reveal that one is planning to, once a firm decision to do so has been formed. It has also been held that employees who are not managers do not owe such duties.[446] Such employees may not be obliged to answer truthfully questions about what they

---

[440] *Sybron Corp v Rochem Ltd* [1984] Ch. 112, Illustration 6. cf. *PennWell Publishing (UK) Ltd v Ornstien* [2007] EWHC 1570 (QB); [2008] 2 B.C.L.C. 246 at [65] (no duty on employee to report misdeeds of more senior staff).

[441] See a valuable discussion of *Bell v Lever* at first instance in *Item Software (UK) Ltd v Fassihi* [2003] EWHC 3116 (Ch); [2003] 2 B.C.L.C. 1, especially at [51].

[442] See *HPOR Servicos De Consultoria Ltda v Dryships Inc* [2018] EWHC 3451 (Comm); [2019] 1 Lloyd's Rep. 260.

[443] *Item Software (UK) Ltd v Fassihi* [2004] EWCA Civ 1244; [2005] 2 B.C.L.C. 91. See Watts (2007) 123 L.Q.R. 21; and Ho and Lee [2007] C.L.J. 348. For criticism, see Berg (2005) 121 L.Q.R. 213. See too *GHLM Trading Ltd v Maroo* [2012] EWHC 61 (Ch) at [192] onwards; *IT Human Resources Plc v Land* [2014] EWHC 3812 (Ch) at [121] (supplying copyright material to a competitor); *Parr v Keystone Healthcare Ltd* [2019] EWCA Civ 1246 at [23].

[444] *British Midland Tool Ltd v Midland International Tooling Ltd* [2003] EWHC 466 (Ch); [2003] 2 B.C.L.C. 523; *QBE Management Services (UK) Ltd v Dymoke* [2012] EWHC 80 (QB) at [169]. But an implied duty to disclose one's own breaches does not, it seems, attach to employees, at least those not serving in a management role: *Ranson v Customer Systems Plc* [2012] EWCA Civ 841; [2012] I.R.L.R. 769 at [55].

[445] *Foster Bryant Surveying Ltd v Bryant* [2007] EWCA Civ 200; [2007] 2 B.C.L.C. 239 (where the duty of disclosure was met); *British Midland Tool Ltd v Midland International Tooling Ltd* [2003] EWHC 466 (Ch); [2003] 2 B.C.L.C. 523; *Shepherds Investments Ltd v Walters* [2006] EWHC 836 (Ch); [2007] F.S.R. 15; [2007] 2 B.C.L.C. 202; not following dicta in *Balston Ltd v Headline Filters Ltd* [1990] F.S.R. 385; and *Framlington Group Plc v Anderson* [1995] 1 B.C.L.C. 475. See too *Berryland Books Ltd v BK Books Ltd* [2009] EWHC 1877 (Ch) at [23]; *G. Attwood Holdings Ltd v Woodward* [2009] EWHC 1083 (Ch); *Gamatronic (UK) Ltd v Hamilton* [2016] EWHC 2225 (QB) at [88] and [151]. *Grace v Biagioli* [2005] EWCA Civ 1222; [2006] 2 B.C.L.C. 70 at [69]–[70] suggests also that where the director's intention becomes apparent, the company may remove the director from office or require him to stand down. See also Companies Act 2006 ss.172 and 175; and *Company Directors: Duties, Liabilities and Remedies* (Mortimore, ed, 3rd edn); Watts (2007) 123 L.Q.R. 21.

[446] *Helmet Integrated Systems Ltd v Tunnard* [2006] EWCA Civ 1735; [2007] I.R.L.R. 126. See too *RBC Dominion Securities Inc v Merrill Lynch Canada Inc* [2008] 3 S.C.R. 79; Brodie (2012) 16 Edinburgh L.R. 198; and *Ranson v Customer Systems Plc* [2012] EWCA Civ 841; [2012] I.R.L.R.

are going to do once their employment ceases,[447] at least where their intentions are not hampering the performance of their duties before their departure.

Statutory requirements   Sometimes disclosure of a conflict is required by statute   **6-055** or statutory instrument. Thus persons engaged in estate agency work are in some circumstances required to disclose to their clients services which they or persons connected with them offer to purchasers[448]; or that they or persons connected with them are seeking to acquire an interest in the land concerned.[449] Statutory requirements would usually be taken as supplemental to, rather than a replacement for, equity's requirements unless the statute were clear on the point.[450]

Modification of duties by contract: common law[451]   Some persons exercising   **6-056** pure agency functions in the old sense may remain in this sphere of activity, but wish to modify the equitable duties that would otherwise apply to them. Yet others who normally act as principals may undertake agency functions, or something like them, but wish to make clear that they do not intend the ordinary incidents of agency to apply to them. An appropriate professional description or contract clause can be used to seek to make clear that, for instance, a securities firm, or a joint venture party, is not an agent, but rather a financial adviser and/or dealer. Although certain fiduciary duties may perhaps attach to them as advisers, these will be more limited than those attaching to pure agents[452]; and of course a dealer would not prima facie be under fiduciary duties at all.

Otherwise, contract terms can purport in some way to exclude or restrict the fiduciary duties which might otherwise arise. It is plain that a fiduciary could not exclude liability for personal fraud (including fraudulent non-disclosure) or deliberate breach of contract[453] though a fiduciary might, if the wording was clear enough, exclude liability for the fraud of an agent.[454] Furthermore, in the absence of the clearest language, it is unlikely that a court would find that a clause permitting a conflict was intended to permit the agent actively to prefer one party over the other, as opposed to attempting to act even-handedly. In *Bristol and West BS v Mothew* Millett LJ referred to what he called the "no inhibition principle",[455] that requires an agent acting with consent for both parties to refrain from putting himself in a

---

769 at [68].

[447] See *MPT Group Ltd v Peel* [2017] EWHC 1222 (Ch) at [86].

[448] Estate Agents (Undesirable Practices) (No.2) Order 1991 (SI 1991/1032) (made under Estate Agents Act 1979 s.18) reg.2; see Murdoch, *The Estate Agents and Property Misdescriptions Acts* (3rd edn), Ch.3A; *Law of Estate Agency* (5th edn), p.290 onwards. The civil remedy is that the contract may be unenforceable: Estate Agents Act 1979 s.18(5).

[449] Estate Agents (Undesirable Practices) (No.2) Order 1991 (SI 1991/1032) Sch.1 para.2; see Murdoch, above, pp.212–213.

[450] See *Barfoot & Thompson Ltd v Real Estate Agents Authority* [2016] NZCA 105.

[451] See Bean, *Fiduciary Obligations and Joint Ventures* (1995), p.84 onwards.

[452] See *Burns v Kelly Peters & Associates Ltd* (1987) 41 D.L.R. (4th) 577; *Alliance Craton Explorer Pty Ltd v Quasar Resources Pty Ltd* [2013] FCAFC 29; Finn, in *Commercial Aspects of Trusts and Fiduciary Obligations* (McKendrick ed., 1992), pp.7 and 10–11.

[453] *S. Pearson & Son Ltd v Dublin Corp* [1907] A.C. 351 at 355 and 362; Treitel, *Law of Contract* (15th edn), para.7-034–7-035.

[454] *HIH Casualty and General Insurance Ltd v Chase Manhattan Bank* [2003] UKHL 6; [2003] 1 All E.R. (Comm) 349, requiring express reference to fraud or very similar wording. But see the Hon. Justice K.R. Handley (2003) 119 L.Q.R. 537.

[455] *Bristol and West BS v Mothew* [1998] Ch. 1 at 19; *Consolidated Finance Ltd v Collins* [2013] EWCA Civ 475 at [59]; *Northampton Regional Livestock Centre Co Ltd v Cowling* [2015] EWCA Civ 651; [2016] 1 B.C.L.C. 431 at [77]. For discussion, see Conaglen (2009) 125 L.Q.R. 111 at 127–140.

position where the agent feels inhibited about doing his best for both parties. Liability for damages might ensue where this principle is not adhered to,[456] and almost certainly will where the fiduciary actively promotes the interests of one party over the other.

As for the general approach to attempts to modify what would otherwise be fiduciary duty, it is usually necessary for there to be an express term to that effect. However, we have seen that recent dicta of high authority suggesting that all agency is contractual and that the rights and duties of the parties to such a contract stem entirely from the contract between them,[457] may be taken to suggest that the background against which intermediaries act, and the general understandings in the type of business, may establish that there are no fiduciary duties, or very limited duties, in certain situations. The principles of interpretation and implied terms may be adequate without express exclusion clauses. It has earlier been noted, however, that this purely contractual approach is not beyond question, certainly as a reason for inferring that obligations implied by law are inapplicable.[458] It was, for example, long ago held in *Robinson v Mollett*[459] that a usage of the market which allowed an agent to buy to become a seller to the principal was inconsistent with the relationship of agency and so invalid against a principal unless the principal was aware of it.

As for express terms, there are some precedents but the case law has until recently been relatively thin.[460] Recent important cases upholding exclusion clauses in respect of the duties of trustees could prima facie be extended to the duties of agents.[461]

This paragraph is principally directed to modification of fiduciary duties in advance of action. Generally speaking, a principal is also able, retrospectively, to excuse what would otherwise have been a breach of duty. In relation to company directors, waiver of breach is referred to as "ratification" (a different usage to that used in agency law in general).[462] Such ratification is now governed by the Companies Act 2006 s.239. As for consent to what would otherwise be a breach of fiduciary duty, see above, para.6-039.

---

[456] *Leeds and Holbeck Building Society v Arthur and Cole* [2002] P.N.L.R. 78; *Nationwide Building Society v Goodwin Harte* [1999] Lloyd's Rep. P.N. 338 at 345.

[457] *Kelly v Cooper* [1993] A.C. 205 at 213–214 (Illustration 9 to Article 43); *Torre Asset Funding Ltd v The Royal Bank of Scotland Plc* [2013] EWHC 2670 (Ch) at [143]; *AP-Fonden v Bank of New York Mellon SA/NV* [2013] EWHC 3127 (Comm) at [177]; cf. above, para.6-034.

[458] See above, para.6-034.

[459] *Robinson v Mollett* (1874) L.R. 7 H.L. 802, Illustration 8 to Article 31. See too *Brandeis (Brokers) Ltd v Black* [2001] 2 Lloyd's Rep. 359.

[460] cf. *Hayim v Citibank NA* [1987] A.C. 730 (clause reducing duties of executor of will towards beneficiaries); *Movitex Ltd v Bulfield* [1988] B.C.L.C. 104 (modification of self-dealing rules in company's articles); see also *Noranda Australia Ltd v Lachlan Resources NL* (1988) 14 N.S.W.L.R. 1.

[461] *Armitage v Nurse* [1998] Ch. 241; *Walker v Stones* [2001] Q.B. 902; Law Com. C.P. No.171 (2003); *Citibank NA v QVT Financial LP* [2007] EWCA Civ 11; [2007] 1 All E.R. (Comm) 475; *Spread Trustee Co Ltd v Hutcheson* [2011] UKPC 13; [2012] 2 A.C. 194; *Lehtimaki v Cooper* [2020] UKSC 33 at [82]. See also *Australian Securities and Investments Commission v Citigroup Global Markets Australia Pty Ltd* (2007) 62 A.C.S.R. 427 (Fed. Ct) (contractual provision avoided any conflict-of-interest disabilities that might have arisen from the fact that one division of the defendant was advising a client on its takeover offer for a company at the same time as another division was independently buying up shares in the company (noted Getzler (2008) 124 L.Q.R. 15; Tuch (2007) 7 J. Corp Leg. Stud. 51); and *Zhang Hong Li v DBS Bank (Hong Kong) Ltd* [2019] HKCFA 45.

[462] See, e.g. *North-West Transportation Ltd v Beatty* (1887) 12 App.Cas. 589; *Burland v Earle* [1902] A.C. 83 PC.

Custom or usage   A custom or usage which converts an agent into a principal or   **6-057**
otherwise gives the agent an interest at variance with duty is prima facie unreasonable,[463] and will therefore be ineffective unless known of and consented to by the
principal.[464]

Unfair Contract Terms Act 1977[465]   A contract clause seeking to make clear that   **6-058**
a person who might be an agent is not, or might in some circumstances not be acting as such, may also be caught by the Unfair Contract Terms Act 1977, which
could require it to be assessed against the "requirement of reasonableness". Here,
however, conceptual problems may arise.[466] The relevant provision will normally
be s.3, which operates where one party deals "as consumer or on the other's written standard terms of business". One of these two requirements may often be satisfied; but then the wording of the section is entirely geared to exclusions or restrictions of "breach of contract", "contractual performance" and "contractual
obligation". The section therefore seems to apply only to such duties as can be
regarded as contractual and normal to the type of transaction; and we are therefore
remitted to the problem, discussed above,[467] as to the extent to which the agent owes
fiduciary duties and the extent to which, in so far as that is the case, these are
contractual.[468] If the duties arise outside the contract, the Act may not affect such
duties at all. Equally, it could be argued that a clause establishing the nature of the
function of a person in question is not an exclusion clause within the Act at all, and
so is immune from the requirement of reasonableness. Reasoning of this type was
rejected, albeit in a slightly different context, by the House of Lords, but may have
recently become more acceptable.[469]

In response to either argument, the strongest part of s.3 is s.3(2)(b)(i), which does
not rely on the idea of existing contractual obligations at all: under it a person cannot "claim to be entitled to render a contractual performance substantially different from that which was reasonably expected of him", except in so far as the clause
is reasonable under the Act. It is this provision which gets nearest to approaching
the problems outlined above and it may accordingly prove to be of most value
where the exclusions used by a person who might be taken to be offering agency
or similar functions are such that a reasonable person using that person's services
would not have anticipated their effect.

A different issue is raised by clauses which seek to limit liability to fraud or gross

---

[463] *Robinson v Mollett* (1875) L.R. 7 H.L. 802, Illustration 8 to Article 31; *Hamilton v Young* (1881) 7
L.R.Ir. 289, Illustration 5; *Tetley v Shand* (1871) 25 L.T. 658; *Anglo-African Merchants Ltd v Bayley*
[1970] 1 Q.B. 311; *North and South Trust Co v Berkeley* [1971] 1 W.L.R. 470; *Cec. McManus Realty
Ltd v Bray* (1970) 14 D.L.R. (3d) 564 at 568; cf. *Jones v Canavan* [1971] 2 N.S.W.L.R. 243.
[464] See Article 31.
[465] See in general *Chitty on Contracts* (33rd edn), para.15-062 onwards. Exclusion of liability for
misrepresentation is covered by s.3 of the Misrepresentation Act 1967.
[466] Sch. 1 cl.1(e) to the Act excludes from its scope "any contract so far as it relates to the creation or
transfer of securities or of any right or interest in securities". This appears on its face to relate to
provisions concerning the transfer of the securities themselves and not to the function performed by
the person effecting the transfer.
[467] See above, para.6-034.
[468] See above, para.6-034.
[469] *Smith v Eric S. Bush* [1990] 1 A.C. 831; cf. *Henderson v Merrett Syndicates Ltd* [1995] 2 A.C. 145;
Titan Steel Wheels Ltd v Royal Bank of Scotland Plc [2010] EWHC 211 (Comm); [2010] 2 Lloyd's
Rep. 92.

negligence or the like.[470] As applied to agents, these would normally be subject to the Act's provisions.

The financial market in the UK is, as has already been stated, regulated by techniques laid down by statute, now the Financial Services and Markets Act 2000.[471] In so far as the 1977 Act, and its "requirement of reasonableness", is applicable, it seems likely that compliance with such provisions would be strong, but should not be conclusive, evidence of the reasonableness of a particular contract term.

6-059   **Consumer Rights Act 2015**[472]   A contract by a private person with a professional agent may involve the supply of services to a consumer and hence be caught by Pt 2 of the Consumer Rights Act 2015. The provisions do not apply to the fairness of a term to the extent that the term specifies the main subject-matter of the contract.[473] Otherwise, the Act could be used to address modifications or exclusions of what would otherwise be equity's control of conflicts of interest or other incidents of the fiduciary relationship. The control is exercised where a term "contrary to the requirement of good faith causes a significant imbalance to the parties' rights and obligations under the contract to the detriment of the consumer".[474] Such terms are not enforceable, but the rest of the contract normally remains.

6-060   **Public law: the Financial Services and Markets Act 2000**[475]   The Financial Services and Markets Act 2000, as substantially amended by the Financial Services Act 2012, rationalised the legislative framework governing banks, building societies, investment firms, insurance companies as well as several other types of regulated financial services entity. Under the legislation, the Financial Conduct Authority ("FCA", replacing the earlier Financial Services Authority) operates as the UK's single statutory financial services regulator.

The Act authorises the making of rules by the FCA which may potentially affect fiduciary duties. Thus, Pt 9A (replacing earlier s.138) contains powers for the FCA to make rules applying to the activities of regulated firms which are necessary or expedient for protecting the interests of consumers. Rules made under this section would include requirements for firms to disclose to their customers details of charges, remuneration and commission.[476] The general rulemaking power in s.137A is supplemented by various other sections. So, for example, additional provision is made in relation to client money (s.137B) and as to the rights and duties of participants in authorised unit trust schemes and openended investment companies (ss.247(1)(b) and 262(2)(e)). Most conspicuous is s.147, which allows for the making of so-called "control of information" rules which relate to "the

---

[470]   See *Armitage v Nurse* [1998] Ch. 241; *Walker v Stones* [2001] 2 Q.B. 902; *Spread Trustee Co Ltd v Hutcheson* [2011] UKPC 13; [2012] 2 A.C. 194.

[471]   See below.

[472]   Formerly, the Unfair Terms in Consumer Contracts Regulations 1999. See *Chitty on Contracts* (33rd edn), Ch.38; Treitel, *Law of Contract* (15th edn), para.7-086 onwards.

[473]   SI 1999/2083, replacing earlier regulations of 1994, SI 1994/3159.

[474]   See s.62. The former Regulations have been treated as potentially applicable to renewal and commission terms in management contracts between real estate agents and landlords in *Office of Fair Trading v Foxtons Ltd* [2009] EWCA Civ 288; [2010] 1 W.L.R. 663.

[475]   The Act is a specialised topic which has generated its own literature. See, for example, Sweet & Maxwell's *Encyclopaedia of Financial Services Law* (Lomnicka and Powell eds); Butterworths *Financial Services Law and Practice* (looseleaf); and Blackstone's *Guide to the Financial Services and Markets Act 2000*.

[476]   See s.137H onwards.

disclosure and use of information held by an authorised person ('A')". Section 137P (replacing earlier s.147) provides that control of information rules may:

"(a)   require the withholding of information which A would otherwise be required to disclose to a person ("B") for or with whom A does business in the course of carrying on any regulated or other activity;
(b)   specify circumstances in which A may withhold information which A would otherwise be required to disclose to B;
(c)   require A not to use for the benefit of B information—
    (i)   which is held by A, and
    (ii)   which A would otherwise be required to use for the benefit of B;
(d)   specify circumstances in which A may decide not to use for the benefit of B information within paragraph (c)."

The section is taken to refer to the setting up of Chinese, or "Ethical", Walls for which rules then provide the details.

The view can be taken that rules so made can alter the rights and duties of the parties as they would otherwise be determined by the rules of private law[477] in the particular context of financial services, for example in the first three conflict situations referred to above. Equally, rules made under s.147(2) might affect situations of the fourth type. Indeed, the UK Government took this view when introducing the Act. It stated that, in light of recent case law[478]:

"It is the Government's firm belief that the courts would be unlikely to hold that someone could successfully sue an authorised person for breach of fiduciary duties where the authorised person has complied with FCA rules, which, of course, are made under Parliament's delegated statutory powers."[479]

It seems very doubtful, however, whether the power to alter basic protective rules of law could be conferred on a rule-making body in this way and by such general wording. Compliance with such standards might, however, as indicated above, be evidence of statutory reasonableness; or be a guide to the extent of the fiduciary obligation; to trade usage; or more simply as to the understandings of the parties to a contract. The provisions as to clients' money, on the other hand, raise no such problems, for the way in which a fiduciary holds money is in any case variable in accordance with the context. In many circumstances, claimants will prefer to use the statutory provisions, the remedies for which are very flexible.[480]

Illustrations

(1)   An agent for sale sells to a company of which he is a director and large shareholder. The sale is not binding on the principal.[481]   **6-061**
(2)   A director of a company may not sell to his company articles which he, or a firm in which he has an interest, manufactures. Any such contract is voidable

---

[477]   Law Com. C.P. No.124, p.176 onwards.
[478]   This was primarily a reference to *Prince Jefri Bolkiah v KPMG* [1999] 2 A.C. 222.
[479]   *Hansard*, H.L., col.1409, May 9, 2000, per Lord McIntosh of Haringey.
[480]   See above, para.6-041. And in relation to the remedies under the statute, *Re Lehman Bros International (Europe) Ltd (in administration)* [2012] UKSC 6; [2012] 3 All E.R. 1; *Allanfield Property Insurance Services Ltd v Aviva Insurance Ltd* [2015] EWHC 3721 (Ch); [2016] Lloyd's Rep. I.R. 217.
[481]   *Salomons v Pender* (1865) 3 H. & C. 639, although the case was primarily reasoned on the basis of the agent selling to the principal (as to which see below, para.6-065).

by the company, quite apart from the question of its fairness, since a director is not permitted to enter into transactions in which his own interest is in conflict with his duty to promote the interests of the company.[482]

(3) Factory owners employed a surveyor to prepare a specification of repairs for submission to the War Damage Commission and to supervise the repair work as it was done by a building company. After the preparation of a specification, but before any repair work was done, the surveyor became the managing director of the building company and told the factory owners of his new position. The surveyor placed himself in a position where his duty and interest conflicted and this was a breach of his contract. But he was entitled to recover his fees since the factory owners had acquiesced in his continuance as their agent.[483]

(4) A solicitor engaged an assistant to undertake, among other business, the work of an important client. During his employment, the assistant agreed with the client to leave the employment of the solicitor in order to set up in practice on his own. The client agreed that, if he did so, the client would transfer his work to the assistant. Held, in so acting, the assistant was in breach of the implied term of his agreement to serve the claimant with good faith and fidelity. He was, accordingly, liable in damages to his principal.[484]

(5) A broker was authorised to sell certain shares, and pay himself certain advances out of the proceeds. A custom whereby he might himself take over the shares at the price of the day, in the event of him being unable to find a purchaser at an adequate price, was unreasonable, and such a transaction was not binding on the principal unless he had notice of the custom at the time when he gave the broker the authority, even if a forced sale of the shares would inevitably have realised less than the price given by the broker.[485] So a custom whereby an agent for sale of a ship may himself purchase at the minimum price if he cannot find a purchaser was held to be unreasonable.[486]

(6) The European zone controller of an international chemical company engages with other employees in setting up and operating rival businesses in competition with the company. He is in breach of duty in not disclosing the misconduct of the other employees, and on the terms of the company's pension scheme the company need not make certain payments to him and can recover sums paid.[487]

(7) Two members of a committee appointed to sell residential units on behalf of joint principals, including themselves, promote a rapid sale, deliberately failing to pursue other potential offers, in order to be able to meet debt obligations on personal loans they had taken out to acquire some of their units. Since the purchaser was aware of the conflict of interest, the sale agreement was set aside.[488]

---

[482] *Aberdeen Ry Co v Blaikie Bros* (1854) 1 Macq. 461.

[483] *Thornton Hall v Wembley Electrical Appliances Ltd* [1947] 2 All E.R. 630.

[484] *Sanders v Parry* [1967] 1 W.L.R. 753. See also *Robb v Green* [1895] 2 Q.B. 315 at 320. This expression is also to be found in *Wessex Dairies Ltd v Smith* [1935] 2 K.B. 80; *Hivac Ltd v Park Royal Scientific Instruments Ltd* [1946] Ch. 169; *Aubanel and Alabaster Ltd v Aubanel* (1949) 66 R.P.C. 343; *State Vacuum Stores v Phillips* [1954] 3 D.L.R. 621.

[485] *Hamilton v Young* (1881) 7 L.R.Ir. 289; *Rothschild v Brookman* (1831) 2 Dow. & Cl. 188. But cf. Article 45, Illustration 9.

[486] *De Bussche v Alt* (1878) 8 Ch.D. 286.

[487] *Sybron Corp v Rochem Ltd* [1984] Ch. 112.

[488] *Ng Eng Ghee v Mamata Kapildev Dave* [2009] SGCA 14.

(8) The outgoing chief executive of a company, X, agrees a remuneration package with an incoming executive director, Y, which is very generous including in its severance entitlements. X had sold Y his shares in the company albeit at no more than market value. Y is later made redundant and invokes the severance terms. X had a conflict of interest and is liable to compensate the company for the severance costs.[489] Similar consequences attach to a director who at a time when his company is insolvent takes steps to ensure that the company discharges a debt to him ahead of paying the company's other creditors.[490]

(9) An insurance broker, acting both for the insured and the reinsured on income insurance policies in the film industry, failed to inform the reinsured of various post-contract breaches of warranty by the insured. The broker's conflict of interest could not excuse it from performing its duty to the reinsured.[491]

Article 45

AGENT DEALING WITH PRINCIPAL[492]

(1) Where an agent purports to enter into a contract or transaction with himself on behalf of the principal the agent will need express authority to do so. In the absence of such authority, the dealing may be void at law[493] and will be voidable *ex debito justitiae* at equity.[494]   **6-062**

(2) Where an agent enters into any other contract or transaction with the principal, or with the principal's representative in interest, the agent must act with perfect good faith, and make full disclosure of all the material circumstances, and of everything known to him respecting the subject-matter of the contract or transaction which would be likely to influence the conduct of the principal or the principal's representative.[495]

---

[489] *PNC Telecom Plc v Thomas* [2007] EWHC 2157 (Ch); [2008] 2 B.C.L.C. 95.

[490] *MacPherson v European Strategic Bureau Ltd* [2000] 2 B.C.L.C. 683; *E-Clear (UK) Plc v Elia* [2013] EWCA Civ 1114 at [33].

[491] *HIH Casualty & General Insurance Ltd v JLT Risk Solutions Ltd* [2007] EWCA Civ 710; [2007] 2 Lloyd's Rep. 278; [2007] 2 All E.R. (Comm) 1106. On the facts, the claimant was unable to establish that the breach caused its loss.

[492] See generally *Snell's Equity* (34th edn), paras 7-020 and 7-021; Conaglen [2006] C.L.J. 366; Edelman, in *Fault Lines in Equity* (Glister and Ridge eds, 2012), Ch.5.

[493] See, e.g. *Salomons v Pender* (1865) 3 H. & C. 639 at 642 (a case denying the agent any commission, when arguably it was not in any event earned on a sale to oneself).

[494] See *Tito v Waddell (No.2)* [1977] Ch. 106 at 241; *York Buildings v MacKenzie* (1795) 8 Bro. P.C. 42; *Kimber v Barber* (1872) L.R. 8 Ch. App. 56. For a collection of other cases, see Conaglen, *Fiduciary Loyalty*, p.126.

[495] *Collins v Hare* (1828) 2 Bli.(N.S.) 106; *Jones v Thomas* (1837) 2 Y. & C.Ex. 498; *Molony v Kernan* (1842) 2 Dr. & War. (Ir.) 31; *Charter v Trevelyan* (1844) 11 C. & F. 714; *Savery v King* (1856) 5 H.L. Cas. 627; *Waters v Shaftesbury* (1866) 14 L.T. 184; *Parker v McKenna* (1874) L.R. 10 Ch.App. 96; *Ward v Sharp* (1884) 53 L.J.Ch. 313; *Demerara Bauxite Co v Hubbard* [1923] A.C. 673; *J.J. Harrison (Properties) Ltd v Harrison* [2001] EWCA Civ 1467; [2002] 1 B.C.L.C. 162; but cf. *Hanson v Lorenz & Jones* [1987] 1 F.T.L.R. 23 (agent enters joint venture with principal). And see Illustrations; Finn, *Fiduciary Obligations* (1977), Ch.20 and pp.223–228; *Meagher, Gummow and Lehane's Equity Doctrines and Remedies* (5th edn), para.5-180 onwards. The problem of "self-contracting" raises in civil law jurisdictions theoretical problems to which the common law, largely concerned with protection of the principal, has paid little attention. See Badr (1982) 30 Am.J.Comp.L. 255.

(3)   Where any question arises as to the validity of any such contract or transaction, or of any gift made by a principal to an agent, the burden of proving that there was no leverage of position by the agent, or of the confidence reposed in the agent, and that the transaction was fair, and entered into in perfect good faith and after full disclosure, lies upon the agent.[496]

Comment

6-063   **Basis of principles**   The foregoing principles reflect what are often called the "self-dealing" and the "fair-dealing" rules. The two concepts are not always kept distinct, but in the context of agency, the former is certainly the appropriate term where agents purport to make contracts with themselves on behalf of their principal, or where an agent is a co-agent and participates in the decision to make the contract.[497] The fair-dealing rule governs where the principal acts in person but is negotiating a contract with the agent. To the extent that self-dealing transactions may be unauthorised at law it is not necessary to have recourse to the fiduciary duties to avoid conflicts of interest and not to profit from position. The relationship of the fair-dealing rule with those duties is, however, not altogether clear.[498] In part this reflects the fact that fact patterns do not fall into neat categories. Particularly where an agent is buying property from the principal, the agent may have received information about the property in his capacity as agent that means he could be profiting from position. In other cases, there could be such a marked degree of confidence reposed by the principal in the agent that a relationship of undue influence exists or can be presumed[499]; this would not be the case with all agency relationships. It seems, however, that the fair-dealing rule, as with the self-dealing rule, does not turn on proof of use of position or on the existence of a relationship of influence, but does require that the dealing be one that has a connection with the subject-matter of the agency. A transaction between principal and agent that relates, for instance, to property which has no connection to the mandate that the agent has, or has had, from the principal would not be caught by the fair-dealing rule, even if in some cases it might otherwise be subject to challenge for undue influence.[500] On this basis, it has been argued that the fair-dealing rule is simply part of the conflicts rule affecting all fiduciaries.[501] If so, the rules reflect a broad version of the concept of conflict of interest. In requiring that a transaction be "open and fair, and free from all objection",[502] the cases seem to require not only that all relevant information be disclosed but that agents conduct themselves with the utmost good faith; a fiduci-

---

[496] See *Bristol and West BS v Mothew* [1998] Ch. 1 at 18, per Millett LJ; and see material cited in fn.495 above.

[497] As to the capacity and the authority of an agent to contract with himself on behalf of his principal, see above, para.2-014.

[498] See Conaglen [2006] C.L.J. 366, a most useful analysis.

[499] *Barnard v Hunter* (1856) 2 Jur. (N.S.) 1213; *Wright v Carter* [1903] 1 Ch. 27 (solicitors). See further below, para.6-069.

[500] *Montesquieu v Sandys* (1811) 18 Ves. 302 at 313; *McPherson v Watt* (1877) 3 App.Cas. 254 at 270–271; *John Youngs Insurance Services Ltd v Aviva Insurance Service UK Ltd* [2011] EWHC 1515 (TCC) at [98] (see further above, para.6-036); *Wollenberg v Casinos Austria International Holding GmbH* [2011] EWHC 103 (Ch) (solicitor enters into business arrangement with former client on basis of share of profits). See further Conaglen [2006] C.L.J. 366 at 381–382.

[501] Conaglen [2006] C.L.J. 366, critically analysing a much-cited dictum of Megarry VC in *Tito v Waddell (No.2)* [1977] Ch. 106 at 341.

[502] *Lewis v Hillman* (1852) 3 H.L. Cas. 607 at 630.

ary has "a heavy duty to show the righteousness of the transactions".[503] The relationship is one uberrimae fidei.

Many of the self-dealing and fair-dealing cases involve sales by an agent to a principal or a purchase from a principal by an agent, and each of those types is treated in the following paragraphs. But the principles are applicable to any transaction between principal and agent. For the potential operation of fair-dealing principles before appointment, see above, para.6-038.

Purchase from principal   A long-established line of cases indicates that a person   **6-064**
who stands in a position of a confidential character in respect of the property of another, which would include many types of agent, cannot purchase it personally without full and fair disclosure of all the facts to the principal.[504] The onus in such a case is on the agent to show that the price was adequate, that the sale was as advantageous to the principal as any other sale the agent could have obtained from a third party, and that all the relevant facts were disclosed to the principal before the purchase and that the principal gave its informed consent.[505] The rule extends to sub-agents, who may themselves be fiduciaries.[506] It also applies to agents who take leases from their principals.[507] In this respect an agent may differ in some degree from a trustee, because a purchase of the trust property by a trustee is voidable at the instance of any beneficiary unless very stringent rules are complied with.[508] Where a solicitor purchases from a client, it is important (if not essential) that the client should have had independent advice; otherwise, the solicitor will have

---

[503] *CIBC Mortgages Plc v Pitt* [1994] 1 A.C. 200 at 209. See too *Re Taylor, Stileman & Underwood* [1891] 1 Ch. 590 CA at 600–601; *Re Morris* [1908] 1 K.B. 473 CA at 477 and 480; and *Candey Ltd v Crumpler* [2020] EWCA Civ 26; [2020] Bus. L.R. 1452 at [56].

[504] *Gibson v Jeyes* (1801) 6 Ves. 266; *Lowther v Lowther* (1806) 13 Ves. 95; *Austin v Chambers* (1838) 6 C. & F. 1, 37; *Rothschild v Brookman* (1831) 2 Dow. & Cl. 188; *Dally v Wonham* (1863) 33 Beav. 154; *Salomons v Pender* (1865) 3 H. & C. 639; *Dunne v English* (1874) L.R. 18 Eq. 524, Illustration 4; *McPherson v Watt* (1877) 3 App.Cas. 254, Illustration 3; *Imeson v Lister* (1920) 149 L.T.Jo. 446; *McKenzie v McDonald* [1927] V.L.R. 143; *Christie v McCann* (1972) 27 D.L.R. (3d) 544; *Lunghi v Sinclair* [1966] W.A.R. 172; *Headway Construction Co Ltd v Downham* (1974) 233 E.G. 675, Illustration 17; *Gathergood v Blundell & Brown Ltd* [1991] 1 N.Z.L.R. 405; *Chen v Marcolongo* (2009) 260 A.L.R. 353.

[505] *Gibson v Jeyes* (1801) 6 Ves. 266; *Holman v Loynes* (1854) 4 De G.M. & G. 270; *Savery v King* (1856) 5 H.L. Cas. 627 at 655–656; *Spencer v Topham* (1856) 22 Beav. 573; *Gresley v Mousley* (1862) 31 L.J.Ch. 537; *Pisani v Att.-Gen. for Gibraltar* (1874) L.R. 5 P.C. 516; *Ward v Sharp* (1883) 53 L.J.Ch. 313; *Wright v Carter* [1903] 1 Ch. 27; *Moody v Cox & Hatt* [1917] 2 Ch. 71; *Demerara Bauxite Co Ltd v Hubbard* [1923] A.C. 673; *Christie v McCann* (1972) 27 D.L.R. (3d) 544; *Bristol and West BS v Mothew* [1998] Ch. 1 at 18 ("he must prove affirmatively that the transaction is fair", per Millett LJ). Such is the authority. But another approach would be to look to the disclosure: if a fully informed principal wishes to deal on terms adverse to himself, he should be allowed to do so—for case law support for this view, see Conaglen [2006] C.L.J. 366.

[506] *Ex p. James* (1803) 8 Ves. 337; *Hobday v Peters* (1860) 28 Beav. 349; *De Bussche v Alt* (1878) 8 Ch.D. 286; *Powell & Thomas v Evan Jones & Co* [1905] 1 K.B. 11; *Blair v Martin* [1929] N.Z.L.R. 225; *Christie v McCann* (1972) 27 D.L.R. (3d) 544; *Palinko v Bower* [1976] 4 W.W.R. 118; Finn, *Fiduciary Obligations* (1977), pp.177–178 and 202–203; and see Article 35.

[507] *Selsey v Rhoades* (1824) 2 S. & St. 41; affirmed (1827) 2 Bli. (N.S.) 1, Illustration 20. See also *Aaran Acceptance Corp v Adam* (1987) 37 D.L.R. (4th) 133 (loan).

[508] *Ex p. Lacey* (1802) 6 Ves. 625; *Ex p. James* (1803) 8 Ves. 337; *Campbell v Walker* (1800) 5 Ves. 678; (1807) 13 Ves. 601; *Cardigan v Moore* [2012] EWHC 1024 (Ch). But cf. *Holder v Holder* [1968] Ch. 353, an unusual case; as to which see *Goff and Jones, Law of Unjust Enrichment* (9th edn) paras 8-175–8-180. See *Lewin on Trusts* (20th edn), para.46-093 onwards; Finn, *Fiduciary Obligations* (1977), pp.182–185, suggesting that there is little difference.

difficulty in showing that the transaction was a fair one.[509] Such advice may be appropriate in other relationships of presumptive undue influence also.

6-065   **Sale to principal**   Similarly, an agent may not sell the agent's own property to the principal without full and fair disclosure and the obtaining of the principal's informed consent[510]; nor may an agent lease his own property to the principal without full disclosure. The agent must also prove that the transaction was fair.[511] But however fair the transaction may be, it can still be set aside by the principal if there has not been full disclosure.[512] Cases suggesting a more lenient rule have not been followed.[513] However, it has been held that a sale to an agent's spouse is not automatically voidable, unless the agent was also the spouse's agent, but the fairness of the transaction is open to scrutiny.[514]

6-066   **Agent with specific instructions**   Where, however, the agent has specific instructions to buy or sell at a particular price and no element of advice or discretion is involved, there may be cases where the agent is free to sell property of the agent's own to the principal or buy the principal's property, there being no possibility of conflicting interest.[515]

6-067   **Person who has ceased to be agent**   Difficult questions arise if the agent deals with the principal after the agent has ceased to be an agent. It appears that the duty to disclose can continue, but whether it does so in any particular case in fact will depend on all the circumstances of the case. For example, if the confidence created by the agency relationship still exists at the time of the transaction,[516] or if the agent has a personal ascendancy over the principal, and certainly if the agent has

---

[509] *Allison v Clayhills* (1907) 97 L.T. 709; *McMaster v Byrne* [1952] 1 All E.R. 1362, Illustration 8; *Wintle v Nye* [1959] 1 W.L.R. 284. See also *Cutts v Salmon* (1852) 21 L.J.Ch. 750; *King v Anderson* (1874) 8 I.R.Eq. 625; *Spector v Ageda* [1973] Ch. 30, where Megarry J said that a solicitor should in ordinary circumstances refuse to act for a client in relation to a transaction when he is himself a party with an adverse interest in that same transaction.

[510] *Massey v Davies* (1794) 2 Ves. 317; *Gibson v Jeyes* (1801) 6 Ves. 266; *Rothschild v Brookman* (1831) 2 Dow. & Cl. 188; *Bentley v Craven* (1853) 18 Beav. 75; *Lucifero v Castel* (1887) 3 T.L.R. 371; *Tetley v Shand* (1871) 25 L.T. 658; *Skelton v Wood* (1894) 71 L.T. 616; *Kuhlirz v Lambert Brothers* (1913) 18 Com.Cas. 217; *Tito v Waddell (No.2)* [1977] Ch. 106 at 240–244. See too *NBH Ltd v Hoare* [2006] EWHC 73 (Ch); [2006] 2 B.C.L.C. 649 (informal unanimous assent by company's shareholders precluded later complaint by company about sale to it made by director).

[511] *Bristol and West BS v Mothew* [1998] Ch. 1 at 18.

[512] *Aberdeen Ry Co v Blaikie Bros* (1854) 1 Macq. 461, Illustration 2 to Article 44; *Transvaal Lands Co v New Belgium (Transvaal) Land and Development Co* [1914] 2 Ch. 488; *Gray v New Augarita Porcupine Mines* [1952] 3 D.L.R. 1 (PC); *Maguire v Makaronis* (1997) 188 C.L.R. 449 (mortgage).

[513] e.g. *Charter v Trevelyan* (1844) 11 C. & F. 714 at 732. Distinguish the doctrine of undue influence, as to which see *Snell's Equity* (34th edn), para.8-009 onwards. But see also *CIBC Mortgages Plc v Pitt* [1994] 1 A.C. 200 at 209, per Lord Browne-Wilkinson. See further below, para.6-069.

[514] *Newgate Stud Co v Penfold* [2004] EWHC 2993 (Ch); [2008] 1 B.C.L.C. 46.

[515] See *Kelly v Enderton* [1913] A.C. 191; *Dalgety & Co v Gray* (1919) 26 C.L.R. 249, 265 (PC) (loan to principal); *Jones v Canavan* [1972] 2 N.S.W.L.R. 236 (stockbroker); *R.H. Deacon & Co v Varga* (1972) 30 D.L.R. (3d) 653; affirmed (1973) 41 D.L.R. (3d) 767 (stockbroker); cf. *Thompson v Meade* (1891) 7 T.L.R. 698 (stockbroker); cf. also *Beer v Lea* (1913) 29 O.L.R. 255; *Bentley v Nasmith* (1912) 46 S.C.R. 477; *McMaster v Byrne* [1952] 1 All E.R. 1362, Illustration 8. And see Finn, *Commercial Aspects of Fiduciary Obligations* (McKendrick ed., 1992), Ch.1, pp.37–39.

[516] *Carter v Palmer* (1842) 8 C. & F. 657. But cf. *Connolly v Brown* 2007 S.L.T. 778 (fiduciary duty had on the facts terminated); *Wollenberg v Casinos Austria International Holding GmbH* [2011] EWHC 103 (Ch) (commercial client of solicitor and no need to advise to take independent advice); *KBL Investments Ltd v KBL Courtenay Ltd* [2016] NZCA 227 at [64] (mortgage broker becomes purchaser from client).

acquired special knowledge during the mandate relating to the subject-matter of the transaction, a court will be inclined to hold that the duty of disclosure is still binding on the agent.[517] Thus a solicitor's duty to disclose may last longer than the duty of a less confidential agent, e.g. a stockbroker.[518] An agent who resigns in order to exploit an appropriate opportunity remains subject to fiduciary obligations at any rate in respect of that matter. An agent cannot, of course, claim that the agent's own breach of duty terminates the agency and that therefore the agent is no longer bound to make full disclosure in any transaction that afterwards takes place with the principal.[519]

Remedies of principal   A number of remedies can arise out of self-dealing and fair-dealing. While most of the relevant case law is at equity, in some cases of self-dealing, at least, the transaction will be unauthorised and treated both at law and equity as a nullity.[520] As to equity, a principal who finds, for instance, that an agent has purported to borrow the principal's money without consent may disown the loan, and either seek an account of the money or treat any asset bought with the money as belonging to the principal.[521] Otherwise, the principal may, in general, rescind any contract affected by the self-dealing and fair-dealing rules.[522] Rescission in equity is, however, a discretionary remedy, it seems, and a court may withhold it, including on the ground that the principal is not fully disowning the transaction.[523] Nonetheless, while the normal rule is that rescission is ab initio, that is a shorthand notion that should not be taken too literally, at least at equity.[524] So, it normally does not matter that the contract has been executed, since equity can make monetary adjustments, nor that the property being returned has meanwhile

6-068

---

[517] *Allison v Clayhills* (1907) 97 L.T. 709; *Demerara Bauxite Co v Hubbard* [1923] A.C. 673. See also *Edwards v Meyrick* (1842) 2 Hare 60; *Montesquieu v Sandys* (1811) 18 Ves. 302; *Learmonth v Bailey* (1875) 1 V.L.R. 122.

[518] Compare Illustrations 8 and 9; and see *Longstaff v Birtles* [2001] EWCA Civ 1219; [2002] 1 W.L.R. 471; *Richards v Law Society* [2009] EWHC 2087 (Admin) at [45].

[519] *Regier v Campbell-Stuart* [1939] Ch. 766, Illustration 16; *McLeod & More v Sweezey* [1944] 2 D.L.R. 145. Quaere whether, if the principal is in breach of duty, the agent's obligation can continue. In some cases it may not: see In *Plus Group Ltd v Pyke* [2002] EWCA Civ 370; [2002] 2 B.C.L.C. 201. If the principal becomes an alien enemy, it may well be that the agent's duties of loyalty come to an end: *Nordisk Insulinlaboratorium v Gorgate Products Ltd* [1953] Ch. 430 at 442, Illustration 11.

[520] See *Rothschild v Brookman* (1831) 5 Bli. (NS) 165 at 191–192 and at 282; *Salomons v Pender* (1865) 3 H. & C. 639.

[521] See *Tang Ying Loi v Tang Ying Ip* [2017] HKCFA 3.

[522] *Maguire v Makaronis* (1997) 188 C.L.R. 449 (mortgage set aside on terms). In relation to companies where there is a director's conflict of interest, see *Fairford Water Ski Club Ltd v Cohoon* [2020] EWHC 290 (Comm) at [104].

[523] *Johnson v EBS Pensioner Trustees Ltd* [2002] EWCA Civ 164; [2002] Lloyd's Rep P.N. 309; *Hurstanger Ltd v Wilson* [2007] EWCA Civ 299; [2007] 1 W.L.R. 2351; [2007] 4 All E.R. 1118 at [50]; *Fenwick v Naera* [2015] NZSC 68; [2016] 1 N.Z.L.R. 354 at [122]; *Gamatronic (UK) Ltd v Hamilton* [2016] EWHC 2225 (QB) at [218]; *Pengelly v Business Mortgage Finance 4 Plc* [2020] EWHC 2002 (Ch). For more detailed treatment of the remedy, see D. O'Sullivan, S. Elliott and R. Zakrzewski, *Law of Rescission* (2nd ed, 2014).

[524] "The words [i.e. rescission ab initio] are sufficient for most purposes, but they should not be taken literally. Neither rescission by a party nor a judge's say so can turn the clock back to have that literal effect, and a contract avoided ab initio is not, in Newspeak, an uncontract": *FAI General Insurance Co Ltd v Ocean Marine Mutual Protection and Indemnity Association* (1997) 41 N.S.W.L.R. 559, per Giles CJ; cited with approval in *Brit Syndicates Ltd v Italaudit SPA* [2006] EWHC 341 (Comm) at [24]. See too *MacKenzie v Royal Bank of Canada* [1934] A.C. 468 PC (guarantee set aside despite lender's reliance by making loan).

decreased in value.[525] However, the intervention of third party interests can preclude rescission.[526] The principal must also take proceedings within a reasonable time after discovering the truth about the transaction or may be taken to have acquiesced or affirmed.[527] Otherwise, the principal can elect to affirm,[528] but where there is doubt, the onus is on the agent to show that the principal has affirmed.[529] The principal will also usually be able to claim the profit any agent has made, for it is deemed to have been made on the principal's behalf.[530] Recent authority further suggests that the principal might, where there is a sale at an undervalue, treat the agent (and affected third parties) as holding the asset on constructive trust for the principal in proportion that the price paid by the agent bears to the true value of the asset purchased.[531] The resulting remedy might be proprietary or personal. Alternatively, if the complaint is of loss the principal may claim damages for breach of contract, or conceivably equitable compensation under the principle of *Nocton v Ashburton*.[532] Thus, where an agent has bought the principal's property, the principal can claim any profit on a resale[533] or the difference between the value of the property and the price the agent gave.[534]

However, where the agent sells property to the principal, it seems that a distinction is to be drawn between the situation in which the agent is instructed to find a seller but secretly buys property which the agent then sells to the principal, making a personal profit, and the situation in which the agent sells property which belonged to the agent before the agency was created. In the first situation the agent will be liable to account for any profit made from the transaction, since the agent will be presumed to have bought on the principal's behalf and to have been holding on trust for the principal.[535] But in the second situation the agent was not acting on the principal's behalf and the orthodox view is that the agent will not be accountable for profits made: the usual remedy will be rescission, for no profit has

---

[525] *Armstrong v Jackson* [1917] 2 K.B. 822.

[526] For sub-purchases pendente lite, see *Trevelyan v White* (1839) 1 Beav. 588.

[527] *De Montmorency v Devereux* (1840) 7 C. & F. 188; *Champion v Rigby* (1830) 1 Russ. & M. 539; affirmed (1840) 9 L.J.(O.S.) Ch. 211; *Flint v Woodin* (1852) 9 Hare 618; *Lyddon v Moss* (1859) 4 De G. & J. 104; *Clanricarde v Henning* (1861) 30 Beav. 175; *Wentworth v Lloyd* (1863) 32 Beav. 467.

[528] *Bentley v Craven* (1853) 18 Beav. 75; *Rea v Bell* (1852) 18 L.T.(O.S.) 312; *Gray v New Augarita Porcupine Mines* [1952] 3 D.L.R. 1 (PC); *Hely-Hutchinson v Brayhead Ltd* [1968] 1 Q.B. 549; *Robinson v Randfontein* [1921] App.D. 168 at 178.

[529] *Cavendish-Bentinck v Fenn* (1887) 12 App.Cas. 652 at 666, Illustration 15. The principal must know the full facts, including the fact that he could rescind the transaction if he so wished: *Crowe v Ballard* (1790) 2 Cox Eq.Cas. 253; *Osry v Hirsch* [1922] Cape P.D. 531; *Holder v Holder* [1968] Ch. 353; *Peyman v Lanjani* [1985] Ch. 457.

[530] For an example of calculation see *Estate Realties Ltd v Wignall (No.2)* [1992] 2 N.Z.L.R. 615; Watts [1992] L.M.C.L.Q. 439.

[531] *Akita Holdings Ltd v Attorney General of Turks and Caicos Islands Is* [2017] UKPC 7; [2017] A.C. 590 (noted Glister (2017) 11 J.Eq. 219; P.G. Turner, "Accountability for profits derived from involvement in breach of fiduciary duty" [2018] C.L.J. 255).

[532] *Nocton v Ashburton* [1914] A.C. 932; *Brickenden v London Loan & Savings Co* [1934] 3 D.L.R. 465 PC; above para.6-042. See Conaglen (2003) 119 L.Q.R. 246.

[533] *Barker v Harrison* (1846) 2 Coll. 546; *De Bussche v Alt* (1878) 8 Ch.D. 286; *Blackham v Haythorpe* (1917) 23 C.L.R. 156; *Headway Construction Co Ltd v Downham* (1974) 233 E.G. 675, Illustration 17.

[534] *Hall v Hallett* (1784) 1 Cox Eq.Cas. 134.

[535] *Massey v Davies* (1794) 2 Ves. 317; *Benson v Heathorn* (1842) 1 Y. & C.Ch.Cas. 326; *Tyrrell v Bank of London* (1862) 10 H.L.Cas. 26; *Kimber v Barber* (1872) L.R. 8 Ch.App. 56; *Regier v Campbell-Stuart* [1939] Ch. 766, Illustration 16; *Tweedvale Investments Pty Ltd v Thiran* (1996) 14 WAR 109.

been made within the scope of the agency.[536] If this remedy is lost for any reason, e.g. because restitutio in integrum is impossible, it seems that the only right is to damages or compensation as above.[537] That right, too, may be lost if the contract is affirmed in such a manner as to show that the principal does not intend to pursue rights against the agent.[538] In any case the agent's right to commission on the transaction is lost.[539]

Gifts The nature of the relationship between a particular principal and agent may   **6-069**
lead to the application of a different, but related, rule, the presumption of undue influence, to a gift received by an agent from the principal,[540] and indeed to other transactions between them. On this basis the gift may be set aside unless it can be proved that undue influence was not exercised. The rule has often been applied between solicitor and client or counsel and lay client.[541] Any gift made to a solicitor by a client is presumed to have been made under undue influence and this presumption is not rebutted merely because the client has employed a completely separate and independent solicitor to advise about the gift.[542] This presumption will be applied although the solicitor-client relationship has come to an end, provided that there is still a relationship of confidence and trust between the parties. But a gift can be supported if the court is satisfied that it is perfectly fair and proper in all the circumstances:

> "The court, in dealing with such a transaction, starts with the presumption that undue influence exists on the part of the donee, and throws upon him the burden of satisfying the court that the gift was uninfluenced by the position of the solicitor. Secondly, this presumption is not a presumption which is entirely irrebuttable, though it is one which is extremely difficult to be rebutted."[543]

---

[536] *Re Cape Breton Co* (1885) 29 Ch.D. 795; affirmed sub nom. *Cavendish-Bentinck v Fenn* (1887) 12 App.Cas. 652, Illustration 15 (see discussion by Conaglen (2003) 119 L.Q.R. 246, at 249–250); *Burland v Earle* [1902] A.C. 83; *Robinson v Randfontein* [1921] App.D. 168 at 179; *Cook v Evatt (No.2)* [1992] 1 N.Z.L.R. 676 (noted Watts [1992] L.M.C.L.Q. 439).

[537] *Jacobus Marler Estates Ltd v Marler* (1913) 85 L.J.P.C. 167n; *P. & OSN Co v Johnson* (1938) 60 C.L.R. 189 at 213. This topic is discussed in *Walden Properties Ltd v Beaver Properties Pty Ltd* [1973] 2 N.S.W.L.R. 815 at 835–837; and in *Aequitas Ltd v Sparad No.100 Ltd* (2001) 19 A.C.L.C. 1006 at [430]. It is strongly argued by Conaglen (2003) 119 L.Q.R. 246, that equitable compensation should be available. See discussion of the *Marler* case at 253–254; but cf. *Meagher, Gummow and Lehane's Equity Doctrines and Remedies* (5th edn), para.5-180.

[538] This would appear to be the effect of *Re Cape Breton Co* (1885) 29 Ch.D. 795, as approved by the PC in *Burland v Earle* [1902] A.C. 83. See also *Cook v Deeks* [1916] 1 A.C. 554; *Tracy v Mandalay Pty Co* (1953) 88 C.L.R. 215; Sealy [1963] C.L.J. 119 at 132–135. But see Finn, *Fiduciary Obligations* (1977), p.225.

[539] *Salomons v Pender* (1865) 3 H. & C. 639; *Keppel v Wheeler* [1927] 1 K.B. 577 at 592; *Lunghi v Sinclair* [1966] W.A.R. 172; Article 60.

[540] *Hunter v Atkins* (1834) 3 Myl. & K. 113; *Barnard v Hunter* (1856) 2 Jur. (N.S.) 1213; *Union Fidelity Trustee Co of Australia Ltd v Gibson* [1971] V.R. 573. See in general *National Westminster Bank Plc v Morgan* [1985] A.C. 686; Snell's *Equity* (34th edn), para.8-009 onwards; Finn, above, Ch.16.

[541] *Broun v Kennedy* (1864) 4 De G.J. & S. 217.

[542] *Morgan v Minnett* (1877) 6 Ch.D. 638; *Saunderson v Glass* (1742) 2 Atk. 296; *Middleton v Welles* (1785) 4 Bro.P.C. 245; *Wright v Proud* (1806) 13 Ves. 136; *Tomson v Judge* (1885) 3 Drew. 306; *O'Brien v Lewis* (1863) 32 L.J.Ch. 569; *Liles v Terry* [1895] 2 Q.B. 679; *Wright v Carter* [1903] 1 Ch. 27. For a solicitor to accept a gift without ensuring that the client has received independent legal advice can amount to professional misconduct: *Re a Solicitor* [1975] Q.B. 475.

[543] *Wright v Carter* [1903] 1 Ch. 27 at 57, per Stirling LJ.

The rule will apply to gifts to near relatives of the solicitor,[544] but it does not apply to trifling gifts.[545] The rule may be applied somewhat less strictly to gifts by will but the solicitor must ensure that the client receives independent legal advice and is fully capable of understanding what the client is doing.[546] The desirability of independent advice can apply to other relationships also.[547]

Illustrations

Purchase from principal

6-070 (1) A solicitor purchases property from his client's trustee in bankruptcy. He must make a full disclosure of all the knowledge acquired by him respecting such property during the time when he was acting as solicitor for the bankrupt.[548]

(2) A solicitor purchased property from a former client, and concealed a material fact. Another solicitor acted for the client in this transaction, but he did not possess all the necessary information and somewhat neglected his duty. The transaction was set aside.[549]

(3) A Scottish attorney purchased four houses from his clients, doing so in the name of his brother. He did not disclose that he was the real purchaser of two of the houses. The House of Lords refused to order specific performance of the contract.[550]

(4) Two persons become partners to sell a mine. One represents to the other that he has found a purchaser. Actually he has arranged to share with the purchaser in the profits made by floating a company to buy and work the mine. He must share the profit he makes with the other.[551]

(5) An auctioneer, who was employed to sell an estate, purchased it himself. The transaction was set aside, after an interval of 13 years.[552] So, an agent of a trustee for sale or of a mortgagee selling under his power of sale, who is employed as agent in the matter of the sale,[553] cannot purchase the property sold[554]; and a solicitor who conducts a sale of property must not purchase it without a full explanation to the vendor.[555]

---

[544] See, e.g. *Willis v Barron* [1902] A.C. 271.
[545] *Rhodes v Bate* (1866) L.R. 1 Ch.App. 252; *Wright v Carter* [1903] 1 Ch. 27 at 57.
[546] See for a discussion of this topic, see Cordery, *Solicitors* (8th ed), pp.17–18; and *Ramcoomarsingh v Administrator-General* [2002] UKPC 67; cf. *Re Tyler* [1967] 1 W.L.R. 1269 at 1276, where it is said that the court will require evidence which will satisfy it beyond doubt. Because the burden of proof in a civil case is never more than the balance of probabilities, this must mean that the presumption to be displaced is a heavy one.
[547] See, e.g. *O'Sullivan v Management Agency and Music Ltd* [1985] Q.B. 428 (musician and manager).
[548] *Luddy's Trustees v Peard* (1886) 33 Ch.D. 500. See also *Boswell v Coaks* (1884) 27 Ch.D. 424 (reversed on the evidence, sub nom. *Coaks v Boswell* (1886) 11 App.Cas. 232).
[549] *Gibbs v Daniel* (1862) 4 Giff. 1; cf. *Guest v Smythe* (1870) L.R. 5 Ch.App. 551 (solicitor's name appeared on particulars of sale only).
[550] *McPherson v Watt* (1877) 3 App.Cas. 254. See also *Lewis v Hillman* (1852) 3 H.L.Cas. 607; *Cane v Allen* (1814) 2 Dow. 289; *Uppington v Bullen* (1842) 2 Dr. & War. 184; *Murphy v O'Shea* (1845) 8 I.Eq.R. 329; *Crowe v Ballard* (1790) 2 Cox.Eq.Cas. 253.
[551] *Dunne v English* (1874) L.R. 18 Eq. 524.
[552] *Oliver v Court* (1820) 8 Price 127. See also *Haywood v Roadknight* [1927] V.L.R. 512. But laches may afford a defence: see *Wentworth v Lloyd* (1863) 32 Beav. 467.
[553] See *Nutt v Easton* [1899] 1 Ch. 873; affirmed on other grounds [1900] 1 Ch. 29.
[554] *Whitcomb v Minchin* (1820) 5 Madd. 91; *Martinson v Clowes* (1882) 21 Ch.D. 857; *Lawrance v Galsworthy* (1857) 3 Jur.(N.S.) 1049; cf. *Bath v Standard Land Co* [1911] 1 Ch. 618 and *Orme v*

(6)   A broker is employed to sell goods. He sells them ostensibly to A, really to A and himself jointly. While the goods are still in possession of the broker, he becomes bankrupt, A also being insolvent. The principal may repudiate the contract and recover the goods specifically from the trustee in bankruptcy of the broker.[556]

(7)   An agent for the management of trust property purchased part of such property from the cestui que trust. Held, that the circumstances being highly disadvantageous to the seller, the burden lay on the agent to prove that the transaction was right and honest, and that in the circumstances the lack of disinterested advice was fatal.[557]

(8)   M owned shares in a Canadian company. He granted X an option to purchase them for $30,000. X assigned the option to B, who was the solicitor to the company and had until recently been solicitor to M. B exercised the option. At that time active negotiations for the take-over of the company were taking place and that fact was known to B when he exercised the option. As a result of the take-over B later sold the shares for $127,000. Held, although B was no longer M's solicitor, the confidential relationship between them still subsisted and B was under a duty to make full disclosure to M before he purchased the shares from him.[558]

(9)   A stockbroker is commissioned to buy for a client. The client is unable to meet the amount due on settlement. In accordance with normal procedures the broker sells the shares. This is a valid closing of the account and he is entitled to indemnity.[559] He also repurchases them himself. This is legitimate[560] unless the repurchase is sufficiently a part of the same transaction that he secures a preferential price because the market-maker does not have to carry the shares. In the latter case the broker may be liable for a secret profit.[561]

(10) Dealers employ agents to grant future options in cocoa. The agents do so and then take the options themselves. They fail to notify the dealers that the options have been declared. This is not merely a breach of their duties as agents, but rather, since their own taking of the options was valid, the options in respect of which no declarations were made by them lapse.[562]

(11) A Danish corporation deposited insulin in an English bank shortly before the outbreak of war. When the Germans invaded Denmark the corporation became an alien enemy and the property vested in the Custodian of Enemy Property, who sold it to the defendants. The defendants had been the English selling agents of the corporation before the war; they now resold the insulin

---

Wright (1839) 3 Jur. 19; *Nutt v Easton* [1899] 1 Ch. 873 at 972.

[555] *Re Bloye's Trust* (1849) 1 Mac. & G. 488; *Ex p. James* (1803) 8 Ves. 337.

[556] *Ex p. Huth, re Pemberton* (1840) Mont. & C. 667.

[557] *King v Anderson* (1874) 8 I.R.Eq. 625. See also *Dally v Wonham* (1863) 33 Beav. 154.

[558] *McMaster v Byrne* [1952] 1 All E.R. 1362. See also *J.J. Harrison (Properties) Ltd v Harrison* [2001] EWCA Civ 1467; [2002] 1 B.C.L.C. 162, Illustration 7 to Article 96.

[559] *Macoun v Erskine, Oxenford & Co* [1901] 2 K.B. 493; *Walter and Gould v King* (1897) 13 T.L.R. 270; *Christoforides v Terry* [1924] A.C. 566. But a direct purchase by the broker personally would be voidable: *Re Finlay* [1913] 1 Ch. 565. See also *Jones v Canavan* [1972] 2 N.S.W.L.R. 236 (custom of "marrying" buying and selling transactions held reasonable).

[560] See cases cited above.

[561] *Erskine, Oxenford & Co v Sachs* [1901] 2 K.B. 504.

[562] *Limako BV v Hentz & Co Inc* [1979] 2 Lloyd's Rep. 23.

at a profit. Held, as the defendants had not acquired any special or secret knowledge about the insulin while they were the corporation's agents, they were under no fiduciary duty regarding it and were not accountable for the profit they made on resale.[563]

Sale to principal

6-071 (12) A firm of brokers were authorised to purchase goods. They delivered bought notes to the principal which purported to be notes of a contract of which the brokers guaranteed performance, but which did not disclose the sellers. The principal paid the brokers their commission and a deposit, and subsequently discovered that one of the brokers intended to perform the contract himself. The principal was held to be entitled to repudiate the contract, and the brokers were ordered to repay the deposit and commission, with interest, since no agent can become a principal and deal on that footing without full and fair disclosure.[564]

(13) A stockbroker was employed to purchase certain shares. He purchased the shares from his own trustee without informing the principal of the fact. The transaction was set aside, after an interval of many years, without inquiry whether or not a fair price was charged.[565]

(14) A director proposes to contract with his company, it being provided by the articles of association that directors may contract with the company on disclosing their interest. It is the director's duty to declare the full extent and exact nature of the interest.[566]

(15) A company was formed to purchase certain coal areas in Newfoundland. It purchased these areas from A, who was a trustee for B and had been so for some time before the formation of the company. B was one of the directors of the company but did not disclose that he was beneficially interested in the coal areas. When the company was wound up, the shareholders, with full knowledge of the circumstances, decided to sell the coal areas. They realised a smaller sum than expected, but rescission of the original contract of purchase was now impossible. Held, any claim to damages had been forfeited by the affirmation of the contract, and any claim to B's profit was unsustainable as B had not acquired the property with a view to selling it to the company but owned it already.[567]

(16) A, an estate agent, agreed with B that A would furnish B with particulars of houses which A might think suitable for purchase by B. A, having found a

---

[563] *Nordisk Insulinlaboratorium v Gorgate Products Ltd* [1953] Ch. 430.

[564] *Wilson v Short* (1848) 6 Hare 366. See also *Robinson v Mollett* (1874) L.R. 7 H.L. 802, Illustration 8 to Article 31; *Skelton v Wood* (1894) 71 L.T. 616; *Stange & Co v Lowitz* (1898) 14 T.L.R. 468; *Nicholson v J. Mansfield & Co* (1901) 17 T.L.R. 259. cf. *Ellis & Co's Trustee v Watsham* (1923) 155 L.T.Jo. 363 ("bought of ourselves as principals"—held sufficient disclosure).

[565] *Gillett v Peppercorne* (1840) 3 Beav. 78. See also *Rothschild v Brookman* (1831) 2 Dow. & Cl. 188; *King, Viall & Benson v Howell* (1910) 27 T.L.R. 114; *Oelkers v Ellis* [1914] 2 K.B. 139; *Armstrong v Jackson* [1917] 2 K.B. 822.

[566] *Imperial Mercantile Credit Co v Coleman* (1873) L.R. 6 H.L. 189; *Gluckstein v Barnes* [1900] A.C. 240. cf. *Chesterfield & Baythorpe Colliery Co v Black* (1877) 37 L.T. 740.

[567] *Re Cape Breton Co* (1885) 29 Ch.D. 795; affirmed sub nom. *Cavendish-Bentinck v Fenn* (1887) 12 App.Cas. 652. See also *Jacobus Marler Estates Ltd v Marler* (1913) 85 L.J.P.C. 167n (on both cases see Conaglen (2003) 119 L.Q.R. 246 at 249 onwards); *Walden Properties Ltd v Beaver Properties Pty Ltd* [1973] 2 N.S.W.L.R. 815 at 836.

suitable house, procured C to purchase it for £2,000, the purchase money being provided by A; and thereupon purported to buy it from C for £4,500. A then informed B that he had purchased the house for £4,500, and offered it to B for £5,000, representing that this price would allow a profit to A of £500. B purchased the house from A for £5,000. Held, that A was the agent of B for the purpose of furnishing particulars of suitable houses; that though an agent might terminate the relationship of principal and agent by selling to his principal property which belonged to himself, it was his duty to act honestly and faithfully, and, if he concealed material facts, the relationship was not terminated by such a transaction; and that A, having concealed the true nature of the transaction, was liable to account to B for all profits obtained by A without B's knowledge and consent.[568]

(17) P engaged A to ascertain the owners of properties adjacent to a site he was developing. A did so but dishonestly told P that he had failed. A then made an agreement with P whereby he agreed for a commission to acquire the properties for P. He then formed a company and acquired the properties for £42,000. This company then sold the properties to P for £57,000. Held, A was liable to P for the profit of £15,000 and damages of £3,000 for loss of the chance to acquire the properties for less than £42,000. P was entitled to avoid the contract with A and was not liable to A for commission in respect of other transactions.[569]

(18) An airport company, X Ltd, develops two hotels and markets units in each of them. The contracts of sale of units in respect of each hotel provide for X Ltd to be the managing agent of the hotels, but on different terms as to remuneration. The fact that there were those differences was not disclosed to investors. There was no breach of the fair dealing rules at the time of the making of the contracts because those contracts pre-dated the creation of the agency relationship. But the differences may yet have to be disclosed once the agency relationship is under way.[570]

Other dealings by agent with principal

(19) If a solicitor lends to a client on mortgage or otherwise takes a security from   **6-072**
a client, the transaction may be rescinded.[571] The court will not enforce any unusual stipulations in the mortgage disadvantageous to the client,[572] and will restrain the solicitor from exercising his rights as mortgagee in an unfair or inequitable manner.[573] Where a power of sale exercisable at any time was inserted in such a mortgage without the usual proviso requiring interest to be in arrear or notice to be given, and the solicitor sold the property under the

[568] *Regier v Campbell-Stuart* [1939] Ch. 766. See Murdoch, *Law of Estate Agency and Auctions* (4th edn), p.63 onwards.
[569] *Headway Construction Co Ltd v Downham* (1974) 233 E.G. 675.
[570] *Sharbern Holding Inc v Vancouver Airport Centre Ltd* [2011] 2 S.C.R. 175; (2011) 331 D.L.R. (4th) 1.
[571] *Maguire v Makaronis* (1997) 188 C.L.R. 449 (set aside on terms). See too cases where a solicitor (or other agent) takes security from a client for fees, and is found consequently to have waived any lien: fully discussed in *Candey Ltd v Crumpler* [2020] EWCA Civ 26; [2020] Bus. L.R. 1452.
[572] *Cowdry v Day* (1859) 1 Giff. 316; *Eyre v Hughes* (1876) 2 Ch.D. 148. See also *Gray v Dalgety & Co Ltd* (1916) 21 C.L.R. 509.
[573] *Macleod v Jones* (1883) 24 Ch.D. 289; *Pearson v Benson* (1860) 28 Beav. 598.

power, he was held liable to the client in damages as for an improper sale, it not being shown that he had explained to the client the unusual nature of the power.[574] Similar principles apply where the solicitor's client is a lender which is encouraged to make a loan that advantages the solicitor.[575]

(20) A steward contracts with his employer for a lease. He must show that he is giving as high a rent as it would have been his duty to obtain from a third party and that his employer was fully informed of every circumstance affecting the value of the property which was, or ought to have been, within the steward's knowledge.[576]

Article 46

AGENT'S DUTY NOT TO PROFIT FROM POSITION

6-073   An agent must not profit from the agent's position as such, except with the principal's consent.

Comment

6-074   This is a principle applicable to all fiduciaries. One of its classic expositions is that of Lord Russell of Killowen in *Regal (Hastings) Ltd v Gulliver*[577]:

> "The rule of equity which insists on those, who by use of a fiduciary position make a profit, being liable to account for that profit, in no way depends on fraud, or absence of bona fides; or upon such questions or considerations as whether the profit would or should otherwise have gone to the plaintiff, or whether the profiteer was under a duty to obtain the source of the profit for the plaintiff, or whether he took a risk or acted as he did for the benefit of the plaintiff, or whether the plaintiff has in fact been damaged or benefited by his action. The liability arises from the mere fact of a profit having, in the stated circumstances, been made. The profiteer, however honest and well-intentioned, cannot escape the risk of being called upon to account."

Lord Russell's compact exposition makes a number of points directed to the stringency of the obligation not to profit, including the fact that honesty in the fiduciary is no defence nor the fact that the principal may have suffered no loss. More detail on these aspects will be found in the succeeding paragraphs.[578]

Commonly, the profit will be derived from use of the principal's property or confidential information, but it need not be so derived, at least directly. In one of the most famous illustrations, *Boardman v Phipps*,[579] it is possible to regard the relevant profit as being derived indirectly from the use of the clients' property, but it is simpler to see it as derived from the defendant solicitor's use of position as

---

[574] *Readdy v Pendergast* (1887) 56 L.T. 790; *Cockburn v Edwards* (1881) 18 Ch.D. 449; *Craddock v Rogers* (1884) 53 L.J.Ch. 968. cf. *Pooley's Trustee v Whetham* (1886) 2 T.L.R. 808. See in general Cordery, *Solicitors* (8th edn), p.13 onwards.

[575] See *Brickenden v London Loan & Savings Co* [1934] 3 D.L.R. 465 PC.

[576] *Selsey v Rhoades* (1824) 2 S. & St. 41; affirmed (1827) 1 Bli.(N.S.) 1. See also *Watt v Grove* (1805) 2 Sch. & Lef. 492; *Waters v Shaftesbury* (1866) 14 L.T. 184; *Molony v Kernan* (1842) 2 Dr. & War. 31; *Ker v Lord Dungannon* (1841) 1 Dr. & War. (Ir.) 509.

[577] *Regal (Hastings) Ltd v Gulliver* [1967] 2 A.C. 134n at 144–145. For discussion of the traditionally strict approach of equity in this field, see Samet (2008) 28 O.J.L.S. 768.

[578] See especially, Article 48.

[579] *Boardman v Phipps* [1967] 2 A.C. 46. For further detail of the facts see Illustration 4 to Article 48.

representative of the clients (trustees of a trust) in respect of their shareholding in a company. In that capacity he attended company meetings, pressured the directors to provide information, and over a three-year period carried on negotiations with the directors and the shareholders of the company in relation both to changing the company's operations and to the acquisition of their shares in the company. Ultimately, he was able, through his own and his clients' shareholding, to have himself appointed director, whereupon he set about further rationalising the company's business assets. By these methods he became privy to confidential information in relation to the company, but that information belonged to the company not to his clients. He was held accountable to his clients (along with a second defendant who also could be said to have used the clients' status) for the profit made on his own shares. Lord Cohen, in particular, rested his judgment on use of position rather than use of confidential information,[580] an analysis found also in the dissenting judgments of Viscount Dilhorne and Lord Upjohn, and less decisively in the judgment of Lord Hodson. The fifth member of the court, Lord Guest, does seem to have considered that liability rested on use of confidential information.

In principle, therefore, a fiduciary is accountable for any gain leveraged from use of position.[581] Complications can arise from the principle that a mere use of position is sufficient for accountability. In particular, it is possible that the agent's profiting might also involve improperly using the property of a third party, or leveraging the position that the agent has with a separate principal. *Boardman*, as noted, was potentially a case of this sort, since the inside information acquired by the defendant belonged to the company not the claimant trustees. Where the agent has already had to account to the third party, the costs of so doing would be taken into account in measuring the account of profits to the principal. Otherwise, the principal who has obtained a full account may need to be joined to proceedings if the agent is later sued by the third party.[582]

Broad though the concept of profiting-from-position is, it has limits. Hence, the mere fact that the agent learns something while acting for the principal would not make the agent liable for exploiting that information, if the information was not confidential but publicly available and the resulting opportunity for profit had no connection to the principal's lines of business.[583] For what is required for consent to be given to profiting see above, para.6-039, and for modification of fiduciary duties, see above, para.6-056.

The application of the principle to use of property and confidential information is dealt with in Article 47, where it will be seen that other remedies such as injunc-

---

[580] *Boardman v Phipps* [1967] 2 A.C. 46 at 102.

[581] For examples of the reach of the principle, see the Illustrations to Article 48; and *The Peppy* [1997] 2 Lloyd's Rep. 722; *Cobbetts LLP v Hodge* [2009] EWHC 786 (Ch) (employee solicitor taking shares in client of firm arising out of work done by the firm for the client); *Sinclair Investments (UK) Ltd v Versailles Trade Finance Group Plc* [2011] EWCA Civ 347; [2012] Ch. 453; *Crown Prosecution Service v Aquila Advisory Ltd* [2019] EWCA Civ 588 at [25] (illegal activity).

[582] See *Adlam v Savage* [2016] NZCA 454; [2017] 2 N.Z.L.R. 309 at [48]; *Faichney v Aquila Advisory Ltd* [2018] EWHC 565 (Ch) at [42]; upheld on different points [2019] EWCA Civ 588 (potential claims by different companies in case where Crown Prosecution Service also claiming).

[583] *Aas v Benham* [1891] 2 Ch. 244 at 255–256; *Boardman v Phipps* [1967] 2 A.C. 46 at 100; *Nottingham University v Fishel* [2000] I.C.R. 146 (university academic not accountable for income from private consulting, but accountable for arranging for other employees to work on his external projects). For other authorities on this point, see below, para.6-081.

tion and compensation for loss can also arise. Other aspects of the duty not to profit from position are then addressed in subsequent Articles.

Article 47

AGENT USING PRINCIPAL'S PROPERTY AND CONFIDENTIAL INFORMATION

6-075   An agent may not, without the informed consent of the principal, use the principal's property, or confidential information acquired during the course of the agency, to acquire a benefit (i.e. a secret profit).[584]

Comment

6-076   **Property**   It has long been established that if the agent makes any secret profit from the use of the principal's property, the agent is accountable to the principal for that profit, unless the principal with full knowledge of the circumstances consents to the retention of it by the agent:

> "It is quite clear that if an agent uses property, with which he has been entrusted by his principal, so as to make a profit for himself out of it, without his principal's consent, then he is accountable for it to his principal ... Likewise with information or knowledge which he has been employed by his principal to collect or discover, or which he has otherwise acquired, for use of his principal, then again if he turns it to his own use, so as to make a profit by means of it for himself, he is accountable ...".[585]

The fact that the agent's liability can be based on holding identifiable property of the principal makes this an obvious example where the duties of a trustee can be said to be extended to the agent. But it can also be regarded as a simple example of the general principle stated in Article 46, that the agent must not without disclosure make a profit from the agent's position. It is not, of course, any use by the agent of the principal's property which attracts this liability: in many circumstances some form of use is contemplated. It is use leading to an undisclosed profit to which the rule applies.

Under this principle can also be brought the case where an agent is treated as holding in trust money the agent has received from the principal, with the result that the agent is liable for interest on it or may be required to account for profits.[586] Such profits would not of course be secret. Where the agent has recourse to the principal's money without authority, the principal can elect as of right to take ownership of any assets bought with it.[587] All these liabilities appear to attract a proprietary remedy; but courts often speak of an account of profits, which is personal.[588]

A person who acts as agent without authority may also be liable under this principle.[589] See further above, para.6-068.

---

[584] See Comment.
[585] *Boardman v Phipps* [1965] Ch. 992 at 1030, per Pearson LJ.
[586] See above, para.6-041.
[587] See above, para.6-040.
[588] See *Warman International Ltd v Dwyer* (1995) 182 C.L.R. 544 at 556 onwards; above, paras 6-042 and 6-043; below, paras 6-079, 6-094.
[589] *English v Dedham Vale Properties Ltd* [1978] 1 W.L.R. 93.

Confidential information[590]   There is also no doubt that if an agent uses   **6-077**
confidential information acquired as a result of the agency the agent may be liable
to the principal in respect of it.[591] On one view, this is explicable on the basis that
such information is property.[592] But:

> "perhaps the most sterile of the debates which have arisen around the subject of informa-
> tion received in confidence is whether or not such information should be classified as
> property."[593]

For it is only in certain circumstances, difficult of definition, that information is
protected, and the criteria for ascertaining this are not the same as those used to
determine whether property reasoning is inherently appropriate:

> "If only some information is described as property, i.e. information protected by the courts,
> to call that information property is merely to add yet another consequence to a decision
> taken for reasons quite unrelated to property considerations."[594]

The principle is not, however, peculiar to the law of agency; if any fiduciary exploits
confidential information which is acquired in the course of the relationship with the
beneficiary, the fiduciary is in breach of fiduciary duty and if, as is usually the case,
the agent has a contract with the principal, the agent will probably be in breach of
contract also.[595] But the duty may be independent of contract or even of a standing
relationship. If any person receives information which that person knows or ought
to know[596] is confidential and uses that information for personal profit, that person
is so liable whether there is any previous relationship with the claimant or not,
although the remedy for breach will depend on the circumstances[597]:

> "The law on this subject does not depend on any implied contract. It depends on the broad
> principle of equity that he who has received information in confidence shall not take unfair

---

[590] See *Restatement, Third*, § 8.05; Finn, *Fiduciary Obligations* (1977), Ch. 19; Jones (1970) 86 L.Q.R. 463; Snell's *Equity* (34th edn), Ch. 7, 9 and para.18-021. The Law Commission (No.110, Cmnd. 8388 (1981)) recommended the creation of statutory tort liability. This would have left much of the liability arising from fiduciary relationships as a separate area of law. There may sometimes be a defence to disclosure under the Public Interest Disclosure Act 1998.

[591] *Boardman v Phipps* [1967] 2 A.C. 46, Illustration 4 to Article 48; *Peter Pan Manufacturing Corpora-tion v Corsets Silhouette Ltd* [1964] 1 W.L.R. 96, Illustration 6; *Att.-Gen. v Guardian Newspapers Ltd (No.2)* [1990] 1 A.C. 109 at 288; Jones [1989] C.L.P. 49.

[592] See *Boardman v Phipps* [1967] 2 A.C. 46 at 89–90, 107 and 115; cf. 102, 127–128; but this was not the basis of the decision, which may simply have been the use by the defendant of his position.

[593] Finn, above, p.131. See also The Rt Hon. Lord Millett [1993] Restitution L.Rev. 7 at 11: "owes more to metaphor than to legal reality".

[594] Finn, above, p.132.

[595] *Lamb v Evans* [1893] 1 Ch. 218, Illustration 5; *Robb v Green* [1895] 2 Q.B. 315; *Duchess of Argyll v Duke of Argyll* [1967] Ch. 302; *Westminster Chemical NZ Ltd v McKinley* [1973] 1 N.Z.L.R. 659; *New Zealand Needle Manufacturers Ltd v Taylor* [1975] 2 N.Z.L.R. 33; *Investors Syndicate Ltd v Versatile Investments Ltd* (1983) 149 D.L.R. (3d) 46; *Prince Jefri Bolkiah v KPMG* [1999] 2 A.C. 222; *Cadbury Schweppes Inc v FBI Foods Ltd* [1999] 1 S.C.R. 142; (1999) 167 D.L.R. (4th) 577; cf. *Arklow Investments Ltd v Maclean* [2000] 1 W.L.R. 594 (PC) (no proof of misuse). See Abdul-lah and Tey (1995) 115 L.Q.R. 376.

[596] *Coco v A.N. Clark (Engineers) Ltd* [1969] R.P.C. 41 at 48; and see *Printers and Finishers Ltd v Hol-loway* [1965] R.P.C. 239 at 252; *Att.-Gen. v Jonathan Cape Ltd* [1976] Q.B. 752; cf. *United Sterling Corp Ltd v Felton* [1974] R.P.C. 162. See also *Union Carbide Corp v Naturin Ltd* [1987] F.S.R. 538; *Att.-Gen. v Guardian Newspapers Ltd (No.2)* [1990] 1 A.C. 109 at 281.

[597] *Saltman Engineering Co Ltd v Campbell Engineering Co* (1948) [1963] 3 All E.R. 413n.; *Talbot v General Television Corp Pty Ltd* [1981] R.P.C. 1; *Fraser v Thames Television Ltd* [1984] Q.B. 44; *Racing Partnership Ltd v Sports Information Services Ltd* [2020] EWCA Civ 1300 at [79].

advantage of it. He must not make use of it to the prejudice of him who gave it without obtaining his consent."[598]

The mere receipt of confidential information does not of itself create a fiduciary relationship.[599] It may therefore be said that the rule is not a special one applicable to fiduciaries, but rather that the receipt of confidential information may impose an obligation not to misuse it.[600] Confidential information can be any non-public information expressly or impliedly imparted in confidence. It can extend beyond trade secrets[601] to such things as lists or databases of customers of the principal.[602]

Once the information is readily available to the public it has ceased to be confidential. It will then no longer be a breach of confidence for the agent to make use of it.[603] However, even in those circumstances, the other duties of some agents, including those relating to the pursuit of business opportunities,[604] may constrain the agent from exploiting the information. Similarly, while the agent remains engaged, damaging and unnecessary dispersal of non-confidential information held on behalf of the principal could conceivably be a breach of an agent's duties of care and skill.

A principal whose confidential information has been used by the agent, or a former agent, has various remedies open to it.[605] It seems indeed that remedies are particularly flexible in this area. It is not impossible that this flexibility may in due course be extended to breach of fiduciary duty in general. The principal may seek an injunction to restrain the agent from making any further use of the information[606]; or may sue for damages for breach of contract in an appropriate case. Where a contractual action is not available, there is authority that damages may be awarded in equity to cover the price which the owner would have charged for the informa-

---

[598] *Seager v Copydex Ltd* [1967] 1 W.L.R. 923 at 931, per Lord Denning MR. The liability extends to persons to whom information is further transmitted. See Finn, *Fiduciary Obligations* (1977), pp.152–156; *Schering Chemicals Ltd v Falkman Ltd* [1982] Q.B. 1, Illustration 7; *Wheatley v Bell* [1982] 2 N.S.W.L.R. 544. But different considerations may arise where information is received in confidence which ought in the public interest to be disclosed to one who has a proper interest to receive it: *Initial Services Ltd v Putterill* [1968] 1 Q.B. 396; *Fraser v Evans* [1969] 1 Q.B. 349; *Hubbard v Vosper* [1972] 2 Q.B. 84; *Church of Scientology v Kaufman* [1973] R.P.C. 635; cf. *Schering Chemicals Ltd v Falkman Ltd* [1982] Q.B. 1; *Lion Laboratories Ltd v Evans* [1985] Q.B. 526.
[599] *Indata Equipment Supplies Ltd v ACL Ltd* [1998] 1 B.C.L.C. 412; *Arklow Investments Ltd v Maclean* [2000] 1 W.L.R. 594 (PC); *Walsh v Shanahan* [2013] EWCA Civ 411 at [38].
[600] cf. above, para.6-061.
[601] See *Faccenda Chicken Ltd v Fowler* [1987] 1 Ch. 117; *Del Casale v Artedomus (Aust) Pty Ltd* (2007) 73 I.P.R. 326.
[602] *Baker v Gibbons* [1972] 1 W.L.R. 693; *Peninsular Real Estate Ltd v Harris* [1992] 2 N.Z.L.R. 216; *Whitmar Publications Ltd v Gamage* [2013] EWHC 1881 (Ch) at [58].
[603] *O Mustad & Son v Dosen (1928)* [1964] 1 W.L.R. 109n.; *Cranleigh Precision Engineering Ltd v Bryant* [1965] 1 W.L.R. 1293 at 1314–1319; *Speed Seal Products Ltd v Paddington* [1985] 1 W.L.R. 1327; *Att.-Gen. v Guardian Newspapers (No.2)* [1990] 1 A.C. 109, esp. at 285.
[604] See below, para.6-081.
[605] See Finn, *Fiduciary Obligations* (1977), p.163 onwards; Davies, in *Consensus ad Idem* (Rose ed., 1996), pp.163–165; Abdullah and Tey (1999) 115 L.Q.R. 376.
[606] *Merryweather v Moore* [1892] 2 Ch. 518; *Lamb v Evans* [1893] 1 Ch. 218, Illustration 5; *Robb v Green* [1895] 2 Q.B. 315; *Peter Pan Manufacturing Co Ltd v Corsets Silhouette Ltd* [1964] 1 W.L.R. 96, Illustration 6; *Coco v A.N. Clark (Engineers) Ltd* [1969] R.P.C. 41; *Dunford & Elliott Ltd v Johnson & Firth Brown Ltd* [1977] 1 Lloyd's Rep. 505; cf. *Amber Size and Chemical Co Ltd v Menzel* [1913] 2 Ch. 239; *Baker v Gibbons* [1972] 1 W.L.R. 693. The grant of an injunction is of course discretionary: see *Att.-Gen. v Guardian Newspapers Ltd (No.2)* [1990] 1 A.C. 109.

tion,[607] and it seems that this award may be independent of damages in lieu of injunction under Lord Cairns' Act.[608] The principal may also sue for an account of the profits made by the agent from use of the confidential information,[609] and where the agency relationship is still subsisting at the time of exploitation an account of profits would usually be granted.[610] The onus of proving that a profit has been derived without the use of confidential information lies on the fiduciary.[611] It seems however that the court will determine the appropriate remedy rather than permit the claimant to elect.[612] Finally, whether or not the information can properly be described as the property of the principal, it seems that an agent who has made profits by making use of it is a trustee of those profits for the principal,[613] though where no fiduciary is involved and the recourse is simply to general principle the matter is more arguable, for the action for an account of profits is in principle in personam.[614] An injunction against a former employee, even a senior one, to prevent the employee working for a competitor (as opposed to an injunction against using the confidential information itself[615]) would not usually be given in the absence of a restraint of trade clause.[616] A principal cannot automatically obtain against a former agent an order for delivery up of all copies of written confidential information held by the agent.[617]

Illustrations

(1)   The master of a ship was authorised to employ the vessel to the best advantage; **6-078**
he could not procure remunerative freight and so loaded her with cargo of his

[607] *Saltman Engineering Co Ltd v Campbell Engineering Co* (1948) [1963] 3 All E.R. 413n. *Seager v Copydex Ltd* [1967] 1 W.L.R. 923 at 932, where Lord Denning MR says that there is to be an inquiry as to damages as "it may not be a case for an injunction"; for the principle upon which the damages were to be assessed see *Seager v Copydex Ltd (No.2)* [1969] 1 W.L.R. 809; *Interfirm Comparison (Australia) Pty Ltd v Law Society of NSW* [1975] 2 N.S.W.L.R. 104; *Dowson & Mason Ltd v Potter* [1986] 1 W.L.R. 1419. cf. *Marathon Asset Management LLP v Seddon* [2017] EWHC 300 (Comm) at [235]. And see Illustration 4.
[608] See *Nicrotherm Electrical Co Ltd v Percy* [1956] R.P.C. 272; [1957] R.P.C. 207; *Seager v Copydex Ltd (No.2)* [1969] 1 W.L.R. 809. But see *English v Dedham Vale Properties Ltd* [1978] 1 W.L.R. 93 at 111–112.
[609] *Peter Pan Manufacturing Corp Ltd v Corsets Silhouette Ltd* [1964] 1 W.L.R. 96, Illustration 6; cf. *Lever v Goodwin* (1887) 36 Ch.D. 1; *Att.-Gen. v Guardian Newspapers Ltd (No.2)* [1990] 1 A.C. 109 at 288; *Dart Industries Inc v Decor Corp Pty Ltd* (1993) 179 C.L.R. 101; *Hoechst Celanese International Corp v BP Chemicals Ltd* [1999] R.P.C. 203 (all profits treated as made on claimants' behalf).
[610] *Walsh v Shanahan* [2013] EWCA Civ 411 at [68].
[611] *United Pan-Europe Communications NV v Deutsche Bank AG* [2000] 2 B.C.L.C. 461 at [34].
[612] *English v Dedham Vale Properties Ltd* [1978] 1 W.L.R. 93; *Walsh v Shanahan* [2013] EWCA Civ 411 at [66].
[613] *United Pan-Europe Communications NV v Deutsche Bank AG* [2000] 2 B.C.L.C. 461.
[614] See *Lees v Nuttall* (1829) 1 Russ. & M. 53; affirmed (1834) 2 My. & K. 819; *Triplex Safety Glass Co Ltd v Scorah* [1938] Ch. 211; *Boardman v Phipps* [1965] Ch. 992; [1967] 2 A.C. 46; *Warman International Ltd v Dwyer* (1995) 182 C.L.R. 544 at 556–557; above, paras 6-042 and 6-043; below, para.6-094.
[615] *Personnel Hygiene Services Ltd v Rentokil Initial UK Ltd* [2014] EWCA Civ 29; *Allfiled UK Ltd v Eltis* [2015] EWHC 1300 (Ch) (interim injunction).
[616] *Caterpillar Logistics Services (UK) Ltd v de Crean* [2012] EWCA Civ 156; [2012] F.S.R. 33.
[617] *Eurasian Natural Resources Corp Ltd v Judge* [2014] EWHC 3556 (QB) at [75].

own. Held, he must account to the owners for the profit to be made on the sale of the cargo and not merely for a reasonable freight.[618]

(2) A telegraph company erected and maintained a "special wire" alongside a railway line in Newfoundland. The railway company were by contract entitled to use the wire in and about their railway business but were not entitled to transmit any commercial messages except for the account of the telegraph company. In fact they used it in part for their shipping business and other commercial undertakings. Held, they were accountable to the telegraph company for all the profits made and that they held these profits in trust for the company.[619]

(3) A client instructs a stockbroker to buy a certain quantity of stock in a company and "carry at 8%". The stockbroker deals with the shares so bought on his own account. He must account for his profits.[620]

(4) B is managing director of a company publishing a trade journal for the timber industry. With the company's consent, he is also manager and principal shareholder of another company which publishes a "Lumberman's Atlas". He inserts in the journal free advertisements for the Atlas. He must refund to his employer company a reasonable charge for doing so.[621]

(5) The proprietor of a trade directory employed canvassers to obtain advertisements from traders for insertion in the directory. He discovered that the canvassers were proposing to assist a rival publication with similar advertisements after their agreement with his had come to an end. Held, the canvassers were not entitled to use material or information obtained while in the claimant's employment for the purpose of this publication.[622]

(6) English licensees of the patents for brassières were shown in confidence new designs not yet on the market. They made use of this information to design their own brassières and then terminated their licence from the claimants. Held, the claimants were entitled: (a) to an injunction restraining the defendants from making and selling brassieres made from the new designs; (b) to an account of the profits from the brassieres already sold; and (c) to an order for delivery-up or destruction of the offending goods.[623]

(7) A drug company, to combat unfavourable publicity as to the side effects of one of its drugs, engages a specialist in television training to train its executives to put the company's point of view effectively when interviewed on television. The person engaged himself engages an experienced broadcaster to assist. During the courses the latter acquires information which he subsequently uses in making a documentary film in conjunction with a television company. The

---

[618] *Shallcross v Oldham* (1862) 2 Johns. & H. 609. See also *Gardner v M'Cutcheon* (1842) 4 Beav. 534; *Diplock v Blackburn* (1811) 3 Camp. 43.

[619] *Reid-Newfoundland Co v Anglo-American Telegraph Co Ltd* [1912] A.C. 555. See as to this unusual case Finn, *Fiduciary Obligations* (1977), p.99. The wire remained the property of the company.

[620] *Thornley v Tilley* (1925) 36 C.L.R. 1; see also *Langton v Waite* (1868) L.R. 6 Eq. 165 (reversed on other grounds (1869) L.R. 4 Ch.App. 402); *McLaughlin v Solloway* [1936] S.C.R. 127; [1938] A.C. 247; cf. *King v Hutton* [1900] 2 Q.B. 504.

[621] *B.C. Timber Industries Journal v Black* [1934] 3 D.L.R. 31.

[622] *Lamb v Evans* [1893] 1 Ch. 218. For the extent to which names and addresses not in a written list may be confidential information which a defendant may be restrained from using, see *Baker v Gibbons* [1972] 1 W.L.R. 693; *Investors Syndicate Ltd v Versatile Investments Inc* (1983) 149 D.L.R. (3d) 46. See also *Faccenda Chicken Ltd v Fowler* [1987] Ch. 117; *Crowson Fabrics Ltd v Rider* [2007] EWHC 2942 (Ch); [2008] I.R.L.R. 288; [2008] F.S.R. 17.

[623] *Peter Pan Manufacturing Corp Ltd v Corsets Silhouette Ltd* [1964] 1 W.L.R. 96.

showing of the film is a breach of confidence and may be restrained by injunction.[624]

Article 48

AGENT ACQUIRING BENEFITS IN BREACH OF DUTY

An agent may not in breach of duty acquire a benefit from a third party without the principal's consent. The agent must account to the principal for any benefit so obtained.[625]   **6-079**

Comment

Scope of principle   On the account here given of the fiduciary duties of an agent, this is a residual principle, insofar as it does not rely on the notion of using the principal's property, information or other attributes, though it can be taken to suggest that acquisitions *become* the principal's property. In part, it addresses the first limb, the "conflicts rule", in the following well-known description of the fiduciary's liability to account for profits, found in the judgment of Deane J in *Chan v Zacharia* (the second limb being the subject of Articles 46 and 47)[626]:   **6-080**

> "Stated comprehensively in terms of the liability to account, the principle of equity is that a person who is under a fiduciary obligation must account to the person to whom the obligation is owed for any benefit or gain (i) which has been obtained or received in circumstances where a conflict or significant possibility of conflict existed between his fiduciary duty and his personal interest in the pursuit or possible receipt of such a benefit or gain or (ii) which was obtained or received by use or by reason of his fiduciary position or of opportunity or knowledge resulting from it."

It is important to note that the principle covers profits derived from the agent's having placed himself in a position where the agent's interests *potentially* conflict with the principal's,[627] as well as cases where there is *actual* conflict and the agent's conduct has clearly been disloyal.[628] The taking of bribes and secret commissions, covered by this principle, is elaborated in Article 49, below. Note that the duty of loyalty is usually applied to the positive exercise of powers conferred on the agent by the principal, but a conflict of interest can arise in relation to an omission to

---

[624] *Schering Chemicals Ltd v Falkman Ltd* [1982] Q.B. 1.

[625] See Comment and Illustrations; *Restatement, Third*, § 8.02; *Meinhard v Salmon* 164 N.E. 545 (1928), per Cardozo CJ. For the possibility of the agent's being accountable for benefits derived by third parties as a result of the agent's breach of duty, see above, para.6-042.

[626] *Chan v Zacharia* (1984) 154 C.L.R. 178 at 198–199, per Deane J, quoted with approval in *Don King Productions Inc v Warren* [2000] Ch. 291. See also *Rothschild v Brookman* (1831) 2 Dow. & Cl. 188; *Parker v McKenna* (1874) L.R. 10 Ch.App. 96 at 118; *Re Birt* (1883) 22 Ch.D. 604; *Bray v Ford* [1896] A.C. 44 at 51–52; *Lindgren v L.&P. Estates Ltd* [1968] Ch. 572; *North and South Trust Co v Berkeley* [1971] 1 W.L.R. 470; the Rt Hon. Lord Millett [1993] Restitution L.Rev. 7 at 16: "A fiduciary will not be allowed to retain any advantage acquired in violation of the rule".

[627] *Imageview Management Ltd v Jack* [2009] EWCA Civ 63; [2009] 2 All E.R. 666 (Illustration 13); *Keogh v Dalgety & Co Ltd* (1916) 22 C.L.R. 402 (defendants appointed agent to procure mortgage loan for claimant, but arrange one whereby, without disclosure, they obtain a commission from the mortgagee for giving a guarantee of the mortgage).

[628] *JD Wetherspoon Plc v Van De Berg & Co Ltd* [2009] EWHC 639 (Ch) (diversion of opportunity to acquire properties to self and subsequent on-sale to competitor of the principal; defendant disguised conflict by inserting an intermediary in his transactions with principal).

exercise those powers.[629]

The principle also makes accountable those agents whose functions include locating assets or business opportunities (either particular or of a class) for their principals, or who have assumed management functions in the principal's business affairs, who proceed to acquire assets or opportunities (often termed "corporate opportunities" or "business opportunities") in their own right which should have been pursued, if at all, for the principal. It is not altogether clear whether this aspect of the principle is merely a particular example of the duty to avoid conflicts of interest, or an independent head of liability. While all fiduciaries have an obligation to avoid conflicts of interest, not all agents have the function of acquiring assets or business opportunities. The reconciliation might be, however, that the application of the conflicts rule can only be determined in each case by identifying the tasks that the relevant agent has undertaken to perform for the principal.

The detail of the relevant case law is treated separately in the succeeding paragraphs, but the body of law can be traced back to *Keech v Sandford*.[630] Here, property was leased to a trust, and when the lease determined the trustee renewed it for his own personal benefit. It was held that the trustee held the benefit of the lease on trust for his beneficiaries. The rule as to renewals has been held to extend also to purchases of the reversion.[631] But the presumption may sometimes be rebuttable.[632] It undoubtedly performs a cautionary role. "I very well see" said Lord King LC "if a trustee on refusal to renew might have a lease to himself, few trust estates would be renewed to cestui que use".[633] As elsewhere, full disclosure of all the material facts and consent by the principal will displace liability that would otherwise ensue.[634] However, a plea that the principal would have consented to the fiduciary's conduct if asked is unlikely to be countenanced by the court.[635]

The principle the subject of this Article is a strict one, and all profits must be accounted for even if, in acquiring them, the agent has incurred a risk of loss,[636] and the principal could not personally have made the profit, has suffered no injury or has even made a profit.[637] However, the court may make an allowance to the fiduci-

---

[629] e.g. *British Midland Tool Ltd v Midland International Tooling Ltd* [2003] EWHC 466 (Ch); [2003] 2 B.C.L.C. 523; *Chan v Zacharia* (1984) 154 C.L.R. 178 (refusal to renew lease).

[630] *Keech v Sandford* (1726) Sel.Cas.Ch. King 61; But cf. Hicks [2010] C.L.J. 287. For the application of *Keech v Sandford* to agents, see *York Buildings v Mackenzie* (1795) 8 Bro. P.C. 42 at 63–64. See too *Chan v Zacharia* (1984) 154 C.L.R. 178 at 201, 203.

[631] *Protheroe v Protheroe* [1968] 1 W.L.R. 519.

[632] See *Re Biss* [1903] 2 Ch. 40; *Chan v Zacharia* (1984) 154 C.L.R. 178 at 201–205; *Lewin on Trusts* (20th edn), Ch 45; Finn, *Fiduciary Obligations* (1977), Ch.23; *Meagher, Gummow and Lehane's Equity Doctrines and Remedies* (5th edn), para.5-055.

[633] See also *Bray v Ford* [1896] A.C. 44 at 51–52; *Chan v Zacharia* (1984) 154 C.L.R. 178.

[634] *New Zealands Netherlands Society "Oranje" Inc v Kuys* [1973] 1 W.L.R. 1126. For further detail, see above, para.6-039. As to modification of fiduciary duties by contract, see above, para.6-056.

[635] *Murad v Al-Saraj* [2005] EWCA Civ 959; [2005] 1 W.T.L.R. 1573. See too *United Pan-Europe Communications BV v Deutsche Bank AG* [2000] 2 B.C.L.C. 461 at [47]; and *Parr v Keystone Healthcare Ltd* [2019] EWCA Civ 1246 at [20].

[636] See e.g. *Burrell v Mossop* (1888) 4 T.L.R. 270; *Williams v Stevens* (1866) L.R. 1 P.C. 352.

[637] *Parker v McKenna* (1874) L.R. 10 Ch.App. 96; *Boardman v Phipps* [1967] 2 A.C. 46, Illustration 4, a case where the principal acquired great benefit as a result of the fiduciaries' action: *Industrial Development Consultants Ltd v Cooley* [1972] 1 W.L.R. 443, Illustration 7; *Warman International Ltd v Dwyer* (1995) 182 C.L.R. 544; *Akita Holdings Ltd v Attorney General of Turks and Caicos Islands* [2017] UKPC 7; [2017] A.C. 590; *Parr v Keystone Healthcare Ltd* [2019] EWCA Civ 1246 at [18].

ary for skill and expenditure in making the profit[638]; and sometimes this appears to approach a share in the profit.[639]

A claim made under the principle set out in this Article is often, of course, advanced in conjunction with a claim that the agent has used property or information belonging to the principal to acquire a benefit[640]: but the present principle is wider, since it is not confined to situations where trust property can be readily identified. Since there is, until it is generated, no property to which the right can attach, it can be said that the only remedy is a duty to account, which is personal[641]; but where an identifiable asset is acquired in most cases the principal will have a proprietary claim.[642] The case for a proprietary remedy is most compelling where the agent was under a positive duty to obtain the asset for the principal.[643]

A person who acts as agent without authority may also be liable under this principle, although this is an unusual situation.[644]

"Business (or corporate) opportunities"[645]   The body of law dealing with li-   **6-081**
ability for diverting business opportunities is in modern times commonly associated with company directors, in which context it is usual to refer to "corporate opportunities", but it is by no means so confined. It applies to any agent who has undertaken, not necessarily as a matter of contract, to locate, or assist in the acquisition of, business opportunities for his principal, or who has assumed management functions in relation to the principal's business affairs.[646] The agent will be held accountable for pursuing opportunities personally which should have been pursued, if at all, for the principal. As remarked already, some examples also involve the

---

[638] *Boardman v Phipps* [1967] 2 A.C. 46; but cf. *Guinness Plc v Saunders* [1990] 2 A.C. 663; *Imageview Management Ltd v Jack* [2009] EWCA Civ 63; [2009] 2 All E.R. 666; *Cobbetts LLP v Hodge* [2009] EWHC 786 (Ch) at [118]. See also *Yates v Finn* (1880) 13 Ch.D. 839; *Re Jarvis* [1958] 1 W.L.R. 815; *Paul A. Davies (Australia) Pty Ltd v Davies* [1983] 1 N.S.W.L.R. 440; *Nottingham University v Fishel* [2000] I.C.R. 146. See further Watts (2009) 125 L.Q.R. 369 at 374.
[639] See *O'Sullivan v Management Agency and Music Ltd* [1985] Q.B. 428; *Re Duke of Norfolk's Settlement Trusts* [1962] Ch. 61; *Re Berkeley Applegate (Investment Consultants) Ltd* [1989] Ch. 32; *Estate Realties Ltd v Wignall* [1992] 2 N.Z.L.R. 615; *Warman International Ltd v Dwyer* (1995) 182 C.L.R. 544.
[640] e.g. *Boardman v Phipps* [1967] 2 A.C. 46; see Article 47.
[641] *Warman International Ltd v Dwyer* (1995) 182 C.L.R. 544 at 557. See above, para.6-041; below, para.6-094. See also paras 6-051, 6-052, 6-075 and 6-094.
[642] See *FHR European Ventures LLP v Cedar Capital Partners LLC* [2014] UKSC 45; [2015] A.C. 250.
[643] e.g. *Cook v Deeks* [1916] 1 A.C. 554; *Aerostar Maintenance International Ltd v Wilson* [2010] EWHC 2032 (Ch) at [193].
[644] *English v Dedham Vale Properties Ltd* [1978] 1 W.L.R. 93. As to "self-appointed" agents: see Beatson, *Use and Abuse of Unjust Enrichment* (1991), pp.241–243; (1978) 94 L.Q.R. 347; (1978) 41 M.L.R. 474; and DeMott, in *Agency Law in Commercial Practice* (Busch, Macgregor and Watts, eds, 2016), Ch.3. See also *HKSAR v Luk Kin* [2016] HKCFA 81 at [34]. cf. *Arklow Investments Ltd v Maclean* [2000] 1 W.L.R. 594 PC.
[645] See *Gower's Principles of Modern Company Law* (10th edn), Chs 5 and 16; Worthington (2000) 116 L.Q.R. 638 at 662 onwards; Kershaw (2005) 25 O.J.L.S. 603.
[646] e.g. *Cook v Deeks* [1916] 1 A.C. 554 (company director); *Thompson's Trustee in Bankruptcy v Heaton* [1974] 1 W.L.R. 605 (partnership); *Don King Productions Inc v Warren* [2000] Ch. 291; *Chirnside v Fay* [2007] 1 N.Z.L.R. 433 (NZSC) (informal joint venture); *Brandeis Brokers Ltd v Black* [2001] 2 Lloyd's Rep. 359 at 368 (broker); *JD Wetherspoon Plc v Van De Berg & Co Ltd* [2009] EWHC 639 (Ch) (purchaser's agent); *Cook v Evatt (No.2)* [1992] 1 N.Z.L.R. 676 (investment adviser); *FHR European Ventures LLP v Cedar Capital Partners* [2014] UKSC 45; [2015] A.C. 250. As to company directors, see now Companies Act 2006 s.175; and above, para.6-080.

agent in using the principal's property, confidential information or other attributes.[647] However, it is not necessary to show that there has been any use of position, property or information; indeed, the agent may have learned of the opportunity casually in "his own time".[648]

Where such an undertaking exists, to divert such opportunities will usually be disloyal conduct, though dishonesty is not necessary. Liability for profits arises even if no liability would have arisen had the agent simply failed to have pursued the opportunity at all[649]—so, non-executive directors may have no positive obligation to pursue a relevant opportunity for their company, but would nonetheless be precluded from pursuing it for themselves, or it may be that the third party is only interested in dealing with the agent.[650] The agent may be liable even though by the time the profit is made the agent has ceased to act for the principal; indeed, the person concerned may often have resigned as agent precisely in order to pursue the profit.[651] Nor does it matter if the parties have been negotiating to terminate their relationship when the opportunity arises.[652]

Some authority appears to support the view that it is only "maturing opportunities", namely those that the principal had already identified for pursuit, that cannot be exploited by the agent, or former agent.[653] Other cases conclude that accountability cannot be so confined.[654] Much turns on the scope of the tasks that the agent has undertaken to perform, and the closeness of the connection of the opportunity to the principal's existing business or businesses. The principle may, however, extend to opportunities that have a close fit with a dormant part of the principal's business,[655] or which relate to new lines of business in which the principal has indicated a firm interest.[656] The mere possibility that the agent might at some time in the future be called on to act for the principal in the relevant matter is, on some authority, sufficient to impose liability.[657] This however is open to doubt, unless the agent is under a pre-existing duty to act in that way.[658]

Conversely, accountability will not extend to opportunities that are not part of the principal's business,[659] or which clearly do not arise until after the agent's appoint-

---

[647] e.g. *Regal (Hastings) Ltd v Gulliver* [1967] 2 A.C. 134n (directors' combining personal capital with that of company capital to obtain shared ownership of assets relevant to company's business). As to use of property and confidential information in general, see Article 47.

[648] e.g. *Bhullar v Bhullar* [2003] 2 B.C.L.C. 241; cf. *Wilkinson v West Coast Capital Ltd* [2005] EWHC 3009 (Ch); [2007] B.C.C. 717 at [306].

[649] Perhaps implicit in *Keech v Sandford* (1726) Sel.Cas.Ch. 61 itself, per Lord King LC.

[650] *Industrial Development Consultants Ltd v Cooley* [1972] 1 W.L.R. 443; *G.E. Smith Ltd v Smith* [1952] N.Z.L.R. 470.

[651] See Illustrations 7 and 8; *Recovery Partners GP Ltd v Rukhadze* [2018] EWHC 2918 (Comm).

[652] *Bhullar v Bhullar* [2003] 2 B.C.L.C. 241; *Pennyfeathers Ltd v Pennyfeathers Property Co Ltd* [2013] EWHC 3530 (Ch) at [58].

[653] See *Island Export Finance Ltd v Umunna* [1986] B.C.L.C. 460 at 482; *Balston Ltd v Headline Filters Ltd* [1990] F.S.R. 385 at 412; *Dranez Anstalt v Hayek* [2002] 1 B.C.L.C. 693 at [76].

[654] *Bhullar v Bhullar* [2003] 2 B.C.L.C. 241; *Canadian Aero Service Ltd v O'Malley* (1973) 40 D.L.R. (3d) 371 at 391; *Pacifica Shipping Co Ltd v Anderson* [1986] 2 N.Z.L.R. 328 at 334.

[655] *Coleman Taymar Ltd v Oakes* [2001] 2 B.C.L.C. 749; *Bhullar v Bhullar* [2003] 2 B.C.L.C. 241.

[656] *Dwyer v Lippiatt* (2004) 50 A.C.S.R. 333.

[657] See *Boardman v Phipps* [1967] 2 A.C. 46 where it was said that the solicitor might at some time be called on to advise whether to apply to the court for permission for the trust to increase its holding in the company. However, liability in this case arose even without this consideration.

[658] See *Tyrrell v Bank of London* (1862) 10 H.L. Cas. 26; *Re Thomson* [1930] 1 Ch. 203; *British Syphon Co v Homewood* [1956] 1 W.L.R. 1190; Finn, *Fiduciary Obligations* (1977), pp.244–246.

[659] See Illustrations 1, 6, 9 and 15. See too *Aas v Benham* [1891] 2 Ch. 244; *Trimble v Goldberg* [1906]

ment has ceased.[660] One case has suggested that for all but partners the corporate opportunity doctrine does not require a connection between the lines of the principal's business and the profit,[661] but the case is readily, and better, explained as involving exploitation of the fiduciary's position, for which there need not be any connection to the business.

In a controversial decision,[662] a majority of the Supreme Court of Canada extended the corporate opportunity doctrine to a person who was a mere adviser of the principal. The solicitor there had a duty to inform the claimant of the availability of a *type* of tax driven scheme, but, as the majority accepted, his undertaking did not preclude him from informing any other client of specific opportunities or from exploiting them himself (putting aside the fact that his colleagues had directed him not to get involved with clients in a scheme). Because he had failed to inform the claimant of the tax opportunity the court held him accountable for all the profits he derived from his own participation in such schemes during the period that the claimant was a client of the firm. This seems wrong. There was insufficient connection between the profits made and the breach of duty. The profits were not a result of an undisclosed conflict (he did not need the client's consent to make them), there was no use of fiduciary position, and he had given no undertaking to direct opportunities the claimant's way. The award was, therefore, punitive. It may have been acceptable to award "springboard damages" to remove any advantage the solicitor gained from suppressing from his client the availability of the schemes, but not more.

The liability to account for the taking of corporate opportunities is, in accordance with principle, subject to there having been no disclosure to, and consent by, the principal to the agent's action.[663] In some cases, it has been held that that consent can be given to a company director by the other directors,[664] but it is not clear that a director's colleagues are the appropriate persons to be giving such an indulgence.

Agent acquiring specific asset in own name   If an agent who agrees to acquire,   **6-082**
to assist in the acquisition of, land or another asset on behalf of the principal

A.C. 494 (partner's purchase of land from company in which partnership held shares not a breach of duty); *Wilkinson v West Coast Capital* [2005] EWHC 3009 (Ch); [2007] B.C.C. 717 at [284]; *Canberra Residential Developments Pty Ltd v Brendas (No.5)* [2009] FCA 34; *Howard v Commissioner of Taxation* [2014] HCA 21; (2014) 253 C.L.R. 83 at [37].

[660] *Nordisk Insulinlaboratorium v Gorgate Products Ltd* [1953] Ch. 430; *National Trust for Places of Historic Interest v Birden* [2009] EWHC 2023 (Ch); *Thermascan Ltd v Norman* [2009] EWHC 3694 (Ch) at [16] (relevant contracts made with former regular customers of principal, but not initiated until after agent's resignation).

[661] *O'Donnell v Shanahan* [2009] EWCA Civ 751; [2009] 2 B.C.L.C. 666 at [55] (criticised Lim (2013) 129 L.Q.R. 242); *Invideous Ltd v Thorogood* [2013] EWHC 3015 (Ch). cf. *Poon Ka Man v Cheng Wai Tao* [2016] HKCFA 23 at [85] (not following *O'Donnell*).

[662] *Strother v 3464920 Canada Inc* [2007] 2 S.C.R. 177 (criticised by Edelman (2008) 124 L.Q.R. 21; Duggan, in *Exploring Private Law* (Bant and Harding eds, 2010), Ch.12). cf. *Colyer Fehr Tallow Pty Ltd v KNZ Australia Pty Ltd* [2011] NSWSC 457 (buying agent held not liable because undertook no implied obligation not to buy for others or for own account).

[663] See above, para.6-039. See also *Robash Pty Ltd v Gladstone Pacific Nickel Pty Ltd* (2012) 86 A.C.S.R. 432.

[664] *Peso Silver Mines Ltd v Cropper* [1966] S.C.R. 673; (1966) 58 D.L.R. (2d) 1, a controversial case: see (1967) 30 M.L.R. 450; Beck (1971) 49 Can.B.R. 80; Prentice (1972) 50 Can.B.R. 623. See also *Mid-Western News Agency Ltd v Vanpinxteren* (1975) 62 D.L.R. (3d) 555; *Evans v Anderson* (1977) 76 D.L.R. (3d) 482; and the cases cited above, para.6-039.

acquires it personally the agent becomes a trustee of it for the principal.[665] The principle is not limited to purchases; it applies, for example, to leases. Thus, where an agent took a lease in his own name which he had been instructed to take jointly for himself and his principal, it was decided that he held it on trust for the benefit of both himself and his principal.[666]

At least in relation to land, the intervention of equity in this context can be explained by the fact that neither a disclosed nor an undisclosed principal can claim that conveyance to the agent vests property in the principal. In the case of chattels, a disclosed principal will often be able to claim that title vested directly in the principal. It is also possible that an undisclosed principal may sometimes claim that property is by transfer to the agent vested in the principal, rather than held on trust,[667] but often recourse to equity would be needed.

If the agent purports to sell to the principal the property which the agent has acquired personally (and which the agent therefore holds on trust), the sale is of no effect in equity, since the agent is already holding it on trust for the principal. Accordingly, the principal can recover from the agent anything the principal has paid in excess of the price paid by the agent for the property. It also follows that the agent holds this excess on trust for the principal until it is claimed by the principal.[668]

Illustrations

6-083   (1)   Commission agents who were also merchants were employed to ship and sell goods abroad. They did so and purchased other goods with the proceeds. They were not bound to account for the profit on the sale of the goods bought with the proceeds, because such profit was not made in the course of or by means of the agency. They were only bound to account for the proceeds of the goods sold on the principal's behalf.[669]

(2)   Three directors of a company which carried on the business of railway construction contractors obtained for themselves a contract to build a railway line to the exclusion of the company. They concealed this from the fourth director until the contract was obtained. Held, they held the benefit of the contract on behalf of the company.[670]

(3)   A company wished to purchase the leases of two cinemas from X which, with a cinema it already owned, were to be transferred to a subsidiary company and then sold to a third party. The intention was that the company should own

---

[665] *Lees v Nuttall* (1829) 1 Russ. & M. 53; (1834) 2 Myl. & K. 819; *Austin v Chambers* (1837) 6 C. & F. 1 at 36–40; *Tyrrell v Bank of London* (1862) 10 H.L. Cas. 26 (discussed in detail in Watts (2013) 129 L.Q.R. 526). In *Bartlett v Pickersgill* (1760) 1 Cox 15; and *James v Smith* [1891] 1 Ch. 384; affirmed (1892) 65 L.T. 544, there was held to be a trust in favour of the principal, but one which he could not enforce as it did not comply with s.7 of the Statute of Frauds. In *Rochefoucauld v Boustead* [1897] 1 Ch. 196 this limitation was overruled but the cases are still authority for the principle expressed in the Article. See also *Taylor v Salmon* (1838) 4 Myl. & Cr. 134 at 139; *Trench v Harrison* (1849) 17 Sim. 111; *Cave v Mackenzie* (1877) 46 L.J.Ch. 564; *Gray v Smith* [2013] EWHC 4136 (Comm); [2014] 2 All E.R. (Comm) 359 at [35]. See further Comment to Article 9; Youdan [1984] C.L.J. 306.
[666] *Atkins v Rowe* (1728) Mos. 39; *Taylor v Salmon* (1838) 4 Myl. & Cr. 134; *Raleigh v McGrath* (1877) 3 V.L.R. 250.
[667] See Article 89.
[668] cf. *Regier v Campbell-Stuart* [1939] Ch. 766, Illustration 16 to Article 45; and *Bentley v Craven* (1853) 18 Beav. 75.
[669] *Kirkham v Peel* (1881) 44 L.T. 195; cf. *Union Government v Chappell* [1918] Cape P.D. 462.
[670] *Cook v Deeks* [1916] 1 A.C. 554.

all the shares in the subsidiary. X required personal guarantees of the rent so long as the subscribed capital of the subsidiary was below a certain amount. It being difficult to secure such guarantees, and the company not having the money to subscribe further, the directors of the company and their solicitor personally subscribed for the remainder of the capital. When the directors sold their shares they made a profit which they could not keep for themselves but held for the benefit of their company, even after the company had been sold. The solicitor was however unaffected.[671]

(4) A will created a trust which included a shareholding in a private company. X, the solicitor who had been acting for the trust, and Y, a beneficiary, decided that the best way to protect the interests of the trust was to gain control of the company and this they did by purchasing sufficient extra shares in the company with their own money. By holding themselves out as acting on behalf of the trust, they acquired both the opportunity to bid for the further shares and also confidential information which satisfied them that the purchase of the shares would be a good investment. As a result of the changes in control of the company, X and Y and the trust made considerable profits. They had made formal disclosure to two trustees but not to the third; and later, when the estate had been administered, disclosure to the beneficiaries had not been complete. Held, X and Y were accountable to the trust for the profit made on the shares which they had purchased with their own money, as they had used their position to make a profit for themselves as well as the trust. X and Y could, however, claim remuneration for their expenses and labour in taking over the company.[672]

(5) Two mine prospectors employed X to stake asbestos mineral claims for them in Manitoba. X received information about the area from them, explored the area and reported that there was no asbestos there. However, in the course of his prospecting he discovered that there were other valuable minerals in the area. Shortly afterwards he staked claims to these minerals for himself and made a considerable profit. Held, he was under a duty to disclose all he had learnt about the area to his principals and he must account for the profits made within the area he agreed to explore.[673]

(6) The board of directors of a mining company considers a proposition put up by an outsider for mining in an area near to the company's holdings, and reject it. Individual directors contact the outsider and put up the money for the venture, taking advice from the company's consulting geologist. They are not liable to account for profits.[674]

---

[671] *Regal (Hastings) Ltd v Gulliver* [1967] 2 A.C. 134n.

[672] *Boardman v Phipps* [1967] 2 A.C. 46. This is a stern decision, and there is considerable force in the dissenting judgment of Lord Upjohn. A crucial reason seems to have been that X and Y purported, at any rate initially, to be acting for the trust: there was certainly no pre-existing agency relationship. The company was also a private one and information could not be obtained from its public documents. The trust could not have purchased shares in the company without leave of the court and in some speeches reliance is placed, perhaps questionably, on the fact that it was possible that at some time in the future the solicitor would be asked to advise in this respect; on the question of remuneration cf. *Guinness Plc v Saunders* [1990] 2 A.C. 663. See Finn, *Fiduciary Obligations* (1977), p.242 onwards; *Chan v Zacharia* (1984) 154 C.L.R. 178 at 204–205, per Deane J.

[673] *McLeod and More v Sweezey* [1944] 2 D.L.R. 145.

[674] *Peso Silver Mines Ltd v Cropper* [1966] S.C.R. 673; (1966) 58 D.L.R. (2d) 1, a controversial case: see (1967) 30 M.L.R. 450; Beck (1971) 49 Can.B.R. 80; Prentice (1972) 50 Can.B.R. 623. See also

(7)   C was managing director of the plaintiffs, a company which carried on busi-
        ness as construction consultants. As such, he was negotiating with E for a
        contract. E made it clear to him that he had no intention of contracting with
        the plaintiffs but indicated that he might be prepared to contract with C
        personally. At a subsequent interview with the chairman of the plaintiffs, C
        did not tell him of E's offer but falsely told him that he was seriously ill. For
        this reason he was given permission by the plaintiffs to resign at once instead
        of working out his contractual period of notice. Having resigned from the
        plaintiff's employment C at once made a contract with E. Held, C had al-
        lowed his personal interest to conflict with his duty as a director of the
        plaintiffs. Notwithstanding that the plaintiffs had sustained no loss (because
        E was not willing to contract with them) C was ordered to account to the
        plaintiffs for all his profits from his contract with E.[675]

(8)   The executive president and vice-president of a company engage in
        preliminary prospecting towards an extensive aerial mapping project to be
        paid for by a government. They subsequently form a separate company and
        obtain the contract in competition with their previous company. They must
        account for profits.[676]

(9)   The managing director of a company formed to exploit mining licences is
        poised to exploit successful negotiations. The collapse of one of the
        company's shareholders leaves it without working capital. The managing
        director takes the licences in his own name, resigns as managing director (but
        not as a director) and forms his own company to exploit the concession. He
        explains the full position and the inherent risks to the board, which decides
        to pursue the concession no further and permit him to do what he wants with
        the licence. He is not liable to account.[677]

(10)   The prospective purchaser of property applies for planning permission in
        respect of it in the vendor's name without telling the vendor. He must ac-
        count for profits made as the result of the application.[678]

(11)   A sergeant in the Army stationed at Cairo, while in uniform, accompanied
        civilian lorries containing illicit goods through Cairo, enabling them to pass
        the civilian police without inspection. He was paid large sums of money for
        his services. The military authorities took possession of the money, and the
        sergeant petitioned the Crown for its return. Held, he could not recover the
        money. He had obtained the money by reason of his employment, but in
        dereliction of his duty—by using his position as a sergeant and the uniform

---

Mid-Western News Agency Ltd v Vanpinxteren (1975) 62 D.L.R. (3d) 555; *Evans v Anderson* (1977)
76 D.L.R. (3d) 482.

[675] *Industrial Development Consultants Ltd v Cooley* [1972] 1 W.L.R. 443. See also *Green & Clara Pty
Ltd v Bestobell Industries Pty Ltd* [1982] W.A.R. 1; *Crowson Fabrics Ltd v Rider* [2007] EWHC
2942 (Ch); [2008] I.R.L.R. 288; [2008] F.S.R. 17.

[676] *Canadian Aero Service Ltd v O'Malley* [1974] S.C.R. 592; (1973) 40 D.L.R. (3d) 371. See also *Abbey Glen Property Corp v Stumborg* (1978) 85 D.L.R. (3d) 35; (1979) 42 M.L.R. 215; and in general
as to those cases *Gower's Principles of Modern Company Law* (10th edn), para.16-84 onwards.

[677] *Queensland Mines Ltd v Hudson* (1978) 52 A.L.J.R. 399 PC; see (1979) 42 M.L.R. 711. See also
Island Export Finance Ltd v Umunna [1986] B.C.L.C. 460.

[678] *English v Dedham Vale Properties Ltd* [1978] 1 W.L.R. 93. For comment on this case, see above,
notes to para.6-080.

to which his rank entitled him; the Crown could retain the money—at least against the sergeant— even though it was earned by a criminal act.[679]

(12) A enters into a joint venture with B and C to buy a hotel for £4.1 million. It is understood that A will contribute £500,000 and B and C together £1 million; the remainder will be borrowed from a bank. In breach of his fiduciary duty A conceals the fact that his contribution is largely by way of deductions to the price in respect of the introduction. Had they known this B and C would have gone ahead, but allowing a smaller profit share to A. The hotel is sold for a profit of £2 million. A must account to B and C for the whole of the profit less the small amount of money genuinely put in by him, subject to an allowance for skill and effort.[680]

(13) A sports agent undertakes to provide advice to and representation for a professional footballer for a two-year period, in return for a commission on salary payable under any resulting employment contracts. The agent procures for the player a position with a Club. At the same time, at the Club's request and for a fee, the agent provides services in obtaining a work permit for the player. Some time into his contract with the Club, the player subsequently disowns the contract with the agent on the basis of the non-disclosure of the work undertaken for the Club, reclaiming all commission, and claiming an account of the fee paid by the Club. Held, the agent must not only account for the fee but must also refund the commission received from the player and forfeit any right to ongoing commission under the Club contract.[681]

(14) A agrees with B to bid at an auction for property which they both want and promises that if he acquires it he will cede part to B. A holds that part on trust for B and cannot claim to own the whole.[682]

(15) An owner of land sells part of it to a company for a golf course and becomes a director, and for a time CEO, of that company. He commences to develop another golf course on his remaining land. He is not obliged to offer this new business to the company. His involvement in managing two competing businesses could in principle involve an actionable conflict of interest, but not where he had resigned from the company before the new business commenced trading.[683]

[679] *Reading v Att.-Gen.* [1951] A.C. 507; but care must be taken in applying the principles of fiduciary obligation in public law situations: see Finn, *Fiduciary Obligations* (1977), pp.214–215. See also *Att.-Gen. v Goddard* (1929) 98 L.J.K.B. 743; *Hawrelak v City of Edmonton* (1975) 54 D.L.R. (3d) 45.
[680] *Murad v Al-Saraj* [2005] EWCA Civ 959; [2005] 1 W.T.L.R. 1573. See also *Gray v New Augarita Porcupine Mines Ltd* [1952] 3 D.L.R. 1 (PC); cf. *Chirnside v Fay* [2007] 1 N.Z.L.R. 433.
[681] *Imageview Management Ltd v Jack* [2009] EWCA Civ 63; [2009] 2 All E.R. 666 (noted Watts (2009) 125 L.Q.R. 369; and Oram [2010] L.M.C.L.Q. 95). For doubt about whether forfeiture of remuneration was appropriate here, see below para.7-050.
[682] *Chattock v Muller* (1878) 8 Ch.D. 177; applied in *Pallant v Morgan* [1953] Ch. 43; considered in *Banner Homes Group Plc v Luff Developments Ltd* [2000] Ch. 372. See also *Chirnside v Fay* [2007] 1 N.Z.L.R. 433.
[683] *Links Golf Tasmania Pty Ltd v Sattler* [2012] FCA 634; (2012) 292 A.L.R. 382.

Article 49

LIABILITY OF AGENTS IN RESPECT OF BRIBES AND SECRET COMMISSIONS

6-084　When an agent receives or arranges to receive any money or property by way of bribe or secret commission in the course of his agency from a person who deals or seeks to deal with the principal, the agent is liable to the principal jointly and severally with that person—

    (1)　in restitution for the amount of the bribe or secret commission; or

    (2)　in tort or contract, for any loss suffered by the principal from entering into the transaction in respect of which the bribe or secret commission was given or promised.[684]

Comment

6-085　**Bribes and secret commissions**[685]　A bribe is a type of secret profit, and a clear breach of fiduciary duty. However, the rules for bribes have special features, and the area has its own specialised group of cases. Courts generally eschew attaching rigid definitions to common law concepts, and this is true of the concept of a bribe. However, two formulations much referred to in other cases follow, the latter more apposite to the broader concept of a secret commission:

> "If a gift be made to a confidential agent with the view of inducing the agent to act in favour of the donor in relation to transactions between the donor and the agent's principal and that gift is secret as between the donor and the agent—that is to say, without the knowledge and consent of the principal—then the gift is a bribe in the view of the law" : *Hovenden & Sons v Millhoff*, per Romer LJ.[686]

> "[F]or the purpose of the civil law a bribe means a payment of a secret commission, which only means (i) that the person making the payment makes it to the agent of the other person with whom he is dealing; (ii) that he makes it to that person knowing that the person is acting as the agent of the other person with whom he is dealing; and (iii) that he fails to disclose to the other person with whom he is dealing that he has made that payment to the person whom he knows to be the other person's agent" : *Industries and General Mortgage Co Ltd v Lewis*, per Slade J.[687]

Where the payment is not for a corrupt purpose, a corrupt purpose being one intended to influence the agent in the performance of the agent's tasks in favour of the payer or some other outside party, it is more appropriate to refer to the arrangement as a secret commission. But absence of corruption on the third party's part makes no difference to the agent's duty to account for an undisclosed

---

[684] *Mahesan v Malaysia Government Officers Co-operative Housing Society Ltd* [1979] A.C. 374, Illustration 8. See further Article 96 as to the position between principal and third party.

[685] See Berg [2001] L.M.C.L.Q. 27 (a valuable article).

[686] *Hovenden & Sons v Millhoff* (1900) 83 L.T. 41 at 43, per Romer LJ. See too *Novoship (UK) Ltd v Mikhaylyuk* [2012] EWHC 3586 (Comm) at [106] reversed on other issues [2014] EWCA Civ 908.

[687] *Industries and General Mortgage Co Ltd v Lewis* [1949] 2 All E.R. 573 at 575. See also *Taylor v Walker* [1958] 1 Lloyd's Rep. 490, Article 96, Illustration 4; *Anangel Atlas Cia. Naviera SA v Ishikawajima-Harima Heavy Industries Co Ltd* [1990] 1 Lloyd's Rep. 167 at 171, per Leggatt J: "More succinctly it may be said that a bribe consists in a commission or other inducement which is given by the third party to an agent as such, and which is secret from the principal".

commission.[688] It is also irrelevant that the agent has not in fact been influenced or departed from duty to the principal,[689] for the acceptance of or agreement to receive a bribe is of itself a breach of the agent's general fiduciary duty, as giving an interest contrary to the agent's duty to the principal.[690] This reasoning applies also to commissions given by way of discount on payment.[691] It is generally as problematic for the third party to promise a bribe or secret commission as to pay it, although inducement will need to be proven by the principal (actual payment supplies it own proof).[692] Agents are liable in respect of bribes and secret commissions in restitution or in tort.[693] It is now also clear that a bribe which comprises money or other property is held on trust for the principal.[694] Bribes may be offered by the third party or sought by the agent,[695] can frequently be in kind (including an offer of future employment),[696] and can be paid to relatives of, trustees for, or otherwise at the direction of, the agent.[697] It is not necessary that the bribe relate to a particular transaction, and the validity of all subsequent transactions may be affected.[698] On the other hand, not all undisclosed profiting from position would amount to a bribe or secret commission. Some gains which an agent might make will be from activities that do not relate directly to the services the agent performs for the principal and their receipt could not realistically be considered as likely to influence those

---

[688] See *Daraydan Holdings Ltd v Solland International Ltd* [2004] EWHC 622 (Ch); [2005] Ch. 119 at [53].

[689] *Harrington v Victoria Graving Dock Co* (1878) 3 Q.B.D. 549; *Shipway v Broadwood* [1899] 1 Q.B. 369; *Re a Debtor* [1927] 2 Ch. 367; *Daraydan Holdings Ltd v Solland International Ltd* [2004] EWHC 622 (Ch); [2005] Ch. 119 at [53]; *Donegal International Ltd v Republic of Zambia* [2007] EWHC 197 (Comm); [2007] 1 Lloyd's Rep. 397 at [275]; *Fiona Trust & Holding Corp v Privalov* [2010] EWHC 3199 (Comm) at [72]; *Otkritie International Investment Management Ltd v Urumov* [2014] EWHC 191 (Comm) at [164]; *Shagang Shipping Co Ltd v HNA Group Co Ltd* [2018] EWCA Civ 1732 at [84]; reversed on the facts [2020] UKSC 34; *HKSAR v Chu Ang* [2020] HKCFA 18 (violin teacher receives undisclosed commission when assisting pupil buy violin).

[690] *Shipway v Broadwood* [1899] 1 Q.B. 369 at 373. Statements that the recipient is conclusively presumed to have been influenced (e.g. *Hovenden v Millhoff* (1900) 83 L.T. 41; *Industries and General Mortgage Co v Lewis* [1949] 2 All E.R. 573 at 578), are therefore beside the point: the Rt Hon. Lord Millett [1993] Restitution L.Rev. 7 at 13.

[691] e.g. *Turnbull v Garden* (1869) 38 L.J.Ch. 331, Illustration 2. Sometimes such transactions can be treated as a sale by the agent to his principal: see *Kimber v Barber* (1872) L.R. 8 Ch.App. 56; Article 45.

[692] *Grant v Gold Exploration & Development Syndicate Ltd* [1900] 1 Ch. 233; though the agent can only be liable in restitution where he has received the money; *Donegal International Ltd v Republic of Zambia* [2007] EWHC 197 (Comm); [2007] 1 Lloyd's Rep. 397 at [274]–[275]; *Otkritie International Investment Management Ltd v Urumov* [2014] EWHC 191 (Comm) at [68] (corrupt purpose need not be proved).

[693] *Mahesan's case* [1979] A.C. 374 at 383.

[694] *FHR European Ventures LLP v Cedar Capital Partners LLC* [2014] UKSC 45; [2015] A.C. 250. See further para.6-087.

[695] *Novoship (UK) Ltd v Mikhaylyuk* [2012] EWHC 3586 (Comm) at [106] (issue not addressed on appeal: [2014] EWCA Civ 908).

[696] See the cases cited below, para.6-087; and *Amalgamated Industrials Ltd v Johnson & Firth Brown Ltd, The Times,* April 15, 1981 (offer of future employment).

[697] *Novoship (UK) Ltd v Mikhaylyuk* [2012] EWHC 3586 (Comm) at [107] (issue not addressed on appeal: [2014] EWCA Civ 908); *Shagang Shipping Co Ltd v HNA Group Co Ltd* [2018] EWCA Civ 1732 at [84]; reversed on the facts [2020] UKSC 34.

[698] *Novoship (UK) Ltd v Mikhaylyuk* [2012] EWHC 3586 (Comm) at [109]; affirmed [2014] EWCA Civ 908 at [54]; *Otkritie International Investment Management Ltd v Urumov* [2014] EWHC 191 (Comm) at [70].

services.[699] In some cases, nonetheless, the agent may be accountable in equity for incidental benefits if they were derived from the agent's fiduciary position without those benefits being considered commissions or bribes.[700] Liability also does not attach to small gifts made after the conclusion of a transaction related to services performed by the agent,[701] unless it appears that such gifts were expected when the transaction was entered into, or are intended to affect future transactions[702]; nor to discounts obtained on transactions independent of the agency relationship.[703] In yet other situations, the intermediary may not be a fiduciary at all if it is clear that the intermediary was not undertaking any obligations of loyalty to the putative principal nor otherwise exercising any powers on the principal's behalf.[704] The label "agent" is not determinative of a person's fiduciary status.

6-086   **Disclosure**   Active concealment is not necessary: it is sufficient that the principal did not know of the bribe.[705] Third parties who pay a commission cannot assert that they thought the agent would disclose it; the only safe approach is for the third party directly to inform the principal of the payment.[706] Furthermore, to free the agent from liability, the disclosure must be such as to enable the principal to understand the implications of the arrangement: thus a partial disclosure may be insufficient.[707] That the principal (including an appropriate other agent of the principal[708]) is aware that the agent is receiving some sort of commission from the third party may preclude the principal's rescinding the transaction with the third party, but leave the agent accountable for incomplete disclosure.[709] Where the contract between agent and principal provides that the agent may receive commission or other remunera-

---

[699] See, e.g. *Anangel Atlas Cia Naviera SA v Ishikawajima-Harima Heavy Industries Co Ltd* [1990] 1 Lloyd's Rep. 167 at 174; *Rowland v Chapman* (1901) 17 T.L.R. 669.

[700] For an example in the context of the criminal law, see *Secretary for Justice v Chan Chi Wan* [2017] HKCFA 15. See also *Fawcett v Whitehouse* (1829) 1 Russ. & M. 132; *Turnbull v Garden* (1869) 38 L.J.Ch. 331.

[701] *The Parkdale* [1897] P. 53, Illustration 1. See also *Meadow Schama & Co v C. Mitchell & Co Ltd* (1973) 228 E.G. 1511 (sum promised after commission earned: not a bribe). See too *Donegal International Ltd v Republic of Zambia* [2007] EWHC 197 (Comm); [2007] 1 Lloyd's Rep. 397 at [277]; *Bank of Ireland v Jaffery* [2012] EWHC 1377 (Ch) at [392] (side deals but for full value and not intended as inducements).

[702] See *Fiona Trust Holding Corp v Privalov* [2010] EWHC 3199 (Comm) at [73] and [1392] ("sufficient to create a 'real possibility' of a conflict between interest and duty"); *Field v R.* [2012] 3 N.Z.L.R. 1 (MP criminally liable for having received free labour on house following assistance to immigrants in electorate). See also Article 96, Illustration 1.

[703] See *London School Board v Northcroft* (1892), Hudson's *Building and Engineering Contracts* (12th edn), para.2.235 (not carried forward to later editions).

[704] See *Eze v Conway* [2019] EWCA Civ 88; *Commercial First Business Ltd v Pickup* [2017] C.T.L.C. 1 at [52]. cf. *McWilliam v Norton Finance (UK) Ltd* [2015] EWCA Civ 186; [2015] 1 All E.R. (Comm) 1026 at [40].

[705] *Temperley v Blackrod Mfg. Co Ltd* (1907) 71 J.P. 341; *Fiona Trust & Holding Corp v Privalov* [2010] EWHC 3199 (Comm) at [1388]

[706] *Daraydan Holdings Ltd v Solland International Ltd* [2004] EWHC 622 (Ch); [2005] Ch. 119 at [53]. For other cases to the same effect, see below, para.8-222.

[707] *Bartram & Sons v Lloyd* (1904) 90 L.T. 357; *McWilliam v Norton Finance (UK) Ltd (t/a Norton Finance)* [2015] EWCA Civ 186; [2015] 1 All E.R. (Comm) 1026 at [49] (credit broker receives commission from both parties). See also *Christie v McCann* (1972) 27 D.L.R. (3d) 544. The onus is on the agent: *Jordy v Vanderpump* (1920) 64 S.J. 324; *FHR European Ventures LLP v Cedar Capital Partners LLC* [2014] UKSC 45; [2015] A.C. 250.

[708] *Rowland v Chapman* (1901) 17 T.L.R. 669 (knowledge of solicitor imputed).

[709] *Hurstanger Ltd v Wilson* [2007] EWCA Civ 299; [2007] 1 W.L.R. 2351; [2007] 4 All E.R. 1118 (lender pays finder's fee to borrower's agent; loan not rescindable, but agent accountable to borrower).

tion from the third party and states that where that happens the amount will be disclosed, it is likely to be misleading conduct for the agent not to disclose the actual receipt of commission since the principal may make the assumption that none has been paid.[710]

If the principal knows that the agent has been paid such a commission and consents, the principal cannot afterwards claim against the agent[711]; similarly, where the principal leaves the agent to look to the other party for remuneration or knows that the agent will receive something from the other party, the principal cannot object on the ground that it did not know the precise particulars of the amount paid. Such situations often occur in connection with usage and custom of trades and markets.[712] The courts are generally most reluctant to recognise any custom or market practice that is asserted in relation to undisclosed benefits received by an agent,[713] but nonetheless the existence of the practice may provide some circumstantial evidence of consent on the part of the principal.[714]

Where the principal is a company and the recipient of the bribe is a director, disclosure by that director to a colleague, rather than to the board as a whole (or the shareholders, which may be necessary in some cases), is insufficient disclosure.[715] Where the issue is notification to the company by the third party that it has given a commission to the director, then it may be sufficient for notice to be given to the managing director (or other independent director), or to the company's solicitors.[716] The third party would still need to show that it had become reasonable to infer that the principal's consent had ensued.

Remedies There are various remedies available to a principal when it discovers **6-087** that the agent has been bribed. If the bribe has been paid and is in money, the principal can sue the agent for its amount[717] in an action which was in earlier cases regarded as lying in equity[718] but was subsequently treated as an action in restitution at common law[719]; and this regardless of whether the principal affirms or disaf-

---

[710] *Pengelly v Business Mortgage Finance 4 Plc* [2020] EWHC 2002 (Ch) at [79]; distinguishing *Hurstanger Ltd v Wilson* [2007] EWCA Civ 299.

[711] *Great Western Insurance Co of New York v Cunliffe* (1874) L.R. 9 Ch.App. 525; *Re Haslam and Hier-Evans* [1902] 1 Ch. 765; *P&O SN Co v Johnson* (1938) 60 C.L.R. 189; cf. *Federal Supply and Cold Storage of South Africa v Angehrn & Piel* (1910) 80 L.J.P.C. 1 (in which an acceptance of an agent's denial that he had received a bribe was held not to be condonation or consent, where he had in fact done so).

[712] See Illustration 9; *Medsted Associates Ltd v Canaccord Genuity Wealth (International) Ltd* [2019] EWCA Civ 83 at [44].

[713] See *McWilliam v Norton Finance (UK) Ltd (t/a Norton Finance)* [2015] EWCA Civ 186; [2015] 1 All E.R. (Comm) 1026 at [54]; and the cases cited in *Secretary of State for Justice v Topland Group Plc* [2011] EWHC 983 (QB); and above, para.6-057.

[714] *Secretary of State for Justice v Topland Group Plc* [2011] EWHC 983 (QB) at [69].

[715] *Ross River Ltd v Cambridge City Football Club Ltd* [2007] EWHC 2115 (Ch); [2008] 1 All E.R. 1004 at [213]; *BFS Group Ltd v Foley* [2017] EWHC 2799 (QB) at [29]. See further, para.6-039, above.

[716] *Ross River Ltd v Cambridge City Football Club Ltd* [2007] EWHC 2115 (Ch); [2008] 1 All E.R. 1004 at [214].

[717] *Morison v Thompson* (1874) L.R. 9 Q.B. 480; *Hay's Case* (1875) L.R. 10 Ch.App. 593; *Boston Deep Sea Fishing and Ice Co v Ansell* (1888) 39 Ch.D. 339; *Lister & Co v Stubbs* (1890) 45 Ch.D. 1; *Att.-Gen. v Goddard* (1929) 98 L.J.K.B. 743 (but see Article 48, Illustration 11); *Ardlethan Options Ltd v Easdown* (1916) 20 C.L.R. 285 at 292.

[718] *Fawcett v Whitehouse* (1829) 1 Russ. & M. 132.

[719] *Mahesan v Malaysia Government Officers' Co-operative Housing Society Ltd* [1979] A.C. 374, Il-

firms the contract with the third party,[720] and whether the principal has suffered any loss.[721] A sub-agent is similarly liable despite the absence of privity of contract.[722] In this action the person who gave the bribe is also liable jointly and severally.[723] If the bribe is given in property, older cases say that the agent is liable for the value of the property at the highest value which it had while in the agent's possession.[724] Interest is payable from the date when the bribe was received.[725] The Supreme Court has now determined that the proceeds of bribetaking, where identifiable, are held on constructive trust for the principal.[726] This brings English law into line with other common law jurisdictions.[727] This topic is dealt with in more detail above.[728]

In addition, the agent and the person giving the bribe are jointly and severally liable in deceit for any loss suffered.[729] This action will be preferable to the restitutionary and proprietary claims where the loss suffered exceeds the amount of the bribe, or the bribe has decreased in value; and as regards the action against the agent, where the bribe has not yet been paid. The agent who makes a lossmaking contract for the principal is also likely to be liable for breach of the contract of agency. The principal cannot however recover under all heads and must elect before judgment.[730]

An agent who takes a bribe or secret commission may also find that the right to commission or remuneration that would have otherwise been received is forfeited,

---

lustration 8.

[720] *Logicrose Ltd v Southend United Football Club Ltd* [1988] 1 W.L.R. 1256 at 1263. See too *Marino v FM Capital Partners Ltd* [2020] EWCA Civ 245; [2020] 3 W.L.R. 109.

[721] See *Daraydan Holdings Ltd v Solland International Ltd* [2004] EWHC 622 (Ch); [2005] Ch. 119 at [53].

[722] *Att.-Gen. v Goddard* (1929) 98 L.J.K.B. 743, above; *Powell & Thomas v Evan Jones & Co Ltd* [1905] 1 K.B. 11, Illustration 6 to Article 35; *Daraydan Holdings Ltd v Solland International Ltd* [2004] EWHC 622 (Ch); [2005] Ch. 119 at [52]. A sub-agent may also not be able to plead the head principal's rights as a defence to a claim brought by the sub-principal: see *FM Capital Partners Ltd v Marino* [2018] EWHC 2905 (Comm) at [106] (varied on appeal on other points: [2020] EWCA Civ 245).

[723] *Mahesan's case* [1979] A.C. 374; see Article 78.

[724] *McKay's Case* (1878) 2 Ch.D. 1; *Pearson's Case* (1877) 5 Ch. D. 336; *Nant-y-glo and Blaina Iron Co v Grave* (1878) 12 Ch.D. 738; *Eden v Ridsdales Railway Lamp & Lighting Co Ltd* (1889) 23 Q.B.D. 368; see Illustration 4. It is not clear on what basis a bribe in services would be quantified. An agent will, it seems, be accountable for the market value of a bribe in kind even if the agent asserts that he would not have been willing to pay for the benefit: *Towers v Premier Waste Management Ltd* [2011] EWCA Civ 923 at [48] (use of dumper and excavator on director's private property). See also *Fiona Trust & Holding Corp v Privalov* [2010] EWHC 3199 (Comm) at [1387] (free holiday).

[725] *Nant-y-glo and Blaina Iron Co v Grave* (1878) 12 Ch.D. 738; *Boston Deep Sea Fishing and Ice Co v Ansell* (1888) 39 Ch.D. 339 at 353 and 372 (Illustration 3).

[726] *FHR European Ventures LLP v Cedar Capital Partners LLC* [2014] UKSC 45; [2015] A.C. 250.

[727] See *Att.-Gen. for Hong Kong v Reid* [1994] 1 A.C. 324; *Grimaldi v Chameleon Mining NL (No.2)* (2012) 27 A.L.R. 22.

[728] See above, para.6-042.

[729] *Mahesan's case* [1979] A.C. 374; *Fyffes Group Ltd v Templeman* [2000] 2 Lloyd's Rep. 643; Article 96; (1978) 41 M.L.R. 603; (1978) 94 L.Q.R. 344; Needham (1979) 95 L.Q.R. 536. In *Petrotrade Inc v Smith* [2000] 1 Lloyd's Rep. 486 at [19] David Steel J considered that the action was one in fraud rather than deceit; but see *Kensington International Ltd v Republic of Congo* [2007] EWCA Civ 1128; [2008] 1 Lloyd's Rep. 161 at [62]–[63]; and *Cavell USA Inc v Seaton Insurance Co* [2009] EWCA Civ 1363 at [25].

[730] *Mahesan's case* [1979] A.C. 374; not following dicta in *Salford Corp v Lever* [1891] 1 Q.B. 168; and *Hovenden & Sons v Millhoff* (1900) 83 L.T. 41. See Tettenborn (1979) 95 L.Q.R. 68.

at least where as a result the services performed are valueless[731]; the agent may also lose the right to indemnity.[732] The principal is justified in terminating without notice the contract of any agent who accepts a bribe in the course of the agency[733] and such a termination will still be justifiable, even if the bribery is not discovered until after the agent has been dismissed.[734]

Where the bribed agent knows that the proposed contract is contrary to the principal's interests, or is reckless on that issue, the agent acts dishonestly, and thereby without authority. The contract is likely to be void in such circumstances, and not merely voidable. It would seem, however, that an arbitration clause in such a contract may nonetheless remain valid.[735] In other cases, the contract with the third party will be voidable at the option of the principal.[736] A bribe paid in relation to one contract, however, will not usually give a right in the principal to rescind both that contract and an independent, though related, agreement with the third party made before the inducement occurred.[737] The liability of the agent persists even if the contract is disowned, and where the principal has recovered the bribe money the principal is entitled to keep it and need not give credit for it in the rescission.[738]

Criminal law   Corrupt dealings with agents are a criminal offence. The Bribery   **6-088**
Act 2010 replaced existing offences in this area, both common law and statutory (principally, at common law, criminal conspiracy,[739] and, in statute, the Prevention of Corruption Act 1906, the Public Bodies Corrupt Practices Act 1889 and the Prevention of Corruption Act 1916).

It is beyond the scope of this work to give a detailed treatment of the 2010 Act, and only a bare outline is provided.[740] The Act creates four offences: the paying of bribes (s.1); the receiving of bribes (s.2); the bribery of foreign public officials (s.6); and the failure of commercial organisations to prevent bribery (s.7). The last of

---

[731] See Article 55 and *Cec. McManus Realty Ltd v Bray* (1970) 14 D.L.R. (3d) 564; *Meadow Schama & Co v C. Mitchell & Co Ltd* (1973) 228 E.G. 1511; *Imageview Management Ltd v Jack* [2009] EWCA Civ 63; [2009] 2 All E.R. 666. But not necessarily in respect of other transactions: cf. *Hippisley v Knee Bros* [1905] 1 K.B. 1; *P & OSN Co v Johnson* (1938) 60 C.L.R. 189 at 216–217. And see Article 60.

[732] *Stange & Co v Lowitz* (1898) 14 T.L.R. 468; *Nicholson v J. Mansfield & Co* (1901) 17 T.L.R. 259. See Article 65.

[733] *Bulfield v Fournier* (1895) 11 T.L.R. 282; *Swale v Ipswich Tannery Ltd* (1906) 11 Com. Cas. 88; *Temperley v Blackrod Manufacturing Co Ltd* (1907) 71 J.P. 341; *Federal Supply and Cold Storage Co of South Africa v Angehrn & Piel* (1910) 80 L.J.P.C. 1.

[734] *Boston Deep Sea Fishing & Ice Co v Ansell* (1888) 39 Ch.D. 339, Illustration 3.

[735] *Fiona Trust and Holding Corp v Privalov* [2007] EWCA Civ 20; [2007] 2 Lloyd's Rep. 267 at [26]; affirmed sub nom. *Premium Nafta Products Ltd v Fili Shipping Co Ltd* [2007] UKHL 40; [2007] 4 All E.R. 951; [2007] 2 All E.R. (Comm) 1053. See further above, para.3-012 and below, para.8-021.

[736] See *Taylor v Walker* [1958] 1 Lloyd's Rep. 490; Article 96. See too *Conway v Eze* [2018] EWHC 29 (Ch) at [156]; affirmed on appeal on different grounds [2019] EWCA Civ 88.

[737] *Ross River Ltd v Cambridge City Football Club Ltd* [2007] EWHC 2115 (Ch); [2008] 1 All E.R. 1004 at [228].

[738] *Logicrose v Southend United Football Club* [1988] 1 W.L.R. 1256.

[739] *R. v Barber* (1887) 3 T.L.R. 491. See also *R. v Whitaker* [1914] 3 K.B. 1283; *R. v De Kromme* (1892) 66 L.T. 301 (incitement to conspire).

[740] For more detail, see *Blackstone's Guide to the Bribery Act 2010* (2011); Shea, *The Bribery Act 2010* (2011). For the philosophical background, see Horder (2011) 127 L.Q.R. 37; Arnell and Evans [2015] Jur. Rev. 167. As to the concept of "corruption" that was central to the former legislation, see *R v J* [2013] EWCA Crim 2287; *Field v R.* [2012] 3 N.Z.L.R. 1 (SC), and for earlier authorities the nineteenth edition of this work.

these has no counterpart in the prior law and has far-reaching implications for businesses.

In paraphrase, the first offence turns on the offering, promising or giving of "financial or other advantages" to another, either knowing or believing that acceptance would involve the "improper performance" of "a relevant function or activity", or intending to induce or reward such improper performance. The second offence makes provision for four alternative types of comparable conduct by any party who requests, agrees to receive or accepts such advantages. The concept of "function or activity" embraces functions of a public nature, any activity connected with business or any activity performed in the course of employment or on behalf of a body of persons (corporate or unincorporate), so long as the relevant person is expected to perform it in good faith or impartially, or is otherwise in a position of trust in performing it (s.3). Improper performance is to be judged by the expectations of a reasonable person in the UK, irrespective of where the conduct takes place (ss.4 and 5), unless relevant written law of the foreign jurisdiction permits it.

The offence of bribery of foreign public officials in large part overlaps with the first offence, given the extraterritorial application of both offences. Bribery, as defined, is an offence where the defendant intends thereby to obtain or retain business, or an advantage in the conduct of business.

The offence of failing to prevent bribery can be committed only by commercial organisations (business incorporations or partnerships) that are formed in the UK or which carry on business in the UK. Liability potentially arises whenever an "associated person" of the defendant commits an offence under s.1 or s.6 (whether or not that person has been prosecuted). An associated person is a person who, in any capacity (including without limitation, an employee, agent or subsidiary of the defendant), performs services for or on behalf of the defendant. The offence is one of strict liability, subject only to a defence that the organisation had in place adequate procedures designed to prevent offences under ss.1 and 6.

Illustrations

6-089 (1) The master of a ship receives three payments totalling £45 by way of gratuity for efficient discharge of cargo. This is not a bribe and he may retain the money.[741]

(2) A requested B to provide an outfit for A's son. B did so, and obtained certain discounts, but charged A the full prices. The discounts were disallowed, although B did not charge any commission as an agent.[742]

(3) A director of a company who was a shareholder in two other companies accepted bonuses from such other companies, in consideration of his giving them orders on behalf of the first company. He also took a commission, which was unknown to his company, on a contract for the building of a number of boats. The articles of association provided that the directors might contract with the company. Held, that he was accountable to the company for the bonuses and the secret commission with interest; and that the bribery justi-

---

[741] *The Parkdale* [1897] P. 53.
[742] *Turnbull v Garden* (1869) 38 L.J.Ch. 331. See also *Hippisley v Knee Bros* [1905] 1 K.B. 1, Illustration 5 to Article 60; *North American Land and Timber Co Ltd v Watkins* [1904] 1 Ch. 242; [1904] 2 Ch. 233, Illustration 3 to Article 29.

fied the dismissal of the director, although it was not discovered until after the dismissal.[743]

(4)   The secretary of a company, when making a contract on behalf of the company with the vendor, stipulated that he should receive, and subsequently did receive, from the vendor 600 fully paid-up shares. Held, that he must account to the company for the highest value borne by the shares during the time they were held by him, which in this case was assumed to be the nominal value.[744]

(5)   A director of a company, before the transactions between the promoter and the company had been finally completed, accepted his qualification shares from the promoter. The director had to account to the company for the highest value attributable to the shares during the time they were held by him, with interest on such value from the date the shares were transferred to him to the date of the action.[745] So, if a director receives the money to pay for his qualification shares, he must account for the amount received, with interest from the date of its receipt.[746] Where a promoter sold shares to a director, the director was compelled to account for the difference between the nominal value of the shares and the price he paid for them.[747]

(6)   A assisted B in the negotiations for the building of a ship by C for B, B agreeing to pay A a sum for his services. The negotiations with C were conducted through D, a shipbroker, who was to receive commission from C. Unknown to B, A and D arranged that A should take half of D's commission. Held, B could recover from A the latter's share of the commission.[748]

(7)   A solicitor, who was retained by A to act for him in negotiation for the purchase of a patent, had previously received a commission note from the owner of the patent agreeing to pay him commission in the event of a purchaser being found. A purchased the patent and the solicitor, with A's knowledge, received the commission from the seller. Held, that he was not accountable to A for the commission, having made full disclosure.[749]

(8)   The agent of a housing society, for a bribe of $122,000 arranges that a third party should buy land at a low price and sell it to the society at a profit. The third party buys the land for $456,000 and sells it to the society for $944,000. The society recovers the $122,000 from the agent and also sues him for $443,000, being the third party's net profit. The society must elect between one claim and the other before judgment is entered.[750]

(9)   It was usual for underwriters to allow all intermediaries, for punctual payment of premiums, a percentage as discount, or 12 per cent calculated on the yearly profits, in addition to the ordinary commission of 5 per cent on each

---

[743] *Boston Deep Sea Fishing & Ice Co v Ansell* (1888) 39 Ch.D. 339; see also *Temperley v Blackrod Manufacturing Co Ltd* (1907) 71 J.P. 341.

[744] *McKay's Case* (1875) 2 Ch.D. 1.

[745] *Nant-y-glo & Blaina Iron Co v Grave* (1878) 12 Ch.D. 738; *Pearson's Case* (1877) 5 Ch.D. 336; *Eden v Ridsdale's Railway Lamp & Lighting Co Ltd* (1889) 58 L.J.Q.B. 579; *Mitcalfe's Case* (1879) 13 Ch.D. 169.

[746] *Hay's Case* (1875) L.R. 10 Ch.App. 593; *McLean's Case* (1885) 55 L.J.Ch. 36; cf. *Archer's Case* [1892] 1 Ch. 322.

[747] *Weston's Case* (1879) 10 Ch.D. 579.

[748] *W.A. Phillips, Anderson & Co v Euxine Shipping Co* [1955] 2 Lloyd's Rep. 512.

[749] *Re Haslam and Hier-Evans* [1902] 1 Ch. 765.

[750] *Mahesan v Malaysia Government Officers' Co-operative Housing Society Ltd* [1979] A.C. 374.

reinsurance. A company, having made no inquiry as to the remuneration paid by the underwriters, and not being aware of the 12 per cent allowance, employed Baring Bros as agent to negotiate business. After the agent (who received no remuneration from the company) had been paid the usual allowance of 12 per cent for more than eight years, the company discovered it and claimed to have it paid over to them as secret profit. It was held that they were not entitled to recover.[751]

(10) An agent accepts a bribe in connection with the grant of a concession. The facts are discovered and the agent accounts for most of the bribe to his principal. The principal rescinds the concession. He may keep the bribe: if he has not received it he can still recover it from the agent. He is under no obligation to give credit for it to the third party in the rescission.[752]

Article 50

DUTY TO KEEP PROPERTY OF PRINCIPAL SEPARATE AND DELIVER BUSINESS RECORDS AND CORRESPONDENCE

6-090   It is the duty of an agent—

(1) where the agent holds money or property belonging to the principal, to keep it separate from the agent's own and from that of other persons[753];

(2) to preserve and be constantly ready with correct accounts of all the agent's dealings and transactions in the course of the agency[754];

(3) to produce to the principal upon request, or to a proper person appointed by the principal, all books, correspondence and documents (including emails and other electronic material) under the agent's control relating to the principal's affairs.[755]

Comment

6-091   **(1) Separation of property**   If an agent is entrusted (as trustee) with the money or property of the principal, it must be kept separate from the agent's own. If the agent is sued for an account and has failed to keep the principal's property separate,

---

[751] *Great Western Insurance Co of New York v Cunliffe* (1874) L.R. 9 Ch.App. 525; see also *Leete v Wallace* (1888) 58 L.T. 577; *Norreys v Hodgson* (1897) 13 T.L.R. 421, where an agent who was instructed to procure a loan from an insurance company which required a policy on the life of the principal was held entitled to retain the commission on the policy; *Baring v Stanton* (1876) 3 Ch.D. 502; cf. *Queen of Spain v Parr* (1869) 39 L.J.Ch. 73; *E. Green & Son Ltd v G. Tughan & Co* (1913) 30 T.L.R. 64; cf. *Copp v Lynch* (1882) 26 S.J. 348; *Hurstanger Ltd v Wilson* [2007] EWCA Civ 299; [2007] 1 W.L.R. 2351; [2007] 4 All E.R. 1118 at [36]; *FHR European Ventures LLP v Mankarious* [2011] EWHC 2308 (Ch) at [81]; reversed on other points [2014] UKSC 45; [2015] A.C. 250; *Secretary of State for Justice v Topland Group Plc* [2011] EWHC 983 (QB) at [65]; *Hobbins v Royal Skandia Life Assurance Ltd* [2012] HKCFI 10.

[752] *Logicrose v Southend United Football Club* [1988] 1 W.L.R. 1256.

[753] *Gray v Haig* (1855) 20 Beav. 219; *Clarke v Tipping* (1846) 9 Beav. 284; *Palette Shoes Pty Ltd v Krohn* (1937) 58 C.L.R. 1 at 30; cf. above, para.6-041.

[754] *Gray v Haig* (1855) 20 Beav. 219; *Clarke v Tipping* (1846) 9 Beav. 284; *Pearse v Green* (1819) 1 J. & W. 135; *Turner v Burkinshaw* (1867) L.R. 2 Ch.App. 488; *Collyer v Dudley* (1823) T. & R. 421; *Utz v Carver* [1972] 1 N.S.W.L.R. 407; cf. *Re Lee Ex p. Neville* (1868) L.R. 4 Ch.App. 43.

[755] *Restatement, Third*, § 8.12; *Dadswell v Jacobs* (1887) 34 Ch.D. 278; *Re Burnand Ex p. Baker, Sutton & Co* [1904] 2 K.B. 68 (bankruptcy of agent); *Re Ellis & Ellis* [1908] W.N. 215; 25 T.L.R. 38 (bankruptcy of principal).

the agent will be liable for the contents of the mixture or anything acquired by expenditure from it, up to the value of the input.[756] This obligation only arises, however, in connection with money or property which is beneficially owned by the principal; in such a case the agent will be in the position of a trustee.[757] In other cases however the court will infer that the parties intended the relationship of debtor and creditor, on the ground that a duty to keep money separate would be an unintended restriction on the agent's commercial activity.[758] The duty to keep the principal's money or property separate from that of other parties, is also only presumptive. It is quite common for an agent, such as a solicitor, to run just one trust account for multiple principals.[759]

(2) Accounts An agent is under an obligation to keep an accurate account of all   **6-092**
transactions entered into on the principal's behalf[760] and must be ready at all time to produce it to the principal.[761] If the agent fails to keep and preserve correct accounts, everything is presumed against the agent:

> "In such a case ... I am compelled to ... presume everything most unfavourable to him, which is consistent with the rest of the facts which are admitted or proved."[762]

The agent need not, however, produce records of transactions which do not concern the principal[763] (but the position is otherwise, it seems, when the agent has made it not possible to extricate those relating to the principal from those of other clients[764]), nor need the agent produce detailed items which the principal has agreed expressly or impliedly are not required.[765]

(3) Documents and electronic records and correspondence The principal is   **6-093**

---

[756] See material cited above, para.6-040.
[757] See, e.g. *Burdick v Garrick* (1870) L.R. 5 Ch.App. 233, Illustration 1 to Article 43. The Estate Agents Act 1979 s.13, requires clients' money to be held on trust (but see Article 53 as to interest). The same is the case with solicitors: Solicitors Act 1974 ss.32–33. See above, paras 6-040–6-041; also Murdoch, *The Estate Agents and Property Misdescriptions Acts* (3rd edn); Cordery, *Solicitors*, Division K.
[758] See *Henry v Hammond* [1913] 2 K.B. 515; *Neste Oy v Lloyd's Bank Plc* [1983] 2 Lloyd's Rep. 658; *Walker v Corboy* (1990) 19 N.S.W.L.R. 398; *Paragon Finance Plc v D.B. Thackerar & Co* [1999] 1 All E.R. 400 at 415; and generally above, para.6-041; Article 43, Illustrations 1–5.
[759] See *Lomas v RAB Market Cycles (Master) Fund Ltd* [2009] EWHC 2545 (Ch) at [54].
[760] *Chedworth v Edwards* (1802) 8 Ves. 46; *White v Lincoln* (1803) 8 Ves. 363; *Tindall v Powell* (1858) 32 L.T.(O.S.) 8; and cases cited at fn.754 above. Some agents are under a statutory obligation to keep special forms of accounts and other records, e.g. solicitors under the Solicitors' Accounts Rules 1998; and estate agents under Estate Agents Act 1979 s.21A, as added by Consumers, Estate Agents and Redress Act 2007 s.54. It may be a breach of duty wrongfully to disclose the account to third parties: see *Fogg v Gaulter and Blane* (1960) 110 L.J. 718; *Yasuda Fire and Marine Ins. Co of Europe Ltd v Orion Marine Ins. Underwriting Agency Ltd* [1995] Q.B. 174 (right still existed though contract terminated by repudiatory breach); *Khouj v Acropolis Capital Partners Ltd* [2016] EWHC 2120 (Comm) at [46] and [76] (no need for contract between agent and principal).
[761] *Pearse v Green* (1819) 1 J. & W. 135; *Turner v Burkinshaw* (1867) L.R. 2 Ch.App. 488; *Equitas Ltd v Horace Holman & Co Ltd* [2007] EWHC 903 (Comm) at [27]; *Barkley v Barkley Brown* [2009] NSWSC 76; *Accidia Foundation v Simon C. Dickinson Ltd* [2010] EWHC 3058 (Ch) at [88] (duty to inform principal of gross sale price).
[762] *Gray v Haig* (1855) 20 Beav. 219 at 226, per Romilly MR; see also *Jenkins v Gould* (1827) 3 Russ. 385; *Malhotra v Dhawan* [1997] EWCA Civ 1096; *Ross River Ltd v Waveley Commercial Ltd* [2013] EWCA Civ 910 at [94]; *Keown v Nahoor* [2015] EWHC 3418 (Ch).
[763] *Gerard v Penswick* (1818) 1 Swan. 533; *Heugh v Garrett* (1875) 44 L.J.Ch. 305.
[764] *Equitas Ltd v Horace Holman & Co Ltd* [2007] EWHC 903 (Comm) at [27].
[765] *Hunter v Belcher* (1864) 2 De G.J. & S. 194.

prima facie entitled to have delivered up upon request, and at the termination of the agency, all documents and electronic records and correspondence (together "records") concerning the principal's affairs which have been prepared by the agent in the course of the agency and are retained.[766] It is not necessary for the principal to prove that it owns the records,[767] although where it does not own particular records it seems likely that only a copy need be furnished. In each case it is necessary (unless, as may be the case, the right to the documents is settled by the contract between the parties) to decide whether the document in question came into existence for the purpose of the agency relationship or for some other purpose, e.g. in pursuance of a duty to give professional advice. Thus land agents have been ordered to hand over memorandum books, a private rental and cash book and a field book[768]; an architect was ordered to deliver up the plans of a house after the work had been completed and paid for.[769] Both the land agents and the architect were considered to be acting as agents. But memoranda prepared by quantity surveyors for their own use in measuring up buildings were held to be their own property[770]; and documents, books, maps and plans prepared by rating valuers employed to give advice and assistance to a county council remained the property of the valuers.[771] In one case[772] the Court of Appeal held that working papers, draft and final accounts, notes and calculations and draft tax computations, brought into being by chartered accountants in the course of auditing a company's accounts, were the property of the accountants, the relationship being that of professional person and client; while correspondence between the accountants and the Inland Revenue relating to the company's tax liability was conducted by the accountants as the company's agents, so that original and copy letters comprising such correspondence belonged to the company. Where a document was prepared by the agent for the third party, the agent, though in breach of his duty to his principal in preparing it, was held not bound or entitled to give his principal inspection or possession of it.[773]

What the duties of agents are to preserve records as they arise is a separate question on which there is little authority. Plainly, Rule (2) of Article 50 asserts an obligation to preserve the basic records of all dealings and transactions. Beyond that, it is suggested that an agent should take reasonable steps to maintain records (including copies of correspondence) that might reasonably be expected to be relevant to the ongoing business of the principal, including in relation to disputes with third parties.

The agent may sometimes exercise a lien over documents and other records.[774]

---

[766] *Fairstar Heavy Transport NV v Adkins* [2013] EWCA Civ 886; [2014] F.S.R. 8.

[767] *Fairstar Heavy Transport NV v Adkins* [2013] EWCA Civ 886; [2014] F.S.R. 8. Normally, emails and other correspondence created in the course of the agency would be accessible to the principal but would not be "owned" by him: *Capita Plc v Darch* [2017] EWHC 1248 (Ch); [2017] I.R.L.R. 718 at [70].

[768] *Beresford v Driver* (1851) 14 Beav. 387.

[769] *Gibbon v Pease* [1905] 1 K.B. 810, in which the Court of Appeal held that a custom to the contrary would be unreasonable.

[770] *London School Board v Northcroft* (1889), Hudson's *Building and Engineering Contracts* (12th edn), para.2.235.

[771] *Leicestershire CC v Michael Faraday & Partners* [1941] 2 K.B. 205.

[772] *Chantrey Martin v Martin* [1953] 2 Q.B. 286; and see *Floydd v Cheney* [1970] Ch. 602; *Equitas Ltd v Horace Holman & Co Ltd* [2007] EWHC 903 (Comm) at [28].

[773] *North and South Trust Co v Berkeley* [1971] 1 W.L.R. 470, Illustration 3 to Article 5.

[774] Article 65.

Article 51

Duty to Account

An agent may be required to account in equity to his principal.   **6-094**

Comment

The action of account: history   The action of account was an ancient common   **6-095**
law action first used against bailiffs and receivers.[775] It fell gradually into disuse
when the Court of Chancery began to exercise jurisdiction in matters of account:
the Chancery procedure could be used to compel a defendant to make discovery on
oath and so was superior. It became settled that the action was available not only
against trustees but also against other fiduciaries such as agents.[776]

Before the fusion of law and equity there were various rules to determine when
an action of account lay in equity. Thus if there was a fiduciary situation between
the principal and the agent, or if there was a suspicion of fraud, or if the accounts
were complicated, the agent could be compelled to account in equity: otherwise,
the principal could only bring an action in the courts of common law.[777] Since the
Judicature Acts, however, any division of the High Court has the jurisdiction
originally vested in the previous courts of Common Law and Chancery. By virtue
of s.61 of and Sch.1 to the Senior Courts Act 1981, actions for an account are usually to be assigned to the Chancery Division.[778]

Substantive significance   The duty to account is in this sense simply a liability   **6-096**
to the exercise of certain sorts of procedures used in courts of equity for the
ascertainment of the true position between trustee or other fiduciary and beneficiary.
As such it can be regarded as no more than a procedure ancillary to the ascertainment of other rights[779]: though the remedy does of course provide a sanction for,
and hence the basis of, the duty to keep accounts and make them available to the
principal.[780] However, the liability to account in equity has also a certain substantive significance in that it may lead to a judgment of the court for payment of the
money shown to be due on the account, whether arising from liabilities for breach
of trust, constructive trust, contract, etc. or on other grounds such as tracing. Further,
when the agent cannot explain exactly what has happened to money or property,
presumptions may be made against the agent which will lead to substantive liabilities in the agent.[781] These old presumptions are founded on an assumption that
it is the agent who in all respects will be in possession of the facts, not the principal.

---

[775] See Fifoot, *History and Sources of the Common Law* (1952), pp.268–277; Jackson, *History of Quasi-Contract* (1936), pp.9–17; Stoljar, pp.299–300; (1964) 80 L.Q.R. 203.
[776] See in general *Snell's Equity* (34th edn), para.20-004 onwards; *Meagher, Gummow and Lehane's Equity Doctrines and Remedies* (5th edn), Ch.26. See too *John Youngs Insurance Services Ltd v Aviva Insurance Service UK Ltd* [2011] EWHC 1515 (TCC); *McGann v Bisping* [2017] EWHC 2951 (Comm) at [295].
[777] See especially *Foley v Hill* (1848) 2 H.L.Cas. 28; *Navulshaw v Brownrigg* (1852) 2 De G.M. & G. 441.
[778] And see *Civil Procedure* (2005), Vol.1, 25.1.38, Vol.2, [1-88].
[779] This is borne out by the wording of s.23 of the Limitation Act 1980, which refers to the "claim which is the basis of the duty to account". See *Libertarian Investments Ltd v Hall* [2013] HKCFA 93 at [167]–[168], per Lord Millett. See also Conaglen (2016) 40 Melb. U.L.R. 126.
[780] Article 50.
[781] See *GHLM Trading Ltd v Maroo* [2012] EWHC 61 (Ch) at [148]; *Re Mumtaz Properties Ltd, Wet-*

It will be the agent who is handling the moneys relating to the principal's business, and in many cases the acts of the agent will also have created the transactions to which the principal is a party. The principal, in other words, will be the vulnerable party. This may not always be the case, such as where it is the principal who stipulates and provides the accounting system to be used by the agent to keep records, and it turns out that the computer software driving the system is defective. Caution is needed to prevent injustice arising from the unquestioning application of these presumptions; records created by the system will not bind the agent if it is unconscionable for them to do so.[782]

It is also frequently said that the agent has a general fiduciary obligation to account for profits. Although on orthodox doctrine claims in pursuance of such an obligation are traditionally regarded as proprietary, and amount to claims to profits attributable to what has been designated as the principal's property,[783] a more general and less precise notion of accounting (which is particularly relied on in some cases relating to confidential information[784]) has assisted also in the development of an equitable action in personam against the agent, which does not carry the sometimes inappropriate consequences on bankruptcy of the agent which would follow from a true proprietary claim.[785]

6-097   **The account**   The actual taking of accounts can be a long and complex matter, and it has been said in the context of dissolution of partnership that such a judgment may be "often oppressive".[786]

An agent will usually be held to be bound by the agent's own accounts; thus if they show that the agent has credited the principal with money received, the agent will be presumed to have received that money and will be liable for it to the principal.[787] But the agent will not be liable if the account shows that the money has not, in fact, been received,[788] or if the principal's accounts show that the agent has not received the money.[789] Similarly, if the agent, after submitting an account which shows money in the agent's hands, later corrects the accounts and the principal does

---

ton v Ahmed [2011] EWCA Civ 610 at [16]; *Ross River Ltd v Waveley Commercial Ltd* [2013] EWCA Civ 910 at [94]. cf. *Exsus Travel Ltd v Turner* [2014] EWCA Civ 1331 at [24] (account should not be an instrument of oppression of agent).

[782] See *Bates v Post Office Ltd (No 3)* [2019] EWHC 606 (QB) at [851] and [1113] (principal owed duties of good faith to its agents).

[783] See above, para.6-042.

[784] See above, paras 6-077 and 6-079.

[785] See above, paras 6-077 and 6-079; *Warman International Pty Ltd v Dwyer* (1995) 182 C.L.R. 544 at 556–557; *Paragon Finance Plc v D.B. Thackerar & Co* [1999] 1 All E.R. 400 at 416. See further the explanation put forward by the Rt Hon. Lord Millett (1998) 114 L.Q.R. 214 at 225–227; but cf. Getzler, in *Restitution and Equity* (Birks and Rose eds, 2000), pp.248–250. See also above, paras 6-040 and 6-041.

[786] *Lindley and Banks on Partnership* (20th edn), para.25-32. See also *Docker v Somes* (1834) 2 My. & K. 655 at 673; *Wedderburn v Wedderburn* (1838) 4 My. & Cr. 41.

[787] *Shaw v Picton* (1825) 4 B. & C. 715. See also *Shaw v Woodcock* (1827) 7 B. & C. 73 (where the submission of accounts showing amounts received and allowing the principal to draw on the agent for the amounts was held sufficient evidence to go to the jury to establish a personal obligation on the agent to pay); *Skyring v Greenwood* (1825) 4 B. & C. 281; *Owens v Kirby* (1861) 30 Beav. 31; *Cave v Mills* (1862) 7 H. & N. 913.

[788] *Shaw v Dartnall* (1826) 6 B. & C. 56 at 65.

[789] *Shaw v Dartnall* (1826) 6 B. & C. 56 at 65–66.

not disagree with such correction,[790] or if the agent shows a mistake was made, the agent will not be accountable to the principal.[791]

In an action of account the agent will be allowed to deduct all reasonable expenses incurred on the principal's behalf,[792] unless such deduction is contrary to the terms of the agency agreement.[793] An account will also take account of any benefits derived by the principal from the agent's activities, but the onus rests on the agent to establish that the principal did derive a benefit.[794]

Account stated   If an account is agreed, the principal can sue on an account stated.   **6-098**
This may be a mere acknowledgment of a debt, and in that case the agent may show that no such debt in fact existed; or it may be an account containing debts on both sides in which the parties have agreed that the debts of one should be set against the debts of the other and only the balance paid. In the latter case the agent may only dispute the account where there are items which, if paid, would be recoverable by the agent on the basis of a total failure of consideration.[795] This second form of account stated is also called a settled account. It is not always clear when an account will be held a settled account.[796] There must be mutual debts, since if all the accounting has to be done by one party, there cannot be a settling of accounts.[797] Once the principal has approved the accounts, they are settled,[798] and if the principal enters the account as agreed in its books and either pays the balance or recognises in some other way that the account is correct, there is also a settled account.[799] It has been held that a principal who received an account and kept it for two years without objection could not later maintain it was not a settled account.[800] But there will not be a settled account where a principal allows part of the agent's claim but is silent as to the rest.[801]

The general rule is that settled accounts will not be reopened,[802] but the principal may be given leave to surcharge and falsify them, if they are drawn up under a mistake.[803] Thus, where a partnership account recorded £1,950 as lent to the

[790] *Shaw v Dartnall* (1826) 6 B. & C. 56 at 65–66.
[791] *Shaw v Picton* (1825) 4 B. & C. 715; *Dails v Lloyd* (1848) 12 Q.B. 531; cf. *Worrall v Peters* (1902) 32 S.C.R. 52.
[792] *Dale v Sollet* (1767) 4 Burr. 2133 (expenses of fighting an action for principal); *East India Co v Blake* (1673) C.Temp.F. 117 (entertainment expenses); cf. *Baring v Stanton* (1876) 3 Ch.D. 502.
[793] See *Bath v Standard Land Co Ltd* [1911] 1 Ch. 618.
[794] *Amaltal Corp Ltd v Maruha Corp* [2007] 3 N.Z.L.R. 192 at [30], Illustration 14 to Article 43.
[795] *Siqueira v Noronha* [1934] A.C. 332; *Laycock v Pickles* (1863) 4 B. & S. 497.
[796] See *Bates v Post Office Ltd (No 3)* [2019] EWHC 606 (QB) at [817] (contract had comprehensive accounting method).
[797] *Anglo-American Asphalt Co Ltd v Crowley Russell & Co Ltd* [1945] 2 All E.R. 324; *Equitas Ltd v Horace Holman & Co Ltd* [2007] EWHC 903 (Comm) at [91].
[798] *East India Co v Mainston* (1676) 2 Cas. in Cha. 218.
[799] *Ovington v Bell* (1812) 3 Camp. 237; *Hunter v Belcher* (1864) 2 De G.J. & S. 194; *McKellar v Wallace* (1853) 8 Moo.P.C. 378.
[800] *Tickel v Short* (1751) 2 Ves.Sen. 239; but see the Canadian case of *Smith v Redford* (1872) 19 Grant 274.
[801] *Farquhar v East India Co* (1845) 8 Beav. 260.
[802] *Parkinson v Hanbury* (1867) L.R. 2 H.L. 1. See also *Re Webb* [1894] 1 Ch. 73.
[803] *Mozeley v Cowie* (1877) 47 L.J.Ch. 271; *Hardwicke v Vernon* (1798–99) 4 Ves. 411; *Gething v Keighley* (1878) 9 Ch.D. 547; *Cheese v Keen* [1908] 1 Ch. 245; the Rt Hon. Lord Millett (1998) 114 L.Q.R. 214 at 225–227.

plaintiff, whereas only £1,000 was in fact advanced, it was held that the amount could be corrected without the whole account being reopened.[804]

But where the agent has been guilty of fraud (whether legal or equitable)[805] or the accounts have been settled under undue influence,[806] the accounts may be reopened from the commencement of the agency. In such cases lapse of time is no defence and proof of one fraudulent overcharge has been held sufficient to entitle the principal to have the agent's accounts reopened for a period of 20 years.[807] When accounts have been drawn up between fiduciaries and their beneficiaries, the courts have been astute to reopen them if there is any suspicion of underhand dealing.[808] So, where there were incorrect entries, and amounts unexplained and unaccounted for in the accounts of a deceased agent of a company, who was also a large shareholder in the company, his accounts were reopened after his death for a period of 25 years.[809]

The illegality of a transaction entered into by an agent is not a bar to an action by the principal for an account,[810] unless the contract of agency is itself illegal, in which case money paid to the agent may be irrecoverable.[811]

Article 52

COMMON LAW DUTY TO PAY OVER MONEY HELD FOR PRINCIPAL

6-099   Subject to the provisions of Article 70, an agent who holds or receives money for the principal is bound to pay over or account for that money at the request of the principal, notwithstanding claims made by third persons, even if the money has been received in respect of a void or illegal transaction.[812]

Comment

6-100   The principle expressed in this Article is a principle of common law which applies wherever an agent holds money for the principal. Thus if the agent has received money on the principal's behalf, or receives it for a particular purpose

---

[804] *Gething v Keighley* (1878) 9 Ch.D. 547; cf. *Daniell v Sinclair* (1881) 6 App.Cas. 181.

[805] *Beaumont v Boultbee* (1800) 5 Ves. 485; *Clarke v Tipping* (1846) 9 Beav. 284, as mentioned by Jessel MR in *Williamson v Barbour* (1877) 9 Ch.D. 529; *Hardwicke v Vernon* (1808) 14 Ves. 504; *Walsham v Stainton* (1863) 1 De G.J. & S. 678.

[806] *Watson v Rodwell* (1879) 11 Ch.D. 150; *Coleman v Mellersh* (1850) 2 Mac. & G. 309; *Lewes v Morgan* (1817) 5 Price 42; *Jones v Moffett* (1846) 3 J. & L. 636; *Ward v Sharp* (1883) 53 L.J.Ch. 313.

[807] *Williamson v Barbour* (1877) 9 Ch.D. 529; *Coleman v Mellersh* (1850) 2 Mac. & G. 309.

[808] *Williamson v Barbour* (1877) 9 Ch.D. 529; *Re Webb* [1894] 1 Ch. 73; *Cheese v Keen* [1908] 1 Ch. 245; cf. *Newman v Payne* (1793) 2 Ves. 199; *Equitas Ltd v Horace Holman & Co Ltd* [2007] EWHC 903 (Comm) at [92].

[809] *Stainton v Carron Co* (1857) 24 Beav. 346.

[810] *Williams v Trye* (1854) 18 Beav. 366; *Close v Wilson* [2011] EWCA Civ 5.

[811] *Knowles v Haughton* (1805) 11 Ves. 168; *Battersby v Smyth* (1818) 3 Madd. 110; *Sykes v Beadon* (1879) 11 Ch.D. 170; and see Article 52.

[812] See this Article discussed in *Martin v Pont* [1993] 3 N.Z.L.R. 25, Illustration 4; *Edgell v Day* (1865) L.R. 1 C.P. 80; *Blaustein v Maltz Mitchell & Co* [1937] 2 K.B. 142, Illustration 7 to Article 56; *Eames v Hacon* (1881) 18 Ch.D. 347, Illustration 6 to Article 54; *Nickolson v Knowles* (1820) 5 Madd. 47; *Harsant v Blaine, Macdonald & Co* (1887) 56 L.J.Q.B. 511; *Eisentrager v Lyneham* [1952] St. R. Qd. 232; *Sharma v Mundath* [2019] NZHC 24 at [97]; *Crown Prosecution Service v Aquila Advisory Ltd* [2019] EWCA Civ 588 at [25].

which the agent does not carry out, the principal can sue the agent in restitution.[813] Further, if the principal has entrusted money to the agent for a particular purpose which the agent has not carried out, the principal can recover that money on the same basis.[814] When available, such common law actions in restitution have long been alternatives to an account.[815] Where the money can be regarded as held in trust, however, a proprietary remedy will be available, and may be more advantageous.[816] Liability to account is prima facie strict, and does not turn on proof of want of care,[817] but a reasonable time to effect payment over may need to be allowed for. Liability in tort on the basis of an assumption of responsibility may in some cases provide an alternative claim.[818] It has been held that, in some circumstances at least, the duty to account is a continuing one, with in consequence a moving limitation date.[819]

The principal cannot make a claim in restitution until the agent has either received the money[820]; or has been credited with it in the agent's own account with a third party.[821] This does not mean that the principal must wait until the agent admits that the money has been received; if, for example, the principal employs an agent to sell goods for it and the agent does not account to the principal within a reasonable time, it may be presumed in the absence of evidence to the contrary that the agent has received money for the goods.[822] It is not settled whether demand has to be made by the principal for the money before it can start its action against the agent, but on general principles it seems that the right to money held to the principal's use accrues as soon as it comes into the agent's hands and that no demand should be necessary.[823] It may be, however, that a claim for interest on such a claim will only run from the date of a demand for payment and its refusal.[824] At

---

[813] See Powell, pp.324–326. Article 48. See, e.g. *Al Khudairi v Abbey Brokers Ltd* [2010] EWHC 1486 (Ch) at [117]; [2010] P.N.L.R. 32 (misapplication by mortgage broker of moneys received for principal).

[814] *Parry v Roberts* (1835) 3 A. & E. 118; *Hill v Smith* (1844) 12 M. & W. 618; *Martin v Pont* [1993] 3 N.Z.L.R. 25; *Napier v Torbay Holdings Ltd* [2016] NZCA 608 at [20]. cf. *Thomas v Da Costa* (1818) 8 Taunt. 345; *Livingstone v Elmslie* (1902) 21 N.Z.L.R. 640 (money paid by husband to be paid to wife on her obtaining a divorce could not be recovered); *Abraaj Investment Management Ltd v Bregawn Jersey Ltd* [2010] EWHC 630 (Comm). Probably an action in restitution will not lie against an agent entrusted with money for a particular purpose until the agent violates his duty by applying it for some other purpose, or otherwise shows an intention not to be bound by his obligation: *Hardman v Bellhouse* (1842) 9 M. & W. 596; *Ehrensperger v Anderson* (1848) 3 Exch. 148; *Whitehead v Howard* (1820) 2 B. & B. 372. See too *Zhong v Wang* (2007) N.Z.C.P.R. 488.

[815] Stoljar, pp.301–302.

[816] See above, paras 6-040 and 6-041.

[817] *Equitas Ltd v Walsham Brothers & Co Ltd* [2013] EWHC 3264 (Comm) at [49].

[818] *Equitas Ltd v Walsham Brothers & Co Ltd* [2013] EWHC 3264 (Comm) at [58].

[819] *Equitas Ltd v Walsham Brothers & Co Ltd* [2013] EWHC 3264 (Comm) at [71], perhaps a rather surprising conclusion, outside cases involving breach of trust.

[820] *Varden v Parker* (1798) 2 Esp. 710.

[821] *Andrew v Robinson* (1812) 3 Camp. 199; but if the principal and the third party have a common agent, an entry in the books of such agent will not be conclusive: see *McLarty v Middleton* (1858) 6 W.R. 379; 9 W.R. 861.

[822] *Hunter v Welsh* (1816) 1 Stark. 224.

[823] There are confusing dicta in actions for money paid under a mistake of fact: see *Freeman v Jeffries* (1869) L.R. 4 Ex. 189; *Baker v Courage & Co* [1910] 1 K.B. 56.

[824] See, e.g. *Edgell v Day* (1865) L.R. 1 C.P. 80; *Harsant v Blaine, Macdonald & Co* (1887) 56 L.J.Q.B. 511. See also Article 52.

the same time, an implied term to account promptly will often be appropriate, for breach of which damages may be available.[825]

Agents usually discharge their liability by handing over the money or property they have received to their principal, but they may also pay a third party in accordance with the principal's instructions[826]; they will also be discharged if they pay a third party in obedience to the instructions of the court.[827] Furthermore, an agent, in accounting for money received for the principal, is entitled to set off all just allowances and any sums expended by the agent in that connection with the authority of the principal,[828] even if they were spent for an unlawful purpose[829]; but if the authority to deal with the money in an unlawful manner is revoked before the agent has used the money, the principal can recover.[830]

Even though the agent receives money for the principal in respect of a transaction which is void or illegal, the principal can sue the agent in restitution. Thus if an agent was employed to make bets and won money, the agent was under a duty to pay it over to the principal, although the betting transactions were themselves void[831]; similarly, if an agent is employed to sell shares, the agent cannot retain the money received by saying that the sale is illegal by Act of Parliament.[832] Even if the contract between the principal and agent is itself illegal, then the principal may be able to recover any money received by the agent. Formerly, the money would have been irrecoverable under the ex turpi causa principle, but the law has now been changed.[833]

Where money is wrongfully obtained by an agent or is paid to the agent under a mistake of fact the agent can resist an action by the principal on the grounds that it has been repaid to the person who paid it to the agent[834]; and where money is paid to an agent in respect of a voidable contract, the agent can show that the contract

825 See *Equitas Ltd v Walsham Brothers & Co Ltd* [2013] EWHC 3264 (Comm) at [47] and [125].
826 *McCarthy v Colvin* (1839) 9 A. & E. 607; *Blyth v Whiffin* (1872) 27 L.T. 330 at 333.
827 *Brown v Farebrother* (1888) 58 L.J.Ch. 3.
828 *Dale v Sollett* (1767) 4 Burr. 2133; *Curtis v Barclay* (1826) 5 B. & C. 141; *Wemys v Greenwood, Cox and Hammersley* (1827) 5 L.J.(O.S.) K.B. 257; *Potter v Fowler* (1837) 6 L.J.Ch. 273; *Cropper v Cook* (1868) L.R. 3 C.P. 194; *Roxburghe v Cox* (1881) 17 Ch.D. 520; cf. *Monkwearmouth Flour Mill Co Ltd v Lightfoot* (1897) 13 T.L.R. 327; *Dorf v Neumann, Luebeck & Co* (1924) 40 T.L.R. 405; *Bath v Standard Land Co Ltd* [1911] 1 Ch. 618. The agent cannot retain money where the agent's right to do so has not yet accrued: *Wilkinson v North Surburban Properties Ltd* [1959] E.G.D. 218. In contracts for work and labour the defendant may have the right to make deductions in respect of defective performance of contractual services: see, e.g. *Hanak v Green* [1958] 2 Q.B. 9. Such deductions cannot be made in respect of a claim for marine freight: *Aries Tanker Corp v Total Transport Ltd (The Aries)* [1977] 1 W.L.R. 185; and this exception has been held to apply also to a claim against an agent for freight: *James & Co v Chinecrest Ltd* [1979] 1 Lloyd's Rep. 126.
829 *Bayntun v Cattle* (1833) 1 Moo. & R. 265.
830 *Bone v Ekless* (1860) 5 H. & N. 925; *Taylor v Bowers* (1876) 1 Q.B.D. 291.
831 *De Mattos v Benjamin* (1894) 63 L.J.Q.B. 248, Illustration 3; *Bridger v Savage* (1885) 15 Q.B.D. 363; overruling *Beyer v Adams* (1857) 26 L.J.Ch. 841. But cf. *A.R. Dennis & Co v Campbell* [1978] Q.B. 365. The basis of these cases is removed by the validation of betting and gaming transactions by the Gambling Act 2005.
832 *Bousfield v Wilson* (1846) 16 M. & W. 185; *Tenant v Elliot* (1797) 1 B. & P. 3; *Farmer v Russell* (1798) 1 B. & P. 296; *Sharp v Taylor* (1849) 2 Ph. 801; see also *Sykes v Beadon* (1879) 11 Ch.D. 170; *Thomson v Thomson* (1802) 7 Ves. 470; *Crown Prosecution Service v Aquila Advisory Ltd* [2019] EWCA Civ 588 at [25].
833 See now *Patel v Mirza* [2016] UKSC 42; [2017] A.C. 46. For the earlier position, see *Booth v Hodgson* (1795) 6 T.R. 405; *Catlin v Bell* (1815) 4 Camp. 183; *Knowles v Haughton* (1805) 11 Ves. 168; *Battersby v Smyth* (1818) 3 Madd. 110, with which cf. *Davenport v Whitmore* (1836) 2 My. & Cr. 177; *Harry Parker Ltd v Mason* [1940] 2 K.B. 590; and, Illustration 2.
834 See Article 111 and Comment.

has been rescinded and the money repaid, even where the contract was rescinded solely on the ground of the agent's own fraud.[835]

Where an agent is appointed by two or more persons jointly, there is no discharge unless the agent accounts to them all, except where the principals are partners.[836] But an agent who has been severally appointed by one person cannot refuse to account separately to that person on the ground that others are jointly interested in the money in the agent's hands.[837]

Illustrations

(1) B granted an annuity to C and D guaranteed the payment of the instalments. **6-101** B was in arrears with his instalments and at the same time owed money for another reason to C's agent, E. E made an application to B and D for the payment of the instalments and as a result of this application and D's insistence B paid a sum of money to E. Held, E could not keep the money as payment for his own debt but had received it on C's behalf and must account for it to C.[838]

(2) An agent sells a horse and receives the purchase money. The sale is subsequently rescinded on the ground of the agent's fraud, and the purchase money is repaid. The agent is not liable to the principal for the amount of the purchase money.[839]

(3) A factor raises money by wrongfully pledging the goods of his principal. The principal may adopt the transaction, and treat the money raised as money had and received to his use.[840]

(4) P gives money to an accountant to invest. The accountant's daughter misappropriates it. The accountant is liable for its return.[841]

Article 53

LIABILITY FOR INTEREST

(1) Where an agent holds money which belongs in law or equity to the principal, **6-102** any interest earned in respect of that money belongs to the principal, and the agent must account to the principal for it.[842]

(2) Subject to the discretion of the court under s.35A of the Senior Courts Act 1981 an agent who receives money in breach of fiduciary duties, or who fails to pay the principal on demand, must pay interest on it from the date of default.

---

[835] *Murray v Mann* (1848) 2 Exch. 538, Illustration 2; cf. *Stevens v Legh* (1853) 2 C.L.R. 251 and *Field v Allen* (1842) 9 M. & W. 694.

[836] *Lee v Sankey* (1872) L.R. 15 Eq. 204; *Innes v Stephenson* (1831) 1 M. & R. 145; *Trajkovski v Simpson* [2019] NSWCA 52. cf. *Husband v Davis* (1851) 10 C.B. 645. See Article 11.

[837] *Roberts v Ogilby* (1821) 9 Price 269; and see *Suart v Welch* (1839) 4 Myl. & Cr. 305; Article 54.

[838] *Shaw v Picton* (1825) 4 B. & C. 715.

[839] *Murray v Mann* (1848) 2 Exch. 538.

[840] *Bonzi v Stewart* (1842) 5 Scott N.R. 1 at 26; 4 M. & G. 295.

[841] *Martin v Pont* [1993] 3 N.Z.L.R. 25: see Stevens [2005] L.M.C.L.Q. 101 at 118.

[842] See a critical analysis by Elliott [2001] Conv. 313.

Comment

6-103 **Rule (1)** If the agent holds money as trustee for the principal, the agent may not keep personally anything earned with that money.[843] The claim for interest is alternative to a proprietary claim for profits[844] and sometimes merely interest is claimed because of the difficulty of establishing what the profits are, or because the result has been not to make a profit but to effect a saving. When the agent is under a duty to invest and does not do so, the agent may under this head be liable for the interest which should have been received.[845] It is not, however, clear exactly when such a duty arises; there are dicta suggesting that a holder of trust money is always liable for interest if the holder knows that the money has this character,[846] but there are cases holding that there is no liability where it is proved that no profit was made.[847]

6-104 **Stakeholders** In *Potters (A Firm) v Loppert*[848] Pennycuick V-C held that an estate agent was under no obligation to account for the interest earned by the agent on a sum deposited with him to hold as stakeholder. The decision related to a precontract deposit, but the reasoning applies equally to contract deposits. The basis of the decision was that the agent was not a trustee and was liable only in contract or restitution. A better reason for the rule might be that although the agent holds as trustee, there is a usage that the agent is entitled to the income in return for the services in holding the deposit.[849] The rule is of ancient origin[850] and it is open to question whether such a rule is appropriate to modern times, particularly in view of the size of some deposits on commercial and other property. In relation to estate agents, it is now however provided by the Estate Agents Act 1979 that money received in the course of estate agency work by way of pre-contract or contract deposit is held on trust[851] and must be paid into a client account[852]; there is provi-

---

[843] See *Att.-Gen. v Alford* (1855) 4 De G.M. & G. 843; *Brown v IRC* [1965] A.C. 244; above, para.6-040 onwards.

[844] *Re Davis* [1902] 2 Ch. 314.

[845] *Burdick v Garrick* (1870) L.R. 5 Ch.App. 233, Illustration 2. As to the amount of interest see *Snell's Equity* (34th edn), para.30-020.

[846] *Moons v De Barnales* (1826) 1 Russ. 301; *Att.-Gen. v Alford* (1855) 4 De G.M. & G. 843 at 851; and see Finn, *Fiduciary Obligations* (1977), pp.114–115.

[847] e.g. *Turner v Burkinshaw* (1867) L.R. 2 Ch.App. 488.

[848] *Potters (A Firm) v Loppert* [1973] Ch. 399; *Manzanilla Ltd v Corton Property and Investments Ltd* Unreported November 13, 1996, CA, per Millett LJ); *The Governor and Company of The Bank of Scotland v Truman* [2005] EWHC 583 (QB).

[849] See Goode (1976) 92 L.Q.R. at 371.

[850] Pennycuick VC followed *Harrington v Hoggart* (1830) 1 B. & Ad. 577, a case concerning an auctioneer decided in the Court of King's Bench which was a claim in assumpsit not based upon principles of equity. However, the court cited an unreported dictum of Lord Eldon and upon this basis said that their decision was not at variance with any rule of equity. (Yet the case had been argued partly on the basis that the agent was a trustee and therefore not obliged to obey the instructions of the vendor to put the money out to earn interest). The defendant auctioneer was treated as if he were a banker and his position was contrasted with that of an agent. See also below, Illustrations 1–3 to Article 111; *Royal Norwegian Government v Calcutta Marine Engineering Co Ltd* [1960] 2 Lloyd's Rep. 431.

[851] Estate Agents Act 1979 ss.12 and 13. "Estate agency work" is defined in s.1 and applies only to some of the work performed by estate agents. See in general Murdoch, *The Estate Agents and Property Misdescriptions Acts* (3rd edn), Ch.13D; *Law of Estate Agency* (5th edn), Ch.6.

[852] Estate Agents Act 1979 s.14.

sion for the making of accounts regulations requiring payment of interest.[853] These
detailed requirements supersede the normal consequences of a trusteeship in such
cases[854]; but the regulations made do not in fact require payment of interest on
money received as stakeholder.[855]

Solicitors A solicitor may hold property on trust, depending on the
circumstances.[856] In many cases however money held for clients is paid into general
client account. In *Brown v IRC*[857] it was held that the solicitor had no right to the
interest earned on such money, whatever the difficulty of accounting as between the
clients concerned. The matter was subsequently regulated by statute[858] under which
rules may be made providing for payment of interest on client accounts[859]: beyond
this no interest is due.[860] It is apparently assumed that these rules are not applicable to money received as stakeholder.
    6-105

Financial services For details on this topic the reader is referred to specialised
works.[861]
    6-106

Rate of interest The rate of interest may vary in accordance with whether the
agent has, or may be presumed to have, made more money by the breach, or
whether the misconduct is serious, as where there is fraud or breach of fiduciary
duty.[862] Old cases used 4 per cent on the basic simple interest rate, with 5 per cent
and compound interest for the special cases. However, in periods where general
interest rates have been higher, such higher rates have been ordered.[863]
    6-107

Rule (2) In general there was no right to interest on money received for a principal
and not held in trust unless the agent was guilty of a breach of fiduciary obligation
or refused to pay the principal on demand. In these latter cases there was such a
right in equity though not at common law,[864] and the same considerations as those
mentioned above were applicable in calculating the rate of interest. The decisions
on this point were largely rendered obsolete by s.3 of the Law Reform (Miscellaneous Provisions) Act 1934, which gave the court a wide discretion to award interest
    6-108

---

[853] Estate Agents Act 1979 s.15.
[854] Estate Agents Act 1979 s.13(3).
[855] See Estate Agents (Accounts) Regulations 1981 (SI 1981/1520) reg.7.
[856] See, e.g. *Burdick v Garrick* (1870) L.R. 5 Ch.App. 233, Illustration 2.
[857] *Brown v IRC* [1965] A.C. 244, Illustration 1.
[858] See Solicitors Act 1974 ss.32 and 33 as amended.
[859] Solicitors' Accounts Rules 1998.
[860] Solicitors Act 1974 s.33(3).
[861] See above, para.6-060.
[862] See *Burdick v Garrick* (1870) L.R. 5 Ch.App. 233 at 241–242; *Wallersteiner v Moir (No.2)* [1975]
Q.B. 373 at 397; *Westdeutsche Landesbank Girozentrale v Islington LBC* [1996] A.C. 669; *Herbert
Equities Ltd v Mamfredos* [2009] NZHC 128; *Herrod v Johnston* [2013] 2 Qd R. 102 at [50];
Libertarian Investments Ltd v Hall [2013] HKCFA 93 at [141] (simple interest only); *Glenn v Watson*
[2018] EWHC 2483 (Ch). *Snell's, Equity* (34th edn), para.30-020; Finn, *Fiduciary Obligations*
(1977), pp.115–117.
[863] *Wallersteiner v Moir (No. 2)*, above. And see *O'Sullivan v Management Agency and Music Ltd*
[1985] Q.B. 428; and *Sempra Metals Ltd v IRC* [2007] UKHL 34; [2008] 1 A.C. 561.
[864] See e.g. *Pearse v Green* (1819) 1 J. & W. 135; *Wolfe v Findlay* (1847) 6 Hare 66; *Edgell v Day* (1865)
L.R. 1 C.P. 80; *Harsant v Blaine, Macdonald & Co* (1887) 56 L.J.Q.B. 511; *Boston Deep Sea Fishing and Ice Co v Ansell* (1888) 39 Ch.D. 339; *Barclay v Harris* (1915) 85 L.J.K.B. 115; *Webster v
British Empire Mutual Life Assurance Co* (1880) 15 Ch.D. 169; *Accidia Foundation v Simon C.
Dickinson Ltd* [2010] EWHC 3058 (Ch) at [97] (compound interest).

on all or any part of any debt or damages for which judgment is given at such rate as it thinks fit for the whole or any part of the period between the date when the cause of action arose and judgment. These powers are now contained in the Senior Courts Act 1981 as amended.[865] The 1934 provision used the words "proceedings tried" and thus did not apply to a default judgment, nor perhaps to certain other situations. In such cases it was sometimes still necessary to rely on the equitable rather than on the statutory jurisdiction.[866] The wording of the (amended) Senior Courts Act, referring simply to "proceedings ... before the High Court", is wider.[867]

Illustrations

6-109 (1) A solicitor held sums of money on deposit in his clients' account. This account earned interest which, in accordance with common practice, the solicitor kept for himself as part of the profits of his firm. Held, the solicitor was in a fiduciary position in relation to his clients and that the interest accordingly belonged to them. The practice of the solicitor retaining the interest for himself could not be permitted.[868]

(2) A solicitor was authorised by power of attorney to sell certain property and invest the proceeds. He paid the proceeds into the account of his firm, who made use of the money. Held, that he must pay interest at the rate of 5 per cent.[869]

(3) An agent, who undertook to invest his principal's money in the funds, kept large balances in his hands. Held, that he must pay interest on such balances.[870]

3. ESTOPPEL AS TO PRINCIPAL'S TITLE

Article 54

AGENT'S ESTOPPEL AS TO PRINCIPAL'S TITLE

6-110 (1) Where an agent is in possession of property in the agent's capacity as such, the agent is estopped from asserting a better title to it than the principal, for the agent's possession is deemed to be that of the principal.[871]

(2) An agent is estopped from asserting that a third party has a better right than the principal to receive money held by the agent for or on account of the principal or otherwise owed by the agent to the principal.[872]

(3) But an agent who is a bailee of chattels from the principal as bailor may in an action by the principal for wrongful interference with them show that a third

---

[865] Senior Courts Act 1981 s.35A, inserted by Administration of Justice Act 1982 s.15. See also County Courts Act 1984 s.69(1), as amended.

[866] See *Wallersteiner v Moir (No.2)* [1975] Q.B. 373; *Gardener Steel Ltd v Sheffield Bros (Profiles) Ltd* [1978] 1 W.L.R. 916.

[867] *President of India v La Pintada Compania Navigacion SA (The La Pintada)* [1985] A.C. 104; cf. *Hungerfords v Walker* (1989) 171 C.L.R. 125. Interest may sometimes also be due under the Late Payment of Commercial Debts (Interest) Act 1998.

[868] *Brown v IRC* [1965] A.C. 244. The problems presented to solicitors by this case are met in part by the Solicitors' Accounts Rules 1998.

[869] *Burdick v Garrick* (1870) L.R. 5 Ch.App. 233. cf. *Chedworth v Edwards* (1802) 8 Ves. Jun. 48.

[870] *Browne v Southouse* (1790) 3 Bro.C.C. 107; *Barwell v Parker* (1751) 2 Ves. 364.

[871] *Cooper v De Tastet* (1829) Tamlyn 177 at 179; *Williams v Pott* (1871) L.R. 12 Eq. 149 at 151.

[872] *Blaustein v Maltz, Mitchell & Co* [1937] 2 K.B. 142, Illustration 7.

party has a better right than the principal as respects all or any part of the interest claimed by the principal or in right of which the principal sues.[873]

Comment

Although the word "estoppel" is not much used in the cases relating to these propositions, the first and second constitute situations where an agent is not allowed to make such allegations against the principal, and they can conveniently be regarded as based on a form of estoppel. The third was formerly a case where estoppel reasoning was articulately applied: but this has been reversed by statute.

6-111

An agent who is in possession of property in the agent's capacity as such cannot acquire title against the principal under the Limitation Act, for the agent is estopped from denying that the principal's right to possession[874]:

"An agent cannot well get an adverse title, unless he can very distinctly shew that what he has done is in respect of title, and not in respect of his agency".[875]

Moreover, an agent may not set up the agent's own title as true owner against a prescriptive title acquired by the principal through the agent. Thus, where an agent received rents for 25 years and paid them to his principal, it was the principal who acquired the statutory title by limitation, since the agent was not permitted to deny that the principal acquired it through him.[876]

Again, if the agent has received money for the principal as a result of the agency the agent cannot assert that a third party has a better right to receive it than the principal[877]:

"The law is perfectly clear that an agent receiving money rightfully for his principal is not liable in respect of that money to the owner of the money even where the principal, upon receiving it, would be bound to pay it over to the owner."[878]

This rule applies where the relationship between principal and agent is merely that of creditor and debtor. A fortiori the agent cannot assert a third party's rights to money which the agent holds as trustee for the principal. However, longstanding authority supports the view that an agent may deny the principal's title to money (or chattels) received by the agent as a result of the principal's fraud on a third party.[879]

There was long a third rule whereby an agent was prevented from making a claim

---

[873] Torts (Interference with Goods) Act 1977 s.8(1).

[874] *Ward v Carttar* (1865) L.R. 1 Eq. 29, Illustration 2; *Smith v Bennett* (1874) 30 L.T. 100; *Lyell v Kennedy* (1889) 14 App.Cas. 437, Illustration 1. He must possess as agent and not in any other capacity, but it is for the agent to prove that he was not acting as agent, and the burden of proof is heavy: *White v Bayley* (1861) 10 C.B.(N.S.) 227; *Markwick v Hardingham* (1880) 15 Ch.D. 339; *Re Hobbs* (1887) 36 Ch.D. 553; *Bell v Marsh* [1903] 1 Ch. 528.

[875] *Att.-Gen. v Corporation of London* (1850) 2 Mac. & G. 247 at 259, per Lord Cottenham LC.

[876] *Williams v Pott* (1871) L.R. 12 Eq. 149, Illustration 3.

[877] *Dixon v Hamond* (1819) 2 B. & A. 310, Illustration 5; *Roberts v Ogilby* (1821) 9 Price 269, Illustration 5; *Suart v Welch* (1839) 4 Myl. & Cr. 305; *Eames v Hacon* (1881) 18 Ch.D. 347, Illustration 6; *Davie v Sachs* [1911] Cape P.D. 992; *Mangena v Moyatusi* [1918] App.D. 650; *Blaustein v Maltz, Mitchell & Co* [1937] 2 K.B. 142, Illustration 7. See too the rules about receipt by an agent of money paid by a third party under mistake, discussed below, Article 111.

[878] *Blaustein v Maltz, Mitchell & Co* [1937] 2 K.B. 142 at 156, per Scott LJ. Sed quaere: see Article 113.

[879] See *Field v Allen* (1842) 9 M.&W. 694; *Murray v Mann* (1848) 2 Ex. 538; *Cheesman v Exall* (1851)

adverse to the principal, and here the term estoppel was more frequently used.[880] Where the agent was also a bailee of the principal, the agent was bound by a rule that a bailee may not assert that a third party has a better right to the property than has the bailor.[881] There were exceptions to this: a bailee might rely on a third party's title if the bailee had handed the goods over to the third party or if the agent defended the bailor's claim by authority of and on behalf of the third party.[882] The exceptions did not apply if the bailee had accepted the bailment or attorned to the bailor with knowledge of the third party's claim.[883]

But by virtue of section 8(1) of the Torts (Interference with Goods) Act 1977:

> "in any action for wrongful interference with goods the defendant is entitled to show, in accordance with rules of court, that a third party has a better right than the plaintiff as respects all or part of the interest claimed by the plaintiff or in right of which he sues, and any rule of law (sometimes called jus tertii) to the contrary is abolished."

The purpose of this legislation was in general to end multiplicity of actions[884]; and to that end the defendant's proper course is to apply for joinder of the named third party.[885]

Illustrations

6-112   (1)   A receives the rents of certain properties as an agent, and pays them into a separate account at his own bank. The principal dies intestate. A continues to receive the rents for more than 12 years after the death of the principal, stating to several of the tenants that he is acting for the heir, whoever he may be. Thirteen years afterwards, a purchaser from the heir brings an action against A, claiming possession of the property and an account of the rents and profits. A claims the property as his own, and pleads the Statute of Limitations. The claimant is entitled to possession of the property, and an account of all the rents and profits received by A, which were held in trust.[886]

  (2)   A solicitor paid off a mortgage debt due from a client, and entered into possession of the mortgaged property. Held, that he must be taken to have acted as the agent of the client, and therefore (a) was not a mortgagee in possession; and (b) was not entitled to set up the Statute of Limitations in an action by the client for redemption.[887]

  (3)   A receives the rents of certain property as B's agent for more than 12 years,

---

6 Ex. 341.

[880] See, e.g. *Kahler v Midland Bank Ltd* [1950] A.C. 24 at 38.

[881] *Clerk and Lindsell on Torts* (22nd edn), para.17-74 onwards; Palmer, *Bailment* (3rd edn), para.4-026 onwards; *Spencer Bower: Reliance-Based Estoppel* (5th edn), paras 9.54 and 9.58–9.61.

[882] *Biddle v Bond* (1865) 6 B. & S. 225; *Rogers, Sons & Co v Lambert & Co* [1891] 1 Q.B. 318; *Ross v Edwards & Co* (1895) 73 L.T. 100; *Kahler v Midland Bank Ltd* [1950] A.C. 24.

[883] *Re Sadler Ex p. Davies* (1881) 19 Ch.D. 86; *Eastern Construction Co Ltd v National Trust Co* [1914] A.C. 197 at 210; *Wilson v Lombank* [1963] 1 W.L.R. 1294 at 1297.

[884] See Law Reform Committee, 18th Report, Cmnd. 4774 (1971), paras 51–78; *Clerk and Lindsell on Torts* (22nd edn), para.17-82; Palmer, *Bailment* (3rd edn), para.4-058 onwards. See also *De Franco v Commissioner of Police for the Metropolis, The Times,* May 8, 1987.

[885] See s.8(2) of the Act.

[886] *Lyell v Kennedy* (1889) 14 App.Cas. 437. And see *Smith v Bennett* (1874) 30 L.T. 100.

[887] *Ward v Carttar* (1865) L.R. 1 Eq. 29.

and duly pays them over to B. B thereby acquires a good prescriptive title to the property, in the absence of fraud, even if A was the true owner.[888]

(4) A makes advances for the purpose of a mine, in order to obtain ore, which he consigns to B for sale, B undertaking to account to him for the proceeds. B cannot set up any paramount title to the ore, or dispute A's right to the proceeds, on the ground that there are rights of third persons existing independently of the contract between A and B.[889]

(5) A ship which is the property of A is transferred to B as security for a debt. B insures the ship for and on behalf of A & Co, and charges them with the premiums. The ship is lost, and B receives the insurance money. B must pay over the money, after deducting the amount of his debt, to A & Co, and cannot set up A's title, having insured for and on behalf of A & Co[890] So an insurance broker who receives money under a policy cannot dispute the claim of his principal on the ground that other persons are interested in the subject-matter of the insurance.[891]

(6) E died intestate in Ireland and letters of administration were granted to P. Part of E's assets were in India and P sent a power of attorney to F & Co, who obtained letters of administration for the benefit of P. They collected his Indian assets, paid his debts and sent the assets to A, their English agents. A refused to hand the assets over to P without the concurrence of E's next of kin. Held (the next of kin making no claim), A could not set up any third party's title against P.[892]

(7) B was engaged to Miss J. Her father, J, gave him a cheque for £172.10s., the amount of the deposit on the intended matrimonial home, as a gift conditional on the marriage taking place. B paid the cheque into his bank account and sent his own cheque for the same sum to the estate agent, B then instructed M (who was J's son-in-law) to act for him as solicitor in the purchase of the house. The engagement between B and Miss J was broken off and B instructed M to reclaim the deposit, which he did. M refused to pay B the amount of the deposit since J had ordered him not to do so and had told M to account to J for it. Held, (i) the relationship between B and M was that of principal (creditor) and agent (debtor); (ii) the principle of jus tertii as applied to bailments had no application to a sum of money; and (iii) M could not plead J's orders and must account to B for the money.[893]

(8) A wrongfully distrains B's goods and delivers them to C, an auctioneer, for sale, C having at the time no knowledge of B's adverse claim. B subsequently gives notice of his title to C, and claims the proceeds.[894] C may now, if sued by A, apply for B to be joined as a party.[895]

---

[888] *Williams v Pott* (1871) L.R. 12 Eq. 149.

[889] *Zulueta v Vinent* (1852) 1 De G.M. & G. 315. But see Illustration 8.

[890] *Dixon v Hamond* (1819) 2 B. & A. 310.

[891] *Roberts v Ogilby* (1821) 9 Price 269. But if money is paid by B to A to hold for P, it cannot be claimed by P until A has acknowledged the agency: *Wedlake v Hurley* (1830) 1 C. & J. 83; *Stephens v Badcock* (1832) 3 B. & Ad. 354; Article 112.

[892] *Eames v Hacon* (1881) 18 Ch.D. 347.

[893] *Blaustein v Maltz, Mitchell & Co* [1937] 2 K.B. 142.

[894] cf. *Biddle v Bond* (1865) 6 B. & S. 225; *Rogers Son & Co v Lambert & Co* [1891] 1 Q.B. 318; *Ross v Edwards & Co* (1895) 73 L.T. 100.

[895] Torts (Interference with Goods) Act 1977 s.8; see Comment.

CHAPTER 7

RIGHTS OF AGENTS AGAINST THEIR PRINCIPALS

INTRODUCTORY NOTE

Duties of co-operation and good faith   Legal systems which categorise types of   **7-001**
agent and seek to lay down the incidents of the various legal relationships may well
prescribe duties of principals towards their agents just as they prescribe duties of
agents towards their principals. English law however has traditionally viewed the
principal as the person requiring protection, against wrongful use of the agent's
powers, and have paid little attention to the position of the agent. Thus it was long
ago held that the principal was under no duty to account on a fiduciary basis to the
agent.[1] In general the view that the principal has fiduciary duties towards the agent
is not one that is often put forward.[2] Equally, the limited body of law relating to the
common law duties owed by agents towards their principals has no obvious
counterpart concerning duties owed towards agents by their principals.

In the absence of fiduciary duties generally being owed by principals to agents,
the most likely candidates for terms implied in law are duties of co-operation and
of good faith. But the almost infinite variety of relationships that involve agency
functions makes it unsafe to assume that a principal always owes an implied duty
of co-operation,[3] or even good faith towards an agent.[4] In some cases, for instance,
a duty to act solicitously to an agent who is an independent contractor might be
incompatible with the principal's duties to its clients or its employees.[5] But there
will be circumstances where duties of co-operation[6] and of good faith will be
appropriate.[7] This is more likely to be the case where the agent is an employee of
the principal.[8] But such duties could also arise without an employment relationship, such as where it is the principal not the agent who is in control of informa-

---

[1]   *Padwick v Stanley* (1852) 9 Hare 627; *Padwick v Hurst* (1854) 18 Beav. 575; *McGann v Bisping*
   [2017] EWHC 2951 (Comm) at [297].
[2]   See *Paper Reclaim Ltd v Aotearoa International Ltd* [2007] 3 N.Z.L.R. 169 (NZSC) (principals do
   not, in general, owe fiduciary duties to agents); *Galambos v Perez* [2009] 3 S.C.R. 247 (SCC).
[3]   See *Mona Oil Equipment Supply Co Ltd v Rhodesia Railways Ltd* [1949] 2 All E.R. 1014; and
   Hospital Products Ltd v United States Surgical Corp (1984) 156 C.L.R. 41 (as to the duties of
   distributors). See too *Luxor (Eastbourne) Ltd v Cooper* [1941] A.C. 108, esp. at 138–139.
[4]   See *Bates v Post Office Ltd (No 3)* [2019] EWHC 606 (QB) at [721]. But cf. *Restatement, Third*, §
   8.15, which propounds a duty on a principal to act "fairly and in good faith, including a duty to
   provide the agent about risks of physical harm or pecuniary loss" that may affect the agent's work.
[5]   See *Wales (t/a Selective Investment Services) v CBRE Managed Services Ltd* [2020] EWHC 16
   (Comm) at [73] (duty of good faith asserted by agent performing services relating to principal's
   employee pension scheme could compromise principal's duties to its employees under the scheme).
[6]   See in general Burrows (1968) 31 M.L.R. 390; Lücke (1973) 5 Adelaide L.Rev. 32; Kerr (1980) 97
   S.A.L. Rev. 550; Brodie (1996) 25 I.L.J. 121; (2001) 117 L.Q.R. 604. As to the application of exclusion clauses in relation to duties of co-operation, see *Axa Sun Life Services Plc v Campbell Martin
   Ltd* [2011] EWCA Civ 133; [2011] 2 Lloyd's Rep. 1; [2011] 1 C.L.C. 312.
[7]   *Bates v Post Office Ltd (No.3)* [2019] EWHC 606 (QB) at [705] onwards.
[8]   See *Mahmud v Bank of Credit and Commerce International SA* [1998] A.C. 20 HL at 45: "the
   employer shall not, without reasonable and proper cause, conduct itself in a manner calculated and

tion vital to the performance of the contract between the parties. For instance, where the information relevant to determining an agent's quantum of commission is solely in the possession of the principal, one can expect the courts to look sternly (if only in the approach to costs) on a failure by the principal to provide the raw information that would enable the agent's entitlements to be determined.[9] Equally, the principal may dictate and control the accounting systems that the agent is obliged to use and ought to bear responsibility for those systems' fitness for purpose.[10] In some circumstances the Unfair Contract Terms Act 1977 may also be available to an agent in respect of the contract of agency.[11]

Other terms implied in law can exist. So, it is implicit that the principal will reimburse and indemnify the agent against expenses incurred in the agency, addressed in Article 62, though this may not always be contractual. Normal contractual principles will also apply in the provision of remedies for a wrongful termination of the agency by the principal.[12] Other cases have had to consider when a term will be implied that the principal will not prevent the agent from earning commission.[13]

Notwithstanding the starting position outlined at the beginning of this paragraph, one also cannot altogether rule out a principal owing fiduciary duties to an agent on particular facts.[14]

There could also be cases where a principal is liable to the agent in tort: the existence of a contractual action between them may regulate or modify the duties owed, but does not exclude tort liability based on general principles.[15] As to contract, however, parties drafting agency contracts (or related contracts such as distributorship contracts) are well advised to deal specifically with the duties of the principal.

The rights of an agent are normally based on a contract between agent and principal. The agent may sometimes however be entitled under the Contracts

---

likely to destroy or seriously damage the relationship of confidence and trust between employer and employee". See also *Eastwood v Magnox Electric Plc* [2004] UKHL 35; [2005] 1 A.C. 503 at [11]; *Scally v Southern Health Board* [1992] 1 A.C. 294; *Spring v Guardian Assurance Plc* [1995] 2 A.C. 296. But cf. *James-Bowen v Commissioner of Police* [2018] UKSC 40; [2018] 1 W.L.R. 4021 (no duty owed by employer to employee in settling third party action based on vicarious liability).

[9] See the inconclusive discussion in *Easyair Ltd (t/a Openair) v Opal Telecom Ltd* [2009] EWHC 339 (Ch) at [47].

[10] *Bates v Post Office Ltd (No.3)* [2019] EWHC 606 (QB) at [705] onwards and at [851] and [1113].

[11] *Bates v Post Office Ltd (No.3)* [2019] EWHC 606 (QB) at [1063] onwards. See also *Axa Sun Life Services Plc v Campbell Martin Ltd* [2011] EWCA Civ 133; [2011] 2 Lloyd's Rep. 1.

[12] See Comment to Article 123.

[13] See Article 58.

[14] Fiduciary duties in a franchisor were denied in *Jirna v Mister Donut of Canada Ltd* (1973) 40 D.L.R. (3d) 303; criticised by Shepherd (1981) 97 L.Q.R. 51 at 59; and see Brown (1971) 49 Tex.L.Rev 650, suggesting that franchising should be regarded as creating a fiduciary relationship. But see *Hospital Products Ltd v US Surgical Corp* (1984) 156 C.L.R. 41, per Mason and Deane JJ (on duties of a distributor). See also *Jani-King (GB) Ltd v Pula Enterprises Ltd* [2007] EWHC 2433; [2008] 1 All E.R. (Comm) 451 (no implied term of trust and confidence in favour of franchisee); cf. above, para.6-015.

[15] *Henderson v Merrett Syndicates Ltd* [1995] 2 A.C. 145, explaining *Tai Hing Cotton Mill Ltd v Liu Chong Hing Bank Ltd* [1986] A.C. 80. A franchisor has been held liable to the franchisee for negligent advice concerning the franchise: see *MGB Printing & Design Ltd v Kall Kwik UK Ltd* [2010] EWHC 624 (QB); *Traderight (NSW) Pty Ltd v Bank of Queensland Ltd* [2015] NSWCA 94 (alleged inaccurate projections of revenue to prospective agent).

(Rights of Third Parties) 1999: for example, a duty to pay commission to a broker is often contained in a charterparty.[16]

Commercial agents   The Commercial Agents (Council Directive) Regulations   **7-002**
1993, however, lay down duties for the principals of commercial agents as there defined. In particular, a principal must act towards the agent "dutifully and in good faith".[17] The Regulations are dealt with in Chapter 11.

1.   REMUNERATION

Article 55

WHETHER AGENT ENTITLED TO ANY REMUNERATION

(1)   An agent is only entitled to remuneration for the agent's services if either the   **7-003**
express or implied terms of the agency contract, if any, so provide or the agent has a right in restitution to claim on a quantum meruit.

(2)   Where the contract contains express terms providing for remuneration to be paid, the agent cannot normally claim remuneration other than in accordance with those terms. In the absence of such express terms the right to claim any remuneration, and the amount and terms of payment of such remuneration, are determined by such terms as may be implied into the contract.

(3)   In deciding what terms are to be implied the court will have regard to all the circumstances of the case, including the nature and length of the services, the express terms of the contract and the customs, usages and practices of the particular area of activity. In the absence of any factors to the contrary, a term will be implied that the agent is entitled to reasonable remuneration.[18]

Comment

Contractual claim   Apart from claims in restitution, the rendering of services to   **7-004**
another, however long continued, creates no right to remuneration unless the agency contract expressly or impliedly makes provision for such payments.[19] If there are no express terms relating to remuneration, terms providing for remuneration will only be implied where the circumstances are such as to indicate that the parties intended that there should be remuneration.[20] In general, however, the mere employment of a professional person raises a presumption that it was intended that that person should be remunerated unless there are circumstances indicating the

---

[16] See *Nisshin Shipping Co Ltd v Cleaves & Co* [2003] EWHC 2602 (Comm); [2004] 1 All E.R. (Comm) 481 (holding that the third party in effect becomes a statutory assignee of the promisee's right of action and hence is subject to a requirement of arbitration as the promisee would be).

[17] Commercial Agents (Council Directive) Regulations 1993 reg.4(1).

[18] See Comment.

[19] Of course, if there is no agency contract at all, there is no duty to pay commission (though there may be restitutionary consequences): see *Lady Manor Ltd v Fat Cat Café Bars Ltd* [2001] 2 E.G.L.R. 1 ("cold calling" by estate agents).

[20] *Reeve v Reeve* (1858) 1 F. & F. 280; *Foord v Morley* (1859) 1 F. & F. 496. See also *Hulse v Hulse* (1856) 17 C.B. 711. See *Benhams Ltd v Kythira Investments Ltd* [2004] EWHC 2973 (QB); *Ian Greenhill Residential Ltd v Asfari* [2007] EWHC 1491 (QB) at [106]; cf. *Primlake Ltd v Matthews Associates* [2006] EWHC 1227 (Ch); [2007] 1 B.C.L.C. 666.

contrary.[21] So, there is no general principle that fiduciaries are not entitled to remuneration without express consent.[22] The position is different with company directors, who, like trustees, are entitled to remuneration only if express provision is made therefor.[23] Consistently with the foregoing principles, it is unlikely that a court would imply a right to remuneration in favour of a relative or friend of the donor under a power of attorney; the relationship would generally be non-contractual.[24] The position would likely be different where the attorney appointed was a professional person.

In respect of some contracts, failure to agree on the price would be a strong indication that no contract had been concluded. In the case of the contract of agency, however, the question of the agent's remuneration is less central, and if it is found that remuneration was intended, its amount can be determined by reference to scales or even by what is reasonable.[25] If the parties have not settled the event which triggers the right to commission—a highly variable element in agency contracts—the court may have to conclude that no contract can be established. However, if intent to create contractual relations is apparent and there can be no doubt what would be the latest possible trigger for commission (such as completion of the contract between principal and third party) then it will not be necessary for the parties to spell that out.[26]

What terms may be implied into the contract will depend upon the normal rules for the implication of terms into contracts.[27] In particular, no terms may be implied which would be inconsistent with the express terms.[28] Thus, if the express terms provide for remuneration which seems unduly low, no term may be implied which will give a more reasonable remuneration.[29] But if the agent performs services at the request of the principal which are outside the duties for which the contract expressly provides for remuneration, a term may exceptionally be implied that a reasonable sum shall be paid for such services.[30] If the contract provides that the amount of remuneration shall be in the discretion of the principal, the court may

---

[21] *Miller v Beale* (1879) 27 W.R. 403, Illustration 6; *Manson v Baillie* (1855) 2 Macq. 80; *Gibbon v Budd* (1863) 2 H. & C. 92; *Landless v Wilson* (1880) 8 R. 289; *Turner v Reeve* (1901) 17 T.L.R. 592; *Corbin v Stewart* (1911) 28 T.L.R. 99 (the former) practice of one doctor charging no fee for attendance on the children of another doctor was a circumstance displacing the general rule); *Way v Latilla* [1937] 3 All E.R. 759, Illustration 3; Supply of Goods and Services Act 1982 s.15.

[22] See *Dale v Inland Revenue Commissioners* [1954] A.C. 11 at 27.

[23] See *Guinness Plc v Saunders* [1990] 2 A.C. 663; *Ball v Hughes* [2017] EWHC 3228 (Ch) at [259]; *Toone v Robbins* [2018] EWHC 569 (Ch).

[24] See *Lincolne v Williams* [2008] TASSC 41 at [15].

[25] cf. Supply of Goods and Services Act 1982 s.15. See *Ian Greenhill Residential Ltd v Asfari* [2007] EWHC 1491 (QB) at [96].

[26] See *Wells v Devani* [2019] UKSC 4; [2020] A.C. 129 at [19] (noted P. Davies, "Interpretation and Implication in the Supreme Court" [2019] C.L.J. 267).

[27] See above, para.7-001.

[28] *Broad v Thomas* (1830) 7 Bing. 99; *Read v Rann* (1830) 10 B. & C. 438; *Phillipps v Briard* (1856) 25 L.J.Ex. 233; *Alder v Boyle* (1847) 4 C.B. 635; *Green v Mules* (1861) 30 L.J.C.P. 343, Illustration 8; *Barnett v Isaacson* (1888) 4 T.L.R. 645; *Lott v Outhwaite* (1893) 10 T.L.R. 76; *Harley & Co v Nagata* (1917) 34 T.L.R. 124; *Moor Line Ltd v Louis Dreyfus & Co* [1918] 1 K.B. 89; *Howard Houlder & Partners Ltd v Manx Islands SS Co* [1923] 1 K.B. 110; *Burrough's Adding Machine Ltd v Aspinall* (1925) 41 T.L.R. 276; *Jones v Lowe* [1945] K.B. 73; *Fairvale Ltd v Sabharwal* [1992] 2 E.G.L.R. 27. But a trade custom or usage may be used to interpret a contract, provided that it is not inconsistent with the express terms: *Caine v Horsefall* (1847) 1 Exch. 519; *Allan v Sundius* (1862) 1 H. & C. 123; *Parker v Ibbetson* (1858) 4 C.B.(N.S.) 346.

[29] *Kofi Sunkersette Obu v Strauss & Co* [1951] A.C. 243, Illustration 1.

[30] *Marshall v Parsons* (1841) 9 C. & P. 656; *Williamson v Hine Bros* [1891] 1 Ch. 390.

not decide what sum should be paid; to do so would be to re-write the contract and usurp the principal from the function which the parties agreed should be the principal's.[31] But if the contract expressly or impliedly provides that a reasonable sum shall be payable, the court will determine what is a reasonable sum and the terms on which it should be paid.[32] In the absence of a contrary indication as to the amount payable, the term which will be implied is for a reasonable sum on reasonable terms. What is reasonable will depend upon all the circumstances of the case.[33] When an agent is charging on an hourly basis, it will often be relevant to consider whether the ends to be obtained justify the hours spent.[34] Where the express or implied understanding of reasonable remuneration is by commission, then evidence of industry norms (rather than hourly rates for work done) will be relevant.[35] Commission based on "income" derived by the principal is likely to be taken as meaning gross income, in the absence of other indications.[36] Permission to sell at a stated price does not imply that the agent can take as commission anything obtained in excess of that price.[37] Rates and other elements of remuneration may be varied as a result of the operation of general legal principles, including those of contract and estoppel.[38]

Scales: implied terms and custom[39]   The fact that a professional person normally   7-005
charges on a fixed scale, such as a scale of charges laid down by the relevant professional body which provides for a varying percentage of the total sum involved, does not ipso facto entitle that person to remuneration according to that scale. It must be shown that the scale was incorporated into the contract either by express term or otherwise. If it is not incorporated expressly it may be possible to show that the scale is to be implied by custom; but the custom must, of course, be reasonable if it is to bind the other party.[40] In the absence of express or implied incorporation of a scale, the implied term will be that the professional person is only entitled to a reasonable sum, although the scale may provide the measure of or an indication of

---

[31] *Kofi Sunkersette v Strauss & Co* [1951] A.C. 243; *Re Richmond Gate Property Co Ltd* [1965] 1 W.L.R. 335, where the articles of a company provided (from Table A in the Companies Act 1948) for "such remuneration as the directors may determine". This was held to exclude any implied term because the contract provided expressly for the directors to determine the sum payable and any implied term would have been contrary to the express terms.

[32] *Way v Latilla* [1937] 3 All E.R. 759, Illustration 3; *Powell v Braun* [1954] 1 W.L.R. 401; *Gross Fine & Krieger Chalfen v Clifton* (1974) 223 E.G. 837; *Harding Maughan Hambly Ltd v CECAR* [2000] 1 Lloyd's Rep. 316.

[33] As to the amount, see *Cohen v Paget* (1814) 4 Camp. 96; *Rucker v Lunt* (1863) 3 F. & F. 959; *Great Western Insurance Co v Cunliffe* (1874) L.R. 9 Ch.App. 525; *Baring v Stanton* (1876) 3 Ch.D. 502; *Stubbs v Slater* [1910] 1 Ch. 632; *Campbell v National Trust Co Ltd* [1931] 1 D.L.R. 705 (PC); *Hugh V. Allen & Co v A. Holmes Ltd* [1969] 1 Lloyd's Rep. 348; *Harding Maughan Hambly Ltd v CECAR* [2000] 1 Lloyd's Rep. 316. As to the conditions, see *Broad v Thomas* (1830) 7 Bing. 99; *Hall v Benson* (1836) 7 C. & P. 711; *Burnett v Bouch* (1840) 9 C. & P. 620.

[34] See *Mirror Group Newspapers Plc v Maxwell (No.2)* [1998] 1 B.C.L.C. 638.

[35] See *ACLBDD Holdings Ltd v Staechelin* [2018] EWHC 44 (Ch) at [160]; affirmed on different points [2019] EWCA Civ 817.

[36] See *McGann v Bisping* [2017] EWHC 2951 (Comm) at [208].

[37] See *Taylor v Smith* (1926) 38 C.L.R. 48.

[38] See *Cellarit Pty Ltd v Cawarrah Holdings Pty Ltd* [2018] NSWCA 213.

[39] For a full discussion of this topic in connection with estate agents, see Murdoch, *Law of Estate Agency* (5th edn), p.134 onwards.

[40] See Article 31.

what a reasonable sum might be.[41] The court may have regard to the negotiations of the parties in order to ascertain the value which each of them put upon the services.[42] It has been suggested that where the agent performs services which are not geared to producing particular results, the sum should be ascertained on the basis of time and trouble, unless a custom incorporating a scale can be established; but that where an agent employed to achieve results achieves those results, assessment of a reasonable sum by reference to a scale may be more appropriate.[43]

7-006 **Fiduciaries** There is no rule that fiduciaries are presumed to work for nothing. There is such a presumption with trustees and directors, but not with fiduciaries, including agents, in general. But the fiduciary nature of an agent's functions may mean that the agent cannot charge for other services without the informed consent of the person or persons to whom the fiduciary duty is owed.[44] There are equitable[45] and statutory[46] exceptions to this rule, often concerning solicitors. Until 2013, barristers had no legal right to receive remuneration for services rendered in an official capacity.[47] Where an agent's remuneration turns on variable factors, such as number of hours worked, then equity will exercise supervision over the agent's rendering of costs to the principal.[48]

7-007 **Estate agents** Under s.18 of the Estate Agents Act 1979 a person who enters into a contract with another under which the agent will engage in estate agency work must give the client certain information regarding the remuneration payable and

---

41 *Upsdell v Stewart* (1793) Peake 255 (in which a surveyor attempted to prove a trade custom that he was entitled to 5 per cent of the cost of the works. Of this custom, Lord Kenyon said: "as to the custom offered to be proved, the course of robbery on Bagshot Heath might as well be proved in a court of justice"); *Footner v Joseph* (1859) 3 L.C.J. 233; affirmed 5 L.C.J. 225 (Canada); *Debenham v King's College, Cambridge* (1884) 1 T.L.R. 170; *Brocklebank v Lancashire & Yorkshire Ry Co* (1887) 3 T.L.R. 575; *Drew v Josolyne* (1888) 4 T.L.R. 717 (in which Lord Coleridge said that he would never sanction surveyors being paid not with reference to the work done but on a percentage of the amount involved. A similar view was expressed by Younger J in *Faraday v Tamworth Union* (1917) 86 L.J.Ch. 436, Illustration 5); *Farthing v Tomkins* (1893) 9 T.L.R. 566; *Wilkie v Scottish Aviation Ltd* 1956 S.C. 198, Illustration 4. See also *Gibbon v Pease* [1905] 1 K.B. 810 (custom that architect can retain plans after payment unreasonable); *Att.-Gen. v Drapers' Co* (1869) L.R. 9 Eq. 69; *Buckland and Garrard v Pawson & Co* (1890) 6 T.L.R. 421; *Turner v Reeve* (1901) 17 T.L.R. 592; *Re Wolfe* [1952] 2 All E.R. 545; *Frank Swain v Whitfield Corp Ltd* (1962) 183 E.G. 479; *Graham & Baldwin v Taylor, Son & Davis* (1965) 109 S.J. 793.
42 *Way v Latilla* [1937] 3 All E.R. 759, Illustration 3, following *Scarisbrick v Parkinson* (1869) 20 L.T. 175; *Berezovsky v Edmiston & Co Ltd* [2011] EWCA Civ 431 at [53].
43 *Murdoch* [1981] Conv 424, doubting the cases cited at Illustration 10.
44 e.g. *Sheriff v Axe* (1827) 4 Russ. 33 (commission agent became executor); *Williams v Barton* [1927] 2 Ch. 9 (stockbroker's clerk was trustee); cf. *Douglas v Archbutt* (1858) 2 De G. & J. 148 (trustee acted as auctioneer); and see *Bath v Standard Land Co Ltd* [1911] 1 Ch. 618; *Re Northcote's Will Trusts* [1949] 1 All E.R. 442 (charge for getting in foreign assets allowable by foreign law). See in general Articles 43–48; Finn, *Fiduciary Obligations* (1977), pp.206–208.
45 The rule in *Cradock v Piper* relating to solicitor trustees: see *Snell's Equity* (34th edn), para.7-028; Cordery, *Solicitors* (8th edn), pp.177–178.
46 Rules made under the Insolvency Act 1986.
47 See *Kennedy v Broun* (1863) 13 C.B.(N.S.) 677; *Broun v Kennedy* (1864) 4 De G.J. & S. 217, affirming 33 Beav. 133; *Re May* (1858) 4 Jur.(N.S.) 1169; *Wells v Wells* [1914] P. 157; *Re Sandiford (No.2)* [1935] Ch. 681; *Gwinnutt v George* [2019] EWCA Civ 656; [2019] Ch. 656 (but barrister's non-contractual rights can vest in the official assignee). See now Standard Contractual Terms for the Supply of Legal Services by Barristers to Authorised Persons 2012, and the Code of Conduct of the Bar of England and Wales.
48 See *Mirror Group Newspapers Plc v Maxwell (No.2)* [1998] 1 B.C.L.C. 638. See also Article 51.

other sums (such as advertising and other expenses) which may become payable.[49] If the agent does not do so, the contract is unenforceable except pursuant to an order of the court.[50] The time at which the information must be given is specified by regulation.[51] This legislative scheme has generated a body of case law which is not fully analysed in this work.[52] There are some uncertainties with it. Hence, it is not altogether clear how the scheme applies to the classic estate agent's agreement, which involves a unilateral offer by the client, and under which the agent enters into no contract until commission is earned by the agent's introducing a purchaser or something similar.[53] The Act contemplates a contract being made before the agent commences work. It seems likely that it will not matter if, on the balance of probabilities, the agent can prove that there was a written contract that complied with the 1979 Act, but it has subsequently been lost.[54]

Unfair Terms in Consumer Contracts Regulations 1999[55]   Some commission agreements in consumer contracts may be caught by these, for example if a higher sum is due on late payment.[56]

7-008

Quantum meruit where no contractual right   If services are rendered by the agent not pursuant to a contract, but they were freely accepted by the principal with full knowledge, or (perhaps) from which the principal incontrovertibly benefits, the courts may, on principles of restitution, award a reasonable sum to the agent as remuneration on a quantum meruit.[57] The leading case is now *Benedetti v Sawiris*,[58] confirming that the basis of the action is unjust enrichment, even if it is arguable

7-009

---

[49]   "Estate agency work" is defined in s.1; it only covers some of the functions normally performed by estate agents. The notice must be in writing: Estate Agents (Provision of Information) Regulations 1991 (SI 1991/859) reg.4 (made under s.30 of the Act). See *Foxtons Ltd v Bicknell* [2008] EWCA Civ 419; [2008] 24 E.G. 142; [2008] N.P.C. 52 (noted Watts [2009] J.B.L. 268).

[50]   As to the court's discretion see: *Benhams Ltd v Kythira Investments Ltd* [2004] EWHC 2973; *Great Estates Group Ltd v Digby* [2011] EWCA Civ 1120; [2012] 2 All E.R. (Comm) 361; *Wells v Devani* [2019] UKSC 4; [2020] A.C. 129. In *Ian Greenhill Residential Ltd v Asfari* [2007] EWHC 1491 (QB) at [96] it was held that the 1979 Act was not inconsistent with the existence of an implied term as to remuneration, but the agreement would not be enforceable without the court's consent. On the facts no agreement as to remuneration was established. As to the possibility of rectification of the agency contract, see *Ballan (CA) Pty Ltd v Oliver Hume (Australia) Pty Ltd* [2017] VSCA 11.

[51]   Estate Agents (Provision of Information) Regulations 1991 reg.3(1): "when communication commences between the estate agent and the client or as soon as is reasonably practicable thereafter provided it is at a time before the client is committed to any liability towards the estate agent".

[52]   See in general Murdoch, *The Estate Agents and Property Misdescriptions Acts 1979* (3rd edn); *Law of Estate Agency* (5th edn); below, paras 7-020 and 7-038.

[53]   See below, para.7-015.

[54]   See in relation to comparable legislation, *Savills (NSW) Pty Ltd v ATF CTH Pty Ltd* [2020] NSWSC 956.

[55]   SI 1999/2083.

[56]   *Bairstow Eves London Central Ltd v Smith* [2004] EWHC 263; [2004] 2 E.G.L.R. 25. But the basic commission charge would not be so subject, by virtue of cl.6(2) of the Regulations. For an example of a penal provision before the Regulations see *Chris Hart (Business Sales) Ltd v Mitchell* 1996 S.C.L.R. 68.

[57]   See *Benedetti v Sawiris* [2013] UKSC 50; [2014] A.C. 938 (noted Virgo [2013] C.L.J. 508; McInnes (2014) 130 L.Q.R. 8; Mitchell [2013] L.M.C.L.Q. 436). See, more generally, *Goff and Jones, Law of Unjust Enrichment* (9th edn), para.1-06, and Ch.17. In some of the authorities quantum meruit is used to describe a claim in contract for a reasonable sum due under an implied term of that contract. It is probably preferable to avoid this terminology, which may lead to confusion between a claim under a contract and a claim in restitution where no contract exists and may, further, cause the normal principles for the implication of terms into a contract to be overlooked. cf. below, para.7-024. See also *Accidia Foundation v Simon C. Dickinson Ltd* [2010] EWHC 3058 (Ch) (remuneration to sub-

that the rejection in this context of the older approach based on implied contract is doctrinaire. Recourse to the law of restitution is likely if the contract under which the services were rendered was a nullity or was subsequently rescinded[59] or made without authority (ratification being impossible),[60] or it contained terms so vague or uncertain as to make it unenforceable,[61] or the parties provided that remuneration shall be such as they shall subsequently agree but they thereafter fail to reach agreement.[62] A quantum meruit may also be available even when there is a valid contract between the parties if it simply fails to address the circumstances that have occurred, and there is no indication that the agent was taking the risk of not being remunerated.[63]

However, agency services performed in the simple hope that a contract on commission may eventuate will not normally meet the requirements for a quantum meruit.[64] Nor will a quantum meruit be awarded when to do so would undermine statutory or other common law policy, such as where barristers work on non-contractual terms,[65] or the policy that trustees and directors prima facie provide their services without reward.[66] The starting point for setting the rate of remuneration under a quantum meruit is the reasonable or market value of the services. In some

---

agent by way of equitable allowance in an account).

58 *Benedetti v Sawiris* [2013] UKSC 50; [2014] A.C. 938.
59 *Faraday v Tamworth Union* (1917) 86 L.J.Ch. 436, Illustration 5. This case may be difficult to reconcile with the earlier Scottish case of *Boyd & Forrest v Glasgow & SW Ry Co*, 1915 S.C. 20 HL (reported also as a note in [1915] A.C. 526). See also *Proactive Sports Management Ltd v Rooney* [2011] EWCA Civ 1444; [2012] F.S.R. 16 at [122] (agency contract void as being in restraint of trade of the principal; quantum meruit not governed by the contractual rate); *CJ Motorsport Consulting Ltd v Bird* [2019] EWHC 2330 (QB) (no quantum meruit warranted).
60 *Craven-Ellis v Canons Ltd* [1936] 2 K.B. 403. See also *William Lacey (Hounslow) Ltd v Davis* [1957] 1 W.L.R. 932.
61 See *Turner v Webster*, 24 Kan. 38 (1880) for a clear illustration of this principle, which was considered in a wider context in *Scammell v Ouston* [1941] A.C. 251. See also *Jaques v Lloyd D. George & Partners Ltd* [1968] 1 W.L.R. 625, where the contract was void for uncertainty and no remuneration was payable; and *John Meacock & Co v Abrahams* [1956] 1 W.L.R. 1463, Illustration 9.
62 *Loftus v Roberts* (1902) 18 T.L.R. 532; *Benourad v Compass Group Plc* [2010] EWHC 1882 (QB) at [132] (insufficient evidence of value adduced). The courts will be keen to find a contract if they can by implying reasonable terms, especially when the parties have proceeded a long way under the supposed contract: *F. & G. Sykes (Wessex) Ltd v Fine Fare Ltd* [1967] 1 Lloyd's Rep. 53. But cf. *Courtney & Fairbairn Ltd v Tolaini Bros (Hotels) Ltd* [1975] 1 W.L.R. 297; *Mallozzi v Carapelli SpA* [1975] 1 Lloyd's Rep. 229; *Whittle Movers Ltd v Hollywood Express Ltd* [2009] EWCA Civ 1189 at [15]. See also *Hillas & Co Ltd v Arcos Ltd* (1932) 38 Com.Cas. 23; *May & Butcher v R.* (1929) reported [1934] 2 K.B. 17n.; *Foley v Classique Coaches Ltd* [1934] 2 K.B. 1; *British Bank of Foreign Trade Ltd v Novinex* [1949] 1 K.B. 623; *National Coal Board v Galley* [1958] 1 W.L.R. 16; *Luanda Exportadora v Wahbe Tamari* [1967] 2 Lloyd's Rep. 353 at 361.
63 *Barton v Gwyn-Jones* [2019] EWCA Civ 1999, Illustration 12 (criticised W. Day and G. Virgo, "Risks on the contract/unjust enrichment borderline" (2020) 136 L.Q.R. 349).
64 *MSM Consulting Ltd v United Republic of Tanzania* [2009] EWHC 121 (QB); *Becerra v Close Brothers Corporate Finance Ltd* [1999] EWHC 289 (Comm); *Moran Yacht & Ship Inc v Pisarev* [2014] EWHC 1098 (Comm); [2014] 2 Lloyd's Rep. 88 at [91]; affirmed [2016] EWCA Civ 317; [2016] 1 Lloyd's Rep. 625 (claimant attempting to assist defendant sell yacht so latter would be in position to buy other yacht for which claimant had an agency); *Beagle v ACT and SNSW Rugby Union Ltd* [2017] ACTCA 29 at [124]; *Moorgate Capital (Corporate Finance) Ltd v HIG European Capital Partners LLP* [2019] EWHC 1421 (Comm). cf. *Cooke v Hopper* [2012] EWCA Civ 175 (investigatory work collateral to otherwise gratuitous assistance awarded quantum meruit).
65 See *Gwinnutt v George* [2018] EWHC 2169 (Ch); [2019] Ch. 52; reversed on other points: [2019] EWCA Civ 656; [2019] Ch. 471 (unenforceable rights to remuneration still "property").
66 See *Langsam v Beachcroft LLP* [2011] EWHC 1451 (Ch) at [253] (appealed on other points, [2012] EWCA Civ 1230); *Guinness Plc v Saunders* [1990] 2 A.C. 663 at 689; *Toone v Robbins* [2018]

circumstances, it might be possible for the recipient of the services to devalue that rate, but it will be rare for above-market rates to be awarded even if there is evidence that under some circumstances, such as a now abandoned contract, the recipient might have been prepared to pay more than market rate[67]; those other circumstances may have reflected bad judgement on the recipient's part, and if the provider of the services has not cemented the terms in contract the windfall has not been secured.

Contractual right   This situation must, of course, be distinguished from that in which P asks A to perform a service and A does so. Request and performance will normally create a contract and, subject to the considerations discussed above, reasonable remuneration will be payable pursuant to an implied term of that contract rather than give rise to a claim upon a quantum meruit in restitution. Equally, the contract may itself provide for reasonable remuneration where for some reason a stipulated commission is not earned.[68] It can also be appropriate to infer a right to remuneration where the express terms deal only with one trigger for remuneration but are silent on what is to happen in other circumstances.[69]   **7-010**

Commercial agents   The Commercial Agents (Council Directive) Regulations 1993 provide in some detail for remuneration of commercial agents in the absence of agreement.[70] The Regulations are discussed in Chapter 11.   **7-011**

Illustrations

(1)   A company engaged A to act as its agent for the purchase and shipment of rubber to the company. The contract of engagement provided that: **7-012**

> "the company has agreed to remunerate my services with a monthly sum of fifty pounds … A commission is also to be paid to me … which I have agreed to leave to the discretion of the company."

A claimed a commission on all rubber purchased by him for the company. The Privy Council held that it could not determine the basis and rate of commission and that to do so would be to vary the existing contract by transferring to the court the exercise of a discretion vested in the company.[71]

(2)   A entered into an agreement which provided:

> "I hereby agree to enter your service as a weekly manager, and the amount of payment I am to receive I leave entirely for you to determine."

EWHC 569 (Ch) at [47]. For the position of partners, whose remuneration is usually by way of sharing in profits, see *Hameed v Packe* [2018] EWHC 3061 (Ch).

[67]   *Benedetti v Sawiris* [2013] UKSC 50; [2014] A.C. 938.

[68]   See Illustration 10; below, para.7-024.

[69]   See *Barton v Gwyn-Jones* [2019] EWCA Civ 1999 at [41] and [75] (but in fact case decided on restitutionary basis).

[70]   Commercial Agents (Council Directive) Regulations 1993 reg.6(1).

[71]   *Kofi Sunkersette Obu v Strauss & Co* [1951] A.C. 243. See also *Taylor v Brewer* (1813) 1 M. & S. 290; *Roberts v Smith* (1859) 4 H. & N. 315; *Mann v Shell Petroleum Ltd* [1961] C.L.Y. 1440; *Re Richmond Gate Property Co Ltd* [1965] 1 W.L.R. 335. But cf. *Sudbrook Trading Estate Ltd v Eggleton* [1983] 1 A.C. 444.

He served in that capacity for six weeks. It was held that he was entitled, in an action on a quantum meruit, to recover such an amount as the employer, acting in good faith, ought to have awarded.[72]

(3)   A alleged that he had agreed with P that he should send P information relating to gold mines and concessions in Africa and that P should give him a reasonable share in the same and pay a reasonable sum for the information. Held, there was no concluded contract between the parties as to the amount of the share and the court could not complete the contract for the parties, but that there was an employment contract between the parties which clearly indicated that A was not to work gratuitously; a term would be implied under which A was entitled to reasonable remuneration. In fixing the amount, the court could have regard to the negotiations between the parties in order to ascertain what value they had themselves placed upon the service.[73]

(4)   W was employed by S to act as valuer, adviser and witness in arbitration proceedings. No provision was made for his fees. After the work was completed W prepared a bill of charges, made up in accordance with the Scale of Professional Charges of the Royal Institution of Chartered Surveyors, amounting to £3,009. S paid him £1,000 and he sued for the balance. Held, fees would be payable according to the Scale if it was customary to pay according to the Scale and if the resulting fee was reasonable. If W could not prove the incorporation of the Scale by custom the court would fix a reasonable fee.[74]

(5)   F was employed by the defendants to act as surveyor for them in connection with an arbitration. The contract provided that he should be paid a percentage fee on Ryde's Scale of Professional Charges, but as a result of an innocent misrepresentation by the defendants, F thought that his percentage would be based on the entire amount in issue whereas the contract provided that it should be based only on the defendants' share. Held, (i) the contract could be rescinded by F for the defendants' innocent misrepresentation; (ii) F was entitled to reasonable remuneration on a quantum meruit; (iii) such remuneration was to be fixed in accordance with the work actually done and not on a percentage of values. Ryde's Scale was therefore ignored.[75]

(6)   A engages an auctioneer to sell property on his behalf. It is implied that A is to pay the auctioneer the usual and reasonable commission.[76]

(7)   A contract provided that an agent should receive commission on all sales effected or orders executed by him. By a custom of the trade, no commission was payable in respect of bad debts. It was held that the agent was entitled to commission on all sales effected by him, including those resulting in bad debts, the trade custom being inconsistent with the express terms of the contract.[77]

---

[72] *Bryant v Flight* (1839) 5 M. & W. 114. The basis of the decision is obscure. See also *Peacock v Peacock* (1809) 2 Camp. 45; *Jewry v Busk* (1814) 5 Taunt. 302; *Bird v M'Gahey* (1849) 2 C. & K. 707; *Powell v Braun* [1954] 1 W.L.R. 401 where it was clear that the parties intended a reasonable sum to be paid.

[73] *Way v Latilla* [1937] 3 All E.R. 759.

[74] *Wilkie v Scottish Aviation Ltd* 1956 S.C. 198.

[75] *Faraday v Tamworth Union* (1917) 86 L.J.Ch. 436.

[76] *Miller v Beale* (1879) 27 W.R. 403. As to the remuneration of auctioneers on a sale by the court, and the relevant practice, see *Re Wolfe, Heller v Wolfe* [1952] 2 All E.R. 545 and CPR 40 PD 40D.

[77] *Bower v Jones* (1831) 8 Bing. 65; cf. *Caine v Horsefall* (1847) 1 Exch. 519; and see *Read v Rann*

(8)   P employed A to find a purchaser or mortgagee for property. A introduced N to P and negotiations started between them. These negotiations flagged and P agreed with A that A should write N a letter and that if N made an advance or purchased *in consequence* of the letter P would pay A £100. N purchased but gave evidence that he was not influenced by the letter. It was held that A was entitled to no remuneration since (i) the subsequent agreement had replaced the original agreement; (ii) the terms of the subsequent agreement left no room for a claim on a quantum meruit; and (iii) the event specified in the subsequent agreement had not taken place.[78]

(9)   P, a second mortgagee, gave A instructions to sell the property by auction. The contract between P and A provided that if a sale was effected between the date of receipt of instructions and the date of the auction, commission was payable on the same scale as for a sale by auction. On the day before the auction the mortgagor redeemed the mortgages and sold the property himself. Held, (i) A was not entitled to commission since the event on which commission was due had not taken place; (ii) no claim on a contractual quantum meruit lay because P had received no advantage and the contract provided for the events on which payment became due.[79]

(10) An agent introduces suitable purchasers to a prospective vendor, but takes no part in negotiations. The relevant scale provides commission for "seeking and negotiating" but not for seeking and finding without negotiating. It also provides for quantum meruit on "abortive work". Remuneration may be assessed on the basis of trouble taken, at considerably less than the scale fee.[80]

(11) An agent entitled to, and paid, commission upon a binding contract being made irrespective of completion, which contract fell through, was not entitled to a further commission when he effected a second sale, since there was no fresh written contract for the second sale as required by local law.[81]

(12) B had, first through a company and then personally, contracted to buy a property from G, both of which sales had fallen through leaving G with rights to forfeit pre-payments required of B under the contracts. G then agrees with B that if he can find another purchaser for the property for £6.5 million he would receive a commission of £1.2 million, a figure designed to allow B to recoup the forfeited sums under the earlier deals. B introduces a buyer who purchases the property from G for £6 million. Held, B was entitled to a reasonable commission on the sale, not measured by reference to the special commission which was obtainable only on procuring a sale at £6.5 million.[82]

(1830) 10 B. & C. 438; *Broad v Thomas* (1830) 7 Bing. 99; *Harley v Nagata* (1917) 34 T.L.R. 124. And see Article 58.

[78] *Green v Mules* (1861) 30 L.J.C.P. 343. This decision may today be regarded as somewhat harsh.

[79] *John Meacock & Co v Abrahams* [1956] 1 W.L.R. 1463. See also *Fairvale Ltd v Sabharwal* [1992] 2 E.G.L.R. 27; cf. *Bernard Marcus & Co v Ashraf* [1988] 1 E.G.L.R. 7; Murdoch, *Law of Estate Agency and Auctions* (4th edn), pp.144–147.

[80] *Sinclair Goldsmith v Minero Peru Comercial* [1978] E.G.D. 194; following *Reif Diner & Co v Catalytic International Inc* (1978) 246 E.G. 743. See also *Hoddell v Smith* [1976] E.G.D. 217; *Hampton & Sons v Trade and General Securities Ltd* (1978) 250 E.G. 451; *Lewis & Graves v Harper* (1978) 250 E.G. 1287. But see Murdoch [1981] Conv. 424; and *Law of Estate Agency* (5th edn), p.124 onwards; above, para.7-005. See further *Debenham Tewson & Chinnocks v Rimington* [1990] 2 E.G.L.R. 21; *Michael Elliott & Partners Ltd v UK Land Plc* [1991] 1 E.G.L.R. 39; *Cooke v Hopper* [2012] EWCA Civ 175 at [42].

[81] *Icon Property Pty Ltd v Wood* [2008] VSCA 123.

[82] *Barton v Gwyn-Jones* [2019] EWCA Civ 1999.

Article 56

AGENTS' REMUNERATION DUE UPON THE HAPPENING OF AN EVENT

7-013   (1) Where an agent is entitled to remuneration upon the happening of a future event, that entitlement does not arise until the event has occurred.

(2) The event upon which the agent's entitlement to remuneration arises is to be ascertained from the terms of the agency contract.

(3) Where the event upon which the agent's entitlement to remuneration arises does not occur, the agent will not be entitled to receive remuneration on a quantum meruit unless provision for this is expressly made in the agency contract, or unless a term to such effect can be implied into the agency contract in order to give it business efficacy or otherwise to give effect to the intentions of the parties.[83]

Comment

7-014 **General rule** This Article should be read in conjunction with Articles 57 and 58. The rule stated above is fundamental to the remuneration of the large number of agents who are paid by way of a commission on transactions which they bring about for their principals. The commission may be payable on many separate transactions, as in the case of a selling agent,[84] or it may be payable on a single transaction, as in the case of an estate agent acting for a private vendor. The principle stated is, however, of general application.[85] The agent must prove that the event has occurred upon which remuneration becomes due. What that event is is a question of law to be determined from the construction of the terms of agency contract.

> "It is a settled rule for the construction of commission notes and the like documents which refer to the remuneration of an agent that a plaintiff cannot recover unless he shows that the conditions of the written bargain have been fulfilled. If he proves fulfilment he recovers. If not, he fails. There appears to be no halfway house, and it matters not that the plaintiff proves expenditure of time, money and skill."[86]

In most instances the question whether the event has occurred presents no great difficulties. For example, if an agent is engaged to bring about a contract for the principal the agent's entitlement to commission will arise if and when the contract

---

[83] See Comment. The Article was cited with approval in *Berkeley Community Villages Ltd v Pullen* [2007] EWHC 1330 (Ch); [2007] N.P.C. 71 at [106].

[84] See, e.g. *Lockwood v Levick* (1860) 8 C.B.(N.S.) 603. *Del credere* commission is due and payable, in the absence of any special terms to the contrary, as soon as the contract is made in respect of which it is claimed: *Solly v Weiss* (1818) 8 Taunt. 371; *Caruthers v Graham* (1811) 14 East 578.

[85] *Lara v Hill* (1863) 15 C.B.(N.S.) 45; *Alder v Boyle* (1847) 4 C.B. 635; *Horford v Wilson* (1807) 1 Taunt. 12; *Platt v Depree* (1893) 9 T.L.R. 194; *Passingham v King* (1898) 14 T.L.R. 392; *Re Sovereign Life Assce. Co, Salter's Claim* (1891) 7 T.L.R. 602; *Skinner v Andrews & Hall* (1910) 26 T.L.R. 340; but cf. *Peacock v Freeman* (1888) 4 T.L.R. 541. Many of the early cases must be regarded with caution in view of the leading decision in *Luxor (Eastbourne) Ltd v Cooper* [1941] A.C. 108, e.g. *Fisher v Drewett* (1878) 48 L.J.Ex. 32; *Fuller v Eames* (1892) 8 T.L.R. 278; *Green v Lucas* (1876) 33 L.T. 584; *Vulcan Car Agency Ltd v Fiat Motors Ltd* (1915) 32 T.L.R. 73; and the dicta on substantial performance in *Rimmer v Knowles* (1874) 30 L.T. 496.

[86] *Howard Houlder & Partners Ltd v Manx Isles SS Co* [1923] 1 K.B. 110 at 113–114, per McCardie J; *Coupers Partnership Ltd v Basarik* [2007] EWCA Civ 40; [2007] R.V.R. 116; *Norton Property Group Pty Ltd v Ozzy States Pty Ltd* [2020] NSWCA 23 (buyer's agent not entitled to commission where buyer entered only into an option contract which option was not exercised).

is made. The agent has then done what he or she was engaged to do. However, owing largely to the number of stages involved in a contract for the purchase of real property, the commission of an estate agent has been the subject of many decisions in the courts; the estate agent frequently wishes to earn commission at a stage earlier than at which the principal enters into the contract the agent was engaged to bring about. Rule (3) may not apply where principal and agent effectively enter upon a new engagement, to which the former arrangements for commission are not applicable.[87]

Estate agents[88]   Much of the law on entitlement to commission derives from cases   **7-015**
of the 1950s and 1960s relating to estate agents. But "commission contracts are subject to no peculiar rules or principles of their own; the law which governs them is the law which governs all contracts and all questions of agency".[89] There are, therefore, no special rules of law relating to estate agents' contracts although the application to these of some of the basic principles of the law of contract has given rise to a considerable body of case law which can, making due allowances, be applied also in other contexts.

Nature of estate agent's contract   The nature of the estate agent's contract was   **7-016**
analysed by Lord Russell of Killowen in *Luxor (Eastbourne) Ltd v Cooper*.[90] He said that:

> "contracts by which owners of property, desiring to dispose of it, put it in the hands of agents on commission terms, are not (in default of specific provisions) contracts of employment in the ordinary meaning of those words. No obligation is imposed on the agent to do anything. The contracts are merely promises binding on the principal to pay a sum of money upon the happening of a specified event, which involves the rendering of some service by the agent. There is no real analogy between such contracts, and contracts of employment by which one party binds himself to do certain work, and the other binds himself to pay remuneration for the doing of it."[91]

The normal estate agent's contract is therefore said to be a unilateral contract, the agent not being bound to do anything. A "sole" or "exclusive" agency agreement is however said to raise a bilateral contract. There are difficulties of analysis which are discussed below.[92]

Entitlement to commission   Whenever an estate agent claims remuneration the   **7-017**
court must determine, as a matter of construction of the particular agency contract concerned, whether the event has occurred upon which the agent's entitlement to remuneration accrues:

> "No general rule can be laid down by which the rights of the agent or the liability of the principal under commission contracts are to be determined. In each case these must

---

[87]   See, e.g. *Benedetti v Sawiris* [2013] UKSC 50; [2014] A.C. 938.
[88]   See Murdoch, *Law of Estate Agency* (5th edn), Ch.3 (also discussing commission and remuneration of auctioneers). The nature of the estate agent's contract was considered in detail, and the then relevant cases reviewed, in Ash, *Willing to Purchase* (1963).
[89]   *Luxor (Eastbourne) Ltd v Cooper* [1941] A.C. 108 at 124, per Lord Russell of Killowen (Illustration 1 to Article 58).
[90]   Above.
[91]   *Luxor (Eastbourne) Ltd v Cooper* [1941] A.C. 108 at 124.
[92]   See Comment to Article 58.

depend upon the exact terms of the contract in question, and upon the true construction of those terms."[93]

A useful statement of the relevant principles is that of Jenkins LJ in *Midgley Estates Ltd v Hand*[94]:

"So far as any general principle is deducible from the authorities, their effect may, I think, be thus summarised: The question depends on the construction of each particular contract, but prima facie the intention of the parties to a contract of this type is likely to be that the commission stipulated for should only be payable in the event of an actual sale resulting ... That is, broadly, speaking, the intention which, as a matter of probability, the court should be disposed to impute to the parties. It follows that general or ambiguous expressions, purporting, for instance, to make the commission payable in the event of the agent 'finding a purchaser' or ... 'selling the property,' have been construed as meaning that the commission is only to be payable in the event of an actual and completed sale resulting, or, at least, in the event of the agent succeeding in introducing a purchaser who is able and willing to purchase the property. That is the broad general principle in the light of which the question of construction should be approached; but this does not mean that the contract, if its terms are clear, should not have effect in accordance with those terms, even if they do involve the result that the agent's commission is earned and becomes payable although the sale in respect of which it is claimed, for some reason or another, turns out to be abortive."

Clear and unambiguous words must, therefore, be used if the commission is to be payable without an actual sale taking place,[95] since it is "the common understanding of men ... that the agent's commission is payable out of the purchase price".[96] A comparable understanding may make a sub-agent's entitlement to commission contingent on the agent's entitlement, or even actual collection by the agent of commission from the principal, though express words would be needed to achieve a pay-if-paid result.[97] A similarly narrow approach to the question whether agents' services *caused* a sale has recently been taken by the Court of Appeal.[98]

But as fast as the courts have held that one particular formula will not entitle the

---

[93] *Luxor (Eastbourne) Ltd v Cooper* [1941] A.C. 108 at 124, per Lord Russell of Killowen.

[94] *Midgley Estates Ltd v Hand* [1952] 2 Q.B. 432 at 435–436. This statement was approved in *Wells v Devani* [2019] UKSC 4; [2020] A.C. 129 at [23].

[95] See also *Luxor (Eastbourne) Ltd v Cooper* [1941] A.C. 108 at 129. The contra proferentem rule was applied in *Price, Davies & Co v Smith* (1929) 141 L.T. 490 at 494; *Jaques v Lloyd D. George & Partners Ltd* [1968] 1 W.L.R. 625 at 632; *Block Bros Realty Ltd v Viktora* (1974) 42 D.L.R. (3d) 474. See also *Mustafa v K.G. Palos* [1972] E.G.D. 797.

[96] *Dennis Reed Ltd v Goody* [1950] 2 K.B. 277 at 284, per Denning LJ; *H.W. Liebig & Co v Leading Investments Ltd* [1986] 1 S.C.R. 70 at 79–82; (1985) 25 D.L.R. (4th) 161 at 176–179; *Wells v Devani* [2019] UKSC 4; [2020] A.C. 129. (But an argument, based on this statement, that a contract contained an implied term that the estate agent was entitled to commission from the purchase money held by the vendor's solicitor was rejected in *W.A. Ellis Services Ltd v Stuart Wood* [1993] 2 E.G.L.R. 43.) See also *Jaques v Lloyd D. George* [1968] 1 W.L.R. 625, where Lord Denning MR said that if the agency contract provided for payment of commission other than on the conclusion of business, it was the agent's duty to inform his principal; if not, the agent might be unable to recover. This statement goes further than other cases and may be difficult to reconcile with the general principle that a person is presumed to have read his contract. The contract provided that commission was payable if the agent should be "instrumental in introducing a person willing to sign a document capable of becoming a contract to purchase at a price which at any stage of the negotiations has been agreed" by the prospective vendor. The court held that these words were too vague to be enforceable: they could cover signature of a blank piece of paper.

[97] *Crema v Cenkos Securities Plc* [2010] EWCA Civ 1444; [2011] 1 W.L.R. 2066.

[98] *Foxtons Ltd v Bicknell* [2008] EWCA Civ 419; [2008] 24 E.G. 142; [2008] N.P.C. 52 (noted Watts

agent to commission before the contract of sale is made, so have estate agents devised new formulae in an endeavour to achieve this result. The reported cases are therefore no more than illustrations of the strict criteria which the courts have applied, and many of the contractual formulae used in them must be regarded as obsolete in so far as they clearly will not achieve what the agent generally desires to do, viz., to secure a right to commission as soon as someone is produced who shows a serious interest in buying the property. It must also be remembered that in the purchase of real property in England and Wales the contractual arrangements have, unlike a normal commercial contract, traditionally fallen into three distinct stages:

(1) *Agreement "subject to contract"* The third party makes an offer "subject to contract" or "subject to survey" and, if this is accepted, pays a deposit to the estate agent. This transaction is not normally, in law, a contract to purchase the property and either party is free to withdraw from further negotiations for any, or even no, reason.[99]

(2) *Contract* The parties sign and, normally through their solicitors, exchange contracts. From the moment of exchange of contracts, but not until then, they are contractually bound to each other[100] (subject to the ordinary rules, such as those relating to void and voidable contracts).

(3) *Completion* This is normally effected through solicitors. The vendor's solicitor transmits the title deeds to the purchaser's solicitor in exchange for a banker's draft for the balance of the purchase price with an adjustment for outgoings from the date of contract.

The estate agent generally wants to be entitled to commission at stage (1); the courts have rarely held that there is an entitlement before stage (2) and sometimes even not until stage (3).

In a work of this nature it is not appropriate to consider every reported case in which an estate agent has claimed commission and, indeed, there is a very large number of such cases.[101] All that is possible is to consider some of the leading cases in which forms of wording then common were used, in order thereby to illustrate the general principle. This Article is therefore not accompanied by Illustrations: it has seemed better to incorporate them into the exposition. It should be noted also that differences and developments in conveyancing practice, and in the functions of an estate agent, lead to differences between jurisdictions. For example, in some countries an estate agent may be expected to procure a purchaser's signature to the contract and take a deposit.[102]

Introduction of a "purchaser" The simplest practical form of estate agent's contract provides that commission shall be payable on the "introduction of a   **7-018**

[2009] J.B.L. 268). See further Article 57.

[99] *Chillingworth v Esche* [1924] 1 Ch. 97; *Eccles v Bryant* [1948] Ch. 93. But as to "subject to survey" and "subject to satisfactory survey", see *Astra Trust v Adams* [1969] 1 Lloyd's Rep. 81, doubted in *The Merak* [1976] 2 Lloyd's Rep. 250 at 254; *Ee v Kakar* (1979) 40 P. & C.R. 223; and in general Treitel, *Law of Contract* (15th edn), paras 2-090.

[100] *Eccles v Bryant* [1948] Ch. 93.

[101] See Murdoch (1982) 264 E.G. 419 at 513. Almost all the older cases of importance were examined in Ash, *Willing to Purchase* (1963). For another account of the modern law see Murdoch, *Law of Estate Agency* (5th edn), p.83 onwards.

[102] See, e.g. *Pemberton v Action Realty Ltd* [1986] 1 N.Z.L.R. 286.

purchaser".[103] Sometimes the agent is merely asked to "find a purchaser"[104] or to "find someone to buy".[105] In these cases there must, it seems, be a binding contract to purchase before there can be any question of entitlement to commission.[106] Moreover, if after contract and before completion the purchaser withdraws for any reason, the agent's entitlement will (unless specific performance is obtained[107]) be lost because the person introduced was not a "purchaser".[108] On the other hand, if the *vendor* defaults after contract but before completion, the agent's entitlement is normally not lost; the vendor may not rely upon the fact that what prevented the contract from proceeding to completion was the vendor's own wrong vis-à-vis the person introduced by the agent.[109] If a purchaser withdraws from a contract owing to the vendor's misrepresentation, the agent, it seems, will not normally be entitled to commission due solely upon a binding contract being made,[110] but the vendor may be liable to the agent for damages for breach of an implied term in the contract of appointment that the vendor will not make fraudulent misrepresentations to the purchaser.[111] Many forms of commission contract provide extending definitions of

---

[103] *Jones v Lowe* [1945] K.B. 73. As to the meaning of "introduce", see *D.C. Wylde & Co v Sparg* 1977 (2) S.A.L.R. 75: in the context the word meant: "to direct the attention of a person who has not applied his mind in that direction to the fact that a property is for sale, or to a material element of the sale not previously appreciated by him". See also *John D. Wood & Co v Dantata* [1987] 2 E.G.L.R. 23 at 25, per Nourse LJ ("the leading or bringing in of the purchaser to that transaction"); *Peter Yates & Co v Bullock* [1990] 2 E.G.L.R. 24; *Estafnous v London & Leeds Business Centres Ltd* [2009] EWHC 1308 (Ch) at [53]; affirmed [2011] EWCA Civ 1157 (introduction does not require personal contact between vendor and purchaser) A clause entitling to commission on introduction will not in the absence of other indications entitle to commission on introductions effected before the making of the contract providing for commission: *Samuel & Co v Sanders Bros* (1886) 3 T.L.R. 145.

[104] *Fowler v Bratt* [1950] 2 K.B. 96.

[105] *McCallum v Hicks* [1950] 2 K.B. 271. See also *Alder v Boyle* (1847) 4 C.B. 635; *Lott v Outhwaite* (1893) 10 T.L.R. 76; *Chapman v Winson* (1904) 91 L.T. 17; *Henry v Gregory* (1905) 22 T.L.R. 53; *Timms v Carofaro* (1989) 53 S.A.S.R. 572 ("effect a sale ... substantially the transaction contemplated by the contract").

[106] See *McCallum v Hicks* [1950] 2 K.B. 271; *James v Smith* (1921) [1931] 2 K.B. 317n; *Blake & Co v Sohn* [1969] 1 W.L.R. 1412; *Phillipson v Indus Realty Pty Ltd* (2004) 8 V.L.R. 446 ("subject to completion of sale"). But the right to commission is not lost because the parties later vary the contract: *Lord v Trippe* (1977) 51 A.L.J.R. 574.

[107] See *Boots v E. Christopher & Co* [1952] 1 K.B. 89 at 98 where Denning LJ also suggests that if the vendor sues, and obtains full damages including commission payable to the agent, commission would be due. In *H.W. Liebig & Co v Leading Investments Ltd* [1986] 1 S.C.R. 70 at 86; (1985) 25 D.L.R. (4th) 161 at 181–182 LaForest J suggests that the agent may in such a case be entitled to some form of restitutionary award. But the vendor is not bound to sue and may settle the case: ibid.

[108] *James v Smith* (1921) [1931] 2 K.B. 317n; *Martin v Perry and Daw* [1931] 2 K.B. 310; *Poole v Clarke & Co* [1945] 2 All E.R. 445. If the contract expressly or impliedly provides that commission is to be paid out of the purchase price, no commission will be due if the purchase price is not paid: *Bull v Price* (1831) 5 M. & P. 2; *Martin v Tucker* (1885) 1 T.L.R. 655; *Beningfield v Kynaston* (1887) 3 T.L.R. 279; *Knight, Frank & Rutley v Gordon* (1923) 39 T.L.R. 399; *Price, Davies & Co v Smith* (1929) 141 L.T. 490; *Boots v E. Christopher & Co* [1952] 1 K.B. 89. See also *Fidcott v Friesner* (1895) 11 T.L.R. 187; *Foster's Agency Ltd v Romaine* (1916) 32 T.L.R. 545.

[109] *Luxor (Eastbourne) Ltd v Cooper* [1941] A.C. 108 at 126, 142; *Dennis Reed Ltd v Goody* [1950] 2 K.B. 277 at 285. See also *Alpha Trading Ltd v Dunnshaw-Patten Ltd* [1981] Q.B. 290, Illustration 3 to Article 58. But cf. *Adler v Ananhall Advisory & Consultancy Services Ltd* [2009] EWCA Civ 586; [2009] N.P.C. 80 (commission only upon completion).

[110] *Peter Long & Partners v Burns* [1956] 1 W.L.R. 1083; *John D. Wood & Co (Residential and Agricultural) Ltd v Craze* [2007] EWHC 2658 (QB); [2008] 1 E.G.L.R. 17; [2008] 6 E.G. 132; [2007] 50 E.G. 108 (C.S.); [2007] N.P.C. 130.

[111] *John D. Wood & Co (Residential and Agricultural) Ltd v Craze* [2007] EWHC 2658 (QB); [2008] 1 E.G.L.R. 17; [2008] 6 E.G. 132; [2007] 50 E.G. 108 (C.S.); [2007] N.P.C. 130 (noted Watts [2009]

the word "purchaser" to include direct and indirect links between the person introduced and the actual purchasers.[112]

Introduction of a person "ready, willing and able to purchase" Use of the above expressions was unsatisfactory to those agents who wanted to be entitled to their commission at an earlier stage than exchange of contracts. Accordingly, some agents provided that their commission was to be earned on the introduction of a person who was "ready, willing and able to purchase".[113] Sometimes one or more of the adjectives was dropped (e.g. a person "willing and able to purchase"[114]). It does not matter what adjectives are used; the principle which the courts have applied in the construction of such contracts is the same. The agent must prove that the person introduced fulfilled the qualifications provided in the contract.

7-019

At first, commission was fairly readily awarded to the agent on such wording,[115] but in the 1950s it became clear that the courts would apply a strict test to decide whether the agent's entitlement had arisen. In *Graham and Scott (Southgate) Ltd v Oxlade*[116] the Court of Appeal held that if a prospective purchaser made an offer which was subject to any conditions, such as "subject to contract" or "subject to survey", this showed that the purchaser was not "willing to purchase" because a *locus poenitentiae* had been reserved. Only an unqualified offer, capable of acceptance by the vendor, would show that the prospective purchaser was "willing". Shortly afterwards, in *Dennis Reed Ltd v Goody*,[117] the Court of Appeal repeated its decision in *Oxlade*'s case, holding that a person who made a conditional offer to purchase was not shown to be "willing" to purchase. This strict approach was subsequently followed. In *Dellafiora v Lester*[118] where, after contract, the vendor's landlord refused to consent to the assignment of the lease to the person introduced and the parties did not proceed further, the Court of Appeal held that this showed that the person introduced was not "able" to purchase and the agent was therefore not entitled to commission. In *Christie, Owen & Davies v Stockton*[119] the contract provided that commission should be payable if, inter alia, the vendor withdrew

---

J.B.L. 268).

[112] See, e.g. *Christie Owen & Davies Plc v Raobgle Trust Corp* [2011] EWCA Civ 1151.

[113] See, e.g. *Keningtons v Regional Properties Ltd* [1946] E.G.D. 86; *Dennis Reed Ltd v Nicholls* [1948] 2 All E.R. 914; *Lewis & Tucker v Lee* (1949) 153 E.G. 342; *Bennett & Partners v Millett* [1949] 1 K.B. 362; *Berry Estates v Burgess* (1949) 153 E.G. 343; *Brown & Co v Michaels* (1949) 153 E.G. 511; *E.P. Nelson & Co v Rolfe* [1950] 1 K.B. 139; *E.P. Nelson v Lyons* (1949) 154 E.G. 376; *Murdoch Lownie v Newman* [1949] 2 All E.R. 783; *Dennis Reed Ltd v Goody* [1950] 2 K.B. 277.

[114] *Graham & Scott (Southgate) Ltd v Oxlade* [1950] 2 K.B. 257.

[115] See, e.g. *Dennis Reed Ltd v Nicholls* [1948] 2 All E.R. 914; *Bennett & Partners v Millett* [1949] 1 K.B. 362; *Knight, Frank and Rutley v Fraser*, 1974 S.L.T. 50.

[116] *Graham and Scott (Southgate) Ltd v Oxlade* [1950] 2 K.B. 257. This involved overruling *Giddys v Horsfall* [1947] 1 All E.R. 460; *Bennett & Partners v Millett* [1949] 1 K.B. 362; and probably by implication disapproving of some of the reasoning in *Dennis Reed Ltd v Nicholls* [1948] 2 All E.R. 914. This latter case was regarded as overruled by Denning LJ in *Dennis Reed Ltd v Goody* [1950] 2 K.B. 277 at 289. Another inconsistent decision, *E.P. Nelson & Co v Rolfe* [1950] 1 K.B. 139 was explained as having turned on a concession.

[117] *Dennis Reed Ltd v Goody* [1950] 2 K.B. 277. A month later the Court of Appeal held in *Bennett, Walden & Co v Wood* [1950] 2 All E.R. 134 that an offer "subject to contract" did not entitle the agent to commission when the agency contract provided that commission was due when the agent "secured an offer".

[118] *Dellafiora v Lester* [1962] 1 W.L.R. 1208. The form of wording in the case was unusual, but the case was decided on whether the potential purchaser was "able". The Court of Appeal expanded the definition given in earlier cases in which it had suggested that the ability to purchase related to financial ability; the potential purchaser must be "able" in every way.

[119] *Christie, Owen & Davies v Stockton* [1953] 1 W.L.R. 1353.

"after having accepted an offer to purchase by a person able and willing to enter into a formal contract". The agents introduced a person and a price was agreed "subject to contract". During negotiations the vendor withdrew. Slade J held that the agent was not entitled to commission. The language was not clear and unequivocal and there were no agreed terms since the whole matter was "subject to contract". Under these circumstances the principle of *Oxlade*'s case applied. A rather similar attempt to claim commission failed in *A.L. Wilkinson Ltd v Brown*.[120] Commission was due on the introduction of a person "prepared to enter into a contract to purchase" at an agreed price. A person was introduced and a price "agreed" but the offer to purchase was conditional on the potential purchaser selling his own house. Before contract the vendor sold elsewhere. The Court of Appeal held that there was only an expectancy that a contract would be signed and that there was therefore no introduction of a suitably qualified person.

In the above cases the agent failed because the event upon which the commission became due had not occurred. That event was defined by the contract as being the introduction of a person having certain qualifications ("ready, willing and able to purchase"). The person introduced did not have those qualifications and the commission thus had not become due. Whether the person introduced did have those qualifications is a question of fact and if an agent does introduce such a person, the agent is entitled to the agreed commission even if no sale contract is thereafter concluded because the potential vendor declines to enter into a contract with that person. Thus in *Christie Owen & Davies Ltd v Rapacioli*[121] the defendant instructed the plaintiff agents to help him find a purchaser of his business and to quote a price of £20,000. The agency contract provided that commission was payable in the event of the plaintiffs "effecting an introduction either directly or indirectly of a person ... ready able and willing to purchase [for £20,000] or any other price". The plaintiffs introduced a person who was prepared to purchase for £17,700 and this offer was accepted "subject to contract". The parties' solicitors thereafter negotiated and a draft contract was prepared, engrossed and signed by the potential purchaser. The defendant then decided to proceed no further with the sale. The Court of Appeal held that the plaintiffs were entitled to succeed in their claim to commission. The person whom they had introduced was willing to contract with the defendant in terms acceptable to him until the moment of his withdrawal. The court expressly approved a passage from the judgment of Bucknill LJ in *Dennis Reed Ltd v Goody*,[122] who said:

"... the plaintiffs' claim to commission is not established merely by showing that the person whom they introduced was able and willing to purchase the property at any one particular moment of time: they must prove that he was ready, able and willing to purchase up to the time when either an enforceable contract for the purchase of the house is made between the parties or, alternatively, up to the time when the vendor refuses to enter into

---

[120] *A.L. Wilkinson Ltd v Brown* [1966] 1 W.L.R. 194. See also *Gerlach v Pearson* [1950] V.L.R. 321 ("secure a purchaser": offer "subject to finance": no commission due).

[121] *Christie Owen & Davies Ltd v Rapacioli* [1974] Q.B. 781. The court followed *A.L. Wilkinson Ltd v O'Neil* (1961) 181 E.G. 137. See also *John E. Trinder & Partners v Haggis* (1951) 158 E.G. 4 (not cited in the *Christie* case but decided on similar principles). The court declined to follow *Martin, Gale & Wright v Buswell* [1961] E.G.D. 418 in view of the different grounds of decision given by the court. See also *Walters v John Crisp Pty Ltd* (1982) 64 F.L.R. 299 (Aus.) ("if you or anyone else obtains a person who is ready, willing and able to purchase the property ... a full fee is payable to the listing agent").

[122] *Dennis Reed Ltd v Goody* [1950] 2 K.B. 277.

such a contract on terms on which the purchaser is willing to purchase and the vendor was at one time willing to sell."[123]

It should be noted that the wording of the contract in *Rapacioli*'s case was particularly precise. Although there were suggestions in the judgments that some of Lord Denning's earlier dicta may have gone too far, it is not clear that this is so.[124]

The problem raised by this case is that the prospective purchaser's willingness must be measured against some terms on which the purchaser is to be "willing to purchase". In theory it might be possible to specify in the agency contract all the terms which the prospective purchaser must be willing to accept; only if those terms were agreed to would there be a "willing" purchaser for the purposes of the agency contract. But in practice this would be unacceptable in view of the fact that negotiations between prospective purchaser and prospective vendor are inevitable. Furthermore, neither party would be willing to accept such provisions before the market has been tested. The prospective purchaser's willingness has therefore been tested by the courts against the terms on which the prospective vendor is prepared to sell. The difficulty is that the "subject to contract" situation is not a simple offer and acceptance situation; at any time until exchange of contracts a prospective vendor can change the terms on which the vendor is prepared to sell and any willingness is thus only a temporary willingness until that time. The most that can be said is that until exchange of contracts the prospective vendor has expressed the view that in due course he or she will be willing to sell on certain terms provided there is no change of mind thereafter. In holding that the prospective purchaser's willingness may be tested against terms which at one time the prospective vendor was prepared to accept, the court was referring only to this temporary manifestation of preparedness to accept which could at any time be altered vis-à-vis the prospective purchaser. A conclusive willingness can only be tested at the moment of exchange of contracts because it is only at this moment that it is known what the prospective vendor's terms are, and thus whether the prospective purchaser is "willing to purchase" on those terms. The Court of Appeal was therefore prepared to look for a willingness on the part of the prospective vendor for the purposes of the agency contract which was not yet a willingness to sell for the purposes of the sale contract.

These difficulties had been foreseen by Denning LJ (as he then was) in *McCallum v Hicks*.[125] He said:

"A person may not properly be said to be 'willing' to purchase, so as to entitle the agent to commission, unless he is irrevocably willing, that is, unless he has given irrevocable proof of his willingness by entering into a binding contract to purchase."[126]

Only then could the prospective purchaser be said to be "willing to purchase" on terms acceptable to the prospective vendor. This remark of Denning LJ was expressly disapproved by the Court of Appeal in *Christie Owen & Davies Ltd v Rapacioli*,[127] as was a similar statement by the same judge in *Dennis Reed Ltd v*

---

[123] *Dennis Reed Ltd v Goody* [1950] 2 K.B. 277 at 283.
[124] See *H.W. Liebig & Co v Leading Investments Ltd* [1987] 1 S.C.R. 70 at 82; (1986) 25 D.L.R. (4th) 161 at 179, per LaForest J.
[125] *Dennis Reed Ltd v Goody* [1950] 2 K.B. 277.
[126] *Dennis Reed Ltd v Goody* [1950] 2 K.B. 277 at 276.
[127] *Christie Owen & Davies Ltd v Rapacioli* [1974] Q.B. 781 at 787, 790, 791. But see *H.W. Liebig &*

Goody.[128] A problem of a similar nature had also arisen indirectly in *Ackroyd & Sons v Hasan*[129]: the agents' contract there provided that their commission was due in the event of their introducing "a party prepared to enter into a contract to purchase [on certain terms set out in the agency contract] or on such other terms to which [the vendor might] assent". The terms of sale were agreed "subject to contract" between the potential purchaser's and the potential vendor's solicitors, but the vendor had not yet agreed to what her solicitors had negotiated. She withheld this agreement and no contract was ever made. The Court of Appeal held that, on the facts, the agents had failed to prove that the vendor had assented to the terms. At first instance, Winn J had said[130] that in his view "assent" meant legally binding assent. In the Court of Appeal Upjohn and Ormerod LJJ expressed their strong disagreement with this view.[131] Upjohn LJ said that whether the vendor had assented[132] was "purely a question of fact" and that, for example, it could be strongly argued that a vendor could be shown to assent by having signed his part of the contract notwithstanding that he withdrew before exchange. Sellers LJ,[133] however, was not satisfied that Winn J's view was wrong or that commission could be due where the assent of the vendor fell short of communicated assent so as to conclude a contract. He reserved consideration of this question until it might arise on another set of facts. The view of the majority of the court was that which was later accepted in *Christie Owen & Davies v Rapacioli*.[134] The court in that case recognised that a situation might well arise where the potential vendor might well have to pay two commissions, one to the agent who introduced a person who was willing to purchase on terms on which the principal had at one time been willing to sell but from which he had withdrawn, and another to the agent through whom he finally sold. Such a conclusion in this context seems however at variance with the statement of Lord Wright in *Luxor (Eastbourne) Ltd v Cooper*[135] that:

> "the commission agreement is, however, subordinate to the hoped for principal agreement of sale. It would be strange if what was preliminary or accessory should control the freedom of action of the principal in regard to the main transaction which everyone contemplates might never materialise."

Where however the agent does introduce a person who signs an offer to purchase, but at the time of doing so the principal has already accepted an offer from another

---

Co v Leading Investments Ltd [1987] 1 S.C.R. 70 at 82; (1986) 25 D.L.R. (4th) 161.

[128] *Dennis Reed Ltd v Goody* [1950] 2 K.B. 277 at 287–288.

[129] *Ackroyd & Sons v Hasan* [1960] 2 Q.B. 144.

[130] *Ackroyd & Sons v Hasan* [1959] 1 W.L.R. 706 at 712: " ... in that context the word assent means: finally 'assent' at the last moment of time at which you, the property owner, will be entitled, when the negotiations have proceeded to that final stage, to say: 'These are the terms precisely to which I give my concluded and considered assent'. I do not think it permissible to construe in favour of the estate agent and against the property owner in such a contract as this the word 'assent' as meaning: 'give a half-considered assent on the basis that it seems at the moment to be all right, but possibly with a mental reservation, due to advice received from the solicitor, that there is no final commitment on this matter until the time comes for exchanging the formal contracts'".

[131] *Ackroyd & Sons v Hasan* [1960] 2 Q.B. 144 at 156 (Upjohn LJ), 162 (Ormerod LJ).

[132] In *Martin Gale & Wright v Buswell* [1961] E.G.D. 418 Upjohn LJ made it clear that what the vendor's solicitor had "agreed" with the potential purchaser's solicitor was not the "assent" which had to be proved since the solicitor, in the absence of express authority could not bind his client. What had to be proved was that the vendor assented to the draft contract prepared by the solicitor.

[133] *Ackroyd & Sons v Hasan* [1960] 2 Q.B. 144 at 166–167.

[134] *Christie Owen & Davies v Rapacioli* [1974] Q.B. 781.

[135] *Luxor (Eastbourne) Ltd v Cooper* [1941] A.C. 108 at 138–139.

buyer introduced by another agent, it has been held that no commission is due, on the basis that the right to commission is subject to an implied restriction that the property has not already been sold. This implication is a natural one for most transactions.[136]

Estate Agents (Provision of Information) Regulations 1991[137]   By these Regula-   **7-020**
tions, an estate agent using in the course of estate agency work[138] the phrase "ready, willing and able purchaser" must explain the intention and effect of these words in writing in a way described in the Regulations.[139] Failure to comply with this obligation makes the contract unenforceable except by order of the court.[140] The explanation required is as follows:

> "A purchaser is a 'ready, willing and able' purchaser if he is prepared and is able to exchange unconditional contracts for the purchase of your property.
> You will be liable to pay remuneration to us, in addition to any other costs or charges agreed, if such a purchaser is introduced by us in accordance with your instructions and this must be paid even if you subsequently withdraw and unconditional contracts for sale are not exchanged, irrespective of your reasons."[141]

Where the contract wording varies, the explanation must be given with appropriate modifications.[142] It may be that this requirement, in calling for clearer drafting, will avoid in the future some of the difficulties of the past. The older cases must, however, be noted as examples of the problems to be avoided. It should be noted that the explanation given by the regulations, while inappropriate to estate agents seeking *tenants*, is more favourable to the estate agent than some of the judicial decisions on similar wording.[143]

Other types of estate agent contracts   Some of the difficulties discussed above   **7-021**
have been avoided where an agent has stipulated for commission upon the introduction by the agent of a person who signs or enters into a legally binding contract to purchase. The event here is clearly defined, even if it may not be sufficiently advanced in time to please all estate agents. Thus, in *Midgley Estates Ltd v Hand*[144]

---

[136] *A.A. Dickson & Co v O'Leary* (1979) 254 E.G. 731, following *E.P. Nelson & Co v Rolfe* [1950] 1 K.B. 139 on this point. But it is certainly possible for a vendor to be liable for two commissions: below, para.7-029.

[137] SI 1991/859, made under s.30(1) of the Estate Agents Act 1979.

[138] As to which see Estate Agents Act 1979 s.1; Murdoch, *Law of Estate Agency and Auctions* (4th edn), p.266 onwards; and in general Murdoch, *The Estate Agents and Property Misdescriptions Acts* (3rd edn).

[139] Estate Agents (Provision of Information) Regulations 1991 reg.5.

[140] Estate Agents Act 1979 s.18(5). Such a contract was enforced in *Benhams Ltd v Kythira Investments Ltd* [2004] EWHC 2973. See further, para.7-007.

[141] Regulations 1991 Schedule. The definition clause defines "purchaser" as "a person to whom an interest in land is transferred or in whose favour it was created". In *Foxtons Ltd v Thesleff* [2005] EWCA Civ 514; [2005] 2 E.G.L.R. 29 it was held that this covered a person who contracted unconditionally to buy, and also that the Regulations could not affect the proper meaning of the contract entered into.

[142] Estate Agents (Provision of Information) Regulations 1991 reg.5(1),(2). As to the time at which notice must be given, see regs 3, 5(3).

[143] It does not require that the transaction proceeds as far as the exchange of contracts. See Murdoch, *Law of Estate Agency and Auctions* (3rd edn), pp.205–206.

[144] *Midgley Estates Ltd v Hand* [1952] 2 Q.B. 432; and see *Foxtons Ltd v Thesleff* [2005] EWCA Civ 514; [2005] 2 E.G.L.R. 29.

and *Scheggia v Gradwell*[145] the agents were held entitled to their commission although, in the former case, the purchaser withdrew after contract and, in the latter, the contract that was signed would not have been enforced by specific performance. In each case the event, the signature of a legally binding contract, had occurred. On the other hand, in *Peter Long & Partners v Burns*[146] the agents' claim to commission failed because the contract was voidable due to an innocent misrepresentation. They had therefore not introduced a person who had entered into a legally binding contract. Another format entitles the agent to commission if a person is introduced "with whom we have not been in prior communication, and who subsequently completes" a contract. This avoids problems of effective cause[147] and appears effective.[148] Where commission contracts with different terms are used, this may result in two commissions being payable.[149] Where the person or group introduced subsequently completes the transaction by means of a newly formed company, subsidiary or syndicate, it may be held that the person introduced has completed the purchase, though by means of others,[150] subject to considerations of effective cause.[151]

The most satisfactory way for an agent to ensure an entitlement to commission upon an introduction seems to be to avoid all references to the ultimate contract or to purchasers. Thus in *Drewery and Drewery v Ware-Lane*[152] the agents' contract provided that commission was to be due when a "prospective purchaser" signed the agents' "purchaser's agreement" and the vendor signed the agents' "vendor's agreement" (both supplied by the agents). Both these documents were "subject to contract" but both were signed. The Court of Appeal held that the agents were entitled to their commission notwithstanding that the prospective purchaser was unable to obtain a mortgage and so never entered into a contract to purchase. The court held that the expression "prospective purchaser" did not require that the person introduced must be ready, willing or able but simply that he must bona fide

---

[145] *Scheggia v Gradwell* [1963] 1 W.L.R. 1049. In *A.L. Wilkinson Ltd v Brown* [1966] 1 W.L.R. 194 at 202–203. Salmon LJ described the *Scheggia* type of contract as "a ridiculous bargain" and said that the scope of that decision ought not to be extended. See also *Jaques v Lloyd D. George & Partners Ltd* [1968] 1 W.L.R. 625 at 632; para.7-017, above.

[146] *Peter Long & Partners v Burns* [1956] 1 W.L.R. 1083; cf. *Chris Hart (Business Sales) Ltd v Currie* 1992 S.L.T. 544 (concluded contract conditional on transfer of licence of public house by licensing board; licence not transferred; commission due). Even a vendor's fraudulent misrepresentation will not entitle the agent to commission on an otherwise unconditional contract. The vendor may, however, be liable to the agent for damages on an implied term: *John D. Wood & Co (Residential and Agricultural) Ltd v Craze* [2007] EWHC 2658 (QB); [2008] 1 E.G.L.R. 17; [2008] 6 E.G. 132; [2007] 50 E.G. 108 (C.S.); [2007] N.P.C. 130 (noted [2009] J.B.L. 268).

[147] See Article 57.

[148] *Brian Cooper & Co v Fairview Estates (Investments) Ltd* [1987] 1 E.G.L.R. 18. See also *Raja v Rollerby Ltd* (1997) 74 P. & C.R. D25 ("in case of selling the above properties to your clients at the sum of £750,000 your commission will be 2 per cent. This offer is valid until the end of this week"); *Glentree Estates Ltd v Favermead Ltd* [2010] EWCA Civ 1473 at [17] (express entitlement to commission even if vendor himself finds purchaser implies that no need for agent to be effective cause of sale when the agent effects an introduction).

[149] See, e.g. *Lordsgate Properties Ltd v Balcombe* [1985] 1 E.G.L.R. 20; *Bernard Marcus & Co v Ashraf* [1988] 1 E.G.L.R. 7 (auctioneer); *Peter Yates & Co v Bullock* [1990] 2 E.G.L.R. 24. It is also possible that there may be two effective causes: *Lordsgate Properties Ltd v Balcombe* [1985] 1 E.G.L.R. 20: see below, para.7-029.

[150] *Di Dio Nominees Pty Ltd v Brian Mark Real Estate Pty Ltd* [1992] 2 V.R. 732.

[151] *Gunn v Showell's Brewery Co Ltd* (1902) 50 W.R. 659, Illustration 12 to Article 57.

[152] *Drewery and Drewery v Ware-Lane* [1960] 1 W.L.R. 1204.

contemplate purchasing.[153] This condition had been fulfilled. But in *Mustafa v K.G. Palos*[154] the contract provided that commission was payable to a mortgage broker in the event of "an offer of mortgage" on terms set out in the agency contract. The agent found a building society which offered to grant a mortgage but the prospective vendor then withdrew from the sale negotiations. The Court of Appeal held that commission was not due because an "offer of mortgage" meant an offer which actually led to a mortgage.

Custom[155]   Just as custom cannot entitle an agent to commission where it is unreasonable or contrary to the express terms of the contract,[156] it also cannot debar an agent from commission where it is unreasonable, or where the terms of the contract entitle the agent to commission.[157]   **7-022**

Conclusion   The cases discussed in this Comment are no more than illustrations of the criteria applied. It cannot be too strongly emphasised that each case falls to be decided with reference to the general principles: **7-023**

> "first, when an agent claims that he has earned the right to commission, the test is whether upon the proper interpretation of the contract between the principal and agent the event has happened upon which commission is to be paid. Secondly, there are no special principles of construction applicable to commission contracts with estate agents. Thirdly, contracts under which a principal is bound to pay commission for an introduction which does not result in a sale must be expressed in clear language."[158]

Claims for work done when commission not earned   In the nineteenth century it was commonly thought that if an agent was prevented from earning commission the agent was nevertheless entitled to receive a reasonable sum on a quantum meruit[159]; but, as was frequently also pointed out,[160] such suggestions were contrary to principle. A claim for a contractual quantum meruit of the type envisaged must   **7-024**

---

[153] Even this difficulty could, it seems, have been overcome by substituting "person" in the agency contract for "prospective purchaser".

[154] *Mustafa v K.G. Palos* [1972] E.G.D. 797. The principles expressed in this case seem entirely at variance with those expressed in *Christie Owen & Davies Ltd v Rapacioli* [1974] Q.B. 781 although the two cases can, perhaps, be reconciled on their particular facts and contractual terms. On "obtain an offer", see *Cash v George Dundas Realty Ltd* [1976] 2 S.C.R. 796; (1975) 59 D.L.R. (3d) 605; on "arrange a mortgage", see *Capital Management Corp v Hackett Development* (1971) 18 F.L.R. 362; and on "subject to our offer being accepted", see *Richard Ellis v Pipe-Chem (Holdings) Ltd* [1981] E.G.D. 222.

[155] See Article 31.

[156] See above, para.3-037.

[157] *Les Affréteurs Reunis Société Anonyme v Leopold Walford (London) Ltd* [1919] A.C. 801. See too *Crema v Cenkos Securities Plc* [2010] EWCA Civ 1444; [2011] 1 W.L.R. 2066.

[158] *Ackroyd & Sons v Hasan* [1960] 2 Q.B. 144 at 154, per Upjohn LJ.

[159] The expression quantum meruit is used in at least two different senses in the cases: (i) to describe a claim in restitution: see above, para.7-009; (ii) to describe a claim in contract for a reasonable sum. Such a claim must be based on an express or implied term in the agency contract. In many of the older authorities no distinction is made between the two different uses of the expression and it is often not clear to which the court intended to refer. The matter is further complicated because the courts have sometimes been referring to the principle expressed in *Planché v Colburn* (1831) 8 Bing. 14 that in certain circumstances, where an innocent party has rendered services under a contract which has been terminated by that party because of the other party's breach, a resulting claim for breach of contract can be waived with the agent suing in restitution on a quantum meruit to recover a reasonable sum for the services: cf. *Goff and Jones, Law of Unjust Enrichment* (9th edn), para.5-40. Because the principle depends essentially on breach of contract and termination, it is doubtful whether it can have any application to the typical estate agent's contract, which is unilateral.

be based on an implied contractual term that a reasonable sum is payable in the circumstances. Where the contract expressly provides for remuneration on the happening of an event, any such implication would be contrary to this express term and so could not be made. "It was said that there was an implied contract to pay the agent a quantum meruit for his services. The answer was that there could be no implied contract when there was an express contract".[161] The principle is, perhaps, most clearly to be found in *Howard Houlder & Partners Ltd v Manx Isles SS Co*[162] and *Bentall, Horsley & Baldry v Vicary*.[163] In the latter case an estate agent claimed on a quantum meruit when the vendor sold the property himself, although the agent had been appointed the sole agent. McCardie J held that the principal was not in breach of contract. Of the agent's claim on a quantum meruit he said[164]:

> "Undoubtedly ... [the agent] did work and incurred expense. But this is quite a usual feature of an estate agent's vocation when he works under a commission note which only gives him a right to recover commission when he fulfils the terms of the note. He runs the risk of losing his labour and expense unless he can comply with the conditions of the bargain. There is no scope in the present case for the operation of the doctrine of quantum meruit."

It may, however, be that the intention of the parties was that the principal should pay the agent a reasonable sum if the event upon the happening of which remuneration was due did not occur. The contract may make express provision to this effect.[165] Alternatively, the implication of a term to this effect might be necessary to give business efficacy to the contract or otherwise to effect the clear intention of the parties. But it is clear that such an implication would only be made in exceptional cases.[166]

7-025 **Overpaid commission** Sometimes advance payments of commission exceed the amounts actually due when the contract is terminated. In such a case it is a matter

---

[160] See, e.g. *Martin v Tucker* (1885) 1 T.L.R. 655; *Peacock v Freeman* (1888) 4 T.L.R. 541; *Barnett v Isaacson* (1888) 4 T.L.R. 645; *Re Sovereign Life Assce Co, Salter's Claim* (1891) 7 T.L.R. 602; *Lott v Outhwaite* (1893) 10 T.L.R. 76.

[161] *Lott v Outhwaite* (1893) 10 T.L.R. 76 at 141, per Lindley LJ.

[162] *Howard Houlder & Partners Ltd v Manx Isles SS Co* [1923] 1 K.B. 110.

[163] *Bentall, Horsley & Baldry v Vicary* [1931] 1 K.B. 253. *Berkeley Community Villages Ltd v Pullen* [2007] EWHC 1330 (Ch); [2007] N.P.C. 71 at [104] onwards.

[164] *Bentall, Horsley & Baldry v Vicary* [1931] 1 K.B. at 262. See also for more modern examples *Fairvale Ltd v Sabharwal* [1992] 2 E.G.L.R. 27; and *Ian Greenhill Residential Ltd v Asfari* [2007] EWHC 1491 (QB).

[165] See, e.g. *Sinclair Goldsmith v Minero Peru Comercial* [1978] E.G.D. 194; *Reif Diner & Co v Catalytic International Co* (1978) 246 E.G. 743, Illustration 10 to Article 55. For the amount payable see para.7-005, above.

[166] See, e.g. *Firth v Hylane Ltd* [1959] E.G.D. 212. The agency contract there provided that if the agent could find a purchaser willing to purchase the property for £35,000 he would receive £1,000 commission. This figure for commission was admitted to be high and in the nature of a bonus. The property was eventually sold for £31,000 to a person introduced by the agent. The Court of Appeal said it did not make sense for the agent to be paid nothing if the property fetched less than £35,000 and held that the parties had merely defined how the commission was to be quantified. They had, therefore, not excluded payment of a reasonable sum for work done by the agent at the principal's request. The court awarded £450 plus £100 expenses. See also *Boots v E. Christopher & Co* [1952] 1 K.B. 89 at 98–99; Article 58.

of interpretation of each contract whether there is or is not an implication that such overpayments must be repaid.[167]

Commercial agents   The Commercial Agents (Council Directive) Regulations   **7-026**
1993 contain provisions as to entitlement to commission.[168] These are discussed in Chapter 11.

Article 57

WHETHER AGENT IS EFFECTIVE CAUSE OF TRANSACTION

Subject to any special terms or other indications in the contract of agency, where   **7-027**
the remuneration of an agent is a commission on a transaction to be brought about, the agent is not entitled to such commission unless the services performed were the effective cause of the transaction.[169]

Comment

The principle stated in this Article is no more than a particular example of the   **7-028**
wider principle stated in the preceding Article, and it has recently been stressed that there are contracts to which it does not apply.[170] But there exists a body of cases on the notion of "effective cause" which is sufficiently discrete to require segregation. Where the agent is to be remunerated upon the happening of an event, the question whether that event has occurred depends upon the facts of the case and the express or implied terms of the agency contract. Many agents are employed upon terms that if a certain transaction is brought about, they will be entitled to a commission calculated by reference to the amount of the consideration passing in that transaction or to a stated fee. Sometimes the transaction is carried out but has not been brought about as a result of the agent's efforts. Sometimes the agent has played a part in bringing about the transaction but only a small part, or the agent has achieved only a partial success. It can be anticipated that the "effective cause" requirement will be attractive to a court where the agency is not exclusive and there might therefore be multiple agents working independently to secure a transaction.[171]

Sometimes the principal has carried out a different transaction from the one the agent was employed to bring about but the substitute transaction was nevertheless the result of the agent's efforts. For example, an agent may have been employed to find a purchaser for a house. He introduces a person who is only willing to take a long lease of the house and the principal thereafter decides to grant such a lease rather than sell. Has the agent earned his commission? The matter may take a more complicated form. For example, an agent is employed to find a purchaser for part

---

[167] See *Rivoli Hats Ltd v Gooch* [1953] 1 W.L.R. 1190; *Clayton Newbury, Ltd v Findlay* [1953] 1 W.L.R. 1194 (Note); *Bronester Ltd v Priddle* [1961] 1 W.L.R. 1294; *Prudential Assurance Co Ltd v Rodriguez* [1982] 2 N.Z.L.R. 54. See *D.O. Ferguson & Associates v Sohl* (1992) 62 Build.L.R. 95; Birks, in *Consensus ad Idem* (Rose ed., 1996), p.199.

[168] Commercial Agents (Council Directive) Regulations 1993 regs 7–12.

[169] See Comment, esp. para.7-029 as to "the" or "an"; Murdoch (1985) 276 E.G. 742 and 877.

[170] *Freedman v Union Group Plc* [1997] E.G.C.S. 28; *Raja v Rollerby Ltd* (1997) 74 P. & C.R. D25, per Evans LJ; *Watersheds Ltd v Simms* [2009] EWHC 713 (QB); *Edmond De Rothschild Securities (UK) Ltd v Exillon Energy Plc* [2014] EWHC 2165 (Comm) at [25].

[171] See *Silvercloud Finance Solutions Ltd (t/a Broadscope Finance) v High Street Solicitors Ltd* [2020] EWHC 878 (Comm) at [93].

of the business being carried on by the principal. The agent introduces a potential purchaser, but after direct negotiations between the principal and the potential purchaser, the two of them agree to establish a new company with the principal as minority shareholder and transfer the business to that company in exchange for shares. The final transaction is different in substance from the sale the agent was employed to achieve but was carried out in substitution for that sale without the agent having caused or even been aware of the change. Has the agent earned a commission?

The answers to these questions depend upon the express or implied terms of the relevant agency contract. But a large number of them interpret the agent's contract in connection with a sale on the basis that to be entitled to commission the agent must be the, or at least an, effective cause of the sale. This seems to result:

> "from the use in the agency agreements of expressions such as 'find a purchaser' or 'introduce a purchaser' … It would have been quite artificial to suppose that the parties intended that the agent should earn his commission simply by finding an individual who, independently of any further action by the agent, later agreed to buy the subject property."[172]

Where the contract is in such terms as "You are employed to find a purchaser of the property", the above result flows as a result of a constructional implication.[173] Where there is no such term, the implication will only be made to give business efficacy to the contract.[174] Where the ultimate transaction is different from and carried out in substitution for the contract which the agent was employed to bring about, the same implication will be made and the court will ask whether the agent was the effective cause of the particular transaction which the principal entered into.[175] The fact of a substitute transaction may be evidence of a break in the chain of causation. But it should be noted that in some cases the terms of the contract or the nature of the transaction mean that there is no room for this implication.[176]

An agency involving "sole selling rights" within the Estate Agents (Provision of

---

[172] *Doyle v Mr. Kidston Mining and Exploration Pty Ltd* [1984] 2 Qd.R. 386 at 392, per McPherson J; *MSM Consulting Ltd v United Republic of Tanzania* [2009] EWHC 121 (QB) at [139]; *Benourad v Compass Group Plc* [2010] EWHC 1882 (QB) at [123]. In *The County Homesearch Co (Thames & Chilterns) Ltd v Cowham* [2008] EWCA Civ 26; [2008] 1 W.L.R. 909 at [16], per Longmore LJ it was tentatively accepted that the presumption of the need for cause may be weaker where the agent is acting for a purchaser. Sed quaere; see Watts [2009] J.B.L. 268.

[173] This is probably the explanation of *Favermead Ltd v FPD Savills* [2002] EWHC 626 (Ch), though the implication was described as an implied term. A winding-up petition by estate agents claiming commission was restrained by injunction on the basis that the question whether there was such an implication was arguable.

[174] See above, para.7-001.

[175] *Gunn v Showell's Brewery Co Ltd* (1902) 18 T.L.R. 659, Illustration 12; *Burchell v Gowrie and Blockhouse Collieries Ltd* [1910] A.C. 614; *Price Davies & Co v Smith* (1929) 141 L.T. 490; *Stewarts & Lloyds Ltd v Zoess, The Times,* July 5, 1955 (HL); *Jack Windle Ltd v Brierley* [1952] 1 All E.R. 398 (doubted [1981] E.G.D. at 245); *Chamberlain and Willows v HBS (Trust) Ltd* [1952] E.G.D. 443; *Poulter v Doggett* (1964) 115 L.J. 76; *Allen v Anderson* [1969] N.Z.L.R. 951; *Levers v Dunsdon* [1968] E.G.D. 280. But cf. *Estafnous v London & Leeds Business Centres Ltd* [2011] EWCA Civ 1157, Illustration 13.

[176] See *David Leahy (Aust.) Pty Ltd v McPhersons Ltd* [1991] 2 V.R. 367, Illustration 18; *Brian Cooper Ltd v Fairview Estates (Investments) Ltd* [1987] 1 E.G.L.R. 18. Also the definition of "sole selling rights" in the Estate Agents (Provision of Information) Regulations 1991 Schedule, does not seem to require effective cause.

Information) Regulations 1991 Schedule, does not require that the agent has been an effective cause of the transaction before being entitled to commission.[177]

General principle   This is well stated in *Millar, Son & Co v Radford*[178] where the defendant employed the plaintiff to find a purchaser of property or, failing that, a tenant. A tenant was found and commission was paid. Fifteen months later the tenant purchased the property and the plaintiff claimed commission on the sale although he had not been concerned with the property since the letting. In holding that the plaintiff was not entitled to commission Collins MR said[179]:

> "It is important to point out that the right to commission does not arise out of the mere fact that agents had introduced a tenant or purchaser. It is not sufficient to show that the introduction was a causa sine qua non. It is necessary to show that the introduction was an efficient[180] cause in bringing about the letting or the sale. Here the plaintiffs fail to establish what is a condition precedent to their right to commission—viz., that they have brought about the sale. It is open to the defendant[181] in an action like this to say either that, though the plaintiffs effected a sale, they were not his agents, or that, though they were his agents, they had not effected the sale. If the defendant proves either the one or the other, the plaintiffs fail to make out their case."[182]

"The" or "an"?   There is doubt as to whether the rule is more helpfully formulated by requiring that the agent's act be "the effective cause" or merely "an effective cause". The word "the" is used in this Article: but it should be noted that in various places, including the passage quoted in the paragraph above, the indefinite article "an" is used.[183] It is certainly true that the agent can be entitled to commission though there are other events which could be called causes of the transaction. In some cases the introduction is crucial.[184] Thus if the agent introduces a person who becomes the purchaser "it is nothing to the point ... that that person would have become the purchaser without the intervention of the agent, or that the principal's own efforts were also an effective cause of the sale".[185] But it is submitted that it is the word "effective" which is the most significant:

> ""Effective cause" means more than simply 'cause'. The inquiry is whether the actions

7-029

7-030

[177] *Dashwood v Fleurets Ltd* [2007] EWHC 1610 (QB) at [43].
[178] *Millar, Son & Co v Radford* (1903) 19 T.L.R. 575. For cases on almost identical facts, see *Toulmin v Millar* (1887) 58 L.T. 96, Illustration 4; *Nightingale v Parsons* [1914] 2 K.B. 621. See too *Seakom Ltd v Knowledgepool Group Ltd* [2013] EWHC 4007 (Ch) at [96].
[179] *Millar, Son & Co v Radford* (1903) 19 T.L.R. 575 at 576.
[180] The word "efficient" has changed its meaning since 1903. The modern equivalent is "effective" (see, e.g. *Allan v Leo Lines Ltd* [1957] 1 Lloyd's Rep. 127 at 133).
[181] The burden of proving entitlement to commission rests on the agent throughout. By using the expression "it is open to the defendant" Collins MR can mean no more than that the defendant may assert; the plaintiff agent must, of course, disprove the assertions. See *Pettigrew v George Wimpey UK Ltd* [2007] EWHC 2559 (QB) at [48] (onus on claimant to show effective cause of sale).
[182] The passage has, for the sake of clarity, been altered from the indirect speech of the original report to direct speech.
[183] See also *Burchell v Gowrie and Blockhouse Collieries Ltd* [1910] A.C. 614 at 624, where both phrases are used.
[184] See *Allan v Leo Lines Ltd* [1957] 1 Lloyd's Rep. 127 per Devlin J.
[185] *L.J. Hooker Ltd v W.J. Adams Estates Pty Ltd* (1977) 138 C.L.R. 52 at 58, per Barwick CJ. For an example see *Doyle v Mt. Kidston Mining & Exploration Pty Ltd* [1984] 2 Qd.R. 386. Both cases are discussed by Waller LJ in *Nahum v Royal Holloway, etc., College* [1999] E.M.L.R. 252, Illustration 20; *Seascape Capital Services Ltd v Anglo-Atlantic SS Co Ltd* [2002] EWHC (Comm) 1277; [2002] 2 Lloyd's Rep. 611. But cf. *Lichtenstein v Clube Atletico Mineiro* [2005] EWHC 1300 (QB).

of the agent really brought about the relation of buyer and seller, and it is seldom conclusive that there were other events which could each be described as a cause of the ensuing sale. The factual inquiry is whether a sale is really brought about by the act of the agent."[186]

In a more recent case where a submission was made that the better usage was "*an effective cause*", Woolf LJ said that this could create problems where there are "two or more effective causes, each of which could be the object of a claim for commission".[187] A situation of two genuinely effective causes of equal potency is possible, though unlikely,[188] and recent judicial authority prefers "an".[189] But a vendor may more easily become liable for two (or more) commissions on the same sale by virtue of the specific terms of two (or more) agency contracts.[190]

Apart from the general principle that in the absence of other indications the agent must be the effective cause of the transaction taking place, no clear principles can be easily derived from the many cases on this topic. No precise definition of "effective cause" in this context has yet been given by an English court.[191] Accordingly, any conclusions to be drawn from these cases must be advanced with hesitation. An agent will normally be entitled to commission if the agent causes a person to negotiate with the principal and contract, no substantial break in the negotiations having taken place.[192] It appears that the agent does not have to complete or even take part in the negotiations,[193] nor arrange any meeting,[194] nor persuade either party to enter into the contract. Further, the agent is still entitled to

---

[186] *L.J. Hooker Ltd v W.J. Adams Estates Pty Ltd* (1977) 138 C.L.R. 52 at 86, per Jacobs J. See also *Tufton Associates v Dilmun Shipping* [1992] 1 Lloyd's Rep. 71 at 78 ("cause which had the greatest efficacy" not the last).

[187] *Brian Cooper & Co v Fairview Estates (Investments) Ltd* [1987] 1 E.G.L.R. 18 at 20.

[188] It occurred in *Lordsgate Properties Ltd v Balcombe* [1985] 1 E.G.L.R. 20, Illustration 19; but many cases simply decide between rival claims to be effective cause, e.g. *Bloom v Yefet* [1982] 2 E.G.L.R. 30; *Anscombe & Ringland Ltd v Watson* [1991] 2 E.G.L.R. 28.

[189] In *Nahum v Royal Holloway, etc., College* [1999] E.M.L.R. 252, Waller LJ used "an" while saying that he doubted whether there was any difference except possibly where "there are two agents with agreements that they are entitled to commission if they introduce a purchaser". "An" was also preferred in *Harding Maughan Hambly Ltd v CECAR* [2000] 1 Lloyd's Rep. 316 at 335, in the context of insurance brokers.

[190] See *Bernard Marcus & Co v Ashraf* [1988] 1 E.G.L.R. 7 (auctioneer); *Peter Yates & Co v Bullock* [1990] 2 E.G.L.R. 24; above, para.7-021.

[191] *Restatement, Second*, § 448, states that: "an agent is an 'effective cause' ... when his efforts have been sufficiently important in achieving a result for the accomplishment of which the principal has promised to pay him, so that it is just that the principal should pay the promised compensation to him". This definition is open to the objection that it begs the question. But see *Harding Maughan Hambly Ltd v CECAR* [2000] 1 Lloyd's Rep. 316 at 334; *Goh Lay Khim v Isabel Redrup Agency Pte Ltd* [2017] SGCA 11 at [37]. Discussion of the earning of commission is omitted from *Restatement, Third* as being a matter of general contract law.

[192] It seems that merely sending out particulars may rank as introduction: *Christie Owen & Davies Plc v Ryelance* [2005] EWHC 148; (2005) 18 E.G. 148 (C.S.); *Christie Owen & Davies Plc v King* 1998 S.C.L.R. 786; Murdoch (2005) E.G. (No.154) 177.

[193] *Re Beale Ex p. Durrant* (1888) 5 Morr. 37, Illustration 8; *Green v Bartlett* (1863) 14 C.B.(N.S.) 681, Illustration 9; *Mansell v Clements* (1874) L.R. 9 C.P. 139; *Barnett v Brown & Co* (1890) 6 T.L.R. 463; *Steere v Smith* (1885) 2 T.L.R. 131; *Burton v Hughes* (1885) 1 T.L.R. 207; *Thompson, Rippon & Co v Thomas* (1896) 11 T.L.R. 304; *Brandon v Hanna* [1907] 2 I.R. 212; *Walker, Fraser and Steele v Fraser's Trustees*, 1910 S.C. 222; *Burchell v Gowrie and Blockhouse Collieries Ltd* [1910] A.C. 614; *Howard Houlder & Partners Ltd v Manx Isles SS Co Ltd* [1923] 1 K.B. 110; *Bow's Emporium Ltd v A.R. Brett & Co Ltd* (1928) 44 T.L.R. 194; *Bartlett v Cole* [1963] E.G.D. 452, Illustration 15; *Burns v Coomber* [1966] E.G.D. 110; *F.P. Rolfe & Co v George* [1969] E.G.D. 331; *McKeag Harris Realty & Development Co Ltd v Builders' Mutual Assets Ltd* (1968) 66 W.W.R. 512; *Knight, Frank & Rutley v Fraser* 1974 S.L.T. 50; *Berezovsky v Edmiston & Co Ltd* [2010] EWHC 1883

commission if the principal contracts at a lower price or on other terms than the agent was authorised to offer, provided that the agent was the effective cause and the express or implied terms of the agency contract are such as to show that the remuneration was payable upon the happening of the transaction which actually resulted.[195]

The agent will not normally be entitled to commission if the third party who ultimately contracts has its attention drawn to the possibility of contracting by means other than those intended by the agent to bring about the contract.[196] Moreover, the fact that one agent introduces a person who ultimately purchases after a later introduction by another agent will not necessarily entitle the first agent to commission.[197] In such a case the court must determine which of the two agents was the effective cause of the transaction taking place.[198] On the whole, it may be said that the first introducer has more often succeeded. But it is possible that a sale might have two effective causes.[199]

Commercial agents   The Commercial Agents (Council Directive) Regulations 1993 contain provisions on entitlement to commission which parallel the "effective cause" rule.[200] The Regulations are discussed in Chapter 11.   **7-031**

Illustrations

(1)   A employs B, a broker, to procure a charter for a ship. B introduces C, who is also a broker, C introduces D, who negotiates for but does not enter into a charterparty. D informs E that the ship is available and E charters her from A. B is not entitled to commission, the transaction being too remote a consequence of his introduction.[201]   **7-032**

(2)   A employs B to find a purchaser for a ship. B, acting on behalf of A, contracts

---

(Comm) at [41] (reversed on one issue, [2011] EWCA Civ 431). But if the agent simply advises the principal, the agent may not be the effective cause: *Hoddell v Smith* [1976] E.G.D. 217.

[194]   See, e.g. *Green v Bartlett* (1863) 14 C.B.(N.S.) 681, Illustration 9.

[195]   *Allan v Leo Lines Ltd* [1957] 1 Lloyd's Rep. 127, Illustration 2; *Poulter v Dogget* (1964) 115 L.J. 76; *Allen v Anderson* [1969] N.Z.L.R. 951. See also *Spiess v Taylor* (1984) 271 E.G. 196 (no effective cause where property offered at wrong price: sed quaere); *Connell Estates v Begej* [1993] 2 E.G.L.R. 35 (commission on sale by part exchange); *Moneywood Pty Ltd v Salamon Nominees Pty Ltd* (2001) 202 C.L.R. 351 (part of land only) (see Fridman (2002) 76 A.L.J. 195); *Glentree Estates Ltd v Favermead Ltd* [2010] EWCA Civ 1473 at [23].

[196]   Illustrations 9, 13 and 16. See also *D.C. Wylde & Co v Sparg* 1977 (2) S.A.L.R. 75 (eventual purchaser knew about property already); *Lichtenstein v Clube Atletico Mineiro* [2005] EWHC 1300 (QB) (football agent authorised to interest clubs in player; club which bought player had previously been interested). But cf. *Cobbs Property Services Ltd v Liddell-Taylor* [1990] 1 E.G.L.R. 49.

[197]   *Murray v Currie* (1836) 7 C. & P. 584; *Barnett v Brown* (1890) 6 T.L.R. 463; *Curtis v Nixon* (1871) 24 L.T. 706, Illustration 3; *Davis v Trollope & Sons* [1943] 1 All E.R. 501; *Bartlett v Cole* [1963] E.G.D. 452, Illustration 15; *Chesterfield & Co Ltd v Zahid* [1989] 2 E.G.L.R. 24; *Egan Lawson Ltd v Standard Life Assurance Co* [2001] 1 E.G.L.R. 27; *Foxtons Ltd v Bicknell* [2008] EWCA Civ 419; [2008] 24 E.G. 142; [2008] N.P.C. 52; *Glentree Estates Ltd v Holbeton Ltd* [2011] EWCA Civ 755. Sometimes the matter may turn on who "introduced": e.g. *Terry Martel Real Estate Ltd v Lovette Investments Ltd* (1981) 123 D.L.R. (3d) 387.

[198]   *John D. Wood & Co v Dantata* [1987] 2 E.G.L.R. 23. See also *Chasen Ryder & Co v Hedges* [1993] 1 E.G.L.R. 47. If two different agents are claiming commission from the principal he cannot normally interplead: *Greatorex & Co v Shackle* [1895] 2 Q.B. 249. See also Article 70.

[199]   *Lordsgate Properties Ltd v Balcombe* [1985] 1 E.G.L.R. 20, Illustration 19.

[200]   Commercial Agents (Council Directive) Regulations 1993 reg.7(1).

[201]   *Wilkinson v Martin* (1837) 8 C. & P. 1. And see *Ellis v May & Co* (1960) 110 L.J. 140 (introduction of mortgage broker: no commission for "arranging mortgage"); cf. *Crema v Cenkos Securities Plc*

with C that C will receive a commission if he finds a purchaser. X, acting through D, asks C to find a ship for purchase and C gives X the name of A's ship. Various offers and counter-offers are passed through C, the last being rejected by A. Shortly afterwards A sells the ship to X privately. C is entitled to his commission, the introduction of X being the effective cause of the sale. The fact that the final sale was at a different figure from any that passed through C did not mean that C was not the real cause of the sale taking place at all.[202]

(3)   An estate agent lets a house for a term of years, the tenant having the option of taking it for a further term. The tenant declines to exercise this option but agrees to take the house for a further term at a lower rent. The first agent is not entitled to commission on the further term since he was not the proximate cause of the reletting.[203]

(4)   An agent is employed to let an estate and procures a tenant. The tenant subsequently buys the estate without any further communication with the agent. The agent is not entitled to commission on the sale.[204]

(5)   An agent employed to sell property on commission is not entitled to commission if he and the principal agree together that he shall be the purchaser himself, unless they expressly agree that commission shall be payable on such a sale.[205]

(6)   An agent, employed to find a purchaser of property at a specified price, brings it to the notice of a government department which, after negotiations to purchase fail, compulsorily acquires it at a lower price and against the wishes of the principal. The agent is not entitled to commission. He was employed only to find a ready and willing purchaser at a price which the principal voluntarily accepts.[206]

(7)   A entered into an agreement with B in the following terms:

> "In case of your introducing a purchaser [of a certain business] of whom I approve, or capital which I should accept, I could pay you 5 per cent commission, provided no one else is entitled to commission in respect of the same introduction."

B introduced C, who advanced £10,000 by way of loan, and B was duly paid his commission in respect of that advance. Some months afterwards, A and C entered into an agreement for a partnership, C advancing a further

---

[2010] EWCA Civ 1444; [2011] 1 W.L.R. 2066.

[202] *Allan v Leo Lines Ltd* [1957] 1 Lloyd's Rep. 127. The facts have been slightly simplified for the sake of clarity.

[203] *Curtis v Nixon* (1871) 24 L.T. 706. See also *Ex p. Chatteris* (1874) 22 W.R. 289; *Lofts v Bourke* (1884) 1 T.L.R. 58.

[204] *Toulmin v Millar* (1887) 58 L.T. 96 (reported on another point (1887) 12 App. Cas. 746). The test there laid down by Lord Watson that "in order to found a legal claim for commission there must not only be a causal, there must also be a contractual relation between the introduction and the ultimate transaction of sale" is difficult to understand and does not seem in practice to have been applied. See also *Millar, Son & Co v Radford* (1903) 19 T.L.R. 575; and *Nightingale v Parsons* [1914] 2 K.B. 621 for cases on almost identical facts.

[205] *Hocker v Waller* (1929) 29 Com.Cas. 296. See also *Barnett v Isaacson* (1888) 4 T.L.R. 645, Illustration 14.

[206] *Hodges & Sons v Hackbridge Park Residential Hotel Ltd* [1940] 1 K.B. 404. See also *Battams v Tompkins* (1892) 8 T.L.R. 707; *Beable v Dickerson* (1885) 1 T.L.R. 654; *Thompson v British Berna Motor Lorries Ltd* (1917) 33 T.L.R. 187; cf. *Price, Davies & Co v Smith* (1929) 141 L.T. 490 and *O'Connor Real Estate Ltd v Flynn* (1969) 3 D.L.R. (3d) 345.

£4,000 by way of capital. Held, that B was not entitled to commission on the £4,000, that amount having been advanced in consequence of the negotiations between A and C for a partnership, with which B had nothing to do.[207]

(8) A, who was employed by B to find a purchaser for certain property, introduced C to B, but C could not accept B's terms. Shortly afterwards B became bankrupt. Further negotiations took place between C and B's trustee in bankruptcy, resulting in a sale of the property three weeks after the original introduction. Held, A's introduction brought about the sale and he was entitled to prove in the bankruptcy for his commission.[208]

(9) A, an auctioneer and estate agent, was employed by P to sell the island of Herm by auction or otherwise. He put it up for auction and the reserve price was not reached. Afterwards T, who had attended the auction, asked A for and was given P's name. T then approached P direct and eventually purchased the island from him. Shortly before the sale P wrote to A withdrawing A's authority to sell. Held, A was the *causa causans* of the sale and was entitled to commission.[209]

(10) A employed B to sell an estate in lots. C bought certain lots and B received commission on them. At this stage C refused to buy further lots. A then withdrew B's authority, and 27 months later C bought the remaining lots by private contract. Held, that the jury were entitled to find that the ultimate sale was not due to B's intervention.[210]

(11) An estate agent, A, was instructed by P to offer a house for sale. It was agreed that he should receive two-and-a-half per cent commission if he found a purchaser or a guinea for his services if the house was sold without his intervention. T called on A and received a card to view the house. T viewed it and after negotiations through a friend of P, he ultimately bought it. Held, there was evidence for the jury that the house was sold through the intervention of A so as to entitle him to commission.[211]

(12) Two brewery companies agreed to pay A a commission on all licensed properties or businesses they might purchase through his introduction. A submitted a brewery for their consideration. The companies decided that the most advantageous course was for them to promote a new company to buy the brewery. Held, the position was the same as if the companies had bought the brewery themselves and sold it to the new company. A was accordingly entitled to his commission.[212]

---

[207] *Tribe v Taylor* (1876) 1 C.P.D. 505. See also *Boyd v Tovil Paper Co Ltd* (1884) 4 T.L.R. 332.

[208] *Re Beale Ex p. Durrant* (1888) 5 Morr. 37; cf. *Egan Lawson Ltd v Standard Life Assurance Co* [2001] 1 E.G.L.R. 27.

[209] *Green v Bartlett* (1863) 14 C.B.(N.S.) 681. See also *Bayley v Chadwick* (1878) 39 L.T. 429; *Wilkinson v Alston* (1879) 48 L.J.Q.B. 733; *Ong Kee Ming v Quek Yong Kang* [1991] 3 M.L.J. 294; *Dashwood v Fleurets Ltd* [2007] EWHC 1610 (QB) at [51].

[210] *Lumley v Nicholson* (1886) 34 W.R. 716. Compare *Jack Windle Ltd v Brierley* [1952] 1 All E.R. 398; *Christie Owen & Davis Plc v King* 1998 S.C.L.R. 786 ("introduced to you").

[211] *Mansell v Clements* (1874) L.R. 9 C.P. 139. See also *Barnett v Brown* (1890) 6 T.L.R. 463; *Steere v Smith* (1885) 2 T.L.R. 131; *Burton v Hughes* (1885) 1 T.L.R. 207; *Thompson, Ripon & Co v Thomas* (1896) 11 T.L.R. 304; *Brandon v Hanna* [1907] 2 I.R. 212; *Howard Houlder & Partners Ltd v Manx Isles SS Co* [1923] 1 K.B. 110; *Burns v Coomber* [1966] E.G.D. 110; *McKeag Harris Realty & Development Co Ltd v Builders Mutual Assets Ltd* (1968) 64 W.W.R. 208; affirmed (1968) 66 W.W.R. 512.

[212] *Gunn v Showell's Brewery Co Ltd & Crosswell's Ltd* (1902) 50 W.R. 659 (see also at first instance (1901) 17 T.L.R. 563); *Di Dio Nominees Pty Ltd v Brian Mark Real Estate Pty Ltd* [1992] 2 V.R.

(13) A company agrees to pay a commission upon the introduction of a buyer for a property. Instead, the potential buyer buys the shares in the vendor. Held, that while the agency contract might have impliedly extended to a sale of shares where the vendor owned the company that owned the property, it did not extend to a sale of the shares in the vendor itself.[213]

(14) A introduced T to P, his principal, as a possible purchaser of certain property belonging to P, but no agreement between them was reached. P subsequently sold the property by auction, T being the purchaser. Held, A was not entitled to his commission.[214]

(15) A agreed to pay B a commission of £5,000 in the event of B introducing a purchaser of A's business. B failed to find a purchaser, but introduced C, an accountant, as a person who might be able to introduce a purchaser. C eventually himself bought the property at the proposed price after deducting the commission which he was to have been paid in the event of his finding a purchaser. Held, that there was no evidence that B had introduced a purchaser of the business, he having introduced C, not as a purchaser, but as an agent to find a purchaser, and that B could not recover either the agreed commission or a quantum meruit, the claim for a quantum meruit being excluded by the express terms of the contract.[215]

(16) A employed B to sell his café. B introduced C, who wanted to buy but could not without a loan, and who eventually went to new agents for a lower-priced business. The new agents also had A's business on their books, and assured C of finance, advising him to employ a solicitor for the purchase. The new agents' finance fell through but C's solicitor found finance and C bought. Held, the removal of the financial problem made B's introduction which had otherwise been successful the effective cause of the purchase. Semble, if the new agents had been able to supply finance they would have been the effective cause.[216]

(17) P, who was the owner of a shop suitable for a pin-table arcade, arranged with A to pay him a commission if A could find a tenant. A telephoned C, a manufacturer of pin-tables, and told him of the shop. C said he wanted to consult his partner. T overheard the telephone conversation and asked C for the address. C merely said it was "in Victoria". T went to Victoria, found the shop, and arranged a lease direct with P. Held, A was not entitled to commission. The deliberate withholding of the address by C broke the chain

732. See also *Glendinning v Cavanagh* (1908) 40 S.C.R. 414; *Stratton v Vachan and Wilson* (1911) 44 S.C.R. 395; *McBrayne v Imperial Loan Co* (1913) 13 D.L.R. 448; *Levers v Dunsdon* [1968] E.G.D. 280; *L.J. Hooker Ltd v W.J. Adams Estates Pty Ltd* (1977) 138 C.L.R. 52; Illustration 17; *Lord v Trippe* (1977) 51 A.L.J.R. 574. See also *Freedman v Union Group Plc* [1997] E.G.C.S. 28.

[213] *Estafnous v London & Leeds Business Centres Ltd* [2011] EWCA Civ 1157.

[214] *Taplin v Barrett* (1889) 6 T.L.R. 30. See also *Green v Mules* (1861) 30 L.J.C.P. 343, Illustration 8 to Article 55; *Lofts v Bourke* (1884) 1 T.L.R. 58; *Coles v Enoch* [1939] 3 All E.R. 327, Illustration 16; cf. *Walker, Fraser and Steele v Fraser's Trustees* 1910 S.C. 222.

[215] *Barnett v Isaacson* (1888) 4 T.L.R. 645; cf. *Burney v London Mews Co Ltd* [2003] EWCA Civ 766, where the agent gave the particulars to another agent, who introduced a purchaser.

[216] *Bartlett v Cole* [1963] E.G.D. 452; cf. *Robert Drummond v Mangles* [1981] E.G.D. 265; *Hartnell v Taylor, Cook v Bromwich* [1982] E.G.D. 436. See also *Rungay v Forrester* (1967) 63 D.L.R. (2d) 338; *Tufnell v Richard Costain Ltd* (1968) 209 E.G. 705; *Christie & Co v Jones* [1966] E.G.D. 439; *Glentree Estates Ltd v Gee* [1981] E.G.D. 235; cf. *Jack Windle Ltd v Brierley* [1952] 1 All E.R. 398 as a case where the finance was provided by the seller; doubted in *Glentree Estates Ltd v Gee* [1981] E.G.D. 235; *Peter Yates & Co v Bullock* [1990] 2 E.G.L.R. 24.

of causation and A was not the direct or efficient cause of T becoming the tenant.[217]

(18) An agent is engaged to locate a satisfactory purchaser for land at a satisfactory price. The agent introduces two persons, L and H, who conduct real property development operations though a number of companies including A Co L makes several unsuccessful offers. The vendor had independently been in touch with another development company of which B Co was a subsidiary. A Co and B Co enter into a joint venture agreement; B Co buys the land and makes an allotment of shares to A Co. The agent had played no part in introducing either company and did not know of the joint venture. He is not entitled to commission.[218]

(19) A "business broker" states terms to company X upon which it will act in the acquisition of other businesses. A fee is payable if a company or business submitted by the broker is acquired by the company. In 1982 the broker introduces a business. Negotiations ensue but are abandoned. In 1985 the business is transferred to a public listed company. In 1987 company X effects a takeover of the listed company. The broker's fee is due.[219]

(20) X engages the services of two agents, each of which introduces the same prospective purchaser. X's son tells the second agents that he has an offer through the first agents, and the second agents tell this to the prospective purchaser, who raises his offer, neither he nor the second agent realising that he is bidding against himself. The two agents are both effective causes of the eventual sale.[220]

(21) A is asked to find a buyer for paintings. He introduces a buyer for one. The second is later sold to the same buyer, but the buyer's agent attempts to cut A out and A plays little role in the sale. He is held entitled to commission in respect of both paintings.[221]

Article 58

AGENT PREVENTED BY PRINCIPAL FROM EARNING REMUNERATION

A principal will only be liable for preventing the agent from earning remuneration when the implication of a promise that the principal will not do so is necessary to give business efficacy to the contract, or otherwise to effect the intention of the parties.[222]   **7-033**

---

[217] *Coles v Enoch* [1939] 3 All E.R. 327. See also *Antrobus v Wickens* (1865) 4 F. & F. 291.

[218] *L.J. Hooker Ltd v W.J. Adams Estates Pty Ltd* (1977) 138 C.L.R. 52. (The judgments in this case repay study.) See too *Aboulsaud v Aboukhater* [2007] EWHC 2122 (QB).

[219] *David Leahy (Aust.) Pty Ltd v McPherson's Ltd* [1991] 2 V.R. 362. See also *Brian Cooper Ltd v Fairview Estates (Investments) Ltd* [1987] 1 E.G.L.R. 18 ("introduce a tenant ... with whom we have not been in previous communication and who subsequently completes a lease"). See also *Harding Maughan Hambly Ltd v CECAR* [2000] 1 Lloyd's Rep. 316 (agent's services dispensed with after most of placing work done: effective cause).

[220] *Lordsgate Properties Ltd v Balcombe* [1985] 1 E.G.L.R. 20.

[221] *Nahum v Royal Holloway and Bedford New College* [1999] E.M.L.R. 252.

[222] See Comment.

Comment

7-034   If the agent claims an entitlement to damages because the principal has wrongfully deprived the agent of the opportunity to earn remuneration, the agent must be able to show some contractual promise of which the principal is in breach. Where there is an express promise on which the agent can rely, no difficulty will arise. But where there is no express promise the question will arise whether any, and if so what, promise can be implied. Ordinary contract principles will apply if a principal renegotiates a reduction in or cancellation of a right to commission, for instance as a condition of the agent's continuing to get work.[223]

7-035   **Earlier case law**   For many years it was thought that the principal was under a duty not to deprive the agent of the opportunity of earning commission. This view was first expressed in *Prickett v Badger*.[224] A series of confused cases followed,[225] the basis of the supposed principle never being fully worked out. Most of the cases concerned agents, e.g. estate agents, who were entitled to receive a commission if they brought about a certain transaction for their principals. It was realised, however, that the principal could not be held liable in the context of sale of land when the principal did *any* act which had the effect of preventing the agent from earning commission; for the vendor may be taken normally to wish to retain some element of discretion. The supposed rule became therefore more and more tenuous. In *G. Trollope & Sons v Martyn Bros*[226] the Court of Appeal held that the principal of an estate agent would be liable in damages to the agent if (but only if) the principal unreasonably withdrew from negotiations with the potential purchaser with the result that the agent could not earn commission. However, the dissenting judgment of Scrutton LJ revealed the fallacies in the reasoning of the majority of the court, and in *Luxor (Eastbourne) Ltd v Cooper*[227] the House of Lords expressly overruled *G. Trollope & Sons v Martyn Bros*.

7-036   **Estate agent's contract**   In *Luxor*'s case the House made a detailed examination of the estate agent's contract. The peculiarity of the usual version of this arrangement is that the agent is not under an obligation to do anything.[228] Hence in the typical situation the principal makes a continuing or single offer of a unilateral contract only, which the agent accepts by introducing a purchaser or whatever else is

[223] See *Times Travel (UK) Ltd v Pakistan International Airlines Corp* [2019] EWCA Civ 828; [2020] Ch. 98 (variation not voidable for economic duress), currently under appeal to UKSC.

[224] *Prickett v Badger* (1856) 1 C.B.(N.S.) 296.

[225] These are considered in detail in Ash, *Willing to Purchase* (1963). They include *Green v Lucas* (1875) 33 L.T. 584; *Fisher v Drewett* (1878) 48 L.J.Q.B. 32; *Roberts v Barnard* (1884) 1 Cab. & El. 336; *Grogan v Smith* (1890) 7 T.L.R. 132; *Fuller v Eames* (1892) 8 T.L.R. 278; *Nosotti v Auerbach* (1899) 15 T.L.R. 140; *Brinson v Davies* (1911) 105 L.T. 134; *Hankinson v Vickers* [1931] E.G.D. 16.

[226] *G. Trollope & Sons v Martyn Bros* [1934] 2 K.B. 436. This case was followed in *G. Trollope & Sons v Caplan* [1936] 2 K.B. 382; *Kahn v Aircraft Industries Corp Ltd* [1937] 3 All E.R. 476; *Harrods Ltd v Geneen* [1938] 4 All E.R. 493; *Way & Waller Ltd v Verrall* [1939] 3 All E.R. 533.

[227] *Luxor (Eastbourne) Ltd v Cooper* [1941] A.C. 108, Illustration 1. Most of the cases cited in fnn.225 and 226 above must now be taken to have been wrongly decided, or at least decided on the wrong principles. In general, any case on this topic before *Luxor*'s case should be regarded with caution. It is suggested that the statement in *J.H. Milner & Son v Percy Bilton* [1966] 1 W.L.R. 1582 at 1588 that "the estate agent who has been employed to sell a particular house can sue for damages if his authority is withdrawn" is now out of date, especially since the judge relied upon *G. Trollope & Sons v Martyn Bros*.

[228] See Comment to Article 56.

required by the terms of the particular offer.[229] Sometimes a letter following the engagement may contain wording purporting to create a bilateral contract, inasmuch as it contains undertakings that the agent will use best endeavours and so forth.[230] Although there can be no objection in principle to a new contract being subsequently formed in this way, or indeed to the initial contract being a bilateral one, the authoritative way in which the normal agency contract is analysed in *Luxor's* case means that such an interpretation of the facts, which might force a bilateral contract on one who has made a unilateral one, would be difficult to establish.

On the unilateral analysis, the next question is whether the principal is to be regarded as promising not to deprive the agent of commission. Although the speeches in the case speak of implied *terms*, it is submitted that if the contract is truly unilateral, the requirement would be for the implication of an implied collateral *contract*.[231] However this be, the House, having interpreted the nature of the transaction, treated the question of implication as a question of business efficacy and held that such implication was not appropriate. It was improbable that a principal would wish to fetter the principal's freedom of choice by promising the agent not to withdraw unreasonably from negotiations when the principal was free vis-à-vis the potential purchaser to withdraw at any time for any reason. Furthermore, the agent earns a considerable commission if successful, and likewise takes the business risk that if the agent's efforts are unsuccessful nothing is earned.[232]

"Sole" and "exclusive" agency   Where the agent is appointed "sole" agent, however, it is established that if the principal then employs a second agent who earns the commission on the transaction which the first agent should have earned, the first agent is entitled to damages.[233] The normal view of such a transaction is that it is a bilateral contract, the consideration for the principal's promise not to sell through another agent being the agent's undertaking to use the agent's best

7-037

---

[229] *L.J. Hooker Ltd v W.J. Adams Estates Pty Ltd* (1977) 138 C.L.R. 52 at 73. A different type of analysis, which tends to discount the conceptual difference between unilateral and bilateral contracts, is however suggested by Lord Wilberforce in *A.M. Satterthwaite & Co v New Zealand Shipping Co Ltd (The Eurymedon)* [1975] A.C. 154 at 167–168; followed by Barwick CJ in *Port Jackson Stevedoring Pty Ltd v Salmond & Spraggon (Australia) Pty Ltd (The New York Star)* [1979] 1 Lloyd's Rep. 298 at 305–306, whose judgment was endorsed by the Privy Council [1981] 1 W.L.R. 138 at 148.

[230] See Murdoch, *Law of Estate Agency* (5th edn), pp.141–144; (1977) 242 E.G. 609; cf. McConnell (1983) 265 E.G. 547. In two cases the confirming letter appears to have been treated as effective: *Way & Waller Ltd v Ryde* [1944] 1 All E.R. 9 and *John E. Trinder & Partners v Haggis* (1951) 158 E.G. 4. Murdoch, above, suggests that they are inconsistent with *Toulmin v Millar* (1887) 58 L.T. 96, Illustration 4 to Article 57.

[231] Contra, Treitel, *Law of Contract* (15th edn), para.2-052, 6-061. And see fn.228 above.

[232] See also *Burns Fry Ltd v Khurana* (1985) 20 D.L.R. (4th) 245.

[233] *Milsom v Bechstein* (1898) 14 T.L.R. 159; *Hampton & Sons Ltd v George* [1939] 3 All E.R. 627; *Newton v Erickson* (1951) 157 E.G. 414; *Nicholas Prestige Homes v Neal* [2010] EWCA Civ 1552. Where the agent was employed to effect a single transaction the damages will be calculated by reference to the sum at which it is proved that the plaintiff agent could have found a purchaser: *Hampton & Sons Ltd v George* [1939] 3 All E.R. 627; *De Coning v Monror Estate and Investment Co (Pty) Ltd* 1974 (3) S.A. 72. Where the agent was employed generally, the damages will, on the principles expressed in *Roberts v Elwells Engineers Ltd* [1972] 2 Q.B. 586, be what he has lost in consequence of breach, i.e. what he would have been expected to earn, less any saved expenses. An account is not the appropriate relief. Nor, under this reasoning, is commission due: but see below, para.7-038.

endeavours to sell the property.[234] Alternatively, it could be said that the contract is still unilateral, but that this is a case where a collateral contract not to revoke will readily be implied, which would not be the case in the first and more general situation.[235] This seems however a more artificial interpretation and where an ordinary bilateral contract can be found it is probably better to use this analysis rather than have recourse to collateral contracts. Normally however the principal will still not be in breach of contract by negotiating the sale of the property personally, for the mere appointment of a sole agent does not imply any prohibition on the principal from so acting.[236] Some agency contracts may, however, expressly prohibit the principal from selling, or at least require the payment of commission on sale, other than through the agent during the period of the sole agency[237]: these are sometimes called "exclusive" or "sole selling" agency contracts.[238] Equally, provision may be made that commission must nevertheless be paid to the agent though the principal sells the property personally.[239] It would seem, however, that the principal can still *withdraw* the property.[240] The question of commission if the principal refuses to sell to a particular buyer, or chooses one over another, is solved by the interpretation of the contract term under which commission is due.[241] Similar problems arise with distributorship contracts, though here a prohibition on the principal selling personally may more easily be inferred.[242] But in all cases the interpretation of the whole contract is crucial: decisions cannot be based entirely on the phrase used.[243]

7-038 **Estate Agents (Provision of Information) Regulations 1991**[244] Where the terms "sole selling rights" or "sole agency" are used in the course of estate agency work[245] the estate agent must give an explanation of their meaning in the way described in the regulations.[246] Failure to do so makes the estate agency contract unenforce-

---

[234] *C. Christopher & Co v Essig* [1948] W.N. 461; *Mendoza & Co v Bell* (1952) 159 E.G. 372; *Hampton & Sons v Chapman* [1952] C.P.L. 24; *Galan v Alekno* [1950] 3 D.L.R. 9; *Fidelity Trust Co v Rudy* (1957) 23 W.W.R. 668; *Bradley-Wilson (1954) Ltd v Canyon Gardens Ltd* (1965) 53 W.W.R. 413; cf. *Midland Business Agency v Apted* (1971) 218 E.G. 1727, where the supposed consideration was illusory.
[235] Murdoch (1975) 91 L.Q.R. 357.
[236] *Bentall, Horsley & Baldry v Vicary* [1931] 1 K.B. 253; *Sadler v Whittaker* (1953) 162 E.G. 404.
[237] See, e.g. *Snelgrove v Ellringham Colliery Co* (1881) 45 J.P. 408; *Chamberlain & Willows v Rose* [1924] E.G.D. 356; *Property Choice Ltd v Fronda* [1991] 2 E.G.L.R. 249; *Harwood v Smith* [1998] 1 E.G.L.R. 5 (interpreting such a provision). They are common in auctioneers' contracts: see *Bernard Marcus & Co v Ashraf* [1988] 1 E.G.L.R. 7. See also *Chinnock v Sainsbury* (1860) 30 L.J.Ch. 409; *Lamb & Sons v Goring Brick Co Ltd* [1932] 1 K.B. 710.
[238] *Brodie Marshall & Co (Hotel Division) v Sharer* [1988] 1 E.G.L.R. 21 at 22.
[239] See, e.g. *Tredinnick v Browne* (1921), cited in *Bentall, Horsley & Baldry v Vicary* [1931] 1 K.B. 253 at 260; *Savills (UK) Ltd v Blacker* [2017] EWCA Civ 68.
[240] See Murdoch, *Law of Estate Agency* (5th edn), pp.127–128.
[241] See above, para.7-029.
[242] *W.T. Lamb & Sons v Goring Brick Co Ltd* [1932] 1 K.B. 710: see above, para.1-033.
[243] *Murphy Buckley & Keogh Ltd v Pye (Ireland) Ltd* [1971] I.R. 57; *G.F. Galvin (Estates) Ltd v Hedigan* [1985] I.L.R.M. 295 at 300, where it was apparently argued that "sole selling agency" allowed the vendor to sell personally, but "exclusive selling rights" did not.
[244] SI 1991/859, made under s.30 of the Estate Agents Act 1979.
[245] As to which, see Estate Agents Act 1979 s.1; Murdoch, *Law of Estate Agency and Auctions* (4th edn), p.266 onwards; and in general Murdoch, *The Estate Agents and Property Misdescriptions Acts* (3rd edn).
[246] Estate Agents (Provision of Information) Regulations 1991 reg.5.

able, except pursuant to an order of the court.[247] It should be noted that the forms prescribed in the Regulations[248] entitle the estate agent to actual commission rather than, as under the common law, to damages for breach of the special contract term. Where a contract does not, however, provide for commission in circumstances where damages would still be available at common law for breach by a vendor of a term as to sole agency, it seems that the right to damages must also be spelt out in the contract in order to comply with the Regulations.[249] It has been held that the word "purchaser" in the phrase "a purchaser introduced by us during the period of our sole agency" means a purchaser who becomes a purchaser as a result of the introduction, thereby engaging something like the "effective cause" requirement that is ordinarily implied as a prerequisite to commission.[250] Where the contract wording varies, the explanation must be given with appropriate modifications.[251]

Principles of general application   It would seem that the principles referred to above are of general application in connection with agents remunerated by commission. Where the transaction is interpreted as a unilateral contract, and the agent has no duty to do anything, the agent could only be protected by an implied collateral contract not to revoke, and although there are dicta in another context that a promise not to revoke the offer of such a contract will in general be implied,[252] it is submitted that these are too wide. Where the contract is bilateral, the question is one of implication of terms. Since the contract for an agent working for commission seems to be too varied to rank as one of which general incidents are worked out,[253] in both cases there will only be implications on the basis of "business efficacy"[254]; and such implications have hitherto been rare.[255] It may however be that the implication of a *term* is easier than the implication of a *contract*, since the lat-

7-039

---

[247] Estate Agents Act 1979 s.18(5). As to the exercise of the court's discretion, see *Great Estates Group Ltd v Digby* [2011] EWCA Civ 1120.

[248] In the Schedule. They are as follows.

"Sole selling rights.
You will be liable to pay remuneration to us, in addition to any other costs or charges agreed, in each of the following circumstances—

- if unconditional contracts for the sale of the property are exchanged, in the period during which we have sole selling rights, even if the purchaser was not found by us but by another agent or by any other person, including yourself;
- if unconditional contracts for the sale of the property are exchanged after the expiry of the period during which we have sole selling rights but to a purchaser who was introduced to you during that period or with whom we had negotiations about the property during that period."

"Sole agency.
You will be liable to pay remuneration to us, in addition to any other costs or charges agreed, if at any time unconditional contracts for the sale of the property are exchanged—

- with a purchaser introduced by us during the period of our sole agency or with whom we had negotiations about the property during that period; or
- with a purchaser introduced by another agent during that period."

[249] *Great Estates Group Ltd v Digby* [2011] EWCA Civ 1120 (Rix and Toulson LJJ; Lloyd LJ dissenting) (noted Murdoch (2012) 1203 E.G. 87).

[250] *Foxtons Ltd v Bicknell* [2008] EWCA Civ 419; [2008] 24 E.G. 142; [2008] N.P.C. 52.

[251] Estate Agents (Provision of Information) Regulations 1991 reg.5(1),(2). As to the time at which notice must be given, see regs 3, 5(3).

[252] *Daulia Ltd v Four Millbank Nominees Ltd* [1978] Ch. 231 at 239, per Goff LJ.

[253] Under the principles laid down in *Liverpool City Council v Irwin* [1977] A.C. 239; see above, para.7-001.

[254] See *Liverpool City Council v Irwin* [1977] A.C. 239; below, para.7-041.

ter is to some extent inconsistent with, or at least modifies the nature of the transaction as already determined.

7-040 **Dismissal and termination of authority** The most obvious way of preventing an agent from earning commission is by terminating the agent's authority or dismissing him or her. Whether or not this constitutes a breach of contract at all turns on the interpretation of the contract (if any) and in particular on its provisions (if any) relating to appointment for a specified period and to termination by either party; or on the interpretation of an offer of a unilateral contract, and any additional promises that may be implied with such an offer. The matter is dealt with under "Termination of authority" in Article 123.

7-041 **Prevention by other means** Terms may by the same techniques be implied against prevention by other means. The nature of the promise will vary from case to case. The term sometimes[256] might be that the principal will not do *anything* to prevent the agent from earning the commission as contemplated. Or it might be that there are certain things which the principal must not do. It has been held that a term was to be implied to prevent a vendor from "playing a dirty trick on the agent ... a term which prevents the vendor from acting unreasonably to the possible gain of the vendor and the loss of the agent"; as by breaking the contract on performance of which the agent is entitled to commission.[257] In another case a term that the vendor will not make fraudulent misrepresentation to the purchaser, which thereby allowed the contract to be cancelled, was implied.[258]

A further implication might be that if the principal does prevent the agent from earning commission on the happening of an event but, as contemplated by the contract, the agent has had to spend money and undertake work, the principal will pay the agent on a quantum meruit for what has already been done.[259] It is clear from *Luxor*'s case that such a contractual promise will not normally be implied into an estate agent's engagement in general, and it is probable that such an implication will be made only in an exceptional case. Where an agent cannot perform the agent's duties under the agency contract without the active cooperation of the principal, a

---

[255] See above, para.7-002 and *Martin-Smith v Williams* [1999] E.M.L.R. 571, where in the present context Mummery LJ said that the cases cited "are only illustrations of a more general principle that a term will be implied in a contract when it is necessary to do so to give it business efficacy"; *Green v Skandia Life Assurance Co Ltd* [2006] EWHC 1626 (Ch) at [30]–[31] (no duty to ensure insurance agent earned commission); *Adler v Ananhall Advisory & Consultancy Services Ltd* [2009] EWCA Civ 586; [2009] N.P.C. 80 (no implied term for commission upon cancellation by principal of contract where commission earned only if contract "completed"). But cf. *Standard Life Health Care Ltd v Gorman* [2009] EWCA Civ 1292; [2010] I.R.L.R. 233 at [21] per Waller LJ (where agent employed on commission basis, obligation on principal not to prevent earning of commission).

[256] But not in an estate agent situation: above, para.7-036.

[257] *Alpha Trading Ltd v Dunnshaw-Patten Ltd* [1981] Q.B. 290 at 306, per Templeman LJ (Illustration 3). See further cases cited at Illustration 3. See also *John D. Wood & Co (Residential and Agricultural) Ltd v Craze* [2007] EWHC 2658 (QB); [2007] 50 E.G. 108 (C.S.); [2007] N.P.C. 130, and above, para.7-018.

[258] *John D. Wood & Co (Residential and Agricultural) Ltd v Craze* [2007] EWHC 2658 (QB); [2007] 50 E.G. 108 (C.S.); [2007] N.P.C. 130 (but see note, Watts [2009] J.B.L. 268).

[259] This is, perhaps, the most satisfactory explanation of *Inchbald v Western Neilgherry Coffee, Tea and Cinchona Plantation Co Ltd* (1864) 17 C.B.(N.S.) 733. In *Luxor (Eastbourne) Ltd v Cooper* [1941] A.C. 108 at 147, Lord Wright said that he could not understand Inchbald's case unless it was treated as analogous to a case of wrongful dismissal. Its authority must be regarded as doubtful.

promise can sometimes be implied that such cooperation will be forthcoming.[260] This implication is an example of the general rule and can again only be made in so far as it is necessary "to make the contract workable".[261]

Remuneration after termination Sometimes the question will arise whether the agent is entitled to remuneration after the contract has been terminated. This remuneration will usually take the form of commission on business introduced before the contract was terminated. Usually the solution is found by interpreting the contract; but sometimes questions of implied terms arise.

7-042

If the fact which renders the commission earned occurs before the termination of the contract, whether the contract is terminated for breach or otherwise,[262] and no matter by which party, the commission has become due and is still payable. So if the contract on its true construction so provides, commission may be earned by a mere introduction effected before termination. This is so even though the contract provides that the agent is actually to be paid on receipt, acceptance or execution of the order, and this occurs after termination.[263]

There may be more difficulty if the commission is, despite an earlier introduction, only earned, on the true interpretation of the contract, by receipt, acceptance, or execution of the order,[264] and this occurs after the termination of the contract. Here, after the initial question of interpretation, if the termination occurs without breach (e.g. by effluxion of time, or by the exercise of a power by principal or agent), the issue may be as to whether the contract is to be regarded as containing an implied term that commission is to remain payable after termination where the business was introduced before termination.[265] To determine this it is "legitimate to have regard to the course of dealing to supplement the express terms".[266] The same inquiry could be relevant if the agent was in breach in terminating, though it is unlikely here that there would be any protection gained from an implied term. If the principal was in breach in terminating, the appropriate course is to sue the principal for depriving the agent of the opportunity to earn commission.[267]

Similar reasoning should be applied where the contract provides for commission on "repeat orders". If it does not do so expressly, an implied term to that ef-

---

[260] *Mona Oil Equipment & Supply Co Ltd v Rhodesia Railways Ltd* [1949] 2 All E.R. 1014. See also *Luxor (Eastbourne) Ltd v Cooper* [1941] A.C. 108 at 118, 148; *Mackay v Dick* (1881) 6 App.Cas. 251; *Colley v Overseas Exporters* [1921] 3 K.B. 302. See also Burrows (1968) 31 M.L.R. 390; Lücke (1973) 5 Adelaide L.Rev. 32.

[261] *Mona Oil Equipment & Supply Co Ltd v Rhodesia Railways Ltd* [1949] 2 All E.R. 1014 at 1018, per Devlin J; and see *Secretary of State for Employment v Associated Society of Locomotive Engineers and Firemen (No.2)* [1972] 2 Q.B. 455; *Coupers Partnership Ltd v Basarik* [2007] EWCA Civ 40; [2007] R.V.R. 116 at [23].

[262] But no commission on a transaction will be payable, it seems, if the contract is terminated for the agent's failure to disclose a conflict of interest in respect of that transaction: *Imageview Management Ltd v Jack* [2009] EWCA Civ 63; [2009] 2 All E.R. 666. See, further Article 76, below.

[263] *Sellers v London Counties Newspapers* [1951] 1 K.B. 784; *Gold v Life Assurance Co of Pennsylvania* [1971] 2 Lloyd's Rep. 164; *Explora Group Plc v Hesco Bastion Ltd* [2005] EWCA Civ 646 at [64], per Rix LJ; *Proactive Sports Management Ltd v Rooney* [2011] EWCA Civ 1444 at [45].

[264] As in *Hilton v Helliwell* [1894] 2 I.R. 94.

[265] See *Explora Group Plc v Hesco Bastion Ltd* [2005] EWCA Civ 646 at [126]–[128], per Longmore LJ; *Bilbee v Hasse & Co* (1889) 5 T.L.R. 677, affirmed *The Times,* January 16, 1890; *Levy v Goldhill* [1917] 2 Ch. 297.

[266] *Explora Group Plc v Hesco Bastion Ltd* [2005] EWCA Civ 646 at [126]–[128] at [67], per Rix LJ.

[267] See *Roberts v Elwells Engineers Ltd* [1972] 2 Q.B. 586; *Faulkner v Cooper & Co Ltd* (1889) 4 Com.Cas. 213; *Great Estates Group Ltd v Digby* [2011] EWCA Civ 1120 (Lloyd LJ dissenting).

fect is unlikely.[268] It may be that on interpretation an entitlement to commission on repeat orders will be found to exist only on orders that come in while the agency subsisted.[269] But if this is not so, and the initial introduction occurred before termination, and the repeat orders came in later, a question may arise as to whether there is an implied term that the repeat order provision should survive termination.[270] If the termination occurs without breach, this could be so.[271] If it is the agent who terminates, the implication of a term that commission on repeat orders continues is less likely.[272]

If it is the principal who terminates and such an interpretation is appropriate, the remedy is again an action for damages for loss of opportunity of earning commission rather than a declaration as to the right to commission.[273]

7-043   **Commercial agents**   The Commercial Agents (Council Directive) Regulations 1993 contain provisions regarding remuneration after termination.[274] They are discussed in Chapter 11.

Illustrations

7-044   (1)   An agent indicates willingness to introduce a purchaser for two cinemas if paid commission. He introduces a prospective purchaser but the vendor decides not to proceed with the sale. The agent is not entitled to commission.[275]

(2)   Shipbrokers procured a charter of a vessel for 18 months which provided for a commission of two-and-a-half per cent on hire paid under it and any continuation of it. After four months the owners sold the vessel. The brokers were unable to recover commission for the remainder of the charter period.[276]

(3)   Agents introduced buyers to sellers, who entered into a contract of sale. A contract between agents and sellers provided, in consideration for the introduction, for commission calculated per metric ton sold on performance of the sale contract, and for certain other payments in connection with the demurrage payable at the port of discharge. The sellers failed to perform the contract, forfeited a performance bond and settled additionally with the buyers. Held, a term was to be implied that:

---

[268] The question of commission on repeat orders is considered in detail in Powell, pp.364–369. See *Weare v Brimsdown Lead Co* (1910) 103 L.T. 429.

[269] *Crocker Horlock & Co Ltd v B. Lang & Co Ltd* [1949] 1 All E.R. 526. See also *Morris v Hunt & Co* (1896) 12 T.L.R. 187; *Barrett v Gilmour & Co* (1901) 17 T.L.R. 292; *Cramb v Goodwin* (1919) 35 T.L.R. 477; also *Bickley v Browning, Todd & Co* (1912) 30 T.L.R. 134 ("half-commission man").

[270] As in *Sellers v London Counties Newspapers* [1951] 1 K.B. 784.

[271] As in *Levy v Goldhill* [1917] 2 Ch. 297; cf. *Marshall v Glanvill* [1917] 2 K.B. 87.

[272] See Longmore LJ in *Explora Group Plc v Hesco Bastion Ltd* [2005] EWCA Civ 646; (2005) 149 S.J.L.B. 924 at [125]; *Personal Touch Financial Services Ltd v Simplysure Ltd* [2016] EWCA Civ 461; [2016] Bus.L.R. 1049 at [47].

[273] See cases cited in fn.267 above.

[274] Commercial Agents (Council Directive) Regulations 1993 reg.8.

[275] *Luxor (Eastbourne) Ltd v Cooper* [1941] A.C. 108.

[276] *L. French & Co Ltd v Leeston Shipping Co Ltd* [1922] 1 A.C. 451. See this case explained by Bingham LJ in *Marcan Shipping (London) Ltd v Polish SS Co* [1989] 2 Lloyd's Rep. 138. See also Article 123 and Illustrations; *Sun Alliance, etc., Ltd v Webster* [1991] 2 Lloyd's Rep. 410.

"the vendors will not deprive the agents of their commission by committing a breach of the contract between the vendors and the purchaser which releases the purchaser from its obligation to pay the purchase price."[277]

Article 59

SPECIFIC ENFORCEMENT OF AGENCY CONTRACT

The performance of a contract of agency will not normally be enforced by an order for specific performance or other similar order.[278]   **7-045**

Comment

Specific performance exceptional   A contract of agency is by its nature a   **7-046** personal contract; the relationship between the parties is of a fiduciary character and depends upon mutual confidence. It has long been established that the courts will not normally enforce the continuation of such a contract, whether directly by an order for specific performance or indirectly by injunction.[279] The normal remedy for breach of contract by the principal is therefore an action for damages. But because these specific remedies are equitable they are discretionary and it is therefore not possible to state that the principle has no exceptions. In this context the contract of agency has many similarities with the contract of employment: indeed some agents may be employees. In *Hill v C.A. Parsons & Co Ltd*[280] the Court of Appeal gave an interim injunction to an employee to restrain his employers from dismissing him.[281] The court made clear the wholly exceptional nature of the case[282]: the employers had full confidence in the employee and were being forced to dismiss

---

[277] *Alpha Trading Ltd v Dunnshaw-Patten Ltd* [1981] Q.B. 290 (see (1982) 45 M.L.R. 220); followed in *Martin-Smith v Williams* [1999] E.M.L.R. 571 (waiver by principal of future royalties on which agent would have earned commission); *George Moundreas & Co SA v Navimpex Centrata Navata* [1985] 2 Lloyd's Rep. 515; *Orient Overseas Management and Finance Ltd v File Shipping Co Ltd (The Energy Progress)* [1993] 1 Lloyd's Rep. 355; cf. *Marcan Shipping (London) Ltd v Polish SS Co* [1989] 2 Lloyd's Rep. 138; *Sun Alliance Pensions Life and Investments Services Ltd v Webster* [1991] 2 Lloyd's Rep. 410; *Micklefield v SAC Technology Ltd* [1990] 1 W.L.R. 1002. Sometimes such events are specifically provided for: see *Christie & Vesey Ltd v Maatschappij, etc., Helvetia NV (The Helvetia-S)* [1960] 1 Lloyd's Rep. 540; cf. *White v Turnbull Martin & Co* (1898) 3 Com.Cas. 183.

[278] See in general *Chitty on Contracts* (33rd edn), Ch.27; Treitel, *Law of Contract* (15th edn), para.21-039 onwards; *Meagher, Gummow and Lehane's Equity Doctrines and Remedies* (5th edn), Ch.20; Spry, *Equitable Remedies* (9th edn); Sharpe, *Injunctions and Specific Performance* (4th edn); Jones and Goodhart, *Specific Performance* (2nd edn).

[279] See Fry, *Specific Performance* (6th edn), p.50; *Chinnock v Sainsbury* (1860) 30 L.J.Ch. 409 (auctioneer); *Mortimer v Beckett* [1920] 1 Ch. 571; *Page One Records Ltd v Britton* [1968] 1 W.L.R. 157; *Denmark Productions Ltd v Boscobel Productions Ltd* [1969] 1 Q.B. 699; *Netline Pty Ltd v Qav Pty Ltd (No.2)* [2015] WASC 113. The leading case is now *Co-operative Insurance Society Ltd v Argyll Stores (Holdings) Ltd* [1998] A.C. 1, which though in a different context may perhaps be taken as authority for a stricter approach to specific enforcement than has sometimes been adopted.

[280] *Hill v C.A. Parsons & Co Ltd* [1972] 1 Ch. 305. See also *Tito v Waddell (No.2)* [1977] Ch. 106 at 321–322; *Posner v Scott-Lewis* [1987] Ch. 25; *Irani v Southampton, etc., Health Authority* [1985] I.C.R. 80.

[281] Trade Union and Labour Relations (Consolidation) Act 1992 s.236 prohibits a court, whether by an order for specific performance or an injunction, from compelling an employee to do any work or attend at any place for the doing of any work.

[282] The exceptional nature of the relief granted in *Hill v C.A. Parsons & Co Ltd* was emphasised in *Sanders v Ernest A. Neale Ltd* [1974] I.C.R. 565; and *Chappell v Times Newspapers Ltd* [1975] 1 W.L.R.

him in breach of contract under pressure from a trade union. However, some cases have indicated a greater readiness to enforce performance.[283] The continuation of confidence is clearly a factor of importance, especially in what may be called the field of pure agency where the agent represents the principal vis-à-vis third parties and can bring the principal into contractual relationship with them.[284] Where the agent is a sole agent, it is particularly hard to envisage the contract being specifically enforced; in that event the principal would be obliged to cease carrying on the business in question or to continue it through the agency of someone in whom the principal may have lost confidence and against whom the principal is currently engaged in litigation. In other cases the principal may have a right to terminate the contract,[285] or the agent may also have only limited rights, e.g. because the agent's contract is unilateral.[286] But a distributorship or franchising contract, and other contracts which may be said to involve a joint venture rather than pure agency, may perhaps more readily be specifically enforced, or at least supported by an injunction against dealing with others.[287]

7-047 **Subsistence of contract** It was formerly considered that, contrary to the principles of the general law of contract, a contract of employment could be unilaterally terminated by either party[288] and that a court would therefore not grant a declaration that such a contract still subsisted. However, after a period of uncertainty in the case law,[289] the position now appears to be, at least in England and Wales, that an employment contract cannot be summarily terminated by one party and that such a contract is therefore not an exception to the general principles

---

482. But see Freedland, below.

[283] See *C.H. Giles & Co Ltd v Morris* [1972] 1 W.L.R. 307, esp. at 318; *Sky Petroleum Ltd v V.I.P. Petroleum Ltd* [1974] 1 W.L.R. 576; *Sudbrook Trading Estate Ltd v Eggleton* [1983] 1 A.C. 444; Freedland, *The Personal Employment Contract* (2006), p.372 onwards (stressing that many cases involve public authorities).

[284] The importance of continued confidence was stressed in *Page One Records Ltd v Britton* [1968] 1 W.L.R. 157 where the manager of a very successful group of young musicians was refused an injunction which would have had the effect of enforcing his agency contract. See too *Angove's Pty Ltd v Bailey* [2016] UKSC 47; [2016] 1 W.L.R. 3179 at [6].

[285] See Article 123.

[286] As in the case of an estate agent: see above, para.7-035. See also *Chinnock v Sainsbury* (1860) 30 L.J.Ch. 409 (auctioneer); *Metropolitan Electric Supply Co Ltd v Ginder* [1901] 2 Ch. 799.

[287] See, e.g. *Decro-Wall International SA v Practitioners in Marketing Ltd* [1971] 1 W.L.R. 361; *Evans Marshall & Co v Bertola SA* [1973] 1 W.L.R. 349, esp. at 379 (injunction cases); but cf. *Co-operative Insurance Co Ltd v Argyll Stores (Holdings) Ltd* [1998] A.C. 1. See also *Donnell v Bennett* (1883) 22 Ch.D. 835; *Atlas Steels (Australia) Pty Ltd v Atlas Steels Ltd* (1948) 49 S.R. (N.S.W.) 157; *Pasen v Dominion Herb Distributors Inc* (1968) 67 D.L.R. (2d) 405; affirmed 69 D.L.R. (2d) 651. cf. *Paxton v Spira* (1965) 54 D.L.R. (2d) 627; *Shell (Petroleum Mining) Co Ltd v Todd Petroleum Mining Co Ltd* [2008] 2 N.Z.L.R. 418 (NZCA) (injunction against action that involved repudiation of agency agreement, where agent a joint venture company). See also *Standard Life Health Care Ltd v Gorman* [2009] EWCA Civ 1292; [2010] I.R.L.R. 233.

[288] e.g. *Vine v National Dock Labour Board* [1957] A.C. 488; *Cranleigh Precision Engineering Ltd v Bryant* [1965] 1 W.L.R. 1293; *Denmark Productions Ltd v Boscobel Productions Ltd* [1969] 1 Q.B. 699; *Roberts v Elwells Engineers Ltd* [1972] Q.B. 586; *Sanders v Ernest A. Neale Ltd* [1974] I.C.R. 565.

[289] See *Francis v Kuala Lumpur Councillors* [1962] 1 W.L.R. 1411 (PC) at 1417–1418; *Decro-Wall International SA v Practitioners in Marketing Ltd* [1971] 1 W.L.R. 361. See also *Gunton v Richmond-upon-Thames LBC* [1981] Ch. 448; *London Transport Executive v Clarke* [1981] I.C.R. 355. cf. *Sport International Bussum BV v Inter-Footwear Ltd* [1984] 1 W.L.R. 776 (no relief against forfeiture); *Wilson v St Helen's BC* [1999] 2 A.C. 52 at 77.

of the law of contract in this respect.[290] The same position applies to an agency contract where the agent is not an employee.[291] The points here made impact on the question of the revocability of the agent's authority, which is considered under Article 120.

Article 60

NO REMUNERATION FOR UNAUTHORISED TRANSACTIONS OR IN CASES OF MISCONDUCT OR BREACH OF DUTY

An agent is not entitled to remuneration—   **7-048**

(1) in respect of any unauthorised transaction[292] which is not ratified by the principal[293];

(2) in respect of transactions in relation to which the agent is in breach of duties as agent, such breach going to the root of the contract or otherwise justifying the principal's repudiation of the liability to pay.[294]

Comment

Unauthorised transactions   Commission is by its nature only payable in respect   **7-049** of transactions expressly or impliedly authorised or ratified. Transactions made by agents with themselves without the consent of their principal may be unauthorised.[295] Where authority is wrongfully withdrawn, however, there may be an action for breach of contract.

Breach of duty by agent   Where the agent commits a serious breach of duty to   **7-050** the principal, the principal may be justified in refusing to pay commission in respect of the transaction as to which the agent is in breach[296]: further, if the agent is appointed by the principal for a fixed time in circumstances entitling the agent to notice[297] the principal may terminate the agent's employment or other contract summarily and decline to pay any remuneration that is not due and payable at the date of dismissal.[298] But commission earned, and retainer, salary or wages already due,

---

[290] *Société Générale, London Branch v Geys* [2012] UKSC 63; [2013] 1 A.C. 523. See further *Chitty on Contracts* (33rd edn), para.40-191 onwards.

[291] See *Atlantic Underwriting Agencies Ltd v Cia. di Assicurazione di Milano SpA* [1979] 2 Lloyd's Rep. 240; *Paper Reclaim Ltd v Aotearoa International Ltd* [2007] 3 N.Z.L.R. 169 (NZSC) at [19] (repudiation by principal of agency agreement to market its products had the effect of determining the agency but not the contract itself until the repudiation had been accepted; the duty to mitigate will frequently lead to acceptance of the repudiation).

[292] Illustrations 1–42.

[293] As in *Keay v Fenwick* (1876) 1 C.P.D. 745. See Articles 13–20.

[294] See Comment.

[295] *Salomons v Pender* (1865) 3 H. & C. 639, Illustration 4.

[296] *Andrews v Ramsay & Co* [1903] 2 K.B. 635, Illustration 4; *Rhodes v Macalister* (1923) 29 Com.Cas. 19.

[297] See Comment to Article 123.

[298] *Boston Deep Sea Fishing & Ice Co v Ansell* (1888) 39 Ch.D. 339; *Rhodes v Macalister* (1923) 29 Com.Cas. 19 at 29; *Shepherd v Felt and Textiles of Australia Ltd* (1931) 45 C.L.R. 359. See further Article 48.

at the time of the breach must normally be paid.[299] This is simply an application of the law as to discharge of contract by breach.[300]

A breach of duty such as to warrant the withholding of remuneration, and in some cases the recovery of remuneration already paid, may be justified in various ways. In some cases it may be sufficient to say that commission has not been earned, without reference to discharge of the contract of agency, if any: this reasoning has been used where the agent has wrongfully delegated the agent's duties[301] or stated a wrong asking price for the property leading to its sale at less than the vendor intended.[302] But in other cases it may be appropriate to say more generally that the agent's breach goes to the root of the contract,[303] or that the agent's dereliction of duty is itself a repudiation of the agent's obligations which may be accepted by the principal.[304]

A breach by an agent of the obligations arising from the agent's fiduciary character, e.g. where the agent accepts a bribe, or personally purchases (without disclosure) the principal's property, can be regarded as fatal to a right to remuneration,[305] and may be described as a breach going to the root of the contract.[306] It is not clear, however, that breach of fiduciary duty is itself an independent basis for forfeiture. In some such cases it may be possible to find, and the courts have so found, that the agent was not acting as agent at all but as buyer, or generally not within the scope of the agent's authority.[307] In other cases, especially of professional agents, it may be said that the agent has been guilty of gross neglect or misconduct,[308] or lack of due diligence,[309] or dishonesty[310] with the result that the services are entirely valueless to the principal and do not therefore qualify the agent

---

[299] *Boston Deep Sea Fishing & Ice Co v Ansell* (1888) 39 Ch.D. 339.

[300] See *Chitty on Contracts* (33rd edn), Ch.24; Treitel, *Law of Contract* (15th edn), Chs 17 and 18. See too *Crocs Europe BV v Anderson (t/a Spectrum Agencies)* [2012] EWCA Civ 1400; [2013] 1 Lloyd's Rep. 1 at [24] (not all breaches of fiduciary duty will warrant termination of agency).

[301] *Beable v Dickerson* (1885) 1 T.L.R. 654; *John McCann & Co v Pow* [1974] 1 W.L.R. 1643.

[302] *Spiers v Taylor* (1984) 271 E.G. 196.

[303] *Thornton Hall & Partners v Wembley Electrical Appliances Ltd* [1947] 2 All E.R. 630 at 634; cf. *Keppel v Wheeler* [1927] 1 K.B. 577 at 592.

[304] *Boston Deep Sea Fishing & Ice Co v Ansell* (1888) 39 Ch.D. 339 at 365. And see *Hurst v Holding* (1810) 3 Taunt. 32 (agent himself prevented performance); *Styles v Rogers Realty Ltd* (1987) 43 D.L.R. (4th) 629 (exclusive agent did not use reasonable efforts to sell land).

[305] *Andrews v Ramsay & Co* [1903] 2 K.B. 635, Illustration 4; *Rhodes v Macalister* (1923) 29 Com.Cas. 19; *Price v Metropolitan House Investment Agency Co Ltd* (1907) 23 T.L.R. 630; *L.S. Harris Trustees Ltd v Power Packing Services (Hermit Road) Ltd* [1970] 2 Lloyd's Rep. 65 (breach of confidence); *Greenwood v Harvey* [1965] N.S.W.R. 1489; *Cec. McManus Realty Ltd v Bray* (1970) 14 D.L.R. (3d) 564; *Ian Scott & Co v Medical Installations Co Ltd* [1981] E.G.D. 228 (attempt to extract extra commission); *Ocean City Realty Ltd v A. & M. Holdings Ltd* (1987) 36 D.L.R. (4th) 94; *Wheen v Smithmann European Homes*, CA June 20, 2000 (where Article 60 was cited by the court). But this is not always so: cf. *Hippisley v Knee Bros* [1905] 1 K.B. 1, Illustration 5; *Keppel v Wheeler* [1927] 1 K.B. 577 at 592.

[306] *Thornton Hall & Partners v Wembley Electrical Appliances Ltd* [1947] 2 All E.R. 630 at 634.

[307] *Salomons v Pender* (1865) 3 Hurl. & C. 639, Illustration 4; and *Boston Deep Sea Fishing & Ice Co v Ansell* (1888) 39 Ch. D. 339.

[308] *White v Lady Lincoln* (1803) 8 Ves. 363 (failure by solicitor to keep accounts; but the principle of this case does not apply when the solicitor is not the general agent of the client: *Re Lee Ex p. Neville* (1868) L.R. 4 Ch.App. 43); *Huntley v Bulwer* (1839) 6 Bing.N.C. 111.

[309] *Moneypenny v Hartland* (1824) 1 Car. & P. 352.

[310] *Rhodes v Macalister* (1923) 29 Com. Cas. 19; *Andrews v Ramsay & Co* [1903] 2 K.B. 635, Illustration 4.

for commission.[311] Again a slight breach of duty or omission may bar the agent from remuneration if the obligation is treated as entire, for such an obligation cannot be sued upon by an agent until it has been completely performed.[312]

In *Imageview Management Ltd v Jack*,[313] forfeiture of an agent's entire remuneration was upheld even though there was no finding of dishonesty in the agent, and even though the services conformed to what was requested and there was no suggestion that their value had been affected by the breach of duty. The reasoning in this case has since been applied to forfeit the profit share of a partner in a limited partnership when the partner had disloyally been seeking to persuade some employees to leave and start a new business with him,[314] and more surprisingly still to a case where the relevant corruption took place some years previously when the agent was acting for an unrelated principal, albeit in a transaction with the same third party.[315] It is strongly arguable that the reasoning in these cases is inconsistent with both common law and equitable principle, since, where there has been no failure of performance, and any collateral profit has (rightly) already been stripped, forfeiture of remuneration is justified neither by the law of contract nor the principles of equity.[316] In particular, the existence of an independent equitable jurisdiction to forfeit remuneration is plainly based on a misunderstanding of the 19th century case law, and rubs against the principle that equity does not act penally. Perhaps only the Supreme Court could now undertake a principled reconsideration of the law. But some recent cases show judges finding the means to take a more restrained approach to forfeiture, looking for a breach which goes to the root of the agency contract (which bad faith and dishonesty will usually do),[317] and otherwise not forfeiting remuneration where to do so would be "disproportionate and

---

[311] *Huntley v Bulwer* (1839) 6 Bing.N.C. 111; *Denew v Daverell* (1813) 3 Camp. 451, Illustration 10; *Hamond v Holiday* (1824) 1 C. & P. 384 (shipbroker); *Hill v Featherstonhaugh* (1831) 7 Bing. 569 (attorney); *Maketu Estates Ltd v Robb* [2014] NZHC 2664.

[312] Such may be the case with solicitors' retainers to conduct actions: *Underwood, Son & Piper v Lewis* [1894] 2 Q.B. 306; *Cachia v Isaacs* (1985) 3 N.S.W.L.R. 366; *Richard Buxton (Solicitors) v Mills-Owens* [2010] EWCA Civ 122; [2010] 1 W.L.R. 1997; *French v Carter Lemon Camerons LLP* [2012] EWCA Civ 1180 at [26]. But cf. *Warmingtons v McMurray* (1937) 52 T.L.R. 381; *Caldwell v Treloar* (1982) 30 S.A.S.R. 202; *Cawdery Kaye Fireman & Taylor v Minkin* [2012] EWCA Civ 546; [2012] 3 All E.R. 1117 (client ends solicitor's retainer).

[313] *Imageview Management Ltd v Jack* [2009] EWCA Civ 63; [2009] 2 All E.R. 666, Illustration 11 (noted P. Watts, "Restitution and Conflicted Agency" (2009) 125 L.Q.R. 369; L. Macgregor, "An agent's fiduciary duties: modern law placed in historical context" (2010) 14 Edinburgh L.R. 121; S. Oram "Forfeiture of fiduciary remuneration following. breach of duty: from contract to conscience" [2010] L.M.C.L.Q. 95). See too *Rahme v Smith & Williamson Trust Corp Ltd* [2009] EWHC 911 (Ch) at [141]; *Stupples v Stupples & Co (High Wycombe) Ltd* [2012] EWHC 1226 (Ch); [2013] 1 B.C.L.C. 729 at [25]; *Avrahami v Biran* [2013] EWHC 1776 (Ch) at [345] (project manager misappropriates sums throughout period of project).

[314] See *Hosking v Marathon Asset Management LLP* [2016] EWHC 2418 (Ch); [2017] Ch. 157. But cf. *Healey v Française Rubastic SA* [1917] 1 K.B. 946; *Item Software (UK) Ltd v Fassihi* [2002] EWHC 3116 (Ch); [2003] 2 B.C.L.C. 1 (discussed on this point on appeal at [2004] EWCA Civ 1244; [2005] 2 B.C.L.C. 91 at [20], [50] and [52]).

[315] See *HPOR Servicos de Consultoria Ltd v Dryships Inc* [2018] EWHC 3451 (Comm); [2019] 1 Lloyd's Rep. 260.

[316] See P. Watts "Forfeiture of Agents' Remuneration" in *Impact of Equity and Restitution in Commerce* (P. Devonshire and R. Havelock eds, 2018), Ch. 10. See the treatment of *Imageview* in *Staechelin v ACLBDD Holdings Ltd* [2019] EWCA Civ 817 at [84].

[317] See *Kelly v Cooper* [1993] A.C. 205 at 216; *Premium Real Estate Ltd v Stevens* [2009] 2 N.Z.L.R. 384 at [90], Illustration 12; *Wright Hassall LLP v Horton Jr* [2015] EWHC 3716 (QB) at [61]; and *Staechelin v ACLBDD Holdings Ltd* [2019] EWCA Civ 817 at [76].

inequitable".[318] But a failure to let basic contract principles do the necessary work (including amongst those the concept of "failure of consideration") has led to undue complexity.

There can obviously however be cases where the agent effects severable transactions, and in these cases the rule depriving the agent of commission will only apply to those in respect of which the agent is in breach of duty[319]; or where the breach does not go to the whole contract.[320] There has also been some tendency to hold commission recoverable when the agent makes an honest mistake, even if that mistake renders the agent liable in damages.[321] And there may be a waiver of the agent's breach[322]: but this is not implied from the fact that the principal takes the benefit of the transaction negotiated by the agent,[323] nor from the fact that the principal recovers a bribe from the agent.[324]

Illustrations

7-051   (1)   A is employed on commission to procure a loan upon certain terms. Before anything is done the principal varies the terms. A is unable to procure the loan on the terms as varied, but obtains an offer on the original terms, which the principal refuses to accept. A is not entitled to any commission, though he may be entitled to damages for breach of contract.[325]

      (2)   An agent is employed on commission to sell certain property. His authority is revoked by the death of the principal, but he subsequently sells the property, and the principal's executors confirm the sale. The agent is not entitled to recover the agreed commission from the executors unless they recognise the terms of his employment, but he may be entitled upon a quantum meruit.[326]

      (3)   An auctioneer, who is employed to sell property by auction, sells it by private contract. He is not entitled to commission.[327]

      (4)   An agent, who is employed to sell certain land, sells it to a company in which he is a director and large shareholder. He is not entitled to commission upon the sale, even if it is adopted and confirmed by the principal.[328] This can be explained on the basis that the agent had no authority to sell to himself or a party in which he held a substantial equity interest. In other cases, the explanation can be that because of the agent's breach of duty, the principal received no benefit from the transaction. So, if an agent for sale fraudulently takes a secret commission from the purchaser, he is not only accountable to the principal for the secret commission, but is not entitled to remuneration

---

[318] See *Bank of Ireland v Jaffery* [2012] EWHC 1377 (Ch) at [373]; *Gamatronic (UK) Ltd v Hamilton* [2016] EWHC 2225 (QB) at [171].

[319] Illustration 5.

[320] See Illustrations 5 and 6. See also *Bank of Ireland v Jaffery* [2012] EWHC 1377 (Ch) at [372]; *Electrosteel Castings (UK) Ltd v Metalpol Ltd* [2014] EWHC 2017 (Ch) at [64].

[321] See Illustrations 6 and 7.

[322] Illustration 8; *Thornton Hall & Partners v Wembley Electrical Appliances Ltd* [1947] 2 All E.R. 630.

[323] *Salomons v Pender* (1865) 3 H. & C. 639; *Rhodes v Macalister* (1923) 29 Com.Cas. 19; *Imageview Management Ltd v Jack* [2009] EWCA Civ 63; [2009] 2 All E.R. 666.

[324] *Andrews v Ramsay & Co* [1903] 2 K.B. 635.

[325] *Toppin v Healey* (1863) 11 W.R. 466.

[326] *Campanari v Woodburn* (1854) 15 C.B. 400. As to quantum meruit see above, paras 7-009 and 7-024.

[327] *Marsh v Jelf* (1862) 3 F. & F. 234; *Gillow & Co v Lord Aberdare* (1892) 9 T.L.R. 12.

[328] *Salomons v Pender* (1865) 3 H. & C. 639.

from the seller; and if the seller pays him commission in ignorance of the facts, he is entitled to recover it.[329]

(5)   An auctioneer, employed to sell property on the terms that he should be paid a certain commission and out-of-pocket expenses, received discounts from printers and advertisers, and charged the principal in full without deducting the discounts, in the honest belief that he was entitled to retain them. It was held that, though he must account for the discounts, he was entitled to commission, as he had not acted fraudulently, and as the receipt of the discount was incidental to his main duty of selling the goods.[330] So, where a commission agent fraudulently overcharged his principal in respect of some transactions, but acted honestly in other separate and distinct transactions, it was held that he was entitled to commission on the transactions in which he had acted honestly.[331]

(6)   An agent, employed to find a purchaser, procured an offer, which the vendor accepted, subject to contract. Subsequently, a higher offer was made by another party to the agent, which, in the bona fide belief that he had fulfilled his duty, he failed to communicate to the vendor, and the vendor concluded a contract with the person whose offer had been accepted. The vendor recovered as damages from the agent the difference between the price fixed by the concluded contract and the higher offer. The agent would have been entitled to commission on the price so fixed and this sum was therefore to be deducted from the damages.[332]

(7)   An agent firm introduces purchasers whose offer is accepted subject to contract. The agents' branch manager hears of difficulties which the vendors are having concerning the house to which they hope to move. He thinks it his duty to tell the prospective purchasers and does so. The sale nearly falls through, but the vendors terminate the agents' instructions and sell the property to the same purchasers directly: they move into rented accommodation. The agents are entitled to commission, though they would have been liable in damages had loss resulted to the vendor.[333]

(8)   The estate department of a company acting for the vendor of a house introduced a purchaser, and, in ignorance of the agency, the building department of the company acted for the purchaser and made a report on the house which had the effect of reducing the price. Subsequently the company discovered that they had been acting in this way and made an offer to the vendor to invite the purchaser to obtain an independent report on the house. The vendor refused and completed the sale at a reduction of the agreed price, the reduction being due to the work required to be done as a result of the report. Held, that although the company had committed a breach of their duty

---

[329] *Andrews v Ramsay & Co* [1903] 2 K.B. 635. cf. *Turner v Laurentide Financial Realty Corp (Western) Ltd* (1979) 97 D.L.R. (3d) 429. See also Articles 48 and 96.
[330] *Hippisley v Knee Bros* [1905] 1 K.B. 1; applied in *The Peppy* [1997] 2 Lloyd's Rep. 722. See (1905) 21 L.Q.R. 102.
[331] *Nitedals Taendstikfabrik v Bruster* [1906] 2 Ch. 671. But cf. *Headway Construction Co Ltd v Downham* (1974) 233 E.G. 675 (whole commission agreement voidable for fraud).
[332] *Keppel v Wheeler* [1927] 1 K.B. 577. See also Murdoch (1974) 232 E.G. 1021, criticising *John McCann & Co v Pow* [1974] 1 W.L.R. 1643; and *Lloyd v Pangani Properties Ltd* [2019] NZCA 314. See also Estate Agents (Undesirable Practices) (No.2) Order 1991 (SI 1991/1032) Sch.3 para.2.
[333] *Robinson Scammell & Co v Ansell* [1985] 2 E.G.L.R. 41; see also *Eric V Stansfield v South East Nursing Home Services Ltd* [1986] 1 E.G.L.R. 29.

as agents, since the principal with full knowledge of this breach had completed the sale at the reduced price, he had affirmed the transaction and the agent was entitled to commission.[334]

(9) An agent was employed by a lessee to find a purchaser of leasehold premises which were subject to a covenant prohibiting the carrying on of any business other than that of a music seller without the consent of the lessor. Several tailors made offers to the lessee to buy the premises for £2,500, but the lessee, believing that the lessor would not consent, did not approach him upon the matter. The agent, having an offer from a tailor of £2,250, and having obtained an assurance from the lessor that he would consent to a tailor's business being carried on upon the premises, concealed from the lessee the fact that the lessor had so assured his consent and the nature of the business of the person making the offer, and induced the lessee to accept £2,250. Held, that the agent was not entitled to any commission.[335]

(10) An auctioneer employed to sell an estate negligently omitted to insert in the conditions of sale a proviso usually inserted in them, and in consequence of the omission the sale was rendered nugatory. Held, that he was not entitled to any compensation or remuneration for his services, although the particulars of the sale had been submitted to the principal and were not objected to by him.[336]

(11) A sports agent under a two-year contract with a professional footballer obtains for him a position with a club, taking a commission on his salary. The agent also receives a fee from the club for procuring a work permit for the player, which fee is not revealed to the player. Held, on account of the failure to disclose the conflict of interest, that the agent both forfeited his commission (even though the principal had no objection to the contract obtained for him by the agent and continued to play for the club) and was accountable for the fee received from the club.[337]

(12) A real estate agency appointed by the vendor leads the vendor to believe that the proposing purchaser intends to live in the house, when it knows that the purchaser is a property developer intent on on-selling the house, a fact that would have been material to the vendor in its negotiating position and who would not have sold to the developer had he known the facts. The agency regularly also acts for the purchaser, and so acts in the subsequent sale of the property at a profit. Held, that the agency was not entitled to any commission on the sale.[338]

Article 61

No Remuneration in Respect of Unlawful Transactions

7-052 (1) An agent may be debarred from recovering remuneration for services if at the

---

[334] *Harrods Ltd v Lemon* [1931] 2 K.B. 157. See also *Dargusch v Sherley Investments Pty Ltd* [1970] Qd.R. 338. cf. *Jones v Canavan* [1972] 2 N.S.W.L.R. 236.

[335] *Heath v Parkinson* (1926) 136 L.T. 128.

[336] *Denew v Daverell* (1813) 3 Camp. 451.

[337] *Imageview Management Ltd v Jack* [2009] EWCA Civ 63; [2009] 2 All E.R. 666. See too *Rahme v Smith & Williamson Trust Corp Ltd* [2009] EWHC 911 (Ch) at [141].

[338] *Premium Real Estate Ltd v Stevens* [2009] 2 N.Z.L.R. 384.

time when the services were rendered the agent was not legally qualified to act in the capacity in which the remuneration is claimed, or if the enforcement of the contract of agency is affected in some other way by statute or statutory instrument.[339]

(2) An agent cannot recover any remuneration in respect of any transaction which is obviously, or to the agent's knowledge, unlawful,[340] or unlawful by virtue of legislation which is to be interpreted as affecting contracts which involve the doing of acts prohibited by it.

Comment

Rule (1): Incapacity to act   There are frequently statutory or other requirements regarding capacity to act in certain professional and similar activities. An obvious example is the Solicitors Act 1974, referred to in Illustration 1. So also in Australia, New Zealand and elsewhere real estate agents may require licences.[341] Unqualified persons cannot normally recover remuneration. But the exact result must in each case turn on the terms of the legal provisions imposing the requirement of qualification. Sometimes the very acting as agent for the particular person in certain ways is unlawful.[342] Some statutes prevent persons exercising agency functions from suing on the agency contract in certain circumstances.[343] Other statutes simply prescribe penalties.

7-053

Rule (2): Illegal transactions   This rule is an application of the common law principles as to illegal contracts, which should be considered, as developed by cases most of which are not relevant to agency, in each situation individually.[344] The formulation in the Article gives no more than the most general of guidelines. Older cases will need to be reconsidered in the light of the flexibility of the approach to illegality adopted in *Patel v Mirza*.[345]

7-054

Wagering transactions   It seems that before 1892 commission was recoverable by agents employed to make wagers[346] just as indemnity was recoverable.[347] But this was reversed by the Gaming Act 1892, which by s.1 provided that:

7-055

"any promise, express or implied ... to pay any sum of money by way of commission, fee, reward or otherwise, in respect of any contract or agreement [rendered null and void

---

[339] Illustrations 1 and 2; and see Comment.
[340] Illustrations 3, 4 and 5; and see Comment. See also *Allkins v Jupe* (1877) 2 C.P.D. 375 (illegal insurance); *Harrington v Victoria Graving Dock Co* (1878) 3 Q.B.D. 549 (corrupt contract, see further below); *North v Marra Developments Ltd* (1981) 148 C.L.R. 42; *RTA (Business Consultants) Ltd v Bracewell* [2015] EWHC 630 (QB) (Money Laundering Regulations 2007).
[341] e.g. Auctioneers and Agents Act 1971 (Qld); Real Estate Agents Act 2008 (NZ).
[342] e.g. Accommodation Agencies Act 1953; see *Saunders v Soper* [1975] A.C. 239; Partington (1975) 125 New L.J. 148; Cartwright (1979) 123 S.J. 577; Szekely (1984) 12 Aus. Bus. Law Rev. 408. See also *Phoenix General Ins. Co of Greece SA v Halvanon Ins. Co* [1988] Q.B. 216 (Insurance Companies Act 1982 s.2, now repealed).
[343] See Illustrations 1 and 2.
[344] See *Chitty on Contracts*, (33rd edn), Ch.16; Treitel, *Law of Contract* (15th edn), Ch.11.
[345] *Patel v Mirza* [2016] UKSC 42; [2017] A.C. 467. Quaere, e.g. whether *Harrington v Victoria Graving Dock Co* (1878) 3 Q.B.D. 549 would be decided the same way (agreement to employ agent with corrupt intention in relation to his principal but agent not in fact corrupted and unsuccessfully seeking remuneration).
[346] *Knight v Fitch* (1855) 15 C.B. 566.
[347] *Read v Anderson* (1884) 13 Q.B.D. 779.

by the Gaming Act 1845], or of any services in relation thereto or connection therewith, shall be null and void, and no action shall be brought or maintained to recover any such sum of money."[348]

The main difficulties occurred in connection with speculative transactions on the Stock Exchange.[349] But the 1892 Act is repealed by the Gambling Act 2005, under which wagers are enforceable.

Illustrations

7-056

(1) No costs are recoverable in respect of anything done by any unqualified person acting as a solicitor.[350]

(2) An estate agent who enters into a contract with another under which he will engage in estate agency work and who fails to supply to his client information as required by the Estate Agents Act 1979 or statutory instrument made under it cannot enforce the contract, whether by legal action or the exercise of a lien over the client's money, except pursuant to an order of the court.[351]

(3) An action was brought for work done and money expended in buying shares in a company which affected to act as a body corporate without authority by charter or statute and was therefore illegal. Held, that the action was not maintainable because it arose out of an unlawful transaction.[352]

(4) Commission was claimed by a broker for procuring freight. Held, that the fact that the charterparty in respect of which commission was claimed would be illegal unless the charterer obtained certain licences was no answer to the action, it not being part of the broker's duty to see that the licences were obtained.[353]

(5) Claims for remuneration for attending auctions for the purpose of "puffing" prices,[354] and claims for remuneration for procuring the sale of public offices,[355] are unenforceable.

---

[348] Note that it is only money that is referred to.

[349] Especially contracts for "differences".

[350] Solicitors Act 1974 s.25(1). "Costs" includes fees, charges, disbursements, expenses and remuneration: Solicitors Act 1974 s.87(1). For "unqualified person" see Solicitors Act 1974 s.87(1) as amended and s.1. See also Solicitors Act 1974 s.25(2); *Kent v Ward* (1894) 70 L.T. 612; *Re Sweeting* [1898] 1 Ch. 268; *Browne v Barber* [1913] 2 K.B. 553; *Hudgell Yeates & Co v Watson* [1978] Q.B. 451; Cordery, *Solicitors* (8th edn), p.35.

[351] Estate Agents Act 1979 s.18(5); above, paras 7-007 and 7-037; *Solicitors' Estate Agency (Glasgow) Ltd v MacIver* 1993 S.L.T. 23; *Connell Estate Agents v Begej* [1993] 2 E.G.L.R. 35; Murdoch, *Law of Estate Agency* (5th edn), p.288 onwards; Murdoch, *The Estate Agents and Property Misdescriptions Acts* (3rd edn). As to lien, see Articles 64–68. For an example of court approval despite there being no such information supplied, see *Benhams Ltd v Kythira Investments Ltd* [2004] EWHC 2973 (QB).

[352] *Josephs v Pebrer* (1825) 3 B. & C. 639.

[353] *Haines v Busk* (1814) 5 Taunt. 521.

[354] *Walker v Nightingale* (1726) 4 Bro.P.C. 193. See too *North v Marra Developments Ltd* (1981) 148 C.L.R. 42.

[355] *Stackpole v Earle* (1761) 2 Wil.K.B. 133; *Parsons v Thompson* (1790) 1 Hy.Bl. 322; *Waldo v Martin* (1825) 4 B. & C. 319.

2. REIMBURSEMENT AND INDEMNITY

Article 62

REIMBURSEMENT OF EXPENSES AND INDEMNITY FROM LIABILITIES INCURRED IN COURSE OF AGENCY

Subject to the provisions of Article 63, every agent has a right against the principal to be reimbursed all expenses and to be indemnified against all losses and liabilities incurred by the agent in the execution of the agent's authority[356]: and where the agent is sued for money due to the principal, the agent has a right to set off the amount of any such expenses, losses or liabilities,[357] unless the money due to the principal is held on trust.[358]

7-057

Comment

The rule here given is normally stated in such general terms,[359] but its juristic basis may require attention. In the nineteenth century, actions at law were based on the common count for money paid, and it was not often necessary to distinguish between contractual and what would now be called restitutionary claims.[360] At the present day it could matter how the claim was classified in a particular case. The case law is unclear as to the extent to which agents are entitled to be indemnified in respect of liabilities in tort incurred by them in the course of carrying out their mandate, and in respect of losses incurred by them as a result of the wrongs of third parties suffered by them in the course of carrying out the mandate. In respect of the former category of case (liabilities incurred to third parties), it seems there will be a right of indemnity,[361] unless the agent's exposure to the liability was the result of a breach of duty owed the principal or the action taken by the agent was obviously unlawful.[362] In respect of the latter category (losses suffered through the wrongs of third parties), where the losses were suffered while carrying out an action specifically directed by the principal there is likely to be a right of indemnity if the agent cannot recover from the wrongdoer.[363] The position in respect of the wrongs of others suffered incidentally in the course of the agency is less clear.

7-058

---

[356] See Comment and Illustrations; *Restatement, Third* § 8.14; Ch.3 above as to authority. See Illustrations 11 and 12 of para.7-062 below.

[357] Illustrations 4 and 5.

[358] See *Stumore v Campbell & Co* [1892] 1 Q.B. 314; *Re Mid-Kent Fruit Factory* [1896] 1 Ch. 567; above, para.6-040 onwards.

[359] See, e.g. *Thacker v Hardy* (1878) 4 Q.B.D. 685 at 687. The principle is also stated in even wider terms that do not confine it to agency: see *Dugdale v Lovering* (1875) L.R. 10 C.P. 196; *Sheffield Corp v Barclay* [1905] A.C. 392; *Secretary of State for India v Bank of India Ltd* [1938] 2 All E.R. 797; *Guaranty Trust Co v James Richardson & Son* (1963) 39 D.L.R. (2d) 517. But cf. *Cory & Son Ltd v Lambton & Hetton Collieries Ltd* (1916) 86 L.J.K.B. 401.

[360] See Stoljar, *Law of Quasi-Contract* (2nd edn), p.152 onwards; *Bowlby v Bell* (1846) 3 C.B. 284; *Pawle v Gunn* (1838) 4 Bing.N.C. 445.

[361] See *Sheffield Corp v Barclay* [1905] A.C. 393; *Re Famatina Development Corp Ltd* [1914] 2 Ch. 271 (no actual liability to third party found, but entitlement to be indemnified for the costs of defending the claim); *Adamson v Jarvis* (1827) 4 Bing. 66, Article 63, Illustration 9. See also other cases in Illustration 8.

[362] See below, Article 63.

[363] See *The James Seddon* (1866) L.R. 1 A. & E. 62; *Benyatov v Credit Suisse Securities (Europe) Ltd* [2020] EWHC 85 (QB) (where the issue is discussed but the point did not need to be decided) cf.

7-059   **Contract**   Where the agency agreement is contractual, the agreement to reimburse and indemnify in return for what has been requested, if not express,[364] can be regarded as an implied term of the contract that operates unless clearly excluded.[365] There is thus no difficulty in such cases in holding that the principal is liable to reimburse and indemnify the agent for all payments made and liabilities incurred within the agent's express or implied authority.[366] This would include not only pay‑ ments that the principal is legally bound to make, but also payments which the agent is legally bound to make though the principal would not be liable for them,[367] cases where the agent is bound by the usage of a market,[368] cases where the agent makes an authorised but gratuitous payment on the principal's behalf,[369] cases where the agent makes a payment which could not have been enforced but which there is a strong and legitimate pressure to make,[370] cases where the agent, though under a li‑ ability, has as yet not had to meet it,[371] and cases where a payment is reasonably but mistakenly made by the agent.[372] Cases where the agent acts beyond instruc‑ tions,[373] or interferes without request, would not however be included.

7-060   **Restitution**   But where the agency is not contractual and the law of contract can‑ not be relied on, the agent's claim is only restitutionary[374] and confined to the reimbursement of payments made by the agent under compulsion, in respect of which the ultimate liability is on the principal, and the benefit of which the principal obtains.[375] It does not, therefore, extend to the full indemnity which the contractual right might give. Normally speaking, agency is contractual: but circumstances can arise where it is not, e.g. because one of the parties is a minor, or because the agent

---

National Roads and Motorists' Association v Whitlam (2007) 25 A.C.L.C. 688, Illustration 12, criticised in *Benyatov*.

[364]   As in *Toplis v Grane* (1839) 5 Bing.N.C. 636; *Moore v Moore* (1611) 1 Bulst. 169.

[365]   Since agency is probably not a generic contract such as to attract the implications developed for such contracts, it is probably a "business efficacy" implied term, perhaps more satisfactorily coming under the wording of the "officious bystander" test. See above, para.7-001. It could also be based on interpretation of the consideration offered. Where there is a separate implied contract, these difficul‑ ties disappear.

[366]   As to whether the right of indemnity can arise before the agent has suffered loss by meeting the li‑ ability, see *Firma C-Trade SA v Newcastle P & I Assn (The Fanti and The Padre Island)* [1991] 2 A.C. 1; *McIntosh v Dalwood (No.4)* (1930) 4 S.R. (N.S.W.) 415.

[367]   *Adams v Morgan & Co* [1924] 1 K.B. 751, Illustration 6; *Brittain v Lloyd* (1845) 14 M. & W. 762.

[368]   See Illustration 11; there were many old cases on the usage of the London Stock Exchange, but most are now obsolete. As to customs and usages of markets, see Article 31.

[369]   *Brittain v Lloyd* (1845) 14 M. & W. 762 at 773; *Pawle v Gunn* (1838) 4 Bing.N.C. 445 at 448–449.

[370]   *Rhodes v Fielder, Jones and Harrison* (1919) 89 L.J.K.B. 15, Illustration 10; *Schneider v Eisovitch* [1960] 2 Q.B. 430; *Gwinnutt v George* [2019] EWCA Civ 656 at [26].

[371]   *Lacey v Hill, Crowley's Claim* (1874) L.R. 18 Eq. 182, Illustration 7. cf. *Cape Distribution Ltd v Cape Intermediate Holdings Plc (No.2)* [2016] EWHC 1786 (QB) at [111] (consideration of when limitation period runs in relation to right to indemnity). Where the agent has incurred a liability, his right to indemnity has arisen, and a purported revocation of his authority to discharge it is ineffective. See below, para.10-010.

[372]   See Illustration 8.

[373]   *Islamic Republic of Iran Shipping Lines v Zannis Cia. Naviera SA (The Tzelepi)* [1991] 2 Lloyd's Rep. 265.

[374]   See *Goff and Jones, Law of Unjust Enrichment* (9th edn), para.19-17 onwards taking a distinction between reimbursement and indemnity, and attributing a special restitutionary meaning to the former.

[375]   See *Brook's Wharf & Bull Wharf Ltd v Goodman Bros* [1937] 1 K.B. 534; *Owen v Tate* [1976] Q.B. 402; *Liberian Insurance Agency Inc v Mosse* [1977] 2 Lloyd's Rep. 560; *The Pindaros* [1983] 2 Lloyd's Rep. 635; *Goff and Jones, Law of Unjust Enrichment*.

has not been properly appointed.[376] In some cases there may still be room for the implication of an independent contract to indemnify, created by the request of one party to another to do something, accompanied by a promise to indemnify against loss incurred by so doing. A widely stated principle permits this[377]; though in the agency context it is doubtful whether it extends to gratuitous agents.[378] But in other cases it may be necessary to rely on the restitutionary remedy, which will normally (though not always, because not limited by the scope of the agent's authority) be narrower in scope. However, the right of indemnity exists also in equity, and where the agent can invoke the assistance of equity,[379] e.g. as trustee[380] or surety,[381] the limitations imposed by the common law rules of restitution will not apply: the right may therefore be wider.

Right of reimbursement superseded by remuneration   It should be borne in   **7-061**
mind that in many cases the right of reimbursement of *expenses* will not apply, because any expense incurred is taken to be covered by the remuneration. Thus in some areas estate agents do not seek to recover the cost of advertising, for this is taken to be included in their commission, if earned, and if no commission is earned the expenditure is a business loss in respect of which no reimbursement can be claimed.[382] Many office and professional expenses are likewise taken to be covered by the remuneration payable.

Illustrations

(1)   A employs B to find a purchaser for certain bark. C agrees with B to purchase   **7-062**
the bark, subject to its being equal to sample. B, being offered a *del credere* commission by A, accepts A's draft for the price of the bark, and in due course pays the amount of the draft. C then refuses the bark, which is not equal to sample. B is entitled to recover from A the amount of the draft paid by him.[383]
(2)   An auctioneer is instructed to sell certain property, and after he has incurred liabilities in reference to his employment, his authority is revoked by the principal. The principal must indemnify him against the liabilities.[384]
(3)   An accommodation bill is drawn and accepted for the purpose of raising

---

[376]   cf. *Craven-Ellis v Canons Ltd* [1936] 2 K.B. 403.
[377]   See *Dugdale v Lovering* (1875) L.R. 10 C.P. 196; *Sheffield Corp v Barclay* [1905] A.C. 392; *Yeung Kai Yung v Hong Kong and Shanghai Banking Corp* [1981] A.C. 787; *Naviera Mogar SA v Soc. Metallurgique de Normandie (The Nogar Marin)* [1988] 1 Lloyd's Rep. 412 (implication turns on form of individual case); *Linklaters v HSBC Bank Plc* [2003] EWHC 1113 (Comm); [2003] 2 Lloyd's Rep. 545; cf. *Guaranty Trust Co of New York v Hannay & Co* [1918] 2 K.B. 623. There are even dicta in these cases suggesting that the obligation is wider than a contractual obligation. But in Yeung Kai Yeung's case it was suggested (at 799–800) that the rule in the Sheffield case might be too wide, and require reconsideration in view of the division of responsibility permitted by the Civil Liability (Contribution) Act 1978: below, para.7-068.
[378]   See *W. Cory & Son Ltd v Lambton and Hetton Collieries* (1916) 86 L.J.K.B. 401 at 405–406.
[379]   See *Lacey v Hill, Crowley's Claim* (1874) L.R. 18 Eq. 182, Illustration 7; *Wallersteiner v Moir (No.2)* [1975] Q.B. 373 (minority shareholder suing on behalf of company).
[380]   cf. *Adams v Morgan & Co* [1924] 1 K.B. 751, Illustration 6; *Campbell v Larkworthy* (1894) 9 T.L.R. 528.
[381]   See *Snell's Equity* (34th edn), para.45-020.
[382]   But see *Bernard Thorpe & Partners v Flannery* (1977) 244 E.G. 129, where such expenses were recoverable on the terms of the contract. It is usually said that neither auctioneers nor estate agents are normally entitled to expenses: see Murdoch, *Law of Estate Agency* (5th edn), pp.150–151.
[383]   *Hooper v Treffry* (1847) 1 Exch. 17; but distinguish *Simpson v Swan* (1812) 3 Camp. 291.
[384]   *Warlow v Harrison* (1859) 1 E. & E. 309 at 317; *Brittain v Lloyd* (1845) 14 M. & W. 762.

money for the benefit of the drawer and acceptor. The drawer instructs a bill broker to get the bill discounted. It is the common practice for bill brokers to give a general guarantee to the bankers who discount their bills, and not to indorse each bill discounted on behalf of their customers. The bill is dishonoured, and the broker becomes liable to the bankers upon such a guarantee. The broker is entitled to recover from the acceptor the amount that he is compelled to pay in pursuance of such guarantee, with interest, it being a liability incurred in the execution of his authority in the ordinary course of his business as a bill broker.[385]

(4) A broker, in accordance with a reasonable custom of the particular market in which he was employed, rendered himself personally responsible for the price of goods bought on behalf of his principal, and duly paid for the goods. Held, that he was entitled to set off the amount so paid, in an action by the principal's trustee in bankruptcy for money due to the principal.[386]

(5) An agent, who had general authority to receive and sell goods on behalf of the principal, in good faith brought an action against a third person who wrongfully withheld possession of the goods. In an action by the principal for the proceeds of the goods it was held that the agent was entitled to set off the amount of the costs incurred by him in the proceedings to recover the goods.[387]

(6) The seller of a business carries it on between the date of contract and the date of completion on the buyer's account, a clause in the contract expressly providing for indemnity. He may obtain indemnity for supertax which he is obliged to pay, even though the buyer, being a corporation, would not be liable for supertax.[388]

(7) A stockbroker incurred liabilities on the Stock Exchange on behalf of his principal. The stockbroker subsequently paid a composition on the amount of his debts (including such liabilities), and by a rule of the Stock Exchange he could not be sued for the balance of such debts without the permission of the committee. The principal was bound to indemnify him to the full extent of the liabilities incurred on his behalf.[389]

(8) An agent incurs damages and expenses in defending an action on behalf of his principal. He is entitled to reimbursement of such damages and expenses if he was acting within the scope of his authority in defending the action, and the loss was not caused by his own default.[390] Where an agent, exercising his best judgment, compromised an action brought against him in respect of a contract made on behalf of the principal, who had notice of the action, and

---

[385] *Re Fox, Walker & Co Ex p. Bishop* (1880) 15 Ch.D. 400.

[386] *Cropper v Cook* (1868) L.R. 3 C.P. 194. And see *Anglo-Overseas Transport Co Ltd v Titan Industrial Corp (United Kingdom)* [1959] 2 Lloyd's Rep. 152; *Perishables Transport Co Ltd v N. Spyropoulos (London) Ltd* [1964] 2 Lloyd's Rep. 379.

[387] *Curtis v Barclay* (1826) 5 B. & C. 141; *Williams, Torrey & Co v Knight* [1894] P. 342 at 349.

[388] *Adams v Morgan & Co* [1923] 2 K.B. 234; [1924] 1 K.B. 751. cf. *Re Hollebone's Agreement* [1959] 1 W.L.R. 536.

[389] *Lacey v Hill, Crowley's Claim* (1874) L.R. 18 Eq. 182; *Fraser v Equitorial Shipping Co Ltd (The Ijaolo)* [1979] 1 Lloyd's Rep. 103.

[390] *Frixione v Tagliaferro & Sons* (1856) 10 Moo.P.C. 175; *The James Seddon* (1866) L.R. 1 A. & E. 62; *Re Wells & Croft Ex p. Official Receiver* (1895) 72 L.T. 359; *Williams v Lister & Co* (1913) 109 L.T. 699; *Re Famatina Development Corp Ltd* [1914] 2 Ch. 271; *Simpson and Miller v British Industries Trust Ltd* (1923) 39 T.L.R. 286.

had not given any instructions as to the course to be pursued, it was held that the agent was entitled to indemnity, although the plaintiff could not, in the circumstances, have succeeded in the action.[391]

(9) A acted as B's agent for the purchase of goods from C. The terms included immediate payment, made by A, of £1,000, which would be forfeited if the contract were cancelled. Subsequently, believing that B would not be able to perform the contract, A without authority cancelled the contract, and the £1,000 was forfeited. A claimed to be reimbursed by B in respect of the £1,000 paid out. Held, that although the cancellation by A was a breach of the contract of agency for which B might obtain damages (though none could be shown here, for, on the facts, the £1,000 would have been lost in any case), yet the £1,000 had been paid by A, and his right to reimbursement accrued when it was paid, before the breach; and the £1,000 was therefore recoverable.[392]

(10) A country solicitor requests his London agent to instruct counsel. The litigation is successful, but some of the costs are disallowed. The country solicitor purports to revoke the authority of the London solicitor to pay fees to counsel. The London solicitor nevertheless pays. Counsel could not have sued for the fees, but the London agent might have been guilty of professional misconduct had he not paid them. He is entitled to an indemnity in respect of the fees paid out, and may retain money in his hands for this purpose.[393]

(11) A freight forwarder is by custom of the market obliged to undertake personal liability for dead freight when his customer provides insufficient cargo. He may recover the sum paid from his customer.[394]

(12) A corporate officer in his capacity as such gives a media interview, which he alleges was later distorted by the media in a way that defamed him. It was held that the director had no implied right to be indemnified by the corporation against the losses caused by the defamation.[395]

(13) P requests a travel agent to buy 42 tickets for international travel on Ansett Airlines. Agent pays for tickets, having first obtained credit card indemnity by P. Airline goes into financial collapse and ceases operations. P cancels credit card payment. Held that the agent retained its right to indemnity from P.[396]

---

[391] *Pettman v Keble* (1850) 9 C.B. 701. See also *Broom v Hall* (1859) 7 C.B.(N.S.) 503; *The Millwall* [1905] P. 155 at 174; *Wallersteiner v Moir (No.2)* [1975] Q.B. 373.

[392] *John Koch Ltd v C. & H. Products Ltd* [1956] 2 Lloyd's Rep. 59; cf. *World Transport Agency v Royte (England) Ltd* [1957] 1 Lloyd's Rep. 381.

[393] *Rhodes v Fielder, Jones and Harrison* (1919) 89 L.J.K.B. 15.

[394] *Anglo Overseas Transport Co Ltd v Titan Industrial Corp (United Kingdom) Ltd* [1959] 2 Lloyd's Rep. 152; *Perishables Transport Co Ltd v N. Spyropoulos (London) Ltd* [1964] 2 Lloyd's Rep. 379; cf. *Wilson v Avec Audio-Visual Equipment Ltd* [1974] 1 Lloyd's Rep. 81 (insurance broker not personally liable to insurance company so not entitled to indemnity).

[395] *National Roads and Motorists' Association v Whitlam* (2007) 25 A.C.L.C. 688. But see the doubt thrown on this case in *Benyatov v Credit Suisse Securities (Europe) Ltd* [2020] EWHC 85 (QB).

[396] *Imaje Events Pty Ltd v Taylor* [2007] VSC 390.

Article 63

Cases Where Reimbursement or Indemnity Not Available

7-063   Subject to contrary agreement and to context:

(1)   An agent may be debarred from recovering reimbursement or indemnity if at the time when the services were rendered the agent was not legally qualified to act in the capacity in which the reimbursement or indemnity is claimed, or if the enforcement of the contract of agency is in some other way affected by statute or statutory instrument.

(2)   An agent is not entitled to reimbursement of expenses incurred, nor to indemnity against losses or liabilities—

    (a)   in respect of any unauthorised act or transaction which is not ratified by the principal, except where the agent has a right of action in restitution[397];

    (b)   incurred solely[398] in consequence of the agent's own negligence, default, insolvency or breach of duty[399];

    (c)   in respect of any act or transaction which is obviously, or to the agent's knowledge, unlawful,[400] or unlawful by virtue of legislation which is to be interpreted as affecting contracts which involve the doing of acts prohibited by it; except where the agent is entitled to contribution towards damages for which the agent is liable in tort[401];

    (d)   where the contract of agency expressly precludes a right to indemnity.[402]

Comment

7-064   **Rule (1)**   The statutory provisions which prevent certain agents and others acting in certain capacities from recovering commission normally apply also to reimbursement and indemnity, at least in so far as claims for these arise in contract.[403]

7-065   **Rule (2): Unauthorised acts**   It is obvious that the contractual duty to reimburse and indemnify cannot operate where the act is unauthorised and not ratified[404]; there

---

[397] See Comment; Illustrations 1, 2; *Frixione v Tagliaferro & Sons* (1856) 10 Moo.P.C. 175 at 196.

[398] This word has been added pursuant to dicta in *Linklaters v HSBC Bank* [2003] EWHC 1113 (Comm); [2003] 2 Lloyd's Rep. 545 at [36], and in conformity with *Restatement, Second*, § 440. On this case however see Ellinger (2004) 120 L.Q.R. 226. See too *Rohr v Kennedy* [2010] NZHC 772 (solicitor in course of acting for client by mistake exposed himself to liability to beneficiary of estate in respect of which he successfully claimed indemnity from his client who would have had the ultimate liability to the beneficiary).

[399] *Thacker v Hardy* (1878) 4 Q.B.D. 685 at 687; *Frixione v Tagliaferro & Sons* (1856) 10 Moo.P.C. 175; Illustrations 3 and 4; and see *Gregory v Ford* [1951] 1 All E.R. 121: there may be circumstances in which an agent can recover his losses by a different cause of action (employee not to be required to do unlawful act).

[400] See Comment; Illustrations 5–9; below, para.7-067.

[401] Under the Civil Liability (Contribution) Act 1978: see Comment.

[402] See *Mega-Top Cargo Pty Ltd v Moneytech Services Pty Ltd* [2015] NSWCA 402.

[403] See Article 61, Illustrations 2 and 3.

[404] See Comment to Article 62.

may however be cases where, though it is not possible to rely on the contractual right, an action in restitution is available.[405]

Where agent at fault   Where the expenses and liabilities arise only because of the agent's fault, including by excessive employment of solicitors and other advisers,[406] it is obvious that there will usually be no liability to indemnify[407]: and this is true also where the liability cannot be said to arise from the performance of the act requested.[408] It should be noted that the reasoning covers liability arising from the agent's bankruptcy, where the bankruptcy was not occasioned by the agent's activities on behalf of the principal.[409] Where the expenses and liabilities do not so arise, but the agent is in repudiatory breach of duty as agent, contractual indemnity may be refused on grounds similar to those relating to refusal of remuneration discussed under Article 62.[410] The principal may sometimes, however, incur a liability in restitution as indicated under Article 64.   **7-066**

Unlawful transactions   Here again, as in Article 63, the wording gives only the most general indication of the applicable rules: too much turns on the nature of the illegality for a more precise formulation to be possible.[411] But it should be noted that provisions forbidding unqualified persons from recovering remuneration may not apply to mere reimbursement and indemnity.[412]   **7-067**

Joint tortfeasors   The old rule was that a tortfeasor could recover neither contribution nor indemnity from the person at whose request or on whose behalf the tort was committed,[413] and this was based on the maxim ex turpi causa non oritur actio. But: **7-068**

> "where one person requests another to commit or where they jointly commit an indifferent act, of which the illegality does not appear, but which may subsequently be proved to be tortious, the contractual relation may arise; and where one party induces another party by fraud to commit a tortious act, and that other party does not in fact know and need not be presumed to know that he was doing an unlawful act, he may have redress or contribution."[414]

---

[405] See above, para.7-060.

[406] See *Mirror Group Newspapers Plc v Maxwell (No.2)* [1998] 1 B.C.L.C. 638 (court-appointed receivers' spending on legal services).

[407] See Illustration 3. But cf. *Cape Distribution Ltd v Cape Intermediate Holdings Plc (No.1)* [2016] EWHC 1119 (QB) at [87] (subsidiary agent for parent company).

[408] See *W. Cory & Son Ltd v Lambton and Hetton Collieries* (1916) 86 L.J.K.B. 401; as explained in *Linklaters v HSBC Banks Plc* [2003] EWHC 1113 (Comm); [2003] 2 Lloyd's Rep. 545 at [36].

[409] *Duncan v Hill* (1873) L.R. 8 Ex. 242, Illustration 4.

[410] See, e.g. *Hurst v Holding* (1810) 3 Taunt. 32 (agent prevented goods reaching principal); *Ellis v Pond* [1898] 1 Q.B. 426 (wrongful sale by stockbroker); *Solloway v McLaughlin* [1938] A.C. 247 (fraud of agent). It can also be said that a person cannot claim an indemnity in respect of the consequences of his own wrong; or that the allowing of an indemnity would promote circuity of action. See *Goulandris Bros Ltd v Goldman & Sons* [1958] 1 Q.B. 74, esp. at 94–98; Comment to Article 60; cf. *J.O. Lund Ltd v Anglo Overseas Transport Co Ltd* [1955] 1 Lloyd's Rep. 142.

[411] See, e.g. Illustration 6.

[412] See Solicitors Act 1974 s.25(2); Cordery, *Solicitors* (8th edn), pp.91–92. But cf. Estate Agents Act 1979 s.18(5).

[413] *Merryweather v Nixan* (1799) 8 T.R. 186; *Shackell v Rosier* (1836) 2 Bing.N.C. 634; *W.H. Smith & Son v Clinton & Harris* (1908) 99 L.T. 840.

[414] *W.H. Smith & Son v Clinton & Harris* (1908) 99 L.T. 840 at 841 (and see Defamation Act 1952 s.11). See *Adamson v Jarvis* (1827) 4 Bing. 66, Illustration 9; *Betts & Drewe v Gibbins* (1834) 2 A. & E.

And even where the act is obviously unlawful, contribution may now be recoverable by statute. By the Civil Liability (Contribution) Act 1978 s.1(1),[415] any person liable in respect of damage suffered by another person may recover contribution from any other person liable in respect of the same damage, whether jointly with that other or otherwise. Nothing in the Act however affects express or implied contractual or other right to indemnity.[416] The amount of contribution is such as the court may find just and equitable having regard to that person's extent of responsibility for the damage; and the court has power to exempt from liability or direct a complete indemnity.[417] But the Act does not render enforceable any agreement for indemnity which would not have been enforceable apart from it.[418] The ready implication of a promise to indemnify by one who requests another to act[419] may sometimes exclude these provisions, and it has been suggested that the cases on such implication may require reconsideration because of the advantages of permitting the court to divide responsibility.[420]

7-069 **Wagering transactions** From the early eighteenth century there have been legal restrictions on gaming and wagering: in particular, the Gaming Act 1845 s.18, provided that all suits by way of gaming or wagering should be null and void. In the context of agency the Gaming Act 1892 excluded the principal's obligation to indemnify by providing that any promise to pay any person any sum of money paid by that person under or in respect of any contract or agreement rendered null and void by the Act of 1845 should itself be null and void. Apart from its central context, this caused difficulties in respect of speculative financial transactions. All this legislation was repealed by the Gambling Act 2005.[421] Part 17 of the Act deals with the legality and enforceability of gambling contracts. Gambling contracts are no longer void, but the Gambling Commission is given powers to avoid particular bets. The financial transactions context is dealt with by the Financial Services and Markets Act 2000.[422]

Illustrations

7-070 (1) A authorises B, a broker, to effect a marine insurance policy. After the underwriters have signed the slip, but before a binding contract is made, A revokes B's authority. B, nevertheless, effects the policy, and pays the premiums. B cannot recover the premiums from A, having acted without authority.[423]

(2) A authorises B and C to insure his life in their names. They insure in the names

---

57; *Toplis v Grane* (1839) 5 Bing.N.C. 636 (cf. *Cory & Son Ltd v Lambton & Hetton Collieries Ltd* (1916) 86 L.J.K.B. 401); *Dugdale v Lovering* (1875) L.R. 10 C.P. 196; *Thacker v Hardy* (1878) 4 Q.B.D. 685 at 687.

[415] Replacing Law Reform (Married Women and Tortfeasors) Act 1935 s.6. See *Clerk & Lindsell on Torts* (22nd edn), para.4-13 onwards.

[416] Civil Liability (Contribution) Act 1978 s.7(3).

[417] Civil Liability (Contribution) Act 1978 s.2(1).

[418] Civil Liability (Contribution) Act 1978 s.7(3).

[419] See above, para.7-060.

[420] *Yeung Kai Yung v Hong Kong and Shanghai Banking Corp* [1981] A.C. 787 at 799–800.

[421] The Act was brought fully into force on September 1, 2007.

[422] See s.412 (which is amended by the Gambling Act 2005 to remove references to the old legislation).

[423] *Warwick v Slade* (1811) 3 Camp. 127.

of B, C and D, and pay the premiums. They are not entitled to recover the amount of the premiums from A, not having strictly pursued their authority.[424]

(3) A solicitor undertook a prosecution for perjury, and agreed that he would only charge out-of-pocket expenses. The prosecution failed in consequence of the negligent way in which the indictment was drawn. Held, that the solicitor was not entitled to recover his disbursements.[425] So, an auctioneer is not entitled to be indemnified against a loss incurred by him in consequence of his own mistake on a point of law as to which he ought to have been competent.[426] And where the manager of the stud stock department of a company conducting activities connected with agriculture is asked to buy "top rams" and because of lack of knowledge of terms used by sheep breeders buys rams which are not "tops" no reimbursement is due.[427]

(4) A stockbroker is instructed by his principal to carry over stock to the next settlement. Before the next settling day the broker becomes insolvent and is declared a defaulter, in consequence of which the stock is sold at a loss. The principal is not bound to indemnify the broker, the loss having been caused by the broker's insolvency.[428]

(5) A purchased shares as a broker, not being duly licensed as the law then required. Held, that he was entitled to recover from the principal the price of the shares, which he was compelled to pay, such payment not being an essential part of the duty of a broker, although, in consequence of not being licensed, he could not recover any commission or remuneration.[429]

(6) A broker effects an illegal insurance on behalf of his principal, and pays the premium. He is not entitled to recover from the principal the amount of the premium, or any other payments made by him in respect of such insurance.[430]

(7) An election agent made payments which were illegal under the Corrupt Practices Acts. He could not recover the amount of any such payments from the candidate employing him.[431]

(8) A employs B to purchase smuggled goods. B purchases the goods and pays for them. B cannot recover the price from A, even if A obtains possession of the goods.[432]

(9) A instructs B, an auctioneer, to sell goods of which A has no right to dispose, B having no knowledge of any defect in A's title. B sells the goods, and duly pays over the proceeds to A. B is afterwards compelled to pay to the true owner the value of the goods. A must indemnify B, the transaction not being obviously, or to B's knowledge, unlawful.[433]

---

[424] *Barron v Fitzgerald* (1840) 6 Bing.N.C. 201. As to instructions given to stockbrokers, see *Johnson v Kearley* [1908] 2 K.B. 514; *Aston v Kelsey* [1913] 3 K.B. 314; *Blaker v Hawes and Brown* (1913) 109 L.T. 320.
[425] *Lewis v Samuel* (1846) 8 Q.B. 685.
[426] *Capp v Topham* (1805) 6 East 392.
[427] *New Zealand Farmers Co-operative Distributing Co Ltd v National Mortgage and Agency Co of New Zealand Ltd* [1961] N.Z.L.R. 969.
[428] *Duncan v Hill* (1873) L.R. 8 Ex. 242. This case is retained here on account of the general significance of the reasoning.
[429] *Smith v Lindo* (1858) 5 C.B.(N.S.) 587.
[430] *Ex p. Mather* (1797) 3 Ves. 373.
[431] *Re Parker* (1882) 21 Ch.D. 408.
[432] *Ex p. Mather* (1797) 3 Ves. 373.
[433] *Adamson v Jarvis* (1827) 4 Bing. 66.

3. LIEN

Article 64

DEFINITIONS OF GENERAL AND PARTICULAR POSSESSORY LIENS

7-071 (1) A possessory lien is the right of a person who has possession of goods or chattels belonging to another to retain possession of them until the satisfaction of some debt or obligation by the owner of the goods or chattels.[434]

(2) Where the right is to retain possession in respect of a general balance of account, or until the satisfaction of debts or obligations incurred independently of the goods or chattels subject to the right, it is called a general lien. Where the right is confined to debts and obligations incurred in respect of the goods and chattels subject to the right, it is called a particular lien.

Comment

7-072 **Introduction** The cases collected in this section go beyond agency law as such; and many of them are old and reflect practices that may no longer obtain. It seems, however, worth preserving the collection and updating it, for they remain the only authority on many of the matters which they decide, and excellent illustrations from which the principles may be understood.

7-073 **Liens** A possessory lien involves the right to retain goods only[435]: it does not involve the right to sell the them except in special circumstances,[436] e.g. where trade usage or statute permit. Indeed, a person who sells thereby destroys the lien and becomes liable in conversion.[437] But such a lien confers not only a defence against the principal (who cannot sue in conversion since the principal has not the immediate right to possess), but also the right to sue in conversion, where the goods are wrongfully removed, against the principal or third parties, for it involves possession and may confer an immediate right to possession.[438]

Strictly speaking, liens are given by law only; but an analogous right can be regarded as arising by contract,[439] and it is a right of this latter type that an agent has. Particular liens are favoured by the law, but general liens are "founded in custom only, and are therefore to be taken strictly".[440]

---

[434] See *Hammonds v Barclay* (1802) 2 East 227 at 235.

[435] This may carry with it the right to direct movement. Thus a shipping agent who had a lien over a bill of lading was held justified in having the goods brought back home: *Edwards v Southgate* (1862) 10 W.R. 528.

[436] *Smart v Sandars* (1848) 5 C.B. 895. Nor, of itself, does it confer the right of stoppage in transit: see Article 69.

[437] *Sibel v Springfield* (1863) 8 New Rep. 36.

[438] *Rogers v Kennay* (1846) 9 Q.B. 592; *Dicas v Stockley* (1836) 7 C. & P. 587; *Bryans v Nix* (1839) 4 M. & W. 775.

[439] *Gladstone v Birley* (1817) 2 Mer. 401 at 404.

[440] *Houghton v Matthews* (1803) 3 B. & P. 485 at 494; *Rushforth v Hadfield* (1805) 6 East 519; (1806) 7 East 224; *Bock v Gorrissen* (1860) 2 De G.F. & J. 434 at 443.

Article 65

POSSESSORY LIEN OF AGENTS

(1) An agent has a possessory lien on the goods and chattels of the principal in respect of all lawful claims the agent may have as such against the principal, for remuneration earned, or advances made, or losses or liabilities incurred, in the course of the agency, or otherwise arising in the course of the agency,[441] provided—

    (a) that the possession of the goods or chattels was lawfully obtained by the agent in the course of the agency, and in the same capacity as that in which the lien is claimed[442];

    (b) that there is no agreement inconsistent with the right of lien; and

    (c) that the goods or chattels were not delivered to the agent with express directions, or for a special purpose, inconsistent with the right of lien.[443]

(2) The possessory lien of an agent is a particular lien only, except where the agent has a general lien by agreement, express or implied, with the principal. Such an agreement may be implied from a course of dealing between the principal and agent, or from an established custom or usage.[444]

7-074

Comment

Clear authority for the general proposition as to the lien of an agent is difficult to find. This is not surprising, for the word agent can be applied in many situations, and no doubt some persons to whom the word could be applied would have no lien. For example, an estate agent will not normally hold property of the principal upon which a lien could be exercised.[445] Equally, there will be many cases where a person who has agency powers holds the principal's property in circumstances quite inconsistent with the agent's having a lien over it.[446] But in general it is established by the cases that an agent is entitled to a lien over the property of the principal in respect of payments, liabilities, etc. relating to matters connected with that property. This seems in many cases to be a development of the older lien of a craftsperson who makes repairs to a chattel[447]; but it was developed by cases on factors, brokers, auctioneers and other undoubted agents.

7-075

When exercisable There is little authority on when the lien is exercisable, and in particular on whether it can only be exercised when the principal's breach is

7-076

---

[441] Illustrations 1 and 2; and see Comment. For a discussion of choice of law problems, see Chesterman (1973) 22 I.C.L.Q. 213; *Benjamin's Sale of Goods* (10th edn), para.26-180 onwards.

[442] Illustrations 3 and 4; and see Comment.

[443] Illustrations 5–9.

[444] *Bock v Gorrissen* (1860) 2 De G.F. & J. 434 at 443; *Rushforth v Hadfield* (1805) 6 East 519; *Holderness v Collinson* (1827) 7 B. & C. 212; *Langley, Beldon & Gaunt Ltd v Morley* [1965] 1 Lloyd's Rep. 297. Custom is not easy to establish: see Article 31.

[445] But he may hold a deposit: see below, para.7-077. For an attempt by an estate agent to claim rights over proceeds of sale held by his principal's solicitor, see *W.A. Ellis Services Ltd v Stuart Wood* [1993] 2 E.G.L.R. 43.

[446] See *Ariston Products Pty Ltd v Egan* (1977) 3 A.C.L.R. 418 (accountant).

[447] See *Woodworth v Conroy* [1976] Q.B. 884 at 890 (accountant); but cf. *Ariston Products Pty Ltd v Egan* (1977) 3 A.C.L.R. 418. See also *R. v South Devon Ry Co* (1850) 15 Q.B. 1043 (arbitrator); *Ridgway v Ley* (1856) 25 L.J.Ch. 584 (Parliamentary agent); *Fraser v Equitorial Shipping Co Ltd (The Ijaolo)* [1979] 1 Lloyd's Rep. 103 (consulting marine engineer).

repudiatory in nature. It does not seem that the contract must be brought to an end before the remedy can be exercised. Where the lien is a particular lien over something worked on or produced by the agent (e.g. documents produced by a solicitor) the analogy of the unpaid seller's lien suggests that the existence of the lien will in many situations indicate no more than that the agent need not deliver except against payment, unless the agent has granted credit. It seems likely however that most agents work on a credit basis; and such reasoning is in any case much more difficult to apply in the case of a general lien. The exercise of the lien requires that payment is due and has not been made.[448] Although late payment is not of itself repudiatory, it has been said that:

> "common sense suggests that where the agency is of a continuing nature, it will not usually survive the exercise by the agent of rights inconsistent with those of the principal over goods which are the very subject-matter of the agency; and this would appear to indicate that the principal's conduct must at least be of a repudiatory nature, even if not formally treated by the agent as such."[449]

In general it would seem that the fiduciary relationship between principal and agent will require the agent to exercise the right with consideration for the principal, and that the agency relationship will not survive its exercise.[450]

7-077   **Goods and chattels**   In principle, a lien operates over goods and chattels only, including those choses in action which are represented by documents, often called securities, which can themselves be treated as goods and chattels—for example, insurance policies, share certificates, bills of exchange. It is sometimes said that the lien extends to funds or money held: thus in connection with bankers it has been said that "[a]ll moneys paid into a bank are subject to a lien",[451] and the auctioneer's lien has been said to be over goods and their proceeds. It is however difficult to see how a lien can be exercised over money, which will normally be the actual property of the holder subject to an obligation to account for it. It seems that reference to a lien over money should in many cases be explained as references to the agent's right to set-off and counterclaim when sued by the principal for the money.[452] In the case of an auctioneer it may also refer to the auctioneer's right to sue for the price upon a separate contract, and then retain it; or to the rule that the third party may not, to the extent of the auctioneer's lien, set off against the auctioneer claims which the third party has against the vendor.[453] In other circumstances it may refer to an equitable assignment by way of charge[454]; or to an equitable lien arising out of the

---

[448] *Crawshay v Homfray* (1820) 4 B. & Ald. 50; *Fisher v Smith* (1878) 4 App.Cas. 1.

[449] *Compania Financiera "Soleada" SA v Hamoor Tanker Corp Inc (The Borag)* [1980] 1 Lloyd's Rep. 111 at 122, per Mustill J (where the agents arrested the principal's ship: reversed on a different point [1981] 1 W.L.R. 274).

[450] See *Restatement, Second*, comment b to § 464.

[451] *Misa v Currie* (1876) 1 App.Cas. 554 at 569.

[452] See *Paget's Law of Banking* (15th edn), Ch.14, esp. para.14.6; *Halesowen Presswork and Assemblies Ltd v Westminster Bank Ltd* [1971] 1 Q.B. 1 at 33–34, 46; the decision was reversed by the House of Lords on another point ([1972] A.C. 785), but see the judgments of Viscount Dilhorne at 802 and of Lord Cross at 810; *Eide UK Ltd v Lowndes Lambert Group Ltd* [1999] Q.B. 199. See also *Richmond Shipping Ltd v D/S and A/S Vestland (The Vestland)* [1980] 2 Lloyd's Rep. 171 at 181.

[453] See Illustration 1; below, para.9-023.

[454] See *Re Welsh Irish Ferries Ltd (The Ugland Trailer)* [1986] Ch. 471; *The Annangel Glory* [1988] 1 Lloyd's Rep. 45; *Itex Italgrani Export SA v Care Shipping Corp (The Cebu (No.2))* [1990] 2 Lloyd's

position of the parties towards each other, as in the case of solicitor and client.[455] In so far as an estate agent has a lien, it is likely to be over a deposit held for his client's account.[456]

Possession The agent must possess the goods: "there can be no lien upon any property unless it is in the possession of the party who claims the lien".[457] But the possession may be held for the agent by another: thus in *Bryans v Nix*[458] an agent's lien was held to arise where the principal delivered a cargo to a bargemaster employed by the principal together with documents indicating that the bargemaster was to hold the cargo for the agent. And it has been held that an agreement, made for valuable consideration, to hand over a bill of lading to an agent for the purpose of giving the agent security over the goods represented by it gives the agent the right in equity to the bill of lading and possession of the goods, as against the principal and the principal's creditors.[459] Further, the lien is not lost by giving the goods to be held by another specifically on behalf of the person entitled to the lien.[460] On the other hand, even though the goods are in the agent's custody and control, they may not be in the agent's possession without performing some overt act taking them into possession, and hence there may be no lien.[461]

7-078

Lawfully obtained A lien cannot be acquired by a wrongful act. Thus if an agent obtains goods from the principal by misrepresentation, the agent has no lien over them, though the circumstances in other respects are such that a lien would have been available if the goods had been obtained lawfully.[462] And where the agent takes goods without authority, or is given goods by the principal after the latter's bankruptcy,[463] the agent acquires no lien. In general, an agent's claim to a lien cannot be more extensive than the principal's powers in relation to the relevant property; hence, it will not be enough if the principal owns the property but is subject to court restrictions as to its use.[464]

7-079

Rep. 316; *Kingscroft Insurance Co v H.S. Weavers (Underwriting) Agencies Ltd* [1993] 1 Lloyd's Rep. 187 at 194–195. These cases refer to the lien on sub-freights in maritime law. This is now said to be "a contractual non-possessory right of a kind which is sui generis": *Agnew v Commissioner of Inland Revenue* [2001] UKPC 28; [2001] 2 A.C. 710 at [41], per Lord Millett.

[455] See *Snell's Equity* (34th edn), Ch.44; *Hewett v Court* (1983) 149 C.L.R. 639, esp. at 663.
[456] See Murdoch, *Law of Estate Agency* (5th edn), pp.152–153. This would usually only be so on completion. An agent's right to exercise the "lien" could be affected by failure to comply with the information requirements of the Estate Agents Act 1979 and statutory instruments made thereunder: see above, para.7-007. As to auctioneers, see ibid.; Harvey and Meisel, *Auctions: Law and Practice* (2006).
[457] *Shaw v Neale* (1858) 6 H.L. Cas. 581 at 601.
[458] *Bryans v Nix* (1839) 4 M. & W. 775, distinguishing *Kinloch v Craig* (1789) 3 T.R. 119; (1790) 3 T.R. 783. See also *Evans & Evans v Nichol & Nichol* (1841) 3 M. & G. 614; *Hammonds v Barclay* (1802) 2 East 227; cf. *Kruger v Wilcox* (1755) Amb. 252; *Taylor v Robinson* (1818) 2 Moo. 730, Illustration 5; *Nichols v Clent* (1817) 3 Price 547.
[459] *Re Evans Ex p. Barber* (1843) 3 M.D. & De G. 174; *Lutscher v Comptoir d'Escompte de Paris* (1876) 1 Q.B.D. 709. This is an equitable charge: see *Benjamin's Sale of Goods* (10th edn), para.18-285.
[460] *McCombie v Davis* (1805) 7 East 5; see Article 67. A more modern example is the trust receipt. Aliter if the delivery is a conversion.
[461] See *Hatton v Car Maintenance Co Ltd* [1915] 1 Ch. 621 (owner could remove car from company's premises at will: company had no lien); cf. *Rose v CMS Operations* [2002] EWHC 59 (Ch).
[462] cf. *Madden v Kempster* (1807) 1 Camp. 12.
[463] *Nichols v Clent* (1817) 3 Price 547; *Copland v Stein* (1799) 8 T.R. 199.
[464] See *Withers LLP v Langbar International Ltd* [2011] EWCA Civ 1419 at [53].

7-080 **In the same capacity** Even a general lien will not extend to the retaining of goods by an agent in satisfaction of debts incurred previous to or outside the agency.[465] Thus a factor's general lien did not entitle the factor to retain goods in respect of rent that was owing but which was unconnected with the factor's operations as such,[466] or in respect of transactions performed by the factor in some other capacity.[467] This requirement to some extent overlaps with those next referred to.

7-081 **No inconsistent agreement and goods not delivered in circumstances inconsistent with lien** The scope of these two requirements, which overlap, will be apparent from the Illustrations.[468] It should be noted that the lien will not easily be displaced.[469]

7-082 **General liens** Factors,[470] marine insurance brokers,[471] stockbrokers,[472] solicitors,[473] bankers,[474] wharfingers[475] and packers[476] are among those who have been held to have a general lien by implication from custom. On the other hand it has been held that a confirming house was not a modern version of the factor, and had no such lien[477]; and the old cases on the packer's lien were based on the packer being to some extent a factor and again may not avail those who conduct for different sorts of business in a modern context, e.g. a freight forwarder[478] or a consolidator[479] in the absence of proof of custom. Further details should be sought in specialised works.

7-083 **Solicitors' charging lien** Solicitors have a lien on the property of the client in

---

[465] *Houghton v Matthews* (1803) 3 B. & P. 485, Illustration 4. See also *Tellrite Ltd v London Confirmers Ltd* [1962] 1 Lloyd's Rep. 236.

[466] *Houghton v Matthews* (1803) 3 B. & P. 485 at pp.494–495.

[467] *Dixon v Stansfield* (1850) 10 C.B. 398, Illustration 5.

[468] See Illustrations 8–11.

[469] See, e.g. *Brandao v Barnett* (1846) 12 C. & F. 787, Illustration 6; *London Chartered Bank of Australia v White* (1879) 4 App.Cas. 413; *Re London & Globe Finance Corp* [1902] 2 Ch. 416.

[470] *Kruger v Wilcox* (1755) Amb. 252; *Godin v London Assurance Co* (1758) 1 W.Bl. 103; *Baring v Corrie* (1818) 2 B. & A. 137; *Re Fawcus Ex p. Buck* (1876) 3 Ch.D. 795; Illustrations 3, 4 and 5.

[471] *Mann v Forrester* (1814) 4 Camp. 60; *Westwood v Bell* (1815) 4 Camp. 349; *Fisher v Smith* (1878) 4 App.Cas. 1.

[472] *Jones v Peppercorne* (1858) John. 430; *Re London & Globe Finance Corp* [1902] 2 Ch. 416; *John D. Hope & Co v Glendinning* [1911] A.C. 419.

[473] *Barratt v Gough-Thomas* [1951] Ch. 242. Money-laundering legislation makes it increasingly unlikely that solicitors will possess a general lien in relation to client money: *Withers LLP v Langbar International Ltd* [2011] EWCA Civ 1419 at [51]. See P. Watts, "Solicitors' Liens and Third Parties" [1996] N.Z. Law Rev. 402.

[474] *Brandao v Barnett* (1846) 12 C. & F. 787; *London Chartered Bank of Australia v White* (1879) 4 App.Cas. 413; *Misa v Currie* (1876) 1 App.Cas. 554.

[475] *Naylor v Mangles* (1794) 1 Esp. 109; *Spears v Hartly* (1800) 3 Esp. 81; cf. *Holderness v Collinson* (1827) 7 B. & C. 212; *Jowitt & Sons v Union Cold Storage Co* [1913] 3 K.B. 1 (lien by contract only).

[476] *Re Witt Ex p. Shubrook* (1876) 2 Ch.D. 489. But in *Toll Logistics (NZ) Ltd v McKay* [2011] 2 N.Z.L.R. 601 at [61] it was held that any custom favouring packers with a general lien has not survived in New Zealand, and that, alternatively, the lien was excluded on the facts by the detailed contractual lien.

[477] *Tellrite Ltd v London Confirmers Ltd* [1962] 1 Lloyd's Rep. 236. See also *Ahlers v Broome & Greene Ltd* (1938) 62 Ll.Rep. 163; *Rolls Razor Ltd v Cox* [1967] 1 Q.B. 552.

[478] See *Langley, Beldon & Gaunt Ltd v Morley* [1965] 1 Lloyd's Rep. 297 at 305.

[479] *Chellaram & Sons (London) Ltd v Butlers Warehousing and Distribution Ltd* [1978] 2 Lloyd's Rep. 412. As to warehousemen, see *Majeau Carrying Co Pty Ltd v Coastal Rutile Ltd* (1973) 129 C.L.R. 48.

their possession and an equitable lien on property recovered or preserved through their instrumentality.[480] Once a solicitor notifies a party to litigation with the solicitor's client that the other is not to pay direct to the client any moneys payable under judgment or a compromise in favour of the client because the client is indebted to the solicitor for fees in respect of the litigation, the other should respect the notification, either by paying over the money owed to the solicitor, or by paying the moneys into court in the case of dispute between solicitor and client.[481] This form of equitable lien can arise without the institution of formal legal proceedings, but there must be a disputed claim before any intervention by a solicitor could lead to a lien.[482] Under s.73 of the Solicitors' Act 1974 a court may also declare a solicitor entitled to a charge upon property recovered or preserved through the solicitor's instrumentality, and conveyances done or operating to defeat that charge are valid except against a bona fide purchaser for value. This latter is often referred to as a "charging lien", but it depends upon the order of the court.[483]

Maritime liens   A shipmaster has a maritime lien over the ship and freight[484] for wages and for disbursements and liabilities properly made or incurred on account of the ship.[485] Maritime liens, which are enforced by Admiralty action in rem, do not depend on possession, and attach to the ship from the moment when the claim arises: they can have effect even against a bona fide purchaser for value.[486]   **7-084**

"Statutory liens"   Certain Admiralty claims can be enforced by proceeding in rem against the ship: by virtue of s.20(2)(p) of the Senior Courts Act 1981 this includes "any claim by a master, shipper, charterer or agent in respect of disbursements made on account of the ship". This procedure in certain respects creates claims enforceable against the ship, and the result is sometimes referred to as a "statutory lien": but the procedure is a special one and connected neither with the general law of liens nor with that of agency.[487]   **7-085**

Illustrations

(1)   An auctioneer who is employed to sell goods has a lien on the goods for his charges and commission.[488]   **7-086**

(2)   An agent was appointed by a company to sell goods on their behalf in a shop

---

[480]   See *Snell's Equity* (34th edn), Ch.44; Cordery, *Solicitors* (9th edn), E [691] onwards; (8th edn), Ch.8; *French v Carter Lemon Camerons LLP* [2012] EWCA Civ 1180 at [27]. But cf. the position where a solicitor is acting as stakeholder: *Rockeagle Ltd v Alsop Wilkinson (a firm)* [1992] Ch. 47.

[481]   *Khans Solicitor (A Firm) v Chifuntwe* [2013] EWCA Civ 481; [2014] 1 W.L.R. 1185; *Gavin Edmondson Solicitors Ltd v Haven Insurance Co Ltd* [2018] UKSC 21; [2018] 1 W.L.R. 2052.

[482]   *Bott & Co Solicitors Ltd v Ryanair DAC* [2019] EWCA Civ 143; [2019] 1 W.L.R. 3375 (leave to appeal to UKSC: [2019] 1 W.L.R. 6640).

[483]   See further Cordery, *Solicitors* (9th edn), E [776] onwards.

[484]   See above, para.7-077.

[485]   Merchant Shipping Act 1995 s.41. See *The Ever Success* [1999] 1 Lloyd's Rep. 824.

[486]   See further Thomas, *Maritime Liens* (1980). An insurance broker's claim for the cost of hull insurance was held not covered in *Bain Clarkson Ltd v Owners of the Ship "Sea Friends"* [1991] 2 Lloyd's Rep. 322. A managing agent may perhaps be an agent for the purposes of this section: see *The Corona Energy* Unreported 1977, folio no.174. See also *The Westport (No.3)* [1966] 1 Lloyd's Rep. 342.

[487]   See in general Thomas, *Maritime Liens* (1980); Meeson, *Admiralty Jurisdiction and Practice* (4th edn). For an example in the agency context see *The Ohm Mariana* [1993] 2 Singapore L.R. 698.

[488]   *Williams v Millington* (1788) 1 H.Bl. 81; *Robinson v Rutter* (1855) 4 E. & B. 954; *Webb v Smith* (1885) 30 Ch.D. 192. (The lien does not apply to land.) As to his lien over any deposit paid, see *Skin-*

taken for that purpose, and it was agreed that he should from time to time accept bills representing the value of the goods in his hands for sale. Goods were consigned to the agent, and he accepted a bill for their value. Before the bill became due, the company was wound up, and the liquidators took possession of and sold the goods. Held, that the agent, having paid the bill, had a lien upon the goods for the amount, and was entitled to be repaid out of the proceeds thereof in preference to the other creditors of the company.[489]

(3) A bought goods as a factor for and on behalf of B, and it was agreed that the goods should remain upon the premises of the seller at a rent to be paid by B. After a time A was requested by the seller to remove the goods, but did not do so. Subsequently, without B's authority or instructions, A removed the goods to his own premises, and about the same time a petition in bankruptcy was presented against B. Held, that the possession of the goods continued in B, and that A had therefore no lien upon them.[490]

(4) A, a factor, sold goods in his own name on B's behalf to C. C subsequently sent goods to A for sale, never having employed him as a factor before. C became bankrupt. A had no lien upon C's goods for the price of the goods sold by him on B's behalf.[491]

(5) A factor insures a ship on his principal's behalf as insurance broker, the transaction being quite distinct and separate from his duties as factor. His general lien does not extend to the policy of insurance, because he did not acquire it in the capacity of factor.[492] So, if a policy is left merely for safe custody in an agent's hands, he has no general lien over it for advances.[493] Where a partner deposited a lease with a banker to secure a particular advance to himself personally, it was held that the banker had no lien over it for the general balance due from the firm.[494]

(6) A life policy was deposited at a bank, with a memorandum charging it with overdrafts not exceeding a specified amount. Held, that the banker's general lien was excluded by the special contract, such contract being inconsistent with the existence of a general lien on the policy.[495] If a factor expressly agrees to deal in a particular way with the proceeds of goods deposited with him for sale, his general lien is excluded.[496] But the lien is not excluded unless the contract is clearly inconsistent with its existence.[497] Thus, where certain securities were deposited with stockbrokers for a specific loan, and they were given a power

---

ner v Trustee of the Property of Reed [1967] Ch. 1194; and above, para.7-077. In Skinner's case the amount outstanding on the mortgage exceeded the purchase price, so the auctioneer had no lien. See in general Murdoch, Law of Estate Agency (5th edn), p.153.

[489] Re Pavy's Patent Felted Fabric Co (1876) 1 Ch.D. 631.

[490] Taylor v Robinson (1818) 2 Moo.C.P. 730.

[491] Houghton v Matthews (1803) 3 B. & P. 485.

[492] Dixon v Stansfeld (1850) 10 C.B. 398.

[493] Muir v Fleming (1822) D. & R.N.P. 29.

[494] Wolstenholm v Sheffield Union Banking Co Ltd (1886) 54 L.T. 746; Withers LLP v Langbar International Ltd [2011] EWHC 1151 (Ch) (solicitor's lien).

[495] Re Bowes, Strathmore v Vane (1886) 33 Ch.D. 586. See also Re Laurence Ex p. M'Kenna, City Bank Case (1861) 3 De G.F. & J. 629.

[496] Walker v Birch (1795) 6 T.R. 258; See also Buchanan v Findlay (1829) 9 B. & C. 738; Bock v Gorrissen (1860) 2 De G.F. & J. 434; Frith v Forbes (1862) 4 De G.F. & J. 409; Rolls Razor Ltd v Cox [1967] 1 Q.B. 552.

[497] Brandao v Barnett (1846) 12 C. & F. 787; Re European Bank, Agra Bank Claim (1872) L.R. 8 Ch.App. 41; Davis v Bowsher (1794) 5 T.R. 488.

of sale, it was held that their general lien extended to such securities.[498] So, an agreement that there shall be monthly settlements does not affect the lien of an insurance broker for premiums upon policies in his hands.[499] And the general lien of a factor is not excluded merely because he acts under special instructions to sell in his principal's name and at a particular price.[500]

(7) A consigns goods to B, who transfers the bill of lading to his factor C, to secure £1,000. B becomes bankrupt. C has no lien on the bill of lading for a general balance due from B, and A may stop the goods in transit, subject to C's claim for £1,000.[501]

(8) Certain exchequer bills were deposited at a bank, to be kept in a box under lock and key, the key being kept by the customer. The bills were subsequently entrusted to the bank, with instructions to obtain the interest on them, and get them exchanged for new bills, and to deposit the new bills in the box as before. Held, that the banker's lien did not attach to the original bills or to those for which they were exchanged, the special purpose for which they were placed in his hands being inconsistent with a right of general lien.[502]

(9) A factor, who acted as such for the owners of a ship, asked the master to let him have the certificate of registry for the purpose of paying certain duties at the custom house. Held, that his general lien as a factor did not attach to the certificate.[503]

Article 66

CONFINED TO RIGHTS OF PRINCIPAL, EXCEPT IN THE CASE OF MONEY OR NEGOTIABLE SECURITIES

(1) The possessory lien of an agent attaches only upon goods or chattels in respect of which the principal has, as against third parties, the power to create the lien, and except in the case of money or negotiable securities, and subject to any statutory provision to the contrary,[504] is confined to the rights of the principal in the goods or chattels at the time when the lien attaches, and is subject to all rights and equities of third parties available against the principal at that time.[505] **7-087**

(2) The lien of an agent over negotiable securities deposited with the agent by or in the name of the principal is not affected by the rights or equities of third parties, and is as effectual as if the principal were the absolute owner of such money or securities, provided that at the time when the lien of the agent attaches the agent has no notice of any defect in the title of the principal to them.[506]

---

[498] *Jones v Peppercorne* (1858) John. 430. See also *Re London & Globe Finance Corp* [1902] 2 Ch. 416.
[499] *Fisher v Smith* (1878) 4 App.Cas. 1.
[500] *Stevens v Biller* (1883) 25 Ch.D. 31; *König v Brandt* (1901) 84 L.T. 748.
[501] *Spalding v Ruding* (1843) 6 Beav. 376.
[502] *Brandao v Barnett* (1846) 12 C. & F. 787.
[503] *Burn v Brown* (1817) 2 Stark. 272.
[504] e.g. Factors Act 1889; Sale of Goods Act 1979 ss.24–26. (See Article 87.)
[505] See Illustrations; *Att.-Gen. v Trueman* (1843) 11 M. & W. 694; *Cuthbert v Robarts, Lubbock & Co* [1909] 2 Ch. 226 at 233.
[506] See Illustration 9.

Comment

7-088   No one can create a lien beyond their own interest.[507] This means that not only does a lien take effect subject to the interests existing in the property concerned at the time that any money first becomes due in respect of which it may be exercised, but also that a subsequent disposition of the goods by the owner, in principle and subject to the circumstances of the disposition, freezes the lien at the sum due at that time: notice of such interests or dispositions to the person having the lien is (in the case of legal interests in ordinary chattels) irrelevant.[508] On the other hand, to the extent to which dispositions are subject to the lien, it is equally irrelevant whether or not the person taking under such disposition had notice of the lien: nor can that person acquire priority to it by giving notice.[509]

The position as regards negotiable instruments depends not on special rules as to liens, but on the normal rules of negotiability. Notice of previous interests in or subsequent dealings as to the goods is therefore relevant, in so far as it may prevent the person claiming the lien from being a holder in due course.[510]

Illustrations

7-089   (1)   A solicitor or other agent can have no lien on the share register or minute book of a company, because the directors have no power to create any lien that could interfere with the use of such register or book for the purposes of the company. So, no lien can attach upon such books of a company as, under the articles of association or the Companies Acts, ought to be kept at the registered office of the company.[511] And where documents come into the hands of a solicitor pending the winding-up of a company, he cannot claim any lien on them that would interfere with the winding-up.[512] But the fact that a company has issued debentures as a floating security does not prevent an agent from acquiring a lien on the title deeds of the company, and such a lien has priority to the claims of the debenture holders.[513]

(2)   The directors of a building society, which has no borrowing powers, overdraw the banking account of the society, and agree that certain deeds deposited at the bank shall be held as security for the general balance. The transaction is ultra vires, and the banker has no lien on the deeds for the overdraft. He is, however, in equity, entitled to hold them as security for so much of the money advanced as he can show to have been actually applied in payment of the debts and liabilities of the society.[514]

---

[507] See e.g. *Eide UK Ltd v Lowndes Lambert Group Ltd* [1999] Q.B. 199. See too *Rockeagle Ltd v Alsop Wilkinson (a firm)* [1992] Ch. 47 (stakeholder).

[508] *Blunden v Desart* (1842) (Ir.) 59 R.R. 753, Illustration 8 (authorities reviewed); see also *Watson v Lyon* (1855) 7 De G.M. & G. 288; *Young v English* (1843) 7 Beav. 10; *Jeffryes v Agra & Masterman's Bank* (1866) L.R. 2 Eq. 674; cases cited at Illustration 4. As to equitable interests see, e.g. *Re Gross Ex p. Kingston* (1871) L.R. 6 Ch.App. 632.

[509] *West of England Bank v Batchelor* (1882) 51 L.J.Ch. 199.

[510] See Bills of Exchange Act 1882 ss.27(3) and 29.

[511] *Re Capital Fire Ins. Assn* (1883) 24 Ch.D. 408; *Re Rapid Road Transit Co* [1909] 1 Ch. 96; Companies Act 2006 ss.113 and 114.

[512] *Re Anglo-Maltese Hydraulic Dock Co Ltd* (1885) 54 L.J.Ch. 730.

[513] *Brunton v Electrical Engineering Corp* [1892] 1 Ch. 434. See also *Re Dee Estates Ltd, Wright v Dee Estates Ltd* [1911] 2 Ch. 85.

[514] *Blackburn Benefit Building Society v Cunliffe* (1884) 9 App.Cas. 857; see Article 93; *Goff and Jones,*

(3)   A solicitor or other agent is employed by trustees. He normally has no lien on the trust funds for his expenses.[515]

(4)   Deeds are deposited with a solicitor by a tenant for life. The solicitor has no lien on the deeds as against the remainderman.[516] The lien of a solicitor upon deeds and papers deposited with him by a client is confined to the rights of the client in them, and is subject to all rights and equities of third persons available against the client.[517] So, a solicitor or other agent has no lien, as such, on the separate property of a partner for the obligations of the firm.[518]

(5)   A mortgage is paid off, and the property is reconveyed to the mortgagor. The mortgagee's solicitor has no lien as against the mortgagor on the title deeds for costs due from the mortgagee, except the cost of the reconveyance, even if such costs were incurred in respect of the mortgaged property, e.g. the costs of an attempted sale by the mortgagee.[519] Where a mortgagor borrowed the title deeds from the mortgagee and sold the property, it was held that the solicitor of the mortgagor, to whom the deeds were handed for the purpose of completing the sale, had no lien over them for costs due from the mortgagor in respect of other transactions.[520]

(6)   A sells goods to B, and ships them to B's order. Before the goods arrive, A and B agree to rescind the contract for sale. The wharfinger cannot, on the arrival of the goods at his wharf, claim a lien on them as against A, for a general balance due from B.[521] So, a wharfinger has no lien on goods, as against a buyer, for charges becoming due from the seller after the sale.[522]

(7)   A, an owner of land, deposits the title deeds at a bank as security for his general balance, and subsequently contracts to sell the land to B, who has notice of the terms of the deposit. The banker has notice of the sale, but continues to account, and makes fresh advances to A, who pays in sums from time to time. B pays the purchase money to A, by instalments, without notice of such advances. A having paid into the bank sums exceeding in the aggregate the amount owing to the bank at the time of the contract of sale, the banker has no lien on the title deeds or charge on the land as against B, though on the general balance there was always a debt due to the bank.[523]

(8)   A client deposits deeds with a solicitor. Judgment is subsequently obtained

---

Law of Unjust Enrichment (9th edn), para.15-42.

[515] *Staniar v Evans* (1886) 3 T.L.R. 215; *Worrall v Harford* (1802) 8 Ves. 4; *Lightfoot v Keane* (1836) 1 M. & W. 745; *Hall v Laver* (1842) 1 Hare 571; *Francis v Francis* (1854) 5 De G.M. & G. 108; Cordery, *Solicitors* (8th edn), pp.60–61. See too *Heslop v Cousins* [2007] 3 N.Z.L.R. 679 at [190] (solicitor no lien or set-off on moneys given him for a particular purpose).

[516] *Turner v Letts* (1855) 20 Beav. 185; 7 De G.M. & G. 243; *Ex p. Nesbitt* (1805) 2 Sch. & Lef. 279.

[517] *Hollis v Claridge* (1813) 4 Taunt. 807; *Furlong v Howard* (1804) 2 Sch. & Lef. 115; *Pelly v Wathen* (1851) 1 De G.M. & G. 16; Cordery, *Solicitors* (8th edn), pp.236–238.

[518] *Turner v Deane* (1849) 3 Exch. 836; *Watts v Christie* (1849) 11 Beav. 546.

[519] *Re Llewellin* [1891] 3 Ch. 145; *Wakefield v Newbon* (1844) 6 Q.B. 276. See also *Franicevich v Strong* [1997] 1 N.Z.L.R. 460.

[520] *Young v English* (1843) 7 Beav. 10.

[521] *Richardson v Goss* (1802) 3 B. & P. 119.

[522] *Barry v Longmore* (1840) 12 A. & E. 639.

[523] *London and County Banking Co Ltd v Ratcliffe* (1881) 6 App.Cas. 722 (a case on mortgage: see now Law of Property Act 1925 s.94. But Lord Blackburn refers also to lien). See *Paget's Law of Banking* (15th edn), Ch. 4.

against the client. The solicitor's lien does not extend to costs becoming due after the date of the judgment.[524]

(9) A banker borrowed a specific sum of money from a stockbroker, with whom he deposited, as security, negotiable instruments belonging to third persons. The banker dealt as a principal with the broker, having had many previous transactions with him, and there was nothing to lead the broker to believe that the securities were not the property of the banker. Held, that the broker's general lien for the balance due to him from the banker attached upon the securities, although the banker had been guilty of gross fraud.[525] So, the general lien of a banker upon negotiable instruments deposited with him is not affected by the circumstance that the customer who deposits them is acting as agent for a third person,[526] nor by equities between the customer and third persons.[527] But an agent has no lien upon a negotiable instrument, as against the true owner, for advances made after notice of a defect in the title of the principal.[528]

Article 67

How Lien Extinguished or Lost

7-090 (1) The lien of an agent is extinguished or lost—
  (a) by tender to the agent of the sum due[529];
  (b) by the agent's entering into any agreement,[530] or acting in any capacity,[531] which is inconsistent with the continuance of the lien;
  (c) by waiver.[532]

(2) The lien of an agent is extinguished by voluntarily[533] parting with the possession of the goods or chattels subject to it,[534] except where the circumstances in which the agent parts with possession are consistent with the continuance of the lien and are such as to show an intention to retain the lien.[535]

(3) The lien of an agent is not affected by the fact that the claim secured by it becomes barred by limitation,[536] or that the principal becomes insolvent, or

---

[524] *Blunden v Desart* (1842) (Ir.) 59 R.R. 753.
[525] *Jones v Peppercorne* (1858) John. 430.
[526] *Brandao v Barnett* (1846) 12 C. & F. 787; *Baker v Nottingham & Nottinghamshire Banking Co Ltd* (1891) 60 L.J.Q.B. 542.
[527] *Misa v Currie* (1876) 1 App.Cas. 554; *Johnson v Robarts* (1875) L.R. 10 Ch.App. 505.
[528] *Solomons v Bank of England* (1791) 13 East 135 (but this is hardly clear authority); Bills of Exchange Act 1882 ss.27(3) and 29.
[529] See Comment.
[530] Illustration 1; *How v Kirchner* (1857) 11 Moo.P.C. 21.
[531] Illustrations 2 and 3.
[532] See Comment; Illustrations 4, 5, 6 and 7; Sale of Goods Act 1979 s.43(1)(c).
[533] See *Tibmor Pty Ltd v Nashlyn Pty Ltd* [1989] 1 Qd.R. 610 (obligatory payment into court did not extinguish lien).
[534] Illustration 8; *Kruger v Wilcox* (1755) Amb. 252; *Bligh v Davies* (1860) 28 Beav. 211.
[535] Illustrations 9, 10 and 11.
[536] *Spears v Hartly* (1800) 3 Esp. 81; *Re Broomhead* (1847) 5 D. & L. 52; *Curwen v Milburn* (1889) 42 Ch.D. 424; *Re Carter, Carter v Carter* (1885) 55 L.J.Ch. 230; *Coshott v Barry* [2016] FCAFC 173 at [14]. The statute can be said to bar the remedy, not the right.

sells or otherwise deals with the goods or chattels subject to the lien, after the lien has attached.[537]

Comment

Tender   Acceptance or refusal of a valid tender extinguishes the lien. But a lien   **7-091**
is not necessarily lost by a claim for more than the sum due, unless the claimant
gives no details from which the correct sum can be calculated, or insists emphati-
cally on an incorrect sum.[538]

Waiver   A waiver is implied whenever the conduct of the agent is such as to   **7-092**
indicate an intention to abandon the lien, or is inconsistent with the continuance of
it.[539] The situations referred to in Rule (1)(b) are in fact no more than examples of
implied waiver. Questions of tender are also sometimes expressed in terms of
waiver.[540]

Parting with possession   The lien of an agent is not affected where the agent was   **7-093**
induced to part with possession of the goods by fraud,[541] or possession was obtained
unlawfully or without the agent's consent.[542] In such cases, the lien continues, and
the person entitled to it can sue in conversion, whether or not possession has been
recovered, and if the agent has recovered possession, even where that was achieved
by a trick[543]: nor is the lien affected by the fact that the goods are given by the agent
to another to hold on the agent's behalf,[544] even where that other is the principal, if
the agreement to retain the lien is clear: an example where this occurs is the commercial situation covered by the trust receipt.[545] Where the agent simply delivers
the goods with a purported unilateral reservation of the lien to which the receiver
has not agreed, it is arguable that the lien is lost, on the grounds that such terms of
receipt cannot be unilaterally imposed. It has however been decided that the lien
is maintained, and that if the receiver does not agree to the terms under which the
goods are delivered the receiver must give notice to the lienor to remove them.[546]
It appears that in some cases, where the subject-matter of the lien comes lawfully
back into the claimant's hands after voluntarily parting with it, the lien revives, even
for sums due before possession was lost.[547]

---

[537] The last two propositions follow from the nature of the lien as a right in rem.
[538] *Albemarle Supply Co Ltd v Hind & Co* [1928] 1 K.B. 307; *Coshott v Barry* [2016] FCAFC 173 at [5].
[539] e.g. Illustrations 4 and 5.
[540] e.g. *Scarfe v Morgan* (1838) 4 M. & W. 270. The principle seems to be similar to that of election: a person may waive a contract term which is to his benefit. Obviously there can also be estoppels as to whether there has been or will be a waiver.
[541] *Wallace v Woodgate* (1824) R. & M. 193.
[542] *Dicas v Stockley* (1836) 7 C. & P. 587; *Re Carter, Carter v Carter* (1885) 55 L.J.Ch. 230.
[543] *Bristol (Earl) v Wilsmore* (1823) 1 B. & C. 514.
[544] *Wilson v Kymer* (1813) 1 M. & S. 157; *McCombie v Davis* (1805) 7 East 5.
[545] See Illustration 10; *Benjamin's Sale of Goods* (10th edn), para.18-279 onwards.
[546] *Caldwell v Sumpters* [1972] Ch. 478, Illustration 11. See also *Bentley v Gaisford* [1997] Q.B. 627, where copying the documents was held a breach of the second holder's duty.
[547] *Levy v Barnard* (1818) 8 Taunt. 149 (marine insurance policy); *Caldwell v Sumpters* [1972] Ch. 478 at 488. But a general lien, at any rate, does not do so where he has meanwhile discovered that the person with whom he is dealing is only an agent, or where dispositions of the goods have meanwhile been made: see *Near East Relief v King, Chasseur & Co Ltd* [1930] 2 K.B. 40 at 44–45; Article 70.

Illustrations

7-094 (1) The holder of a lien allows the owner of the goods free access to the goods for the purpose of using and returning them: he may be held to have lost his lien.[548]

(2) A solicitor acts for both mortgagor and mortgagee in carrying out a mortgage. The solicitor thereby loses his lien on the title deeds of the mortgaged property for costs due from the mortgagor, even if the costs were incurred prior to the mortgage, and even if the deeds are not permitted to be taken out of the solicitor's possession.[549]

(3) A solicitor prepares a marriage settlement, on the instructions of the intended husband, and retains it in his possession after the marriage. He has no lien on the settlement as against the trustees, the cost of preparing it being payable by the husband.[550]

(4) An agent causes goods upon which he has a lien to be taken in execution at his own suit. He thereby waives the lien, though the goods are sold to him under the execution, and are never removed from his premises.[551]

(5) Upon a demand being made against an agent by his principal for a chattel upon which the agent has a lien, the agent claims to retain the chattel on some other ground, without mentioning the lien. He thereby waives the lien.[552]

(6) A solicitor, having a lien for costs, takes a security for them, and does not tell the client that he intends to reserve the lien. He is deemed to waive the lien, it being the duty of a solicitor, if he intends to reserve his lien in such a case, to explain to the client that such is his intention.[553]

(7) An agent entitled to a lien takes other security for the claim. He may be deemed to waive the lien,[554] but only if the nature of the security,[555] or the circumstances in which it is taken,[556] are inconsistent with the continuance of the lien, or indicate an intention to abandon it. The taking of a bill of exchange will usually be no more than conditional acceptance of a particular mode of payment.[557]

(8) An agent delivers goods, on which he has a lien, on board a ship, to be conveyed on account and at the risk of the principal. The agent thereby sur-

---

[548] *Forth v Simpson* (1849) 13 Q.B. 680; cf. *Albermarle Supply Co Ltd v Hind & Co* [1928] 1 K.B. 307. See also *Hatton v Car Maintenance Co Ltd* [1915] 1 Ch. 621.

[549] *Re Nicholson Ex p. Quinn* (1883) 53 L.J.Ch. 302; *Re Snell* (1877) 6 Ch.D. 105; *Re Mason and Taylor* (1878) 10 Ch.D. 729.

[550] *Re Lawrance, Bowker v Austin* [1894] 1 Ch. 556.

[551] *Jacobs v Latour* (1828) 5 Bing. 130.

[552] *Weeks v Goode* (1859) 6 C.B.(N.S.) 367; *Boardman v Sill* (1808) 1 Camp. 410n. The rule is different from that applicable to discharge of contract by breach, where a person who gives an invalid reason for treating the contract as discharged may subsequently justify his conduct by a valid reason.

[553] *Re Morris* [1908] 1 K.B. 473; *Re Taylor, Stileman & Underwood* [1891] 1 Ch. 590; *Bissill v Bradford & District Tramway Co Ltd* (1893) 9 T.L.R. 337; *Re Douglas Norman & Co* [1898] 1 Ch. 199; *Candey Ltd v Crumpler* [2020] EWCA Civ 26; [2020] Bus. L.R. 1452. It seems, therefore, that the solicitor's position is somewhat unfavourable. See Cordery, *Solicitors* (8th edn), p.249.

[554] *Cowell v Simpson* (1809) 16 Ves. 275 (note payable three years later); *Hewison v Guthrie* (1836) 2 Bing.N.C. 755 (bill at 12 months); *Mason v Morley (No.1)* (1865) 34 Beav. 471.

[555] *Angus v McLachlan* (1883) 23 Ch.D. 330.

[556] See *The Albion* (1872) 27 L.T. 723.

[557] *Gunn v Bolckow, Vaughan & Co* (1875) L.R. 10 Ch.App. 491; cf. *Tamvaco v Simpson* (1866) L.R. 1 C.P. 363; *W.J. Alan & Co Ltd v El Nasr Export & Import Co* [1972] 1 Q.B. 189.

renders his lien on the goods, and he has no power to revive it by stopping the goods in transit.[558]

(9)   A, as a solicitor, on the instructions of a mortgagor, prepares and engrosses a reconveyance, which he sends to the solicitor of the mortgagee with a request that he will hold it on A's account, he having a lien thereon. The mortgagee executes the reconveyance. A's lien is not, in the circumstances, prejudiced by his parting with the possession of the engrossment, nor by its being executed by the mortgagee as a deed, and he can restrain the mortgagee's solicitor from transferring the deed to a subsequent purchaser of the land.[559]

(10)   An agent gives up a chattel in order that the principal may sell it and account for the proceeds to the agent; he does not thereby lose his lien on the chattel.[560]

(11)   The intending vendor of property changes her solicitor during negotiations. The former solicitor claims a lien on the deeds. The new solicitor requires the deeds in connection with the sale. At the request of the new solicitor, the former solicitor gives them up, accompanying them by a letter saying that they are sent "on the understanding that you will hold them to our order". The new solicitor immediately writes refusing to agree to these terms, but does not offer the deeds back. The former solicitor's lien continues: if the new solicitors were not willing to hold the deeds on these terms they should have told the former solicitors to come and take them back.[561]

Article 68

LIEN OF SUB-AGENTS

(1)   Except where otherwise expressly provided by statute,[562] a sub-agent who is employed by an agent in circumstances where the agent has no actual or apparent authority to delegate the agent's functions has no lien over the goods or chattels of the principal as against the principal.[563]   **7-095**

(2)   Where a sub-agent is employed by an agent in circumstances where the agent has actual or apparent authority to delegate without creating privity of contract between principal and sub-agent, the sub-agent—

(a)   has the same right of lien, general or particular, against the principal, over the goods and chattels of the principal, in respect of claims arising in the course of the sub-agency, as the sub-agent would have had against the

---

[558] *Sweet v Pym* (1800) 1 East 4; *Hathesing v Laing* (1873) 17 Eq. 92. See, however, Article 69.

[559] *Watson v Lyon* (1855) 7 De G.M. & G. 288.

[560] *North Western Bank Ltd v Poynter, Son & Macdonalds* [1895] A.C. 56; see also *Albemarle Supply Co Ltd v Hind & Co* [1928] 1 K.B. 307; *Rose v CMS Operations* [2002] EWHC 59 (Ch); See too *Coshott v Barry* [2016] FCAFC 173 at [4].

[561] *Caldwell v Sumpters* [1972] Ch. 478. See Comment.

[562] See Article 87 as to the Factors Act.

[563] Illustration 1. As to when the agent has the power to affect the legal position of the principal, see Ch.3. And see in general *Restatement, Second*, § 465. As to cases where bailees have authority to place goods in the hands of persons who may subsequently claim a lien against the owner, see *Cassils & Co v Holden Wood Bleaching Co* (1914) 84 L.J.K.B. 834; *Tappenden v Artus* [1964] 2 Q.B. 185; *Chellaram & Sons (London) Ltd v Butlers Warehousing and Distribution Ltd* [1978] 2 Lloyd's Rep. 412; Article 27, Illustration 10.

agent if the agent had been the owner of the goods and chattels; and such right of lien is not liable to be defeated by any settlement between the principal and the agent to which the sub-agent is not a party[564];

(b) has the same right of general lien over the goods and chattels of the principal in respect of all claims, whether arising in the course of the sub-agency or not, as the sub-agent would have had against the agent if the agent had been the owner of the goods and chattels; provided that, as against the principal, such right of lien is available only to the extent of the lien, if any, to which the agent would have been entitled if the goods and chattels had been in the agent's possession[565]; and

(c) has the same right of lien, general or particular, over the goods and chattels of the principal, as the sub-agent would have had against the agent if the agent had been the owner of the goods and chattels, where that at the time when the lien attaches the sub-agent believes on reasonable grounds that the agent is the owner of the goods and chattels and is acting in the matter on the agent's own behalf.[566]

Comment

7-096   **Unauthorised delegation**   Where an agent for a disclosed principal delegates the agent's duties but has no authority, actual or apparent, to do so, it is obvious that the principal's position cannot be affected.[567] The remainder of the Article applies to cases where delegated performance is authorised, but the creation of privity between principal and sub-agent is not.[568] In cases where such privity does exist, the so-called sub-agent is actually an agent of the principal and entitled to an agent's normal remedies against the principal.[569]

7-097   **General rule**   But where delegation to a sub-agent is authorised by virtue of actual or apparent authority, the principal can be regarded as having authorised the agent to subject the property to a lien. The general rule, therefore, set out in Rule (2)(a), is that the sub-agent's lien against the principal is confined to claims arising in the course of performance of the duties properly delegated to the sub-agent. However, where the agent personally has an interest in the principal's property by way of lien,[570] the sub-agent is entitled to exercise a lien to that extent against the principal, as stated in Rule (2)(b). Both these rules can be regarded as applications of the principle that no one can create a lien beyond that person's own interest.[571]

Against the agent, of course, the sub-agent has the normal rights of an agent against the principal.

7-098   **Undisclosed principal**   It has long been established that, as stated in Rule (2)(c), when the agent does not disclose the existence of the principal, the sub-agent may exercise against such principal the full lien that would have been available against the agent had that agent in fact been principal, to the extent that such lien had ac-

---

[564] Illustration 2.
[565] Illustration 3.
[566] Illustration 4–6.
[567] Illustration 1.
[568] See Article 35.
[569] See Article 35.
[570] Illustration 3.
[571] See Comment to Article 66.

crued up to the time of discovery of the principal[572] provided, of course, that the delegation was within the authority of the agent. The basis of this rule seems to be the notion that an undisclosed principal intervenes on the contract of the agent subject to equities already accrued,[573] and there is no tendency in the cases regarding lien to require some fault in the principal that could be treated as raising an estoppel.[574] However, since the agent is authorised, it would seem that on discovery of the principal the sub-agent is remitted to the position under Rule (2)(a).

Although a lien revives, at any rate in some cases, where possession of the goods is recovered,[575] it has been held that the general lien of a marine insurance broker on a policy does not revive when at the time that possession is recovered the broker has notice that the person with whom the broker had dealt was only an agent,[576] and this seems to be a rule applicable to all general liens, based on the fact that the regained possession is a new possession.[577] It would not, however, apply where the first possession is lost not voluntarily, but by fraud or a trick.[578]

Illustrations

(1) A factor delegated his authority to a sub-agent, without the assent of the principal. The sub-agent, who knew that the goods did not belong to the factor, had no lien on the principal's goods, even for duties paid in respect of those goods.[579]   **7-099**

(2) An agent, with the authority of his principal, employs an insurance broker to effect a policy for his principal, the broker being aware that the agent is acting for a principal. The principal pays the agent the amount of the premiums due in respect of the policy. Notwithstanding such payment, the broker has a lien upon the policy for premiums paid by him in respect of it, or for which he is liable.[580] But he has no lien, as against the principal, for a general balance due from the agent in respect of other transactions.[581]

(3) As against the country solicitor employing him, a London agent has a general lien upon all moneys received and documents deposited with him in the course of his employment,[582] but as against the client, his general lien is limited to the amount due from the client to the country solicitor.[583] As against both the country solicitor and the client, he has a lien upon money recovered and docu-

---

[572] *Westwood v Bell* (1815) 4 Camp. 349; Marine Insurance Act 1906 s.53(2).

[573] *Montagu v Forwood* [1893] 2 Q.B. 350 at 355–356.

[574] Compare the position as regards set-off: see Comment to Article 81.

[575] *Levy v Barnard* (1818) 2 Moo.C.P. 34 (marine insurance policy).

[576] *Near East Relief v King, Chasseur & Co Ltd* [1930] 2 K.B. 40; *Eide UK Ltd v Lowndes Lambert Group Ltd* [1999] Q.B. 199 at 209–210 and see Marine Insurance Act 1906 s.53.

[577] Powell, pp.375–376.

[578] See Comment to Article 67.

[579] *Solly v Rathbone* (1814) 2 M. & S. 298; *Snook v Davidson* (1809) 2 Camp. 218. And see *Chellaram & Sons (London) Ltd v Butlers Warehousing and Distribution Ltd* [1978] 2 Lloyd's Rep. 412 (uncontemplated sub-bailment).

[580] *Fisher v Smith* (1878) 4 App.Cas. 1; Marine Insurance Act 1906 s.53(2).

[581] *Mildred v Maspons* (1883) 8 App.Cas. 874; *Maanss v Henderson* (1801) 1 East 335; *Man v Shiffner* (1802) 2 East 523; Marine Insurance Act 1906 s.53(2); *Fairfield Shipbuilding & Engineering Co Ltd v Gardner Mountain & Co Ltd* (1911) 104 L.T. 288.

[582] *Lawrence v Fletcher* (1879) 12 Ch.D. 858; *Bray v Hine & Fox* (1818) 6 Price 203; *Re Jones and Roberts* [1905] 2 Ch. 219.

[583] *Ex p. Edwards* (1881) 8 Q.B.D. 262; *Moody v Spencer* (1822) 2 D. & R. 6; *Waller v Holmes* (1860) 1 John. & H. 239; *Peatfield v Barlow* (1869) L.R. 8 Eq. 61.

ments deposited with him in a particular suit, for the amount of his agency charges and disbursements in connection with that suit.[584]

(4) An agent, on behalf, and with the authority, of his principal, employs an insurance broker to effect a policy, the broker having no notice, and being unaware, that he is dealing with an agent. The broker has a lien on the policy for the general balance due to him from the agent, and is entitled to apply the proceeds of the policy in payment of such balance, notwithstanding that he has, in the meantime, received notice of the principal's rights.[585]

(5) A, a commission agent, employed B, a broker, to buy certain goods, B having no knowledge that A was acting as an agent. B bought and paid for the goods and retained the warrants relating to them. A was in fact acting for C, and C paid A for the goods. B, on A's instructions, resold the goods, and applied the proceeds in reduction of a running account between himself and A. In an action by C against B for converting the goods, it was held that B was not liable, because at the time of the sale he had a lien on goods for the balance due to him from A.[586]

(6) A employed B to collect general average contributions under an insurance policy. B, in the ordinary course of business, employed C, an insurance broker, to collect the contributions, C being unaware that B was acting as an agent. C collected the contributions, and B became bankrupt. Held, in an action by A against C for the contributions, as money had and received to his use, that C was entitled to set off the amount of a debt due to him from B.[587]

4. OTHER MISCELLANEOUS RIGHTS

Article 69

RIGHTS IN RESPECT OF GOODS BOUGHT IN OWN NAME

7-100   Where an agent, by contracting personally,[588] becomes solely liable for the price of goods bought on behalf of the principal, the property in the goods, as between the principal and the agent, vests in the agent, and does not pass to the principal until the principal pays for the goods, or the agent intends that it shall pass[589]; and the agent has the same rights with regard to the disposal of the goods, and with regard to stopping them in transit, as the agent would have had if the relation with the principal had been that of seller and buyer.[590]

Comment

7-101   A person who is in general an agent and obtains goods for the principal may on a particular occasion genuinely buy them from the third party and resell them to the

---

[584] *Dicas v Stockley* (1836) 7 C. & P. 587; *Lawrence v Fletcher* (1879) 12 Ch.D. 858. See Cordery, *Solicitors* (8th edn), p.242.

[585] *Mann v Forrester* (1814) 4 Camp. 60; *Westwood v Bell* (1815) 4 Camp. 349; Marine Insurance Act 1906 s.53(2).

[586] *Taylor v Kymer* (1832) 3 B. & Ad. 320.

[587] *Montagu v Forwood* [1893] 2 Q.B. 350. And see *New Zealand, etc., Land Co v Watson* (1881) 7 Q.B.D. 374; Article 81.

[588] See Comment and Article 98.

[589] *Cassaboglou v Gibb* (1883) 11 Q.B.D. 797 at 803–804, 806–806, Illustration 4.

[590] Sale of Goods Act 1979 s.38(2); and see Comment; *Restatement, Second,* § 466.

principal.[591] In such a case the agent has all the normal remedies of a seller, and is under the liabilities of a seller, except in so far as circumstances indicate otherwise.

But another interpretation of the agent's functions is possible: the agent may deal with the third party as principal, while remaining in the status of agent towards his or her own principal—i.e. the agent's remuneration will (normally[592]) be by commission rather than by profit on resale, and the agent's duty would not be the absolute one of a seller, but rather that of an agent to exercise due diligence in carrying out the principal's instructions.[593] This is one of the interpretations put on the function of a commission merchant in the leading case of *Ireland v Livingston*.[594] It is referred to elsewhere in this work as "indirect representation" and associated with the civil law notion of *commissionnaire*.[595] The specialised group of cases on which this Article is based concern nineteenth-century examples of (what appears to be) this situation: they are indeed among the only cases which can be said to concern it, and so are of considerable importance. The assumptions behind them are not easy to get into.

In such a case the agent may nevertheless have, as against the principal, some of the remedies regarding the goods which are available to unpaid vendors. It has long been established that the right of stoppage in transit could apply, not being confined to genuine vendors[596]: the unpaid vendor's lien has also been extended to such a case.[597] In any case the agent has a lien as such, but the unpaid vendor's rights may be exercised by a person who has never acquired property or possession.[598] The effect of these cases was put into statutory form in s.38(2) of the Sale of Goods Act 1979 which extends the rights of the unpaid seller against the goods to "any person who is in the position of a seller, as, for instance ... a consignor or agent who has himself paid, or is directly responsible for, the price". This indicates that such a person has not only the rights of lien and stoppage in transit but also that of resale.

Whether an agent in such a position can reserve property so as to be able to exercise the right of withholding delivery, as opposed to a lien, is open to argument. It used to be said that the normal rule for agents is that the goods become the property of the principal as soon as they are consigned to the principal.[599] On one view, an agent who does something that would normally reserve property, e.g. takes a bill of lading to the agent's own order, reserves a lien only: if the agent is to reserve property he or she must be acting not as agent but as seller, as it is difficult to see under what transaction the goods would otherwise eventually become the

---

[591] See above, para.1-036 onwards. Provided that he is not in breach of his fiduciary duties in doing so: see Article 31, Illustration 9; Articles 45 and 47.

[592] See above, para.1-036.

[593] See *Cassaboglou v Gibb* (1883) 11 Q.B.D. 797; *Bolus & Co Ltd v Inglis Bros Ltd* [1924] N.Z.L.R. 164 at 174; *Witt & Scott Ltd v Blumenreich* [1949] N.Z.L.R. 806; *Anglo-African Shipping Co of New York Inc v J. Mortner Ltd* [1962] 1 Lloyd's Rep. 610 (but note the dissenting opinion of Diplock LJ). See above, para.1-017.

[594] *Ireland v Livingston* (1872) L.R. 5 H.L. 395 at 404–405, 412, 416 (Illustration 1 to Article 26).

[595] See above, para.1-021. But compare expressions used elsewhere; and see *Ex p. Miles* (1885) 15 Q.B.D. 39 at 42; *Brown & Gracie v F.W. Green Pty Ltd* [1960] 1 Lloyd's Rep. 289, per Lord Denning. See further Hill (1972) 3 J. Maritime Law and Commerce, 307, esp. at 318–324 (a valuable article); (1968) 31 M.L.R. 623.

[596] *Feise v Wray* (1802) 3 East 93, Illustration 1; cf. *Siffken v Wray* (1805) 6 East 371. See also *The Tigress* (1863) 32 L.J.Ad. 97; *Hawkes v Dunn* (1831) 1 C. & J. 519.

[597] See *Imperial Bank v London & St. Katharine Docks Co* (1877) 5 Ch.D. 195, Illustration 2.

[598] *Jenkyns v Usborne* (1844) 7 M. & G. 678.

[599] *Hathesing v Laing* (1873) L.R. 17 Eq. 92 at 101; *Re Tappenbeck Ex p. Banner* (1876) 2 Ch.D. 278 at 287, Illustration 3. And see Article 89.

property of the principal.[600] On another view, the agent may in appropriate cases still be an agent, but may reserve and subsequently transmit property nevertheless.[601] There may be little difference in practice, for even where an agent would be for the above purposes treated as a seller, it is clear that the agent cannot act as a seller to the exclusion of the agent's instructions and sue the principal for non-acceptance of goods bought[602]; the agent cannot sue for the price of goods as on a sale[603]; the measure of damages for breach of contract is not that of a contract of sale[604]; and the agent will often not answer for breach of warranty of quality.[605] Property will presumably pass by intention,[606] but not in accordance with the rules for sales laid down in the Sale of Goods Act 1979 as such. In view of these points, it is doubtful whether there is much utility in calling the agent a seller, and it is submitted that the second view is preferable.

A third way in which an agent who contracts personally may act is by making a contract between the principal and the third party and adding the agent's own liability to it: the possibilities in this respect are discussed elsewhere.[607] The cases cited for the propositions above do not apply to such a situation. If appropriate, the agent can here presumably reserve property, and may certainly exercise an agent's lien. If the agent discharges the principal's liability, it seems that the agent also has the unpaid vendor's rights.[608] It is not clear whether or not the agent has these rights when the agent is liable but has not been called upon to pay, e.g. where the principal is insolvent.[609]

Illustrations

7-102 (1) P instructs A, a factor in Hamburg, to procure and ship wax for him. A buys wax in his own name, ships to P's order, and draws on P for the price. P becomes insolvent. A can stop in transit.[610]

(2) D, a broker, buys goods lying in a warehouse from C for unnamed principals. D obtains a delivery order, and delivers it to Z, his principals. Z pledge their interest in the goods to X and indorse the order to X. X requests the warehouse to attorn to him. Before the warehouse has done so Z becomes insolvent, and

---

[600] See *Benjamin's Sale of Goods* (10th edn), Ch. 18; Blackburn, *Contract of Sale* (3rd edn), p.352.

[601] See *Cassaboglou v Gibb* (1883) 11 Q.B.D. 797 at 804, 806 (Illustration 4); see also *Jenkyns v Brown* (1849) 14 Q.B. 496; *Schuster v McKellar* (1857) 7 E. & B. 704; *Falk v Fletcher* (1865) 18 C.B.(N.S.) 403; *Re Tappenbeck Ex p. Banner*(1876) 2 Ch.D. 278; *The Prinz Adelbert* [1917] A.C. 586 at 590; Sale of Goods Act 1979 s.38(2).

[602] *Tetley v Shand* (1871) 25 L.T. 658, Illustration 5; *White v Benekendorff* (1873) 29 L.T. 475; cf. *Robinson v Mollett* (1875) L.R. 7 H.L. 802, Illustration 8 to Article 31.

[603] *Seymour v Pychlau* (1817) 1 B. & A. 14.

[604] *Cassaboglou v Gibb* (1883) 11 Q.B.D. 797.

[605] See *J.S. Robertson (Australia) Pty Ltd v Martin* (1950) 94 C.L.R. 30.

[606] See *Cassaboglou v Gibb* (1883) 11 Q.B.D. 797 at 803–804.

[607] See Comment to Article 98.

[608] See Sale of Goods Act 1979 s.38(2); *Imperial Bank v London & St Katharine Docks Co* (1877) 5 Ch.D. 195. See further as to this case, and especially as to the reference to the Mercantile Law Amendment Act, *Benjamin's Sale of Goods* (10th edn), para.15-013.

[609] See Blackburn, *Contract of Sale* (3rd edn), p.352; *Cassaboglou v Gibb* (1883) 11 Q.B.D. 797 at 804; Sale of Goods Act 1979 s.38(2).

[610] *Feise v Wray* (1802) 3 East 93.

D, knowing nothing of X, pays C and obtains another delivery order. D can exercise the unpaid vendor's lien against X and Z.[611]

(3) P employs A in South America to buy goods. A buys goods in his own name using money raised by bills drawn on P. A ships the goods, taking a bill of lading to P's order. The bills of exchange are not all paid. A has the right to stop in transit, but no further rights against the goods once the transit is ended.[612]

(4) P requests A in Hong Kong to buy and ship a certain kind of opium. A ships the wrong kind of opium. P sues A. The measure of damages is not the difference between the value of the opium ordered and that shipped, as on a sale, but the loss actually sustained by P in consequence of the opium not being as ordered, the contract being one of agency.[613]

(5) P requests A, a cotton broker, to buy cotton gradually at eight-and-a-quarter d if A cannot do better. A purchases in his own name at 81/16d and 713/15d and sends P a bought note for the cotton at eight and a quarter d. P discovers what has happened and repudiates the transaction. The contract is not one of sale and A cannot sue for non-acceptance: also, he is in breach of his duties as agent.[614]

Article 70

RIGHT TO INTERPLEAD

(1) Where adverse claims whether legal or equitable, are made upon an agent in respect of any money, goods, or chattels in the agent's possession, and the agent claims no interest in the subject-matter of the dispute other than for costs or charges, the agent may claim relief by way of interpleader,[615] even as against the principal whose title the agent has acknowledged,[616] provided that the agent had no notice of the adverse claim at the time of the acknowledgment.[617]   **7-103**

(2) Where the agent claims a lien on property as against the owner, whoever that person may be, the lien is not such an interest as deprives the agent of the right to interplead in respect of the ownership of the property[618]; but where the agent claims a lien or any other interest in the property, or part of it, other than for costs or charges, as against a particular claimant, the agent is not permitted to interplead.[619]

---

[611] *Imperial Bank v London & St Katharine Docks Co* (1877) 5 Ch.D. 195.

[612] *Re Tappenbeck, Ex p. Banner* (1876) 2 Ch.D. 278.

[613] *Cassaboglou v Gibb* (1883) 11 Q.B.D. 797.

[614] *Tetley v Shand* (1871) 25 L.T. 658.

[615] See PD RSC 17 (CPR Sch. 1).

[616] *Tanner v European Bank Ltd* (1866) L.R. 1 Ex. 261; *Attenborough v St Katharine Docks Co* (1878) 3 C.P.D. 450; *Ex p. Mersey Docks and Harbour Board* [1899] 1 Q.B. 546; Illustrations 1 to 6. As to interpleader on claims by agent and undisclosed principal, see *Meynell v Angell* (1863) 32 L.J.Q.B. 14.

[617] *Re Sadler Ex p. Davies* (1881) 19 Ch.D. 86. If he had such notice he would formerly have been estopped from denying his principal's title. But by virtue of s.8(1) of the Torts (Interference with Goods) Act 1977 he may now apply for joinder of the third party in such a situation. See Article 56 and Comment.

[618] *Attenborough v St Katharine's Dock Co* (1878) 3 C.P.D. 450; *Cotter v Bank of England* (1833) 3 Moo. & S. 180.

[619] *Mitchell v Hayne* (1824) 2 Sim. & S. 63; *Moore v Usher* (1835) 7 Sim. 383. But cf. *Best v Hayes* (1863) 1 H. & C. 718, Illustration 6.

Illustrations

7-104 (1) An agent has funds in his hands, upon which a third person claims to have been given a lien by the principal. The agent may interplead as against his principal and the third person.[620]

(2) A instructs a stockbroker to sell shares, and sends him the share certificate and blank transfers. The shares are claimed by B, who alleges that they were obtained from him by fraud. A sues the broker, claiming the return of the certificate and transfers. The broker may interplead.[621]

(3) A, a part-owner of a vessel, instructs B, a broker, to insure the vessel. B receives an amount due under the policy in respect of a loss, and the whole of the amount is claimed by A. A sues B for the whole amount, and certain other part-owners sue him for part thereof. B may interplead.[622]

(4) A deposits goods with B, a wharfinger, and afterwards requests him to transfer them to the name of C, reserving to himself a right to draw samples. B enters the goods in C's name. D then claims them as paramount owner, and A acquiesces in his claim. C also claims them. B may interplead as against C and D.[623]

(5) A entrusted a policy to B for a specified purpose. C, who had pledged the policy with A, and A each brought an action against B for the policy. Held, that B was entitled to interplead.[624]

(6) A, an auctioneer, sells goods on behalf of B, and whilst a portion of the proceeds is still in his hands, receives notice of a claim by C. B sues A for the balance of the proceeds. A may deduct his expenses and charges and interplead as to the residue.[625]

(7) Two estate agents claim commission in respect of the sale of the same property. There is a possibility that the vendor may be under an obligation to pay commission to both. He may not interplead.[626]

---

[620] *Smith v Hammond* (1833) 6 Sim. 10.

[621] *Robinson v Jenkins* (1890) 24 Q.B.D. 275.

[622] *Suart v Welch* (1839) 4 My. & C. 305.

[623] *Mason v Hamilton* (1831) 5 Sim. 19; *Pearson v Cardon* (1831) 2 Russ. & M. 606; *Ex p. Mersey Docks and Harbour Board* [1899] 1 Q.B. 546.

[624] *Tanner v European Bank* (1866) L.R. 1 Ex. 261.

[625] *Best v Hayes* (1863) 1 H. & C. 718; cf. *Mitchell v Hayne* (1824) 2 Sim. & S. 63; *Wright v Freeman* (1879) 48 L.J.Q.B. 276; *Ingham v Walker* (1887) 3 T.L.R. 448 (claims against auctioneer not co-extensive; seller claims price paid, buyer claims damages).

[626] *Greatorex & Co v Shackle* [1895] 2 Q.B. 249; *Dominion Factors Pty Ltd v L.J. Hooker Ltd* [1963] N.S.W.R. 573.

Chapter 8

RELATIONS BETWEEN PRINCIPALS AND THIRD PARTIES

1. Contract

Article 71

Disclosed Principal: General Rule

(1) A disclosed principal, whether identified or unidentified, may sue or be sued   **8-001**
on any contract made on the principal's behalf by an agent acting within the
scope of the agent's actual authority or whose acts are validly ratified.[1]

(2) So far as concerns deeds, bills of exchange, promissory notes and cheques, this
Article must be read subject to Articles 77 and 78.

Comment

Rule (1) This Article states the basic principle of contractual agency—that an   **8-002**
agent acting within the scope of the agent's actual authority, express or implied,
binds and entitles the principal. As such it does no more than link up this section
with Chapter 3, where many relevant authorities will be found. Ratification will
also, subject to the rules peculiar to that branch of the law, achieve the same result.[2]
The usual explanation of the rights and liabilities of the principal is that on an objective interpretation of the dealings involved the principal has in fact made the
contract, and this explanation is, if the action used be regarded as contractual,
indeed made necessary by the doctrine of consideration and the related rules of privity of contract.[3] But it is by no means clear that it disposes of all the difficulties. The
plain fact is that business convenience requires that one person be in some cases
liable and entitled on the contract of another; it is potentially to the benefit of both
parties that the dealings of an authorised agent are mutually binding. The historical evolution of the above rule has been complex.[4]

Rule (1), though stating a standard principle, applies only where the agent acted
as such. It is not always clear on the facts when this is so. If the agent acts specifically, whether orally or in writing, on behalf of a principal whom the agent names,
then the conclusions inherent in the principle will normally follow. If the principal

---

[1] cf. *Restatement, Third*, § 6.01. See also Article 92. In the case of an unidentified principal, there may
occasionally be difficulty in determining for whom the agent acted. The problem is referred to under
the heading of "Ratification", above, para.2-067.

[2] See Ch.2, Section 3.

[3] See *Freeman & Lockyer v Buckhurst Park Properties (Mangal) Ltd* [1964] 2 Q.B. 480 at 502.

[4] See Ch.1; Powell, pp.148–150; Stoljar, pp.32–41.

is unidentified, it may be necessary to prove who the principal was and that the agent intended to act for that person.[5] If a person who might be an agent is simply named without more in a contract (which in such circumstances is more likely to be in writing) the first assumption will usually be that that person is in fact acting as a party to the contract and will be liable and entitled on it.[6] It is possible, however, that that party may, despite a lack of indication in the writing, be acting not as principal but as agent: and it may be argued that the contractual matrix surrounding the agent's dealing with the third party gave the third party reason to know that the agent dealt only as the principal's representative.[7] Even if the parol evidence rule were applied to the document,[8] evidence may be given as to the capacity in which the parties acted. Clear evidence would be required of the understanding of the parties and of the identity of the principal for whom the agent was acting.

The situations described above should not be confused with a true undisclosed principal situation. The latter occurs where a party undoubtedly makes a contract as principal, but in doing so is in fact authorised by a further principal the existence or relevance of whom the agent does not disclose. In such a case, unless the contract is one impliedly confined to the parties,[9] the undisclosed principal is liable and entitled on the contract in addition to (or perhaps alternatively to) the agent. In such a case proof that the agent had actual authority, and that the contract is not confined to the parties, will be crucial. The specialised doctrine of the undisclosed principal is considered in Article 76.

In recent cases it has been common to make a reservation for situations referred to above, where the name of the principal is established by extrinsic evidence supplementing or displacing a name in a (usually written) contract, and suggest that the interpretation does not apply where the terms of the contract unequivocally and exhaustively define the parties to it, or some similar phrase.[10] This is plainly connected with the rule excluding the intervention of an undisclosed principal referred to above.[11] The situations are however different.[12] In the undisclosed principal situation the contract is by definition with the agent, and the question is whether its terms are inconsistent with the intervention of another person as principal, bearing in mind that the first or original principal, who turns out to be an agent, is certainly

---

[5] See *Teheran-Europe Co Ltd v ST Belton (Tractors) Co Ltd* [1969] 2 Q.B. 545 at 355–356; below, para.9-016. The latter problem of intention is discussed in connection with ratification, above para.2-067, and the undisclosed principal, below, para.8-072. The agent might sometimes be liable and entitled as well as the principal: see Article 98.

[6] See Articles 99 and 100. See also *Magellan Spirit ApS v Vitol SA* [2016] EWHC 454 (Comm); [2016] 1 Lloyd's Rep. 1 at [28].

[7] See, e.g. *Filatona Trading Ltd v Navigator Equities Ltd* [2020] EWCA Civ 109 (where however some of what is said by Simon LJ refers to undisclosed principals, who attract different rules: see below). See also *Humfrey v Dale* (1857) 7 E.&B. 266 at 275 (affirmed (1858) E.B.&E. 1004); *Internaut Shipping GmbH v Fercometal SARL* [2003] 2 Lloyd's Rep. 430 at [56]; *Hamid v Francis Bradshaw Partnership* [2013] EWCA Civ 470; [2013] B.L.R. 447 at [50]–[57]; *Aspen Underwriting Ltd v Kairos Shipping Co Ltd* [2018] EWHC 590; [2019] 1 Lloyd's Rep. 221 at [46] (point not in issue [2020] UKSC 110); *Turks Shipyard Ltd v Owners of the Vessel November* [2020] EWHC 661 (Admlty); *Bell v Ivy Technology Ltd* [2020] EWCA Civ 1563; *Restatement, Third, Agency*, para.6.01 at p.9.

[8] As to which, see *Chitty on Contracts* (33rd edn, 2018), paras 13-109 onwards.

[9] As to which see below, para.9-079.

[10] See the *Filatona* case [2020] EWCA Civ 109 at [62].

[11] See the *Filatona* case at first instance, [2019] EWHC 173 (Comm) at [64] where Teare J suggests that substantially the same principle should apply for cases involving disclosed principals.

[12] A complicating feature is that the "beneficial assumption" of Diplock LJ that the third party would normally be prepared to deal with anyone (below, para.8-079) treats all these situations together.

still liable and entitled on the contract. In the disclosed principal situation referred to above, the evidence establishes who the principal is, and (usually) that the agent is not liable: the question is whether there is any clause[13] or other feature of the contract which makes such an interpretation not possible.[14] It has been suggested that this would be difficult to establish.[15] But other dicta suggest that where the document is clear the proposition that external evidence can be deployed to contradict it may not be beyond argument.[16] It seems undesirable that courts encourage claimants to add parties to contract claims simply because those parties have a legal (e.g. shareholding) or economic connection to the named party in the hope of finding more evidence by the time of trial.[17] It is quite common, for instance, for an asset the subject of a contract to be owned by a party other than the promisor.[18] There should be no presumption that the promisor is the agent, disclosed or undisclosed, of the owner, especially where it is known that the named party is not the owner and the owner has done nothing to encourage a belief that it backs the promise.

Though it is often said that the agent "drops out" of an authorised transaction, there are in fact circumstances in which the agent is liable as well as the principal. These matters are considered in Articles 97 and 98.

Written evidence: Statute of Frauds. The old law   Under s.40 of the Law of **8-003** Property Act 1925, contracts for the sale of land and certain similar contracts were unenforceable without a note or memorandum, signed by the party to be charged. Such a document might instead be signed by an agent "thereunto by him lawfully authorised".[19] The cases on this provision and its predecessor, s.4 of the Statute of Frauds 1677, "decide that to satisfy the statute the agreement or memorandum must name or identify two parties who are contractually bound to each other".[20] Therefore, if an agent made an agreement in such terms that the agent was person-

---

[13] Examples are given in the *Filatona* case at [90]. But "entire agreement" clauses are not necessarily efficacious for either of the above two types of case: see *Aspen Underwriting Ltd v Kairos Shipping Co Ltd* [2018] EWCA Civ 2590; [2019] 1 Lloyd's Rep. 221 at [53] (point not in issue [2020] UKSC 11); *Kaefer Aislamientos SA de CV v AMS Drilling Mexico SA de CV* [2019] EWCA Civ 10; [2019] 1 W.L.R. 3514 at [113].
[14] For a clear explanation of this difference, see the judgment of Males LJ in the *Filatona* case, [2020] EWCA Civ 109.
[15] See the *Filatona* case in the Court of Appeal [2020] EWCA Civ 2590 at [126]; at first instance [2019] EWHC 173 (Comm) at [294].
[16] See *Taylor v Rhino Overseas Inc* [2020] EWCA Civ 353; [2020] Bus. L.R. 1486 at [46], per Arnold LJ; who contrasted the dicta of Jackson LJ in *Hamid v Francis Bradshaw Partnership* [2013] EWCA Civ 470; [2013] B.L.R. 447, above (a "more relaxed approach") with the dicta of Blair J in *Barbudev v Eurocom Cable Management Bulgarian Food* [2011] EWHC 1560 (Comm); [2011] 2 All E.R. (Comm) 951 at [114] (against admission of extrinsic evidence). See too *Americas Bulk Transport Ltd (Liberia) v Cosco Bulk Carrier Ltd (China) MV Grand Fortune* [2020] EWHC 147 (Comm) at [19]. The dicta of Jackson LJ are followed in *Gregor Fisken Ltd v Carl* [2020] EWHC 1385 (Comm); and *Maftoon (t/a Fm Construction Services) v Sayed* [2020] EWHC 1801 (TCC) at [66].
[17] See further above, para.1-030.
[18] See, e.g. *Foster v Action Aviation Ltd* [2014] EWCA Civ 1368 at [38]–[39]; *Taylor v Rhino Overseas Inc* [2020] EWCA Civ 353; [2020] Bus. L.R. 1486 at [51]. cf. *Turks Shipyard Ltd v Owners of the Vessel November* [2020] EWHC 661 (Admlty) at [16]; *The Swan* [1968] 1 Lloyd's Rep. 5 at 14, Illustration 6 to Article 98 (dealings directly with owner, but see footnote on this case in para.9-034, below).
[19] As to authorisation of such an agent, see above, para.2-019.
[20] *Basma v Weekes* [1950] A.C. 441 at 454, per Lord Reid.

ally liable as a contracting party, the memorandum would satisfy the statute,[21] and would not cease to do so because the other party knew that the agent was acting as an agent.[22] In such a case, and also in the case where the principal was undisclosed, the contract was enforceable by or against either principal or agent, for the effect of the introduction of the principal was to add the liability of a new party to the agent's already existing liability.[23] But where the agreement was made by the agent in such terms that the agent was not personally liable as a contracting party, the principal could sue or be sued only if the principal's name appeared in the memorandum, or if, from the description therein, the principal's identity as a party was clear.[24] Thus where an agent signed as agent for an unnamed principal, there might be no memorandum satisfying the statute, unless a custom existed making the agent personally liable in a manner not inconsistent with the form of signature, so that the agent's signature alone could suffice.[25]

The same rules presumably applied and still apply to contracts of guarantee, which were also governed by the Statute of Frauds, and remain so governed, the wording of which regarding authorisation is the same as that later reproduced in s.40.[26]

8-004   **The new law**   Section 40 of the 1925 Act was however repealed and replaced by s.2 of the Law of Property (Miscellaneous Provisions) Act 1989, which requires that such contracts actually be in writing, signed by each party. This provision also allows signature by agents, but in different words: it requires that the signature be "by or on behalf of each party to the contract". It does not require that the agent has written authority.[27] Although the Law Commission Working Paper which eventually led to the Act avowed an intention to "let the ordinary principles of agency operate"[28] it is not clear how they do so. If the agent signs for a principal who is named, the matter is straightforward.[29] At the other extreme, if the agent signs "as agent only" and no principal is named in or identifiable from the document, the contract is presumably not in writing, the name of one of the parties being missing. But if the agent signs in such a way as to be personally liable, but is also stated to be acting on behalf of an unidentified principal, or is in fact acting on behalf of a completely undisclosed principal, situations where the memorandum may have been adequate under the previous law, the situation is more difficult of analysis. It can be said that

---

[21]   *Filby v Hounsell* [1896] 2 Ch. 737, as interpreted by Younger LJ in *Lovesey v Palmer* [1916] 2 Ch. 233.

[22]   *Basma v Weekes* [1950] A.C. 441; disapproving dicta of Luxmoore LJ in *Smith-Bird v Blower* [1939] 2 All E.R. 406; *Davies v Sweet* [1962] 2 Q.B. 300.

[23]   *Higgins v Senior* (1841) 8 M. & W. 834; *Calder v Dobell* (1871) L.R. 6 C.P. 486; *Basma v Weekes* [1950] A.C. 441. See also *Morris v Wilson* (1859) 5 Jur.(N.S.) 168.

[24]   *Lovesey v Palmer* [1916] 2 Ch. 233.

[25]   See *Dale v Humfrey* (1857) 7 E. & B. 266; affirmed (1858) E.B. & E. 1004; Article 100.

[26]   See *Bateman v Phillips* (1812) 15 East 272; *Garrett v Handley* (1825) 4 B. & C. 664. See also *Marginson v Ian Potter & Co* (1976) 136 C.L.R. 161 (where principal already liable, his promise to pay was not a guarantee). An agent may have authority to sign for both parties: above, para.2-014. As to a solicitor's authority see above, para.3-023, Illustration 9 and para.3-032, Illustrations 5 and 6; as to estate agents, para.3-032, Illustration 7.

[27]   See *McLaughlin v Duffill* [2008] EWCA Civ 1627; [2010] Ch.1.

[28]   *Law Com.W.P. No. 92* (1985), s.5.16.

[29]   For the position where an agent signs on behalf of a company not yet formed and is liable under s.51 of the Companies Act 2006, see *Braymist Ltd v Wise Finance Ltd* [2002] EWCA Civ 127; [2002] Ch. 273. A signature as agent was held sufficient to enable the agent (a solicitor) to sign: the agent was the "statutory deemed vendor". See below, para.9-086.

the change from a mere requirement of authorisation to the wording "by or on behalf of" means that the signature must now be avowedly "on behalf of" the party concerned, and hence that in neither of the above cases can the principal now sue or be sued. This seems consonant with the policy of the Act of requiring that the full terms of the contract be in writing, rather than merely evidenced by a note or memorandum.[30] But it can be argued alternatively that an agent signs "on behalf of" the principal whenever the agent signs with authority to do so and intending to act for the principal. On this basis the previous law remains valid, and unnamed or undisclosed principals may enforce the contract or have it enforced against them. If that is so, it is then, however, necessary to inquire whether or not the unnamed or undisclosed principal is a party to the contract entered into by the agent, or to some other contract: for if it was to some other contract, writing and signature would be required for that. It seems clear that the undisclosed principal is a party to the same contract as the agent[31]; and although doubt may now be cast on whether the unidentified principal of an agent who undertakes personal liability is a person alternatively as opposed to cumulatively liable, as older cases suggest, it is clear that the principal's liability, whether joint or joint and several, is normally on the same contract as that of the agent.[32] The view that the law has been changed (albeit without this being stated in the relevant Law Commission reports[33]) seems the more natural reading of the provision, but that result could cause considerable inconvenience, since purchasers of land often wish to remain incognito.

The provisions of s.2 do not apply to sales by public auction[34] and hence it appears that no writing is needed for such sales.[35]

Cases where agent also liable and entitled In this context, the fact that the principal instructs an agent who operates in a market by the rules or customs of which the agent is personally liable and entitled on contracts which the agent makes within it does not of itself exclude the principal's right to sue and be sued, for the agent's rights and duties are simply additional to those of the principal and not inconsistent with them.[36] If the rules or customs require that the agent be solely liable and entitled, and the principal knows of them, the principal may be regarded as instructing the agent on that basis.[37] If, however, the principal does not know of them, assent is assumed to be only to such rules or customs as are reasonable,[38] and such a rule may as against an outsider sometimes not be.[39]

8-005

Foreign principal Certain nineteenth-century cases held that a foreign principal

8-006

---

[30] *Spiro v Glencrown Properties Ltd* [1991] Ch. 537 at 541. The requirements for satisfying s.2 are laid down in *Commission for the New Towns v Cooper (GB) Ltd* [1995] Ch. 259.
[31] Article 76.
[32] See Comment to Article 98.
[33] See *Law Com.W.P. No.92* (1985); *Law Com. No. 164* (1987).
[34] 1989 Act s.2(5)(b).
[35] It is arguable that s.40 of the 1925 Act is not repealed in the case of public auctions, since the repealing provision (s.2(8)) appears in s.2, which by its own wording does not apply to sales by public auction. But s.2(8) also states in brackets that it supersedes s.40 and this is probably enough to prevent what would be a surprising result.
[36] See, e.g. *Levitt v Hamblet* [1901] 2 K.B. 53 as an example of many cases concerning the former rules of the London Stock Exchange. And see in general below, para.9-016.
[37] As in *Morrison, Kekewich & Co v Mendel* (1888) 5 T.L.R. 153.
[38] Article 31.
[39] See *Morrison, Kekewich & Co v Mendel* (1888) 5 T.L.R. 153, above. But cf. *Cunliffe-Owen v Teather & Greenwood* [1967] 1 W.L.R. 1421 (usage that only members can declare options reasonable).

could neither sue nor be sued on an agent's contracts. The rule was based on the notions that such a principal did not authorise an English agent to establish privity of contract between the principal and English contracting parties; and that the English contracting party did not authorise its agent to establish privity of contract with foreign dealers. Therefore the agent was personally the contracting party and there was not in form any exception to normal agency principles. The rule, if such it was, is now obsolete, though the fact that the principal is foreign may be relevant to the question whether the agent is liable in addition to the principal. Since the case law was, and what remains still is, principally relevant to the liability of the agent rather than that of the principal, it is dealt with under Article 98.

8-007 **Knowledge of third party that agent not authorised** If the principal does something indicating the withdrawal of authority, but does not communicate this to the agent, between the agent and the principal the agent still has actual authority and is not liable to the principal for exercising it. But if in such circumstances that withdrawal of authority comes to the notice of the third party, the third party probably cannot hold the principal liable, not only as regards apparent authority[40] but also on principles of actual authority.[41]

8-008 **Rule (2)** The general rule is displaced in the case of deeds and negotiable instruments, where special significance is attached to the wording of the documents used. These are therefore dealt with separately in Articles 77 and 78.

Article 72

APPARENT (OR OSTENSIBLE) AUTHORITY

8-009 Where a person, P, by words or conduct, represents or permits it to be represented that another person, A, has authority to act on P's behalf, P is bound by the acts of A with respect to anyone dealing with A as an agent on the faith of any such representation, to the same extent as if A had the authority that A was represented to have, even though A had no such actual authority.[42]

Comment

8-010 **Doctrine of apparent authority** This Article seeks to formulate the general doctrine of apparent (sometimes called alternatively ostensible) authority. It should be read together with the three Articles following, and with Article 121 that deals with apparent authority lingering after an agent's authority has been terminated.

---

[40] Article 72.

[41] See Wright (1937) 15 Can.B.R. 196, criticising *Robert Simpson Co v Godson* [1937] 1 D.L.R. 454 (to the contrary effect); *Restatement, Second,* § 7, Comment *d,* § 144, Comment *e.* (cf. *Restatement, Third,* § 3.11). See also above, para.2-032.

[42] See *Pickering v Busk* (1812) 15 East 38; *Pickard v Sears* (1837) 6 A. & E. 469; *Reynell v Lewis* (1846) 15 M. & W. 517; *Freeman v Cooke* (1848) 2 Exch. 654; *Smith v M'Guire* (1858) 3 H. & N. 554; *Robinson v Tyson* (1888) 9 L.R. (N.S.W.) 297; *International Paper Co v Spicer* (1906) 4 C.L.R. 739; *Freeman & Lockyer v Buckhurst Park Properties (Mangal) Ltd* [1964] 2 Q.B. 480; *Hely-Hutchinson v Brayhead Ltd* [1968] 1 Q.B. 549; *R. v Charles* [1977] A.C. 177 at 183; *Armagas Ltd v Mundogas SA (The Ocean Frost)* [1986] A.C. 717 at 777. For consideration of policy issues, see Hetherington (1966) 19 Stanford L.Rev. 76; Rubenstein (1958) 44 A.B.A.J. 849; Lipson (1999) 33 Georgia L.Rev. 1219; Watts [2015] L.M.C.L.Q. 36.

Under this doctrine a principal may be bound by the acts of an agent which the principal has not authorised, and has even forbidden. Most western systems of law have found the necessity for some type of reasoning which at least imposes liability, if it does not confer the right to sue, in situations such as those covered by this doctrine. The English version is plainly based on the notion of a representation by the principal. The leading case, which is constantly cited, is *Freeman & Lockyer v Buckhurst Park Properties (Mangal) Ltd*,[43] in which Diplock LJ said:

> "An 'apparent' or 'ostensible' authority ... is a legal relationship between the principal and the contractor created by a representation, made by the principal to the contractor, intended to be and in fact acted upon by the contractor, that the agent has authority to enter on behalf of the principal into a contract of a kind within the scope of the 'apparent' authority, so as to render the principal liable to perform any obligations imposed upon him by such contract. To the relationship so created the agent is a stranger. He need not be (although he generally is) aware of the existence of the representation but he must not purport to make the agreement as principal himself. The representation, when acted upon by the contractor by entering into a contract with the agent, operates as an estoppel, preventing the principal from asserting that he is not bound by the contract. It is irrelevant whether the agent had actual authority to enter into the contract."[44]

Restatement, Third distances itself from the notion of representation used above by referring to situations "where the third party reasonably believes that the actor has authority to act on behalf of the principal and that belief is traceable to the principal's manifestations".[45] This, with its use of the more neutral word "manifestation"[46] is probably, because it is less specific, a better formulation of the notion, common to most legal systems but uneasy in its justification, that apparent authority stems in some way from the principal's conduct.[47]

Applicable outside contract   The above dictum concerns contract, where the   **8-011**
main application of the doctrine is to be found. While the operation of the doctrine arises most often in connection with the formation of contracts, it also arises in relation to the performance of an existing contract.[48] The doctrine can also apply in respect of transfers of property[49]; and sometimes in other contexts as well, including in a limited way in tort[50] and the giving and receiving of notices.[51] However, subject to true estoppel and restitutionary defences, the recipient of a gift from an

---

[43]   *Freeman & Lockyer v Buckhurst Park Properties (Mangal) Ltd* [1964] 2 Q.B. 480, Illustration 31. See also *East Asia Co Ltd v PT Satria Tirtatama Energindo* [2019] UKPC 30 at [41]–[43].
[44]   *Freeman & Lockyer v Buckhurst Park Properties (Mangal) Ltd* [1964] 2 Q.B. 480 at 503.
[45]   §§ 2.03 and 3.03.
[46]   Discussed in § 1.03.
[47]   See below, para.8-028. See PECL, art.3:201; UNIDROIT Principles, art.2.2.5(2); DCFR, II, 6:103. As to the UNIDROIT Principles, see *Commentary on the UNIDROIT PICC* (Vogenauer and Kleinhesterkamp eds, 2009), Ch.2, Section 2; *The Unauthorised Agent* (Busch and Macgregor eds, 2009); and Reynolds (2009) 13 Eur. Rev. Private Law 975.
[48]   See, e.g. *Martin v Artyork Investments Ltd* [1997] 2 S.C.R. 290 (apparent authority to borrow, but lender needs also to ensure that draw down is by an authorised person); *Acute Property Developments Ltd v Apostolou* [2013] EWHC 200 (Ch) (manager's authority to direct payment of debt owed to principal to other person); *Pourzand v Telstra Corp Ltd* [2014] WASCA 14 (lessee's property manager authorising lessor to make building alterations); *Lo v Russell* [2016] VSCA 323 (estate agent's apparent authority to receive cooling-off notice).
[49]   Article 83.
[50]   Article 90.
[51]   See, e.g. *Aldford House Freehold Ltd v Grosvenor (Mayfair) Estate* [2019] EWCA Civ 1848; [2020] 2 W.L.R. 116 at [53] (giving of notice); and Article 94 (receiving notice). See also *Ciban Manage-*

agent purportedly on behalf of a principal needs to prove actual authority in the agent, not apparent.[52]

8-012 **Liability only** Normally, of course, the actual and apparent authority will coincide, and it will be unnecessary for the doctrine of apparent authority to be invoked. But when it is, the full consequences of the agency relationship do not flow, for the doctrine is primarily concerned with the question whether the principal is bound,[53] and the burden of proof is on the person alleging it.[54] Apparent authority is not therefore the same as implied authority, though older cases did not always make the distinction now recognised, or at least in the form in which it is now recognised: in the judgments, recourse was more often had to the notion of the wide implied authority of a general agent.[55] Even some more recent cases have tended to confuse the two.[56] Therefore, although apparent authority has twice been mentioned, and juxtaposed with actual authority, in the discussion of the agent's authority,[57] its main treatment is here. It is further developed in the specialised context of dispositions of property by the agent in Article 83. Reference should also be made to Article 121, where the application of the doctrine in cases of termination of authority is discussed.

It will be seen also that the formulation is redolent of estoppel, and that this explanation of the doctrine receives articulate support from the dictum of Diplock LJ quoted. There are however some difficulties with this explanation in modern times, as will appear: the matter is reverted to after the formulation has been analysed.[58]

8-013 **Represents by words or conduct (including course of dealing)** There must be a representation, or in *Restatement, Third* terms, a manifestation.[59] This seems to occur in three main ways. It may be express (whether orally or in writing)[60]; or implied from a course of dealing[61]; or it may be made "by permitting the agent to act in some way in the conduct of the principal's business with other persons".[62]

---

ment Corp v Citco (BVI) Ltd [2020] UKPC 21; [2020] 3 W.L.R. 705 at [28].

[52] See *High Commissioner for Pakistan in the United Kingdom v Prince Muffakham Jah* [2019] EWHC 2551 (Ch); [2020] 2 W.L.R. 699 at [247]. See further, Articles 83 and 88.

[53] But see below, para.8-029.

[54] See above, para.3-007.

[55] See above, para.1-045.

[56] See, e.g. *Ryan v Pilkington* [1959] 1 W.L.R. 403; and explanations of that case in *Burt v Claude Cousins & Co Ltd* [1971] 2 Q.B. 426 at 438, 448–449, 454; *Barrington v Lee* [1972] 1 Q.B. 326 at 336, 341; and *Sorrell v Finch* [1977] A.C. 728.

[57] Comments to Articles 1 and 22.

[58] Below, para.8-027.

[59] See above, para.8-010. See also Dal Pont, para.20.18 onwards.

[60] Illustrations 13 and 22.

[61] See the cases collected in Illustrations 7 and 21. See too *International Sponge Importers Ltd v Watt & Sons* [1911] A.C. 279 at 285; *Pharmed Medicare Private Ltd v Univar Ltd* [2002] EWCA Civ 1569; [2003] 1 All E.R. (Comm) 321 (larger order than usual: principal still liable); *Lovett v Carson Country Homes Ltd* [2009] EWHC 1143 (Ch); [2009] 2 B.C.L.C. 19; *Russell Gould Pty Ltd v Ramangkura (No.2)* [2015] NSWCA 14 at [10]; *Ukraine v Law Debenture Trust Plc* [2018] EWCA Civ 2026; [2019] 2 W.L.R. 655 at [99]; *Ciban Management Corp v Citco (BVI) Ltd* [2020] UKPC 21; [2020] 3 W.L.R. 705 at [27] (course of conduct in issuing powers of attorney for a company).

[62] *Freeman & Lockyer v Buckhurst Park Properties (Mangal) Ltd* [1964] 2 Q.B. 480 at 503 (managing director); *East Asia Co Ltd v PT Satria Tirtatama Energindo* [2019] UKPC 30 at [43]. See, e.g. *Collen v Gardner* (1856) 21 Beav. 540 (steward); *Howard v Sheward* (1886) 2 C.P. 148; *Baldry v*

There is a statement of Lord Cranworth in *Pole v Leask*,[63] and another of Robert Goff LJ in *Armagas Ltd v Mundogas SA*,[64] which suggest that a mere course of dealing is not sufficient to establish apparent authority, at least with an agent who is not an employee or has not held a standing position. Lord Cranworth's judgment in *Pole v Leask* is undoubtedly an important one in the development of agency law, but on this issue (crucial to the outcome of the case) the judgment was a dissenting one. The remarks of Robert Goff LJ on the point were certainly obiter dicta. The weight of authority supports a course of dealing being sufficient to create apparent authority, at least where it can be inferred that the principal must have become aware of the earlier transactions and the transactions are of a consistent type.[65] But the position will be different where it is no part of the agent's role to be representing anything on behalf of the principal, such as where the agent is a mere conduit or messenger.[66] There will be other cases where circumstances will make it unsafe to assume that an agent holds any ongoing authority.[67] A further way in which such a representation may be made, by entrusting the agent with the indicia of ownership of property, is dealt with in connection with dispositions of property; suffice to say that mere possession of property or documents of title is not usually by itself a sufficient representation of an entitlement to deal with them.[68] The representation need not identify the principal by name, and can refer to a trading name used by the principal.[69]

Two types of case   If the doctrine is based on the idea of representation, it may **8-014** be suggested that the cases can be divided into two types. First, and this category embraces the first two types of representation above, cases where there is something that can be said to be something like a genuine representation (orally, in writing, by course of dealing or by allowing the agent to act in certain ways, e.g. entrusting him with the conduct of particular negotiations[70] or allowing him to run a business that appears to be the principal's business[71]) by the principal of the agent's authority, on which the third party relies: such cases could be called cases of "genuine apparent authority" and more easily (but not always perfectly) based on estoppel. Secondly, cases where the representation is only of a very general nature, and arises only from the principal's putting the agent in a specific position carrying with it a usual authority,[72] e.g. placing the agent in a certain physical position

---

Bates (1885) 52 L.T. 620 (horse dealers).
[63] *Pole v Leask* (1863) 33 L.J. Ch. 155 at 162 HL.
[64] *Armagas Ltd v Mundogas SA* [1986] A.C. 717 at 732–733.
[65] See further, Watts [2015] L.M.C.L.Q. 36.
[66] See *Spooner v Browning* [1898] 1 Q.B. 528, Article 75, Illustration 1 (mere authority of junior clerk to communicate acceptance did not by repeat dealings away from principal's premises create representation that there had in fact been a further acceptance); *Marme Inversiones 2007 SL v Natwest Markets Plc* [2019] EWHC 366 (Comm) at [421].
[67] See Article 121. cf. *Barrett v Irvine* [1907] 2 I.R. 462.
[68] See Articles 83–85.
[69] See *Winter v Hockley Mint Ltd* [2018] EWCA Civ 2480; [2019] 1 W.L.R. 1617 at [78].
[70] *Crabb v Arun DC* [1976] Ch. 179 at 183; *IRC v Ufitec Group Ltd* [1977] 3 All E.R. 924; *Egyptian International Foreign Trade Co v P.S. Refson & Co Ltd (The Raffaella)* [1985] 1 Lloyd's Rep. 36 at 41 (Illustration 11); *Magripilis v Baird* [1926] St.R.Qd. 89 at 96 (HC of A.: "accredited as his legal agents and medium of communication").
[71] *Gurtner v Beaton* [1993] 2 Lloyd's Rep. 369, Illustration 5.
[72] See Articles 29 and 30.

on the principal's business premises, or making the agent a partner[73] or managing director,[74] or using the services of a professional agent, viz. someone whose occupation normally gives an agent a usual authority to do things of a certain type, e.g. a solicitor.[75] It is said that:

> "by so doing the principal represents to anyone who becomes aware that the agent is so acting that the agent has authority to enter on behalf of the principal into contracts with other persons of the kind which an agent so acting in the course of his principal's business has usually 'actual' authority to enter into."[76]

Here the notion of representation to the third party is more tenuous and the connection of the principal's liability with estoppel more difficult to maintain.[77] It seems further that in this category the authority which the third party is entitled to infer is that which would normally be implied between principal and agent, and it is of this that the court receives evidence. But the third party may be quite ignorant of what authority would be so implied, e.g. of what authority a "branch manager" of an insurance company normally has,[78] and is not required to testify to the third party's own knowledge.

8-015 **Representation need not be deliberate** The foregoing analysis suggests that the words of Diplock LJ, which appear to require that the representation be deliberate, and certainly say that it must be actually intended to be acted on, are too narrow. This wording does not appear elsewhere in the judgment.

8-016 **Totality of conduct to be looked at** It is important to note that the above two categories are not mutually exclusive. There may be additional representations by the principal, peculiar to the case in question, over and above the putting into a position carrying usual authority. Where it is not clear what authority a person in the particular position would normally have, such factors may be crucial:

> "But where, as in the present case, the holding out is alleged to consist of a course of conduct wider than merely describing the agent as holding a particular office, although the authority normally found in the holder of such an office is very material, it must be looked at as part and parcel of the whole course of the principal's conduct in order to decide whether the totality of the principal's actions constitute a holding out of the agent as possessing the necessary authority."[79]

The representation will normally be of an authority of some generality: although there is no reason why there should not be a representation of authority to enter into

---

[73] Partnership Act 1890 ss.5 and 14.

[74] *Hely-Hutchinson v Brayhead Ltd* [1968] 1 Q.B. 549 at 583.

[75] *Waugh v H.B. Clifford & Sons Ltd* [1982] Ch. 374, Illustration 16; *Seiwa Australia Pty Ltd v Beard* (2010) 75 N.S.W.L.R. 74 at [257] (usual business of accountancy partnership).

[76] *Freeman & Lockyer v Buckhurst Park Properties (Mangal) Ltd* [1964] 2 Q.B. 480 at 503, per Diplock LJ.

[77] See below. See further as to this distinction above, para.3-005.

[78] See *British Bank of the Middle East v Sun Life Insurance Co of Canada (UK) Ltd* [1983] 2 Lloyd's Rep. 9 HL (Illustration 10 to Article 75), a harsh decision for this reason. See also *Restatement, Third*, § 3.03 Comment *d*; *Cleveland Manufacturing Co v Muslim Commercial Bank Ltd* [1981] 2 Lloyd's Rep. 646 (shipping agent); *Ricci Burns Ltd v Toole* [1989] 1 W.L.R. 993 at 1007.

[79] *Egyptian International Foreign Trade Co v Soplex Wholesale Supplies Ltd (The Raffaella)* [1985] 2 Lloyd's Rep. 36, Illustration 11; *Gurtner v Beaton* [1993] 2 Lloyd's Rep. 369 at 379; *Pacific Carriers Ltd v BNP Paribas* (2004) 218 C.L.R. 451 at [35], Illustration 2 to Article 21 (a case that on the facts took a very generous view of what was a holding out—see above, para.2-106).

a specific transaction only, such a case would be rare, especially where the third party knows of the lack of general authority.[80] It is implicit in the above statement that, in considering the totality of the circumstances, a court will have as much regard to negative indicators of authority as to positive ones.[81]

Ingredients of representation must be sufficient to warrant reliance It has **8-017** been seen in the preceding paragraphs that the range of facts that might be used to establish a representation of authority is very broad indeed. It has also been seen that more than one indicium of authority may be needed to constitute an effective representation. What is implicit in that conclusion is that the evidence used to justify an assertion of authority in an agent must be adequate, which carries the further implication that reliance on that evidence must have been reasonable: "[T]he starting point is that the principal must be shown to have made a representation, which the third party could and did reasonably rely on, that the agent had the necessary authority".[82]

Beyond the criterion of adequacy or reasonableness, much will turn on the facts of the particular case. Guidance is best obtained by examples and a wide range of Illustrations is provided at the end of this Article. However, the case law has thrown up a number of issues of broad application. Hence, mere possession of a principal's property, even by someone who has some agency functions, does not amount to a holding out of any right to deal with the property. This issue and a number of others are dealt with in the paragraphs which follow. The incremental way in which the common law develops has meant that there are other issues that remain unsettled. Some of these involve written communications. The ubiquity of letterhead (paper or electronic) within most businesses means that it would not normally be safe to rely on letterhead alone as representing that the writer has authority to bind the principal whose letterhead it is.[83] A business card that is genuine and gives an agent's status may, however, be an adequate representation,[84] and uniforms have similarly been treated as having at least some effect as a representation.[85] Less clarity attends the issue of a document (paper or electronic) which has been written by the principal or by someone who had actual authority to write it but that is then sent off or handed over prematurely (by accident or

[80] See *Armagas Ltd v Mundogas SA (The Ocean Frost)* [1986] A.C. 717 at 777.
[81] See, e.g. *Kop-Coat New Zealand Ltd v Incodo Ltd* [2018] NZCA 430 at [52] (no holding out of general manager where form of contract contemplated signature of directors); *Stavrinides v Bank of Cyprus Public Co Ltd* [2019] EWHC 1328 (Ch) at [107].
[82] *Egyptian International Foreign Trade Co v Soplex Wholesale Supplies Ltd (The Raffaella)* [1985] 2 Lloyd's Rep. 36 at 41; *Pourzand v Telstra Corp Ltd* [2014] WASCA 14 at [83]; *East Asia Co Ltd v PT Satria Tirtatama Energindo* [2019] UKPC 30; [2020] 2 All E.R. 294 at [42].
[83] *Kooragang Investments Pty Ltd v Richardson & Wrench Ltd* [1982] 1 A.C. 462 at 475; *Harvey v State of New South Wales* [2006] NSWSC 1436 at [176] (government stationery); *Quikfund (Australia) Pty Ltd v Chatswood Appliance Spare Parts Pty Ltd* [2013] NSWSC 646 (possession of lender's blank loan forms with authority to distribute them did not confer any authority to make representations); *Anderson v Sense Network Ltd* [2018] EWHC 2834 (Comm); [2019] Bus. L.R. 1601 at [217] (affirmed without reference to this point [2019] EWCA Civ 1395). cf. *F. Mildner & Sons v Noble* [1956] C.L.Y. 32; *The Times*, March 8, 1956, Illustration 2, where other cases are collected.
[84] *Martin v Britannia Life Ltd* [2000] Lloyd's Rep. P.N. 412 at [5.3.4]; *Derham v Amev Life Insurance Co Ltd* (1981) 56 F.L.R. 34; *Moneyworld NZ 2000 Ltd v Lee* (2005) 8 N.Z. Business L.C. 101,638; *Heperu Pty Ltd v Morgan Brooks Pty Ltd (No.2)* [2007] NSWSC 1438; reversed on other points in *Perpetual Trustees Australia Ltd v Heperu Pty Ltd* [2009] NSWCA 84 (holding out by webpage, letterhead and business cards).
[85] See *Rimell v Sampayo* (1824) 1 Car. & P. 253; *Aste v Montague* (1858) 1 F. & F. 264.

design) by another agent without actual authority to deliver it.[86] Modern technology will throw up other new issues. Information on genuine webpages might amount to a holding out as might an email from an appropriate person from a genuine e-address,[87] but it would not be safe to assume that correspondence with a contact-us address entitles one to rely on any response to an inquiry or on an assumption that the message has been passed on to the appropriate personnel for dealing with it.[88] It has been held that the mere fact that someone has access to one's password for the purpose of effecting electronic signatures does not create a representation that the person with access to the password has authority to apply the signature.[89]

8-018   **Authority to make representations as to authority of others**   The representation as to authority need not be made by the principal personally: it may obviously be made by an intermediate agent with actual authority to do so. More difficulties arise if the authority is apparent. It seems correct in principle to say that an agent can have apparent authority to make representations as to the authority of other agents, provided that agent's own authority can finally be traced back to a representation by the principal or to a person with actual authority from the principal to make it.[90] However, such apparent authority would in general only be attributed to a person who would normally have actual authority to act within that particular sphere of activity.[91] An agent would, therefore, not usually be regarded as having apparent authority, simply because the agent is or appears to be permitted to answer inquiries, or to attribute authority to another agent, unless involvement by the agent in the conduct of that business, or that part of the business to which the transaction related, was or appeared to be authorised.[92]

---

[86]   Compare *Smith v Prosser* [1907] 2 K.B. 735 (attorney in possession of promissory notes signed in blank but with instructions not to use them without telegraphed instructions, confers no rights when he fraudulently negotiates them) with the dicta in *Shearson Lehman Hutton Inc v Maclaine Watson & Co Ltd* [1988] 1 W.L.R. 16 at 28 HL.

[87]   See *Heperu Pty Ltd v Morgan Brooks Pty Ltd (No 2)* [2007] NSWSC 1438, above.

[88]   See *Goyal v Florence Care Ltd* [2020] EWHC 659 (Ch) at [138].

[89]   See *Williams Group Australia Pty Ltd v Crocker* [2016] NSWCA 265; *Frederick v Positive Solutions (Financial Services) Ltd* [2018] EWCA Civ 431 (agent's power to use principal's access to bank's online portal does not make principal liable for acts otherwise lacking apparent authority); *Ramsay v Love* [2015] EWHC 65 (Ch) at [117] (access to signing machine). See too *Colonial Bank v Cady and Williams* (1890) 15 App.Cas. 267 (signed share certificates not create an estoppel); *Ruben v Great Fingall Consolidated* [1905] A.C. 439 at 444 (possession of company seal no longer creating representation). cf. *Gurtner v Beaton* [1993] 2 Lloyd's Rep. 369 at 381 (agent answering company's listed telephone number held one factor in establishing a holding out).

[90]   There are, however, dicta appearing to require actual authority in the agent whose representation is relied on as creating apparent authority, in cases connected with companies. It is submitted that *Crabtree-Vickers Pty Ltd v Australian Direct Mail Advertising Co Ltd* (1975) 133 C.L.R. 72 may go too far in following these and requiring such actual authority, which need not exist except at the ultimate level: see [1983] J.B.L. 409; *Cromwell Corp Ltd v Sofrana Immobilier (NZ) Ltd* (1992) 6 N.Z. Company L.C. 67,997; *AJU Remicon Co Ltd v Alida Shipping Co Ltd* [2007] EWHC 2246 (Comm); and below, para.8-019.

[91]   This seems clear from *British Bank of the Middle East v Sun Life Assurance Co of Canada Ltd* [1983] 2 Lloyd's Rep. 9 (HL) (Illustration 10 to Article 75); see esp. 17. See, however, *Canadian Laboratory Supplies Ltd v Engelhard Industries of Canada Ltd* [1979] 2 S.C.R. 787; (1979) 97 D.L.R. (3d) 1, where the Supreme Court of Canada differed as to the effect of an inquiry as to an employee's authority to sell, made to a company's purchasing agent, while agreeing on the effect of that made to a Vice-President (Operations).

[92]   See also below, paras 8-019 and 8-020; *BP Oil International Ltd v Target Shipping Ltd* [2012]

No representation by agent personally, unless permitted by principal As **8-019**
already stated, the essence of apparent authority is an appearance emanating from
the principal. Therefore, the representation must be made by the principal, or by
another agent authorised to act for the principal, as described above. An agent cannot ordinarily self-authorise.

> "All 'ostensible" authority involves a representation by the principal as to the extent of
> the agent's authority. No representation by the agent as to the extent of his authority can
> amount to a 'holding out' by the principal."[93]

In the leading modern case, *Armagas Ltd v Mundogas SA (The Ocean Frost)*[94] the
agent was known to have no relevant authority and did not claim to have it, but
wrongly stated that he had gone away and obtained authority from his managing
director. It was held that there was no apparent authority.

The position can be different where the principal has in some way instigated or
permitted an agent to appear to have authority of the scope in question.[95] Routinely,
there will be some sort of representation by the principal present, if only in
maintaining business premises where the agent appears to be performing a role of
a usual type. But it may be sufficient if the principal has conferred a general authority of the precise type in question on the agent, which the principal is aware the
agent is regularly exercising, and there is nothing to indicate to the third party that
the transaction in question was other than routine.[96]

There will also be situations where the agent has usual authority, or has been
permitted by the principal, to communicate that those with actual authority have
exercised that authority.[97] Again, in many such cases there will have been a holding out by the principal. Otherwise, it is to be expected that the situations where
what might be termed a "communicating agent" has usual authority to bind a

---

EWHC 1590 (Comm) at [222]. But cf. *Kelly v Fraser* [2012] UKPC 25; [2013] 1 A.C. 450 (trustees
of company pension fund hold out company as their messenger for their decisions).

[93] *Att.-Gen. for Ceylon v Silva* [1953] A.C. 461 at 479, per Mr. L.M.D. de Silva. See also *Lanyon v
Blanchard* (1811) 2 Camp. 597; *Fay v Miller, Wilkins & Co* [1941] Ch. 360 at 365; *New Zealand
Tenancy Bonds Ltd v Mooney* [1986] 1 N.Z.L.R. 280; *Essfood v Crown Shipping (Ireland) Ltd* [1991]
I.L.R.M. 97; *East Asia Co Ltd v PT Satria Tirtatama Energindo* [2019] UKPC 30 at [61].

[94] *Armagas Ltd v Mundogas SA (The Ocean Frost)* [1986] A.C. 717, Illustration 11 to Article 75; *Savill
v Chase Holding (Wellington) Ltd* [1989] 1 N.Z.L.R. 257 CA affirmed PC; *British Bank of the Middle East v Sun Life Assurance Co of Canada (UK) Ltd* [1983] 2 Lloyd's Rep. 9 HL, Article 75, Illustration 10.

[95] *Colonial Bank v Cady and Williams* (1890) 15 App.Cas. 267 at 273; *De Tchihatchef v Salerni
Coupling Ltd* [1932] 1 Ch. 330 at 342; *Fay v Miller, Wilkins & Co* [1941] Ch. 360 at 365; *Freeman
& Lockyer v Buckhurst Park Properties (Mangal) Ltd* [1964] 2 Q.B. 480 at 505. cf. Partnership Act
1890 s.14(1). But see *Hely-Hutchinson v Brayhead Ltd* [1968] 1 Q.B. 549 at 563–564 (affirmed on
another ground at 573); *Canadian Laboratory Supplies Ltd v Engelhard Industries of Canada Ltd*
[1979] 2 S.C.R. 787 at 800; (1979) 97 D.L.R. (3d) 1 at 10. The latter dictum is discussed by Fridman (1983) 13 Manitoba L.J. 1.

[96] This is a possible explanation for *Hambro v Burnand* [1904] 2 K.B. 10, discussed above, para.3-
012, although the actual holding in that case is problematic on any basis. cf. *Farquharson Brothers
& Co v King & Co* [1902] A.C. 325, Illustration 6 to Article 84, where agency was undisclosed and
the third party was not an eligible counterparty; *Shortal v Buchanan* [1920] N.Z.L.R. 103, Illustration 5 to Article 25 where it was held land agents had no general authority to settle price for vendors.

[97] See *Kelly v Fraser* [2012] UKPC 25; [2013] 1 A.C. 450 at [12]; *Australia and New Zealand Banking Group Ltd v Frenmast Pty Ltd* [2013] NSWCA 459. See further, Watts [2015] L.M.C.L.Q. 36.
cf. *Allco Finance Group Ltd v Gothard* [2014] FCAFC 6 (director has no apparent authority to communicate more than receivers of company actually decided). See further in relation to companies,
para.8-039 below.

principal on the basis of reporting the decisions of others will be confined and likely to involve senior personnel, such as the role of company secretary.[98] There has been a suggestion, as yet not fully considered, that in such cases the third party may be entitled only to recovery for reliance losses.[99] The basis for drawing a distinction between negotiating agents and communicating agents, in this way, is not clear. The normal remedy, it is suggested, will be to recognise a contract and enforce it.[100]

8-020   **Qualifications and exceptions**   Qualifications, and perhaps exceptions, can be said to eat into such an apparently clear principle as that just addressed. Hence, there will be cases where an agent would normally have authority but only if certain facts were true, and the agent gives the impression that they are. The agent may have apparent authority to confirm that the preconditions are met. Some examples follow:

(1)   The master of a ship has authority to sign bills of lading, but frequently only if they are in accordance with mate's receipts, in particular as to date of shipment and condition on loading. A third party holder of the bill is entitled to rely on the master's signature as to such matters.[101] Equally, the master is only entitled to sign for goods that are on board: but his attestation that they were can be relied on.[102]

(2)   A manager of a business directs one of its debtors to pay a third party rather than the owner of the business. The debtor might be expected to ask for a reason why he is being asked not to pay the owner, but is entitled to believe the manager when a plausible answer is given.[103]

(3)   A solicitor may have actual authority to enter into a guarantee on behalf of his partners or employers if the firm holds the client's money or has good reason to expect that it will do so: the third party cannot know whether the underlying facts are true, yet may be able to rely on the solicitor's apparent authority if a reasonably careful and competent lender would have concluded that there was an appropriate underlying transaction.[104] There is also authority that finds that it is not usually necessary to go behind a

---

[98]   See, e.g. *Spooner v Browning* [1898] 1 Q.B. 528, Article 75, Illustration 1 (messenger too junior to bind principal).

[99]   See *Stavrinides v Bank of Cyprus Public Co Ltd* [2019] EWHC 1328 (Ch) at [100], adopting an argument in S. Worthington, "Corporate Attribution and Agency: Back to Basics" (2017) 133 L.Q.R. 118 at 142.

[100] See *Kelly v Fraser* [2012] UKPC 25; [2013] 1 A.C. 450 at [17].

[101] *The Starsin* [2000] 1 Lloyd's Rep. 85 at 93–98 (point not considered on appeal [2001] 1 Lloyd's Rep. 437). cf. *George Whitechurch Ltd v Cavanagh* [1902] A.C. 117 (company secretary's authority to certify share transfers conditional on sighting share certificates; false certification by fraudulent secretary not binding on company).

[102] Carriage of Goods by Sea Act 1992 s.4. But it was not always so: see below, para.8-067, Illustration 2.

[103] *Acute Property Developments Ltd v Apostolou* [2013] EWHC 200 (Ch) at [38].

[104] *United Bank of Kuwait Ltd v Hammoud* [1988] 1 W.L.R. 1051, Illustration 10; but cf. *Hirst v Etheringtons* [1999] Lloyd's Rep. P.N. 938, where it is suggested (against the background of a transaction needing inquiry) that some of the dicta in the first case may go too far in suggesting that a solicitor must normally be believed; and that a mere inquiry whether the transaction is within the course of business may not be enough. Another example of the same problem (a serious one) may be found in connection with officials the normal authority of whom would not necessarily be known to a third party: see *British Bank of the Middle East v Sun Life Assurance Co of Canada (UK) Ltd* [1983] 2 Lloyd's Rep. 9 (HL), Illustration 10 to Article 75; cf. Article 21, Illustration 2.

solicitor's representation in the conduct of litigation, including as to whether the principal has agreed to a compromise of it.[105]

(4) More generally, there are cases that have found that an agent who has no authority to contract may sometimes have authority to say whether particular contract terms will be enforced,[106] or even to say whether the principal is performing the contract, or whether or not a proposal is accepted.[107]

(5) An agent may be found to have sufficient apparent authority to bind the purported principal to a collateral contract of arbitration, or to a collateral contract designating a jurisdiction for determining disputes, without necessarily having such authority to conclude the main contract.[108]

From these examples it might be argued that it is only a small step to say that agents may have authority to say whether they have been authorised. But it is this final step which is not approved in *The Ocean Frost*.[109] The case *First Energy (UK) Ltd v Hungarian International Bank Ltd*,[110] the facts of which are summarised in Illustration 12, gets quite near to taking this step. The case involved a misstatement that the agent's superiors had approved a contract. The result was supported in the judgment of Steyn LJ on the basis of the importance of protecting third parties. It is submitted that the decision can be supported without invoking any exception to general principle (it was only the manager in question who had qualified the usual authority he otherwise would have had and in such circumstances he should be able to reinstate it; it appears that the third party had attended at the manager's office, and there had been a course of dealing).[111] Any ready admission of the agent's statement of his or her own authority as creating apparent authority involves a departure from the basic principles of apparent authority, for which no general justifying principle seems ready to hand. Although cases where an agent is authorised to say whether facts which confer authority on the agent can occur and have occurred, situations where this reasoning is legitimate should be specialised and unusual.[112]

---

[105] *Waugh v H.B. Clifford & Sons Ltd* [1982] Ch. 374, Article 30, Illustration 5. For commentary on this case and for other authorities, see above, paras 3-004 and 3-030.

[106] *State Rail Authority of New South Wales v Heath Outdoor Pty Ltd* (1987) 7 N.S.W.L.R. 170 at 184, per McHugh JA (albeit in a dissenting judgment). See also *Legione v Hateley* (1983) 152 C.L.R. 406; compare different reasoning in *Waltons Stores (Interstate) Ltd v Maher* (1988) 164 C.L.R. 387. But cf. *New Zealand Tenancy Bonds Ltd v Mooney* [1986] 1 N.Z.L.R. 280 (no authority to accept deposit late).

[107] See *International Paper Co v Spicer* (1906) 4 C.L.R. 739.

[108] See *Premium Nafta Products Ltd v Fili Shipping Co Ltd* [2007] UKHL 40; [2007] 4 All E.R. 951; [2007] 2 All E.R. (Comm) 1053; [2008] 1 Lloyd's Rep. 254 (arbitration clause); and *Deutsche Bank AG v Asia Pacific Broadband Wireless Communications Inc* [2008] EWCA Civ 1091; [2008] 2 Lloyd's Rep. 619 at [25] (jurisdiction clause). See Rushworth (2008) 124 L.Q.R. 195.

[109] Above, para.8-020. See especially per Robert Goff LJ in the Court of Appeal, [1986] A.C. at 730–735; quoted by Lord Keith of Kinkel in the House of Lords: ibid. at 777.

[110] *First Energy (UK) Ltd v Hungarian International Bank Ltd* [1993] 2 Lloyd's Rep. 194, Illustration 12: applied in *HSBC Ltd v Jurong Engineering Ltd* [2000] 2 Singapore L.R. 54. See also *Dale v Govt of Manitoba* (1997) 147 D.L.R. (4th) 605. cf. *Kilcran v Gothard* [2014] FCAFC 6 at [78] (receiver's limited delegation to superseded manager not extendable by manager); Watts [2015] L.M.C.L.Q. 36.

[111] See *Sun Life Assurance Co of Canada v CX Reinsurance Co Ltd* [2003] EWCA Civ 283; [2004] Lloyd's Rep I.R. 58 at [39].

[112] See *Armagas Ltd v Mundogas SA* [1986] A.C. 717, at 777; *Restatement, Third*, § 3.03. See also *Berryere v Firemans Fund Insurance Co* (1965) 51 D.L.R. (2d) 603 (doubted in *The Ocean Frost*); *Jensen v South Trail Mobile Ltd* (1972) 28 D.L.R. (3d) 233; *Cypress Disposal Ltd v Inland Kenworth Sales (Nanaimo) Ltd* (1975) 54 D.L.R. (3d) 598; *Savill v Chase Holdings (Wellington) Ltd* [1989]

8-021 **Representation of law** Until recently it would have been said on general grounds that the representation must be one of fact: a pure representation of law would not be sufficient to create apparent authority. A situation in which there was such a representation may be unlikely to arise in this context,[113] but the decision of the House of Lords in *Kleinwort Benson Ltd v Lincoln CC*,[114] allowing recovery in restitution of money paid under mistake of law, prompts reconsideration of all situations in which the distinction arises.[115]

8-022 **No estoppel through simple negligence** It is plain that if the third party does not know of the existence of any principal, there cannot be apparent authority, as when the agent purports to deal as principal.[116] A representation that does not come to the notice of the third party is no representation.[117] The mere fact that the principal enables the agent to commit fraud by putting the agent in a position where the agent can do so is not, without more, decisive.[118] The common law has avoided, so far at least, a concept of estoppel by negligence.[119] The mere possession of another's goods or documents (including those of title) creates no representation of entitlement to deal with them, since there can be any number of reasons why a bailment of them subsists. The doctrine does not apply even if the principal represents that the agent is the owner of goods or of a business where the third party was unaware of the representation, though in many such cases the related doctrine of apparent ownership[120] may apply, or there may be evidence that permits an inference of a grant of actual authority by the undisclosed principal.[121]

8-023 **On the faith of any such representations** This involves three elements:

  (1) The representation must be made to a third party or to a number of third parties. Old cases speak of holding out to the world,[122] but this is a loose expression[123]:

---

1 N.Z.L.R. 257 at 304–306, 313–314 (affirmed PC); *AJU Remicon Co Ltd v Alida Shipping Co Ltd* [2007] EWHC 2246 (Comm) at [16].

[113] See *De Tchihatchef v Salerni Coupling Ltd* [1932] 1 Ch. 330; below, para.9-066.

[114] *Kleinwort Benson Ltd v Lincoln CC* [1999] 2 A.C. 349.

[115] Contra in this context Treitel, *Law of Contract* (15th edn), para.16-026.

[116] *A.L. Underwood Ltd v Bank of Liverpool* [1924] 1 K.B. 775; *Farquharson Brothers & Co v King & Co* [1902] A.C. 325, Illustration 6 to Article 84; *Freeman & Lockyer v Buckhurst Park Properties (Mangal) Ltd* [1964] 2 Q.B. 480 at 503. But it is possible that the doctrine of undisclosed principal may apply: see Article 76. As to the possibility of a principal's being unable to deny the authority of a sub-agent who has relied on the head agent's apparent authority to appoint him, see *AJU Remicon Co Ltd v Alida Shipping Co Ltd* [2007] EWHC 2246 (Comm); and para.5-015 above.

[117] See para.8-024.

[118] *Farquharson Brothers & Co v King & Co* [1902] A.C. 325; *Morris v C.W. Martin & Sons Ltd* [1966] 1 Q.B. 716; Article 74.

[119] *Johnson Matthey (Aust.) Ltd v Dascorp Pty Ltd* (2003) 9 V.R. 171 at 185 (negligent failure to detect employee's theft of gold); *Williams Group Australia Pty Ltd v Crocker* [2016] NSWCA 265 at [69]. See Watts (2005) 26 Aust. Bar Rev. 185.

[120] Article 84.

[121] Article 76.

[122] e.g. *Whitehead v Tuckett* (1812) 15 East 400 at 411.

[123] *Dickinson v Valpy* (1829) 10 B. & C. 128 at 140.

"the 'holding out' must be to the particular individual who says he relied on it, or under such circumstances of publicity as to justify the inference that he knew of it and acted upon it."[124]

Nevertheless, the holding out may be quite general. If the analogy of estoppel were followed strictly, it is arguable that there could be no apparent authority where the principal at the time of making the representation by words or conduct had no third party or parties in contemplation, for it would be difficult to say that the principal had made a representation with the intent that it should be acted on, as the dictum of Diplock LJ quoted above seems to require[125]: it is clear however, that in many cases a third party can simply rely on the agent's having the authority usual to a person in the agent's position, without needing to testify to personal knowledge of what is usual[126], unless that third party knew that the agent had no such authority. It is not therefore necessary, though it is sufficient, that the representation be to a specific person. In relation to partnerships, the Partnership Act 1890 s.14(1) specifies that persons holding themselves out, or knowingly allowing themselves to be held out, as partners do not need to know who among the firm's creditors has relied on the representation.[127]

(2) The third party must have relied on the representation.[128] This is of course another aspect of the same point. Thus the third party cannot hold the principal liable if that party: did not believe that or care whether the agent had authority[129]; knew that the agent did not have authority[130] despite the appearance of authority; or had no dealings with the agent or was not aware of the circumstances giving rise to apparent authority.[131] The third party may also be unable to do so where informed of the terms of the agent's authority: this is discussed under Article 73.[132] A third party cannot rely on a docu-

---

[124] *Farquharson Brothers & Co v King & Co* [1902] A.C. 325 at 341, per Lord Lindley. A third party cannot rely on a representation that he knows was meant solely for others: *Ing Re (UK) Ltd v R & V Versicherung AG* [2006] EWHC 1544 (Comm); [2006] Lloyd's Rep. I.R. 653 at [119].

[125] See Comment to Article 21.

[126] See above, para.8-014; Powell, p.37; Articles 22, 29 and 30.

[127] See further, *Lindley and Banks on Partnership* (20th edn), para.12-06; *UCB Home Loans Corp Ltd v Soni* [2013] EWCA Civ 62.

[128] *Farquharson Brothers & Co v King & Co* [1902] A.C. 325 (written warrant given to warehouse but that was unknown to third party); *East Asia Co Ltd v PT Satria Tirtatama Energindo* [2019] UKPC 30 at [59].

[129] *Tinkler v Revenue & Customs* [2019] EWCA Civ 1392; [2019] 4 W.L.R. 138 at [46] (no intention of using agent as method of serving notice).

[130] *Home Owners Loan Corp v Thornburgh* 106 P. 2d 511 at 512 (SC Okl., 1940): "Apparent authority loses all of its apparency when the third party knows that actual authority is lacking"; *Bloomenthal v Ford* [1897] A.C. 156 at 168; *Galaxy Aviation v Sayegh Group Aviation* [2015] EWHC 3478 (Comm) at [101]; *Stavrinides v Bank of Cyprus Public Co Ltd* [2019] EWHC 1328 (Ch) at [105]. Reliance is not precluded by the fact that the third party subsequently attempts to get the principal also to sign a memorandum of the agreement, out of precaution: see below, para.8-060.

[131] See, e.g. *Farquharson Brothers & Co v King & Co* [1902] A.C. 325; *Technology Leasing Ltd v Lennmar Pty Ltd* [2012] FCA 709 at [153]; *UCB Home Loans Corp Ltd v Soni* [2013] EWCA Civ 62; *Anderson v Sense Network Ltd* [2018] EWHC 2834 (Comm); [2019] Bus. L.R. 1601 at [222] (affirmed without reference to this point [2019] EWCA Civ 1395); *Marme Inversiones 2007 SL v Natwest Markets Plc* [2019] EWHC 366 (Comm) at [424]; *East Asia Co Ltd v PT Satria Tirtatama Energindo* [2019] UKPC 30 at [59]. See further above, para.8-022.

[132] Where the third party has written notice from the principal as to the extent of the agent's authority, it requires a strong case to establish an apparent authority beyond this: *Australian Bank of Com-*

ment as creating a representation of apparent authority when that party knows that he or she was not supposed to have seen the document.[133]

Further, it is often said that the third party must in some way have acted on the representation. Again, if the analogy of common law estoppel by representation is followed, the acting must have been to that party's detriment, and this requirement is stated in several cases.[134] Others, however, speak simply of alteration of position, or acting on the faith of the representation,[135] and it seems in fact that there need be no more than an entering into a contract in reliance on the representation.[136] This tends to make this aspect of the doctrine merge with the previous one.

(3) The reliance must have been reasonable. There are in turn, two aspects to this. First, as already discussed, the grounds used to establish the representation of authority must be adequate to justify a belief that the agent had authority.[137] Secondly, even where there are such grounds, there may be other evidence that undermines what would otherwise be an adequate representation of authority. The latter class of case is dealt with in Article 73.

Within partnership law, there appears to be a specialised rule that enables a third party to sue persons who have allowed themselves to appear to be members of the firm even though the third party cannot show but-for reliance on that holding out.[138]

8-024 **Effect of representations where third party also acts through agents** The foregoing paragraphs are premised on a third party who acts directly. It is, however, part of regular commerce for both sides to the transaction to act through agents, and this will necessarily be the case where the third party is a company. It is obvious that for the purposes of those paragraphs it is sufficient if the agent acting for the third party was aware of the existence of the representations even if that agent's own principal was not. It will not normally matter that the third party's agent gained the

---

merce v Perel [1926] A.C. 737.

[133] *Ing Re (UK) Ltd v R & V Versicherung AG* [2006] EWHC 1544 (Comm); [2006] Lloyd's Rep. I.R. 653 at [118].

[134] *Howard v Hudson* (1853) 2 E. & B. 1; *George Whitechurch Ltd v Cavanagh* [1902] A.C. 117; *Farquharson Brothers & Co v King & Co* [1902] A.C. 325; *Mac Fisheries Ltd v Harrison* (1924) 93 L.J.K.B. 811; *Wilson & Meeson v Pickering* [1946] K.B. 422; *Norfolk County Council v Secretary of State for the Environment* [1973] 1 W.L.R. 1400. The situation seems to be similar in the US: see *Restatement, Third*, § 2.03, reporter's note a.

[135] *Pickard v Sears* (1837) 6 A. & E. 469; *Freeman v Cooke* (1848) 2 Exch. 654; *Cornish v Abington* (1859) 4 H. & N. 549; *Rama Corp v Proved Tin and General Investments* [1952] 2 Q.B. 147; *Freeman & Lockyer v Buckhurst Park Properties (Mangal) Ltd* [1964] 2 Q.B. 480 at 503; *Kelly v Fraser* [2012] UKPC 25; [2013] 1 A.C. 450 at [17].

[136] *Freeman & Lockyer v Buckhurst Park Properties (Mangal) Ltd* [1964] 2 Q.B. 480; *Cleveland Mfg. Co Ltd v Muslim Commercial Bank Ltd* [1981] 2 Lloyd's Rep. 646 at 650; *Polish SS Co v A.J. Williams Fuels (Overseas Sales) Ltd (The Suwalki)* [1989] 1 Lloyd's Rep. 511 at 514; *Arctic Shipping Co Ltd v Mobilia AB (The Tatra)* [1990] 2 Lloyd's Rep. 51 at 59. In *Silver v Ocean Steamship Co Ltd* [1930] 1 K.B. 416 it was held that the taking up of a bill of lading was sufficient evidence of reliance on it to raise an estoppel: see at 428, 434, 441. See also *Thanakharn Kasikorn Thai Chamchat v Akai Holdings Ltd (In Liquidation)* (2010) 13 H.K.C.F.A.R. 479 at [75].

[137] See above, para.8-017.

[138] See Partnership Act 1890 s.14, as construed in *Lynch v Stiff* (1943) 68 C.L.R. 428 at 435. cf. *Nationwide Building Society v Lewis* [1998] Ch. 482. See further *Lindley & Banks on Partnership* (20th edn), para 5-44.

relevant knowledge before being appointed.[139] Equally, if the third party is aware of the representation, it will not matter if the agent appointed to effect the transaction is not. The key principle is that the third party needs to show reliance on the representation, and one cannot rely if one does not know. That principle will need to guide the situation where a third party uses multiple agents in a transaction (as will be common where the third party is a company). It follows that it would not normally be sufficient that an agent of the third party who was not in any way engaged in the transaction was aware of the representation, if the parties so engaged were not. As to the position where the third party's agent knows that the other agent lacks actual authority, see below, para.8-051.

Scope of the doctrine   The general doctrine here stated applies to cases where the person concerned is not, apart from the estoppel, an agent at all (an unusual situation)[140]; to cases where the agent has some authority, but not authority to do what has in fact been done; to cases where the agent would have such authority but for the existence of reservations unknown to the third party; and to cases where the agent previously had authority, but this has, unknown to the third party, been terminated.[141] There is no reason of principle why it should not apply to the agent of an unidentified principal. If the principal appoints an agent who acts as such but does not reveal the principal's identity and the third party is willing to deal on this basis, apparent authority may be created.[142]   **8-025**

Doctrine does not validate act for all purposes   The doctrine of apparent authority validates the agent's act as regards the third party.[143] But it does not necessarily make it valid as regards the agent personally, who may be liable to the principal for breach of duty if the breach is not waived.[144]   **8-026**

Relationship of apparent authority with estoppel   There is much argument as to whether apparent authority should be regarded as based on estoppel or not.[145] The passage from Diplock LJ cited at the beginning of this Comment indicates that it should, and there are other judicial statements to the same effect. An example is: **8-027**

"Ostensible or apparent authority ... is merely a form of estoppel, indeed, it has been termed agency by estoppel, and you cannot call in aid an estoppel unless you have three

---

[139] *Racing UK Ltd v Doncaster Metropolitan District Council* [2005] EWCA Civ 999; [2005] L.L.R. 701 at [33]. See too *Cramaso LLP v Ogilvie-Grant, Earl of Seafield* [2014] UKSC 9; [2014] A.C. 1093 (noted Macgregor (2014) 19 Edin. L.R. 112) (representation as to facts relevant to subject matter of contract made to agent of third party before appointment).

[140] See Illustrations 1–6; Article 121.

[141] As to hidden reservations, see Illustrations 13–23, 26; as to termination of authority, see Illustrations 24 and 25 and Article 121.

[142] The problem can arise in connection with ship's agents. See *Lake Charles Stevedores v M/V Professor Vladimir Popov* 199 F. 3d 220 (5th Cir., 1999); cf. *N. & J. Vlassopulos Ltd v Ney Shipping Ltd (The Santa Carina)* [1977] 1 Lloyd's Rep. 478, Illustration 3 to Article 101; *Restatement, Third*, § 2.13, Comment *f* and reporter's notes thereto.

[143] It does not simply give rise to liability for the reliance interest on the basis of *culpa in contrahendo*, as, it appears, may sometimes be the case in German law.

[144] See Comments to Articles 20 and 36.

[145] Powell, pp.68–72; Stoljar, pp.25–36; Seavey (1920) 29 Yale L.J. 859; Montrose (1938) 16 Can.B.R. 757; Mechem, *Principles of Agency* (4th edn), §§ 84 onwards.

ingredients: (i) a representation, (ii) a reliance on the representation, and (iii) an alteration of your position resulting from such reliance."[146]

The main difficulties with this approach have already been referred to. They are,
first, the fact that the representation giving rise to the estoppel is in this area permitted to be very general indeed,[147] and second, that the detriment incurred by the
representee may be small.[148] Of these, the first is clearly the more important. The
idea that by allowing the agent to act in certain ways the principal is making
representations to third parties is an artificial one, especially where the "representation" simply amounts to putting someone in a position which carries usual authority, or using the services of a professional person whose activities carry a usual
authority.[149] If a genuine estoppel is looked for, the category would indeed be even
narrower than that marked off above as "genuine apparent authority".[150] In the editions of this work edited by Bowstead himself it can be said that a distinction
between two types of case was in fact made, though later writings have enabled it
to be more clearly stated. The Article above, which now stands for all apparent
authority, by its reference to "representations" may be regarded as having been
intended to refer to "genuine" estoppel cases. The broader notion was dealt with in
Article 80 of the eighth edition of 1932 (the last edited by Bowstead himself) as
follows:

"Every act done by an agent in the course of his employment on behalf of his principal,
and within the apparent scope of his authority, binds the principal, unless the agent is in
fact unauthorised to do the particular act, and the person dealing with him has notice that
in doing such act he is exceeding his authority."[151]

It will be noted that this last formulation approaches the terminology now reserved
for the liability of an employer for the torts of his employee. Though it can be connected with the notion of usual authority,[152] it is not in accord with current thinking in contract law.

8-028   **Alternative analyses**   Those common lawyers who reject the idea of estoppel
have indeed mostly argued for some sort of extension of the tort principles of this

---

[146] *Rama Corp v Proved Tin and General Investments* [1952] 2 Q.B. 147 at 149–150, per Slade J; see
also *R. v Charles* [1977] A.C. 177 at 183; *Egyptian International Foreign Trade Co v Soplex
Wholesale Supplies Ltd (The Raffaella)* [1985] 2 Lloyd's Rep. 36 at 41; *Armagas Ltd v Mundogas
SA (The Ocean Frost)* [1986] A.C. 717 at 777; *Lloyd's Bank v Independent Insurance* [2000] Q.B.
110 at 122; *The Starsin* [2000] 1 Lloyd's Rep. 85 at 95 (unconscionability: final proceedings [2004]
1 A.C. 715); *AMB Generali, etc. v SEB Trygg, etc.* [2005] EWCA Civ 1237; [2006] 1 Lloyd's Rep.
318 at [31]; Ewart, *Estoppel* (1900), Ch.XXVI; *Spencer Bower: Reliance-Based Estoppel* (5th edn),
para.9.2 onwards; Mechem, *Outlines of Agency* (4th edn), §§ 86 onwards; Tan Cheng Han (2020)
136 L.Q.R. 315.
[147] See above, para.8-014.
[148] See above, para.8-023; Dal Pont, pp.549–550.
[149] See Articles 29 and 30; e.g. *Waugh v H.B. Clifford & Sons Ltd* [1982] Ch. 374, Illustration 16, where
the dicta go some way towards attributing an independent position to the agent.
[150] See above, para.8-014.
[151] cf. Partnership Act 1890 s.5. This Article, in the form in which it appeared in the 4th edn, was relied
on by counsel in *Lloyd v Grace, Smith & Co* [1912] A.C. 716. It was also cited with approval by
the Court of Appeal in *Navarro v Moregrand Ltd* [1951] 2 T.L.R. 674; and *Ryan v Pilkington* [1959]
1 W.L.R. 403. But it was severely criticised by Falconbridge in (1939) 17 Can. B.R. 248 at 255–
256; and see *Armagas Ltd v Mundogas SA (The Ocean Frost)* [1986] A.C. 717 at 779 onwards; cf.
Brown [2004] J.B.L. 391.
[152] See above, para.3-005.

type[153]; or based themselves on the objective analysis applicable to the formation of contract and argued that it applies equally to the formation of contracts through agents.[154] The former view is certainly one that could be adopted, but is not in accord with the present accepted approach to common law agency, at least in England.[155] The latter has much to commend it. It explains the weak requirements as to representation and reliance in respect of authority, which are difficult to reconcile with the requirements of common law estoppel by representation as normally stated, which are usually taken to require an unequivocal representation[156] and action in reliance on it.[157] Recent developments in estoppel have also tended to stress that the consequences of the estoppel should only be sufficient to satisfy the equity raised[158] which if applied to apparent authority would create serious uncertainties in a doctrine designed to satisfy commercial certainty. Finally, to explain apparent authority in a different way would enable true estoppel situations, which can certainly be found in this area and are discussed under Article 21, to be separated off.[159] The distinction between objective interpretation and estoppel is in fact made in connection with formation of contract situations, where sometimes the normal objective interpretation techniques, which were themselves once attributed to estoppel,[160] give way to true estoppel reasoning.[161] In the US the distinction was taken in *Restatement, Second*[162] and is emphasised in *Restatement, Third*.[163]

As to English law, it is certainly true that cases on master and servant and cases on principal and agent have not always been clearly separated, that some of the old cases on what is now called apparent authority reached their results without reference to estoppel, on broader notions such as that of the implied authority of a general agent.[164] But cases on agency and the related notion of apparent ownership which use what would now be called estoppel reasoning can also be traced back many years, and indeed some of them even seem to figure among the origins of the general doctrine of estoppel.[165] There can be little doubt that the prevailing approach in England has been in terms of representation and estoppel, at any rate as regards the agent's contracts.

---

[153] Wright (1935) 1 U. Toronto L.J. 40; Mearns (1962) 48 Va.L.Rev. 50; Bester (1972) 89 S.A.L.J. 49; Comment to Article 22.

[154] Cook (1905) 5 Col.L.R. 36; (1906) 6 Col.L.R. 34; Conant (1968) 47 Neb.L.Rev. 678; Krebs, in *Contract Formation and Parties* (Burrows and Peel eds, 2010), Ch.10.

[155] See above, para.1-026.

[156] *Low v Bouverie* [1891] 3 Ch. 82 at 106.

[157] *Carr v L & NW Ry* (1875) L.R. 10 C.P. 307 at 317.

[158] See, e.g. *Commonwealth v Verwayen* (1990) 170 C.L.R. 394, per Brennan J; Dal Pont, pp.520–521 (paras 20.12–20.13).

[159] See para.2-105 above. Contra, Mechem, *Outlines of Agency* (4th edn), § 90.

[160] See, e.g. Hughes (1930) 54 L.Q.R. 370. See also Lord Bingham in *The Starsin* [2003] UKHL 12; [2004] 1 A.C. 715 at [8], suggesting that in commercial contracts a process of reasoning similar to that used for interpretation should be used for questions of who was a contracting party.

[161] See Treitel, *Law of Contract* (15th edn), paras 2-044–2-046 (estoppel where offer met by silence).

[162] See §§ 140 and 141; 8 and Comment *d*; 8B and Comment.

[163] § 2.05, Comment *d* ("Estoppel does not require as close a fit between affirmative acts of the principal and the third party's belief"). Contra, Mechem, *Outlines of Agency* (4th edn), § 90 ("The distinction is relatively unimportant").

[164] See *Smith v M'Guire* (1858) 3 H. & N. 554; Stoljar, Ch.3. See also Partnership Act 1890 s.5; Thomas (1971) 6 Victoria U. of Wellington L.Rev. 1. Development on the continent of Europe was certainly not based on any principle like that of estoppel: Müller-Freienfels (1964) 13 Am.J.Comp.L. 193 at 341. See also Articles 2 and 29.

[165] See, e.g. *Pickering v Busk* (1812) 15 East 38 (a case on actual authority); *Pickard v Sears* (1837) 6 A. & E. 469; *Freeman v Cooke* (1848) 2 Exch. 654. See also *VLM Holdings Ltd v Ravensworth*

But there are also difficulties with the alternative theory mentioned, that of the objective basis of contract. It is not easy to see how this can avoid the conclusion that not only has the principal made a manifestation to the third party by means of the agent, but also that the third party who contracts has made a (usually much clearer) manifestation to the principal. This logically requires that principals must be able, without subjecting themselves to the ratification rules and their safeguards, to sue the third party for non-performance of an executory contract, simply because the third party could sue on it under the doctrine of apparent authority. This logical conclusion was indeed adopted in *Restatement, Second*,[166] and is continued in *Restatement, Third*,[167] though the sole case cited is hardly strong authority.[168] It seems preferable therefore, and in accordance with English authority, to retain the estoppel justification; but to treat it as invoking a special (and weak) type of estoppel relevant only in the agency context.[169] This still enables what may be called true estoppels (where the full requirements as normally stated are complied with) in the agency context to be separated off, though not so clearly as the *Restatement* position allows. If it is unsatisfactory, it is probably no more so than solutions found elsewhere for a problem which causes difficulty in many legal systems.

It has already been pointed out under Article 21 that true estoppel reasoning can be used in agency situations, outside the doctrine of apparent authority. Examples of such cases are there given.

8-029   **Can the principal sue on the contract?**   No doubt where the principal is sued on a contract within the apparent authority of an agent, the principal can make counterclaims as well as adduce defences. But if the doctrine of apparent authority is based on any form of estoppel, it seems clear that the principal cannot personally sue on such a contract without ratifying it.[170] As stated above, this view is not however taken in the US, where it seems to be assumed that the principal can sue independently of ratification.[171] If the doctrine is based on estoppel, this view is impossible. Even if it is not, the juristic basis of this analysis is not easy to see. Ratification, which would solve the problem, would not in any case normally be a difficult matter, and could presumably be inferred from the bringing of a

---

Digital Services Ltd [2013] EWHC 228 (Ch) at [69].

[166]   § 292.

[167]   § 2.03, Comment and reporter's notes thereto.

[168]   *Equitable Variable Life Insurance Co v Wood* 362 S.E.2d 741 (Va., 1987), where an assured cancelled a life insurance policy, notifying only a person with apparent but (as it transpired) not actual authority to receive the notice. She was killed in an air crash one day later. It was held that the policy had been cancelled.

[169]   In *Pole v Leask* (1863) 33 L.J.Ch. 155 at 162, Lord Cranworth refers to "this agency by estoppel, if I may so designate it". See too the 2nd edn of *Anson on Contract* (1882). As to the variety of estoppels, see Hon. K. Handley, *Estoppel by Conduct and Election* (2nd edn, 2016), p.20: "Each form of estoppel has its own elements, although some are common to others. The similarities warrant their recognition as a form of estoppel but the differences make each a distinct form with its own history and requirements".

[170]   Contra, Powell, p.70. Different views were expressed on the point by the Ontario Court of Appeal in *Canadian Laboratory Supplies Ltd v Engelhard Industries of Canada Ltd* (1977) 78 D.L.R. (3d) 232. On appeal the case was decided on different grounds: [1979] 2 S.C.R. 787; (1979) 97 D.L.R. (3d) 1. In general, a third party is not precluded from taking the point that an agent has acted without authority: see, e.g. *Smith v Henniker-Major & Co* [2002] EWCA Civ 762; [2003] Ch. 182; *Sherlock Holmes International Society Ltd v Aidiniantz* [2016] EWHC 1076 (Ch) at [113]; affirmed [2017] EWCA Civ 1875; [2018] 1 B.C.L.C. 188 (proceedings brought without authority). See too the cases cited in the notes to para.3-007, above.

[171]   See above, para.8-028.

counterclaim. The question will only be of practical significance where ratification is for some reason impossible, e.g. because of difficulties about ratification in part[172] or as to the time of ratification.[173] The present law is that ratification is possible though the third party has meanwhile purported to withdraw from the contract.[174] Were it otherwise, the question whether the principal can sue on a contract binding the principal under the doctrine of apparent authority might assume more practical significance. In general it seems appropriate to apply the safeguards on ratification[175] to such actions by principals; and if this is correct, it provides also a practical reason for adhering to the rule that the doctrine of itself only operates against the principal.

Some special cases are now discussed.

Agents of companies[176]   In general, companies can only act through agents, except   **8-030**
in the comparatively rare situations where a contractual or statutory provision by its wording precludes the operation of attribution through agency.[177] Yet it may be extremely difficult for a person dealing with another who purports to be the agent of a company to know whether that person can be or is in fact authorised to do what the agent purports to do. The question of the apparent authority of agents of companies is therefore correspondingly important. But it is, not surprisingly, complicated by special factors peculiar to company law. The complications which previously existed have now been reduced, but not eliminated, by statutory provisions. Full guidance should be sought in works on company law: what follows seeks only to give general indications as to the impact on agency law of these special factors.[178]

Ultra vires doctrine   The first complication is the doctrine of ultra vires. Under   **8-031**
this doctrine a company was not bound by a contract or (in some cases) other act into which by virtue of the objects clause in its memorandum it had no capacity to enter, or which it similarly had no capacity to perform.[179] This doctrine was sometimes interpreted rather widely so as to cover situations where the activity was not precluded but the motive for the doing of it was improper, or where the exercise of a power was in the circumstances illegal, or where delegation to particular officers was not authorised by the memorandum or articles. More recent case law has produced the opposite problem of removing from the ambit of the concept of vires the use of a power of a type that the corporation undoubtedly has to pursue objects

---

[172] As in the *Canadian Laboratory Supplies Ltd v Engelhard Industries of Canada Ltd* (1977) 78 D.L.R. (3d) 232.

[173] Above, para.2-092; Article 19.

[174] *Bolton Partners v Lambert* (1889) 41 Ch.D. 295; see Article 18.

[175] See Article 19.

[176] See above, para.1-028; and *Gower's Modern Company Law* (10th edn), Ch.7. See also the leading cases *Freeman & Lockyer v Buckhurst Park Properties (Mangal) Ltd* [1964] 2 Q.B. 480; and *Hely-Hutchinson v Brayhead Ltd* [1968] 1 Q.B. 549. Compare the situation with that in partnerships, where every partner is an agent of the firm for carrying on the partnership business in the normal way: Partnership Act 1890 s.5.

[177] See above, para.1-028. See too *Stone & Rolls Ltd v Moore Stephens Ltd* [2009] UKHL 39; [2009] 1 A.C. 1391 (noted Watts (2010) 126 L.Q.R. 14; Halpern (2010) 73 M.L.R. 487).

[178] There are special rules with respect to charitable companies: see Charities Act 1993 ss.63, 65, 67 and 68. See also Companies Act 2006 s.42, in relation to charities incorporated under that Act.

[179] *Ashbury Railway Carriage and Iron Co v Riche* (1875) L.R. 7 H.L. 653 (unanimous vote of ratification by the shareholders could not validate an ultra vires transaction).

outside those for which the corporation was formed.[180] This has turned the original ultra vires doctrine on its head, where the focus had been not (principally) on absence of powers but the use of them to divert the corporation's business from the ends stipulated in its founding documents. This misunderstanding of the ultra vires doctrine seems, however, to have cemented itself into English law. The practical effect may not be great, since as a result of implementing the EC First Directive on Company Law,[181] very few trading companies now have any limits on the objects that they can pursue. Where there are limits to a corporation's powers or objects, the directors or other officers will lack actual authority, even under the modern approach.[182]

8-032   **Constructive notice of company's public documents**   There was also a doctrine, of rather uncertain scope, under which a person dealing with a company was deemed to have constructive notice of what appeared in its public documents. It was not clear exactly what these documents were, but they certainly included its memorandum and articles. Thus the third party might in particular be deemed to know not only of limitations on the company's authorised activities but also of restrictions on delegation contained in its articles. As stated above, sometimes such matters of delegation had been taken into the ultra vires rule; but if it was wrong to do so, the significance of the constructive notice rule for such situations became greater. The third party might not be able to rely on what would otherwise be apparent authority under agency law because that party was deemed to have constructive notice of the company's objects and of restrictions on the power to delegate to agents. The rule only applied against the third party: it did not apply in in that party's favour.[183]

8-033   **Common law: the rule in Turquand's case**   The public documents of a company may provide that a power can be delegated: but they may require some special procedure, for example a resolution of a general meeting; or special procedures may be laid down by the directors for the exercise of ordinary powers, for example a requirement that a cheque on the company's account needs signatures of persons authorised in particular ways.[184] The third party may have no way of finding out whether or not these procedures may have been followed. This problem was dealt with, after the introduction of the system of incorporation by registration, by judicial decision. Under the rule in *Royal British Bank v Turquand*[185] a third party acting in good faith is entitled to assume that the relevant procedures of "indoor management", the details of which were not available to that party, have been complied with. The third party is not, however, entitled to assume from the mere fact that

---

[180] *Rolled Steel Products (Holdings) Ltd v British Steel Corp* [1986] Ch. 246; *Charles Terence Estates Ltd v Cornwall Council* [2012] EWCA Civ 1439; [2013] 1 W.L.R. 466 at [47]. For criticism, see P. Watts, "The *Rolled Steel* Case and the Memorandum of Association" [1986] N.Z.L.J. 270.

[181] Directive 68/151 art.9.

[182] For the residual relevance of lack of corporate capacity, see above, para.2-021.

[183] *Rama Corp Ltd v Proved Tin & General Investments Ltd* [1952] 2 Q.B. 147 at 149; *Freeman & Lockyer v Buckhurst Park Properties (Mangal) Ltd* [1964] 2 Q.B. 480 at 504, 508.

[184] e.g. *Mahony v East Holyford Mining Co* (1875) L.R. 7 H.L. 869.

[185] *Royal British Bank v Turquand* (1856) 6 El. & Bl. 327, Illustration 27; *Mahony v East Holyford Mining Co* (1875) L.R. 7 H.L. 869. A director might in some circumstances rank as a third party for the purposes of this rule: *Hely-Hutchinson v Brayhead Ltd* [1968] 1 Q.B. 549; affirmed on other grounds [1968] 1 Q.B. 549 at 573.

authority was possible that it had actually been conferred.[186] This could only be assumed where under the general principles of agency there would normally be apparent authority. This requires that the company, by a representation traceable back to an authorised officer,[187] has held out the agent as having authority: either by appointing the agent to a position which would normally carry such authority, or by representing that the agent has been appointed to it, or by some more specific holding out.[188] If this was so, compliance with internal procedures might be assumed. In other words, the rule is not designed to eliminate the need to deal with persons of sufficient standing to make the relevant contract, but only to protect against failure by such persons to comply with procedural rules.[189]

No need for actual or apparent authority if contract in attested deed form?   The actual holding in *Turquand*'s case was not concerned with ordinary contracts but with those in deed form.[190] The case, applying ancient law, supports the conclusion that a deed, when correct in its manner of execution (i.e. the sealing, if required, is genuine, and the correct witnesses by number and identity have signed the document), can be relied upon by an outside party for what it provides even if that party has not attempted to establish that entry into the deed was properly authorised, so long as there was nothing to put that party on notice of irregularity.[191] That is not the position for dealings that are not in deed form; there, as seen above, actual or apparent authority has first to be established by the third party, before advantage can be taken of any presumption of regularity (or presumption against knowledge of irregularity) in respect of procedural requirements. The result is that *Turquand* has become relevant to two different sets of circumstances, ordinary contracts and deeds. This aspect of the common law has been reinforced by the provisions of the Companies Act 2006.[192] It seems that trust deeds can create in favour of third parties a similar presumption of regularity in their dealings with a trustee.[193]   **8-034**

Statutory reforms: ultra vires   Limited provisions protecting third parties dealing with companies in s.9(1) of the European Communities Act 1972, later re-enacted as s.35 of the Companies Act 1985, proved inadequate to abolish the ultra   **8-035**

---

[186] See *Houghton & Co v Nothard, Lowe & Wills Ltd* [1927] 1 K.B. 246 at 266–267; affirmed on other grounds [1928] A.C. 1; *Northside Developments Ltd v Registrar-General* (1990) 170 C.L.R. 146 at 195–198; *East Asia Co Ltd v PT Satria Tirtatama Energindo* [2019] UKPC 30 at [64]–[65].

[187] *Freeman & Lockyer v Buckhurst Park Properties (Mangal) Ltd* [1964] 2 Q.B. 480 at 504, 508 at 506 (representation) must be made by person possessing "actual authority to manage the affairs of the company generally or with respect to the matter to which the contract relates". See also below, para.8-040.

[188] cf. above, para.8-014.

[189] *Northside Developments Pty Ltd v Registrar-General* (1990) 170 C.L.R. 146 at 198; *East Asia Co Ltd v PT Satria Tirtatama Energindo* [2019] UKPC 30 at [64]. This paragraph was approved in *Business Mortgage Finance 6 Plc v Roundstone Technologies Ltd* [2019] EWHC 2917 (Ch) at [55].

[190] See P. Watts, "Deeds and the Principles of Authority in Agency Law" (2002) 2 O.U.C.L.J. 93.

[191] See *Royal British Bank v Turquand* (1855) 5 El. & Bl. 248 at 260, per Lord Campbell CJ; and (1856) 6 El. & Bl. 327 (ExCh) at 332, per Jervis CJ. See too *Agar v Athenaeum Life-Assurance Society* (1858) 1 C.B. (NS) 729 at 749–750, 756; *South Yorkshire Railway and River Dun Co v Great Northern Railway* (1853) 9 Ex. 55 at 84; *Burkinshaw v Nicolls* (1878) 3 App.Cas. 1004 at 1026–1027; *County of Gloucester Bank v Rudry Merthyr Steam & House Coal Colliery Co* [1895] 1 Ch. 629; *Northside Developments Ltd v Registrar-General* (1990) 170 C.L.R. 146 at 164, per Mason CJ. But cf. the majority view in the *Northside* case.

[192] See Companies Act 2006 ss.44 and 46, discussed below, para.8-040.

[193] See *Staechelin v ACLBDD Holdings Ltd* [2019] EWCA Civ 817; [2019] 3 All E.R. 419 at [106].

vires doctrine completely,[194] particularly in that they failed to distinguish between issues of corporate capacity and directors' authority. Further reform in 1989 has now been carried through into the Companies Act 2006. Section 31 of the 2006 Act confirms as a starting point that companies have unrestricted objects. Rather oddly, the Act does not expressly also confirm that companies have unconstrained *powers* (subject again to the constitution) but it seems likely that this is implicit within s.31. Incorporators are then free to depart from that starting point by choosing through the constitution to limit a company's objects. Where, however, a company does so choose, s.39 of the 2006 Act provides that "the validity of an act done by a company shall not be called in question on the ground of lack of capacity by reason of anything in the company's constitution". This provision removes any possibility of argument that an act that would otherwise be ultra vires is automatically invalid. It was never clear, in any event, that an act beyond a company's capacity was void irrespective of the third party's state of knowledge or means of knowledge.[195] Section 40 then protects persons dealing with the company in good faith from any limitation there may be on directors' powers in the constitution. A person is not to be treated as acting in bad faith "by reason only of his knowing that an act is beyond the powers of the directors under the company's constitution".[196] In theory at least, the drafting still seems to envisage both that a company might choose to limit its capacity and that such limits would preclude a third party enforcing any contract where acting in bad faith. It is not clear, however, just when someone would be viewed as acting in bad faith. Section 40(4) seems to envisage that shareholders can also intervene in advance of action to prevent what would otherwise be an ultra vires act (consistently with the common law position), but not once legal rights have arisen under the transaction.[197] Section 40(5) also preserves the right of the company to bring suit against the directors for exceeding their powers. These issues will arise infrequently because most incorporators simply do not opt to limit their company's objects or powers.

8-036 **Constructive notice** As indicated above, mere abolition of the ultra vires rule would not protect third parties adequately unless the constructive notice rule was also abolished, for that could lead to the conclusion that the third party was deemed to know that the act was outside the objects and could not be authorised. Protection was also needed against the constructive notice rule for cases where the articles gave no power to delegate, or actually prohibited delegation, either at all or to particular persons. Provisions protecting third parties were first enacted in s.9(1) of the European Communities Act 1972, but these proved not only inadequate to abolish the ultra vires rule, as stated above, but also unsatisfactory in general. Improved provisions were inserted in the Companies Act 1985 in 1989, and have in turn been replaced by s.40 of the 2006 Act.

8-037 **Companies Act 2006 section 40** Section 40(1) provides:

"In favour of a person dealing with a company in good faith, the power of the directors

---

194 For discussion of s.9(1), see Prentice (1973) 89 L.Q.R. 518; Sealy [1973] C.L.J. 1; Farrar and Powles (1973) 36 M.L.R. 270; Hirtenstein (1973) 123 N.L.J. 312. Special provisions apply to ultra vires acts by companies that are charities: Companies Act 2006 s.42.
195 See above, para.2-011.
196 See s.40(2)(b)(iii).
197 Intervention by shareholders might involve an injunction to prevent a contract being entered into in breach of constitutional limits, but could also involve the proposed exercise by the company of an option that would be inconsistent with such restrictions.

to bind the company, or authorise others to do so, is deemed to be free of any limitation under the constitution."

This provision, in the rare instance that a company might now choose to limit its capacity, would in most circumstances protect outside parties. The section also abolishes constructive notice of any limitations on directors' powers. So, s.40(2)(b)(i) provides that a person dealing with the company is not bound to inquire as to any limitation on directors' powers. As will be seen below, s.40(2) goes on to provide that even actual knowledge of any limitations does not preclude a plea of good faith.

In *Smith v Henniker-Major & Co*,[198] Robert Walker LJ held that the phrase "limitation under the constitution" in the predecessor to s.40(1) (s.35A of the Companies Act 1985) was capable of covering the case where a decision was made by less than the required quorum for a board meeting (in fact only one director). However, this was a dissenting judgment. The other members of the Court held that, whatever the reach of the section, it could not protect a transaction where the counterparty was the very director who was purporting to cause the company to contract with him. Given that the majority of the Court did not rule on the issue, Robert Walker LJ's judgment cannot, and should not, be regarded as authoritative on the point. The section has its origin in the problematic ultra vires doctrine, not in procedural requirements for the exercise of authority.[199] In terms, it is concerned with the powers of the directors as a composite body.[200] A quorum requirement is not a limitation on directors' powers, but defines what constitutes a board for the purpose of its exercising those powers. There are no indications that the section was intended to change the starting point that directors acting outside their collective authority have limited usual authority to bind the company.[201] It has elsewhere been held that the section (again in its earlier guise) does not apply to a director who does not purport to be acting as the board at the time.[202]

The company's constitution for the purposes of the section includes not only its articles, but also any resolution of the shareholders or agreement between the members of the company (or relevant class)[203] Section 40(1) applies to a "person" dealing with a company, but it has been held that this does not cover directors.[204]

Central to the operation of the section are the concepts of dealing and good faith. Both these concepts are defined. As regards dealing, the definition is framed broadly

[198] *Smith v Henniker-Major & Co* [2002] EWCA Civ 762; [2003] Ch. 182. See also *Ford v Polymer Vision Ltd* [2009] EWHC 945 (Ch) (failure to notify all directors of meeting, and meeting held in wrong country).
[199] Article 9 of the First Council Directive 68/151/EEC was not concerned with procedural elements of corporate governance.
[200] This was the view taken by Rimer J at first instance: [2002] B.C.C. 544. There is no significance, it is suggested, in s.40(1) referring to "the directors" rather than the "board of directors" as appeared in s.35A of the 1985 Act.
[201] See para.3-030, Illustration 4.
[202] *Wrexham Associated Football Club Ltd v Crucialmove Ltd* [2006] EWCA Civ 237; [2008] 1 B.C.L.C. 508 at [47]. cf. *TCB Ltd v Gray* [1986] Ch. 621 at 637; affirmed [1987] Ch. 458 where all directors had informally approved the transaction.
[203] Companies Act 2006 s.40(3). And see ss.17 and 29 of the 2006 Act. See, e.g. *Cane v Jones* [1980] 1 W.L.R. 1451.
[204] *Smith v Henniker-Major & Co* [2002] EWCA Civ 762; [2003] Ch. 182 (a majority decision). This replicates the common law as expressed in *Morris v Kanssen* [1946] A.C. 459.

so as to cover any transaction or other act to which the company is a party.[205] However, it has been held that a bonus issue of shares did not constitute a dealing as there was no bilateral transaction.[206] The definition of good faith is not so straightforward. First, a person will be presumed to be acting in good faith.[207] Secondly, a person will not be regarded as acting in bad faith by reason only of knowing that the act is beyond the powers of the directors.[208] The adverb "only" is critical. It is intended to distinguish situations where the directors are exceeding their authority from those where they are actually abusing it, a not altogether easy dichotomy. In the first situation mere knowledge of this fact will not result in a person dealing with the company being unable to enforce the transaction; and this goes further than the normal rules of apparent authority. But where the third party knows or is to be taken to know that the directors are abusing their authority, there will be no such protection.[209] There are also provisions curtailing a shareholder's internal right to enforce the memorandum and articles against the directors.[210] However, if one of the third parties is a director of the company or its holding company, or is associated with such a director, or is a company with which such a director is associated, the transaction is in certain circumstances voidable against that party.[211] In this respect, it can be said that the ultra vires doctrine survives. This provision gives effect to a policy that the protection against ultra vires given to third parties in general should normally not be extended to third parties who are also directors or otherwise involved with the company.

8-038   **The overall position: dealing with directors**   Where the third party deals with the board of directors, or with a person actually authorised by it, the transaction will usually be effective. The default position under the 2006 Act is that the board is given "the management of the company's business, for which purpose they may exercise all the powers of the company."[212] The board's powers of delegation are also virtually unlimited,[213] but directors could be personally liable for loss caused by an irresponsible delegation. Outside parties are otherwise well protected by s.40. This is further reinforced by s.161 of the 2006 Act, under which "The acts of a director or manager are valid notwithstanding any defect that may afterwards be discovered in his appointment or qualification".[214] Where a company has only one

---

[205] Companies Act 2006 s.40(2).
[206] *EIC Services Ltd v Phipps* [2004] EWCA Civ 1069; [2005] 1 W.L.R. 1377. This is open to doubt: see Payne and Prentice [2005] L.M.C.L.Q. 447.
[207] Companies Act 2006 s.40(2)(b)(ii). But on the authority of *International Sales and Agencies Ltd v Marcus* [1982] 3 All E.R. 551, on the 1972 wording, the burden is on the third party to establish that he dealt with the company within the wording.
[208] Companies Act 2006 s.40(2)(b)(iii). A person acts in good faith if he acts genuinely and honestly in the circumstances, i.e. the test is subjective; *Barclays Bank Ltd v TOSG Trust Fund Ltd* [1984] B.C.L.C. 1 at 18 (on the predecessor provision to the current s.40).
[209] This distinction is required by art.9(2) of the First Directive.
[210] Companies Act 2006 s.40(4).
[211] Companies Act 2006 s.41. This section supersedes Companies Act 1985 s.322A. It seems on the strength of the *Smith v Henniker-Major & Co* [2002] EWCA Civ 762; [2003] Ch. 182, that in some circumstances a dealing with a director might be void, and not merely voidable; s.322A was not discussed in the case.
[212] See Companies (Model Articles) Regulations 2008 (SI 2008/3229) Sch.3 art.3 (public companies); Sch.1 art.3 (private companies).
[213] See Companies (Model Articles) Regulations 2008 (SI 2008/3229) Sch.3 art.5.
[214] This provision is not excluded by s.160 (void resolution to appoint), replacing s.292 of the 1985 Act. However, it only applies where there is a defect in an appointment made by persons who had the

director, that director will have authority orally to override earlier general instructions to a bank that it is to act on written instructions only.[215]

Dealings with other agents of the company   In respect of other agents, including individual directors, the agreement will be enforceable by the application of the normal rules of agency. The third party cannot be affected by anything in the company's constitution. The third party is also entitled, if acting in good faith, to assume by virtue of s.40 that the board of directors has power to authorise others to bind the company. But that party can only assume that it has actually exercised this power by virtue of the common law rules. In particular there must, as before, be a holding out by the company, which might then be reinforced by the indoor management rule.[216] This may be by appointing a person to an office carrying a usual authority,[217] e.g. managing director, or representing that it has done so.[218] In such a case all acts within that authority will bind the company,[219] but not acts outside it. The holding out may also, as in apparent authority generally, be by more specific conduct, as by granting powers of attorney without restriction,[220] or regularly accepting the acts of the agent in question.[221] But pursuant to the general doctrine, there is no protection, even in such a case, for a third party who has notice of the lack of authority[222] or is put on inquiry by the facts of the transaction.[223]

    In the leading case on apparent authority, which also relates to the agents of companies, Diplock LJ said that in such cases:

> "the representation must be made by a person or persons who had 'actual' authority to manage the business of the company either generally or in respect of those matters to which the contract relates."[224]

This must now be read subject to s.40 of the Companies Act 2006, above. But on the general principle, the High Court of Australia has followed this wording and

8-039

---

    ability to make the appointment had they complied with proper procedures, and does not apply to appointments made by persons without the ability to make the appointment: *Morris v Kanssen* [1946] A.C. 459; *Re Northwestern Autoservices Ltd* [1980] 2 N.Z.L.R. 302; *OBG Ltd v Allan* [2007] UKHL 21; [2008] 1 A.C. 1 at [91]; *New Falmouth Resorts Ltd v International Hotels Jamaica Ltd* [2013] UKPC 11 at [25].

[215] *Hill Street Services Co Ltd v National Westminster Bank Plc* [2007] EWHC 2379 (Ch) at [17].

[216] See *Kreditbank Cassel GmbH v Schenkers* [1927] 1 K.B. 826 at 842–843; *Wrexham Associated Football Club Ltd v Crucialmove Ltd* [2006] EWCA Civ 237; [2008] 1 B.C.L.C. 508 at [47].

[217] See Articles 22 and 29.

[218] *Freeman & Lockyer v Buckhurst Park Properties (Mangal) Ltd* [1964] 2 Q.B. 480, Illustration 28.

[219] *Mahony v East Holyford Mining Co* (1875) L.R. 7 H.L. 869; *Biggerstaff v Rowatt's Wharf* [1896] 2 Ch. 93, Illustration 25; *British Thomson-Houston Co Ltd v Federated European Bank Ltd* [1932] 2 K.B. 176, as explained in *Freeman & Lockyer v Buckhurst Park Properties (Mangal) Ltd* [1964] 2 Q.B. 480; *Clay Hill Brick & Tile Co Ltd v Rawlings* [1938] 4 All E.R. 100; *Freeman & Lockyer v Buckhurst Park Properties (Mangal) Ltd* [1964] 2 Q.B. 480, (Illustration 31); *Panorama Developments (Guildford) Ltd v Fidelis Furnishing Fabrics Ltd* [1971] 2 Q.B. 711, Illustration 30. cf. *Kreditbank Cassel GmbH v Schenkers* [1927] 1 K.B. 826; *Rama Corp Ltd v Proved Tin and General Investments Ltd* [1952] 2 Q.B. 147.

[220] *Mercantile Bank of India Ltd v Central Bank of India Ltd* [1938] 1 All E.R. 52.

[221] See *First Energy (UK) Ltd v Hungarian International Bank Ltd* [1993] 2 Lloyd's Rep. 194, Illustration 12.

[222] *Morris v Kanssen* [1946] A.C. 459; *Howard v Patent Ivory Co* (1888) 38 Ch.D. 156. cf. *Hely-Hutchinson v Brayhead Ltd* [1968] 1 Q.B. 549; affirmed on other grounds at 573.

[223] *A.L. Underwood Ltd v Bank of Liverpool* [1924] 1 K.B. 775; *Liggett v Barclays Bank* [1928] 1 K.B. 48; *Houghton & Co v Nothard, Lowe & Wills* [1927] 1 K.B. 246, Illustration 26; and see Article 75.

[224] *Freeman & Lockyer v Buckhurst Park Properties (Mangal) Ltd* [1964] 2 Q.B. 480 at 506.

refused to find apparent authority in a person whose authority was represented by a person who only had apparent authority to do so.[225] It is submitted, however, that whether or not the decision is correct on the facts, this goes too far: so long as the authority ultimately traces back to a person with actual authority (subject to s.40), that should be sufficient.[226]

Case law as to what usual authority should be attributed to the various company officials other than directors is limited and mostly out of date. As in the case of solicitors, accountants and the like, modern evidence should be required as to what can be regarded as normal.[227] Old cases tended to attribute limited authority to persons designated as "managers", and to company secretaries. But more recent decisions recognise greater authority in such persons[228]; and the role of the chairman of the directors has developed since the nineteenth century, though it varies from company to company.[229]

8-040   **Execution of documents**   Section 44 of the Companies Act 2006, which re-enacts earlier legislation abolishing the necessity for a corporate seal,[230] further provides that in favour of a purchaser (defined as a "purchaser in good faith for valuable consideration ... who ... acquires an interest in property") a document shall[231] be deemed to be duly executed if it purports to be signed by a director and the secretary or by two directors, or by a single director whose signature is witnessed.[232] This provision is then supplemented by ss.46 and 47 in relation to deeds and documents signed under a power of attorney. As seen above,[233] it is strongly arguable that at common law the unauthorised use of the company seal is a special matter of indoor management of the company and does not turn on the relevant agents' possession of actual or apparent authority to enter into the transaction in question (the deed, however, would have to be correct in form and the signatures those of genuine officers, even if unauthorised). On this basis, a company's deed can be binding without the normal requirements of the law of agency being met, as indeed may deeds generally. Whatever the position at com-

---

[225] *Crabtree-Vickers Pty Ltd v Australian Direct Mail Advertising and Addressing Co Pty Ltd* (1975) 133 C.L.R. 72.

[226] See *British Bank of the Middle East v Sun Life Assurance Co of Canada (UK) Ltd* [1983] 2 Lloyd's Rep. 9 HL, Illustration 10 to Article 75, where the apparent authority of an intermediate agent was discussed. See also above, para.8-018.

[227] See above, para.3-032.

[228] e.g. *Panorama Developments (Guildford) Ltd v Fidelis Furnishing Fabrics Ltd* [1971] 2 Q.B. 711, Illustration 30 (company secretary); *First Energy (UK) Ltd v Hungarian International Bank Ltd* [1993] B.C.L.C. 1409 at 1422; *Kelly v Fraser* [2012] UKPC 25; [2013] 1 A.C. 450 at [13]; *Australia and New Zealand Banking Group Ltd v Frenmast Pty Ltd* [2013] NSWCA 459. See too *Montreal and St Lawrence Light and Power Co v Robert* [1906] A.C. 196 at 203 (joint representation of president and secretary).

[229] See *Hely-Hutchinson v Brayhead Ltd* [1968] 1 Q.B. 549; *Deutsche Bank AG v Asia Pacific Broadband Wireless Communications Inc* [2008] EWCA Civ 1091; [2008] 2 Lloyd's Rep. 619 at [27].

[230] Companies Act 1985 s.36A, which was superseded on October 1, 2008.

[231] As to good faith in this context, see *LNOC Ltd v Watford Association Football Club Ltd* [2013] EWHC 3615 (Comm) at [91].

[232] See s.44(2); *Re Armstrong Brands Ltd* [2015] EWHC 3303 (Ch) (director resigns before secretary also signs); *Signature Living Hotel Ltd v Sulyok* [2020] EWHC 257 (Ch) (no deed where single signature not witnessed). See further *Buckley on the Companies Acts* (2006). In relation to contracts and the execution of documents by overseas companies, see the Overseas Companies (Execution of Documents and Registration of Charges) Regulations 2009 (SI 2009/1917) promulgated under Companies Act 2006 s.1045. As to Scottish companies, see s.48 of the 2006 Act.

[233] See above, para.8-034.

mon law, s.44 does appear to give prima facie validity in favour of "purchasers"[234] to company documents executed in accordance with the section whether or not with proper authority. It is possible under s.44 for a director to execute a document both for the company and in a personal capacity,[235] but a single signature cannot operate for more than one company at once.[236] A contract not executed in accordance with the requirements of s.44 can still take effect as an ordinary contract if entered into by a person with actual or apparent authority.[237] The provision in s.44 that a document executed by a single director binds if the signature is witnessed is remarkably generous to third parties, since it seems that the witness need have no connection to the company. It is one thing to have to answer for the acts of two dishonest directors, but quite another to do so for just one, the signature of whom is witnessed by a stranger. This surprising reform somewhat undermines the standard position that a single director, without management functions, has modest apparent authority to bind a company.[238]

As to the use of powers of attorney by corporations, see below, para.8-087.

Forgery   As under apparent authority generally,[239] the company can be bound, though the agent effects a forgery in the sense of executing an unauthorised signature. But an actual counterfeit signature would simply be a nullity.[240] There may, however, be an estoppel against setting up a forgery in either sense, if the elements of a holding out and reliance can be established.[241] It has also been suggested, in relation to companies, that s.44 of the Companies Act 2006 might give effect to forged signatures.[242] In particular, s.44(5) provides: "[i]n favour of a purchaser a document is deemed to have been duly executed by a company if it purports to be signed in accordance with subsection (2)". Forged directors' signatures do *purport* to be official signatures. However, this would lead to the most surprising, and not very just, conclusion that a company could be bound by forged signatures that were placed on a document by persons who had no connection whatsoever with the company. It is difficult to believe that this outcome was contemplated by the section.[243] **8-041**

---

[234] As to which, see *Lovett v Carson Country Homes Ltd* [2009] EWHC 1143 (Ch); [2009] 2 B.C.L.C. 196 (noted by Payne [2010] L.M.C.L.Q. 197).

[235] See *Williams v Redcard Ltd* [2011] EWCA Civ 466; [2011] 2 B.C.L.C. 350.

[236] See s.44(6).

[237] See *Signature Living Hotel Ltd v Sulyok* [2020] EWHC 257 (Ch) at [34]; and see above, para.2-042.

[238] For the common law position, see above, para.3-031.

[239] See Article 74.

[240] *Northside Developments Pty Ltd v Registrar-General* (1990) 170 C.L.R. 146 at 199.

[241] *Greenwood v Martin's Bank Ltd* [1933] A.C. 51; *M'Kenzie v British Linen Co* (1881) 6 App.Cas. 82; *Fung Kai Sun v Chan Fui Hing* [1951] A.C. 489; *Rowe v B. & R. Nominees Pty Ltd* [1964] V.R. 477; *Welch v Bank of England* [1955] Ch. 508; *Spiro v Lintern* [1973] 1 W.L.R. 1002.

[242] *Lovett v Carson Country Homes Ltd* [2009] EWHC 1143 (Ch); [2009] 2 B.C.L.C. 196 at [99], where, however, the forging party was also a real director. He was also held to have had apparent authority to bind the company. cf. *Skandinaviska Enskilda Banken v Asia Pacific Breweries* [2009] 4 Singapore L.R. 788; affirmed [2011] SGCA 22.

[243] cf. *Kreditbank Cassel GmbH v Schenkers* [1927] 1 K.B. 826 at 842–843, per Atkin LJ.

8-042   **The Crown**   Employees of the Crown are all servants of the Crown and do not employ each other.[244] Apparent authority may be extremely difficult to prove in a Crown or other public agent, for in *Att.-Gen. for Ceylon v Silva*[245] it was said that:

> "no public officer, unless he possesses some special power, can hold out on behalf of the Crown that he or some other public officer has the right to enter into a contract in respect of the property of the Crown when in fact no such right exists."[246]

However, this was a clear case, inasmuch as the agent's powers were limited by delegated legislation, and to hold otherwise would have been to give a Crown official a dispensing power to validate ultra vires acts. Apparent authority in a Crown agent, even a Minister of Finance, cannot be established in the face of a constitutional restriction on powers,[247] unless infraction of the restriction was not apparent.[248] Another clear case occurs where to bind the Crown would be to permit an officer of the Crown to fetter the Crown's freedom of action to do its public duty.[249] Subject to these important reservations, however, it may be possible to establish apparent authority, including usual authority,[250] in the normal way[251]; though where it is argued that one officer held out another as having authority, it will be necessary to establish the actual (or sometimes apparent) authority of that officer to do so.[252] It may also be difficult to distinguish this form of estoppel from other estoppels, e.g. as to whether the relevant authority has taken a decision or an

---

[244] *Raleigh v Goschen* [1898] 1 Ch. 73; *Bainbridge v Postmaster-General* [1906] 1 K.B. 178; *Moukataff v BOAC* [1967] 1 Lloyd's Rep. 396 at 423–424; *Commissioner of Inland Revenue v Chesterfields Preschools Ltd* [2013] NZCA 53; [2013] 2 N.Z.L.R. 679 at [47].

[245] *Att.-Gen. for Ceylon v Silva* [1953] A.C. 461. See also *Comeau v Province of New Brunswick* (1973) 36 D.L.R. (3d) 763 (welfare official); *Director of Posts and Telegraphs v Abbott* (1974) 22 F.L.R. 157 (clerk in telephone office); *Donegal International Ltd v Republic of Zambia* [2007] EWHC 197 (Comm); [2007] 1 Lloyd's Rep. 397 at [450]; *Tipperary Developments Pty Ltd v The State of Western Australia* (2009) 38 W.A.R. 488.

[246] *Att.-Gen. for Ceylon v Silva* [1953] A.C. 461 at 479, per Mr L.M.D. de Silva. cf. *Robertson v Minister of Pensions* [1949] 1 K.B. 227; see as to this case *Howell v Falmouth Boat Construction Co* [1951] A.C. 837 at 845, 849; and *Commissioners of Crown Lands v Page* [1960] 2 Q.B. 274.

[247] *Donegal International Ltd v Republic of Zambia* [2007] EWHC 197 (Comm); [2007] 1 Lloyd's Rep. 397 at [451].

[248] *Ukraine v Law Debenture Trust Corp Plc* [2018] EWCA Civ 2026; [2019] 2 W.L.R. 655 at [111].

[249] See *Southend-on-Sea Corp v Hodgson (Wickford) Ltd* [1962] 1 Q.B. 416; *Union SS Co of New Zealand Ltd v CIR* [1962] N.Z.L.R. 656; *Director of Posts and Telegraphs v Abbott* (1974) 22 F.L.R. 157.

[250] There are a number of cases involving foreign governments where usual authority has been found to exist or been considered: see *Marubeni Hong Kong & South China Ltd v Government of Mongolia* [2004] EWHC 472 (Comm); [2004] 2 Lloyd's Rep. 198; affirmed on other grounds [2005] EWCA Civ 395; [2005] 2 Lloyd's Rep. 231; *Donegal International Ltd v Republic of Zambia* [2007] EWHC 197 (Comm); [2007] 1 Lloyd's Rep. 397 at [450]; *Charles Terence Estates Ltd v Cornwall Council* [2012] EWCA Civ 1439; [2013] 1 W.L.R. 466 at [49]; *Law Debenture Trust Corp Plc v Ukraine* [2018] EWCA Civ 2026; [2019] 2 W.L.R. 655. As to usual authority separate from apparent authority, see Treitel [1957] P.L. 335, suggesting that *Robertson v Minister of Pensions* [1949] 1 K.B. 227 may be an example of this. The possibility of usual authority was ignored in *Miles v McIlwraith* (1883) 8 App.Cas. 120 but that was a criminal case.

[251] Liability of the Crown in contract was facilitated by the Crown Proceedings Act 1947 s.1. See *J.E. Verreault et Fils Ltée v Att.-Gen. for Quebec* [1977] 1 S.C.R. 41; (1975) 57 D.L.R. (3d) 403; Hilliard (1976) 54 Can.B.R. 401; *Commonwealth v Crothall Hospital Services (Aust.) Ltd* (1981) 54 F.L.R. 439; *PEC Ltd v Asia Golden Rice Co Ltd* [2014] EWHC 1583 (Comm) at [57]; *Pascoe Properties Ltd v Att.-Gen.* [2014] NZCA 616 at [54]. cf. *Director of Posts and Telegraphs v Abbott* (1974) 22 F.L.R. 157. As to the apparent authority of a Consul-General, see *Tasita Pty Ltd v Sovereign State of Papua New Guinea* (1991) 34 N.S.W.L.R. 691.

[252] See above, para.8-029.

immunity has been waived.[253] The interaction of public and private law principles makes the area a difficult one.

Illustrations

Creation of an agent

(1) A was in B's counting-house, apparently entrusted with the conduct of B's business. Held, that a payment to A on B's account operated as a payment to B, although A was not, in fact, employed by B.[254]

(2) A professional organiser of fairs and exhibitions ordered supplies for a fair using note paper on which the defendant's names appeared as an "executive committee". They were held liable for the supplies notwithstanding that the fair was a proprietary concern belonging to the organiser, since the suppliers were led to believe that the committee was responsible for the management of the fair.[255]

(3) Goods are ordered for an unincorporated charitable institution on behalf of the person who first managed the institution. A committee of governors is later formed which tacitly acquiesces in the continued supply of goods. A member of the committee is liable.[256]

(4) A, the tenant and licensee of a public house, agreed with B and the owners of the public house that B should become tenant in place of A, but the licence was not transferred to B, and A's name remained painted over the doorway. C, not knowing that A was the licensee, supplied goods at the public house to B; and afterwards discovered that A was the licensee and sued him for the price of the goods. Held, that the agreement that B should occupy a position as tenant which could only be lawfully occupied by A did not make B the agent of A in relation to C; and that there was no estoppel in the matter between A and C,

8-043

---

[253] See *Miles v McIlwraith* (1883) 8 App.Cas. 120; *Att.-Gen. for Ceylon v Silva* [1953] A.C. 461 at 480; *P. v P.* [1957] N.Z.L.R. 854; *P. v P. (No.2)* [1958] N.Z.L.R. 349; *Wells v Minister of Housing and Local Government* [1967] 1 W.L.R. 1000; *Lever Finance Ltd v Westminster (City) London BC* [1971] 1 Q.B. 222; *Norfolk CC v Secretary of State for the Environment* [1973] 1 W.L.R. 1400; *Co-operative Retail Services Ltd v Taff-Ely BC* (1979) 39 P. & C.R. 223; *Rootkin v Kent CC* [1981] 1 W.L.R. 1186; *Western Fish Products Ltd v Penwith DC* [1981] 2 All E.R. 204; Craig, *Administrative Law* (7th edn), para.22-027 onwards.

[254] *Barrett v Deere* (1828) Moo. & M. 200. The situation is obviously an unusual one. See also *Galbraith & Grant v Block* [1922] 2 K.B. 155; *Bocking Garage v Mazurk*, *The Times*, February 4, 1954; *Hoddesdon v Koos Bros* 135 A.2d 702 (N.J., 1957) (Illustration 1 to Article 21) (bogus salesman in shop); *Luken v Buckeye Parking Corp* 68 N.E.2d 217 (Ohio, 1945) (bogus parking attendant: cf. *Mendelssohn v Normand Ltd* [1970] 1 Q.B. 177). Some of these cases come close to contravening the principle that one does not become liable merely because one provides facilities within which others can commit fraud: see Comment to Article 21.

[255] *F. Mildner & Sons v Noble* [1956] C.L.Y. 32; *The Times,* March 8, 1956; see also *Pilot v Craze* (1888) 52 J.P. 311; *Royal Albert Hall Corp v Winchilsea* (1891) 7 T.L.R. 362; *Povey v Taylor* (1966) 116 New L.J. 1656; *Winter v Hockley Mint Ltd* [2018] EWCA Civ 2480; [2019] 1 W.L.R. 1617 at [76].

[256] *Glenester v Hunter* (1831) 5 C. & P. 62; *Luckombe v Ashton* (1862) 2 F. & F. 705; *Harper v Granville-Smith* (1891) 7 T.L.R. 284. cf. *Royal Albert Hall Corp v Winchilsea* (1891) 7 T.L.R. 362; *Draper v Earl Manvers* (1892) 9 T.L.R. 73. See further Article 107; Keeler (1971) 34 M.L.R. 615; Fletcher (1979) 11 U.Qd.L.J. 53 and material there cited.

because whatever misrepresentations had been made, they had not reached C nor caused him to act to his detriment.[257]

(5)   A person is employed by a company to service their aircraft and teach some of its employees to fly. The company permits him to run an air taxi business under a name which gives the impression that the business is part of theirs. Neither the company nor the person concerned is licensed to do such work. An aircraft crashes while on such work. The company has held out the person concerned as its agent and is the carrier.[258]

(6)   The holder of a stolen cheque card and cheque book may, by virtue of the statements on the card, have apparent authority to communicate to a third party the offer of the card issuer to honour a cheque supported by it.[259]

Extension of existing authority

8-044   (7)   A occasionally employed B to purchase goods from C and duly recognised such purchases. Subsequently, B purchased goods from C for his own use, C believing him to be buying them on behalf of A, and giving credit to A. Held, that it was a question of fact whether A had, by his conduct, held out B as his agent to purchase the goods.[260]

(8)   The assignee of a life policy which was voidable if the assured went beyond Europe, in paying the premiums to the local agent of the assurance company, told him that the assured was in Canada. The agent said that that would not avoid the policy, and continued to receive the premiums until the death of the assured. Held, that the company was estopped by the representation of its agent from saying that the policy was avoided by the absence of the assured.[261] So, where a shipmaster signed a bill of lading containing a statement that the freight had been paid, it was held that the owners were estopped from claiming the freight from an indorsee for value of the bill of lading.[262]

---

[257] *Mac Fisheries Ltd v Harrison* (1924) 93 L.J.K.B. 811; cf. *Smith v M'Guire* (1858) 3 H. & N. 554; *Dunn v Shanks* [1932] N.I. 66. See also *Charrington Fuel Oils Ltd v Parvant Co, The Times,* December 28, 1988, CA (property changes hands; new owners request previous suppliers, who have no notice of change, to continue; no apparent authority to bind former owners).

[258] *Gurtner v Beaton* [1993] 2 Lloyd's Rep. 369. See also *Lease Management Services Ltd v Purnell Secretarial Services Ltd* [1994] C.C.L.R. 127 (finance company estopped from saying employee of supplying company not its agent). Such an explanation could be applied to the famous but puzzling case of *Watteau v Fenwick* [1893] 1 Q.B. 346, considered below, para.8-077. See Tettenborn [1998] C.L.J. 274.

[259] *First Sport Ltd v Barclays Bank Plc* [1993] 1 W.L.R. 1229.

[260] *Todd v Robinson* (1825) 1 Ry. & M. 217; *Gilman v Robinson* (1825) 1 Ry. & M. 226; *Haughton v Ewbank* (1814) 4 Camp. 188; *Watkins v Vince* (1818) 2 Starke 368. See also *International Paper Co v Spicer* (1906) 4 C.L.R. 739; *International Sponge Importers Ltd v Watt & Sons* [1911] A.C. 279; *Swiss Air Transport Co Ltd v Palmer* [1976] 2 Lloyd's Rep. 604; *Pharmed Medicare Private Ltd v Univar Ltd* [2002] EWCA Civ 1569; [2003] 1 All E.R. (Comm) 321; *Lovett v Carson Country Homes Ltd* [2009] EWHC 1143 (Ch); [2009] 2 B.C.L.C. 19; *CRJ Services Ltd v Lanstar Ltd (t/a CSG Lanstar)* [2011] EWHC 972 (TCC) (agent regularly hiring equipment short term for principal has apparent authority to hire larger capital items for longer periods); cf. *Spooner v Browning* [1898] 1 Q.B. 528. Article 75, Illustration 1; *Bailey & Whites Ltd v House* (1915) 31 T.L.R. 583 (carelessness over paying for unordered goods did not constitute a course of dealing); *Slingsby v District Bank Ltd* [1932] 1 K.B. 544 at 566; *PEC Ltd v Asia Golden Rice Co Ltd* [2014] EWHC 1583 (Comm) at [67] (relevant contract on a grander scale than any previous dealings).

[261] *Wing v Harvey* (1854) 5 De G.M. & G. 265. See Clarke, *Law of Insurance Contracts* (6th edn), paras 8-2A1 and 20-7C. cf. Article 75, Illustration 8.

[262] *Howard v Tucker* (1831) 1 B. & Ad. 712. See also *Compania Naviera Vasconzada v Churchill &*

(9)   A was in debt to a company for goods supplied by its branch at X, and also for goods supplied by its branch at Y. He entered into a deed of assignment for the benefit of his creditors. The company's agent at X branch assented to the deed, but its agent at Y branch refused to assent. The company sued A for the debt incurred at Y branch. Held, that the company was bound by the first assent given by its agent at X branch as to all debts due from A, and was precluded from maintaining the action.[263]

(10)   E, in one case as a salaried partner of a firm of solicitors, and in the other as an employed solicitor of a different firm, makes representations that funds becoming available to his firm will be transferred to a bank or to a customer of the bank: on the security of these undertakings the bank makes loans. The firms are bound.[264]

(11)   The documentary credits manager of a trading bank signs a guarantee without, as he should have done, obtaining a director's assent and a counter-signature. Evidence indicates that practice regarding the authority of such officials is varied, but there are other indications from which it appears that the bank has entrusted the handling of this particular matter to the manager. The bank is bound.[265]

(12)   The senior manager in charge of the Manchester office of a foreign bank operating in London who would have usual authority to enter into debt contracts of the type requested, but in fact did not have actual authority, informs the borrower of the fact that any facilities would need to be approved by head office. Pending approval of a loan facility, a valid ad hoc hire purchase agreement was entered into between the parties. The manager writes a letter accepting the borrower's request for further hire purchase finance. He has apparent authority to notify the prospective borrower that his superiors in London have approved the finance and is interpreted as having done so: the bank is bound.[266]

Reservations in authority not known to third party

(13)   An agent was entrusted by his principal with a document containing a writ- **8-045**
ten consent signed by the principal to do a particular act, but the agent was told not to give the consent, except on certain conditions which were not specified in the document. The agent consented unconditionally. Held, that the principal was bound, though he had signed the document without having read it.[267] So, where A gave B a power of attorney to charge and transfer in any form whatever any estate, etc. "following A's letters of instructions and private advices which, if necessary", should "considered part of these

Sim [1906] 1 K.B. 237; *Silver v Ocean Steamship Co Ltd* [1930] 1 K.B. 416 (statements as to apparent order and condition of goods shipped); *The Nea Tyhi* [1982] 1 Lloyd's Rep. 606 (shipment under deck); Article 75, Illustration 2.

[263] *Dunlop Rubber Co Ltd v Haigh & Sons* [1937] 1 K.B. 347.

[264] *United Bank of Kuwait Ltd v Hammoud* [1988] 1 W.L.R. 1051; see [1989] J.B.L. 63 and above, para.8-020. But cf. *Hirst v Etheringtons* [1999] Lloyd's Rep. P.N. 938; and see *Hammoud's* case criticised in *Lindley and Banks on Partnership* (20th edn), para.12-06.

[265] *Egyptian International Foreign Trade Co v Soplex Wholesale Supplies Ltd (The Raffaella)* [1985] 2 Lloyd's Rep. 36. cf. Article 21, Illustration 2.

[266] *First Energy (UK) Ltd v Hungarian International Bank Ltd* [1993] 2 Lloyd's Rep. 194.

[267] *Duke of Beaufort v Neeld* (1845) 12 C. & F. 248.

presents", it was held that A was bound by a mortgage on his property executed by B, although as between A and B the mortgage was not authorised.[268] So, where a principal wrote: "I have authorised A to see you, and, if possible, to come to some amicable arrangement" and gave A private instructions not to settle for less than a certain amount, it was held that he was bound by A's settlement for less than that amount, the instructions not having been communicated to the other party.[269]

(14) A gives B a signed form of promissory note or acceptance in blank, with authority on certain conditions to fill it up and convert it into a bill of exchange or promissory note for a certain amount. B fills it up in breach of the conditions and for a larger amount than was authorised, and negotiates it to C, who takes it in good faith and for value, without notice of the circumstances. A is liable to C on the bill or note as filled up, for he is estopped from denying its validity as between himself and C.[270] It would be otherwise if C had had notice of the circumstances in which the document was issued[271] or if B had not been authorised to issue the document as a negotiable instrument except on the receipt of instructions from A on that behalf.[272]

(15) An agent was given authority, in cases of emergency, to borrow money on exceptional terms outside the ordinary course of business. A third person, in good faith and without notice that the agent was exceeding his authority, lent money to him on such exceptional terms. Held, that the principal was bound, although in the particular case the emergency had not arisen.[273]

(16) A solicitor is entrusted with the conduct of litigation for clients who are defendants. A compromise is contemplated involving the purchase of property by the defendants at a valuation. The clients tell him not to agree to the appointment of a valuer, but these instructions do not reach the person handling the matter, who agrees the terms of the compromise and the appointment of a valuer. The client is bound.[274]

(17) An auctioneer is instructed to sell goods by auction, a reserve price being fixed. By mistake he sells without reserve. The principal is bound by the sale,[275] unless the conditions of sale expressly provide that the lot is offered subject to a reserve price.[276]

---

[268] *Davy v Waller* (1899) 81 L.T. 107. cf. *Industrial and Commercial Bank of China Ltd, Mumbai Branch v Ambani* [2019] EWHC 3436 (Comm) at [87].

[269] *Trickett v Tomlinson* (1863) 13 C.B.(N.S.) 663.

[270] *Lloyd's Bank Ltd v Cooke* [1907] 1 K.B. 794. But quaere whether this and related cases should be regarded as agency cases: they are more properly to be attributed to general estoppel principles. See also Bills of Exchange Act 1882 s.20. See further *Chalmers and Guest on Bills of Exchange* (18th edn), para.2-139; below, para.8-134; *General & Finance Facilities Ltd v Hughes* (1966) 110 S.J. 847.

[271] *Hatch v Searles* (1854) 24 L.J.Ch. 22.

[272] *Smith v Prosser* [1907] 2 K.B. 735; see also *Baxendale v Bennett* (1878) 3 Q.B.D. 525; *Perpetual Trustees Australia Ltd v Heperu Pty Ltd* [2009] NSWCA 84.

[273] *Montaignac v Shitta* (1890) 15 App.Cas. 357.

[274] *Waugh v H.B. Clifford & Sons Ltd* [1982] Ch. 374. But this may not always be so: see above, para.3-005. See also *Thompson v Howley* [1977] 1 N.Z.L.R. 16; Kenny (1982) 126 S.J. 663; Foskett (1982) 79 L.S.Gaz. 57.

[275] *Rainbow v Howkins* [1904] 2 K.B. 322.

[276] *McManus v Fortescue* [1907] 2 K.B. 1. See also *Fay v Miller, Wilkins & Co* [1941] Ch. 360 (bidders need not have read the conditions). cf. *Szembrener v Pepper (New Zealand) Custodians Ltd* [2014] NZHC 324 (vendor ratified auctioneer's action by signing memorandum of sale).

(18) A solicitor is authorised to sue for a debt. A tender of the debt to his managing clerk operates as a tender to the client, although the clerk was instructed not to receive payment of the particular debt, unless at the time of the tender the clerk disclaims any authority to receive the money.[277]

(19) At a meeting of the provisional directors of a proposed company it was resolved that the company should be advertised, and the secretary was directed to take the necessary steps for that purpose. The secretary employed an advertising agent and upon being asked on what authority he was acting, showed the agent the prospectus and resolution. Held, that the jury were justified in finding the directors who were parties to the resolution liable for the expenses of the advertising agent, though they had allowed their names to appear as provisional directors on the faith of a promise by the secretary to find all the preliminary expenses.[278]

(20) A charterparty provides that the master, who is appointed by the owners, shall sign bills of lading as the agent of the charterers only. The owners are liable on a bill of lading signed on their behalf by the master, to a person who ships goods with notice of the charterparty but without notice of its terms.[279]

(21) A man who has regularly paid bills in respect of contracts made by his wife[280] or otherwise shown his acquiescence in such contracts, as by directing alterations to goods supplied,[281] revokes his wife's authority to pledge his credit. His wife nevertheless orders further goods from a supplier who does not know of the prohibition. The man is liable. The same would be true if the debt was incurred in similar circumstances by a person who lived with him but was not his wife.[282] But apparent authority does not necessarily arise merely because he has met one bill,[283] or accompanied the person concerned shopping,[284] nor did it arise where the goods were supplied to a different address from that originally used.[285]

(22) A signs an underwriting agreement purporting to give B authority to apply for shares in a company in A's name and on his behalf, and hands it to an agent of the promoters, with a letter stating that the agreement was signed, and is only to hold good, on certain conditions. The agreement is delivered to B, who applies for the shares, and they are duly allotted to A, neither B nor the company having any notice of the letter or conditions. A is bound as a shareholder, though the conditions were not complied with.[286]

---

[277] *Moffat v Parsons* (1814) 1 Marsh. 55; *Kirton v Braithwaite* (1836) 1 M. & W. 310; *Finch v Boning* (1879) 4 C.P.D. 143. cf. *Bingham v Allport* (1833) 1 N. & M. 398. And see *Re Buckley and Bienefelt* (1976) 13 A.L.R. 291; Cordery, *Solicitors* (8th edn), p.82.

[278] *Maddick v Marshall* (1864) 17 C.B.(N.S.) 829; *Riley v Packington* (1867) L.R. 2 C.P. 536; cf. *Burbidge v Morris* (1865) 3 H. & C. 664. As to company promoters, see further *Gower's Principles of Modern Company Law* (10th edn), Ch.5.

[279] *Manchester Trust v Furness* [1895] 2 Q.B. 539; cf. *Baumwoll Manufactur von Carl Scheibler v Furness* [1893] A.C. 8, where the master was appointed by the demise charterer.

[280] *Debenham v Mellon* (1880) 16 App.Cas. 24 at 36; *Drew v Nunn* (1879) 4 Q.B.D. 661; *Hawthorne Bros v Reilly* [1949] V.L.R. 137.

[281] *Jetley v Hill* (1884) C. & E. 239.

[282] *Ryan v Sams* (1848) 12 Q.B. 460.

[283] *Durrant v Holdsworth* (1886) 2 T.L.R. 763.

[284] *Seymour v Kingscote* (1922) 38 T.L.R. 586.

[285] *Swan & Edgar Ltd v Mathieson* (1910) 103 L.T. 832; cf. *Filmer v Lynn* (1835) 4 N. & M. 559. See also Illustration 7; Article 75, Illustration 1.

[286] *Ex p. Harrison, re Bentley & Co & Yorkshire Breweries Ltd* (1893) 69 L.T. 204.

[429]

(23) A ship requires salvage services. Its owners arrange for a salvage tug. Coincidentally, another tug appears and offers assistance. The master takes it to be the tug ordered by the owners and signs a salvage agreement. He would normally have actual authority to do so, but on this occasion has not because other arrangements have been made. The owners are bound.[287]

Agents of companies

8-046 (24) By the articles of association of a company, the directors are authorised to borrow on bond as may from time to time be authorised by general resolution of the company. The directors borrow £1,000 on a bond to which the corporate seal was attached, no such resolution having been passed. Held, that the company is liable on the bond, the lender having no notice of the irregularity.[288]

(25) The directors of a company had power, by the articles of association, to delegate such of their powers as they thought fit to a managing director. Held, that the company was bound by the acts, with the scope of such powers, of a person who acted to their knowledge as managing director, though there was no evidence that he had been duly appointed or that the powers of the directors had been delegated to him, the person dealing with him having acted in good faith and without notice of any want of authority.[289]

(26) By the articles of a fruit importing company the directors were authorised to delegate their powers. One of the directors, acting without authority, purported to make an agreement on behalf of the company whereby a loan was made (by a fruit broker) to another fruit importing company of which he was also a director, and the lender was granted the right to sell on commission the fruit imported by both companies, retaining the commission against the loan to the second company. The lender required confirmation from the secretary of the first company, who, also acting without authority, gave it. The first company was not bound by the agreement, as the acts concerned were not within the usual authority of a director and a secretary, and the articles not having been read by the lender, no apparent authority arose.[290]

(27) A trading company, having power by its memorandum of association to borrow money and give security and to act through agents, gave a power of attorney to an agent empowering him to borrow and give security. Held, that the company was bound by the acts of the agent acting within the apparent scope of the authority so constituted, notwithstanding that the agent may have exceeded the authority actually given to him as between himself and the company, provided that (as the law then stood) nothing in the articles of association prohibited the company from borrowing through such an agent.[291]

(28) A and B formed a company to purchase and resell a large estate. A and B,

---

[287] *The Unique Mariner* [1978] 1 Lloyd's Rep. 438. See above, para.4-008.

[288] *Royal British Bank v Turquand* (1856) 6 E. & B. 327.

[289] *Biggerstaff v Rowatt's Wharf Ltd* [1896] 2 Ch. 93.

[290] *Houghton & Co v Nothard, Lowe & Wills* [1927] 1 K.B. 246; affirmed on other grounds [1928] A.C. 1.

[291] *Mercantile Bank of India Ltd v Chartered Bank of India, Australia and China* [1937] 1 All E.R. 231. The headnote is misleading in suggesting that the estoppel arose from the articles rather than the power of attorney: see *Gower's Modern Company Law* (10th edn), para.7-26. For the present position see above, para.8-033.

together with a nominee of each of them were the directors of the company. A agreed to pay the running expenses of the company and to reimburse himself out of profits. A instructed architects to apply for planning permission and to do other work in connection with the estate. The company was held liable for the architects' fees, though A had never been appointed managing director.[292]

(29) Directors of a company accept a loan and execute a guarantee and a debenture over all the company's assets for an inadmissible purpose. The execution of the guarantee and the debenture come within the company's corporate capacity, but the directors have no authority to enter into the guarantee for such a purpose. The third party is aware of this. The transaction is void.[293]

(30) A company secretary hires cars, saying that they are needed to meet customers of the company at London Airport and drive them to the company's factory at Leeds. He uses the cars for purposes of his own. The company is bound by the contracts of hire, since the secretary has apparent authority to act in such matters of administration.[294]

(31) The chairperson and head of the company's remuneration committee authorises the chief executive to instruct solicitors to prepare remuneration contracts for himself and an executive colleague. The chief executive includes in his instructions to the solicitors terms that would confer large bonuses to be paid to the executives on the occurrence of certain events. The solicitors act on those instructions and send the prepared contracts to the chairperson for approval and signature. There was a holding out of the chief executive to give instructions to the solicitors in relation to drafting the terms of his own remuneration given that the final version of the contract would go before the remuneration committee.[295]

Article 73

No Unauthorised Act Binding with Respect to Persons with Notice

No act done by an agent in excess of actual authority is binding on the principal with respect to persons having notice that in doing the act the agent may be exceeding the agent's authority.[296] **8-047**

---

[292] *Freeman & Lockyer v Buckhurst Park Properties (Mangal) Ltd* [1964] 2 Q.B. 480.
[293] *Rolled Steel Products (Holdings) Ltd v British Steel Corp* [1986] Ch. 246. See further Payne and Prentice [2005] L.M.C.L.Q. 447; Article 23.
[294] *Panorama Developments (Guildford) Ltd v Fidelis Furnishing Fabrics Ltd* [1971] 2 Q.B. 711. Earlier decisions giving a very limited authority to a company secretary were said to be obsolete in view of changed practice: see *Barnett, Hoares & Co v South London Tramways Co* (1887) 18 Q.B.D. 815; *Ruben v Great Fingall Consolidated* [1905] A.C. 439; *Kleinwort, Sons & Co v Associated Automatic Machine Corp* (1934) 50 T.L.R. 244. See [1972A] C.L.J. 44; cf. Article 75, Illustration 3. See other cases referred to above, para.8-039.
[295] *Newcastle International Airport Ltd v Eversheds LLP* [2013] EWCA Civ 1514; [2014] 1 W.L.R. 3073.
[296] cf. Partnership Act 1890 s.5. See *Lysaght Bros & Co Ltd v Falk* (1905) 2 C.L.R. 421; *Combulk Pty Ltd v TNT Management Pty Ltd* (1993) 113 A.L.R. 214. This Article and the following Article are cited with approval in *Albright & Wilson UK Ltd v Biachem Ltd* [2001] EWCA 301; [2001] 2 All E.R. (Comm) 537 at [16] (on appeal [2002] UKHL 37; [2002] 2 All E.R. (Comm) 753); *Knightsbridge Property Development Corp (UK) Ltd v South Chelsea Properties Ltd* [2017] EWHC 2730 (Ch) at [65] (noted E. Lees, "Agency, knowledge and good faith in land registration: Knightsbridge

Comment

8-048   This proposition is mainly relevant to apparent authority: but it seems also true of the perfectly possible situation where the third party knows that the agent's authority has been withdrawn but the agent does not.[297] It arises naturally from the formulation of the doctrine of apparent authority, which requires that the third party deal with the agent on the faith of the principal's representation.[298] Situations of express notice cause no difficulty.[299] The problem is to know what constitutes notice, and when there is a duty to inquire. It is often said that neither constructive[300] nor presumed[301] notice apply in commercial transactions. This certainly excludes the full doctrine of constructive notice of equitable interests in land, whereby a person is expected to take the initiative and make inquiries, being deemed to have notice of property interests which would have come to that person's knowledge if such inquiries and inspections had been made as ought reasonably to have been made.[302] But there can be no doubt that in many situations where it is relevant to know whether one person has knowledge of facts, including those raising the doctrine of apparent authority, the court may infer from the circumstances that the person concerned must have known of the facts in question or at least ought to have been suspicious to the extent that further inquiries would have been appropriate in the context.[303]

It seems that the proper approach in commercial cases is to apply the objective interpretation which one person is entitled to put on another's words and conduct in the light of the facts known to the former. The matter was well elucidated in a judgment of Neill J relating to the imposition of a constructive trust on a person who buys goods which are being sold in breach of duty at undervalue—admittedly a different context.[304] He said:

"In deciding whether a person in the position of the defendants had actual notice, (a) the

---

Property Development Corporation (UK) Limited v South Chelsea Properties Limited" [2018] Conv. 76).

[297] See above, para.8-007.

[298] See above, para.8-023. Continental European systems, from a different starting-point, may tend towards a different result and may even conclude that a third party can hold the principal liable though he knows of the lack of authority, simply because of the position of the agent. The principal's remedy is to remove the agent. But efforts may also be made to avoid such results by the use of other doctrines such as that of good faith. See Schmitthoff, 1970 *I Hague Recueil des Cours*, pp.120–121; Müller-Freienfels (1964) 13 Am.J. Comp.L. 192 at 211 onwards and 341 onwards. See too *The Unauthorised Agent* (Busch and Macgregor eds, 2009).

[299] See Illustration 1.

[300] *Manchester Trust v Furness* [1897] 2 Q.B. 539.

[301] *Eagle Star Insurance Co Ltd v Spratt* [1971] 2 Lloyd's Rep. 116 at 128.

[302] See Law of Property Act 1925 s.199(1).

[303] This passage was approved and applied in *Combulk Pty Ltd v TNT Management Pty Ltd* (1993) 113 A.L.R. 214. See also *Macmillan Inc v Bishopsgate Investment Trust Plc* [1993] 1 W.L.R. 837 at 1000 and 1014–1015; *Alliance & Leicester BS v Edgestop Ltd* [1993] 1 W.L.R. 1462; and *Skandinaviska Enskilda Banken v Asia Pacific Breweries* [2009] 4 Singapore L.R. 788; affirmed [2011] SGCA 22. In *Hirst v Etheringtons* [1999] Lloyd's Rep. P.N. 938, Smedley J refers to "a reasonably acute, experienced and suspicious banker"; but in *Waugh v H.B. Clifford & Sons Ltd* [1982] Ch. 374 at 387, Brightman LJ points out that in some situations an inquiry by one solicitor of another might be "officious". This shows the variable nature of the duty. It appears that in French law the approach tends to concentrate on the reasonableness of the behaviour of the third party rather than the manifestations of the principal, which may enable a more careful scrutiny of questions such as these than the common law might allow: See Saintier in *The Unauthorised Agent* (Busch and Macgregor eds, 2009) Ch.2. But as to equity see below. See also Dal Pont, p.539 onwards.

[304] *Feuer Leather Corp v Frank Johnston & Sons Ltd* [1981] Com.L.Rep. 251, Illustration 7; and see

court will apply an objective test and look at all the circumstances; (b) if by an objective test clear notice was given liability cannot be avoided by proof merely of the absence of actual knowledge; (c) a person will be deemed to have had notice of any fact to which it can be shown that he deliberately turned a blind eye ... ; (d) on the other hand, the court will not expect the recipient of goods to scrutinise commercial documents such as delivery notes with great care; (3) there is no general duty on the buyer of goods in an ordinary commercial transaction to make inquiries as to the right of the seller to dispose of the goods; (f) the question becomes, looking objectively at the circumstances which are alleged to constitute notice, do those circumstances constitute notice? This must be a matter of fact and degree to be determined in the particular circumstances of the case .... The burden of proving a bona fide purchase for value without notice rests on the person who asserts it."

This particular dictum is cited here because, although uttered in the context of the constructive trust where later case law has intervened,[305] it remains appropriate to the sort of commercial situations in which the doctrines of apparent authority and apparent ownership are relied on. It is plain that the demands of commerce are a very significant factor in determining what a reasonable third party would do (note, not "might do") given the information available to him.[306] However, in another case concerned with liability in equity it has been pointed out that the exigencies of commerce cannot be an excuse for tolerating conduct regarded as unreasonable by persons in the same market or line of business[307]:

"The good sense of the general rule in relation to ordinary commercial transactions where there is no time or opportunity to make inquiries is obvious. But it would be very surprising if the law today was that the mere fact that a transaction was a commercial transaction was sufficient to prevent any duty of inquiry ever arising whatever the circumstances, particularly so many years after the confluence of the separate streams of equity and common law."

Many things might be sufficient to put an outsider on inquiry as to an agent's authority. The third party's knowledge that the agent has a substantial conflict of interest in respect of the transaction is one of the more common examples,[308] but unusual aspects of the transaction are another.[309]

Standard Bank v Bank of Tokyo [1995] 2 Lloyd's Rep. 167 at 175; *Macmillan Inc v Bishopsgate Investment Trust Plc* [1995] 1 W.L.R. 978 at 1000 and 1014–1015.

[305] See below, para.9-136.

[306] See e.g. *Lexi Holdings Plc v Pannone & Partners* [2009] EWHC 2590 (Ch) at [98] (solicitor not expected to question instructions of managing director of client); *Stavrinides v Bank of Cyprus Public Co Ltd* [2019] EWHC 1328 (Ch) at [104].

[307] *Baden Delvaux v Société Générale & Co SA* [1993] 1 W.L.R. 509 at 581, per Peter Gibson J; affirmed [1985] B.C.L.C. 258; below, para.9-132. See also *London Joint Stock Bank v Simmons* [1892] A.C. 201 at 223, per Lord Herschell: "And I do not think the law lays upon [the purchaser of bills] the obligation of making any inquiry into the title of the person whom he finds in possession of them; of course, if there is anything to arouse suspicion, to lead to a doubt whether the person purporting to transfer them is justified in entering into the contemplated transaction the case would be different, the existence of such suspicion or doubt would be inconsistent with good faith. And if no inquiry were made, or if on inquiry the doubt were not removed and the suspicion dissipated, I should have no hesitation in holding that good faith was wanting in a person thus acting".

[308] See *Lysaght Bros & Co Ltd v Falk* (1905) 2 C.L.R. 421 at 432; *John v Dodwell & Co Ltd* [1918] A.C. 563 (PC) at 569; *A.L. Underwood Ltd v Bank of Liverpool* [1924] 1 K.B. 775 (CA) at 788 and 794; *Reckitt v Barnett, Pembroke & Slater Ltd* [1929] A.C. 176 at 190; *Midland Bank Ltd v Reckitt* [1933] A.C. 1; *Rolled Steel (Holdings) Ltd v British Steel Corp* [1986] Ch. 246 (CA) at 306–307; *Heinl v Jyske Bank (Gibraltar) Ltd* [1999] Lloyd's Rep. Bank. 511 at 521; *Wrexham Association*

8-049   **Recent developments**   The foregoing paragraph retains, with small additions, the text of previous editions.[310] Doubt was thrown on these principles by Lord Neuberger of Abbotsbury in the Hong Kong Court of Final Appeal in *Akai Holdings Ltd v Thanakharn Kasikorn Thai Chamchat ("Akai")*.[311] He was persuaded by an argument that once apparent authority is established, the ability to rely on the representation so made out will be lost only if the third party has actual knowledge of the lack of actual authority or if that party's belief in the agent's authority was dishonest or irrational. The new concept, in this context anyway, of "irrationality" was preferred to the older test of unreasonable reliance on the holding out. Lord Neuberger distinguished a line of cases supporting the unreasonable reliance test on the basis that the cases involved promisors that were companies, and dated from a time when the law was especially protective of companies (since changed by statute). His Lordship then relied upon the idea that at common law it is no defence to a claim founded on a representation to show that the representee might have discovered its falsity by the exercise of reasonable care. The reasoning in *Akai* was then followed in a number of English cases.[312] However, orthodoxy appears to have been restored by the Privy Council decision in *East Asia Co Ltd v PT Satria Tirtatama Energindo*,[313] where the *Akai* case was expressly not followed on this issue.

8-050   Given that Privy Council decisions are not ordinarily binding in England and Wales,[314] it may be as well to retain in the meanwhile the following commentary, which was largely approved in the *East Asia* case. It is respectfully suggested that the reasoning in *Akai* was based on a misunderstanding of prior authorities and of general principle. For most practical purposes, what is at issue is whether the principal is bound to a contract with the third party. In principal-to-principal contracting it is very clear that the issue whether the parties have intended to contract, and the terms on which they have contracted, are judged from the position of the reasonable person, with such person's knowledge of observable facts,

---

    Football Club Ltd v Crucialmove Ltd [2006] EWCA Civ 237; [2008] 1 B.C.L.C. 508 at [46]; *Re Moulin Global Eyecare Holdings Ltd, Active Base Ltd v Sutton* [2009] HKCFA 14, Illustration 8; *Thanakharn Kasikorn Thai Chamchat v Akai Holdings Ltd (In Liquidation)* (2010) 13 H.K.C.F.A.R. 479 at [85]; *East Asia Co Ltd v PT Satria Tirtatama Energindo* [2019] UKPC 30; [2020] 2 All E.R. 294 at [58] and [94]. cf. *Hambro v Burnand* [1904] 2 K.B. 10 CA at 25 (mere knowledge of conflict of duty-and-duty did not put on inquiry).

[309] See, e.g. *Business Mortgage Finance 6 Plc v Roundstone Technologies Ltd* [2019] EWHC 2917 (Ch) at [69] (invalidly appointed receiver).

[310] See further Watts [2015] L.M.C.L.Q. 36.

[311] *Akai Holdings Ltd v Thanakharn Kasikorn Thai Chamchat ("Akai")* (2010) 13 H.K.C.F.A.R. 479 at [51] onwards (noted Lee and Ho (2012) 75 M.L.R. 91) (absence of apparent benefit and known conflict of interest meant the irrationality test was met on the facts).

[312] *Quinn v CC Automotive Group Ltd* [2010] EWCA Civ 1412; [2011] 2 All E.R. (Comm) 584 at [23(ii)] (noted Roberts [2011] L.M.C.L.Q. 457), Article 73, Illustration 10; *Newcastle International Airport Ltd v Eversheds LLP* [2012] EWHC 2648 (Ch) at [109]; reversed on other points [2013] EWCA Civ 1514; [2014] 1 W.L.R. 3073; *Gaydamak v Leviev* [2012] EWHC 1740 (Ch) at [252]; *Acute Property Developments Ltd v Apostolou* [2013] EWHC 200 (Ch) at [39]; *LNOC Ltd v Watford Association Football Club Ltd* [2013] EWHC 3615 (Comm) at [92]; *PEC Ltd v Asia Golden Rice Co Ltd* [2014] EWHC 1583 (Comm) at [73].

[313] *East Asia Co Ltd v PT Satria Tirtatama Energindo* [2019] UKPC 30; [2020] 2 All E.R. 294 (noted I. Sin, "Corporate Contracting, Ostensible Authority and Constructive Notice" (2020) 136 L.Q.R. 364); followed in *Business Mortgage Finance 6 Plc v Roundstone Technologies Ltd* [2019] EWHC 2917 (Ch) at [64].

[314] cf. *Willers v Joyce* [2016] UKSC 44; [2018] A.C. 843 (noted P. Mirfield, "A Novel Theory of Privy Council Precedent" (2017) 133 L.Q.R. 1).

not the unreasonable yet rational person.[315] The same approach, as we have seen, is taken in establishing a representation of authority.[316] It would be surprising to look for reasonableness in assessing whether a representation was made in the first place, but throw that over when assessing whether there were counter-signs. The cases prior to *Akai* drew no such distinction.[317] In so far as many of these cases involved companies, it is not the case that the courts were taking a stricter stance (in favour of corporate principals) than they would with individuals. The courts were simply insisting that companies should not be in a *worse* position than individuals through a mechanistic invocation of the rule in *Turquand*'s case.[318] As is explained above, that rule is concerned only with procedural irregularity and does not affect the ordinary requirement that third parties show that they dealt with someone with actual or apparent authority from the company to make the contract. The company cases, therefore, are mainstream agency cases. Nor is there a universal principle that a representee is not required to look behind a representation. If there were, it would be inconsistent with the rules for contract formation. Indeed, the notion of not needing to look behind a representation operates mainly in the law of misrepresentation, where the representee is using the representation to deny or alter what might otherwise be a contractual obligation, not to create a contractual obligation.[319] This is the position with most of the cases on which Lord Neuberger relied in the *Akai* case.[320] Otherwise, in the absence of evidence of actual intention that a representation be relied upon, as in cases of fraud,[321] reliance on a representation needs to be reasonable.[322] In short, the no-inquiries rule operates at common law only where what is sought is rescission (or other form of restitution), or, in cases of fraud, damages for reliance loss.[323] It cannot be relied upon to make a contract. Even within the sphere of its operation, the cases conclude that, in the absence of obfuscation,

---

[315] See *Smith v Hughes* (1871) L.R. 6 Q.B. 597 at 607; *Gissing v Gissing* [1971] A.C. 886 at 906; *Rainy Sky SA v Kookmin Bank* [2011] UKSC 50; [2011] 1 W.L.R. 2900 at [14]; *Toll (FGCT) Pty Ltd v Alphapharm Pty Ltd* (2004) 219 C.L.R. 165 at [40].

[316] *Egyptian International Foreign Trade Co v Soplex Wholesale Supplies Ltd (The Raffaella)* [1985] 2 Lloyd's Rep. 36 at 41. See further above, para.8-018.

[317] *Houghton & Co v Nothard, Lowe & Wills* [1927] 2 K.B. 28 at 36; *AL Underwood Ltd v Bank of Liverpool & Martins* [1924] 1 K.B. 775 at 788–789; *Morris v Kanssen* [1946] A.C. 459 at 475; *Rolled Steel Products (Holdings) Ltd v British Steel Corp* [1986] 1 Ch. 246 at 30. See too *Egyptian International Foreign Trade Co v Soplex Wholesale Supplies Ltd (The Raffaella)* [1985] 2 Lloyd's Rep. 36 at 44; *Hopkins v TL Dallas Group Ltd* [2004] EWHC 1379 (Ch); [2005] 1 B.C.L.C. 543 at [94]; *Pharmed Medicare Private Ltd v Univar Ltd* [2002] EWCA Civ 1569; [2003] 1 All E.R. (Comm) 321 at [7]; *Wrexham Association Football Club Ltd v Crucialmove Ltd* [2006] EWCA Civ 237; [2008] 1 B.C.L.C. 508 at [45]; *Smith v Peter & Diana Hubbard Pty Ltd* [2006] NSWCA 109 at [74] (transaction pursuant to power of attorney); *Pourzand v Telstra Corp Ltd* [2014] WASCA 14 at [115].

[318] As to which rule, see above, para.8-033. See now *East Asia Co Ltd v PT Satria Tirtatama Energindo* [2019] UKPC 30; [2020] 2 All E.R. 294 at [92].

[319] See *East Asia Co Ltd v PT Satria Tirtatama Energindo* [2019] UKPC 30 at [87] and [89].

[320] *Greer v Downs Supply Co* [1927] 2 K.B. 28 at 36; *Bloomenthal v Ford* [1897] A.C. 156. See too *Redgrave v Hurd* (1881) 20 Ch.D. 1; and *Versloot Dredging BV v HDI Gerling Industrie Versicherung AG* [2014] EWCA Civ 1349; [2015] Q.B. 608 (misrepresentation by agent in insurance claim).

[321] See, e.g. *Standard Chartered Bank v Pakistan National Shipping Corp (No.2)* [2002] UKHL 43; [2003] 1 A.C. 959 at [14].

[322] See *Jorden v Money* (1854) 5 H.L.C. 185 at 212; *Sidney Bolsom Investment Trust Ltd v E Karmios & Co (London) Ltd* [1956] 1 Q.B. 529 at 540–541; *Thornton Springer v NEM Ins Co Ltd* [2000] 2 All E.R. 489 at 518. See, more generally, *Spencer Bower: Reliance-Based Estoppel* (5th edn), pp.195–196.

[323] As to damages under the Misrepresentation Act 1967, see *Peekay Intermark Ltd v Australia and New*

the no-inquiries rule applies only to unequivocal representations, not to ones where there is ambiguity or a series of inconsistent statements.[324]

Finally, it should be recalled that the operation of estoppel by representation within the concept of apparent authority is a somewhat tenuous one.[325] It would be remarkable, therefore, if the law were to treat a representation founded solely on the principal's conduct—there being no verbal communication directly between the principal and third party—as virtually conclusive even though a reasonable person would have spotted counter-signals and inquired about them. This point was well made by Brennan J in *Northside Developments Pty Ltd v Registrar-General*[326]:

> "Although such representations by the company seem a slender foundation on which to build an estoppel, the indoor management rule treats them as sufficient unless the party relying on the rule is put on notice to inquire into the authority of the officers or agents to do what they did in the transaction. The slenderness of the foundation enhances the importance of the qualification."

In this regard, it is suggested that the process of determining whether apparent authority is made out is ultimately a single process, rather than a rigid two-step process of finding a holding out, and then inquiring as to the third party's state of knowledge of absence of authority.[327]

8-051 **Knowledge of agent of third party**   The knowledge of an agent of the third party will often be attributed to the third party: this is dealt with in Article 96.[328] If however the third party knows of the lack of authority, the third party cannot sue even if the agent does not know of it.

8-052 **Powers of attorney**   In the case of a disposition of land by an agent stating that the agent acts under a power of attorney, there will doubtless be a duty to examine the power. But even in other situations the power itself will often constitute the only holding out by the principal; therefore third parties who know of a power can only rely on it if they have examined it,[329] unless there are other circumstances creating apparent authority, such as the position or profession of the agent, or other acts by

---

Zealand Banking Group Ltd [2006] EWCA Civ 386; [2006] 2 Lloyd's Rep. 511.

[324] See *Smith v Chadwick* (1884) 9 App.Cas. 187 at 200, per Lord Blackburn: "I should think that a reasonable man reading this prospectus would hardly act on the faith of such an obscure statement without further inquiry". See too an earlier passage at p.199; *Capel & Co v Sim's Composition Co* (1888) 58 L.T. 808 at 808–809; *Peekay Intermark Ltd v Australia and New Zealand Banking Group Ltd* [2006] EWCA Civ 386 at [25]–[28] and [52]; and *East Asia Co Ltd v PT Satria Tirtatama Energindo* [2019] UKPC 30 at [89].

[325] See above, paras 8-014 and 8-027.

[326] See (1990) 170 C.L.R. 146 at 178.

[327] See *Stavrinides v Bank of Cyprus Public Co Ltd* [2019] EWHC 1328 (Ch) at [107].

[328] See, e.g. *Knightsbridge Property Development Corp (UK) Ltd v South Chelsea Properties Ltd* [2017] EWHC 2730 (Ch) at [65].

[329] See *Jacobs v Morris* [1902] 1 Ch. 816, Illustration 3; *National Bolivian Navigation Co v Wilson* (1880) 5 App.Cas. 176 at 209; *Xie v Huang* [2012] NZHC 960 at [43]. There used to be statutory requirements for the filing of powers of attorney: see Law of Property Act 1925 s.125(1); Trustee Act 1925 s.25. By virtue of s.2 of the Powers of Attorney Act 1971 filing is no longer possible, but lasting powers of attorney made under the Mental Capacity Act 2005 must be registered: see below, para.10-009. As to less formal written authority, see *Suncorp Insurance & Finance v Milano Assecurazioni SpA* [1993] 2 Lloyd's Rep. 225 at 233 ("onus on the third party to ask to see that authority where the agent is acting close to the border of what is usual": per Waller J). It would seem that where a third party has seen the authorising document once, he should, if active over a period, ask to see it again if there is a serious possibility of its terms being changed.

the principal indicating authority, e.g. acceptance of similar acts by the agent in the past.[330] However, where such an inspection would not reveal the want of authority, failure to make it has been held not to be fatal. It is not clear that this conclusion is consistent with the general reluctance of the law to let parties avoid making standard inquiries on the basis that if they had made them they would not have learned the truth.[331] However, where there is otherwise a basis for believing the act to be authorised, the third party cannot be expected to inquire further into the agent's motives for doing it unless there are special reasons (e.g. some irregular practice) for doubt.[332]

Acts within usual authority Where the agent is acting within the usual author-   **8-053** ity of a person holding the position which the agent holds, e.g. that of managing director,[333] or of a professional agent exercising such functions as the agent is exercising, e.g. in former days, a factor,[334] or where the agent exercises functions combining the two, e.g. a solicitor conducting litigation[335] there will not normally be any duty to inquire[336] unless the transaction is abnormal or there are further circumstances giving grounds for suspicion—for instance, in the area of banking practice, where the agent pays the principal's money into the agent's own personal bank account,[337] or uses a signed blank transfer for what might well, to an outsider, be the agent's own purposes.[338]

Acts outside usual authority An agent acting outside such authority as that   **8-054** indicated above is acting abnormally, and in the absence of other indications of authority there may well be a duty to inquire. Thus a contract of sale of goods by a commodity broker in the broker's own name would not, at any rate according to former usage, normally be authorised, and apparent authority might not be easy to establish.[339] So also where it is notorious that usual authority is specially limited by trade usage, e.g. in particular markets, there may be no apparent authority, though some of the cases applying such reasoning are open to criticism.[340]

Representation of limited authority only If the representation is of limited   **8-055** authority only, there will obviously be no liability where that authority is exceeded.[341]

---

[330] See, e.g. Article 72, Illustration 7.

[331] See *Jones v Williams* (1857) 24 Beav. 47 at 62. See further above, para.3-012.

[332] *Hambro v Burnand* [1904] 2 K.B. 10, Illustration 1 to Article 74.

[333] See Articles 29 and 72.

[334] See Articles 2 and 30.

[335] *Waugh v H.B. Clifford & Sons Ltd* [1982] Ch. 374, Illustration 16 to Article 72 (compromise: "officious" of other side to demand to be satisfied as to authority).

[336] *Borries v Imperial Ottoman Bank* (1873) L.R. 9 C.P. 38; see also *Smith v M'Guire* (1855) 3 H. & N. 554; *Knight v Matson & Co* (1902) 22 N.Z.L.R. 293 (horse dealer); *Lexi Holdings Plc v Pannone & Partners* [2009] EWHC 2590 (Ch) (managing director). Some of the cases used the concept of general agent in this connection: see Comments to Articles 2 and 29.

[337] *Midland Bank Ltd v Reckitt* [1933] A.C. 1, Illustration 3 to Article 74.

[338] *Sheffield v London Joint Stock Bank Ltd* (1888) 13 App.Cas. 333; *Levy v Richardson* (1890) 5 T.L.R. 236; *Colonial Bank v Cady and Williams* (1890) 15 App.Cas. 267.

[339] *Cooke & Sons v Eshelby* (1887) 12 App.Cas. 271, Illustration 7 to Article 81; *Baring v Corrie* (1818) 2 B. & A. 137.

[340] See Article 75, Illustration 2. See also the cases on solicitors, above, para.8-020.

[341] *Forman & Co Pty Ltd v The Liddesdale* [1900] A.C. 190; *Russo-Chinese Bank v Li Yau Sam* [1910] A.C. 174; *Doey v L & NW Ry Co* [1919] 1 K.B. 623.

8-056 **Bills of exchange**   In the case of bills of exchange, promissory notes and cheques, it has been long established that a signature per procurationem operates as notice that the agent has but a limited authority to sign, and the principal is only bound if the agent in so signing was acting within the limits of the agent's actual authority.[342]

8-057 **Public documents: companies**   It was formerly possible to say that registration of the public documents of a company was notice of limitations of authority contained in them. The matter is a specialist part of company law now regulated by statute.[343]

8-058 **Agents of the Crown**   A person dealing with an agent whose powers are fixed by statute or statutory instrument or other delegated legislation ought to inquire into them, for such an agent can by law have no authority to contract beyond such limits; unless there is some holding out, which can only be effected by an official with power to do so, and would be difficult to establish.[344]

8-059 **Statutes**   The inquiries made by a third party may also be relevant to the application of statutes, under which the third party may need to establish that he acted in good faith.[345]

8-060 **Response to inquiries**   Sometimes the response to an inquiry may be indecisive. For example, the person of whom the inquiry as to the authority of an agent is made may, if not himself the principal (as in the case of a company), say that that person will investigate and make further contact but may not do so.[346] In such a case there may be apparent authority if the person's conduct is such as to give the impression that the authority questioned exists. Any response, whether indirect in this way or direct, will however only bind the principal if given by the principal personally or by an agent with authority to make it. Such authority will normally only be attributed to a person authorised to act in connection with the particular business in question[347]: it is difficult to believe that authority to give answers to inquiries which bind the employer will easily be inferred.[348] Where apparent authority is otherwise established, the mere fact that the third party seeks unsuccessfully to get confirmation from the principal of the agent's authority, and does not renew its efforts, will not remove its ability to rely on the apparent authority.[349]

---

[342] Bills of Exchange Act 1882 s.25. See *Chalmers and Guest on Bills of Exchange* (18th edn), para.3-095 onwards. See *Bryant, Powis & Bryant v Quebec Bank* [1893] A.C. 170; Article 21; Article 74, Illustration 1.

[343] See above, para.1 onwards.

[344] See *Att.-Gen. for Ceylon v Silva* [1953] A.C. 461; above, para.8-042.

[345] e.g. Sale of Goods Act 1979 ss.25 and 26; Factors Act 1889 s.2 (see Article 89); Bills of Exchange Act 1882 s.29. As to the Companies Act 2006, see above, para.8-039.

[346] See *Canadian Laboratory Supplies Ltd v Engelhard Industries of Canada Ltd* [1979] 2 S.C.R. 787; (1979) 97 D.L.R. (3d) 1.

[347] See *British Bank of the Middle East v Sun Life Assurance Co of Canada (UK) Ltd* [1983] 2 Lloyd's Rep. 9, Illustration 10 to Article 75; above, para.8-019.

[348] But see Grönfors [1962] *Scandinavian Studies in Law* 97 at 104, discussing the position of a person "to whom telephone customers are referred".

[349] See *Flexirent Capital Pty Ltd v EBS Consulting Pty Ltd* [2007] VSC 158 at [219]; *Golden Ocean Group Ltd v Salgaocar Mining Industries PVT Ltd* [2011] EWHC 56 (Comm); [2011] 1 W.L.R. 2575 at [128]; affirmed [2012] EWCA Civ 265; [2012] 1 W.L.R. 3674.

Illustrations

(1)   General conditions of sale state that auctioneers have no authority to make   **8-061**
representations in relation to the property sold. Contrary to this, the
auctioneers state that no schemes for compulsory purchase or the like affect
the property. Such representations are not within their apparent authority.[350]

(2)   A authorised his son to take delivery of a mare, provided that a certain warranty was given, and told the owner so. The son took away the mare without
the warranty in question. Held, that the son's act did not amount to an acceptance of the mare, so as to bind the father.[351]

(3)   An agent, purporting to act under a power of attorney, which he represented
gave him full power to borrow, borrowed money from A, and misapplied it.
The agent produced the power, which did not in fact authorise the loan, but
A acted on his representation, and did not read the power. Held, that A must
be taken to have had notice of the terms of the power, and that the principal
was not bound by the loan.[352]

(4)   Cattle are brought to an auctioneer for sale by a dealer who normally buys
and resells on his own account, but has on one previous occasion, to the
auctioneer's knowledge, sold on account of another. The auctioneer is not
fixed with notice that on this occasion the dealer is again acting for that
other.[353]

(5)   A accepts a bill of exchange drawn by B, and delivers it to B to be held by
him for A's use. B indorses the bill to C for a loan, having told C that it
belongs to A, and that he (B) has no authority to deal with it. A is entitled to
recover the bill or its value from C.[354]

(6)   A indorses a bill of exchange "pay B or order for my use". B's bankers
discount the bill and pay the proceeds to B's account. The bankers are liable
to A for the amount, because the restrictive indorsement operated as notice
that the bill did not belong to B.[355]

(7)   A dealer in an established market buys goods which are sold at undervalue
in circumstances suggesting that the seller is in difficulties. The dealer is not
thereby fixed with notice that the seller is selling goods which are not his own
in breach of his obligations to the owner.[356]

(8)   A lender which has been approached by A for a large personal loan, agrees
to make the loan to the company in which A is a director. The company then
asserts that the borrowing was unauthorised. The lender knew (through one
of its own directors and its solicitor) who the directors of the company were,

---

[350] *Overbrooke Estates v Glemcombe Properties Ltd* [1974] 1 W.L.R. 1335, holding also that such a
clause is not within Misrepresentation Act 1967 s.3. *Mendelssohn v Normand Ltd* [1970] 1 Q.B. 177
is somewhat difficult to reconcile with this decision: see Coote [1975] C.L.J. 17. It was followed in
Collins v Howell-Jones [1981] E.G.D. 207.

[351] *Jordan v Norton* (1838) 4 M. & W. 155.

[352] *Jacobs v Morris* [1902] 1 Ch. 816.

[353] *Knight v Matson & Co* (1902) 22 N.Z.L.R. 293; see also *Curlewis v Birkbeck* (1863) 3 F. & F. 894.

[354] *Evans v Kymer* (1830) 1 B. & Ad. 528.

[355] *Lloyd v Sigourney* (1829) 5 Bing. 525; Bills of Exchange Act 1882 s.35. See *Chalmers and Guest
on Bills of Exchange* (18th edn), para.5-031 onwards.

[356] *Feuer Leather Corp v Frank Johnston & Sons Ltd* [1981] Com.L.Rep. 251 (a case on constructive
trust: see above, para.8-048 and Comment to Article 115). See also *Re Funduk and Horncastle*
(1973) 39 D.L.R. (3d) 94 (car).

but was requested by the company treasurer to prepare a board minute that named as those to be present only half the board, all of whom were family members related to A. Held, that although ordinarily the lender might be able to rely on the company treasurer's certificate that a proper board meeting had been held, it was put on inquiry by the oddity that only a conflicted quorum was expected to be present.[357]

(9)　A, the manager of property-owning company C Ltd, has general authority to engage letting agents. He re-engages D Ltd as agent when its manager, X, knows that the directors of C Ltd had previously terminated its agency for dissatisfaction with X's services. Somewhat surprised, X asks A to confirm that his superiors are happy for D Ltd to be reappointed, which A does. Held, D Ltd cannot rely on A's usual authority.[358]

(10)　Claimants seeking to buy a new red Jaguar car are persuaded by a sales agent at the defendant's showrooms to agree to buy, on hire purchase, a blue one (not yet in the showroom) in exchange for the claimants' existing silver Jaguar. Later the same day, the agent contacts the claimants to say that he has located a red Jaguar in another town. Some days later, he arranges to meet the claimants at a motorway service station, closer to the claimants' home, in order formally to cancel the agreement for the blue car and substitute new documentation for the red one. A further week later, the agent meets the claimants at the same service station and the silver Jaguar is exchanged for the red one together with a sum of money. The agent is fraudulent; neither he nor the defendant has authority to sell the red car, and the agent on-sells the silver one without arranging for discharge of the outstanding hire purchase debt. The defendant is held vicariously liable for the deceits; the agent's apparent authority was not lost by the off-premises dealings.[359]

Article 74

FRAUD OF AGENT IS NOT INCOMPATIBLE WITH APPARENT AUTHORITY

8-062　An act of an agent within the scope of the agent's apparent authority does not cease to bind the principal merely because the agent was acting fraudulently and in furtherance of the agent's own interests.

---

[357] *Re Moulin Global Eyecare Holdings Ltd, Active Base Ltd v Sutton* [2009] HKCFA 14. See too *Acute Property Developments Ltd v Apostolou* [2013] EWHC 200 (Ch) (put on inquiry by manager's direction to debtor to pay not his principal but his wife).

[358] *IH Wedding & Sons Ltd v Buy-Sell Realty NZ Ltd* [2009] NZHC 1717.

[359] *Quinn v CC Automotive Group Ltd* [2010] EWCA Civ 1412; [2011] 2 All E.R. (Comm) 584.

Comment

This principle is applicable to cases of contract[360]; in tort[361]; in the disposition of property[362]; a similar result even appears in criminal cases.[363] But for the principal to be responsible under agency principles the agent must normally have been acting within the scope of the agent's actual or apparent authority.[364] It is a well-known proposition that the mere fact that the principal by appointing an agent gives that agent the opportunity to steal or otherwise to behave fraudulently does not without more make the principal liable.[365] Furthermore, the fact that an agent is acting in furtherance of personal interests may negative actual authority[366] and may, if known to the third party or such that the third party ought to know it, put that party on notice as regards apparent authority.[367] As regards forgery, a forger may profess not to act for but as the person whose document is forged[368]; and a counterfeit document may of itself be ineffective. The forger may nonetheless have apparent authority to warrant the genuineness of the document, but the normal requirements for a holding out must to that effect be established.[369]

8-063

Illustrations

(1) A is authorised in writing to act as the agent of B for the purpose of underwriting policies of insurance, and carrying on the ordinary business of underwriting, at Lloyd's, in the name and on behalf of B, in accordance with the usual custom of Lloyd's. A, in his own interests, and in abuse of his authority, underwrites a guarantee policy in B's name, the assured acting in good faith, but having no knowledge of the existence of the written authority or of its terms. It is in the ordinary course of business at Lloyd's to underwrite such

8-064

---

[360] Illustrations 1 and 2; *Bryant, Powis & Bryant v Quebec Bank* [1893] A.C. 170 at 180; *A.L. Underwood Ltd v Bank of Liverpool* [1924] 1 K.B. 775 at 791–792; *Lloyds Bank v Chartered Bank of India, Australia & China* [1929] 1 K.B. 40; *Uxbridge Permanent Benefit Building Society v Pickard* [1939] 2 K.B. 248; *Alliance and Leicester BS v Edgestop Ltd* [1993] 1 W.L.R. 1462.

[361] *Lloyd v Grace, Smith & Co* [1912] A.C. 716; *Uxbridge Permanent Benefit Building Society v Pickard* [1939] 2 K.B. 248; *Morris v C.W. Martin & Sons Ltd* [1966] 1 Q.B. 716.

[362] Many of the cases involve fraud on the part of the agent: see, e.g. *Oppenheimer v Attenborough & Son* [1908] 1 K.B. 221; *Canadian Laboratory Supplies Ltd v Engelhard Industries of Canada Ltd* [1979] 2 S.C.R. 787; (1979) 97 D.L.R. (3d) 1; *Lexi Holdings Plc v Pannone & Partners* [2009] EWHC 2590 (Ch); cf. *De Gorter v Attenborough & Son* (1904) 21 T.L.R. 19.

[363] See *Moore v Bresler Ltd* [1944] 2 All E.R. 515.

[364] See *Ruben v Great Fingall Consolidated* [1906] A.C. 439; *Morris v C.W. Martin & Sons Ltd* [1966] 1 Q.B. 716; *Polkinghorne v Holland* (1934) 51 C.L.R. 143 (partner). But see the next paragraph and also Articles 72 and 83–85. As to vicarious liability in tort, see Article 90.

[365] *Farquharson Bros & Co v King & Co* [1902] A.C. 325, Illustration 6 to Article 84; *Ruben v Great Fingall Consolidated* [1906] A.C. 439; *Morris v C.W. Martin & Sons Ltd* [1966] 1 Q.B. 716 at 726, 737, 740–741; *Leesh River Tea Co v British India Steam Navigation Co* [1967] 2 Q.B. 250; *Koorangang Investments Pty Ltd v Richardson & Wrench Ltd* [1982] A.C. 462, Illustration 4.

[366] See Article 23; Article 95, Illustration 11. Especially when the agent is practising a fraud on the principal himself: *Kwei Tek Chao v British Traders and Shippers Ltd* [1954] 2 Q.B. 459; below, para.8-213.

[367] Illustration 3; and see Article 73.

[368] A possible explanation of *Ruben v Great Fingall Consolidated* [1906] A.C. 439.

[369] For the ways in which forgery may be committed, see Forgery and Counterfeiting Act 1981 ss.1 and 2–5; also above, para.2-057. As to estoppel against setting up a forgery, see cases cited above, para.8-041.

policies, and A was therefore acting within the scope of his apparent authority, though in fraud of B. B is bound by the policy.[370]

(2) A was entrusted by B with the letting of B's flat. A, as a condition of granting C a tenancy of the flat, demanded an illegal premium which C paid to A. The premium was recoverable by C by virtue of the Landlord and Tenant (Rent Control) Act 1949 s.2(5). Held, that C could recover the premium from B.[371]

(3) A gave B a power of attorney authorising him to draw cheques on A's banking account and apply the money for A's purposes. B fraudulently drew cheques on A's account, signing the cheques "A by B his attorney", and paid the cheques into his own banking account to meet an overdraft. B's bankers applied the cheques in reduction of the overdraft without making inquiries as to B's authority. Held, that B's bankers were bound by the terms of B's actual authority, which did not extend to paying B's debts with A's money; that they had converted the cheques; and as, from the form of the cheques, they had notice that the money was not B's money, they were negligent in not making inquiry as to B's authority and therefore could not avail themselves of the protection of the Bills of Exchange Act 1882 s.82, and were liable to A for the amount of the cheques.[372]

(4) An employee of valuers is told not to issue valuations for a particular group of companies. He nevertheless does so, on his employer's headed notepaper, and signs it with his employer's name, it not appearing on the valuation who prepared it. The valuation is negligent. His employers are not liable.[373]

(5) The company secretary of the claimant funds manager, and authorised signatory on its bank account, in fraud of the company, drew cheques in favour of a futures trader, using the funds thereby obtained for his personal futures trading with the trader. The paying and collecting bank was the same bank. The trader was not told by the bank who the drawer of the cheques was. The bank was protected from liability in conversion by the apparent authority of the secretary, but not the trader which was put on inquiry because it was deemed to know through the collecting bank, as its agent, that the cheques were drawn on the claimant, rather than its client, and thus had the means of knowing that the client was using other people's money to fund personal dealing.[374]

---

[370] *Hambro v Burnand* [1904] 2 K.B. 10, a famous and controversial case which can be and has been taken to refer also to actual authority. See Comment to Article 23 for further discussion; see (1903) 17 HarvL.Rev. 56; (1934) 50 L.Q.R. 228–230; (1935) 1 U Toronto L.J. 42–43; (1972) 89 S.A.L.J. 60; Watts (2002) 2 O.U. Commonwealth L.J. 93 at 96–98; Watts [2017] J.B.L. 269; see also *Refuge Ass. Co Ltd v Kettlewell* [1909] A.C. 243.

[371] *Navarro v Moregrand Ltd* [1951] 2 T.L.R. 674; cf. *Barker v Levinson* [1951] 1 K.B. 342. See also *Credit Services Investments Ltd v Evans* [1974] 2 N.Z.L.R. 683; *Gordon v Selico Co Ltd* [1986] 1 E.G.L.R. 71.

[372] *Midland Bank Ltd v Reckitt* [1933] A.C. 1; *John v Dodwell and Co Ltd* [1918] A.C. 563; *Nelson v Larholt* [1948] 1 K.B. 339. See Article 73; Cheques Act 1957 s.4 as amended.

[373] *Kooragang Investments Pty Ltd v Richardson & Wrench Ltd* [1982] A.C. 462; criticised, [1982] C.L.J. 36.

[374] *NIML Ltd v Man Financial Australia Ltd* (2006) 15 V.R. 156 (Vic CA).

Article 75

A disclosed principal is not bound by an act of an agent which is outside the **8-065**
scope of the agent's implied or apparent authority unless the principal in fact
authorised the agent to do the particular act or ratified it. This Article is subject to
the provisions of Articles 79 and 84–87.[375]

Comment

This Article simply completes the account of actual and apparent authority by **8-066**
further examples of principals who are not bound. It should be read in conjunction
with Article 23 and with the Article following, Article 76, concerning the doctrine
of the undisclosed principal. It should also be noted that the common law reasoning that an act that is unauthorised makes it a nullity, i.e. void, will not usually
preclude recourse by the principal to equitable causes of action and remedies against
the third party.[376] Where money or other property is transferred under a void transaction, the principal will usually have a choice of common law or equitable remedies.

Illustrations

(1) A, a stockbroker, employed B, a clerk, to whom he allowed a commission on **8-067**
orders obtained by him and accepted by A. B was not authorised to accept
orders on A's behalf. On three occasions C gave orders to B away from A's
premises, which were passed on to A, and executed by him, A sending
contract notes to C. C made payment in respect of the first two orders by
cheques payable to A's order, and in respect of the third order by a cheques
payable to B's order. The cheques were delivered to B, and passed on to A,
who duly credited C. Subsequently, C gave orders to B, who did not transmit
them to A, but made out bought notes on which he forged A's signature, and
handed them to C. C gave cheques in payment to B, who misapplied them.
It was held that there was no evidence that A had held out B as authorised to
accept orders on his behalf, and that A was under no liability in respect of the
orders subsequent to the first three.[377]

(2) The master of a ship signs a bill of lading on behalf of the owner stating that
goods of a particular mercantile quality have been received on board. The
goods are of a different quality. The owner is not bound by the statement; for

---

[375] cf. Partnership Act 1890 s.7. As to ratification see Ch.2, section 3. See too para.8-097 below, indicating that the position may be different where it is a question of the rights of the principal, rather than
his liabilities.

[376] See *John v Dodwell & Co* [1918] A.C. 563 at 569; *Rolled Steel Products (Holdings) Ltd v British
Steel Corp* [1986] Ch. 246 at 298; *Guinness Plc v Saunders* [1990] 2 A.C. 663 at 702, Illustration
13. cf. *Trustee of the Property of F.C. Jones & Sons v Jones* [1997] Ch. 159 at 164. As to actions,
both real and personal, to recover money or other assets transferred without authority or in bad faith,
see Articles 88 and 116. As to equitable remedies in general against third parties, see Article 96, and
esp. para.8-221.

[377] *Spooner v Browning* [1898] 1 Q.B. 528. As to course of dealing generally, see also para.8-013 and
Article 72, Illustrations 7 and 21.

to ascertain such matters is outside the scope of the functions and capacities of a ship's master.[378]

(3)   The secretary of a company fraudulently, and without the knowledge of the directors, represented to A that if he took certain shares he would be appointed solicitor to the company, and subsequently that he had been so appointed. A, on the faith of the representations, applied for the shares, which were allotted to him. Held, that A was bound by the contract to take the shares, the representations being outside the scope of the secretary's authority.[379] So, where the secretary of a tramway company made a representation as to the financial relations of the company, and it was not shown that he was authorised to make the representation, it was held that the company was not bound, it not being part of the ordinary duties of such an official to make such representations on behalf of the company.[380]

(4)   Where an estate agent who is employed to procure a purchaser at a certain price enters into a contract of sale, the principal is not bound unless he in fact authorised the agent to make the contract on his behalf, because it is not within the ordinary scope of such an agent's authority to enter into binding contracts on his principal's behalf.[381]

(5)   An estate agent, not being authorised to do so, takes a deposit from a prospective purchaser of land in a transaction "subject to contract". The prospective vendor is not liable.[382]

(6)   The manager of a tied public-house, who had authority to deal with particular persons only, bought spirits from a person with whom he had no authority to deal. Held, that the principal was not bound, it being usual for such managers to be restricted to particular persons from whom to purchase spirits.[383]

(7)   A bank manager guaranteed the payment of a draft. It was not within the ordinary scope of a bank manager's authority to give such a guarantee, and the bank therefore was not liable on it unless he was expressly authorised to give it.[384]

(8)   The local agent of an insurance company contracted on behalf of the company to grant a policy. Held, that it was not within the ordinary scope of the authority of such an agent to make such a contract (as opposed to issuing a cover

---

[378] *Cox, Patterson & Co v Bruce & Co* (1886) 18 Q.B.D. 147. The reasoning seems valid despite the fact that the case on which this decision was based, *Grant v Norway* (1851) 10 C.B.(N.S.) 665, which held that a master did not bind his owner if he signed for goods not on board, was reversed in England by s.4 of the Carriage of Goods by Sea Act 1992. The reasoning of that case had appeared obsolete for a long time; yet there was substantial authority which made it difficult for any tribunal but the House of Lords to establish this. The application of the decision could however be restricted to its facts, i.e. signature when goods not on board. See *The Nea Tyhi* [1982] 1 Lloyd's Rep. 606; *The Starsin* [2000] 1 Lloyd's Rep. 85 at 93–98 ("aberrant reasoning": point not considered on appeal [2003] UKHL 12; [2004] 1 A.C. 715).

[379] *Newlands v National Employers' Accident Association Ltd* (1885) 54 L.J.Q.B. 428.

[380] *Barnett, Hoares & Co v South London Tramways Co* (1887) 18 Q.B.D. 815; *Ruben v Great Fingall Consolidated* [1906] A.C. 439. The authority of a company secretary in administrative matters was, however, considerably enlarged by *Panorama Developments (Guildford) Ltd v Fidelis Furnishing Fabrics Ltd* [1971] 2 Q.B. 711, Illustration 30 to Article 72; and though these examples do not concern administration they may require reconsideration in view of what was said in that case as to changing practice.

[381] See Article 30, Illustration 6.

[382] *Sorrell v Finch* [1977] A.C. 728. See Articles 92 and 111; below, para.9-026.

[383] *Daun v Simmins* (1879) 41 L.T. 783.

[384] *Re Southport & West Lancashire Banking Co* (1885) 1 T.L.R. 204.

note[385]), and that the company was not bound unless it could be shown that the agent had actual authority.[386] So an insurance company has been held not bound by the acceptance of a premium by its agent after the time for payment of the premium had expired.[387]

(9) An insurance broker, being authorised to effect an insurance, agreed with a company for a policy on certain terms. The policy was duly executed by the company and the broker was debited with the amount of the premium. The broker, having been paid the premium by his principal, told the company that the insurance was a mistake, and fraudulently cancelled without the principal's authority. The principal was entitled to enforce the contract against the company, it being no part of a broker's usual authority to cancel contracts made by him.[388]

(10) The "unit manager" of an insurance company, whose only authority is to transmit proposals for life assurance or loans on mortgage to higher officers of the company, purports to bind the company to guarantee a loan. The lender writes to the "general manager" of the company asking whether the "unit manager" is authorised to do this. There is no "general manager": the letter is answered by a "branch manager", who describes himself as such, and whose authority is similar to that of a unit manager. He purports to confirm the authority. He has neither actual nor apparent authority to do so and the company is not bound.[389]

(11) The Chartering Manager and Vice-President (Transportation) of a company, authorised to negotiate the sale of a ship belonging to the company, purports to enter into a simultaneous agreement to take it back on charter, the charter containing unusual terms. The third party knows that the Vice-President has no authority to enter into such a charter without approval from higher in the company. The Vice-President falsely states that he has obtained such approval. The company is not bound.[390]

(12) A shipping agent is authorised to arrange for the shipment of goods and prepare the necessary documents, including those to be presented under a letter of credit. An employee prepares a draft, signs and indorses it in blank on behalf of the customer, and the money is paid to the agency firm. The authority to prepare the documents does not represent that the firm has authority to receive payment under the credit, and payment to the firm is invalid: the bank must pay again.[391]

(13) A committee of directors of a company agreed that the company would pay one of their number £5.2 million for his services in connection with a

[385] See, e.g. *Wilkinson v General Accident Fire and Life Assurance Corp Ltd* [1967] 2 Lloyd's Rep. 182; and see *Stockton v Mason* [1978] 2 Lloyd's Rep. 430 (broker) (a puzzling case: see [1979] J.B.L. 169).

[386] *Linford v Provincial, etc., Ins Co* (1864) 34 Beav. 291.

[387] *Acey v Fernie* (1840) 7 M. & W. 151. See Clarke, *Law of Insurance Contracts* (6th edn), para.8-2A1 onwards.

[388] *Xenos v Wickham* (1866) L.R. 2 H.L. 296.

[389] *British Bank of the Middle East v Sun Life Assurance Co of Canada (UK) Ltd* [1983] 2 Lloyd's Rep. 9 (HL) (a harsh decision). See above, para.8-018.

[390] *Armagas Ltd v Mundogas SA (The Ocean Frost)* [1986] A.C. 717. But cf. *Egyptian International Foreign Trade Co v Soplex Wholesale Supplies Ltd* [1985] 2 Lloyd's Rep. 36, Illustration 11 to Article 72; cf. *First Energy (UK) Ltd v Hungarian International Bank Ltd* [1993] 2 Lloyd's Rep. 194, Illustration 12 to Article 72.

[391] *Cleveland Mfg. Co Ltd v Muslim Commercial Bank Ltd* [1981] 2 Lloyd's Rep. 646.

takeover bid being made by the company, and made the payment. The articles of association required any such contract to be made by the whole board, and not by a committee. The contract was void, and the money held recoverable in equity.[392]

Article 76

UNDISCLOSED PRINCIPAL: RIGHTS AND LIABILITIES

8-068   (1)   An undisclosed principal may sue or be sued on a contract made on the principal's behalf, or in respect of money paid or received on his or her behalf, by an agent acting within the scope of the agent's actual authority. Where a contract is involved, the agent on entering into it must have intended to act on the principal's behalf.[393]

(2)   (Perhaps), an undisclosed principal may also be sued on any contract made, or in respect of money received, on the principal's behalf, by an agent acting within the authority usually confided to an agent of that character, notwithstanding limitations put upon that authority as between principal and agent.[394]

(3)   Where an agent enters into a contract, oral or written, without reference to agency, evidence is admissible to show who is the real principal, in order to charge the principal or entitle the principal to sue on the contract.[395]

(4)   The terms of the contract may, expressly or impliedly, exclude the principal's right to sue and the principal's liability to be sued. The contract itself, or the circumstances surrounding the contract, may show that the agent is the true and only principal.[396]

---

[392] *Guinness Plc v Saunders* [1990] 2 A.C. 663.

[393] *Siu Yin Kwan v Eastern Insurance Co Ltd* [1994] 2 A.C. 199 at 207 (Illustration 12), per Lord Lloyd of Berwick; *Taylor v Van Dutch Marine Holding Ltd* [2019] EWHC 1951 (Ch) at [277]. See Comment; Illustrations 1, 2 and 3; *Thomson v Davenport* (1829) 9 B. & C. 78 at 90; *Sims v Bond* (1833) 5 B. & Ad. 389; *Browning v Provincial Insurance Co of Canada* (1873) L.R. 5 P.C. 263 at 272; *Moto Vespa SA v Mat (Britannia Express) Ltd* [1979] 1 Lloyd's Rep. 175. cf. *Restatement, Third*, § 6.03. As to what is an undisclosed principal in this context, see below, para.8-071. As to money paid, see *Duke of Norfolk v Worthy* (1808) 1 Camp. 337, Illustration 3 (action by principal); *Transvaal & Delagoa Bay Investment Co v Atkinson* [1944] 1 All E.R. 579 (liability of principal); Articles 92, 93 and 111. The doctrine is considered against the background of the unsatisfactory drafting of s.14(5) of the Sale of Goods Act 1979 in *Boyter v Thomson* [1995] 2 A.C. 628: see Brown (1996) 112 L.Q.R. 225.

[394] *Watteau v Fenwick* [1893] 1 Q.B. 346 at 348. See Comment; Illustrations 4, 5 and 6; cf. *Restatement, Third*, § 2.06.

[395] See Comment; Illustrations 7 and 8.

[396] *Siu Yin Kwan v Eastern Insurance Co Ltd* [1994] 2A.C. 199 at 207 (Illustration 12), per Lord Lloyd of Berwick; *Taylor v Van Dutch Marine Holding Ltd* [2019] EWHC 1951 (Ch) at [277]. See Comment; Illustrations 1, 2 and 3; *Thomson v Davenport* (1829) 9 B. & C. 78 at 90; *Sims v Bond* (1833) 5 B. & Ad. 389; *Browning v Provincial Insurance Co of Canada* (1873) L.R. 5 P.C. 263 at 272; *Moto Vespa SA v Mat (Britannia Express) Ltd* [1979] 1 Lloyd's Rep. 175. cf. *Restatement, Third*, § 6.03. As to what is an undisclosed principal in this context, see below, para.8-071. As to money paid, see *Duke of Norfolk v Worthy* (1808) 1 Camp. 337, Illustration 3 (action by principal); *Transvaal & Delagoa Bay Investment Co v Atkinson* [1944] 1 All E.R. 579 (liability of principal); Articles 92, 93 and 111. The doctrine is considered against the background of the unsatisfactory drafting of s.14(5) of the Sale of Goods Act 1979 in *Boyter v Thomson* [1995] 2 A.C. 628: see Brown (1996) 112 L.Q.R. 225.

(5)   So far as concerns deeds, bills of exchange, promissory notes and cheques, this
Article must be read subject to Articles 77 and 78.[397]

Comment

Rule (1): Undisclosed principal doctrine   Rule (1) is a statement of the com-   **8-069**
mon law doctrine of undisclosed principal. The leading modern formulation of the
features of the doctrine is that of Lord Lloyd of Berwick in *Siu Yin Kwan v Eastern
Insurance Co Ltd*[398]:

> "For present purposes the law can be summarised shortly. (1) An undisclosed principal
> may sue and be sued on a contract made by an agent on his behalf, acting within the scope
> of his actual authority. (2) In entering into the contract, the agent must intend to act on
> the principal's behalf. (3) The agent of an undisclosed principal may also sue and be sued
> on the contract. (4) Any defence which the third party may have against the agent is avail-
> able against his principal. (5) The terms of the contract may, expressly or by implication,
> exclude the principal's right to sue, and his liability to be sued. The contract itself, or the
> circumstances surrounding the contract, may show that the agent is the true and only
> principal."

The proposition that a principal, someone of whose existence or connection with
the transaction the third party was totally unaware, can in appropriate circumstances
sue and be sued on a contract made by an agent may be surprising, but is well
established. Its origin is said to lie in the right of the principal of a factor to intervene
in the factor's bankruptcy, to claim the principal's goods or the unpaid price of
them; and later to sue in respect of the whole contract.[399] This somehow led to more
generalised reasoning whereby such a principal was entitled to sue on the agent's
contracts in general; and it became established that the principal was liable also.
Such a conclusion is certainly difficult to accommodate within standard theories of
contract, which emphasise, even though under objective criteria, the consent of the
parties. It should be remembered however that the doctrine was formed before such
theories had acquired prominence.[400] There are judicial dicta to the effect that the
contract is that of the undisclosed principal, just as in cases of disclosed principal,[401]
and some decisions can only be justified on this reasoning.[402] But, subject to the
intervention of the principal, it seems that the agent also can sue on such a contract
and even recover the principal's loss by way of damages; and can be sued on it.[403]
There are also special rules whereby a third party cannot be prevented by the
intervention of the principal from exercising that party's rights against the agent[404]
nor (normally) from using against the principal defences which the party had against

---

[397] For the position as between agent and undisclosed principal, see above, para.6-082.
[398] *Siu Yin Kwan v Eastern Insurance Co Ltd* [1994] A.C. 199 at 207.
[399] Stoljar, pp.203–211; Goodhart and Hamson (1932) 4 C.L.J. 320. As to factors, see above, para.1-
045.
[400] Müller-Freienfels (1953) 16 M.L.R. 299.
[401] *Keighley, Maxsted & Co v Durant* [1901] A.C. 240 at 261; *Said v Butt* [1920] 3 K.B. 497 at 500 (Illustration 11).
[402] e.g. *Cooke & Sons v Eshelby* (1887) 12 App.Cas. 271, Illustration 7 to Article 81; below, para.8-
112.
[403] See below, para.9-012; as to measure of damages, see below, para.9-013.
[404] *O'Herlihy v Hedges* (1803) 1 Sch. & Lef. 123 (specific performance in favour of a principal may
be refused unless the agent will enter into or continue personal covenants with third party);
Montgomerie v United Kingdom Mutual Steamship Assn [1891] 1 Q.B. 370 at 372; *Mooney v Williams* (1906) 3 C.L.R. 1 at 8. See below, paras 8-098 and 9-012.

the agent.[405] These cast doubt on such dicta and decisions[406] and highlight an uneasy tension between two organising theories, that the contract is that of the agent and that the contract is that of the principal. It is difficult to deny that the undisclosed principal is really a third party intervening on a contract which the principal did not make, and this view has been accepted in the Court of Appeal.[407]

If it were treated as an exception to the rules of privity of contract, the doctrine would still be unusual, since the third party is not mentioned, nor indeed contemplated by one of the parties, and furthermore takes liabilities as well as rights. Another suggestion is that the basis of the doctrine is similar to that of assignment[408]: but there is no evidenced transfer, formal or informal, nor are the rights of the agent extinguished; and the principal receives liabilities as well as rights. It can be said further that the undisclosed principal takes burdens because the principal receives benefits: but this does not explain why the principal receives benefits. Sometimes it is argued that the agent is trustee for the undisclosed principal, but it has been held in the context of the res judicata doctrine that, as regards the third party, the agent is not to be so regarded,[409] and in any case the principal who intervenes has control over litigation in a way that a trust beneficiary would not.[410] Nevertheless, some aspects of the relation between principal and agent are undoubtedly to be accounted for, here as elsewhere, on the basis of trust, or at least of analogous fiduciary duties.[411] The doctrine is probably best explained simply as one of commercial convenience, and its justice is disputable.[412] "It has often been doubted" said Blackburn J "whether it was originally right so to hold: but doubts of this kind come now too late".[413] The Privy Council has in recent years rejected the analogy of assignment.[414] This throws the law back on the tensions between the two approaches described above—that the contract is that of the principal, or that the principal intervenes on the agent's contract. Reasoning based on the notion, at first glance straightforward, that the contract is that of the principal should however be regarded with caution.

It has been suggested in a leading judgment on apparent authority that the rule "can be rationalised as avoiding circuity of action".[415] It is true that in continental systems similar results can sometimes be achieved by circuitous routes: the principal may sue as assignee of the agent's rights, or directly, and the third party

---

[405] *Siu Yin Kwan v Eastern Insurance Co Ltd* [1994] 2 A.C. 199 at 207 (Illustration 12); Article 79.

[406] See Comments to Articles 80 and 81.

[407] *Welsh Development Agency v Export Finance Co Ltd* [1992] B.C.L.C. 148.

[408] Goodhart and Hamson (1932) 4 C.L.J. 320.

[409] *Pople v Evans* [1969] 2 Ch. 255; and see *Allen v F. O'Hearn & Co* [1937] A.C. 213.

[410] See below, para.9-012.

[411] Higgins (1965) 28 M.L.R. 167; and see Comment to Article 43.

[412] See Pollock (1887) 3 L.Q.R. 358; (1896) 12 L.Q.R. 204; (1898) 14 L.Q.R. 2; Ames (1909) 18 Yale L.J. 443; Lewis (1909) 9 Col.L.Rev. 116; Mechem (1910) 23 Harv.L.Rev. 513; Seavey (1920) 29 Yale L.J. 859; Montrose (1938) 16 Can.B.R. 770–771; Weinrib (1975) 21 McGill L.J. 298; Barak (1976) 2 Tel Aviv U. Studies in Law 45; Geva (1979) 25 McGill L.J. 32; Stoljar, pp.228–233; Rochvarg (1989) 34 McGill L.J. 286; Barnett (1987) 75 Calif. L.Rev. 1969; Tan Cheng Han (2004) 120 L.Q.R. 480; G. Fridman, "Undisclosed Principals and the Sale of Goods" in *Agency Law in Commercial Practice* (Busch, Macgregor and Watts eds, 2016), Ch. 5.

[413] *Armstrong v Stokes* (1872) L.R. 7 Q.B. 598 at 604; *VTB Capital Plc v Nutritek International Corp* [2013] UKSC 5; [2013] 2 W.L.R. 398 at [141].

[414] *Siu Yin Kwan v Eastern Insurance Co Ltd* [1994] 2 A.C. 199, Illustration 12.

[415] *Freeman & Lockyer v Buckhurst Park Properties (Mangal) Ltd* [1964] 2 Q.B. 480 at 503, per Diplock LJ. cf. Ames (1909) 18 Yale L.J. 443; Higgins (1965) 28 M.L.R. 167.

may exercise the agent's right of indemnity against the principal.[416] It is said indeed that the simplicity of the common law doctrine is admired by some continental jurists.[417] But the principal's right to sue is perhaps more easily justified on this basis than the liability to be sued.[418] Indeed, the generalisation of what was apparently in origin a limited right of intervention into an arm of general agency principle causes serious problems, many of which are in England at least still unsolved.[419]

Authority and ratification   The agent must have actual authority to act so as to bind and entitle the principal,[420] though this may of course be express or implied. It has been held that the doctrine of ratification does not apply to undisclosed principals.[421] The reason usually given is that if it did, one person could too easily intervene on the contracts of another. This is certainly true where the person whose acts another seeks to ratify initially had no authority at all. Indeed, in such a case there would be no one who could be called an undisclosed principal, and the proposition would simply mean that a person cannot become an undisclosed principal by purporting to ratify the act of another, which is doubtless correct. It is not clear however that such reasoning is so appropriate where the agent already has some authority, but exceeds it. It is arguable that in such a situation a principal who chooses to ratify should be liable; and that the should also be able to sue, the third party being protected by the various safeguards against unfair operation of the doctrine of ratification.[422] Of these, the case for the liability of the principal, which can hurt no one but the principal, is obviously the stronger. The leading case,[423] however, which is a decision of the House of Lords, concerns just this situation and holds the principal not liable.[424]

8-070

Undisclosed principal doctrine compared with indirect representation   It is necessary to keep the concept of the undisclosed principal separate from that of indirect representation. The latter concept has already been outlined.[425] It is not uncommon for civil law trained comparative lawyers to assume that the concept of the undisclosed principal is a version of indirect representation.[426] For the undisclosed principal doctrine to operate the principal must have authorised the agent to bring the principal into contractual privity with the third party. So long as that basic requirement is met, it does not matter whose ends are being pursued by concealing the existence of the principal from the third party. Sometimes, it is the

8-071

---

[416] Müller-Freienfels (1955) 18 M.L.R. 33: Schmitthoff, 1970 I *Hague Recueil des Cours* 115 at 114–145. cf. UNIDROIT Principles Article 2.2.4; criticised by Krebs [2009] L.M.C.L.Q. 57.

[417] Müller-Freienfels (1953) 16 M.L.R. 299.

[418] Zweigert and Kötz, *Introduction to Comparative Law* (tr. Weir) (3rd edn), p.439 onwards; cf. Ames (1909) 18 Yale L.J. 443 at 449; Geva (1975) 25 McGill L.J. 32.

[419] e.g. as to capacity, see below, para.8-074; in connection with indirect representation, para.8-071; connection with unidentified principal, para.8-073; exclusion of the doctrine, para.8-079 onwards; and in connection with dispositions of property, see Article 89.

[420] See further below, para.8-071.

[421] *Keighley, Maxsted & Co v Durant* [1901] A.C. 240, Illustration 3 to Article 15. Schmitthoff calls this a "remarkable restriction": 1970 I *Hague Recueil des Cours* at p.148. See also Seavey (1954) 21 U.Chi.L.Rev. 248; Rochvarg (1989) 34 McGill L.J. 286. As to ratification in general, see Ch.2, section 3.

[422] Article 19.

[423] *Keighley, Maxsted & Co v Durant* [1901] A.C. 240: see above, para.2-063.

[424] Ratification by an undisclosed principal is envisaged by the wording of *Restatement, Third*, Agency: § 4.01 and reporter's note a.

[425] See above, paras 1-021 and 1-022.

[426] See e.g. Hamel, *Le Contrat de Commission* (Paris, 1949), pp.310–327.

principal who wishes to conceal that it is a party to the contract, perhaps because it does not wish it to be known that it has entered the market.[427] Otherwise, it might be the agent who does not tell the third party who is the principal because the agent does not wish the third party on the next transaction to bypass the agent and go direct to the principal; and the principal either acquiesces in this or makes no inquiry as to the agent's practice.[428] These examples are far from exhaustive. Once the conferral of authority is established, the principal can both sue and be sued on any resulting contract. On this basis, the liability of the undisclosed principal is one that is voluntarily assumed, as in agency generally.[429] Subject to the doubtful deployment of the concept of usual authority in *Watteau v Fenwick*,[430] discussed below, an undisclosed principal cannot be liable for the unauthorised acts of the agent, including by a wrongful delegation by the agent to another.[431] Equally, the mere fact that a person "operates" a company does not make that person an undisclosed principal to its transactions.[432]

In contrast, under the concept of indirect representation, although the intermediary works on an "agency" basis in respect to the principal, viz. undertakes only to use best endeavours, does not act as an independent merchant or supplier of services but takes a commission on the transaction arranged, and so forth,[433] the intermediary nonetheless has no authority to bring the principal into contractual privity with the third party and does not do so. Under European legal systems, despite the lack of privity, the principal is in certain circumstances, mainly upon the insolvency of the intermediary, entitled to intervene to claim the price of goods or services directly from the third party. In some jurisdictions there is a (more controversial) reciprocal right given the third party against the principal.[434] These entitlements are, however, introduced ab extra, and do not depend, as does the common law doctrine, on normal principles of authority.

Some dicta suggest that a category of indirect representation does not exist at all in English law: either there is true agency or a contract (usually of sale) between principals.[435] However, other dicta, including the formidable authority of Lord

---

[427] This is particularly the case with land transactions. As to the US, see Hynes and Loewenstein, *Agency, Partnership and the LLC* (7th edn, Charlottesville, Va.) p.361.

[428] There may even be cases where the agent acts contrary to instructions in not disclosing his principal's name: *Ex p. Dixon, re Henley* (1876) 4 Ch. D. 133. Swedish law differentiates between cases where the principal is undisclosed in his own interest and cases where he is undisclosed in the interests of the agent. In the former case it seems that he will be liable and entitled; in the latter, entitled but not liable: Grönfors [1962] Scandinavian Studies in Law 97 at 100, 122–123.

[429] For arguments that agency liability can be imposed, see above, paras 1-025 and 1-026.

[430] *Watteau v Fenwick* [1893] 1 Q.B. 346, discussed below, para.8-077.

[431] See *Hutton v Bulloch* (1874) L.R. 9 Q.B. 572; *New Zealand and Australian Land Co v Watson* (1881) 7 Q.B.D. 374; *Kaltenbach, Fischer & Co v Lewis and Peat* (1885) 10 App.Cas. 617, Illustration 9 to Article 81; Goodhart and Hamson (1932) 4 C.L.J. 320 at 330–335. See also *The Astyanax* [1985] 2 Lloyd's Rep. 109.

[432] See *Yukong Line Ltd v Rendsburg Investments Corp (The Rialto) (No.2)* [1998] 1 W.L.R. 294; and see *Atlas Maritime Co SA v Avalon Maritime Ltd (The Coral Rose) (No.1)* [1991] 1 Lloyd's Rep. 563; *Peterson Farms Inc v C&M Farming Ltd* [2004] EWHC 121 (Comm); [2004] 1 Lloyd's Rep. 603 at [62]; *Magellan Spirit ApS v Vitol SA* [2016] EWHC 454 (Comm) at [27], [28].

[433] See above, paras 1-020 and 1-021.

[434] Kortmann and Kortmann, in *Agency Law in Commercial Practice* (Busch, Macgregor and Watts eds), Ch.6. See also PECL Article 3.3-1(b).

[435] e.g. *Anglo-African Shipping Co of New York Ltd v J. Mortner Ltd* [1962] 1 Lloyd's Rep. 610, per Diplock LJ; *Scrimshire v Alderton* (1743) 2 Str. 1182.

Blackburn,[436] have been willing to recognise the notion of indirect representation.[437] Lord Blackburn was also clear that where such an analysis was not appropriate, the undisclosed principal doctrine might still operate where its requirements were met.[438] The now obsolete cases on foreign principals[439] also operated on a concept of indirect representation; they are based on the idea that a foreign principal does not authorise an English agent to bring the principal into contractual privity with English third parties (and the converse). They recognise clearly, as did Lord Blackburn,[440] that a person acting in such a way does not rank as an undisclosed principal. But the absence of contractual privity in such circumstances precludes the principal from intervening directly on the contracts made by the intermediary or "commissionnaire".

Intention of the agent   Although the intention of one party not communicated to   **8-072** the other is not usually relevant to the legal effect of a transaction, it is plain that if the agent has, as is required for the doctrine to operate, actual authority, the agent's subjective intention will frequently be relevant to the question whether in this particular situation the agent has acted for the principal, or for some other principal, or personally.[441] In particular, where the agent's instructions do not relate to a unique transaction, or the agent has not undertaken to act exclusively for the principal (when an estoppel may run in favour of the principal), it may not be possible, without the agent's personal testimony, to tell whether the agent intended to exercise a mandate for the principal in relation to the transaction in dispute. The other possibilities are that the agent was intending to act personally or for some other principal who has given authority under similar instructions. Whether the agent so intended is a matter of evidence.[442] There are recent dicta doubting this position and suggesting that objective evidence is always required.[443] It might be accepted that objective evidence of the *existence* of an undisclosed principal might be necessary, but it ought not to be necessary that in addition there be objective evidence, contemporary or otherwise, that there has been an *exercise* of the authority.[444] Similar issues arise where it is an unidentified principal that is at issue, rather than

---

[436] *Armstrong v Stokes* (1872) L.R. 7 Q.B. 598, Illustration 7 to Article 80; also *Elbinger Actiengesellschaft v Claye* (1873) L.R. 8 Q.B. 313.

[437] See *Robinson v Mollett* (1875) L.R. 7 H.L. 802 at 809–810 (but the majority regarded the arrangement as inconsistent with the nature of agency: see Article 31, Illustration 8); *Ireland v Livingston* (1872) L.R. 5 H.L. 395.

[438] *Armstrong v Stokes* (1872) L.R. 7 Q.B. 598 at 605–606. But cf. *Maspons y Hermano v Mildred, Goyeneche & Co* (1882) 9 Q.B.D. 530; affirmed on other grounds (1883) 8 App.Cas. 874 which could be said to apply ordinary agency analysis to such a situation. See Reynolds [1983] C.L.P. 119 at 128–133.

[439] See below, para.9-020.

[440] See *Armstrong v Stokes* (1872) L.R. 7 Q.B. 598 at 605–606.

[441] *Siu Yin Kwan v Eastern Insurance Co Ltd* [1994] 2 A.C. 199 at 207 (Illustration 12); *Rolls Royce Power Engineering Plc v Ricardo Consulting Engineers Ltd* [2003] EWHC 2871 (TCC); [2004] 2 All E.R. (Comm) 129; *Gray v Smith* [2013] EWHC 4136 (Comm); [2014] 2 All E.R. (Comm) 359 at [34]; *Sackville UK Property Select II (GP) No.1 Ltd v Robertson Taylor Insurance Brokers Ltd* [2018] EWHC 122 (Ch) at [49] (break notice in relation to lease not given on behalf of lessee). cf. *Restatement, Third*, § 6.03, Comment *d*.

[442] See above, para.2-067. For examples of the sort of evidence that may be used, see *National Oilwell (UK) Ltd v Davy Offshore Ltd* [1993] 2 Lloyd's Rep. 582 at 596–597.

[443] See *Magellan Spirit ApS v Vitol SA* [2016] EWHC 454 (Comm) at [17] and [19], per Leggatt J. cf. *Haberdashers' Aske's Federation Trust Ltd v Lakehouse Contracts Ltd* [2018] EWHC 558 (TCC) at [54].

[444] For example, in the leading case of *Keighley Maxsted & Co v Durant* [1901] A.C. 240 the agent

an undisclosed principal.[445] If it were necessary in such cases that there be objective evidence of the party for whom the agent was acting in the particular transaction, it would follow that in the absence of such evidence there would be no contract at all. Naturally, where objective evidence is available (such as communications between principal and agent, business records, evidence of past practice) it is likely to be preferred over contradictory personal testimony from the agent at trial. In the last resort, however, the question will turn on whether the trier of fact believes the agent when the agent asserts that in this particular instance he or she was acting for the principal or personally or for a different principal.

8-073 **Degree of knowledge of the third party** Many decisions on the undisclosed principal doctrine could be analysed as, or as very close to, cases of disclosed but unidentified principals, and it is useful to bear this in mind when they are considered. The obvious situation for the operation of the doctrine is that where the third party does not know of the involvement of any principal. Many cases suggest or imply that a third party dealing with an apparent principal has no duty of inquiry as to whether that person has anyone behind them[446]; that the third party need not prove lack of knowledge of a principal's existence[447]; and that constructive notice of it is not to be attributed to the third party.[448] But there are several decisions which go further and apply the undisclosed principal doctrine to situations where the third party is actually aware that the agent sometimes deals personally and sometimes on behalf of others but does not know which is true on this occasion[449]; to situations where the third party is aware of the existence (possibly even the name) and involvement of the principal, but is not clear as to the principal's exact relationship with the agent,[450] and even to situations where the third party is aware that the principal is using the intermediary's services on an agency basis and that the principal does not wish to become a party to the agent's contract.[451] In all these cases the first requisite would of course be that the agent was liable as a

---

certainly had authority, and had he stayed within it there would surely (in the absence of other indications) have been no need to communicate to the principal or otherwise manifest an intention that he intended to exercise it.

[445] See *National Oilwell (UK) Ltd v Davy Offshore Ltd* [1993] 2 Lloyd's Rep. 582 at 597; above, para.2-067; *Americas Bulk Transport Ltd (Liberia) v Cosco Bulk Carrier Ltd (China) MV Grand Fortune* [2020] EWHC 147 (Comm) at [23]. See also *A. Tomlinson (Hauliers) Ltd v Hepburn* [1966] A.C. 451; and *Lai Wo Heung v Cheung Kong Fur Pty Co Ltd* [2004] 1 H.K.L.R.D. 959 (subjective intention of agent important where principal unidentified).

[446] *Fish v Kempton* (1849) 7 C.B. 687; *Ex p. Dixon, re Henley* (1876) 4 Ch.D. 133; *Gothard v Davey* [2010] FCA 1163 at [236].

[447] *Borries v Imperial Ottoman Bank* (1873) L.R. 9 C.P. 38. See also *Semenza v Brinsley* (1865) 18 C.B. (N.S.) 467; *Knight v Matson & Co* (1902) 22 N.Z.L.R. 293.

[448] *Greer v Downs Supply Co* [1927] 2 K.B. 28.

[449] *Baring v Corrie* (1818) 2 B. & A. 137; *Cooke & Sons v Eshelby* (1887) 12 App. Cas. 271, Illustration 7 to Article 81; and perhaps *Armstrong v Stokes* (1872) L.R. 7 Q.B. 598, Illustration 7 to Article 80.

[450] *Addison v Gandassequi* (1812) 4 Taunt. 574; *Paterson v Gandasequi* (1812) 15 East 62; *Teheran-Europe Co Ltd v S.T. Belton (Tractors) Ltd* [1986] 2 Q.B. 545 (where the Court of Appeal was undecided whether the case was one of unidentified or of undisclosed principal); and perhaps *Pyxis Special Shipping Co Ltd v Dritsis & Kaglis Bros Ltd (The Scaplake)* [1978] 2 Lloyd's Rep. 380.

[451] *Maspons y Hermano v Mildred, Goyeneche & Co* (1882) 9 Q.B.D. 530; affirmed on other grounds (1883) 8 App.Cas. 874. *Browning v Provincial Insurance Co of Canada* (1873) L.R. 5 P.C. 263 also seems to concern such a person. See Busch, *Indirect Representation in European Contract Law* (2005), pp.171–172.

contracting party: otherwise the transaction would lack certainty.[452] It is possible that the first two situations would really be better analysed as involving disclosed but unidentified principals, if a rule that the agent of such a principal was prima facie personally liable could be adopted, for they seem to be brought within the undisclosed principal doctrine by the desire to hold the agent liable and entitled as well as the principal, or otherwise to use reasoning applicable to undisclosed rather than fully disclosed principals.[453] Whether the third situation invokes the undisclosed principal rules has already been discussed.[454] Here again there are significant uncertainties as to the application of the doctrine.

Capacity of agent   Although the doctrine is here explained on the general basis that the principal intervenes on the agent's contract, this need not mean that the agent who acts for an undisclosed principal must, contrary to the normal rule for agents,[455] have capacity. There are sufficient inelegancies in the doctrine for it to be appropriate to examine each situation on its merits rather than by reference to formulae. If the agent's contract is unenforceable for lack of capacity, it is possible that the principal may nevertheless be able to intervene, and is liable, although the agent could not sue or be sued.[456]   **8-074**

Contract in writing   The question whether an undisclosed principal can intervene on a contract signed only by the agent and the third party is undetermined. The principal certainly was able to do so under s.40 of the Law of Property Act 1925, which re-enacting the Statute of Frauds 1677 required a note or memorandum of the contract. But s.2 of the Law of Property (Miscellaneous Provisions) Act 1989 requires that the contract actually be in writing and signed by or on behalf of the parties. The matter is discussed elsewhere.[457]   **8-075**

Merger and election   It seems to have been at least in part unease about the justifiability of the undisclosed principals' doctrine which led to the application of rules as to merger and election, whereby the third party may be able to sue principal or agent, but not both.[458] These are separately discussed under Article 82. They operate in one direction only: the third party cannot elect as to by whom the party is sued; though that party may be able to insist on exercising rights against the agent   **8-076**

---

[452] See *Public Trustee v Taylor* [1978] V.R. 289 ("for himself or as agent for an undisclosed principal"—agent personally liable so transaction valid).

[453] See below, para.9-016.

[454] See above, para.8-071.

[455] Article 5.

[456] See Weinrib (1975) 21 McGill L.J. 298, criticising *Commonwealth Trust Co v De Witt* (1973) 40 D.L.R. (3d) 113, in which the fact that it acted for an undisclosed principal was held actually to confer capacity on a corporate agent. The case is also criticised in (1976) 40 Sask.L.Rev. 291. In *Danziger v Thompson* [1944] K.B. 654, Illustration 8, specific performance was decreed against an undisclosed principal whose agent was a minor: but the facts and decision are not clear, and the contract was probably one of those binding minors.

[457] See Comment to Article 71.

[458] e.g. *Kendall v Hamilton* (1879) 4 App.Cas. 504 at 544.

despite the principal's intervention,[459] and, as explained below, there are cases where the principal may not be permitted to intervene at all.[460]

8-077   **Rule (2): Watteau v Fenwick**   This Rule represents the proposition to be derived from a Divisional Court case of 1893 which has achieved a surprising prominence. The interest that it has generated among commentators, and the fact that its result is regarded as acceptable doctrine in the US,[461] justify its continued statement here. Its correctness is however most doubtful. Liability under the undisclosed principal's doctrine arises because the principal voluntarily authorised the very transaction. It is not a doctrine designed to impose liability, as if it were a species of vicarious liability.

In *Watteau v Fenwick*[462] the owner of a hotel sold his business to a firm of brewers, who retained him as their manager. The licence was taken out in his name and his name was painted over the door. It was agreed that he should buy all supplies other than bottled ales and mineral waters from the brewers. In breach of this stipulation he bought cigars on credit from the plaintiffs, and the brewers were held liable on this contract. The case cannot be explained on the basis of apparent authority, since the principal was undisclosed,[463] and there was no actual authority. It was in fact based on a wider principle. Wills J said[464]:

> "Once it is established that the defendant was the real principal, the ordinary doctrine as to principal and agent applies—that the principal is liable for all the acts of the agent which are within the authority usually confided to an agent of that character, notwithstanding limitations, as between the principal and the agent, put upon that authority. It is said that it is only so where there has been a holding out of authority—which cannot be said where the person supplying the goods knew nothing of the existence of a principal. But I do not think so. Otherwise in every case of undisclosed principal, or at least in every case where the fact of there being a principal was undisclosed, the secret limitation of authority would prevail and defeat the action of the person dealing with the agent and then discovering that he was an agent and had a principal."

This proposition, which can be regarded as suggesting a special form of usual authority,[465] is however extremely dubious. It was supported by two arguments: an analogy with the law of partnership, and an earlier case in the Queen's Bench, *Edmunds v Bushell and Jones*.[466] The analogy with the law of partnership has long since been shown to be wrong.[467] *Edmunds v Bushell and Jones* is a case where the

---

[459] See *O'Herlihy v Hedges* (1803) 1 Sch. & Lef. 123; *Finmoon Ltd v Baltic Reefers Management Ltd* [2012] EWHC 920 (Comm); [2012] 2 Lloyd's Rep. 388 at [76] (undisclosed principal entitled to join arbitration action).
[460] See below, para.8-079.
[461] See below, text to fn.481.
[462] *Watteau v Fenwick* [1893] 1 Q.B. 346, Illustration 5; criticised (1893) 9 L.Q.R. 111; (1893) 7 HarvL.Rev. 49; (1893) 37 S.J. 280; Ewart, *Estoppel* (1900), p.246 onwards.
[463] Though Goodhart and Hamson seek so to explain it: see (1932) 4 C.L.J. 320 at 336, but cf. Wright (1935) 13 Can.B.R. 116 at 120; Montrose (1939) 17 Can.B.R. 693 at 696; Powell, pp.75–76.
[464] *Watteau v Fenwick* [1893] 1 Q.B. 346 at 348–349.
[465] See Comment to Article 22.
[466] *Edmunds v Bushell and Jones* (1865) L.R. 1 Q.B. 97, Illustration 4.
[467] See *Lindley and Banks on Partnership* (20th edn), para.12-11 onwards; Pollock (1893) 9 L.Q.R. 111; Montrose (1939) 17 Can.B.R. 693 at 699 onwards (but as to some of the points made, see Thomas (1971) Vic.U. of Wellington L.R. 1); Powell, pp.76–77; *Construction Engineering (Aust.) Pty Ltd v Hexyl Pty Ltd* (1985) 155 C.L.R. 541.

facts are not clear[468] and there may have been apparent authority: in any case the dicta in the short judgments cast doubt on the reasoning employed. Thus Shee J said[469]:

> "The natural inference when a person allows an agent to carry on a particular business as an ostensible principal, is that he clothes him with every authority incidental to a principal in the business."

But this involves confusion: a principal has no authority and deals on his own account.[470]

The case was followed, and indeed preferred to other authority which might appear contrary,[471] by the Divisional Court in a case subsequently reversed on other grounds,[472] and it has been distinguished.[473] The supposed doctrine of *Watteau v Fenwick*[474] is therefore tentatively reproduced here. But the Supreme Court of Ontario[475] and the Court of Appeal of British Columbia[476] have refused to follow it; and doubt has been cast on it in the High Court of Australia[477] and in England.[478] It may be that a careful study of the facts would enable a conclusion that the case was really one of unidentified principal. It is submitted that it is in fact inconsistent with the basic principles of agency law as subsequently established.[479] If the doctrine is adopted, therefore, this should only be done on the basis of a conscious advance on the previous accepted theories of agency, made for the purpose of extending liability.[480]

Restatement, Second regarded this as an example of "inherent agency power": that is to say, as a rule not justifiable on orthodox linking theory, but creating a satisfactory result.[481] In *Restatement, Third* the notion of "inherent agency power" is eliminated, but a rule similar to the effect of *Watteau v Fenwick* is retained under the heading of "Estoppel of Undisclosed Principal". Article 2.06 reads:

> "An undisclosed principal may not rely on instructions given to an agent that qualify or reduce the agent's authority to less than the authority a third party would reasonably believe the agent to have under the same circumstances if the principal had been disclosed."

---

[468] See Montrose (1939) 17 Can.B.R. 693 at 697–699; (1893) 37 S.J. 280.
[469] *Edmunds v Bushell and Jones* (1865) L.R. 1 Q.B. 97 at 100.
[470] cf. Ewart, *Estoppel* (1900), Ch.XVII.
[471] *Daun v Simmins* (1879) 41 L.T. 783.
[472] *Kinahan & Co v Parry* [1910] 2 K.B. 389; reversed [1911] 1 K.B. 459, Illustration 6.
[473] See *Johnston v Reading* (1893) 9 T.L.R. 200; *Lloyd's Bank Ltd v Swiss Bankverein* (1912) 107 L.T. 309 (affirmed 108 L.T. 143); *Jerome v Bentley* [1952] 2 All E.R. 114.
[474] *Watteau v Fenwick* [1893] 1 Q.B. 346.
[475] *McLaughlin v Gentles* (1919) 51 D.L.R. 383; see also *Becherer v Asher* (1896) 23 Ont.App. 202.
[476] *Sign-o-Lite Plastics Ltd v Metropolitan Life Insurance Co* (1990) 73 D.L.R. (4th) 541.
[477] *International Paper Co v Spicer* (1906) 4 C.L.R. 739 at 763. The Privy Council made no attempt to use such reasoning in the earlier case of *Miles v McIlwraith* (1883) 8 App.Cas. 120.
[478] See *The Rhodian River* [1984] 1 Lloyd's Rep. 373. See also *Re Att.-Gen.'s Reference (No.1 of 1985)* [1986] Q.B. 491 at 506.
[479] See Comment to Article 22; Hornby [1961] C.L.J. 239. In *A.L. Underwood Ltd v Bank of Liverpool* [1924] 1 K.B. 775 at 792, Scrutton LJ said: "Just as you cannot ratify the act of an agent who did not profess to act for you ... so in my view you cannot rely on the apparent authority of an agent who did not profess in dealing with you to act as agent". See also above, para.1-026.
[480] Montrose (1939) 17 Can.B.R. 693; Bester (1972) 89 S.A.L.J. 49.
[481] § 8A: "the power of an agent which is derived not from authority, apparent authority or estoppel, but solely from the agency relation, and exists for the protection of persons harmed by or dealing with a servant or other agent". See also above, para.3-005.

The Comment states that:

"Liability will result only when a third party deals with an agent but has no notice that the agent represents the interests of another and when the third party would not have reason to inquire into the scope of the agent's authority if the third party knew the agent acted on behalf of a principal."

In justifying the rule, the injustice of allowing a principal who has chosen to deal through an agent but to remain undisclosed to have the benefit of restrictions on an agent's authority is stressed, and also the fact that the third party would not think to inquire. Although the UNIDROIT Principles in general abolish the doctrine of the undisclosed principal altogether, an exception is puzzlingly retained for cases where the owner of a business sells the business but continues as manager while appearing as owner and enters into a contract which would not be queried were he still the owner.[482] Some protection for third parties in such situations may well be justified; and indeed for any case where a person disposes of assets to which that party's creditors might expect recourse. But it is not easy to see why this should be obtained by applying rules of agency to a person who has indeed changed the capacity in which that person acts to that of agent, yet as such has neither actual nor apparent authority. If relief is to be given under the law of contract, it should rather be under the law of mistake as to the person.[483]

Although such an extension of liability such as that which could be taken to follow from *Watteau v Fenwick* might on the face of it appear progressive, it is not easy to justify a rule of liability on such a loose basis. Contemporary decisions of the House of Lords[484] and Privy Council,[485] while not adverting expressly to the point, are not consistent with any trend to extend liability beyond situations where authority exists or appears to exist. In a fairly recent case Bingham J said that the argument advanced for the unsuccessful defendant in *Watteau v Fenwick* seemed to him in principle correct.[486] It is submitted that the supposed doctrine is too vague to be satisfactorily employed.[487] It is sometimes suggested that the actual decision in *Watteau v Fenwick* can be explained on the basis of apparent ownership[488]: but this would be an extension of that doctrine, which only applies to dispositions of property and perhaps to contracts to dispose of property, and which requires not only that the owner of property must have given another possession of the property, but also done something more, so as to raise an estoppel against him.[489] Had execution been sought against the property, that doctrine might conceivably have applied: but it would not (again unless the case indicates an extension of the doctrine) make

---

[482] Article 2.2.4(2): "However, where such an agent, when contracting with the third party on behalf of a business, represents itself to be the owner of that business the third party, upon discovery of the real owner of the business, may also exercise against the owner the rights it has against the agent".

[483] cf. *Lake v Simmons* [1927] A.C. 487.

[484] *Moorgate Mercantile Co Ltd v Twitchings* [1977] A.C. 890, Illustration 7 to Article 84; *British Bank of the Middle East v Sun Life Assurance Co of Canada (UK) Ltd* [1983] 2 Lloyd's Rep. 9, Illustration 10 to Article 77.

[485] *Kooragang Investments Pty Ltd v Richardson & Wrench Ltd* [1982] A.C. 462, Illustration 4 to Article 74.

[486] *Rhodian River Shipping Co SA v Holla Maritime Corp (The Rhodian River)* [1984] 1 Lloyd's Rep. 373 at 379.

[487] See also Comment to Article 22.

[488] Hornby [1961] C.L.J. 239; Conant (1968) 47 Neb.L.Rev. 678; Mechem, *Outlines of Agency* (4th edn), §§ 173–176. This receives some support from the cases dealing with set-off against the agent: see Article 81.

[489] Article 84.

the brewer liable for the money.[490] Other explanations of the decision, e.g. that the brewer had received and used the goods and was liable on that basis only,[491] or that the owners were estopped from establishing that they were a separate entity from the person with whom the supplier did business,[492] are possible, should they be thought necessary.

It does not appear that the supposed doctrine of this case enables the principal to sue, any more than does that of apparent authority: and the principal being undisclosed, there can be no ratification.[493]

Rule (3): Contract in writing: evidence to show who is the real principal In **8-078** *Humble v Hunter*[494] the argument was accepted that where the contract was in writing, the intervention of the undisclosed principal might be prevented under the parol evidence rule, as being inconsistent with the written contract.[495] This was contrary to the rationale of the cases on the Statute of Frauds, referred to above, which is that where the effect of the principal's intervention is to add a contracting party, not to exclude one, the writing is adequate.[496] Though the case has been followed,[497] it has more often been distinguished,[498] and it has also been judicially questioned.[499] It is obvious that if such a view was readily taken, the intervention of an undisclosed principal would be almost impossible. It is therefore submitted that the undisclosed principal can only be excluded from intervening under the proposition stated in Rule (4) of this Article, and that evidence of such a principal will be admitted unless the exclusion of such a principal is expressed or implied by the terms of the contract,

---

[490] Ewart, *Estoppel* (1900), p.247.

[491] Ferson (1951) 4 Vand.L.Rev. 260 at 280.

[492] Tettenborn [1998] C.L.J. 274. Such reasoning would be similar to that in *Gurtner v Beaton* [1993] 2 Lloyd's Rep. 369, Illustration 5 to Article 72, and *Lease Management Services v Purnell Secretarial Services* [1994] C.C.L.R. 127. See the discussion of other estoppels, above, para.8-027.

[493] See above, para.8-070.

[494] *Humble v Hunter* (1848) 12 Q.B. 310, Illustration 7.

[495] But compare the arguments of counsel with the judgment given. However, such was the interpretation put on the case in *Formby Brothers v Formby* (1910) 102 L.T. 116. The argument had been rejected in *Wilson v Hart* (1817) 1 Moo.C.P. 45.

[496] See above, para.8-075; Comment to Article 71.

[497] *Formby Brothers v Formby* (1910) 102 L.T. 116 ("proprietor"), where the court would have followed *Humble v Hunter* but was prevented by the fact that the matter had not been raised in the lower court (and see on this case Stoljar, p.22); *Rederiaktiebolaget Argonaut v Hani* [1918] 2 K.B. 247 ("as charterer") (but see Lord Shaw in *Drughorn v Rederiaktiebolaget Transatlantic* [1919] A.C. 203); *Fawcett v Star Car Sales Ltd* [1960] N.Z.L.R. 406 at 420–425.

[498] *Killick & Co v Price & Co & Lingfield SS Co Ltd* (1896) 12 T.L.R. 263; *Drughorn Ltd v Rederiaktiebolaget Transatlantic* [1919] A.C. 203 ("charterer"); *Danziger v Thompson* [1944] K.B. 654, Illustration 8 ("tenant"); *Epps v Rothnie* [1945] K.B. 562 ("landlord"); *O/Y Wasa SS Co & N.V Stoomschip Hannah v Newspaper Pulp & Wood Export* (1949) 82 Ll.L.Rep. 936 ("disponent owner") (where there is a full review of the authorities); *Murphy v Rae* [1967] N.Z.L.R. 103 ("vendor"); *The Astyanax* [1985] 2 Lloyd's Rep. 109 ("disponent owner"; held to act personally); *White v Baycorp Advantage Business Information Services Ltd* (2006) 200 F.L.R. 125 at [83] (plaintiff claimed that defendant credit reference bureau incorrectly listed it as a defaulting debtor in relation to certain creditors; defendant countered that named creditors were undisclosed principals of parties with whom plaintiff had contracted).

[499] *Killick & Co v Price & Lingfield SS Co Ltd* (1896) 12 T.L.R. 263 at 264 (but see *Formby Brothers v Formby* (1910) 102 L.T. 116); *Drughorn Ltd v Rederiaktiebolaget Transatlantic* [1919] A.C. 203 at 209; *Epps v Rothnie* [1945] K.B. 562 at 565; *Diamond Stud Ltd v New Zealand Bloodstock Finance Ltd* [2010] NZCA 423 (para.8-078 expressly approved).

written or unwritten, as explained below.[500] Indeed the dicta of Lord Denman CJ in *Humble v Hunter* itself afford some support for this view,[501] and *Humble v Hunter* may be explained as an example, if a curious one, of such exclusion. This would be a true application of the parol evidence rule to this situation. The relation between the two rules—the rule of law dealing with exclusion of the principal by the express or implied terms of the contract, and the rule of evidence against variation of written contracts by extrinsic evidence—has often been misunderstood.[502] *Humble v Hunter* is frequently simply not referred to, the court looking to the evidence to see if an unidentified or unnamed principal exists outside the writing.[503]

8-079   **Rule (4): Express or implied exclusion of undisclosed principals**[504]   It is to be expected that there should be some limitations on the principal's intervention, but it is not clear what these are. First, older case law finds that where the agent contracts for a named principal, no other principal may intervene.[505] But this is not a rigid rule. Where a company is the named principal and there is no restriction on the personnel who may act for the company, the third party already has little control over who actually carries out the performance of the contract. In such cases, the intervention of an undisclosed principal may not inconvenience the third party[506] Secondly, where there is an express term of the contract that the agent is the only party to it, there can be no intervention by an undisclosed principal.[507] It may indeed be prudent to insert such clauses into contracts where it is desired to exclude the possibility of intervention.[508] As Rule (4) states, there can however be cases where the agent impliedly contracts that he or she is principal, or that no other party is directly involved.[509] Sometimes this implication is derived from the interpretation of words descriptive of the agent personally, and of the contract as a whole, that the

---

[500] *Finzel, Berry & Co v Eastcheap Dried Fruit Co* [1962] 1 Lloyd's Rep. 370 at 375; *Murphy v Rae* [1967] N.Z.L.R. 103; *Teheran-Europe Co Ltd v S.T. Belton (Tractors) Ltd* [1968] 2 Q.B. 545 at 552; Davies (1968) 8 U. of W.A.L.Rev. 534; Fridman (1968) 84 L.Q.R. 224 at 239–244; McLauchlan, *The Parol Evidence Rule* (Wellington, NZ, 1976), Ch.13.

[501] See the case explained by a court containing two of the same judges in *Schmaltz v Avery* (1851) 12 Q.B. 655 at 660. See also *Drughorn Ltd v Rederiaktiebolaget Transatlantic* [1919] A.C. 203 at 207 ("a term of the contract that he should contract as owner of that property"); *O/Y Wasa SS Co v Newspaper Pulp & Wood Export* (1949) 82 Ll. L. Rep. 936.

[502] See Landon (1945) 61 L.Q.R. 130; (1946) 62 L.Q.R. 20; McLauchlan, above.

[503] See *Filatona Trading Ltd v Navigator Equities Ltd* [2020] EWCA Civ 109 at [78] (parties to shareholders' agreement).

[504] Ivamy (1951) 18 *Solicitor* 245; Goodhart and Hamson (1932) 4 C.L.J. 320; Powell, pp.154–166; Glanville Williams (1945) 23 Can.B.R. 397–416; *Restatement, Third*, § 6.03, Comment *d*; Dal Pont, para.19.34 onwards.

[505] *Phillips v Duke of Bucks* (1683) 1 Vern. 227; cf. *M'Auliffe v Bicknell* (1835) 2 Cr.M. & R. 263. But see Article 108.

[506] See *Foster v Action Aviation Ltd* [2014] EWCA Civ 1368 (but parent company of seller was disclosed principal).

[507] *United Kingdom, etc., Assn v Neville* (1887) 19 Q.B.D. 110, Illustration 9; *J.A. Rayner (Mincing Lane) Ltd v Department of Trade and Industry* [1990] 2 A.C. 418 at 516 ("The contract is made between ourselves and yourselves as principals, we alone being liable to you for its performance"); *Filatona Trading Ltd v Navigator Equities Ltd* [2020] EWCA Civ 109 at [89]. This exception was criticised as illogical by Williston, *Contracts* (rev. ed.), § 286. See also *Bart v British West Indian Airways* [1967] 1 Lloyd's Rep. 239 at 243–249, 284–287 (contract regulated by Warsaw Convention).

[508] A non-assignment clause would not necessarily be effective: see below.

[509] See *Finzel, Berry & Co v Eastcheap Dried Fruit Co* [1962] 1 Lloyd's Rep. 370 at 375; *Foster v Action Aviation Ltd* [2014] EWCA Civ 1368 at [38] (legal owner disclosed principal; no room for beneficial owner as undisclosed principal); *Aspen Underwriting Ltd v Kairos Shipping Ltd* [2018]

agent alone answers the description in question: this is probably the best interpretation of the cases cited in the preceding paragraph, and it seems that (if the cases are all to be treated as correct) whereas the words "owner" or "proprietor" may perhaps raise such an implication,[510] descriptions of the agent as "landlord", "tenant", "disponent owner", "charterer" or "vendor" are less likely to do so.[511] In these cases intervention by an undisclosed principal would be inconsistent with the contract on which the principal seeks to intervene. "The principle applied is clearly sound, whether or not as a matter of interpretation the contracts were properly construed".[512]

It was formerly arguable that where the benefit of a contract is not assignable or its burden could not be vicariously performed[513] the undisclosed principal cannot intervene.[514] That there is a rule to this effect was however rejected by the Privy Council in the leading modern case of *Siu Yin Kwan v Eastern Insurance Co Ltd*.[515] The mere fact that a contract by its terms excluded subsequent assignment was said not to be crucial as to whether an undisclosed principal already existing at that time could intervene.[516] Nonetheless, it is clear from *Siu Yin Kwan* itself that weight was placed on the fact that, whoever was the formal party, the insurer was fully aware of the exact vessel and the number of crew that the insurance was intended to, and in fact could only, protect. In most cases where the undisclosed-principals doctrine has been successfully invoked the nature and scope of the third party's obligations would not have much varied whoever was the principal.

It is suggested, therefore, that the fact that a third party has undertaken a fixed or determinate liability has to be borne in mind when reading the dictum of Diplock LJ, approved in *Siu Yin Kwan*, that in an "ordinary commercial contract" it may be assumed that a person is:

"willing to treat as a party to the contract anyone on whose behalf the agent may have been authorised to contract … unless either the other party manifests his unwillingness or there

---

EWCA Civ 2590; [2019] 1 Lloyd's Rep. 221 at [51]; *Kaefer Aislamientos SA de CV v AMS Drilling Mexico SA de CV* [2019] EWCA Civ 10; [2019] 1 W.L.R. 3514 at [113] (relevance of entire-agreement clause). It is possible that *Greer v Downs Supply Co* [1927] 2 K.B. 28 and *Collins v Associated Greyhound Racecourses* [1930] 1 Ch. 1 could be so explained, but see fn.522 below. See *Talbot Underwriting Ltd v Nausch, Hogan & Murray Inc (The Jascon 5)* [2006] EWCA Civ 889; [2006] 2 Lloyd's Rep. 195, finding the undisclosed principal doctrine excluded, distinguishing *Siu Yin Kwan v Eastern Insurance Co Ltd* [1994] 2 A.C. 199. For argument that the undisclosed principal doctrine is readily excluded in insurance contracts, see Merkin (2006) 17 K.C.L.J. 111.

[510] e.g. *Davis v Capel* [1959] N.Z.L.R. 825; *Construction Engineering (Aust.) Pty Ltd v Hexyl Pty Ltd* (1985) 155 C.L.R. 541 at 546–547; *White v Baycorp Advantage Business Information Services Ltd* (2006) 200 F.L.R. 125 at [83] (see above, para.8-078).

[511] See above, para.8-078. Goodhart and Hamson describe such implied exclusion as arising only in "highly peculiar circumstances": (1932) 4 C.L.J. 320 at 356. But the decision as to "tenant" can be criticised: see fn.538 below.

[512] *Restatement, Second*, Appendix, p.520 (Seavey).

[513] See *Chitty on Contracts* (33rd edn) para.19-043 onwards and para.19-082 onwards. Intervention on a sale would under this rule rarely be disallowed, for both in the case of assignment and in the case of undisclosed principal, the liability of the original contracting party to the third party remains. But intervention on a loan would rarely be permitted.

[514] This was the view of Goodhart and Hamson (1932) 4 C.L.J. 320.

[515] *Siu Yin Kwan v Eastern Insurance Co Ltd* [1994] 2 A.C. 199, Illustration 12. Had it not been for findings of fact, the case would be a straightforward one of unidentified principal: the insurers knew the occupation of the agents and that they did not own the ship. The case may in fact be another where facts appropriate to unidentified principals distort the rules for undisclosed principals: see Reynolds, in *Consensus ad Idem* (Rose ed., 1997), pp.92–95; and above, para.8-073.

[516] See *Restatement, Third*, § 6.03, Comment *d*.

are other circumstances which would lead the agent to realise that the other party was not so willing."[517]

Lord Lloyd of Berwick described Diplock LJ's approach as a "beneficial assumption".[518] But it is at best an assumption rather than a prescription: unwillingness does not have to be manifested by a term in the contract.[519] So, it may be inferred that obligations of a personal nature, which could not be vicariously performed, will not permit intervention. Equally, intervention may be precluded where it is clear that the third party cannot have intended to expose itself to open-ended liability to unknown parties. It is for this reason that there is little, if any, role for the concept of the undisclosed principal in relation to the tort of negligent misstatement.[520] The absence of reciprocity would not encourage an assumption that the utterer of a statement was content for unknown parties to rely upon it. The fact that losses in tort tend to be highly individualised also counts against any assumption of responsibility to undisclosed parties.

Other, less satisfactory, approaches to the right (or not) for an undisclosed principal to intervene have been suggested. In *Said v Butt*[521] a theatre critic bought, as undisclosed principal through an agent, a ticket for a first night performance. He was refused admission. He was held not entitled to sue for breach of contract, apparently on the ground that the formation of the contract was affected by mistake. But this reasoning involves the assumption that the contract is between third party and undisclosed principal, and as we have seen the validity of this reasoning is limited.[522] Further, it does not provide useful guidance: if the contract is made (as this was) with a named person, on such reasoning no other person can ever be a party to it. Since the first night was largely by invitation, this may have been a case where an implied exclusion of the, or any, principal was appropriate: and this may be the best explanation of the decision.

The simpler explanation for *Said v Butt* is one that an undisclosed principal cannot intervene when the principal knew or should have known at the time of the contract that the third party would not have dealt with him or her.[523] It might be answered to this that it would be sufficient in such circumstances for the law to

---

[517] *Teheran-Europe Co Ltd v S.T. Belton (Tractors) Ltd* [1968] 2 Q.B. 545 at 555.

[518] *Siu Yin Kwan v Eastern Insurance Co Ltd* [1994] 2 A.C. 199 at 209. See too *Diamond Stud Ltd v New Zealand Bloodstock Finance Ltd* [2010] NZCA 423 (term expressly making bidder at auction liable despite any undisclosed agency did not impliedly exclude liability of undisclosed principal).

[519] *Rolls Royce Power Engineering Plc v Ricardo Consulting Engineers Ltd* [2003] EWHC 2871 (TCC); [2004] 2 All E.R. (Comm) 129.

[520] *Playboy Club London Ltd v Banca Nazionale del Lavoro SpA* [2018] UKSC 43; [2018] 1 W.L.R. 4041 (noted J. Grower and P. Sherman, "Equivalent to Contract?" (2019) 135 L.Q.R. 177).

[521] *Said v Butt* [1920] 3 K.B. 497, Illustration 11. The action was actually against the manager of the theatre for inducing breach of contract. See also *Smith v Wheatcroft* (1878) 9 Ch.D. 223 at 230; *Nelthorpe v Holgate* (1844) 1 Col.C.C. 203.

[522] See above, para.8-069; Glanville Williams (1945) 23 Can.B.R. 397–414; Goodhart and Hamson (1932) 4 C.L.J. 320. *Said v Butt* is to some extent supported by *Greer v Downs Supply Co* [1927] 2 K.B. 28, where a third party made a contract with an agent because the agent owed him money which could be set off, and the undisclosed principal was not permitted to intervene. But the judgments in the case are unsatisfactory (see (1945) 23 Can.B.Rev. 411) since it is clear that the setoff could have been used against the principal in any case: see Article 81. See also *Collins v Associated Greyhound Racecourses Ltd* [1930] 1 Ch. 1, below, para.8-099; *Campbellville Gravel Supply Co Ltd v Cook Paving Co Ltd* (1968) 70 D.L.R. (2d) 354.

[523] Treitel, *Law of Contract* (15th edn), para.16-065 onwards; see also *Smith v Wheatcroft* (1878) 9 Ch.D. 223 at 230; *Humble v Hunter* (1848) 12 Q.B. 310 at 313 (the undisclosed principal "shall not come forward so as unfairly to prejudice the party sued"). It derives some support from the judg-

withhold specific performance without denying the existence of the right to intervene on the contract. Given, however, that the "beneficial assumption" must surrender to the parties' intentions, it is not clear that the law should strive overly to favour the principal.

The question whether a principal could, if sued, personally plead that the contract was one excluding intervention does not appear to have been considered; but if the question depends on the terms of the contract there seems no reason why that could not be possible. If a misrepresentation was involved, as discussed below, the matter would be different.

Intervention is not permitted in respect of deeds and negotiable instruments for reasons connected with the nature of those documents. These are discussed in the following two Articles.

Misrepresentation   Where the contract is procured by misrepresentation by the   **8-080**
agent, whether fraudulent or innocent, on general principles the contract can be rescinded if it is not too late to do so; and specific performance may be refused. The representation must be material to the representee.[524] Where the agent or the principal, or both, knew or must have known that the third party would not deal with the particular principal, or would only deal with the agent, a specific representation that that principal was not involved, or that no one else but the agent was involved, could be material.[525] Greater difficulties arise if the agent simply does not disclose the principal's involvement. Rescission should only be available where the situation is one of those in which non-disclosure constitutes a misrepresentation[526]; though there are cases in this context where specific performance has been refused though rescission might not perhaps have been granted.[527] It would seem however that an innocent misrepresentation or non-disclosure is not to be regarded as material if the only facts are that the agent was thereby seeking to secure better terms for the principal.[528]

Discovery against principal   It has been held that where it is alleged that the   **8-081**
claimant agent acted for an undisclosed principal, proceedings by the agent may be stayed unless the principal discloses documents (or the agent procures that the principal does so) which the principal would be required to do if the principal were an express party to the contract.[529] As a matter of disclosure this may be correct, for what is revealed may well be relevant to the claimant's damages. But it seems to have been assumed that the agent in such a case had no interest in the proceedings other than the right to bring them in the agent's own name. In view of the interest

---

ment of Diplock LJ in *Teheran-Europe Co Ltd v S.T. Belton (Tractors) Ltd*, quoted above.
[524] See Treitel, *Law of Contract* (15th edn), paras 9-023–9-026.
[525] See *Restatement, Third*, § 6.03, Comment *d*; (1931) 44 Harvard L.R. 1271.
[526] See *Chitty on Contracts* (33rd edn), para.7-018 onwards; (1927) 75 U.Pa.L.R. 761 at 764.
[527] e.g. *Archer v Stone* (1898) 78 L.T. 34; *Phillips v Duke of Bucks* (1683) 1 Vern. 227.
[528] e.g. *Dyster v Randall & Sons* [1926] Ch. 932, Illustration 10 (criticised, *Restatement, Second*, Appendix, p.524); *Smith v Wheatcroft* (1878) 9 Ch.D. 223; and see the well known judgment of Cardozo J in *Kelly Asphalt Block Co v Barber Asphalt Paving Co* 105 N.E. 88 (Ct.App.N.Y. 1914). cf. *Nash v Dix* (1898) 78 L.T. 445, where it was held that there was no agency but a purchase for resale. See J.C. Smith [1972B] C.L.J. 197 at 219 onwards, considering the relationship between these cases and *Berg v Sadler and Moore* [1937] 2 K.B. 158. See also *Garnac Grain Co Inc v H.M.F. Faure & Fairclough Ltd* [1966] 1 Q.B. 650 (at first instance); [1966] 1 Q.B. 650 at 685–686 (in CA); affirmed by HL [1968] A.C. 1130 (fraud of undisclosed principal: below, para.8-096).
[529] *Abu Dhabi National Tanker Co v Product Star Shipping Co (The Product Star)* [1992] 2 All E.R. 20. And see below, para.9-015.

of the agent of an undisclosed principal in the contract made, as explained above, this seems doubtful.[530]

Illustrations

8-082   (1)   S, a solicitor, practised in the name of S and C (which was not a partnership). C was also a solicitor, but acted as clerk to S. Held, that S, being the real principal, was entitled to sue alone upon a contract made in the name of the firm.[531]

(2)   Gunpowder is bought by a person who appears to be acting on his own account. At a later stage the seller discovers that the buyer was agent for certain mineowners. He may sue the mine-owners.[532]

(3)   An agent entered into a contract in his own name for the purchase of property, and paid a deposit. Held, that on the default of the vendor, the agent's principal was entitled to sue for the return of the deposit.[533]

(4)   A owned a business, which was carried on in the name of B with B as manager. B appeared to be the principal. The drawing and accepting of bills of exchange were incidental to the ordinary conduct of such a business. A forbade B to draw or accept bills. B accepted a bill in the name in which the business was carried on. Held, A was liable on the bill.[534] Sed quaere.

(5)   The owner of a hotel sold it but continued to act as manager and licensee, and dealt as such in his own name, the new owner being undisclosed. The manager was forbidden by the new owner to buy cigars on credit, but he bought cigars on credit. Held, the new owner was liable as undisclosed principal for the price of the cigars, it being within the authority usually confided to the manager of a hotel to buy such goods on credit.[535] Sed quaere.

(6)   A appointed B as the manager of an hotel owned by A, and the licence was taken out in the name of B, who appeared to be the principal. A told B to order spirits from a certain brewery only, but B disregarded this instruction and ordered whisky from C. Held, A was liable to C for the price of the whisky.[536] Sed quaere.

(7)   An agent executed a charterparty in his own name, and was described in the contract as the owner of the vessel. It was held that the principal was not entitled to give evidence to show that the agent contracted on his behalf, so as to enable him to maintain an action on the contract, because such evidence was inconsistent with the statement that the agent was the owner of the vessel.[537]

(8)   The expression "tenant" does not negative agency, and oral evidence has been

---

[530] See above, para.8-069.
[531] *Spurr v Cass, Cass v Spurr* (1870) L.R. 5 Q.B. 656. See also *Cothay v Fennell* (1830) 10 B. & C. 671.
[532] See *Curtis v Williamson* (1874) L.R. 10 Q.B. 57.
[533] *Duke of Norfolk v Worthy* (1808) 1 Camp. 337.
[534] *Edmunds v Bushell and Jones* (1865) L.R. 1 Q.B. 97. See Comment.
[535] *Watteau v Fenwick* [1893] 1 Q.B. 346. See Comment.
[536] *Kinahan & Co v Parry* [1910] 2 K.B. 389. See Comment. But the decision was reversed [1911] 1 K.B. 459, on the ground that there was no evidence that the manager had not bought the goods for his own use.
[537] *Humble v Hunter* (1848) 12 Q.B. 310.

held admissible to show that a person described in a tenancy agreement as the tenant in fact entered into the agreement as agent for another.[538]

(9) A is the managing part-owner of a ship. He becomes a member of a mutual insurance association, and insures the ship under the rules and regulations of that association. By the terms of the policy and rules of the association, the right to recover in respect of losses, and the liability for contributions in the nature of premiums, are confined to members of the association. The other partowners, not being members of the association, cannot, as undisclosed principals of A, sue for any losses, nor can they be sued for contributions due in respect of the policy, even if A fails to pay them, because the right and liability of the principals to sue and be sued are excluded by the terms of the contract.[539] It would be otherwise, if the liability for contributions is thrown by the policy on the persons assured, without reference to whether or not they are members of the association; or if it is provided that the persons assured shall be liable therefore as if they were members.[540]

(10) P, a developer, knew that T would not sell land to him, and therefore bought it through A, who did not disclose that he was acting as agent. A later requested T to cancel the contract, but P sued for specific performance. Held, he was entitled to succeed.[541] So also when in a similar case the persons wishing to buy the land (a committee of Roman Catholics) knew that the sellers (trustees of a Congregational chapel) would not sell to them, and offered an intermediary a commission to buy the land and resell it to them: but here there was no agency.[542]

(11) P wished to see the first night of a play at a theatre of which T was managing director, but knew that T would not allow a ticket to be sold to him on account of allegations he had previously made about T. He bought a ticket through an intermediary, but when he appeared at the theatre he was refused admission on T's instructions. Held, he could not sue T for inducing a breach of contract by the company that owned the theatre, for there was no breach of contract in refusing him admission: the contract was one on which he had no right to intervene as undisclosed principal.[543]

(12) Shipping agents take out workmen's compensation insurance on the crew of a vessel owned by others. The policy is not assignable, but it is not established that the insurers knew that the agents were not the employers of the crew, and it is found as a fact that the identity of the employers of the crew is a matter

---

[538] *Danziger v Thompson* [1944] K.B. 654; *Hanstown Properties Ltd v Green* (1977) 246 E.G. 917 CA. The reasoning is criticised by McLauchlan, *The Parol Evidence Rule* (Wellington, NZ, 1976), p.137 on the grounds that the identity of a tenant is likely to be of importance. cf. *Carberry v Gardiner* (1936) 36 S.R. (N.S.W.) 559 (assignment of lease).

[539] *United Kingdom Mutual Steamship Assurance Assn v Nevill* (1887) 19 Q.B.D. 110; *Montgomerie v United Kingdom Mutual Steamship Assn* [1891] 1 Q.B. 370.

[540] *Ocean Iron Steamship Insurance Assn Ltd v Leslie* (1889) 22 Q.B.D. 722n; *Great Britain 100 A1 Steamship Insurance Assn v Wyllie* (1889) 22 Q.B.D. 710; *British Marine Mutual Insurance Co v Jenkins* [1900] 1 Q.B. 299.

[541] *Dyster v Randall & Sons* [1926] Ch. 932; criticised, *Restatement, Second*, Appendix, at p.524; *Williams v Bulat* [1992] 2 Qd.R. 566.

[542] *Nash v Dix* (1898) 78 L.T. 445.

[543] *Said v Butt* [1920] 3 K.B. 497. See Comment. As to the tort liability, see below, para.9-121.

of indifference to them. The owners of the vessel can claim under the policy.[544]

(13) A demise charterer sues the defendant alleging it is liable for causing the death of a senior crewman. The defendant defends by arguing that the claimant was not the employer of the crewman and not entitled to damages. It was held that the charterer was the undisclosed principal of the employment agency which was the nominal employer of the crewman.[545]

Article 77

DEEDS

8-083 (1) Subject to the following exceptions, a principal may not sue or be sued on any deed inter partes, even if it is expressed to be executed on his behalf, unless he is described as a party to it and it is executed in his name.[546]

(2) Where an agent who has entered into a deed in his own name is a trustee for his principal of the rights under the deed, the principal may enforce such rights in proceedings to which the agent is a party as plaintiff or defendant.[547]

(3) By virtue of the Law Property Act 1925 s.56(1), a person may take an immediate interest in land or other property, or the benefit of any condition, right of entry, covenant or agreement over or respecting land or other property, although he is not named as a party to the conveyance or other instrument.

(4) By virtue of the Contracts (Rights of Third Parties) Act 1999 a person who is not a party to a contract may in his own right enforce a term of the contract if (a) the contract expressly provides that he may; or (b) the term purports to confer a benefit on him.[548]

(5) By virtue of the Powers of Attorney Act 1971 s.7(1),[549] if the donee of a power of attorney is an individual he may, if he thinks fit, execute any instrument with his own signature, and, where sealing is required, with his own seal, by the authority of the donor of the power; and every document executed in that manner shall be as effective as if executed or done by the donee with the signature and seal of the donor of the power. Consistently with deeds executed personally, the attorney's signature must be witnessed in accordance with the provisions of the Law of Property (Miscellaneous Provisions) Act 1989 s.1.[550]

---

[544] *Siu Yin Kwan v Eastern Insurance Co Ltd* [1994] 2 A.C. 199, a case on Third Parties (Rights against Insurers) legislation. See fn.515 above; Reynolds, in *Consensus ad Idem* (Rose ed., 1997), pp.92–95. See also *Ferryways NV v Associated British Ports* [2008] EWHC 225 (Comm); [2008] 1 Lloyd's Rep. 639.

[545] *Ferryways NV v Associated British Ports* [2008] EWHC 225 (Comm); [2008] 1 Lloyd's Rep. 639; affirmed on appeal on other points [2009] EWCA Civ 189; [2009] 1 Lloyd's Rep. 595.

[546] Illustrations 1–4. The formalities required for deeds are now laid down by the Law of Property (Miscellaneous Provisions) Act 1989 s.1. For companies, see Companies Act 2006 ss.44–46.

[547] *Harmer v Armstrong* [1934] Ch. 65, Illustration 5.

[548] Contracts (Rights of Third Parties) Act 1999 s.1.

[549] As amended by Law of Property (Miscellaneous Provisions) Act 1989.

[550] 1989 Act s.7(1A) as added in 2005.

Comment

Rule (1)   Rule (1) is an exception to the general principles stated in Articles 71   **8-084**
and 72, and to the rules as to undisclosed principal stated in Article 76, and results
from the strict rules concerning deeds. It requires signature in a form such as "A,
by B his attorney".[551] But the exact form might not matter, for example "B for A"
is acceptable.[552] The rules are to some extent modified by statute: and where the
deed is not inter partes the principal may, if a covenantee, sue in any case.[553] And
in general a right of action may be assigned by the normal procedures. *Restatement, Third* makes no reference to such a rule, which has been abolished by statute
in many American states, judicial decisions having taken the view that abolition was
not within the judicial function.[554] But the Supreme Court of Canada has affirmed
the rule on the same grounds, though not without casting doubt on it.[555] It can be
argued that a party wishing to exclude undisclosed principals can do so by the terms
of the document.

Rule (2)   Rule (2) is straightforward from the point of view of principle: if the   **8-085**
trustee will not sue, the beneficiary may, joining the trustee as co-defendant. The
question when a trust arises, of course, causes more difficulty.[556] When the
beneficiary sues, the beneficiary does not do so as such, but to enforce the agreement according to its tenor in favour of the trustee.[557]

Rules (3) and (4)   Rules (3) and (4) embody the effect of s.56 of the Law of   **8-086**
Property Act 1925 and the general effect of the Contracts (Rights of Third Parties)
Act 1999. Their details are beyond the scope of this work[558] but they may clearly
entitle the principal to sue on the agent's deed in some situations.

Rule (5): Powers of attorney   The effect of s.7(1) of the Powers of Attorney Act   **8-087**
1971[559] is not clear. The previous rule was that the holder of a power of attorney
should exercise it in the principal's name, i.e. sign the principal's name and use his
seal.[560] Otherwise the principal, at any rate, would not at common law be bound or

---

[551]   *Combe's Case* (1613) 9 Co.Rep. 75a; *Frontin v Small* (1726) 2 Ld.Raym. 1418; *White v Cuyler*
(1795) 6 T.R. 176; *Wilks v Back* (1802) 2 East 142; cf. above, para.2-020.
[552]   *Wilks v Back* (1802) 2 East 142; and see *Lawrie v Lees* (1880) 14 Ch. D. 249.
[553]   *Cooker v Child* (1673) 2 Lev. 74; *Sunderland Marine Insurance Co v Kearney* (1851) 16 Q.B. 925.
[554]   § 6.03: see Comment *f*.
[555]   *Friedmann Equity Developments Inc v Final Note Ltd* [2000] 1 S.C.R. 842; (2005) 188 D.L.R. (4th)
269 ("to effect such a change would have unwarranted, far-reaching and complex consequences both
in the law of contract and the law of property": per Bastarache J at [48]).
[556]   See *Snell's Equity* (34th edn), para.21-003.
[557]   See *Harmer v Armstrong* [1934] Ch. 65 at 88 (Illustration 5), as explained in the *Friedmann Equity
Developments Inc v Final Note Ltd* [2000] 1 S.C.R. 842; (2005) 188 D.L.R. (4th) 269.
[558]   As to s.56, see *Beswick v Beswick* [1968] A.C. 58; Chitty on *Contracts* (33rd edn), para.18-127
onwards. As to the 1999 Act, see ibid., para.18-090, reaching the conclusion that the Act probably
applies to contracts by deed. The 1999 Act operates without prejudice to s.56: s.7(1). Section 56 is
narrower in that it requires that the instrument purport to contain a grant to or covenant with the third
party. As to the agent's liability on a deed, see below, para.9-047.
[559]   Superseding s.123(1) of the Law of Property Act 1925, itself re-enacting Conveyancing Act 1881
s.46.
[560]   The requirement of sealing was abolished by the Law of Property (Miscellaneous Provisions) Act
1989 s.1, which also provides that in certain circumstances solicitors and licensed conveyancers are
conclusively presumed to be authorised to deliver the instrument.

entitled, though in some cases the agent himself might be bound.[561] It is clear that the agent may now in certain circumstances use the agent's own name and seal and nevertheless render the principal liable and entitled. The first problem is as to whether the section by its words requires that the agent should have specific authority to act in the agent's own name. Earlier editions of this book took the view (on the former legislation) that it does, but the wording of the section is not clear and it seems unlikely that such authority is required.[562] The second problem is whether the principal must in such a case be named in the deed. It is clear that one of the purposes of the original reform was to permit an attorney to sign in the attorney's own name, but beyond that the provision is quite generic and not aimed specifically at deeds. It is not obvious that the old rule that an undisclosed principal cannot intervene on a deed (to the extent that a deed is necessary for the efficacy of the transaction) was intended to be abrogated by the reform.[563] On this assumption, the section allows execution by an attorney in the attorney's own name: but the principal should be mentioned in the body of the deed, and though it may not be strictly necessary,[564] it is highly desirable that deed should state that the attorney executes as such or on behalf of the principal, though the attorney need not be so careful in the formula used as under the old law. It is not clear whether the agent is personally discharged from liability in cases where the agent would hitherto have been bound. The former provision said that the deed "shall be as effectual to all intents" as if the agent had executed it in the principal's name. This made it arguable that the agent was discharged. The removal of these words may be thought to make such a construction less likely. If the provision does have this effect, it would assimilate the law as to deeds with that as to other written contracts.

The provision operates without prejudice to any statutory direction that an instrument is to be executed in the name of an estate owner, and is an alternative to the procedure prescribed by s.74(3) and (4) of the Law of Property Act 1925 (as amended), which deal with execution of conveyances by or on behalf of corporations.[565]

Illustrations

8-088   (1)   An agent entered into a contract by deed in his own name, the principal not being named in it. It was held that the principal was not liable to be sued on the contract.[566]

(2)   A shipmaster executed a charterparty by deed in his own name "as agent for the owners". Held, that the owners were not entitled to sue for the freight, because they were not parties to the deed.[567]

(3)   An attorney, who was authorised in writing to execute a lease, signed and sealed the lease in and with his own name and seal. It was held that the

---

[561] See *Appleton v Binks* (1804) 5 East 148, Illustration 1 to Article 102. It would be more difficult for him to show that he was entitled to sue: see *Frontin v Small* (1726) 2 Ld.Raym. 1418.

[562] Powell, p.178; *Davidson's Concise Precedents in Conveyancing* (21st edn), Vol.2, p.447.

[563] But cf. J. Nitikman "Section 7 of the BC Power of Attorney Act: What Does it Say and Why Does it Say it?" (2020) 26 *Trusts & Trustees* 307.

[564] See *Re Whitley Partners Ltd* (1886) 32 Ch.D. 337 at 338; but cf. Wolstenholme and Turner, *The Conveyancing Acts* (3rd edn, 1883), p.99.

[565] 1925 Act s.7(2), as amended, s.7(3). As to s.74 of the Law of Property Act 1925, see *Skelwith (Leisure) Ltd v Armstrong* [2015] EWHC 2830 (Ch); [2016] Ch. 345 at [73].

[566] *Re International Contract Co, Pickering's Claim* (1871) L.R. 6 Ch.App. 525.

[567] *Schack v Anthony* (1813) 1 M. & S. 573. A charterparty would not be made by deed nowadays.

principal was not entitled to sue on the covenants in the lease, though they were expressed to be made by the tenant with the landlord, because the deed was not executed in his name.[568]

(4) A by deed transferred shares to B. In consequence of the winding up of the company, the transfer could not be registered, and A was compelled to pay a call. A had no right of action for indemnity against B's principal, for whom B acted in taking the transfer.[569]

(5) By a contract under seal made between A and B, A agreed to purchase the copyright in certain periodicals from B. A in fact entered into the contract as agent and trustee for himself and C. Held, in an action brought by C against A and B for a declaration that A was agent and trustee as stated above and for specific performance, that as the agency and trusteeship of A had been established and all necessary parties were before the court, there was jurisdiction to decree specific performance.[570]

Article 78

BILLS, NOTES AND CHEQUES

(1) A principal is not liable on a bill of exchange, promissory note or cheque unless the principal's signature appears on it[571]: but it is not necessary that the principal should sign it personally; it is sufficient if the signature is written by some person by or under the principal's authority.[572]   **8-089**

(2) No person can be liable as acceptor of a bill except the person on whom it is drawn, except where it is accepted for honour.[573]

Comment

These rules can be justified on the ground that negotiable instruments are likely to come into the hands of persons who have no knowledge of the circumstances in which they were issued. Such persons must be able to rely on what appears on the face of the instrument. Hence undisclosed principals are not liable.   **8-090**

Rule (1)   Rule (1) provides another exception to the general rules as to the liability of a principal on an agent's transactions stated in Articles 71, 72 and 76: the principal cannot be liable on a bill without being named on it, although the principal's signature may be effected by an agent. If the agent simply writes the principal's name, there is no difficulty. In other cases, the form of representative signature is regulated by s.26 of the Bills of Exchange Act 1882, which reads: **8-091**

  "(1)   Where a person signs a bill as drawer indorser or acceptor, and adds words to his

[568] *Berkeley v Hardy* (1826) 5 B. & C. 355; *Lord Southampton v Brown* (1827) 6 B. & C. 718. But the result might now be different by virtue of s.56 of the Law of Property Act 1925.
[569] *Viscount Torrington v Lowe* (1868) L.R. 4 C.P. 26.
[570] *Harmer v Armstrong* [1934] Ch. 65.
[571] Bills of Exchange Act 1882 ss.23 and 89.
[572] Bills of Exchange Act 1882 s.91(1).
[573] Bills of Exchange Act 1882 s.17(1); *Polhill v Walter* (1832) 3 B. & Ad. 114; *Steele v M'Kinlay* (1880) 5 App.Cas. 754. As to acceptance for honour, see Bills of Exchange Act 1882 ss.65–68. Section 1 of the Contracts (Rights of Third Parties) Act 1999 confers no rights in respect of such instruments: s.6(1).

signature, indicating that he signs for or on behalf of a principal, or in a representative character, he is not personally liable thereon; but the mere addition to his signature of words describing him as an agent, or as filling a representative character, does not exempt him from personal liability.

(2)   In determining whether a signature on a bill is that of the principal or that of the agent by whose hand it is written, the construction most favourable to the validity of the instrument shall be adopted."

Subsection (1) lays down the standard rule for representative signatures. In cases of drawing or indorsing the question is usually as to whether the principal or the agent is the drawer or indorser; to this subsection (2) is not normally relevant, and the matter is decided by application of the main rule, which is discussed elsewhere.[574]

It should be noted that forged and unauthorised signatures do not bind principals,[575] though a principal may be precluded from setting up the forgery,[576] and may ratify an unauthorised signature.[577] A signature by procuration operates as notice that the agent has but a limited authority to sign, and the principal is only bound by such signature if the agent in so signing was acting within the limits of the agent's authority.[578]

8-092 **Rule (2)**   Since only the drawee can be liable as acceptor, it may be important to know whether or not a signature is valid as an acceptance; and here s.26(2) may be more often relevant. It seems that where the bill is drawn on an agent, the principal cannot be liable on the agent's acceptance, even though the agent accepts in the principal's name or in a representative character, and with the principal's authority.[579] Where the bill is drawn on the principal, if the agent accepts in the principal's name or using representative words the principal will be liable: but if the agent accepts in his or her own name or using descriptive words, the principal will not be liable (and nor will the agent). In either case s.26(2), with its presumption of validity, assists in doubtful cases only: it does not reverse the rule as to representative signatures, nor does it prevent clearly inappropriate signatures from being inoperative.[580]

As regards partnerships, the signature of the firm is equivalent to those of the partners[581]: otherwise, the names of all partners sought to be held liable would have to appear in accordance with s.23 of the Bills of Exchange Act 1882.

The above rules relate to the suing of the principal: whether or not the principal can sue depends on whether the principal is the payee, or a holder of the bill, in accordance with the general law.

---

[574] See Article 103. For full citation of the many cases relevant to this section, see *Byles on Bills of Exchange* (30th edn), para.7-007 onwards; *Chalmers and Guest on Bills of Exchange* (18th edn), para.3-105 onwards.

[575] Bills of Exchange Act 1882 s.24. But as to the meaning of this provision, see Chalmers and Guest, above, para.3-043 onwards.

[576] *Greenwood v Martins Bank Ltd* [1933] A.C. 51. See further above, para.8-041.

[577] Ch.2, Section 3.

[578] Bills of Exchange Act 1882 s.25.

[579] Bills of Exchange Act 1882 s.17; *Polhill v Walter* (1832) 3 B. & Ad. 114; *Steele v M'Kinlay* (1880) 5 App.Cas. 754. For the liability of the agent in this case, see Article 103.

[580] *Britannia Electric Lamp Works v D. Mandler & Co Ltd* [1939] 2 K.B. 129.

[581] Partnership Act 1890 s.6. As regards companies, see Companies Act 2006 s.52.

Illustrations

(1) A bill of exchange is drawn on "Artitalia", a partnership. One partner accepts   **8-093**
it with the authority of the other but signs her own name. The other partner is
not liable on the bill.[582]

(2) A duly authorised agent draws or indorses a bill, or indorses a note or cheque,
in his own name. The principal is not liable on it.[583]

(3) A promissory note is signed "The JS Laundry Ltd, JS, Managing Director".
JS is not liable; the company would be.[584]

(4) A promissory note in the form "We promise to pay … etc." is signed "C D,
Director, E F, Secretary, The FE Ltd". The signatories are personally liable and
the company is not.[585]

(5) A bill of exchange is addressed to A B, and is accepted "A B for and on behalf
of C D". C D is not liable as acceptor, even if A B was expressly authorised
to accept the bill on his behalf.[586]

Article 79

DEFENCES TO ACTION BY OR AGAINST PRINCIPAL

(1) Where a principal, whether disclosed or undisclosed, sues the other party to a   **8-094**
contract made by the principal through an agent, the other party has all the
defences which that party would have had against the principal if the principal
had personally made the contract in the same circumstances.[587]

(2) Where an undisclosed principal sues the other party to a contract, the other
party may, in addition to the defences mentioned above, plead all defences
which had accrued against the agent before the party had reasonable notice that
the agent was not acting personally.[588]

(3) Where the other contracting party sues the principal, the principal, whether
disclosed or undisclosed, can plead against the party all defences arising out
of that party's transaction with the agent, and defences personal to the
principal, but not defences personal to the agent.[589]

Comment

Rule (1): General rule   The third party should be able to use all defences aris-   **8-095**
ing out of the contract itself, and all defences available against the principal personally (e.g. set-off, the fact that the principal is an alien enemy)[590] but not defences

---

[582] *Geo. Thompson (Aust.) Pty Ltd v Vitadello* [1978] V.R. 199.

[583] *Ducarrey v Gill* (1830) M. & M. 450. And see *Leadbitter v Farrow* (1816) 5 M. & S. 345 at 350.

[584] *Chapman v Smethurst* [1909] 1 K.B. 927. See also *Britannia Electric Lamp Works Ltd v D. Mandler & Co Ltd* [1939] 2 K.B. 129.

[585] *Brebner v Henderson* 1925 S.C. 643.

[586] *Polhill v Walter* (1832) 3 B. & Ad. 114.

[587] See Comment. cf. *Restatement*, §§ 298, 299 and 308.

[588] See Comment; *Siu Yin Kwan v Eastern Insurance Co Ltd* [1994] 2 A.C. 199 at 207.

[589] See Comment.

[590] The application of this rule to undisclosed principals is criticised by Busch (1999) 3 Eur.Rev. Private Law 319 at 332–333 on the basis that in such cases the third party never expected the benefit of such defences. The criticism is however made against the background of the action directe of the civil

and set-offs[591] which the party may have against the agent but which are not connected with the instant transaction. It is clear that the third party can allege fraud,[592] misrepresentation,[593] non-performance, illegality and mistake, where these are attributable to the agent, just as could be done if the agent were a contracting party. And where the third party has such a defence, he or she can also take proceedings for rescission and restitution.[594] Where there is fraud or misrepresentation by the principal personally, a fortiori this will be a[595] defence to the third party.[596] It was held at first instance in *Garnac Grain Co Inc v HMF Faure and Fairclough Ltd*[597] that where an agent sued on a contract made on behalf of an undisclosed principal, it would be a defence to prove that the contract was induced by the fraud of the undisclosed principal. The decision was reversed on other grounds, but this view was accepted in the Court of Appeal.[598] A fortiori such fraud could be pleaded if the undisclosed principal was a plaintiff.

8-096 **Rescission for misrepresentation** It is not yet clear whether the third party's defence under Rule (1), where based on an agent's misrepresentation, requires that the misrepresentation have been made within the agent's actual or apparent authority, so long as the agent had some authorised role in the transaction.[599] If the relevant contract was entirely negotiated by the agent, the principal may find it difficult to deny the agent's apparent authority to make the statements that induced it if the principal wishes to enforce the contract. In such circumstances, it is unlikely to matter that at the time the misrepresentation was made the agent had not yet been appointed, so long as the representation can be regarded as continuing after the appointment.[600] Obviously, the third party will be in a weaker position where the misrepresenting agent had a lesser role to play in the process. However, it has been suggested that there is a general principle that "no person can take advantage of the fraud of his agent",[601] which precludes the principal from enforcing a contract induced by deceit whether or not the agent had express or apparent authority to have made the statement.[602] In *New Brunswick Railway v Conybeare*,[603] both Lord Westbury and Lord Chelmsford adverted to the possibility of a contract procured by the fraud of an agent being rescindable even though no action for damages would lie against the principal (actual or apparent authority normally being required before

---

law in the case of indirect representation, which is more closely linked to the agent's contract than is the common law action of the principal.

[591] As to payment to or set-off with agent on the same transaction, see Article 81.

[592] *Archer v Stone* (1898) 78 L.T. 34 (action by agent); *Raphael v Goodman* (1838) 8 A. & E. 565; *Foster v Green* (1862) 7 H. & N. 881; *Ludgater v Love* (1881) 44 L.T. 694.

[593] *Mullens v Miller* (1882) 22 Ch.D. 194; *Winch v Winchester* (1812) 1 V. & B. 375; *Myers v Watson* (1851) 1 Sim.(N.S.) 523. As to liability in tort, see below, para.8-185.

[594] *Wilde v Gibson* (1848) 1 H.L. Cas. 605; *Stevens v Legh* (1853) 2 C.L.R. 251; *Wauton v Coppard* [1899] 1 Ch. 92; *Whurr v Devenish* (1904) 20 T.L.R. 385.

[595] But see above, para.8-077.

[596] See *Mullens v Miller* (1882) 22 Ch.D. 194.

[597] *Garnac Grain Co Inc v HMF Faure and Fairclough Ltd* [1966] 1 Q.B. 650.

[598] *Garnac Grain Co Inc v HMF Faure and Fairclough Ltd* [1966] 1 Q.B. 650 at 685–686. See also [1968] A.C. 1130n.

[599] As to rescission by a principal on the basis of a bribe paid or promised by an unauthorised agent of the third party to the principal's agent, see below, para.8-221.

[600] See *Briess v Woolley* [1954] A.C. 333. cf. *Cramaso LLP v Ogilvie-Grant, Earl of Seafield* [2014] UKSC 9; [2014] 1 A.C. 1093.

[601] *Mair v Rio Grande Rubber Estates Ltd* [1913] A.C. 853 at 872–873, per Lord Moulton.

[602] See Hon. K. Handley (2003) 117 L.Q.R. 537.

[603] *New Brunswick Railway v Conybeare* (1862) 9 H.L. Cas. 711 at 726 and 749.

tortious liability for an agent's misstatements arises[604]). There are other dicta,[605] although it is difficult to find a case which has in fact turned on this point.[606] The principle being suggested appears to be an example of the idea that a principal should not be permitted to approbate and reprobate.[607] Although the cases relied upon involve fraud, it is not clear that the principle, if it exists, should be confined to fraud.[608] On the other hand, where the agent had no actual or apparent authority to make the statement, and neither the principal nor any agent whose approval was needed for the making of the contract knew of the misrepresentation, it seems likely that rescission would be permitted only where the principal could adequately be put back in its pre-contractual position.[609]

Rule (2): Undisclosed principal   As a starting-point, the same position as pertains under rule (1) should apply where the principal is undisclosed, mutatis mutandis. But as the contract is initially made between third party and agent, the third party should not be prejudiced by the intervention of the undisclosed principal. Therefore the third party should in addition be able to plead against the principal all defences against the agent, including personal defences such as set-offs which accrued before that party had reasonable notice of the principal's existence.[610] In the case of settlement with the agent and set-off against the agent, however, some English cases indicate that these can only be pleaded against the principal where the principal was in some way at fault in misleading the third party: the matter is dealt with in Article 81. 8-097

Rule (3): Defences available to principal   The principal should be able to plead defences arising out of the transaction, and defences personal to himself (e.g. that he is a minor, set-off in his favour)[611] but not defences personal to the agent (e.g. 8-098

---

[604] See below, para.8-180. See too *Savash v CIS General Insurance Ltd* [2014] EWHC 375 (TCC) at [59] (father makes fraudulent insurance claim on behalf of son).

[605] See *Swift v Jewsbury* (1874) L.R. 9 Q.B. 301 at 312–313; *Weir v Bell* (1878) 3 Ex.D. 238 at 245; *Mackay v Commercial Bank of New Brunswick* (1874) L.R. 5 P.C. 394 at 416; *Daniell v Griffiths* (1883) 1 N.Z.L.R. (CA) 340; *Refuge Assurance Co Ltd v Kettlewell* [1909] A.C. 243 at 244; *Hughes v Liverpool Victoria Legal Friendly Society* [1916] 2 K.B. 482 at 493–494; *Briess v Woolley* [1954] A.C. 333 at 348–349; less clearly, *Bradford Third Equitable Building Society v Borders* [1941] 2 All E.R. 205 at 228. See too *Armagas Ltd v Mundogas SA* [1986] A.C. 717 at 745, per Robert Goff LJ; and *Bank of Credit and Commerce International SA v Aboody* [1990] 1 Q.B. 923 at 972. See also Watts [2017] L.M.C.L.Q. 385 at 405.

[606] *Refuge Assurance Co Ltd v Kettlewell* [1909] A.C. 243 comes closest, but the House of Lords simply affirmed the Court of Appeal ([1908] 1 K.B. 545), where two of the three judges thought that damages would have been available against the principal had they been sought. But see [1907] 2 K.B. 242 at 246–247, per Phillimore J.

[607] See *Lloyd v Grace, Smith & Co* [1912] A.C. 716 at 738, per Lord Macnaghten. See too above, para.2-081.

[608] cf. *Versloot Dredging BV v HDI Gerling Industrie Versicherung AG* [2014] EWCA Civ 1349; [2015] Q.B. 608 (avoidance of otherwise valid insurance claim by reason of agent's misrepresentation on incidental matter).

[609] For discussion of cognate issues, see P. Watts, [2002] C.L.J. 301; P. Watts, "The Acts and States of Knowledge of Agents as Factors in Principals' Restitutionary Liability" [2017] L.M.C.L.Q. 385 at 410.

[610] *Siu Yin Kwan v Eastern Insurance Ltd* [1994] 2 A.C. 199; *Sims v Bond* (1833) 5 B. & Ad. 389 at 393; *Browning v Provincial Insurance Co of Canada* (1873) L.R. 5 P.C. 263 at 272–273; *Rabone v Williams* (1785) 7 T.R. 360. And see above, para.8-069; below, para.9-012.

[611] See *Restatement, Second*, § 203.

that the agent is a minor, set-off in favour of the agent), which only the agent could plead.[612]

In *Collins v Associated Greyhound Racecourses Ltd*[613] it was held that an undisclosed principal could not rescind, for misrepresentation in the prospectus, a contract to underwrite part of an issue of shares when he alone, and not the agent, was proved to have relied on the misrepresentation. This seems correct, and probably follows from the proposition that the third party cannot by the principal's intervention be deprived of his rights against the agent should he desire to exercise them[614]: the principal cannot therefore deprive him of them by rescinding the whole contract unless it is clear that the agent could do so, or at least that the agent would have a valid defence to proceedings against him.[615]

8-099 **Rectification** Although a remedy that is not always defensive in operation, it is convenient to deal here with the role of agents in the rectification of written contracts and other documents. This is a subject that has only relatively recently attracted the attention of the courts. Where the principal is a company any decision to enter into a written contract will involve agents, but even where the principal is an individual, the principal may not have had any active role in the making of the contract or may have left most of the negotiations to an agent. In these circumstances, whose intention counts where a written contract fails to record the terms as negotiated? It may also be necessary to consider separately cases where it is asserted that both parties reached an agreement or understanding with which the written terms are inconsistent (sometimes inaptly called cases of "common mistake"), from cases of "unilateral mistake" where it is asserted that the counter-party knew that the party seeking rectification was mistaken as to what the written terms provided. In relation to common mistake, it has been argued that prima facie it is the intentions and actions of parties who have actual authority to conclude a contract that matter, not the intentions and actions of parties who have authority only to negotiate.[616] However, where the principal or the agents taking the formal steps to bind the principal (such as passing resolutions and executing the document) have left all the negotiations of the relevant contract to an agent then the understandings reached between that agent and the third party (and their comparable agents, if any) may justify rectification.[617] In the case of unilateral mistake, the same principles ought to apply to the position of the party seeking rectification, but the position of the party resisting rectification is potentially different. Unilateral rectification requires proof that the third party actually knew of the counter-party's misunderstanding of the written terms. Is it sufficient to show actual

---

[612] The exclusion of defences personal to the agent is criticised in respect of undisclosed principals by Busch (1999) 3 Eur.Rev. Private Law 319 at 333–334 as unduly favourable to the third party.

[613] *Collins v Associated Greyhound Racecourses Ltd* [1930] 1 Ch. 1.

[614] See above, para.8-098; *O'Herlihy v Hedges* (1803) 1 Sch. & Lef. 123; see also *Montgomerie v United Kingdom etc., Ass.* [1891] 1 Q.B. 370 at 372.

[615] See Goodhart and Hamson (1932) 4 C.L.J. 320 at 353 onwards. Despite dicta in the case to the contrary, it is however doubtful whether this was correctly assessed as a situation where the undisclosed principal could not intervene, for shares are transferable, and the agent would be liable for any loss.

[616] P.S. Davies, "Agency and Rectification" (2020) 136 L.Q.R. 77; relying principally on *Barnet LBC v Barnet Football Club Holdings Ltd* [2004] EWCA Civ 1191; *George Wimpey UK Ltd v VI Construction Ltd* [2005] EWCA Civ 77; [2005] B.L.R. 135.

[617] *Hawksford Trustees Jersey Ltd v Stella Global UK Ltd* [2012] EWCA Civ 55; [2012] 2 All E.R. (Comm) 748; *Murray Holdings Investments Ltd v Oscatello Investments Ltd* [2018] EWHC 162 (Ch); *Univar UK Ltd v Smith* [2020] EWHC 1596 (Ch) at [211].

knowledge in an agent of the third party when that agent was not the person who concluded the contract? It has been suggested that it is.[618] However, it may be that the only correct remedy in such a case is rescission, not rectification.[619]

Article 80

SETTLEMENT BETWEEN PRINCIPAL AND AGENT AFFECTING RECOURSE TO PRINCIPAL

(1) Except as provided in this Article, a principal is not discharged by the circumstances that the principal has paid or settled or otherwise dealt to its prejudice with the agent.   **8-100**

(2) Where a debt or obligation has been contracted through an agent, and the principal is induced by the conduct of the creditor reasonably to believe that the agent has paid the debt or discharged the obligation or that the creditor has elected to look to the agent alone for its payment or discharge, and in consequence of such belief pays, or settles or otherwise deals to its prejudice with the agent, the creditor is not permitted to deny, as between itself and the principal, that the debt has been paid or the obligation discharged or that it has elected to give exclusive credit to the agent so as to discharge the principal.[620]

(3) (Perhaps) where an undisclosed principal settles with an agent at a time when the third party still does not know that the agent acted for a principal, the principal is discharged.[621]

Comment

General rule In general, the right of a third party is not affected by the fact that the principal has paid or otherwise adjusted accounts with the agent[622]: this is a transaction with which the third party has no concern, and the mere fact that the third party delays in enforcing its claim, or in making application to the principal for payment of the debt or discharge of the obligation, is irrelevant, unless there are special circumstances rendering the delay misleading.[623]   **8-101**

Exceptions But there may be cases where such third party is precluded from suing the principal, other than under the rules relating to merger and election (though the two overlap).[624] Two different lines of reasoning are to be found in the cases: (i) the principal may be discharged in such a case where the third party has led the principal to suppose that settlement with the agent was satisfactory; (ii) the principal is discharged where hardship would result if the principal were forced to pay the third party.   **8-102**

First view: estoppel The first view, a form of estoppel, has been more generally accepted. Thus the principal is discharged from liability by paying the agent where   **8-103**

---

[618] P.S. Davies, above, (2020) 136 L.Q.R. 77 at 97.

[619] As to rescission, see above, para.8-096.

[620] See Comment; *Restatement, Third*, § 6.07; as to election, see Article 82.

[621] See Comment.

[622] *Kymer v Suwercropp* (1807) 1 Camp. 109; *Waring v Favenck* (1807) 1 Camp. 85; *Heald v Kenworthy* (1855) 10 Exch. 739; *Macfarlane v Giannacopulo* (1858) 3 H. & N. 860; *Irvine & Co v Watson & Sons* (1880) 5 Q.B.D. 414.

[623] See *Davison v Donaldson* (1882) 9 Q.B.D. 623, Illustration 6.

[624] See Article 82, esp. at para.8-119.

the third party requests payment by the agent,[625] or leads the principal to believe that the agent has paid,[626] or that the third party looks to the agent alone for payment.[627] If this view is correct, since the discharge of the principal is based on the action of the third party in misleading the principal,[628] it is difficult to see how there can be such discharge while the principal is undisclosed, for the third party could not make any representation to someone of whose existence that party was ignorant at the time of making the supposed representation.[629] The argument is however not found to be conclusive in other situations.[630] *Restatement, Third* applies it to undisclosed principals as a matter of policy—that the principal should take the risk.[631]

8-104   **Second view: prejudice of principal**   The second view is that the third party cannot sue the principal where the principal would be unfairly prejudiced were that party to do so.[632] This is a looser formulation which stresses the position of the principal rather than that of the third party and has its origin in old cases,[633] some of which can now be, and have been, re-explained in terms of the first view.[634] But this second view, if correct, could of course apply to undisclosed principals, and it was so applied in *Armstrong v Stokes*,[635] where it was held that a third party could not sue an undisclosed principal who had in good faith paid the agent at a time when the third party still knew of no principal. In that case a reconciliation of the two views previously attempted by Parke B,[636] that it would only be an unfair prejudice to the principal for the third party to sue where the third party's conduct had induced the principal to believe that a settlement had been made with the agent, was specifically rejected by Blackburn J.

But in the leading cases of *Irvine & Co v Watson & Sons*[637] and *Davison v*

---

[625] *Smyth v Anderson* (1849) 7 C.B. 21. When the agent paid by the principal is also the agent of the third party, normal principles of agency law must be invoked to ascertain whether the agent has authority to receive payment for the third party. See *Miller v Douglas* (1886) 56 L.J.Ch. 91.

[626] *Horsfall v Fauntleroy* (1830) 10 B. & C. 755; *Wyatt v Hertford* (1802) 3 East 147, Illustration 1; *MacClure v Schemeil* (1871) 20 W.R. 168, Illustration 3; but cf. *Irvine & Co v Watson & Sons* (1880) 5 Q.B.D. 414, Illustration 5.

[627] *Smith v Ferrand* (1827) 7 B. & C. 19, Illustration 2; *Smethurst v Mitchell* (1859) 1 E. & E. 623, as explained in *Davison v Donaldson* (1882) 9 Q.B.D. 623; cf. *Hopkins v Ware* (1869) L.R. 4 Ex. 268, Illustration 4. A further line of reasoning appears here which is not clearly distinguished: that of taking the agent's bill in satisfaction of the principal's debt. See below, para.8-121.

[628] *Kymer v Suwercropp* (1807) 1 Camp. 109; *Heald v Kenworthy* (1855) 10 Exch. 739; *Irvine & Co v Watson & Sons* (1880) 5 Q.B.D. 414; *Davison v Donaldson* (1882) 9 Q.B.D. 623.

[629] See *Campbell v Hicks* (1858) 28 L.J.Ex. 70. cf. below, para.8-109. It is possible that this could be said to occur where a document is issued which might come into the hands of third parties, e.g. a freight prepaid bill of lading. See *Restatement, Third*, § 6.07, Comment *b*.

[630] See Articles 76(2), 81, 84 and 85.

[631] § 6.07; see Comments *b* and *d*.

[632] Some cases even refer to an alteration of the accounts between principal and agent as avoiding the principal's liability: *Thomson v Davenport* (1829) 9 B. & C. 78; *Curtis v Williamson* (1874) L.R. 10 Q.B. 57. But this must be too wide: see, e.g. *Waring v Favenck* (1807) 1 Camp. 85 (principal cannot set off against third party money owed to him by agent).

[633] Principally the judgment of Bayley J in *Thomson v Davenport* (1829) 9 B. & C. 78.

[634] See *Smyth v Anderson* (1849) 7 C.B. 21; and *Wyatt v Hertford* (1802) 3 East 147, Illustration 1; explained in *Heald v Kenworthy* (1855) 10 Ex. 739; *Smethurst v Mitchell* (1859) 1 E. & E. 623, explained in *Davison v Donaldson* (1882) 9 Q.B.D. 623.

[635] *Armstrong v Stokes* (1872) L.R. 7 Q.B. 598, Illustration 7.

[636] In *Heald v Kenworthy* (1855) 10 Exch. 739.

[637] *Irvine & Co v Watson & Sons* (1880) 5 Q.B.D. 414, Illustration 5.

Donaldson[638] the views of Parke B were preferred, and *Armstrong v Stokes* was explained as a special case where the third party, by virtue of local usage,[639] dealt with the agent as sole principal and it was reasonable for the principal to believe that the third party had so dealt.

Different rule for undisclosed principals   It is submitted that any difficulty there **8-105** may be is caused by an assumption that the same rule should be applied to disclosed and to undisclosed principal cases, and in particular by a failure to distinguish between disclosed but unidentified principals and true undisclosed principals. As has already been pointed out, the true undisclosed principal's position is a very special one.[640] Where the principal is disclosed, the first, or estoppel view is clearly appropriate: and this is so whether the principal is identified or unidentified. It seems to be the latter situation which *Irvine & Co v Watson & Sons*[641] and *Davison v Donaldson*[642] concern. In a true undisclosed principal situation, however, the third party deals on the credit of the agent alone and reasoning based on the notion that the contract is that of the principal (the estoppel view) is inappropriate. Rather it may be said that the principal "has done his duty to customers of the agent if he has seen to it that the agent is properly kept in funds to meet his obligations".[643] Thus where at the time of payment the third party still gave credit to the agent and knew of no principal, it may be right to hold the principal discharged. This was in fact the situation to which Blackburn J confined his decision in *Armstrong v Stokes*[644]; he specifically excluded "the case of the broker, who avowedly acts for a principal (though not necessarily named)". Of the three judges in *Irvine & Co v Watson & Sons*[645] only one, Bramwell LJ, doubted whether the undisclosed principal case was rightly distinguished from the general rule.[646] A special rule for undisclosed principal situations is therefore tentatively formulated above.

Illustrations

(1)   A creditor takes a security from the agent of his debtor, and gives the agent a **8-106** receipt for the debt. The principal deals to his detriment with the agent on the faith of the receipt. The principal is discharged from liability to the creditor.[647]

(2)   An agent of a debtor offers to pay the debt either in cash or by a bill of exchange. The creditor takes a bill in payment, and it is dishonoured. If the agent had funds of the principal's with which to pay the debt, or if the principal

---

[638]   *Davison v Donaldson* (1882) 9 Q.B.D. 623, Illustration 6.
[639]   Among Manchester commission merchants: see above, para.1-021 as to commission agents and indirect representation; also Article 69.
[640]   See above, para.8-071 onwards.
[641]   *Irvine & Co v Watson & Sons* (1880) 5 Q.B.D. 414.
[642]   *Davison v Donaldson* (1882) 9 Q.B.D. 623. Also *Thomson v Davenport* (1829) 9 B. & C. 78. See further *Sopwith Aviation & Engineering Co Ltd v Magnus Motors Ltd* [1928] N.Z.L.R. 433 (principal disclosed).
[643]   Mechem, *Principles of Agency* (4th edn), § 186. See Reynolds [1983] C.L.P. 119 at 133–135. See also (1947) 18 Mississippi L.J. 436.
[644]   *Armstrong v Stokes* (1872) L.R. 7 Q.B. 598. But cf. Higgins (1965) 28 M.L.R. 167 at 175–178.
[645]   *Irvine & Co v Watson & Sons* (1880) 5 Q.B.D. 414.
[646]   See *Irvine & Co v Watson & Sons* (1880) 5 Q.B.D. 414 at 417–418; cf. Baggallay LJ at 419 and Brett LJ at 421. See also the judgment of Jessel MR in *Davison v Donaldson* (1892) 9 Q.B.D. 623 at 628.
[647]   *Wyatt v Hertford* (1802) 3 East at 147; *Smyth v Anderson* (1849) 7 C.B. 21.

deals to his prejudice with the agent on the faith of his having paid it, the principal is discharged from liability to the creditor.[648]

(3) Goods were sold, on the terms that they should be paid for cash on delivery, to an agent who appeared to be buying on his own account. The seller omitted to enforce cash payment, and the principal, not knowing that the seller had not been paid, paid the agent for the goods. Held, that the principal was discharged.[649]

(4) The agent of a debtor paid the debt by means of his own cheque, and the creditor neglected to present the cheque for four weeks, when it was dishonoured and the agent absconded. There was a reasonable chance that the cheque would have been honoured if it had been presented within three weeks, and the principal had dealt to his detriment with the agent on the faith of the payment. Held, that the principal was discharged.[650]

(5) A employed a broker to buy oil. The broker bought from B, telling him that he was acting for a principal, the terms being that the oil should be paid for by "cash on or before delivery". B delivered the oil without payment, and A, not knowing that B had not been paid, in good faith paid the broker. The broker soon afterwards became insolvent, and B sued A for the price of the oil. It was proved that it was not the invariable custom in the oil trade to insist on prepayment in the case of a sale for "cash on or before delivery". Held, that, in the absence of such an invariable custom, the mere omission to insist on prepayment was not such conduct as would reasonably induce A to believe that the broker had paid for the oil, and that, therefore, A was liable to B for the price.[651]

(6) Stores are sold to the managing owner of a ship. The supplier applies for payment but does not obtain it. The managing owner's principal settles accounts with his agent three months after the goods were supplied, and again two years later. More than three years after the supply of the goods, the agent becomes bankrupt. There has been no such conduct on the part of the supplier as to prevent his suing the principal.[652]

(7) Commission merchants, who act sometimes for themselves and sometimes as agents, regularly buy shirting from X on credit. X never inquires whether the commission merchants are acting for themselves or not. They subsequently stop payment. It is discovered that the shirting was bought for Y on a commission basis and sent to him after being bleached. Y had paid for the shirtings the day after receipt and before the commission merchant stopped payment. Y is not liable to pay again.[653]

Article 81

SETTLEMENT WITH OR SET-OFF AGAINST AGENT AFFECTING RIGHTS OF PRINCIPAL

8-107   (1)   Except as provided in this Article, the third party, in an action by the principal,

---

[648] *Smith v Ferrand* (1827) 7 B. & C. 19. But see fn.627 above.
[649] *MacClure v Schemeil* (1871) 20 W.R. 168 (but the judgments proceed principally on the basis of election); cf. *Kymer v Suwercropp* (1807) 1 Camp. 109.
[650] *Hopkins v Ware* (1869) L.R. 4 Ex. 268; cf. *Everett v Collins* (1810) 2 Camp. 515.
[651] *Irvine & Co v Watson & Sons* (1880) 5 Q.B.D. 414.
[652] See *Davison v Donaldson* (1882) 9 Q.B.D. 623.
[653] *Armstrong v Stokes* (1872) L.R. 7 Q.B. 598. But see discussion above.

has no right to set off any claim that party may have against the agent personally[654]; and the principal is not bound by a payment to or settlement with the agent unless that payment or settlement was made in the ordinary course of business and in a manner actually or apparently authorised by the principal.[655]

(2) A person who, in dealing with an agent, reasonably believes that the agent is the principal in the transaction is discharged from liability by payment to or settlement with the agent in any manner which would have operated as a discharge if the agent had been the principal, and is entitled, as against the principal, to the same right of set-off in respect of any debt due from the agent personally as that person would have been entitled to if the agent had been the principal; provided that such third party had not, at the time when the payment to or settlement took place, or the set-off accrued, received notice that the agent was not in fact the principal.[656]

Comment

Rule (1): General rule A set-off against an agent is a defence against the agent personally: therefore the third party cannot use it against a disclosed principal by virtue of the rules stated in Article 79, unless this is authorised by the principal.[657] And the third party is only discharged by settlement with the agent if the latter had authority, actual or apparent, to receive it, in accordance with the principles explained in Chapter 3.[658] Hence payment by set-off, under which the money is not readily available to the payee, is normally unauthorised.[659] However, if the money is paid over to the principal the third party is, obviously, discharged. And there are cases where an agent, for example an auctioneer, may be regarded as contracting independently with the third party.[660] In such a case, the right of the principal to sue on the contract is subservient to that of the agent: and a payment to or settlement with the agent may operate as a discharge, notwithstanding that the person making the payment or settlement has had notice from the principal or trustee in bankruptcy not to pay the agent; and such payment or settlement may be by way of set-off or settlement of accounts between the agent and the person making the settlement.[661]

8-108

Rule (2): Undisclosed principal[662] Where the principal is undisclosed, and the third party therefore believes that the agent is dealing on his or her own account, the third party may use all the defences, including set-offs and other matters personal to the agent,[663] which had already arisen[664] (whether or not on the original

8-109

---

[654] i.e. unconnected with the instant transaction. See Illustrations 6–10.

[655] See Comment and Illustrations 1–3. See also *Mooney v Williams* (1905) 3 C.L.R. 1.

[656] See Comment; *Restatement, Third*, § 6.07. § 6.07(3)(a) provides that a third party who receives notice of the principal's existence may demand reasonable proof of the principal's identity, and is in general not affected until it is given.

[657] As in *Barker v Greenwood* (1837) 2 Y. & C.Ex. 414, Illustration 2 to Article 28; *Stewart v Aberdein* (1838) 4 M. & W. 211; cf. *Young v White* (1844) 7 Beav. 506.

[658] See especially Article 28.

[659] See *Pearson v Scott* (1878) 9 Ch.D. 198, Illustration 3 to Article 28.

[660] See below, paras 9-009 and 9-023.

[661] Illustrations 4 and 5. See also below, para.10-010.

[662] See valuable discussions in Derham, *Law of Set-Off* (4th edn), para.13.79 onwards; Wood, *English and International Set-Off* (1989), Ch.19.

[663] See Article 79, Illustrations 1 and 3; *Rabone v Williams* (1785) 7 T.R. 360n.; *George v Clagett* (1979)

account, and whether previously or subsequently to the original transaction[665]) against the agent prior to the discovery of the principal,[666] and is discharged by payment to the agent prior to such time.[667] So also the third party, before receiving notice of the principal's existence, may vary the contract by agreement with the agent.[668] But if the principal intervenes, the third party should no longer pay the agent.[669]

All this is obviously reasonable, but the principle justifying it is not certain, and there may be differences of application, depending upon what that principle is. One approach, which, it is submitted, is the better, concentrates on the position of the third party, and holds that party entitled to take advantage of such defences while believing the agent to be principal, on the ground that the principal intervenes on the agent's contract and must do so, like an assignee, subject to equities.[670] This would be contrary to the Privy Council's caveat as to the assignment analogy in *Siu Yin Kwan v Eastern Insurance Co Ltd*,[671] but in its favouring of the third party is in accord with modern approaches to agency.

The other approach concentrates on the position of the principal[672] and holds principals bound by such defences only if they have done something towards misleading the third party, as by giving the agent possession of goods. The fact that the principal is bound is said to depend on estoppel.[673] This reasoning seems to arise to some extent from a confusion with the rules as to apparent ownership,[674] where the validity of a disposition of property is in issue and an estoppel is required to displace the operation of the property—protecting *maxim nemo dat quod non habet*. In the present case, however, the validity of the contract is not disputed and no special reasoning is therefore required: a person contracting with another is surely entitled to assume that the other contracts personally and that he or she can therefore safely pay the other or plead set-off against the other unless there is reason to believe the contrary, and to this the fault, or lack of it, of a person unknown to that person is not conclusive. Further, as with the situation of the third party indicating

---

7 T.R. 359; *Ex p. Dixon, re Henley* (1876) 4 Ch.D. 133. Where there are mutual credits between the agent and the other contracting party, in order to constitute a right of set-off as against the principal, each of the debts must be liquidated: *Turner v Thomas* (1871) L.R. 6 C.P. 610.

664 As to the meaning of this word see Derham, *Law of Set-Off* (4th edn), para.13.84; cf. Wood, *English and International Set-off* (1989), p.985 onwards. It seems likely that the debt need not be payable, but perhaps it must be payable by the time the money is actually demanded, or the third party would be able to get satisfaction in respect of a debt not yet payable.

665 It is submitted that this is the best view, though there seems to be no clear authority. For an exhaustive, though now dated, summary of English and American cases on this and related topics, see 53 A.L.R. Annotated 414 (1928).

666 Illustrations 9 and 10; *Mann v Forrester* (1814) 4 Camp. 60.

667 *Coates v Lewes* (1808) 1 Camp. 444; *Curlewis v Birkbeck* (1863) 3 F. & F. 894.

668 *Blackburn v Scholes* (1810) 2 Camp. 341. See *Restatement, Third*, § 6.08.

669 See below, para.9-012.

670 cf. *Rabone v Williams* (1785) 7 T.R. 360n.; *George v Clagett* (1797) 7 T.R. 359; *Ramazotti v Bowring* (1859) 7 C.B.(N.S.) 851 at 856; *Turner v Thomas* (1871) L.R. 6 C.P. 610 at 613; *Montgomerie v UK Mutual Steamship Assn* [1891] 1 Q.B. 370 at 372. And see Article 79(2).

671 *Siu Yin Kwan v Eastern Insurance Co Ltd* [1994] 2 A.C. 199; above, para.8-079.

672 See *Baring v Corrie* (1818) 2 B. & A. 137.

673 *Cooke & Sons v Eshelby* (1887) 12 App.Cas. 271 at 278 (Illustration 7); cf. p.283. See also *Fish v Kempton* (1849) 7 C.B. 687; *Ramazotti v Bowring* (1859) 7 C.B.(N.S.) 851; *Drakeford v Piercy* (1866) 7 B. & S. 515.

674 Article 84. See the same confusion in *Lloyds & Scottish Finance Ltd v Williamson* [1965] 1 W.L.R. 404. But cf. Mechem, *Outlines of Agency* (4th edn), §§ 177–183.

that it has received payment, discussed above,[675] it is difficult to see how a person can ever rely on the representation of someone of whom that person has not heard. The same criticism applies to the doctrine of apparent ownership, and this has therefore to receive a special and somewhat involved justification in terms of estoppel by conduct,[676] which can here be avoided. It also seems clear that the supposed estoppel can arise even where the principal told the agent to disclose the agency.[677] Finally, the conditions giving rise to estoppel in this case appear to fall short of those required to give rise to apparent ownership: it is now settled that apparent ownership is not created by merely giving the possession of goods to another,[678] whereas it seems that the estoppel in this situation can be raised by such conduct without more.[679]

Notice as to principal's existence   Under each approach it is clear that, while it is said that the doctrine of constructive notice is not applicable in commercial transactions,[680] the third party may be taken to have notice that the agent has or may have a principal, e.g. by the nature of the agent's occupation[681] or because the fact or possibility is known to that party's own agent.[682] Under the first approach there would not be an equity in favour of the third party: under the second, this prejudice would not have been caused by the principal's conduct.   **8-110**

Preferable approach   Although the second approach was adopted by the House of Lords in *Cooke & Sons v Eshelby*[683] it is submitted that, as in the case of settlement by the principal with the agent, previously discussed,[684] the difficulty arises partly from the failure to distinguish between disclosed principal cases and   **8-111**

---

[675] Para.8-103.

[676] See Article 84 and Comment.

[677] *Ex p. Dixon, re Henley* (1876) 4 Ch.D. 133; *Knight v Matson & Co* (1903) 22 N.Z.L.R. 293.

[678] See Article 84.

[679] *Borries v Imperial Ottoman Bank* (1873) L.R. 9 C.P. 38; *Rabone v Williams* (1785) 7 T.R. 360n; *George v Clagett* (1797) 7 T.R. 359; *Ex p. Dixon, re Henley* (1876) 4 Ch.D. 133; *Knight v Matson & Co* (1903) 22 N.Z.L.R. 293. The old cases usually required that possession be given to a factor, who had authority to and often did sell in the factor's own name, as opposed to a broker who should not—indeed the distinction between them was largely worked out in this connection: see *Baring v Corrie* (1818) 2 B. & Ald. 137; *Semenza v Brinsley* (1865) 18 C.B.(N.S.) 467; *Drakeford v Piercy* (1866) 7 B. & S. 515; *Cooke & Sons v Eshelby* (1887) 12 App.Cas. 271; above, para.1-046. If these were the only cases, this could rank as an extra feature over and above delivery of possession (see Comment to Article 84). But the doctrine was also applied to brokers; see *Coates v Lewes* (1808) 1 Camp. 444; *Blackburn v Scholes* (1810) 2 Camp. 341; and in any case, decisions could not turn on that distinction today. This difference seems to have been ignored in *Lloyds & Scottish Finance v Williamson* [1965] 1 W.L.R. 404, where these cases were cited, but passing of property was in issue.

[680] *Manchester Trust v Furness* [1895] 2 Q.B. 539; *Greer v Downs Supply Co* [1927] 2 K.B. 28; *Borries v Imperial Ottoman Bank* (1873) L.R. 9 C.P. 38; but see Article 73 and above, para.8-073.

[681] Notably if he is a broker: *Baring v Corrie* (1818) 2 B. & A. 137, which was a leading case on the position of brokers as opposed to factors; *Cooke & Sons v Eshelby* (1887) 12 App.Cas. 271. It is not, of course, necessary that the actual principal is known: *Maanss v Henderson* (1801) 1 East 335; *Semenza v Brinsley* (1865) 18 C.B. N.S. 467: *Mildred v Maspons* (1883) 8 App.Cas. 874.

[682] *Dresser v Norwood* (1864) 17 C.B.(N.S.) 446, Illustration 6. See the cases discussed in Derham, *Law of Set-Off* (4th edn), para.13.85 onwards.

[683] *Cooke & Sons v Eshelby* (1887) 12 App.Cas. 271, Illustration 7: treated as correct in *Cooper v Strauss & Co* (1898) 14 T.L.R. 233; and *Wester Moffat Colliery v Jeffrey* 1911 S.C. 346. See also *Owens v Harris Bros* (1932) 34 W.A.L.R. 110. In *Montagu v Forwood* [1893] 2 Q.B. 350, Illustration 10, the emphasis on fault is not so strong, and indeed on the facts stated in the official report it is not easy to see how the principal was at fault. But further facts appear in the report at 69 L.T. 371. See also Powell, pp.174–178.

[684] Article 80.

undisclosed principal cases. The latter type of case is a very special one and may not be rightly subsumed under normal agency principles.[685] The estoppel approach is based on the notion that the contract is that of the principal, and hence is again only appropriate to the case of the disclosed principal, whether named or unnamed.

Where the third party knows of no principal and this is reasonable in the circumstances it seems inappropriate and indeed unfair to that party to require fault in the principal before set-off against the agent may be valid or settlement with the agent effective. The third party may have dealt with the agent precisely because the agent was indebted to him or her. Where the principal cannot be said to have been at fault, the principal's intervention could on the estoppel approach only be prevented under the rules preventing an intervention which is inconsistent with the express or implied terms of the contract,[686] rules which are of rare application.[687] It is therefore submitted that in the case of undisclosed principals, the analogy of the assignee intervening subject to equities should again be followed, and Rule (2) has been modified to permit this.[688] *Cooke & Sons v Eshelby*[689] is a marginal decision (albeit a common fact situation) where the agent (a broker) sometimes dealt personally and sometimes as an agent: the third party said that he had no belief one way or the other as to which was the case on this occasion. It is thus not clear whether the principal should have been treated as undisclosed or merely as unidentified. The decision against the third party may or may not have been a fair one on the facts.[690]

The two approaches will normally yield the same result: for principals who use the services of an agent whom they direct not to disclose their name, or who they know does not disclose the existence of the principals, can be regarded as leading the third party to suppose that the agent acts personally.[691] The same is true where, as often, a principal gives the agent possession of goods. But there can be a difference. Where the principal does not transfer such possession, and does not do anything that facilitates the deception of the third party, but simply tells the agent to contract in the principal's name, and the agent disobeys and contracts personally, the principal might on the estoppel view not be bound by set-offs against, and payments to, the agent.[692]

Illustrations

8-112 (1) A traveller offers a sample of goods to a tradesman with whom he has had previous dealings: the tradesman knows that the traveller is probably acting for someone else. The tradesman orders coats as per sample, and they are sent to him by the supplier. The traveller was working for the supplier on this occasion only, having represented to the supplier that he could obtain an order

---

[685] See Comment to Article 76.

[686] As in *Greer v Downs Supply Co* [1927] 2 K.B. 28.

[687] See above, para.8-079.

[688] The wording in earlier editions was "A person who, in dealing with an agent, is led by the conduct of the principal to believe, and does in fact believe … etc." But Derham, *Law of Set-Off* (4th edn), simply regards this as an anomaly upon a doctrine already anomalous: see para.13.99.

[689] *Cooke & Sons v Eshelby* (1887) 12 App.Cas. 271, Illustration 7.

[690] It was criticised by Pollock (1887) 3 L.Q.R. 358. See also Reynolds [1983] C.L.P. 119 at 122–125.

[691] See *Semenza v Brinsley* (1865) 18 C.B.(N.S.) 467; *Ex p. Dixon, re Henley* (1876) 4 Ch.D. 133 (where the agent acted contrary to instructions).

[692] *Restatement*, § 306, Comment *a*, rejected in *Restatement, Third*, § 6.06, Comment *a* and reporter's notes thereto. But cf. *Ex p. Dixon, re Henley* (1876) 4 Ch.D. 133.

from the tradesman. Payment to the traveller, there being an invoice bearing the supplier's name, is no discharge to the tradesman.[693]

(2)   A firm employed A, a traveller, to carry with him for sale parcels of sponges. It was A's duty, on concluding a bargain, to forward particulars of the transaction to the firm. The firm would then send to the customer an invoice and (monthly) a statement of account. The statement of account contained three notices: (1) "Cheques to be crossed". (2) "All cheques to be made payable to the firm". (3) "No receipt valid unless on firm's printed form to be attached hereto". B dealt thus with the firm for some years. Between 1905 and 1908 A sold three parcels of sponges to B. In respect of two of these sales A induced B to pay by cheque payable to him. For the third parcel B paid A in cash. A had no authority to receive in payment anything except crossed cheques in favour of the firm. A fraudulently appropriated the three sums to himself. Held, that the payments to A were valid against the firm, for the notices in the statements of accounts did not contain sufficient intimation to their customer that A was not authorised to receive payment for goods delivered in cash or by a cheque in his favour cashable at once.[694]

(3)   A broker sells goods in the name of his principal to A, who pays the broker for them. The broker absconds without paying over the money to the principal. A is liable to the principal for the price of the goods, unless the broker had authority, or was held out by the principal as having authority, to receive payment, and the mere fact that the principal had on previous occasions authorised him to receive payment for goods sold on his behalf is not sufficient evidence of such authority or holding out.[695]

(4)   A factor who has a lien on goods for advances sells the goods in his own name. The buyer, though he knew that the factor was acting as an agent, is, to the extent of the factor's lien, discharged by a payment to him, even if the payment be by way of set-off,[696] or be made after the bankruptcy of the principal, and after notice from the trustee in bankruptcy not to pay the factor.[697]

(5)   A factor who had a lien on goods in excess of the value sold the goods to A, to whom he was indebted. The factor became bankrupt. A gave credit for the price of the goods, and proved in the bankruptcy for the residue of his debts against the factor. Held, that this settlement was a good answer to an action by the principal against A for the price.[698]

(6)   A broker bought goods on behalf of A from a factor who sold them on behalf of B. The broker knew that the factor sold the goods on behalf of a principal, but A thought that he was selling his own goods. B sued A for the price. Held, that A was bound by the knowledge of his broker, and therefore had no right to set off a debt to him from the factor.[699]

(7)   A broker who was entrusted by his principal with the possession of goods sold

[693] *Butwick v Grant* [1924] 2 K.B. 483. See also Article 28.
[694] *International Sponge Importers Ltd v Andrew Watt & Sons* [1911] A.C. 279. See also Article 28.
[695] *Linck, Moeller & Co v Jameson & Co* (1885) 2 T.L.R. 206.
[696] *Warner v M'Kay* (1836) 1 M. & W. 591.
[697] *Drinkwater v Goodwin* (1775) Cowp. 251.
[698] *Hudson v Granger* (1821) 5 B. & A. 27. These cases, like that of the auctioneer, are nowadays best explained as involving collateral contracts. See below, paras 9-009 and 9-021.
[699] *Dresser v Norwood* (1864) 17 C.B.(N.S.) 466. See the same case, Article 95, Illustration 3.

them in his own name without disclosing the principal. The buyer knew that the broker sometimes sold goods in his own name, though acting as a broker, and sometimes sold goods of his own, and in this case had no particular belief one way or the other. Held, that the buyer was not entitled, in an action by the principal for the price, to set off a debt due from the broker personally.[700]

(8) A, who acted as shipping agent for B, a merchant in Havana, consigned in his own name to C a cargo of tobacco C, according to his instructions, insured the cargo for the benefit of all concerned, having had notice that there was a principal. The cargo was lost, and the insurance money was paid to C after he had received notice that B claimed it. Held, that C was not entitled to set off, as against B, debts due to him from A personally.[701]

(9) Goods were consigned to an agent for sale. The agent pledged the goods to brokers as security for a specific advance, and authorised them to sell. The broker sold the goods, but before receiving the proceeds had notice that the principal was the owner, and that he claimed the proceeds. Held, that the principal was entitled to the balance of the proceeds after deducting the amount of the advance, and that the brokers were not entitled to set off such balance against a general account due to them from the agent.[702] It would be otherwise, if they had received the proceeds in the bona fide belief that they belonged to the agent, and had credited the amount in the account with the agent before receiving notice of the principal's claim.[703]

(10) A employed B to collect general average contributions under an insurance policy. B instructed a broker to collect the contributions, the broker believing him to be the principal. B became bankrupt. In an action by A against the broker for the contributions, as money received to his use, it was held that the broker was entitled to set off a debt due from B.[704]

Article 82

MERGER AND ELECTION: RELEASE OF PRINCIPAL

8-113 (1) Where an agent enters into a contract personally, and judgment is obtained against the agent on it, the judgment, though unsatisfied is, so long as it subsists,[705] a bar to any proceedings against the principal, undisclosed or (perhaps) disclosed, on the contract.[706]

(2) (Perhaps), where an agent enters into a contract on behalf of an undisclosed principal or on such terms that the agent is personally liable on it together with the principal, and the other contracting party, knowing or discovering who is the real principal, elects to pursue a claim against the agent, that party is bound

---

[700] *Cooke & Sons v Eshelby* (1887) 12 App.Cas. 271.

[701] *Mildred, Goyeneche & Co v Maspons y Hermano* (1883) 8 App.Cas. 874.

[702] *Kaltenbach, Fischer & Co v Lewis and Peat* (1885) 10 App.Cas. 617. See on this case (1932) 4 C.L.J. 320 at 333–334.

[703] ibid.; *New Zealand and Australian Land Co v Watson* (1881) 7 Q.B.D. 374.

[704] *Montagu v Forwood* [1893] 2 Q.B. 350. See also *Knight v Matson & Co* (1903) 22 N.Z.L.R. 293; *Curlewis v Birkbeck* (1863) 3 F. & F. 894.

[705] As to the position where the first judgment is set aside, see *C Inc Plc v L* [2001] 2 Lloyd's Rep. 459 at [107].

[706] But see below, paras 8-116 and 8-117.

by that election and cannot afterwards sue the principal on the contract. The question whether or not election has occurred is a question of fact.

(3) Except as provided in this Article, the liability of a principal, whether disclosed or undisclosed, upon a contract made on the principal's behalf is not affected by fact that the agent is personally liable on the contract.[707]

Comment

Questions of principle   The propositions stated above represent a conservative at-   **8-114**
tempt to state the law emerging from the many and rather confused decisions on this topic. They are, however, difficult propositions to justify in principle.[708] It is difficult to see in principle why, where principal and agent are both liable on a contract, any doctrine of merger or election should bar a person who has proceeded against one from proceeding against the other. Only satisfaction of the claim should normally be a bar.

The real basis of such notions of merger and election seems to be an assumption, common in older cases, that the contract was either with the principal or with the agent. In cases of disclosed principal these were in effect alternative interpretations of the facts: but it seems to have been applied also to undisclosed principals and their agents on the basis that there was alternative liability as a matter of substantive law. But it is now clear that there can be cases where the agent is liable together with the disclosed principal[709]: and there seems no real reason why this should not be so in the case of the undisclosed principal also. To such analysis, the idea of merger or election in respect of alternative liabilities seems inappropriate.

Only three lines of reasoning appear available to justify the results stated in the Article as formulated. The first is that the principal and the agent are liable jointly. If there is only one obligation, it can be said that judgment against one can release the other. This would be solely a doctrine of merger: any notion of election would be irrelevant. This is certainly a possible interpretation of some cases where disclosed principal and agent are both liable on a contract. But it is by no means the only one: indeed, it is an unlikely one.[710] Further, there seems no reason at all to apply it to undisclosed principals and their agents, and indeed it has not been applied to them. In any case, the rule that judgment against one person jointly liable releases the other was abolished in England by statute in 1978, so that the reasoning now fails, at any rate in England.[711]

The second possible justification is that the liability of principal and agent is, where they are both liable to the third party, as a matter of substance an alternative

---

[707] See Comment. For an extended treatment of the problems in this area, see Reynolds (1970) 86 L.Q.R. 318 (on which, however, the present text represents some advance). See also Clayton (1925) 3 Texas L. Rev. 384; Merrill (1933) 12 Nebr.L.Bull. 100; (1953) 34 Nebr.L.Rev. 613; Hill [1967] J.B.L. 125–128; Sargent and Rochvarg (1982) 36 U. Miami.L.Rev. 411; Richmond (1983) 66 Marq.L.Rev. 745; Seavey, *Studies in Agency* (1949), pp.215–219 and 330–331; Stoljar, pp.216–219. cf. Indian Contract Act s.233, the interpretation of which has caused difficulties: Pollock and Mulla, *Indian Contract and Specific Relief Acts* (14th edn). As to the position in Scotland, see Phillips, 1993 J.R. 133.

[708] See a valuable discussion of this topic by Thomas J in *L.C. Fowler & Sons Ltd v St Stephen's College Board of Governors* [1991] 3 N.Z.L.R. 304.

[709] See below, para.9-006.

[710] See below, para.9-006.

[711] Civil Liability (Contribution) Act 1978 s.3.

liability. The leading case of *United Australia Ltd v Barclays Bank Ltd*,[712] concerning waiver of tort, accepts a distinction as to choice between inconsistent rights and choice between alternative remedies. In the first, election is required; but in the second the right to proceed is (probably[713]) only lost by satisfaction of the claim. The standard example of the first is the right to treat a contract as discharged for breach, or to forfeit a lease: once this is done, the party concerned cannot proceed on the basis that the contract or lease subsists. An example in the context of agency is the right or power to ratify.[714] It is possible, and indeed is assumed in the *United Australia* case itself,[715] that the liabilities of agent and undisclosed principal are inconsistent in such a way as to require election between rights. This can only really be justified as a special analysis applicable in this context to situations of undisclosed principals. But as to disclosed principals, although a third party could enter into a contract with a disclosed principal and agent on the basis that their liability was alternative, it is difficult to see that in normal situations there would be any reason for doing so,[716] and hence for a court to put such an interpretation on the facts. The problem in the disclosed principal situation seems rather to be one of alternative remedies against persons who are both liable. Modern analysis of the situation where the agent is liable together with the principal has made this clearer than it was before.[717] As stated above, older cases tended to assume that either the principal or the agent was liable. Such reasoning more easily raises the possibility of an argument that the third party must choose. There has also sometimes been, as in other areas, a lack of clarity in distinguishing a true undisclosed principal from a mere unidentified though disclosed principal,[718] which may have added to the confusion.

It does, however, seem that the liability of agent and undisclosed principal is on present authority to be regarded as an alternative one: and since the whole doctrine of the undisclosed principal can be said to be anomalous anyway,[719] it cannot be said that such a view is demonstrably wrong, even if there is not much to commend it.[720] If this is so, the governing principle could be regarded either as one of merger or as one of election. If it is one of merger, manifestation of choice to sue one or the other would have no relevance; but a judgment against one would discharge the other, and where it is against the agent, even where it was taken without knowledge of the principal. If the principle is the broader one of election, the third party has an election or choice as to with whom that party wishes to regard the contract as having been made. When this choice has been manifested, the third party cannot thereafter change course. Until the third party realises the existence of the undisclosed principal, of course, that party is not able to make a valid election, for on general principles a choice cannot be exercised by one who does not know that

---

[712] *United Australia Ltd v Barclays Bank Ltd* [1941] A.C. 1.
[713] cf. *United Australia Ltd v Barclays Bank Ltd* [1941] A.C. 1 at 3, 21 and 30.
[714] See Article 17; *Verschures Creameries Ltd v Hull and Netherlands SS Co Ltd* [1921] 2 K.B. 608, Illustration 6 to Article 20. But this is probably distinct from election.
[715] See *United Australia Ltd v Barclays Bank Ltd* [1941] A.C. 1 at 30.
[716] But see below, para.9-023 as to certain types of brokerage arrangements.
[717] See Comment to Article 98.
[718] See above, para.8-073.
[719] See Comment to Article 76.
[720] See *L.C. Fowler & Sons Ltd v St Stephen's College Board of Governors* [1991] 3 N.Z.L.R. 304; *Taylor v Van Dutch Marine Holding Ltd* [2019] EWHC 1951 (Ch) at [222].

there is a choice.[721] Though the narrower, merger principle predominates, the election approach has been taken in some cases, including the *United Australia* case itself.[722] A compromise position is that judgment is the only true election.[723]

The third justification is this. There are many situations where a person does not allege that both agent and principal were liable, but cannot decide on the correct interpretation of the facts whether a contract was with one or the other; and therefore sues both in the alternative and leaves the court to decide the question. Or again, that person may allege one interpretation and the other party may in defence allege another. Here the court is asked to decide between two mutually inconsistent legal interpretations of the facts. Once a final judgment has been obtained on this issue of fact, the matter is res judicata. This is obviously not a matter of merger; but neither is it one of election between inconsistent rights. In this situation, at least in theory, one interpretation is right and the other simply wrong. The matter is rather one of finality of decision as to the proper legal analysis of facts; or sometimes as to restrictions on the advancing of mutually inconsistent allegations. Difficulties arise in particular when it is sought to reopen the issue in connection with judgments subject to appeal, and as to default and summary judgments, and some of the leading cases concern procedural problems arising in such situations.[724] In such situations there is an element of choice in a rather special sense. The third party may choose which interpretation to allege, and sue on that basis. If the action is undefended, or summary judgment is given, that interpretation is in theory adopted by the court. But this happened merely at the choice of the plaintiff. Had the case proceeded to trial the court might have decided on a different interpretation of the facts. So the third party has certainly made a choice of a sort; but it is not an election between inconsistent rights, to each of which he is entitled, it is, rather, a pragmatic choice as to against whom to start proceedings in an uncertain situation. However, the dicta in these cases are sometimes uncompromisingly general. Both for default and summary judgments, the procedural decisions are given on the apparent basis that the liability in issue is alternative. This, it is submitted, is not correct. It is these cases which are productive of the most confusion.[725]

It may be added that there are other situations where third parties may do an act

---

[721] See below, para.8-121.

[722] See *United Australia Ltd v Barclays Bank Ltd* [1941] A.C. 1 at 30.

[723] See cases cited below, para.8-119.

[724] e.g. *Morel Bros & Co Ltd v Earl of Westmorland* [1904] A.C. 11; *Moore v Flanagan* [1920] 1 K.B. 919. See also the cases on default judgments cited below, para.8-118. The leading Australian case of *Petersen v Moloney* (1958) 84 C.L.R. 91 may be of this type. Here the purchaser of land paid the vendor's estate agent and the question was whether the agent had authority to receive payment: the eventual answer was "no". The vendor sued the purchaser and his agent in the alternative: and it was held that a judgment against the agent which was subject to appeal did not prevent judgment against the purchaser. Here the inconsistent interpretations were that the purchaser had paid and the agent was liable to the vendor; or that the purchaser had not paid and was still liable to pay, and hence the agent not liable to the vendor. However, it can be said that the action against the agent was a ratification of the agent's act in receiving the money, which would have involved a need to elect between inconsistent rights. But ratification was not argued: see at 93. In any case, the decision concerns an action by a principal against his own agent—not by the third party (despite some argument to the contrary: see at 93 and 97–98). It accepts the view that judgment alone constitutes election. It was followed in *Bain Securities Ltd v Curmi* (1990) 1 A.C.S.R. 794, which was a true case of a third party suing agent and undisclosed principal. See also *Con-Stan Industries of Australia Pty Ltd v Norwich Winterthur Insurance (Australia) Ltd* (1986) 160 C.L.R. 226.

[725] Obtaining a default judgment will not usually constitute an election: *Pendlteton v Westwater* [2001] EWCA Civ 1841; *Balgobin v South West Regional Health Authority* [2012] UKPC 11; [2013] 1 A.C. 582 (not agency cases). In *Lang Transport Ltd v Plus Factor International Trucking Ltd* (1997) 143

which is relevant to the establishment of liability at a much earlier stage, e.g. enter principal or agent in their books as debtor. This is even less an election in respect of legal rights: it is simply an act which may assist in interpreting the initial intentions of all possible parties with respect to any contractual position between them.[726]

The last technique which may be applied is that of estoppel. By the principle of equitable estoppel, a person who represents that he or she intends to take a particular course of action may be debarred from going back on that representation if there is some element of reliance making it inequitable to do so.[727] By other forms of estoppel, for example estoppel by convention, a person who acts on the basis of a particular assumption of facts or interpretation may be debarred from going back on it.[728] These and similar lines of reasoning may sometimes debar a person who has taken one course of action in such a dispute from going back on it. They are not, however, the same as election.

8-115 **The Restatements** It will be seen that the clearest case for the application of some doctrine of merger or election is the specialised one of the undisclosed principal, where the view that the liability is substantively alternative certainly can, though it need not, be taken. The alternative liability can, as has been stated, be attributed either to a merger rule, or to a wider rule of election. *Restatement, Second*, of 1958 accordingly provided, in deference to the case law of the time, but contrary to the inclinations of the Reporter, Professor Seavey,[729] for release of the agent of an undisclosed principal by judgment against the principal.[730] This was a rule of merger only: no role was left for election.[731] But it only provided for release of the undisclosed principal by judgment against the agent where it was taken with knowledge of the principal's connection with the transaction[732]—an exception which, as the Reporter recognised[733] could be justified under a principle of election, but is contrary to the principle of merger on an alternative liability. It is nevertheless a gloss which can readily be understood. The *Restatement* also preserved the application of estoppel.[734] In the area of disclosed principal it allowed for loss of the right of action only if the parties contracted jointly, in which case there was a merger once judgment is given.[735] This is not now relevant in English law. It also again allowed for estoppel.[736] *Restatement, Third*,[737] by reference to more recent case law,[738] simply provides that judgment against principal or

---

D.L.R. (4th) 672, the Ontario Court of Appeal by a majority held that where a default judgment was obtained against an agent who was not liable at all, it could be set aside.

[726] See below, para.8-120.

[727] See *Société Italo-Belge, etc. v Palm and Vegetable Oils (M) Sdn Bhd (The Post Chaser)* [1982] 1 All E.R. 19; note the reference to election reasoning (though in a different context) at the end of the judgment.

[728] See above, para.8-027.

[729] See Comment to § 210; 7 Proc. Am. Law Inst. 257 (1929) (on the first *Restatement*): "We do not think that it is a sound theory, sound common sense or good justice".

[730] § 337.

[731] §§ 209 and 237.

[732] § 210.

[733] See Comment to § 210.

[734] § 337.

[735] § 184(1).

[736] § 336.

[737] § 6.09.

[738] Especially *Grinder v Bryans Road Building and Supply Co* 432 A.2d 453 (Md. 1981), where it is

agent does not discharge the liability unless satisfied. Estoppel is again preserved.[739] However, the English cases are such and so numerous as to require special treatment: it is (unfortunately) difficult to say that they at present justify the formulation in this Article of rules even such as those of either *Restatement*.[740]

These general points being made, discussion follows of the case law on which the actual wording of the Article is based.

Rule (1): Judgment. Undisclosed principal   It is well established in England that if the third party obtains judgment against the agent of an undisclosed principal, that party can no longer sue the principal, even though the judgment was obtained in ignorance of the fact that the agent had been acting for another, and so of that party's full rights, and even though the judgment is unsatisfied.[741] The rule seems to be based on two arguments. The first is that there is only one obligation, which is merged in the judgment.[742] The analogy is with the case of joint debtors[743]; but the reasoning seems rather that the obligation is an alternative one. This is reinforced by a rather rough and ready argument, that the liability of the undisclosed principal involves an interpretation of the facts inconsistent with that involving the agent's liability, and the third party cannot have it both ways: the principal's liability is in a sense a windfall, and the third party cannot complain if the windfall turns out to be of limited value.[744] But, as stated above, this rule relating to joint debtors has been changed by statute.[745] And what may be called the "windfall" argument can be regarded as reneging on the doctrine of undisclosed principal itself. It seems that in the late nineteenth century the doctrine came to be thought of as inconsistent with basic contract theory, and limitations were consequently placed on it. Such inconsistency was not of itself a valid reason for the limitations imposed. It seems clear, however, that the present rule for undisclosed principals, that the obligation is alternative, can only be changed by the Supreme Court. There is now considerable authority in the US rejecting such a rule.[746]

8-116

Disclosed principal   The cases indicate that the same doctrine of merger applies to situations where both agent and principal are liable on the contract, but where the existence of the principal is disclosed: it has been applied to cases of identified

8-117

---

said (at 463) that "The foregoing reasoning is unassailable on any ground other than its lack of strict adherence to the precedents". See also fn.746 below.
[739] See § 6.09, Comment *d*.
[740] See Rix J in *The Nea Tyhi* [1999] 2 Lloyd's Rep. 497 at 534.
[741] *Priestly v Fernie* (1863) 3 H. & C. 977, Illustration 1; *Kendall v Hamilton* (1879) 4 App.Cas. 504 at 513–515. See too *Antonio Gramsci Shipping Corp v Stepanovs* [2011] EWHC 333 (Comm); [2011] C.L.C. 396 at [28]; *Taylor v Van Dutch Marine Holding Ltd* [2019] EWHC 1951 (Ch) at [222].
[742] *Kendall v Hamilton* (1879) 4 App.Cas. 504 at 515; *M. Brennen & Sons Mfg. Co Ltd v Thompson* (1915) 33 Ont.L.T. 465 at 471–472; *Marginson v Ian Potter & Co* (1976) 136 C.L.R. 161; *Taylor v Van Dutch Marine Holding Ltd* [2019] EWHC 1951 (Ch).
[743] *Kendall v Hamilton* (1879) 4 App.Cas. 504 was in fact the leading case on joint debtors, though paradoxically it takes the position of the undisclosed principal as a paradigm.
[744] *Kendall v Hamilton* (1879) 4 App.Cas. 504 at 544.
[745] Civil Liability Contribution Act 1978 s.3.
[746] A leading case is *Grinder v Bryans Road Building and Supply Co* 432 A.2d 453 (CA Md., 1981); see also *Crown Controls Inc v Smiley* 756 P.2d 717 (Wash., 1988); *Engelstat v Cargill Inc* 336 N.W. 2d 284 (Minn., 1983); *Tower Cranes of America v Public Service Co* 702 F.Supp.371 (DNH, 1988). See above, para.8-115.

principals[747] and a fortiori would apply to cases of unidentified principals, who are in any case nearer to undisclosed principals. It has also been applied to recovery of judgment for part only of an undivided debt.[748] In the disclosed principal situation, however, the doctrine is even more difficult to justify. The "windfall" argument is completely inapplicable. The "one obligation" argument, though relied on,[749] is as regards joint obligations again now rendered obsolete by statute,[750] and there seems in the case of a disclosed principal little reason to regard the obligation as alternative.[751] In those circumstances where the third party may be regarded as having stipulated for the liability of both agent and principal, it may be thought that that party does so in order to make sure of satisfaction: the dual liability would be of much reduced utility if lost by a mere unsatisfied judgment against one party. It has been suggested above that the extension of the merger doctrine to disclosed principal situations is due to two things: a failure, as in other contexts,[752] to distinguish an unidentified principal situation from a true undisclosed principal situation[753]; and a failure to analyse adequately the nature of the agent's liability in cases where the agent is liable together with the principal.

Older cases tended to assume that either the principal or the agent was liable. But modern analysis[754] indicates that an agent liable together with the principal may in principle be liable jointly, jointly and severally, as surety, on a separate contract, or in the alternative. Joint liability, with its technical rules, is rarely appropriate: it applies to partners,[755] but not normally to husband and wife.[756] The possibilities of suretyship[757] and separate contracts[758] are also recognised. But in this context of the taking of proceedings against one or the other, there are a surprising number of as-

---

[747] *Morel Bros & Co Ltd v Earl of Westmorland* [1904] A.C. 11, Illustration 2; *Sullivan v Sullivan* [1912] 2 I.R. 116 at 127–128; *Moore v Flanagan* [1920] 1 K.B. 919; *RMKRM (A Firm) v MRM VL (A Firm)* [1926] A.C. 761, Illustration 3; *Debenhams Ltd v Perkins* (1925) 133 L.T. 252 at 254; *Barrington v Lee* [1972] 1 Q.B. 326. See also the leading Australian case of *Petersen v Moloney* (1958) 84 C.L.R. 91; as to which see fn.724 above.

[748] *French v Howie* [1906] 2 K.B. 674.

[749] *Moore v Flanagan* [1920] 1 K.B. 919 at 925–926.

[750] See Civil Liability (Contribution) Act 1978. See too *1196303 Inc v Glen Grove Suites Inc* 2015 ONCA 580.

[751] See *L.C. Fowler & Sons Ltd v St Stephen's College Board of Governors* [1991] 3 N.Z.L.R. 304 at 311–312 (Illustration 7); *Taylor v Van Dutch Marine Holding Ltd* [2019] EWHC 1951 (Ch) at [226]; and para.8-114.

[752] cf. above, paras 8-073, 8-105 and 8-111.

[753] cf. above, para.8-114. See also *Priestly v Fernie* (1863) 3 Hurl. & C. 977.

[754] See Comment to Article 98.

[755] Partnership Act 1890 s.9.

[756] *Morel Bros & Co Ltd v Earl of Westmorland* [1904] A.C. 11. cf. *Swanton Seed Service Ltd v Kulba* (1968) 68 D.L.R. (2d) 38.

[757] *Imperial Bank v London & St Katharine Docks Co* (1877) 5 Ch.D. 195 at 200; *Fleet v Murton* (1871) L.R. 7 Q.B. 126 at 132. See also *Young v Schuler* (1883) 11 Q.B.D. 651; *Rutherford v Ounan* [1913] 2 I.R. 265 at 268.

[758] *Barclays Bank Ltd v Williams* (1971) 115 S.J. 674 (breach of warranty of authority); *M. Brennen & Son Mfg Co Ltd v Thompson* (1915) 33 Ont.L.R. 465 at 469–470; *1196303 Inc v Glen Grove Suites Inc* 2015 ONCA 580. But cf. *Benton v Campbell, Parker & Co* [1925] 2 K.B. 410 at 414, where it is contemplated that election may apply between the separate causes of action against the auctioneer and his vendor. Sometimes the agent's liability comes to an end by its terms on the acceptance of a contract by the third party with the principal. This could formerly occur on the Stock Exchange: see *Grissell v Bristowe* (1868) L.R. 4 C.P. 36; *Maxted v Paine* (1869) L.R. 4 Ex. 203; affirmed (1871) L.R. 6 Ex. 132; (1929) 39 Yale L.J. 265; below, para.9-023.

sertions against joint and several liability and in favour of alternative liability.[759] Indeed the doctrine of merger has in some cases been applied where it might appear that the agent against whom judgment was obtained was in fact not liable at all,[760] so that the judgment should have been regarded as abortive and as being no bar to subsequent proceedings against a person who was liable.[761] It has also been extended to actions in restitution in respect of deposits paid to estate agents in "subject to contract" situations.[762] But many cases[763] where the doctrine of merger has been held to operate should probably be explained by the proposition that where claims are made against principal and agent in the alternative, on the basis that the facts justify the liability of one or the other, but not both, judgment against one, unless set aside, involves res judicata in favour of the other. Whatever the arguments, the true interpretation of the facts is now settled.[764] This is based on the idea, not that both are substantively liable in the alternative, but that one is and the other is not. But it is submitted that the law urgently requires clarification. There should be no scope for merger in most disclosed principal cases. But it may be that in England, because of the weight of authority, again only the Supreme Court can say so.[765]

There can, of course, be cases where on any criterion the agent's liability is separate. Thus a wife may order goods for herself, and other, identifiably different, goods as agent for her husband.[766] In another case an agent negotiated a sale of patents by the principal, and received the price, which the agent retained. The principal later agreed to repurchase the patents and gave the third party a cheque, which was dishonoured. It was held that the third party had separate causes of action against the agent as stakeholder, and against the principal on the cheque and the agreement to repurchase.[767] It has also been held that where judgment had been obtained against a firm (Salbstein Bros) which was never proved to exist or to be liable, this was no bar to a subsequent action on the same facts against a person (H.

---

[759] See cases cited in notes to para.8-117 above; *Murray v Delta Copper Co Ltd* [1925] 4 D.L.R. 1061 at 1067; *Lang Transport Ltd v Plus Factor International Trucking Ltd* (1997) 143 D.L.R. (4th) 672.

[760] See the (then) RSC Ord.14 cases cited on the liability of husband and wife: *Morel Bros & Co Ltd v Earl of Westmorland* [1904] A.C. 11 (discussed (1970) 86 L.Q.R. at 338–340); *French v Howie* [1906] 2 K.B. 674; *Sullivan v Sullivan* [1912] 2 I.R. 116; *Moore v Flanagan* [1920] 1 K.B. 919. See also *Cross & Co v Matthews and Wallace* (1904) 91 L.T. 500 (default judgment: discussed (1970) 86 L.Q.R. at 341–342); *Cyril Lord (Carpet Sales) v Browne* (1966) 111 S.J. 51 (default summons: discussed at 342–343). But cf. *Longman v Hill* (1891) 7 T.L.R. 639; *Petersen v Moloney* (1951) 84 C.L.R. 91; *Goodey v Garriock* [1972] 2 Lloyd's Rep. 369 (Ord. 14).

[761] On the basis of *Isaacs & Sons v Salbstein* [1916] 2 K.B. 139, discussed below; *Longman v Hill* (1891) 7 T.L.R. 639.

[762] *Barrington v Lee* [1972] 1 Q.B. 326, Illustration 6. But on this fact situation see *Sorrell v Finch* [1977] A.C. 728, Illustration 4 to Article 92.

[763] Perhaps the Ord.14 cases on husband and wife, cited above.

[764] See above, para.8-114; *Reardon Smith Line Ltd v Cayzer, Irvine & Co Ltd* (1929) 35 Com.Cas. 270; see also *Beadon v Capital Syndicate* (1912) 28 T.L.R. 427; *Clark v Urquhart* [1930] A.C. 28. As to setting aside of judgments, see below.

[765] But see *L.C. Fowler & Sons Ltd v St Stephen's College Board of Governors* [1991] 3 N.Z.L.R. 304, where a bold line was taken.

[766] *Debenham's Ltd v Perkins* (1925) 133 L.T. 252.

[767] *B.O. Morris Ltd v Perrott & Bolton* [1945] 1 All E.R. 567. See also *Bucknell v O'Donnell* (1922) 31 C.L.R. 40; *Goldrei Foucard & Son v Russian Chamber of Commerce* [1918] 1 K.B. 180.

Salbstein) who was liable.[768] And where the actions are in tort the position is different: principal and agent are joint tortfeasors.[769]

8-118   **Setting aside of judgments**   It seems in principle correct to say that where a judgment against the agent is set aside on the merits, i.e. as being wrong, it is no bar to another action against the principal[770]; but that a judgment may not simply be set aside by consent for this purpose.[771] But the cases are not clear.[772]

8-119   **Rule (2): Election. Undisclosed principal**   Some cases state the doctrine under which the third party may not sue both agent and undisclosed principal as applying to situations short of judgment.[773] If this is correct, the bar must be caused by the notion of election, or manifestation of choice, rather than merger. The basis of such a doctrine must again be that the obligations of agent and principal are as a matter of substantive law alternative at the election of the third party. There are, however, cases which speak of judgment as the only proof of election.[774] Here also the famous case of *Scarf v Jardine*,[775] which requires election between inconsistent liabilities in partnership law, is sometimes invoked. But, as in the case of judgment against joint debtors, the situation here is not quite the same and need not be treated in the same way.[776] "Elective liability" between two parties is a strange concept for the law. The problem is made easier, however, by the fact that though many cases speak of election, virtually every case in the field of undisclosed principal holds that the acts in question are insufficient to constitute election.[777] Only two have been traced which purport to hold that there has been a binding election short of judgment, and both can also be explained on the basis that the third party, after learning of the principal's existence, did an act which induced the principal to settle with, or alter position as to the agent, and thereby debarred the third party

---

[768] *Isaacs & Sons v Salbstein* [1916] 2 K.B. 139; followed in *Maxform SpA v Mariani and Goodville* [1979] 2 Lloyd's Rep. 385; affirmed [1981] 2 Lloyd's Rep. 54.

[769] See below, para.8-191; *Derham v Amev Life Assurance Co Ltd* (1981) 56 F.L.R. 34.

[770] See *Partington v Hawthorne* (1888) 52 J.P. 807 (explained in *Brennen & Sons Mfg Co Ltd v Thompson* (1915) 33 Ont. L.R. 465 at 470–471); *Buckingham v Trotter* (1901) I.S.R.(N.S.W.) 253; *Petersen v Moloney* (1951) 84 C.L.R. 91; *Goodey v Garriock* [1972] 2 Lloyd's Rep. 369 (Ord.14); *Lang Transport Ltd v Plus Factor International Trucking Ltd* (1997) 143 D.L.R. (4th) 672.

[771] *Hammond v Schofield* [1891] 1 Q.B. 453 (Ord. 14).

[772] Difficulty is caused by *Cross & Co Ltd v Matthews & Wallace* (1904) 91 L.T. 500 (default summons: discussed (1970) 86 L.Q.R. at 341–342); *Cyril Lord (Carpet Sales) v Browne* (1966) 111 S.J. 51 (default summons: discussed (1970) 86 L.Q.R. at 342–343); and the cases on husband and wife cited above. A default judgment was set aside in *Kohn v Devon Mortgage Ltd* (1983) 3 D.L.R. (4th) 466 (reversed on other grounds (1985) 20 D.L.R. (4th) 480).

[773] *Curtis v Williamson* (1874) L.R. 10 Q.B. 57, Illustration 4; *United Australia Ltd v Barclays Bank Ltd* [1941] A.C. 1 at 30; *Clarkson Booker Ltd v Andjel* [1964] 2 Q.B. 775 at 794, Illustration to Article 104; *Chestertons v Barone* [1987] 1 E.G.L.R. 15 at 17; *Adams v Atlas International Property Services Ltd* [2016] EWHC 2680 (QB); [2017] Bus. L.R. 287 (but claimant also pleading agent solely liable).

[774] *Priestly v Fernie* (1863) 3 Hurl. & C. 977 at 983–984; *Buckingham v Trotter* (1901) 1 S.R.(N.S.W.) 253, at 259, 261; *Petersen v Moloney* (1951) 84 C.L.R. 91; *Morgan v Lifetime Building Supplies Ltd* (1967) 61 D.L.R. (2d) 178; *Bain Securities Ltd v Curmi* (1990) 1 A.C.S.R. 794.

[775] *Scarf v Jardine* (1882) 7 App.Cas. 345; see also *Fell v Parkin* (1882) 52 L.J.Q.B. 99.

[776] See (1970) 86 L.Q.R. at 321–322, 327; *Spencer Bower: Reliance-Based Estoppel* (5th edn), para.13.44 onwards.

[777] *Nelson v Powell* (1784) 3 Doug. 410; *Taylor v Sheppard* (1835) 1 Y. & C.Ex. 271; *Curtis v Williamson* (1874) L.R. 10 Q.B. 57, Illustration 4; *Clarkson Booker Ltd v Andjel* [1964] 2 Q.B. 775, Illustration to Article 104.

from looking to the principal.[778] Such cases are part of a well-established group which is not normally associated with the idea of election at all,[779] but rather with estoppel, the hallmark of which is some form of reliance. It is submitted therefore that though there is in a Court of Appeal case concerning an undisclosed principal[780] extensive discussion on the basis that the rights against principal and agent are inconsistent and subject to election (though the decision was that there had been no election), a third party should only be debarred from suing an undisclosed principal, short of an actual judgment against the agent, by an act which raises an estoppel against that party, e.g. where after discovery of the principal the third party does an act leading the principal to suppose that that party relied on the agent, or has been paid by the agent, or in some other way waives the liability of the principal in a manner relied on.[781] There are, however, fairly recent dicta in the Court of Appeal maintaining the notion of election.[782]

Disclosed principal   Again, in the case of disclosed principal there are clear dicta   **8-120** that where both principal and agent are liable, the third party must elect.[783] The criticisms made above of the merger doctrine for such cases apply a fortiori to any requirement of election. Only if the liabilities are in the alternative does the idea of election make sense[784]; and of the many possible interpretations which can be given to the situation where agent and principal are liable, alternative liability is an unlikely one.[785] In this area however most of the cases appear fairly obviously not to be based on election between two liabilities on an alternative contract at all, but on problems of formation of contract. The typical situation is that discussed in several nineteenth-century cases, where a third party deals with an agent in circumstances where either agent or principal might reasonably be regarded as the other contracting party. In principle the law of agency assumes that the third party is dealing with the principal, unless there are clear indications to the contrary,[786] but these there may be.[787] It is also clear that the third party may contract on the basis that both are liable to that party.[788] Thus invoicing and debiting the agent or the like, which are sometimes spoken in terms of election, should perhaps really be classified in terms of offer or counter-offer.[789] There are many cases dealing with this

---

[778] *MacClure v Schemeil* (1871) 20 W.R. 168, Illustration 3 to Article 82; *Smethurst v Mitchell* (1859) 1 E. & E. 622 (explained in *Davison v Donaldson* (1882) 9 Q.B.D. 623).

[779] See Article 80.

[780] *Clarkson Booker Ltd v Andjel* [1964] 2 Q.B. 775.

[781] See *MacClure v Schemeil* (1871) 20 W.R. 168; *Taylor v Van Dutch Marine Holding Ltd* [2019] EWHC 1951 (Ch) at [242]; and the other cases, above. But the taking of a bill or cheque from the agent will not normally produce such an estoppel: see cases cited in fn.801 below; cf. *Restatement, Third*, § 6.09, Comment *d*; see also Corbin (1909) 19 Yale L.J. 221 at 239.

[782] *Chestertons v Barone* [1987] 1 E.G.L.R. 15 at 17, per May LJ. See also *Adams v Atlas International Property Services Ltd* [2016] EWHC 2680 (QB); [2017] Bus. L.R. 287; *Taylor v Van Dutch Marine Holding Ltd* [2019] EWHC 1951 (Ch) at [243].

[783] *Calder v Dobell* (1871) L.R. 6 C.P. 486 at 499 (Illustration 5); *Benton v Campbell Parker & Co* [1925] 2 K.B. 410 at 414; *Murray v Delta Copper Co* [1925] 4 D.L.R. 1061 at 1067; *Tedrick v Big T Restaurants of Canada Ltd* [1983] 2 W.W.R. 135.

[784] *L.C. Fowler & Sons Ltd v St Stephen's College Board of Governors* [1991] 3 N.Z.L.R. 304 at 309 (Illustration 7).

[785] See above, para.8-114.

[786] *Thomson v Davenport* (1829) 9 B. & C. 78 at 90.

[787] e.g. *Addison v Gandassequi* (1812) 4 Taunt. 574; cf. *Paterson v Gandasequi* (1812) 15 East 62.

[788] *Calder v Dobell* (1871) L.R. 6 C.P. 486 at 494; Comment to Article 98.

[789] e.g. *Thomson v Davenport* (1829) 9 B. & C. 78. See also cases on building subcontracts: *Young &*

point where the idea of election is not employed at all.[790] Such situations may of course give rise to estoppels as in the case of undisclosed principals. It is therefore submitted that in this area also a supposed election (short of judgment) to have recourse to the agent does not bind the third party unless it again gives rise to some form of estoppel.[791] This does not, of course, remove any authority from the cases referred to above dealing with the question with whom the contract was made.

8-121 **What constitutes election?** If, however, contrary to what is suggested above, any doctrine of election (as opposed to one of estoppel) is applicable, on general grounds the person electing must know the facts,[792] and the election must be clear and unequivocal[793] and voluntary.[794] It may also be that it must occur within a reasonable time,[795] though cases on this point seem better attributed to estoppel.[796] The question is certainly one of fact.[797] The following have been held not to constitute election: debiting the agent in the third party's books[798]; demanding payment of the agent[799]; receipt of part payment from the agent[800]; taking a bill of exchange or cheque from the agent[801]; proving in the agent's bankruptcy[802]; pursu-

---

Co v White (1911) 28 T.L.R. 87; *Beigtheil & Young v Stewart* (1900) 16 T.L.R. 177; cases on husband and wife: *Jewsbury v Newbold* (1857) 26 L.J.Ex. 247; *Bentley v Griffin* (1814) 5 Taunt. 356; *Metcalfe v Shaw* (1811) 3 Camp. 22; *Callot v Nash* (1923) 39 T.L.R. 292; shipping cases of various sorts: *Eastman v Harry* (1875) 33 L.T. 800; *Whitwell v Perrin* (1858) 4 C.B.(N.S.) 412; *Lamont v Hamilton* 1907 S.C. 628; *Beliard, Crighton (Belgium) & Co Ltd v Charles Lowe & Partners Ltd* (1922) 13 Ll. L. Rep. 567; *The Huntsman* [1894] P. 214; and other cases regularly cited in this connection: *Bottomley v Nuttall* (1858) 5 C.B.(N.S.) 122; *Dramburg v Pollitzer* (1873) 28 L.T. 470; *Re Bowerman Ex p. Vining* (1836) 1 Deac. 555.

[790] e.g. as to husband and wife: *Lea Bridge District Gas Co v Malvern* [1917] 1 K.B. 803; as to ship stores: *Dawson (Ship Stores) v Atlantica Co Ltd* (1931) 40 Ll. L. Rep. 63; *Evans & Reid Coal Co v McNabb, Rougier & Co Ltd* (1924) 18 Ll. L. Rep. 471; *Fraser-Johnston Engineering, etc., Co v Sam Isaacs (Aberdeen) Ltd* (1922) 12 Ll. L. Rep. 233; *Freimuller (Ships Stores) Ltd v Ocean Carriers (London) Ltd* [1961] 2 Lloyd's Rep. 309; *Pearson v Nell* (1860) 12 L.T. 607; *Thompson v Finden* (1829) 4 C. & P. 158. See also *Williamson v Barton* (1862) 7 H. & N. 899; *Gardiner v Heading* [1928] 2 K.B. 284; *Pennell v Alexander* (1854) 3 E. & B. 283; *Thomas v Edwards* (1836) 2 M. & W. 215; *Mortimer v M'Callan* (1840) 6 M. & W. 58 (cf. *Stoneham v Wyman* (1901) 6 Com.Cas. 174); *Format International Security Printers Ltd v Mosden* [1975] 1 Lloyd's Rep. 37. As to ship repairs and stores see Article 99, Illustration 8; Article 101, Illustration 2.

[791] cf. *Restatement, Third*, reporter's notes to § 6.09. See too *Bell v Ivy Technology Ltd* [2020] EWCA Civ 1563 at [37].

[792] *Dunn v Newton* (1884) C. & E. 278; *Clarkson Booker Ltd v Andjel* [1964] 2 Q.B. 775 at 792; *Pyxis Special Shipping Co Ltd v Dritsas & Kaglis Bros Ltd (The Scaplake)* [1978] 2 Lloyd's Rep. 380; *Kammins Ballrooms Co Ltd v Zenith Investments (Torquay) Ltd* [1971] A.C. 850 at 882–883; *Peyman v Lanjani* [1985] Ch. 457; *L.C. Fowler & Sons v St Stephen's College Board of Governors* [1991] 3 N.Z.L.R. 304.

[793] *Clarkson Booker Ltd v Andjel* [1964] 2 Q.B. 775 at 792.

[794] *L.C. Fowler & Sons Ltd v St Stephen's College Board of Governors* [1951] 3 N.Z.L.R. 304.

[795] Powell, p.272.

[796] e.g. *Smethurst v Mitchell* (1859) 1 E. & E. 622.

[797] *Clarkson Booker Ltd v Andjel* [1964] 2 Q.B. 775.

[798] *Thomson v Davenport* (1829) 9 B. & C. 78; *Calder v Dobell* (1871) L.R. 6 C.P. 486, Illustration 5; *Eastman v Harry* (1875) 33 L.T. 800; *Young & Co v White* (1911) 28 T.L.R. 87. This is really a matter of formation of contract: see above.

[799] *Calder v Dobell* (1871) L.R. 6 C.P. 486; *Beigtheil & Young v Stewart* (1900) 16 T.L.R. 177; *Eastman v Harry* (1875) 33 L.T. 800; cf. *MacClure v Schemeil* (1871) 20 W.R. 168, Illustration 3 to Article 80.

[800] *Ex p. Pitt* (1923) 40 T.L.R. 5.

[801] *Robinson v Read* (1829) 9 B. & C. 449. Unless it is received in full satisfaction, which would be difficult to establish. See *Everett v Collins* (1810) 2 Camp. 515; *Marsh v Pedder* (1815) 4 Camp.

ing a claim in arbitration against the agent[803]; serving a writ on the agent[804]; or obtaining leave to sign judgment against the agent under the then RSC Ord.14.[805] It has, however, recently been said that "the clearest evidence of election is at least the commencement of proceedings against one or other of the two relevant parties".[806]

Rule (3)   The strength of this residual rule obviously varies in accordance with the validity of the doctrine of election above discussed. But the cases deciding that there has been no election far outnumber those holding that there has been.   **8-122**

Substance or procedure?   A difficult question is whether the above rules are to be classified as rules of substance or procedure for the purposes of the conflict of laws. In general, the rules for undisclosed principal do appear to represent rules of substance whereby the principal is liable alternatively with the agent. Much of the law as to disclosed principals, on the other hand, seems to derive from procedural considerations concerning summary and default judgments; though questions of guarantee and joint and several liability would be substantive. The question which of two persons is a party to a contract is of course one of substance. The confused bases of the rules make generalisation extremely difficult.   **8-123**

Illustrations

(1)   The master of a ship signs a bill of lading in his own name. The consignee obtains judgment against him on it, but the judgment is not satisfied. The consignee cannot thereafter sue the shipowner.[807]   **8-124**

(2)   The Earl and Countess of Westmorland are sued jointly by a tradesman for wines and provisions ordered by the Countess. The Countess submits to summary judgment but the Earl obtains leave to defend. It is held that there is no evidence of joint liability; and that having signed judgment against the wife the plaintiff cannot sue the husband as her principal.[808]

(3)   The agent of a moneylender sues the agent of another moneylender on a debt

---

257; *Strong v Hart* (1827) 6 B. & C. 160; *Smith v Ferrand* (1827) 7 B. & C. 191; *The Huntsman* [1894] P. 214.

[802] *Curtis v Williamson* (1874) L.R. 10 Q.B. 57, Illustration 4; cf. *MacClure v Schemeil* (1871) 20 W.R. 168; *Scarf v Jardine* (1882) 7 App.Cas. 345; *Fell v Parkin* (1882) 52 L.J.Q.B. 99; *Con-Stan Industries of Australia Pty Ltd v Norwich Winterthur Insurance (Australia) Ltd* (1986) 160 C.L.R. 226.

[803] *Pyxis Special Shipping Co Ltd v Dritsas & Kaglis Bros Ltd (The Scaplake)* [1978] 2 Lloyd's Rep. 380.

[804] *Clarkson Booker Ltd v Andjel* [1964] 2 Q.B. 775 (actually here served on principal).

[805] *C. Christopher (Hove) Ltd v Williams* [1936] 3 All E.R. 68.

[806] *Chestertons v Barone* [1987] 1 E.G.L.R. 15 at 17, per May LJ. Contrast *Bain Securities Ltd v Curmi* (1990) 1 A.C.S.R. 794.

[807] *Priestly v Fernie* (1863) 3 Hurl. & C. 977. This leading case reads strangely to modern eyes. In present times the master (who appears to have been imprisoned for the debt in Melbourne) would not be liable at all. The assumption seems to have been that he was the sole contracting party; the argument put was that in the case of shipmasters the owners were, by maritime law and contrary to principle, liable also. The court applied what it said was a general rule that principal and agent were liable in the alternative.

[808] *Morel Bros & Co Ltd v Earl of Westmorland* [1904] A.C. 11 (where the husband's liability was affected by the rules as to presumptions of authority: see above, para.3-041). See also *Sullivan v Sullivan* [1912] 2 I.R. 116, where the court regretted the conclusion to which it regarded itself as bound to come; *Moore v Flanagan* [1920] 1 K.B. 919, a claim by a milliner and dressmaker, where Scrut-

and obtains judgment. Later the first moneylender sues the second moneylender on the same debt. The action is barred.[809]

(4)   A bought goods in his own name on behalf of B. The seller discovered that B was the principal, and subsequently, A having filed a liquidation petition, a clerk of the seller, for the purpose of proving in the liquidation, made an affidavit treating A as the debtor, and the affidavit was duly filed. The seller could still sue B for the price of the goods.[810]

(5)   A broker is authorised to buy cotton, but not to disclose his principal's name. Being unable to obtain a contract on his own credit, he reveals the principal's name and bought and sold notes are exchanged between him and the seller naming the principal as the buyer. The goods are invoiced to the broker, but, the market falling, he refuses to accept the goods. The seller threatens both with legal proceedings, but subsequently sues the principal. He is not precluded from doing so.[811]

(6)   The seller of a house instructs two estate agents. B makes an offer subject to contract and pays a deposit to each agent. The sale does not proceed. One estate agent returns the deposit, the other does not. B obtains judgment against the second agent, but it is unsatisfied. Even if the principal is liable in respect of the deposit, an action against him is barred by the judgment against the agent.[812]

(7)   An agent acting for a school contracts on the school's behalf, with a firm which arranges such tours, for a sporting tour for the school. The school pays its agent, who passes on some of the money to the firm and disappears. The firm obtains a default judgment against the agent for the remainder, but it is not satisfied. Later the firm sues the school. The school is liable and the firm's action is not barred by election or judgment, the judgment against the agent being against one who was not liable to the firm at all.[813]

2.   DISPOSITIONS OF PROPERTY AND RESTITUTIONARY CLAIMS

Article 83

DISPOSITIONS OF PRINCIPAL'S PROPERTY BY AGENT ACTING WITHIN ACTUAL OR APPARENT AUTHORITY

8-125   A principal is bound by dispositions of property made by an agent acting within the scope of such agent's actual authority or which are ratified, and, where for value, within the scope of the agent's apparent authority.[814]

---

ton LJ said that the rule was "extremely technical" but Atkin LJ robustly said that "[a]ny ill result to the plaintiff arises from her abuse of the procedure under Order XIV".

[809] *RMKRM (A Firm) v MRMVL (A Firm)* [1926] A.C. 761 (discussed (1970) 86 L.Q.R. at 337–338).

[810] *Curtis v Williamson* (1874) L.R. 10 Q.B. 57.

[811] *Calder v Dobell* (1871) L.R. 6 C.P. 486.

[812] *Barrington v Lee* [1972] 1 Q.B. 326 (noted (1972) 88 L.Q.R. 184). But as to the principal's liability, see *Sorrell v Finch* [1977] A.C. 728, Illustration 4 to Article 92.

[813] *L.C. Fowler & Sons Ltd v St Stephen's College Board of Governors* [1991] 3 N.Z.L.R. 304.

[814] See Comment. The rules as to principal and agent are preserved by s.62(2) of the Sale of Goods Act 1979. As to actual authority, see Ch.2; as to apparent authority, see Article 72; as to ratification, see Articles 13–20. For extended discussion of this difficult topic, see Powell, pp.80–97; Stoljar, Ch.5; Fridman, Ch.7.

Comment

It is obvious that a disposition within an agent's actual authority, express or implied, transfers property, whether the principal is disclosed or not[815]; and that an unauthorised disposition can be ratified, the ratification ranking as a transfer from the time at which it occurs.[816] The position with apparent authority is, however more complex.

8-126

Where the disposition is made by the agent and received by the donee as a gift, the broad concept of apparent authority does not operate to protect the donee.[817] In such cases, while a true representation by the principal of entitlement in the agent to make a gift that is actually then relied upon by the donee might suffice to defeat the principal's ownership, the weak form of estoppel that lies behind apparent authority would not. In particular, the reliance element within apparent authority is nominal where there is a contract, but could not be allowed to be nominal where the third party has given no value.[818] Where, however, the recipient of the property is not a volunteer but purports to be contracting with the principal, then naturally the concept of apparent authority will operate. There may also be room for apparent authority to operate where the third party is contracting with a party other than the principal, but expecting to receive ownership from the principal.[819]

There follows a further issue. In so far as estoppel is relied on, an estoppel in general only operates between two parties and their privies. Yet the result of a disposition which is effective under estoppel is apparently to confer "a real title and not merely a metaphorical title by estoppel",[820] viz. a title which can be transmitted to a person unable to rely on the estoppel, and which will bind not only a volunteer but also a bona fide purchaser from the person estopped.[821] This is recognised in s.21(1) of the Sale of Goods Act 1979, which gives as an exception to the maxim *nemo dat quod non habet* the case where "the owner of goods is by his conduct precluded from denying the seller's authority to sell".[822] This again

---

[815] An example would be a distributor of goods which he holds under a "Romalpa" clause: he is generally authorised to resell them. Such a person is not usually however a true agent. See above; below, para.8-165.

[816] For examples, see Illustrations to Article 17. On principle, the ratification should operate from the time of the act ratified: see Article 20. But in any case there could often be an estoppel from alleging that an act had not been ratified: see Article 21.

[817] *High Commissioner for Pakistan in the United Kingdom v Prince Muffakham Jah* [2019] EWHC 2551 (Ch); [2020] 2 W.L.R. 699 at [247].

[818] See above, para.8-023.

[819] e.g. *Pickering v Busk* (1812) 15 East 38, Illustration 1; *Quinn v CC Automotive Group Ltd* [2010] EWCA Civ 1412; [2011] 2 All E.R. (Comm) 584.

[820] *Eastern Distributors Ltd v Goldring* [1957] 2 Q.B. 600 at 611, per Devlin J (Illustration 4 to Article 84). cf. W.H. Goodhart (1957) 73 L.Q.R. 455.

[821] *Eastern Distributors Ltd v Goldring* [1957] 2 Q.B. 600 at 611. But where the interests of the person concerned are adverse to those of the person estopped, e.g. as a creditor, he may not be bound by the estoppel; see *Heane v Rogers* (1820) 9 B. & C. 577; *Richards v Johnston* (1859) 4 H. & N. 660; *Richards v Jenkins* (1887) 18 Q.B.D. 451; *Geddes v M'Donnell* (1896) 22 V.L.R. 330; *Curtis v Perth & Fremantle Bottle Exchange Co Ltd* (1914) 18 C.L.R. 17 at 23, 28; Ewart, *Estoppel* (1900), pp.196–221; *Spencer Bower: Reliance-Based Estoppel* (5th edn), Ch.6. The solution to this difficulty turns on the extent to which apparent ownership and apparent authority are separate from the general rules of estoppel.

[822] This provision only applies to a sale as opposed to an agreement to sell: *Shaw v Commissioner of Police of the Metropolis* [1987] 1 W.L.R. 1332.

causes difficulties of theory, at least where there is no abstract transfer by deed, where the notion of apparent authority may validate the document itself.[823]

A third general point should be noted, though this is a point of application rather than theory. A basic tenet of this part of the law is that the mere entrusting of goods or documents of title to an agent does not confer apparent authority to make a disposition of them, for otherwise "no one would be safe in parting with possession of anything".[824] Even carelessness in an owner is not fatal; it would, in any event, be an unsafe assumption that the third party dealing with the non-owner is more innocent of blame than the owner. As Lord Macnaghten put the matter in one of the leading cases:

> "If it were permissible it would be interesting to inquire which of the two firms parties to this litigation was the more blameworthy in a moral point of view. The plaintiffs trusted a man whom they had long known and whom they believed to be honest. The defendants trusted a man they had never seen, whom a breath of suspicion and the most ordinary inquiries would have unmasked. But we have nothing to do with this matter ... The right of the true owner is not prejudiced or affected by his carelessness in losing the chattel, however gross it may have been."[825]

A person in possession of goods may be a bailee; a person in possession of documents of title may be a mortgagee or a mere depositary. The cases therefore constantly indicate the necessity for some further act on the part of the owner beyond the mere parting with possession.

Returning to apparent authority,[826] an agent may have such authority by virtue of a representation by the principal. This can occur in the property context where the principal regularly acquiesces in transfers by an agent; or where the agent is entrusted with goods or documents of title together with a further indication that the agent has authority to dispose of them. It is difficult to find a clear case of this where the disposition is not binding by virtue of a contract,[827] but if an agent is given goods and a written authority to pledge them, the agent's disposition would surely be valid notwithstanding that there are secret limits on his or her authority which

---

[823] See *Northside Developments Pty Ltd v Registrar-General* (1990) 170 C.L.R. 146; Watts (2002) 2 O.U. Commonwealth L.J. 93; and see Companies Act 2006 ss.44 and 45.

[824] *Weiner v Gill* [1905] 2 K.B. 172 at 182; *Cole v North Western Bank* (1872) L.R. 10 C.P. 354 at 362; *Colonial Bank v Cady* (1890) 15 App.Cas. 267; *Farquharson Brothers & Co v King & Co* [1902] A.C. 325, Illustration 6 to Article 84; *Johnson v Crédit Lyonnais* (1877) 3 C.P.D. 32; *Fry v Smellie* [1912] 3 K.B. 282, Illustration 3 to Article 85; *Jerome v Bentley & Co* [1952] 2 All E.R. 114; *Central Newbury Car Auctions Ltd v Unity Finance Ltd* [1957] 1 Q.B. 371, Illustration 3 to Article 84; *Moorgate Mercantile Co Ltd v Twitchings* [1977] A.C. 890 at 902–904 (Illustration 7 to Article 84); *Yu v Brownvalley Investments Pty Ltd* [2010] NSWSC 253 at [22] (possession of signed guarantee but without authority to deliver it, did not give any entitlement to lender upon wrongful delivery); *Bassano v Toft* [2014] EWHC 377 (QB) at [56] (pledgee does not lose pledge by delivering to an agent); *Ramsay v Love* [2015] EWHC 65 (Ch) at [117].

[825] *Farquharson Brothers & Co v King & Co* [1902] A.C. 325 at 335–336. See also *Sorrell v Finch* [1977] A.C. 728 HL at 754; *Shogun Finance Ltd v Hudson* [2003] UKHL 62; [2004] 1 A.C. 919 at [192], per Lord Walker of Gestingthorpe.

[826] See above, para.8-014.

[827] A possible example is *Davy v Waller* (1899) 81 L.T. 107, but the case does not distinguish clearly between actual and apparent authority as now understood. See also *Robinson v Montgomeryshire Brewery Co Ltd* [1896] 2 Ch. 841; cf. *Jameson v Union Bank of Scotland* (1913) 109 L.T. 850. The third party must of course rely on the appearance of authority: see *Raffoul v Esanda Ltd* [1970] 3 N.S.W.R. 8.

are not disclosed.[828] Again, in the second category the entrusting of goods to an agent, e.g. in former times a factor, who in the way of business normally had authority to sell, will create apparent authority,[829] and a disposition in the ordinary course of business of such an agent will be effective: but here a clear modern case is difficult to find because such an agent would normally come under the wider protections of the Factors Act.[830] It is also possible for an estoppel to occur in relation to land through the actions of an agent.[831]

There are two other ways in which the courts have sought to validate unauthorised dispositions by agents in possession of goods or documents of title. **8-127**

(1) *Apparent ownership* Where the owner has allowed an agent to have possession of goods or documents of title and also in some further way let the agent appear to be *owner* of the goods or the property represented by the document of title, the agent's unauthorised disposition may be valid. This is not really a rule of agency, inasmuch as the person concerned is not thought to be an agent and need not in fact be such: but the reasoning in the cases is virtually identical to that relating to apparent authority and indeed the majority of the cases on property dispositions by agents lie in this area rather than in that of true apparent authority. The interconnection between the two is shown by the fact that Chalmers, in his first commentary on the Sale of Goods Act,[832] cited cases on apparent ownership as cases where the owner is under s.21 precluded from denying the seller's authority to sell.[833] One difference however should be noted. The fact that a sale is not in the ordinary course of business may be evidence that it is not within the apparent authority: but this point would not be relevant where the agent actually appeared to own the goods.[834] The doctrine of apparent ownership is dealt with in the following Article.

(2) *Delivery plus some actual authority to make a disposition.* A number of cases, mostly dealing with land, tend to suggest a proposition that where the principal delivers possession of documents of title, and authorises the agent to make certain property dispositions, the principal may in certain circumstances be bound when the agent makes other, unauthorised dispositions. Though this may be a reasonable idea, it does not accord with central agency doctrines,

---

[828] See Illustration 2.
[829] *Pickering v Busk* (1812) 15 East 38, Illustration 1 (actually a case on a broker). As to the distinction between brokers and factors see above, para.1-046.
[830] Article 87. A possible modern example is *Fuller v Glyn, Mills, Currie & Co* [1914] 2 K.B. 168, as explained in *Mercantile Bank of India Ltd v Central Bank of India Ltd* [1938] A.C. 287 and in *Tobin v Broadbent* (1947) 75 C.L.R. 378. In *Shearson Lehman Brothers Inc v Maclaine, Watson & Co Ltd* [1988] 1 W.L.R. 16 at 28 it was said that authority to pass property may be more easily inferred than authority to enter into an obligation: "business would come to a standstill if persons who receive documents from clerks and secretaries, acting in the course of their employment, were not entitled to assume that these documents were sent with the authority of the employer": per Lord Bridge of Harwich.
[831] *Fielden v Christie-Miller* [2015] EWHC 87 (Ch) at [26].
[832] *Sale of Goods* (2nd edn, 1894).
[833] A common root for both doctrines is *Pickering v Busk* (1812) 15 East 38: see Stoljar, p.113 onwards; *Eastern Distributors Ltd v Goldring* [1957] 2 Q.B. 600, Illustration 4 to Article 84 likewise is relevant to both doctrines. The relevant section of the Sale of Goods Act is sometimes cited in apparent ownership cases: see *J. Sargent (Garages) Ltd v Motor Auctions (West Bromwich) Ltd* [1977] R.T.R. 121.
[834] *Motor Credits (Hire Finance) Ltd v Pacific Motor Auctions Pty Ltd* (1963) 109 C.L.R. 87; reversed on other grounds [1965] A.C. 867; but cf. *General Distributors Ltd v Paramotors Ltd* [1962] S.A.S.R. 1.

inasmuch as there is in these cases no actual or apparent authority (or apparent ownership), and the position between principal and agent should not be relevant to the position of the third party (though references to that position tend to creep into cases in all categories). It seems to be based on reasoning applicable to problems of priority in land law, and any more general validity is doubtful. It is dealt with in Article 85.

Other estoppels   It should be noted finally that even though a disposition is not valid under any of the above rules, the principal may by conduct subsequent to it be estopped from alleging its invalidity; or from alleging in general that the property is the principal's. This conduct may take the form of a positive representation; in other cases there must be a duty to speak or disclose.[835]

Illustrations

8-128   (1)   The purchaser of hemp lying at wharves in London has, at the time of the purchase, the hemp transferred into the wharfinger's books in the name of the broker who effected the purchase, and whose ordinary business it is to buy and sell hemp. An unauthorised sale by the broker passes property.[836]

(2)   Stockbrokers have a loan account with their bankers, with whom they deposit stocks, shares and bonds belonging to various clients en bloc as security for the bankers' advances. These are transferred to and held by trustees for the bank. A client alleges that the authority which he had given to the brokers to repledge his securities authorised them to do so only for an amount not exceeding what was due from him to them. On the evidence of Stock Exchange practice there was nothing to make the bank think that the stocks and shares were not the broker's own property, and a pledge for a greater sum was valid.[837]

(3)   A person purports to sell a leasehold interest in land, and the agreement is signed for him by a land agent. The agent has no authority to sign, but the owner knows of the sale, and allows the purchaser to pay rent and rates on the land. It is held that whether he had assented or not, he is estopped by his conduct from denying that he had so assented, and he is ordered to do what is necessary to give effect to the rights of the purchaser.[838]

Article 84

DOCTRINE OF APPARENT OWNERSHIP

8-129   Where a principal, by words or conduct, represents or permits it to be represented that an agent is the owner of any property, any sale, pledge, mortgage or other

---

[835]   See above, Article 21.

[836]   *Pickering v Busk* (1812) 15 East 38, really a case on implied authority, though a root for both implied and apparent authority. See Stoljar, p.113 onwards.

[837]   *Bentinck v London Joint Stock Bank* [1893] 2 Ch 120. See this case explained by Dixon J in *Tobin v Broadbent* (1947) 75 C.L.R. 378 at 404–407 (a useful discussion).

[838]   *West v Dillicar* [1920] N.Z.L.R. 139; [1921] N.Z.L.R. 617; see also *Fung Kai Sun v Chan Fui Hing* [1951] A.C. 489; *Spiro v Lintern* [1973] 1 W.L.R. 1002; *Worboys v Carter* [1987] 2 E.G.L.R. 1; *M'Kenzie v British Linen Co* (1881) 6 App.Cas. 82; *Greenwood v Martin's Bank Ltd* [1933] A.C. 51. See in general Article 21; above, para.8-027.

disposition for value of the property by the agent is as valid against the principal as if the agent were its owner, with respect to anyone dealing with the agent on the faith of such representation.[839]

Comment

Where, in such a case, the agent's disposition is authorised, it is valid under ordinary doctrine; if necessary, the principal can be referred to as undisclosed.[840] But the above proposition embraces also more complex cases which do not strictly depend on agency principles, for there is no actual authority, and the third party does not think that the agent is an agent, but the owner. The proposition in the Article is in fact a specific formulation of a more general proposition which is not confined to disposition by persons who are already agents. But the cases are usually confused with cases on agency, and agency terminology used.[841] **8-130**

The rule is regarded, by longer pedigree than that of apparent authority in contract, as based on estoppel,[842] though it is an even looser application, for, apart from the fact that the estoppel confers title,[843] it is difficult to see that a third party can rely on the representation of someone of whose existence that party may not be aware. The estoppel is therefore usually said to be based on representation in a very loose sense, or on negligent conduct. Although the two are often difficult to distinguish, e.g. in the case of signature of a document, the latter is usually more appropriate, since the word "representation" implies a manifestation or communication from the principal to the third party, and, as stated above, in many cases the third party does not know of the principal at all. The rules seem to be effectively the same whichever is relied on.[844] Where the notion of representation is employed, it is said that it must be made to a person or group of persons,[845] though as the group can apparently be quite a wide one this is necessarily vague in its application. Where negligent conduct is relied on, it is often said that there must be a duty of care,[846]

---

[839] See Comment.

[840] See *VLM Holdings Ltd v Ravensworth Digital Services Ltd* [2013] EWHC 228 (Ch) at [65] (grant of copyright licence).

[841] See *Rimmer v Webster* [1902] 2 Ch. 163, Illustration 5; *Central Newbury Car Auctions Ltd v Unity Finance Ltd* [1957] 1 Q.B. 371, Illustration 3; *Eastern Distributors Ltd v Goldring* [1957] 2 Q.B. 600, Illustration 4; *Jerome v Bentley & Co* [1952] 2 All E.R. 114; *Stoneleigh Finance Ltd v Phillips* [1965] 2 Q.B. 537; above, para.8-127; Sale of Goods Act 1979 s.21 (referred to in such a situation in *J. Sargent (Garages) Ltd v Motor Auctions (West Bromwich) Ltd* [1977] R.T.R. 121).

[842] See cases cited below, fnn.846 and 851; indeed some of these cases are seminal for the doctrine of estoppel in general. But cf. *Eastern Distributors Ltd v Goldring* [1957] 2 Q.B. 600 at 611.

[843] But see Comment to Article 83, esp. para.8-126.

[844] *Mercantile Bank of India Ltd v Central Bank of India Ltd* [1938] A.C. 287 at 298–299. See also *Bell v Marsh* [1903] 1 Ch. 528 at 541; Dal Pont, paras 21.18–21.19.

[845] "The 'holding out' must be to the particular individual who says he relied on it, or under such circumstances of publicity as to justify the inference that he knew of it and acted upon it": *Dickinson v Valpy* (1829) 10 B. & C. 128 at 140; approved in *Farquharson Bros & Co v King & Co* [1902] A.C. 325 at 341 (Illustration 6). As to representation through an agent, see *Moorgate Mercantile Co Ltd v Twitchings* [1977] A.C. 890, Illustration 7.

[846] *Swan v North British Australasian Co Ltd* (1863) 2 Hurl. & C. 175 at 182; *R.E. Jones Ltd v Waring & Gillow Ltd* [1926] A.C. 670 at 693; *Mercantile Bank of India Ltd v Central Bank of India Ltd* [1938] A.C. 287; disapproving dicta in *Commonwealth Trust v Akotey* [1926] A.C. 72; *Wilson & Meeson v Pickering* [1946] K.B. 422 at 425; *Mercantile Credit Co Ltd v Hamblin* [1965] 2 Q.B. 242 at 271; *Moorgate Mercantile Co Ltd v Twitchings* [1977] A.C. 890; *Beverley Acceptances Ltd v Oakley* [1982] R.T.R. 434 at 439 (Illustration 8); *Haines Bros Earthmoving Pty Ltd v Rosecell Pty Ltd* [2016] NSWCA 112 (manager of owner victim of duress to the person).

breach of which is the proximate cause of the deception of the third party,[847] and detrimental reliance. But again it seems that the duty can be owed to a wide class of persons, and indeed some cases speak of it being owed to all the world.[848] The loss must however be foreseeable, and one which the principal is culpable in failing to guard against: there cannot be negligence in the air. Moreover, it seems that negligence is not of itself sufficient to create apparent ownership, because the common law has long taken the view that mere negligence in parting with possession of goods does not imperil one's ownership.[849]

Hence, a principal is not bound merely because the principal has let the agent have goods and/or documents of title[850]: more must have been done, e.g. allowed property to stand in the agent's name,[851] given the agent an acknowledgment that the agent has bought and paid for the goods,[852] signed a document offering to buy the goods from the agent or a third party[853]; or (perhaps) entrusted the goods to a person who in the normal course of business sells goods that are that person's own.[854] Further, in all these cases the representation must be relied on: a person who did not believe that the agent was owner cannot found on this doctrine.[855] But it is not at all clear how far this goes: in particular, the question of the duty of care owed by those who sign documents in blank, which is not of course confined to agency situations, is a vexed one.[856] It seems that no estoppel will normally arise against a person who gives an agent share certificates accompanied by signed blank transfers,[857] for this could be used as a method of effecting a mortgage. It has been suggested that, apart from cases of specific representation and (possibly) entrust-

---

[847] *Swan v North British Australasian Co Ltd* (1863) 2 Hurl. & C. 175, where this was not so because the agent stole share certificates from the principal.

[848] *Swan v North British Australasian Co Ltd* (1863) 2 Hurl. & C. 175; *Gallie v Lee* [1969] 2 Ch. 17 at 36, 48; (affirmed sub nom. *Saunders v Anglia Building Society* [1971] A.C. 1004). But see *Thomas Australia Wholesale Vehicle Trading Co Pty Ltd v Marac Finance Australia Ltd* (1985) 3 N.S.W.L.R. 452 esp. at 458–459, per Kirby P (dissenting); *Leonard v Ielassi* (1987) 46 S.A.S.R. 495.

[849] See the cases in fn.824 above.

[850] cf. Illustrations 6–8; *Motor Credits (Hire Finance) Ltd v Pacific Motor Auctions Pty Ltd* (1963) 109 C.L.R. 87 at 99 (reversed on other grounds [1965] A.C. 867). A car registration document is not such a document of title: *J. Sargent (Garages) Ltd v Motor Auctions (West Bromwich) Ltd* [1977] R.T.R. 121; *Beverley Acceptances Ltd v Oakley* [1982] R.T.R. 417, Illustration 8. Lord Denning MR consistently took a different view: ibid.

[851] Illustration 2; *Dyer v Pearson* (1824) 3 B. & C. 38; *Pickard v Sears* (1837) 6 A. & E. 469; *Freeman v Cooke* (1848) 2 Exch. 654; *Henderson & Co v Williams* [1895] 1 Q.B. 521; *Leonard v Ielassi* (1987) 46 S.A.S.R. 495. See also *Lloyds & Scottish Finance v Williamson* [1965] 1 W.L.R. 404; sed quaere what was the extra feature in that case. The court seems to have applied the rules as to settlement with an agent discussed in Article 80; but these do not require more than possession of goods, and the principal seeks to affirm the transfer and require a second payment. Unless the case can be justified on the basis of *Brocklesby v Temperance Building Society*, discussed under Article 85, it is probably best treated, as it seems to have been at first instance, as a case of actual authority.

[852] Illustration 5.

[853] Illustrations 3 and 4.

[854] *Motor Credits (Hire Finance) Ltd v Pacific Motor Auctions Pty Ltd* (1963) 109 C.L.R. 87.

[855] *Motor Credits (Hire Finance) Ltd v Pacific Motor Auctions Pty Ltd* (1963) 109 C.L.R. 87; *Pickering v Busk* (1812) 15 East 38; *Motor Finance and Trading Co Ltd v Brown* [1928] S.A.S.R. 153. Sed quaere.

[856] See Pickering (1939) 55 L.Q.R. 400; Ewart, *Estoppel* (1900), p.438 onwards.

[857] *France v Clark* (1884) 26 Ch.D. 257; *Hutchison v Colorado Mining Co* (1886) 3 T.L.R. 265; *Fox v Martin* (1895) 64 L.J.Ch. 473, Illustration 2 to Article 85; cf. cases on the negligent custody of company seals: *Bank of Ireland v Evans' Trustees* (1855) 5 H.L. Cas. 389; *Merchants of Staple v Bank of England* (1888) 21 Q.B.D. 160; *Lewes Sanitary Steam Laundry v Barclay & Co Ltd* (1906) 22 T.L.R. 737. But a duty of care was held to exist in *Fuller v Glyn, Mills, Currie & Co* [1914] 2 K.B. 168. This case is difficult to reconcile with *Fox v Martin* (1895) 64 L.J.Ch. 473, and the mat-

ing to persons who normally sell goods that are their own, any estoppel is confined to the case of negotiable instruments,[858] viz. (presumably), instruments intended to become negotiable instruments[859]: where incomplete documents are deposited merely for custody there is apparently no actionable negligence.[860] More recent authority however indicates doubt as to whether it should be so limited, even if cases in other areas would be rare.[861] The formulation of principles is so difficult that the courts have frequently been forced back on the famous dictum of Ashurst J: "Whenever one of two innocent persons must suffer by the acts of a third, he who has enabled such third person to occasion the loss must sustain it".[862] But this hardly furnishes a precise guide: whether a person has "enabled" seems to turn on the criteria indicated above.[863]

Agent as trustee   The doctrine is inapplicable where the principal vests property in the agent as trustee,[864] for "a person is entitled to leave his property, whatever it may be, in the name of a trustee".[865] But in such a case the principal's interest could of course be defeated by a bona fide purchaser for value of the legal estate without notice.[866]

8-131

Notice   The question of notice is discussed under Article 73.

8-132

Illustrations

(1)   A, though the agency of B, a broker, obtained a loan on a mortgage of stock, and afterwards permitted the security to be transferred to B's banker, who had no notice of A's title and believed that B was the owner of the stock. B sold

8-133

---

ter turns on the correct propositions to be derived from *Colonial Bank v Cady and Williams* (1890) 15 App.Cas. 267. It was explained in *Mercantile Bank of India Ltd v Central Bank of India Ltd* [1938] A.C. 287 at 302–303 as a case where the agent, a stockbroker, had a usual authority to pledge: this explanation was accepted by Starke and Dixon JJ in *Tobin v Broadbent* (1947) 75 C.L.R. 378, but Latham CJ thought the case "not satisfactorily supported by authority". See further *Chomley v Union Bank of Australia Ltd* [1951] S.A.S.R. 152; *Pan-Electric Industries Ltd v Sim Lim Finance Ltd* [1993] 3 Singapore L.R. 242 (authorities reviewed).

[858] *Wilson & Meeson v Pickering* [1946] K.B. 422 at 427; *Swan v North British Australasian Co Ltd* (1863) 2 Hurl. & C. 175. This, if correct, would explain *Lloyds Bank v Cooke* [1907] 1 K.B. 794; but cf. (1945) 9 M.L.R. 298. That case can also be based on the doctrine of *Brocklesby v Temperance Building Society*, but this doctrine is itself doubtful: see Article 85. See also Bills of Exchange Act 1882 s.20; Article 72, Illustration 14.

[859] Powell, p.90.

[860] *Smith v Prosser* [1907] 2 K.B. 735, Illustration 14 to Article 72; *Perpetual Trustees Australia Ltd v Heperu Pty Ltd* [2009] NSWCA 84.

[861] *Mercantile Credit Co Ltd v Hamblin* [1965] 2 Q.B. 242 at 279; *Gallie v Lee* [1967] 2 Ch. 17 at 48; affirmed sub nom. *Saunders v Anglia Building Society* [1971] A.C. 1004; *Union Credit Bank Ltd v Mersey Docks and Harbour Board* [1899] 2 Q.B. 205 at 210; *United Dominions Trust Ltd v Western* [1976] Q.B. 513; *Gator Shipping Corp v Trans-Asiatic Oil Ltd SA (The Odenfeld)* [1978] 2 Lloyd's Rep 357 at 375–378.

[862] *Lickbarrow v Mason* (1787) 2 T.R. 63 at 70.

[863] *Farquharson Bros & Co v King & Co* [1902] A.C. 325 at 342 (Illustration 6); *R.E. Jones Ltd v Waring & Gillow Ltd* [1926] A.C. 670 at 693; *Jerome v Bentley & Co* [1952] 2 All E.R. 114 at 118; *Central Newbury Car Auctions Ltd v Unity Finance Ltd* [1957] 1 Q.B. 371 at 389 (Illustration 4); *Johnson Matthey (Aust.) Ltd v Dascorp Pty Ltd* (2003) 9 V.R. 171 at 185 (see above, para.8-022).

[864] *Shropshire Union Railways and Canal Co v R.* (1875) L.R. 7 H.L. 496; *Burgis v Constantine* [1908] 2 K.B. 484.

[865] *Burgis v Constantine* [1908] 2 K.B. 484 at 498.

[866] The above cases involved subsequent equitable mortgagees, who were postponed to the equitable owners.

the stock, which was transferred by the banker to the purchaser, and, having paid off the loan, converted the balance to his own use. Held, that A had no remedy against the banker.[867]

(2) A broker, having effected an insurance policy in his own name, was permitted to retain possession of it for the purpose of receiving the proceeds. The broker pledged the policy. Held, that the pledgee was entitled, as against the principal, to retain the advance out of the proceeds of the policy.[868]

(3) B agrees to buy A's car on hire-purchase and signs documents proposing to buy it from a finance company. A lets B have car and registration document and drive away. Later B sells the car, with the registration document, to a third party who is ignorant of B's lack of title. The third party does not acquire title, since possession of the car is not apparent ownership of it and the registration document contains a warning that the person holding it may or may not be the owner.[869]

(4) A wishes to borrow money on the security of his car. He agrees to a dealer representing to a finance company that he (the dealer) owns the car, and signs in blank documents agreeing to buy the car on hire-purchase from the finance company. The dealer fills in the documents and purports to sell the car to the company, who duly hire it to A. A is estopped from denying the dealer's authority to sell the car to the finance company.[870]

(5) R gives a broker a mortgage bond and instructs him to sell it. The broker induces R to execute transfers of the bond to him, acknowledging receipt of purchase money (though R has received nothing). The broker sub-mortgages the bond to W. The sub-mortgage binds R.[871]

(6) F, timber merchants, warehouse timber with a dock company and instruct the company to accept all orders signed by their clerk. The clerk gives orders transferring timber to himself under an assumed name and under that name fraudulently sells it to K. F would be estopped against the warehouse company but not against K. He can recover the timber from K.[872]

(7) A finance company transferring a car on hire purchase negligently fails to register the transaction with H.P. Information Ltd, an independent organisation to which 95 per cent of such finance companies belong and which maintains a central register of hire-purchase agreements. The hirer offers it to a motor dealer who is also a member. That dealer inquires as to the existence of any agreement on the car, and on being told none is recorded, buys it. Held

---

[867] *Marshall v National Provincial Bank* (1892) 61 L.J.Ch. 465; cf. *Tobin v Broadbent* (1947) 75 C.L.R. 378.

[868] *Callow v Kelson* (1862) 10 W.R. 193. See also *Williams v Allsup* (1861) 10 C.B.(N.S.) 417.

[869] *Central Newbury Car Auctions Ltd v Unity Finance Ltd* [1957] 1 Q.B. 371 (see (1957) 73 L.Q.R. 309); *Astley Industrial Trust Ltd v Miller* [1968] 2 All E.R. 36; *J. Sargent (Garages) Ltd v Motor Auctions (West Bromwich) Ltd* [1977] R.T.R. 121.

[870] *Eastern Distributors Ltd v Goldring* [1957] 2 Q.B. 600, a leading case on apparent authority also; *Stoneleigh Finance Ltd v Phillips* [1965] 2 Q.B. 537; *Snook v London & West Riding Investments Ltd* [1967] 2 Q.B. 786; cf. *Mercantile Credit Co Ltd v Hamblin* [1965] 2 Q.B. 242.

[871] *Rimmer v Webster* [1902] 2 Ch. 163; *Abigail v Lapin* [1934] A.C. 491. See also *Shaw v Commissioner of Police of the Metropolis* [1987] 1 W.L.R. 1332. Contrast *Debs v Sibec Developments Ltd* [1990] R.T.R. 91 (document signed under duress does not found estoppel by representation).

[872] *Farquharson Bros & Co v King & Co* [1902] A.C. 325; see (1902) 18 L.Q.R. 18 and 159. See also *Mercantile Bank of India Ltd v Central Bank of India Ltd* [1938] A.C. 287; cf. *Canadian Laboratory Supplies Ltd v Engelhard Industries of Canada Ltd* [1979] 2 S.C.R. 787; (1979) 97 D.L.R. (3d) 1.

by a majority that there was no estoppel. The first company can assert its interest because (a) the answer does not allege that there is no such agreement; (b) H.P.I. are independent suppliers of information and not agents for their members (in this case the finance company); (c) the members owe no duty to each other to register agreements.[873]

(8) The pledgee of two valuable motor cars who keeps them in a shed in the yard of his premises lends the owner the keys, and the registration document of one, supposedly to enable the owner to show the cars to insurers. The owner executes bills of sale on the cars. The first pledgee is not estopped from setting up his prior interest.[874]

Article 85

Dispositions By Agents Entrusted with Indicia of Property

(Perhaps) where a principal entrusts an agent with the possession of the indicia of title to property, and authorises the agent to raise money on their security, any security given by the agent on the property for money advanced, though for a higher amount than he was authorised to raise, is valid against the principal, provided that the person taking the security acts in good faith, and without notice that the agent is exceeding authority.[875]   **8-134**

Comment

A person who holds the indicia of title to another's property has no apparent authority to sell or mortgage it merely from possession, for that person may well, for example, be a mortgagee; nor is there apparent ownership.[876] The cases on which this Article is based seek to find an additional element that validates an unauthorised disposition in the fact that the principal has, unknown to the third party, given the agent authority to effect some sort of disposition of the property in the agent's possession. It is however difficult to justify such a proposition on principle. The underlying notion seems to be that where a person is given documents of title with authority to use them for the purpose of raising money, the owner of the documents cannot take advantage of any limitation in point of amount placed on the agent's authority as against a lender who had no notice of such limitation.[877] This may be a reasonable idea, but it is not in accord with well-established rules of agency to the effect that where an agent acts outside actual authority, the principal   **8-135**

---

[873] *Moorgate Mercantile Co Ltd v Twitchings* [1977] A.C. 890. See also *Cadogan Finance Ltd v Lavery* [1982] Com.L.Rep. 248 (aircraft); *Leonard v Ielassi* (1987) 46 S.A.S.R. 495; *Debs v Sibec Developments Ltd* [1990] R.T.R. 91 (failure to report robbery to police).

[874] *Beverley Acceptances Ltd v Oakley* [1982] R.T.R. 417 (Lord Denning MR dissenting). See also *McManus v Eastern Ford Sales Ltd* (1981) 128 D.L.R. (3d) 246.

[875] *Brocklesby v Temperance Building Society* [1895] A.C. 173, Illustration 1; *Perry-Herrick v Attwood* (1857) 2 De G. & J. 21; *Rimmer v Webster* [1902] 2 Ch. 163; *Fry v Smellie* [1912] 3 K.B. 282, Illustration 3. *Brocklesby*'s case was followed in *Lloyd's Bank v Cooke* [1907] 1 K.B. 794, but this difficult case should probably be explained on the grounds of estoppel by conduct. (See *Wilson & Meeson v Pickering* [1946] K.B. 422; above, para.8-130.) It was also referred to with approval by the Court of Appeal in *Abbey National BS v Cann* [1989] 2 F.L.R. 265; affirmed on other grounds [1991] 1 A.C. 56.

[876] Articles 83 and 84.

[877] *Brocklesby v Temperance Building Society* [1895] A.C. 173 at 180–181.

is only bound where there is apparent authority, or where the contract is ratified.[878] The fact that the agent, unknown to the third party, has some limited authority in the relevant direction should, if principle were adhered to, make no difference in the absence of ratification, apparent authority, or apparent ownership. The cases seem to have developed a pragmatic exception based on an aggregation of possession and a limited degree of actual authority to dispose of the property.

One of the leading cases, *Brocklesby v Temperance Building Society*,[879] could be explained on the ground that the agent had, in addition to the deeds, a document conferring on him an apparent authority to pledge them,[880] but the relevance of this was discounted in the judgments and emphasis placed on the existence of some initial authority, and the possible injustice to third parties if the unauthorised pledge was not valid. In another leading case, *Fry v Smellie*,[881] an agent who was given share certificates and a signed blank transfer, and instructed to borrow not less than a certain sum, borrowed less than the stipulated sum, and the owner of the shares was held bound. It could be argued that the deposit of share certificates together with such a transfer gives apparent ownership, or gives an apparent authority to borrow on their security,[882] but there was authority against this,[883] based on a practice of effecting mortgages by the use of such documents. Again the initial authority was held to make the difference. It is indeed difficult to escape the significance of the initial authority if this line of cases is to be accepted. The rule seems to originate from cases of priority of mortgages of land,[884] where it takes the form that if a mortgagee of property permits the mortgagor to have possession of the title deeds for the purpose of giving a security on the property, any security given for value by the mortgagor thereon has priority to the claim of the mortgagee, provided that the person taking the security acts in good faith and without notice of the mortgage.[885] But in this rather different area, priority is largely regulated by conduct rendering the equities unequal as between the parties, or displacing the superiority of the legal estate, and it is obvious that conduct of one party, even where unknown to the other, could be taken into account in this sort of inquiry.[886] Thus gross negligence with regard to the deeds has been said to displace the claim of a prior

---

[878] cf. *Keighley Maxsted & Co v Durant* [1901] A.C. 240. And the distinction between exceeding authority and doing an act right outside the authority would be difficult to operate. It is, however, defended by Atiyah [1965] J.B.L. 130 at 136; Sale of Goods (12th edn). cf. Ewart, *Estoppel* (1900), pp.244–246. It could never apply to an agent to sell goods.
[879] *Brocklesby v Temperance Building Society* [1895] A.C. 173, Illustration 1.
[880] Powell, p.84.
[881] *Fry v Smellie* [1912] 3 K.B. 282, Illustration 3; criticised by Powell, pp.82–83.
[882] See per Farwell LJ at p.296. See also *Tobin v Broadbent* (1947) 75 C.L.R. 378 at 405–406.
[883] *Fox v Martin* (1895) 64 L.J.Ch. 473, Illustration 2.
[884] See the doctrine discussed by Millett J in *Macmillan Inc v Bishopsgate Investment Trust Plc (No.3)* [1995] 1 W.L.R. 978 (where counsel had described it as "the arming principle"). Millett J said that it was "indeed part of the law of priorities and not of agency" (at 1012).
[885] *Perry-Herrick v Attwood* (1857) 2 De G. & J. 21; *Briggs v Jones* (1870) L.R. 10 Eq. 92; *Clarke v Palmer* (1882) 21 Ch.D. 124; cf. *Colyer v Finch* (1856) 5 H.L.Cas. 905; *Northern Counties Insurance Co v Whipp* (1884) 26 Ch.D. 482; *Hunt v Elmes* (1861) 30 L.J.Ch. 255; *Cottey v National Provincial Bank Ltd* (1904) 20 T.L.R. 607. The connection between the rule and these mortgage cases is supported by the fact that in *Northern Counties Insurance Co v Whipp* (1884) 26 Ch.D. 482, at 492–493 it is suggested that it is only where the delivery was for the purpose of raising money that a prior mortgagee who fails to retain the deeds (as opposed to one who fails to obtain them) is postponed.
[886] "To hold that a person who advances money on an estate, the title deeds of which are under such circumstances left in the hands of the mortgagor, is not to have preference would be to shut our eyes to the plainest equity": *Perry-Herrick v Attwood* (1857) 2 De G. & J. 21 at 39, per Lord Cranworth

or legal mortgagee.[887] Although it is said that the cases involving agents are not based on negligence,[888] their rationale is most imprecisely stated,[889] and their relation to agency cases not fully worked out.[890] Further, many mortgage cases can also be explained on the ground of apparent ownership, in that the mortgagee, by returning the mortgagor's own deeds to the mortgagor (or allowing him or her to hold them), whether simpliciter or with some false acknowledgment of receipt of the mortgage debt,[891] has enabled the mortgagor to appear as the owner of unencumbered property. Similar reasoning can be applied to other mortgage cases.[892]

The leading cases contain dicta which are very difficult to reconcile with the normal principles of agency law.[893] One case, *Rimmer v Webster*,[894] suggests that where the agent has authority to sell, an unauthorised pledge may be effective. This is however even more difficult to reconcile with other authority,[895] and the case is probably best explained on its other ground of decision, that of apparent ownership.[896] Another view, however, is that the cases referred to in this Article and

---

LC. "A person who puts it in the power of another to deceive and to raise money must take the consequences; he cannot afterwards rely on a particular or a different equity": *Briggs v Jones* (1870) L.R. 10 Eq. 92 at 98, per Lord Romilly MR.

[887] See in general Waldock, *Law of Mortgages* (2nd edn), p.392 onwards and 420 onwards (though the interpretation given of the cases here discussed at p.393 is, it is submitted, erroneous). Quaere to what extent this differs from estoppel by conduct: see, e.g. *Rimmer v Webster* [1902] 2 Ch. 163 at 172; Ashburner, *Principles of Equity* (2nd edn), p.453 onwards. For an argument that the weight of authority does not support gross negligence as being sufficient to disturb equitable priorities, see Watts (1998) 18 N.Z.U.L.R. 46.

[888] *Perry-Herrick v Attwood* (1857) 2 De G. & J. 21 at 37 and 39.

[889] See *Perry-Herrick v Attwood* (1857) 2 De G. & J. 21; discussed in *Briggs v Jones* (1870) L.R. 10 Eq. 92 at 98; *Hunter v Walters* (1870) L.R. 11 Eq. 292 at 318; *Clarke v Palmer* (1882) 21 Ch.D. 124 at 129; *Manners v Mew* (1885) 29 Ch.D. 725 at 732; *Northern Counties Insurance Co v Whipp* (1884) 26 Ch.D. 482 at 492–493; *Fox v Hawks* (1879) 13 Ch.D. 822 at 834; *National Provincial Bank v Jackson* (1886) 33 Ch.D. 1 at 12; *Jones v Rhind* (1869) 17 W.R. 1091; *Lloyds Bank v Bullock* [1896] 2 Ch. 193 at 198.

[890] In land cases the tendency is to think in terms of priority of estates and to consider what conduct will displace the holder of an earlier title. In chattel cases, the reasoning used is more likely to follow the maxim *nemo dat quod non habet* unless there is apparent authority or apparent ownership. Cases involving shares may employ either type of reasoning.

[891] e.g. *Rice v Rice* (1854) 2 Drew. 73; cf. *Martinez v Cooper* (1826) 2 Russ. 198.

[892] e.g. *Robinson v Montgomeryshire Brewery Co* [1896] 2 Ch. 841; cf. *Jameson v Union Bank of Scotland* (1913) 109 L.T. 850.

[893] Including references to "equitable estoppel": *Fry v Smellie* [1912] 3 K.B. 282 at 299; cf. *Eastern Distributors Ltd v Goldring* [1957] 2 Q.B. 600 at 611. The doctrine seems to have been nurtured by Farwell LJ, who sat in most of the cases.

[894] *Rimmer v Webster* [1902] 2 Ch. 163, Illustration 5 to Article 84. See also *Wishart v Credit & Mercantile Plc* [2015] EWCA Civ 655; [2015] 2 P. & C.R. 15. Here, the disposition was also outside the class of transactions authorised. This again makes the case difficult to square with general principle, but the result may be justified by the fact that the claimant's rights were equitable only and he was relying on an exception to override a legal interest. See the critical notes by Sampson [2016] C.L.J. 21 and Televantos [2016] Conv. 181.

[895] See *Fox v Martin* (1895) 64 L.J.Ch. 473, Illustration 2; *Hutchison v Colorado Mining Co* (1886) 3 T.L.R. 265. This situation will often be covered by s.2 of the Factors Act 1889; see *Lloyd's Bank Ltd v Bank of America, etc.* [1938] 2 K.B. 147, Illustration 6 to Article 87, and this seems to be the proper approach to it.

[896] See *Tsang Chuen v Li Po Kwai* [1932] A.C. 715 at 728–729; *Abigail v Lapin* [1934] A.C. 491 at 508; Article 84. The case was distinguished in *Jerome v Bentley & Co* [1952] 2 All E.R. 114; and there are signs of a similar approach in *Lloyds & Scottish Finance v Williamson* [1965] 1 W.L.R. 404. This case was, however, treated also as a case of apparent authority, and is probably even better explained as a case of actual authority. There are similar suggestions in *Mercantile Credit Co Ltd v Hamblin* [1965] 2 Q.B. 242 at 276, 277. See also *Union Credit Bank Ltd v Mersey Docks & Harbour Board*

in Article 84 constitute pragmatic qualifications to the generality of the *nemo dat* rule and to the general principles of agency law.[897] They do not in themselves justify reopening those principles, nor do they support the result in *Watteau v Fenwick*.[898]

8-136 **Forgery** Forged instruments do not confer rights at common law (though statutory registration regimes can give effect to forged documents), and if the agent counterfeits a signature, seal or document in a situation such as those above, no rights are transferred by the forged document.[899] But if the forgery consists only in signing or sealing as agent but without authority it may be ratified.[900]

8-137 **Notice** The question of notice is discussed under Article 73.

Illustrations

8-138 (1) The owner of deeds entrusts them to an agent, with authority to pledge them for a certain sum. The agent pledges them for a larger sum to a person who takes them in good faith and without notice of the limit on the agent's authority. The owner is not entitled to recover the deeds except on repayment of the full amount advanced on them.[901]

(2) A authorises B, stockbroker, to sell certain shares and entrusts him with the certificates and a blank transfer of the shares for that purpose. B deposits the blank transfer and certificates with his banker as security for an advance to himself. The banker has no title to the shares as against A.[902]

(3) A gives B share certificates and a signed blank transfer, authorising him to borrow not less than £250. B borrows £100. The mortgage is valid, because B was authorised to borrow.[903]

(4) A solicitor is employed to obtain a loan of £100 on a mortgage of certain property, and is entrusted with the title deeds for that purpose. He forges a mortgage deed for £400, and misappropriates the whole sum. The mortgage is void, and the client is not liable to the mortgagee, even to the extent of £100.[904]

Article 86

DEALINGS WITH MONEY AND NEGOTIABLE SECURITIES

8-139 (1) Where an agent, in consideration of an antecedent debt or liability, or for any other valuable consideration, pays or negotiates money or negotiable securities in the agent's possession to a person who receives the same in good faith

---

[1899] 2 Q.B. 205.

[897] See Watts (2002) 2 O.U. Commonwealth L.J. 93 at 99–100. Compare Seavey's notion of inherent agency power, above, para.3-005.

[898] *Watteau v Fenwick* [1893] 1 Q.B. 346, fully discussed above, para.8-077.

[899] Illustration 4.

[900] See above, para.2-059. And a person may be estopped from setting up forgery: ibid.

[901] *Brocklesby v Temperance Building Society* [1895] A.C. 173.

[902] *Fox v Martin* (1895) 64 L.J.Ch. 473; *Hutchison v Colorado Mining Co* (1886) 3 T.L.R. 265. But cf. *Rimmer v Webster* [1902] 2 Ch. 163, Illustration 5 to Article 84; *Fuller v Glyn, Mills, Currie & Co* [1914] 2 K.B. 168 (see above, para.8-126). See also *Tobin v Broadbent* (1947) 75 C.L.R. 378.

[903] *Fry v Smellie* [1912] 3 K.B. 282.

[904] *Painter v Abel* (1863) 2 H. & C. 113; see also *Fox v Hawks* (1879) 13 Ch.D. 822.

and without notice that the agent has not authority so to pay, title in the money or negotiable securities passes that person.

(2) A thing is deemed to be done in good faith within the meaning of this Article when it is in fact done honestly, whether it is done negligently or not.

Comment

Bills of exchange   The position is here regulated by statute: the holder in due course of a negotiable instrument, i.e. a person who receives it in the circumstances specified in Rule (1) of this Article, acquires title to it free from defects in title of prior parties,[905] and subsequent transferees deriving title through a holder in due course have the same rights unless parties to fraud or illegality affecting the bill.[906] The doctrine of constructive notice does not apply in this branch of the law.[907]   **8-140**

Money   Money has been called a "negotiable chattel",[908] and partakes both of the nature of chattels and of the nature of negotiable instruments. When the principal's money is transferred by the agent to a third party but has not yet passed into currency (e.g. coins of a set kept in a case), and the agent has no actual or apparent authority to transfer the property, and none of the exceptions to the maxim *nemo dat quod non habet* apply, it can be recovered at common law, no property having passed.[909] But where it is paid as money for valuable consideration to a person having no notice of the lack of authority (both of these requirements applying in the modified form laid down for bills of exchange[910]), it cannot be recovered, because it has passed into currency.[911] Such money could not normally be identified in any case: but even if it could, the rule would apply.[912]   **8-141**

Illustrations

(1) A, having bought on the Stock Exchange scrip which was issued in England by the agent of a foreign government, and which purported to entitle the bearer, on payment of £100, to receive a bond for that amount, entrusted the scrip to a broker. The broker pledged the scrip as security for a debt owing by himself, the pledgee taking it in good faith and without notice that the broker was not authorised so to pledge it. Held, that the scrip being negotiable in the same   **8-142**

---

[905] Bills of Exchange Act 1882 ss.38 and 29(2); but see s.81 ("not negotiable" crossing). For definition of "holder in due course", see s.29(1) and (2); for definition of "valuable consideration", see s.27(1). For special rules as to bankers, see ss.60, 80, 81A and 82; Cheques Act 1957 s.4 (all as amended by Cheques Act 1992).

[906] Bills of Exchange Act 1882 s.29(3).

[907] Bills of Exchange Act 1882 s.90; see Rule (2) above; *Goodman v Harvey* (1836) 4 A. & E. 870; *Raphael v Bank of England* (1855) 17 C.B. 161; *Jones v Gordon* (1877) 2 App.Cas. 616; Illustration 2. But this simply means that there is no duty to inquire: it may be found as a fact that a person must have been suspicious: cf. Article 73.

[908] *Banque Belge pour l'Etranger v Hambrouck* [1921] 1 K.B. 321 at 329. See Proctor, *Mann on the Legal Aspect of Money* (7th edn), Ch.1.

[909] See Article 88.

[910] As to consideration, see Rule (1) above. As to notice, see Rule (2); *Raphael v Bank of England* (1855) 17 C.B. 161; *Lloyds Bank Ltd v Swiss Bankverein* (1913) 108 L.T. 143; *Nelson v Larholt* [1948] 1 K.B. 339 at 343–344.

[911] *Miller v Race* (1758) 1 Burr. 452 at 457; *Clarke v Shee & Johnson* (1774) 1 Cowp. 197 at 200; *Wookey v Pole* (1820) 4 B. & A. 1 at 7; *Lipkin Gorman v Karpnale Ltd* [1991] 2 A.C. 548. But its proceeds may be recovered from the agent if they are identifiable: see Article 88.

[912] *Miller v Race* (1758) 1 Burr. 452 at 457.

manner as the bond which it represented would be, the pledgee acquired a good title, as against A, to the extent of the pledge.[913]

(2) A broker fraudulently pledged with a banker negotiable securities belonging to various principals, as security for an advance. The banker acted in good faith, but had no knowledge whether the securities were the property of the broker, or whether he had authority to pledge them, or not, and made no inquiries. Held, that the banker had a good title to the securities, as against the principals, to the extent of the advance.[914]

(3) An agent fraudulently applies moneys of his principal in the purchase of overdue bills, which he sells to a company. The company has no title to the bills as against the principal, overdue bills not being negotiable instruments.[915]

Article 87

DISPOSITIONS PROTECTED BY THE FACTORS ACT 1889

8-143   Where a mercantile agent is, with the consent of the owner, in possession of goods, or of the documents of title to goods, any sale, pledge or other disposition of the goods made by the agent when acting in the ordinary course of business of a mercantile agent is as valid as if the agent were expressly authorised by the owner of the goods to make the same: provided that the person taking under the disposition acts in good faith and has not, at the time of the disposition, notice that the agent has not authority to make the same.[916]

Comment

8-144   **Historical**   The Factors Act 1889 is a consolidation, with changes and improvements, of a series of Acts dating from 1823, the general purpose of which was to protect bona fide purchasers in mercantile transactions.[917] It should be noted that it involves making a distinction between such transactions and nonmercantile transactions, a distinction familiar in civil law countries but not prominent in the common law. In general it may be said that the Act both confirmed and altered the law, the latter principally by validating not only unauthorised sales by agents, which would often have been effective at common law if the agent was a person in the business of selling,[918] but also unauthorised pledges, which would not normally be effective under the common law rules.[919] The Acts take their name from the factor, a well-known type of commercial agent of the nineteenth century who regularly

---

[913] *Goodwin v Robarts* (1876) 1 App.Cas. 476; *Rumball v Metropolitan Bank* (1877) 2 Q.B.D. 194; *Edelstein v Schuler* [1902] 2 K.B. 144; *Bechuanaland Exploration Co v London Trading Bank Ltd* [1898] 2 Q.B. 658.

[914] *London Joint Stock Bank v Simmons* [1892] A.C. 201; *Bentinck v London Joint Stock Bank* [1893] 2 Ch. 120; *Mutton v Peat* [1900] 2 Ch. 79; *Lloyds Bank Ltd v Swiss Bankverein* (1913) 108 L.T. 143; cf. *Sheffield v London Joint Stock Bank* (1888) 13 App.Cas. 333.

[915] *Re European Bank Ex p. Oriental Commercial Bank* (1870) L.R. 5 Ch.App. 358. And see Article 90.

[916] Factors Act 1889 s.2(1). cf. Uniform Commercial Code s.2-403(2), a much simpler and wider provision.

[917] See Munday (1977) 6 Anglo-Am.L.Rev. 221 at 243 onwards.

[918] Under the doctrines of apparent authority and apparent ownership: see Articles 83 and 84.

[919] See Stoljar, Ch.5; *Cole v North Western Bank* (1875) L.R. 10 C.P. 354.

dealt with goods in the factor's own name,[920] though that operation was not confined to factors. But the operations of business intermediaries are now conducted in different ways from those in use in the nineteenth century, and the main application of the Act seems nowadays to be in respect of situations of much more casual agency, such as that of a motor car dealer obtaining offers for a customer, or a commercial traveller carrying samples. The term "Factors Act" is therefore in some ways misleading[921]: "Mercantile Agents Act" would give a better indication of the ambit of the legislation, and in some common law jurisdictions titles of this sort are adopted.

It is tempting to think of this provision as a statutory form of the doctrine of apparent authority. This is only true in the most general sense, as it contains specific requirements, connected with a need for fault in the owner, compliance with which would usually be outside the knowledge of the third party. (The same is true of the traditional doctrine of agency of necessity, except that here the requirements do not link to fault in the principal, but rather, to the existence of necessity: this is one of the reasons for doubting it.[922]) The protection conferred by the Act is detailed and specific, and even when combined with the doctrines of apparent authority, apparent ownership and other possible lines of reasoning do not constitute a complete protection for bona fide purchasers such as is found in the laws of some countries.

Alongside the Factors Act existed the common law concept of "market overt". Under this concept a bona fide purchaser in certain markets could acquire title to goods even though they were stolen. It was of very limited application and has now been abolished by statute.[923]

Mercantile agent   The term was introduced by the 1889 Act.[924] The notion of   **8-145**
"mercantile agent" is defined in partly circular terms as "a mercantile agent having, in the customary course of his business as such agent, authority either to sell goods, or to consign goods for the purpose of sale, or to buy goods, or to raise money on the security of goods".[925] This excludes, e.g. mere servants of the owner (such as shop assistants), carriers and warehousemen.[926] But it does not appear that such a person need follow a recognised occupation as commercial agent of a known sort,[927] and a person may be a mercantile agent though acting for one principal only, or for an isolated transaction.[928] However, a person who agrees to find a purchaser

---

920   See above, para.1-046; *Heyman v Flewker* (1863) 13 C.B.(N.S.) 519 at 527–528.
921   See *Rolls Razor Ltd v Cox* [1967] 1 Q.B. 552 at 578.
922   See above, para.4-007.
923   Sale of Goods (Amendment) Act 1994. For the old law see *Benjamin's Sale of Goods* (4th edn), para.7-016 onwards.
924   Previous statutes used the words "agent entrusted". Therefore cases on such statutes should be viewed with caution, though it has been said that the wording of the 1889 Act represents the results of decisions on the earlier wording: *Oppenheimer v Attenborough & Son* [1907] 1 K.B. 510 at 514. Statutes in other jurisdictions also may use the older wording.
925   1889 Act s.1(1).
926   *Lowther v Harris* [1927] 1 K.B. 393, Illustration 3; *Cole v North Western Bank* (1875) L.R. 10 C.P. 354; *Lamb v Attenborough* (1862) 1 B. & S. 831, Illustration 1; *Heyman v Flewker* (1863) 13 C.B.(N.S.) 519.
927   There are dicta to the contrary in *Heyman v Flewker* (1863) 13 C.B.(N.S.) 519; and *Hastings Ltd v Pearson* [1893] 1 Q.B. 62; but the latter case was disapproved in *Weiner v Harris* [1910] 1 K.B. 285. See also *Davey v Paine Bros (Motors) Ltd* [1954] N.Z.L.R. 1122.
928   *Lowther v Harris* [1927] 1 K.B. 393; *Weiner v Harris* [1910] 1 K.B. 285; *Heyman v Flewker* (1863) 13 C.B.(N.S.) 519; *Mortgage Loan & Finance Co of Australia Ltd v Richards* (1932) 32

for goods for another as a friend is not a mercantile agent on these facts alone,[929] nor is a person who only buys and sells personally.[930] If a person receives goods when not a mercantile agent and subsequently becomes one, the section will not apply unless there is further consent to that person's possession of the goods subsequent to the acquisition of the character of mercantile agent.[931]

8-146 **With the consent of the owner** Such consent is presumed in the absence of evidence to the contrary.[932] Where the agent has, with such consent, been in possession of the goods themselves or documents, a disposition which would have been valid if the consent had continued is valid notwithstanding determination of the consent, provided that the person taking under the disposition had not, at the time thereof, notice that the consent had been determined.[933] Where an agent has obtained possession of documents of title through being or having been, with such consent, in possession of the goods themselves or of other documents of title to them, the agent's possession of the former documents is deemed to be with such consent.[934] Where the owner consents to possession by the agent, the operation of the Act is not defeated by the fact that the consent was obtained by deception or fraud,[935] unless the owner did not intend the agent to have possession at all.[936]

The word "owner" may cover a person who would not strictly be so called, but without whose concurrence the goods cannot be sold even by the true owner, e.g. a pledgee whose right of sale has not arisen who returns documents of title to the pledgor under a trust receipt.[937]

8-147 **In possession** It is provided that a person is deemed to be in possession of goods or documents when they are in that person's actual custody, or are held by any other person subject to his control, or on that person's behalf.[938] It has been held that a person who pledges goods for less than their value retains sufficient control to make a further pledge for the balance valid against the principal.[939] But if that person simply pledges the goods twice and the first pledgee has possession, this provision

S.R.(N.S.W.) 50; *Thoresen v Capital Credit Corp Ltd* (1962) 37 D.L.R. (2d) 317 at 327 (decision reversed (1964) 43 D.L.R. (2d) 94); *Fairfax Gerrard Holdings Ltd v Capital Bank Plc* [2006] EWHC 3439 (Comm); [2007] 1 Lloyd's Rep. 171 at [31]; reversed on other grounds [2007] EWCA Civ 1226; [2008] 1 Lloyd's Rep. 297; [2008] 1 All E.R. (Comm) 632.

[929] *Budberg v Jerwood & Ward* (1934) 51 T.L.R. 99; *Kendrick v Sotheby & Co* (1967) 111 S.J. 470.
[930] *Belvoir Finance Co Ltd v Harold G. Cole & Co Ltd* [1969] 1 W.L.R. 1877; *Fadallah v Pollak* [2013] EWHC 3159 (QB) at [35].
[931] *Heap v Motorists Advisory Agency Ltd* [1923] 1 K.B. 577 at 588.
[932] 1889 Act s.2(4).
[933] See s.2(2); cf. Article 121.
[934] 1889 Act s.2(3).
[935] *Whitehorn Bros v Davison* [1911] 1 K.B. 463; *Pearson v Rose & Young Ltd* [1951] 1 K.B. 275; *Folkes v King* [1923] 1 K.B. 282; *Du Jardin v Beadman Bros* [1952] 2 Q.B. 712; *Ingram v Little* [1961] 1 Q.B. 31 at 70.
[936] *Pearson v Rose & Young Ltd* [1951] 1 K.B. 275; *Stadium Finance Ltd v Robbins* [1962] 2 Q.B. 664. This might be the case where the agent obtains the goods as the result of a mistake on the part of the owner as to the agent's identity, where such identity is material: see *Lake v Simmons* [1927] A.C. 487. See also Illustration 4.
[937] *Lloyds Bank Ltd v Bank of America National Trust and Savings Association* [1938] 2 K.B. 147, Illustration 6; see also *Beverley Acceptances Ltd v Oakley* [1982] R.T.R. 417, Illustration 10.
[938] 1889 Act s.1(2). See *Brown & Co v Bedford Pantechnicon Co* (1889) 5 T.L.R. 449.
[939] *Portalis v Tetley* (1867) L.R. 5 Eq. 140.

cannot be used to validate the second pledge against the first pledgee.[940] The possession must be held by the agent in the capacity as a mercantile agent: the fact that the person in possession is a mercantile agent makes no difference if the agent is not in possession of the goods for a purpose in some way connected with being a mercantile agent, e.g. where goods are deposited for repair with a person who is also a dealer, or let to a dealer on hire purchase.[941] This is a strong limitation: but if it were not so, when a furnished house was let to an auctioneer he or she might acquire power to dispose of the furniture.[942] But it does not seem that it is necessary for the owner to have contemplated that the agent would dispose of all the goods: thus where pictures were sent to the owner of a gallery, some for sale but some for display only, the Act was held to apply to all.[943]

Goods The term includes wares and merchandise,[944] but not certificates of stock.[945] It was suggested in *Pearson v Rose & Young Ltd*[946] that where a person obtained possession of a car with the consent of the owner but of the registration document without such consent, that person had not obtained "goods" with the owner's consent because "goods" in the Act means in this connection the car together with the registration document.[947] But this reasoning was not accepted in *Stadium Finance Ltd v Robbins*[948] and *Pearson v Rose & Young Ltd* can be otherwise explained (though the alternative explanation is equally unsatisfactory).[949]

8-148

Documents of title to goods This expression includes any bill of lading, dock warrant, warehouse keeper's certificate, and warrant or order for the delivery of goods, and any other document used in the ordinary course of business as proof of the possession or control of goods, or authorising, or purporting to authorise, either by indorsement or by delivery, the possessor of the document to transfer to receive the goods thereby represented.[950] This is wider than the notion of "document of title" at common law, which is effectively confined to bills of lading, in that it could cover

8-149

---

[940] *Beverley Acceptances Ltd v Oakley* [1982] R.T.R. 417.

[941] *Staffs Motor Guarantee Ltd v British Motor Wagon Co Ltd* [1934] 2 K.B. 305; *Lowther v Harris* [1927] 1 K.B. 393; *Pearson v Rose & Young Ltd* [1951] 1 K.B. 275; *Stadium Finance Ltd v Robbins* [1962] 2 Q.B. 664; *Astley Industrial Trust Ltd v Miller* [1968] 2 All E.R. 36; *Belvoir Finance Co Ltd v Harold G. Cole & Co Ltd* [1969] 1 W.L.R. 1877; *Henderson v Prosser* [1982] C.L.Y. 21 (car left for valeting); *Schafhauser v Shaffer and National Finance Co* [1943] 3 D.L.R. 656; *Universal Guarantee Pty Ltd v Metters Ltd* [1966] W.A.R. 74 ("display or return"); *McManus v Eastern Ford Sales Ltd* (1981) 128 D.L.R. (3d) 246; *Fadallah v Pollak* [2013] EWHC 3159 (QB) at [53]. The criticism of the *Staffs Motor Guarantee* case in *Pacific Motor Auctions Pty Ltd v Motor Credits (Hire Finance) Ltd* [1965] A.C. 867 applies only to the point in relation to s.25(1) of the Sale of Goods Act 1893 (now s.24 of 1979 Act).

[942] See *Cole v North Western Bank* (1875) L.R. 10 C.P. 354 at 369, per Blackburn J.

[943] *Moody v Pall Mall Deposit & Fowarding Co Ltd* (1917) 33 T.L.R. 306; sed quaere (an inadequately reported case). See also *Fuentes v Montis* (1868) L.R. 3 C.P. 268 at 284; *Turner v Sampson* (1911) 27 T.L.R. 200, Illustration 5; *Pearson v Rose & Young Ltd* [1951] 1 K.B. 275 at 288. But cf. *Stadium Finance Ltd v Robbins* [1962] 2 Q.B. 664 at 674, on which see Hornby (1962) 25 M.L.R. 719.

[944] 1889 Act s.1(3).

[945] *Freeman v Appleyard* (1862) 32 L.J.Ex. 175.

[946] *Pearson v Rose & Young Ltd* [1951] 1 K.B. 275.

[947] See esp. at 290.

[948] *Stadium Finance Ltd v Robbins* [1962] 2 Q.B. 664. See also (1951) 67 L.Q.R. 3; Powell, pp.228–229; *Paris v Goodwin* [1954] N.Z.L.R. 823.

[949] See below, para.8-153.

[950] 1889 Act s.1(4).

documents incapable of transferring constructive possession even by attornment.[951] A motor vehicle registration document is in England not a document of title.[952]

8-150   **Sale, pledge or other disposition**   The meaning of "sale" is clear from the Sale of Goods Act 1979.[953] It should be noted that there is not, as there is in other provisions,[954] any requirement of delivery.[955] "Pledge" includes any contract pledging or giving a lien or security on goods, whether in consideration of an original advance, or of any further or continuing advance, or of any pecuniary liability.[956] A pledge of the documents of title to goods is deemed to be a pledge of the goods.[957] The Act thus applies to pledges for antecedent debts: but where the goods are pledged, without authority, for an antecedent debt or liability of the pledgor, the pledgee acquires no further right to the goods than could have been enforced by the pledgor at the time of the pledge.[958] Where the goods are pledged without authority in consideration of the delivery or transfer of other goods or documents of title to goods, or of a negotiable security, the pledgee acquires no right or interest in the goods so pledged in excess of the value of the goods, documents or security when so delivered or transferred in exchange.[959] It has been held in Canada that the Act applies where the goods are pledged along with other goods to secure a loan based on the total value of all the goods so pledged.[960]

8-151   **Other disposition**   Sales and pledges have consideration: but it seems that "other dispositions" must equally not be gratuitous, for it is provided that the consideration necessary for the validity of a sale, pledge or other disposition may be any valuable consideration.[961] But it would in any case be rare for a gratuitous transfer to be in the normal course of business of a mercantile agent. Entrusting goods to an auctioneer for sale is not a pledge or other disposition within the meaning of the Act, though the auctioneer makes advances on the goods.[962]

8-152   **Time and effect of disposition**   It seems that the sale, pledge or other disposi-

---

[951] See *Benjamin's Sale of Goods* (10th edn), para.7-036.
[952] *Joblin v Watkins & Roseveare Motors Ltd* [1949] 1 All E.R. 47; see also *Pearson v Rose & Young Ltd* [1951] 1 K.B. 275; *Central Newbury Car Auctions Ltd v Unity Finance Ltd* [1957] 1 Q.B. 371, Illustration 3 to Article 84; *Moorgate Mercantile Co Ltd v Twitchings* [1977] A.C. 890, Illustration 7 to Article 84; *J. Sargent (Garages) Ltd v Motor Auctions (West Bromwich) Ltd* [1977] R.T.R. 121; *Beverley Acceptances Ltd v Oakley* [1982] R.T.R. 417. Lord Denning MR consistently took a different view: ibid.
[953] Sale of Goods Act 1979 s.2.
[954] e.g. Sale of Goods Act 1979 ss.24 and 25.
[955] But it may be that the property would only pass by delivery: *Benjamin's Sale of Goods* (10th edn), para.7-048.
[956] 1889 Act s.1(5).
[957] 1889 Act s.3; Illustration 8. The transfer of a document may be by indorsement, or where the document is by custom or by its express terms transferable by delivery, or makes the goods deliverable to the bearer, then by delivery: s.11.
[958] 1889 Act s.4; Illustration 8.
[959] 1889 Act s.5.
[960] *Thoresen v Capital Credit Corp* (1964) 43 D.L.R. (2d) 94; and see *Kaltenbach, Fischer & Co v Lewis and Peat* (1885) 10 App.Cas. 617; but cf. *City Bank of Sydney v Barden* (1908) 9 S.R. (N.S.W.) 41. See further *Benjamin's Sale of Goods* (10th edn), para.7-049 onwards.
[961] See s.5. "Consideration" includes exchange: ibid. As to "disposition", see *Worcester Works Finance Ltd v Cooden Engineering Co Ltd* [1972] 1 Q.B. 210.
[962] *Waddington & Sons v Neale & Sons* (1907) 96 L.T. 786; *Roache v Australian Mercantile Land & Finance Co Ltd (No.2)* [1966] 1 N.S.W.L.R. 384.

tion must occur at the same time as the possession is held.[963] It also seems that the effect of the Act is only to transfer such title as the person who entrusted the goods had.[964]

Acting in the ordinary course of business of a mercantile agent[965]   This require-   **8-153**
ment must be distinguished from the requirement that the agent have authority to deal with goods in the customary course of business as a mercantile agent. If an agent has no such authority, the agent is not a mercantile agent within the Act: but even if the agent is, the section may not apply, because the agent acts outside the ordinary course of business, e.g. by selling outside business premises, or out of business hours.[966] But it is irrelevant whether or not the agent sells in his or her own name, and it seems that provided the general requirements relating to sales by mercantile agents are fulfilled, it is not relevant whether the agent is acting within the ordinary course of business of the particular type of mercantile agent, nor whether the circumstances of the transaction in question are normal.[967] Thus a diamond broker may be acting in the ordinary course of business of a mercantile agent within the meaning of the Act in pledging diamonds entrusted to the broker for sale, although by the custom of the trade such a broker has no authority to pledge diamonds so entrusted.[968] But it is not in the ordinary course of business for a mercantile agent to ask a friend to pawn goods entrusted to the agent: in order that the pledgee may be protected, the agent must pledge the goods personally, or by a servant or agent employed in the ordinary course of business.[969] A sale by a dealer on terms that the price is to be paid direct to one of the dealer's creditors would probably not be in the ordinary course of business[970] nor a forced sale to provide security for a debt owed by the agent,[971] nor a sale the profits of which went to the agent,[972] nor a sale of an entire stock-in-trade[973]; nor, perhaps, in some cases, the sale of a car in England without the registration document.[974]

In each case the special facts of the transaction may, however, be evidence that

---

[963] *Beverley Acceptances Ltd v Oakley* [1982] R.T.R. 417, Illustration 10; *Fairfax Gerrard Holdings Ltd v Capital Bank Plc* [2006] EWHC 3439 (Comm); [2007] 1 Lloyd's Rep. 171 at [31]; reversed on other grounds [2007] EWCA Civ 1226; [2008] 1 Lloyd's Rep. 297; *Fadallah v Pollak* [2013] EWHC 3159 (QB) at [55].

[964] cf. *National Employers' Mutual General Insurance Ltd v Jones* [1990] 1 A.C. 24, a case on s.25(1) of the Sale of Goods Act 1979; *Cook v Rodgers* (1946) 46 S.R.(N.S.W.) 229.

[965] Ivamy (1951) 18 *Solicitor* 28 at 31; Dal Pont, para.21.26 onwards.

[966] *Oppenheimer v Attenborough & Son* [1908] 1 K.B. 221 at 230–231 (Illustration 7). But see *Newtons of Wembley Ltd v Williams* [1965] 1 Q.B. 560, where the sale of a second-hand car in Warren Street in London was held to be within the ordinary course of business.

[967] *Janesich v Attenborough & Son* (1910) 102 L.T. 605; *Ceres Orchard Partnership v Fiatagri Australia Pty Ltd* [1995] 1 N.Z.L.R. 112 (citing further authority).

[968] *Oppenheimer v Attenborough & Son* [1908] 1 K.B. 221.

[969] 1889 Act s.6; *De Gorter v Attenborough & Son* (1904) 21 T.L.R. 19.

[970] See *Lloyds & Scottish Finance Ltd v Williamson* [1965] 1 W.L.R. 404; *Biggs v Evans* [1894] 1 Q.B. 88 (the other point on which the Act was excluded was doubted in *Turner v Sampson* (1911) 27 T.L.R. 200). But a sale on credit could be: *Tingey v Chambers* [1967] N.Z.L.R. 785.

[971] *Motor Credits (Hire Finance) Ltd v Pacific Motor Auctions Pty Ltd* (1963) 109 C.L.R. 87 (reversed on other grounds [1965] A.C. 867); *Nash v Barnes* [1922] N.Z.L.R. 303.

[972] *Raffoul v Esanda Ltd* [1970] 3 N.S.W.R. 8.

[973] *Mortimer-Rae v Barthel* (1979) 105 D.L.R. (3d) 289.

[974] *Pearson v Rose & Young Ltd* [1951] 1 K.B. 275; *Stadium Finance Ltd v Robbins* [1962] 2 Q.B. 664; *Lambert v G. & C. Finance Corp* (1963) 107 S.J. 666. Sed quaere: should this be a matter relevant to the buyer's good faith? cf. *Folkes v King* [1923] 1 K.B. 282; *Oppenheimer v Attenborough & Son* [1908] 1 K.B. 221; *Janesich v Attenborough & Son* (1910) 102 L.T. 605; *Durham v Asser* (1968) 67 D.L.R. (2d) 574; *Astley Industrial Trust v Miller* [1968] 2 All E.R. 36 (document left with licens-

the receiver did not act in good faith, e.g. if there is an unduly high rate of interest,[975] the price was unduly low,[976] or it is well known that such an agent has not authority to make the type of disposition involved.[977] Indeed, the demarcation between matters of ordinary course of business and good faith is not clear, and they do not always operate as separate requirements.

In *Pearson v Rose & Young Ltd*[978] it was suggested that where a car dealer obtains possession of a car with the consent of the owner, but obtains the registration document without such consent, a sale by him of car and registration document is not in the ordinary course of business. This is dubious: provided the book was supplied to the buyer, its provenance should be irrelevant, for the sale is perfectly regular on its face.[979] The case can be explained on other grounds, but these are equally unsatisfactory.[980] It was followed in *Stadium Finance Ltd v Robbins*,[981] but in this case it appears that the buyer was given neither the registration document nor the ignition key (which the owner had retained) when he bought the car, which might perhaps indicate that the sale was not in the ordinary course of business.[982]

8-154   **Good faith and absence of notice**   This must be proved by the third party.[983] "Good faith" is not defined, but on the analogy of the Sale of Goods Act[984] it may be assumed that the standard is one of honesty: a thing is done in good faith if it is done honestly, whether or not negligently. It is often said that constructive notice is not relevant in commercial transactions.[985] The court may, however, infer that the third party must have known of the lack of authority, e.g. in the circumstances discussed above; and in general the courts have in other contexts, especially that of constructive trust, imposed something akin to a duty to inquire.[986] In the case of a disposition by two or more persons who are acting in the transaction as partners, want of good faith on the part of any one of them may deprive all of the protection

---

ing authority for taxing purposes). As to different practice in Australia, see *Magnussen v Flanagan* [1981] 2 N.S.W.L.R. 926. As to sale on part-exchange basis, see *Davey v Paine Bros (Motors) Ltd* [1954] N.Z.L.R. 1122.

975 *Janesich v Attenborough & Son* (1910) 102 L.T. 605.

976 *Heap v Motorists Advisory Agency Ltd* [1923] 1 K.B. 577 at 591; *Davey v Paine Bros (Motors) Ltd* [1954] N.Z.L.R. 1122 at 1130; *Summers v Havard* [2011] EWCA Civ 764; [2011] 2 Lloyd's Rep. 283.

977 *Oppenheimer v Attenborough & Son* [1908] 1 K.B. 221, Illustration 7.

978 *Pearson v Rose & Young Ltd* [1951] 1 K.B. 275.

979 See (1951) 67 L.Q.R. 3.

980 See above, para.8-148.

981 *Stadium Finance Ltd v Robbins* [1962] 2 Q.B. 664. See Hornby (1962) 25 M.L.R. 719; Thornely [1962] C.L.Y. 139; (1972) 78 L.Q.R. 468.

982 See above, fn.974 and text.

983 *Heap v Motorists Advisory Agency Ltd* [1923] 1 K.B. 577; *Stadium Finance Ltd v Robbins* [1962] 2 Q.B. 664 at 673. Yet under s.23 of the Sale of Goods Act 1979, the burden is on the original owner: *Whitehorn Bros v Davison* [1911] 1 K.B. 463. See in general Dal Pont, para.21.30; *Fairfax Gerrard Holdings Ltd v Capital Bank Plc* [2006] EWHC 3439 (Comm); [2007] 1 Lloyd's Rep. 171 at [31]; reversed on other grounds [2007] EWCA Civ 1226; [2008] 1 Lloyd's Rep. 297; [2008] 1 All E.R. (Comm) 632.

984 Sale of Goods Act s.61(3). See also *Barclays Bank Ltd v TOSG Trust Fund Ltd* [1984] B.C.L.C. 1 at 18 ("genuinely and honestly in the circumstances of the case"); *Ceres Orchard Partnership v Fiatagri Australia Pty Ltd* [1995] 1 N.Z.L.R. 112 at 117 ("must have known or must have suspected and wilfully shut his eyes to the means of knowledge available").

985 See Article 73; *Re Funduk and Horncastle* (1973) 39 D.L.R. (3d) 94.

986 See *Summers v Havard* [2011] EWCA Civ 764; [2011] 2 Lloyd's Rep. 283. Comments to Articles 73 and 116. As to knowledge of adverse claims as preventing bona fides see *Carl Zeiss Stiftung v Herbert Smith & Co (No.2)* [1969] 2 Ch. 276.

of the statute.[987] It has been held that if the disponee has had possession of documents that would, if read, have pointed to a lack of authority in the disponor, the disponee will not get the protection of the Act.[988]

Undisclosed principal It should be noted that the Act applies notwithstanding that the third party believes the agent to be the owner of the goods: what is relevant is that the agent is a mercantile agent in possession, etc. not that the third party thinks the person is.[989] Thus the Act applies to agents of undisclosed as well as disclosed principals.

8-155

Miscellaneous An agreement made with a mercantile agent through a clerk or other person authorised in the ordinary course of business to make contracts of sale or pledge on the agent's behalf is deemed to be an agreement with the agent.[990] The Act is in amplification and not in derogation of other powers of an agent.[991] But nothing in it authorises agents to exceed or depart from their authority as between them and their principals, or exempts them from any liability, civil or criminal, for so doing[992]; or prevents the owner from recovering goods from an agent or a trustee in bankruptcy of the agent before a sale or pledge; or from redeeming pledged goods, before sale, on satisfying the claim for which they were pledged and paying to the agent, if required, money in respect of which the agent would have a lien; or from recovering from a pledgee any balance in the pledgee's hands as the proceeds of sale, after deducting the amount of any lien[993]; or from recovering the price agreed to be paid by the buyer.[994]

8-156

The protection given by ss.24 and 25 of the Sale of Goods Act 1979 to dispositions by sellers and buyers in possession after sale extends to dispositions by them through mercantile agents; and the peculiar wording of s.25(1) leads to the apparent conclusion that where a buyer is in possession after sale, advantage can only be taken of its provisions if the buyer sells, though a private person, in the ordinary course of business of a mercantile agent.[995] Therefore cases on the application of this section may be relevant to the interpretation of s.2 of the Factors Act 1889.[996]

Where an owner of goods has given possession of the goods to an agent for the purpose of consignment or sale, or has shipped goods in the name of the agent, and the consignee of the goods has not had knowledge that the agent is not the owner of the goods, the consignee, in respect of advances made to or for the use of the

---

[987] *Oppenheimer v Frazer & Wyatt* [1907] 2 K.B. 50.

[988] *Fairfax Gerrard Holdings Ltd v Capital Bank Plc* [2006] EWHC 3439 (Comm): [2007] 1 Lloyd's Rep. 171 at [31]; reversed on other grounds [2007] EWCA Civ 1226; [2008] 1 Lloyd's Rep. 297.

[989] *Oppenheimer v Attenborough & Son* [1908] 1 K.B. 221 at 229 (Illustration 7); cf. *Boyter v Thomson* [1995] 2 A.C. 628. *Greer v Downs* [1927] 2 K.B. 28 might have been another example, had the defendant chosen to rely on the Factors Act 1889.

[990] 1889 Act s.6.

[991] 1889 Act s.13.

[992] 1889 Act s.12(1).

[993] 1889 Act s.12(2).

[994] 1889 Act s.12(3).

[995] See *Newtons of Wembley Ltd v Williams* [1965] 1 Q.B. 560, a case on s.9 of the Factors Act 1889, which is largely reproduced in s.25(1) of the Sale of Goods Act 1979. But cf. *Langmead v Thyer Rubber Co Ltd* [1947] S.A.S.R. 29; *Jeffcott v Andrew Motors Ltd* [1960] N.Z.L.R. 721.

[996] e.g. *Newtons of Wembley Ltd v Williams* [1965] 1 Q.B. 560 (sale of second-hand car in street market); *Pacific Motor Auctions Pty Ltd v Motor Credits (Hire Finance) Ltd* [1965] A.C. 867; *Fadallah v Pollak* [2013] EWHC 3159 (QB) at [49]. See in general *Benjamin's Sale of Goods* (10th edn), para.7-055 onwards.

agent, has the same lien on the goods as if the agent were the owner of the goods, and may transfer any such lien to another person; but this does not limit or affect the validity of any sale, pledge or other disposition by a mercantile agent.[997]

8-157 **Exclusion of the Act** It is not possible to contract out of the provisions of the Factors Act; but if a mercantile agent is in possession as buyer of the goods and not as mercantile agent they will not apply.[998]

Illustrations

8-158 (1) A wine merchant's clerk, permitted to have the possession for the purpose of his master's business of dock warrants for wine belonging to his master, fraudulently pledges the warrants for an advance to himself. The transaction is not protected by the Factors Act, because the clerk is not a mercantile agent within the meaning of the Act.[999]

(2) A, a manufacturing jeweller, supplies jewellery to B, a retail jeweller, on sale or return, on the terms that it is to remain the property of A until it is sold or paid for—B, after selling it, to retain half the difference between the cost price and selling price, by way of remuneration, and to remit the balance of the proceeds to A. B is merely A's agent for sale, and therefore a mercantile agent within the meaning of the Act.[1000]

(3) L wishes to sell furniture and a tapestry. He stores it in a house and engages P, an art dealer who has a shop nearby, to sell it on commission: he permits P to occupy a flat in the house and to show the items to customers. P is a mercantile agent but is not in possession of the goods. P pretends that he has sold the tapestry to W, and L permits him to remove it. P sells it to H. He was at the time of sale in possession of the tapestry with L's consent and the sale is valid.[1001]

(4) An agent employed by a foreign principal to negotiate sales in London obtains an offer from A, which the principal accepts. The principal specially indorses to A the bill of lading for the goods, and sends it to the agent to be exchanged for A's acceptance. The agent, without the principal's authority, agrees with A to cancel the contract, and subsequently induces him to indorse the bill of lading by representing that it was specially indorsed by mistake, and then, having obtained possession of the goods by means of the bill of lading, pledges them for an advance. The pledge is not protected by the Factors Act, because the agent did not obtain possession of the goods with the consent of the principal. The principal, therefore, is entitled to recover the goods from the pledgee.[1002]

(5) The owner of a picture asks a dealer to hang it in his gallery and report any

---

[997] Factors Act 1889 s.7. See *Mildred, Goyeneche & Co v Maspons y Hermano* (1883) 8 App.Cas. 874 at 883; see Article 69.

[998] See *Weiner v Gill* [1906] 2 K.B. 574; *Kempler v Bravingtons* (1925) 41 T.L.R. 519; cf. *Weiner v Harris* [1910] 1 K.B. 285, Illustration 2. This distinction can be criticised: see Stoljar, p.124.

[999] *Lamb v Attenborough* (1862) 1 B. & S. 831. See also *Farquharson Bros & Co v King & Co* [1902] A.C. 325, Illustration 6 to Article 84.

[1000] *Weiner v Harris* [1910] 1 K.B. 285; cf. *Weiner v Gill* [1906] 2 K.B. 574; *Universal Guarantee Pty Ltd v Metters Ltd* [1966] W.A.R. 74 (electrical goods "on consignment").

[1001] *Lowther v Harris* [1927] 1 K.B. 393.

[1002] *Vaughan v Moffatt* (1868) 38 L.J.Ch. 144.

offers he may receive for it. The dealer sells it and disappears. The sale is valid.[1003]

(6) A company pledged bills of lading with A, a bank, as security for bills of exchange or advances. A handed the bills of lading back to the company upon terms contained in trust receipts, whereby the company was authorised to sell the goods and undertook to hold the proceeds in trust for A. The company pledged the bills of lading with B, a bank, to secure advances. B acted in good faith and without notice that the company was not entitled so to pledge the bills of lading. A claimed the bills of lading from B. Held, that A was owner of the goods represented by the bills of lading within the meaning of the Factors Act; but that the company was a mercantile agent in possession of the bills of lading within the meaning of the Act and that the pledge to B was valid.[1004]

(7) A diamond broker asks a diamond dealer to let him have some diamonds to show to two firms of diamond merchants to whom he says he thinks he can sell them. The dealer lets him have diamonds for this purpose, but the broker, instead of showing them to any merchant, pledges them. The pledge is valid.[1005]

(8) A broker is authorised to sell goods, and is entrusted with the bill of lading for them by their owner. By means of the bill of lading he obtains dock warrants for the goods, and without the authority of the principal, pledges the warrants with his banker as security for an overdraft, the banker taking them in good faith, and without notice that in so pledging them he is exceeding his authority. Before receiving notice of the want of authority, the banker, on the faith of the pledge, permits the overdraft to be increased. So far as concerns the overdraft existing at the time of the pledge, the principal is only bound by the pledge to the extent of any lien the broker had on the goods at that time, and may redeem the goods upon payment to that extent, and payment of the amount overdrawn since the date of the pledge. If the broker has a lien in excess of the full amount of the overdraft, the principal must, if required, also pay to the broker the amount of the excess before he is entitled to redeem the goods.[1006]

(9) A factor is entrusted with the possession of goods for sale. The principal revokes his authority, and demands the return of the goods. The factor refuses to return the goods, and then fraudulently sells and delivers them to a person who purchases them in good faith, and without notice that the factor has no authority to sell them, or that he is in possession of the goods without the consent of the owner. The principal is bound by the sale, but may sue in his own name for the price, subject to any right of set-off the purchaser may have against the factor.[1007]

(10) A person pledges two cars and possession is transferred to the pledgee. He subsequently asks to borrow the keys and one registration document (the other not being available), ostensibly to show them to insurance

---

[1003] *Turner v Sampson* (1911) 27 T.L.R. 200.
[1004] *Lloyds Bank Ltd v Bank of America National Trust and Savings Association* [1938] 2 K.B. 147. See *Benjamin's Sale of Goods* (10th edn), para.18-288.
[1005] *Oppenheimer v Attenborough & Son* [1908] 1 K.B. 221.
[1006] 1889 Act s.12(2).
[1007] 1889 Act s.12(3).

representatives. He actually shows the car to representatives of a finance house; and by virtue of having done so he is later able to execute a bill of sale in favour of the finance house. The disposition is not protected by the Factors Act as (a) he never regained possession of the goods; (b) the registration document is not a document of title; (c) the disposition did not occur at the same time as any possession that he might have had.[1008]

Article 88

PRINCIPAL'S RIGHTS TO RECOVER PROPERTY, MONEY, AND IN RESPECT OF OTHER BENEFITS CONFERRED—RESTITUTIONARY CLAIMS

8-159   (1)   Subject to the provisions of Articles 83–87, where an agent disposes of the property or money of the principal in a manner not authorised, ratified or otherwise valid, the principal is entitled, as against the agent and third parties, to recover that property or money, or the proceeds of that property or money, wherever they may be found, provided that they can be traced in accordance with the rules of common law and equity,[1009] and the recipient can make out no defence to the claim.

(2)   Subject again to Articles 83–87, where an agent otherwise disposes of property or money on behalf of the principal under circumstances that, if made by the principal, would give rise to a restitutionary claim in the principal, the principal may assert such a claim against the third party.

Comment

8-160   The circumstances in which a third party might claim to retain property the subject of an unauthorised disposition by an agent have been covered in the preceding Articles. This Article is concerned with the other side of the coin, when can a principal succeed in a restitutionary claim against a third party? In theory, at least, such claims could include not only property and money but other types of benefit conferred by an agent at the principal's expense. It is not practicable to treat in any depth here the substantive requirements of the range of claims that might be brought within the law of restitution. The use of the phrase "restitutionary claims" to cover the group of claims available for the recovery of both property and money is itself controversial, since not all commentators treat property claims as restitutionary, but it is a convenient expression and there are undoubted connections between them.[1010] But no attempt is made here to engage with the idea that a concept of unjust enrichment can be used to claim mere increases in a defendant's general wealth causally connected with the claimant, without the claimant needing to show a particular transfer of property or a particular payment made by or on behalf of the claimant and a corresponding receipt by the defendant. An expanded concept of unjust

---

[1008] *Beverley Acceptances Ltd v Oakley* [1982] R.T.R. 417.

[1009] See Comment. The literature on this topic is extensive. See *Lewin on Trusts* (20th edn), Ch.44; Goff and Jones, *Law of Unjust Enrichment* (9th edn), Ch.7; Burrows, *Law of Restitution* (3rd edn), Chs 6 and 7; Lionel Smith, *Law of Tracing* (1997); Birks, "The Necessity of a Unitary Law of Tracing", in *Making Commercial Law* (Cranston ed., 1997), p.239; Lionel Smith (2009) 125 L.Q.R. 338; Burrows (2001) 117 L.Q.R. 412. As to the distinction between "following" and "tracing", see *Foskett v McKeown* [2001] 1 A.C. 102 at 127.

[1010] See P. Watts "Unjust Enrichment—The Potion that Induces Well-Meaning Sloppiness of Thought" [2016] C.L.P. 289.

enrichment of that sort appears now to have gone into retreat.[1011] Reflecting the underlying analytical controversies of the field, the material in this Article should be read with that in Article 96, dealing with particular aspects of the rights of a principal where third parties become implicated in an agent's breach of duty. Finally by way of introduction, it should be noted that previous editions of this book addressed in this section the risks that principals were exposed to when their agents became subject to the law of distress. All this law in relation to commercial tenancies has, from April 6, 2014, been swept away by the Tribunals, Courts and Enforcement Act 2007 s.71, and the replacement regime does not permit the seizure of goods not owned by the tenant.

Rule (1): Common law Where an agent holds the property or money of the principal and disposes of it in a manner authorised, title passes. So also it passes by virtue of the special rules of the law of agency in cases of apparent authority,[1012] and where one of the exceptions to the rule *nemo dat quod non habet* applies.[1013] Otherwise where the dealing is unauthorised the property or money remains the property of the principal, who may have the right to recover it (and in some circumstances its traceable substitutes) at common law not only from the original recipient but from subsequent recipients.[1014] It matters not whether the agent exceeds the agent's mandate dishonestly or mistakenly.[1015] The principal's rights to reclaim remain so long as the property remains identifiable,[1016] whether tangible[1017] or intangible,[1018] and in some cases if it is converted into a different form of property,[1019] provided that there is no admixture of other property or money (when it may be necessary to have recourse to equity[1020]). The primary action for enforcing the principal's rights in relation to chattels is that of conversion,[1021] and in the case of money an action in money had and received, though this latter action really affirms property in the defendant, because money is not normally identifiable.[1022] Either of these actions lies against recipients who have parted with what they have received; but in the case of the restitutionary action a defence of

8-161

[1011] See *Swynson v Lowick Rose LLP* [2017] UKSC 32; [2018] A.C. 313 (noted P. Watts, "Lucky escapes" (2017) 133 L.Q.R. 542). cf. P. Birks, *Unjust Enrichment*, 2nd edn (Oxford Univerty Press, 2005), Ch.4; and *Menelaou v Bank of Cyprus UK Ltd* [2015] UKSC 66; [2016] A.C. 176.

[1012] Articles 72 and 83.

[1013] Articles 83–87.

[1014] *Lang v Smyth* (1831) 7 Bing. 284 at 292; *Farquharson Bros & Co v King & Co* [1902] A.C. 325. The principal may have sufficient title to trace where the agent draws money from the principal's bank account, for the bank's indebtedness is a chose in action belonging to the principal: see *Lipkin Gorman v Karpnale Ltd* [1991] 2 A.C. 548. Where the transfer is authorised or ratified, the principal may of course sometimes be able to trace against the *agent*; but that is not relevant in this context. See Article 43.

[1015] For instances of mistaken excess of authority, see *R v Vincent* (1852) 16 Jur. 457; and *J.S. Brooksbank & Co (Australasia) Ltd v EXFTX Ltd* (2009) 10 N.Z.C.L.C. 264,520, Illustration 8.

[1016] *Taylor v Plumer* (1815) 3 M. & S. 562 at 575 (Illustration 1). (It is by no means clear that this is really a common law case, though it is normally treated as such.) See Smith [1995] L.M.C.L.Q. 240.

[1017] e.g. coins in a bag: *Taylor v Plumer* (1815) 3 M. & S. 562 at 565.

[1018] *Banque Belge pour l'Etranger v Hambrouck* [1921] 1 K.B. 321 (unmixed bank balance); *Agip (Africa) Ltd v Jackson* [1990] Ch. 265; [1991] Ch. 547 (effect of bank clearing mechanisms).

[1019] e.g. *Taylor v Plumer* (1815) 3 M. & S. 562 (draft converted into stock and bullion). An unpaid debt in respect of the sale of the property would presumably be recoverable: cf. *Re Wood Ex p. Boden* (1873) 28 L.T. 174; and see Illustration 8.

[1020] See below, para.8-162.

[1021] e.g. *Farquharson Bros & Co v King & Co* [1902] A.C. 325; *Gompertz v Cook* (1903) 20 T.L.R. 106.

[1022] See *Calland v Lloyd* (1840) 6 M. & W. 26; *Marsh v Keating* (1834) 1 Bing.N.C. 198; *Scott v Sur-*

change of position is available to a recipient who has changed position in good faith in such a way that it would be inequitable to require him or her to make restitution in whole or in part.[1023] In the past there have been doubts in relation to money claims as to whether they can lie against a recipient subsequent to the first.[1024] If they do, as now seems likely in relation to unauthorised payments, they should not lie against a person who gave value in good faith[1025] or against such a recipient who was only a conduit of the funds.[1026] Nor should there be an entitlement to profits made. Recent authority however suggests that profits can be recovered, at least where these result from a mere increase in the value of what is traced.[1027] It is easier to justify such a result against knowing recipients than innocent volunteers who by having to account for profits or capital gains may be deprived of the benefits of their skill (or luck).

Claims more readily classifiable as in rem may also be asserted in other ways, such as bankruptcy proceedings, in an action for a declaration,[1028] by way of defence to an action in conversion[1029] and in proceedings regarding the registration of shares.[1030] There is however no general common law action of a proprietary nature, and many of the problems here discussed arise from the difference between the right vindicated and the common law remedies available to support it.

8-162   **Equity**   In equity there is a historically separate right to recover unauthorised distributions of property or money, and to trace into substitute property, and the significance of the latter is greater because equity's mechanisms, which include a lien, can be applied to a mixed fund. It has often been said that equitable restitutionary claims are only triggered by a breach of trust or fiduciary duty. Although that

---

man (1742) Willes 400; *Banque Belge pour l'Etranger v Hambrouck* [1921] 1 K.B. 321, per Atkin L.J; *Primlake Ltd v Matthews Associates* [2006] EWHC 1227 (Ch); [2007] 1 B.C.L.C. 666 at [335]; *Napier v Torbay Holdings Ltd* [2016] NZCA 608. In *Relfo Ltd v Varsani* [2012] EWHC 2168 (Ch) at [88] it was accepted that money had and received might be available against a downstream recipient of the claimant's funds on the basis of but-for causation without using the rules of tracing. This is a surprising conclusion, and the subsequent reasoning in the Court of Appeal is somewhat more cautious: [2014] EWCA Civ 360; [2015] 1 B.C.L.C. 14 (noted Nolan (2015) 131 L.Q.R. 8). This case needs now to be considered in the light of *Investment Trust Companies (In Liquidation) v Revenue and Customs Commissioners* [2017] UKSC 29; [2017] 2 W.L.R. 1200 at [37] and [48].

[1023] *Lipkin Gorman v Karpnale Ltd* [1991] 2 A.C. 548. See McKendrick (1992) 55 M.L.R. 377; Goff and Jones, *Law of Unjust Enrichment* (9th edn), Chs 27 and 30; Burrows, *Law of Restitution* (3rd edn), Chs 21 and 22; Bant, *Change of Position* (2009), pp.204–209.

[1024] See the Rt Hon. Lord Millett (1991) 107 L.Q.R. 71 at 77–79; and McKendrick [1991] L.M.C.L.Q. 378 at 384–386; *Goff and Jones, Law of Unjust Enrichment* (9th edn), para.6-63. See the controversial case, *Banque Belge* [1921] 1 K.B. 321; and the discussion in *Agip (Africa) Ltd v Jackson* [1990] Ch. 265 and [1991] Ch. 547. The case seems to be regarded as correct in *Lipkin Gorman v Karpnale Ltd* [1991] 2 A.C. 548. See too *Shalson v Russo* [2003] EWHC 1637; [2005] Ch. 281; *Spangaro v Corporation Investment Funds Management Ltd* (2003) 47 A.C.S.R. 285 at [50].

[1025] Unless this is to be regarded as a manifestation of the change of position defence, as to which see Birks [1989] L.M.C.L.Q. 296 at 301–302; [1991] L.M.C.L.Q. 473 at 490–492; the Rt Hon. Lord Millett (1991) 107 L.Q.R. 71 at 82.

[1026] *Agip (Africa) Ltd v Jackson* [1990] 1 Ch. 265 at 287.

[1027] *Trustee of the Property of F. C. Jones & Co v Jones* [1997] Ch. 159; see Andrews and Beatson (1997) 113 L.Q.R. 21. See too Rt Hon. Lord Millett, in *Equity in Commercial Law* (Degeling and Edelman eds, 2005), at p.305.

[1028] e.g. *Banque Belge pour l'Etranger v Hambrouck* [1921] 1 K.B. 321.

[1029] e.g. *Taylor v Plumer* (1815) 3 M. & S. 562, Illustration 1.

[1030] e.g. *France v Clark* (1884) 26 Ch.D. 257; *Hutchison v Colorado United Mining Co & Hamill, Hamill v Lilley* (1887) 3 T.L.R. 265; *Colonial Bank v Cady and Williams* (1890) 15 App. Cas. 267; *Fox v Martin* (1895) 64 L.J.Ch. 473, Illustration 2 to Article 85.

may at first sight seem reasonable, such a requirement is paradoxical, since it attributes greater force to a principal's equitable title than the principal's legal ownership, though equity always recognised legal ownership. However, fiduciary relationships have been detected on extremely slender bases[1031] and it seems likely that the need to find such a relationship will disappear as the historically distinct tracing rules of common law and equity are assimilated.[1032] In the agency context the matter is of less importance, since where an agent holds property entrusted to the agent by the principal the agent often does so as fiduciary and an unauthorised disposition may involve a breach of the equitable duties of loyalty[1033]; and in other cases the agent may have control over the principal's money as fiduciary in a way that gives equal access to the right to trace.[1034] Plainly, where the principal's title to an asset is only equitable, the principal's rights to follow and trace the asset will only be equitable (whether or not the agent has the legal title).[1035]

The principal's right in equity consists of an entitlement at the claimant's option to assert beneficial ownership of the property concerned or a proportionate share of it, even where it has increased in value[1036]; or to enforce a lien (sometimes referred to as a charge) for the amount of misapplied money[1037] against the fund or property, whether mixed or not,[1038] held by the agent or by a subsequent holder. The right operates against one who takes with notice[1039] or a volunteer,[1040] but not against a bona fide purchaser for value without notice,[1041] nor where the property or (more usually) money sought to be traced has ceased to be identifiable, e.g. because, being money, it has been spent without identifiable proceeds,[1042] or has passed into an overdrawn bank account.[1043]

Constructive trust/knowing receipt   Whether or not there exists a proprietary   **8-163**
claim and an accompanying right to trace, a person receiving trust property or

---

[1031] e.g. the right to rescind for fraud: see *El Ajou v Dollar Land Holdings Plc* [1993] 3 All E.R. 717 at 734; *National Crime Agency v Robb* [2014] EWHC 4384 (Ch); [2015] Ch. 520 (post-formation fraud) (noted Turner [2016] C.L.J. 206). cf. *Twinsectra Ltd v Yardley* [1999] Lloyd's Rep. Bank 438 at 461–462; [2000] Lloyd's Rep.P.N. 239; *Chase Manhattan Bank NA v Israel British Bank (London) Ltd* [1981] Ch. 105; cf. *Bank of America v Arnell* [1999] Lloyd's Rep. Bank, 399.

[1032] See material cited at fn.1009 above. See also *Bank of New Zealand v Elders Pastoral Ltd* [1992] 1 N.Z.L.R. 536.

[1033] See Comment to Article 43.

[1034] *Agip (Africa) Ltd v Jackson* [1990] Ch. 265.

[1035] See, e.g. *Gray v Smith* [2013] EWHC 4136 (Comm); [2014] 2 All E.R. (Comm) 359.

[1036] *Foskett v McKeown* [2001] 1 A.C. 102 at 131–132.

[1037] *Foskett v McKeown* [2001] 1 A.C. 102 at 131–132; *Re Hallett's Estate* (1880) 13 Ch.D. 696 at 709; *Clark v Cutland* [2003] EWCA Civ 810; [2004] 1 W.L.R. 783; *Primlake Ltd v Matthews Associates* [2006] EWHC 1227 (Ch); [2007] 1 B.C.L.C. 666 at [334].

[1038] See *Lupton v White* (1808) 15 Ves. Jun. 432.

[1039] *Re Diplock, Diplock v Wintle* [1948] Ch. 465 at 539; affirmed [1951] A.C. 251; *Crédit Agricole Corp and Investment Bank v Papadimitriou* [2015] UKPC 13; [2015] 1 W.L.R. 4265 (noted Watts (2015) 131 L.Q.R. 511).

[1040] *Re Diplock, Diplock v Wintle* [1948] Ch. 465 at 539 at 539.

[1041] *Re Diplock, Diplock v Wintle*[1948] Ch. 465 at 539 at 539; *Thorndike v Hunt* (1859) 3 De G. & J. 563. As to the meaning of "notice" in this context, see *Polly Peck International Plc v Nadir (No.2)* [1992] 4 All E.R. at 781–782 (but see Bryan (1993) 109 L.Q.R. 368); *Gray v Smith* [2013] EWHC 4136 (Comm); [2014] 2 All E.R. (Comm) 359.

[1042] *Re Diplock, Diplock v Wintle* [1948] Ch. 465 at 539 at 546–550.

[1043] *Bishopsgate Investment Management Ltd v Homan* [1995] Ch. 211; *Moriarty v Various Customers of BA Peters Plc* [2008] EWCA Civ 1604; *Federal Republic of Brazil v Durant International Corp* [2015] UKPC 35; [2016] A.C. 297. See Smith [1995] C.L.J. 290; cf. Conaglen (2011) 127 L.Q.R. 432.

property affected by some other fiduciary interest with knowledge of the trust or fiduciary interest may nevertheless be liable to account as constructive trustee.[1044] It is usually assumed that this is a separate head of liability, effectively in personam, based on different principles, and it might be thought that it is only on this ground that a recipient who has parted with the property would still be liable, and could be required to account for profits made. The action is usually called one for "knowing receipt". The relationship of this part of the law with that of tracing is however controversial at present.[1045] The matter is discussed in connection with the liability of the agent to the principal[1046] and again in connection with the liability of the agent to third parties[1047]; but of course the principles apply equally to third parties who receive money *from* agents, and some aspects of this type of liability are dealt with in Article 96.[1048]

8-164   **Bankruptcy**   Bankruptcy of the agent involves the clearest case where a claim in rem may be needed. The principal will seek to assert that money or goods are the principal's and, the agent's authority to deal with them having ceased, the principal is entitled to extricate them from the agent's bankruptcy. The basic rule is that property held by the bankrupt the legal title to which is in the principal, and property held by the agent in trust, or as a fiduciary, is not liable to be seized: this extends to property that can be traced at law or in equity.[1049] But once the property can no longer be traced, the principal becomes an ordinary creditor with the rest. Debts owed to the principal are not owed to the agent and so can be recovered by the principal.[1050] Some debts owed to the agent could be regarded as held in trust for the principal and so rank as property held on trust.

8-165   **"Romalpa" clauses**   Considerable difficulties can be caused by the use of so-called "Romalpa" clauses, whereby a supplier of goods may seek to protect itself against the bankruptcy of the person to whom it supplies them by reserving title not only in the goods themselves, but also sometimes in the proceeds of their resale, and even into the product of mixing and manufacturing processes to which they may be subjected. Sometimes such provisions contain a "current account" clause, which reserves title not only pending payment in respect of the goods concerned, but also so long as any debt is outstanding between the parties. Apart from problems of identification of goods and appropriation of payments to particular consignments, the main danger from the point of view of the supplier is that they may be held to create some sort of charge and hence be void for non-registration. Therefore, though such arrangements are not normally related to agency relationships at all but rather to that of seller and buyer, attempts may be made to draft or interpret them as creating agency features, even though the transaction concerned is inappropri-

---

[1044] See, e.g. *Vernon v Public Trustee* [2016] NZCA 388 (receipt of funds misapplied by holder of power of attorney). See further below, para.9-136.

[1045] See *Re Montagu's Settlement Trusts* [1987] Ch. 264 at 285; but cf. the Rt Hon. Lord Millett (1991) 107 L.Q.R. 71 at 80–81; and by the same author (1998) 114 L.Q.R. 399.

[1046] Article 43.

[1047] Article 116.

[1048] See below, para.9-138 as to the duties and liabilities of banks.

[1049] See Insolvency Act 1986 s.283(3); Williams and Muir Hunter, *Bankruptcy* (19th edn), pp.260–280 (not reproduced in the subsequent *Muir Hunter on Personal Insolvency* (looseleaf)). A number of old illustrations concerning bankruptcy of agents were collected in the 15th edition of the present work (1985).

[1050] See *Angove's Pty Ltd v Bailey* [2016] UKSC 47; [2016] 1 W.L.R. 3179.

ate to such interpretation. Thus it may be suggested that a buyer of goods under such a clause resells as agent and holds the proceeds as trustee. The concept of agency can be made to work in this context, but the generally arm's-length nature of the sales setting makes it a marginal case, and its invocation may create unexpected and unsatisfactory side-effects. For example, the supplier may be liable as undisclosed principal on a resale by his purchaser.[1051]

Rule (2): Other restitutionary claims   A principal, disclosed or undisclosed, is entitled to sue for the recovery of money paid by an agent on the principal's behalf where the payment is made under a mistake of fact or any other circumstances ordinarily entitling a person paying money to recover it from the payee.[1052] It is sufficient that the payment is made on the principal's behalf even if not with money belonging to the principal.[1053]   **8-166**

The question has arisen of the effect on the principal's right to recover money paid by an agent under a mistake of fact of the circumstance that, when the payment is made, some other agent has knowledge of the true facts. It has been said that:

> "where ... a limited liability company is concerned and payments are made under a bona fide mistake ... by an authorised agent of the company, the fact that some other agent of the company may have had full knowledge of all the facts does not disentitle the company to recover the money so paid, provided that the agent with the full knowledge does not know that the payments are being made on an erroneous basis."[1054]

Presumably this principle applies also where the payment is made on behalf of any other kind of corporation or natural person. It seems likely that not only the state of knowledge of the other agent but the scope of the agent's authority, actual or apparent, will be relevant since what the recipient will essentially be asserting against the principal is some sort of estoppel.[1055] It has been suggested that (in the absence of estoppel) so long as the paying agent is mistaken, the mere fact that other, even more senior agents, are aware of the facts and of the payment will not be fatal to a restitutionary action.[1056]

[1051] See further above, para.1-035. More generally, see general *Chitty on Contracts* (33rd edn), para.44-173 onwards; *Benjamin's Sale of Goods* (10th edn), para.5-143 onwards; Watts (1986) 6 O.J.L.S. 456.

[1052] See *Goff and Jones, Law of Unjust Enrichment* (9th edn); Mitchell, "Banks, Agency and Unjust Enrichment" in *Commercial Law: Perspectives and Practice* (Lowry and Mistelis eds, 2006), Ch.8; S. Watterson, "Agents and organisations: attribution rules in unjust enrichment claims" [2017] R.L.R. 254.

[1053] See *Agip (Africa) Ltd v Jackson* [1991] Ch. 547; *Argyle UAE Ltd v Par-La-Ville Hotel & Residences Ltd* [2018] EWCA Civ 1762 at [49].

[1054] See *Turvey v Dentons (1923) Ltd* [1953] 1 Q.B. 218 at 224; and *BP Oil International Ltd v Target Shipping Ltd* [2012] EWHC 1590 (Comm) at [226]. For the right of the agent to recover money, see Article 110.

[1055] *Turvey v Dentons* (1923) Ltd [1953] 1 Q.B. 218 at 224, per Pilcher J; applying the stronger case of *Anglo-Scottish Beet Sugar Corp Ltd v Spalding UDC* [1937] 2 K.B. 607, where "the carelessness of the various officials of the company was more pronounced than any carelessness" existing in the later case; *BP Oil International Ltd v Target Shipping Ltd* [2012] EWHC 1590 (Comm) at [239]; *Astex Therapeutics Ltd v Astrazeneca AB* [2017] EWHC 1442 (Ch) at [392] (person inducing mistaken view need not be agent making the payment). See also below, para.8-185.

[1056] See *HKSAR v Luk Kin* [2016] HKCFA 81 at [36], per Lord Hoffmann.

Illustrations

8-167 (1) A broker misapplied his principal's money by purchasing stock and bullion, and absconded. He was adjudicated bankrupt on the day upon which he received and misapplied the money. On being arrested he surrendered the securities for the stock and bullion to the principal. Held, that the principal was entitled to retain the securities as against the trustee in bankruptcy.[1057]

(2) An agent who was entrusted with bills to get discounted mixed them with his own property, absconded, and became bankrupt. He was arrested with money in his possession which was the produce of portions of the mixed property. Held, that the principal was entitled, in preference to the other creditors, to a first charge on such money for the amount of the bills.[1058]

(3) Money is paid to a broker by his principal for application in a particular way. The broker pays the money into his own account at a bank, and becomes bankrupt before applying it as directed. The principal is entitled to the money as against the broker's trustee in bankruptcy.[1059] If, in such a case, the agent has drawn on the account, the principal has a charge on the balance in the banker's hands, the amounts so drawn being deemed to be drawn out of the agent's own moneys, whenever they were paid in,[1060] so long as the balance exceeds the trust moneys.[1061] Where the moneys of several principals have been paid into the account, their charges have priority in the inverse order of the payments, the balance being deemed to consist of the trust moneys most recently paid in.[1062]

(4) An agent who was employed to sell certain goods mixed them with goods of his own, and consigned the whole of the goods together to a factor for sale, representing to his principal that he had sold his goods, and debiting himself with the amount of the supposed prices. The agent having become bankrupt, the principal was held entitled to have the proceeds of the mixed property marshalled, so as to throw advances made by the factor, as far as possible, on to the agent's own goods.[1063]

(5) A factor becomes bankrupt. Goods in his hand for sale, fresh goods directly bought with the proceeds of sale of such goods, and unmatured bills and notes received by him as the price of goods sold, must, subject to his lien, be returned

---

[1057] *Taylor v Plumer* (1815) 3 M. & S. 562; *Re Hulton Ex p. Manchester and County Bank* (1891) 39 W.R. 303. See also *Marsh v Keating* (1834) 1 Bing. (N.C.) 198.

[1058] *Frith v Cartland* (1865) 34 L.J.Ch. 301.

[1059] *Re Strachan Ex p. Cooke* (1876) 4 Ch.D. 123; *Hancock v Smith* (1889) 41 Ch.D. 456; *Re Arthur Wheeler* (1933) 102 L.J.Ch. 341. See also *Re Cotton Ex p. Cooke* (1913) 108 L.T. 310 (auctioneer); cf. *Re Hallett & Co, Ex p. Blane* [1894] 2 Q.B. 237; *Re Mawson Ex p. Hardcastle* (1881) 44 L.T. 523; *King v Hutton* [1900] 2 Q.B. 504; *Wilsons & Furness-Leyland Line Ltd v British & Continental Shipping Co Ltd* (1907) 23 T.L.R. 397.

[1060] *Re Hallett's Estate* (1880) 13 Ch.D. 696; *Re Wreford* (1897) 13 T.L.R. 153; *Banque Belge pour l'Etranger v Hambrouck* [1921] 1 K.B. 321. See also *Re Oatway* [1903] 2 Ch. 356.

[1061] *James Roscoe (Bolton) Ltd v Winder* [1915] 1 Ch. 62; and see *Campden Hill Ltd v Chakrani* [2005] EWHC 911; [2005] N.P.C. 65.

[1062] *Re Stenning* [1895] 2 Ch. 433. See also *Re Diplock* [1948] Ch. 465; affirmed [1951] A.C. 251. This is subject to contrary intention: see *Barlow Clowes International Ltd v Vaughan* [1992] 4 All E.R. 22; *Commerzbank Aktiengesellschaft v IMB Morgan Plc* [2004] EWHC 2771 (Ch); [2005] 1 Lloyd's Rep. 298.

[1063] *Broadbent v Barlow* (1861) 3 De G.F. & J. 570; *Re Holland Ex p. Alston* (1868) L.R. 4 Ch.App. 168; *Re Burge, Woodall & Co Ex p. Skyrme* [1912] 1 K.B. 393.

to the principal, and may be recovered by him from the trustee in bankruptcy.[1064] The price of goods already sold may, subject to the agent's lien, be recovered by the principal from the purchaser,[1065] and, if paid to the trustee in bankruptcy, may be recovered from him by the principal.[1066]

(6) The chief accountant of a company fraudulently alters a cheque duly signed on the company's behalf, with the effect that it is credited to another company with which the paying company has no connection, and from there the money is paid out on instructions. It is assumed that the directors of the latter company have no knowledge of the reason behind the transaction. They are liable for money still in their possession.[1067]

(7) A partner in a firm of solicitors fraudulently draws money from the company's account and spends it gambling at a casino. The firm may recover the money from the casino subject to a defence of change of position.[1068]

(8) A warehouse holding wool on behalf of a seller with strict instructions not to deliver it to the buyer without express confirmation from the seller of receipt of payment, mistakenly delivers the wool to the buyer when it has not been paid for. The seller is entitled to recover the wool or its value in conversion from the buyer (and its receivers).[1069]

(9) A custom-house officer took exorbitant fees from a shipmaster. Held, that the owner of the vessel had a right to sue to recover the amount paid in excess of the proper fees.[1070]

Article 89

DISPOSITIONS AND PAYMENTS TO AGENT

(1) Where a purported transfer of property in goods[1071] is made to the agent of a disclosed principal, and the agent receives it as such acting within the agent's actual or apparent authority, the property in the goods is transferred to the principal if such is the intention of the parties to the transfer.   **8-168**

(2) (Perhaps) where a purported transfer of property in goods is made to the agent of an undisclosed principal and the agent is authorised to receive it and does so intending to act as agent, the property in the goods is transferred to the undisclosed principal if such is the intention of the agent and the principal, unless the principal knows that the transferor would not have transferred the property in the goods to the principal.

(3) (Perhaps), where there is an attornment by the holder of goods to the agent of an undisclosed principal and the agent is authorised to receive it and does so intending to act as agent, the principal has the right to treat the attornment as

[1064] *Scott v Surman* (1742) Wiles 400 (see as to this case *Triffit Nurseries v Salads Etcetera Ltd* [2000] 1 All E.R. (Comm) 737 at 742–743); *Whitecomb v Jacob* (1710) 1 Salk. 160; *Godfrey v Furzo* (1733) 3 P. Wms. 186. See also *Ex p. Sayers* (1800) 5 Ves. 169.
[1065] *Scott v Surman; Re Wood Ex p. Boden* (1873) 28 L.T. 174.
[1066] See *Scott v Surman* (1742) Wiles 400 and the other cases cited with it, above.
[1067] *Agip (Africa) Ltd v Jackson* [1990] Ch. 265; [1991] Ch. 247.
[1068] *Lipkin Gorman v Karpnale Ltd* [1991] 2 A.C. 548.
[1069] *J.S. Brooksbank & Co (Australasia) Ltd v EXFTX Ltd* (2009) 10 N.Z.C.L.C. 264,520.
[1070] *Stevenson v Mortimer* (1778) Cowp. 805; see also *Holt v Ely* (1853) 1 E. & B. 795; *Taylor v Smith* (1926) 38 C.L.R. 48.
[1071] The position as to land would be different: see above, para.2-037.

being to the principal unless the principal knows that the holder of the goods would not have attorned to him or her.[1072]

(4) A disclosed principal can be subject to restitutionary claims brought in respect of money paid (and sometimes other property transferred) to an agent in connection with transactions effected within the agent's actual or apparent authority, even though the principal has not personally received it.

Comment

8-169   The question of the effect of dispositions *by* an agent of the principal's property raises problems of transfer of property by a non-owner. That of the effect of dispositions *in favour* of the agent, on the other hand, raises quite different problems regarding the relevance of the intention of the parties to the transfer of property and possession, and in some circumstances, the law of restitution.

8-170   **Disclosed principal**   Property in goods is transferred by delivery, and in some cases (particularly contracts of sale of goods[1073]) by intention. There is no objection to the acquisition of property through an agent. Hence a transfer of goods, whether by delivery or mere intention, to an agent who in receiving possession or assenting to receive property without possession acts for a disclosed principal, named or unnamed, will pass property to the principal, provided that all the other conditions normally required for the passing of property[1074] are satisfied. It would of course be necessary that the agent was acting within the agent's actual or apparent authority: since the acquisition of property is usually an advantage, cases where there was no authority of either sort would be the exception rather than the rule. Where *possession* is also transferred to the agent, however, this rests with the agent, though by a pre-existing intention the agent may immediately choose to become a bailee for the principal. As bailee the agent possesses: the principal does not.[1075]

8-171   **Undisclosed principal**   When however there is a transfer to a person who is acting as agent for an undisclosed principal and intends to receive for the principal, the position becomes very difficult to analyse. The operation of the undisclosed principal doctrine outside the realm of pure contract raises many problems, the solutions to which have hardly been considered. On one view, transfer of property is not the same as contract, and the passage of property does not necessarily occur in pursuance of a contract. Hence the intentions of the parties must be looked at in isolation from any contractual implications. On this basis the intention of the transferor is only to transfer to the agent, and a concealed intention of the agent to acquire for another should not be able to produce a different effect. If the agent wishes to make a further transfer to the principal this can be instantly effected, as regards property, by intention alone (at least where there is consideration for the disposition): but the property will have passed through the agent for a *scintilla temporis*, which may have legal significance, e.g. for bankruptcy or tax purposes.

[1072] See Comment; Goode, *Proprietary Rights and Insolvency in Sales Transactions* (3rd edn), Ch.III.

[1073] Sale of Goods Act 1979 s.17.

[1074] e.g. that the goods are ascertained: see Sale of Goods Act 1979 s.16 (as modified by Sale of Goods (Amendment) Act 1995).

[1075] See Paton, *Bailment in the Common Law* (1952), pp.6–9; Pollock and Wright, *Possession in the Common Law* (1888), pp.57–60. As to possession of documents by an agent for the purpose of subpoena *duces tecum*, see *Rochfort v Trade Practices Commission* (1982) 153 C.L.R. 134 and cases there cited.

Again, *possession* will pass to the agent, though the agent may immediately, by virtue of intention, become bailee to the principal.

It may furthermore be argued that in a contract situation the undisclosed principal doctrine involves an element of intervention. The undisclosed principal intervenes on a transaction entered into by the agent which is valid in itself; and the third party may elect to sue the principal on such a transaction, but need not do so. Such an element of choice can be said to be inappropriate in property transactions: there cannot be a right to possess in both principal and agent. It is also true that agents taking conveyances of land are held to act as trustees for their principals and not to vest property in their principals directly[1076]: but these cases seem to depend on the fact that written instruments are used which by their words purport to vest the land in the agent.

As against these arguments it may be said that the formation of obligation is, at least prima facie, of an even more personal nature than the transfer of property. The latter rids the transferor of obligations rather than creates them, and does not produce a continuing relationship: it is often, perhaps usually, a matter of indifference to a transferor who receives the goods with which the transferor intends to part. If an undisclosed principal can intervene on an obligation, a fortiori such a principal should be able to intervene on a transfer of property, which usually occurs in pursuance of an obligation. It may even be argued that in the case of sale of goods the requirement of intention of the parties[1077] is supplied by the transferor's intention to transfer and the undisclosed principal's intention to receive, though these have no reference to each other. These propositions are strengthened by the usual view that the origin of the undisclosed principal doctrine lay in the desire to protect the principal in the agent's bankruptcy.[1078] For that purpose it is obviously important that the principal's title should be protected from the moment of acquisition of goods for the principal by the agent.

If the principal has the right to intervene and claim property, that right is presumably subject to the exception to which intervention on a contract is subject: that it must not be excluded by the express or implied terms of the transaction.[1079] It is arguable also that the exception goes further than this and that a principal cannot claim that property vested in the principal automatically (rather than by a further transfer from the agent) where the principal knows that the transferor would not have transferred to him or her.[1080]

An agent who has no authority to create privity with the third party, but nevertheless acts for a principal (the *commissionnaire* of the civil law)[1081] may probably (though the question is unsolved) receive and transmit the property to the principal. A group of old cases involving this problem is considered in Article 71.

Attorment   An attornment in respect of goods occurs where a possessor of **8-172** goods, whether personally the transferor or the bailee of the transferor, acknowledges that he or she holds, and possesses, for another. There is authority that such

---

[1076] Article 53.
[1077] Sale of Goods Act 1979 s.17.
[1078] See above, para.8-069.
[1079] See above, para.8-078; *Maynegrain Pty Ltd v Compafina Bank Ltd* [1982] 2 N.S.W.L.R. 141 at 153: "unless the terms of the attornment or of the arrangements for the making of that attornment require A.N.Z. to be treated as the only attornee".
[1080] See above, para.8-078.
[1081] See above, para.1-029.

an attornment creates a fresh bailment by means of a constructive delivery and redelivery.[1082] It may be used to pass property to a buyer: but it may instead create a pledge in favour of the attornee. Attornment to the agent of a disclosed principal acting as such may plainly rank as attornment to the principal. If intention is the key to the effect of attornment, the intention where the agent's principal is undisclosed is, however, only to attorn to the agent. Indeed, any other conclusion could be said to lead to there being a constructive delivery to two persons, each of whom effects a redelivery. But again it can be argued that, since attornment will usually occur in pursuance of a contract, the undisclosed principal's intervention should not be disallowed in such a case when it is allowed in the case of contract; and that not only should attornment be capable of passing property to an undisclosed principal, it should also (subject to the same provisos regarding cases where the attornor did not or would not have attorned to the principal) be capable of constituting the principal a pledgee. Such a conclusion has been reached by the Court of Appeal of New South Wales in *Maynegrain Pty Ltd v Compafina Bank*,[1083] the facts of which are summarised below.

8-173   **Estoppel**   In the above case there was an additional complication: the goods in respect of which an attornment (for the purposes of creating a security) was made were part of an undivided bulk, and the court assumed[1084] that there can be no possession, and hence no bailment, of such unascertained goods. Therefore as a pure attornment, viz. a constructive delivery and redelivery, the act concerned (the issue of a warehouse receipt) was ineffective. In such cases however there is authority that an attornment also operates by way of estoppel, in that it prevents persons attorning from denying that they in fact hold goods as described for the attornee.[1085] A further doctrinal point therefore arises: can a warehouse owner be estopped against someone whose existence it has not contemplated? This turns on the scope of the owner's representation, not on any notion of intervention. Again there is a choice. On one view, it may be immaterial to a holder of goods to whom they are transferred, for whom they are held or to whom the receipt which the holder has signed is shown. On another, estoppel raises the question of who is contemplated as likely to rely on the representation, and a statement specifically addressed to one person may well not be intended to be relied on by another, at any rate where a document of title is not involved.[1086] The analogy of share certificates,[1087] which are not documents of title, suggests the adoption of the first view, and indeed to dif-

---

[1082] *Dublin City Distillery Ltd v Doherty* [1914] A.C. 823 at 852; *Official Assignee of Madras v Mercantile Bank of India Ltd* [1935] A.C. 53 at 58.

[1083] *Maynegrain Pty Ltd v Compafina Bank* [1982] 2 N.S.W.L.R. 141, Illustration 1; reversed on the facts (1984) 58 A.L.J.R. 389 PC. See Goode, *Proprietary Rights and Insolvency in Sales Transactions* (3rd edn), at pp.11–12.

[1084] But see *Hayman & Son v M'Lintock* (1907) S.C. 936; *Benjamin's Sale of Goods* (10th edn), para.18-339. It is possible that the position is altered by the Sale of Goods (Amendment) Act 1995, which allows ownership of part of a bulk to arise in new circumstances: see *Benjamin's Sale of Goods*, para.18-335 onwards. The position as regards possession is unsolved. See Gullifer [1999] L.M.C.L.Q. 93.

[1085] *Knights v Wiffen* (1870) L.R. 5 Q.B. 660; *Coventry, Sheppard & Co v GE Ry Co* (1883) 11 Q.B.D. 776. See also *Alicia Hosiery Ltd v Brown, Shipley & Co Ltd* [1970] 1 Q.B. 195 at 206.

[1086] cf. *V/O Rasnoimport v Guthrie & Co* [1966] 1 Lloyd's Rep 1, where a signature as agent was held to constitute a contractual offer of authority to persons taking up the document.

[1087] *Re Bahia and San Francisco Ry Co Ltd* (1868) L.R. 3 Q.B. 584; see *Gower's Principles of Modern Company Law* (10th edn), paras 27-5–27-6; *Spencer Bower: Reliance-Based Estoppel* (5th edn), Ch.6.

ferentiate in result between cases where the goods are specific and cases where they are part of a bulk seems wrong. The court not surprisingly held that the estoppel applied likewise: granted the first decision, it would have been unsatisfactory to decide differently on this issue.

Rule (4): Restitutionary claims in relation to payments to agent Rule (4) touches on a wide subject, the law of restitution, a close scrutiny of which is beyond this book.[1088] Plainly, where a claimant wishes to assert a restitutionary right, the claimant may often prefer to sue the principal of the actual recipient of the money, or other property, for the usual reason that there are stronger chances of enforcing judgment against that person. As with many other areas of the law of restitution, the precise bounds of a principal's liability in such circumstances are still being settled. It is reasonably clear that if the payment was made to a person who received the payment for a principal, disclosed or undisclosed, within the agent's actual authority, or for a disclosed principal within the agent's apparent authority, the principal will be prima facie liable.[1089] If the money is in fact accounted for by the agent to the principal, and accepted as such, the principal is also likely to be liable to a restitutionary claim, if only on the basis of ratification, even when the initial receipt was without authority. Where the claimant has a proprietary claim, the mere receipt by the principal may well be sufficient to expose the principal to an action, even without ratification. Less clear are the circumstances in which the principal might be able to raise defences such as change of position and bona fide purchase for value without notice, especially where the receiving agent was aware of the circumstances that might give rise to a claim but the principal was not. Another defence that might arise to protect the principal is the defence of "ministerial receipt", arising where an agent on a frolic of the agent's own has simply used the principal as a receiving box, and the money has merely gone in and out of the principal's accounts. In cases of that sort the agent will usually have initiated the transaction, and relevant commentary and cases are found in Article 92.

8-174

Illustrations

(1) A warehouseman, holding imported goods for a customer at the customer's request, for purposes of creating a security, issues a warehouse receipt for a quantity of goods, part of an undivided mass, for the account of a local bank. He subsequently delivers some of the goods at the customer's direction. The local bank to whom he issued the receipt was in fact agent for another bank which has actually advanced money to the owner of the goods. The lending bank can intervene and, as bailor, sue the warehouseman in conversion.[1090]

(2) An agent appointed by the managing owner of a ship demanded too much freight from the consignees of certain goods, and refused to deliver the goods until payment. The consignees paid the amount demanded, under protest, and

8-175

[1088] See *Goff and Jones, Law of Unjust Enrichment* (9th edn); Watts [2017] L.M.C.L.Q. 385.

[1089] *Coulthurst v Sweet* (1866) L.R. 1 C.P. 649, Illustration 2; *Portman Building Society v Hamlyn Taylor Neck* [1998] 4 All E.R. 202 at 207; *Marsfield Automotive Inc v Siddiqi* [2017] EWHC 187 (Comm); *Sixteenth Ocean GmbH & Co Kg v Société Générale* [2018] EWHC 1731 (Comm); [2018] 2 Lloyd's Rep. 465.

[1090] *Maynegrain Pty Ltd v Compafina Bank* [1982] 2 N.S.W.L.R. 141. But the decision was reversed on the facts on the basis that the local bank had assented to the delivery: (1984) 58 A.L.J.R. 389 (PC).

sued one of the part-owners of the ship for the excess. Held, that he was liable, though no portion of the money had come to his hands.[1091]

3. WRONGS

Introductory Note

8-176 **Torts** The primary application of the principles of agency is in the fields of contract, dispositions of property and the law of restitution. The law of tort, in general, uses different techniques. Anyone considering the application of agency principles in the law of tort is initially faced with the fact that when that branch of the law deals with liability of one person for the acts of another, the question normally turns not on the authority of the person who committed the tort, but on whether the tortfeasor was the servant (or employee) of the person sought to be held liable, or an independent contractor. An agent may be either (or indeed, in some situations, such as the case of a gratuitous agent, neither). A very rough summary of the usual view would be to say that people are liable for torts committed by another which they specifically instigate or authorise, or which are committed by their servants acting within the course of employment, or which involve a breach of a non-delegable duty owed by them, though the acts leading to such breach were actually performed by another (usually an independent contractor). Vicarious liability in the law of tort seems also to have a different basis from agency in contract, and elsewhere. In contract, the agent is not liable as a matter of course, and the effect of agency rules is, in the majority of cases, to establish the primary liability of the person with whom the third party intended to deal. But with most torts the actual tortfeasor is in principle liable, and the effect of vicarious liability is to add a defendant, often unknown to and uncontemplated by the victim; on one view its purpose is simply to find a defendant who can pay.[1092]

However, the law of agency appears to be important in the operation of some torts, especially those involving liability for statements, including deceit, negligent misstatement and, more doubtfully, defamation.[1093] It may also be relevant to tortious claims for negligent performance of services, where, as with negligent misstatement, the underlying explanation is, arguably anyway, the near-contractual one

---

[1091] *Coulthurst v Sweet* (1866) L.R. 1 C.P. 649.

[1092] Atiyah, *Vicarious Liability in the Law of Torts* (1967), Chs 1, 2; and see *Rose v Plenty* [1976] 1 W.L.R. 141 at 147. See too *Dubai Aluminium Co Ltd v Salaam* [2002] UKHL 48; [2003] A.C. 366 at [107], per Lord Millett; *Majrowski v Guy's & St. Thomas's NHS Trust* [2006] UKHL 34; [2007] 1 A.C. 224 at [9], per Lord Nicholls of Birkenhead. The orthodox view is that vicarious liability works by making the employer (or, in some cases, principal) secondarily liable for the tort or other wrong of the employee (or agent): *Majrowski v Guy's & St. Thomas's NHS Trust* [2006] UKHL 34; [2007] 1 A.C. 224, at [15], [56], [68], and [81]. But cf. Stevens (2007) 123 L.Q.R. 30; and Stevens, *Torts and Rights* (2007), Ch.11. See too Neyers (2005) 43 Alberta L.R. 287.

[1093] See *Mercantile Credit Co v Garrod* [1962] 3 All E.R. 1103 (a case on partnership); *Armagas Ltd v Mundogas SA (The Ocean Frost)* [1986] A.C. 717 (deceit); *Williams v Natural Life Health Foods Ltd* [1998] 1 W.L.R. 830 (negligent misstatement); *Colonial Mutual Life Assurance Society Ltd v Producers and Citizens Cooperative Co of Australia Ltd* (1931) 46 C.L.R. 41 (defamation). The latter three cases are discussed below. For general discussion, see Ferson (1948) 2 Vand.L.Rev. 1; Watts (2012) 128 L.Q.R. 260. cf. liability under the Misrepresentation Act 1967 s.2(1); and as to the tort of inducement of breach of contract, see below, para.9-121; *Kallang Shipping SA Panama v Axa Assurances Senegal* [2008] EWHC 2761 (Comm) at [92]; *New South Wales v Lepore* (2003) 212 C.L.R. 511.

of assumption of responsibility.[1094] The deployment of agency law in these torts may have both a narrowing and a broadening effect compared to other torts. On the one hand, a claimant may need to show that the agent's conduct was authorised or appeared to be authorised (rather than simply that the conduct took place "in the course of employment"). On the other hand, in such cases it would not usually matter that the agent was not an employee of the defendant.

Apart from the important situations just mentioned, there are various ways in which agency concepts can appear in connection with torts or other wrongs. They may be enumerated as follows, with the reservation that, as is obvious, the categories are not mutually exclusive:

(a) Parallels from one part of the law have long been cited in the other[1095] and the terminologies of master and servant and principal and agent have been and still are sometimes interchanged: the same applies to the phrases "course of employment" and "scope of authority".[1096]

(b) The clear dichotomy between contract and tort which was made from the late nineteenth century was not made in earlier times,[1097] and is now again subject to considerable reservations and qualifications.

(c) Ancillary notions primarily related, according to modern ideas, to contractual agency, e.g. ratification, have on occasion been useful in the field of tort.[1098] Another example arises where a party instigates or authorises a third party, not necessarily an employee, to commit a tort on its behalf.[1099]

(d) Certain persons whom the law of tort, as expounded above, might for the sake of consistency describe as servants seem in common speech more appropriately described as agents, especially where their duties involve commercial matters such as the making of contracts, dispositions of property, etc. Thus a shipmaster who sells the cargo wrongfully,[1100] a solicitor's managing clerk dealing with a mortgage who defrauds the person with

---

[1094] See *Williams v Natural Life Health Foods Ltd* [1998] 1 W.L.R. 830 at 834; *Sainsbury's Supermarkets Ltd v Condek Holdings Ltd* [2014] EWHC 2016 (TCC); [2014] B.L.R. 574 at [17]; *P&P Property Ltd v Owen White and Catlin LLP* [2018] EWCA Civ 1082; [2019] Ch. 273 at [65], [72] and [75].

[1095] "There has never been a time when cases on master and servant were not cited as authority in the law of principal and agent, and vice versa": Street, *Foundations of Legal Liability* (1906), Vol.2, p.454.

[1096] Had there been separate commercial courts, the result might have been otherwise; the terminology of agency is a commercial one, but that of master and servant has long been rooted in the common law. See Holdsworth, *H.E.L. VIII*, p.227. See also e.g. Pollock, *Contracts* (15th edn), p.58 onwards; *Barwick v English Joint Stock Bank* (1867) L.R. 2 Ex. 259 at 266; *Swire v Francis* (1877) 3 App.Cas. 106; *Holdsworth v City of Glasgow Bank* (1880) 5 App.Cas. 317 at 326–327; *Lloyd v Grace, Smith & Co* [1912] A.C. 716 at 734–735; *Uxbridge Permanent Benefit Building Society v Pickard* [1939] 2 K.B. 248 at 254; *Navarro v Moregrand Ltd* [1951] 2 T.L.R. 674; *Morris v C.W. Martin & Sons Ltd* [1966] 1 Q.B. 716 at 726; *Heaton Transport (St Helens) Ltd v T&GWU* [1973] A.C. 15 at 99; *Rose v Plenty* [1976] 1 W.L.R. 141. Statutes relating to tort may use the term "agent": see Crown Proceedings Act 1947 s.2(1)(a).

[1097] Especially as regards representations: Stoljar, pp.64–67.

[1098] Indeed ratification may be older than the idea of agency. But it is probably now confined to cases of conversion and trespass: see Comment to Article 14. Agency terminology may also be used where a servant does acts upon which the tortiousness of further acts may depend, e.g. invites persons on to land where they would otherwise be trespassers: *Hillen & Pettigrew v ICI Alkall Ltd* [1936] A.C. 65; *Young v Box & Co* [1951] 1 T.L.R. 789.

[1099] See below, para.8-177.

[1100] *Ewbank v Nutting* (1849) 7 C.B. 797.

whom the clerk is dealing,[1101] or a bailiff levying distress wrongfully[1102] may well be servants (or independent contractors), but the term "agent" may nevertheless be used when the principal is made liable for their torts committed in the course of their professional activities. On the other hand, though a bus driver could be an agent for buying petrol, the driver is certainly more likely to be called a servant if involved in a collision on the way to get it.[1103] In some cases the term used may depend simply on whether a tort leading to personal injuries is involved, or an economic tort, e.g. deceit.

(e) In one unique line of cases one person is held liable for the tort of another who is certainly neither that person's servant nor independent contractor, but who can be said in some sense to be acting that person—in most cases by driving a car. These cases, often referred to as involving the notion of casual delegation, are sometimes (unsatisfactorily) explained as based on agency.[1104]

(f) Some statutory sources of civil liability are drafted using the concepts of the law of agency, rather than vicarious liability.[1105]

(g) Sometimes it is the *principal* that wishes to invoke agency concepts in a suit in tort against a third party. So, a misrepresentation made to an agent where the maker of the statement intends that it will be passed on to the principal or relied upon by the agent in acting for the principal can found a suit by the principal even if the agent is not an employee.[1106] It is not clear, however, that it matters in such cases whether or not the receiving intermediary is an agent in the technical sense, so agency concepts may not be doing the work.[1107] The focus of this section is, however, on a principal's liability, not rights.

Attempts can be and have been made to unify all agency in contract and tort into one set of principles,[1108] and even, abandoning the terminology of master and servant, to seek to establish the types of authority as the guiding criteria in tort as well as contract.[1109] If there is a separate notion of usual authority,[1110] it is plainly of much assistance for this: some of the rules relating to independent contractors would be incorporated here and some related to the personal duty of the principal. Though there is some support in the cases,[1111] such an exercise is a creative and theoretical

---

[1101] *Lloyd v Grace, Smith & Co* [1912] A.C. 716, Illustration 12 to Article 90; *Uxbridge Permanent Benefit Building Society v Pickard* [1939] 2 K.B. 248, Illustration 13 to Article 90.

[1102] Article 90, Illustration 17.

[1103] *Limpus v London General Omnibus Co Ltd* (1862) 1 H. & C. 526.

[1104] See below, para.8-187.

[1105] See, e.g. *Giltrap City Ltd v The Commerce Commission* [2004] 1 N.Z.L.R. 608 (price-fixing); *Alfred v Wakelin (No.2)* [2008] FCA 1543 (proscribed industrial action).

[1106] See, e.g. *OMV Petrom SA v Glencore International AG* [2015] EWHC 666 (Comm) at [139]; *Libyan Investment Authority v King* [2020] EWHC 440 (Ch) at [125]; *Ras Al Khaimah Investment Authority v Azima* [2020] EWHC 1327 (Ch) at [152].

[1107] See, e.g. *Clef Aquitaine Sarl v Laporte Materials (Barrow) Ltd* [2001] Q.B. 488 at 502–503.

[1108] cf. *Restatement, Second*, § 2. And see above, para.1-026 onwards.

[1109] See Powell, pp.184–194; Fridman, Ch.7; cf. Ferson (1951) 4 Vand.L.Rev. 260; Conant (1968) 48 Neb.L.Rev. 42; Tedeschi (1969) 4 Israel L.Rev. 1; Atiyah, *Vicarious Liability in the Law of Torts* (1967), Ch.9.

[1110] See Comment to Article 22; above, para.8-077.

[1111] See material cited at fn.1096 above; cases relating to false imprisonment cited at Article 90, Illustration 5; cases on solicitors and bailiffs cited at Article 90, Illustration 18. cf. Partnership Act 1890

one involving a development of the law beyond the form in which it is at present stated and understood in England and Wales. It has already been suggested that such attempts are of doubtful validity in pure contract situations,[1112] and they do not seem to illuminate tort situations either.

For the elucidation of the law as at present applied it is more appropriate to set out briefly an indication of the basic rules as to liability in tort, based on the distinction between servants and independent contractors, and to suggest the ways in which agency reasoning may be regarded as supplementing the results which the orthodox tort reasoning might reach. More attention is then given to those torts where the use of agency reasoning, arguably at least, performs a more substantive role.

Article 90

LIABILITY OF PRINCIPAL FOR TORTS COMMITTED BY AGENT

(1) In general,[1113] if an agent is the employee of the principal, the principal is li-   **8-177**
able for loss, damage or injury caused by the wrongful act of the agent when acting in the course of employment.[1114] Partners are similarly liable for wrongful acts of one another.[1115]

(2) A principal is liable in tort for loss or injury caused by an agent, whether or not an employee, and if not an employee, whether or not the agent can be called an independent contractor, in the following cases:

    (a) if the wrongful act was specifically instigated, authorised[1116] or ratified[1117] by the principal.

    (b) (semble) in the case of a statement made in the course of representing the principal within the actual or apparent authority of the agent: and for such a statement the principal may be liable notwithstanding that it was made for the benefit of the agent alone and not for that of the principal.[1118]

    (c) where the principal can be taken to have assumed a responsibility for the actions of the agent.[1119]

---

s.10.

[1112] See Comment to Article 22.

[1113] This is an important qualification; see, for instance, torts based on statements, discussed below, para.8-180.

[1114] See Comment: *Salmond and Heuston on the Law of Torts* (21st edn), Ch.21; *Clerk and Lindsell on Torts* (22nd edn), Ch.6; Atiyah, *Vicarious Liability in the Law of Torts* (1967); P. Giliker, *Vicarious Liability in Tort* (2010); P. Giliker "A Revolution in Vicarious Liability" in *Revolution and Evolution in Private Law* (Worthington, Robertson and Virgo eds, 2018), Ch.7. See a not dissimilar formulation in *Restatement, Third*, §7.03. In *New South Wales v Ibbett* (2006) 231 A.L.R. 485 (HCA) exemplary damages were awarded against an employer who was vicariously liable only, see para.8-192, Illustration 7. In *S v Att.-Gen.* [2003] 3 N.Z.L.R. 450 at 472–475 CA (abuse of foster children by foster parents under state control) exemplary damages were held to be generally inappropriate where liability was only vicarious, but the case of abuse of official status was left open. cf. *Kuddus v Chief Constable of Leicestershire Constabulary* [2002] 2 A.C. 122; and *Blackwater v Plint* (2005) 258 D.L.R. (4th) 275 (SCC) (noted Neyers (2006) 122 L.Q.R. 195).

[1115] See Partnership Act 1890 s.10. See *Lindley and Banks on Partnership* (20th edn), Ch.12.

[1116] Illustrations 14 to 16; Atiyah, above, Ch.27. See *C. Evans & Sons Ltd v Spritebrand Ltd* [1985] 1 W.L.R. 317 (director) and the collection of cases below, paras 8-194 and 9-120.

[1117] See Article 14.

[1118] See Comment; Article 74. cf. Partnership Act 1890 s.10. As to apparent authority, see Article 72.

[1119] See Comment.

(3) In some circumstances, the owner of a business or organisation may owe duties of care, usually in relation to the personal safety and wellbeing of others, that apply whether or not the owner performs the services personally or through employees, or by engaging independent contractors. Such duties are termed "non-delegable". These duties do not necessarily invoke agency concepts.

(4) Where principal and agent are both liable for a wrongful act committed by the agent they are joint tortfeasors.[1120]

(5) In this Article, save where the context requires, "act" includes "omission".

Comment

8-178 **Rule (1): Employees and partners** This rule gives a brief indication of the liability of a principal for the acts of an employee, and of one partner for the acts of another. A definition of "servant" or "employee" is given in Article 2. In the context of the present article it should be taken to embrace company directors, who as officers will not necessarily also be employees.[1121] The usual corollary is that a party, P, is not liable for torts committed by persons who do not fit into the categories of employee, director or partner.[1122] This would generally be so even if, apart from the actions constituting the tort, the tortfeasor were for some purposes an agent of P.[1123] The Supreme Court has recently reaffirmed this orthodoxy.[1124] Relationships akin to employment, are discussed below.

As for liability for the acts of employees, the traditional view is that an employee acts in the course of employment if the employee commits any wrongful act authorised by the employer or does an act within the scope of the employee's duties in a wrongful and unauthorised manner.[1125] It is established that the employee may act in the course of employment notwithstanding that the employer has expressly prohibited the act done[1126]: whether the prohibited act is or is not in the course of the employee's employment depends upon whether the prohibition is such as merely regulates the conduct of the employee within the scope of employment or is such as limits the sphere of that employment itself.[1127] An employee may act in the course of employment notwithstanding that the act is done for the benefit of

---

[1120] *Jones v Manchester Corp* [1952] 2 Q.B. 852 at 869. See below, para.8-191.

[1121] *Bellman v Northampton Recruitment Ltd* [2018] EWCA Civ 2214; [2019] I.C.R. 459 (managing director).

[1122] The leading case is *Quarman v Burnett* (1840) 6 M.&W. 499. See also *Emmanuel v DBS Management Plc* [1999] Lloyd's Rep P.N. 593 at 594; *Woodland v Swimming Teachers Association* [2013] UKSC 66; [2014] A.C. 537 at [3]; *Scott v Davis* (2000) 204 C.L.R. 333 at [18] and [301]; *Hollis v Vabu Pty Ltd* (2001) 207 C.L.R. 21 at [40]; *Ng Huat Seng v Munib Mohammad Madni* [2017] SGCA 58 (noted D. Tan (2018) 134 L.Q.R. 193).

[1123] See *Holdnerness v Goslin* [1975] 2 N.Z.L.R. 46 at 50–51; *Emmanuel v DBS Management Plc* [1999] Lloyd's Rep P.N. 593 at 594. As to Scotland, see *M v Hendron* [2007] CSIH 27 at [132].

[1124] *Barclays Bank Plc v Various Claimants* [2020] UKSC 13; [2020] 2 W.L.R. 960.

[1125] See *Poland v John Parr & Sons Ltd* [1927] 1 K.B. 236 at 240; *Bugge v Brown* (1919) 26 C.L.R. 110; *Salmond and Heuston on the Law of Torts* (21st edn), p.443; *Stevens v Brodribb Sawmilling Company Pty Ltd* (1986) 160 C.L.R. 16.

[1126] Illustrations 7–10.

[1127] See *Plumb v Cobden Flour Mills Co Ltd* [1914] A.C. 62 at 66–67; *Canadian Pacific Ry Co v Lockhart* [1942] A.C. 591 at 599; *Rose v Plenty* [1976] 1 W.L.R. 141; *Harrison v Michelin Tyre Co Ltd* [1985] 1 All E.R. 918; *Kooragang Investments Pty Ltd v Richardson & Wrench Ltd* [1982] A.C. 462, Illustration 9.

the employee alone and not for that of the employer.[1128] The leading modern case of *Lister v Hesley Hall Ltd*[1129] uses a looser test of connection between the acts in question and the employment in the context of the liability of the employer of a warden of a school for sexual abuse of the pupils by the warden. Lord Steyn said that "The test is whether the [person concerned's] torts are so closely connected with his employment that it would be fair and just to hold the employers vicariously liable".[1130] This was said in the context of intentional torts against the person. However, similar reasoning has been applied in the context of the equitable wrong of accessory liability to breach of trust ("dishonest assistance"[1131]); where useful consideration of criteria to be applied can be found.[1132] A firm of solicitors was held liable under s.10 of the Partnership Act 1890 in respect of "any wrongful act or omission" of a partner acting in such a way.[1133] It was said that:

> "[i]f regard is paid to the closeness of the connection between the employee's wrongdo-ing and the class of acts which he was employed to perform or to the underlying rationale of vicarious liability, there is no relevant distinction to be made between performing an act in an improper manner and performing it for an improper purpose or by improper means."[1134]

Such reasoning now seems likely to be deployed in respect of vicarious liability generally. It was applied but the test held not to be satisfied (again for the purposes of s.10 of the Partnership Act) where the act of a partner in indorsing an unlikely investment plan was quite outside the normal function of a solicitor.[1135] More recently, the Supreme Court has held that the close connection test, away at least from cases of sexual assault on persons within the defendant's care, requires that the connection be to the tasks that the employee was engaged to perform.[1136] It is not enough that there be a close temporal or even but-for causal connection between

---

[1128] Illustrations 11–13. cf. Article 74.

[1129] *Lister v Hesley Hall Ltd* [2001] UKHL 22; [2002] 1 A.C. 215. See also not dissimilar discussion in the High Court of Australia in *New South Wales v Lepore* (2003) 212 C.L.R. 511. But cf. *Prince Alfred College Inc v ADC* [2016] HCA 37 (noted H. Crawford (2017) 24 Torts L.J. 179).

[1130] *Lister v Hesley Hall Ltd* [2001] UKHL 22; [2002] 1 A.C. 215 at [28]. See also *Majrowski v Guy's & St. Thomas's NHS Trust* [2006] UKHL 34; [2007] 1 A.C. 224 at [10], per Lord Nicholls of Birkenhead; *Maga v The Trustees of the Birmingham Archdiocese of the Roman Catholic Church* [2010] EWCA Civ 256; [2010] 1 W.L.R. 1441; *Brink's Global Services Inc v Igrox Ltd* [2010] EWCA Civ 1207; [2011] I.R.L.R. 343 (employer vicariously liable for theft by employee whilst fumigating claimant's containers) (noted Morgan [2011] L.M.C.L.Q 172); *Weddall v Barchester Healthcare Ltd* [2012] EWCA Civ 25 (assault by junior employee on more senior); *Bellman v Northampton Recruitment Ltd* [2018] EWCA Civ 2214; [2019] I.C.R. 459 (company liable for managing director's assault of employee outside work hours); *Mohamud v Wm Morrison Supermarkets Plc* [2016] UKSC 11; [2016] A.C. 677 (assault by employee on supermarket forecourt); *Axon v Ministry of Defence* [2016] EWHC 787 (QB); [2016] E.M.L.R. 20 at [95] (potential breach of privacy by employee in respect of information available only through employer). See also *Hickey v McGowan* [2017] IESC 6.

[1131] See Article 116.

[1132] See *Group Seven Ltd v Notable Services LLP* [2019] EWCA Civ 614; [2020] Ch. 129 at [143]–[146].

[1133] *Dubai Aluminium Co Ltd v Salaam* [2002] UKHL 48; [2003] 2 A.C. 366. (It should be noted that the liability of the actual solicitor was posited in the context of the matter in dispute and had never been admitted.)

[1134] *Dubai Aluminium Co Ltd v Salaam* [2002] UKHL 48; [2003] 2 A.C. 366 at [124], per Lord Millett.

[1135] *J.J. Coughlan Ltd v Ruparelia* [2003] EWCA Civ 1057; [2004] P.N.L.R. 4. See too *The Northampton Regional Livestock Centre Co Ltd v Cowling* [2015] EWCA Civ 651; [2016] 1 B.C.L.C. 431 at [96] (vicarious liability found).

[1136] *Wm Morrison Supermarkets Plc v Various Claimants* [2020] UKSC 12; [2020] 2 W.L.R. 941, Il-

those tasks and the tortious acts; employees can still be on a "frolic of their own" in such circumstances. While the fact that the employee is acting for personal benefit is not inconsistent with vicarious liability, it is not irrelevant that the employee acted to spite the employer.

For a period, the traditional dichotomy in the case law between employee and independent contractor appeared to be breaking down,[1137] in part on a conjectured premise that the use of independent contractors rather than employees is more prevalent in modern commerce than formerly. But the Supreme Court in *Barclays Bank Plc v Various Claimants* has now clarified that the "akin to employment" phraseology, which had been one of the engines for expansion, is not intended to erode the key role that the concept of employment plays in vicarious liability.[1138] The Court noted that in some of the cases where vicarious liability had been imposed without a formal employment contract between the tortfeasor and defendant, the deciding court had observed that the parties were more closely and continuously connected (including with powers of direction) than would be true of many employment relationships. Examples include the relationship between Christian brothers and their institution,[1139] and that between a prison and prisoners while undertaking prison work.[1140] The Supreme Court also counselled against reliance on the five general factors, or incidents (including the relative wealth of the defendant), that had appeared in the case involving the Christian brothers and had been another vehicle for over-expansion of vicarious liablity. Those factors may be useful at the margin, but the key will lie in the details of the parties' relationship. "Where it is clear that the tortfeasor is carrying on his own independent business it is not necessary to consider the five incidents."[1141] Although it did not surface in the reasoning in *Barclays Bank*, it may be that where there is a pre-existing relationship between the claimant and the defendant (especially where that relationship is closer than that between the defendant and the tortfeasor) it may be possible to conclude that the defendant had assumed responsibility for the loss that the claimant has suffered.[1142] Such an analysis is often called, somewhat obscurely, one involving a "non-delegable duty", and is further discussed below.[1143]

Even during the period where the scope of vicarious liability appeared to be expanding, it was not suggested that the mere existence of an agency relationship between two parties was sufficient to warrant the imposition of vicarious liability.[1144] Nor traditionally has a mere power to appoint another to (and remove from) a posi-

---

lustration 15 at [23].

[1137] See *Barclays Bank Plc v Various Claimants* [2018] EWCA Civ 1670 (noted P. Watts "The Travails of Vicarious Liability" (2019) 135 L.Q.R. 7), now reversed: [2020] UKSC 13; [2020] 2 W.L.R. 960.

[1138] *Barclays Bank Plc v Various Claimants* [2020] UKSC 13; [2020] 2 W.L.R. 960, particularly at [24]. See too *Kafagi v JBW Group Ltd* [2018] EWCA Civ 1157 at [21] and [56].

[1139] *Various Claimants v The Catholic Child Welfare Society* [2012] UKSC 56; [2013] 2 A.C. 1 at [58].

[1140] *Cox v Ministry of Justice* [2016] UKSC 10; [2016] A.C. 660 at [35] (noted Morgan [2016] C.L.J. 202; J. Plunkett "Taking stock of vicarious liability" (2016) 132 L.Q.R. 556).

[1141] *Barclays Bank Plc v Various Claimants* [2020] UKSC 13; [2020] 2 W.L.R. 960 at [27].

[1142] Such an analysis might have provided an explanation for the result in *Armes v Nottinghamshire CC* [2017] UKSC 60; [2018] A.C. 355 (noted S. Deakin, "Organisational torts: vicarious liability versus non-delegable duty" [2018] 77 C.L.J. 15; A. Dickinson, "Fostering uncertainty in the law of tort" (2018) 134 L.Q.R. 359), described in the *Barclays Bank* case: [2020] UKSC 13; [2020] 2 W.L.R. 960 at [23] as "perhaps the most difficult" of the cases to be considered. It may also have had application in *Cox v Ministry of Justice* [2016] UKSC 10; [2016] A.C. 660, and *Barclays Bank* itself: see P. Watts (2019) 135 L.Q.R. 7.

[1143] See paras 8-183 and 8-184, below.

[1144] But cf. *Heaton's Transport (St Helens) v Transport and General Workers Union* [1973] A.C. 15; and

tion been considered sufficient. *Kuwait Asia Bank EC v National Mutual Life Nominees Ltd*,[1145] for instance, remains authority for the proposition that a shareholder of a company is not vicariously liable for the wrongs of its appointees as directors of a company, even when those appointees are its employees, so long as there is no attempt to direct them in that capacity. In that context, the employees exercise their powers qua directors independently of their employer.

Transferred employment[1146]   An employee, X, may be in the general employ- **8-179** ment of A, but, as the result of arrangements made between A and B, X may be acting as the employee of B, so as to make B, and not A, responsible for X's tort at the relevant time.[1147] The test is whether X is transferred, or only the use and benefit of X's work,[1148] and this depends upon the extent to which A places X under the control and at the disposition of B.[1149] The question of control will be determined by deciding where the authority lies to direct, or to delegate to, the employee the manner in which the work is to be done.[1150] Where an employee is lent with a machine, such as a crane, "it is easier to infer that the general employer continues to control the method of performance", since the driver remains responsible to the employer for the safe keeping of the machine.[1151] The agreement between the principals does not determine the question, although it may help to determine such relevant matters as, e.g. who pays or can dismiss the employee, how long the alternative service is to last, and (where relevant) what machinery is to be employed.[1152] Each case must depend on its own circumstances.[1153] Prima facie, responsibility for the negligence of the employee rests upon the employer who engaged and generally employs the employee, and the burden upon the general employer to shift that responsibility to the hirer is a heavy one.[1154] But the Supreme Court has now confirmed that two different levels of employer may each be liable for a person transferred to their control.[1155]

S v Attorney General [2003] 3 N.Z.L.R. 450 (CA) (abuse of foster children by foster parents under state control; arguably better analysed as an example of non-delegable duty).

[1145] *Kuwait Asia Bank EC v National Mutual Life Nominees Ltd* [1991] 1 A.C. 187 PC.

[1146] See *Clerk and Lindsell on Torts* (22nd edn), paras 6-03 and 6-22.

[1147] *Century Insurance Co Ltd v Northern Ireland Road Transport Board* [1942] A.C. 509 at 513.

[1148] *Century Insurance v Northern Ireland RTB* [1942] A.C. 509 at 509, 513 and 516.

[1149] *Cameron v Nystrom* [1893] A.C. 308 at 312; *Century Insurance Co Ltd v Northern Ireland Road Transport Board* [1942] A.C. 509 at 517. See also *Chua Chye Leong Alan v Grand Palace De-luxe Nite Club Pte Ltd* [1993] 3 Singapore L.R. 449 ("parking jockey" supplied by independent contractor to night club for valet parking held "servant or agent" of night club).

[1150] *Mersey Docks and Harbour Board v Coggins & Griffith* [1947] A.C. 1 at 12.

[1151] *Mersey Docks and Harbour Board v Coggins & Griffith* [1947] A.C. 1 at 17; *Ready Mixed Concrete (East Midlands) Ltd v Yorkshire Traffic Area Licensing Authority* [1970] 2 Q.B. 397 at 404. See also *Garrard v A.E. Southey & Co* [1952] 2 Q.B. 174; *Denham v Midland Employers Mutual Ass. Ltd* [1955] 2 Q.B. 437; *Bhoomidas v Port of Singapore Authority* [1978] 1 All E.R. 956 PC; *Royal Bank of Scotland v Bannerman Johnstone Maclay*, 2005 S.C. 437 (financial controller).

[1152] *Mersey Docks and Harbour Board v Coggins & Griffith* [1947] A.C. 1.

[1153] *Ready Mixed Concrete (East Midlands) Ltd v Yorkshire Traffic Area Licensing Authority* [1970] 2 Q.B. 397 at 406.

[1154] *Mersey Docks and Harbour Board v Coggins & Griffith* [1947] A.C. 1 at 10; *Ready Mixed Concrete (East Midlands) Ltd v Yorkshire Traffic Area Licensing Authority* [1970] 2 Q.B. 397 at 404; *Biffa Waste Services Ltd v Maschinenfabrik Ernst Hese GmbH* [2008] EWCA Civ 1257; [2009] Q.B. 725.

[1155] *Various Claimants v The Catholic Child Welfare Society* [2012] UKSC 56; [2013] 2 A.C. 1; approving *Viasystems (Tyneside) Ltd v Thermal Transfer (Northern) Ltd* [2005] EWCA Civ 1151; [2005] 4 All E.R. 181 (sub-contractor and sub-sub-contractor liable for negligence of employee of subsubcontractor). cf. *Day v The Ocean Beach Hotel Shellharbour Pty Ltd* [2013] NSWCA 250;

8-180 **Torts involving misstatements** Torts of misrepresentation, unlike most torts where the claimant will be a hapless victim, involve reliance by the claimant. This suggests that the principal should not be liable for the misstatements of an agent who is also an employee unless the third party was justified in relying on them, viz. unless they were made within the agent's actual or apparent authority, which of course they may be.[1156] This approach, consistent with that employed in *Lloyd v Grace, Smith & Co*,[1157] was adopted by the House of Lords in *Armagas Ltd v Mundogas SA* as regards the tort of deceit.[1158] On this approach it will not matter whether or not the agent is an employee; liability arises if, but only if, the relevant misstatement was made within the agent's actual or apparent authority. The corollary of this that non-employer principals could be liable for the misstatements of their agents is addressed in para.8-182, below.

However, the Court of Appeal in *So v HSBC Bank Plc*[1159] held that the reasoning in *Armagas* on the issue of vicarious liability is confined to deceit, and that the standard "course of employment" test applies to an action in negligent misstatement. It is difficult to see on what basis an employer should be more readily liable for an employee's negligent statements than for his deceits, and cases prior to *So v HSBC* provide no support for such a conclusion. Hence, in *Kooragang Investments Pty Ltd v Richardson & Wrench Ltd*,[1160] not cited in *So v HSBC*, the Privy Council declined to make an employer liable for an employee's negligent valuations of land expressly on the basis that the employee had no actual or apparent authority to furnish them to the particular claimant, even though it was part of the employee's general functions to provide valuations. In *Williams v Natural Life Health Foods Ltd*,[1161] a case also not referred to in *So v HSBC*, the House of Lords held that an employee is himself not liable for his negligent statements made in the course of employment without an assumption of responsibility for their accuracy, and the court went on to conclude that the employer can be liable only on the same

---

(2013) 85 N.S.W.L.R. 335.

[1156] See *NRAM Ltd v Steel* [2018] UKSC 13; [2018] 1 W.L.R. 1190. For an example of justified reliance involving an agent's deceit, see *Breiss v Woolley* [1954] A.C. 333, Illustration 20. cf. *Bank of Montreal v Young* (1966) 60 D.L.R. (2d) 220 (bank manager not authorised to advise on investments).

[1157] *Lloyd v Grace, Smith & Co* [1912] A.C. 716 at 725, 736 and 742.

[1158] *Armagas Ltd v Mundogas SA (The Ocean Frost)* [1986] A.C. 717, Illustration 27. See also *Kleinwort, Sons & Co v Associated Automatic Machine Corp Ltd* (1934) 151 L.T. 1 (authority needed before liability for deceit, but company secretary not an employee); *Sorrell v Finch* [1977] A.C. 728 at 751; *Quinn v CC Automotive Group Ltd* [2010] EWCA Civ 1412; [2011] 2 All E.R. (Comm) 584; *Pioneer Mortgage Services Pty Ltd v Columbus Capital Pty Ltd* [2016] FCAFC 78 at [66]; *Winter v Hockley Mint Ltd* [2018] EWCA Civ 2480; [2019] 1 W.L.R. 1617.

[1159] *So v HSBC Bank Plc* [2009] EWCA Civ 296; [2009] 1 C.L.C. 503. See Watts (2012) 128 L.Q.R. 260 for critique of this case and for more detailed analysis of the relevant principles and authorities; P. Watts [2015] L.M.C.L.Q. 36; Tan Cheng Han [2012] S.J.L.S. 92. cf. *Skandinaviska Enskilda Banken AB v Asia Pacific Breweries (Singapore) Pte Ltd* [2011] SGCA 22 (noted Chan and Tjio (2012) 128 L.Q.R. 27); *Ong Han Ling v American International Assurance Co Ltd* [2017] SGHC 327 at [175]. All these cases are hard to square with English law.

[1160] *Kooragang Investments Pty Ltd v Richardson & Wrench Ltd* [1982] A.C. 462. See too *Chudley v Clydesdale Bank Plc* [2017] EWHC 2177 (Comm); distinguishing *So v HSBC* [2009] EWCA Civ 296.

[1161] *Williams v Natural Life Health Foods Ltd* [1998] 1 W.L.R. 830. See too *Standard Chartered Bank v Pakistan National Shipping Corp (No.2)* [2002] UKHL 43; [2003] 1 A.C. 959 at [21]; *Deslauriers v Guardian Asset Management Ltd* [2017] UKPC 34 at [22]; *NRAM Ltd v Steel* [2018] UKSC 13; [2018] 1 W.L.R. 1190 at [24]. cf. *Customs and Excise Commissioners v Barclays Bank Plc* [2006] UKHL 28; [2007] 1 A.C. 181.

basis.[1162] These holdings reinforce the view that, if an employer is to be liable for an employee's statements, some form of authorisation of the relevant statement, including by way of holding out, is needed. Such reasoning is as applicable to principals and agents who are not in an employment relationship as to those who are. Under this approach, the liability of the employer is direct, not vicarious.[1163] Dicta in the House of Lords in *Dubai Aluminium Co Ltd v Salaam*[1164] also support the view that the rules governing employer liability are not uniform for all torts, and in particular that torts founded on reliance on an agent's statements require that those statements be made with actual or apparent authority before a principal, including an employer, can be liable for them. Liability for other wrongs committed in connection with authorised activities where the claimant has less control over events (e.g. assault, negligent driving) remains; in this respect the course of employment test is wider than "authority" reasoning.[1165]

Certainly, the old saying that "he who trusts most should suffer most"[1166] is an unreliable guide given that the outside party, who will usually be present when the relevant dealing is made whereas the principal usually will not be, will often in a better position to sense the employee's overreach than the principal: "It has been said that 'in justice' the one of two innocent people to suffer should be the vendor who chose the estate agent. But this seems to me too loose an approach to the problem, which should be solved by analysis of legal rights and relationships".[1167] Similar ideas lie behind the nemo dat principle.[1168]

Rule (2)(a): Authorising and procuring wrongs The principal's liability where **8-181** the tort is specifically authorised or ratified is obvious: the principal has effectively committed the tort personally, and the liability is not truly vicarious.[1169] By similar reasoning, a person who appoints an independent contractor to undertake a task without making that contractor an agent can become liable for that person's wrongful acts in performing the task if the appointer gives directions to the contractor, or otherwise interferes in the contractor's work.[1170]

Rule (2)(b): Liability for statements based only on agency reasoning The **8-182**

[1162] *Williams v Natural Life Health Foods Ltd* [1998] 1 W.L.R. 830 at 838. See also *Foster v Action Aviation Ltd* [2014] EWCA Civ 1368 (company that legally owned aeroplane being sold was sole party liable for negligent misrepresentation by chairman and beneficial owner of company); *Frederick v Positive Solutions (Financial Services) Ltd* [2018] EWCA Civ 431 at [77]. cf. *Playboy Club London Ltd v Banca Nazionale del Lavoro SpA* [2018] UKSC 43; [2018] 1 W.L.R. 4041 at [7]; *CGL Group Ltd v The Royal Bank of Scotland Plc* [2017] EWCA Civ 1073; [2018] 1 W.L.R. 2137 at [82]; *Anderson v Sense Network Ltd* [2019] EWCA Civ 1395; [2020] Bus. L.R. 1 at [65].
[1163] See Roberts [2013] N.Z. Law Rev. 625, arguing that even for deceit a principal's liability, being based on authorisation, should be direct not vicarious.
[1164] *Dubai Aluminium Co Ltd v Salaam* [2002] UKHL 48; [2003] 2 A.C. 366 at [29]–[30] and [127].
[1165] See *Navarro v Moregrand Ltd* [1951] 2 T.L.R. 674 at 680, Illustration 23, per Denning LJ. But cf. *Heaton Transport Ltd (St Helen) v T&GWU* [1973] A.C. 15 at 99. See also Illustrations 3, 4, 11 and 12. As to defamation, see *Riddick v Thames Board Mills Ltd* [1977] Q.B. 881.
[1166] Usually associated with *Hern v Nichols* (1701) 1 Salk. 289.
[1167] *Sorrell v Finch* [1977] A.C. 728 at 754, per Lord Russell of Killowen (but non-employee agent). See too *Slingsby v District Bank* [1932] 1 K.B. 544 at 560; *Armagas Ltd v Mundogas SA (The Ocean Frost)* [1986] A.C. 717 at 780.
[1168] See above, para.8-126; see also *Farquharson Bros & Co v C King & Co* [1902] A.C. 325 at 335; *Shogun Finance Ltd v Hudson* [2004] A.C. 919 at [181]–[182].
[1169] Illustrations 15 and 16. See further below, para.9-120.
[1170] See the discussion in *Ventra Investments Ltd v Bank of Scotland Plc* [2019] EWHC 2058 (Comm) at [73] onwards.

second category causes more difficulty. As has been seen above, para.8-180, where an employee commits a tort involving misstatements, the terminology of authority is appropriate: the employee renders the employer liable when making a misstatement within the scope of the employee's actual or apparent authority and the statement is acted on. In the case of an employee it has been argued above that this authority terminology controls the normal tort "course of employment" test, which cannot be used to invoke a wider vicarious liability.[1171] But it is almost the corollary of that reasoning that "authority" may also be used to *create* liability in one person for the misstatements of another who is not the former's employee but merely an agent (i.e. independent contractor), and for whom there is no liability under the normal principles of non-delegable duty[1172] relating to independent contractors. The reasoning is somewhat limited. It should apply to an agent:

> "when the function entrusted is that of representing the person who requests his performance in a transaction with others, so that the very service to be performed consists in standing in his place and assuming to act in his right and not in an independent capacity."[1173]

Thus it has been held that an estate agent, who is not an employee, may have authority to make representations about property for which the agent is seeking a buyer or tenant, so that the principal is liable for their falsity.[1174] So also the vendor of land may be liable for false statements wilfully or negligently made by the vendor's solicitor in answer to inquiries.[1175] Cases involving negligent representations seem relatively straightforward, at least where there has been a holding out of authority by the principal to make them. The tortious liability, based on an assumption of responsibility, closely parallels contractual liability. The liability is also direct, and frequently agents who make actionable statements will not be personally liable unless they too can be taken as undertaking an assumption of responsibility.[1176] So much is apparent from *Williams v Natural Life Health Foods*,[1177] discussed above.

Much more controversial is the imposition of liability on a principal for defamatory statements made by an agent who is not an employee. In *Colonial Mutual Life Assurance Society Ltd v Producers' and Citizens' Cooperative Co of Australia*

[1171] *Armagas Ltd v Mundogas SA (The Ocean Frost)* [1986] A.C. 717; see above, para.8-180. See also *Brockway v Pando* (2000) 22 W.A.R. 405.

[1172] See *Clerk and Lindsell on Torts* (22nd edn), para.6-62 onwards; *Gladman Commercial Properties v Fisher Hargreaves Proctor* [2013] EWHC 25 (Ch) at [125]; affirmed [2013] EWCA Civ 1466.

[1173] *Colonial Mutual Life Assurance Society Ltd v Producers and Citizens Cooperative Co of Australia Ltd* (1931) 46 C.L.R. 41, per Dixon J. See also *The Litsion Pride* [1985] 1 Lloyd's Rep. 437 at 513–514; *NZ Guardian Trust Ltd v Brooks* [1995] 1 W.L.R. 4 PC.

[1174] See Illustrations 19–22.

[1175] *Cemp Properties (UK) Ltd v Dentsply Research and Development Corp* [1989] 2 E.G.L.R. 196, Illustration 24 (Misrepresentation Act 1967 s.2(1)); *Gran Gelato Ltd v Richcliff Group Ltd* [1992] Ch. 560 (Misrepresentation Act 1967 s.2(1)); criticised Cane (1992) 108 L.Q.R. 539; and see *Derham v Amev Life Insurance Co Ltd* (1981) 56 F.L.R. 34 (fraud of insurance agent).

[1176] See *Gran Gelato Ltd v Richcliff Group Ltd* [1992] Ch. 560; *NRAM Ltd v Steel* [2018] UKSC 13; [2018] 1 W.L.R. 1190. cf. *McCullagh v Lane Fox & Partners Ltd* [1996] 1 E.G.L.R. 35 at 41–44; *Punjab National Bank Ltd v de Boinville* [1992] 1 W.L.R. 1138, where employees of insurance brokers were held to owe a duty of care to an assignee of the policy brokered. In *Dean v Allin & Watts* [2001] EWCA Civ 758; [2001] 2 Lloyd's Rep. 249 the *Gran Gelato* case was accepted as laying down a general rule for solicitors, though the solicitor was in fact held liable to the third party. For further discussion, see below, para.9-117.

[1177] *Williams v Natural Life Health Foods* [1998] 1 W.L.R. 830. See too *Challinor v Juliet Bellis & Co* [2013] EWHC 347 (Ch) at [732] (reversed on other points, sub nom. *Bellis v Challinor* [2015] EWCA Civ 59).

Ltd,[1178] from which the above quotation is taken, the High Court of Australia held an insurance company liable for defamation of another company committed by its agent (not an employee) in the course of soliciting business. The victim of the defamation will not usually have relied on the agent as having had authority to make the defamatory statement, and there will not normally be an assumption of responsibility by the agent, or the principal, for its accuracy. An English case in which similar suggestions appear is *Uxbridge Permanent Benefit Building Society v Pickard*,[1179] where a solicitor was held liable for the fraud (involving forgery) of his managing clerk, though this could be explained on the basis of the established rules as to master and servant. There are also cases where the agent was not an employee, and the possibility of the agent's nevertheless having acted within authority so as to render the principal liable was discussed, but negatived on the facts.[1180] More recently, it has been suggested in Australia that the reasoning in *Colonial Mutual* might be confined to agents who have full contracting authority.[1181] It is also reasonably clear that agency is not a basis for imposing vicarious liability outside the context of statements. Thus it has been held in South Africa that an insurance company was not liable for the negligent driving of its agent who was taking a doctor to examine a prospective client.[1182]

Rule (2)(c): Wider use of the concept of an assumption of responsibility   The   **8-183** concept of an assumption of responsibility, which, as seen, has had a prominent role in the development of tortious liability for negligent misstatement, has gradually been invoked in a wider range of circumstances, particularly where services have been performed negligently. However pragmatic the development has been as a method of avoiding perceived shortcomings in the law of contract,[1183] especially when there is concurrent contractual liability, its role seems established.[1184] The concept has perhaps as great a role in limiting tortious liability for economic loss

---

[1178] *Colonial Mutual Life Assurance Society Ltd v Producers' and Citizens' Cooperative Co of Australia Ltd* (1931) 46 C.L.R. 41, Illustration 25. See also *Monir v Wood* [2018] EWHC 3525 (QB), a doubtful decision; *Thiessen v Clarica Law Reinsurance Co* (2002) 219 D.L.R. (4th) 98 (insurance agent steals money given to him for investment); *Cornwall v Rowan* (2004) 90 S.A.S.R. 269 (consultant responsible for report issued by others not liable for defamation). The principle has been held not to apply to make the client of a solicitor conducting litigation liable for contempt of court by the solicitor: *Forestview Nominees Pty Ltd v Perron Investments Pty Ltd* (1999) 93 F.C.R. 117 (Aus.)— see valuable discussion at 134–140, per R.D. Nicholson J.

[1179] *Uxbridge Permanent Benefit Building Society v Pickard* [1939] 2 K.B. 248, Illustration 12.

[1180] *Bradford Third Equitable BS v Borders* [1941] 2 All E.R. 205; *Kwei Tek Chao v British Traders and Shippers Ltd* [1954] 2 Q.B. 459; *Strover v Harrington* [1988] Ch. 390, Illustration 8 to Article 94 (Misrepresentation Act 1967 s.2(1)).

[1181] See *Hallmark Construction Pty Ltd v Harford* [2020] NSWCA 41 at [75]. See also *Sweeney v Boylan Nominees Pty Ltd* [2006] HCA 19; (2006) 226 C.L.R. 161 at [24].

[1182] *Colonial Mutual Life Assurance Society Ltd v Macdonald* [1931] A.D. 412, Illustration 26. See also *Eggington v Reader* [1936] 1 All E.R. 7, Illustration 6; and *Sweeney v Boylan Nominees Pty Ltd* (2006) 226 C.L.R. 161 (defendant owner of commercial refrigerator not vicariously liable for negligent repair by repairman who was an independent contractor). But cf. *Dobson v Holderness* [1975] 2 N.Z.L.R. 749; *Nelson v Raphael* [1979] R.T.R. 437, cases, however, which move into the area of "casual delegation": see below, para.8-187.

[1183] See *Cramaso LLP v Ogilvie-Grant, Earl of Seafield* [2014] UKSC 9; [2014] A.C. 1093. cf. *Robinson v PE Jones (Contractors) Ltd* [2011] EWCA Civ 9; [2012] Q.B. 44.

[1184] See *Hedley Byrne & Co Ltd v Heller & Partners Ltd* [1964] A.C. 465; *Kooragang Investments Pty Ltd v Richardson & Wrench Ltd* [1982] A.C. 462; *Henderson v Merrett Syndicates Ltd* [1995] 2 A.C. 145; *Dunlop Haywards Ltd v Erinaceous Insurance Services Ltd* [2008] EWHC 520 (Comm); [2008] Lloyd's Rep. I.R. 676 at [66]; reversed on other points [2009] EWCA Civ 354; *P&P Property Ltd v Owen White and Catlin LLP* [2018] EWCA Civ 1082; [2019] Ch. 273 at [72] and [75]. See further

as expanding it.[1185] But persistent optimism as to the role of the courts in making one person compensate for the economic loss of another means doubt remains as to whether the assumption of legal responsibility is a necessary, as opposed to a sufficient,[1186] element in tortious liability for causing loss that is exclusively economic, and, if so, whether the assumption needs to be a genuine one.[1187] In many cases where a genuine assumption exists, it will be appropriate to regard as agents those employees and independent contractors who are engaged by the principal to perform the relevant tasks.[1188] It is not so obvious that all persons whose tasks are merely part of the process by which the principal intends to perform his undertaking, for example a contractor engaged to make technical drawings or to make a valuation, would be regarded as an agent, in the strict sense. The mere performance of work by such persons may not, for instance, itself change their principals' legal position, since at the time it was performed it may not be certain that the product of their work will ever be delivered to the third party. There may also not be much room of the application of fiduciary obligations in some of these cases. It can be expected, nonetheless, that the label agent will often be applied to such persons, particularly those who are not employees.

8-184   **Non-delegable duties**[1189]   The concept of assumption of responsibility to take due care is potentially capable of resulting in direct liability on the owners of businesses in a wide range of circumstances. Such liability can run in parallel with express or implied contractual duties of care. Having connections to assumption of responsibility, but not exclusively explained by that rationale (the duty may, for example, be based on statutory implication), is a body of law that turns on a person being liable as principal for what is called a "non-delegable duty of care". The performance of that duty may be delegated to others who need not be employees, but the principal remains responsible for injury or damage caused by the actions of the delegate. The leading case is now the decision of the Supreme Court in *Woodland v Essex County Council*.[1190] In this case Lord Sumption referred to the long recognition of a non-delegable duty of care in "a large, varied and anomalous class of case" concerned with physical harm resulting from the operation of hazardous activities, especially in public places. A second line of cases has developed within the law of nuisance to impose liability on a building owner for the negligent

---

above, para.6-016.

[1185] See *NRAM Ltd v Steel* [2018] UKSC 13; [2018] 1 W.L.R. 1190; *James-Bowen v Commissioner of Police* [2018] UKSC 40; [2018] 1 W.L.R. 4021 at [24]; *Poole Borough Council v GN* [2019] UKSC 25; [2019] 2 W.L.R. 1478 at [67] and [88]; *Seddon v Driver and Vehicle Licensing Agency* [2019] EWCA Civ 14; [2019] 1 W.L.R. 4593 at [57].

[1186] *Caparo Industries Plc v Dickman* [1990] 2 A.C. 605 at 628 and 637; *Customs and Excise Commissioners v Barclays Bank Plc* [2006] UKHL 28; [2007] 1 A.C. 181; *CGL Group Ltd v The Royal Bank of Scotland Plc* [2017] EWCA Civ 1073; [2018] 1 W.L.R. 2137 at [82].

[1187] See, e.g. *Chandler v Cape Plc* [2012] EWCA Civ 525; [2012] 1 W.L.R. 3111 at [64]; *P&P Property Ltd v Owen White and Catlin LLP* [2018] EWCA Civ 1082; [2019] Ch. 273 at [76].

[1188] See, e.g. *Gempride Ltd v Bamrah* [2018] EWCA Civ 1367 at [97] (solicitor responsible for misstatements of independent costs draftsperson).

[1189] See Stevens, in *Emerging Issues in Tort Law* (Neyers, Chamberlain and Pitel eds, 2007), Ch.13; Beuermann (2013) 20 Torts L.J. 265; Foster in *Divergences in Private Law* (Robertson and Tilbury eds, 2016), Ch.7; Todd (2016) 23 Torts LJ 105.

[1190] *Woodland v Essex County Council* [2013] UKSC 66; [2014] A.C. 537 (noted Morgan [2015] C.L.J. 109). See also *Riverstone Meat Co Pty Ltd v Lancashire Shipping Co Ltd (The Muncaster Castle)* [1961] A.C. 807; *Biffa Waste Services Ltd v Maschinenfabrik Ernst Hese GmbH* [2008] EWCA Civ 1257; [2009] Q.B. 725; *Central Darling Shire Council v Greeney* [2015] NSWCA 51.

actions of the owner's independent contractors in damaging the claimant's property, whether or not the activities were inherently dangerous. Occupiers' liability can also be regarded as involving non-delegable duties.[1191]

Woodland confirms that there is another category of case—that where there is an antecedent relationship between claimant and defendant, but where, for one reason or another, a contractual route to finding a duty of care does not exist.[1192] The relevant services (in *Woodland*, school swimming lessons) may, for example, be provided by the state or a local authority without a contract with the claimant. This category of case is based on an assumption of responsibility for the exercise of due care in relation to the relevant activity.[1193] The claimant will usually have been in the custody, charge or care of the defendant, and will have had little control over the way in which the care was discharged. As with other cases based on a voluntary assumption of responsibility, it is probably not necessary to regard the independent contractor as the agent of the defendant, although some of the cases concerned with the duties of an employer to his own workforce have used the language of agency.[1194] In *Woodland*, Lord Sumption cautioned about finding an assumption of a non-delegable duty too readily, lest it swallow the general rule that one is not liable for the tortious actions of others.[1195] The concept might, however, be regarded as having a role to play to the extent that an employer has a duty to provide employees with a safe working environment, and some of the more difficult vicarious liability cases might also be better appraised on this basis.[1196]

Deceit: division of ingredients[1197]   The tort of deceit, where because of its con-   **8-185**
nection with contract situations agency terminology is frequently used, raises special problems where agents are involved, in so far as it requires a false statement made, with the intention that it should be acted on, "knowingly, or without belief in its truth, or recklessly, careless whether it be true or false".[1198] Is the principal to be liable to a third party where (for instance) the agent made a representation innocently, believing it to be true, and the principal knew of the untruth of the statement but did not know that it was being made? In such case no individual is guilty of personal fraud: there is an "innocent division of ingredients".[1199] But are the acts and minds of principal and agent to be regarded as so far one that, by taking the agent's statement and the principal's knowledge together, the principal can be held liable to the third party in deceit? There was some

---

[1191] See *Libra Collaroy Pty Ltd v Bhide* [2017] NSWCA 196 (independent contractor an agent but owner's liability not derived from contractor's agency functions).

[1192] For a comparable situation where a contractual action was available, see *Wong Mee Wan v Kwan Kin Travel Services* [1996] 1 W.L.R. 38 (package tour operator liable for negligence of subcontractors).

[1193] *Woodland v Swimming Teachers Association* [2013] UKSC 66; [2014] A.C. 537 at [7].

[1194] *Wilsons & Clyde Coal Co Ltd v English* [1938] A.C. 57 at 75.

[1195] *Woodland v Swimming Teachers Association* [2013] UKSC 66; [2014] 1 A.C. 537 at [22].

[1196] For discussion, see P. Watts "The Travails of Vicarious Liability" (2019) 135 L.Q.R. 7 at 10–11, with particular reference to *Armes v Nottinghamshire CC* [2017] UKSC 60; [2018] A.C. 355.

[1197] Powell, pp.200–207; *Salmond and Heuston on the Law of Torts* (21st edn), pp.376–377; Devlin (1937) 53 L.Q.R. 344; Wright (1937) 15 Can.B.R. 716; Gower (1952) 15 M.L.R. 232; Unger (1952) 15 M.L.R. 508; Müller-Freienfels in *Civil Law in the Modern World* (Yiannopoulos ed., 1965), pp.77 and 120–124. See also Article 21, Illustration 2; Dugdale (2006) 12 N.Z. Business L.Q. 3.

[1198] *Derry v Peek* (1889) 14 App. Cas. 337 at 374, per Lord Herschell.

[1199] The language of Devlin J in (1937) 53 L.Q.R. 344; and in *Armstrong v Strain* [1951] 1 T.L.R. 856 (at first instance).

authority that they were[1200]: but the law was later clarified by the decision of the Court of Appeal in *Armstrong v Strain*[1201] and is best stated in a series of propositions.

(a) P, the principal, is liable if P authorised the agent, A, to make the false representation which P knew to be untrue (or did not believe to be true), whether or not A knew the truth.[1202]

(b) P, the principal, is liable if, while not expressly authorising the agent, A, to make the false representation, P knew it to be untrue and was guilty of some positive wrongful conduct, as by consciously permitting A to remain ignorant of the true facts, so as to prevent the disclosure of the truth to the third party, if the third party should ask A for information, or in the hope that A would make some false representation.[1203] A's representation when made would of course require to be within the scope of A's actual or apparent authority.[1204]

(c) The principal, P is liable if the agent, A, made the false representation fraudulently, it being within the scope of A's actual or apparent authority and within the course of A's employment, to make such a representation,[1205] sometimes even where the representation reached the third party by way of another innocent agent,[1206] or by way of the P, albeit innocently,[1207] because

---

[1200] See the confusing discussion in *Woyka & Co v London & Northern Trading Co* (1922) 10 Ll. L. Rep. 110.

[1201] *Armstrong v Strain* [1952] 1 K.B. 232; affirming [1951] 1 T.L.R. 856, Illustration 22 (not considering *Woyka & Co v London & Northern Trading Co* (1922) 10 Ll. L. Rep. 110).

[1202] If the agent knew the truth, they are jointly and severally liable; if not, the principal is alone liable for the principal's own tort committed through the agent as an innocent instrument.

[1203] *Ludgater v Love* (1881) 44 L.T. 694; *Cornfoot v Fowke* (1840) 6 M. & W. 358 at 370, 372 and 373–374; *Gordon Hill Trust Ltd v Segall* [1941] 2 All E.R. 379 at 390; *Awaroa Holdings Ltd v Commercial Securities & Finance Ltd* [1976] 1 N.Z.L.R. 19; *The Siboen and The Sibotre* [1976] 1 Lloyd's Rep. 293 at 320–321. Presumably this would be equally so if the failure to act was of another agent of the principal acting in the course of his employment, the principal being innocent: *UBS AG (London Branch) v Kommunale Wasserwerke Leipzig GmbH* [2014] EWHC 3615 (Comm) at [757] (affirmed [2017] EWCA Civ 1567).

[1204] See *MCI WorldCom International Inc v Primus Telecommunications Inc* [2003] EWHC 2182; [2004] 1 All E.R. (Comm) 138 at [58], [59]; reversed on other grounds [2004] EWCA Civ 957; [2004] 2 All E.R. (Comm) 833.

[1205] *Barwick v English Joint Stock Bank* (1867) L.R. 2 Ex. 259; *Briess v Woolley* [1954] A.C. 333, Illustration 21; *Egger v Viscount Chelmsford* [1965] 1 Q.B. 248 at 261; *Mackay v Commercial Bank of New Brunswick* (1874) L.R. 5 P.C. 394. See also *Hern v Nichols* (1701) 1 Salk. 289; *Udell v Atherton* (1861) 7 H. & N. 172, per Pollock CB and Wilde B. Unless perhaps the fraud of the agent is primarily practised on the principal himself: *Kwei Tek Chao v British Traders & Shippers Ltd* [1954] 2 Q.B. 459. See also *Credit Lyonnais Bank Nederland NV v ECGD* [2000] 1 A.C. 486 (no liability for employee not himself committing deceit but assisting external tortfeasor to do so; liability in conspiracy not relied upon); *Frederick v Positive Solutions (Financial Services) Ltd* [2018] EWCA Civ 431 at [74]. In *Frederick*, not only were any agency powers exercised by the relevant rogue merely tangential to the deceit carried out on the claimant, but the rogue's actions were not within his actual or apparent authority, nor did the claimant rely on any holding out.

[1206] *London County Freehold & Leasehold Properties Ltd v Berkeley Property & Investment Co Ltd* [1936] 2 All E.R. 1039; as explained in *Anglo-Scottish Beet Sugar Corp Ltd v Spalding UDC* [1937] 2 K.B. 607; approved by the Court of Appeal in *Armstrong v Strain* [1952] 1 K.B. 232. See also *UBS AG (London Branch) v Kommunale Wasserwerke Leipzig GmbH* [2014] EWHC 3615 (Comm) at [757] (affirmed [2017] EWCA Civ 1567).

[1207] *S. Pearson & Son Ltd v Dublin Corp* [1907] A.C. 351; as explained in *Anglo-Scottish Beet Sugar Corp Ltd v Spalding UDC* [1937] 2 K.B. 607.

in such a case the innocent second agent or principal may be no more than a conduit pipe for the fraud of the guilty agent, A.[1208]

(d) The principal, P, is not liable if the agent, A, made the false representation innocently, P knowing the true facts but not having authorised A to make the representation, nor knowing that it would be made, nor being guilty of fraudulent conduct as in (b) above.[1209]

(e) Conversely, the principal, P, is not liable if P made the false representation innocently, notwithstanding that an agent knew the true facts.[1210]

The question whether the principal can exclude liability for an agent's fraud has only recently been articulated addressed. It is normally assumed that a principal cannot exclude liability for personal fraud; and that the principal can provide that the agent has no authority to speak for him or her.[1211] It appears that liability for an agent's fraud in the making of the contract can probably be excluded, but the wording would need to be very clear.[1212] Such a clause would however be subject to the unfair contract terms legislation in so far as that applied in the context.[1213]

Negligence The problems centred around *Armstrong v Strain* arose from attempts to invoke the tort of deceit in respect of actions that were in substance in respect of negligent misrepresentation—largely in respect of misrepresentations made by the agents of companies. Since 1964[1214] it has been established that an action in negligence may in principle lie in such cases (at least where the agents had apparent authority to be making the statements), and the rules stated above are therefore of less importance. It is possible in appropriate cases to sue the principal where the statement was negligently made by an agent[1215]; or where, though no one person can be said to have been negligent, the totality of the operations of the principal in the particular respect can be regarded as involving an assumption of responsibility for the relevant loss.[1216] The same is true of actions under s.2 of the Misrepresentation Act 1967.[1217] Exclusion clauses raise the same considerations as elsewhere in the law.[1218]

8-186

[1208] *S. Pearson & Son Ltd v Dublin Corp* [1907] A.C. 351 at 367.

[1209] *Armstrong v Strain* [1952] 1 K.B. 232; *Cornfoot v Fowke* (1840) 6 M. & W. 358; *Gordon Hill Trust v Segall* [1941] 2 All E.R. 379.

[1210] See *Anglo-Scottish Beet Sugar Corp Ltd v Spalding UDC* [1937] 2 K.B. 607. "You cannot add an innocent state of mind to an innocent state of mind and get as a result a dishonest state of mind": per Devlin J in *Armstrong v Strain* [1951] 1 T.L.R. 856 at 872. The same reasoning would apply where the relevant knowledge was possessed by another agent.

[1211] cf. *Overbrooke Estates Ltd v Glencombe Properties Ltd* [1974] 1 W.L.R. 1335.

[1212] *HIH Casualty and General Insurance Ltd v Chase Manhattan Bank* [2003] UKHL 6; [2003] 1 All E.R. (Comm) 349; but see Lord Hobhouse of Woodborough at [98]. Previous authority (*S. Pearson & Son Ltd v Dublin Corp* [1907] A.C. 351; *Mair v Rio Grande Rubber Estates Ltd* 1913 S.C.(H.L.) 74; and *Boyd and Forrest v Glasgow & SW Ry Co* 1915 S.C.(H.L.) 20 was regarded as inconclusive. See also *Satyam Computer Services Ltd v Upaid Systems Ltd* [2008] EWCA Civ 487; [2008] 2 All E.R. (Comm) 465 at [82].

[1213] See *Chitty on Contracts* (33rd edn), Chs 15 and 38.

[1214] *Hedley Byrne & Co Ltd v Heller & Partners Ltd* [1964] A.C. 465.

[1215] Thus in *Mutual Life and Citizen's Assurance Co v Evatt* [1971] A.C. 793 it was alleged that the defendant company gave advice "by itself, its servants and agents". See also *Ministry of Housing and Local Government v Sharp* [1970] 2 Q.B. 223; *Esso Petroleum Co Ltd v Mardon* [1976] Q.B. 801; *Box v Midland Bank Ltd* [1979] 2 Lloyd's Rep. 391.

[1216] See *W.B. Anderson & Sons v Rhodes (Liverpool) Ltd* [1967] 2 All E.R. 850; *McInerny v Lloyd's Bank Ltd* [1974] 1 Lloyd's Rep. 246. See also Article 21, Illustration 2.

[1217] *Howard Marine and Dredging Co Ltd v A. Ogden & Sons (Excavations) Ltd* [1978] Q.B. 574. But

8-187 Casual delegation A distinct line of tort cases holds the owner or bailee of a motor car or other conveyance, and sometimes some other type of chattel, liable for the negligence of one whom the owner permits to use it. The cases mostly concern cars, and from the policy point of view there is obviously some relevance in the owner's or bailee's insurance. The cases have been the subject of numerous explanations, each of which imposes its own limits on the doctrine: one of them has been that the driver or user is in some sense an agent of the owner or bailee in that the driver is carrying out that person's purposes: though in the leading English case[1219] Lord Wilberforce said that in the present context agency "is merely a concept, the meaning and purpose of which is to say 'is vicariously liable'".[1220] In an Australian leading case Dixon J said that "it is easier to see the direction in which the branch grows than to understand the support it derives from the main trunk of traditional doctrine governing vicarious responsibility".[1221] The doctrine and its history have recently been exhaustively reconsidered by the High Court of Australia in a case involving a private aeroplane, the owner of which was held not liable.[1222] What seems to emerge clearly from the decision is that the cases do not link to agency, at least in the central sense of that word.[1223] Further details should therefore be sought in works on tort.[1224]

8-188 Contributory negligence The attribution to a principal of acts, omissions and knowledge that might be relevant to a defence of contributory negligence remains a subject of considerable uncertainty. It is widely assumed that attribution ought to occur in the same way as for liability.[1225] It is not yet clear that this is the correct approach. For many torts, a principal is vicariously liable only for the acts and omissions of employees, and not liable for the acts and omissions of independent contractors even if they are agents.[1226] On the other hand, to the extent that a principal is expected to take due care of its own interests, it could be argued that if it uses an independent contractor to do that, it carries the risk of that party's failures. Some of the cases concern claims in negligent misstatement and for pure economic loss, where there is, in any event, more room for the operation of agency models.[1227] Otherwise, there are some cases that have in relation to companies used *alter ego*

---

the state of mind of the "reasonable belief" defence must be that of the principal: see *MCI WorldCom International Inc v Primus Telecommunications Inc* [2003] EWHC 2182; [2004] 1 All E.R. (Comm) 138 at [58], [59]; reversed on other grounds [2004] EWCA Civ 957; [2004] 2 All E.R. (Comm) 833. See also *Gosling v Anderson* (1972) 223 E.G. 1743 at 1745, per Lord Denning MR Although this section uses the analogy of fraud in imposing liability, it seems that the fraud rules as to division of ingredients will not be applied: cf. Atiyah and Treitel (1967) 30 M.L.R. 369 at 374.
[1218] See *Chitty on Contracts* (33rd edn), Chs 15 and 38.
[1219] *Launchbury v Morgans* [1973] A.C. 127.
[1220] *Launchbury v Morgans* [1973] A.C. 127 at 135.
[1221] *Soblusky v Egan* (1960) 103 C.L.R. 215 at 229.
[1222] *Scott v Davis* (2000) 204 C.L.R. 333.
[1223] See especially para.227 onwards (Gummow J) and 299 onwards (Hayne J). See too *Lloyd v Borg* [2013] NSWCA 245; (2013) 84 N.S.W.L.R. 652 (control held necessary).
[1224] See *Clerk and Lindsell on Torts* (22nd edn), paras 6-80–6-83.
[1225] See a valuable article by Bartlett (1998) 114 L.Q.R. 460. See also *Daniels v Anderson* (1995) 37 N.S.W.L.R. 438 at 569–570.
[1226] See above, para.8-178.
[1227] See, e.g. *O'Hagan v Body Corp 189855* [2010] 3 N.Z.L.R. 445 at [141] (claimants suing local authority found contributorily negligent on basis of their solicitor's failure to undertake proper search of property records); *Zurich Australian Insurance Ltd v Withers* [2016] NZCA 618; [2017] 2 N.Z.L.R. 745 at [58] (contributory negligence of non-employee agent under statutory liability for "misleading conduct in trade").

reasoning for the attribution of contributory negligence[1228]; or whether in relation to companies or not, have used the supposed fraud exception to the rules as to imputation of the agent's knowledge to the principal, whereby such an imputation is not made where the agent is acting in fraud of the principal.[1229] The resolution of the difficulties in this area is unlikely to be assisted by creating special rules for companies. As for the fraud exception, this is difficult to reconcile with the principle that makes the principal liable for the agent's fraud.[1230] The problems in this area are of fairly recent development and await clarification.

Corporations Corporate principals can be liable in tort like individuals, though **8-189** the torts must necessarily be committed through employees or agents. Arguments based on the notion of ultra vires have long been rejected or evaded in the tort context,[1231] and are now removed by legislation which has primary applicability in contract but is also relevant to torts.[1232] Thus corporations can be sued for conversion,[1233] wrongful distress,[1234] false imprisonment,[1235] trespass to land or goods[1236] and, as regards cases where a specific mental element may be involved, defamation,[1237] malicious prosecution,[1238] fraud[1239] and conspiracy.[1240] In general, corporations are liable for the torts of their employees, independent contractors and agents in accordance with the principles already discussed above. The difficulties caused by the use of reasoning that the acts of certain persons may rank as the acts of the corporation itself ("*alter ego*" reasoning) have already been referred to.[1241] Other difficulties arise where it is asserted that a parent company owes direct duties in tort for the activities of its subsidiaries.[1242] Some conduct or omission on the part of the parent company's employees will be required, but it may not be necessary for any formal link such as agency to exist between the two companies.[1243] In principle, the position of a parent company should not be any different from that of a human shareholder who owns the majority or all the shares in the company.

[1228] See *British Racing Drivers' Club Ltd v Hextall Erskine & Co* [1996] 3 All E.R. 667.
[1229] This may be the explanation of *Dairy Containers Ltd v NZI Bank Ltd* [1995] 2 N.Z.L.R. 30: see criticism by Bartlett (1998) 114 L.Q.R. 460. See also *Edwards Karwacki Smith & Co Pty Ltd v Jacka Nominees Pty Ltd* (1994) 15 A.C.S.R. 502.
[1230] *Lloyd v Grace Smith & Co* [1912] A.C. 716. As to the fraud exception, see below, para.8-214.
[1231] e.g. *Campbell v Paddington Corp* [1911] 1 K.B. 869.
[1232] Companies Act 2006 ss.39 and 40, considered above, para.8-035 onwards.
[1233] *Yarborough v Bank of England* (1812) 16 East 6; *Giles v Taff Vale Ry* (1853) 2 E. & B. 822; *Barnett v Crystal Palace Co* (1861) 4 L.T. 403.
[1234] *Eastern Counties Ry Co v Broom* (1851) 6 Exch. 314; *Smith v Birmingham Gas Co* (1834) 3 L.J.K.B. 165.
[1235] Illustration 5.
[1236] *Maund v Monmouthshire Canal Co* (1842) 4 Man. & G. 452.
[1237] Illustration 23.
[1238] *Cornford v Carlton Bank* [1899] 1 Q.B. 392.
[1239] *Ranger v Great Western Ry Co* (1854) 5 H.L.Cas. 72; *Barwick v English Joint Stock Bank* (1867) L.R. 2 Ex. 259; *Mackay v Commercial Bank of New Brunswick* (1874) L.R. 5 P.C. 394.
[1240] See *Barclay Pharmaceuticals Ltd v Waypharm LP* [2012] EWHC 306 (Comm); [2013] 2 B.C.L.C. 551 at [229]; *Muduroglu v Reddish LLP* [2015] EWHC 1044 (Ch). But see Watts in *Agency Law in Commercial Practice* (Busch, Macgregor and Watts eds, 2016), p.109.
[1241] See above, paras 1-028 and 8-184.
[1242] See *Chandler v Cape Plc* [2011] EWHC 951 (QB) at [75]; affirmed [2012] EWCA Civ 525; [2012] 1 W.L.R. 3111; *Lungowe v Vedanta Resources Plc* [2017] EWCA Civ 1528. cf. *Thompson v Renwick Group Plc* [2014] EWCA Civ 635; *Okpabi v Royal Dutch Shell Plc* [2018] EWCA Civ 191; *AAA v Unilever Plc* [2018] EWCA Civ 1532 (see too *NRAM Ltd v Steel* [2018] UKSC 13; [2018] 1 W.L.R. 1190).
[1243] See further para.1-030, above.

8-190   **The Crown**   The Crown Proceedings Act 1947 provides that the Crown is subject to all those liabilities in tort to which, if it were a private person of full age and capacity, it would be subject in respect of torts committed by its servants or agents: provided that no proceedings lie against the Crown by virtue of this provision in respect of any act or omission of a servant or agent of the Crown unless the act or omission would apart from the provisions of the Act give rise to a cause of action in tort against that servant or agent or his estate.[1244] The words "servant or agent" cause some difficulty. It is arguable that there is nowadays no such person as a servant of the Crown in the strict sense, but it has been said that there is a large category of persons, including civil servants, whom "the Crown (through or with the advice of a Minister) controls ... and directs their activities in a way which ... makes the term 'servant' quite appropriate".[1245] As regards agents, it is provided that "agent ... includes an independent contractor",[1246] but the inference from this is that the word covers also persons other than independent contractors. It is submitted that the effect of the use of the word is to leave it in no doubt that the Crown is to be liable in those cases in which an ordinary person would be liable for the torts of his agent. It seems that the word covers also those public bodies that act on behalf of the Crown, though there is little authority on which bodies are to be regarded as agents of the Crown for this purpose.[1247] Further discussion should be sought in specialised works.[1248]

8-191   **Rule (3): Judgment against principal or agent: contribution[1249]**   Where the principal is liable for the torts of his agent, or the master for those of his servant, they are in principle to be regarded as joint tortfeasors.[1250] At common law judgment against one such tortfeasor released the others[1251] and there was no general right of contribution between them.[1252] The Law Reform (Married Women and Tortfeasors) Act 1935[1253] abolished the first rule; and also made provision for contribution between such tortfeasors. The Civil Liability (Contribution) Act 1978[1254] repealed the relevant part of the 1935 Act, extending the right to contribution to situations where one wrongdoer was not liable in tort (but rather for breach

---

[1244] Crown Proceedings Act 1947 s.2(1)(b) and proviso. See *New South Wales v Ibbett* (2006) 231 A.L.R. 485 (exemplary damages for unlawful acts of police officers); *Cox v Ministry of Justice* [2016] UKSC 10; [2016] A.C. 660; *Axon v Ministry of Defence* [2016] EWHC 787 (QB) at [81].

[1245] *Bank voor Handel en Scheepvaart NV v Administrator of Hungarian Property* [1954] A.C. 584 at 616, per Lord Reid, rejecting dicta of Devlin J at first instance, [1952] 1 All E.R. 314 at 319.

[1246] Crown Proceedings Act 1947 s.38(2).

[1247] Treitel [1957] P.L. 320 at 327 onwards. See also Griffith (1952) 9 U. Toronto L.J. 169; *Moukataff v BOAC* [1967] 1 Lloyd's Rep. 396.

[1248] e.g. *Clerk and Lindsell on Torts* (22nd edn), para.5-02 onwards.

[1249] See in general a valuable article by Mitchell [1997] Restitution L.R. 27; Glanville Williams, *Joint Torts and Contributory Negligence* (1951); *Salmond and Heuston on the Law of Torts* (21st edn), p.423 onwards; *Clerk and Lindsell on Torts* (22nd edn), para.3-57 onwards; *NZ Guardian Trust Ltd v Brooks* [1995] 1 W.L.R. 96 (PC).

[1250] *Jones v Manchester Corp* [1952] 2 Q.B. 852 at 869.

[1251] *Merryweather v Nixan* (1788) S.T.R. 186. As to release as a result of settlement with one of the parties, see *Gladman Commercial Properties v Fisher Hargreaves Proctor* [2013] EWCA Civ 1466; *Starlight Shipping Co v Allianz Marine and Aviation Versicherungs AG* [2014] EWHC 3068 (Comm); [2015] 2 All E.R. (Comm) 747 at [58].

[1252] *Brinsmead v Harrison* (1872) L.R. 7 C.P. 547.

[1253] Law Reform (Married Women and Tortfeasors) Act 1935 s.6.

[1254] See *Law Com. No.79* (1977).

of contract or in equity)[1255] and also making improved provision for the right to contribution,[1256] dealing with two cases which previously had been controversial. These were whether a tortfeasor who had settled a claim against the claimant was entitled to contribution: and whether contribution could be recovered from a person who had been sued to judgment and held not liable in circumstances in which that person would have been liable had he or she been sued at some other time or in some other way.[1257] The Act binds the Crown.[1258]

The employer can often, however, recover an indemnity at common law apart from statute,[1259] for employees are under a duty to take reasonable care in the execution of their duties, and if they break this duty the measure of damages may be the loss they have caused the employer, who has had to answer for their torts.[1260] Where an agent can be brought under this reasoning, the agent may similarly be liable.[1261] But if the employer or principal is personally at fault, the agent or employee may not be liable under this head.[1262] However, even if an employer or principal was at fault, that person may be able to recover such sum as the court considers just and equitable by way of contribution under the Act: and where not at fault such person can equally sue under the statute, instead of at common law, and may recover 100 per cent contribution.[1263] But a principal has no right to recover contribution where the agent is completely innocent, for here the principal is under a duty to indemnify the agent.[1264]

Illustrations

The course of the employee's employment

(1) The driver of a tanker, whose duty included the delivery of petrol into stor- **8-192** age tanks, while transporting petrol from the tanker to a storage tank at a garage, struck a match to light a cigarette and threw the lighted match on the floor, thereby causing a fire. Held, that his employer was liable for the damage so caused by the negligent act of the driver, which was done in the course of his employment.[1265]

(2) An assistant storekeeper at a warehouse is inconvenienced by a lorry belonging to a customer, which is blocking the entrance. Without making any inquir-

---

[1255] Civil Liability (Contribution) Act 1978 ss.2, 4 and 6. But release of one joint tortfeasor still releases the others. For application of the Act to equitable wrongs, see *Dubai Aluminium Co Ltd v Salaam* [2002] UKHL 48; [2003] 2 A.C. 366.

[1256] Civil Liability (Contribution) Act 1978 ss.1, 2 and 7(3).

[1257] The Act creates, however, considerable difficulties; see *Clerk and Lindsell on Torts*, above.

[1258] Civil Liability (Contribution) Act 1978 s.5.

[1259] The right to do so is preserved by s.7(3).

[1260] *Lister v Romford Ice & Cold Storage Co* [1957] A.C. 555. But the effect of this case has been circumvented in practice: see Gardiner (1959) 22 M.L.R. 652; *Clerk and Lindsell on Torts* (22nd edn), para.4-37 onwards.

[1261] See Articles 40 and 42 as to the duties owed by contractual and non-contractual agents.

[1262] See *Jones v Manchester Corp* [1952] 2 Q.B. 852 at 865. But cf. Atiyah, *Vicarious Liability in the Law of Torts* (1967), pp.428–430. See also *Adamson v Jarvis* (1827) 4 Bing. 66, Illustration 9 to Article 63 for the converse case where an agent recovers indemnity because innocent.

[1263] *Ryan v Fildes* [1938] 3 All E.R. 517; *Semtex v Gladstone* [1954] 1 W.L.R. 945; *Harvey v R.G. O'Dell* [1958] 2 Q.B. 78. This may be useful where for some reason the common law action is not available, as in *Harvey v R.G. O'Dell*.

[1264] See *Adamson v Jarvis* (1827) 4 Bing. 66; and Article 63 generally.

[1265] *Century Insurance Co Ltd v Northern Ireland Road Transport Board* [1942] A.C. 509; *Jefferson v Derbyshire Farmers Ltd* [1921] 2 K.B. 281; *Staton v National Coal Board* [1957] 1 W.L.R. 893.

ies of anyone he attempts to move the lorry and causes personal injuries to another. His employers are liable.[1266]

(3) The manager of a branch of a furniture business, while repossessing goods under a hire-purchase contract, assaults the hirer. His employer is liable.[1267]

(4) An employee of a garage, after serving a customer with petrol, incorrectly thinking that the customer was about to depart without paying or giving up the necessary coupons, pursued him and abused him. The customer paid and delivered the coupons and then said that he would report the employee to his employers. The employee struck the customer. Held, the assault had no connection with the discharge of the employee's duty to his employers, who were therefore not liable.[1268]

(5) The manager of a shop detains a person suspected of shoplifting. The person detained is innocent. The manager's employer may be liable for false imprisonment.[1269]

(6) A commission agent uses his own car for the purpose of getting orders for his principal. The principal is not liable for damage caused by the agent's negligent driving. The agent was not the servant of the principal.[1270]

(7) Two non-uniformed and armed police officers pursuing someone against whom only a driving offence can be charged enter without lawful right private property waking the pursued's mother at 2 a.m. and brandishing a pistol at her. Held, Crown vicariously liable for aggravated damages and exemplary damages for assault and trespass.[1271]

Prohibited acts

8-193   (8)   A bus driver, in order to prevent a rival bus from overtaking him, drove his bus across the road and caused the rival bus to overturn. The driver had instructions from his employers not to race with or obstruct other buses. Held,

---

[1266] *Kay v ITW Ltd* [1968] 1 Q.B. 140; cf. *Beard v London General Omnibus Co* [1900] 2 Q.B. 530; and see *Ilkiw v Samuels* [1963] 1 W.L.R. 991; *Nelson v Raphael* [1979] R.T.R. 437 (person demonstrating controls of car to buyer).

[1267] *Dyer v Munday* [1895] 1 Q.B. 742. cf. Illustration 17. And see *Hamlyn v John Houston & Co* [1903] 1 K.B. 81 (bribery).

[1268] *Warren v Henlys* [1948] 2 All E.R. 935; But cf. *Pettersson v Royal Oak Hotel Ltd* [1948] N.Z.L.R. 136; *Deatons Pty Ltd v Flew* (1949) 79 C.L.R. 370; *Keppel Bus Co Ltd v Salad bin Ahmed* [1974] 1 W.L.R. 1082; *Auckland Workingmen's Club v Rennie* [1976] 1 N.Z.L.R. 278; *Brown v Robinson* [2004] UKPC 56; *Bellman v Northampton Recruitment Ltd* [2018] EWCA Civ 2214; [2019] I.C.R. 459;); *Mohamud v Wm Morrison Supermarkets Plc* [2016] UKSC 11; [2016] A.C. 677; and *Wm Morrison Supermarkets Plc v Various Claimants* [2020] UKSC 12; [2020] 2 W.L.R. 941 at [41]. See further as to assaults by servants and agents Rose (1977) 40 M.L.R. 420; *Clerk and Lindsell on Torts* (22nd edn), para.6-47; Atiyah, *Vicarious Liability in the Law of Torts* (1967), pp.276–280.

[1269] See *Neville v C & A Modes Ltd* 1945 S.C. 175 (a case of slander). An account of such a case heard in York is reported in *The Times* on September 30, 1983. The older cases often concerned the giving of a person into custody, and drew a distinction between preservation of the employer's property and a mere desire to punish. See e.g. *Bank of New South Wales v Owston* (1879) 4 App.Cas. 270; *Abrahams v Deakin* [1891] 1 Q.B. 516. Police officers are more likely nowadays to arrest on their own responsibility: see *Meering v Graham-White Aviation Co Ltd* (1919) 122 L.T. 44; but cf. *Martin v Watson* [1996] A.C. 74 (malicious prosecution). See further Atiyah, above, at pp.266–267.

[1270] *Eggington v Reader* [1936] 1 All E.R. 7; cf. Illustration 24.

[1271] *New South Wales v Ibbett* (2006) 231 A.L.R. 485. See, however, para.8-177, above.

that the employers were liable, the wrongful act being done in the course of the driver's employment.[1272]

(9) The driver of a vehicle had authority to carry his employer's servants, but had been expressly forbidden to carry other persons, and a notice to this effect was displayed in the vehicle. The driver gave a lift to a person who was not a fellow employee and who, in dismounting, suffered injury. Held, the driver acted outside the course of his employment, so that the employer was not liable.[1273]

(10) The employee of a firm of valuers is instructed not to make valuations for certain companies. He nevertheless does so on the vendor's headed notepaper, it not appearing who made the valuation. The valuation is negligent. The valuers are not liable for it.[1274]

(11) An employee of A, in disregard of a written notice issued to A's employees prohibiting the use of privately owned cars for the purpose of A's business unless adequately protected by insurance, used his own uninsured car for the purpose of ordinary work, and by negligent driving injured the plaintiff. Held, that the means of transport was incidental to the execution of what the servant was employed to do; that the prohibition merely limited the way in which, or means by which, the servant was to execute the work; and that A was liable to the plaintiff.[1275]

Wrong of employee or agent committed for his own benefit

(12) A solicitor's managing clerk who had a general authority to conduct conveyancing business induced a widow to give him instructions to realise properties with a view to reinvestment of the proceeds. For that purpose she handed him her title deeds, for which he gave her a receipt in his principal's name; and, at his request, she signed two documents, which were not read over or explained to her, and which were in fact conveyances of the properties to the clerk. He afterwards disposed of the properties for his own benefit. The principal was liable for the fraud.[1276]   **8-194**

(13) A solicitor's managing clerk was authorised to carry out conveyancing business and to borrow money from building societies, on behalf of clients, upon security of mortgage. He obtained an advance from a building society by producing a deed which he knew to be forged. Held, he was acting within the scope of his apparent authority and his principal was liable for the fraud, despite the fact that it involved a forgery.[1277]

(14) A, at the request of B, a transport contractor, committed goods to B's serv-

---

[1272] *Limpus v London General Omnibus Co* (1862) 1 H. & C. 526.

[1273] *Conway v George Wimpey & Co (No.2)* [1951] 2 K.B. 266; *Twine v Bean's Express Ltd* [1946] 1 All E.R. 202. cf. *Young v Edward Box & Co Ltd* [1951] 1 T.L.R. 789.

[1274] *Kooragang Investments Pty Ltd v Richardson & Wrench Ltd* [1982] A.C. 462 (criticised, [1982] C.L.J. 36; but see Watts (2012) 128 L.Q.R. 260).

[1275] *Canadian Pacific Ry Co v Lockhart* [1942] A.C. 591; *LCC v Cattermoles (Garages) Ltd* [1953] 1 W.L.R. 997.

[1276] *Lloyd v Grace, Smith & Co* [1912] A.C. 716.

[1277] *Uxbridge Permanent Benefit Building Soc. v Pickard* [1939] 2 K.B. 248. As to the liability of a solicitor to the disciplinary action of the court for the misdeeds of his clerk, see *Myers v Elman* [1940] A.C. 282.

ants for carriage by road. In the course of their employment B's servants stole the goods so received. Held, B was liable to A for the value of the goods.[1278]

(15) A, a senior employee with internal audit functions was requested by the external auditors to provide a file of payroll data in respect of all the company's employees. A supplies it, but then out of spite arranges for it to be made publicly available. Held, the employer was not vicariously liable to the employees whose privacy was invaded.[1279]

Authority to commit the wrongful act

8-195 (16) A, the chairman at a meeting, at the request of B, who took part in the meeting, made a defamatory statement concerning C, and both A and B expressed a desire that the reporters present would take notice of "this very scandalous case". Correct reports having been published, it was held, in an action by C for libel, that there was evidence for the jury of publication by A and B through the reporters, whom they had made their agents.[1280]

(17) A, being hired to sing at a music hall, and being permitted to choose his own song, sang a song infringing B's copyright. No control was exercised by the proprietor of the music hall to prevent infringement of copyright. Held, that there was sufficient evidence of authority to sing the song complained of to justify a verdict for B in an action against the proprietor for the infringement.[1281]

Liability for acts of agent

8-196 (18) An unnecessary sale by a shipmaster of any part of the cargo, where the sale, though unauthorised, is within the general scope of the authority conferred upon the master by the owners of the ship, is a conversion for which the owners are liable.[1282]

(19) A landlord is liable for wrongful distress committed by a bailiff acting on the landlord's behalf and within the scope of the bailiff's authority.[1283] But he is not liable for an unauthorised assault committed by the bailiff in levying a

---

[1278] *United Africa Co Ltd v Saka Owoade* [1955] A.C. 130; *Morris v C.W. Martin & Sons* [1966] 1 Q.B. 716; overruling *Cheshire v Bailey* [1905] 1 K.B. 237; *Mendelssohn v Normand Ltd* [1970] 1 Q.B. 177.

[1279] *Wm Morrison Supermarkets Plc v Various Claimants* [2020] UKSC 12; [2020] 2 W.L.R. 941.

[1280] *Parkes v Prescott* (1869) L.R. 4 Ex. 169. cf. *Lucas v Mason* (1875) L.R. 10 Ex. 251. See *Gatley on Libel and Slander* (12th edn), para.6-52 onwards. See too *Body Corporate 366611 v Wu* [2012] NZCA 614; [2013] 3 N.Z.L.R. 522 (liability for authorised nuisance), varied on appeal [2014] NZSC 137; [2015] 1 N.Z.L.R. 215 (liability for trespass).

[1281] *Monaghan v Taylor* (1886) 2 T.L.R. 685; *Marsh v Conquest* (1864) 17 C.B. 418; cf. *Performing Rights Society Ltd v Ciryl Theatrical Syndicate Ltd* [1924] 1 K.B. 1; *Fish & Fish Ltd v Sea Shepherd UK* [2015] UKSC 10; [2015] A.C. 1229; and further cases cited below, para.9-120. For commentary, see Cornish and Llewelyn, *Intellectual Property* (9th edn), Ch. 12.

[1282] *Ewbank v Nutting* (1849) 7 C.B. 797. And see Illustration 19.

[1283] See, e.g. *Hurry v Richman and Sutcliffe* (1831) 1 M. & Rob. 126; *Freeman v Rosher* (1849) 13 Q.B. 780; *Hasseler v Lemoyne* (1858) 5 C.B.(N.S.) 530. But the basis of liability is not clear: some cases put it on the basis of express authorisation or ratification only, also sheriffs are liable for the acts of their officers: *Hooper v Lane* (1857) 6 H.L.Cas 443. But the sheriff himself is the agent of the court and the execution creditor is not liable for his acts unless he specifically authorised them: *Barclays Bank v Roberts* [1954] 1 W.L.R. 1212. However, a solicitor is the agent of the execution creditor, so that if he by indorsement of the writ directs the sheriff to seize the goods of the wrong party, the client is liable for the acts of the sheriff as so directed: *Jarmain v Hooper* (1843) 6 Man. & G. 827;

distress, at any rate if the person assaulted was not interfering with the distress.[1284]

(20) A principal is liable for infringement by his employee or agent, acting in the course of his employment or within the scope of his authority, of a patent,[1285] trade mark[1286] or copyright.[1287]

(21) A director starts negotiations to sell the shares in the company without authority, and makes fraudulent misrepresentations. He is later authorised to negotiate by the shareholders in general meeting, and takes no steps to correct the misrepresentations. The shareholders are liable.[1288]

(22) An estate agent tells a prospective purchaser of a bungalow that any building society will lend £1,200 on a mortgage of it. The bungalow is in fact structurally unsound, but the estate agent was not fraudulent in making such statements. The owners of the bungalow, for whom the estate agent was acting, knew of the unsoundness, but not that the estate agent had made such a representation. The owner is not liable in deceit for the agent's false statement, it not having been proved that he deliberately kept the agent in ignorance of the facts.[1289]

(23) An estate agent demands a premium from a person who wishes to acquire the tenancy of a flat. The premium is illegal. It is recoverable from the landlord though the agent kept the money himself and the taking of the premium was not within his actual authority.[1290]

(24) A solicitor acting for the vendor in a conveyancing transaction negligently makes false statements in answer to inquiries. The vendor is liable in respect of the statements but the solicitor is not.[1291]

(25) A canvasser and agent was engaged by an insurance company under an agreement one of the terms of which prohibited him from defaming any other person or institution. While attempting to obtain business, he made defamatory statements concerning another assurance company. It was held that in do-

---

Morris v Salberg (1889) 22 Q.B.D. 614; *Lee v Rumilly* (1891) 55 J.P. 519; cf. *Condy v Blaiberg* (1891) 55 J.P. 580. The same applies if the solicitor issues execution after the debt has been paid: *Bates v Pilling* (1826) 6 B. & C. 38; *Clissold v Cratchley* [1910] 2 K.B. 244. But he has no authority to direct the seizure of particular chattels, and the client will not be liable if he does this: *Smith v Keal* (1882) 9 Q.B.D. 340; *Hewitt v Spiers & Pond* (1896) 13 T.L.R. 64; and see *Williams v Williams & Nathan* [1937] 2 All E.R. 559; *Barclays Bank v Roberts* [1954] 1 W.L.R. 1212. These lines of cases are well established, but their basis and their reconciliation with more recent authorities on vicarious liability are a difficult matter. See Atiyah, *Vicarious Liability in the Law of Torts* (1967), pp.136–142. Note that the right of distraint in relation to commercial tenancies has been abolished by the Tribunals, Courts and Enforcement Act 2007 s.71.

[1284] *Richards v West Middlesex Waterworks Co* (1885) 15 Q.B.D. 660. See Illustrations 3 and 4 above.
[1285] *Betts v Neilson* (1868) L.R. 3 Ch.App. 429.
[1286] *Tonge v Ward* (1869) 21 L.T. 480.
[1287] Illustration 17 above.
[1288] *Briess v Woolley* [1954] A.C. 333.
[1289] *Armstrong v Strain* [1952] 1 K.B. 232. See above, para.8-185.
[1290] *Navarro v Moregrand Ltd* [1951] 2 T.L.R. 674. See also *Credit Services Investments Ltd v Evans* [1974] 2 N.Z.L.R. 653. cf. *Kabel v Ronald Lyon Espanola SA* (1968) 208 E.G. 265.
[1291] *Cemp Properties (UK) Ltd v Dentsply Research and Development Corp* [1989] 2 E.G.L.R. 196 (Misrepresentation Act 1967 s.2(1)); see also *Strover v Harrington* [1988] Ch. 390 (Misrepresentation Act 1967 s.2(1), Illustration 8 to Article 94; no liability on facts); *Gran Gelato Ltd v Richliff Group Ltd* [1992] Ch. 560 (Misrepresentation Act and common law negligence: see above, para.8-180); as to surveyors *Thompson v Henderson & Partners Pty Ltd* (1989) 51 S.A.S.R. 43 (negligence); and as to insurance agents *Derham v Amev Life Insurance Co Ltd* (1981) 56 F.L.R. 34 (fraud).

ing so he was acting not independently but as a representative of the first assurance company conducting negotiations for that company, and that the company was liable for his statements.[1292]

(26) An agent employed by an assurance company drives a doctor to make the necessary examination of a person who wishes to propose for life insurance. He drives negligently and the doctor is injured. The company is not liable.[1293]

(27) The Chartering Manager and Vice-President (Transportation) of a company, authorised to negotiate the sale of a ship belonging to the company, purports to enter into a simultaneous agreement to take it back on charter. The third party knows that the Vice-President has no authority to enter into such a charter without approval from higher in the company, but believes the Vice-President when he falsely says that he has obtained such approval. There is no apparent authority; nor therefore is the company vicariously liable for the deceit of its agent.[1294]

Article 91

MISREPRESENTATIONS BY AGENT AS TO CREDIT OF THIRD PARTIES

8-197   No action can be maintained against a principal in deceit or under s.2(1) of the Misrepresentation Act 1967 in respect of any representation as to the character, conduct, credit, ability, trade or dealings of another person, to the intent that such other person may obtain credit, unless such representation is in writing signed by the principal[1295]; the signature of an agent is not sufficient, even if expressly authorised by the principal, except in the case of a limited company.[1296]

Comment

8-198   This Article reproduces the effect of the Statute of Frauds Amendment 1828 (Lord Tenterden's Act), the purpose of which was to prevent a person against whom the Statute of Frauds was pleaded in respect of a guarantee evading the protection

---

[1292] *Colonial Mutual Life Assurance Society Ltd v Producers' and Citizens Co-operative Assurance Co Ltd of Australia* (1931) 46 C.L.R. 41; *Citizens Life Assurance Co Ltd v Brown* [1904] A.C. 423 (PC). See the first case discussed by McHugh J in *Scott v Davis* (2000) 204 C.L.R. 333, para.56 onwards. See also *Derham v Amev Life Assurance Co Ltd* (1981) 56 F.L.R. 34. See further as to defamation *Whitfield v SE Ry Co* (1858) E.B. & E. 115; *Nevill v Fine Arts Assurance Co* [1895] 2 Q.B. 156; [1897] A.C. 68; *Ellis v National Free Labour Assn* (1905) 7 F. 629; *Finburgh v Moss Empires Ltd* 1908 S.C. 928; *Fitzsimons v Duncan and Kemp & Co* [1908] 2 I.R. 483; *Glasgow Corp v Lorimer* [1911] A.C. 209; *Aiken v Caledonian Ry Co* 1913 S.C. 66; *Egger v Viscount Chelmsford* [1965] 1 Q.B. 248; Atiyah, *Vicarious Liability in the Law of Torts* (1967), pp.274–276. As to partners see *Meekins v Henson* [1964] 1 Q.B. 472. Liability was imposed on a person employing a debt collection agency which used extremely threatening methods in *Wong Wai Hing v Hui Wei Lee* [2001] 1 H.K.L.R.D. 736.

[1293] *Colonial Mutual Life Assurance Society Ltd v Macdonald* [1931] A.D. 412.

[1294] *Armagas Ltd v Mundogas SA (The Ocean Frost)* [1986] A.C. 717.

[1295] Statute of Frauds Amendment Act 1828 (Lord Tenterden's Act) s.6. The actual wording reads: "May obtain credit, money or goods upon, unless etc,": see *Lyde v Barnard* (1836) 1 M. & W. 101 at 104 (explaining the background of the Act). For a case on similar Scottish legislation, see *Clydesdale Bank Ltd v Paton* [1896] A.C. 381. See *Contex Drouzhba Ltd v Wiseman* [2007] EWCA Civ 1201; [2008] 1 B.C.L.C. 631. The representation may be made in an email provided that the email includes a written indication of who is sending it: *Lindsay v O'Loughnane* [2010] EWHC 529 (QB) at [95].

[1296] See Comment. There is a useful discussion of this provision (which led to its repeal in New South Wales) in Report LRC 57 of the *New South Wales Law Reform Commission* (1988).

of the Statute by suing in tort.[1297] It was subsequently established that it applied only to actions in deceit, the form of action which would have been used at the time, and not to those in negligence, where the gist of the tort is said to lie not in the representation but in the breach of a duty of care.[1298] It is also confined to representations as to creditworthiness.[1299] However, the wording of s.2(1) of the Misrepresentation Act 1967, which uses the referent of fraud liability, appears to produce the result that s.6 applies also to claims under that provision.[1300]

It was held in *Swift v Jewsbury and Goddard*[1301] that signature of an agent was not sufficient under the Act:

"If you mean to charge a person with a fraudulent act ... you shall not charge that person unless you can produce his own handwriting for the statement of fraud by which you say you have been misled."[1302]

However, this caused difficulties with the emerging doctrine of corporate personality. A corporation can only sign by agents, and hence it might appear that a fraudulent misrepresentation signed by the agent of a corporation would never render the corporation liable. In *Hirst v West Riding Union Banking Co Ltd*[1303] it was therefore argued that the Act only applied to natural persons and not to corporations at all. The proposition was rejected, but the Act held effective to protect the Bank against liability for a fraudulent representation as to credit signed by a local manager. On this basis companies would not be liable except perhaps where reasoning that the signature ranks as that of the company itself can be deployed. This was done in *UBAF Ltd v European American Banking Corp Ltd*,[1304] where a company was held liable for a fraudulent misrepresentation as to credit signed by its assistant secretary. As to the relevance of Lord Tenterden's Act to an agent's liability in deceit for misrepresentation as to the principal's creditworthiness, see below, para.9-114.

Article 92

MONEY, ETC., MISAPPROPRIATED BY AGENT

Where the money of a third party is received by an agent while acting within the scope of the agent's authority or in respect of a transaction ratified by the principal, **8-199**

[1297] See *Williams v Mason* (1873) 28 L.T. 232. See further below, para.9-119.
[1298] *Banbury v Bank of Montreal* [1918] A.C. 626; *W.B. Anderson & Sons v Rhodes (Liverpool) Ltd* [1967] 2 All E.R. 850; *Diamond v Bank of London and Montreal Ltd* [1979] Q.B. 333.
[1299] *Diamond v Bank of London and Montreal Ltd* [1979] Q.B. 333; *Roder UK Ltd v West* [2011] EWCA Civ 1126; [2012] Q.B. 752 (statute does not extend to renewals of existing credit). See discussion in *Clerk and Lindsell on Torts* (22nd edn), paras 18-52–18-53.
[1300] *UBAF v European American Banking Corp* [1984] Q.B. 713; *LBI HF v Stanford* [2014] EWHC 3921 (Ch) at [184].
[1301] *Swift v Jewsbury and Goddard* (1874) L.R. 9 Q.B. 301.
[1302] *v Jewsbury and Goddard* (1874) L.R. 9 Q.B. 301, per Lord Coleridge CJ at 312.
[1303] *Hirst v West Riding Union Banking Co Ltd* [1901] 2 K.B. 560.
[1304] *UBAF Ltd v European American Banking Corp Ltd* [1984] Q.B. 713; *Contex Drouzhba Ltd v Wiseman* [2007] EWCA Civ 1201; [2008] 1 B.C.L.C. 631, treated further below, para.9-119. See also above, paras 1-028 and 8-189.

and misapplied by the agent, or is received by the principal and misapplied by the agent, the principal is liable to repay the third party.[1305]

Comment

8-200   The authority of the agent may of course be actual or apparent.[1306] This rule, which is based on s.11 of the Partnership Act 1890, is placed here for convenience, since it relates to the liability of a principal for the wrongs of the agent, but it does not follow that the liability is always in tort. Sometimes situations arise where the liability of the principal is indeed in tort for the fraud or conversion of an agent[1307]: but sometimes the action may be in restitution, whether in money had and received, or at equity in the form of the constructive trust and the action for knowing receipt,[1308] and sometimes it is sufficient to say that a payment made in respect of a contract is binding whatever may have happened to it,[1309] or that there is a breach of contract, whether or not the facts also constitute a tort.[1310] Liability will not arise in respect of receipts of money paid by an agent into a principal's bank account then withdrawn where the agent had no actual or apparent authority to pay the money into the account.[1311]

Illustrations

8-201   (1)   A local manager, acting as agent for a bank, induced a lady to invest money in paying off a certain mortgage. The money was paid to him for that purpose, and he misappropriated it. Held, that he was acting within the scope of his apparent authority in receiving the money, which must therefore be deemed to have been received by the bank, and that the bank was liable to repay it.[1312]

          (2)   An agent, acting apparently in the ordinary course of business, sent an account to A, representing that certain advances had been made on his account, and drew on him for the amount. It was within the scope of the agent's authority to make advances of that kind, but he had in fact misappropriated the

---

[1305] See Illustrations. cf. Partnership Act 1890 s.11, which refers to "money or property", as to which see Atiyah, *Vicarious Liability in the Law of Torts* (1967), pp.119–121. As to the agent's liability, see Article 111.

[1306] *Trott v National Discount Co* (1900) 17 T.L.R. 37.

[1307] *Swire v Francis* (1877) 3 App.Cas. 106, Illustration 2.

[1308] *Thompson v Bell* (1854) 10 Exch. 10, Illustration 1; cf. *Russo-Chinese Bank v Li Yau Sam* [1910] A.C. 174. Again, the principal may be a trustee: see *Hackney v Knight* (1891) 7 T.L.R. 254. See also Article 71, Illustration 2; Article 111. More detailed treatment of equitable claims, including that for knowing receipt, is found in Article 116.

[1309] *Thompson v Bell* (1854) 10 Exch. 10 at 14 ("the money is still in the hands of the bank").

[1310] *National Bank of Lahore v Sohan Lal, A.I.R.* 1965 S.C. 1663.

[1311] *General Accident Fire & Life Assurance Corp Ltd v Midland Bank Ltd* [1940] 2 K.B. 388 at 415–416; *National Commercial Banking Corporation of Australia Ltd v Batty* (1986) 160 C.L.R. 251; *Heperu Pty Ltd v Belle* (2009) 76 N.S.W.L.R. 230, Illustration 5; *Jones v Churcher* [2009] EWHC 722 (QB); [2009] 2 Lloyd's Rep. 94; *Perpetual Trustee Co Ltd v El-Bayeh* [2010] NSWSC 1487. cf. *Law Society of England and Wales v Habitable Concepts Ltd* [2010] EWHC 1449 (Ch) at [14] (beneficial receipt as principal).

[1312] *Thompson v Bell* (1854) 10 Exch. 10. cf. *Bishop v Jersey (Countess)* (1854) 2 Drew. 143; *Russo-Chinese Bank v Li Yau Sam* [1910] A.C. 174. See also *Royal Globe Life Assurance Co Ltd v Kovacevic* (1979) 22 S.A.S.R. 78.

money, and had not made the advances. A accepted and paid the bill. Held, that the principal was liable to A for the amount.[1313]

(3) An auctioneer receives a deposit in connection with a concluded contract, and does not pay it over to the vendor. The vendor is liable whether the auctioneer received it as agent for the vendor or as stakeholder.[1314]

(4) An estate agent receives a deposit on a transaction "subject to contract," whether expressly "as stakeholder" or without any indication of the capacity in which he was to hold it, and does not pay it over to the prospective vendor. The vendor is not liable unless the agent received it as agent for him, having authority to do so.[1315]

(5) A husband has signing authority on his wife's bank accounts, and uses those accounts for temporary lodgement of funds obtained by him by fraud. The wife is unaware of the movement of the funds through her accounts and has given no authority to her husband to use them for purposes unrelated to her own finances. She is not liable at law or in equity for the receipt or withdrawal of the funds.[1316]

Article 93

MONEY APPLIED BY AGENT FOR BENEFIT OF PRINCIPAL

Where, by any wrongful act of an agent, or by an unauthorised act which is not ratified, the money of the third party is obtained and applied for the benefit of the principal, the principal is liable in equity to restore such money to the extent that it has been so applied.[1317] **8-202**

Comment

This applies notwithstanding that the third party knew that the agent was not authorised to obtain or receive money,[1318] for its basis is not liability for the acts of the agent, but a wider principle akin to a doctrine of subrogation, whereby the third party is entitled to stand in the same position as the principal's creditor when the money has been paid over. There is no full subrogation, however, because the third party is not entitled to the benefit of the securities of the creditor,[1319] at least where the third party did not intend itself to be a secured creditor. It has been suggested that the true basis of the principle is rather, that an unauthorised loan is adopted or validated pro tanto.[1320] The main application of the wider principle lay in cases of ultra vires borrowing by companies, where the view could have been taken that the transaction, though ultra vires, had not added to the liabilities of the company, which **8-203**

[1313] *Swire v Francis* (1877) 3 App.Cas. 106.
[1314] See Article 111, Illustrations 2 and 3 and cases cited.
[1315] *Sorrell v Finch* [1977] A.C. 728. cf. *Branwhite v Worcester Works Finance Ltd* [1969] 1 A.C. 552. See Article 111, Illustration 3 and cases cited.
[1316] *Heperu Pty Ltd v Belle* (2009) 76 N.S.W.L.R. 230.
[1317] See Comment.
[1318] *Reversion Fund & Insurance Co v Maison Cosway Ltd* [1913] 1 K.B. 364, Illustration 1, interpreting *Bannatyne v D. & C. McIver* [1906] 1 K.B. 103; accepted in *Rolled Steel Products (Holdings) Ltd v British Steel Corp* [1986] Ch. 246 at 300 and 307.
[1319] *Reversion Fund & Insurance Co v Maison Cosway Ltd* [1913] 1 K.B. 364 at 377.
[1320] See *Hazlewood v West Coast Securities Ltd* (1974) 49 D.L.R. (3d) 46; affirmed (1976) 68 D.L.R. (3d) 172; and cf. *Orakpo v Manson Investments Ltd* [1978] A.C. 95.

remained unchanged[1321]: but there is a similar rule in the case of loans for necessaries purchased by minors[1322] and in some cases the doctrine, or a similar doctrine, has been applied to situations of money obtained by fraud.[1323] The money must be used by the defendant personally or by an authorised agent: the principle does not apply where a third party discharges the defendant's debt without authority.[1324] It is uncertain how far the words "for the principal's benefit" in this Article should be stretched: the cases concern discharge of legal liabilities, but it is possible that the principle can apply wherever the money is used on any purpose authorised by the defendant,[1325] e.g. in making authorised but gratuitous payments.

It should be noted that a similar result may sometimes be obtained without the aid of equity, by invoking the doctrine of tracing at common law. If the money has been paid into the principal's bank account, the principal may be liable to an action in restitution.[1326]

Illustrations

8-204   (1)   The managing director of a company borrows money on the company's behalf without authority. The lender knows that he has no authority, but expects that the company will adopt the loan. The company does not do so, but the money is spent by the managing director in discharging existing legal debts of the company. The company must repay the money.[1327]

(2)   The secretary of a company forges and discounts certain bills of exchange, and pays the proceeds to his own account, upon which he draws cheques in favour of the company. The company is liable to the discounter to the extent that the proceeds of the bills have been applied for its benefit.[1328]

(3)   A manager who had no authority to borrow money or overdraw his principal's account, having overdrawn the account and misapplied the money, borrowed £20 for the alleged purpose of paying the principal's workmen (but really to make up the defalcations), paid it into the principal's account, and drew on the account to pay the workmen. Held, that the £20 having been applied for the benefit of the principal, he was liable to repay the amount to the lender.[1329]

4.   NOTIFICATION TO AND KNOWLEDGE ACQUIRED THROUGH AGENT[1330]

Article 94

NOTIFICATION TO AGENT

8-205   A notification given to an agent is effective as such if the agent receives it within the scope of the agent's actual or apparent authority,[1331] whether or not it is

---

[1321] *Blackburn Building Society v Cunliffe, Brookes & Co* (1882) 22 Ch.D. 61 at 71 (see also (1884) 9 App.Cas. 857). The scope of this doctrine is now much reduced: see above, para.8-035 onwards.

[1322] *Marlow v Pitfield* (1719) 1 P.Wms. 558. See also *City Bank of Sydney v McLaughlin* (1909) 9 C.L.R. 615 (person of unsound mind).

[1323] Illustration 2. See also *Barrow v Bank of New South Wales* [1931] V.R. 323, deriving a wider doctrine from *Refuge Assurance Co Ltd v Kettlewell* [1909] A.C. 243.

[1324] *Re Cleadon Trust Ltd* [1939] Ch. 286.

[1325] See *Lindley and Banks on Partnership* (20th edn), paras 12–178.

[1326] Illustration 3; see Article 88.

[1327] *Reversion Fund & Insurance Co v Maison Cosway Ltd* [1913] 1 K.B. 364. See also *Bannatyne v*

subsequently transmitted to the principal, unless the person seeking to charge the principal with notice knew that the agent intended to conceal the notification from the principal.[1332]

Comment

The notion that the knowledge of an agent is that of the principal is frequently invoked in cases of varying types and its full applications are not clearly determined: "When a question of notice, or knowledge, arises, we find ourselves overwhelmed in a sea of authorities, not altogether reconcilable with each other".[1333] *Restatement, Second* sought to lay down exhaustive rules,[1334] but *Restatement, Third* adopts a more general approach.[1335] This Article is the first part of an initial division between cases of notification and mere notice or knowledge. This distinction has been forcefully argued by academic writers,[1336] is adopted in both Restatements,[1337] and has received judicial support in England[1338] and elsewhere.[1339] It is based on the fact that in some cases of the formal giving or disclosure of information, use of the notion of authority to receive it, not only actual but also apparent, seems natural and appropriate.

8-206

Restatement, Third[1340] defines notification as:

"a manifestation that is made in the form required by agreement among parties or applicable law, or in a reasonable manner in the absence of any agreement or applicable law,

---

D. & C. McIver [1906] 1 K.B. 103; and *Campden Hill Ltd v Chakrani* [2005] EWHC 911; [2005] N.P.C. 65 at [90].

[1328] *Ex p. Shoolbred* (1880) 28 W.R. 339. See also *Hazlewood v West Coast Securities Ltd* (1974) 49 D.L.R. (3d) 46; affirmed (1976) 68 D.L.R. (3d) 172.

[1329] *Reid v Rigby & Co* [1894] 2 Q.B. 40.

[1330] Some older editions contained an Article on the question when admissions by agents were evidence against the principal. The case law on this constituted, as did the rules as to admissions by the principal himself, an exception to the Hearsay Rule. Since the abolition of that rule by the Civil Evidence Act 1995 this body of authority is of little relevance in civil law in England, the matter being now one of reliability and weight of evidence. They may sometimes be relevant in criminal cases, and similar reasoning may apply in some other common law jurisdictions (e.g. Australian Evidence Act 1995 (Cth.) s.87; Singapore Evidence Act s.18). A full account was given in the 16th edition of this work, and an abbreviated account is given in *Cross and Tapper on Evidence* (13th edn). Problems may arise in connection with admissions by solicitor and counsel in litigation: an account is given in *Phipson on Evidence* (19th edn), Ch. 4.

[1331] *Tanham v Nicholson* (1872) L.R. 5 H.L. 561, Illustration 3; *Sino Channel Asia Ltd v Dana Shipping and Trading PTE Singapore* [2017] EWCA Civ 1703; [2018] Bus. L.R. 532 (service of arbitration proceedings); and see Comment.

[1332] *Restatement, Third*, § 5.02; *Blackley v National Mutual Life Assn of Australasia Ltd* [1972] N.Z.L.R. 1038, Illustration 7. See also *Norwegian American Cruises A/S v Paul Mundy Ltd (The Vistafjord)* [1988] 2 Lloyd's Rep. 343 at 354.

[1333] *Taylor v Yorkshire Insurance Co Ltd* [1913] 2 Ir.R. 1 at 21, per Palles CB.

[1334] See §§ 9–11 and 268–282.

[1335] §§ 5.01–5.04.

[1336] Powell, pp.236–244; Wright (1935) 1 U. Toronto L.J. 17 at 52; Falconbridge (1939) 17 Can.B.R. 248 at 259; Seavey (1916) 65 U.Pa.L.Rev. 1 (a valuable article); but cf. Fridman, para.10.6, who rejects the distinction.

[1337] *Restatement, Second*, §§ 9 and 268–271; *Restatement, Third*, § 5.01(1)(3).

[1338] *El Ajou v Dollar Land Holdings Ltd* [1994] 2 All E.R. 685; see below.

[1339] *Blackley v National Mutual Life Assn of Australasia Ltd* [1972] N.Z.L.R. 1038, per Turner P. (Illustration 7); *QBE Underwriting Ltd v Southern Colliery Maintenance Pty Ltd* [2018] NSWCA 55 at [94].

[1340] § 5.01(1).

with the intention of affecting the legal rights and duties of the notifier in relation to rights and duties of persons to whom the notification is given."

An obvious example is the notice to quit, and this and other examples appear in the Illustrations. In England Hoffmann LJ referred to a category of cases:

"in which the agent has actual or ostensible authority to receive communications, whether informative (such as the state of health of an insured) or performative (such as a notice to quit)."[1341]

Whether something is intended as a notice is generally to be assessed using objective criteria.[1342] A notice, once communicated, is not normally permitted to be forgotten, whereas mere knowledge it seems can be forgotten or otherwise cease to be imputed to a principal.[1343] While a notice will normally be intended to take immediate effect, it is possible that the parties anticipate that some passage of time will be needed for the agent to communicate the information to the principal before it is effective. Otherwise, the standard principles applicable to actual and apparent authority should apply to notices.[1344]

The fact that cases involving notification, notice or knowledge have until fairly recently been run together does however mean that the sort of reasoning applied in knowledge cases, for example a presumption that information has been passed on, is sometimes found in notification cases.[1345] The leading case of *Blackley v National Mutual Life Association of Australasia Ltd*,[1346] the facts of which are given in Illustration 7, depends for its distinction from the insurance cases referred to in Illustrations 1 and 2 to Article 95 on the interpretation that the assured's wife gave the agent notification of new information as to the assured's health in accordance with the requirements of the policy.[1347]

It is clear on principle that where the third party *knows* (as opposed to merely suspects) that, in breach of duty, the information will not be passed on by the agent, the notification is ineffective.[1348]

Illustrations

8-207 (1) An underwriter sought to avoid a policy on the ground of the non-disclosure

---

[1341] *El Ajou v Dollar Land Holdings Ltd* [1994] 2 All E.R. 685, at 703. See too *Ng Hock Kon v Sembawang Capital Pte Ltd* [2010] 1 S.L.R. 307.

[1342] But cf. *HLB Kidsons (a firm) v Lloyd's Underwriters Subscribing To Lloyd's Policy No. 621/PK1D00101* [2008] EWCA Civ 1206 at [64] and [137].

[1343] See *MCP Pension Trustees Ltd v Aon Pension Trustees Ltd* [2010] EWCA Civ 377; [2012] Ch. 1 (this case was concerned with the concept of "notice" within the Trustee Act 1925 s.27, which may be broader than that of notification, but the reasoning therein would apply, with perhaps more force, to the common law concept of notification). As to knowledge, see below, para.8-209.

[1344] See, e.g. *Goyal v Florence Care Ltd* [2020] EWHC 659 (Ch) (contact-us email address not available for all notices).

[1345] See, e.g. the speeches of Lord Westbury and Lord Colonsay in *Tanham v Nicholson* (1872) L.R. 5 H.L. 561, Illustration 3; *A/S Rendal v Arcos Ltd* [1937] 3 All E.R. 577 (HL); and see below, para.8-210.

[1346] *Blackley v National Mutual Life Association of Australasia Ltd* [1972] N.Z.L.R. 1038, Illustration 7.

[1347] *Blackley v National Mutual Life Association of Australasia Ltd* [1972] N.Z.L.R. 1038 at 1051.

[1348] *Blackley v National Mutual Life Association of Australasia Ltd* [1972] N.Z.L.R. 1038 at 1049; citing *Sharpe v Foy* (1868) L.R. 4 Ch.App. 35; *Re Fitzroy Bessemer Steel Co Ltd* (1884) 50 L.T. 144, Illustration 9 to Article 95—neither of them notification cases however. See also *The Vistafjord* [1988] 2 Lloyd's Rep. 343.

of a material fact. The fact had been disclosed to his solicitor, but had not been communicated to him. Held, that he was not bound by the disclosure to his solicitor, it not being in the ordinary course of a solicitor's employment to receive notice as to mercantile business.[1349]

(2) Notice of withdrawal of an application for shares was given during business hours to a clerk at the registered office of the company, the clerk stating that the secretary was out. Held, that it operated as notice to the company.[1350]

(3) A notice to quit is served at the house of a tenant upon a servant whose duty it is to deliver it to the tenant. That is good service on the tenant though the servant does not deliver the notice to him.[1351]

(4) Notice of a bankruptcy petition against an execution debtor is given to a man left in possession by the sheriff. That does not operate as notice to the sheriff, because the man in possession is only his agent for the purpose of levying, selling the goods, and handing over the proceeds.[1352]

(5) Notice of an incumbrance was given to a solicitor who had been employed by trustees in all matters relating to the trust in which professional assistance was required, but who had not been authorised to receive notices on their behalf, and the solicitor wrote formally acknowledging receipt on behalf of the trustees. Held, that the notice to the solicitor did not operate as notice to the trustees, solicitors not being, as such, standing agents of their clients to receive notices on their behalf.[1353]

(6) A car dealer may be the agent of the finance company for whom he acts, to receive notification of revocation of offer from a prospective hirer.[1354]

(7) B proposes for life insurance. After a medical examination the company accepts the proposal, acceptance not to be completed till the first premium is paid and a banker's order signed. The agent who communicates this acceptance knows at the time of doing so, and is also told by B's wife, that B has just been admitted to hospital and has undergone an apparently successful operation. The premium is paid and a banker's order signed (by B's wife). The agent does not tell the company of the operation. Later B's situation deteriorates. The company cannot repudiate the policy for non-disclosure,

---

[1349] *Tate v Hyslop* (1885) 15 Q.B.D. 368. See too *JL Builders & Son v Naylor and Naylor* [2008] EWCA Civ 1621 (notice to quantity surveyor). Disclosure to insurance agent in relation to insurance policy would be different: see Illustration 7.

[1350] *Re Brewery Assets Corp, Truman's Case* [1894] 3 Ch. 272.

[1351] *Tanham v Nicholson* (1872) L.R. 5 H.L. 561; *Townsend Carriers Ltd v Pfizer Ltd* (1977) 33 P. & C.R. 361. See further, Article 6, Illustration 8.

[1352] *Re Holland Ex p. Warren* (1885) 1 T.L.R. 430.

[1353] *Saffron Walden Second Benefit Building Society v Rayner* (1880) 14 Ch.D. 406. See also *IVI Pty Ltd v Baycrown Pty Ltd* [2005] QCA 205 at [33] (notice of revocation of offer given to purchaser's solicitor ineffective where negotiations had principally been face-to-face and otherwise solicitor had not been appointed to receive notices); and *Vaughan v Von Essen Hotels 5 Ltd* [2007] EWCA Civ 1349 (notice had to be to firm of solicitors expressly stipulated; it was hence not sufficient to give notice to a different firm that was acting in relation to some matters under the contract); *Nakanishi Marine Co Ltd v Gora Shipping Ltd* [2012] EWHC 3383 (Comm) at [16].

[1354] *Financings Ltd v Stimson* [1962] 1 W.L.R. 1184; *CF Asset Finance Ltd v Okonji* [2014] EWCA Civ 870 at [22]. See Consumer Credit Act 1974 ss.57, 69 and 102. See also *HLB Kidsons (a firm) v Lloyd's Underwriters Subscribing to Lloyd's Policy No.621/PK1D00101* [2007] EWHC 1951 (Comm) at [89]; and see clarification judgment [2007] EWHC 2699 (Comm) (partnership was held in default under insurance policy by failing to file in time notice of claim when secretary to partnership had, within authority, received notice of circumstances that could justify claim); varied on appeal [2008] EWCA Civ 1206; [2009] 1 Lloyd's Rep. 8.

there having been notification of circumstances affecting the risk, in accordance with the policy terms, to the agent, who had apparent authority to receive it. Suspicion, short of actual knowledge or positive belief, by B's wife that the information would not be passed on does not vitiate the notification.[1355]

(8) In negotiations for the sale of a house, a misrepresentation is made in the particulars that it is on main drainage. This is subsequently corrected by the vendor's agent in a letter to the purchaser's solicitor. The solicitor does not pass on the information. The purchaser is deemed to have notice for the purposes of an action by him under s.2(1) of the Misrepresentation Act 1967: his loss was caused not by reliance on the continuing representation but by his solicitor's failure to communicate the correction to him.[1356]

(9) An agent with a power of attorney for several principals to purchase racehorses borrows money for the purpose from a bank. The bank makes disclosures requisite under credit contract legislation to the attorney. It has made the disclosure to his principals thereby.[1357]

(10) A vendor's solicitor receives tender of a personal cheque as deposit on a land transaction. He does not have implied authority to accept payment by that method, but he does have implied authority to receive it for the purposes of communicating to the vendor the fact of its tender. The purchaser can assume that that fact has been communicated and can further assume that the tender has been accepted if a prompt rejection does not follow.[1358]

(11) An insurer is prepared to renew a policy only on the basis of adding a terrorism exclusion to the policy, and communicates that fact to the broker acting for the insured, the latter not communicating this change to the insured. Held, the insured is bound by the notification to the broker of the change of terms.[1359]

Article 95

KNOWLEDGE ACQUIRED THROUGH AGENT

8-208 (1) A principal is generally imputed with knowledge relating to the subject matter of the agency which an agent acquired while acting for the principal.[1360]

[1355] *Blackley v National Mutual Life Association of Australasia Ltd* [1972] N.Z.L.R. 1038. The distinction between this case and cases such as those discussed under Illustration 2 to Article 95 is explained at 1051. See also *Marsden v City and County Assurance Co* (1865) L.R. 1 C.P. 232; *QBE Underwriting Ltd v Southern Colliery Maintenance Pty Ltd* [2018] NSWCA 55.

[1356] *Strover v Harrington* [1988] Ch. 390, See too *Gabriel v Little* [2013] EWCA Civ 1513 at [37] (affirmed on other issues sub nom. *Hughes-Holland v BPE Solicitors* [2017] UKSC 21; [2018] A.C. 599).

[1357] *National Australia Finance Ltd v Fahey* [1990] 2 N.Z.L.R. 482.

[1358] *Southbourne Investments Ltd v Greenmount Manufacturing Ltd* [2008] 1 N.Z.L.R. 30 (NZSC) at [20].

[1359] *Axa Corporate Solutions SA v National Westminster Bank Plc* [2010] EWHC 1915 (Comm).

[1360] *Taylor v Yorkshire Insurance Co Ltd* [1913] 2 Ir.R. 1 at 21, per Palles CB. See also *Merry v Abney* (1663) 1 Ch. Cas. 38; *Jennings v Moore* (1708) 2 Vern. 609; affirmed sub nom. *Blenkarne v Jennens* (1709) 2 Bro. P.C. 278 (HL); *Le Neve v Le Neve* (1748) 1 Ves. Sen. 64, Illustration 22; (1748) 3 Atk. 646; *Doe d. Willis v Martin* (1790) 4 T.R. 39; *Boursot v Savage* (1866) L.R. 2 Eq. 134; *Rolland v Hart* (1871) L.R. 6 Ch.App. 678; *Rowland v Chapman* (1901) 17 T.L.R. 669 (solicitor's knowledge of payment to other agent imputed); *Real Estate Opportunities Ltd v Aberdeen Asset Managers Jersey Ltd* [2007] EWCA Civ 197; [2007] 2 All E.R. 791 at [49]; *UBS AG (London Branch) v Kom-*

(2) Where an agent is authorised to enter into a transaction in which the agent's own knowledge is material, knowledge which the agent acquired before appointment or outside the scope of his or her authority may also be imputed to the principal.[1361]

(3) Where a principal has a duty to investigate and make disclosure, the principal may be imputed not only with facts which the principal knows but also with material facts that relevant agents might have been expected to tell the principal.[1362]

(4) Knowledge is not attributed to the principal where the principal is claiming in respect of a breach of duty by an agent that relates to the information in question.[1363] Otherwise, whether a fraudulent or miscreant agent's knowledge is imputable to the principal depends upon the type of legal issue that arises.[1364] There is, therefore, no general fraud exception to imputation to the principal of the knowledge, or the acts, of an agent.

Comment

Introduction   The law on this topic is constituted by a plethora of cases in differ-   **8-209**
ent contexts, which are extremely difficult to reduce to any order. It may be useful therefore to draw attention initially to some main points that may be found lying within them.[1365] Assuming as a starting point that the knowledge of an agent can and must sometimes be imputed to the principal, and for the present cutting through the undergrowth of the cases, the main points that need to be considered are as follows:

(a) It is always necessary to consider the context of the particular legal issue to which imputation of knowledge might be pertinent. There is no overarching principle that a principal is deemed to know at all times and for all purposes that which an agent knows. In this regard the rules of imputation do not exist in a state of nature, such that some reason has to be found to disapply them.[1366] Hence, a principal might be deemed to possess an agent's knowledge for the purpose of liability to outside parties (or for exposure to regulatory or criminal sanction), but not deemed to know those same facts (let alone have condoned any action by the agent) for the purpose of action by the principal against the agent personally.[1367] Further, a distinction needs

---

munale *Wasserwerke Leipzig GmbH* [2014] EWHC 3615 (Comm) at [762]; *McFee v Reilly* [2019] NSWCA 322 (solicitor's knowledge).

[1361] See *El Ajou v Dollar Land Holdings Ltd* [1994] 2 All E.R. 685 at 702; but see Comment.

[1362] See *El Ajou v Dollar Land Holdings Ltd* [1994] 2 All E.R. 685; but see Comment.

[1363] See, e.g. *Belmont Finance Corp Ltd v Williams Furniture Ltd* [1979] 1 Ch. 250 at 261–262. See *Bilta (UK) Ltd v Nazir (No.2)* [2015] UKSC 23; [2016] A.C. 1 at [7], [202] and for more detail, below, para.8-214.

[1364] *Bilta (UK) Ltd v Nazir (No.2)* [2015] UKSC 23; [2016] A.C. 1 at [9], [41]–[45], [181]–[182], [191], [202], [207]. See further below, para.8-214.

[1365] See Watts, in *Unjust Enrichment in Commercial Law* (Degeling and Edelman eds, 2008), Ch.21. For the US position, see DeMott, (2003) 13 Duke J.Comp. and Int.L. 291; Scordato (2004) 10 Fordham J. Corporate and Financial L. 129; Loewenstein (2013) 85 U. Colorado L.R. 305.

[1366] A passage approved in *Bilta (UK) Ltd v Nazir (No.2)* [2015] UKSC 23; [2016] A.C. 1 at [44] and [191]. See also *Moulin Global Eyecare Trading Ltd v CIR* [2014] HKCFA 22 at [106], per Lord Walker of Gestingthorpe; *HKSAR v Luk Kin* [2016] HKCFA 81 at [41], per Lord Hoffmann.

[1367] See *Bilta (UK) Ltd v Nazir (No.2)* [2015] UKSC 23; [2016] A.C. 1 at [7], [43], and [208]; *Mobile Sourcing Ltd v Revenue and Customs Commissioners* [2016] UKUT 274 (TCC) at [48]; *Faichney*

to be drawn between imputation of knowledge in the context of the forma-tion or execution of a contract between arm's length parties, and imputa-tion in the context of the imposition of tortious or restitutionary liability. Cases of the former sort turn on the express or implied understandings between the parties, and, in the absence of express agreement, can usually be reduced to determining what a party could reasonably expect the counterparty to know, given the state of knowledge of their respective agents.[1368] This type of case is always very fact specific. Certainly, the principles of apparent authority cannot be end run by the third party assert-ing that the principal is bound to a contract as a result of being deemed to know of the unauthorised conduct of its undoubted employees or agents.[1369] Cases in tort and restitution, on the other hand, involve *imposed* obliga-tions, and require the law to formulate relatively firm principles. Some ques-tions in tort as to the state of a party's knowledge will not turn on the concept of agency; for instance, the knowledge of an employee who has no agency functions might still be imputed to an employer and preclude an ac-tion in tort by the employer.[1370] Questions of the knowledge of agents do, however, play a particularly prominent role in restitutionary liability, either as an element of the cause of action or as a factor in the application of defences.[1371] The position is the same when rectification of a written contract is at issue.[1372] There can be cases of a third sort, where the operation of a statutory rule turns on the state of a party's knowledge. There, it is a ques-tion of statutory construction what rules of imputation were intended; the context of the provision will be highly relevant, as in the contractual context, but the inference may also be that the legislature intended to borrow the rules used in tortious and restitutionary situations.[1373] Normally, however, it is unsatisfactory to borrow case law from one context for use in another.

(b)   Is knowledge acquired outside the agency attributed to the principal? Again, this issue is dependent on context. Where the only relevant parties are those

---

v Aquila Advisory Ltd [2018] EWHC 565 (Ch) at [53].

[1368] See *Jafari-Fini v Skillglass Ltd* [2007] EWCA Civ 261 at [97], per Moore-Bick LJ, Illustration 20; *Bilta (UK) Ltd v Nazir (No.2)* [2015] UKSC 23; [2016] A.C. 1 at [198]; *Hut Group Ltd v Nobahar-Cookson* [2014] EWHC 3842 (QB) at [226]; affirmed on other points [2016] EWCA Civ 128. For an example where, as a matter of construction, imputation was found inapplicable, see *Infiniteland Ltd v Artisan Contracting Ltd* [2005] EWCA Civ 758; [2006] 1 B.C.L.C. 632.

[1369] See, e.g. *Taylor v Smith* (1926) 38 C.L.R. 48, Article 16, Illustration 8.

[1370] See, e.g. *Howmet Ltd v Economy Devices Ltd* [2016] EWCA Civ 847; (2016) 168 Con. L.R. 27 at [72] and [95] (claimant fails in tort action in respect of losses caused by defective product when its employee became aware of defect).

[1371] On this, see Watts [2017] L.M.C.L.Q. 385; see also *Lewski v Commissioner of Taxation* [2017] FCAFC 145 at [142] (agent's knowledge forecloses right to disclaim property); *Knightsbridge Property Development Corp (UK) Ltd v South Chelsea Properties Ltd* [2017] EWHC 2730 (Ch) (imputed knowledge of wrongful removal of charge and transfer of land).

[1372] For discussion, see above, para.8-099.

[1373] See, e.g. *Meridian Global Funds Management Asia Ltd v Securities Commission* [1995] 2 A.C. 500; *G-Star Raw CV v Rhodi Ltd* [2015] EWHC 216 (Ch) at [167] (civil liability for knowingly import-ing items that infringe copyright); *Jeanswest Corp (New Zealand) Ltd v G-Star Raw CV* [2015] NZCA 14 at [111] (copyright); *Reformation Publishing Co Ltd v Cruiseco Ltd* [2018] EWHC 2761 (Ch) (aggravated damages for breach of copyright); *Julien v Evolving Technologies and Enterprise Development Co Ltd* [2018] UKPC 2 (concept of "discovery" of facts by company for purposes of statute of limitations); *Sandham v Revenue and Customs Commissioners* [2020] UKUT 193 (TCC) at [14].

negotiating a contract, whether it is reasonable to expect a principal to be burdened by an agent's pre-mandate knowledge will very much turn on the context. It is perhaps less likely to be reasonable to burden a principal with imposed obligations (i.e. those owed to outside parties) on the basis of knowledge acquired by an agent before appointment. In the latter context, English law tends to utilise the notion of the agent's authority and not impute pre-mandate knowledge; but it can recognise exceptions which prove extremely difficult to formulate. *Restatement, Third*, follows the view (which was held by Seavey[1374]) that how the knowledge was acquired is irrelevant, provided that it is "material to the agent's duties to the principal".[1375] It will be seen below that much is likely to turn on the scope of the agent's mandate. Sometimes an intermediary may be found not to be agent at all but rather agent for another party to the transaction,[1376] while at the other end of the spectrum the agent may have been delegated the whole carriage of the transaction, with solicitors and canvassing agents often performing roles lying between these two extremes. In the latter case, pre-mandate knowledge might be imputable.

(c)   Should there be an exception for cases where the agent is acting in fraud of the principal in the very transaction in which the knowledge is sought to be imputed, with the result that the agent is unlikely, or certain not, to pass on the knowledge? This is often referred to as the "fraud exception". Until recently it had been thought that there should be such an exception. In fact, despite many references to it in the case law, it had always been open to serious question, especially as a defence to tortious or restitutionary claims.[1377] It is undoubtedly true that where an agent has acted in breach of duty to the principal, the law needs to preclude the agent and parties associated with him from asserting that they cannot be sued by the principal because the principal must be deemed to know what the miscreant agent knew. But imputation of knowledge simply does not operate in such circumstances. No exception is therefore necessary there, and even if it were it would need to cover any breach of duty owed the principal by the agent, and not just fraud. For that reason it would be misleading to refer to it as "the *fraud* exception".[1378] The judgments in *Bilta (UK) Ltd v Nazir (No.2)* now establish, in England at least, that there is no general fraud exception to imputation.[1379]

(d)   It is not clear how to deal with situations where the agent (and through the agent the principal) may claim to have forgotten the information in question. In some circumstances it might seem reasonable to plead forgetfulness, if the knowledge came to the agent a long time before, or the agent dealt with sufficient such transactions to confound them. It is not just a problem of the law of agency, but it has seldom been addressed specifically.[1380] Sometimes

---

[1374] The Reporter for *Restatement, Second*: (1916) 65 U.Pa.L.Rev. 1 at 23 onwards.
[1375] § 5.03.
[1376] *Salkeld Investments Ltd v West One Loans Ltd* [2012] EWHC 2701 (QB) at [45]; *Cassegrain v Gerard Cassegrain & Co Pty Ltd* [2015] HCA 2; (2015) 254 C.L.R. 425 at [41] (husband not agent for wife in fraudulent transfer of property to her).
[1377] See below, para.8-214.
[1378] See further below, para.8-214.
[1379] *Bilta (UK) Ltd v Nazir (No.2)* [2015] UKSC 23; [2016] A.C. 1. For details, see below, para.8-214.
[1380] There is some discussion of the question in the corporate context in *Beach Petroleum NL v Johnson*

recourse might be had to the burden of proof. Many of the old cases concern solicitors dealing with mortgages in their locality in a way that is less common nowadays.[1381] Similar unsettled questions arise in relation to the knowledge of an agent who has ceased to work for the principal before the relevant transaction arises. If the relevant transaction takes place after the departure, the knowledge may no longer be imputed.[1382]

(e) In what circumstances can the knowledge of more than one agent be aggregated in the principal? In causes of action where it is necessary to establish dishonesty in the defendant, it is not, in general, possible to aggregate in the defendant bits of knowledge held separately by the defendant's otherwise innocent agents. The main exemplars are the torts of deceit, and interference with contractual relations, and the equitable action for dishonest assistance in a breach of fiduciary duty.[1383] The position may be different if there is evidence that the principal deliberately structured its business to avoid being affected by inconvenient knowledge.[1384] Aggregation is, it seems, possible where the cause of action does not require proof of dishonesty, as in actions for knowing receipt of trust property in breach of trust.[1385] But again the position may be different where what is at issue are discrete transactions with different employees acting for the principal on each occasion, with no single transaction in itself sufficiently indicating anything amiss.[1386]

Issues of imputed knowledge need to be kept separate from constructive knowledge. Imputed knowledge is concerned with deeming a principal to know that which an agent actually knows. Constructive knowledge is concerned not with things that the principal and agents know but with things the principal ought to have known about by reason of being put on inquiry. The two concepts can, however, operate in tandem. Such actual knowledge as an agent has can generate in the principal a duty

---

(1993) 115 A.L.R. 411 at para.22.36. See also, albeit in a slightly different context, *Re Montagu's ST* [1987] Ch. 264.

[1381] See e.g. *Warrick v Warrick* (1745) 3 Atk. 291; *Worsley v Earl of Scarborough* (1746) 3 Atk. 392.

[1382] *Crossco No.4 Unltd v Jolan Ltd* [2011] EWHC 803 (Ch) at [172]; affirmed [2011] EWCA Civ 1619.

[1383] cf. *Real Estate Opportunities Ltd v Aberdeen Asset Managers Jersey Ltd* [2007] EWCA Civ 197; [2007] 2 All E.R. 791 at [50]. As to deceit, see above, para.8-185. See generally Dugdale (2006) 12 N.Z. Business L.Q. 3. See too *Progressive Enterprises Ltd v Commerce Commission* (2009) 9 N.Z. Business L.C. 102,485 (no aggregation for offence requiring mens rea); affirmed (2010) 9 N.Z. Business L.C. 103,060 at [38]; *McNamara v Auckland City Council* [2012] 3 N.Z.L.R. 701 at [161] and [176] (NZSC) (defence of good faith not circumventable by aggregating knowledge).

[1384] See *Australian Competition and Consumer Commission v Radio Rentals Ltd* (2006) 146 F.C.R. 292 at [179].

[1385] See *National Provincial Bank of England v Jackson* (1886) 33 Ch.D. 1 at 12; *Efploia Shipping Corp Ltd v Canadian Transport Co Ltd* [1958] 2 Ll. L. Rep. 449 at 457; *Krakowski v Eurolynx Properties Ltd* (1995) 183 C.L.R. 563 at 583; *NIML Ltd v Man Financial Australia Ltd* (2006) 15 V.R. 156 at [38]; *Public Trustee v Guardian Trust & Executors Co of New Zealand Ltd* [1939] N.Z.L.R. 613 at 644; affirmed [1942] N.Z.L.R. 115 (PC). cf. *Commonwealth Bank of Australia v Kojic* [2016] FCAFC 186.

[1386] *Australian Competition and Consumer Commission v Radio Rentals Ltd* (2006) 146 F.C.R. 292 at [179] (no unconscionability in retailer where mildly mentally impaired man buys many items of electrical goods on different visits to the retailer's two stores, dealing with a range of sales people, none of whom appreciates the extent of his disability); *Glencore International AG v MSC Mediterranean Shipping Co SA* [2015] EWHC 1989 (Comm); [2015] 2 Lloyd's Rep. 508 at [23] (knowledge on part of prior agents of third party's practices not imputed for purpose of construction of contract made by later agents).

to make further inquiry. Whether the agent's actual knowledge triggers a duty of further inquiry turns on the facts and on the source of the duty to inquire.[1387]

What follows is intended as an account of the English cases. The Article is based in part on the judgment of Hoffmann LJ in *El Ajou v Dollar Land Holdings Ltd*.[1388] This appears to accept the separation off of notification cases as stated in Article 94 above, and to lay down the two categories of cases for the imputation of knowledge stated in Rules (2) and (3) above. It would be misleading in a practitioner's work not to state these categories, which are stated in other books also[1389]; but some reservations are expressed about them below. Rule (1), which was perhaps too obvious to figure in Hoffmann LJ's account, preserves a general rule of imputation for the reasons stated below; and Rule (4) addresses the relevance of fraud in an agent.

Rule (1): Rationales for imputation   This Rule gives a general indication of an **8-210** often stated approach to this part of the law. Apart from general pragmatic justifica- tions,[1390] two main reasons are given for imputing knowledge to the principal for the purposes of a common law rule. The first is that of the identity of principal and agent. This rather conceptual approach can be explained on the basis that principals should not be able by using an agent to put themselves in a better position than that in which they would have been if they had dealt personally. This is a very old idea in the case law, well illustrated by a dictum of Lord Northington LC's in *Sheldon v Cox*: "[It] is a fixed and settled principle that notice to an agent is notice to the principal. If it were otherwise it would cause great inconvenience, and notice would be avoided in every case by employing agents".[1391] Consistently, knowledge acquired by an agent after the relevant contract has been completed will no more bind the principal than if the principal had itself acquired the knowledge at that stage.[1392] *Aliter*, where the knowledge is acquired before the contract becomes unconditional.[1393] The position is less clear where knowledge is acquired before the principal has provided its consideration and the principal can withdraw from the contract.[1394]

The second explanation is that where an agent receives information which it would be the agent's duty to pass on to the principal, it may be assumed or presumed in favour of the third party, at least in the absence of explicit indications to the contrary, that the agent has done so.[1395] This explanation may permit the imputation of knowledge acquired outside the agency, which is a key problem of

---

[1387] For further discussion, see Watts, *Unjust Enrichment in Commercial Law* (Degeling and Edelman eds, 2008), Ch.21.

[1388] *El Ajou v Dollar Land Holdings Ltd* [1994] 2 All E.R. 685.

[1389] e.g. *Lewin on Trusts* (20th edn), para.42-065.

[1390] e.g. "Policy and the safety of the public": per Lord Brougham LC in *Kennedy v Green* (1834) 3 Myl. & K. 699 at 719.

[1391] *Sheldon v Cox* (1764) 2 Eden 224 at 228. See too *Boursot v Savage* (1866) L.R. 2 Eq. 134 at 142, per Kindersley VC: "I confess my own impression is, that the principle on which the doctrine rests is this: that my solicitor is alter ego; he is myself; I stand in precisely the same position as he does in the transaction, and therefore his knowledge is my knowledge; and it would be a monstrous injustice that I should have the advantage of what he knows without the disadvantage"; *Vane v Vane* (1873) L.R. 8 Ch.App. 383 at 400. See further Watts (2001) 117 L.Q.R. 300 at 301.

[1392] *Kettlewell v Watson* (1882) 21 Ch.D. 685 at 712.

[1393] *MBF Australia Ltd v Malouf* [2008] NSWCA 214. See also *Forsyth v Blundell* (1973) 129 C.L.R. 477.

[1394] See *Atterbury v Wallis* (1856) 8 De G.M. & G. 454 at 466.

[1395] See, e.g. *Boursot v Savage* (1866) L.R. 2 Eq. 134 at 142; *Rolland v Hart* (1871) L.R. 6 Ch.App. 678.

this part of the law. It has been said that such reasoning is "rather a justification of the rule than a reason for it".[1396] It links with the so-called fraud exception discussed below.[1397] With varying indications as to the strength of the supposed presumption, it has a long history in the cases, but there are as many cases that do not support it, and it was rejected in *El Ajou*.[1398] Hoffmann LJ admitted that there were situations in which a weak presumption that information had been passed on might be applied, but no more, and he treated the reasoning as primarily applicable to notification cases.[1399] On analysis, it is an unsatisfactory explanation for imputation. In the first place, it is apparent from the case law that imputation can occur even though it is clear beyond doubt that the principal was personally unaware of the relevant fact, and that therefore there has not been any communication by the agent. In such circumstances, the rationale would have to work as an irrebuttable presumption,[1400] which is an artifice. Secondly, it is not obvious how obligations as between principal and agent can confer rights on third parties, who are strangers to that relationship. Thirdly, it is unrealistic to assume that there is in fact a duty as between principal and agent that the agent will inform the principal of all matters of relevance to the principal's business that the agent learns; one of the reasons for using agents is to free the principal's time for other things. The first rationale is, therefore, the more satisfactory one.

8-211 **Only knowledge acquired while performing mandate prima facie imputed**   It is implicit in Rule (1) that only knowledge acquired by an agent whilst carrying out tasks for the principal will be imputed.[1401] Knowledge acquired when not acting for the principal, whether acquired before or even during the period of appointment, would not be imputed. Such an approach has been taken in decisions over many years[1402]; though it is rejected by both *Restatement, Second* and *Restatement, Third*.[1403] Rule (1) is consistent with either general rationale discussed in the previous paragraph, but arguably not dictated by them. Another explanation that has been given from time to time, particularly in priority disputes and other restitutionary contexts, is that it is unreasonable to expect a busy agent, such as a solicitor, to recall all information that might be relevant to a client's affairs when it was learned while

---

[1396] Mechem, *Law of Agency* (2nd edn), § 1806.

[1397] See below, para.8-214.

[1398] See *Espin v Pemberton* (1859) 3 De G. & J. 547 at 555; *Rolland v Hart* (1871) L.R. 6 Ch.App. 678 at 681–682; *Boursot v Savage* (1866) L.R. 2 Eq. 134 at 142. For other cases not supporting the presumption as the basis of imputation, see (2001) 117 L.Q.R. 300 at 304–308.

[1399] *El Ajou v Dollar Land Holdings Ltd* [1994] 2 All E.R. 685 at 703–704. *Mobile Sourcing Ltd v Revenue and Customs Commissioners* [2016] UKUT 274 (TCC) at [51].

[1400] See *Kettlewell v Watson* (1882) 21 Ch.D. 685 at 705 (presumption irrebuttable).

[1401] For discussion, see Watts [2005] N.Z.L. Rev. 307; Watts [2017] L.M.C.L.Q. 385.

[1402] See, e.g. *Taylor v Yorkshire Insurance Co Ltd* [1913] 2 Ir.R. 1 at 21 and other cases there cited; *Mountford v Scott* (1818) 3 Madd. 34 at 40; *Williamson v Barbour* (1877) 9 Ch.D. 529 (knowledge of new partner that defendant had been defrauding firm not imputed); *Farah Constructions Pty Ltd v Say-Dee Pty Ltd* (2007) 236 C.L.R. 89 at [125] (assumption by court that only knowledge acquired within mandate is imputable); *Hickman v Turn and Wave Ltd* [2011] 3 N.Z.L.R. 318 at [192]; reversed on other grounds [2013] 1 N.Z.L.R. 741; *Steel Co Ltd v Pipes NZ Ltd* [2016] NZCA 175 at [28] (knowledge of counterparty's standard terms acquired when agent was acting for former owner of business not carried forward to new owner).

[1403] See *Restatement, Third*, § 5.03.

acting for other clients. This rationale emerged early in judgments of Lord Harwicke LC, in particular *Warrick v Warrick*[1404]:

"[N]otice should be in the same transaction: this rule ought to be adhered to, otherwise it would make purchasers and mortgagees' titles depend altogether on the memory of their counsellors and agents, and oblige them to apply to persons of less eminence as counsel, as not being so likely to have notice of former transactions."

This led some later judges to suggest that if two matters for separate principals took place so close to one another that the knowledge acquired in the first matter must have been still present in the agent's mind, imputation could occur. So, Lord Eldon LC stated in *Mountford v Scott*[1405]:

"The Vice-Chancellor in this case appears to have proceeded upon the notion that notice to a man in one transaction is not to be taken as notice to him in another transaction; in that view of the case it might fall to be considered, whether one transaction might not follow so close upon the other, as to render it impossible to give a man credit for having forgotten it. I should be unwilling to go so far as to say, that if an attorney has notice of a transaction in the morning, he shall be held in a Court of Equity to have forgotten it in the evening; it must in all cases depend upon the circumstances."

The tendency nonetheless has been to conform to the understanding that knowledge needs to have been acquired by the agent whilst acting for the principal.[1406] There are, however, some very important notes and qualifications that need to be made about Rule (1). First, the rule is about knowledge acquired by an agent outside any agency for the principal, so that imputation could still occur where the knowledge was acquired while acting for the same principal, albeit in an earlier transaction (subject to issues of forgetfulness).[1407] It will be seen below that there is an important statutory exception to that position. Secondly, the knowledge of an agent who is acting for more than one party to the same transaction is not generally compartmentalised, and is likely to be imputed to both (or more) principals.[1408] There may be circumstances where the agent's duties of confidentiality might

---

[1404] *Warrick v Warrick* (1745) 3 Atk. 291 at 293. See also *Preston v Tubbin* (1684) 1 Vern. 286; *Worsley v The Earl of Scarborough* (1746) 3 Atk. 392: "It is settled, that notice to an agent or counsel who was employed in the thing by another person, or in another business, and at another time, is no notice to his client, who employs him afterwards; and it would be very mischievous if was so, for the man of most practice and greatest eminence would then be the most dangerous to employ".

[1405] *Mountford v Scott* (1818) 3 Madd. 34. See also *Hargreaves v Rothwell* (1836) 1 Keen 154; *Williamson v Barbour* (1877) 9 Ch.D. 529 at 535; *Burnard v Lysnar* [1927] N.Z.L.R. 757.

[1406] See *Fuller v Benett* (1843) 2 Hare 394; *O'Keefe v London & Edinburgh Insurance Co Ltd* [1928] N.I. 85 at 97, per Andrews LJ: "The danger of making the agent's memory of bygone transactions a jury question is obvious, and recollection or forgetfulness by the agent of matters known to him previous to that relation is not allowed to affect the liability of the principal except in certain well-recognised cases".

[1407] See *Brotherton v Hatt* (1706) 2 Vern. 574; *Jennings v Moore* (1708) 2 Vern. 609; affirmed sub nom. *Blenkarne v Jennens* (1709) 2 Bro. P.C. 278 HL; *Le Neve v Le Neve* (1748) 1 Ves. Sen. 64; (1748) 3 Atk. 646; *Doe d. Willis v Martin* (1790) 4 T.R. 39; *Rolland v Hart* (1871) L.R. 6 Ch.App. 678; *Left Bank Investments Pty Ltd v Ngunya Jarjum Aboriginal Corp* [2020] NSWCA 144 at [103].

[1408] In addition to the cases in the preceding footnote, see *Dresser v Norwood* (1864) 17 C.B.(N.S.) 466; *Boursot v Savage* (1866) L.R. 2 Eq. 134; *Belmont Finance Corp v Williams Furniture Ltd (No.2)* [1980] 1 All E.R. 393 at 404 (common director); *Bank of Credit and Commerce International SA v Aboody* [1990] 1 Q.B. 923 at 974–975; *David Browne Contractors Ltd v Petterson* [2017] NZSC 116; [2018] 1 N.Z.L.R. 112 at [121]. See also the cases in fn.1413 below.

provide a reason for not imputing the knowledge to both principals,[1409] but where the knowledge relates to the position of some outside claimant (e.g. possession of an equitable interest in an asset) it is unlikely that the agent's duties of confidentiality could justify prejudicing the position of that party. Thirdly, courts will be resistant to arguments that two connected transactions were nonetheless discrete for the purposes of the rules of imputation. Fourthly, the rule is, in any event, only a starting point. Most of the cases that created the rule have involved solicitors, the scope of whose authority is normally limited. Other case law suggests that where an agent is given responsibility for the carriage of the transaction at issue, the principal may be burdened with whatever knowledge the agent possesses wherever acquired. For example, if it is only through the auspices of the agent that the principal could have obtained the property or rights that are now contested by the claimant, it would be wrong to allow the principal to adopt the agent's actions whilst disowning the agent's knowledge of the claimant's prior rights.[1410] The well-known dictum of Lord Halsbury LC in *Blackburn, Low & Co v Vigors* provides support for such an approach[1411]:

> "Some agents so far represent the principal that in all respects their acts and intentions and their knowledge may truly be said to be the acts, intentions, and knowledge of the principal. Other agents may have so limited and narrow an authority both in fact and in the common understanding of their form of employment that it would be quite inaccurate to say that such an agent's knowledge or intentions are the knowledge or intentions of his principal ...".

This would provide an explanation for the actual result in the *El Ajou* case, itself a case concerned with knowledge acquired outside the agency, and more convincing than the reasoning actually used in that case, which was to fashion a special rule for companies.[1412] Hoffmann LJ alluded to other situations where a principal can be affected by an agent's knowledge acquired before or outside the agency. These are also somewhat problematic and are the subject of Rules (2) and (3).[1413]

There is relatively little case law on the somewhat different situation where a principal has agents who hold knowledge relevant to a transaction (and acquired that knowledge while acting for the principal) but who are not involved in it. Again, where the only parties involved are those negotiating a contract, the issue will be

---

[1409] See *Harkness v Commonwealth Bank of Australia Ltd* (1993) 32 N.S.W.L.R. 543 at 555.

[1410] See, e.g. *Jessett Properties Ltd v UDC Finance Ltd* [1992] 1 N.Z.L.R. 138; *Permanent Trustee Australia Co Ltd v FAI General Insurance Co Ltd* (2001) 50 N.S.W.L.R. 679 at 692–697 (reversed on other issues (2003) 214 C.L.R. 514). cf. *Cassegrain v Gerard Cassegrain & Co Pty Ltd* [2015] HCA 2; (2015) 254 C.L.R. 425 at [41] (where the defendant was (puzzlingly) held to be the purely passive recipient of property, deputing no agency tasks to obtain it).

[1411] *Blackburn, Low & Co v Vigors* (1887) 12 App. Cas. 531 at 537–538. See too *Brittain v Brown* (1871) 24 L.T. 504 at 506, per Cockburn CJ: "I quite agree that where a man employs an attorney or agent, and places him in his own place and treats him as alter ego, there the doctrine contended for would apply, viz., that a principal is bound by the knowledge of his agent. But it is very different when the contract itself is not placed in the hands of an agent, but the agent is, as here, employed about a matter entirely subsidiary and accessory to the contract"; *Grand Trunk Railway Co of Canada v Robinson* [1915] A.C. 740 at 747.

[1412] *El Ajou v Dollar Land Holdings Ltd* [1994] 2 All E.R. 685 at 705, Illustration 16. See further below, para.8-215.

[1413] e.g. Illustrations 7–11 and 15; and *Bank of Credit and Commerce International SA v Aboody* [1990] 1 Q.B. 923 at 974–975. But see Law of Property Act 1925 s.199(i)(ii), below, para.8-216.

governed by the reasonable expectations of the parties.[1414] Where, however, what is at issue is the rights of outside parties, the law is less likely to tolerate a situation where a principal would be advantaged by a mere change of personnel.[1415] Plainly, no tolerance is likely to be shown if there were evidence that the principal had deliberately excluded an agent with prior knowledge from participating in the transaction. The position is also different where it is a defendant who is resisting an otherwise valid claim on the basis that the claimant had agents not involved in the transaction who knew the truth as to some matter. So, a principal may bring an action in deceit so long as the agent acting for it was deceived by the defendant, even though another of the principal's agents knew the truth.[1416] Similarly, it has already been seen that a principal may have a restitutionary claim to recover a mistaken payment when the paying agent made a mistake, even though some other agent was aware of the true facts.[1417]

Rule (2): Agent's own knowledge material   This category, the first mentioned   **8-212**
by Hoffmann LJ in which previously acquired knowledge or knowledge acquired outside the agency is attributed to the principal, is said to refer to situations where the agent's knowledge affects "the terms or performance" of an authorised contract.[1418] It is said not to rest on imputation, but rather on a special duty resting on agents to insure, who are apparently treated as central examples of the category. This duty is derived from a dictum of Lord Macnaghten in *Blackburn, Low & Co v Vigors*[1419] but although a category of this nature has much to commend it, difficulties of detail were subsequently pointed out by Handley JA in the Court of Appeal of New South Wales in a case in which knowledge of agents acquired outside the agency was imputed to the principal.[1420] First, the view of Lord Macnaghten was a minority view and the majority proceeded by more traditional reasoning in not treating the knowledge of a former agent as that of the principal.[1421] Too much should not however be read into the wording of short judgments in a dispute the answer to which was fairly obvious. Secondly, and more important, non-disclosure by an agent to insure does not affect the "terms or performance" of the contract of insurance, but rather its validity.[1422] Thirdly, one of two other (and older) cases cited[1423] can be said plainly to have been based on general imputation of knowledge rather

---

[1414] See, e.g. *Aste v Montague* (1858) 1 F.&F. 264 (principal able to rely on apparent authority even though some employees not involved in transaction aware of termination of authority). See too the discussion in para.8-215, below.

[1415] See the discussion in para.8-214, below.

[1416] See *Nationwide Building Society v Dunlop Haywards Ltd* [2007] EWHC 1374 (Comm); *Baturina v Chistyakov* [2017] EWHC 1049 (Comm) at [149].

[1417] See above, para.8-166.

[1418] See the *El Ajou* case [1994] 2 All E.R. 685 at 702.

[1419] *Blackburn, Low & Co v Vigors* (1887) 12 App.Cas. 531 at 542–543 (Illustration 5), cited in the *El Ajou* case [1994] 2 All E.R. 685 at 703. cf. *Blackburn, Low & Co v Haslam* (1888) 21 Q.B.D. 144. This speech is often said to be the basis of s.19 of the Marine Insurance Act 1906 (replaced from August 2016 by the Insurance Act 2015).

[1420] *Permanent Trustee Australia Co Ltd v FAI General Insurance Co Ltd* (2001) 50 N.S.W.L.R. 679: see esp. para.76 onwards; reversed on other grounds (2003) 214 C.L.R. 514.

[1421] See pp.537–538 and 540–541. This was accepted by Phillips J in *Deutsche Ruckversicherung AG v Walbrook Insurance Co Ltd* [1995] 1 W.L.R. 1017 at 1034, though not as a central point of his judgment. But in *SA d'Intermediaries Luxembourgeois v Farex Gie* [1995] L.R.L.R. 116, Hoffmann LJ adhered to his earlier view: see also Dillon LJ at 142–143, but cf. Saville LJ at 156.

[1422] See *Banque Keyser Ullmann SA v Skandia (UK) Insurance Co Ltd* [1990] 1 Q.B. 665 at 777–781; [1991] 2 A.C. 249 at 280.

[1423] *Dresser v Norwood* (1864) 17 C.B.(N.S.) 466 at 481 (Illustration 3).

than on any more limited principle; and neither, though both are in fact examples of an agent entrusted with carrying through a transaction, relates to the agent to insure first mentioned.[1424] In the Australian case the principal was in the end held liable on the basis of an exception where the agent was an "agent to know" or that his knowledge had been purchased.[1425] This however seems rather a vague formula and it may be that a better analysis of this category would base it more generally on the idea that the making of a contract is entrusted to an agent—an instance of the argument raised in the previous paragraph. In such a case the agent's entire knowledge would be relevant, whether acquired during the agency or not. It can also be said that in such situations it is simply the knowledge of the agent that is relevant to the transaction: there is no need to assume it communicated with the principal.[1426] However, it has since been said in the English Court of Appeal that knowledge of an agent to insure acquired otherwise than in the agent's capacity as such was not attributable to the principal.[1427] The variation of result and reasoning in these cases can in some cases be explained by the fact that many of them fall into the category of case, alluded to above, concerned with the scope of the obligations of disclosure undertaken between parties to a contract; imputation in such a setting is ultimately a matter of determining what the parties reasonably expected of one another.[1428]

8-213 **Rule (3): Duty to investigate** Hoffmann LJ's second category is addressed to situations where the principal "has a duty to investigate or make disclosure": if the principal employs an agent to discharge such a duty, the agent's knowledge will be imputed to the principal.[1429] The cases on which this category is based however are disparate and raise considerable difficulties. The first case cited is part of a group concerning knowledge of the dangerous characteristics of animals for the purposes of the *scienter* action in tort.[1430] A scrutiny of them does not suggest any principle useful for the other types of case mentioned.

The second type of case covers situations where "there may be something about a transaction by which the principal is 'put on inquiry'".[1431] This can be taken to refer to a very long line of cases involving solicitors. These cases (mostly in the context of priority disputes) have taken the view that if a principal engages the same solicitor as the counterparty, then the principal can be affected by the solicitor's knowledge of an extraneous party's interests acquired by the solicitor whilst act-

---

[1424] The other is *Turton v L & NW Ry Co* (1850) 15 L.T. (O.S.) 92 (agent to conclude contract of carriage).

[1425] See (2001) 50 N.S.W.L.R. 679 at [94]–[96]; *Allianz Australia Ltd v Taylor* [2018] VSC 78 (daughter agent to insure for mother); see further below, para.8-213. This is based on the *Blackburn, Low* case (1887) 12 App.Cas. 531 at 537. See also *Taylor v Yorkshire Insurance Co Ltd* [1913] 2 I.R. 1 at 20–21 (a valuable judgment of Palles CB); *Jessett Properties Ltd v UDC Finance Ltd* [1992] 1 N.Z.L.R. 138; *Body Corporate 398983 v Zurich Australian Insurance Ltd* [2013] NZHC 1109 (reversed on other points [2014] NZSC 147). cf. *Stevenson Brown Ltd v Montecillo Trust* [2017] NZCA 57 at [30].

[1426] See *Permanent Trustee Australia Ltd v Fai General Insurance Co Ltd* (2001) 50 N.S.W.L.R. 679 at [88]–[89].

[1427] *PCW Syndicates v PCW Reinsurers* [1996] 1 W.L.R. 1136 at 1145; see also at 1148; cf. at 1151–1152. But the matter largely turned on s.19 of the Marine Insurance Act 1906, referred to above, which deals with agents to insure, replaced from August 2016 by the Insurance Act 2015. See Macgregor, in *Agency Law in Commercial Practice* (Busch, Macgregor and Watts eds, 2016), Ch.11; Merkin and Gürses (2016) 132 L.Q.R. 445.

[1428] See above, para.8-209; and (2001) 117 L.Q.R. 300; discussing *Arab Bank Plc v Zurich Insurance Co* [1999] 1 Lloyd's Rep. 262, and a number of the other cases referred to above.

[1429] See *El Ajou v Dollar Land Holdings Ltd* [1994] 2 All E.R. 685 at 702.

[1430] *Baldwin v Casella* (1872) L.R. 7 Ex. 325; see Illustration 6.

[1431] *El Ajou v Dollar Land Holdings Ltd* [1994] 2 All E.R. 685 at 703.

ing for the counterparty even if acquired in an earlier retainer for that counterparty.[1432] The application of these cases in relation to land transactions has now been confined by statute law, because the positive duties of inquiry formerly applied to such transactions were, when coupled with imputation of knowledge, regarded as leading to harsh results.[1433] The standards of inquiry expected of persons dealing in assets other than land are lower, so the mere fact that the solicitor has some relevant knowledge would not necessarily adversely affect the principal. On the other hand, where the solicitor's knowledge is sufficient, for instance, to mean that proceeding with the transaction would involve wilful blindness to a third party's protected interests, imputation may still occur.[1434] The duty of loyalty the agent owes other clients does not extend to suppressing knowledge that, if held by the principal, would involve the dishonest destruction of the property interest of a third party. As for the rationale for imputing knowledge acquired for the other client in an earlier matter, it seems to turn on the difficulty, if not the absurdity, of requiring a claimant to prove that the agent re-acquired knowledge in the current transaction of something the agent well knew from the prior transaction for that same client.[1435]

The third type of case is that of disclosure in connection with insurance: where a principal is under a duty to make disclosure, the principal may have to disclose not only facts which are known personally to the principal, but also facts "which he could expect to have been told by his agent", for example the master of the ship to be insured.[1436] But, again as pointed out by Handley JA, "the imputation to the principal ... has hitherto been based on the agent's duty to communicate his knowledge to the principal and not the latter's duty of disclosure"[1437]; though for the reasons given above this reasoning is itself unsatisfactory. Cases of this sort,[1438] usually involve only the principal and the insurer, and are essentially cases of construction; the question is, do the parties expect that the insured will have systems in place for receiving information relevant to the insurance and the risks to be insured against? Whether this should extend to knowledge acquired before, or otherwise outside, the agency is problematic. The general assumption in this area seems again to be that it should not do so[1439] unless the agent's knowledge can be

[1432] *Brotherton v Hatt* (1706) 2 Vern. 574; *Jennings v Moore* (1708) 2 Vern. 609; affirmed sub nom. *Blenkarne v Jennens* (1709) 2 Bro. P.C. 278 (HL); *Le Neve v Le Neve* (1748) 1 Ves. Sen. 64; (1748) 3 Atk. 646; *Doe d. Willis v Martin* (1790) 4 T.R. 39; *Fuller v Benett* (1843) 2 Hare 394; *Rolland v Hart* (1871) L.R. 6 Ch.App. 678, Illustration 8.
[1433] See below, para.8-216.
[1434] *Bank of Credit and Commerce International SA v Aboody* [1990] 1 Q.B. 923.
[1435] *Dresser v Norwood* (1864) 17 C.B. (N.S.) 466 at 481.
[1436] *El Ajou v Dollar Land Holdings Ltd* [1994] 2 All E.R. 685 at 703.
[1437] *Permanent Trustee Australia Ltd v Fai General Insurance Co Ltd* (2001) 50 N.S.W.L.R. 679 at [76].
[1438] An example given by Hoffmann LJ is *Gladstone v King* (1813) 1 M. & S. 35, Illustration 4; but see this case criticised in the House of Lords in *Blackburn, Low & Co v Vigors* (1887) 12 App.Cas. 531, and by Lord Esher MR in the Court of Appeal (1886) 17 Q.B.D. 553 at 567. A better example is perhaps *Proudfoot v Montefiore* (1867) L.R. 2 Q.B. 511, also summarised in Illustration 4. See in general Marine Insurance Act 1906 ss.18 and 19; *MacGillivray on Insurance Law* (14th edn), para.18-014 onwards. These sections were replaced from August 2016 by the Insurance Act 2015. But the situation must be one where there is a duty to pass on information: see *Australia and New Zealand Bank Ltd v Colonial and Eagle Wharves Ltd* [1960] 2 Lloyd's Rep. 241; *Simner v New India Assurance Co Ltd* [1995] L.R.L.R. 240. See also *Det Danske Hedeselskabet v KDM International Plc* [1994] 2 Lloyd's Rep. 534 (relevance of knowledge in the answer of interrogatories: reference to a person "for whose knowledge" the interrogated party "is responsible", at 538).
[1439] See the *Permanent Trustee* case (2001) 50 N.S.W.L.R. 679 at [87].

said to have been "bought", or he is an "agent to know",[1440] as where a shipmaster is engaged who has prior knowledge of the ship.

8-214 **Rule (4): Claims by principal against own agent, and fraud of agent** Rule (4) is a modification of the wording that has appeared in editions of this work before the 20th. The earlier wording spoke of a single "fraud exception" to the imputation of knowledge. However, it is clear that the so-called exception has been raised, if not actually applied, in some four different types of situation, in none of which is it straightforward.[1441] The judgments in *Bilta (UK) Ltd v Nazir (No.2)* now make it clear, in England and Wales at least, that there is no general fraud exception to imputation.[1442]

The first relates to complaints by a principal that an agent has broken duties owed the principal; the claim may be against the agent, or a third party which has promoted[1443] or otherwise assisted in, or benefited from, the breach.[1444] Or the claim may be against a third party whose very duty was to detect the fraud or other misconduct of the agent.[1445] The principal is then met with an allegation that the principal must be deemed to have known what the agent knew or has done, and by inference to have condoned the agent's actions. The fraud exception has been used to reject this argument. This version of the exception is often associated with *Re Hampshire Land Co*,[1446] although the facts of the case do not in fact furnish a good example of it. It is not surprising that defences of this sort have been routinely rejected,[1447] for they have no merit. However, it is suggested that to invoke a fraud exception to deal with them is misconceived. First, there is no reason to limit the

---

[1440] See cases cited infn.1425 above.

[1441] See in general *Moulin Global Eyecare Trading Ltd v CIR* [2014] HKCFA 22 at [106].

[1442] See *Bilta (UK) Ltd v Nazir (No.2)* [2015] UKSC 23; [2016] A.C. 1 at [9], [41]–[45], [181]–[182], [191], [202], [207].

[1443] See *Wells v Smith* [1914] 3 K.B. 722 at 726, per Scrutton J: "[A] man who tells a lie to another cannot protect himself by saying 'Your agent should have warned you of my lie'" (defendant to deceit action cannot rely on fact one dishonest agent of claimant knew of the untruth); *Renault UK Ltd v Fleetpro Technical Services Ltd* [2007] EWHC 2541 (QB); [2008] Bus. L.R. D17 at [124]; *OMV Petrom SA v Glencore International AG* [2015] EWHC 666 (Comm) at [152] (affirmed on different points, [2016] EWCA Civ 778).

[1444] See *Brinks-Mat Ltd v Noye* [1991] 1 Bank L.R. 68; *Nationwide Building Society v Dunlop Haywards Ltd* [2007] EWHC 1374 (Comm) (action in deceit); *Bilta (UK) Ltd v Nazir (No.2)* [2015] UKSC 23; [2016] A.C. 1 at [95], [207]; *Burnden Holdings (UK) Ltd v Fielding* [2016] EWCA Civ 557; [2017] 1 W.L.R. 39 at [49]; affirmed on different points [2018] UKSC 14; [2018] A.C. 857 (knowledge of dishonest agents not imputed for purposes of limitation period in action by principal); *UBS AG (London Branch) v Kommunale Wasserwerke Peipkiz GmbH* [2017] EWCA Civ 1567 at [151]; *Singularis Holdings Ltd v Daiwa Capital Markets Europe Ltd* [2019] UKSC 50; [2019] 3 W.L.R. 997 at [34]; *Skandinaviska Enskilda Banken AB (Publ) v Conway* [2019] UKPC 36 at [124].

[1445] See *Singularis Holdings Ltd v Daiwa Capital Markets Europe Ltd* [2019] UKSC 50; [2019] 3 W.L.R. 997 at [34] (albeit that the *Quincecare* duty is not an obvious one: see above, para.5-016). The position will be different if all the persons to whom the duty was owed were complicit in the misconduct: this is the best explanation of the result in *Stone & Rolls Ltd v Moore Stephens (a firm)* [2009] UKHL 39; [2009] 1 A.C. 1391.

[1446] [1896] 2 Ch. 743, Illustration 21. See note to Illustration 21 below, and Watts (2001) 117 L.Q.R. 300 at 319–320 and in *Unjust Enrichment in Commercial Law* (Degeling and Edelman eds, 2008), Ch.21.

[1447] See *Sharpe v Foy* (1868) L.R. 4 Ch.App. 35; *Re Fitzroy Bessemer Steel Co Ltd* (1884) 50 L.T. 144, Illustration 9; *Houghton v Nothard, Lowe & Wills* [1928] A.C. 1; *Belmont Finance Corp v Williams Furniture Ltd* [1979] Ch. 250; *Nationwide Building Society v Dunlop Haywards Ltd* [2007] EWHC 1374 (Comm) at [75]; *Moore Stephens v Stone & Rolls* [2008] EWCA Civ 644; [2009] 1 A.C. 1391; [2008] 2 Lloyd's Rep. 319; [2008] 2 B.C.L.C. 461 at [71]–[72]; affirmed [2009] UKHL 39; [2009] 1 A.C. 1391; *Soods Solicitors v Dormer* [2010] EWHC 502 (QB); *Moulin Global Eyecare Trading Ltd v CIR* [2014] HKCFA 22 at [106]; *Grimaldi v Chameleon Mining NL (No.2)* (2012) 287

"exception" to fraudulent breaches of duty. If this defensive argument had had any merit it would have been equally applicable to honest breaches of duty. The simple point is that, were the principal deemed to possess an agent's knowledge of the agent's own breaches of duty, and thereby to have condoned them, the principal could never successfully vindicate his or her rights.[1448] Secondly, there is no need for an exception as such. The putative defence that the exception is used to rebut is premised on the fallacy that a principal is prima facie deemed to know at all times and for all purposes that which his agents know. As observed already, imputation has never operated in such a way.[1449] Before imputation occurs, there needs to be some purpose for deeming the principal to know what the agent knows. There is none in this type of case. Reasoning of this sort has now been adopted in the *Bilta* case; there is no exception, rather there is no reason to impute knowledge in these cases.[1450]

The second situation where a fraud exception has appeared is as a defence to property-based claims, including those involving conflicting priorities, and to restitutionary claims.[1451] Where the defendant has also been the victim of the agent's fraud, he or she invokes the exception to deny being burdened with the agent's knowledge of the claimant's rights. However, it is most doubtful whether such a defence should be allowed in such circumstances. In very few cases has such a defence been decisive, and as far as England and Wales is concerned, anyway, it is not supported by the weight of authority,[1452] nor is it consistent in that context with the principles of vicarious liability.[1453] In this fact pattern, the claimant will usually know nothing of the transaction which might defeat the claimant's interests, but the agent of the acquiring party, the defendant, does know of the claimant's

---

A.L.R. 22 at [285]; *JSC BTA Bank v Ablyazov* [2013] EWHC 510 (Comm) at [166]; *Faichney v Aquila Advisory Ltd* [2018] EWHC 565 (Ch) at [55].

[1448] See *Stone & Rolls Ltd v Moore Stephens Ltd* [2009] UKHL 39; [2009] 1 A.C. 1391 at [198]; *Tonto Home Loans Australia Pty Ltd v Tavares* [2011] NSWCA 389 at [209]. See further Watts (2001) 117 L.Q.R. 300 at 316–318. See now *Bilta (UK) Ltd v Nazir (No.2)* [2015] UKSC 23; [2016] A.C. 1 at [7], [202].

[1449] cf. *El Ajou v Dollar Land Holdings Plc* [1994] 2 All E.R. 685 at 715, per Hoffmann LJ: "English law has never taken the view that the knowledge of a director [is] ipso facto imputed to the company—see *Powles v Page* (1846) 3 C.B. 16".

[1450] *Bilta (UK) Ltd v Nazir (No.2)* [2015] UKSC 23; [2016] A.C. 1 at [9], [37], [181].

[1451] *Kennedy v Green* (1834) 3 My. & K. 699; *Thompson v Cartwright* (1863) 33 Beav. 178 at 185 (but see the better reasoning on appeal: (1863) 2 De G.J. & S. 10); *Waldy v Gray* (1875) L.R. 20 Eq. 238 at 251–252; *Cave v Cave* (1880) 15 Ch.D. 639 at 644; *Re European Bank Ex p. Oriental Commercial Bank* (1870) L.R. 5 Ch.App. 358 (exception not decisive); *Kwei Tek Chao v British Traders & Shippers Ltd* [1954] 2 Q.B. 459; *Stoneleigh Finance Ltd v Phillips* [1965] 2 Q.B. 537; *Abbey National Plc v Tufts* [1999] 2 F.L.R. 399. See each of these cases criticised or explained: (2001) 117 L.Q.R. 300.

[1452] See *Jennings v Moore* (1708) 2 Vern. 609; affirmed sub nom. *Blenkarne v Jennens* (1709) 2 Bro. P.C. 278 (HL); *Le Neve v Le Neve* (1747) 1 Ves. Sen. 64; *Doe d. Willis v Martin* (1790) 4 T.R. 39; *Atterbury v Wallis* (1856) 25 L.J.Ch. 792; *Boursot v Savage* (1866) L.R. 2 Eq. 134; *Bradley v Riches* (1878) 9 Ch.D. 189; *Rolland v Hart* (1871) L.R. 6 Ch.App. 678; *Kettlewell v Watson* (1882) 21 Ch.D. 685; *Ex p. Batham* (1888) 6 N.Z.L.R. 342; *Bank of Credit and Commerce International SA v Aboody* [1990] 1 Q.B. 923; *Nathan v Dollars & Sense Ltd* [2008] 2 N.Z.L.R. 557 (noted Watts (2008) 124 L.Q.R. 529); *Permanent Trustee Co Ltd v O'Donnell* [2009] NSWSC 902 at [369], reversed, but not on this point, sub nom. *Tonto Home Loans Australia Pty Ltd v Tavares* [2011] NSWCA 389; *UBS AG (London Branch) v Kommunale Wasserwerke Leipzig GmbH* [2014] EWHC 3615 (Comm) at [616] (affirmed [2017] EWCA Civ 1567).

[1453] See *Doe d. Willis v Martin* (1790) 4 T.R. 39 ("without imputing any fraud to Martin, and indeed it is negatived by the verdict, the maxim, that the principal is civilly responsible for the acts of his agent, universally prevails both in Courts of Law and Equity").

interests. There, the mere fact that the recipient's agent was intending also to defraud that principal cannot justify the principal's taking advantage of the agent's actions whilst disowning the agent's knowledge. The principal cannot approbate and reprobate.[1454] It makes no difference that the dishonest agent might not be benefiting personally but aiming to benefit some third party. Where, however, the principal has simply been a post-box for the agent's fraud, the principal may be permitted to disown the transaction altogether by invoking the concept of "ministerial receipt".[1455]

The third type of case arises in the context of duties of disclosure in the formation and performance of contracts. As noted above,[1456] in this type of case the courts are essentially attempting to provide a solution to issues the parties might themselves have expressly provided for. The court's task is one of construction, and in such circumstances it might well be appropriate to conclude that it was unreasonable for one party to expect the other to know about something that that other's agent was deliberately suppressing.[1457] Each example needs to be decided on its facts, and the cases are strictly of no application outside the contractual context.[1458]

The fourth type of case embraces those where an agent's knowledge is potentially relevant in the operation of a statutory provision. This type of case raises similar issues to the last category, namely it is impossible to know whether knowledge should be imputed or not without considering the purpose of the provision and how it was intended to operate.[1459] Because the answer turns on the construction of particular statutory wording, which in turn requires regard to statutory context, it is doubtful whether there is utility in invoking a generalised "fraud exception".

Each of the foregoing categories poses a discrete problem. To the extent that in each category there might be grounds for not burdening a principal with an agent's knowledge, it is necessary in each case to determine whether it is only actual dishonesty that suffices to avoid imputation or other degrees of wrongdoing. In the first category, as seen, dishonesty is not necessary. In the second, it is argued that even dishonesty should not preclude imputation of knowledge, but, in any event, the cases make clear that mere suppression of information by the agent will not suffice,[1460] and that one should look to the effect of the acts when committed and not

---

[1454] See *Lloyd v Grace, Smith & Co* [1912] A.C. 716 at 738, per Lord Macnaghten; *Nathan v Dollars & Sense Ltd* [2008] 2 N.Z.L.R. 557 at [48]; *Mobile Sourcing Ltd v Revenue and Customs Commissioners* [2016] UKUT 274 (TCC); [2016] B.V.C. 524 at [49]; *Sandham v Revenue and Customs Commissioners* [2020] UKUT 193 (TCC) at [28].

[1455] See above, para.8-174, and Article 92.

[1456] See above, para.8-209.

[1457] See, e.g. *Group Josi Re v Walbrook Insurance Co Ltd* [1996] 1 Lloyd's Rep. 345; *PCW Syndicates v PCW Reinsurers* [1996] 1 Lloyd's Rep. 241; *SA d'Intermediaries Luxembourgeois v Farex Gie* [1995] L.R.L.R. 116; *Arab Bank Plc v Zurich Insurance Co* [1999] 1 Lloyd's Rep. 262. But cf. *Moore Stephens v Stone & Rolls Ltd* [2008] EWCA Civ 644; [2009] 1 A.C. 1391; [2008] 2 Lloyd's Rep. 319; [2008] 2 B.C.L.C. 461 at [72], doubting *Arab Bank Plc v Zurich* on this point (upheld [2009] 1 A.C. 1391).

[1458] For recognition of this, see *Re Bank of Credit and Commerce International SA (No.15); Morris v Bank of India* [2005] EWCA Civ 693; [2005] 2 B.C.L.C. 328 at [124]; *Bilta (UK) Ltd v Nazir (No.2)* [2015] UKSC 23; [2016] A.C. 1 at [198]; *Hut Group Ltd v Nobahar-Cookson* [2014] EWHC 3842 (QB) at [226]; affirmed on other points [2016] EWCA Civ 128.

[1459] See, e.g. *McNicholas Construction Co Ltd v Customs and Excise Commissioners* [2000] S.T.C. 553 at [55]; *Greener Solutions Ltd v HMRC* [2012] S.T.C. 1056 at [41]; *Moulin Global Eyecare Trading Ltd v CIR* [2014] HKCFA 22 at [106]; *Sandham v Revenue and Customs Commissioners* [2020] UKUT 193 (TCC) at [30].

[1460] *Atterbury v Wallis* (1856) 25 L.J.Ch. 792; *Rolland v Hart* (1871) L.R. 6 Ch.App. 678 at 682–683;

to the result once the fraud is revealed.[1461] In the third and fourth categories, everything turns on the particular contractual or statutory context.

Agents of companies and large organisations In applying common law principles there is unlikely to be any call for special rules for the attribution of acts or states of knowledge to companies and other corporations, but statutory and contract drafting may occasionally be based on the inconvenient assumption that only sole traders own businesses.[1462] But where a business owner employs or engages large numbers of people, questions often arise with how to deal with, for instance, the fact that the information relevant to a transaction is available to some employees or agents in the business but not others.[1463] In most such cases, the business owner will be a corporation, but the issues could arise with unincorporated organisations. Again, it is difficult yet to see clear answers emerging from the case law on how to deal with dispersed responsibility. In some such cases it may, because of a time gap or a gap between departments (for example, an insurer may have different teams selling new business and dealing with renewals of policies)\, not be appropriate to attribute the information to the organisation when the person handling the particular matter on its behalf was ignorant of it.[1464] Some assistance in such cases may be derived from the cases that have held that a principal is entitled in some circumstances to have forgotten facts.[1465] There may also be cases where one part of the organisation may have a duty not to disclose to the other.[1466] On the other hand, it has been held that the mere fact that an employee or other agent has left the organisation will not necessarily terminate imputation.[1467] It is again likely to be useful to bear in mind the distinction between imputation in the context of the formation and performance of contracts, and imputation in the law of property and restitution.[1468]

An issue that has arisen quite frequently, but once more without clear resolution, is the situation where one director of a company knows a relevant fact but others do not. The same issue could arise with other organisations that use committees.

8-215

Espin v Pemberton (1859) 3 De G. & J. 547 at 555; *Bunbury v Hibernian Bank* [1908] 1 I.R. 261; *Beach Petroleum NL v Johnson* (1993) 115 A.L.R. 411 at [22.34]; *Lebon v Aqua Salt Co Ltd* [2009] UKPC 2; [2009] 1 B.C.L.C. 549 at [26]. See too *Kirschner v KPMG LLP* (2010) 15 N.Y.3d 446.

[1461] *McNicholas Construction Ltd v HMRC* [2000] S.T.C. 523 at [55]; *Greener Solutions Ltd v HMRC* [2012] S.T.C. 1056 at [41].

[1462] See further above, para.1-028.

[1463] For application of the basic rules to companies see Illustrations 9, 12, 13 and 14.

[1464] *Malhi v Abbey Life Assurance Co Ltd* [1996] L.R.L.R. 237; distinguishing *Evans v Employers Mutual Life Assn Ltd* [1936] 1 K.B. 505 and other authority; see also *FAME Ins. Co Ltd v Spence* [1958] N.Z.L.R. 735; *Grimaldi v Chameleon Mining NL (No. 2)* (2012) 287 A.L.R. 22 at [675]. See in general Clarke, *Law of Insurance Contracts* (6th edn), para.20-7C1.

[1465] See above, para.8-209.

[1466] See above, para.6-047 onwards. As to partnerships, see ibid.; Partnership Act 1890 s.16; *Lindley and Banks on Partnership* (20th edn), para.12-24 onwards.

[1467] *Bury v Bury* (1748) noted E. Sugden, *A Practical Treatise of the Law of Vendors and Purchasers of Estates* (2nd edn, 1806) at 493; *Rolland v Hart* (1871) LR 6 Ch. App. 678 at 683; *El Ajou v Dollar Land Investments Plc* [1994] 2 All E.R. 685 at 697–698; *Dollars & Sense Finance Ltd v Nathan* [2007] 2 N.Z.L.R. 747 CA at [89]; *Real Estate Opportunities Ltd v Aberdeen Asset Managers Jersey Ltd* [2007] EWCA Civ 197; [2007] 2 All E.R. 791 at [50]. cf. *Crossco No.4 Unltd v Jolan Ltd* [2011] EWHC 803 (Ch) at [172]; affirmed [2011] EWCA Civ 1619 (knowledge not imputed when director left company before relevant transaction took place); *Premier Motorauctions Ltd v Pricewaterhousecoopers LLP* [2016] EWHC 2610 (Ch); [2017] Bus. L.R. 490 at [54] (company in liquidation negotiating insurance contract not affected by knowledge of ex-director).

[1468] See above, para.8-209.

The starting point seems to be that knowledge held by one director relevant to the position of a third party will generally be imputed to the company.[1469] This may reflect the general idea that the more senior the agent the less appropriate it is to permit the principal to disown inconvenient knowledge. But this is only a starting point, and as usual the question turns on the issue at stake. The same categories of case as are discussed in the preceding paragraph need to be considered. Hence, where it is an issue of a wrong done to a company in respect of which the company is now claiming, the knowledge of a director implicated in the wrongdoing would not be imputed for the purposes of defeating the claim; imputation in such circumstances would operate as a rogue's charter. Similarly, in the context of the creation and performance of contracts, it may in the particular context be unreasonable for one party to assert that the other knew something, let alone agreed to something, by reason of one director's knowledge.[1470] In the context of consent to an agent's receiving what would otherwise be a secret commission, usually that consent would need to be given by someone more senior than the recipient[1471]; where the recipient is a director that may require that the consent be given by the board and even in some circumstances by the shareholders, and those persons will need to know the facts. There can be other reasons for not imputing the knowledge of one or more directors. In two well-known cases where imputation did not occur the knowledge related to a matter that was only tangential to a claim being brought by the relevant company. In particular, the defendant, also a company, wanted to deny liability on a contract of loan because it asserted that its management was intending to use the proceeds for ultra vires activity, and that one of the lender's directors, being also a director of the borrower, was aware of the intended use of the funds.[1472] It is, perhaps, not surprising that imputation did not occur in those circumstances. These cases do not create a general principle, contrary to the assumption made in *El Ajou*. In a third case, the issue of law related to the giving of notice, not knowledge, and it was held that no notice was given to a company, Co B, which shared a common officer with the party that might have given notice, Co A, in circumstances where Co A had no wish to give a notice.[1473]

Another approach, applicable only to companies involves asking whether the

---

[1469] See *Belmont Finance Corp v Williams Furniture Ltd (No.2)* [1980] 1 All E.R. 393 at 404; *Marr v Arabco Traders Ltd* (1987) 1 N.Z. Business L.C. 102,732; *ZBB (Australia) Ltd v Allen* (1991) 4 A.C.S.R. 495 at 506–507; *Farrow Finance Co Ltd v Farrow Properties Pty Ltd* (1998) 26 A.C.S.R. 544 at 587; *Jafari-Fini v Skillglass Ltd* [2007] EWCA Civ 261 at [98]; *Lebon v Aqua Salt Co Ltd* [2009] UKPC 2 at [26]; *Tonto Home Loans Australia Pty Ltd v Tavares* [2011] NSWCA 389 at [212]; *Stockman Interhold SA v Arricano Real Estate Plc* [2017] EWHC 2909 (Comm) at [198] (non-executive director).

[1470] See, e.g. *Sycamore Bidco Ltd v Breslin* [2012] EWHC 3443 (Ch) at [388] (directors of company the shares of which were being sold became directors of purchaser; knowledge of transferred directors not imputed to preclude purchaser from complaining about breaches of warranty and misrepresentations made by and on behalf of seller); *Jafari-Fini v Skillglass Ltd* [2007] EWCA Civ 261 at [97]; *PEC Ltd v Asia Golden Rice Co Ltd* [2014] EWHC 1583 (Comm) at [58] (majority of board's knowledge of more junior employee's actions did not bind company where formal resolution of board needed for actual authority); *Sanpoint Pty Ltd v V8 Supercars Holding Pty Ltd* [2019] NSWCA 5.

[1471] See *Ross River Ltd v Cambridge City Football Club Ltd* [2007] EWHC 2115 (Ch) at [213]; *BFS Group Ltd v Foley* [2017] EWHC 2799 (QB) at [29]. See further, para.6-086, above.

[1472] *Re Marseilles Extension Railway Co Ex p. Crédit Foncier and Mobilier of England* (1871) L.R. 7 Ch.App. 161; *Re David Payne & Co Ltd* [1904] 2 Ch. 608. See the discussion in Watts [2005] N.Z.L. Rev. 307 at 329. As for *Re Hampshire Land Co* [1896] 2 Ch. 743, Illustration 21, see fn.1512, below.

[1473] *Re Fenwick, Stobart & Co, Deep Sea Fishery Co's Claim* [1902] 1 Ch. 507 (notice of dishonour of a bill of exchange).

company *itself* has information. For this purpose the "directing mind" reasoning[1474] has been used and it may be held that since a person of sufficient significance in the company's operations is aware of something, the company itself is. It has been held that the "directing mind" need not (as earlier cases had suggested) be a person with general management and control: it may be necessary only to identify the person who had management and control in relation to the act or omission in point.[1475] But as was suggested earlier in this book, recourse to this sort of reasoning should only be required when construing statutes and other documents[1476]; there may be specific contractual or statutory wording which will work only if a company is identified with particular actors.[1477]

As noted already, the deployment of directing-mind reasoning in the *El Ajou* case was unnecessary because the court assumed that the ultra vires cases, above, were of more general application than they were.

Law of Property Act 1925 s.199(1)(II)[1478]   This section provides that a purchaser   **8-216**
of property[1479] for valuable consideration shall not be prejudicially affected by notice of any instrument, fact or thing unless it is within his own knowledge, or would have come to his knowledge if such inquiries or inspections had been made as ought reasonably to have been made by him; or *in the same transaction*[1480] with respect to which a question of notice to the purchaser arises, it has come to the knowledge of his counsel, as such[1481]; or of his solicitor, or other agent, as such, or would have come to the knowledge of his solicitor or other agent, as such, if such inquiries and inspections had been made as ought reasonably to have been made by the solicitor or other agent.[1482] In its own context, particularly of land, it very clearly adopts the traditional position that knowledge acquired outside the scope of the agency will not be imputed.[1483] In one respect it goes further than the common law, since at common law knowledge acquired by an agent in an earlier transac-

---

[1474] See above, paras 1-028 and 8-189. See too *The Dolphina* [2012] 1 Lloyd's Rep. 304 at 341 (Sing. HC); *Sandham v Revenue and Customs Commissioners* [2020] UKUT 193 (TCC) at [33].

[1475] *Meridian Global Funds Management Asia Ltd* [1995] 2 A.C. 500 at 507; *El Ajou v Dollar Land Holdings Plc* [1994] 2 All E.R. 685 at 706; *Lebon v Aqua Salt Co Ltd* [2009] UKPC 2; [2009] 1 B.C.L.C. 549 (knowledge of single director imputed) See too *Stone & Rolls Ltd v Moore Stephens Ltd* [2009] UKHL 39; [2009] 1 A.C. 1391.

[1476] See above, para.1-028. See now *Moulin Global Eyecare Trading Ltd v CIR* [2014] HKCFA 22 at [106]; and *Bunnings Group Ltd v CHEP Australia Ltd* [2011] NSWCA 342 at [110] (knowledge relevant to aspects of company's liability in tort of conversion did not require knowledge in a "directing mind and will").

[1477] See, e.g. *Meridian Global Funds Management Asia Ltd v Securities Commission* [1995] 2 A.C. 500; *Re BCCI (No.15): Morris v Bank of India* [2005] EWCA Civ 836; [2005] 2 B.C.L.C. 328; *Man Nutsfahrzeuge AG v Ernst & Young* [2005] EWHC 2347 at [154]; affirmed on other points [2007] EWCA Civ 910; [2007] B.C.C. 986; [2008] 2 B.C.L.C. 22; *Jafari-Fini v Skillglass Ltd* [2007] EWCA Civ 261; *Lebon v Aqua Salt Co Ltd* [2009] UKPC 2; [2009] 1 B.C.L.C. 549; and *Regent Leisuretime Ltd v NatWest Finance Ltd* [2003] EWCA Civ 391 at [105]. cf. *Julien v Evolving Tecknologies and Enterprise Development Co Ltd* [2018] UKPC 2.

[1478] Re-enacting Conveyancing Act 1882 s.3. See Nield [2000] Conv. 196; and Watts in *Unjust Enrichment in Commercial Law* (Degeling and Edelman eds, 2008), p.431.

[1479] Unless the context otherwise requires, "property" includes any thing in action and any interest in real or personal property: s.205(1)(xx).

[1480] Emphasis added.

[1481] i.e. as his agent; see *Re Cousins* (1886) 31 Ch.D. 671; *Taylor v London & County Banking Co* [1901] 2 Ch. 231; cf. *Meyer v Charters* (1918) 34 T.L.R. 589.

[1482] See *Maxfield v Burton* (1873) L.R. 17 Eq. 15.

[1483] See the provision applied in *Halifax Mortgage Services Ltd v Stepsky* [1996] Ch. 207; and *Barclays Bank Plc v Thomson* [1997] 4 All E.R. 816.

tion could be imputed if the agent was acting for the same principal in both transactions.[1484] The rule in the 1925 Act puts the principal who uses agents in a better position than if acting personally. If the principal acted personally he or she would not be permitted to disown knowledge acquired in an earlier transaction, but an agent's knowledge is not carried forward even when the agent was acting for the same principal both times and indubitably has not forgotten the relevant information. This seems insupportable but a remedy would require statutory amendment.

Illustrations

8-217 (1) An agent of an insurance company negotiated a contract of insurance with a man who had lost the sight of an eye. Held, that company must be deemed to have had notice that the assured had lost the sight of an eye, and that it could not avoid the contract on the ground of non-disclosure by him of that fact.[1485]

(2) An insurance proposal form signed by the proposer contained untrue answers which were warranted to be true and which formed the basis of the contract. The answers were filled in by the insurance company's agent, whom the proposer had required or permitted to fill in the form after informing him of the true facts. Held, that the company were entitled to repudiate liability on the ground of the untrue answers. The agent, in filling in the form, was the agent of the proposer. If the agent knew that the answers were untrue, he was committing a fraud which prevented his knowledge being the knowledge of the company; if he did not know, he had no knowledge to be imputed to the company.[1486]

[1484] See, e.g. *Le Neve v Le Neve* (1747) 1 Ves. Sen. 64.

[1485] *Bawden v London, Edinburgh & Glasgow Ass. Co* [1892] 2 Q.B. 534. And see *Hough v Guardian Fire & Life Ass. Co* (1902) 18 T.L.R. 273; *Holdsworth v Lancashire & Yorkshire Insurance Company* (1907) 23 T.L.R. 521; *Thornton-Smith v Motor Union Insurance Co Ltd* (1913) 30 T.L.R. 139; *Golding v Royal London Auxiliary Insurance Co Ltd* (1914) 30 T.L.R. 350; *Keeling v Pearl Life Ass. Co Ltd* (1923) 129 L.T. 573. But these cases became doubtful after *Newsholme Bros v Road Transport & General Ins. Co Ltd* [1929] 2 K.B. 356, Illustration 2, and represent a view of the facts which was subsequently less easily taken. Thus in *Newsholme*'s case Scrutton LJ said: "The decision in *Bawden*'s case is not applicable to a case where the agent himself, at the request of the proposer, fills up the answers in purported conformity with information supplied by the proposer". See Clarke, *Law of Insurance Contracts* (6th edn), para.10-2 onwards; *MacGillivray on Insurance Law* (14th edn), para.18-029 onwards.

[1486] *Newsholme Bros v Road Transport & General Ins. Co Ltd* [1929] 2 K.B. 356 (where there is a review of earlier authorities); *Biggar v Rock Life Ass. Co* [1902] 1 K.B. 516; *Jumna Khan v Bankers and Traders Insurance Co Ltd* (1925) 37 C.L.R. 451; *Dunn v Ocean Accident & Guarantee Ltd* (1933) 50 T.L.R. 32; *Facer v Vehicle & General Insurance Co* [1965] 1 Lloyd's Rep. 113; *O'Connor v BDB Kirby & Co* [1972] 1 Q.B. 90. This is perhaps the prevailing view. But it does not always yield just results, and in some contexts and countries, e.g. where illiteracy is prevalent, it must yield most unfair results. Attempts are sometimes therefore made to evade it, on grounds which are not very clear: see *Stone v Reliance Mutual Insurance Society Ltd* [1972] 1 Lloyd's Rep. 469 (noted (1972) 88 L.Q.R. 462; Tan Lee Meng (1975) 17 Malaya L.Rev. 104); *Blanchette v CIS Ltd* [1973] S.C.R. 833, following *Stone*'s case; *Woolcott v Excess Insurance Co Ltd* [1979] 1 Lloyd's Rep. 231; *Deaves v CML Fire & General Insurance Co Ltd* (1978) 143 C.L.R. 24; *Moxness v Cooperative Fire and Casualty Co* (1979) 95 D.L.R. (3d) 365; Jeyeretnam [1991] 2 M.L.J. lxvii, suggesting a distinction between situations where the information disclosed to the agent is contradicted by the signed proposal form and situations where the information supplements or clarifies the contents of the form; Clarke, above; Adams [1999] J.B.L. 215. Clauses providing that the person filling in the form is the agent of the

(3)   A broker bought goods from a factor, knowing from other experience that he
      was selling on behalf of a principal. Held, that the principal for whom the
      broker acted must be deemed to have had notice that the factor was not sell-
      ing his own goods.[1487]

(4)   A ship was driven on a rock and damaged. The master afterwards wrote a let-
      ter to the owner, but did not communicate the fact of the ship having been
      damaged, and, subsequent to the receipt of the letter, the owner insured the
      ship. Held, that the master ought to have communicated the fact, and that
      therefore the owner must be deemed to have had knowledge of it at the time
      of the insurance.[1488] So, where an agent shipped goods, and, having heard of
      a loss, purposely refrained from telegraphing to the principal because he
      thought it might prevent him from insuring, it was held that it was his duty
      to have telegraphed, and that an insurance effected by the principal after the
      time when he would have received the telegram was void on the ground of
      non-disclosure of material facts.[1489]

(5)   A broker was employed to effect an insurance, but did not effect it.
      Subsequently, another broker effected a policy in respect of the same risk on
      behalf of the same principal. It was sought to avoid the policy on the ground
      of the non-disclosure of material fact which had come to the knowledge of
      the firstmentioned broker in the course of his employment, but which he had
      not communicated to the principal, and which was not known either to the
      principal or to the broker who effected the policy. Held, that the policy was
      valid, there being no duty on the first broker to communicate the knowledge
      he had acquired.[1490]

(6)   A had a dog, which was kept at his stables under the care and control of his
      coachman. The coachman's knowledge of the ferocity of the dog was
      equivalent to A's knowledge.[1491] So, where the wife of A occasionally at-
      tended to his business, which was carried on upon premises where a dog was
      kept, and B made a complaint to her, for the purpose of its being com-
      municated to A, that the dog had bitten B's nephew, it was held that that was
      evidence of scienter on the part of A.[1492] So also, where complaints were made
      of a publican's dog to his barman.[1493] But the mere fact that a servant knows

---

proposer are probably not caught by s.3 of the Misrepresentation Act 1967, which gives the court
discretion to disallow reliance on certain exemption clauses: cf. *Overbrooke Estates Ltd v Glencombe
Properties Ltd* [1974] 1 W.L.R. 1335; *Collins v Howell-Jones* [1981] E.G.D. 207. It is not yet clear
just how much reform of this older law has resulted from the Insurance Act 2015 ss.3 to 6.

[1487] *Dresser v Norwood* (1864) 17 C.B.(N.S.) 466. See this case explained in *El Ajou v Dollar Land
Holdings Plc* [1994] 2 All E.R. 685 at 702. See also *Apthorp v Neville & Co* (1909) 23 T.L.R. 575
(printing contract: agent knew manuscript defamatory).

[1488] *Gladstone v King* (1813) 1 M. & S. 35 But see para.8-213 above.

[1489] *Proudfoot v Montefiore* (1867) L.R. 2 Q.B. 511.

[1490] *Blackburn, Low & Co v Vigors* (1887) 12 App.Cas. 531; cf. *Blackburn, Low & Co v Haslam* (1888)
21 Q.B.D. 144. See Comment above. See also *Wilson v Salamandra Ass. Co of St Petersburg* (1903)
88 L.T. 96 (knowledge of Lloyd's agents not imputed to underwriters); *Glencore International AG
v MSC Mediterranean Shipping Co SA* [2015] EWHC 1989 (Comm); [2015] 2 Lloyd's Rep. 508 at
[23].

[1491] *Baldwin v Casella* (1872) L.R. 7 Ex. 325; Animals Act 1971 s.2(2). See North, *The Modern Law of
Animals* (1972), p.58 onwards.

[1492] *Gladman v Johnson* (1867) 36 L.J.C.P. 153. It seems that this and the following case are still relevant
despite the wording of s.2(2) of the Animals Act 1971; North, above, p.66 onwards.

[1493] *Applebee v Percy* (1874) L.R. 9 C.P. 647.

a dog to be dangerous is no evidence of scienter on the part of the master, where the servant has nothing to do with the care or control of the dog, and has not the control of the premises or place where it is kept.[1494]

(7) The solicitor of a judgment creditor, having issued execution against the debtor, instructed A, a solicitor at the place where the execution was levied, to take an assignment of the goods seized from the sheriff. A did so, after having received notice of an act of bankruptcy by the debtor. Held, that the creditor must be deemed to have taken the assignment with notice of the act of bankruptcy.[1495] So, if a solicitor, with the consent of his client, puts his managing clerk in his place to conduct and manage a matter, notice of an act of bankruptcy to the clerk operates as notice to the solicitor and to the client.[1496]

(8) A solicitor induced a client to advance money on a mortgage of land which he held as trustee and afterwards induced another client to advance money on the same land. Held, that the last-mentioned client must be deemed to have had notice of the prior mortgage.[1497]

(9) Where the directors of a company took part in a misfeasance against the company, it was held that their knowledge did not operate as notice to the company of the misfeasance.[1498]

(10) A solicitor sells or mortgages property, and himself draws the purchase or mortgage deed and carries the transaction through on behalf, and with the consent, of the purchaser or mortgagee. The purchaser or mortgagee is deemed to have notice of all incumbrances known to the solicitor, even if the solicitor fraudulently conceals them.[1499] But the mere fact that the purchaser or mortgagee employs no solicitor does not mean that, when the vendor or mortgagor is a solicitor and prepares the documents, he constitutes such vendor or mortgagor his solicitor.[1500]

(11) A solicitor who was employed to transfer a mortgage knew that there were incumbrances on the property subsequent to such mortgage. Held, that his knowledge did not operate as notice of the incumbrances to the transferee, because the incumbrances were not material to the transfer, for which alone the solicitor was employed.[1501]

[1494] *Stiles v Cardiff Steam Navigation Co* (1864) 33 L.J.Q.B. 310; *Cleverton v Uffernel* (1887) 3 T.L.R. 509; *Colget v Norrish* (1886) 2 T.L.R. 471; North, above, p.62 onwards. See also *The Cawood III* [1951] P. 270 (knowledge of lightermen as to warning notice on jetty not attributed to employers); *Diment v N.H. Foot Ltd* [1974] 1 W.L.R. 1927 (knowledge of agents regarding user of right of way not attributed to absent owner of land). cf. *The Gudermes* [1991] 1 Lloyd's Rep. 456 (knowledge of appointed inspectors that ship had no cargo heating arrangements attributed to principals: decision reversed [1993] 1 Lloyd's Rep. 311).

[1495] *Brewin v Briscoe* (1859) 2 E. & E. 116; *Rothwell v Timbrell* (1842) 1 Dowl.(N.S.) 778.

[1496] *Re Ashton Ex p. McGowan* (1891) 64 L.T. 28; *Pike v Stephens* (1848) 12 Q.B. 465; *Pennell v Stephens* (1849) 7 C.B. 987.

[1497] *Rolland v Hart* (1871) L.R. 6 Ch.App. 678.

[1498] *Re Fitzroy Bessemer Steel Co Ltd* (1884) 50 L.T. 144.

[1499] *Atterbury v Wallis* (1856) 25 L.J.Ch. 792; *Re Weir, Hollingworth v Willing* (1888) 58 L.T. 792; *Boursot v Savage* (1866) L.R. 2 Eq. 134 (see (1916) 65 U. Pa.L.Rev. 34); *Dryden v Frost* (1837) 3 M. & C. 670; *Sheldon v Cox* (1764) 2 Eden 224; *Dixon v Winch* [1900] 1 Ch. 736. Some of the distinctions taken are not convincing. See also *Burnard v Lysnar* [1927] N.Z.L.R. 757 (knowledge by solicitor of true nature of transaction).

[1500] *Espin v Pemberton* (1859) 3 De G. & J. 547; *Hewitt v Loosemore* (1851) 9 Hare 449. But he may be affected by such notice as he would have had had he employed a solicitor: *Kennedy v Green* (1834) 3 Myl. & K. 699; *Boursot v Savage* (1866) L.R. 2 Eq. 134.

[1501] *Wyllie v Pollen* (1863) 32 L.J.Ch. 782; *Brittain v Brown & Millar* (1871) 24 L.T. 504. See also *Wythes*

(12) The secretary of a company, while attending a funeral as a relative of the deceased, acquires at a subsequent meeting of relatives at which the will and other documents are read out by a solicitor, knowledge of an equitable assignment relevant to the company's business. That does not operate as notice to the company of such facts.[1502]

(13) A company, X Ltd, buys assets from Y at an overvalue in order that Y would thereby have funds that could be used to buy shares in X Ltd. It is illegal for X Ltd to give financial assistance in the purchase of its shares in this way. Y uses the money received to buy shares in X Ltd from Z Ltd. Z Ltd is sued as a knowing receiver of the X Ltd's money under an illegal scheme. Z Ltd was held imputed with the knowledge of J, who was one of the directors of both X Ltd and Z Ltd. X Ltd is not, however, deemed to have consented to J's actions.[1503]

(14) Directors of a banking company who had no voice in the management of the accounts acquired knowledge of certain circumstances relating to the accounts. Held, that this did not operate as notice of such circumstances to the company.[1504]

(15) On the sale of land, one firm of solicitors acts for the vendor, another for the purchaser. The two firms are in fact constituted by the same two partners. Knowledge acquired by one firm in acting for the vendor is not to be attributed via the other firm to the purchaser.[1505]

(16) Money which in fact consists of misappropriated trust funds is lent to a company. It is sought to charge the company with knowing receipt of trust property.[1506] The fact that the funds were misappropriated is known for other reasons to a Swiss "fiduciary agent" who acts as broker in the transaction. He is also a director and chairman of the company, is claimed to be the ultimate beneficial owner of the company and signed the relevant agreement regarding the loan. Although as broker he has a duty to disclose the facts to the company and does not do so, the company itself has no duty to inquire into their provenance and hence has no notice through him as their broker in the matter. But his position as a director and chairman of the company acting in connection with this transaction means that he is for this purpose the "directing mind and will" of the company, and the company itself has direct knowledge, not through an agent, that trust funds are involved, sufficient to make it liable for knowing receipt.[1507]

(17) A barrister's knowledge that the judge hearing a case was the brother of a partner of a law firm that was party to indirectly connected proceedings was

---

v Labouchere (1859) 3 De G. & J. 593; Wells v Smith [1914] 3 K.B. 722; Wilkinson v General Accident, etc., Corp [1967] 2 Lloyd's Rep. 182; The Hayle [1929] P. 275.

[1502] Société Générale de Paris v Tramways Union Co (1884) 14 Q.B.D. 424.

[1503] Belmont Finance Corp v Williams (No.2) [1980] 1 All E.R. 393. See too Lebon v Aqua Salt Co Ltd [2009] UKPC 2; [2009] 1 B.C.L.C. 549; David Browne Contractors Ltd v Petterson [2017] NZSC 116; [2018] 1 N.Z.L.R. 112 at [121].

[1504] Powles v Page (1846) 3 C.B. 16; Re Carew's Estate Act (1862) 31 Beav. 39. cf. Ex p. Agra Bank, Re Worcester (1868) L.R. 3 Ch.App. 555.

[1505] Campbell v M'Creath 1975 S.C. 81.

[1506] See Article 116.

[1507] El Ajou v Dollar Land Holdings Plc [1994] 2 All E.R. 685; following on the first point Re David Payne & Co Ltd [1904] 2 Ch. 608. See above, para.8-215.

imputed to the client, precluding the client from later raising an issue of bias against the judge.[1508]

(18) A building society lends on the basis of property valuations that proved fraudulent. One of the society's employees, but not the person who approved the loans, may have been aware of the fraudulent basis to the valuations. The knowledge of that employee was not imputed to the society, which remained able to sue the company that prepared the valuations in the tort of deceit.[1509]

(19) An employer is sued for breach of a duty of care to take reasonable steps to prevent psychiatric injury to an employee. Such injury results from severe racial harassment and intimidatory conduct by a colleague. Knowledge of other employees who were not, however, in the chain of command that the harassment was taking place was not imputed to the employer. Vicarious liability for intentional infliction of emotional harm was, however, upheld, in relation to which imputation was not a requirement.[1510]

(20) A loan contract required the borrower to disclose all facts relevant to the fulfilment of conditions attached to the contract. A bribe was found to have been paid by an employee of the borrower to get officers of the lender to waive certain conditions. The sole director of the borrower was aware of the bribe, and his knowledge entailed that the borrower was in breach of its contractual disclosure obligations. The issue of imputation was a question of construction of the contract.[1511]

(21) A loan made between related companies, which had four directors and a company secretary in common, was challenged some 12 years later on the basis that the borrowing had not been formally approved by the shareholders of the borrower as its articles of association required. The secretary's knowledge of the failure to follow correct procedures was not imputed to the lending company.[1512]

(22) X makes a marriage settlement under which the children of the marriage will inherit upon X's death. Twenty-five years' later, following the death of X's wife, X marries Y purporting to settle the same property on the same terms. This may have been a fraud on Y by X, as well as on the children of the first marriage, X hoping no one would know of the double settlement before he died. It was held that Y was bound by her solicitor's knowledge of the first settlement, she having used the same solicitor as her husband.[1513]

(23) A son residing in London uses his father, resident in Leicestershire, to negotiate the purchase of land in the county. The father learns that the vendor has

---

[1508] *Smits v Roach* (2006) 228 A.L.R. 262 (HCA). The case may simply have raised issues of a barrister's apparent authority to waive objections to the composition of the tribunal.

[1509] *Nationwide Building Society v Dunlop Haywards Ltd* [2007] EWHC 1374 (Comm).

[1510] *Nationwide News Pty Ltd v Naidu* (2007) 71 N.S.W.L.R. 471.

[1511] *Jafari-Fini v Skillglass Ltd* [2007] EWCA Civ 261.

[1512] *Re Hampshire Land Co* [1896] 2 Ch. 743. This is treated as a leading authority on the fraud exception to imputation, above, para.8-215, though it is difficult to see how the company's secretary's failures were fraudulent in any way, nor was he the only officer in common between the companies. A better explanation of the case would seem to be that after some 12 years all shareholders in the borrower had become aware of, and informally approved, the loan. The borrower could also have been subject to a restitutionary claim.

[1513] *Le Neve v Le Neve* (1748) 1 Ves. Sen. 64.

already agreed to sell the land to C. In action by C to restrain the sale, the father's knowledge is imputed to the son.[1514]

5. Interference with Agent By Third Party and Involvement in Agent's Breach of Duty

Article 96

Rights of Principal Where Third Party Implicated in Agent's Breach of Duties

(1) A contract made or act done by an agent which is, to the knowledge of the other party involved, in violation of the agent's equitable duties to the principal entitles the principal to equitable remedies against the third party.[1515]   **8-218**

(2) Where an agent is induced by bribery to depart from the agent's duty to the principal, the third party who bribed or promised the bribe to the agent is liable at common law and equity jointly and severally with the agent to the principal:

    (a) in restitution, for the bribe; or

    (b) in tort, for any loss sustained by the principal from entering into the transaction in respect of which the bribe was given;[1516]

Comment

Relationship between equitable and common law claims The material covered   **8-219** in this Article is mainly addressed to aspects of the equitable liability of third parties for involvement in breaches of duty by an agent. It should be observed that many of the cases where equity intervenes are ones where there will also be common law liability. This is apparent from Rule (2), addressed to bribes. It is obvious too that where agents act in breach of their duty of loyalty they may also act without authority, including by reason of dishonesty.[1517] In such circumstances, the relevant dealing will, in the absence of apparent authority or some other exception, be ineffective either to create a contract or to pass property at law in assets intended to be subject to the dealing. The principal may have claims against a third party in conversion or money had and received.[1518] Another potentially relevant common law claim against a third party is the action for inducing a breach of contract, in this case the

---

[1514] *Merry v Abney* (1663) 1 Ch. Cas. 38.

[1515] *Panama & South Pacific Telegraph Co v India Rubber, etc., Co* (1875) L.R. 10 Ch.App. 515. See Comment and Illustrations 1–4. There are terse but similar provisions entitling the principal to avoid the contract in the PECL Article 3:205 (where part of the statement about common law on p.211 is incorrect), in the UNIDROIT Principles Article 2.2.7; and in the DCFR, II, 6:109.

[1516] *Mahesan v Malaysian Government Officers' Co-operative Housing Society Ltd* [1979] A.C. 374; see below. Much litigation on bribery has occurred in the context of the conflict of laws. See, e.g. *Lemenda Trading Co Ltd v African Middle East Petroleum Co Ltd* [1988] Q.B. 448; *Arab Monetary Fund v Hashim* [1996] 1 Lloyd's Rep. 589; *Dubai Aluminium Co Ltd v Salaam* [2002] UKHL 48; [2003] 2 A.C. 366; *Grupo Torras SA v Al Sabah (No.5)* [2001] Lloyd's Rep. Bank. 36. For a valuable survey of civil liability in respect of bribery, see Berg [2001] L.M.C.L.Q. 27.

[1517] See Article 23.

[1518] See e.g. *Matthews v Gibbs* (1860) 30 L.J.Q.B. 55; *Heinl v Jyske Bank (Gibraltar) Ltd* [1999] Lloyd's Rep. Bank. 511 at 521, per Nourse LJ; citing dicta of Slade and Browne-Wilkinson LJJ in *Rolled Steel Products (Holdings) Ltd v British Steel Corp Ltd* [1986] Ch. 246 at 295, 297 and 304. See also Article 88.

contract between principal and agent. But the development over time of parallel claims in equity has assumed increasing importance. So, in many cases where there have been dispositions without authority, the principal may prefer to use equitable claims to follow the property, or to sue the third party in what is usually called "knowing receipt". Commonly, the basis of equity's intervention in such cases has been breach of fiduciary duty, but breach of fiduciary duty is probably not essential to equitable intervention, except perhaps where the most that can be alleged against the third party is dishonest assistance in the agent's wrongdoing. More is said on these topics in Article 88 and in Article 116, the latter Article being concerned with an agent's liabilities, but in circumstances where the agent is that of the third party, not of the original principal. Much of this material is as applicable to third parties as to agents, but for convenience, it is treated in the next chapter.

8-220   **Equitable claims, including "the proper purpose" duty**   Apart from those just addressed, there are a number of circumstances in which third parties can find themselves implicated in an agent's breach of equitable duty. The most serious of these is involvement in an agent's breach of the duty of loyalty—a failure (not merely one of negligence) to act in the principal's best interests.[1519] A transaction, not necessarily disloyal but affected by a conflict of interest, including one under which an agent receives an incidental benefit, is another example. A third type of case has traditionally been called a "fraud on a power", although again dishonesty need not be shown.[1520] This concept responds to an exercise of powers that is not disloyal but which involves action that equity concludes is contrary to the purposes for which the relevant power was given (hence, the alternative label, "proper purposes doctrine"). The concept of authority, the central focus of agency, turns on the terms of the mandate given by the principal, and on honesty in the exercise of the mandate, whereas the duty of loyalty and the proper purposes doctrine seek to control the use of the mandate for purposes not expressly precluded by the mandate but foreign to what is perceived as its underlying purposes.[1521] Clear distinctions between the two concepts are not always easy to draw, and certainly conscious failure to act in the principal's best interests will usually involve a finding of dishonesty, thereby triggering liability at common law as well.[1522] Historically, the principal applications of the proper purposes doctrine have involved trustees and company directors.[1523] In principle, the doctrine could apply to any fiduciary, although in practice the issue is most likely to arise with those in positions that

---

[1519] See above, para.6-034. As to dishonesty not being an essential element, see *State of South Australia v Clark* (1996) 66 S.A.S.R. 199; *Bishopsgate Investment Management Ltd v Maxwell (No.2)* [1994] 1 All E.R. 261.

[1520] See *Farwell on Powers* (Farwell and Archer eds, 3rd edn); Thomas, *Powers* (2nd edn); Nolan [2009] C.L.J. 293; J. Hudson, "One Thicket in Fraud on a Power" (2019) 39 O.J.L.S. 577; R. Flannigan, "Fraud on a Power, Improper Purpose and Fiduciary Accountability" (2019) 62 Can.Bus.L.J. 133; Rt Hon. Lord Sales, "Use of Powers for Proper Purposes in Private Law" (2020) 136 L.Q.R. 384.

[1521] See the valuable discussion by Nolan in [2009] C.L.J. 293 at 297 onwards. See too above, para.3-011; *Senex Holdings Ltd v National Westminster Bank Plc* [2012] EWHC 131 (Comm); [2012] 1 All E.R. (Comm) 1130, Illustration 9.

[1522] See, e.g. *Criterion Properties Plc v Stratford UK Properties LLC* [2004] UKHL 28; [2004] 1 W.L.R. 1846 at [2] and [30] (noted Watts (2005) 120 L.Q.R. 4). At first instance this case was argued on the basis of fraud on a power, but in the House of Lords it became apparent that questions of actual authority were at issue.

[1523] In relation to directors, the leading cases are *Howard Smith Ltd v Ampol Petroleum Ltd* [1974] A.C. 821, Illustration 8; and *Eclairs Group Ltd v JKX Oil & Gas Plc* [2015] UKSC 71; [2016] 1 B.C.L.C.

confer broad discretionary powers.[1524] The onus of proving an improper purpose lies on the claimant.[1525] Where there are co-agents, such as a board of directors, it seems that the improper purpose must have actuated a majority of the board.[1526] The necessary causative connection between the improper purpose and the transaction being impugned remains unsettled.[1527]

Effect of breach of equitable duty   Although it is common to say that a contract   **8-221**
affected by a breach of equitable duty is voidable, it seems that something may turn on the type of duty infringed by the agent. While a simple undisclosed conflict of interest makes the contract merely voidable,[1528] active disloyalty in the agent,[1529] and, it seems, fraud on a power, make the contract void at equity.[1530] In the latter situations, it would normally be possible for the claimant to follow money or other property transferred, or to sue for knowing receipt, without first needing to rescind any contract with the third party.[1531] Apart from declaring a contract void, or setting it aside,[1532] equity can respond in a variety of ways against third parties who involve themselves in an agent's breaches of equitable duty, including withholding specific performance of a contract,[1533] permitting a set-off against debts owed

---

1 (noted Nolan (2016) 132 L.Q.R. 369; Worthington [2016] C.L.J. 213). See too *Re Sherborne Park Co Ltd* [1987] B.C.L.C. 82; *Roadchef (Employee Benefits Trustees) Ltd v Hill* [2014] EWHC 109 (Ch) at [123] (directors of trustee company transfer shares to another company for purpose foreign to trust); *British Airways Plc v Airways Pension Scheme Trustee Ltd* [2018] EWCA Civ 1533 (pension scheme trustees). For further detail, see *Gower's Principles of Modern Company Law* (10th edn), at para.16-22 onwards; Nolan, in *The Realm of Company Law* (Rider ed., 1998).

[1524] For the possible application of the doctrine to others than fiduciaries, see Nolan [2009] C.L.J. 293 at 313.

[1525] *Australian Metropolitan Life Assurance Co Ltd v Ure* (1923) 33 C.L.R. 199 at 206 and 219.

[1526] *Howard Smith Ltd v Ampol Petroleum Ltd* [1974] A.C. 821 at 831; *Roadchef (Employee Benefits Trustees) Ltd v Hill* [2014] EWHC 109 (Ch) at [129]. cf. the position at common law in relation to conflict of interest: *Benson v Heathorn* (1842) 1 Y. & C. Ch. Cas. 326.

[1527] See *Eclairs Group Ltd v JKX Oil & Gas Plc* [2015] UKSC 71; [2016] 1 B.C.L.C. 1.

[1528] *Hely-Hutchinson v Brayhead Ltd* [1968] 1 Q.B. 549 at 595; *Guinness Plc v Saunders* [1990] 2 A.C. 663 at 697; *Charles Terence Estates Ltd v Cornwall Council* [2012] EWCA Civ 1439; [2013] 1 W.L.R. 466 at [47] (exercise of local authority powers).

[1529] *Rolled Steel Products (Holdings) Ltd v British Steel Corp* [1986] Ch. 246; *Guinness Plc v Saunders* [1990] 2 A.C. 663 at 702, Illustration 13 to Article 75; *Houghton v Fayers* [2000] 1 B.C.L.C. 511; *J.J. Harrison (Properties) Ltd v Harrison* [2001] EWCA Civ 1467; [2002] 1 B.C.L.C. 162; *GHLM Trading Ltd v Maroo* [2012] EWHC 61 (Ch) at [171].

[1530] For authorities and discussion, see Nolan [2009] C.L.J. 293 at 316 onwards; *Roadchef (Employee Benefits Trustees) Ltd v Hill* [2014] EWHC 109 (Ch) at [131]. The position in relation to issues of company shares appears to be different: see *Bamford v Bamford* [1970] Ch. 212 (voidable only); cf. *Residues Treatment & Trading Co Ltd v Southern Resources Ltd (No.4)* (1989) 14 A.C.L.R. 569; and the discussion in Nolan [2009] C.L.J. 293 at 319–320.

[1531] See, e.g. *Belmont Finance Corp v Williams Furniture Ltd (No.2)* [1980] 1 All E.R. 393; *Rolled Steel Products (Holdings) Ltd v British Steel Corp* [1986] Ch. 246; *Houghton v Fayers* [2000] 1 B.C.L.C. 511.

[1532] *Re Panama and South Pacific Telegraph Co v India Rubber, Gutta Percha and Telegraph Works Co* (1875) L.R. 10 Ch.App. 515; *Smith v Sorby* (1875) 3 Q.B.D. 552n, Illustration 2; *Taylor v Walker* [1958] 1 Lloyd's Rep. 490, Illustration 4; *Armagas Ltd v Mundogas SA (The Ocean Frost)* [1986] A.C. 717 at 742–743; *Logicrose Ltd v Southend United Football Club* [1988] 1 W.L.R. 1256 at 1260 (Illustration 6); *Hurstanger Ltd v Wilson* [2007] EWCA Civ 299; [2007] 1 W.L.R. 2351 at [47]; *UBS AG (London Branch) v Kommunale Wasserwerke Peipkiz GmbH* [2017] EWCA Civ 1567 at [155]. This can be done even though it has previously been treated as discharged on inadequate grounds: *Alexander v Webber* [1922] 1 K.B. 642, and perhaps the *Panama* case, above. But the person seeking to do so must of course come in time. See *Lewin on Trusts* (20th edn), para.45-067.

[1533] *Galloway v Pedersen* (1915) 34 N.Z.L.R. 513. cf. *Odessa Tramways Co v Mendel* (1878) 8 Ch.D.

the third party,[1534] declaring a constructive trust of assets in the third party's possession,[1535] imposing liability for knowing receipt[1536] and imposing compensatory liability for dishonest assistance in the agent's breach of duty.[1537] In all cases, a third party is unlikely to be affected by an agent's breach of equitable duty unless that third party has a sufficient degree of knowledge of the breach to warrant equity's attention.[1538] It is clear now that only dishonesty, in an objective sense (itself a difficult concept), is sufficient for liability for dishonest assistance.[1539] The dishonesty can be in an employee or partner, whereupon the usual principles of vicarious liability apply.[1540] There remains uncertainty as to the applicable tests for liability to rescission, for the invocation of the defence of bona fide purchaser for value in relation to proprietary actions and for liability for knowing receipt.[1541] Knowledge of one agent's breach of fiduciary duty may be fatal even if even greater corruption existed within the principal's organisation of which the third party was unaware.[1542]

8-222　**Bribery and secret commissions**　Bribery is a particularly obvious form of corruption, and one that has attracted much attention since the nineteenth century from both common law and equity. A small group of core cases before and after the beginning of the twentieth century lay down and repeat stern rules in respect of bribery, which dominate the area and appear to have had some element of deterrent purpose. Definitions of bribery and of the wider concept of a secret commission, together with an account of the internal effect of the applicable rules as between principal and agent have been addressed in Article 49. This Article concerns the external effect, but should be read in conjunction with the commentary to Article 49. The breadth of the concept of a secret commission means that a third party who offers or confers money or some other personal benefit on an agent (knowing the facts giving rise to that person's fiduciary capacity[1543]) cannot escape legal repercussions merely because the third party avers that he or she thought that the agent would tell or had told the principal of the payment[1544]; or was unaware of the agent's exact intention but aware that the agent did not intend to

---

235.
[1534] *Clark v Cutland* [2003] EWCA Civ 810; [2004] 1 W.L.R. 783.
[1535] See the cases referred to in commentary to Article 88.
[1536] See, e.g. *Aerostar Maintenance International Ltd v Wilson* [2010] EWHC 2032 (Ch) at [194]. See also the cases in fn.1532, above, and the discussion in Article 116. In cases of receipt of corporate opportunities, as opposed to receipt of existing assets of the principal, it seems that a higher test of knowledge is required for liability: see *Satnam Investments Ltd v Dunlop Heywood* [1999] 3 All E.R. 652; *Farah Constructions Pty Ltd v Say-Dee Pty Ltd* (2007) 230 C.L.R. 89 at [118]; and as to Scotland, *Commonwealth Oil & Gas Co Ltd v Baxter* [2009] CSIH 75 at [95].
[1537] *Aerostar Maintenance International Ltd v Wilson* [2010] EWHC 2032 (Ch) at [185] and [197] (recipient of corporate opportunity (and others) also liable for dishonestly assisting director to divert opportunity); *Group Seven Ltd v Notable Services LLP* [2019] EWCA Civ 614; [2020] Ch. 129. See too below, para.8-225. For general discussion of the dishonest assistance action, see Article 116.
[1538] See *Chancery Client Partners Ltd v MRC 957 Ltd* [2016] EWHC 2142 (Ch) at [22].
[1539] See *Royal Brunei Airlines Sdn Bhd v Tan* [1995] 2 A.C. 378; *Group Seven Ltd v Notable Services LLP* [2019] EWCA Civ 614; [2020] Ch. 129.
[1540] See *Dubai Aluminium Co Ltd v Salaam* [2002] UKHL 48; [2003] 2 A.C. 366; and *Group Seven Ltd v Notable Services LLP* [2019] EWCA Civ 614; [2020] Ch. 129. See further para.8-178.
[1541] For discussion, see commentary to Article 116. See too *UBS AG (London Branch) v Kommunale Wasserwerke Peipkiz GmbH* [2017] EWCA Civ 1567 at [110].
[1542] See *UBS AG (London Branch) v Kommunale Wasserwerke Peipkiz GmbH* [2017] EWCA Civ 1567 at [113] and [154].
[1543] *Pengelly v Business Mortgage Finance 4 Plc* [2020] EWHC 2002 (Ch) at [54].
[1544] *Shipway v Broadwood* [1899] 1 Q.B. 369 at 373 (Illustration 3); *Grant v Gold Exploration and*

disclose the dealing to the principal.[1545] The third party is also liable where having arranged for the payment not knowing of the agency, that party continued and entered into the contract with the principal after he or she had learned of it.[1546] It is not necessary for the principal to show that the third party had an intention to influence the agent.[1547] Although it is true that the objectionable feature of bribery is the general one that it gives rise to a conflict of interest,[1548] factors such as those above distinguish bribes from the more general idea of undisclosed profit, which need not involve the complicity of a third party.[1549]

Forms of relief and remedy   The material that follows addresses both Rule (1)   **8-223** and (2) above. The principal who learns of a bribe or secret commission is presented with a wide range of legal options against the inculpated third party. Certainly where the payment was corrupt, and therefore a bribe in the technical sense, the principal has the right to rescind, or cancel, any contract with the third party. Such rights arise at common law and equity. Where the agent's authority extended to binding the principal to the relevant contract, and the agent was as corrupt as the briber, the contract is likely to be void for lack of authority, under the principle discussed in Article 23. Equity then takes a wider view of what constitutes a conflicting interest sufficient to warrant curial intervention. Relevant case law is found above, and in the commentary to Article 49. Where bribery is involved, it will also not generally be necessary that the briber be placed back in its pre-contract position.[1550] In cases where the agent is not dishonest, albeit receiving a secret commission, the contract will be voidable only. Avoidance is less likely where the agent has disclosed the inducement but not given as complete an account as should have been given.[1551] Rescission might be denied in such cases where it is no longer possible fully to return the payer to its pre-contract position.[1552]

Otherwise, the principal may, at common law, claim from the third party the amount of the bribe or damages for loss flowing from the agent's involvement with the bribing party. These are alternative remedies: "(1) to recover from [the third party] the amount of the bribe as money had and received, or (2) to recover, as damages for tort, the actual loss which he has sustained as a result of entering into the

---

Development Syndicate Ltd [1900] 1 Q.B. 233 at 248–250; *Taylor v Walker* [1958] 1 Lloyd's Rep. 490, Illustration 4, at 509–513; *Daraydan Holdings Ltd v Solland International Ltd* [2004] EWHC 622 (Ch); [2005] Ch. 119 at [53]; *Otkritie International Investment Management Ltd v Urumov* [2014] EWHC 191 (Comm) at [68]; *Shagang Shipping Co Ltd v HNA Group Co Ltd* [2018] EWCA Civ 1732 at [84] (intention to influence need not be shown); reversed on the facts [2020] UKSC 34; *Pengelly v Business Mortgage Finance 4 Plc* [2020] EWHC 2002 (Ch) at [55] and [78].

[1545] *Logicrose Ltd v Southend United FC* [1988] 1 W.L.R. 1256 at 1260–1262.

[1546] *Grant v Gold Exploration and Development Syndicate Ltd* [1900] 1 Q.B. 233 at 248.

[1547] *Industries and General Mortgage Co Ltd v Lewis* [1949] 2 All E.R. 573.

[1548] *Anangel Atlas Cia. Naviera SA v Ishikawajima-Harima Heavy Industries Co Ltd* [1990] 1 Lloyd's Rep. 167 at 171.

[1549] As to secret profits, see Articles 45–47.

[1550] See *UBS AG (London Branch) v Kommunale Wasserwerke Leipzig GmbH* [2017] EWCA Civ 1567 at [225]. See also P. Watts, "Rescission of Guarantees for Misrepresentation and Actionable Non-disclosure" [2002] C.L.J. 301.

[1551] See *Hurstanger Ltd v Wilson* [2007] EWCA Civ 299; [2007] 1 W.L.R. 2351; [2007] 4 All E.R. 1118 at [47]. See too above, para.6-085. cf. *Pengelly v Business Mortgage Finance 4 Plc* [2020] EWHC 2002 (Ch) at [80] (undertaking to disclose payments from third party not kept, so rescission the appropriate remedy).

[1552] cf. *Barry v The Stony Point Canning Co* (1917) 55 S.C.R. 51 at 77.

transaction in respect of which the bribe was given".[1553] Older case law suggested that the third party's liability was without taking into account any sum recovered from the agent.[1554] Such a rule was almost penal in operation and surprising, inasmuch as it seemed to allow double recovery[1555] and its origin may have been influenced by the rule, applicable at the time of the leading case, that judgment against one tortfeasor released the others[1556]: it was important to establish the briber's liability as separate from the restitutionary liability of the agent for the bribe. The law however was clarified in *Mahesan v Malaysian Government Officers' Co-operative Housing Society Ltd*[1557] in which it was held that the notion that there could be cumulation was unjustified and inconsistent with the principle as to election laid down in *United Australia Ltd v Barclays Bank Ltd.*[1558] It has since been held, however, that the principal may rescind the contract with the third party, whilst maintaining the principal's rights to strip the agent of the benefits received by way of bribe; otherwise the agent would remain unjustly enriched.[1559] In other cases, the principal will be required to elect between alternative remedies, but the election need not be made before judgment has been entered in the principal's favour in one or other of them.[1560] Affirmation by the principal of the contract with the third party will not usually preclude the former from pursuing monetary remedies against the latter.[1561]

Some difficulties have arisen in categorising the rights of the principal against the third party, especially those at common law. One view has been that the action for damages should be regarded as lying in deceit, and that that cause of action might also embrace liability for the amount of the bribe. Where no clear loss could be proved, such liability was to be explained on the basis that the damages would be presumed to be at least the amount of the bribe.[1562] This would however involve tort liability without actual loss or damage and is contrary to principle. Further, this analysis involves a claim in deceit without representation (except at best by inference) or reliance on a representation; hence the suggestion that the relevant tort is

---

[1553] *Mahesan v Malaysian Government Officers' Co-operative Housing Society Ltd* [1979] A.C. 374 at 383, per Lord Diplock. As to money had and received, see *Hovenden & Sons v Millhoff* (1900) 83 L.T. 41.

[1554] *Salford Corp v Lever* [1891] 1 Q.B. 168; *Morgan v Elford* (1876) 4 Ch.D. 352; *Phosphate Sewage Co v Hartmont* (1877) 5 Ch.D. 394; cf. *Lands Allotment Co v Broad* (1895) 13 R. 699; *Grant v Gold Exploration & Development Syndicate Ltd* [1900] 1 Q.B. 233; *Cohen v Kuschke & Co and Koenig* (1900) 83 L.T. 102.

[1555] Pollock (1891) 7 L.Q.R. 99. But there does not seem to have been actual double recovery in any of the cases; cf. however Tettenborn (1979) 95 L.Q.R. 68, who defends this possibility.

[1556] *Brinsmead v Harrison* (1872) L.R. 7 C.P. 547 (abolished by the Law Reform (Married Women and Tortfeasors) Act 1935). See the argument in *Salford Corp v Lever* [1891] 1 Q.B. 168.

[1557] *Mahesan v Malaysian Government Officers' Co-operative Housing Society Ltd* [1979] A.C. 374, Illustration 8 to Article 49; see Needham (1979) 95 L.Q.R. 536; (1978) 94 L.Q.R. 344; (1978) 41 M.L.R. 603. cf., however, Tettenborn, above.

[1558] *United Australia Ltd v Barclays Bank Ltd* [1941] A.C. 1. The agent is also liable on a proprietary basis: see above, para.6-085. But there is no indication that this extinguishes the personal liability of agent or third party.

[1559] *Logicrose Ltd v Southend United FC* [1988] 1 W.L.R. 1256. See too *Grant v Gold Exploration and Development Syndicate Ltd* [1900] 1 Q.B. 233.

[1560] *Mahesan* [1979] A.C. 374 at 383.

[1561] See *Motortrak Ltd v FCA Australia Pty Ltd* [2018] EWHC 990 (Comm).

[1562] See *Hovenden & Sons v Millhoff* (1900) 83 L.T. 41; *Industries & General Mortgage Co v Lewis* [1949] 2 All E.R. 573; *Grant v Gold Exploration and Development Syndicate Ltd* [1900] 1 Q.B. 233.

the broader one of "fraud".[1563] Then, in relation to the third party's liability for the amount of the bribe in an action for money had and received, the difficulty is that the third party will have paid the bribe, not received it. The action seems to be based on the proposition that "he is entitled to treat the benefit obtained by or promised to the agent as part of the consideration which should have been received by the principal (if he is a vendor) or as excess consideration provided by the principal (if he is a purchaser)".[1564] A conclusive presumption of enrichment appears to be in operation. The cause of action in tort will be advantageous where there is loss which exceeds the amount of the bribe. It might also be more easily available when the bribe has not been paid but merely promised: though it appears that the action in money had and received may still lie in such a case.[1565]

Where the payment is made or agreed upon (or, when originally unauthorised, adopted) after the making of the contract, the effect of a bribe probably turns on the general principles of breach of contract, viz. the payment will be a breach of contract and the consequences of that fact will turn in the ordinary way on what significance the arrangement had for the due performance of the contract.[1566] The appropriate remedy in such circumstances may be cancellation of the contract rather than rescission ab initio.[1567]

The foregoing describes the main claims used by the principal against the third party. A range of other options have been invoked in particular circumstances, including declaring the contract between the parties to be inoperative for failure of a required condition,[1568] or discharged for breach,[1569] holding a promissory note not provable in a bankruptcy[1570] and determining that a particular transaction was not for the best rent under the Settled Land Act.[1571] In these latter situations, common law and equity reasoning is not always distinguished. A transaction involving some

---

[1563] See *Petrotrade Inc v Smith* [2000] 1 Lloyd's Rep. 486 at [19], per David Steel J. But cf. *Kensington International Ltd v Republic of Congo* [2007] EWCA Civ 1128; [2008] 1 Lloyd's Rep. 161 at [62]–[63] (the offering and receiving of bribes involves deception of the principal); and *Cavell USA Inc v Seaton Insurance Co* [2009] EWCA Civ 1363 at [25]. See too Mitchell (2001) 117 L.Q.R. 207; but contra the Hon. Justice K.R. Handley, ibid., 536.

[1564] *Logicrose Ltd v Southend United FC* [1988] 1 W.L.R. 1256 at 1263, per Millett J.

[1565] See *Nelmes v NRAM Plc* [2016] EWCA Civ 491; [2016] C.T.L.C. 106 at [36] (relief under Consumer Credit Act 1974 s.140A); *Grant v Gold Exploration and Development Syndicate* [1900] 1 Q.B. 233 (but see on this case *Mahesan*'s case [1979] A.C. 374 at 382–383); and the dictum of Millett J quoted above ("or promised to"). As to mere promises to pay a bribe or attempts to suborn, see also *Whaley Bridge Calico Printing Co v Green* (1879) 5 Q.B.D. 109; *Donegal International Ltd v Republic of Zambia* [2007] EWHC 197 (Comm); [2007] 1 Lloyd's Rep. 397; and *Nayyar v Sapte* [2009] EWHC 3218 (QB).

[1566] *Armagas Ltd v Mundogas SA (The Ocean Frost)* [1985] 1 Lloyd's Rep. 1 at 18–22, following the view of Mellish LJ in *Panama & South Pacific Telegraph Co v India Rubber, etc., Co* (1875) L.R. 10 Ch.App. 515 at 531–532; and applying *Hong Kong Fir Shipping Co Ltd v Kawasaki Kisen Kaisha Ltd* [1962] 2 Q.B. 26. The decision was reversed on other grounds: [1986] A.C. 717 (CA and HL). See also *Tigris International NV v China Southern Airlines Co Ltd* [2014] EWCA Civ 1649 at [143] (third party innocently thought agency for claimant had terminated).

[1567] *Panama & South Pacific Telegraph Co v India Rubber, etc., Co* (1875) L.R. 10 Ch.App. 515 to the contrary, may need reconsideration in the light of the now favoured principle that post-contract breaches permit cancellation *de futuro* only: see, e.g. *Thornton Hall v Wembley Electrical Appliances Ltd* [1947] 2 All E.R. 630 at 634; *Manifest Shipping Co Ltd v Uni-Polaris Insurance Co Ltd* [2001] UKHL 1; [2003] 1 A.C. 469 at [52]; *Tigris International NV v China Southern Airlines Company Ltd* [2014] EWCA Civ 1649 at [143]. See Watts (2009) 125 L.Q.R. 369 at 372.

[1568] *Shipway v Broadwood* [1899] 1 Q.B. 369, Illustration 3.

[1569] *Bartram & Sons v Lloyd* (1904) 90 L.T. 357.

[1570] *Re a Debtor* [1927] 2 Ch. 367.

[1571] *Chandler v Bradley* [1897] 1 Ch. 315.

forms of corruption may also be unenforceable under the rules for illegal contracts.[1572]

8-224 **Bribery by agent of third party**   The discussion so far has been concerned with bribes paid or promised by third parties themselves, or readily imputable to such third parties. Where a bribe is paid or promised by an *agent*[1573] of the third party without that party's knowledge, the position is likely to be affected by the remedy being sought by the third party. If only rescission is being sought, it may be that the third party cannot maintain the contract because that would be both to adopt and disown the agent's conduct.[1574] If damages are being sought, then probably the standard tort rules should be applied, meaning that usually the principal would be liable only if the agent were an employee, or cognate and the conduct took place in "the course of employment".[1575] There may also be cases where the third party uses an intermediary but does not know exactly what the intermediary will do. In such cases the act of such party may still be attributed to the third party[1576]; or that party may at least be subject to the rescissionary remedy on the grounds that it would be inequitable to insist on the transaction in the circumstances.[1577] It will not usually matter that the agent also performs some role for the other party; the party whose agent received the bribe is nonetheless entitled to rescind the transaction.[1578] This liability would not preclude the third party suing its agent for having embroiled it in corrupt activity.[1579] Conversely, where the third party knows that its own agent is attempting to bribe the agents of the principal, it is likely to find itself unable to plead any default against the agent by reason of the principle ex turpi causa non oritur action.[1580]

8-225 **Action for dishonest assistance**   Now that the basis of accessory liability in respect of breach of fiduciary duty has been clarified,[1581] it is possible that claimants, apprised of their agents' corruption, may prefer to rely on the action for dishon-

---

[1572] For the general law, see *Chitty on Contracts* (33rd edn), Ch.16. For particular difficulties in this context, see Berg [2001] L.M.C.L.Q. 27 at 41 onwards. See too *Hurstanger Ltd v Wilson* [2007] EWCA Civ 299; [2007] 1 W.L.R. 2351; [2007] 4 All E.R. 1118; *Medsted Associates Ltd v Canaccord Genuity Wealth (International) Ltd* [2019] EWCA Civ 83; [2019] 1 W.L.R. 4481 at [49] cf. *Honeywell International Middle East Ltd v Meydan Group LLC* [2014] EWHC 1344 (TCC); [2014] 2 Lloyd's Rep. 133 at [185].

[1573] See the discussion above, para.6-087. See too *FM Capital Partners Ltd v Marino* [2018] EWHC 1768 (Comm) at [449] (procuring payment by company controlled by briber); affirmed on different points [2020] EWCA Civ 245; [2020] 3 W.L.R. 109.

[1574] See above, paras 8-097 and 8-222.

[1575] See *Armagas Ltd v Mundogas SA* [1986] A.C. 717 at 744–745 (in CA, bribing party a joint venturer, perhaps partner), following *Barry v Stoney Point Canning Co* (1917) 55 S.C.R. 51. See also *Hamlyn v John Houston & Co* [1903] 1 K.B. 81; *UBS AG (London Branch) v Kommunale Wasserwerke Leipzig GmbH* [2014] EWHC 3615 (Comm) at [589] (affirmed [2017] EWCA Civ 1567). The payment of bribes is normally outside the authority of the agent: *E. Hannibal & Co Ltd v Frost* (1988) 4 B.C.C. 3, Illustration 4 to Article 29; see further above, para.2-026. But that would not preclude the operation of vicarious liability in appropriate cases.

[1576] See Berg [2001] L.M.C.L.Q. 27 at 46–47. See too *UBS AG (London Branch) v Kommunale Wasserwerke Peipkiz GmbH* [2017] EWCA Civ 1567 at [113].

[1577] *Armagas Ltd v Mundogas SA* [1986] A.C. 717 at 745, per Robert Goff LJ.

[1578] *UBS AG (London Branch) v Kommunale Wasserwerke Leipzig GmbH* [2014] EWHC 3615 (Comm) at [616] (affirmed [2017] EWCA Civ 1567).

[1579] *Ho Kang Peng v Scintronix Corp Ltd* [2014] SGCA 22.

[1580] *Nayyar v Sapte* [2009] EWHC 3218 (QB).

[1581] See *Royal Brunei Airlines Sdn Bhd v Tan* [1995] 2 A.C. 378; *Secretary of State for Justice v Topland Group Plc* [2011] EWHC 983 (QB) at [94]; and Article 116.

est assistance in a breach of fiduciary duty than rely on the law of tort and the action for money had and received, though the remedies would be slightly different; it has been said that "the difference lies not in the factual background but in the remedy sought".[1582] An unsettled issue is whether accessory liability can apply where there is no misappropriation of existing trust assets.[1583] However, there is some authority that it can,[1584] and it seems that the action can extend to stripping the briber of profits.[1585] The use of this action would also enable use of the more generalised principles as to the knowledge required, recently developed in connection with accessory liability, instead of some of the awkward quasi-presumptions which dicta in the common law cases have sometimes seemed to apply. More commentary on the action can be found in Article 116.

Illustrations

(1)   A company awards to another company a sub-contract for the laying of cable. **8-226** The performance of the sub-contract is subject to certification by an engineer appointed by the first company. The sub-contractor employs the same engineer as sub-sub-contractor to lay the cable. The financing of the project goes wrong. The first company discovers the involvement of its engineer in the sub-contract and claims that it should be set aside. The company is successful.[1586]

(2)   A person who dealt with an agent gave him a gratuity in order to influence him generally in favour of the giver. The agent was in fact so influenced in making a contract with the giver on the principal's behalf. Held, that the contract was voidable by the principal, although the gratuity was not given in direct relation to the particular contract.[1587]

(3)   A agreed to buy a pair of horses from B, provided a veterinary surgeon who had been employed by A to find such horses certified that they were sound. B secretly offered the vet a certain sum if the horses were sold, and the vet accepted the offer. The vet certified that the horses were sound. Held, that A

[1582] *Logicrose Ltd v Southend United FC* [1988] 1 W.L.R. 1256 at 1261, per Millett J. As to the monetary remedies available in equity, see Comment to Article 115.

[1583] See Comment to Article 116; *Lewin on Trusts* (20th edn), Ch. 43.

[1584] See ibid.; *Fyffes Group Ltd v Templeman* [2000] 2 Lloyd's Rep. 643, per Toulson J; *Secretary of State for Justice v Topland Group Plc* [2011] EWHC 983 QB. cf. *Petrotrade Inc v Smith* [2000] 1 Lloyd's Rep. 486 to the contrary; Mitchell (2001) 118 L.Q.R. 207.

[1585] See *Novoship (UK) Ltd v Mikhaylyuk* [2012] EWHC 3586 (Comm) at [99]; affirmed [2014] EWCA Civ 908 at [84]; *Australian Careers Institute Pty Ltd v Australian Institute of Fitness Pty Ltd* [2016] NSWCA 34; (2017) 340 A.L.R. 580; cf. *Ancient Order of Foresters in Victoria Friendly Society Ltd v Lifeplan Australia Friendly Society Ltd* [2018] HCA 43 (noted A. Douglas, "Dishonest Assistance, Causation and Account of Profits" (2019) 135 L.Q.R. 214). In *Sinclair Investment Holdings SA v Versailles Trade Finance Ltd* [2007] EWHC 915 (Ch); [2007] 2 All E.R. (Comm) 993 at [133]–[134]; affirmed [2011] EWCA Civ 347; [2012] Ch. 453 it was doubted whether the liability of the briber would extend to liability for incidental profits gained beyond the amount of the bribe itself, and the view was strongly expressed that, if it did, the profits would not be held on trust for the claimant. The third party is unlikely to be liable to the principal for remuneration forfeited by an agent as a result of an improper conflict of interest: *Electrosteel Castings (UK) Ltd v Metalpol Ltd* [2014] EWHC 2017 (Ch) at [65].

[1586] *Panama and South Pacific Telegraph Co v India Rubber, Gutta Percha and Telegraph Works Co* (1875) L.R. 10 Ch.App. 515.

[1587] *Smith v Sorby* (1875) 3 Q.B.D. 552n; *Hough v Bolton* (1885) 1 T.L.R. 606. See also *Galloway v Pedersen* (1915) 34 N.Z.L.R. 513 (specific performance refused).

was not bound by the contract whether the vet was in fact biased by the offer made to and accepted by him or not.[1588]

(4)   A person injured in a road accident employs a "claims service" to negotiate a tort claim. The service uses an assessor, who tells the insurer that he will recommend acceptance of the insurer's offer if the insurer pays his fee. The claimant settles. The sum is a bribe and he can rescind the settlement and pursue his claim for damages.[1589]

(5)   By paying a bribe of $18,000, third parties sell land to a Government and make a profit of $67,940. They are liable for the latter sum, but the $18,000 is subsumed into it. The fact that the Government resold the land at prices whereby it recovered its costs is irrelevant.[1590]

(6)   An agent accepts a bribe in connection with the grant of a licence to operate a market on his principal's land. On learning of this the principal rescinds the contract. He need not give credit for the amount of the bribe, which he is entitled to recover from the agent whether or not he adopts the transaction, and which he can treat as a gift to him.[1591]

(7)   A director bought land from his company not revealing his knowledge that the land had the potential to be re-zoned and indeed that he had already taken steps to apply for planning permission. Held, that the director held the proceeds of on-sale of the relevant property on constructive trust.[1592]

(8)   Company directors exercise their powers to allot unissued shares in the company in favour of shareholder X for the purpose of thereby diluting the voting power of shareholder Y. They act in good faith, believing that Y's business intentions are inimical to the company's best interests. Held, that the allotment was made for an improper purpose and was voidable in equity.[1593]

(9)   A claimant, company A, is one of the holders of a joint account at the defendant bank, a local authority being the other joint holder. The sole director of company A gives a direction to the bank to change the party to the joint account from company A to its parent company, company B, and the bank does so. Company A is arguably insolvent at the time. Held, the bank was entitled to rely on the instructions of the director, who had actual authority to give them, even if the director had failed to comply with equitable duties to take account of the interests of creditors of company A upon its insolvency. He had acted honestly, and in what he thought were the interests of company A.[1594]

(10)   Directors of a company sign a "poison pill" agreement with another company, under which the other company can demand to be bought out from an interest in a joint venture company on terms that are deliberately highly favourable to it. The agreement may be voidable as having been made for an improper purpose.[1595] But if the directors had neither actual nor apparent

[1588] *Shipway v Broadwood* [1899] 1 Q.B. 369.
[1589] *Taylor v Walker* [1958] 1 Lloyd's Rep. 490.
[1590] *Att.-Gen. for Nova Scotia v Christian* (1974) 49 D.L.R. (3d) 742.
[1591] *Logicrose v Southend United FC* [1988] 1 W.L.R. 1256.
[1592] *J.J. Harrison (Properties) Ltd v Harrison* [2001] EWCA Civ 1467; [2002] 1 B.C.L.C. 162.
[1593] *Howard Smith Ltd v Ampol Petroleum Ltd* [1974] A.C. 821. See too *Hogg v Cramphorn* [1967] Ch. 254; *Whitehouse v Carlton Hotel Pty Ltd* (1987) 162 C.L.R. 285.
[1594] *Senex Holdings Ltd v National Westminster Bank Plc* [2012] EWHC 131 (Comm); [2012] 1 All E.R. (Comm) 1130.
[1595] *Criterion Properties Plc v Stratford UK Properties LLC* [2002] EWHC 496 (Ch); [2002] 2 B.C.L.C. 151.

authority to make the agreement, the transaction would be void. The third party's liability in such circumstances does not turn on unconscionability in equity.[1596]

[1596] *Criterion Properties Plc v Stratford UK Properties LLC* [2004] UKHL 28; [2004] 1 W.L.R. 1846.

CHAPTER 9

RELATIONS BETWEEN AGENTS AND THIRD PARTIES

1. CONTRACT

Article 97

GENERAL RULE

In the absence of other indications, when an agent makes a contract, purporting   **9-001**
to act solely on behalf of a disclosed principal, whether identified or unidentified,
the agent is not liable to the third party on it. Nor can the agent sue the third party
on it.[1]

Comment

"There is no doubt whatever as to the general rule as regards an agent, that where a person   **9-002**
contracts as agent for a principal, the contract is the contract of the principal and not that
of the agent; and, prima facie, at common law the only person who may sue is the principal
and the only person who can be sued is the principal."[2]

This is so even where the principal is not in fact bound because the agent was not
authorised; and even where the agent is a *del credere* agent and as such liable to
the principal for the third party's debt.[3] This basic prima facie result is often
expressed in the maxim that the agent "drops out" of the transaction, an expression which, though convenient, may be seriously misleading if pushed too far,[4] and
certainly if pushed beyond contract. In truth, the reason why the agent is not liable
or entitled, when this is so, is that the objective interpretation of the dealings
between the between the parties indicate a contract between principal and third party
only.

When actual authority is present, the contract may be seen as the principal's

---

[1] See Comment.
[2] *Montgomerie v UK Mutual SS Assn Ltd* [1891] 1 Q.B. 370 at 371, per Wright J. (But see the continuation of this passage quoted below, para.9-005.) See also *Paquin v Beauclerk* [1906] A.C. 148;
Restatement, Third, § 6.01. For the apparently different starting point in Scots law, at least where
the principal is disclosed but unidentified, see *Ruddy v Marco* [2008] CSIH 47 at [21]. PECL
art.3:202; UNIDROIT Principles art.2.2.3; DCFR, II, 6:105 all appear to have the same starting point
as the common law.
[3] *Bramwell v Spiller* (1870) 21 L.T. 672. See above, para.1-042.
[4] See Müller-Freienfels (1963) 12 Am.J.Comp.L. 272 at 278.

contract. Where the authority is merely apparent, the principal (unless there is ratification) is only liable, on the basis of a form of estoppel.[5]

But, the mere fact that a person acts as agent and is known to do so does not necessarily negate that person's involvement in the transaction. It has been said that:

"it is not the case that, if a principal is liable, his agent cannot be. The true principle of law is that a person is liable for his engagements (as for his torts) even though he acts for another, unless he can show that by the law of agency he is to be held to have expressly or impliedly negatived his personal liability."[6]

The possibilities had in fact earlier been listed as follows:

"An agent can conclude a contract on behalf of his principal in one of three ways:

(a) *By creating privity of contract between the third party and his principal without himself becoming a party to the contract* The principal need not be named but the contract must show clearly that the agent was acting as such. Familiar examples are contracts made by X as agents and signed by X, the signature being claused 'as agents only. The consequence of such an arrangement is that the third party can only sue, and be sued by, the principal.

(b) *By creating privity of contract between the third party and the principal, whilst also personally becoming a party to the contract* The consequence of this arrangement is that the third party has an option whether to sue the agent or the principal, although this is of little practical value if that party does not know of the principal's existence ...

(c) *By creating privity of contract between himself and the third party, but no such privity between the third party and the principal* In other words, in relation to the third party the agent is a principal, but in relation to the principal he or she is an agent.

The consequence of this arrangement is that the only person who can sue the third party or be sued by the third party is the agent."[7]

Thus it is possible for an agent to be a contracting party instead of or in addition to the principal, as explained in the next Article. Agents are also normally held by a separate contract to warrant their authority to act even when they are not liable on the main contract itself[8]; and they may be liable on other collateral contracts.[9] Agents may also of course be liable in tort.[10] Sometimes agents seek advice as to

---

5 See above, para.8-028.
6 *Yeung Kai Yung v Hong Kong and Shanghai Banking Corp* [1981] A.C. 787 at 795, per Lord Scarman. See also *The Swan* [1968] 1 Lloyd's Rep. 5, Illustration 6 to Article 98; *Ex p. Hartop* (1806) 12 Ves. Jun. 349 at 352: "for the application of that rule, the agent must name his principal as the person to be responsible", per Lord Erskine LC. This quotation makes the same point; but it should not be taken to require that the agent actually give the name of the principal, merely that the agent indicate that he or she acts as agent for a principal.
7 *Teheran-Europe Co Ltd v S.T. Belton (Tractors) Ltd* [1968] 2 Q.B. 53 at 59–60, per Donaldson J; decision affirmed on this point ibid., 545; approved in *Australian Trade Commission v Goodman Fielder Industries Ltd* (1992) 36 F.C.R. 517.
8 Articles 105 and 106.
9 See *Yeung Kai Yung v Hong Kong and Shanghai Banking Corp* [1981] A.C. 787, Illustration 5 to Article 98.
10 Article 113.

their own duties, and in so doing would normally contract as principals; their principals would not normally have any right to rely on that advice.[11]

Illustrations

(1) A solicitor is prima facie not personally liable for the expenses of skilled or other witnesses retained or subpoenaed by him.[12] Nor is he personally liable for sheriff's fees merely because in the course of his duty he lodges a writ at the sheriff's office for execution.[13] In such matters he is deemed to act merely as the agent of his client, unless he expressly pledges his personal credit. But a solicitor who employs a particular bailiff to levy execution may be prima facie personally liable to the bailiff for the fees, if it is the usual course of business for the solicitor to pledge his personal credit in such a case.[14] The same is true where he employs another solicitor.[15]   **9-003**

(2) A broker sent a contract note in the following form: "I have this day sold you, on account of B, etc." (signed) "A B, broker". Held, that the broker had no right of action in his own name against the buyer for refusing to accept the goods.[16] So, where a broker sent a contract note as follows: "Mr. L, I have this day bought in my own name for your account, of AKT, etc." (signed) "A B, broker", it was held that he was acting as agent of AKT; that the words "bought in my own name" were inserted to inform the purchaser that the broker was liable to the vendor; and that the broker had no right to sue L for the price.[17]

(3) A shipmaster signs bills of lading as agent for the owners. He can sue for freight neither under the bills nor on an implied contract.[18] Nor can he sue on an implied contract to pay demurrage.[19]

(4) The manager of a mutual insurance association subscribes a policy on behalf of the members of the association. He cannot sue in his own name for contributions due from the member effecting the policy, though the rules of the association purport to give him such a power.[20]

---

[11] See e.g. *Edenwest Ltd v CMS Cameron McKenna (A Firm)* [2012] EWHC 1258 (Ch) at [77] (receiver not agent of company in obtaining advice in personal capacity).

[12] *Robins v Bridge* (1837) 3 M. & W. 114; *Lee v Everest* (1857) 2 H. & N. 285; *Wakefield v Duckworth* [1915] 1 K.B. 218 (order for photographs to be used in connection with a trial). cf. *Cocks v Bruce, Searl and Good* (1904) 21 T.L.R. 62 (shorthand writer: solicitor liable).

[13] *Royle v Busby* (1880) 6 Q.B.D. 171, following *Mayberry v Mansfield* (1846) 9 Q.B. 754.

[14] *Newton v Chambers* (1844) 13 L.J.Q.B. 141; *Maile v Mann* (1848) 2 Exch. 608 as explained in *Royle v Busby* (1880) 6 Q.B.D. 171. See further Cordery, *Solicitors* (8th edn), p.98–99.

[15] *Scrace v Whittington* (1823) 2 B. & C. 11; and see *Porter v Kirtlan* [1917] 2 I.R. 138.

[16] *Fairlie v Fenton* (1870) L.R. 5 Ex. 169.

[17] *Fawkes v Lamb* (1862) 31 L.J.Q.B. 98.

[18] *Repetto v Millar's Karri and Jarrah Forests Ltd* [1901] 2 K.B. 306. A signature without qualification anywhere else in the document (see Article 101) could perhaps still make the master a contracting party: see at 310; and *Atkinson v Cotesworth* (1825) 3 B. & C. 647. But such a signature would be rare in a commercial context today. See also *Smith v Plummer* (1818) 1 B. & A. 575; cf. *Cawthron v Trickett* (1864) 15 C.B.(N.S.) 754.

[19] *Brouncker v Scott* (1811) 4 Taunt. 1; *Evans v Forster* (1830) 1 B. & Ad. 118; cf. *Jesson v Solly* (1811) 4 Taunt. 52.

[20] *Evans v Hooper* (1875) 1 Q.B.D. 45; *Gray v Pearson* (1870) L.R. 5 C.P. 568.

Article 98

When Agent Has Rights and Liabilities

9-004   An agent who makes a contract on the principal's behalf is liable to or entitled to sue the third party in accordance with the terms of any contractual engagement, whether upon the same contract or upon some independent contract, into which the agent has entered.[21]

Comment

9-005   **Agent may be liable or entitled**   As has been stated in the Comment to the previous Article, there is no reason why an agent should not be entitled and/or liable on the contract which the agent has made for the principal, or upon a separate but related contract if that is what has been agreed. "In all cases the parties can by the express contract provide that the agent shall be the person liable either concurrently with or to the exclusion of the principal."[22] The question whether an agent who has made a contract on behalf of the principal is to be deemed to have contracted personally, and, if so the extent of the agent's liability, depends on the intention of the parties, to be deduced from the nature and terms of the particular contract and the surrounding circumstances, including any binding custom.[23] As in all matters of formation of contract, the test is objective.[24] The rules can be most easily articulated in relation to written contracts, where the use of a particular form of words may constitute an agent a contracting party though it is on the underlying facts doubtful whether the agent intended to become such.[25]

It is sometimes said that an agent can be liable to the third party without being entitled to sue, but cannot be entitled to sue without being liable, for then there would be no consideration to support the agent's right to sue.[26] This is true in the sense that a collateral contract can more easily be constructed on the basis that the agent, in return for the third party's dealing with the principal, undertakes also personal liability on the main contract. But the converse position can also exist,

---

[21] See Comment.

[22] *Montgomerie v UK Mutual SS Assn* [1891] 1 Q.B. 370 at 372, per Wright J (in a later part of the judgment some of which is cited in para.9-002 above). See also *Fawkes v Lamb* (1862) 31 L.J.Q.B. 98 at 100; *The Swan* [1968] 1 Lloyd's Rep. 5, Illustration 6; *Carminco Gold & Resources Ltd v Findlay & Co Stockbrokers (Underwriters) Pty Ltd* (2007) 243 A.L.R. 472, Illustration 24 to Article 98; *Felty v Ernst & Young LLP* [2015] BCCA 445.

[23] This sentence was quoted with approval in *Maritime Stores Ltd v H.P. Marshall & Co Ltd* [1963] 1 Lloyd's Rep. 602 at 608. See too *Temple Legal Protection Ltd v QBE Insurance (Europe) Ltd* [2009] EWCA Civ 453; [2009] Lloyd's Rep. I.R. 544; *CIFAL Groupe SA v Meridian Securities (UK) Ltd* [2013] EWHC 3553 (Comm). In some cases statutory provisions may make the position of the agent different to that of the principal: see, e.g. *Domsalla (t/a Domsalla Buildings Services) v Dyason* [2007] EWHC 1174 (T.C.C.); (2007) 112 Con. L.R. 95 (construction contract entered into by owner on instructions of insurer, found to bind insurer and owner, but owner entitled to invoke the Unfair Terms in Consumer Contracts Regulations 1999).

[24] *The Swan* [1968] 1 Lloyd's Rep. 5 at 12; *Carminco Gold & Resources Ltd v Findlay & Co Stockbrokers (Underwriters) Pty Ltd* (2007) 243 A.L.R. 472 at [23], Illustration 24 to Article 98.

[25] See *Fisher v Marsh* (1865) 6 B. & S. 411; *Sika Contracts Ltd v B.S. Gill* (1978) 9 Build. L.R. 11, Illustration 10 to Article 99; *Foxtons Ltd v Thesleff* [2005] EWCA Civ 514, [2005] 2 E.G.L.R. 29 (estate agent's contract by its wording made signatory of contract liable though in fact an agent); Articles 99–101 and 102–103.

[26] *Fawkes v Lamb* (1862) 31 L.J.K.B. 98 at 101; *Fairlie v Fenton* (1870) L.R. 5 Ex. 169 at 172. See criticism of the dicta in these cases by Stoljar, pp.245–247.

though it may be less likely: a third party may, in return for being introduced to the principal or for some other benefit, be held to make the same promise to the agent as that party does to the principal. Thus a person buying goods at auction is liable to the auctioneer for the price: but the auctioneer's reciprocal promise to that person may be extremely limited and certainly does not involve liability on the contract of sale itself.[27]

Agent's liability   Where an agent is potentially liable, the terms of that liability may require careful analysis. Except as regards the undisclosed principal, discussed below, no specific rules have been laid down by the courts. The possibilities seem to be as follows.   **9-006**

(1)   Sole liability of agent   An agent may be solely liable, i.e. although perhaps authorised to do so, the agent has not created any contract binding the principal at all but has made the contract personally. The majority of the cases seem to assume this as the main interpretation of a situation involving the agent's personal liability[28]: other interpretations have often been justified by reference to special circumstances such as trade custom,[29] or (as in the case of the auctioneer) lien or special property.[30] In such a case the agent's position vis-à-vis the principal may still be regulated by the general part of the law of agency, viz. the agent is remunerated on a commission basis, undertakes only to use best endeavours, must not accept discounts or bribes, etc.; this is the position of the *commissionnaire* of civil law, referred to earlier.[31] Alternatively, it may be regulated by some other set of rules, e.g. those governing the relationship of buyer and seller or consignor and carrier. This is not the concern of the third party.

There are however other possibilities. "There is nothing to prevent an agent entering into a contract on the basis that he is himself to be liable to perform it as well as his principal."[32] Other possibilities may have been too easily overlooked in the

---

[27]   In some cases the consideration would seem to be the release by the auctioneer of his lien when he delivers the goods; see *Chelmsford Auctions v Poole* [1973] Q.B. 542, Illustration 17; below, para.9-023.

[28]   See in general *Parker v Winslow* (1857) 7 E. & B. 942 at 947 ("An agent is liable personally if he is the contracting party; and he may be so though he names his principal"); *Gadd v Houghton* (1876) 1 Ex.D. 357 at 360 ("It seems extraordinary that there should be any doubt whether this binds the principal or the agent"); *H.O. Brandt & Co v H.N. Morris & Co Ltd* [1917] 2 K.B. 784 at 793 ("Prima facie when a person signs a document in his own name … he is the person liable on the contract"). For specific examples may be cited cases on solicitors: *Hall v Ashurst* (1883) 1 C. & M. 714 at 718; *Iveson v Conington* (1823) 1 B. & C. 160 at 162; *Tanner v Christian* (1855) 4 E. & B. 591 at 597–598, all of which should be considered with *Lavan v Walsh* [1964] I.R. 87; and cases on ship repairs and stores, where the contract is often with the local agent placing the order. See Article 101, Illustration 2. See also *Salsi v Jetspeed Air Services Ltd* [1977] 2 Lloyd's Rep. 57 (air freightage broker); *Tranton v Astor* (1917) 33 T.L.R. 383 (advertising agent), not followed by *CFTO-TV Ltd v Mr Submarine Ltd* (1994) 108 D.L.R. (4th) 517; affirmed (1997) 151 D.L.R. (4th) 382. There are also cases involving companies, where it has been concluded that a shareholder or director has in fact undertaken personal responsibility but not the company: see, e.g. *Hamid v Francis Bradshaw Partnership* [2013] EWCA Civ 470.

[29]   See below, para.9-016.

[30]   As to which see below, para.9-009.

[31]   See above, para.1-021 onwards.

[32]   *International Ry v Niagara Parks Commission* [1941] A.C. 328 at 342, per Luxmoore LJ. See also *Young v Schuler* (1887) 11 Q.B.D. 651; *Elbinger Actiengesellschaft v Claye* (1873) L.R. 8 Q.B. 313 at 317; *Calder v Dobell* (1871) L.R. 6 C.P. 486 at 494; *Montgomerie v UK Mutual SS Assn* [1891] 1 Q.B. 370 at 372; *The Swan* [1968] 1 Lloyd's Rep. 5; *Scottish and Newcastle International Ltd v*

past,[33] though there are signs that they may be more readily recognised in the future.[34] It is suggested below that they may be particularly relevant in considering unidentified principal situations. The remainder of this list enumerates them.

(2) Joint or joint and several obligation   The agent may be held to contract jointly or jointly and severally together with the principal.[35] Joint liability applies to partners,[36] but not normally to husband and wife.[37] Joint liability is subject to certain technical rules which may make it inappropriate to an agency relationship[38]: so, though to a lesser degree, is joint and several liability.[39]

(3) Suretyship   The agent may be a surety for the principal, that is to say the agent may guarantee the principal's obligation; or contract to indemnify the third party in respect of its non-performance. This is to be distinguished from *del credere* agency, where the agent's liability is to the principal, not to the third party. Here again suretyship in general, and guarantee in particular, are subject to special rules which may not be appropriate to the particular situation.[40] The possibility is however occasionally referred to.[41]

(4) Collateral contract   The agent may undertake a separate liability on a separate or collateral contract which is not one of suretyship. A contract of indemnity is of course a specialised form of such a contract. Consideration can often be found by the entry into the main contract with the principal. Examples of such

---

Othon Ghalanos Ltd [2008] UKHL 11; [2008] 1 Lloyd's Rep. 462 at [45].

[33] Stoljar, p.234–238. And see Blackburn, *Contract of Sale* (3rd edn), p.352.

[34] See *The Swan* [1968] 1 Lloyd's Rep. 5, Illustration 6; *Gardiner v Heading* [1928] 2 K.B. 284; *Teheran-Europe Co Ltd v S.T. Belton (Tractors) Ltd* [1968] 2 Q.B. 53 at 59–60; [1968] 2 Q.B. 545 at 558; *Wolfe Stevedores (1968) Ltd v Joseph Salter's Sons Ltd* (1971) 16 D.L.R. (3d) 334; *Burt v Claude Cousins & Co Ltd* [1971] 2 Q.B. 426 at 455; *Format International Security Printers Ltd v Mosden* [1975] 1 Lloyd's Rep. 37; *Et Biret Cie SA v Yukiteru Kaiun KK (The Sun Happiness)* [1984] 1 Lloyd's Rep. 381; *Stag Line Ltd v Tyne Shiprepair Group Ltd (The Zinnia)* [1984] 2 Lloyd's Rep. 211; *The Starsin* [2001] 1 Lloyd's Rep. 437 at 452. But cf. *Wilson v Avec Audio-Visual Equipment Ltd* [1974] 1 Lloyd's Rep. 81 at 83, where such liability is said to require "clear and precise evidence of a very special relationship"; *N. & J. Vlassopulos Ltd v Ney Shipping Ltd (The Santa Carina)* [1977] 1 Lloyd's Rep. 478, Illustration 3 to Article 101; *Foalquest Ltd v Roberts* [1990] 1 E.G.L.R. 50; *Belleli SpA v AIG (Europe) Ltd*, QBD (Rix J), May 22, 1996. See also below, para.9-016.

[35] See, e.g. *Middle East Tankers and Freighters Bunker Services SA v Abu Dhabi Container Lines* [2002] EWHC 957 (Comm); [2002] 2 Lloyd's Rep. 643; *Savills (UK) Ltd v Blacker* [2017] EWCA Civ 68 at [46], Illustration 15. See too *Air Tahiti Nui Pty Ltd v McKenzie* [2009] NSWCA 429 (subsidiary company agent of parent; both liable); *Rabiu v Marlbray Ltd* [2016] EWCA Civ 476; [2016] 1 W.L.R. 514 (husband severally liable on contract of purchase when lacked authority also to bind wife).

[36] Partnership Act 1890 s.9.

[37] *Morel Bros & Co Ltd v Earl of Westmorland* [1904] A.C. 11; cf. *Hoare v Niblett* [1891] 1 Q.B. 781; *Swanton Seed Service Ltd v Kulba* (1968) 68 D.L.R. (2d) 38; *Rabiu v Marlbray Ltd* [2016] EWCA Civ 476; [2016] 1 W.L.R. 514.

[38] See Glanville Williams, *Joint Obligations* (1949); but see Civil Liability (Contribution) Act 1978 s.3; and *David Moore Builders Ltd v Preddy* Unreported October 24, 1995 CA; *Goei Tsusho Co Ltd v Leader Engineering & Construction Ltd* [2010] 2 H.K.L.R.D. 1084.

[39] e.g. release of one debtor releases all: see Glanville Williams, *Joint Obligations* (1949), p.135.

[40] e.g. giving time to the principal debtor releases the surety: *Chitty on Contracts* (33rd edn), para.45-104 onwards. See also Rowlatt, *Principal and Surety* (7th edn); Glanville Williams, *Joint Obligations* (1949), p.121 onwards. Guarantees may require written evidence under the Statute of Frauds.

[41] *Imperial Bank v London and St Katharine Docks Co* (1877) 5 Ch.D. 195 at 200; *Fleet v Murton* (1871) L.R. 7 Q.B. 126 at 132; see also *Young v Schuler* (1883) 11 Q.B.D. 651; *Rutherford v Ounan* [1913] 2 I.R. 265 at 268.

contract are found in cases of warranty of authority[42] and auctioneers.[43] It has been held that stockbrokers may warrant the genuineness of a share transfer which they present for registration.[44]

(5) Alternative liability The agent may undertake a liability alternative to that of the principal, the choice to lie with the third party. Though this interpretation seems to be assumed by some of the cases on election, it is submitted that there is little to commend it.[45] Such cases as do recognise the liability of the agent do not usually consider further the nature of that liability, because the question is not relevant. Many old cases raise questions of the Statute of Frauds or of parol evidence, and concern the question whether the fact that a written contract mentions only principal or agent necessarily excludes the other.[46] Others are simply concerned with the question whether the agent can be sued, regardless of whether the principal can, or whether the agent who has paid on a contract is entitled to indemnity as having discharged a legal liability resting on the principal: they go no further than is necessary for the particular decision. The area is therefore not yet fully mapped.

Election When principal and agent are both liable, the doctrines of merger and election may apply, and the third party may be debarred from suing one by obtaining judgment against, or even perhaps simply electing to look to, the other. But this only operates where the two remedies available to the third party are inconsistent, and this may not be so in all cases. The nature of the liability assumed by the agent may therefore be crucial, but it has received insufficient attention in the cases. The value of the doctrine is also doubtful.[47]   **9-007**

Agent's right to sue The question of an agent's right to sue certainly arises less frequently than that of the agent's liability,[48] and it seems that the incorporation of the agent into the contract has more normally the purpose of securing personal liability. In any case, the right to sue can often be specifically assigned to the agent when this is thought desirable. On the analysis given above of the possible interpretations of the agent's liability, headings (1), (2) and (4) could also involve the right to sue. Plainly, the agent who makes the contract as sole contracting party can sue on it as well as be held liable.[49] An agent who is a party to a joint or joint and several obligation can sue on it, subject to the technical rules applicable.[50]   **9-008**

And a collateral contract made by agent with the third party may give the agent

---

42 Article 105.
43 Below, paras 9-009 and 9-023; Illustrations 11–14 and 18–20. It may be that the position of the nineteenth-century factor would today be explicable in such terms, but it is no longer relevant to seek to explain it.
44 *Yeung Kai Yung v Hong Kong & Shanghai Banking Corp* [1981] A.C. 787, Illustration 5.
45 See Comment to Article 82.
46 See Article 102; *Higgins v Senior* (1841) 8 M. & W. 834; *Calder v Dobell* (1871) L.R. 6 C.P. 486; *Basma v Weekes* [1950] A.C. 441; *Davies v Sweet* [1962] 2 Q.B. 300.
47 See Articles 82 and 104.
48 See above, para.9-006. It has arisen where the principal is fictitious or non-existent, or where the agent is his own principal: see Articles 107 and 108.
49 e.g. *Short v Spackman* (1851) 2 B. & Ad. 962. For a more modern example where this was probably the case, see *Anglo-African Shipping Co of New York Inc v J. Mortner Ltd* [1962] 1 Lloyd's Rep. 610; *Carminco Gold & Resources Ltd v Findlay & Co Stockbrokers (Underwriters) Pty Ltd* (2007) 243 A.L.R. 472, Illustration 24.
50 e.g. a partner: cf. Co Litt. 182A. See also *Jung v Phosphate of Lime Co Ltd* (1868) L.R. 3 C.P. 139;

the right to sue on it: a conspicuous example is that of the auctioneer, who can sue for the price of the goods or land sold.[51] On the other hand, a contract of surety-ship does not, and a contract of indemnity would not normally, confer a right to sue; and the cases suggesting alternative liability do so in connection with the *third party's* right to choose between principal and agent. In so far as any question arises between these two as to who should sue, it would probably be solved by reference to the subordinate position of the agent vis-à-vis the principal.[52] Where a party has assigned absolutely contractual rights, that party cannot usually avoid the rule requiring the assignee to be joined by asserting that the suit is brought as agent of the assignee.[53]

9-009   **Lien and special property**   A number of cases, mostly on nineteenth-century fac-tors and auctioneers, suggested that certain types of agent could sue because they have a special property in or lien upon the subject-matter of the contract or a beneficial interest in the completion thereof.[54] It is however clear that the mere fact that an agent has an interest in the completion of the contract, e.g. because the agent hopes to earn commission on it, does not entitle the agent to sue upon it.[55] The cases are in the modern context best explained as particular collateral contracts, upon which there is long-standing authority conferring specific rights and imposing specific duties upon these types of agent. The case law on the factor may be obsolete, but the auctioneer's contract is still of importance.[56] The possibility of detecting such contracts in new circumstances is not of course closed.

9-010   **Agent suing on behalf of principal**   A further group of old cases can be read as suggesting that the agent can in general sue on behalf of a disclosed principal and recover the principal's loss.[57] They should be viewed with extreme caution. Many date from a time when there was no method of assigning legal choses in action, communications did not make it easy for foreign contracting parties to sue in England, contract rights under bills of lading were not transferable,[58] and the central contractual doctrines now accepted had not been fully worked out. The distinction between a right of suit and a right to recover substantial damages was not taken in some of these early cases. However the matter would have been viewed at the time,

---

Perpetual Trustee Co Ltd v Nebo Road Pty Ltd [2011] QSC 283 (contract recognises lead lender as having power to sue for all lenders); *HSBC Bank Plc v Rondônia Transportes Cayman* [2019] EWHC 30 (Comm) at [52].

[51]   See below, para.9-023; Illustrations 11–14 and 18–20.
[52]   See below, para.9-012.
[53]   *Bexhill UK Ltd v Razzaq* [2012] EWCA Civ 1376 at [58] (no evidence of authority).
[54]   The wording of Article 119 of the 1st edition of this book.
[55]   e.g. *Bramwell v Spiller* (1870) 21 L.T. 672 (*del credere* agent); *Fairlie v Fenton* (1870) L.R. 5 Ex. 169; *Turnbull & Jones Ltd v Amner & Sons* [1923] N.Z.L.R. 673.
[56]   See below, para.9-023; also above, para.1-046; Reynolds, in *Contemporary Issues in Commercial Law* (Lomnicka and Morse eds, 1997), p.161 onwards.
[57]   *Davis v James* (1770) 5 Burr. 2680; *Moore v Wilson* (1787) 1 T.R. 659; *Joseph v Knox* (1813) 3 Camp. 320; *Atkinson v Cotesworth* (1825) 3 B. & C. 647; *Dunlop v Lambert* (1839) 6 Cl. & F. 600; *Mead v SE Ry* (1870) 18 W.R. 735. The nearest to a strong case is *Joseph v Knox*. Also cases indicat-ing that admissions by principal or agent are admissible against the other: *Bauerman v Radenius* (1792) 7 T.R. 663; *Smith v Lyon* (1813) 3 Camp. 465; *Welstead v Levy* (1831) 1 M. & Rob. 138; and on discovery: *Willis & Co v Baddeley* [1892] 2 Q.B. 324 (but cf. *James Nelson & Sons Ltd v Nelson Line (Liverpool) Ltd* [1906] 2 K.B. 217); *Abu Dhabi National Tanker Co v Product Star Shipping Ltd* [1992] 2 All E.R. 20.
[58]   A problem dealt with by the Bills of Lading Act 1855 (now replaced by the Carriage of Goods by Sea Act 1992).

it is submitted that most of them would not now be followed or would be otherwise explained. An action brought for another by an agent authorised to do so should nowadays be brought in the name of the principal.[59]

Insurance cases   There are also cases in the context of insurance law in which an **9-011** assured is held entitled to recover loss though another party has actually suffered it; and agency reasoning has sometimes been invoked to justify this.[60] However, it is not clear that this is the correct analysis for such cases. Where the assured is a bailee of goods, the assured's right can be explained by reference to its interest in them. The leading case on such facts is *A. Tomlinson (Hauliers) Ltd v Hepburn*[61] where it was stressed that goods may be insured by a person with an interest in them so as to cover the interests of others. In such a case the assured would have an insurable interest in the full value of the goods, and would recover on *its own* contract; it would then be under an obligation to account to any person actually suffering loss.[62] Where actions are brought by agents and brokers, reliance is often placed on wide dicta regarding actions by agents on insurance policies in *Provincial Insurance Co of Canada v Leduc*[63]; but the case itself still concerned insurance by a part-owner for the other part-owner. Other situations and dicta can be explained on the basis that the agent is in some circumstances a *trustee* for others[64]; but this is by no means true of every agency situation.[65] The person suffering loss may also be able to sue under the Contracts (Rights of Third Parties) Act 1999. But though it has been held at first instance that the principle permitting actions by agents and brokers is a general one[66] it is not in fact clear that there is such a principle, or that it is needed.[67] If it existed it might also make such agents liable, as well as entitled on the contract, which may be contrary to expectation. Where normal agency requirements are satisfied, the principal can of course sue.[68] If however the principal is undisclosed and does not wish to sue, or was excluded by the terms of the contract,[69] the agent as the ostensible contracting party would be able to sue (and also liable).[70] In this special case it may be that the agent could recover the principal's loss as an exception to the normal rules for *damages*: the problem is discussed below.[71] Some special situations are now discussed.

---

[59] *Jones v Gurney* [1913] W.N. 72; *PM Law Ltd & Motorplus Ltd* [2016] EWHC 193 (QB); [2016] 1 Costs L.R. 143 at [45]. See too *Moores v Hopper* (1807) 2 B. & P.N.R. 411.
[60] See, e.g. *Waters v Monarch Fire and Life Insurance Co* (1856) 5 E. & B. 870.
[61] *A. Tomlinson (Hauliers) Ltd v Hepburn* [1966] A.C. 451. The principle can be extended beyond bailment: see *Petrofina (UK) Ltd v Magnaload Ltd* [1984] Q.B. 127 (multi-participant construction project).
[62] See *Re E. Dibbens & Sons Ltd* [1990] B.C.L.C. 577.
[63] *Provincial Insurance Co of Canada v Leduc* (1874) L.R. 6 P.C. 224 at 244.
[64] See *Woodar Investment Development Ltd v Wimpey Construction UK Ltd* [1980] 1 W.L.R. 277 at 294 HL; referring to *Lloyd's v Harper* (1880) 16 Ch.D. 290.
[65] See *Allen v F. O'Hearn & Co* [1937] A.C. 213 at 218.
[66] *Transcontinental Underwriting Agency SRL v Grand Union Insurance Co Ltd* [1987] 2 Lloyd's Rep. 409 at 415.
[67] See Lord Millett in *Alfred McAlpine Construction Ltd v Panatown Ltd* [2001] 1 A.C. 518 at 582; Reynolds, in *Consensus ad Idem* (Rose ed., 1996), pp.84–88. Insurance textbooks do not clearly commit themselves: see *MacGillivray on Insurance Law* (14th edn), Ch. 38; Clarke, *Law of Insurance Contracts* (6th edn), para.5-5 onwards.
[68] See *National Oilwell (UK) Ltd v Davy Offshore Ltd* [1993] 2 Lloyd's Rep. 582 (unidentified principal).
[69] See above, para.8-081.
[70] See below, para.9-012.
[71] See below, para.9-013.

9-012   **Undisclosed principal**   Where the principal is undisclosed at the time of contracting, the contract is made with the agent, and the agent is personally liable and entitled on it. There is no need for the agent to join the principal as a party. However, the principal also may intervene to sue, and may be sued, but the latter only subject to the general rule that nothing must prejudice the right of the third party to sue the agent if that party so wishes.[72] This is therefore a case where both agent and principal are liable and entitled. The doctrine of election, referred to above, may raise problems when the agent is sued.

In this context it is often said that the right of the principal is superior to that of the agent, and it is a defence for the third party to prove that the principal has intervened and claimed payment or damages, or that the agent's authority to sue is otherwise terminated. On principle this seems correct[73]; though some of the cases usually cited for the proposition would now be otherwise explained.[74] This subordination may also apply where the agent of a *disclosed* principal is a joint and several creditor of the third party; the agent's right is presumably secondary to that of the principal.[75]

9-013   **Damages**[76]   The fact that the agent of the *undisclosed* principal appears to be and is regarded as a party to the contract can raise serious problems in the law of damages. An agent can certainly sue for specific performance, at any rate in the agent's own favour[77]: but if the agent sues for damages the problem arises that in general the victim of a breach of contract (or indeed a tort) can in general only recover the victim's own loss.[78] In the case under consideration, any loss may be suffered by the agent's principal. If the agent was a trustee, the agent could recover a beneficiary's loss; but it has been held that the agent of an undisclosed principal cannot be regarded as a trustee for this purpose.[79]

Exceptions to the main rule have long existed, and were recognised in the leading case of *The Albazero*,[80] which concerned an action by a person who was the shipper of goods and charterer of a vessel to recover the loss of the consignee. The exceptions were principally identified in the context of goods in transit which were likely to pass into hands other than those of the original contracting party.[81] More recently decisions in the context of construction have permitted contracting parties to sue for loss suffered by others. The first case involved land changing hands

---

[72]   See Comment to Article 76; *O'Herlihy v Hedges* (1803) 1 Sch. & Lef. 123; *Montgomerie v UK Mutual SS Assn* [1891] 1 Q.B. 370 at 372. See also *Sargent v Morris* (1820) 3 B. & Ald. 277 at 281. As to principal's liability where agent lacks capacity, see above, para.8-074.

[73]   cf. *Restatement, Second*, § 302, Comment c; § 368, Comments d, e, f; § 370; *Maynegrain Pty Ltd v Compafina Bank Ltd* [1982] 2 N.S.W.L.R. 141 at 150 (reversed without reference to this point (1984) 58 A.L.J.R. 389 PC). See Dal Pont, para.19.2.

[74]   e.g. *Rogers v Hadley* (1821) 2 H. & C. 227.

[75]   cf. *Restatement, Second*, § 370.

[76]   See Tan Cheng Han [2013] J.B.L. 799.

[77]   A claim for an order in favour of another might be met by the defence that the third party had not promised to perform in favour of that party.

[78]   A proposition accepted in the leading case, *Alfred McAlpine Construction Ltd v Panatown Ltd* [2001] 1 A.C. 518 at 522–523, 575, 580–581, discussed below.

[79]   *Allen v F. O'Hearn & Co* [1937] A.C. 213 at 218 ("the supposed agent's rights would be to recover the damage suffered by him on the footing that he had been principal"): but this is a puzzling passage.

[80]   *The Albazero* [1977] A.C. 774.

[81]   See *The Albazero* [1977] A.C. 774 at 847, per Lord Diplock.

in a way that had parallels with goods in transit,[82] but the next case did not.[83] The matter came to a head in *Alfred McAlpine Construction Ltd v Panatown Ltd*,[84] where the House of Lords accepted in principle[85] the availability of an action for defective performance by the party engaging a construction firm where the person doing so was in effect a nominee and the loss was suffered by another, associated firm which owned the land on which the building was erected.

Unfortunately the reason for permitting such recovery was not agreed. The majority view was that the contracting party had an interest in the performance which enabled that party to sue when it was defective.[86] The minority view was that the loss was that of a third party but that in this and other exceptional cases the contracting party could sue for loss suffered by another. He would then be accountable to that other[87]; which would not be so (in the absence of other special arrangements) under the first view. Either view, but especially the first, can encounter difficulties with the basic rule of remoteness of damage in contract, which confines damages to what had been in the contemplation of the parties when the contract was made. Where the contract has a value which can be assessed objectively, its breach, whether by way of supply of inferior goods or services, can be assessed on the basis of that value and the problem can be met.[88] Similarly, the costs of obtaining alternative performance of what was promised will usually be reasonably apparent to the promisee. But when what is claimed is loss idiosyncratic to the third party, it may be difficult to say that such loss was in the contemplation of the parties. There are nevertheless in the *Panatown* case suggestions that, whichever view is adopted, the rule is one of law, and that such loss can be taken in on an objective basis.[89] In the context of undisclosed principal such theoretical problems are potentially acute, as the third party has no contemplation of the existence of another party to the contract, let alone of special losses which that party might suffer. It is however assumed that some sort of objective assessment is to be applied as a matter of law,[90] though it cannot be said that the matter is exhaustively argued. There is Scottish authority to that

---

[82] *Linden Gardens Trust Ltd v Lenesta Sludge Disposals Ltd* [1994] 1 A.C. 85.

[83] *Darlington BC v Wiltshire Northern Ltd* [1995] 1 W.L.R. 68.

[84] *Alfred McAlpine Construction Ltd v Panatown Ltd* [2001] 1 A.C. 518. See in general *Chitty on Contracts* (33rd edn), para.18-049 onwards. See also Unberath, *Transferred Loss* (2003), Ch.7, indicating (at p.178) similar difficulties in German law.

[85] The majority also held the action excluded because of the presence of a separate contract between contractor and site owner.

[86] A view strongly put forward by Coote [1997] C.L.J. 537; (2001) 117 L.Q.R. 81; see also Ian Duncan Wallace QC (1999) 115 L.Q.R. 394; and Friedmann (1995) 111 L.Q.R. 628.

[87] A proposition for which there is surprisingly little authority. See however *The Albazero* [1977] A.C. 774 at 846; *Joseph v Knox* (1813) 3 Camp. 320; *Allen v F. O'Hearn & Co* [1937] A.C. 213 at 218.

[88] See *Leif Hoegh & Co v Petrolsea Inc (The World Era)* [1992] 1 Lloyd's Rep. 45 at 52–53, per Hobhouse J.

[89] See *Alfred McAlpine Construction Ltd v Panatown Ltd* [2001] 1 A.C. 518 at 535–536 (Lord Clyde), 554–555 (Lord Goff), 591 (Lord Millett).

[90] See *Alfred McAlpine Construction Ltd v Panatown Ltd* [2001] 1 A.C. 518 at 530 and 535–536 (Lord Clyde), 555–556 (Lord Goff), 591–592 (Lord Millett). See also at 581, where Lord Millett cites *L/M International Construction Inc (now Bovis International Inc) v The Circle Ltd Partnership* (1995) 49 Con.L.R. 12 (see below), as authority for the undisclosed principal situation. Despite this, in *Rolls-Royce Power Engineering Plc v Ricardo Consulting Engineers Ltd* [2003] EWHC 2871 (TCC): [2004] 2 All E.R. (Comm) 129 it was held that recovery was limited to situations where the third party was aware of the interest of the principal. This seems doubtful: see Tettenborn, *Amicus Curiae*, Issue 60, July/August 2005. See also *Welburn v Dibb Lupton Broomhead* [2002] EWCA Civ 1601; [2003] P.N.L.R. 28; *Family Food Court v Seah Boon Lock* [2008] SGCA 31.

effect, albeit conditioned by procedural considerations.[91] The so-called "beneficial assumption" that an undisclosed principal can intervene may not be as unqualified a principle as is sometimes suggested.[92]

9-014　**Indirect representation**[93]　In this situation the principal specifically did not authorise the agent to bring the principal into privity with the third party (as with the old foreign principal rule[94]) or the contract with the third party excluded the intervention of anyone else.[95] Here again the agent may wish to sue for the principal's loss. In this context a rather vague reference to agency has been used to give the same result as that above.[96] The proper analysis of both situations awaits further development.

9-015　**Interrogatories as to existence of undisclosed principal**　It has been held that in an action by the vendor for specific performance of a contract of sale of land, the plaintiff is not entitled to interrogate the defendant for the purpose of ascertaining whether the defendant was acting as agent for an undisclosed principal.[97] And in general it would seem that, the contract being that of the agent, the agent is under no duty when suing or sued to disclose the existence of the principal.[98]

9-016　**Unidentified principal**　Difficult problems must frequently occur in the case of unidentified principals. Where an agent gives the third party to understand that the agent acts for another, as by reference to "our principals", "our clients", "the trustees", etc. there may indeed be cases where the third party can be regarded as being willing to deal with the principal, whoever that person is. Indeed it has been said that in an ordinary commercial transaction such willingness may be assumed by the agent in the absence of other indications.[99] But this may sometimes be an improbable construction to put on the situation; at the other end of the scale, therefore, such facts may give rise, or assist in giving rise, to the inference that the third party deals only with the agent (the problem of the agent's position vis-à-vis the principal being irrelevant to the third party). But there is a middle course. The *Restatement, Third*[100] provides that when the agent acts for a principal whose existence is known but who is not identified at the time of contracting, the agent is unless otherwise agreed a party to the contract, and the inference is that the agent is liable in addition to and not in substitution for the principal (though sometimes the

---

[91]　*Craig & Co v Blackater* 1923 S.C. 472; *James Laidlaw & Sons v Griffin* 1968 S.L.T. 278; and see *Corfield v Grant* (1992) 29 Con.L.R. 58.

[92]　See further above, para.8-079.

[93]　See above, paras 1-021 and 1-022.

[94]　See below, para.9-020.

[95]　See above, para.8-079.

[96]　See *L/M International Construction Inc (now Bovis International Inc) v The Circle Ltd Partnership* (1995) 49 Con.L.R. 12 at 23–24 (Staughton LJ), 32–33 (Millett LJ). In the *Panatown* case, Lord Millett referred to the *Bovis* case as a case of undisclosed principal: [2001] 1 A.C. 518 at 581.

[97]　*Sebright v Hanbury* [1916] 2 Ch. 245. But as to discovery against the principal, see above, para.8-081.

[98]　See below, para.9-017; *IVI Pty Ltd v Baycrown Pty Ltd* [2007] 1 Qd R. 428 at [26] and [98] (no duty to reveal identity of undisclosed principal in pleadings, nor during trial).

[99]　*Teheran-Europe Co Ltd v S.T. Belton (Tractors) Ltd* [1968] 2 Q.B. 545 at 555, per Diplock LJ; referred to as a "beneficial assumption in commercial cases" by Lord Lloyd of Berwick in *Siu Yin Kwan v Eastern Insurance Co Ltd* [1994] 2 A.C. 199 at 209. See also *Thomson v Davenport* (1829) 9 B. & C. 78.

[100]　§ 6.02.

agent's liability may cease on disclosure of the principal's identity). Though the fact that the agent does not name the principal is obviously relevant in determining whether the agent contracts personally, such a general proposition has actually been rejected in England in respect of unwritten contracts,[101] and in the Supreme Court of Canada in respect of a written contract.[102] In view of the weakness, or at least uncertainty, of the law as to demanding to know the identity of the principal,[103] this is perhaps unfortunate. But the wording of written contracts may certainly give rise to the agent being a party to the contract in such a case.[104] And there are many cases showing that in such situations the court will recognise a trade usage that a commercial agent, e.g. a broker, is personally liable, particularly if the principal is unidentified.[105] Here again the exact terms of the agent's engagement with the third party require careful analysis. The trade custom cases, which arise mostly in the context of the rules of evidence, on the whole do seem to assume that the agent's liability is additional to that of the principal[106]: a collateral contract[107] and suretyship[108] are also sometimes suggested. The doctrine of election, referred to above,[109] may again cause problems.

The most difficult cases may perhaps be those where the third party deals with an agent who is known normally to act for principals or in a situation where persons dealing frequently act for principals, but there is no indication as to whether or not that is so on this occasion. This was of course a common situation with the nineteenth-century factor, who was distinguished from a broker on the basis that a broker could be *assumed* to be dealing on behalf of a principal[110]; and cases of this type are associated with the growth of the undisclosed principal doctrine.[111]

---

[101] *N. & J. Vlassopulos Ltd v Ney Shipping Co (The Santa Carina)* [1977] 1 Lloyd's Rep. 478, Illustration 3 to Article 101. But equally it may make clear that he acts as agent: see *Chartwell Shipping Ltd v Q.N.S. Paper Co Ltd* [1989] 2 S.C.R. 683; (1989) 62 D.L.R. (4th) 36; *Southwell v Bowditch* (1876) 1 C.P.D. 374.

[102] *Chartwell Shipping Ltd v Q.N.S. Paper Co Ltd* [1989] 2 S.C.R. 683; (1989) 62 D.L.R. (4th) 36, Illustration 9 to Article 99, on the basis that "to add a burden of proof on the mandatary would blur the focus of analysis: the goal is to identify the intentions of the parties" (per L'Heureux Dubé J at pp.745 and 78).

[103] See below, para.9-017.

[104] e.g. *Tudor Marine Ltd v Tradax Export SA (The Virgo)* [1976] 2 Lloyd's Rep. 135, Illustration 6 to Article 99; *Seatrade Groningen BV v Geest Industries Ltd (The Frost Express)* [1996] 2 Lloyd's Rep. 375, Illustration 7 to Article 99.

[105] *Dale v Humfrey* (1858) E.B. & E. 1004 (oil); *Cropper v Cook* (1868) L.R. 3 C.P. 194 (wool); *Fleet v Murton* (1871) L.R. 7 Q.B. 126 (fruit); *Hutchinson v Tatham* (1873) L.R. 8 C.P. 482 (charterparty); *Imperial Bank v London & St Katharine Docks Co* (1877) 5 Ch.D. 195 (fruit); *Bacmeister v Fenton, Levy & Co* (1883) C. & E. 121 (rice); *Pike v Ongley* (1887) 18 Q.B.D. 708 (hops); *Thornton v Fehr & Co* (1935) 51 Ll. L. Rep. 330 (tallow); *Anglo Overseas Transport Ltd v Titan Industrial Corp (United Kingdom) Ltd* [1959] 2 Lloyd's Rep. 152; *Perishables Transport Co v N. Spyropoulos (London) Ltd* [1964] 2 Lloyd's Rep. 379; *Cory Bros Shipping Ltd v Baldan* [1997] 2 Lloyd's Rep. 58 (forwarding agents); cf. *Wilson v Avec Audio-Visual Equipment Ltd* [1974] 1 Lloyd's Rep. 81 (no such custom as to insurance brokers). See further Article 98.

[106] See, e.g. *Pike v Ongley* (1887) 18 Q.B.D. 708.

[107] *Hutchinson v Tatham* (1873) L.R. 8 C.P. 482 (collateral contract coming into effect if name of principal not given; *Reid v Dreaper* (1861) 6 H. & N. 813.

[108] *Imperial Bank v London and St Katharine Docks Co* (1877) 5 Ch.D. 195.

[109] Para.9-007.

[110] *Baring v Corrie* (1818) 2 B. & A. 137. The factor's contract could perhaps also be treated as collateral: above, para.9-009.

[111] e.g. *Armstrong v Stokes* (1872) L.R. 7 Q.B. 598; see Articles 76 and 80.

Problems may also arise in connection with bidders at auction sales.[112] Such cases may indeed fall to be considered under the undisclosed principal doctrine, in which case the contract is with the agent, subject to the principal's right to intervene and liability to be sued. But more rigorous analysis may require them to be considered in connection with the possible rules for unidentified principal cases.[113]

If there is in unidentified principal cases not even a prima facie rule that the agent is liable together with the principal, the agent may sometimes appear to be free from liability in cases where the agent should arguably be regarded as undertaking it. In such cases the courts have sometimes classified the principal as undisclosed rather than unidentified in order to secure the liability of the agent. The undisclosed principal rules may then themselves be confused by considerations which are really relevant to the unidentified principal situation. For example, it has been held that a third party cannot set off against the principal a debt accruing before the third party had notice of the principal's existence unless the principal was in some way at fault in misleading that party[114]—a rule appropriate to unidentified principal situations where the existence of a principal is from the start envisaged, but not to true undisclosed principals. An inference of personal liability in the agent of an unidentified principal is readily drawn.[115] In such cases, an action by the agent would be an action in accordance with the contract into which the agent had entered. It would not involve the problems of recovery of another's loss discussed in connection with undisclosed principals.[116]

9-017   **Interrogatories as to name of unidentified principal**   It is not clear whether an agent acting for an unidentified principal can be compelled to disclose the principal's name by interrogatory.[117] In some countries an agent who does not name the principal becomes personally liable[118]; but outside trade custom this would in England require legislation. Even if the question can usually be answered in practice, the lack of a proper formal mechanism for ascertaining the principal of a person who acts "for principals" or equivalent is a weakness of English common law, particularly in view of the lack of any presumption that such a person contracts together with his principal.[119]

9-018   **Fictitious or non-existent principal**   Such situations have given rise to

---

[112] See Illustration 4.

[113] See the differing views taken by Lord Denning MR and Diplock LJ in *Teheran-Europe Co Ltd v S.T. Belton (Tractors) Ltd* [1968] 2 Q.B. 545; *Marsh & McLennan Pty Ltd v Stanyers Transport Pty Ltd* [1994] 2 V.R. 232; Comment to Article 76.

[114] *Cooke & Sons v Eshelby* (1887) 12 App.Cas. 271: see Comment to Article 80.

[115] See Reynolds [1983] C.L.P. 119. See *Ferryways NV v Associated British Ports* [2008] EWHC 225 (Comm); [2008] 1 Lloyd's Rep. 639 at [69]; cf. *Lundie v Rowena Nominees Pty Ltd* (2007) 32 W.A.R. 404 (standard form loan agreement was expressed as an agreement to lend money to the plaintiff by defendant as agent for unnamed lender pursuant to a power of attorney; it was held that the defendant could itself be the lender where there was no principal in fact, nor valid power of attorney from any principal).

[116] See above, para.9-013.

[117] See *Hersom v Bernett* [1955] 1 Q.B. 98; *Thöl v Leask* (1855) 10 Exch. 704; *Hancocks v Leblache* (1878) 3 C.P.D. 197; *Sebright v Hanbury* [1916] 2 Ch. 245; *McBride v Christie's Australia Pty Ltd* [2014] NSWSC 1729 at [131]. See also *Santander UK Plc v National Westminster Bank Plc* [2014] EWHC 2626 (Ch) (duty on receiving bank to reveal who account holder is where claimant makes mistaken payment). But cf. *Santander UK Plc v Royal Bank of Scotland Plc* [2015] EWHC 2560 (Ch).

[118] See PECL Article 3:203 and material there cited.

[119] See above, para.9-016.

specialised case law in the context of companies in the course of formation and unincorporated associations. This is discussed separately.[120]

Agent as own principal   Some cases suggest that where the agent has no principal, viz. is his or her own principal, the agent is personally liable and entitled. A firm rule to this effect, as opposed to a presumption, would be contrary to general principle; but since such a proposition is not infrequently put forward, this topic also is separately discussed.[121] It may certainly assist in providing a remedy in situations where the name of the principal is difficult or impossible to discover.   **9-019**

Foreign principal[122]   There long existed a strong presumption of fact[123] (so strong that a court was "justified in treating it as a matter of law"[124]) that in the context of sale where an agent in England contracted on behalf of a foreign principal, disclosed or undisclosed, the agent assumed personal liability to the English suppliers and had no authority to pledge the principal's credit by establishing privity of contract between the principal and the third party[125]; and conversely, where a merchant in England contracted for a principal abroad, that merchant was not to be regarded as having authority to bring the principal into privity of contract with the home supplier. Several of the cases associate this rule with the "commission merchant", in some respects an equivalent of the civil law *commissionnaire*.[126] The presumption could be displaced by clear evidence of authority. Further the effect of the presumption was to render the agent alone liable and entitled on the contract; so that when it was clear that the agent contracted only as agent, and that it was not intended that there be personal liability, there was no room for the presumption, which could not operate inconsistently with the clear purport of the contract.[127] The presumption was not affected by the fact that the contract was in writing: most, if not all, of the cases concern such contracts.   **9-020**

The status of this presumption was discussed in many cases, and though it could be questioned,[128] it was said to reflect both a preference by foreign merchants to use an intermediary who did not bring them into privity of contract with a merchant in another country, especially where the contract involved bulk supplies from several foreign sources; and also the reluctance of English merchants to enter into transactions which might involve them in problems of the conflict of laws or the possibil-

---

[120] See Article 107.
[121] See Article 108.
[122] Hudson (1957) 35 Can.B.Rev. 336; (1960) 23 M.L.R. 695; (1966) 29 M.L.R. 353; (1969) 32 M.L.R. 207. The term "foreign principal" does not seem to be a very precise one, but it is normally taken to mean a principal who does not reside or carry on business in England or Wales. However, the purpose of the rule indicates what sort of person might be regarded as a foreign principal, and it is very doubtful whether principals in Scotland, Northern Ireland or even the Irish Republic should be treated as foreign.
[123] *Paterson v Gandasequi* (1812) 15 East 62; *Smyth v Anderson* (1849) 7 C.B. 21; *Dramburg v Pollitzer* (1872) 28 L.T. 470; *Glover v Langford* (1892) 8 T.L.R. 628; *Malcolm Finn & Co v Hoyle* (1893) 63 L.J.Q.B. 1; *Harper & Sons v Keller, Bryant and Co Ltd* (1915) 84 L.J.K.B. 1696.
[124] *Armstrong v Stokes* (1872) L.R. 7 Q.B. 598 at 605.
[125] *Armstrong v Stokes* (1872) L.R. 7 Q.B. 598; *Elbinger, etc. v Claye* (1873) L.R. 8 Q.B. 313; *Hutton v Bulloch* (1874) L.R. 9 Q.B. 572; and see cases cited in fn.123 above.
[126] See above, paras 1-021 and 1-022; and the cases cited in fnn.124 and 125 above. See also Munday (1977) 6 Anglo-Am.L.Rev. 221 at 232–242.
[127] *Miller, Gibb & Co v Smith & Tyrer Ltd* [1917] 2 K.B. 141.
[128] See *Miller, Gibb & Co v Smith & Tyrer Ltd* [1917] 2 K.B. 141 at 162; *Holt & Moseley v Cunningham & Partners* (1949) 83 Ll.Rep. 141.

ity of having to sue in a foreign jurisdiction, or both,[129] especially where the contract concerned bulk supplies from overseas sources. The latter reasoning seems more significant to modern eyes, since the foreign merchant's contract with the English intermediary may not be governed by English law. The banker's commercial credit system performs a similar function in to some extent localising the transaction. Later cases tended to treat the fact that the principal was foreign as one to be taken into account but no more.[130] In *Teheran-Europe Co Ltd v S. T. Belton (Tractors) Ltd*,[131] where air compressors were ordered for use in Iran, the Court of Appeal finally held that the presumption itself no longer exists, for "the usages of the law merchant are not immutable". But the fact that the principal is foreign is not irrelevant. Diplock LJ said[132]:

> "The fact that the principal is a foreigner is one of the circumstances to be taken into account in determining whether or not the other party to the contract was willing, or led 'the agent to believe' that he was willing, to treat as a party to the contract the agent's principal, and, if he was so willing, whether the mutual intention of the other party and the agent was that the agent should be personally entitled to sue and liable to be sued on the contract as well as his principal. But it is only one of many circumstances, and as respects the creation of privity of contract between the other party and the principal its weight may be minimal, particularly in a case such as the present where the terms of payment are cash before delivery and no credit is extended by the other party to the principal. It may have considerably more weight in determining whether the mutual intention of the other party and the agent was that the agent should be personally liable to be sued as well as the principal, particularly if credit has been extended by the other party."[133]

9-021 **Confirming houses in international sales**[134] A confirming house provides specialised agency functions for an overseas buyer who wishes to import goods. The normal purpose of the intervention of a confirming house is so that a seller, in a transaction with an overseas buyer, will have someone in the seller's own country to look to in respect of performance of the contract: like the banker's commercial credit, it performs the function of reducing the possibility of becoming involved in questions of the conflict of laws or of suing in foreign jurisdictions. A confirming house may, on instructions, act for the buyer as agent only, and if so is not liable to the seller.[135] Alternatively, it may act as merchant, viz. by buying from the seller and reselling to its principal, the buyer.[136] Neither of these arrangements really involves confirmation. A transaction involving confirmation will normally be intended to result in privity of contract being established between seller and confirming

---

[129] See *Armstrong v Stokes* (1872) L.R. 7 Q.B. 598 at 605; Hill (1968) 31 M.L.R. 623 at 637–639; Munday (1977) 6 Anglo-Am.L.Rev. 221 at 235 onwards.

[130] *H.O. Brandt & Co v Morris & Co* [1917] 2 K.B. 784; *Rusholme and Bolton and Roberts Hadfield v S.G. Read & Co* [1955] 1 W.L.R. 146; *Cox v Sorrell* [1960] 1 Lloyd's Rep. 471; *Anglo African Shipping Co of New York Inc v J. Mortner Ltd* [1962] 1 Lloyd's Rep. 610 at 617, 621; *Maritime Stores v H.P. Marshall & Co Ltd* [1963] 1 Lloyd's Rep. 602.

[131] *Teheran-Europe Co Ltd v S. T. Belton (Tractors) Ltd* [1968] 2 Q.B. 545.

[132] *Teheran-Europe Co Ltd v S. T. Belton (Tractors) Ltd* [1968] 2 Q.B. 545 at 558.

[133] As to which see *Fraser v Equitorial Shipping Co Ltd (The Ijaolo)* [1979] 1 Lloyd's Rep. 103.

[134] Hill (1972) 3 J. Maritime Law and Commerce 307; Schmitthoff (1970) 1 *Hague Recueil des Cours* at p.154–157; *Schmitthoff's Export Trade* (12th edn), Ch. 27; [1957] J.B.L. 17.

[135] cf. *Bolus & Co Ltd v Inglis Bros Ltd* [1924] N.Z.L.R. 164; *Stunzi Sons Ltd v House of Youth Pty Ltd* [1960] S.R.(N.S.W.) 220.

[136] See the dissenting judgment of Diplock LJ in *Anglo-African Shipping Co of New York Inc v J. Mortner Ltd* [1962] 1 Lloyd's Rep. 610.

house.[137] In some cases the confirming house may be liable on a collateral contract whereby it answers in some way for the performance of the buyer's contract.[138] In other cases the confirming house may be solely liable to the seller, creating no privity between buyer and seller, but still remaining as an agent in relation to the buyer rather than a seller to its own principal: this possibility, which again involves the notion of what is sometimes called the commission merchant or *commissionnaire*, has not been fully explored.[139] It is clear that the fact that a confirming house acts as principal in one respect does not mean that it cannot act as agent in another, e.g. as a forwarding agent, and vice versa.[140] A confirming house that does undertake liability to the seller may answer for more than the mere solvency of the buyer: subject to the terms of the particular contract and to the commercial understanding of the transaction, it is subject to litigation on the contract in general.[141] So also it may sue the seller, or assign its rights of action to the buyer.

Del credere agents   The position of a *del credere* agent is to be contrasted with   **9-022**
that of a confirming house. A *del credere* agent is normally the agent of the seller, not of the buyer. Thus, though such agents answer to the seller, they do not undertake to the third party that their principal will perform a contract, but undertake to the principal that the third party will.[142] Equally, such an agent cannot sue the third party.[143] A confirming house on the other hand is normally agent of the buyer, and thus answers to the seller not as agent but as a party to a contract with the seller.[144] Its duty to the buyer is therefore usually greater than that of a *del credere* agent, whose obligation is confined to answering for the failure by the other contracting parties, owing to insolvency or the like, to pay ascertained sums which may become due from them as debts.[145] However, situations may occur where it is difficult to distinguish between the two.[146]

Auctioneers   Auctioneers provide examples of liability on what must be explained   **9-023**
in modern terms (however the matter is put in old cases) as collateral contracts.[147] Where an auctioneer sells a specific chattel by auction for a disclosed principal, the

---

[137] *Sobell Industries Ltd v Cory Bros & Co* [1955] 2 Lloyd's Rep. 82 at 89.

[138] *Sobell Industries Ltd v Cory Bros & Co* [1955] 2 Lloyd's Rep. 82 (Illustration 7).

[139] *Rusholme and Bolton and Roberts Hadfield v S.G. Read & Co* [1955] 1 W.L.R. 146; and *Anglo-African Shipping Co of New York Inc v J. Mortner Ltd* [1962] 1 Lloyd's Rep. 610, may be examples of this. See paras 1-021 and 1-022 above; Hill (1972) 3 J. Maritime Law and Commerce 307, at 318–324; (1968) 31 M.L.R. 623; *Bolus & Co Ltd v Inglis Bros Ltd* [1924] N.Z.L.R. 164 at 174–175; *Downie Bros v Henry Oakley & Sons* [1923] N.Z.L.R. 734; *Scott v Geoghegan & Sons Pty Ltd* (1969) 43 A.L.J.R. 243; *Isaac Gundle v Mohanlal Sunderji* (1939) 18 Kenya L.Rep. 137; Comment to Article 69.

[140] *Anglo-African Shipping Co of New York Inc v J. Mortner Ltd* [1962] 1 Lloyd's Rep. 610 at 616–617; *Sobell Industries Ltd v Cory Bros & Co* [1955] 2 Lloyd's Rep. 82 at 90.

[141] *Sobell Industries Ltd v Cory Bros & Co* [1955] 2 Lloyd's Rep. 82 (Illustration 7); *Rusholme, etc., v Read* [1955] 1 W.L.R. 146.

[142] *Churchill & Sim v Goddard* [1937] 1 K.B. 92.

[143] *Bramwell v Spiller* (1871) 21 L.T. 672; Article 2. But sometimes a *del credere* agent may by special arrangement or by the usage of trade answer to both parties to a sale: see Hill (1968) 31 M.L.R. 623 at 639 note 64. And see Illustration 23.

[144] See above, para.9-021.

[145] *Thomas Gabriel & Sons v Churchill & Sim* [1914] 3 K.B. 1272; *Rusholme, etc., v Read* [1955] 1 W.L.R. 146.

[146] See Hill, above. See further as to *del credere* agents, Comment to Article 2.

[147] See above, para.9-009.

auctioneer is not liable upon the contract of sale,[148] nor does he or she impliedly warrant the title of the principal, although the name of the principal has not been disclosed to the buyer.[149] But an auctioneer warrants authority to sell, and that he or she knows of no defect in the title of the principal.[150] The auctioneer's contract with the buyer makes the buyer liable to the auctioneer for the price,[151] and is independent of the contract of sale, which the auctioneer makes on behalf of the seller and to which the auctioneer is not a party.[152] The auctioneer's lien over or special property in the goods is said to be based on this contract, and for this reason seems inappropriate to the sale of land,[153] though no doubt in such cases he may still be subject to contractual duties.[154] Liability of an auctioneer on a collateral contract has also arisen where an auctioneer declines to knock down an item to the highest bidder when the item was said to be without reserve.[155]

Another example was provided by the jobber on the Stock Exchange, who contracted, through the broker, with the seller of shares, to find a purchaser to whom no legitimate objection could be taken. When the jobber had done so, a contract was effected between seller and buyer and the jobber's own collateral undertaking was performed.[156] This method of trading is no longer used in England.

9-024   **Freight forwarders**[157]   The obvious function of freight forwarders is to make contracts of carriage, often several, on behalf of a shipper. For this reason they were often formerly called "forwarding agents". There is however no objection to a person conducting business of this sort acting as carrier, i.e. undertaking to carry and actually performing by means of employees or independent subcontractors, and many do so (and indeed perform various other related functions also). The difficulty is then to determine exactly what is the appropriate legal analysis of what has been arranged.[158] Although in 1920 it was said that a forwarding agent was not a carrier,[159] and in 1965 it was said that the interpretation under which the freight

---

[148] *Elder Smith Goldsbrough Mort Ltd v McBride* [1976] 2 N.S.W.L.R. 631, Illustration 14; cf. *Fraser v Dalgety & Co Ltd* [1953] N.Z.L.R. 126.

[149] *Benton v Campbell, Parker & Co* [1925] 2 K.B. 410; *Chelmsford Auctions Ltd v Poole* [1973] Q.B. 542. The special situation where a sale merely goes through an auctioneer's books was analysed as a sale to the auctioneer and a resale by him in *Murphy v Howlett* [1960] E.G.D. 231.

[150] *Peto v Blades* (1814) 5 Taunt. 657; *Pollway Ltd v Abdullah* [1974] 1 W.L.R. 493 (warranty of authority to sign memorandum and accept deposit entitled auctioneer to sue upon cheque for deposit). See further below, para.9-029; Illustrations 11–14 and 18–20; Murdoch, *Law of Estate Agency* (5th edn), pp.172–173; Reynolds, in *Contemporary Issues in Commercial Law* (Lomnicka and Morse eds, 1997), p.161 onwards.

[151] See Illustration 18.

[152] *Benton v Campbell, Parker & Co* [1925] 2 K.B. 410 at 416.

[153] See *Cherry v Anderson* (1876) I.R. 10 C.L. 204; *Fisher v Marsh* (1865) 6 B. & S. 411; *Evans v Evans* (1834) 3 A. & E. 132; cf. *Cleave v Moore* (1857) 3 Jur.(N.S.) 48.

[154] See *Pollway Ltd v Abdullah* [1974] 1 W.L.R. 493.

[155] *Barry v Davies* [2000] 1 W.L.R. 1962 (noted by Coote [2001] NZ Law Rev. 277; Scott [2001] L.M.C.L.Q. 334). See Illustration 11.

[156] *Grissell v Bristowe* (1868) L.R. 4 C.P. 36; *Maxted v Paine* (1869) L.R. 4 Ex. 203; affirmed (1871) L.R. 6 Ex. 132. See on these cases (1929) 39 Yale L.J. 265–271.

[157] See in general Reynolds, "The Liability of Freight Forwarders", Ch.14 in *Carriage of Goods by Land, Sea and Air: Unimodal and Multimodal Transport in the 21st Century* (Soyer and Tettenborn eds, 2014).

[158] For a case where both forwarder and actual carrier issued a bill of lading for the same goods, and the effect of the forwarder's document was not clear, see *Carrington Slipways Pty Ltd v Patrick Operations Pty Ltd (The Cape Comorin)* (1991) 24 N.S.W.L.R. 745.

[159] *Jones v European & General Express Co Ltd* (1920) 4 Ll.L.Rep. 127, per Rowlatt J.

forwarder was a carrier as opposed to an agent was exceptional,[160] this seems no longer to be so.[161] No doubt this is at least in part connected with the increased possibility of consolidating consignments which was created by the use of containers. The matter is not assisted however by many sets of standard terms the meaning (and sometimes application) of which is not clear, and an alleged tendency of freight forwarders to fight cases seeking to impose responsibility on them.[162] There certainly can be freight forwarders who act as agents for the main contract of carriage but also undertake liability towards the carrier.[163] Beyond the roles of agent and carrier, however, there is at least in theory a third possibility for analysis, based on the notion of indirect representation explained elsewhere in this book[164]: the forwarder is as regards the client an agent, working on an agency basis and owing a duty of best endeavours only, but as regards the carrier a principal. This reduces the forwarder's liability and also makes it difficult for the client to proceed against the carrier. One unreported case accepts this interpretation in the context of the CMR.[165] A more recent case,[166] while casting doubt on some of the reasoning in the earlier case,[167] accepts such an interpretation as a possibility, but states that clear evidence (not present in the case) would be required regarding the assumption of such a role.[168] In some countries, notably Germany, there is recent legislation determining the status and duties of freight forwarders.[169] Such an approach would have many advantages, but is not very likely to be adopted in large common law countries, where an opportunity for such legislation is unlikely to arise.

Deposits: receipt as agent for vendor   An agent, particularly an estate agent,   **9-025**
auctioneer or solicitor acting in connection with the sale of land, may receive money from a third party to hold by way of deposit. Sometimes this money is received as agent for the vendor: this is the assumption in the case of solicitors[170] and estate agents[171] unless there are indications to the contrary. Old cases suggest that auctioneers, on the other hand, prima facie receive money in such circumstances

---

[160] *Lengley, Beldon & Gaunt Ltd v Morley* [1965] 1 Lloyd's Rep. 297 at 306, per Mocatta J.

[161] For examples of freight forwarders as carriers, see *Ulster-Swift Ltd v Taunton Meat Haulage Ltd* [1977] 1 Lloyd's Rep. 346; *Elektronska Industrija Oour v Transped Oour Kontinentalna Spedicna* [1986] 1 Lloyd's Rep. 49; *Vastfame Camera Ltd v Birkart Glogistics* [2005] 4 H.K.C. 117.

[162] See Tetley, *Marine Cargo Claims* (4th edn, 2008), Vol.2. Ch.33.

[163] *Anglo Overseas Transport Ltd v Titan Industrial Corp (UK) Ltd* [1959] 2 Lloyd's Rep. 152 (liable for dead freight); *Perishables Transport Co Ltd v N. Spyropoulos (London) Ltd* [1964] 2 Lloyd's Rep. 379; *Cory Bros Shipping Ltd v Baldan Ltd* [1997] 2 Lloyd's Rep. 58.

[164] See above, para.1-021.

[165] *Bardiger v Halberg Spedition Aps*, Evans J, Unreported October 26, 1990, only available on LEXIS.

[166] *Aqualon (UK) Ltd v Vallana Shipping Corp* [1994] 1 Lloyd's Rep. 669.

[167] See at p.664 per Mance J.

[168] A possible example is *Salsi v Jetspeed Air Services Ltd* [1977] 2 Lloyd's Rep. 57. See also *Royal & Sun Alliance Insurance Plc v MK Dgital (Cyprus) Ltd* [2006] EWCA Civ 629 (interpretation as commissionaire de transport).

[169] See Reynolds, "The Liability of Freight Forwarders", Ch.14 in *Carriage of Goods by Land, Sea and Air: Unimodal and Multimodal Transport in the 21st Century* (Soyer and Tettenborn eds) at 257–258.

[170] *Ellis v Goulton* [1893] 1 Q.B. 350 at 352–353 (Illustration 1 to Article 111); *Tudor v Hamid* [1988] 1 E.G.L.R. 251 at 255. This has the advantage for the purchaser that he has a lien on the property to the extent of the deposit: *Whitehead & Co Ltd v Watt* [1902] 1 Ch. 835; cf. *Combe v Lord Swaythling* [1947] Ch. 625. See also *Skinner v Trustee of the Property of Reed* [1967] Ch. 1194.

[171] *Ojelay v Neosale Ltd* [1987] 2 E.G.L.R. 167 at 168.

not as agents but as stakeholders[172] though it is not clear why the rule for them should be different, and hence whether this interpretation is still correct. The consequence of receipt as agent is that it is the vendor who is liable if the sale goes off and the money is not returned.[173] Statute law may, in some circumstances, govern the use of deposits, and make agents liable for non-compliance with those requirements.[174]

9-026 **Agent as stakeholder**   Whatever the prima facie rule, circumstances frequently arise where persons in these categories receive money as stakeholders. A person receiving money as stakeholder must hold or at least account for it pending the oc-currence of the relevant event, and when this has occurred, pay it across in accord-ance with instructions. A stakeholder must not accede to the unilateral instructions of one of the parties to do otherwise, though he or she must accept the instructions of both of them, for example, to transfer the deposit to another stakeholder.[175] A stakeholder does not, as a general rule, hold the deposit in trust[176] and must pay it to one of the parties, usually the vendor, when the relevant event occurs. If a stakeholder takes the view that it has occurred, but is wrong, the stakeholder is li-able, but in personam.[177] It is sometimes said that in such a case the stakeholder is agent of both parties[178]; but it seems rather that such a person receives the money from the purchaser under a specific and separate obligation as principal.[179] It ap-pears from the auctioneer cases that the vendor also is liable if the stakeholder defaults[180]: but the agent's obligation is clearly a separate one from that of the principal. The obligation is probably contractual, the consideration for a stakeholder's promise being that the stakeholder has the use of the money without

---

[172] *Harington v Hoggart* (1830) 1 B. & Ad. 577; *Furtado v Lumley* (1890) 6 T.L.R. 168.

[173] See Article 111.

[174] See in relation to tenancies of houses, the liabilities of landlords' agents under the Housing Act 2004 ss.214–215, considered in *Draycott v Hannells Letting Ltd (t/a Hannells Letting Agents)* [2010] EWHC 217 (QB); [2011] 1 W.L.R. 1606.

[175] *Rockeagle Ltd v Alsop Wilkinson* [1992] Ch. 47 (despite solicitors having an interest in retaining it against debts owed by vendor). His lien is confined to so much as becomes the property of the vendor: *Skinner v Trustee of the Property of Reed* [1967] Ch. 1194. As to interest, see Article 52.

[176] *Hastingwood Property Ltd v Saunders Bearman Anselm* [1991] Ch. 114; *Potters (A Firm) v Loppert* [1973] Ch. 399.

[177] *Hastingwood Property Ltd v Saunders Bearman Anselm* [1991] Ch. 114; *Merchant International Co Ltd v Natsionalna Aktsionerna Kompaniia Naftogaz Ukrainy* [2014] EWHC 391 (Comm); [2014] 1 C.L.C. 271 at [34].

[178] *Collins v Stimson* (1883) 11 Q.B.D. 142 at 144.

[179] *Hastingwood Property Ltd v Saunders Bearman Anselm* [1991] Ch. 114 at 123. See also *Berry v Hodson* [1989] 1 Qd.R. 361 (knowledge of stakeholder not imputed to vendor); *Bank of Scotland v Truman* [2005] EWHC 583 (QB) at [54]; *Bristol Alliance Nominee No.1 v Bennett* [2013] EWCA Civ 1626 at [24].

[180] *Fenton v Browne* (1807) 14 Ves. 144; *Annesley v Muggridge* (1816) 1 Madd. 593 at 596; *Rowe v May* (1854) 18 Beav. 613; *Christie v Robinson* (1907) 4 C.L.R. 1338; *Swindle v Knibb* (1929) 29 S.R.(N.S.W.) 325; *Grant v O'Leary* (1955) 93 C.L.R. 587; *Goding v Frazer* [1967] 1 W.L.R. 286 at 290–291; *Barrington v Lee* [1972] 1 Q.B. 326 at 335; *Ojelay v Neosale Ltd* [1987] 2 E.G.L.R. 167 at 168; *Thomson Hill Pte. Ltd v Chang Erh* [1992] 2 Singapore L.R. 769; Murdoch, *Law of Estate Agency* (5th edn), p.235 onwards. The rule seems to be based on the idea that the vendor ap-points the stakeholder: quaere whether it should apply when he cannot easily be said to have done so, as where it is the purchaser's solicitor who holds the money. But in the *Thomson Hill* case, above, it was held that the same result ensued because the parties in such a case have by mutual consent made the purchaser's solicitor the stakeholder.

accounting for interest[181]; but alternatively it may lie in restitution, though this head of restitution is not yet well worked out in English law.[182]

Where an agent receives money under a pre-contract situation in the sale of land "subject to contract", as estate agents sometimes do, the agent is often also said to hold as stakeholder, and it has indeed been said that this is the appropriate interpretation where there are no other indications.[183] In this context the term "stakeholder" has at best a specialised meaning, however, and would be better avoided,[184] for the holder is under a duty to return the money to the prospective purchaser on demand at any time before it is paid away on the completion of the contract in accordance with instructions.[185] Such a person is probably better described as agent of the purchaser, authorised to hold and pay away the money unless that authority is revoked. Here the fact that the agent must be ready to return the money on mere demand is more plausibly treated as consideration for an entitlement to interest.[186] In such cases the vendor is not liable if the estate agent defaults.[187]

Express restriction of liability Where an agent contracts personally, the agent's liability may be expressly restricted to certain events. The cesser clause in a charterparty may be cited as an example.[188] Older forms of the clause provide that the charterer signs as agent for others, and that its liability to the shipowner is to cease as soon as the cargo is shipped, the shipowner holding a lien for unpaid charges. Under it the charterer's liability may cease as specified and be superseded by the liability of the holders of the bills of lading.[189] Such clauses, which are the subject of extensive case law,[190] do not necessarily involve true agency by the charterer, for it may not at the time of contracting have a principal or principals as required. The charterer may simply intend to procure that other shippers fill the ship with general cargo and pay the freight between them. Indeed the charterer may in the end ship personally. Later forms of the clause do not refer to agency.   9-027

Agents of the Crown Prior to 1947, no action for breach of contract lay against the Crown, except where permitted by statute. However, as the Crown was to all intents and purposes liable in contract by Petition of Right, no special rule was avowedly applied to agents of the Crown, who were therefore, like other agents, not liable unless they had contracted personally. But they would rarely be held to   9-028

[181] *Potters (A Firm) v Loppert* [1973] Ch. 399; following *Harington v Hoggart* (1830) 1 B. & Ad. 577; and see *Smith v Hamilton* [1951] Ch. 174 at 184. See also Article 52.
[182] See *Chillingworth v Esche* [1924] 1 Ch. 97. See also as to this point *Burt v Claude Cousins & Co Ltd* [1975] 1 Q.B. 426 at 449; *Barrington v Lee* [1972] 1 Q.B. 326 at 337; *Potters (A Firm) v Loppert* [1973] Ch. 399; (1976) 92 L.Q.R. 484; Article 111, Illustration 2.
[183] *Burt v Claude Cousins & Co Ltd* [1975] 1 Q.B. 426, per Lord Denning MR and Sachs LJ. But see *Desmond v Brophy* [1985] I.R. 449, where it was held on the facts that a solicitor received such a deposit as agent for the prospective vendor.
[184] *Maloney v Hardy and Moorsehead* [1971] 2 Q.B. 442n.
[185] *Sorrell v Finch* [1977] A.C. 728 at 749 (Illustration 4 to Article 92). See a recent but rather inconclusive discussion of the role of stakeholders and of vendors and purchaser in a pre-contract situation in *Gribbon v Lutton* [2001] EWCA Civ 1956; [2002] Q.B. 902.
[186] See *Potters (A Firm) v Loppert* [1973] Ch. 399 at 414–415.
[187] *Sorrell v Finch* [1977] A.C. 728. See also Article 111, Illustration 3.
[188] See below, para.9-096.
[189] *Oglesby v Yglesias* (1858) E.B. & E. 930; *Milvain v Perez* (1861) 3 E. & E. 495.
[190] See in general *Scrutton on Charterparties* (24th edn), para.9-168 onwards.

do so,[191] which is doubtless fair when the magnitude of commitment involved in some government contracts is considered. Cases of personal liability are however not impossible,[192] and indeed where the "agent" is a public body there is no particular difficulty about them: in such a case at any rate it is also possible for the Crown and the agent to be liable together.[193] The Crown can now be sued directly by virtue of the Crown Proceedings Act 1947, but the rules as to the liability and entitlement to sue an agent of the Crown remain unchanged.

9-029 **Defences**[194]   Where an agent, being liable on it, is sued on the main contract, the agent can presumably plead defences arising out of the contract, and personal defences, but not defences personal to the principal. Where the agent sues, the third party can likewise plead defences on the main transaction, but not defences against the agent personally unless the principal was undisclosed.

But where an agent sues on a separate or collateral contract, defences available on the main contract may not be available against the agent, depending on the terms of the contract as interpreted by the court. The best example of this is the case of auctioneers.[195] Auctioneers, as stated above, make a separate and quite independent contract with the buyer which renders them subject to certain liabilities and also entitles them to sue. Payment to or set-off against the principal are therefore normally no defence to the auctioneer's claim.[196] But it may sometimes be a defence if the auctioneer knew of such a set-off, for then the collateral contract may be otherwise interpreted, or if the auctioneer apparently waived the right by allowing goods to be taken away contrary to normal practice without asking for payment.[197] And if the auctioneer's principal did not own the goods, the auctioneer has no one from whom to derive an interest in the goods, and payment to the true owner will discharge a purchaser.[198] Further, the auctioneer's right to sue may sometimes be extinguished if the auctioneer has received the agreed commission, for here an equity may be raised against him or her.[199] Similar reasoning was applied to nineteenth-century factors, who likewise had a lien, and sometimes (less obviously) to brokers.[200]

The contract on which an agent sues may be independent of the main contract to such an extent that defences against the agent may be pleaded though the underlying transaction is with the principal. Thus it has been held that an underwriter may

---

[191] See *Palmer v Hutchinson* (1881) 6 App.Cas. 619; *Macbeath v Haldimand* (1786) 7 T.R. 172; also *Kenny v Cosgrave* [1926] I.R. 517. As to the liability of agents of the Crown for breach of warranty of authority, see below, para.9-074.

[192] Illustrations 8–10. But these are special cases: a private individual contracting on behalf of the Crown (as opposed to a public body specially incorporated by statute, or a private person making personal arrangements) does not seem to be liable, and dicta that the individual is free from liability have been couched in strong terms: see, e.g. *Gidley v Palmerston* (1822) 3 B. & B. 275 at 286–287.

[193] *International Ry Co v Niagara Parks Commission* [1941] A.C. 328 (again a case on a public body, incorporated by statute with the power to sue and be sued).

[194] See Derham [1985] C.L.J. 384; *Law of Set-Off* (4th edn), para.13-75; Wood, *English and International Set-Off* (1989), Ch.19.

[195] See Derham [1985] C.L.J. 384, at [13.93], [13.94]; Reynolds, in *Contemporary Issues in Commercial Law* (Lomnicka and Morse eds, 1997), p.161 onwards.

[196] Illustration 19.

[197] Illustration 20.

[198] *Dickenson v Naul* (1833) 4 B. & Ad. 638; and see *Fraser v Dalgety & Co Ltd* [1953] N.Z.L.R. 126.

[199] Illustration 20; but cf. Illustration 19.

[200] See Illustrations 21 and 22; Reynolds, above; para.9-009 above.

set off, in an action by a broker for insurance money due to a client, debts owed by the broker to the underwriter.[201]

Estoppel as to whether a party to contract   There may be circumstances when, although an agent is not on true analysis a party to the contract, the agent's conduct towards the third party creates a representation of personal liability on the contract. In such circumstances an estoppel may be raised against him. This has been held to occur in connection with the demise or "identity of carrier" clause, a bill of lading clause which purports to create a contract with the shipowner where the ship is not owned by or chartered by demise to the party issuing the bill of lading.[202] Under such clauses the party issuing the bill of lading acts as agent only. But where such a party has acted as if a contracting party, and the third party proceeded on this basis with the result that its action against the true principal became time-barred, it was held that the party issuing the bill was estopped from alleging that it was not a party to the contract.[203]   **9-030**

Warranty of authority   An agent who contracts on behalf of a principal is normally regarded as warranting the agent's authority to do so. This special collateral contract is treated separately in Article 105.   **9-031**

Tort   An agent may of course be liable to the third party in deceit. There may also be circumstances in which the agent assumes a duty of care towards the third party. This would not involve liability on the promise, but in respect of negligent representation, or sometimes negligent conduct.[204]   **9-032**

Statute   Section 21 of the Estate Agents Act 1979, in combination with regulations made under the Act,[205] impose on estate agents certain duties of disclosure to third parties of any personal interest in a transaction.[206] These have, however, no civil sanction and are only enforceable in so far as they may trigger the enforcement powers of the Director General of Fair Trading. Persons who undertake contractual liability for package holidays or are organisers of them will be subject to the Package Travel and Linked Travel Arrangements Regulations 2018.[207] These Regulations may not capture all persons who act as travel agents.   **9-033**

Illustrations

Liability of agent

(1)   A acted as the London agent of C & Co, who were paper manufacturers in   **9-034**

---

[201] *Gibson v Winter* (1833) 5 B. & Ad. 96.
[202] See *Scrutton on Charterparties* (24th edn), para.6-032 onwards.
[203] *Pacol Ltd v Trades Lines Ltd (The Henrik Sif)* [1982] 1 Lloyd's Rep. 456, applying reasoning in *Amalgamated Investment & Property Co Ltd v Texas Commerce International Bank Ltd* [1982] Q.B. 84; *Taylors Fashions Ltd v Liverpool Victoria Trustee Co Ltd*, ibid. 133n. See further *The Stolt Loyalty* [1993] 2 Lloyd's Rep. 281 at 289–291; [1995] 1 Lloyd's Rep. 598; above, para.8-028.
[204] See Article 113.
[205] Estate Agents (Undesirable Practices) (No.2) Order 1991 (SI 1991/1032).
[206] See Murdoch, *Law of Estate Agency* (5th edn), p.297 onwards; *The Estate Agents and Property Misdescriptions Acts* (3rd edn), Ch.3C.
[207] SI 2018/634. For cases under the predecessor regulations, see *Hone v Going Places Leisure Travel Ltd* Unreported November 16, 2000, QBD; affirmed [2001] EWCA Civ 947; and *Titshall v Qwerty Travel Ltd* [2011] EWCA Civ 1569 at [16]; [2012] 2 All E.R. 627.

Vienna. B, by letter, ordered paper from A, who in his own name acknowledged the letter, and promised to supply the paper in certain quantities at
certain times. A portion of the paper was delivered, and on B complaining to
A respecting the non-delivery of the remainder, A stated that it was the default
of C & Co B then wrote to C & Co telling them of the position of affairs, and
the excuses made by A. Subsequently B sued A for breach of contract. Held,
that A, having contracted personally, was liable, and that B's letter to C & Co
did not amount to an election by B to substitute C & Co for A as the contracting parties.[208] Some weight was attached to the circumstance that the
principals were foreign.[209]

(2)   Where solicitors instructed stockbrokers to sell stock belonging to A, and
enclosed a blank transfer signed by A, it was held that the instructions to sell
were given by the solicitors as principals and that they were liable when A
objected to the registration of the transfer.[210]

(3)   An agent signed in his own name, without mentioning his principal, an
undertaking to accept shares in a company, and the shares were allotted to
him. Subsequently, the principal took a larger number of shares, in satisfaction, as the agent said, of his undertaking. Held, that the agent, having personally accepted the shares, was liable as a contributory.[211]

(4)   An agent buys goods at a sale by auction, and gives his own name, which is
entered as that of the buyer. He is personally liable, unless it is clearly proved
that he did not intend to bind himself, and that the auctioneer knew that.[212]

(5)   A stockbroker in Hong Kong presenting share transfers for registration has
been held to promise that he will indemnify the person to whom he presents
them against the consequences of registering them; and may also be held to
warrant their genuineness.[213]

(6)   A fishing vessel is owned by R, who forms a company to hire it from him and
operate it. Repairs are ordered by R on the company's notepaper, signed "R,
Director". Although R undoubtedly contracts as agent for the company, he
also, as owner of the vessel, undertakes personal liability.[214]

---

[208] *Dramburg v Pollitzer* (1873) 28 L.T. 470; cf. *J.S. Robertson (Aust.) Pty Ltd v Martin* (1956) 94
C.L.R. 30. See Articles 82 and 104. The "election" reasoning would not be so expressed today: see
above, paras 8-119 and 9-030.
[209] See above, para.9-020.
[210] *Hichens, Harrison Woolston & Co v Jackson & Sons* [1943] A.C. 266; and see *Lavan v Walsh* [1964]
I.R. 87; *Saxon v Blake* (1861) 29 Beav. 438; *Hobhouse v Hamilton* (1826) 1 Hog. 401 (Ir.); and see
Article 97. As to the enforcement of solicitors' undertakings, see *Geoffrey Silver & Drake v Baines*
[1971] 1 Q.B. 396 at 402; Cordery, *Solicitors* (8th edn).
[211] *Re Southampton, Bird's Case* (1864) 4 De G.J. & S. 200.
[212] *Williamson v Barton* (1862) 7 H. & N. 899; *Chadwick v Maden* (1851) 9 Hare 188. Presumably commercial usage in the type of auction sale in question would be relevant.
[213] *Yeung Kai Yung v Hong Kong and Shanghai Banking Corp* [1981] A.C. 787; cf. *Guaranty Trust Corp
of New York v Hannay & Co* [1918] 2 K.B. 623. And see below, para.9-062.
[214] *The Swan* [1968] 1 Lloyd's Rep. 5; see also *R. & J. Bow Ltd v Hill* (1930) 37 Ll.Rep. 46; *Format
International Security Printers Ltd v Mosden* [1975] 1 Lloyd's Rep. 37; cf. *Badgerhill Properties
Ltd v Cottrell* [1991] B.C.L.C. 805, Illustration 16 to Article 99. Compare comments by Legh-
Jones (1969) 32 M.L.R. 325 and Reynolds (1969) 85 L.Q.R. 92. See also Prentice (1973) 89 L.Q.R.
518 at 531, suggesting that the case is inconsistent with *Newborne v Sensolid (Great Britain) Ltd*
[1954] 1 Q.B. 45, Illustration 6 to Article 107; and *Henry Browne & Sons Ltd v Smith* [1964] 2
Lloyd's Rep. 276. It could also be said that some of the dicta are inconsistent with what was
subsequently said in *N. & J. Vlassopulos Ltd v Ney Shipping Co (The Santa Carina)* [1977] 1 Lloyd's
Rep. 478. Illustration 3 to Article 101. As regards repairs to and stores for ships, see further cases

(7)   A buyer in Turkey orders radio sets from an English manufacturer. The order is confirmed by an English confirming house and accepted by the seller. The buyer fails to accept full delivery. The confirming house is liable for the buyer's breach of contract.[215]

(8)   A naval commander, when employing a cook, undertook to pay him a certain sum per annum in addition to the government pay. Held, that the commander was personally liable to pay that sum, he having contracted personally, and not as an agent for the government.[216]

(9)   A clerk of a county court gave orders for the fitting up, etc., of the courthouse. Held, that it was properly left to the jury to say whether he had contracted personally, and that, if he had, he was personally liable on the contract.[217]

(10)   The Commissioners of Public Works and Buildings entered into a contract with certain builders for the erection of public buildings. It was held that the Commissioners must be taken to have contracted for themselves, and not merely as agents for the Crown, and that they were liable to be sued by the builders for damages for breach of the contract.[218]

(11)   An auctioneer sold goods on behalf of a disclosed principal, the conditions of sale providing that the lots should be cleared within three days, and that if from any cause the auctioneer was unable to deliver, etc. the purchaser should accept compensation. Held, that the auctioneer, being in possession of the goods, and having contracted to deliver, was personally liable to the purchaser for nondelivery.[219]

(12)   In a case of a sale of standing corn with straw, to be removed at the purchaser's expense, it was held that the auctioneer contracted to give proper authority to enter and carry away the corn and straw, and undertook that he was in fact authorised to sell, but that he did not warrant the title.[220] Upon a sale of shares, which required transfer by deed, the auctioneers, who were acting on behalf of an unnamed principal, were held liable in damages for failure to procure a transfer of the shares, upon the ground that they had agreed to do so.[221]

(13)   Where a sale by auction is advertised as being "without reserve" it may be that the auctioneer impliedly contracts to accept the offer of the highest bona fide bidder, and is liable in damages for breach of such implied contract if he accepts a bid from the vendor.[222] But an advertisement to the effect that certain

cited above; Article 99, Illustration 7; Article 101, Illustration 2; *H.J. Lyons & Sando Ltd v Houlson* [1963] S.A.S.R. 29; *Stag Line Ltd v Tyne Shiprepair Group Ltd (The Zinnia)* [1984] 2 Lloyd's Rep. 211. For a case where there was express provision for joint and several liability, see *Middle East Tankers and Freighters Bunker Services SA v Abu Dhabi Container Lines* [2002] EWHC 957 (Comm); [2002] 2 Lloyd's Rep. 643.

[215]   *Sobell Industries Ltd v Cory Bros & Co Ltd* [1955] 2 Lloyd's Rep. 82; see above, para.9-021.

[216]   *Clutterbuck v Coffin* (1842) 3 M. & G. 842. See also *Cunningham v Collier* (1785) 4 Doug. 233; cf. *Unwin v Wolseley* (1787) 1 T.R. 674 (cases on deeds); *Rice v Chute* (1801) 1 East 579.

[217]   *Auty v Hutchinson* (1848) 6 C.B. 266.

[218]   *Graham v Public Works Commrs* [1901] 2 K.B. 781; *Roper v Public Works Commrs* [1915] 1 K.B. 45. The Commissioners were a public body incorporated by statute.

[219]   *Woolfe v Horne* (1877) 2 Q.B.D. 355.

[220]   *Wood v Baxter* (1883) 49 L.T. 45; *Benton v Campbell Parker & Co* [1925] 2 K.B. 410.

[221]   *Franklyn v Lamond* (1847) 4 C.B. 637; *Hanson v Roberdeau* (1792) Peake 163.

[222]   *Warlow v Harrison* (1858) 1 E. & E. 295 at 309; followed in *Barry v Davies* [2000] 1 W.L.R. 1962. See Slade (1952) 68 L.Q.R. 238; (1953) 69 L.Q.R. 21; Gower (1952) 68 L.Q.R. 457; *Johnston v Boyes* [1899] 2 Ch. 73. See also *Wright v Madden* [1992] 1 Qd. R. 343; cf. *Rainbow v Howkins*

goods will be sold on certain days does not amount to a contract to sell them, so as to entitle a person who acts on the advertisement to recover damages for loss of time or expense if the goods are not put up at all.[223]

(14) An auctioneer sells a bull at an auction of stud cattle. The bull proves infertile. The auctioneer is not liable for breach of the implied condition as to description and may sue for the price.[224]

(15) A director instructs estate agents to sell land, most of which is owned by his company but part of which he owns personally. Both he and his company are jointly and severally liable for the agents' commission.[225]

Agent's right to sue

9-035 (16) A contract was made in the following form: "It is mutually agreed between J. & R. W., of the one part, and S J C, on behalf of G. & M. Rail Co, of the other part, etc." (signed) "J & R W, S J C". Held, that S J C was entitled to sue in his own name for breach of the contract, he having contracted personally.[226]

(17) A broker contracted in writing in his own name to buy goods, the seller being told that there was a principal. The broker then, under a general authority from the principal, contracted to resell. On hearing of the last-mentioned contract, the principal refused to have anything to do with the goods, and the broker acquiesced. The seller then refused to deliver. Held, that the broker, having contracted personally, had a right to recover damages for the non-delivery, and that the principal's renunciation of the contract did not affect that right.[227]

(18) An auctioneer sells A's goods to a buyer who knows that they are A's property. The auctioneer may, nevertheless, sue in his own name for the price,[228] even where he has already been paid a sum sufficient to cover his commission and charges.[229] But if the contract can be treated by the buyer, who has not paid, as discharged for breach, it may be that the auctioneer cannot sue.[230]

(19) An auctioneer sued for the price of goods sold and delivered. The defendant pleaded that the plaintiff acted as an auctioneer, and that the defendant had paid the principal for the goods before action. Held, that the plea was bad, because the auctioneer would have had, as against the principal, a lien on the proceeds for charges, etc.[231] The defendant should have shown that, either by

---

[1904] 2 K.B. 322; *McManus v Fortescue* [1907] 2 K.B. 1; *Richards v Phillips* [1969] 1 Ch. 39. Compare the auctioneer's liability for breach of warranty of authority: Article 105.

[223] *Harris v Nickerson* (1873) L.R. 8 Q.B. 286. On these auctioneer cases see in general Murdoch, *Law of Estate Agency* (5th edn), p.167 onwards.

[224] *Elder Smith Goldsbrough Mort Ltd v McBride* [1976] 2 N.S.W.L.R. 631; cf. *Fraser v Dalgety & Co Ltd* [1953] N.Z.L.R. 126.

[225] *Savills (UK) Ltd v Blacker* [2017] EWCA Civ 68.

[226] *Cooke v Wilson* (1856) 1 C.B.(N.S.) 153; *Clay & Newman v Southern* (1852) 7 Exch. 717; *H.O. Brandt & Co v H.N. Morris & Co* [1917] 2 K.B. 784; cf. *Sharman v Brandt* (1871) L.R. 6 Q.B. 720.

[227] *Short v Spackman* (1831) 2 B. & Ad. 962.

[228] *Williams v Millington* (1788) 1 H.Bl. 81.

[229] *Chelmsford Auctions Ltd v Poole* [1973] Q.B. 542. See also *Fisher v Marsh* (1865) 6 B. & S. 411. But this does not apply to the sale of land: above, para.9-023.

[230] See *Dickenson v Naul* (1833) 4 B. & Ad. 638; see also discussion in *Elder Smith Goldsbrough Mort Ltd v McBride* [1976] 2 N.S.W.L.R. 631 at 648; above, para.9-023.

[231] *Robinson v Rutter* (1855) 4 E. & B. 954.

the conditions of sale or by facts accruing subsequently, payment to the principal was permitted in discharge of the plaintiff's claim.

(20) An auctioneer, on behalf of A, sold goods to B. A was indebted to B, and there was an agreement between them before the sale that the price of any goods bought by B should be set off against the debt, but the auctioneer had no notice of the agreement. The auctioneer permitted B to take away the goods, thinking that he was going to pay for them, B thinking that he was taking them in pursuance of his agreement with A. The auctioneer paid A on account and after receiving notice of the agreement between A and B, paid A the balance of the proceeds of the sale, such balance exceeding the amount of B's purchases. The auctioneer subsequently sued B for the price of the goods. Held, that the auctioneer's charges having been paid before action, and he having had notice of the agreement between A and B at the time of his payment to A (exceeding the amount for which he was suing B), the settlement between A and B constituted a good defence.[232] Here, the auctioneer was not really prejudiced by the settlement with the principal.

(21) A factor sold, in his own name, goods on which he had a lien for advances. While the advances were unpaid, the factor's right to sue the purchaser and compel payment had priority to that of the principal or his trustee in bankruptcy.[233]

(22) A broker sold, in his own name, goods on which he had made advances. The buyer had no right, in an action by the broker for the price, to set off a debt due to him from the principal.[234]

(23) A, acting as *del credere* agent on behalf of B, a timber exporter, sold a cargo of timber to C. A, in accordance with the contract of agency, paid to B the price of the timber, less A's commission; and, in accordance with the contract of sale, C accepted bills of exchange drawn by A for the price of the timber. When the timber arrived, C rejected it on the ground that it was not as specified, and it was found that he was entitled so to do. C dishonoured his acceptances. Held, that A was not the trustee or agent of B in respect of A's rights as holder of the bills of exchange; that there was no failure of consideration for the bills, which were separate contracts between A and C, and were not affected by the failure of consideration under the contract for sale of the timber; and that C was liable to A for the amount of the bills.[235]

(24) A stockbroking company as agent for unidentified and unascertained principals ("clients of the company") made a contract to lend money on conditions including that the borrower would make an Initial Public Offering ("IPO") by set date. The money was advanced but the IPO did not occur.

---

[232] *Grice v Kenrick* (1870) L.R. 5 Q.B. 340; *Holmes v Tutton* (1855) 5 E. & B. 65; see explanation of these cases in *Chelmsford Auctions Ltd v Poole* [1973] Q.B. 542 at 549; cf. *Manley & Sons Ltd v Berkett* [1912] 2 K.B. 329. On these auctioneer cases, see in general Murdoch, *Law of Estate Agency* (5th edn), p.167 onwards; Derham, *Law of Set-Off* (4th edn), paras 13.101–13.102.

[233] *Drinkwater v Goodwin* (1775) 1 Cowp. 251. See above, para.1-046.

[234] *Atkyns and Batten v Amber* (1796) 2 Esp. 493. But this case was doubted in *Bramwell v Spiller* (1870) 21 L.T. 672.

[235] *Churchill & Sim v Goddard* [1937] 1 K.B. 92; *Hindle v Brown* (1908) 98 L.T. 791; *Pollway Ltd v Abdullah* [1974] 1 W.L.R. 493; *Pendergrast v Chapman* [1988] 2 N.Z.L.R. 177. cf. *Barton, Thompson & Co v Vigers Bros* (1906) 19 Com.Cas. 175; *Jordeson & Co v London Hardwood Co* (1913) 110 L.T. 666; *Flatau, Dick & Co v Keeping* (1931) 39 Ll.L.Rep. 42; *Turnbull & Jones Ltd v Amner & Sons* [1923] N.Z.L.R. 673.

Properly construed, the agent alone was party to the contract (its principals each to provide part of the funds), and hence entitled to sue to recover the loan funds.[236]

Article 99

WRITTEN CONTRACTS

9-036   The question whether the agent is to be deemed to have contracted personally, in the case of a contract in writing other than a deed, bill of exchange, promissory note or cheque, depends upon the intention of the parties, as appearing from the terms of the written agreement as a whole, the construction of which is a matter of law.[237] The party concerned may act as agent in some respects and as principal (including as trustee) in others.[238]

Comment

9-037   In the context of a written contract, an agent may be held liable and entitled rather more easily than in unwritten contracts, because of the interpretation put by the court on words used. There is also a sizeable body of case law in this area which can be cited as precedent in disputes. This is particularly the case in relation to small companies, the owner-managers of which frequently fail to make clear whether they are signing personally or on behalf of their company.[239]

The cases on this topic should only be treated as single instances exemplifying the application of a rather imprecise principle; much turns on the particular context of each contract. Some of the older cases have been overruled,[240] and some may not be able to stand—in particular those which turned on the assumption, at one time held, that the agent must be liable if the principal was not,[241] for it has been clear that in such cases the agent's liability is based on a separate contract,[242] a warranty of authority.[243] Generalisations about particular formulae are dangerous.[244]

The following rules have, however, appeared in previous editions and still seem valid starting points:

(a)   If the contract is signed by the agent personally without qualification, the

---

[236] *Carminco Gold & Resources Ltd v Findlay & Co Stockbrokers (Underwriters) Pty Ltd* (2007) 243 A.L.R. 472.

[237] See *Universal Steam Navigation Co v McKelvie* [1923] A.C. 492; *Bowes v Shand* (1877) 2 App.Cas. 455; *The Swan* [1968] 1 Lloyd's Rep. 5, Illustration 6 to Article 98; Illustrations. See also criticism of the decisions in Stoljar, pp.251–256.

[238] *British Energy Power & Trading Ltd v Credit Suisse* [2008] EWCA Civ 413; [2008] 1 Lloyd's Rep. 413 ("as agent and security trustee" in context of syndicated loan agreement).

[239] See, e.g. *Badgerhill Properties Ltd v Cottrell* [1991] B.C.L.C. 805, Illustration 16 to Article 99; *Hamid v Francis Bradshaw Partnership* [2013] EWCA Civ 470.

[240] e.g. *Lennard v Robinson* (1855) 5 E. & B. 125; overruled in *Universal Steam Navigation Co v McKelvie* [1923] A.C. 492; *Paice v Walker* (1870) L.R. 5 Ex. 173; disapproved in *Gadd v Houghton* (1876) 1 Ex.D. 357. It was formerly thought that the form of the signature was conclusive.

[241] *Downman v Williams* (1845) 7 Q.B. 103, Illustration 2; *Harper v Williams* (1843) 4 Q.B. 219.

[242] *Lewis v Nicholson* (1852) 18 Q.B. 503; *Jenkins v Hutchinson* (1849) 13 Q.B. 744.

[243] Article 105.

[244] Two cases worth particular study are *Gadd v Houghton* (1876) 1 Ex.D. 357, Illustration 11; and *Universal Steam Navigation Co v McKelvie* [1923] A.C. 492, Illustration 13.

agent is deemed to have contracted personally[245] unless a contrary intention plainly appears from other portions of the document.[246]

(b)   The mere fact that the agent is described as an agent, director, secretary,
manager, broker, etc. whether by words connected with or forming part of
the signature,[247] or in the body of the contract,[248] and whether or not the
principal is named, raises no presumption that the agent did not intend to
contract personally; but here again an intention to contract as agent only
may be gathered from the whole document and surrounding
circumstances.[249]

(c)   But if the agent adds to a signature words indicating that he or she signs as
agent, or for or on behalf or on account of a principal, the agent is deemed
not to have contracted personally,[250] unless it is plain from other portions of
the document that, notwithstanding such qualified signature, the agent
intended to be bound.[251] This is so even though the principal is unnamed.[252]
But this proposition should be read subject to Article 102(2) regarding the
liability of agents under trade custom.

As in other cases, care should be taken to ascertain exactly what liability an agent
undertakes, if the agent does appear to contract personally.[253] Although most of the
cases assume that the agent is the only party to the contract, this need not necessarily be so.[254] Extrinsic evidence is admissible to clarify a written contract,[255] provided

---

[245]   Illustration 5. And see *Lavan v Walsh* [1964] I.R. 87; and *Transcontinental Underwriting Agencies
Srl v Grand Union Insurance Co Ltd* [1987] 2 Lloyd's Rep. 409, where this formulation is approved; *Farncombe v Sperling* (1922) 66 S.J. 312; *Ernest Scragg & Son Ltd v Perserverance Banking and Trust Co Ltd* [1973] 2 Lloyd's Rep. 101; *Sika Contracts Ltd v B.S. Gill* (1978) 9 Build. L.R.
11, Illustration 10.

[246]   Illustrations 6 and 11; *Concordia Chemische Fabrik auf Actien v Squire* (1876) 34 L.T. 824. But cf.
Illustration 12, where the indications in the document were not sufficiently clear.

[247]   *Hutcheson v Eaton* (1884) 13 Q.B.D. 861 ("brokers"). As to the term "agent", see *Universal Steam
Navigation Co v McKelvie* [1923] A.C. 492, at 501: "When people add 'agent' to a signature to a
contract, they are trying to escape personal liability, but are unaware that the attempt will fail". But
see Comment to Article 100(1).

[248]   Illustrations 1, 2 (first part), 4 and 5.

[249]   Illustrations 2 (second part) and 3.

[250]   Illustrations 12 and 13. In *Gadd v Houghton* (1876) 1 Ex.D. 357 at 359 James LJ said: "When a man
says that he is making a contract 'on account of' someone else, it seems to me that he uses the very
strongest terms the English language affords to shew that he is not binding himself, but is binding
his principal".

[251]   Illustration 14; *Paice v Walker* (1870) L.R. 5 Ex. 173 (but this case was disapproved in *Gadd v
Houghton* (1876) 1 Ex.D. 357); *Weidner v Hoggett* (1876) 1 C.P.D. 533. But such a contingency is
unlikely: see *Universal Steam Navigation Co v McKelvie* [1923] A.C. 492 at 499, per Lord Shaw:
"But I desire to say that in my opinion the appending of the word 'agents' to the signature of a party
to a mercantile contract is, in all cases, the dominating factor in the solution of the problem of
principal or agent. A highly improbable and conjectural case (in which this dominating factor might
be overcome by other parts of the contract) may by an effort of the imagination be figured, but, apart
from that, the appending of the word 'agent' to the signature is a conclusive assertion of agency, and
a conclusive rejection of the responsibility of a principal, and is and must be accepted in that twofold
sense by the other contracting party".

[252]   *Southwell v Bowditch* (1876) 1 C.P.D. 374, Illustration 3; *Chartwell Shipping Ltd v Q.N.S. Paper
Co Ltd* [1989] 2 S.C.R. 683; (1989) 62 D.L.R. (4th) 36, Illustration 9.

[253]   *Universal Steam Navigation Co v McKelvie* [1923] A.C. 492 at 501. See Comment to Article 100.

[254]   See, e.g. *Stag Line Ltd v Tyne Shiprepair Group Ltd (The Zinnia)* [1984] 2 Lloyd's Rep. 211 at 216;
Seatrade Groningen BV v Geest Industries Ltd (The Frost Express) [1996] 2 Lloyd's Rep. 375, Illustration 7; above, para.9-006.

[255]   See *McCollin v Gilpin* (1881) 6 Q.B.D. 516, Illustration 2; *Young v Schuler* (1883) 11 Q.B.D. 651;

that it is not inconsistent with the contract.[256] It is not impossible for a person to sign both personally and also as agent of another.[257]

In the case of signatures for companies, a further distinction must be taken between cases where an agent signs as agent, which are governed by the above rules, and those where that person signs as the company, viz. simply purports to authenticate the company's signature and so does not even sign as agent. In this latter case the agent's liability or right to sue will be difficult to establish.[258]

Illustrations

9-038   (1)   An agent entered into a written agreement to grant a lease of certain premises. He was described in the agreement as making it on behalf of the principal, but in a subsequent portion of the document it was provided that he (the agent) would execute the lease. Held, that the agent was liable for a breach of the agreement, though the premises belonged to the principal.[259]

(2)   The directors of a company signed a contract in the following terms: "We, the undersigned, three of the directors, agree to repay £500 advanced by A to the company", and at the same time assigned to A, as security, certain property belonging to the company. Held, that the directors were personally liable.[260] But when an agent signed a contract in the following form: "I undertake, on behalf of A [the principal], to pay, etc." it was held that he was not personally liable.[261]

(3)   A broker sent a contract note in the following terms: "Messrs. S.—I have this day sold by your order and for your account to my principal, etc., one per cent. brokerage"; (signed) "W A B". Held, that W A B was not personally liable in an action for goods sold.[262]

(4)   A solicitor wrote: "I hereby undertake to pay on behalf of these creditors [his clients] two-thirds" of certain expenses. Held, that he was personally liable.[263] So, the solicitor of the assignees of a bankrupt tenant was held personally liable on an undertaking as follows: "I, as solicitor to the assignees, undertake to pay the landlord his rent, provided it does not exceed the value of the effects distrained".[264]

Automobiles Renault Canada Ltd v Maritime Import Autos Ltd (1961) 31 D.L.R. (2d) 592.

[256] See Article 100.

[257] See Illustration 14; Article 98.

[258] See *Newborne v Sensolid (Great Britain) Ltd* [1954] 1 Q.B. 45, Illustration 6 to Article 107; *Black v Smallwood* (1966) 117 C.L.R. 52 at 61–62 (Illustration 7 to Article 107); above, para.1-029; below, para.9-082.

[259] *Norton v Herron* (1825) 1 C. & P. 648; *Tanner v Christian* (1855) 4 E. & B. 591; cf. *Spittle v Lavender* (1821) 5 Moo.C.P. 270.

[260] *McCollin v Gilpin* (1881) 6 Q.B.D. 516. See also *H.O. Brandt & Co v H.N. Morris & Co* [1917] 2 K.B. 784.

[261] *Downman v Williams* (1845) 7 Q.B. 103; *Glover v Langford* (1892) 8 T.L.R. 628; *W.T. Avery Ltd v Charlesworth* (1914) 31 T.L.R. 52.

[262] *Southwell v Bowditch* (1876) 1 C.P.D. 374; *Sunnyvale Property Trust v Liu* [2015] NZHC 2804 (agent not liable on contract for sale of land between named parties when signed for principal without reference to his being an agent).

[263] *Hall v Ashurst* (1833) 1 C. & M. 714; *Lavan v Walsh* [1964] I.R. 87 ("sale to the writer in trust for a client"). See also *Weidner v Hoggett* (1876) 1 C.P.D. 533; cf. *Allaway v Duncan* (1867) 16 L.T. 264.

[264] *Burrell v Jones* (1819) 3 B. & A. 47; *Harper v Williams* (1843) 4 Q.B. 219; cf. *Lewis v Nicholson* (1852) 18 Q.B. 503.

(5)   A charterparty was expressed to be made between A B and C D, agent for E F & Son, and was signed by C D, without qualification. Held, that C D was personally liable, though the principals were named, there being nothing in the terms of the contract clearly inconsistent with an intention to contract personally.[265]

(6)   A charterparty states that it is entered into between "A, owners" and "B, charterers". A clause in it provides "This vessel was chartered on behalf of C". B is liable as charterer.[266]

(7)   A charterparty is signed "SG as agents to owners or as disponent owners". SG is personally liable; the actual vessel owners may be also.[267]

(8)   Repairs are arranged for a vessel by telex and a document is signed headed "Agreement between 'Cape Hatteras' and 'Astican'" (the repairers). The contract is with the owners of the Cape Hatteras, whoever they may be.[268]

(9)   Ship's agents write to two firms "As Managing Operators for the charterers we are again pleased to appoint you as agents for the vessel's forthcoming call"; "On behalf of our principals we are again pleased to appoint you as agent for the above-mentioned vessel". The first letter is signed by them "C Shipping Ltd", the second "C Shipping Ltd as agents". They are not personally liable on either contract.[269]

(10)   A tender is accepted in these words: "We have pleasure in informing you that your tender dated 19th July 1974 has been accepted ... Yours faithfully, BS, Chartered Civil Engineer". The signer is personally liable.[270]

(11)   Fruit brokers in Liverpool signed in their own names without qualification a contract in the following form: "We have this day sold to you on account of J M & Co, Valencia, etc.". Held, the brokers were not personally liable, the word "on account" clearly showing that there was no intention to contract personally.[271]

(12)   A charterparty is signed "for A B, of L, C Bros, as agents". C Bros are not

[265] *Parker v Winslow* (1857) 7 E. & B. 942. See also *Cooke v Wilson* (1856) 1 C.B.(N.S.) 153; *Hick v Tweedy* (1890) 63 L.T. 765. cf. Illustration 12. See also *The Elikon* [2003] EWCA Civ 812; [2003] 2 Lloyd's Rep. 430 (charterparty named owners as "A c/o B": signed by B without qualification: B, but not A, party to contract).

[266] *Tudor Marine Ltd v Tradax Export SA (The Virgo)* [1976] 2 Lloyd's Rep. 135. See also *Pyxis Special Shipping Co Ltd v Dritas & Kaglis Bros Ltd (The Scaplake)* [1978] 2 Lloyd's Rep. 380 (noted [1979] J.B.L. 150); *Jugoslavenska Linijska Plovidba v Hulsman (The Primorje)* [1980] 2 Lloyd's Rep. 74; *Et. Biret et Cie SA v Yukiteru Kaiun KK (The Sun Happiness)* [1984] 1 Lloyd's Rep. 381. See also *Electrosteel Castings Ltd v Scan-Trans Shipping and Chartering Sdn. Bhd* [2002] EWHC 1993 (Comm); [2003] 1 Lloyd's Rep. 190 (chartering: later booking note signed as agents superseded earlier recap telex).

[267] *Seatrade Groningen BV v Geest Industries Ltd (The Frost Express)* [1996] 2 Lloyd's Rep. 375.

[268] *Astilleros Canarios SA v Cape Hatteras Shipping Co Inc (The Cape Hatteras)* [1982] 1 Lloyd's Rep. 518; *Armour v Duff & Co* 1912 S.C. 120. Importance may be attached to the fact that if the contract is with the owner, it will often be possible to arrest a ship; cf. *Dawson (Ship Stores) v Atlantica Co Ltd* (1931) 40 Ll.Rep. 63 (contract with agent); *The Swan* [1968] 1 Lloyd's Rep. 5, Illustration 6 to Article 98 (contract with both: above, para.9-006). As to oral contracts see Article 101, Illustration 3.

[269] *Chartwell Shipping Ltd v Q.N.S. Paper Co Ltd* [1989] 2 S.C.R. 683; (1989) 62 D.L.R. (4th) 36.

[270] *Sika Contracts Ltd v B.S. Gill* (1978) 9 Build. L.R. 11. See also *Fraser v Equitorial Shipping Co Ltd (The Ijaola)* [1979] 1 Lloyd's Rep. 103.

[271] *Gadd v Houghton* (1876) 1 Ex.D. 357; disapproving *Paice v Walker* (1870) L.R. 5 Ex. 173 (but see *Hough & Co v Manzanos & Co* (1874) 4 Ex.D. 104); *Ogden v Hall* (1879) 40 L.T. 751; *Mercer v Wright, Graham & Co* (1917) 33 T.L.R. 343, *Lester v Balfour Williamson & Co* [1953] 2 Q.B. 168; cf. *H.O. Brandt & Co v H.N. Morris & Co* [1917] 2 K.B. 784.

liable, unless it clearly appears from the body of the contract that they intended to bind themselves.[272] So, where a contract was signed "G W, J L, for C J M & Co", it was held that G W and J L were not personally liable.[273]

(13) A charterparty was signed "For and on behalf of James McKelvie and Co as agents, J.A. McKelvie", but James McKelvie & Co were described in the body of the agreement as charterers. Held, that James McKelvie & Co were not personally liable, the qualified signature indicating an intention to exclude personal liability.[274]

(14) An agent signed a contract—"p p A, J A & Co, A B". The contract contained a clause providing that A B should guarantee moneys due from his principal to the other contracting party. Parol evidence was admitted to show that A B intended to sign, not only as an agent, but also as a surety. Held, that such evidence was rightly admitted, and that he must be taken to have signed in both capacities.[275]

(15) An insurance policy is issued to "PN Bank, a/c E (Commodities) Ltd". The contract is with the bank.[276]

(16) A contract is signed "The Plumbing Centre, BT, Director". "The Plumbing Centre" is in fact the trade name of BP Ltd, whose name appears (inaccurately) at the foot of the page. The contract is with BP Ltd under its trade name and BT is not liable on it.[277]

Article 100

ADMISSIBILITY OF EXTRINSIC EVIDENCE

9-039 (1) Where it is clear from the terms of a written contract made by an agent that the agent is contracting personally, extrinsic evidence is not admissible to show that, notwithstanding the terms of the contract, it was the intention of the parties that the agent should not be personally liable on it, because such evidence would be contradictory to the written contract.[278]

(2) But where it appears from the terms of a written contract made by an agent that the agent is contracting as agent, extrinsic evidence is nevertheless admis-

---

[272] *Deslandes v Gregory* (1860) 30 L.J.Q.B. 36; *Green v Kopke* (1856) 18 C.B. 549; *Miller, Gibb & Co v Smith & Tyrer* [1917] 2 K.B. 141.

[273] *Redpath v Wigg* (1866) L.R. 1 Ex. 335; *Mahony v Kekulé* (1854) 14 C.B. 390.

[274] *Universal S.N. Co v McKelvie* [1923] A.C. 492; overruling *Lennard v Robinson* (1855) 5 E. & B. 125. See also *Kimber Coal Co v Stone & Rolfe Ltd* [1926] A.C. 414; *Dragages et Travaux Publics v Gladhover Ltd* [1988] 1 H.K.L.R. 298 ("between G for and on behalf of N and the contractors").

[275] *Young v Schuler* (1883) 11 Q.B.D. 651; *Ontario Marble Co Ltd v Creative Memorials Ltd* (1963) 39 D.L.R. (2d) 149; affirmed (1964) 45 D.L.R. (2d) 244; *VSH Ltd v BKS Air Transport Ltd* [1964] 1 Lloyd's Rep. 460; *Sun Alliance Pensions Life & Investments Services Ltd v Webster* [1991] 2 Lloyd's Rep. 410; *Elpis Maritime Co Ltd v Marti Chartering Co Inc (The Maria D)* [1992] 1 A.C. 21.

[276] *Punjab National Bank v de Boinville* [1992] 1 W.L.R. 1138.

[277] *Badgerhill Properties Ltd v Cottrell* [1991] B.C.L.C. 805. See also *Vic Spence Associates v Balchin* 1990 S.L.T. 10.

[278] *Higgins v Senior* (1841) 8 M. & W. 834, Illustration 1; *Magee v Atkinson* (1837) 2 M. & W. 440; *Sobell Industries v Cory Bros* [1955] 2 Lloyd's Rep. 82 Illustration 7 to Article 98; *Sika Contracts Ltd v B.S. Gill* (1978) 9 Build. L.R. 11, Illustration 10 to Article 99; *Transcontinental Underwriting Agency Srl v General Union Insurance Co Ltd* [1987] 2 Lloyd's Rep. 409; *K v S* [2015] EWHC 1945 (Comm). But see Comment.

sible to show that, by custom or usage in the particular trade or business, an agent so contracting is liable either absolutely or conditionally in addition to the principal,[279] provided that such custom or usage is not inconsistent with nor repugnant to the express terms of the written contract.[280]

Comment

Rule (1) It is sometimes said that parol or other extrinsic evidence may not be admitted to add to, vary or contradict a deed or written contract.[281] Such evidence may therefore not be adduced to delete an apparent contracting party (though it may be adduced to *add* a party, e.g. to establish the liability of the principal as well as the agent[282]). But this reasoning is only appropriate where the contract is exclusively contained in a document or documents: there may be documents (e.g. invoices) which do not purport to constitute the complete contract, and in such cases extrinsic evidence will certainly be admissible.[283]

9-040

Further, where a written document can be established not to represent the intention of the parties as clearly agreed, it can be rectified in equity: and there are a few cases holding that the fact that it would be rectified could be pleaded as a defence to a common law action.[284] This can apparently be pleaded even by a plaintiff,[285] and a party can plead that he is not liable, even though it is not established who, if anyone, is liable, provided it is clear that the true intention of the parties was that the person concerned should not be. Thus where an agent made a charterparty and signed it "for X Co A, agents" on the express undertaking that the signatory was acting only as agent and that the use of this formula was the correct way of expressing this, the agent was held to have a good defence to an action on the charterparty.[286] Even if these cases are correct, situations where such clear evidence is available will be rare. It is not clear to what extent the defence is subject to the normal rules relating to the availability of rectification (e.g. that a third party must not be prejudiced), and, of course, the extent to which equity will relieve against mistakes of law as opposed to fact is in general by no means clear.[287] On general principles, any operative mistake would have to be common to the parties, or there

---

[279] Illustrations 2 to 4.

[280] Illustrations 5 and 6. And see Article 31.

[281] *Jacobs v Batavia & General Plantations Trust Ltd* [1924] 1 Ch. 287 at 295 (an extreme formulation). See *Chitty on Contracts* (33rd edn), para.13-109 onwards; McLauchlan, *The Parol Evidence Rule* (Wellington, NZ, 1976); *Law Com. No.154* (1986) for full discussion of this often misunderstood topic.

[282] *Higgins v Senior* (1841) 8 M. & W. 834 at 844. See further Comment to Article 71. As to cases where the principal is undisclosed, see Comment to Article 76.

[283] *Rogers v Hadley* (1861) 2 H. & C. 227; *Holding v Elliott* (1860) 5 H. & N. 117.

[284] *Wake v Harrop* (1862) 1 H. & C. 202; affirming 6 H. & N. 768; *Cowie v Witt* (1874) 23 W.R. 76. And see *Breslauer v Barwick* (1876) 36 L.T. 52; *Mostyn v West Mostyn Coal & Iron Co* (1876) 1 C.P.D. 145; Senior Courts Act 1981 s.49. The possibility of a collateral contract to the same effect is discussed in a note on *Farncombe v Sperling* (1922) 66 S.J. 312; it is possible that breach of a collateral contract might bar an action on the main contract (see *Benjamin's Sale of Goods* (10th edn), para.10-014). *Wake v Harrop* was applied at first instance in Australia in *Alliance Acceptance Co Ltd v Oakley* (1987) 45 S.A.S.R. 148; but on appeal the decision was reversed on grounds which made *Wake v Harrop* irrelevant: (1988) 48 S.A.S.R. 337.

[285] *Breslauer v Barwick* (1876) 36 L.T. 52.

[286] *Wake v Harrop* (1862) 1 H. & C. 202.

[287] See Kerr, *Fraud and Mistake* (7th edn), p.133 onwards; uncertainty now arises as to the reach of the decision of the House of Lords in *Kleinwort Benson Ltd v Lincoln CC* [1999] 2 A.C. 349, concerning money paid under mistake of law.

would have to be some unconscionable conduct on the part of the person not mistaken.[288]

9-041 **Rule (2)**   Where a person signs a contract as agent only, that person is prima facie not liable. However, the rules referred to above do not prevent evidence being adduced to establish who the principal is (though if the case is one regulated by the Statute of Frauds, the principal's identity must be clear from the memorandum[289]); or to establish that, notwithstanding the fact that the agent signed as agent, it was intended that he or she should in fact additionally be liable to some extent not inconsistent with the primary liability of the principal (in which case the agent's signature would satisfy the Statute of Frauds[290]). The cases in this area suggest that the agent may fairly readily be held liable together with, as opposed to instead of, the principal: usages that hold the agent liable have always been common[291] and may be increasing.[292]

Illustrations

9-042 (1) An iron commission agent receives an order to purchase iron from a named company but sends in return a sold note saying "We have this day sold ... to Messrs H & Sons ... " and signs it "JB & Co, WS". Although JB & Co are "notoriously an agent" they are in this instance personally liable.[293]

(2) An agent signed a charterparty expressly "as agent to merchants", the principals being unnamed. It was held that, although it plainly appeared that he did not intend to contract as principal, it might nevertheless be proved that, by a general custom, an agent so signing was, in the ordinary course of trade, personally liable on the contract in the event of his not identifying the principals within a reasonable time. Such a custom was not inconsistent with the terms of the contract as the primary liability was that of the unnamed principals.[294]

(3) A broker entered into a contract in the following terms: "Sold by A to Messrs. B, for and on account of owner, 100 bales of hops". An action was brought against A for not delivering the hops according to sample. Evidence of a custom in the hop trade, whereby a broker who does not identify his principal at the time of the contract is personally liable, was admitted, and the broker was held liable on the contract.[295]

(4) A and B, who were brokers, contracted in the following terms: "We have this day sold for your account to our principal, etc." (signed) "A and B, brokers".

---

[288] As to rectification in general, see Snell's Equity (34th edn), Ch.16.

[289] See *Lovesy v Palmer* [1916] 2 Ch. 233; above, paras 8-003 and 8-004.

[290] See *Dale v Humfrey* (1858) E.B. & E. 1004.

[291] See Illustrations; Marine Insurance Act 1906 ss.53 and 54. As to proof of custom or usage, see Article 31. Sometime the agent's liability ceases on naming a principal. As to the 1906 Act, see Hon. Mrs Justice Gloster [2007] L.M.C.L.Q. 302.

[292] See Comment to Article 98.

[293] *Higgins v Senior* (1841) 8 M. & W. 834.

[294] *Hutchinson v Tatham* (1873) L.R. 8 C.P. 482 (collateral contract).

[295] *Pike v Ongley* (1887) 18 Q.B.D. 708; *Dale v Humfrey* (1858) E.B. & E. 1004 (similar custom in fruit trade); *Thornton v Fehr* (1935) 51 Ll. L. Rep. 330 (tallow trade); *Anglo Overseas Transport Ltd v Titan Industrial Corp* [1959] 2 Lloyd's Rep. 152 (forwarding agents); *Perishables Transport Co v Spyropoulos* [1964] 2 Lloyd's Rep. 379 (air forwarding agents); cf. *Wilson v Avec Audio-Visual Equipment Ltd* [1974] 1 Lloyd's Rep. 81 (no such usage for insurance broker).

Some of the goods were accepted by the principal, whose name was declared by A and B before delivery, and an action was subsequently brought against A and B for not accepting the residue. Held, that they were personally liable, it being proved that by a custom in the particular trade, the broker was personally liable for his principal's default unless the name of the principal was inserted in the written contract.[296] So, by the usage of the London dry goods market, where a broker bought goods for an unnamed principal, he was personally liable for the price.[297]

(5) Brokers entered, as such, into a contract which contained a clause providing that they should act as arbitrators in the event of any dispute between the parties. Held, that evidence of a custom rendering them personally liable on the contract was inadmissible, because the custom was inconsistent with the clause appointing them arbitrators.[298]

(6) Agents sign a contract in a clearly representative capacity. It is argued that since their principals are foreign, they are personally liable. Even when such a custom existed, it would here be inconsistent with the contract.[299]

Article 101

ORAL CONTRACTS

Where an agent makes a contract which is not reduced to writing, the question whether the agent contracted personally, together with the principal or solely as agent is a question of fact.[300] **9-043**

Comment

The proposition contained in this Article means nowadays little more than that general rules or presumptions cannot be laid down for such cases, whereas precedents can be cited on the interpretation of documents.[301] An appellate tribunal may also be more reluctant to interfere with findings of fact as to oral contracts[302]; and in many cases an appeal only lies on point of law. **9-044**

Unidentified principals One area in which a rule might be thought to exist is that of unidentified principals. *Restatement, Third* provides that where an agent acts for an unidentified principal the principal and the third party are parties to the contract and the agent is (also) a party to the contract unless the agent and the third party agree otherwise.[303] Such a rule would to some extent avoid problems about the third **9-045**

---

[296] *Fleet v Murton* (1871) L.R. 7 Q.B. 126 (fruit trade and colonial market). Similar custom in the rice trade: *Bacmeister v Fenton Levy & Co* (1883) Cab. & El. 121.
[297] *Imperial Bank v London & St Katharine Docks Co* (1877) 5 Ch.D. 195 (agent held a surety).
[298] *Barrow & Bros v Dyster, Nalder & Co* (1884) 13 Q.B.D. 635.
[299] *Miller, Gibb & Co v Smith & Tyrer Ltd* [1917] 2 K.B. 141. As to the alleged custom, see above, para.9-020.
[300] See Illustrations; *Castle v Duke* (1832) 5 C. & P. 359; *Gurney v Womersley* (1854) 4 E. & B. 133; *Lakeman v Mountstephen* (1874) L.R. 7 H.L. 17; *Blake v Melrose* [1950] N.Z.L.R. 781.
[301] *The Swan* [1968] 1 Lloyd's Rep. 5 at 12.
[302] e.g. *Gardiner v Heading* [1928] 2 K.B. 284.
[303] § 6.02(2).

party's right to ascertain the name of the principal.[304] In *The Santa Carina* (Illustration 2), however, the Court of Appeal refused to accept such a proposed rule formulated in similar terms to those of *Restatement, Second*[305] and said that the question was entirely one of fact; and that for the agent's additional liability there would have to be some indication, whether from trade custom[306] or special facts,[307] which did not exist in that case. This means that the presumption is that the agent is not liable unless there are indications to displace it.[308] It has already been suggested, however,[309] that the close connection of such cases with undisclosed principal cases, where the agent is liable and entitled, mean that there is a good case for a prima facie rule as in the *Restatement*.

Illustrations

9-046 (1) Brokers sell goods by auction and invoice them in their own names as sellers. It is a question of fact whether the invoice was intended to be the contract. If it was, the brokers are personally liable. If not, it is a question of fact whether they intended to contract personally.[310]

(2) Stores are supplied to, or repairs effected on, a ship on the oral orders of the ship's agent. In appropriate cases the agent may be held to have assumed personal liability.[311]

(3) Brokers on the Baltic Exchange order bunkers from other brokers, also members of the Baltic, for a ship at Penang. The order is given on the telephone without indication of the capacity in which either party is acting. The bunkers are not paid for. The first broker does not expect the second broker to effect the bunkering himself: the second broker knows that the first broker does not own ships. The first broker is not personally liable.[312]

---

[304] See above, para.9-017.

[305] § 321, to similar effect to *Restatement, Third*, § 6.02(2), above.

[306] See Article 100.

[307] e.g. that the principal is foreign: see *Fraser v Equitorial Shipping Co Ltd (The Ijaolo)* [1979] 1 Lloyd's Rep. 103; above, para.9-020.

[308] See also *Wilson v Avec Audio-Visual Equipment Ltd* [1974] 1 Lloyd's Rep. 81 at 83.

[309] See above, para.9-016.

[310] *Holding v Elliott* (1860) 5 H. & N. 117.

[311] See *Fraser-Johnston Engineering, etc., Co v Sam Isaacs (Aberdeen) Ltd* (1922) 12 Ll. L. Rep. 233; *Beliard, Crighton (Belgium) Ltd v Charles Lowe & Partners Ltd* (1922) 13 Ll. L. Rep. 567; *Evans & Reid Coal Co Ltd v McNabb, Rougier & Co (Italy) Ltd* (1924) 18 Ll. L. Rep. 471; *J.D. McLaren & Co v Nomikos* [1961] 1 Lloyd's Rep. 318; *Freimuller (Ship Stores) v Ocean Carriers (London) Ltd* [1961] 2 Lloyd's Rep. 309; *Victory Shipchandlers v Leslie & Anderson Ltd* [1972] E. Africa L.Rep. 42. Sometimes the agent is made liable by statute: see New Zealand Carriage of Goods Act 1979 s.29 (ship's agents). See also *Lamont v Hamilton* 1907 S.C. 628 (insurance); *H.J. Lyons & Sando Ltd v Houlson* [1963] S.A.S.R. 29 (car repairs); cf. *Whitwell v Perrin* (1858) 4 C.B.(N.S.) 412; *Eastman v Harry* (1875) 33 L.T. 800. As to written contracts see Article 99, Illustration 8. The liability of a local agent may be an advantage: on the other hand where the contract is with the shipowner there may be a right to arrest a ship; cf. Article 98, Illustration 6; Article 99, Illustration 8.

[312] *N. & J. Vlassopulos Ltd v Ney Shipping Ltd (The Santa Carina)* [1977] 1 Lloyd's Rep. 478. See also *Marina Shipping Ltd v Laughton* [1982] Q.B. 1127; *A/S Hansen-Tangens Rederi III v Total Transport Corp (The Sagona)* [1984] 1 Lloyd's Rep. 194 at 198–199 (shipping agent arranging port facilities acts for charterer); *Shipping Co Uniform Inc v Intl Transport Workers' Fedn (The Uniform Star)* [1985] 1 Lloyd's Rep. 173.

Article 102

DEEDS

Where an agent is a party to a deed and executes it personally, the agent is person- **9-047**
ally liable and entitled on it, even when described in the deed as acting for and on
behalf of a named principal.[313]

Comment

This rule, which is an application of the strict rules relating to deeds, applies even **9-048**
though the agent executes it specifically on behalf of the principal: a fortiori if it is
executed personally, merely adding descriptive words. To escape liability the agent
must purport to execute the deed as the principal's deed.[314] However, by virtue of
s.7(1) of the Powers of Attorney Act 1971[315] an agent with a power of attorney may
execute a deed by personal signature, and it may be that the agent is exempt from
liability in such circumstances, at least so long as the agent's representative capacity is indicated. If so, the rules for deeds are now in these circumstances the same
as for other written contracts. The matter is discussed elsewhere.[316]

Illustrations

(1) A, on behalf of B, contracted by deed to purchase certain houses, and **9-049**
covenanted that he (A) would pay £800 for them. The houses were destroyed.
Held, that A was personally liable to pay the £800, although he had no effects
in his hands belonging to B.[317] If A covenants under his own hand and seal for
the act of B, A is personally liable, though he describes himself as covenant-
ing for and on behalf of B.[318]

(2) A person signs a deed "signed as agent for and on behalf of CIC". CIC is a
French company, but its corporate title is not given. The signer is personally
liable.[319]

(3) A mortgagee by deed contracted for a tenancy of the mortgaged property, the
contract being expressed to be made between the mortgagee "as agent,
hereinafter called the landlord", and the tenant. Held, that it was a question of
construction who was the lessor, and on the true construction the contract was
that of the mortgagee, and that the mere use of the words "as agent" was not
sufficient to prevent the demise operating on the legal estate of the
mortgagee.[320]

---

[313] See Illustrations; *Plant Engineers (Sales) Ltd v Davies* (1969) 113 S.J. 484 (liquidator); Article 77.
[314] See Article 77; *Lundie v Rowena Nominees Pty Ltd* (2007) 32 W.A.R. 404 (see para.9-016, above).
[315] Replacing Law of Property Act 1925 s.123; as amended by Law of Property (Miscellaneous Provisions) Act 1989.
[316] Article 77.
[317] *Cass v Rudele* (1692) 2 Vern. 280.
[318] *Appleton v Binks* (1804) 5 East 148; *Bacon v Dubarry* (1697) 1 Ld.Raym. 246.
[319] *Bailey v de Kerangat*, CA, December 7, 1993 (but the case was actually decided on general agency
principles).
[320] *Chapman v Smith* [1907] 2 Ch. 97.

Article 103

BILLS, NOTES AND CHEQUES

9-050   (1)   An agent is not personally liable on a bill of exchange, promissory note or cheque unless the agent's name appears on it.[321]

(2)   Where a person signs a bill as drawer, indorser or acceptor, and adds words to the signature indicating that he or she signs for or on behalf of a principal, or in a representative character, that person is not personally liable on it; but the mere addition to the signature of words "agent", or as filling a representative character, does not exempt the signatory from personal liability.[322]

(3)   But no person can be liable as acceptor of a bill except the person on whom it is drawn, except where it is accepted for honour.[323]

(4)   In determining whether the signature on a bill is that of the principal or that of the agent by whose hand it is written, the construction most favourable to the validity of the instrument will be adopted.[324]

Comment

9-051   **Rule (1)**   These rules are to be justified on the ground that negotiable instruments are likely to come into the hands of persons who have no knowledge of the circumstances in which they were issued; such persons must be able to rely on what appears on the fact of the instrument.

9-052   **Rule (2)**   In this case the Bills of Exchange Act 1882 provides when the agent contracts personally and when for the principal. In cases of drawing or indorsement the question is usually merely whether principal or agent is liable, and the problem therefore is as to whether additional words are merely descriptive or indicate that the agent signs solely in a representative capacity for another, viz. "says plainly 'I am the mere scribe'".[325] If the agent signs solely in such a capacity and has authority, the principal is bound; if the agent has no authority, the principal is not bound, and the agent is liable for breach of warranty of authority.

9-053   **Rule (3)**   Rule (3) raises difficulties. Where a bill is drawn on an agent but accepted by the agent in the principal's name and with its authority, the principal nevertheless cannot be bound[326]; but since the agent has not purported to act personally, it seems that the agent cannot be bound either.[327] Where the bill is drawn on the principal and accepted by the agent personally without qualification, equally the agent cannot be liable.[328]

9-054   **Rule (4)**   Where however in acceptance cases such as those above it is not clear

---

[321] Bills of Exchange Act 1882 ss.23 and 89. See e.g. *Maxform SpA v Mariani and Goodville* [1981] 2 Lloyd's Rep. 54. But see also Companies Act 2006 ss.82 and 84, and regulations made thereunder.

[322] Bills of Exchange Act 1882 s.26(2). See *Rolfe Lubbell & Co v Keith* [1979] 1 All E.R. 80.

[323] Bills of Exchange Act 1882 s.17(1). As to acceptance for honour, see ss.65–68.

[324] Bills of Exchange Act 1882 s.26(2).

[325] *Leadbitter v Farrow* (1816) 5 M. & S. 345 at 349. For full citation of the main cases on signatures, see *Byles on Bills of Exchange* (29th edn); *Chalmers and Guest on Bills of Exchange* (18th edn).

[326] Bills of Exchange Act 1882 s.17(1); *Polhill v Walter* (1832) 3 B. & Ad. 114; *Steele v M'Kinlay* (1880) 5 App.Cas. 754.

[327] Bills of Exchange Act 1882 s.26(1).

[328] Bills of Exchange Act 1882 s.17(1).

how the signature should be regarded, the presumption in favour of validity may assist in construing it as the signature of the drawee. The presumption only operates in cases of ambiguity,[329] and it is difficult to see that it can have much relevance in cases of drawing or indorsement, where the question is simply as to whether principal or agent is liable, for in both cases the signature will normally (i.e. in the absence or incapacity of one of the parties or the like) be operative.[330]

Trade, firm and company names Where an agent signs in a trade or assumed name, the agent is liable as if he or she had signed personally[331]; and the signature of a firm is equivalent to the signature by the person so signing of the names of all the persons liable as partners in that firm.[332] Whether the director or other officer of a company who signs on behalf of the company is personally liable depends on ordinary principles of construction.[333] Under former companies legislation,[334] if an officer of a company or a person on its behalf signed or authorised to be signed on behalf of the company any bill of exchange, promissory note, endorsement, cheque or order for money or goods in which the name of the company was not mentioned in legible characters, the signatory was liable to a fine and became personally liable on it unless payment was made by the company.[335] Only the criminal consequences were preserved in the Companies Act 2006 ss.82–84, leaving the civil law consequences to be determined by the common law.

9-055

Illustrations

(1) An agent draws a bill in his own name. He is personally liable as drawer, even to a holder who knows that he is merely an agent, unless words are added to the signature, indicating that he signs merely as an agent.[336]

9-056

(2) A shipmaster draws a bill on his owners in payment for necessaries, the bill concluding with the words "value received in 300 tons coal and disbursements ... supplied to my vessel to enable her to complete her voyage ... for which I hold my vessel, owners and freight responsible". The master is personally liable as drawer, there being nothing in the concluding words excluding such liability.[337]

(3) An agent draws a bill in the name of his principal. The agent is not liable on the bill as drawer.[338]

(4) A bill directed to a company was accepted in the following form: "Accepted ... A B and C D, directors—F F E Ltd". This was the acceptance of the company. The drawer, however, required the bill to be indorsed by the company's directors. Accordingly, A B and C D signed on the back of the bill, "F F E Ltd, A B and C D, directors". Held, A B and C D were personally li-

---

[329] See *Britannia Electric Lamp Works Ltd v D. Mandler & Co Ltd* [1939] 2 K.B. 129.
[330] But see *Elliott v Bax-Ironside* [1925] 2 K.B. 301, Illustration 4, for an example where the presumption was invoked in such a case.
[331] Bills of Exchange Act 1882 s.23(1).
[332] Bills of Exchange Act 1882 s.23(2). See *Ringham v Hackett* [1980] C.L.Y. 158.
[333] See *Ferguson v Wilson* (1866) L.R. 2 Ch.App. 77.
[334] See Companies Act 1985 s.349, now repealed.
[335] As to liability as a matter of contract construction, see *Badgerhill Properties Ltd v Cottrell* [1991] B.C.L.C. 805, Illustration 16 to Article 99; *Hamid v Francis Bradshaw Partnership* [2013] EWCA Civ 470.
[336] *Leadbitter v Farrow* (1816) 5 M. & S. 345; *Sowerby v Butcher* (1834) 4 Tyr. 320.
[337] *The Elmville* [1904] P. 319.
[338] *Wilson v Barthrop* (1837) 2 M. & W. 863.

able on the indorsement, because unless the indorsement was read as the personal indorsement of the directors, it added nothing to the validity of the bill.[339]

(5) Directors have been held personally liable on promissory notes in the following forms:

   (a) "We, directors of A B Company Limited, do promise to pay J D, etc ...";
sealed and signed by four directors without qualification.[340]

   (b) "We, directors of A B Company, for ourselves and other shareholders of the company, jointly and severally promise to pay, etc., on account of the company", signed without qualification.[341]

   (c) "We promise to pay ... C D, Director, E F, Secretary, the F E Ltd ... "[342]

   (d) "We, being members of the executive committee, on behalf of X Cooperative Society, do jointly promise to pay ... "[343]

(6) The secretary of a company signed a note in the following form: "I promise to pay, etc ... (signed)—For M T and W Railway Company, J S, secretary ...". Held, that he was not personally liable.[344]

(7) A note was signed "The J S Laundry Ltd, J S, Managing Director ... " J S was not personally liable: the company would have been.[345]

Article 104

MERGER AND ELECTION: RELEASE OF AGENT

9-057 Any liability of an agent on any contract made on behalf of the principal is discharged by the obtaining of judgment against the principal, and may perhaps be discharged where the third party elects to pursue its rights against the principal, in accordance with the principles stated in Article 82.

Comment

9-058 The situations in which an agent may be liable on a contract made by the agent for the principal are discussed under Article 98. The relevant authorities mainly concern the release of the principal by the obtaining of judgment against, or electing to look to the agent, and are discussed critically under Article 82, where considerable doubts are expressed as to their correctness. But the considerations applicable where the agent seeks to be discharged are obviously the same; thus, subject to the reservations there expressed, the obtaining of judgment against the principal releases the agent,[346] and a clear manifestation of an intention to hold the

[339] *Elliott v Bax-Ironside* [1925] 2 K.B. 301, applying Bills of Exchange Act 1882 s.26(2). See also *Rolfe, Lubell & Co v Keith* [1979] 1 All E.R. 860, where parol evidence was admitted to displace the operation of s.26(1) in case of ambiguity. cf. *Kettle v Dunster and Wakefield* (1927) 43 T.L.R. 770.

[340] *Dutton v Marsh* (1871) L.R. 6 Q.B. 361; *Courtauld v Saunders* (1867) 16 L.T. 562.

[341] *Penkivil v Connell* (1850) 5 Exch. 381.

[342] *Brebner v Henderson* 1925 S.C. 643. See also *Landes v Bradwell* (1909) 25 T.L.R. 478.

[343] *Gray v Raper* (1861) L.R. 1 C.P. 694.

[344] *Alexander v Sizer* (1869) L.R. 4 Ex. 102.

[345] *Chapman v Smethurst* [1909] 1 K.B. 927; see also *Britannia Electric Lamp Works Ltd v D. Mandler & Co Ltd* [1939] 2 K.B. 129; *Bondina Ltd v Rollaway Shower Blinds Ltd* [1986] 1 W.L.R. 517.

[346] *LGOC v Pope* (1922) 38 T.L.R. 270.

principal liable might perhaps have the same effect.[347] But where there are separate causes of action, the rule would not apply,[348] for it is based on there being two inconsistent rights.[349] And, of course, where the principal is not liable at all, the agent cannot be released by any attempt to make the principal liable.

Illustration

Travel agents supply and credit A with tickets, which he buys in his own name. Subsequently they are informed by B Ltd that A was B Ltd's agent in the transaction. They write to both demanding payment, and threatening proceedings, and subsequently issue a writ against B Ltd. Hearing that B Ltd is going into liquidation, they discontinue these proceedings and sue A. A is liable, there having been no election on these facts.[350] **9-059**

Article 105

WARRANTY OF AUTHORITY

(1) Where a person, by words or conduct, represents that he or she has actual authority to act on behalf of another, and a third party is induced by such representation to act in a manner in which that party would not have acted if that representation had not been made, the first-mentioned person is deemed to warrant that the representation is true, and is liable for any loss caused to such third party by a breach of that implied warranty, even if the would-be agent acted in good faith, under a mistaken belief that authority existed.[351] **9-060**

(2) Every person who purports to act as an agent is deemed by that conduct to represent that he or she is in fact duly authorised so to act,[352] except where the purported agent expressly disclaims authority[353] or where the nature and extent of that person's authority, or the material facts from which its nature and extent may be inferred, are known to the other contracting party.[354]

Comment

Historical background Early nineteenth-century cases found great difficulty in identifying a basis of liability for the agent who acted without authority, and there was at one time a tendency to hold that the agent had contracted personally wherever it turned out that there was no authority.[355] This solution was not sustain- **9-061**

---

[347] *Clarkson Booker Ltd v Andjel* [1964] 2 Q.B. 775, Illustration.

[348] See for the nature of the possible causes of action, Comment to Article 98.

[349] See Comment to Article 82.

[350] *Clarkson Booker Ltd v Andjel* [1964] 2 Q.B. 775; cf. *Beigtheil & Young v Stewart* (1900) 16 T.L.R. 177. See also *Format International Security Printers Ltd v Mosden* [1975] 1 Lloyd's Rep. 37.

[351] *Collen v Wright* (1857) 7 E. & B. 301; affirmed (1857) 8 E. & B. 647; *Yonge v Toynbee* [1910] 1 K.B. 215; and see Comment; *Restatement, Third,* § 6.10. But see below as to powers of attorney.

[352] *Collen v Wright* (1857) 7 E. & B. 301.

[353] *Halbot v Lens* [1901] 1 Ch. 344, Illustration 10.

[354] Illustrations 8 and 9; see also *Beattie v Ebury* (1872) L.R. 7 Ch.App. 777 at 810; affirmed L.R. 7 H.L. 102.

[355] *Downman v Williams* (1845) 7 Q.B. 103; *Thomas v Hewes* (1834) 2 C. & M. 519 at 530n. See also the cases on contracts made on behalf of companies in the course of formation, below, para.9-085; Radcliffe (1902) 18 L.Q.R. 364; *Randell v Trimen* (1856) 18 C.B. 786; the judgment of Cockburn

able in principle,[356] except where the agent could genuinely be regarded as undertaking personal liability on the contract,[357] or conceivably where the agent was really acting personally.[358] An agent who fraudulently professed authority would always be liable in deceit,[359] but the basis of an innocent agent's liability was not settled till *Collen v Wright*,[360] where it was decided by a majority that the agent was liable on a separate, implied warranty of authority.

Willes J said:

> "I am of the opinion that a person, who induces another to contract with him as the agent of a third party by an unqualified assertion of his being authorised to act as such agent, is answerable to the person who so contracts for any damages which he may sustain by reason of the assertion of authority being untrue ... The fact that the professed agent honestly thinks that he has authority affects the moral character of his act; but his moral innocence, so far as the person whom he has induced to contract is concerned, in no way aids such person or alleviates the inconvenience and damage which he sustains. The obligation which arises in such a case is well expressed by saying that a person, professing to contract as agent for another, impliedly, if not expressly, undertakes to or promises the person who enters into such contract, upon the faith of the professed agent being duly authorised, that the authority which he professes to have does in point of fact exist."[361]

Where the agent is entirely innocent, this action is the only one available: where he is fraudulent, the plaintiff can sue for deceit or breach of warranty of authority at his option. Where he is negligent, it might be thought that a similar choice obtains in those cases where the negligence gives rise to liability in tort.[362] But the Court of Appeal of New Zealand has ruled against the existence of a duty of care in such circumstances,[363] on the ground that the contractual remedy is adequate and that to permit a tort remedy would create a vicarious liability in a principal who had not authorised the agent.[364] But it seems appropriate to conclude that an agent assumes a responsibility to be careful in representing the extent of his authority, which liability need not also lead to vicarious liability in the principal. Granted therefore the general co-existence of actions in contract and tort, it seems doubtful whether the complete denial of a duty of care is necessary or appropriate, bearing in mind that there may be other advantages of tort actions.

9-062 **Nature of liability** The nature of the liability arising under this rule has been

---

CJ, dissenting, in *Collen v Wright* (1857) 8 E. & B. 647; discussion in *Black v Smallwood* (1966) 117 C.L.R. 52.

[356] *Lewis v Nicholson* (1852) 18 Q.B. 503; *Jenkins v Hutchinson* (1849) 13 Q.B. 744; see Article 108. For a modern example of what could be taken as similar reasoning, see *Savills v Scott* [1988] 1 E.G.L.R. 20, as to which see also [1989] J.B.L. 62.

[357] See Articles 98 and 107.

[358] See Article 108.

[359] *Randell v Trimen* (1856) 18 C.B. 786; *Polhill v Walter* (1832) 3 B. & Ad. 114; *West London Commercial Bank v Kitson* (1884) 13 Q.B.D. 360. And he may commit the offence of obtaining a pecuniary advantage by deception: *R. v Charles* [1977] A.C. 177.

[360] *Collen v Wright* (1857) 7 E. & B. 301; affirmed (1857) 8 E. & B. 647.

[361] *Collen v Wright* (1857) 7 E. & B. 301; affirmed (1857) 8 E. & B. 647 at 657–658.

[362] On the basis of *Hedley Byrne & Co Ltd v Heller & Partners Ltd* [1964] A.C. 465. See further para.9-061.

[363] *Kavanagh v Continental Shelf (No. 46) Ltd* [1993] 2 N.Z.L.R. 648. See however *Fong Maun Yee v Yoong Weng Ho* [1997] 2 Singapore L.R. 297, where a different view appears to have been taken.

[364] See too *Heskell v Continental Express Ltd* [1950] 1 All E.R. 1033, Illustration 5 to Article 106. But cf. *Hedley Byrne & Co Ltd v Heller & Partners Ltd* [1964] A.C. 465 at 532.

much discussed.[365] There are dicta in many of the cases which to modern eyes leave it doubtful whether the cause of action is to be classified as contractual or tortious. But in the absence of fraud an action in tort did not seem appropriate at the time: indeed, the possibility of an action for negligent misstatement has only become apparent comparatively recently. The assumption in the later nineteenth century that all actions must be classifiable into one group or the other eventually led to these actions being regarded as contractual, and contractual rules being applied.[366] The contract is normally unilateral, viz., the agent offers to warrant the existence of authority in exchange for the third party entering into a contract with the principal or otherwise acting as requested; the offer is accepted by the third party acting accordingly.[367] The result of the cause of action being classified as contractual is the strict liability customarily placed on parties who make contractual promises: the agent is in effect a guarantor of his or her authority. There are repercussions as regards the damages obtainable, which are not limited to reliance loss.[368] Perhaps surprisingly, international codifications appear to take the same view.[369]

Cessation of authority unbeknown to agent There was at one time a tendency   **9-063**
to confine the remedy for false profession of agency, as if on a tort, to cases where the agent was negligent[370]: but this, as stated above, does not square with the supposed contractual nature of the liability. The premise of strict liability has been applied in cases where, unknown to the agent, the agent's authority has terminated. The leading case has been *Yonge v Toynbee*.[371] That case was concerned with supervening mental incapacity, and it is now in doubt whether the mere intervention of mental incapacity does automatically terminate an agent's authority.[372] But it is likely that the general premise still applies, and that it could lead to an agent's liability on the warranty in cases of death and, in the case of a company, its

---

[365] Radcliffe (1902) 18 L.Q.R. 364; Holdsworth (1924) 40 L.Q.R. 1 (suggesting that the liability is quasi-contractual); Seavey (1920) 29 Yale L.J. 859 at 886 onwards; *Edwards v Porter* [1923] 2 K.B. 538 at 545–546 (but cf. on appeal, [1925] A.C. 1 at 23, 45); *Leggo v Brown & Dureau Ltd* (1923) 32 C.L.R. 95. See too Reynolds [2012] L.M.C.L.Q. 189.

[366] See *Dickson v Reuter's Telegram Co Ltd* (1877) 3 C.P.D. 1 at 5; *The Piraeus* [1974] 2 Lloyd's Rep. 266 (action contractual for the purposes of RSC Ord.11 r.1(f) (g)); *Commonwealth Bank of Australia v Hamilton* [2012] NSWSC 242 at [304] (plea of contributory negligence not available); *Zoya Ltd v Sheikh Nasir Ahmed (t/a Property Mart)* [2016] EWHC 2249 (Ch); [2016] 4 W.L.R. 174 at [30]; *P&P Property Ltd v Owen White and Catlin LLP* [2018] EWCA Civ 1082; [2019] Ch. 273 at [35] (noted F.M.B. Reynolds, "Of warranty of authority and related topics" (2018) 134 L.Q.R. 511).

[367] See *Yonge v Toynbee* [1910] 1 K.B. 215 at 227–228, discussed further below, para.9-063; *Permanent Custodians Ltd v Geagea* [2014] NSWSC 562.

[368] See Article 106.

[369] *Restatement, Third, Agency*, § 6.10; PECL Article 3:024; UNIDROIT Principles Article 2.2.6; DCFR, II, 6:107(2). See also *The Unauthorised Agent* (Busch and Macgregor eds, 2009); and Verhagen (2009) 6 *European Review of Private Law* 1003. For a view that the whole issue requires reconsideration, see Faulkner (2000) 74 A.L.J. 465. See also below, paras 12-026 and 12-027.

[370] *Salton v New Beeston Cycle Co* [1900] 1 Ch. 43; following *Smout v Ilbery* (1842) 10 M. & W. 1. In relation of *Smout* itself, the case may perhaps be supported on the grounds that on the facts there was no warranty: "the continuance of the life of the principal was ... a fact equally within the knowledge of both contracting parties": at 11. See *Yonge v Toynbee* [1910] 1 K.B. 215 at 227–228; *Randall v Trimen* (1856) 18 C.B. 786 at 793.

[371] *Yonge v Toynbee* [1910] 1 K.B. 215, Illustration 12. See also *Starkey v Bank of England* [1903] A.C. 114 at 119.

[372] See *Blankley v Central Manchester and Manchester Children's University Hospitals NHS Trust* [2015] EWCA Civ 18; [2015] 1 W.L.R. 4307, and para.10-020.

dissolution.[373] There remains a degree of flexibility in the implication of the warranty,[374] and in relation to powers of attorney, the position has been mitigated by statute.[375]

9-064 **Warranty not confined to misrepresentation resulting in contract** The implication of a warranty is not confined to cases where the transaction with the person purporting to have authority results in a contract with the principal[376]:

> "The rule to be deduced is, that where a person by asserting that he has the authority of the principal induces another person to enter into any transaction which he would not have entered into but for that assertion, and the assertion turns out to be untrue, to the injury of the person to whom it is made, it must be taken that the person making it undertook that it was true, and he is liable personally for the damage that has occurred."[377]

Thus the doctrine has been applied where directors purported to pay a creditor by the use of debentures which the company had no power to issue, and to the presentation of a transfer under a forged power of attorney.[378] Nor is the rule confined to cases where the person sought to be held liable is the person who was thought to have authority: there may be liability for a representation that another person has authority.[379] And there may be liability to a person unknown to the defendant who relies on the warranty, e.g. the indorsee of a bill of exchange or bill of lading containing a false representation of authority.[380] But there are limits: the mere fact that X misrepresents a fact relevant to a third party does not mean that X asserts authority to do so.[381]

9-065 **Warranty to third persons** It has further been held in England that the warranty can extend to a party other than the counter-party to a putative contract with the principal. In the decision, the party suing was a lender under a mortgage to a purchaser whose vendor had not given the putative agent authority to sell.[382] It was said that such a party would certainly not have proceeded had it known that the vendor's solicitor was not authorised by the vendor (in fact by one of two co-

---

[373] See *Yonge v Toynbee* [1910] 1 K.B. 215 at 227–228; below, para.10-032. This was the situation dealt with in *Salton v New Beeston Cycle Co* [1900] 1 Ch. 43, the actual decision in which has not been questioned; see also *Schlieske v Overseas Construction Co Pty Ltd* [1960] V.R. 195; *Babury Ltd v London Industrial Plc* (1989) 139 N.L.J. 1596.

[374] See below, para.9-070.

[375] See below, Article 122 (the legislation dating back to Law of Property Amendment Act 1859 s.26).

[376] See Illustrations 3 and 6; *Brown v Law* (1895) 72 L.T. 779; *British Russian Gazette Ltd v Associated Newspapers Ltd* [1933] 2 K.B. 616; *Heskell v Continental Express Ltd* [1950] 1 All E.R. 1033 at 1042, where an attempt to put a limit on the rule was rejected.

[377] *Firbank's Exors v Humphreys* (1886) 18 Q.B.D. 54 at 60, per Lord Esher MR; but cf. the slightly narrower formulation by Lindley LJ at 62.

[378] See Illustrations 3 and 6.

[379] Illustrations 1, 4 and 9 can be so explained.

[380] *V/O Rasnoimport v Guthrie & Co Ltd* [1966] 1 Lloyd's Rep. 1, Illustration 11; following wide dicta in textbooks (mostly to be justified by reference to the words used in *Starkey v Bank of England* [1903] A.C. 114) and dicta of A.L. Smith J at first instance in *West London Commercial Bank v Kitson* (1883) 12 Q.B.D. 157 at 161 (treated by the Court of Appeal as a case of fraud: (1884) 13 Q.B.D. 360). However, the result seems correct, for the agent knows that such a contract is transferable. See also *New Georgia National Bank v Lippman* 249 N.Y. 307, 164 N.E. 108 (1928); Reynolds (1967) 80 L.Q.R. 189.

[381] *Salvesen v Rederi A/B Nordstjernan* [1905] A.C. 302; *Jones v Still* [1965] N.Z.L.R. 1071.

[382] *Penn v Bristol & West BS* [1997] 1 W.L.R. 1356 (leave to appeal to House of Lords was refused). See Reynolds [2012] L.M.C.L.Q. 189.

vendors). It can certainly be said that the dictum of Lord Esher cited above, and other dicta,[383] do not require that the third party actually enter into a contract with the vendor, but refer only to a "transaction": but they do suggest directness of relationship and it is probably going too far to say that the whole scenario of purchase funded by mortgage is one transaction,[384] for events may happen at different times. The reasoning was in fact based on general warranty reasoning of a broader nature than that which justified the basic type of breach of warranty of authority,[385] supported by reference to the bill of lading case referred to above[386] (where the agent was necessarily aware of the fact that the contract was transferable by statute) and the well-known case of *Carlill v Carbolic Smoke Ball Co*,[387] concerning reliance on an advertisement expressed in general terms. Such an extension does not seem to be envisaged by *Restatement, Third*, or the various European codifications referred to above.[388] Though it is well established in England it may be doubted whether such an extension of strict liability is appropriate. As it stands, however, such reasoning can be applied also to purchasers' solicitors acting on behalf of them as borrowers,[389] or in general, to solicitors acting for both borrower and lender,[390] despite the fact that in other respects the latter may be under a retainer to the lender which on normal practice makes them liable for negligence only.[391]

The question that would then arise is as to the test for determining when such a warranty is deemed to be given. It is submitted that this should only be so where, in accordance with normal contractual principles, the warranty of authority can be regarded as inducing an act[392]; and there must then be corresponding reliance on it.[393] Mere knowledge in the warrantor that certain persons can be foreseen as relying on the warranty is redolent of tort liability and should not be sufficient in this context. Thus some flexibility can be derived from this feature.

Scope of warranty The basic warranty is only that the agent has authority from the principal: this is something peculiarly within the agent's knowledge. If the principal proves unreliable, that is something in respect of which the third party could have made inquiries. Merely as agent, therefore, the agent does not warrant that the principal is solvent,[394] or will perform the contract (if any). As can be seen below, in the context of litigation, the warranty is similarly limited in that the agent

9-066

---

[383] See *Starkey v Bank of England* [1903] A.C. 114 at 119, per Lord Davey.
[384] Despite Lord Diplock's reference to the "real-property-mortgaged-to-a-building-society-owning democracy": *Pettitt v Pettitt* [1970] A.C. 777 at 824 (we are grateful to Mark West for this reference).
[385] *Penn v Bristol & West BS* [1997] 1 W.L.R. 1356 at 1363.
[386] *V/O Rasnoimport v Guthrie & Co Ltd* [1966] 1 Lloyd's Rep. 1.
[387] *Carlill v Carbolic Smoke Ball Co* [1893] 1 Q.B. 156.
[388] See above, para.9-062.
[389] See *Bristol & West B.S. v Fancy & Jackson* [1997] 4 All E.R. 582. In such a case the warranty might be of authorisation of certain conveyancing procedures, but there would be little difference: see at 613. But solicitors may sign contracts themselves, as in *Suleman v Shahsavari* [1988] 1 W.L.R. 1181.
[390] See *Excel Securities Plc v Masood*, Mercantile Court, Manchester, June 10, 2009, HH Judge Hegarty QC, below, para.9-068.
[391] A case sometimes cited in this context is *Midland Bank Plc v Cox McQueen* [1999] P.N.L.R. 593, where, however, the relevance of a warranty was rejected.
[392] See the dictum of Lord Esher MR quoted above, para.9-064.
[393] See *Leggo v Brown & Dureau Ltd* (1923) 32 C.L.R. 95 at 106: "The essentials are (1) assertion of authority; (2) inducement by asserting; (3) transaction which but for that assertion the other party would not have entered into"; *Zoya Ltd v Sheikh Nasir Ahmed (t/a Property Mart)* [2016] EWHC 2249 (Ch); [2016] 4 W.L.R. 174 at [39]. See on the whole topic, West (2009) 25 J. Prof. Negligence 131; Reynolds, ibid., 142.
[394] See Article 106.

(normally a solicitor) does not promise that a claim is valid. The difficulty arises however when the cause of lack of authority is that the principal has never existed, no longer exists, or lacks capacity. In England the leading case has been *Yonge v Toynbee*,[395] where the agent was held liable in the context of litigation when the principal had without the agent's knowledge become incapable. As stated above, there is now considerable doubt that the mere intervention of mental incapacity automatically terminates an agent's authority (with the result that the agent's warranty would not be broken), but an agent might remain exposed should the principal have died, or ceased to exist.[396] If an agent warrants that the principal still exists, a fortiori the agent may be held to warrant that the principal has at some time existed.[397] Hence problems of the liability of promoters of companies not yet formed could sometimes perhaps be solved by the implication of this warranty.[398] In many situations where the principal, whether supposedly human or corporate, is non-existent, however, there is some degree of knowledge on both sides, so that the warranty may be excluded,[399] and in some cases, e.g. unformed companies and unincorporated associations, the agent has in fact been held liable on the contract itself.[400]

Cases holding the agent liable where the contract would be ultra vires the corporate principal, and certain other cases such as that of the non-existent principal, may require to be analysed as an extension of the warranty of authority. For in some of them the agent is held liable though the act would, even if authorised by the supposed principal, be a nullity, with the result that there would be no loss caused by the lack of authority.[401] Though *Collen v Wright*[402] is frequently cited in these cases, it may sometimes be necessary to say that what is warranted is that, e.g. there is a power to issue debentures, that the document presented is genuine, and so forth.[403] In the absence of evidence, an agent would not ordinarily be taken to warrant that the principal has been named correctly, but only that the principal existed and had given authority.[404]

9-067   **Warranty in litigation**   A specialised application of the warranty of authority is

---

[395] *Yonge v Toynbee* [1910] 1 K.B. 215, Illustration 12. See also *Scott v J.B. Livingston & Nicol* 1990 S.L.T. 305; cf. *Nelson v Nelson* [1997] 1 W.L.R. 233, where the principal was an undischarged bankrupt, with the result that the cause of action vested in his trustee. This went to its validity, which the solicitor did not warrant.
[396] See above, para.9-063.
[397] See *Simmons v Liberal Opinion Ltd* [1911] 1 K.B. 966; *Russian & English Bank v Baring Bros & Co Ltd* [1935] Ch. 120; *Salter v Cormie* (1993) 108 D.L.R. (4th) 372.
[398] Such an action was successful in *Delta Construction Co Ltd v Lidstone* (1979) 96 D.L.R. (3d) 457; but failed on the issue of damages. See Article 106; Article 107; *Brownett v Newton* (1941) 64 C.L.R. 439 (company not entitled to commence business); *Black v Smallwood* (1966) 117 C.L.R. 52 at 64; *Fernée v Gorlitz* [1915] 1 Ch. 177 (principal a minor); cf. *Newborne v Sensolid (Great Britain) Ltd* [1954] 1 Q.B. 45 at 47; *Hawke's Bay Milk Corp Ltd v Watson* [1974] 1 N.Z.L.R. 236. The argument was successful in *Lomax v Dankel* (1981) 29 S.A.S.R. 68. But there can be problems as to damages. See below, para.9-085.
[399] See below, para.9-070.
[400] Article 107.
[401] Article 106; *Heskell v Continental Express Ltd* [1950] 1 All E.R. 1033; Radcliffe (1902) 18 L.Q.R. 364; cf. *British Russian Gazette v Associated Newspapers Ltd* [1933] 2 K.B. 616 at 649.
[402] *Collen v Wright* (1857) 8 E. & B. 647.
[403] See Illustrations 2–5; *Sheffield Corp v Barclay* [1905] A.C. 392. But as to the presentation of bills of exchange, see *Guaranty Trust Co of New York v Hannay & Co* [1918] 2 K.B. 623; *Greenwood v Martins Bank Ltd* [1933] A.C. 51 at 59–60; cf. *Yeung Kai Yung v Hong Kong and Shanghai Banking Corp* [1981] A.C. 787, Illustration 5 to Article 98.
[404] *Knight Frank LLP v Du Haney* [2011] EWCA Civ 404.

that given by a solicitor or other representative who issues process in litigation. It has been truly said that "this contractual theory presents some conceptual problems in the case of a solicitor conducting litigation".[405] In general, a solicitor only warrants that the solicitor has been authorised by a client who exists[406]; it has been held that the solicitor does not warrant that the name given for that client is correct,[407] and certainly does not warrant the client's solvency or the validity, or even arguability, of the client's claim. A solicitor whose client in litigation purports to have authority to act for another party to the litigation does not thereby assert or warrant that the solicitor is instructed by that other party.[408] Further, solicitors will not be liable for costs where it was the third party who took the point that the litigation was unauthorised and the costs relate to proving that fact. So, solicitors do not warrant their authority where the authority of the agent instructing the firm is known to be controversial and the parties are engaged in litigation to find the answer.[409] The agent who purported to have authority to commence the litigation will often be made liable for the costs.[410]

Cases of identity fraud   The narrow warranty applied to solicitors in litigation has recently been applied to the warranty given by the solicitor for a prospective mortgagor of land to the prospective mortgage lender. These cases have held solicitors against whom identity fraud has been practised by the prospective mortgagor not liable, on the basis that the warranty which they give is in such situations very limited, namely that they have been authorised by a person who reasonably appears to them to be the person that person asserted he or she was.[411] So, agents will not normally promise that a named principal is not impersonating another or has a particular qualification, e.g. owns the property concerned,[412] though this could also

9-068

---

[405] *AMB Generali Holding AG v SEB Trygg Liv* [2005] EWCA Civ 1237; [2006] 1 Lloyd's Rep. 318 at [60], per Buxton LJ. The matter is commonly relevant to the court's jurisdiction to award costs: see e.g. *Bank of Scotland v Qutb* [2012] EWCA Civ 1661; *Re Sherlock Holmes International Society Ltd* [2016] EWHC 1392 (Ch); [2016] 4 W.L.R. 173; *Zoya Ltd v Sheikh Nasir Ahmed (t/a Property Mart)* [2016] EWHC 2249 (Ch); [2016] 4 W.L.R. 174.
[406] See *Nelson v Nelson* [1997] 1 W.L.R. 233.
[407] *AMB Generali Holding AG v SEB Trygg Liv* [2005] EWCA Civ 1237; [2006] 1 Lloyd's Rep. 31. See too *Knight Frank LLP v Du Haney* [2011] EWCA Civ 404.
[408] *Bronze Monkey LLC v Simmons & Simmons LLP* [2017] EWHC 3097 (Comm) (client in effect pleading derivative suit).
[409] *Aidiniantz v The Sherlock Holmes International Society Ltd* [2016] EWHC 1392 (Ch); [2016] 4 W.L.R. 173 at [30]; *Zoya Ltd v Shaikh Nasir Ahmed* [2016] EWHC 2249 (Ch); [2016] 4 W.L.R. 174 at [58].
[410] *Aidiniantz v The Sherlock Holmes International Society Ltd* [2016] EWHC 1392 (Ch); [2016] 4 W.L.R. 173 at [77]; *Zoya Ltd v Shaikh Nasir Ahmed* [2016] EWHC 2249 (Ch); [2016] 4 W.L.R. 174 at [67].
[411] *Excel Securities Plc v Masood* [2010] Lloyd's Rep. P.N. 165; *Cheshire Mortgage Corp Ltd v Grandison* [2012] CSIH 66 (noted Macgregor (2013) 17 Edin. L.R. 398); *Stevenson v Singh* [2012] EWHC 2880 (QB), Illustration 14. cf. *Knight Frank LLP v Du Haney* [2011] EWCA Civ 404, Illustration 14; *P&P Property Ltd v Owen White & Catlin LLP* [2016] EWHC 2276 (Ch); [2016] Bus. L.R. 1337 (where there is a good discussion by Dicker QC of the earlier authorities); reversed in part on different grounds [2018] EWCA Civ 1082; [2019] Ch. 273. See Reynolds [2012] L.M.C.L.Q. 189; Tan Cheng Han (2012) 30 J.C.L. 92.
[412] *Houlgate Investment Co Ltd v Biggart Baillie LLP* [2011] CSOH 160; [2012] P.N.L.R. 2; *P&P Property Ltd v Owen White & Catlin LLP* [2016] EWHC 2276 (Ch); [2016] Bus L.R. 1337 at [126]; reversed in part on different grounds [2018] EWCA Civ 1082; [2019] Ch. 273; *Balan v Lee Moi Moi* Malaysian CA, March 29, 2017 at [53]. cf. *LSC Finance Ltd v Abensons Law Ltd* [2015] EWHC 1163 (Ch).

be so for an unnamed principal, for example on whose behalf a car is sold.[413] There may also be difficulty in finding that an agent, including a solicitor, has undertaken a duty of care to a non-client in cases such as this.[414] However, ultimately the scope of the warranty turns on construction of the words used by the agent, and it has been held that where the agent signed the contract of sale on behalf of the party whose identity has been fraudulently assumed, the agent may be taken to have warranted that he or she was authorised by that party.[415]

9-069   **Mistake of law**   The traditional view has been that the warranty will not be implied where the representation is one of law.[416] There may however be difficulty in distinguishing representations of fact from representations of law.[417] Thus a representation that a company has power to borrow may be one of law if on the true construction of its memorandum it has no such power: but if the power could have been conferred by resolution, the representation may be of fact, that such a resolution has been passed.[418] Again, there may be a representation of the fact that the borrowing limit has not been exceeded.[419] Though there is no clear authority, it seems on principle that a wilfully false statement of law would give rise to liability in deceit, provided the other requirements (e.g. that the statement is likely to be acted on) were satisfied.[420]

9-070   **Rebuttal of the warranty**   The circumstances in which the warranty is implied create the possibility of considerable flexibility, and the strictness of the liability placed on the agent is in effect tempered by this technique. Thus where an agent disclaims authority, the agent avoids such liability,[421] unless the case is one where there is a promise to obtain authority.[422] If the third party does not think that authority can be obtained, this may be a ground for negativing the implication of a warranty, though the fact that A does not think that B can perform a contractual promise made to A does not usually affect B's liability.[423] In some cases the third party may be taken to know of the limitation or lack of authority, so that there are no grounds

---

[413] See two notes doubting a South African decision to the contrary, (1985) 102 S.A.L.J. 596 and 603. See also *Scott v J.B. Livingston & Nicol*, 1990 S.L.T. 305 at 307.

[414] See *P&P Property Ltd v Owen White & Catlin LLP* [2016] EWHC 2276 (Ch); [2016] Bus. L.R. 1337 at [176]. See further below, para.9-117.

[415] See *P&P Property Ltd v Owen White and Catlin LLP* [2018] EWCA Civ 1082; [2019] Ch. 273.

[416] Illustration 5; *Beattie v Ebury* (1872) L.R. 7 Ch.App. 777; affirmed L.R. 7 H.L. 102; *Saffron Walden Second Benefit Building Society v Rayner* (1880) 14 Ch.D. 406.

[417] See *Eaglesfield v Londonderry* (1876) 4 Ch.D. 693 at 703 (affirmed (1876) 38 L.T. 303), Illustration 5.

[418] See *Beattie v Ebury* (1872) L.R. 7 Ch.App. 777 at 800–803.

[419] *Weeks v Propert* (1873) L.R. 8 C.P. 427.

[420] See *Beattie v Ebury* (1872) L.R. 7 Ch.App. 777; *Eaglesfield v Londonderry* (1876) 4 Ch.D. 693; *Hirschfeld v London, Brighton & South Coast Ry Co* (1876) 2 Q.B.D. 1; *West London Commercial Bank v Kitson* (1884) 13 Q.B.D. 360 (but none of these are clear authorities).

[421] *Halbot v Lens* [1901] 1 Ch. 344, Illustration 10; *Re Sherlock Holmes International Society Ltd* [2016] EWHC 1392 (Ch); [2016] 4 W.L.R. 173; *Zoya Ltd v Sheikh Nasir Ahmed (t/a Property Mart)* [2016] EWHC 2249 (Ch); [2016] 4 W.L.R. 174 at [50] (no warranty in litigation where authority to bring the proceedings was the very matter in contention). In *McManus v Fortescue* [1907] 2 K.B. 1 it was held that if the purchaser had notice that there might be a reserve the auctioneer who knocked down an item short of the reserve was not liable for breach of warranty of authority when he refused to sign a memorandum of the sale. Sed quaere: see Murdoch, *Law of Estate Agency* (5th edn), pp.174–178.

[422] *Halbot v Lens* [1901] 1 Ch. 344 at 351.

[423] Powell, pp.256–257.

for implying a warranty by the agent.[424] There will not, however, usually be any duty on a third party to inquire,[425] for the third party is entitled to assume that a person purporting to act as agent warrants the possession of authority. Ultimately, however, if the third party did not rely upon the agent's having authority there will not be liability.[426]

Apparent authority   Where an agent has no actual authority, but contracts in circumstances in which the principal would be bound under the doctrine of apparent authority, it seems that the agent should be prima facie liable, for there was no authority: the fact that the principal could be held liable, however, would mean that the third party could prove no loss. It has been said that this is "but a reflection of the principle that a claim for breach of warranty cannot put the claimant in a better position than if the warranty had been true".[427] However, the expense of proving this could perhaps be recoverable: certainly, the costs of an abortive action in which apparent authority is *not* established can.[428] Even if the principal were insolvent, the agent would not be liable, for the agent is liable only for loss arising out of the absence of authority.[429] However, there are dicta that in a case of apparent authority there is no breach of warranty of authority at all.[430] These can be justified only on the rather doubtful ground that the agent warrants that he or she has actual *or apparent* authority.[431]

9-071

Ratification   It may be assumed that the agent is not liable where the principal ratifies. Here again there is no loss to the third party, but it may be more plausibly argued that there was no breach of warranty at all, on the basis that the agent warrants authority or that the principal will ratify. The third party may, however, be

9-072

---

[424] Illustrations 8 and 9; and see *Beattie v Ebury* (1872) L.R. 7 Ch.App. 777; *Dillon v Macdonald* (1902) 21 N.Z.L.R. 45 (third party ought to have assumed authority expired); *Cook v Williams* (1897) 14 T.L.R. 31 (third party ought to have known estate agent had no authority to sell); *Zoya Ltd v Sheikh Nasir Ahmed (t/a Property Mart)* [2016] EWHC 2249 (Ch). cf. *Austin v Real Estate Listing Exchange* (1912) 2 D.L.R. 324 (list of properties for sale guaranteed by issuers).

[425] See *V/O Rasnoimport v Guthrie & Co Ltd* [1966] 1 Lloyd's Rep. 1, esp. at 11: though there are dicta to the contrary concerning the public documents of companies. And see *Schlieske v Overseas Construction Co Pty Ltd* [1960] V.R. 195 where it was held that solicitors should have realised that the defendant company might have been dissolved. cf., however, *Leggo v Brown & Dureau Ltd* (1923) 32 C.L.R. 95 (plaintiff need not affirmatively establish reliance).

[426] See *Donsland Ltd v van Hoogstraten* [2002] EWCA Civ 253; [2002] P.N.L.R. 26 at [14]; *P&P Property Ltd v Owen White and Catlin LLP* [2018] EWCA Civ 1082; [2019] Ch. 273 at [59].

[427] *Aidiniantz v The Sherlock Holmes International Society Ltd* [2016] EWHC 1392 (Ch); [2016] 4 W.L.R. 173 at [44].

[428] See below, para.9-081. Contra, *Restatement, Third*, § 6.10, Comment b.

[429] See Article 106. It is difficult to see why this point was not considered in *Yonge v Toynbee* [1910] 1 K.B. 215 in view of *Drew v Nunn* (1879) 4 Q.B.D. 661, in which it had been held that there was apparent authority in an agent whose principal had become incapable: see Article 121. cf. Powers of Attorney Act 1971 s.5(1) and (2); see Article 122.

[430] See *Rainbow v Howkins* [1904] 2 K.B. 322 at 326; *Aidiniantz v The Sherlock Holmes International Society Ltd* [2016] EWHC 1392 (Ch); [2016] 4 W.L.R. 173 at [44]. Some doubt was cast on *Rainbow* in *McManus v Fortescue* [1907] 2 K.B. 1, but as regards the apparent authority of an auctioneer to sell without reserve, and in the later case there was notice that there might be a reserve. See also *V/O Rasnoimport v Guthrie* [1966] 1 Lloyd's Rep. 1, at 10; *Mitsui & Co Ltd v Marpro Industrial Ltd* [1974] 1 Lloyd's Rep. 386.

[431] See *Restatement, Second*, § 329, Comment f; *Restatement, Third*, § 6.10, Comment b.

entitled to costs in defending proceedings commenced without authority but later ratified.[432]

9-073   **Powers of attorney**   There is statutory protection for an agent where the agent acts in pursuance of a power of attorney which has been revoked: this is set out in Article 122.

9-074   **Agents of the Crown**   It was held in *Dunn v Macdonald*[433] that an agent of the Crown was not liable for breach of warranty of authority where the agent purported to engage an employee on behalf of the Crown for a fixed period of three years and the plaintiff was dismissed, in accordance with the powers of the Crown to dismiss, within this period. This case is usually taken as authority for a general exemption from liability for breach of warranty of authority on the part of such agents on grounds of public policy: the implication of a warranty is "utterly inconsistent with the facts".[434] Though the majority of the judges involved in the case[435] took this view, the case can be explained as one involving a mistake of law.[436] Further, it could be argued that the defendant had in fact authority to engage the plaintiff, that the contract was impliedly subject to the Crown's right of dismissal, and that all that was held was that the agent did not warrant that the right of dismissal would not be exercised[437] not a matter of authority at all. However, though an agent of the Crown can no doubt expressly warrant his or her authority, it is very doubtful whether such an agent should be regarded as impliedly doing so in the same circumstances as other agents. The agent's non-liability may be explained as based on the other party's being presumed to know of this; but such a presumption is somewhat artificial, and public policy may provide the best explanation.

9-075   **Procedure**   Where the authority of the agent is disputed by the person on whose behalf the contract is made, the person who made the contract may be joined with the agent as co-defendant and relief claimed against them alternatively.[438]

Illustrations

9-076   (1)   The directors of a company wrote a letter to the company's bankers representing that A had been appointed manager and had authority to draw cheques on the company's account, which, to the knowledge of the directors, was already overdrawn. A further overdrew the account, the directors having, in fact, no authority to overdraw. Held, that the directors were liable to the bankers for

---

[432] Unless perhaps the principal initially refused to ratify, thereby causing expense to the third party. See *Yifung Developments Ltd v Liu Chi Keung Ricky* [2017] HKCA 341 at [9]; affirming [2016] HKCFI 2170 (directors commencing proceedings without authority).

[433] *Dunn v Macdonald* [1897] 1 Q.B. 401; ibid., 555; followed in *The Prometheus* (1949) 82 Ll. L. Rep. 859. See also *Kenny v Cosgrave* [1926] I.R. 517. See Street, *Governmental Liability* (1953), p.93; Nettheim [1975] C.L.J. 253.

[434] *Dunn v Macdonald* [1897] 1 Q.B. 401 at 558.

[435] Charles J at first instance; Lopes and Chitty LJJ in the Court of Appeal.

[436] See arguments before Charles J.

[437] See the judgment of Lord Esher MR.

[438] *Honduras Inter-Oceanic Ry Co v Lefevre & Tucker* (1877) 2 Ex.D. 301; *Massey v Heynes* (1888) 21 Q.B.D. 330; *Bennetts v McIlwraith* [1896] 2 Q.B. 464; *Sanderson v Blyth Theatre Co* [1903] 2 K.B. 533. In such a case the court would, in the exercise of its discretion, normally order the unsuccessful defendant to pay the successful defendant's costs by making either a "Bullock Order" or a "Sanderson Order": see *Civil Procedure 2010*, Vol.1, § 44.3.8.

breach of an implied warranty that they had authority to overdraw.[439] But the mere fact that directors of a company in that capacity sign cheques drawn on the company's bankers after the account is overdrawn does not amount to a representation that they have authority to overdraw the account, or to borrow money on the company's behalf.[440]

(2)　A lent £70 to a building society, and received a certificate of the deposit, signed by two directors. The society had no borrowing powers. Held, that the directors were personally liable to A on an implied warranty that they had authority to borrow on behalf of the society.[441]

(3)　The directors of a company issued a certificate for debenture stock, which A agreed to accept in lieu of cash due to him from the company, all the debenture stock that the company had power to issue having already been issued. Held, that the directors were liable to A on an implied warranty that they had authority to issue valid debenture stock, although they had acted in good faith, not knowing that all the stock had been issued.[442] So, where directors of a company which had already fully exercised its borrowing powers issued a debenture bond, it was held that the directors thereby impliedly warranted that they had authority to issue a valid debenture.[443]

(4)　The directors of an unincorporated society held out the secretary as having authority to borrow in excess of the amount prescribed by the rules of the society. The secretary borrowed in excess of such amount, and misappropriated the money. Held, that the directors were personally liable to the lenders on an implied warranty of authority, though they had not acted fraudulently.[444]

(5)　The directors of a company having no borrowing powers induce A to advance money on the security of a Lloyd's bond, which they in good faith represent to be a valid security, A being aware that the company has no borrowing powers. The directors are not liable on an implied warranty of authority, though the bond is invalid, because its validity is a question of law.[445] So, where directors issued certain stock and described it as No.1 Preference Stock, in the erroneous belief that they had power to issue stock to rank with the No.1 Preference Stock already issued, and A purchased some of the new stock, knowing that it was new stock, but believing that it would rank with the No.1 Preference, it was held that the directors were not liable to make good the misrepresentation, because it was a misrepresentation as to a matter of law, and A had not been deceived by any misrepresentation of fact.[446]

(6)　A stockbroker, acting in good faith, induces the Bank of England to transfer consols to a purchaser under a forged power of attorney. He is liable, in an action for breach of warranty of authority, to indemnify the Bank against the claim of the stockholder for restitution.[447]

---

[439] *Cherry & M'Dougall v Colonial Bank of Australasia* (1869) 38 L.J.P.C. 49.

[440] *Beattie v Ebury* (1872) L.R. 7 Ch.App. 777; affirmed L.R. 7 H.L. 102.

[441] *Richardson v Williamson* (1871) L.R. 6 Q.B. 276.

[442] *Firbank's Exors v Humphreys* (1886) 18 Q.B.D. 54; criticised (1902) 18 L.Q.R. 364; cf. *Elkington & Co v Hürter* [1892] 2 Ch. 452 and Illustration 5.

[443] *Weeks v Propert* (1873) L.R. 8 C.P. 427; *Whitehaven Joint Stock Banking Co v Reed* (1886) 2 T.L.R. 353. cf. Illustration 5.

[444] *Chapleo v Brunswick Building Society* (1881) 6 Q.B.D. 696. cf. *Smith v Reed* (1886) 2 T.L.R. 442.

[445] *Rashdall v Ford* (1866) L.R. 2 Eq. 750.

[446] *Eaglesfield v Londonderry* (1876) 38 L.T. 303; affirming (1874) 4 Ch.D. 693.

[447] *Starkey v Bank of England* [1903] A.C. 114; affirming decision of CA sub nom. *Oliver v Bank of*

(7) A acts as broker for both buyer and seller. He impliedly warrants to each that he is duly authorised to act on behalf of the other.[448]

(8) A ship-broker signs a charterparty—"by telegraphic authority; as agent". It is proved that such a form of signature is commonly adopted to negative the implication of any further warranty by the agent than that he has received a telegram which, if correct, authorises such a charterparty as he is signing. The ship-broker is not answerable for a mistake in the telegram.[449]

(9) H, a ship-broker, professes to make a charterparty on behalf of A, and signs it—"by telegraphic authority of B, G H as agent". B is A's agent, but A did not authorise the charterparty. H is liable for breach of an implied warranty that he has authority to make the charterparty on behalf of A, though he acted in good faith, believing that the telegram from B gave him such authority.[450]

(10) A signs a composition agreement with B on behalf of X, both A and B being aware that X has refused to enter into such an agreement, and taking the risk that X would again refuse to be bound. A does not warrant that X will accept the agreement.[451]

(11) A loading broker signed a bill of lading covering goods some of which were never shipped. As regards the goods not shipped his principal, the shipowner, was as the law then stood not bound. The loading broker was liable for breach of warranty of authority.[452]

(12) Solicitors enter an appearance in an action on behalf of a client who has unknown to them become mentally incapable and hence lacks capacity to instruct them. They are liable for the claimant's costs (which their client could not be) as having warranted their authority to act.[453] A solicitor warrants that he has a client who has instructed him. He does not however warrant that he has correctly named the client, nor that the client is solvent or has a good cause of action.[454]

(13) Where a solicitor, without authority, prosecutes or defends an action, the action will in general be dismissed or the defences struck out on the motion of either the plaintiff or the defendant, and the solicitor so acting without authority will be ordered to pay all the costs occasioned thereby.[455]

England [1902] 1 Ch. 610; *Commonwealth Bank of Australia v Hamilton* [2012] NSWSC 242 at [296].

[448] *Hughes v Graeme* (1864) 33 L.J.Q.B. 335. See above, paras 2-013, 6-046 and 6-060.

[449] *Lilly, Wilson & Co v Smales, Eeles & Co* [1892] 1 Q.B. 456.

[450] *Suart v Haigh* (1893) 9 T.L.R. 488.

[451] *Halbot v Lens* [1901] 1 Ch. 344.

[452] *V/O Rasnoimport v Guthrie & Co Ltd* [1966] 1 Lloyd's Rep. 1 (noted (1967) 83 L.Q.R. 189). cf. Article 106, Illustration 5. The principal could now be bound by virtue of Carriage of Goods by Sea Act 1992 s.4.

[453] *Yonge v Toynbee* [1910] 1 K.B. 215—actually a case on the summary jurisdiction in respect of solicitors. This is a different way of raising the same issue: no formal action is required and hence expense is saved, but the considerations taken into account appear to be the same. See *Civil Procedure 2010*, Vol.2, 7C-208; Cordery, *Solicitors* (8th edn), p.113 onwards, 9th (looseleaf) edn, F2A; *Skylight Maritime SA v Ascot Underwriting* [2005] EWHC 15 (Comm).

[454] *AMB Generali Holding AG v SEB Trygg Liv Holding, etc.* [2005] EWCA Civ 1237; [2006] 1 Lloyd's Rep. 318 at [56] onwards; explaining *Nelson v Nelson* [1977] 1 W.L.R. 233, above, para.9-066. See also below, para.10-032.

[455] *Hubbart v Phillips* (1845) 13 M. & W. 702; *Simmons v Liberal Opinion Ltd* [1911] 1 K.B. 966; *Babury Ltd v London Industrial Plc* (1989) 139 N.L.J. 1596. And see Cordery, above. cf. *Zoya Ltd v Sheikh Nasir Ahmed (t/a Property Mart)* [2016] EWHC 2249 (Ch); [2016] 4 W.L.R. 174 (litigation to contest right to sue on behalf of company).

(14) A solicitor has a client who is impersonating the owner of land. The client engages the solicitor to act in a purported sale of the land, which is naturally ineffective. The solicitor signs the contract of sale on behalf of the client. The purchasers sue the solicitor asserting a warranty of authority. It is held as a matter of construction that the solicitor warranted that she was acting for the true owner but that the purchaser had not on the facts relied on the warranty.[456]

Article 106

MEASURE OF DAMAGES FOR BREACH OF WARRANTY OF AUTHORITY

(1) The measure of damages for breach of warranty of authority is the loss which the parties should reasonably have contemplated as liable to result from the breach of warranty.[457]

(2) Where a contract is repudiated by the person on whose behalf it was made on the ground that it was made without authority, such loss is prima facie the amount of damages that could have been recovered from that person in an action if the contract had been duly authorised and subsequently repudiated, together with the costs and expenses (if any) incurred in respect of any legal proceedings reasonably taken against that person on the contract.[458]

9-077

Comment

Contractual principle The cause of action for breach of warranty of authority being eventually classified as contractual, the damages were eventually settled as those required to put the plaintiff in the position in which the plaintiff would have been had the warranty been made good, viz. had the representation of authority been true:

9-078

"The damages, under the general rule, are arrived at by considering the difference in the position [the plaintiff] would have been in had the representation been true and the position he is actually in consequence of it being untrue."[459]

---

[456] *P&P Property Ltd v Owen White and Catlin LLP* [2018] EWCA Civ 1082; [2019] Ch. 273. cf.*Stevenson v Singh* [2012] EWHC 2880 (QB).

[457] See *C. Czarnikow Ltd v Koufos (The Heron II)* [1969] 1 A.C. 350; Illustrations; *Restatement, Third*, § 6.10; *McGregor on Damages* (20th edn), Ch.36.

[458] See Comment and Illustrations. But cf. *Chitholie v Nash & Co* (1973) 229 E.G. 786 (measure of damages available in lieu of specific performance in an action against principal under Lord Cairns' Act not applicable to claim against agent: but see *McGregor on Damages* (20th edn), Ch.36 and Illustration 10).

[459] *Firbank's Executors v Humphreys* (1886) 18 Q.B.D. 54 at 60, per Lord Esher MR. But cf. *Doyle v Olby (Ironmongers) Ltd* [1969] 2 Q.B. 158 at 168, where Winn LJ used this passage to distinguish liability for breach of warranty of authority from liability for breach of contract and to liken it to liability in deceit. This does not seem to be correct, though of course in actions in respect of statements the question of loss actually incurred often has more prominence than the expectation interest, viz. the profit that might have been made: see, e.g. *Kwei Tek Chao v British Traders and Shippers Ltd* [1954] 2 Q.B. 459; *McRae v Commonwealth Disposals Commission* (1951) 84 C.L.R. 377. *Salvesen v Rederi A/B Nordstjernan* [1905] A.C. 302 seems contrary to Winn LJ's suggestion. The statement above is in accord with the PECL Article 3:204 and the UNIDROIT Principles Article 2.2.6.

The claimant must establish loss and not leave it to the court to infer it.[460] Where an agent only warrants authority to negotiate a contract, the damages may be confined to the third party's wasted expenditure.[461]

9-079 **Insolvent principal** Thus it has often been stated that when the principal is insolvent only nominal damages may be given, for a successful action against the principal would have produced no money.[462] However, the fact that the principal is insolvent does not necessarily mean that there will be no damages, if the result of the transaction would, if the agent had had authority, have been to make the third party a preferred creditor of the principal. In *Firbank's Executors v Humphreys*[463] the plaintiffs were induced by the directors of a company to accept debenture stock in lieu of payment for services rendered, but such stock was null because the amount which the company had power to borrow had been exceeded. Had the company been solvent, the loss recoverable from the directors would probably have been nothing, as the plaintiffs could have sued the company on the original debt: but as it was insolvent, this right was valueless, so that the loss was the par value of the debentures, since valid stock of this type retained its value.[464]

9-080 **Transaction unenforceable against principal** Where no redress could be obtained from the principal even if the agent had been authorised, there is again no loss.[465] Thus in *Heskell v Continental Express Ltd*[466] (Illustration 5) even express authorisation of the signature by the principal would not have created a contract with the principal, since no goods had ever been shipped. The same result could follow where the contract is unenforceable against the principal because the principal is a company not yet formed,[467] or for lack of writing under the Statute of Frauds. The latter point arose in *Fay v Miller, Wilkins & Co*[468] and the agent was held liable specifically because it could be held that there was a sufficient memorandum, the argument that if there had been no such memorandum no damage could be shown being apparently accepted. However, the absence of a memorandum could between the contracting parties be outweighed by an act or acts of part performance. Can these be pleaded against the agent, to show that the contract with the principal

---

[460] *McIntosh v Linke Nominees Pty Ltd* [2008] QCA 275 at [20].
[461] *Stevenson v Singh* [2012] EWHC 2880 (QB) at [101].
[462] *Simons v Patchett* (1857) 7 E. & B. 568 at 574; *Spedding v Nevell* (1869) L.R. 4 C.P. 212 at 226; *Goodwin v Francis* (1870) L.R. 5 C.P. 295 at 308; *Richardson v Williamson* (1871) L.R. 6 Q.B. 276 at 279–280; *Weeks v Propert* (1873) L.R. 8 C.P. 427 at 439; *Re National Coffee Palace Co Ex p. Panmure* (1883) 24 Ch.D. 367 at 372; *Skylight Maritime SA v Ascot Underwriting* [2005] EWHC 15 (Comm).
[463] *Firbank's Executors v Humphreys* (1886) 18 Q.B.D. 54, Illustration 3 to Article 105.
[464] cf. *Weeks v Propert* (1873) L.R. 8 C.P. 427 at 439; *Whitehaven Joint Stock Banking Co v Reed* (1886) 2 T.L.R. 353. In neither case was there a pre-existing debt. See also *Alvin's Auto Service Ltd v Clew Holdings Ltd* (1997) 3 B.L.R. (2d) 11 (Canada), where the supposed principal, though insolvent, was amenable to a decree of specific performance.
[465] Quaere whether out-of-pocket expenses could be recovered. On general principle they should: see *Chitty on Contracts* (33rd edn), para.26-025 onwards.
[466] *Heskell v Continental Express Ltd* [1950] 1 All E.R. 1033. cf. *Cro Travel Pty Ltd v Australia Capital Financial Management Pty Ltd* [2018] NSWCA 153 (flaws in contractual position not fatal if third party would nonetheless have obtained rights against principal).
[467] *Delta Construction Co Ltd v Lidstone* (1979) 96 D.L.R. (3d) 457. See above, para.9-066; below, para.9-085.
[468] *Fay v Miller, Wilkins & Co* [1941] Ch. 360. See also *Pow v Davies* (1861) 1 B. & S. 220 (seven-year lease without deed: defence of ejectment action held unreasonable). But cf. *British Russian Gazette Ltd v Associated Newspapers Ltd* [1933] 2 K.B. 616 at 649.

would have been enforceable? It was held in 1876 that this could not be pleaded because the notion of part performance is one that affects the equities between two parties to a suit for specific performance.[469] This is a narrow view; but in England the Statute of Frauds now only applies to guarantees, so the matter is not of importance. It has also been held that if the third party was not in a position to perform, no loss is suffered by the lack of authority and the third party is thus not entitled to damages.[470] Equally, if the principal would have had grounds for seeking to have a putative loan contract reopened under the Consumer Credit Act 1974, the agent can invoke this possibility against the third party.[471]

Costs of legal proceedings   The costs of unsuccessful legal proceedings may also be recovered, provided that they were reasonable[472] and the fact that they might be brought was within the contemplation of the parties.[473] These will usually be proceedings against the principal, but the costs of defending proceedings brought by an unauthorised agent may also be recovered,[474] as may the cost of defending proceedings brought by the supposed principal.[475] Persisting with proceedings after it has become clear that the agent was unauthorised may not however be reasonable.[476] The cost of successfully establishing liability of the principal under the doctrine of apparent authority would not however be recoverable (though it should be recoverable from the principal). It is not clear whether such expenses can be recovered in those cases where the transaction is unenforceable against the principal. In the case of an insolvent principal, it is submitted that they might be, on the basis that a claimant in an action for breach of contract may abandon the claim for the expectation interest and claim expenses only.[477] In the other two cases discussed above, those of the purported transaction that is a nullity and of the contract unenforceable for lack of writing, it is submitted that expenses will not often be regarded as reasonably incurred. An attempt under the same principles to obtain the full loss caused to the claimant in such situations would be met by the defence that the loss was too remote,[478] for otherwise the rules as to the contractual measure of damages would be circumvented.   **9-081**

---

[469] *Warr v Jones* (1876) 24 W.R. 695; but in land contracts the doctrine of part performance is no longer relevant in England by virtue of the Law of Property (Miscellaneous Provisions) Act 1989.

[470] *Singh v Sardar Investments Ltd* [2002] EWHC 380 (Ch) at [58] ("on principle an agent sued for breach of warranty of authority ought to be able to rely on any defences which would have been available to his principal had the contract in fact been authorised"); affirmed [2002] EWCA Civ 1706 at [23]. cf. *Habton Farms v Nimmo* [2003] EWCA Civ 68, Illustration 11 below.

[471] *Campden Hill Ltd v Chakrani* [2005] EWHC 911 (Ch) at [62].

[472] See *Hughes v Graeme* (1864) 33 L.J.Q.B. 355, Illustration 7; cf. *Godwin v Francis* (1870) L.R. 5 C.P. 295, Illustration 9. See also *Hammond & Co v Bussey* (1887) 20 Q.B.D. 79.

[473] See *Spedding v Nevell* (1869) L.R. 4 C.P. 212, Illustration 8.

[474] *Yonge v Toynbee* [1910] 1 K.B. 215, Illustration 12 to Article 105; *Fernée v Gorlitz* [1915] 1 Ch. 177.

[475] *Pow v Davis* (1861) 1 B. & S. 220; *Oliver v Bank of England* [1901] 1 Ch. 562; affirmed on different grounds sub nom. *Starkey v Bank of England* [1903] A.C. 114.

[476] Illustration 9. In *Greenglade Estates v Chana* [2012] EWHC 1913 (Ch) it was held that pursuing proceedings against both the agent and the supposed principal had been reasonable. The costs of such proceedings are not discussed, but it was held that the property concerned must be valued at the date of trial.

[477] See *Anglia Television Ltd v Reed* [1972] 1 Q.B. 60; *Collen v Wright* (1857) 7 E. & B. 301; affirmed (1857) 8 E. & B. 647; *Pow v Davis* (1861) 1 B. & S. 220 (seven-year lease not under seal: cost of repairs allowed); *Lloyd v Stanbury* [1971] 1 W.L.R. 535; *McGregor on Damages* (20th edn), Ch.4; *CCC Films (London) Ltd v Impact Quadrant Films Ltd* [1985] Q.B. 616.

[478] cf. *Heskell v Continental Express Ltd*, para.9-080 above (Illustration 5).

9-082 **Other warranties** These propositions concern the warranty of authority. If the agent is held liable on some *other* warranty, as is suggested in the comment to the previous Article,[479] the damages would require to be calculated by reference to that warranty.

Illustrations

9-083 (1) Directors of a building society represent that they have authority to borrow money on behalf of the society, and A is induced to lend £70. The society being solvent, the measure of damages for breach of warranty of authority is £70, with interest at the rate agreed upon.[480]

(2) A contracted, on behalf of B, to buy a ship. A was not authorised so to do, and B repudiated the contract. The seller having resold the ship at a lower price (which was the best price that, acting reasonably, he could get), it was held that the measure of damages recoverable against A was the difference between the contract price and the price at which the vessel was resold.[481]

(3) A instructed B to apply for shares in a certain company. B by mistake applied for shares in another company, and they were duly allotted to A. The lastmentioned company was ordered to be wound up, and A's name was removed from the list of contributories on the ground that he had not authorised the application for shares. Held, that, A being solvent and the shares unsaleable, the liquidator of the company was entitled to recover from B the full amount payable on the shares.[482]

(4) A brought an action against a company in the US, and recovered judgment for £1,000. An agent of the company in good faith represented that he had authority to settle for £300, and A agreed to accept that sum. The agent was, in fact, not authorised to settle. Held, that, the judgment against the company being, in the circumstances, unenforceable, A was entitled to recover £300 from the agent for the breach of warranty of authority.[483]

(5) Under a contract to sell goods to a foreign buyer, A, the seller, had to procure shipment of the goods. He registered cargo space for the goods, but did not enter into a contract of carriage. He arranged for the dispatch of the goods to the ship, but they were not dispatched. A did not know this, and applied for a bill of lading. A bill of lading was negligently issued by B, the shipowners' broker, the goods never having been received. A later had to pay damages to the buyer for non-delivery. A claimed damages against B for breach of warranty of authority to issue the bill of lading. Held, that A could not have recovered against the shipowners even if the bill of lading had been issued with their authority, for only receipt of the goods on behalf of the shipowner would here have concluded a contract; as they had never been received, there was no contract of carriage and the bill was a nullity. A's rights upon the bill

---

[479] See above, para.9-066; below, para.9-085.

[480] *Richardson v Williamson* (1871) L.R. 6 Q.B. 276.

[481] *Simons v Patchett* (1857) 7 E. & B. 568.

[482] *Re National Coffee Palace Co Ex p. Panmure* (1883) 24 Ch.D. 367. See also *Habton Farms v Nimmo*, Illustration 11 below.

[483] *Meek v Wendt* (1888) 21 Q.B.D. 126. As to an unauthorised settlement, see further *British Russian Gazette Ltd v Associated Newspapers Ltd* [1933] 2 K.B. 616.

was therefore not affected by B's lack of authority, and he could recover nothing against B.[484]

(6)   A bought goods, professedly on behalf of B. The seller brought an action for the price against B, which was dismissed with costs, on the ground that A was not authorised by B. Held, that the seller was entitled to recover from A the price of the goods, and also the costs incurred in the action against B.[485]

(7)   A professed to sell property on behalf of B. Held, that A, not being authorised to sell, was liable to the purchaser for the taxed costs of a suit for specific performance against B, as well as for the value of the contract.[486]

(8)   Where an agent without authority granted a lease, and the lessee agreed to sell his interest, it was held that damages and costs recovered against the lessee for breach of such agreement to sell could not be recovered by him in an action against the agent for breach of warranty of authority; but that the lessee was entitled to recover the value of the lease, and the costs of a suit for specific performance against the principal.[487]

(9)   A contracted to sell an estate to B, and sent him an abstract of title, representing that he had the authority of the owners to sell. The owners repudiated the contract and sold the estate at a higher price to C. B sued the owners, continued the action after they had sworn answers to interrogatories that A had no authority, and was nonsuited. In an action by B against A, it was held that the measure of damages for the breach of warranty of authority was (a) the costs of investigating the title; (b) the costs of the action up to the time when the answers to the interrogatories had been received and considered by the claimant's legal advisers; and (c) the difference between the contract and market prices of the estate, the price at which it was resold to C being prima facie evidence of the market price; but that the loss on a resale of horses, which were bought to stock the land before the investigation of the title and without notice to A, was too remote, it not appearing that the purchase of stock was contemplated by the parties when the contract was made.[488]

(10)   A solicitor falsely warrants that he has authority to sell land, and the vendor refuses to complete. The land rises in value between the date for completion and the date of the action against the solicitor. He is liable for the difference in value between the purchase price and the value of the property at the date of judgment.[489]

(11)   A bloodstock agent purported to buy a racehorse on behalf of his principal

[484] *Heskell v Continental Express Ltd* [1950] 1 All E.R. 1033 (on which see Grunfeld (1950) 13 M.L.R. 516); said to require reconsideration as regards the decision on negligence in *Hedley Byrne & Co Ltd v Heller & Partners Ltd* [1964] A.C. 465 at 532; cf. *V/O Rasnoimport v Guthrie & Co Ltd* [1966] 1 Lloyd's Rep. 1, Illustration 11 to Article 105, where there was a contract of carriage and the plaintiff recovered the value of the goods not delivered plus interest.

[485] *Randall v Trimen* (1856) 18 C.B. 786. See also *Farley Health Products v Babylon Trading Co* [1987] C.L.Y. 1126 (damages included cost of manufacturing, packing and shipping goods not paid for).

[486] *Hughes v Graeme* (1864) 33 L.J.Q.B. 335; *Collen v Wright* (1857) 8 E. & B. 647.

[487] *Spedding v Nevell* (1869) L.R. 4 C.P. 212.

[488] *Godwin v Francis* (1870) L.R. 5 C.P. 295. See also *Schlieske v Overseas Construction Co Pty Ltd* [1960] V.R. 195 (action continued after indications received that principal, a company, dissolved); *McDonnell v McGuinness* [1939] I.R. 223 (principal unable to make title: damages against agent limited by rule (no longer applicable in England) in *Bain v Fothergill* (1874) L.R. 7 H.L. 158).

[489] *Suleman v Shahsavari* [1988] 1 W.L.R. 1181, distinguishing and in part not following *Chitholie v Nash & Co* (1973) 229 E.G. 786. *Suleman* was doubted in *Greenglade Estates Ltd v Chana* [2012] EWHC 1913 (Ch); [2012] 42 E.G. 138 at [12].

for £70,000, subject to certain tests. The tests proved satisfactory and the horse was made available for collection. The agent was not authorised and principal refused to proceed; but the third party seller refrained from selling the horse to anyone else and continued to demand the price. The horse then contracted peritonitis and had to be destroyed. The agent was liable for the full price which the third party would have received without deduction of the value of the horse, since the third party's decision to refrain from reselling the horse on the ground that it was already sold was caused by the agent's breach of warranty of authority.[490]

(12) A co-owner of land, A, has authority to sell land on behalf of both owners, but has no actual authority to make a commission agreement with real estate agent that would bind both owners. A is found to warrant to the real estate agent his authority to engage the agent on behalf of both owners and is liable for the full commission on the sale of the land.[491]

Article 107

PRINCIPAL FICTITIOUS OR NON-EXISTENT

9-084   (1) At common law, where a person purports to contract on behalf of a principal, and the principal is a fictitious or non-existent person or entity, the person so purporting to contract may sometimes be regarded as having contracted personally.[492]

(2) By statute, where a contract purports to be made by or on behalf of a company at a time when the company has not been formed, then subject to any agreement to the contrary, the contract has effect as a contract made with the person purporting to act for the company or as agent for it, and the person is personally liable on the contract and entitled to enforce it accordingly.[493]

Comment

9-085   **Rule (1)**   The situation referred to in this Article normally arises where a person purports to act for a company not yet formed, or for an unincorporated association, which has no legal existence, neither of which can be bound. Where both parties were aware of the position at the time of contracting, it may sometimes be appropriate to conclude that the transaction was intended to have legal effect[494] and hence that the agent contracted personally, viz. is liable, and also entitled to sue. The only alternative interpretation would be that the third party knowingly entered into a transaction of the "subject to contract" or "subject to ratification" type.[495] Where the parties are not aware of the true position there will be more difficulty in apply-

---

[490] *Habton Farms v Nimmo* [2003] EWCA Civ 68; [2004] Q.B. 1.
[491] *Mathews v CD Realty (PN) Ltd* [2010] NZHC 1881.
[492] See Comment; *Kelner v Baxter* (1866) L.R. 2 C.P. 174, Illustration 1; *Black v Smallwood* (1966) 117 C.L.R. 52, Illustration 7; *Marblestone Industries Ltd v Fairchild* [1975] 1 N.Z.L.R. 529; Gross (1971) 87 L.Q.R. 367; (1972) 18 McGill L.J. 512; Shapira (1975) 3 Otago L.Rev. 309.
[493] Companies Act 2006 s.51, replacing Companies Act 1985 s.36C(1) (inserted by Companies Act 1989 s.130(4)). See Comment; Prentice (1973) 89 L.Q.R. 518 at 530–533; Farrar and Powles (1973) 36 M.L.R. 270; Collier and Sealy [1973] C.L.J. 1; Griffiths [1993] L.S. 241; *Gower's Principles of Modern Company Law* (10th edn), paras 5-23–5-28.
[494] See *Kelner v Baxter* (1866) L.R. 2 C.P. 174 at 85.
[495] As to which see Article 18.

ing either of these interpretations,[496] and in any case the agent cannot be treated as contracting personally where clearly contracting as such.[497] The cases on companies to be formed[498] have perhaps been more lenient towards allowing the third party to establish liability than those on unincorporated associations.[499] But even in the case of companies there is no actual rule of law that a person purporting to contract for an unformed company is necessarily (as opposed to by interpretation) personally liable on the contract[500]; it is all a matter of interpretation, sometimes said to be aided by a presumption,[501] of law in the case of a written contract, and of fact in the case of an oral contract.[502] Much of the force of a presumption in these circumstances is derived from the fact that the purporting agent is leading the third party to believe that it is bound; reciprocity suggests that the agent should also be bound. There is some suggestion that this reasoning applies only to a person who purports to act *for* the company: if X purports to act *as* the unformed company, X's act is simply a nullity and X cannot be held personally liable on it.[503] But where in the latter situation X knows that the company does not exist, and the third party does not, it may be a more compelling conclusion to find a contractual obligation than one in deceit.

The alternative analysis, that the party acting is liable only on a warranty of authority, is scarcely more satisfactory.[504] Such an action would probably yield no more than the cost of any abortive proceedings brought against the principal, because since the company has no existence and so no funds it might well not be possible affirmatively to prove further loss arising from the lack of authority.[505] In the case of a signature not on behalf of the company but as the company, to

---

[496] See *Wickberg v Shatsky* (1969) 4 D.L.R. (3d) 540; *Jones v Hope* (1880) 3 T.L.R. 247n., Illustration 4; *Coral (UK) Ltd v Rechtman* [1996] 1 Lloyd's Rep. 235; *Restatement, Third*, § 6.04.

[497] *Hollman v Pullin* (1884) C. & E. 254, Illustration 5; *Coral (UK) Ltd v Rechtman* [1996] 1 Lloyd's Rep. 235.

[498] Illustrations 1 and 2. But cf. *Re Banque du Marchands de Moscou* [1952] 1 All E.R. 1269 as to a company that had been dissolved.

[499] Illustrations 3, 4 and 5. See Powell, pp.263–265; Lloyd, *Law of Unincorporated Associations* (1938); Keeler (1971) 34 M.L.R. 615; Fletcher (1979) 11 U. Qd.L.J. 53 and material there cited.

[500] *Newborne v Sensolid (Great Britain) Ltd* [1954] 1 Q.B. 45 at 50; *Black v Smallwood* (1966) 117 C.L.R. 52; *Stott Land Development Corp v Dean* [1967] W.A.R. 86; *Re Whiteley Insurance Consultants* [2008] EWHC 1782 (Ch). For cases where there was no liability, see e.g. *Dairy Supplies Ltd v Fuchs* (1959) 18 D.L.R. (2d) 408; *Hawke's Bay Milk Corp Ltd v Watson* [1974] 1 N.Z.L.R. 236; *Lomax v Dankel* (1981) 29 S.A.S.R. 68.

[501] See *Marblestone Industries Ltd v Fairchild* [1975] 1 N.Z.L.R. 529 at 539–540; *Vickery v Woods* (1952) 85 C.L.R. 336. But presumptions are perhaps out of fashion nowadays, and the tendency is to rely on interpretation only. See Oliver LJ in *Phonogram Ltd v Lane* [1982] Q.B. 938 at 945–946.

[502] *Summergreene v Parker* (1950) 80 C.L.R. 304 at 323–324.

[503] *Newborne v Sensolid (Great Britain) Ltd* [1954] 1 Q.B. 45, Illustration 6; *Black v Smallwood* (1966) 117 C.L.R. 52, Illustration 7; *Miller Associates (Australia) Pty Ltd v Bennington Pty Ltd* (1975) 7 A.L.R. 144; *Western Radio Group Ltd v McIsaac* (1989) 63 D.L.R. (4th) 433. See Fridman (1966) 116 New L.J. 1605; Baxt (1967) 30 M.L.R. 328. But a company can only act through agents, and *Newborne v Sensolid* is open to criticism as turning on a technicality: see Gray (1953) 17 Conv. 217–219; Shapira (1975) 3 Otago L.Rev. 309; the judgment of Windeyer J in *Black v Smallwood*; and cf. *Elliott v Bax-Ironside* [1925] 2 K.B. 301.

[504] For this approach, see *Black v Smallwood* (1966) 117 C.L.R. 52 at 64–65, per Windeyer J; above, para.9-066. See also *Scott v J.B. Livingston & Nichol*, 1990 S.L.T. 305 at 307.

[505] See Article 105. This argument was accepted in *Delta Construction Co Ltd v Lidstone* (1979) 96 D.L.R. (3d) 457 in a case where the principal came into existence but was insolvent; see also *Wickberg v Shatsky* (1969) 4 D.L.R. (3d) 540; *General Motors Acceptance Corp of Canada Ltd v Weisman* (1979) 96 D.L.R. (3d) 159. An action succeeded in *Lomax v Dankel* (1981) 29 S.A.S.R. 68 but damages were not in issue. It also succeeded in *Alvin's Auto Service Ltd v Clew Holdings Ltd* (1997) 33 B.L.R. (2d) 11 (Canada); but although the supposed principal was insolvent it was

authenticate the company's signature, there is the further difficulty that the signer arguably does not profess agency. It may however be possible in either case to imply some sort of warranty that there is or is still an extent company as described, on the analogy of the cases in which directors were held liable in respect of transactions which even if authorised would have been ultra vires their companies.[506] This depends on the scope of the agent's warranty, which is discussed elsewhere[507]; and would again raise problems of proof of loss.[508] But in the leading case of *Kelner v Baxter*[509] Willes J did not suggest using the reasoning he had employed nine years earlier in *Collen v Wright*,[510] the leading case on warranty of authority.

Should it transpire that an agent is in fact acting personally, the agent might perhaps be held liable under the anomalous rule stated in the next Article. But it would be necessary to prove that the agent was acting personally: such a conclusion would not follow from the mere fact that the supposed principal was not liable.[511]

9-086   *Rule (2)* reproduces s.51(1) of the Companies Act 2006,[512] the successor section to that which originally gave effect to a provision of the first EEC directive on company law. The purport of this directive was that any person who enters into a transaction on behalf of a company not yet formed[513] shall be personally liable on it unless the company on formation assumes the obligation, or there is "a clear exclusion of personal liability".[514] It is now clear that the words "person purporting to act for the company or as agent for it" impose liability regardless of whether at common law the agent might have been held to sign as agent for the company or as authenticating the company's own signature.[515] It does not apply when a contract is made on behalf of a company which exists but is in the process of changing its name to that used[516]; nor when the company existed but has been dis-

---

amenable to an order of specific performance.

[506] See Article 105, Illustrations 2, 3, 4 and 5; *Black v Smallwood* (1966) 117 C.L.R. 52 at 64–65; Palmer (1975) 9 U.Qd.L.J. 123. But cf. *Newborne v Sensolid (Great Britain) Ltd* [1954] 1 Q.B. 45 at 47; *Hawke's Bay Milk Corp Ltd v Watson* [1974] 1 N.Z.L.R. 236; cf. the warranties by solicitors commencing proceedings described in Article 106, Illustration 12.

[507] See above, para.9-066.

[508] The cases referred to in fn.505 above do not touch on this, as they concern situations where the insolvency of the supposed principal was accepted. They tend also to be concerned with the availability of the action rather than the damages recoverable.

[509] *Kelner v Baxter* (1866) L.R. 2 C.P. 174, Illustration 1.

[510] *Collen v Wright* (1857) 8 E. & B. 647; see Article 105.

[511] *Newborne v Sensolid (Great Britain) Ltd* [1954] 1 Q.B. 45, Illustration 6.

[512] The original provision was s.9(2) of the European Communities Act 1972. See *Gower's Principles of Modern Company Law* (10th edn), paras 5-23–5-28.

[513] The relevant EC Directive refers to a company "en formation", i.e. already in the process of formation, which would by English law be liable and entitled in any case. In *Phonogram Ltd v Lane* [1982] Q.B. 938, Illustration 8, the Court of Appeal noted the different wording of the then English statute and followed it.

[514] *Phonogram Ltd v Lane* [1982] Q.B. 938 at 944. An argument that the provision only applies to a person who is the "alter ego" of the company (see above, para.1-029) was rejected in *Braymist Ltd v Wise Finance Co Ltd* [2002] EWCA Civ 127; [2002] Ch. 273; *Royal Mail Estates Ltd v Maple Teesdale* [2015] EWHC 1890 (Ch); [2016] 1 W.L.R. 942 (the contract stating that it is "personal to the company" did not preclude agent being bound by, and able to enforce, the contract).

[515] *Phonogram Ltd v Lane* [1982] Q.B. 938.

[516] *Oshkosh B'Gosh Inc v Dan Marbel Inc Ltd* [1989] B.C.L.C. 507; *Vic Spence Associates v Balchin*, 1990 S.L.T. 10. See also *Badgerhill Properties Ltd v Cottrell* [1991] B.C.L.C. 805 (company not properly named).

solved[517]; and it applies only to companies formed and registered under the Companies Act 2006, or its predecessors.[518] In some such cases, the company, though mis-named, may as a matter of fact be a party to the contract.[519]

Section 51(1) by virtue of its final words "and he is personally liable on the contract accordingly" may be interpreted as referring only to the agent's liability. However, the words immediately preceding state that the contract has effect as a contract made with the person concerned, which suggests that the agent can sue also; and it has been so held. In the case concerned, *Braymist Ltd v Wise Finance Co Ltd*,[520] which involved signature by a solicitor as agent for a company not formed, two of the judges derived this effect from the statute, with the result that the solicitor could sue on a contract for the sale of land. The third judge, Arden LJ, however, was of the opinion that the statute could not be given this effect, and that the matter must be solved by the applicable common law principles, and that these made the agent entitled to sue. It is however not clear on what basis they did so. If the interpretation of the contract led to the inference that the solicitor was a party to it, then the solicitor could sue: but it is not easy without more to derive support for such an interpretation from a signature "as agents". The only other available reasoning was that the solicitor was his own principal; but this is not an easy interpretation of the situation. It is considered in Article 108 below. Statutory provisions drafted to meet this problem in other common law jurisdictions are often more clearly formulated, and may deal also with the problem of ratification by the company when it is formed,[521] which is not possible under English law.[522]

Illustrations

(1) A enters into a written contract on behalf of a company not yet incorporated. A is personally liable on the contract, even if he expresses himself as contracting on behalf of the future company; and parol evidence is not admissible to show that he did not intend to contract personally, because it is only by holding him personally liable that any effect at all can be given to the contract, which refers to "the proposed company".[523]

9-087

(2) The promoters of a future company borrowed money from a bank, to be repaid out of calls on shares. Held, that the promoters must be taken to have

---

[517] *Cotronic (UK) Ltd v Dezonie* [1991] B.C.L.C. 721.

[518] *Rover International Ltd v Cannon Film Sales Ltd* [1987] B.C.L.C. 540; decision varied on other grounds [1989] 1 W.L.R. 912.

[519] See *Coral (UK) Ltd v Rechtman* [1996] 1 Lloyd's Rep. 235 at 238–239.

[520] *Braymist Ltd v Wise Finance Co Ltd* [2002] EWCA Civ 127; [2002] Ch. 273 (holding also that the agent's signature was sufficient for the purposes of the Law Reform (Miscellaneous Provisions) Act 1989 s.2). This is subject to the common law restrictions applicable where other party can assert that he would not have entered into the contract: at [62].

[521] e.g. Companies Act (Singapore) cap. 50 s.41; Companies Ordinance (Hong Kong) s.32A; Corporations Act 2001 (Cth) ss.131–132; Companies Act 1993 (NZ) ss.182–185. See too *Rolle Family & Co Ltd v Rolle* [2017] UKPC 35; [2018] A.C. 205.

[522] See above, para.2-069.

[523] *Kelner v Baxter* (1866) L.R. 2 C.P. 174 (further facts, 36 L.J.C.P. 94); *Wilson & Co v Baker Lees & Co* (1901) 17 T.L.R. 473; *Rita Joan Dairies Ltd v Thompson* [1974] 1 N.Z.L.R. 285; *Marblestone Industries Ltd v Fairchild* [1975] 1 N.Z.L.R. 529. But cf. *Black v Smallwood* (1966) 117 C.L.R. 52, Illustration 7. A company cannot ratify a contract made on its behalf before its incorporation: see Article 15.

contracted that the money would be repaid out of calls, if the calls should prove sufficient, and if not, to pay personally.[524]

(3) The managing committee of a club authorises the steward to order provisions for the use of the club. A supplies provisions on his orders, and invoices them to the club. If A looked to the funds of the club alone for payment, and contracted on the terms that if there were no such funds he should not be paid, the committee is not personally liable. But it is personally liable if he gave credit to them. Whether A gave credit to the committee or looked to the funds of the club alone is a question of fact.[525]

(4) A, a colonel of a volunteer corps, contracts on behalf of the corps with B. A does not intend to pledge nor does B intend to accept, his personal credit, but both think that the corps as an entity may be bound. The corps cannot be bound. A is not personally liable on the contract.[526]

(5) H makes a contract with P and signs it "on behalf of the Tunbridge Wells Medical Association, H". The association is un-registered at the time of the contract. H cannot sue on the contract since he contracted as agent only.[527] Nor can he be sued upon it.[528]

(6) N enters into a contract for the sale of goods to S and signs the contract: "LN (London) Ltd, LN". LN (London) Ltd was not incorporated at the date of the contract. LN cannot sue on this contract, since he made it neither as agent nor as principal.[529] Nor can he be sued on it.[530]

(7) S and C enter into a contract for the sale of land. They sign the contract: "Western Suburbs Holdings Pty Ltd S, C, Directors". The company was not incorporated at the date of the contract. They cannot be sued personally on the contract.[531]

(8) A written letter of contract is signed by the recipient "Signed by BL for and on behalf of Fragile Management Ltd". The company is never formed and the contract never performed. BL is personally liable by virtue of s.9(2) of the European Communities Act 1972 (now s.51 of the Companies Act 2006).[532]

---

[524] *Scott v Ebury* (1867) L.R. 2 C.P. 255; *Coutts & Co v Irish Exhibition in London* (1891) 7 T.L.R. 313; *Drew, Wood & Son v Heath* (1899) 8 T.L.R. 111. cf. *Royal Albert Hall Corp v Winchilsea* (1891) 7 T.L.R. 362.

[525] *Steele v Gourley* (1887) 3 T.L.R. 772; *Collingridge v Gladstone* (1890) 7 T.L.R. 60; *Harper v Granville-Smith* (1891) 7 T.L.R. 284; *Bradley Egg Farm Ltd v Clifford* [1943] 2 All E.R. 378. See also *Carlton Cricket and Football Social Club v Joseph* [1970] V.R. 487; cf. *Peckham v Moore* [1975] 1 N.S.W.L.R. 353. The members of the committee do not normally act as agents for the members: *Flemyng v Hector* (1836) 2 M. & W. 172; *Todd v Emly* (1841) 8 M. & W. 505; *Wise v Perpetual Trustee Co Ltd* [1903] A.C. 139; cf. *Cockerell v Aucompte* (1857) 2 C.B.(N.S.) 440; *Ideal Films Ltd v Richards* [1927] 1 K.B. 374; *Campbell v Thompson* [1953] 1 Q.B. 445. See in general Keeler (1971) 34 M.L.R. 615; Fletcher (1979) 11 U.Qd.L.J. 53; *Davies v Barnes Webster & Sons Ltd* [2011] EWHC 2560 (Ch).

[526] *Jones v Hope* (1880) 3 T.L.R. 247n; and as to clubs see *Overton v Hewett* (1887) 3 T.L.R. 246; cf. *Cross v Williams* (1862) 31 L.J.Ex. 145; *Samuel Bros Ltd v Whetherly* [1908] 1 K.B. 184; *Lascelles v Rathbun* (1919) 35 T.L.R. 347.

[527] *Hollman v Pullin* (1884) C. & E. 254 at 257.

[528] Semble; but see the judgment in *Hollman v Pullin* (1884) C. & E. 254 at 257.

[529] *Newborne v Sensolid (Great Britain) Ltd* [1954] 1 Q.B. 45.

[530] *Newborne v Sensolid* [1954] 1 Q.B. 45 at 47; Illustration 7. But see *Hollman v Pullin* (1884) C. & E. 254 at 257.

[531] *Black v Smallwood* (1966) 117 C.L.R. 52, discussed by Fridman (1966) 116 N.L.J. 1605; *Hawke's Bay Milk Corp Ltd v Watson* [1974] 1 N.Z.L.R. 236.

[532] *Phonogram Ltd v Lane* [1982] Q.B. 938. See above, para.9-086.

Article 108

(1) Where a person professes to contract as agent, whether in writing or orally, and **9-088**
it is shown that that person is, in fact, the principal, and was acting personally, that person is (perhaps) liable on the contract.[533]
(2) Where a person who enters into a contract professedly as an agent is in fact
the real principal, that person may (perhaps) sue on the contract:
  (a) where the identity of the contracting party is not a material element in the
  making of the contract, provided that notice is given to the other contracting party, before action, that that person is the real principal;
  (b) where it has been partly performed or otherwise affirmed by the other
  contracting party with knowledge that that person is the real principal.[534]

Comment

The substance of these propositions has appeared in all editions of this book and **9-089**
the propositions are probably generally accepted[535] despite the slender authority in
their support.

Rule (1): Liability The cases usually cited in support of the agent's liability date **9-090**
from a time when the courts were searching for a way of holding the unauthorised
agent personally liable.[536] At one time it was thought that if an agent had no authority the agent was always to be regarded as having contracted personally[537]: but this
was not supportable,[538] and later decisions made it clear that the agent's liability,
where it could not be regarded as being a second, parallel liability on the contract

---

[533] See Comment.
[534] See Comment.
[535] See *Leigh and Sillivan Ltd v Aliakmon Shipping Ltd (The Aliakmon)* [1983] 1 Lloyd's Rep. 203 at 207 (where counsel accepted the agent's right to sue in such a case) (for further proceedings see [1986] A.C. 785); *Fraser v Thames Television Ltd* [1984] Q.B. 44 at 54–55 (where Hirst J appears to accept it). But in *Electrosteel Castings Ltd v Scan-Trans Shipping and Chartering Sdn. Bhd* [2002] EWHC 1993 (Comm); [2003] 1 Lloyd's Rep. 190 Gross J, though clear that he should follow a relevant decision, referred to the view here expressed as raising "very cogent doubts". See too *Lundie v Rowena Nominees Pty Ltd* (2007) 32 W.A.R. 404 (see above, para.8-087).
[536] They are *Railton v Hodgson* (1804) 4 Taunt. 576n; *Jenkins v Hutchinson* (1849) 13 Q.B. 744; *Carr v Jackson* (1852) 7 Exch. 382; *Adams v Hall* (1877) 37 L.T. 70; and *Gardiner v Heading* [1928] 2 K.B. 284. In *Railton v Hodgson* there seems to have been no clear indication of agency, and it appears that the liability of the agent might have been together with that of the supposed principal, the example of a factor being cited. The relevance of *Jenkins v Hutchinson* is confined to the words "unless it be shown that he was the real principal". *Carr v Jackson* contains similar dicta, but concerns a foreign principal (see above, para.9-020) and a cesser clause (below, para.9-096). These dicta are perhaps the strongest: but they seem contrary to later dicta of Brett J in *Hutchinson v Tatham* (1873) L.R. 8 C.P. 482 (which were only partly withdrawn by him in *Pike v Ongley* (1887) 18 Q.B.D. 708). In any case the agent was held not liable. *Adams v Hall* seems to be a straightforward case of the personal liability of an agent. *Gardiner v Heading* is a case where it was not clear that the agent did contract as agent, though the third party thought that he was doing so: it contains dicta discussed below.
[537] *Thomas v Hewes* (1834) 2 Cr. & M. 519 at 530n; *Downman v Williams* (1845) 7 Q.B. 103. And see discussion in *Black v Smallwood* (1966) 117 C.L.R. 52.
[538] See *Lewis v Nicholson* (1852) 18 Q.B. 503; *Jenkins v Hutchinson* (1849) 13 Q.B. 744; *Black v Smallwood* (1966) 117 C.L.R. 52.

itself,[539] was on a collateral warranty of authority.[540] However, when it could be established that the agent was the real principal, the case was naturally a simpler one, and views were sometimes expressed, even after the establishment of an action for breach of warranty of authority, that in such a case such a person was personally liable.[541]

9-091 **Identified principal** If the agent in fact acts personally, but outwardly for a named principal from whom there is no authority, and that principal is not liable on the basis of apparent authority,[542] any liability of the agent (unless the principal ratifies[543]) ought prima facie to be for breach of warranty of authority or in tort (most obviously, deceit if the representation is false to the agent's knowledge). If the agent has not expressly undertaken personal liability on the contract, it is contrary to the principle of objective interpretation in contract to find the agent a party. The main possible justification of the agent's liability on the contract is that an undisclosed principal can be sued when discovered.[544] But the anomalies of the undisclosed principal rules could be cited as authority for many breaches of principle, and this situation comes under no established rule relating to the undisclosed principal, whose liability is additional to the agent's: the analogy can go no further than providing another case where facts initially unknown to the third party can be invoked in that party's aid.

In *Gardiner v Heading*[545] a builder did work on the orders of H, the director of a company for which the builder had previously done work on H's order. The builder addressed estimates to the company and after completing the work was paid some of his charges by the company. He was then told that the work was not for the company but for other principals. He sued H. H was held liable as the person who ordered the work, on the facts found by the judge of first instance. Scrutton LJ asked[546]:

> "If a man who contracts with another thinking he is a principal may, on finding he is in truth an agent, sue the real principal, why should not the reverse hold good also? Why should not a man who contracts with another, thinking he is an agent, sue him when he finds out that he is the real principal?"

But it should be noted that the reference is to "the real principal", and the passage goes on to exclude where "the supposed agent ... has expressly contracted as agent so as to exclude his liability as a principal party to that contract" and the dicta seem wider than was necessary for the decision of the case, which may be regarded as a straightforward decision on the objective interpretation of the facts surrounding the formation of the contract.[547]

The only other justification for the agent's liability seems to be the agent's right to sue in such a situation, but this is equally disputable, as appears below.

From the third party's point of view there are of course advantages in the agent's

---

[539] See Comment to Article 98.

[540] *Collen v Wright* (1857) 8 E. & B. 647; see Article 105.

[541] See cases cited at fn.536 above.

[542] Article 72.

[543] *Re Tiedemann and Ledermann Freres* [1899] 2 Q.B. 66, Illustration 4 to Article 15.

[544] See *Gardiner v Heading* [1928] 2 K.B. 284 at 290; Article 76.

[545] *Gardiner v Heading* [1928] 2 K.B. 284.

[546] *Gardiner v Heading* [1928] 2 K.B. 284 at 290.

[547] The case was followed by the majority in *Salim v Ingham Enterprises Pty Ltd* (1998) 55 N.S.W.L.R. 7, a case concerning the personal liability of the operator of a one-person company.

personal liability on the contract. Where the purported principal is bankrupt, an action for breach of warranty of authority would produce limited damages, for the loss caused to the third party by the agent's lack of authority is small.[548] If the agent is really the principal, it seems unfair that he or she should be able to take advantage of such a fortuitous circumstance.[549] But it can be argued that the third party's reliance was on the financial standing of the supposed principal, not on that of the agent.[550] If the fact that the agent was acting personally can be genuinely established, however, liability would normally lie in deceit, which would be immune from the limits of the action for breach of warranty of authority.

Unidentified principal   If the agent does not name a principal, there is a possibil-   **9-092**
ity that the agent will be held to have contracted personally. This is another situation where, as previously suggested,[551] a rule of prima facie liability of the agent in such situations would, by reason of the unsatisfactory nature of the authorities on demanding to know the name of the principal,[552] yield fairer results. However that be, where there is a trade usage to that effect this may override the appearance of having contracted as agent only.[553] But where such a person clearly does contract as agent only, and has no principal, analytically liability should again be on a collateral contract that that person has a principal fitting the description (if any) given,[554] and the danger of that person producing an insolvent person is met by the fact that proof was be needed that he or she was in fact acting as agent for such person—otherwise that person would be presumed to have acted for a solvent principal. Analogies from the law as to undisclosed principal are again unconvincing. Alternatively, such a person may be liable in tort (most obviously again, deceit).

The notion that an agent would be liable on the contract in such a case was however apparently accepted in *Hersom v Bernett*,[555] where a defendant gave evidence that his principal was X: this was rejected as false and he himself was held liable. Roxburgh J said that[556]:

> "a fundamental principle of justice requires that a defendant who has given false evidence that his principal was X should not be heard to say ... that his principal may have been somebody else, but must thereafter be treated as having no principal; or, in other words, as being himself the principal."

The latter two propositions are not, with respect, equivalent, and it is submitted that the first proposition is the one properly applicable. The judge however seems to have applied the second: although he was not willing to find as a fact that the defendant was himself the principal,[557] he held that he should be treated as such because of his conduct. If the liability of the agent on the contract is to be accepted, this can only be on the somewhat tenuous basis that it provides a quick route

---

[548]   See Article 106.
[549]   See *Railton v Hodgson* (1804) 4 Taunt. 576n, where this situation arose: but see fn.536 above.
[550]   cf. Mechem, *Outlines of Agency* (4th edn), p.221.
[551]   See Article 98, esp. at para.9-016.
[552]   See above, paras 9-016 and 9-017.
[553]   Article 100(2).
[554]   *Restatement, Second*, § 329, Comment e.
[555]   *Hersom v Bernett* [1955] 1 Q.B. 98; following a dictum in *Owen v Gooch* (1797) 2 Esp. 567 at 568.
[556]   *Hersom v Bernett* [1955] 1 Q.B. 98 at 103.
[557]   *Hersom v Bernett* [1955] 1 Q.B. 98 at 100.

to a desired result.[558] But the mere fact that an agent's act does not bind the purported principal does not mean that the agent is to be regarded as acting personally[559]: there must be evidence that the agent actually is doing so, or (as in *Hersom v Bernett*[560]) other circumstances preventing a denial of personal liability. There is now obiter support for the view that ordinarily an agent who contracts on behalf of a non-existent principal will be liable on a warranty that there is a principal, rather than directly liable for the contract purportedly made.[561]

9-093   **Rule (2): Right to sue**   Whereas the liability on the contract itself of the agent who, despite purporting to name a principal, intended personally to be the principal is an advantage to the third party, the agent's right to sue in such a case is not so and is even more difficult to justify.

9-094   **Identified principal**   Although there is a strong dictum by Lord Ellenborough that "Where a man assigns to himself the character of agent to another whom he names, I am not aware that the law will permit him to shift his situation, and to declare himself the principal, and the other to be a mere creature of straw",[562] it was held in *Rayner v Grote*[563] that a person who had purported to sell goods as agent for such a principal but who was really himself the seller could sue for nonacceptance where the third party had become aware of the true position and nevertheless continued with the contract. On this basis it might be argued that such a person can do so in any case, if notice is given that he or she is the principal,[564] and provided that the third party is not clearly prejudiced.[565] But in such a case the contract is with the named principal, an identified person different from the agent, the agent being by the wording of the contract excluded from being a party, and it is extremely difficult to see how the agent can then intervene and claim the benefit of such a contract. For although mistake is not relevant in the formation of contract where it is not material, it should not be difficult for the third party to show that it intended to contract with the named principal only.[566] That party should not be left to establish prejudice, which, in view of the fact that the benefit of contracts is usually assignable, might not be easy. It is submitted therefore that the case itself should be explained on the basis of novation. The agent having disclosed a personal interest in the transaction, the third party accepted the agent as seller. In other circumstances it is highly doubtful whether the purported agent could intervene as

---

[558] "I am sure it is justice. It is probably the law for that reason": *Gardiner v Heading* [1928] 2 K.B. 284 at 290, per Scrutton LJ; "It is not worth while to be learned on very plain matters": *Layng v Stewart*, 1 Watts & S. (Pa.) 222 (1841), quoted by Mechem, *Outlines of Agency* (4th edn), p.221. See, however, above, para.9-017.

[559] cf. *Newborne v Sensolid (Great Britain) Ltd* [1954] 1 Q.B. 45, Illustration 6 to Article 107; *Black v Smallwood* (1966) 117 C.L.R. 52, Illustration 7 to Article 107.

[560] *Hersom v Bernett* [1955] 1 Q.B. 98.

[561] See *Knight Frank LLP v Du Haney* [2011] EWCA Civ 404 at [27]. See also above, para.9-066.

[562] *Bickerton v Burrell* (1816) 5 M. & S. 383 at 386; *Galaxy Aviation v Sayegh Group Aviation* [2015] EWHC 3478 (Comm) at [76].

[563] *Rayner v Grote* (1846) 15 M. & W. 359, Illustration 2. See also *Fellowes v Lord Gwydyr* (1829) 1 Russ. & M. 83.

[564] *Bickerton v Burrell* (1816) 5 M. & S. 383; *Fellowes v Lord Gwydyr* (1829) 1 Russ. & M. 83. But cf. *Rogers v Hadley* (1861) 2 H. & C. 227.

[565] *Rayner v Grote* (1846) 15 M. & W. 359. This view appears to be accepted by Arden LJ in *Braymist v Wise Finance Co Ltd* [2002] EWCA Civ 127; [2002] Ch. 273 at [60]–[63]. But the case was one where there was no principal, and was dealt with by the other members of the court in a different way: see above, para.9-086.

[566] cf. *Hardman v Booth* (1863) 1 H. & C. 803.

principal: this is supported by a dictum of Alderson B in the case,[567] which has since been cited with approval[568]:

> "In many such cases, such as, for instance, the case of contracts in which the skill or solvency of the person who is named as the principal may reasonably be considered as a material ingredient in the contract, it is clear that the agent cannot then shew himself to be the real principal, and sue in his own name; and perhaps it may be fairly urged that this, in all executory contracts, if wholly unperformed, or if partly performed without the knowledge of who is the real principal, may be the general rule."

Unidentified principal   It was decided in *Schmaltz v Avery*[569] that an agent who   **9-095**
signed a charterparty containing a cesser clause purportedly as agent for an unidentified principal could show that he was himself the principal and sue on the contract, on the grounds that it was not of moment to the third party who contracted on such terms to whom he was liable, and that the agent could say that he was his own principal. Such a right is in danger of being inconsistent with the terms of the contract, especially where the contract can be said to be embodied in a document.[570] It is therefore submitted that, even on the most favourable view of the situation, the true analysis is that the contract in such cases is with the unidentified principal,[571] and that the agent can only intervene if the agent fits such description (if any) as has been given of the supposed principal.[572] Further, if the third party can establish that, with whomsoever it was willing to contract, it was not willing to contract with the agent, it should equally be able to say that it had no agreement with the agent.[573] In *Harper & Co v Vigers Bros*[574] the claimant was allowed to sue on a charterparty which he had signed "as agent for owner", though the third party gave evidence that he would not have made the contract had he known that the agent was acting on his own behalf. Although the claimant was refused costs, it is submitted that the case goes further than necessary in following *Schmaltz v Avery*. In both cases it is arguable that the agent was excluded by the terms of the contract, at least unless a trade usage was proved whereby persons so contracting could nevertheless declare themselves their own principals.[575]

Supposed rule doubtful   *Schmaltz v Avery* is a case arising in the context of a   **9-096**
particular form of the cesser clause, a very specialised charterparty provision on which there is much case law. The purpose of such a clause is that the charterer can substitute for itself shippers or consignees of cargo whose positions are regulated by bills of lading and against whom the shipowner can recover outstanding charges

---

[567] *Rayner v Grote* (1846) 15 M. & W. 359 at 365.
[568] In *Gewa Chartering BV v Remco Shipping Lines Ltd (The Remco)* [1984] 2 Lloyd's Rep. 205, Illustration 3.
[569] *Schmaltz v Avery* (1851) 16 Q.B. 655, Illustration 1.
[570] See Article 100.
[571] See Glanville Williams (1945) 23 Can.B.R. at 397 onwards; cf. *Hardman v Booth* (1863) 1 H. & C. 803.
[572] cf. *Restatement, Second*, § 369, Comment b. See too *Carminco Gold & Resources Ltd v Findlay & Co Stockbrokers (Underwriters) Pty Ltd* (2007) 243 A.L.R. 472, Illustration 24 to Article 98.
[573] cf. *Sowler v Potter* [1940] 1 K.B. 271 (but this case is often criticised); *Hill SS Co Ltd v Hugo Stinnes Ltd* 1941 S.C. 324 at 337.
[574] *Harper & Co v Vigers Bros* [1909] 2 K.B. 549. See criticism by Parker J at first instance in *Newborne v Sensolid (Great Britain) Ltd* [1954] 1 Q.B. 45 at 48.
[575] See *Hill SS Co Ltd v Hugo Stinnes Ltd* 1941 S.C. 324 at 333; cf. Article 100.

by the exercise of a lien.[576] A charterer who uses such a clause may well have no principals: it may hope to procure others to ship or receive goods on bill of lading terms. Indeed, modern forms of the clause make no reference to agency. If the charterer cannot achieve its object, it may ship itself and/or consign to itself[577] in the absence of indications that it would not be an acceptable shipper or receiver of the cargo on bill of lading terms (which is unlikely if it is acceptable as charterer). Even if the clause contains a reference to agency, it implies initial involvement of the charterer. In *Schmaltz v Avery* itself the dispute arose because the cargo was not taken on board, so that the question of the charterer's initial liability did not arise: but it was held that he could sue. The general reasoning of the case has been criticised in Scotland[578] as being obsolete in view of the restatement of the rules as to interpretation of written contracts by the House of Lords in *Universal Steam Navigation Co v McKelvie*,[579] and is difficult to reconcile with the principles of law established since that time. The right to sue of an agent purporting to act for a *disclosed* principal is even more difficult to justify. It is equally difficult to support the agent's liability in such cases: indeed in the context of the cesser clause that liability can be regarded as contrary to other authority.[580] Analogies to the case of the undisclosed principal are misleading, as in that case the third party thinks that it is dealing with the agent, and the effect of the doctrine is to add a further right and liability of a further person.[581] The whole of this Article should therefore be viewed with caution and even suspicion, and the cases approached on the basis that in many if not all of them different reasoning would be used today.[582] In view of the existing case law, however, it does not seem appropriate to omit these propositions at present.

Even if the third party cannot plead that it made no contract with the agent, it can presumably plead misrepresentation in appropriate cases[583]; and all authorities agree that the agent cannot intervene when such intervention would prejudice the third party,[584] e.g. where the third party could show that it relied on liability of both agent and principal, or where the agent's liability as principal is by the terms of the contract less onerous than the agent's liability as such.[585] But this is similar to the rule preventing the intervention of the undisclosed principal in some situations,[586] and it might well be more difficult for the third party to establish such prejudice than merely to plead that the contract was made with the supposed principal and not with the agent. *Harper & Co v Vigers Bros*,[587] indeed, shows clearly the difficulty of establishing prejudice.

Whatever the correct view on this matter, agents can sue only if they purported

---

[576] See *Scrutton on Charterparties* (24th edn), Article 108. The more modern form there given makes no reference to agency. See also above, para.9-027.

[577] See *Gullischen v Stewart Bros* (1884) 13 Q.B.D. 317; *Hill SS Co v Hugo Stinnes Ltd*, 1941 S.C. 324.

[578] *Hill SS Co Ltd v Hugo Stinnes Ltd*, 1941 S.C. 324. And see *Sharman v Brandt* (1871) L.R. 6 Q.B. 720. But it has been followed in Australia: see *MacCormac v Bradford* [1927] S.A.S.R. 152; *Marzo v Land and Homes (W.A.) Ltd* (1931) 34 W.A.L.R. 62.

[579] *Universal Steam Navigation Co v McKelvie* [1923] A.C. 492; see Article 99.

[580] *Oglesby v Yglesias* (1858) E.B. & E. 930; see Scrutton, above, para.9-175.

[581] Article 76.

[582] But see *Restatement, Second*, § 372 and Comment.

[583] See *Newborne v Sensolid (Great Britain) Ltd* [1954] 1 Q.B. 45 at 48.

[584] *Rayner v Grote* (1846) 15 M. & W. 359; *Hill SS Co Ltd v Hugo Stinnes Ltd*, 1941 S.C. 324.

[585] *Hill SS Co Ltd v Hugo Stinnes Ltd*, 1941 S.C. 324.

[586] See above, para.8-079.

[587] *Harper & Co v Vigers Bros* [1909] 2 K.B. 549; above.

to contract as agent: if purporting to contract, for example, as a company which was in fact not yet formed, they cannot sue as principal.[588]

Application in other contexts   In *Braymist v Wise Finance Ltd*[589] this reasoning was extended by Arden LJ (but not by the other members of the court) to solicitors who signed as agents for a company which had not been incorporated, and allowed them to sue on the contract. Although it is true that the solicitors had, for technical reasons, no principals, it does not follow that they were their own principals. The purported contract was between two purported parties, one of whom did not exist. It is not easy to see why there was a contract at all, unless the agent could be interpreted as being a party to it: but any use of such an interpretation, which would accord with the view taken in *Restatement, Third*,[590] was not discussed. The reasoning seems to have been that unless there was a reason why the identity of the contracting counterparty was material to the third party, a party who had only signed as agent could sue. But considerations of materiality of mistake in contract, and questions of assignability of the right of action, only arise where there is a party to the contract the materiality of whose actual identity may be considered. Where there is no such party, there is simply no transaction, and the rights and liabilities of an agent must be dealt with by asking the question what the agent has undertaken. The dictum of Diplock LJ as to the assumption that the identity of the counterparty is irrelevant in an ordinary commercial contract[591] applies to an agent who acts for an unidentified principal, and also to an agent who purports to act on his own account but has an undisclosed principal. It is far from clear that it should apply to an agent who actually gives the name of a principal, even if the name given is not that of a legal entity. If there is no principal, such a person may well be liable for breach of warranty of authority or otherwise, but that does not confer a right to sue. Furthermore, the reasoning that the agent is his or her own principal is only appropriate to an agent who had no authority, actual or apparent, from any principal and simply contracted as agent, perhaps because the agent believed that the third party would not contract with him or her personally.

Illustrations

(1) A signed a charterparty "as agent for the freighter", a cesser clause being inserted therein limiting A's liability to certain events in view of his being an agent. A was himself the freighter. Held, that he might sue on the contract (the clause limiting his liability would be inoperative). It would be otherwise, if the other contracting party had relied on his character as agent, and would not have contracted with him had he known him to be the principal. The freighter, whoever he might have been, would have had a right to sue.[592]

(2) A, professedly as agent for a named principal, contracted in writing to sell certain goods. The buyer, with notice that A was the real principal, accepted

9-097

---

[588] *Newborne v Sensolid (Great Britain) Ltd* [1954] 1 Q.B. 45, Illustration 6 to Article 107.
[589] *Braymist v Wise Finance Ltd* [2002] EWCA Civ 127; [2003] Ch. 273; above, para.9-086.
[590] § 6.02. The position is similar to that as to whether an undisclosed principal should be treated as a party to the contract: see above, para.8-079.
[591] See *Teheran-Europe Co Ltd v S.T. Belton (Tractors) Ltd* [1968] 2 Q.B. 545 at 555: above, para.8-079.
[592] *Schmaltz v Avery* (1851) 15 Q.B. 655. But see Comment.

and paid for part of the goods. Held, that A might sue for non-acceptance of the residue.[593]

(3) The chartering broker of a firm conducting various maritime commercial activities charters a vessel, the owners of which are given the impression that the charterers are a large trading group known to the owners' broker. The chartering broker actually intended to charter for his own firm and arrange by back-to-back charters a recharter to the trading group. The chartering broker's firm is not a party to the contract, which is between the owners and the trading group.[594]

Article 109

NO RIGHT OF ACTION FOR PROMISED BRIBES OR SECRET COMMISSIONS

9-098   No action can be maintained by an agent for recovery of any property or money promised to be given to the agent by way of a bribe whether or not the agent was in fact induced by such promise to depart from duty or not.[595]

2.   RESTITUTION

Article 110

RIGHT OF AGENT TO SUE FOR MONEY PAID BY MISTAKE, ETC

9-099   Where an agent pays money on the principal's behalf under a mistake of fact, or in respect of a consideration which fails, or in consequence of some fraud or wrongful act of the payee or otherwise under such circumstances that the payee is liable to repay the money, the agent may sue the payee for its recovery.[596]

Comment

9-100   In such cases the proper claimant is normally the principal[597]: but the agent can sue also.[598] There is some authority that suggests that where the restitutionary claim is for a failure of consideration, whether brought by an innocent party or a party who was in breach of contract, the agent may not sue even where the agent provided

---

[593] *Rayner v Grote* (1846) 15 M. & W. 359. But see Comment.

[594] *Gewa Chartering BV v Remco Shipping Lines Ltd (The Remco)* [1984] 2 Lloyd's Rep. 205.

[595] *Harrington v Victoria Graving Dock Co* (1878) 3 Q.B.D. 549; *Laughland v Millar* (1904) 6 F. 413; *Lemenda Trading Co Ltd v African Middle East Petroleum Co Ltd* [1988] Q.B. 448. But cf. *Meadow Schama & Co v C. Mitchell & Co Ltd* (1973) 228 E.G. 1571 (sum promised after commission earned: not a bribe). And see Articles 48, 49 and 96. Nor, of course, can the agent be sued for not performing the act which the agent was bribed to do: nor (normally) for return of the bribe to its donor. These are applications of the rules as to illegal contracts. See *Chitty on Contracts* (33rd edn), Ch.16.

[596] *Stevenson v Mortimer* (1778) 2 Cowp. 805; *Langstroth v Toulmin* (1822) 3 Stark. 145; *Holt v Ely* (1853) 1 E. & B. 795; *Colonial Bank v Exchange Bank of Yarmouth, Nova Scotia* (1885) 11 App.Cas. 84; *Royal Securities Corp v Montreal Trust Co* (1966) 59 D.L.R. (2d) 666 (citing this Article) (affirmed (1967) 63 D.L.R. (2d) 15). As to the principal's right to sue, see Article 71.

[597] See above, para.8-166; and Article 88.

[598] *Duke of Norfolk v Worthy* (1808) 1 Camp. 337.

the consideration, but only the principal.⁵⁹⁹ There is also older authority that where the agent is mistaken as to authority to pay, but the money was owed by the principal, the agent would not be able to recover, as the mistake was not one as between claimant and defendant⁶⁰⁰: nor, of course, could the principal recover. But if the principal did not ratify the payment the debt would not be discharged and the principal would still be liable: in such a case it would be strange if the agent could not recover, and authority now takes the view that a claim is available to the agent.⁶⁰¹

Article 111

DUTY OF AGENT TO REPAY MONEY RECEIVED FOR USE OF PRINCIPAL

(1) Except as provided below, an agent is not personally liable to repay money received by the agent for the use of the principal.⁶⁰² **9-101**
(2) Where money is paid to an agent for the use of the principal, and the circumstances are such that the person paying the money is entitled to recover it back, the agent is personally liable to repay such money in the following cases:
  (a) Where the agent contracts or acts personally, and the money is paid in respect of or pursuant to that contract or transaction.⁶⁰³
  (b) Where the money is obtained by duress or by means of any fraud or wrongful act to which the agent is party or privy.⁶⁰⁴
  (c) Where the money is paid under a mistake of fact, or under duress or in consequence of some fraud or wrongful act to which the agent is not party, or generally under circumstances in which an immediate right of recovery arises, and repayment is demanded of the agent, or notice is given to the agent of the intention of the payer to demand repayment, before the agent has in good faith paid the money over to, or otherwise dealt to the agent's detriment with, the principal in the belief that the payment was a good and valid payment.⁶⁰⁵
  (d) Where the receipt of the money is outside the actual and apparent authority of the agent and is not ratified by the principal.⁶⁰⁶

---

⁵⁹⁹ *Hepworht Group Ltd v Stockley* [2006] EWHC 3626 (Ch); [2007] 2 All E.R. (Comm) 82 (consideration took the form of land, not money).
⁶⁰⁰ *Barclay & Co Ltd v Malcolm & Co* (1925) 133 L.T. 512.
⁶⁰¹ See *Barclays Bank Ltd v W. J. Simms Son & Cooke (Southern) Ltd* [1980] Q.B. 677; doubting *Barclay & Co Ltd v Malcolm* (1925) 133 L.T. 512; *Agip (Africa) Ltd v Jackson* [1990] Ch. 265 at 283–284; affirmed [1991] Ch. 547 at 561–562; *Customs & Excise Commissioners v National Westminster Bank* [2002] EWHC 2204 (QB); [2003] 1 All E.R. (Comm) 327. See *Goff and Jones, Law of Unjust Enrichment* (9th edn), para.5-59. See too *Walter v James* (1871) L.R. 6 Ex. 124; *Colonial Bank v Exchange Bank of Yarmouth, Nova Scotia* (1885) 11 App.Cas. 84.
⁶⁰² See Comment. As to the principal's liability, see Articles 71, 92 and 93.
⁶⁰³ See Comment; Article 98.
⁶⁰⁴ See Comment.
⁶⁰⁵ See Comment.
⁶⁰⁶ See, e.g. *Sorrell v Finch* [1977] A.C. 728, Illustration 4 to Article 94. With slight modifications and a change of order this Article dates from the 2nd edition of this work (1898).

Comment

9-102   **Questions of principle**   The cases on this subject indicate two different lines of reasoning which could be taken in respect of recovery of money from an agent.[607] The first uses the notion that payment to an agent for the principal in respect of a matter on which the agent has actual or apparent authority to receive it is payment to the principal. Under this reasoning, unless there is a separate liability in the agent (as where the principal is undisclosed,[608] or where the agent is liable together with the principal, or where the agent commits a wrong), the proper defendant is the principal and the agent is not liable even where the money has not been passed on to the principal.[609] The money is in contemplation of law in the hands of the principal: for example, in the case of a deposit.

The second line of reasoning uses the notion that where an agent holds money to which neither the agent nor the principal is entitled, it can be intercepted and recovered at this stage unless without knowledge of the claim the agent has paid it over to the principal. The case law on payment over is of considerable antiquity and has developed its own rules. It was formerly criticisable on the basis that if the agent was liable in personam, the fact that the money was no longer retained should make no difference. It could now be justified as an example of the notion of change of position now recognised in restitution cases[610]; but the cases certainly have their own, and anterior, existence and it seems that they should still be treated separately.[611] The origin of the approach probably lies in a pragmatic response to cases where the agent was based in England but the principal resided abroad.

There is, however, a place for two lines of reasoning. Where there was no basis for the payment, as where it was paid under mistake or duress, the money may be recovered from the agent before there has been any accounting to the principal.[612] Where, however, the ground of restitution is simply a failure of consideration, and the agent received as a disclosed agent, the action is against the principal only. Here the money is rightly regarded as paid to the principal (even if the agent still has it) because the principal may be permanently entitled to it; but by virtue of subsequent events it becomes repayable, as where a deposit correctly paid is justifiably reclaimed, or there is a total failure of consideration on a contract.[613] The matter

---

[607] Mechem, *Treatise on the Law of Agency* (2nd edn), §§ 1432–1433. See in general *Goff and Jones, Law of Unjust Enrichment* (9th edn), Ch.27.; Burrows, *Law of Restitution* (3rd edn), p.558 onwards; Virgo, *Principles of the Law of Restitution* (3rd edn), p.674 onwards; Stevens [2005] L.M.C.L.Q. 101 at 109 onwards (a careful study of the area). See also Mitchell, in Lowry and Mistelis *Commercial Law: Perspectives and Practice* (2006), Ch.6; Bant [2007] L.M.C.L.Q. 225; W. Day "'At the Expense of' in Unjust Enrichment" [2017] L.M.C.L.Q. 588 at 595.

[608] See *Agip (Africa) Ltd v Jackson* [1990] 2 Ch. 265 at 289; affirmed [1991] Ch. 547; the Rt Hon. Lord Millett (1991) 107 L.Q.R. 71 at 77. But the defence succeeded in *Transvaal and Delagoa Bay Investment Co v Atkinson* [1944] 1 All E.R. 579.

[609] *Ellis v Goulton* [1893] 1 Q.B. 350, Illustration 1.

[610] *Lipkin Gorman v Karpnale Ltd* [1991] 2 A.C. 548; see *Goff and Jones, Law of Unjust Enrichment* (9th edn), Ch.27; Burrows, *Law of Restitution* (3rd edn), Ch.21. Virgo, *Principles of the Law of Restitution* (3rd edn), p.674 onwards.

[611] See below, para.9-107; *Australia and New Zealand Banking Group Ltd v Westpac Banking* (1988) 164 C.L.R. 662 at 684; Burrows, *Law of Restitution* (3rd edn), p.558 onwards.

[612] *Buller v Harrison* (1777) 2 Cowp. 565; *Kleinwort, Sons & Co v Dunlop Rubber Co* (1907) 97 L.T. 263; *Kerrison v Glyn, Mills, Currie & Co* (1911) 81 L.J.K.B. 465 (HL); *Santander UK Plc v National Westminster Bank Plc* [2014] EWHC 2626 (Ch). See also *Owen & Co v Cronk* [1895] 1 Q.B. 265 (receiver not involved in duress by company).

[613] *Ellis v Goulton* [1893] 1 Q.B. 350; *Marsfield Automotive Inc v Siddiqi* [2017] EWHC 187 (Comm).

should therefore be disputed between the principal and the third party.[614] It is sometimes sought to solve such problems on the basis of a supposed principle of agency that the agent "drops out".[615] This is an oversimplification in the context of restitution: even in respect of contract, it is not always so[616]; and in tort it is not so at all.[617]

Rule (1)   It is most convenient to start with the general agency-based rule that money paid to an agent for the principal and received within the agent's actual or apparent authority, or the receipt of which is ratified, is regarded as having been paid to the principal and is recoverable from the principal, for "in contemplation of law the payment is made to the principal and not to the agent".[618] It will normally still be recoverable from the principal even when it is also recoverable from the agent. Thus where a deposit is paid to an agent and the transaction falls through, the money must be recovered from the principal even though the agent has not paid it across,[619] unless the agent was a stakeholder, in which case the agent assumes personal liability.[620]

9-103

Rule (2)(a)   Where an agent acts personally, however, the agent is obviously liable to repay,[621] and such liability is not confined to cases of contract.[622] The question of when an agent contracts personally is discussed in Article 98. In particular, an agent acting for an undisclosed principal contracts personally and so is liable.[623] A bare trustee also normally acts in its own right, even if it is obliged to follow directions from the beneficiary.[624] So also a stakeholder is personally liable unless the money has been paid away in accordance with instructions.[625] But where both agent and principal are liable, the third party may sometimes be prevented from suing the agent by reason of merger or election[626]; and the agent may in appropriate cases have a defence of change of position. A recipient of money paid into a joint bank account will be assumed to receive personally, and not as agent or conduit, in the absence of evidence to the contrary.[627]

9-104

Rule (2)(b)

9-105

---

[614] Mechem, *Treatise on the Law of Agency* (2nd edn), § 438.
[615] See Birks (ed.), *English Private Law* (1st edn, 2000), Vol.1, paras 15.259 and 15.310.
[616] See above, para.9-002.
[617] See Article 113. See Stevens, [2005] L.M.C.L.Q. 101.
[618] *Portman B.S. v Hamlyn Taylor Neck* [1998] 4 All E.R. 202 at 207, per Millett LJ.
[619] See *Ellis v Goulton* [1893] 1 Q.B. 350, Illustration 1; *Sadler v Evans* (1766) 4 Burr. 1984; *Duke of Norfolk v Worthy* (1808) 1 Camp. 337.
[620] See Illustrations 2 and 3; above, paras 9-025 and 9-026.
[621] Illustrations 4 and 5; *Continental Caoutchouc & Gutta Percha Co v Kleinwort, Sons & Co* (1904) 90 L.T. 474.
[622] See *Baylis v Bishop of London* [1913] 1 Ch. 127; *Wakefield v Newbon* (1844) 6 Q.B. 276.
[623] Illustration 5 (though the principal here may have been unnamed rather than undisclosed). But see *Transvaal and Delagoa Bay Investment Co v Atkinson* [1944] 1 All E.R. 579, where the point was not argued.
[624] See *King v Stewart* (1892) 66 L.T. 339; *Skandinaviska Enskilda Banken AB (Publ) v Conway* [2019] UKPC 36 at [88]–[89]; and *AWH Fund Ltd v ZCM Asset Holding Co (Bermuda) Ltd* [2019] UKPC 37 at [84].
[625] See above, para.9-026.
[626] Article 104.
[627] *OEM Plc v Schneider* [2005] EWHC 1072 (Ch).

"If any person gets money into his hands illegally, he cannot discharge himself by paying it over to another."[628]

Therefore, where an agent is a party or privy to a wrong in respect of which money is paid to the agent, the action lies against the agent and it is no defence to allege that the money has been paid over to the principal.[629] This applies whether the agent receives the money on his or her own account[630] or on behalf of the principal.[631] In *Snowdon v Davis*,[632] Mansfield CJ said that the reason that the agent was liable in that case (a case of duress of goods) was that the third party did not pay the money for the purpose of its being paid over to the principal, but "under the terror of process, to redeem his goods". But this would be so in a case where the agent was not the party applying the duress, yet in such cases recovery is barred where the agent has paid the money over.[633] The true explanation is therefore that quoted at the beginning of this paragraph, that the agent as a party to the wrong is personally liable.[634] The principal may also be liable to effect restitution, at least where the agent has accounted for the money to the principal, subject to the rules of merger and election.[635]

9-106   Rule (2)(c)

"Where money has been paid under a mistake of fact to an agent, it may be recovered back from that agent, unless he has in the meantime paid it to his principal, or done something equivalent to payment to him, in which cases the recourse of the party who has paid the money is against the principal only."[636]

This rule has been applied to a wide variety of agents.[637] Although the majority of the decisions and dicta concern money paid under mistake, the formulation of this Article has been extended to all cases where the very fact of payment creates an im-

---

[628] *Townson v Wilson* (1808) 1 Camp. 396 at 397, per Lord Ellenborough.

[629] See Illustrations 6–9; *Steele v Williams* (1853) 8 Exch. 625; *Wakefield v Newbon* (1844) 6 Q.B. 276; *Chappell v Poles* (1837) 2 M. & W. 867; *Keegan v Palmer* [1961] 2 Lloyd's Rep. 449.

[630] *Smith v Sleap* (1844) 12 M. & W. 585, Illustration 9.

[631] *Oates v Hudson* (1851) 6 Exch. 346.

[632] *Snowdon v Davis* (1808) 1 Taunt. 359, Illustration 6. See also *Steele v Williams* (1853) 8 Exch. 625 at 632; *Oates v Hudson* (1851) 6 Exch. 346 at 348.

[633] e.g. *Owen & Co v Cronk* [1895] 1 Q.B. 265.

[634] The statement by Baggallay LJ in *Ex p. Edwards, re Chapman* (1884) 13 Q.B.D. 747 at 751 (Illustration 7) is also probably too wide.

[635] Article 104.

[636] *Pollard v Bank of England* (1871) L.R. 6 Q.B. 623 at 630, per Blackburn J; and see *Portman BS v Hamlyn Taylor Neck* [1998] 4 All E.R. 202 at 207, per Millett LJ. See also *Buller v Harrison* (1777) 2 Cowp. 565; *Continental Caoutchouc and Gutta Percha Co v Kleinwort, Sons & Co* (1904) 90 L.T. 474; *Kleinwort, Sons & Co v Dunlop Rubber Co* (1907) 97 L.T. 263; *Kerrison v Glyn, Mills, Currie & Co* (1911) 81 L.J.K.B. 465; *Transvaal and Delagoa Bay Investment Co Ltd v Atkinson* [1944] 1 All E.R. 579; *Australia and New Zealand Banking Group Ltd v Westpac Banking Corp* (1988) 164 C.L.R. 662; *Agip (Africa) Ltd v Jackson* [1990] Ch. 265 at 288–289.

[637] e.g. clerks: *Cary v Webster* (1721) 1 Str. 480; solicitors: *Davys v Richardson* (1888) 21 Q.B.D. 202; bankers: *Gowers v Lloyds, etc., Foreign Bank* [1938] 1 All E.R. 766, Illustration 12; *Egyptian Intl Foreign Trade Co v Soplex Wholesale Supplies Ltd (The Raffaella)* [1984] 1 Lloyd's Rep. 102; affirmed on other grounds [1985] 2 Lloyd's Rep. 36; *B.M.P. Global Distribution Inc v Bank of Nova Scotia* [2009] 1 S.C.R. 504; (2009) 304 D.L.R. (4th) 292; auctioneers: *Galland v Hall* (1888) 4 T.L.R. 761, Illustration 11 (but cf. Illustration 2); one railway company collecting money for another: *Taylor v Metropolitan Ry* [1906] 2 K.B. 55; cotton brokers: *Re Bourne, Ex p. Bird* (1851) 4 De G. & S. 273; excise collectors: *Greenway v Hurd* (1792) 4 T.R. 553; churchwardens: *Horsfall v Handley* (1818) 8 Taunt. 136. See also Illustrations.

mediate liability to repay; in such cases, the agent is liable, and can only escape by proving payment over in the circumstances mentioned.[638] The principal is however also liable, subject to the rules of merger and election.[639] Where the liability to repay arises subsequently, however, e.g. because of breach of contract, it seems that the more general rule (Rule (1)) applies and the agent is not liable even though still possessed of the money.[640] A recent case has exonerated a bank on the basis of an argument that a bank (or other agent) is not enriched when it receives money for a customer.[641] This decision is *per incuriam*.[642] A preferable analysis might have been that a payment made to a disclosed agent is intended as a payment only to the principal, but the convenience of being able to sue the agent (the principle may have developed as a response to the prevalence of offshore principals) has meant that this has never been the law. It remains possible that where an agent acts in a merely ministerial capacity, e.g. as a bank cashier, the agent is not the proper defendant in an action.[643] Rule 2(c) does not enable an action to be maintained against the agent in a situation where the principal, as a foreign sovereign, is immune from suit.[644]

Payment over   It could be said that this should now be regarded as an example of the defence of change of position[645]; but the rules are long-established and quite fully worked out, and there is recent authority that this view is not correct.[646] For the agent to be immune from suit by reason of payment over, the mere fact that the agent has credited the principal with the amount is not sufficient to avoid liability: the agent must have: **9-107**

> "paid over the money which he received to the principal, or settled such an account with the principal as amounts to payment, or done something which so prejudiced his position that it would be inequitable to require him to refund."[647]

---

[638] cf. *Goff and Jones, Law of Unjust Enrichment* (9th edn), para.9-128 onwards. See *Cox v Prentice* (1815) 3 M. & S. 344 at 348; *Davys v Richardson* (1888) 21 Q.B.D. 202; *Galland v Hall* (1888) 4 T.L.R. 761; *Owen & Co v Cronk* [1895] 1 Q.B. 265; *Sixteenth Ocean GmbH & Co Kg v Societe Generale* [2018] EWHC 1731 (Comm); [2018] 2 Lloyd's Rep. 465. But the agent may sometimes be liable in conversion in any case, e.g. in respect of a cheque: see Article 114. The position in equity may be more complex, where a receiving agent becomes a trustee for the agent's client: see *Goyal v Florence Care Ltd* [2020] EWHC 659 (Ch) at [141].

[639] Article 104.

[640] See cases cited at fn.619 above; *North Eastern Timber Importers v Ch. Arendt & Sons* [1952] 2 Lloyd's Rep. 513.

[641] *Jeremy D. Stone Consultants Ltd v National Westminster Bank Plc* [2013] EWHC 208 (Ch) at [243] (criticised Watts, [2016] C.L.P. 289 at 315). See too *Bellis v Challinor* [2015] EWCA Civ 59 at [114] (but point conceded). See now *High Commissioner for Pakistan in the United Kingdom v Prince Muffakham Jah* [2019] EWHC 2551 (Ch); [2020] 2 W.L.R. 699 at [289]–[290].

[642] cf. *Investment Trust Companies v Revenue and Customs Commissioners* [2017] UKSC 29; [2018] A.C. 275 at [40].

[643] cf. *Restatement, Second*, § 339, Comment g.

[644] *Rahimtoola v Nizam of Hyderabad* [1958] A.C. 379.

[645] See *Lipkin Gorman v Karpnale Ltd* [1991] 2 A.C. 548; cf. *Australia and New Zealand Banking Group Ltd v Westpac Banking Corp* (1988) 164 C.L.R. 662; *Goff and Jones, Law of Unjust Enrichment* (9th edn), Ch.27. cf. Burrows, *Law of Restitution* (3rd edn), Ch.21; Virgo, *Principles of the Law of Restitution* (3rd edn), p.678 onwards. In *Abou-Rahmah v Abacha* [2006] EWCA Civ 1492; [2007] 1 All E.R. (Comm) 827; [2007] 1 Lloyd's Rep. 115 the defendant bank relied only on the change of position defence.

[646] *Portman BS v Hamlyn Taylor Neck* [1998] 4 All E.R. 202 at 207, per Millett LJ. See too *Citigroup Pty Ltd v National Australia Bank Ltd* [2012] NSWCA 381; (2012) 82 N.S.W.L.R. 391.

[647] *Kleinwort, Sons & Co v Dunlop Rubber Co* (1907) 97 L.T. 263 at 265, per Lord Atkinson. See *Australia and New Zealand Banking Group Ltd v Westpac Banking Corp* (1988) 164 C.L.R. 662,

Thus the agent may have given new credit,[648] or credited the sum to the principal in a settled account, or spent it on the instructions of the principal.[649] But where the agent has paid the money to the principal and received it back again for the very purpose of returning it to the claimant, the agent again becomes liable.[650]

9-108   **Rule (2)(d)**   If the agent is not authorised to receive the money and the principal is not bound under the doctrine of apparent authority and does not ratify the payment, even though it is said to be received for the principal, there is no basis on which the principal can be liable, and it is the agent who must be sued.

Illustrations

9-109   (1)   The solicitor of the vendor at a sale by auction receives a contract deposit as agent for the vendor.[651] The sale goes off through the vendor's default. The purchaser cannot maintain an action against the solicitor for its return whether or not it has been paid over to the vendor. The purchaser's action is against the vendor.[652]

(2)   The auctioneer at a sale by auction receives a deposit as stakeholder[653] and pays it over to the vendor. He is personally liable to refund the amount on the default of the vendor, because it was his duty to hold it until the completion of the contract.[654] In such a case the principal is liable also.[655]

(3)   An estate agent arranges an agreement for the sale of land "subject to contract" and takes a deposit. The sale never comes into effect and thus no contract is ever made. If he expressly took the deposit as stakeholder he is liable to the payer for its return,[656] and if he accepts it without indication as to the capacity in which he has taken it he is likewise liable,[657] though in both cases the term "stakeholder" is an unsatisfactory one.[658] It is irrelevant that

---

at 682–684; Watts (1991) 107 L.Q.R. 521 at 525. And see *Buller v Harrison* (1777) 2 Cowp. 565; *Cox v Prentice* (1815) 3 M. & S. 344; *Scottish Met. Ass. Co v P. Samuel & Co* [1923] 1 K.B. 348: *Bavins, Jnr. & Sims v London & South Western Bank* [1900] 1 Q.B. 270; *Jones v Churcher* [2009] EWHC 722 (QB); [2009] 2 Lloyd's Rep. 94; *Citigroup Pty Ltd v National Australia Bank Ltd* [2012] NSWCA 381; (2012) 82 N.S.W.L.R. 391. See also *M'Carthy v Colvin* (1839) 9 A. & E. 607.

[648]   See *Buller v Harrison* (1777) 2 Cowp. 565.

[649]   See *Holland v Russell* (1861) 1 B. & S. 424; affirmed (1863) 4 B. & S. 14, Illustration 10: see also Illustrations 11–12.

[650]   *British American Continental Bank v British Bank of Foreign Trade* [1926] 1 K.B. 328.

[651]   The prima facie rule is that an agent does so: see the cases cited in the next footnote and *Tudor v Hamid* [1988] 1 E.G.L.R. 251 at 255. This is also true of estate agents: *Ojelay v Neosale Ltd* [1987] 2 E.G.L.R. 167 at 168 as regards contract deposits. See also above, para.9-025.

[652]   *Ellis v Goulton* [1893] 1 Q.B. 350; *Bamford v Shuttleworth* (1840) 11 A. & E. 926; *Edgell v Day* (1865) L.R. 1 C.P. 80; *Burt v Claude Cousins & Co Ltd* [1971] 2 Q.B. 426 at 435 (estate agent); *Goodey v Garriock* [1972] 2 Lloyd's Rep. 369; *Arnhem Technology Ltd v Dudley Joiner*, ChD, January 31, 2001; but cf. *Wilder v Pilkington* [1956] J.P.L. 739, where *Ellis v Goulton* was distinguished on grounds that are not clear.

[653]   The prima facie rule seems to be that an agent does so, though quaere whether this is appropriate: see the cases cited below; and above, paras 9-025 and 9-026.

[654]   *Burrough v Skinner* (1770) 5 Burr. 2639; *Edwards v Hodding* (1814) 5 Taunt. 815; *Gray v Gutteridge* (1828) 3 C. & P. 40; *Furtado v Lumley* (1890) 6 T.L.R. 168.

[655]   cf. Illustration 3; see also above, para.9-026.

[656]   See *Burt v Claude Cousins & Co Ltd* [1971] 2 Q.B. 426 at 435–436; *Rayner v Paskell and Cann*, ibid., 439n; *Brodard v Pilkington*, ibid., 442n; *Barrington v Lee* [1972] 1 Q.B. 326.

[657]   *Burt v Claude Cousins & Co Ltd* [1971] 2 Q.B. 426, per Lord Denning MR and Sachs LJ.

[658]   See *Maloney v Hardy and Moorsehead* [1971] 2 Q.B. 442n; above, para.9-026.

he has paid the deposit over to his principal, for he would act wrongly if he did so. His liability is a personal one to the payor, whether in contract or in restitution. If he defaults, the principal is in such a case not liable.[659]

(4) An agent discounts certain bills, and in good faith pays over the proceeds to his principal. The bills turn out to be forgeries. The discounter has no remedy against the agent unless he indorsed or guaranteed the bills, or dealt as a principal with the discounter.[660] But the agent is personally liable to repay the amount, as upon a total failure of consideration, if he dealt as a principal with the discounter.[661]

(5) A bought goods from B, a broker acting for an undisclosed principal, and by mistake paid him too much. B gave his principal, who was largely indebted to him, credit for the amount received. Held, that B was liable to repay to A the amount paid in excess, on the grounds (a) that B dealt as principal with A, and (b) that the mistake accrued to B's personal benefit.[662]

(6) A sheriff issued a warrant of distress against A. The bailiff levied the debt on the goods of B, and, under pressure of the illegal distress, B paid the debt. Held, that the bailiff was personally liable to repay B, though he had paid the amount over to the sheriff.[663]

(7) Pending a bankruptcy petition, and with notice of the act of bankruptcy, a solicitor, as the agent of the petitioning creditor, received from the debtor various sums of money in consideration of the adjournment of the petition, and paid such sums over to his principal. Held, that the solicitor was personally liable to repay the amount to the trustee in bankruptcy, notwithstanding the payment over, because the money was obtained wrongfully.[664]

(8) An agent who acts for an executor de son tort is himself an executor de son tort and personally liable to account for assets collected by him, even after he has paid them over to his principal. Payment over is no defence in the case of wrongdoers.[665]

(9) An agent demands more money than is due, and wrongfully withholds documents from T, who pays him the amount demanded, under protest, in order to recover the documents. The agent is personally liable to T in respect of the amount overpaid, even after he has paid the money over to the principal.[666]

(10) An insurance broker received money from an underwriter in respect of a voidable policy, and settled with his principal for the amount, amongst other matters, without notice of the underwriter's intention to dispute the policy, and without fraud. Held, that the agent was not liable to repay the amount to the underwriter, who had paid it to him under a mistake of fact.[667]

(11) An auctioneer sold certain shares by private contract, and received a deposit. The purchaser declined to complete, on the ground that the contract was void

[659] *Sorrell v Finch* [1977] A.C. 728, Illustration 4 to Article 92.
[660] *Re Bourne Ex p. Bird* (1851) 4 De G. & S. 273.
[661] *Gurney v Womersley* (1854) 4 E. & B. 133; *Royal Exchange Ass. v Moore* (1863) 8 L.T. 242.
[662] *Newall v Tomlinson* (1871) L.R. 6 C.P. 405.
[663] *Snowdon v Davis* (1808) 1 Taunt. 359; cf. *Goodall v Lowndes* (1844) 6 Q.B. 464.
[664] *Ex p. Edwards, re Chapman* (1884) 13 Q.B.D. 747.
[665] *Sharland v Mildon, Sharland v Loosemore* (1846) 5 Hare 469; *Padget v Priest* (1787) 2 T.R. 97. See Williams, Mortimer and Sunnucks, *Executors, Administrators and Probate* (21st edn), para.5-46.
[666] *Smith v Sleap* (1844) 12 M. & W. 585; *Oates v Hudson* (1851) 6 Exch. 346.
[667] *Holland v Russell* (1863) 4 B. & S. 14; *Shand v Grant* (1863) 15 C.B.(N.S.) 324.

as not complying with the provisions of Leeman's Act,[668] and sued the auctioneer for the return of the deposit. Held, that, the auctioneer having paid over the amount of the deposit to the vendor before the repudiation of the contract, the purchaser was not entitled to recover, because the auctioneer was authorised to pay over the deposit to the vendor either on the completion of the contract or on the purchaser's refusal to complete, and such authority had not been revoked.[669]

(12) A, a pensioner, collected his pension from the Crown Agents for the Colonies through the defendant bank by means of receipt forms sent to him by the Crown Agents. Each receipt form contained a certificate that A was still alive. The forms when completed were sent by A to the bank, who obtained payment on A's behalf from the Crown Agents and credited A's account with the amount so obtained. A died. Thereafter, receipt forms containing a forged signature, purporting to be that of A, and a false certificate that A was still living, were sent to the bank by a person pretending to be A, and the bank, believing that the signatures and certificates were genuine and that A was still alive, collected the pension from the Crown Agents and credited the amount to A's account, from which it was withdrawn. The Crown Agents, having discovered that A was dead, sued the bank for the amount of the pension so collected after A's death. Held, that the money could not be recovered as money paid under a mistake of fact, as the bank had paid it over to a person who was their principal, and their belief that such person was A made no difference in this respect.[670]

Article 112

MONEY HELD TO USE OF THIRD PARTIES

9-110 (1) Except as is provided in this Article, an agent is not liable or accountable to any third party in respect of money in the agent's hands which the agent has been directed or authorised by the principal to pay to any third party.[671]

(2) Where a specific fund existing or accruing in the hands of an agent to the use of the principal is assigned or charged by the principal to or in favour of a third party, the agent is bound, upon receiving notice of the assignment or charge, to hold the fund, or so much thereof as is necessary to satisfy the charge, to the use of such third party.[672]

(3) Where an agent is directed or authorised by the principal to pay to a third party money out of a fund existing or accruing in the agent's hands to the use of the principal, and the agent expressly or impliedly promises to pay the third party, or to receive or hold such money on the third party's behalf or for that party's use, the is personally liable to pay such third party, or to receive or hold such

---

[668] Banking Companies (Shares) Act 1867; repealed by Statute Law Revision Act 1966.

[669] *Galland v Hall* (1888) 4 T.L.R. 761.

[670] *Gowers v Lloyds, etc., Foreign Bank* [1938] 1 All E.R. 766; *Vella v Permanent Mortgages Pty Ltd* [2008] NSWSC 505 at [460]; *Citigroup Pty Ltd v National Australia Bank Ltd* [2012] NSWCA 381; (2012) 82 N.S.W.L.R. 391 at [121].

[671] See Comment; Illustration 5; *Gibson v Minet* (1824) 2 Bing. 7.

[672] Illustration 1.

money for the third party, as the case may be, even if the agent has had fresh instructions from the principal not to pay such third party.[673]

Comment

Rule (1)   Rule (1) is the general rule: there is no privity of contract with such third party, and therefore no third party can sue. **9-111**

Rule (2)   This rule refers to cases where the chose in action has been assigned, whether simpliciter or by way of charge. The same rule would therefore apply to mere debts owed by the agent to the principal, though here of course the money could not be regarded as held to the use of the third person, whose action would be contractual. The reference to a "specific fund" in this rule is therefore dictated only by the subject of this section of the chapter: although the assignment must of course be of a specific chose in action[674]; it is not necessary that the chose in action be a fund as opposed to a debt (though the distinction is probably relevant for the purposes of Rule (3)). The complexities of the law of assignment of choses in action are beyond the scope of this work, but once an assignment has been duly made the assignee can sue for the money and the debtor must not pay the assignor, and is not discharged by doing so.[675] But an assignee takes subject to equities, and therefore the agent can plead against the third party set-offs the agent had against the principal before the assignment.[676] An assignment should be sharply distinguished from a mere authority to pay money out of a fund, which is revocable and gives no right to any third party[677] except as provided in Rule (3). **9-112**

Rule (3)   This refers to an "intractable mass of conflicting authority ... contradictory and unintelligible".[678] A large group of mainly nineteenth-century cases establishes that where an agent holds a fund for the principal and is directed by that principal to pay it to a third party, and notifies the third party that he or she is willing to do so, the agent becomes liable to the third party, and the principal's authority becomes irrevocable. It is now clear that the liability is in restitution, and it is submitted that the only way in which the cases can be justified in the light of modern notions is as a sort of attornment of money,[679] whereby the agent holds a fund for the principal and then attorns to the third party, this being evidenced by the promise to pay the third party. And it seems that such was the original doctrine: but the rule was extended in *Israel v Douglas* (1789)[680] to cases where the agent was merely a debtor to the principal. This, of course, causes theoretical complications regarding what is now called privity of contract: but the modern notions of consideration, privity and assignment were not then fully worked out, and there fol- **9-113**

---

[673] See Comment and Illustrations 2–4.

[674] See *Citizens' Bank of Louisiana v First National Bank* (1874) L.R. 6 H.L. 352.

[675] *Brandt's Sons & Co v Dunlop Rubber Co* [1905] A.C. 454; *Brice v Bannister* (1878) 3 Q.B.D. 569.

[676] *Roxburghe v Cox* (1881) 17 Ch.D. 520, Illustration 1.

[677] *Brandt's Sons & Co v Dunlop Rubber Co* [1905] A.C. 454; *Ex p. Hall, Re Whitting* (1879) 10 Ch.D. 615; *Rodick v Gandell* (1852) 1 De G.M. & G. 763. And see Illustrations 1 and 5 and cases there cited.

[678] Jackson, *History of Quasi-Contract* (1936), pp.99 and 103. See ibid., p.31 onwards and p.93 onwards; Davies (1959) 75 L.Q.R. 220; Winfield, *Province of the Law of Tort* (1931), p.135 onwards; Yates (1977) 41 Conv. 49; Comment to Article 118.

[679] See *Goff and Jones, Law of Unjust Enrichment* (9th edn); *FTV Holdings Cairns Pty Ltd v Smith* [2014] QCA 217 at [32].

[680] *Israel v Douglas* (1789) 1 H.Bl. 239.

lowed a large number of cases purporting to explain the rule on the basis of nova-tion,[681] assignment,[682] trust[683] or declaration of agency in favour of the third party.[684] The rule was in the mid-nineteenth century again confined to the case of a fund, and recognised as involving an action not in contract but in restitution, in *Liversidge v Broadbent*[685] and *Griffin v Weatherby*.[686] More than a century later it was discussed in *Shamia v Joory*,[687] where the full complexities were apparently not cited to Barry J, who decided that there was for this purpose no difference between a debt and a fund. But it is only this distinction, unsatisfactory though it may be, that prevents the rule from subverting many of the fundamental principles of the law of contract as now understood. It is submitted that the rule should therefore be confined to the case of a fund: but if it were extended to the case of a debt, it would provide a rather curious type of appropriation or quasi-assignment operating at common law. It does not follow logically that the arrangement should be irrevocable by the principal, especially where the third party is a mere donee, but this irrevocability seems too firmly rooted in the cases to be questioned.

The illustrations that follow have been left, apart from the addition of *Shamia v Joory*, in the arrangement in which they appeared in the second edition of this work (1898), though a few that seem to have no modern relevance have been omitted. But it should be noted that the proper assessment of the cases cited is today a doubt-ful matter. The doctrine of privity of contract and the rules of assignment and consideration are now established with reasonable clarity: therefore the issues should be looked at as being of principle, and the old cases viewed critically. In particular, cases that refuse to distinguish between a debt and a fund could be regarded as wrong in view of *Liversidge v Broadbent* and *Griffin v Weatherby* were it not for the authority of *Shamia v Joory*. Many cases purporting to find an assign-ment[688] or a novation[689] can now be regarded as outdated: and cases refusing to al-low a third party to sue unless there is consideration or assignment[690] should prob-ably be regarded as wrong where a fund is involved, and possibly, if *Shamia v Joory* is correct, where a debt is involved.

The Article, however, which also dates from the second edition, is submitted as being a correct reconciliation of the cases as they stand.[691]

Illustrations

9-114   (1) A principal assigns to another money held by an agent to the principal's use, and the assignee gives notice to the agent of the assignment. The agent is

---

[681] *Walker v Rostron* (1842) 9 M. & W. 411, Illustration 3; *Hodgson v Anderson* (1825) 3 B. & C. 842; *Hamilton v Spottiswoode* (1849) 4 Exch. 200.

[682] *Crowfoot v Gurney* (1832) 9 Bing. 372, Illustration 2; *Hutchinson v Heyworth* (1838) 9 A. & E. 375; *Gardner v Lachlan* (1838) 4 Myl. & C. 129; *Burn v Carvalho* (1839) 4 Myl. & C. 690.

[683] See *Re Douglass Ex p. Cotterill* (1837) 3 Mont. & Ayr. 376 at 385.

[684] See *Lilly v Hays* (1836) 5 A. & E. 548 at 551.

[685] *Liversidge v Broadbent* (1859) 4 H. & N. 603. Of course, the term "restitution" is of modern usage.

[686] *Griffin v Weatherby* (1869) L.R. 3 Q.B. 753.

[687] *Shamia v Joory* [1958] 1 Q.B. 448, Illustration 6; followed in a case involving a fund in *Dellas v Kourtessis* [1962] V.R. 456.

[688] e.g. *Crowfoot v Gurney* (1832) 9 Bing. 372, Illustration 2; *Hutchinson v Heyworth* (1838) 9 A. & E. 375; *Gardner v Lachlan* (1838) 4 Myl. & C. 129; *Burn v Carvalho* (1839) 4 Myl. & C. 690.

[689] e.g. *Walker v Rostron* (1842) 9 M. & W. 411, Illustration 3; *Hodgson v Anderson* (1825) 3 B. & C. 842; *Hamilton v Spottiswoode* (1849) 4 Exch. 200.

[690] e.g. *Wharton v Walker* (1825) 4 B. & C. 163.

[691] The formulation in the first edition was in terms of the third party suing in contract.

bound to account for the money to the assignee,[692] subject to any right of lien or set-off the agent may have against the principal at the time when he receives notice of the assignment.[693] So, if a debtor charges money in the hands of his agent with payment of the debt, the agent is liable to the creditor upon receiving notice of the charge.[694]

(2) A principal gives his agent authority to pay money to T, a third person. The agent promises T that he will pay him when the amount is ascertained. The agent is liable to T for the amount when it is ascertained, though in the meantime the principal has become bankrupt,[695] or has countermanded his authority.[696]

(3) A principal writes a letter authorising his agent to pay to A the amounts of certain acceptances, as they become due, out of the proceeds of certain assignments. A shows the letter to the agent, who assents to the terms of it. Before the acceptances fall due, the principal becomes bankrupt, and the agent pays the proceeds of the assignments to the trustee in bankruptcy. The agent is personally liable to A for the amounts of the acceptances as they become due.[697]

(4) A bill drawn on an agent is made payable out of a particular fund, and the agent promises to pay the holder when he receives money for the principal. The agent is liable to the holder, if he subsequently receives the money.[698]

(5) An acceptor of a bill pays money to a banker for the purpose of taking up the bill, and the banker promises to apply the money accordingly. The banker refuses to take up the bill, and claims to retain the money for a balance due to him from the acceptor. The drawer of the bill has no right of action, either at law or in equity, against the banker to compel him to apply the money to the payment of the bill, there being no privity of contract between them.[699] So, where an agent is authorised to pay a debt out of moneys in his hands, and there is no assignment of or charge on such moneys to or in favour of the creditor, the agent is not liable to the creditor, unless he expressly or impliedly contracts to pay him, or agrees to hold the money to his use.[700]

(6) A owes P money. Ps who lives abroad, wishes to make a gift to T, and instructs A to pay some of the debt to T. A agrees, tells T that he will do so, and sends him a cheque, which is, however, incorrectly drawn. The cheque is returned by T to A for correction, but A makes no further effort to pay T. T can sue A in restitution.[701]

---

[692] *Webb v Smith* (1885) 30 Ch.D. 192; *Row Ex p. South* (1818) 3 Swan. 392; *Rodick v Gandell* (1852) 1 De G.M. & G. 763; *Greenway v Atkinson* (1881) 29 W.R. 560.
[693] *Roxburghe v Cox* (1881) 17 Ch.D. 520; *Webb v Smith* (1885) 30 Ch.D. 192.
[694] See *Webb v Smith*, and the other cases, above.
[695] *Crowfoot v Gurney* (1832) 9 Bing. 372.
[696] *Robertson v Fauntleroy* (1823) 8 Moo. C.P. 10.
[697] *Walker v Rostron* (1842) 9 M. & W. 411; *Fruhling v Schroder* (1835) 7 C. & P. 103; *Hamilton v Spottiswoode* (1849) 4 Exch. 200; *Noble v National Discount Co* (1860) 5 H. & N. 225.
[698] *Stevens v Hill* (1805) 5 Esp. 247; *Langston v Corney* (1815) 4 Camp. 176.
[699] *Moore v Bushell* (1857) 27 L.J.Ex. 3; *Hill v Royds* (1869) L.R. 8 Eq. 290; *Johnson v Robarts* (1875) L.R. 10 Ch.App. 505.
[700] *Williams v Everett* (1811) 14 East 582; *Howell v Batt* (1833) 5 B. & Ad. 504; *Malcolm v Scott* (1850) 5 Exch. 601; *Brind v Hampshire* (1836) 1 M. & W. 365; *Wedlake v Hurley* (1830) 1 C. & J. 83; *Bell v London & Northern Western Ry Co* (1852) 15 Beav. 548; *Morrell v Wotten* (1852) 16 Beav. 197; *Scott v Porcher* (1817) 3 Meriv. 652.
[701] *Shamia v Joory* [1958] 1 Q.B. 448; *Dellas v Kourtessis* [1962] V.R. 456. But see Comment above.

3. TORTS

Article 113

AGENT PERSONALLY LIABLE FOR TORTS AND OTHER WRONGS

9-115   Where loss, damage or injury is caused to any third party by any act or omission of an agent that constitutes a civil wrong[702] while the agent is acting on behalf of the principal, the agent is, in general, personally liable, whether or not acting with the authority of the principal, to the same extent as if the agent was acting personally,[703] unless the authority of the principal justifies the wrong.[704]

Comment

9-116   **General**   It is in general no defence to an action against a tortfeasor for the tortfeasor to prove that he or she acted under the authority, instructions or orders of another.[705] In this respect liability for most torts differs from contract liability, where it is sometimes (misleadingly[706]) said that the agent "drops out". But, of course, where such authority, instructions or orders make legal what might otherwise be tortious, there will be no liability; and ratification also may make non-tortious what was tortious when it was done.[707] Again, there are many cases where a person who follows the instructions or orders of a person who has superior status or skill may for that reason, not be negligent,[708] and a person who acts purely ministerially may sometimes not be liable.[709] It must also be borne in mind that the text of Article 113 refers to acts and omissions that are sufficient to constitute a wrong that the law recognises. Mere fault or carelessness in a person, including an agent, where there is no duty of care will not found liability, even if there were liability in others. Hence, some forms of tortious liability turn not merely on fault but on the presence of an assumption of responsibility for the outcomes of the conduct. In such cases, a careless agent who has assumed no responsibility to the claimant commits no wrong, even where the agent had authority to make the principal liable for the same conduct. In the next paragraph it will be seen that liability for negligent state-

---

[702] Civil liability of an agent for a criminal wrong in the tort of breach of statutory duty will usually turn on statutory intention: see *Campbell v Peter Gordon Joiners Ltd* [2016] UKSC 38; [2016] A.C. 1513.

[703] See Illustrations; *Restatement, Third*, § 7.01: "An agent is subject to liability to a third party harmed by the agent's tortious conduct. Conduct otherwise tortious is not privileged simply because an actor acts as an agent or an employee, with actual or apparent authority, or within the scope of employment". The agent may be liable as joint tortfeasor with the principal: see below, para.9-123.

[704] Illustrations 9 and 10.

[705] *Bennett v Bayes* (1860) 5 H. & N. 391, Illustration 1; *Heugh v Earl of Abergavenny* (1874) 23 W.R. 40; *Carey v Laiken* 2015 SCC 17; [2015] 2 S.C.R. 79 (solicitor liable for contempt of court for releasing frozen fund on client's instructions).

[706] See above, para.9-002.

[707] Illustrations 9 and 10. The reverse does not apply: an agent sued for defamation who pleads qualified privilege is not affected by the malice of the principal: *Egger v Viscount Chelmsford* [1965] 1 Q.B. 248. State immunity under the State Immunity Act 1978 extends to the agents of a foreign state party: *Koo Golden East Mongolia v Bank of Nova Scotia* [2007] EWCA Civ 1443; [2008] Q.B. 717 (bank, as agent of central bank of Mongolia, not subject to order for disclosure of details of its customer's affairs, in relation to alleged tort by the central bank).

[708] See *Gold v Essex CC* [1942] 2 K.B. 293.

[709] See Article 114 (conversion).

ments that are made on behalf of a disclosed principal within the agent's actual or apparent authority and are intended to create legal responsibility rests directly with the principal, rather than with the agent, unless the agent has also assumed responsibility for their accuracy. English law has also been more resistant than some other jurisdictions to the imposition of liability in tort for economic loss, for example in relation to liability for defective products,[710] but should such liability develop it too may result in direct liability on the owner of the relevant business without liability on the part of the employees and others who are responsible for the actual manufacture of the products.[711] This is not centrally an issue of agency law, and it is not further treated here.

Torts connected with contract—deceit and negligent misstatement　In **9-117** contractual situations it is clear that an agent may be liable to the third party in deceit, e.g. when the agent deliberately misrepresents the agent's authority[712] or knowingly signs a false bill of lading.[713] It is also now clear that an action in negligence may be brought within a pre-contractual[714] and also a contractual situation[715] against a contracting party personally. By the same token, the existence of a contractual situation does not bar an action against the agent of one of the contracting parties. The mere fact that the agent acts for one party does not always prevent the agent's owing, in appropriate cases, a duty of care to the other. Such liability is most likely to occur in connection with negligent misrepresentation.[716] Although earlier authority on the leading case of *Hedley Byrne & Co Ltd v Heller & Partners Ltd*[717] suggested a narrow scope for the duty of care in respect of statements,[718] later authority expanded this.[719] In Commonwealth cases, estate agents have been held liable for negligent misrepresentations, not made within the scope of their authority on behalf of the vendor, to prospective purchasers of land.[720] Beyond this specialised context, other decisions have found agents liable to third parties for misstatements.[721] However, except to the extent that these authorities rest on a finding that the agent assumed responsibility for a statement's accuracy, they

---

[710] See, e.g. *Murphy v Brentwood District Council* [1991] 1 A.C. 398.

[711] See, e.g. *Body Corporate 202254 v Taylor* [2009] 2 N.Z.L.R. 17.

[712] *Polhill v Walter* (1832) 3 B. & Ad. 114; *Randell v Trimen* (1856) 18 C.B. 786; *West London Commercial Bank v Kitson* (1884) 13 Q.B.D. 360.

[713] *Standard Chartered Bank v Pakistan National Shipping Corp* [2002] UKHL 43; [2003] 1 A.C. 959.

[714] *Esso Petroleum Co Ltd v Mardon* [1976] Q.B. 801.

[715] *Henderson v Merrett Syndicates Ltd* [1995] 2 A.C. 145; *Midland Bank Trust Co Ltd v Hett, Stubbs & Kemp* [1979] Ch. 384.

[716] But as to Misrepresentation Act 1967, see below, para.9-118.

[717] *Hedley Byrne & Co Ltd v Heller & Partners Ltd* [1964] A.C. 465.

[718] *Mutual Life and Citizens' Assurance Co Ltd v Evatt* [1971] A.C. 793 (PC).

[719] *Esso Petroleum Co Ltd v Mardon* [1976] Q.B. 801.

[720] *Dodds v Dodds and Millman* (1964) 45 D.L.R. (2d) 472; *Bango v Holt* (1971) 21 D.L.R. (3d) 66; *Avery v Salie* (1972) 25 D.L.R. (3d) 495; *Olsen v Poirier* (1978) 91 D.L.R. (3d) 123; *Chand v Sabo Bros Realty Ltd* (1979) 96 D.L.R. (3d) 445; *Komarniski v Marien* (1979) 100 D.L.R. (3d) 81; *Roberts v Montex Development Corp* 100 D.L.R. (3d) 660; *Barrett v J.R. West Ltd* [1970] N.Z.L.R. 789; *Richardson v Norris Smith Real Estate Ltd* [1977] 1 N.Z.L.R. 152; *Roots v Oentory Pty Ltd* [1983] 2 Qd.R. 745. But cf. *Alessio v Jovica* (1973) 34 D.L.R. (3d) 107, reversed in part (1973) 42 D.L.R. (3d) 242; *Jones v Still* [1965] N.Z.L.R. 1071; *Presser v Caldwell Estates Pty Ltd* [1971] 2 N.S.W.L.R. 471; *Shing v Ashcroft* [1987] 2 N.Z.L.R. 154. As to the possibility that an agent may undertake no duty beyond that of passing on what the principal wishes to communicate, see *Butcher v Lachlan Realty Pty Ltd* (2004) 218 C.L.R. 592.

[721] *Allied Finance and Investments Ltd v Haddow & Co* [1983] N.Z.L.R. 22, Illustration 13 (solicitor); *Computastaff Ltd v Ingledew Brown Bennison & Garrett* (1983) 268 E.G. 906 (solicitors and estate

would need, in the UK, to be reviewed in the light of the decision of the House of Lords in *Williams v Natural Life Health Foods Ltd*.[722] Here the principal director of a small company was held not liable for negligent projections in an advisory memorandum to a third party on the basis that the director himself had assumed no responsibility to the claimant. The basis of the case was the orthodox one that no tort is committed by the agent, because, as in the case of the solicitor answering inquiries,[723] there is in the particular case no personal assumption of responsibility for the purposes of a duty of care in respect of pure economic loss.[724] The principal might be liable in such circumstances, though this itself may give rise to difficulties.[725] No assumption of responsibility is, however, necessary for liability in deceit.[726] As regards actions under s.2(1) of the Misrepresentation Act 1967, its wording is confined to representations made by a party to a contract and does not cover misrepresentations by their agents, unless they also are parties to the contract.[727] The position with claims for pure economic loss not founded on an alleged misstatement is less clear.[728]

---

agents); *Garland v Ralph Pay & Ransom* (1984) 271 E.G. 106 (selling agent employed by mortgagee liable to mortgagor); *Al-Kandari v J.R. Brown & Co* [1988] Q.B. 665, Illustration 13; *Punjab National Bank Ltd v de Boinville* [1992] 1 W.L.R. 1138 (insurance broker liable to assignee of policy); *McCullagh v Lane Fox & Partners Ltd* [1996] 1 E.G.L.R. 35 (estate agent); *Woodward v Wolferstans* [1997] N.P.C. 51, *The Times,* April 8, 1997 (solicitor); *BCCI (Overseas) Ltd v Price Waterhouse (No.2)* [1998] Lloyd's Rep. Bank. 85 (auditor); *J. Jarvis & Sons Ltd v Castle Wharf Developments Ltd* [2001] EWCA Civ 19; [2001] Lloyd's Rep. P.N. 308 (quantity surveyor); *Dean v Allin & Watts* [2001] 2 Lloyd's Rep. 249, Illustration 16 (solicitor); *European International Reinsurance Co v Curzon Insurance Ltd* [2003] EWCA Civ 1074; [2003] Lloyd's Rep. I.R. 793 (insurance intermediary); *Crowson v HSBC Insurance Brokers Ltd* Unreported January 26, 2010, ChD; cf. *James McNaughton Paper Group Ltd v Hicks Anderson & Co* [1991] 2 Q.B. 113 (accountant); *Connolly-Martin v Davis* [1999] Lloyd's Rep. P.N. 790; *A. & J. Fabrications (Batley) Ltd v Grant Thornton* [1997] T.L.R. 588 (solicitor); *BDG Roof-Bond v Douglas* [2000] 1 B.C.L.C. 401 (solicitor); *Noel v Poland* [2001] 2 B.C.L.C. 645 (director of Lloyd's underwriting firm); *Avrora Fine Arts Investment Ltd v Christie, Manson & Woods Ltd* [2012] EWHC 2198 (Ch) at [123] (auctioneer, but disclaimer effective); *Smith v Eric S. Bush* [1990] 1 A.C. 831 (valuer); *Merrett v Babb* [2001] EWCA Civ 214; [2001] Q.B. 1174; *Propell National Valuers (WA) Pty Ltd v Australian Executor Trustees Ltd* [2012] FCAFC 31 (valuer); *Walsh v Jones Lang Lasalle Ltd* [2017] IESC 38 (estate agent and disclaimer).

[722] *Williams v Natural Life Health Foods Ltd* [1998] 1 W.L.R. 830 (HL); and see *NRAM Ltd v Steel* [2018] UKSC 13; [2018] 1 W.L.R. 1190 (Scot). See also *Gran Gelato Ltd v Richcliff (Group) Ltd* [1992] Ch. 560 at 569; and *Spring v Guardian Assurance Plc* [1995] 2 A.C. 296 at 316, per Lord Goff of Chieveley; *Foster v Action Aviation Ltd* [2014] EWCA Civ 1368 (fact director was beneficial owner of asset being sold by his company not important).

[723] *Gran Gelato Ltd v Richcliff (Group) Ltd* [1992] Ch. 560, Illustration 15; *NRAM Ltd v Steel* [2018] UKSC 13; [2018] 1 W.L.R. 1190; *P&P Property Ltd v Owen White and Catlin LLP* [2018] EWCA Civ 1082; [2019] Ch. 273. cf. *McCullagh v Lane Fox & Partners Ltd* [1996] 1 E.G.L.R. 35 at 43–44, per Hobhouse LJ.

[724] Quaere whether the same reasoning could be applied to cases of negligence causing physical damage, as is suggested in the judgment of LaForest J in *London Drugs Ltd v Kuehne & Nagel International Ltd* [1992] 3 S.C.R. 299; but McLachlin J did not agree: see at 461. A lone English case is *Fairline Shipping Corp v Adamson* [1975] Q.B. 180, Illustration 12.

[725] See above, paras 8-180 and 8-182.

[726] See *Standard Chartered Bank v Pakistan National Shipping Corp (No.4)* [2002] UKHL 43; [2003] 1 A.C. 959; *Smith Kline & French Laboratories Ltd v Long* [1989] 1 W.L.R. 1 CA.

[727] *Resolute Maritime Inc v Nippon Kaiji Kyokai (The Skopas)* [1983] 1 W.L.R. 857, Illustration 16; and see *MCI WorldCom International Inc v Primus Telecommunications Inc* [2003] EWHC 2182 (Comm); [2004] 1 All E.R. (Comm) 138; reversed on a different point [2004] EWCA Civ 957; [2004] 2 All E.R. (Comm) 833. But an agent may be a genuine party to the contract: see Article 98; and *Avrora Fine Arts Investment Ltd v Christie, Manson & Woods Ltd* [2012] EWHC 2198 (Ch) at

Statute law may also in some cases provide a basis for suit against an agent for misstatement or for failing to reveal relevant information known to the agent, and for other misconduct (such as failure to comply with codes of conduct). In particular, the Consumer Protection from Unfair Trading Regulations 2008[729] are apt to impose wide-ranging duties on businesses and individuals, including estate agents, engaged in the sale of property, including an active duty to reveal material adverse information about the property known to the agent. Liability can be both criminal and civil.

Misrepresentation as to another's creditworthiness   In relation to representa-   **9-118**
tions as to another's creditworthiness, an agent may be protected by the Statute of Frauds Amendment Act 1828 s.6 ("Lord Tenterden's Act"), which requires a representation as to another's creditworthiness to be in writing in order to be actionable. In *Contex Drouzhba Ltd v Wiseman*,[730] however, it was held that the section did not protect a director and principal controller of a company where the director purported to be speaking on behalf of the company as to its own state of credit; the representation was treated as the company's own, albeit procured by the director. This decision was upheld on appeal but on the narrower basis that the director's signature to relevant documents on the company's behalf met both the representation and writing requirements of the 1828 Act.[731] No comment was offered on the broader ground adopted by Irwin J at first instance, a ground which perhaps places undue weight on the particular words the director adopts in contracting on the company's behalf. It has been held that the writing requirement of the 1828 Act could be established by a document that impliedly represented that a third party was creditworthy.[732]

Companies   For a short period, it was thought that the position of company direc-   **9-119**
tors was different to that of agents in general in relation to torts and other wrongs; they were to be identified with the company and not personally liable.[733] There was, however, no reason to privilege directors over employees and other agents,[734] and it has been affirmed that the general principles applicable to unincorporated

---

[134] where potential liability under the Act was conceded. For a case where a principal was held liable under the Act, see *Gosling v Anderson* (1972) 223 E.G. 1743.

[728] See *Henderson v Merrett Syndicates Ltd* [1995] 2 A.C. 145, assumption of responsibility necessary for liability for negligent performance of services. But cf. *Customs and Excise Commissioners v Barclays Bank Plc* [2006] UKHL 28; [2007] 1 A.C. 181 at [37], per Lord Hoffmann. The other judgments in *Customs and Excise v Barclays* also suggest that an assumption of responsibility is not necessary in all cases, particularly those not involving misstatement. See too *CGL Group Ltd v The Royal Bank of Scotland Plc* [2017] EWCA Civ 1073 at [82].

[729] These Regulations have replaced, and go beyond, the Property Misdescriptions Act 1991, which has now been repealed. In relation to estate agents engaged in transactions involving residential property, see also ss.23A–23C of the Estate Agents Act 1979, inserted by the Consumers, Estate Agents and Redress Act 2007 Sch.6. For an illustrative case under the Property Misdescriptions Act 1991, see *Norfolk County Trading Standards Service v Bycroft* [2012] EWHC 4417 (Admin); [2012] 45 E.G. 95 (C.S.).

[730] *Contex Drouzhba Ltd v Wiseman* [2006] EWHC 2708 (Comm); [2007] 1 B.C.L.C. 758.

[731] *Contex Drouzhba Ltd v Wiseman* [2007] EWCA Civ 1201; [2008] 1 B.C.L.C. 631.

[732] *Lindsay v O'Loughnane* [2010] EWHC 529 (QB).

[733] See *Trevor Ivory Ltd v Anderson* [1992] 2 N.Z.L.R. 517 at 524, 528; *Standard Chartered Bank v Pakistan National Shipping Corp (No.2)* [2000] 1 Lloyd's Rep. 218 CA; reversed [2002] UKHL 43; [2003] 1 A.C. 959.

[734] See above, para.1-029; and Watts (2001) 116 L.Q.R. 525; Flannigan (2002) 81 Can.Bar Rev. 247; Campbell and Armour [2003] C.L.J. 290; Reynolds (2003) 33 H.K.L.J. 51; Stevens [2005]

principals and their agents are as applicable to companies and directors.[735] Where tortious liability turns on an assumption of responsibility, it may be found that directors, like other agents, have not assumed any personal liability, but rather have acted solely on behalf of the company, their principal.[736] Otherwise, directors can be liable in tort in the same way as anyone else. They may, however, be liable for procuring the commission of a tort or other wrong by the company or one of its employees, a subject discussed next. There is some authority that a company may commit the tort of conspiracy by conspiring with its sole director.[737] This is a difficult notion. At the least, it would require that the director (or directors, if more than one is involved) purport to perform some acts necessary for the tort in a personal capacity and not merely as agent of the company, since conspiracy requires not only agreement between two or more persons but acts performed by, or perhaps on behalf of, each of them.[738] Further, if a company were to be a direct party to the common design, as opposed to merely vicariously liable for the acts of others, it would need to be shown that the relevant director had authority to commit the wrongful conduct on the company's behalf.[739]

9-120 **Procuring of, and other involvement in, wrongs** Agents, including directors, can be liable for procuring or authorising the commission of torts or other wrongs by others.[740] Again, this is simply part of the general law, and by no means limited to agents. Many of the leading cases, however, have involved directors who have directed more junior agents to do things which are actionable.[741] There are numer-

---

L.M.C.L.Q. 101.

[735] *Standard Chartered Bank v Pakistan National Shipping Corp (No.2)* [2002] UKHL 43; [2003] 1 A.C. 959 (deceit); *Lewis v Yeeles* [2010] EWCA Civ 326 at [26] (procuring a breach of contract by a third party); *Body Corporate 202254 v Taylor* [2009] 2 N.Z.L.R. 17; *Eco3 Capital Ltd v Ludsin Overseas Ltd* [2013] EWCA Civ 413 at [125].

[736] *Williams v Natural Life Health Foods Ltd* [1998] 1 W.L.R. 830; *Foster v Action Aviation Ltd* [2014] EWCA Civ 1368.

[737] *Barclay Pharmaceuticals Ltd v Waypharm LP* [2012] EWHC 306 (Comm); [2013] 2 B.C.L.C. 551 at [229] (criticised by Watts, in *Agency Law in Commercial Practice* (Busch, Macgregor and Watts eds), pp.108–113). See too *O'Brien v Dawson* (1942) 66 C.L.R. 18 at 32 and 34.

[738] See Carty, *An Analysis of the Economic Torts* (2010), Ch.6; Carty (1999) 19 L.S. 489.

[739] As to authority to act illegally, see above, paras 2-026 and 6-023. See also *Digicel (St Lucia) Ltd v Cable & Wireless Plc* [2010] EWHC 774 (Ch), Annex I at [77] (alleged conspiracy as between related companies).

[740] See *Clerk & Lindsell on Torts* (22nd edn), para.5-79 onwards; Carty (1999) 19 L.S. 489; Stevens, *Torts and Rights* (2007), Ch.7; Davies [2011] C.L.J. 353; Davies, *Accessory Liability* (2015).

[741] e.g. *Yuille v B&B Fisheries (Leigh) Ltd* [1958] 2 Lloyd's Rep. 596 (sending unseaworthy vessels to sea); *Wah Tat Bank Ltd v Chan Cheng Kum* [1975] A.C. 507 (PC) (conversion for delivery of goods without bill of lading); *Anderson Antiques (UK) Ltd v Anderson Wharf (Hull) Ltd* [2007] EWHC 2086 (Ch) (procuring company to wrongly register notices against registered title); *Marex Financial Ltd v Garcia* [2017] EWHC 918 (Comm); [2017] 4 W.L.R. 105 (liability for stripping company of assets to defeat judgment). cf. *Rainham Chemical Works v Belvedere Fish Guano Ltd* [1921] 2 A.C. 465 (no liability for factory explosion); *CBS Songs Ltd v Amstrad Consumer Electronics Plc* [1988] A.C. 1013. As to the concept of "authorising" infringement, see the cases cited in para.8-195; and *Ellis v Sheffield Gas Consumers Co* (1853) 2 E. & B. 767; *Southwark LBC v Mills* [2001] 1 A.C. 1 at 22; *Twentieth Century Fox Film Corp v Newzbin Ltd* [2010] EWHC 608 (Ch); [2010] F.S.R. 21; *Body Corporate 366611 v Wu* [2014] NZSC 137; [2015] 1 N.Z.L.R. 215 (owner of property authorised agent to commit trespass), varied on appeal [2014] NZSC 137; [2015] 1 N.Z.L.R. 215 (liability for trespass); *Twentieth Century Fox Film Corp v Sky UK Ltd* [2015] EWHC 1082 (Ch); cf. *Coventry v Lawrence (No.2)* [2014] UKSC 46; [2015] A.C. 106 (landlord did not authorise nuisance merely by collecting rent from known tortfeasor).

ous cases on each side of the line in relation to patent and copyright infringement.[742] Where the agent has actually committed the central acts constituting the wrong, thereby making the employer liable, it will not normally be appropriate to plead that the agent has procured the employer to commit the wrong; the agent will be a primary tortfeasor not a secondary one in such cases.[743] It would also be unnecessary, as a rule, to use the concept of procurement where the defendant uttered a fraudulent, or defamatory, statement intending that some other party, innocent or not, would pass on the inaccurate information to the claimant; the utterer would be directly liable in deceit, or defamation.[744] Apart from liability for procurement or authorisation, agents can also find themselves subject to liability for participating in a common design to commit a tort or other wrong.[745] Where there is an intention to injure there is also the possibility of liability in the separate tort of conspiracy.[746] In English law, there is, at present anyway, no concept of merely facilitating the commission of the tort of another.[747]

Inducement of breach of contract?   In *Said v Butt*[748] it was held that an agent   **9-121**
could not be liable for inducing a breach of contract by the principal. A major reason given was that the liability of the principal, for whom the agent acted, and who

---

[742] e.g. *Performing Rights Society v Ciryl Theatrical Syndicate Ltd* [1924] 1 K.B. 1; *British Thomson-Houston Co Ltd v Stirling Accessories Ltd* [1924] 2 Ch 33; *Mentmore Manufacturing Co Ltd v National Merchandising Co Ltd* (1978) 89 D.L.R. (3d) 195; *Hoover Plc v George Hulme (Stockport) Ltd* [1992] F.S.R. 565; *White Horse Distillers Ltd v Gregson Associates Ltd* [1984] R.P.C. 61; *C. Evans & Sons Ltd v Spritebrand Ltd* [1985] 1 W.L.R. 317; *PLG Research Ltd v Ardon International Ltd* [1993] F.S.R. 197; *Root Quality Pty Ltd v Root Control Technologies Pty Ltd* (2001) 177 A.L.R. 231; *MCA Records Inc v Charly Records Ltd* [2001] EWCA Civ 1441; [2002] F.S.R. 26; [2003] 1 B.C.L.C. 93; *Societa Esplosivi Industriali Spa v Ordnance Technologies (UK) Ltd* [2007] EWHC 2875 (Ch); [2008] 2 B.C.L.C. 428; *Football Association Premier League Ltd v QC Leisure* [2008] EWHC 1411 (Ch); *JR Consulting & Drafting Pty Ltd v Cummings* [2016] FCAFC 20; *Phonographic Performance Ltd v CGK Trading Ltd* [2016] EWHC 2642 (Ch). See Hon. R. Arnold and P. Davies (2017) 133 L.Q.R. 442.

[743] *Williams v Natural Life Health Foods Ltd* [1998] 1 W.L.R. 830 at 838–839; *Standard Chartered Bank v Pakistan National Shipping Corp (No.2)* [2002] UKHL 43; [2003] 1 A.C. 959 at [38]. cf. *Watson v Dolmark Industries Ltd* [1992] 3 N.Z.L.R. 311.

[744] See, e.g. *Cornfoot v Fowke* (1840) 6 M. & W. 358 at 373–374; *Egger v Viscount Chelmsford* [1965] 1 Q.B. 248 at 261; *Clef Aquitaine Sarl v Laporte Materials (Barrow) Ltd* [2001] Q.B. 488 at 502–503.

[745] *The Koursk* [1924] P. 140; *Brooke v Bool* [1928] 2 K.B. 578; *Unilever Plc v Chefaro* [1994] F.S.R. 135; *Fish & Fish Ltd v Sea Shepherd UK* [2015] UKSC 10; [2015] A.C. 1229 (noted McMeel [2016] L.M.C.L.Q. 29); *Glaxo Wellcome UK Ltd (t/a Allen & Hanburys) v Sandoz Ltd* [2017] EWCA Civ 227. cf. *Kalma v African Minerals Ltd* [2020] EWCA Civ 144.

[746] See, in general, *Kuwait Oil Tanker Co SAK v Al Bader* [2000] 2 All E.R. (Comm) 271; *OBG Ltd v Allan* [2007] UKHL 21; [2008] 1 A.C. 1; *Meretz Investments NV v ACP Ltd* [2007] EWCA Civ 1303; [2008] Ch. 244; *Revenue and Customs Commissioners v Total Network SL* [2008] UKHL 19; [2008] A.C. 1174; *JSC BTA Bank v Khrapunov* [2018] UKSC 19; [2018] 2 W.L.R. 1125. For recent cases involving directors and agents, see *Digicel (St Lucia) Ltd v Cable & Wireless Plc* [2010] EWHC 774 (Ch) at Annex I; *Baldwin v Berryland Books* [2010] EWCA Civ 1440; *Stevenson v Singh* [2012] EWHC 2880 (QB) at [18]; *Alpstream AG v PK Airfinance Sarl* [2013] EWHC 2370 (Comm) at [110]; *Emerald Supplies Ltd v British Airways Plc* [2015] EWCA Civ 1024; [2016] Bus. L.R. 145; *Cullen Investments Ltd v Brown* [2017] EWHC 1586 (Ch). cf. Stevens, *Torts and Rights* (2007), Ch.7. P. Davies and Rt Hon. Sir Philip Sales, "Intentional harm, accessories and conspiracies" (2018) 134 L.Q.R. 69.

[747] See, e.g. *Credit Lyonnais v Export Credit Guarantee Department* [1998] 1 Lloyd's Rep. 19; affirmed [2000] 1 A.C. 486; *Fish & Fish Ltd v Sea Shepherd UK* [2015] UKSC 10; [2015] A.C. 1229.

[748] *Said v Butt* [1920] 3 K.B. 497; *Welsh Development Agency v Export Finance Co Ltd* [1992] B.C.L.C. 148 at 171–173, 179–182 and 191. See Oditah [1992] J.B.L. 541 at 565–569; Tan (2011) 23 Sing. Ac. L.J. 816.

would be responsible, could not lie in tort but would rather be for breach of contract. This ground is not convincing.[749] It would be equally unconvincing, however, simply to conclude that all torts must be governed by the same rules.[750] The tort of inducing breach of contract is itself problematic, given that deliberate breach of contract does not itself engage the law of tort. Imposing liability on agents for inducing breach of contract would be to place them in an invidious position when their duty is to act in the best interests of their principal and they conclude that breaching the contract is in their principal's interests. Principals should not be disadvantaged because they have employed agents and relied on them to assess their interests.[751] Where the principal is a company, absent the immunity, directors could find themselves personally liable for any deliberate breach of contract that they cause the company to commit.[752] For these reasons the identity of interest between the promisor and its agents is a qualification to the concept of inducement of a breach of contract, not an exception or defence.[753] *Said v Butt* has been followed in later decisions.[754] It may however be possible to claim where the defendant did not purport to act as agent or acted in clear breach of duty to the principal or employer[755] or not in good faith.[756] A shareholder of a company, including a parent company, would not automatically be protected by the agency qualification.[757] But even a parent company can be the agent of a subsidiary if so authorised, and

---

[749] See *Welsh Development Agency v Export Finance Co Ltd* [1992] B.C.L.C. 148 at 173, 191.

[750] See in respect of conversion, below para.9-126. The first basis for the decision concerned the doctrine of the undisclosed principal: see above, para.8-079.

[751] See *PT Sandipala Arthaputra v ST Microelectronics Asia Pacific Pte Ltd* [2018] SGCA 17 at [64].

[752] *PT Sandipala Arthaputra v ST Microelectronics Asia Pacific Pte Ltd* [2018] SGCA 17 at [63].

[753] *PT Sandipala Arthaputra v ST Microelectronics Asia Pacific Pte Ltd* [2018] SGCA 17 at [65].

[754] *G. Scammell & Nephew Ltd v Hurley* [1929] 1 K.B. 419 at 443 and 449; *D.C. Thomson & Co Ltd v Deakin* [1952] Ch. 646 at 680, 681; *O'Brien v Dawson* (1942) 66 C.L.R. 18 at 32, 34; *Rutherford v Poole* [1953] V.L.R. 130 at 135–136; *Official Assignee v Dowling* [1964] N.Z.L.R. 578 at 580–581; *Telemetrix Plc v Modern Engineers of Bristol (Holdings) Plc* [1985] B.C.L.C. 213 at 217; *Holding Oil Finance Inc v Marc Rich & Co AG* [1996] C.L.Y. 1085; *Cook Strait Skyferry Ltd v Dennis Thompson International Ltd* [1993] 2 N.Z.L.R. 72; *Ridgeway Maritime Inc v Beulah Wings Ltd* [1991] 2 Lloyd's Rep. 611; *Goodacre v Meyer* [2002] EWHC 1785 (Ch) (no liability for procurement of alleged breach of commission-sharing agreement); *Johnson Matthey (Aust.) Ltd v Dascorp Pty Ltd* (2003) 9 V.R. 171; *Dargaville Farms Ltd v Webster* [2017] NZHC 1790 at [45]. But cf. *Thames Valley Housing Association Ltd v Elegant (Guernsey) Ltd* [2011] EWHC 1288 (Ch) at [110], where, however, *Said v Butt* and the foregoing cases were not referred to. It was suggested therein that the position may be different for directors who are performing their constitutional role in good faith. But, there is, it is submitted, no good reason to protect directors at the expense of employees and other agents who are also attempting to do their best for their principal; they are all immune from action.

[755] See *The Leon* [1991] 2 Lloyd's Rep. 611 at 624–625, per Waller J; *SPL Private Finance (PF1) IC Ltd v Arch Financial Products LLP* [2014] EWHC 4268 (Comm) at [288]; *Antuzis v DJ Houghton Catching Services Ltd* [2019] EWHC 843 (QB); [2019] Bus. L.R. 1532 (a difficult decision involving judicial review of directors' decision-making and applying an inapt analogy to the position in deceit, where agents will always be liable). See also *Official Assignee v Dowling* [1964] N.Z.L.R. 578 at 580–581; *Clerk & Lindsell on Torts* (22nd edn), para.24-36.

[756] *Official Assignee v Dowling* [1964] N.Z.L.R. 578 at 580–581; *Bromley Industries Ltd v Martin & Judith Fitzsimons Ltd* [2009] NZHC 1992; *Knights Capital Group Ltd v Bajada and Associates Pty Ltd* [2016] WASC 69 at [76]; *Turf Club Emporium Pte Ltd v Yeo Boong Hua* [2018] SGCA 44 at [316].

[757] See *Esso Petroleum Co Ltd v Kingswood Motors (Addleston) Ltd* [1974] Q.B. 142 at 155; *Stocznia Gdanska SA v Latvian Shipping Co (No.3)* [2002] EWCA Civ 889; [2002] 2 All E.R. (Comm) 768; [2002] 2 Lloyd's Rep. 436 (parent company liable for inducing subsidiary's breach)(noted by Edmundson (2008) 30 M.U.L.R. 62); *Lewis v Yeeles* [2010] EWCA Civ 326 at [26] (director of third party company not immune from personal liability for inducing breach of contract by a fourth party). But cf. *Bumi Armada Offshore Holdings Ltd v Tozzi Srl* [2018] SGCA(I) 05, per Lord Neuberger IJ

therefore protected by the above principles. In such circumstances, it would seem not to matter that both principal and agent have the same directors, so long as regard is had to the capacity in which they have acted.[758] Even without an agency, a shareholder ought not to be liable for acts of its agents taken in a different capacity, including as directors of a subsidiary.[759] On that basis, it is likely to be rare in practice that a parent company would be liable for the tort of inducement; it is an outsider's wrong.[760] It is also possible for a contract between the parties to exclude the possibility of suit against agents for inducing a breach by any of the parties.[761]

Vicarious immunity[762] It might be expected that where a principal has an immunity conferred by contract, an agent working for the principal in respect of that contract would be entitled to the same immunity towards the third party.[763] The notion of privity of contract, however, has prevented this result being easily achieved. It was held by the House of Lords in 1962 that there is no general doctrine of vicarious immunity in English law.[764] On the other hand the agent will be protected where a contract can be construed between agent and third party under which the agent is entitled to the immunities conferred by the main contract on the principal,[765] and the principal can sometimes be regarded as having, acting in the capacity of agent for his or her own agent, negotiated such a contract of immunity for the agent.[766] Although difficulties might be expected in finding the consideration supplied by the agent, the Privy Council brushed these aside and held that there was an implied contract between a consignor of goods and the stevedore at the port of discharge entitling the stevedore to the limitations and immunities of the bill of lading.[767] There may also be other ways of conferring immunity on the agent. In particular, a principal can contract to indemnify an agent against claims made on the agent, and insert into the main contract a clause whereby the third party promises not to sue the agent. If the third party is made aware of the indemnity provision, the liability under it will become the measure of loss caused to the principal if the third party does sue the agent. In such a case the principal may be able to have the third

9-122

(noted P Koh (2020) 136 L.Q.R. 30; Lau Kwan Ho [2020] L.M.C.L.Q. 13).

[758] *LMI Australasia Pty Ltd v Baulderstone Hornibrook Pty Ltd* [2003] NSWCA 74; *Bumi Armada Offshore Holdings Ltd v Tozzi Srl* [2018] SGCA(I) 05.

[759] See *Kuwait Asia Bank EC v National Mutual Life Nominees Ltd* [1991] 1 A.C. 187 (PC) at 221–222; *Bumi Armada Offshore Holdings Ltd v Tozzi Srl* [2018] SGCA(I) 05.

[760] See *O'Brien v Dawson* (1941) 41 S.R.(N.S.W.) 295 at 307–308; affirmed (1942) 66 C.L.R. 18 at 32 and 34: wrongdoers have to be "*outsiders* who are influencing the independent volition of a contracting party who is capable of exercising volition for himself".

[761] *Mir Steel UK Ltd v Morris* [2012] EWCA Civ 1397 at [39].

[762] Treitel, *Law of Contract* (15th edn), para.14-064 onwards; *Chitty on Contracts* (33rd edn), para.15-042 onwards.

[763] *Restatement, Second*, § 347, esp. Comment *b*.

[764] *Scruttons Ltd v Midland Silicones Ltd* [1962] A.C. 446; *Dunlop Pneumatic Tyre Co v Selfridge* [1915] A.C. 847.

[765] This is a possible explanation of *Elder Dempster & Co v Paterson Zochonis & Co* [1924] A.C. 522; discussed in *Scruttons v Midland Silicones* [1962] A.C. 446; but see *The Pioneer Container* [1994] 2 A.C. 324.

[766] *Hall v North Eastern Ry Co* (1875) L.R. 10 Q.B. 437; *Starlight Shipping Co v Allianz Marine and Aviation Versicherungs AG* [2014] EWHC 3068 (Comm); [2015] 2 All E.R. (Comm) 747 at [72].

[767] *New Zealand Shipping Co Ltd v A.M. Satterthwaite & Co Ltd (The Eurymedon)* [1975] A.C. 154; *Port Jackson Stevedoring Pty Ltd v Salmond & Spraggon (Australia) Pty Ltd (The New York Star)* [1981] 1 W.L.R. 138. See too *Sheehan v Watson* [2011] 1 N.Z.L.R. 314 (statutory immunity for lessees impliedly extended to agents of lessees).

party's action against the agent stayed,[768] or even, if all the parties are before the court, dismissed.[769] A broader rule still is to say that the agent, when sued in tort, owes a duty no higher than that prescribed in the main contract, and perhaps in some circumstances no duty at all.[770]

Similar considerations apply where an agent seeks to rely as against the third party on an immunity conferred by the agent's contract with the principal. If a contract with the third party on such terms can be inferred, the agent will be protected.[771] And here there is more recent authority that if the owner of goods expressly or impliedly authorises sub-bailment of them on the sub-bailee's terms (as where the owner authorises sub-bailment "on any terms") and the sub-bailee has sufficient notice that a person other than the bailee (the bailor) is interested in the goods, the subbailee's terms may be invoked against the owner.[772]

For England and Wales the law was changed by the Contract (Rights of Third Parties) Act 1999, which allows a third party to sue on contracts where the contract expressly provides that that party may, or the term purports to confer a benefit on that party.[773] The third party must be expressly identified in the contract by name, as a member of a class or as answering a particular description, but need not be in existence when the contract is entered into.[774] Where a term in a contract excludes or limits liability, references to enforcement are to be construed as references to the third party obtaining the benefit of the exclusion or limitation.[775] In effect therefore a properly drafted clause protecting employees and/or agents can now be effective without reference to the devices mentioned above.

9-123   **Effect of judgment against principal or agent: contribution**   Where the principal is liable for the torts of an agent they are in principle joint tortfeasors. Questions relating to the effect of judgment and contribution have been considered in Chapter 8.[776]

9-124   **The Crown**   Agents of the Crown are liable for their torts[777]; indeed, until the Crown Proceedings Act 1947, they alone were liable, and the Crown was not, and

---

[768] cf. *Gore v Van Der Lann* [1967] 2 Q.B. 31; and see *Nippon Yusen Kaisha v Intl Import and Export Co Ltd (The Elbe Maru)* [1978] 1 Lloyd's Rep. 206.

[769] *Snelling v John G. Snelling Ltd* [1973] Q.B. 87. Quaere whether the agent himself could plead the promise as a defence by virtue of the reasoning in *Hirachand Punamchand v Temple* [1911] 2 K.B. 330; Birks (1975) 1 Poly.L.Rev. 39.

[770] See *London Drugs Ltd v Kuehne & Nagel International Ltd* [1992] 3 S.C.R. 299; (1992) 97 D.L.R. (4th) 261.

[771] *Pyrene Co Ltd v Scindia Navigation Co Ltd* [1954] 2 Q.B. 402; as explained in *Scruttons Ltd v Midland Silicones Ltd* [1962] A.C. 446 at 471.

[772] *The Pioneer Container* [1994] 2 A.C. 324; following dicta in *Morris v C.W. Martin & Sons* [1966] 1 Q.B. 716 at 730. See also *The Mahkutai* [1996] A.C. 650, where there was no decision on an argument based on the terms of the main contract.

[773] Contract (Rights of Third Parties) Act 1999 s.1(1). See, e.g. *Laemthong International Lines Company Ltd v Abdullah Mohammed Fahem & Co* [2005] EWCA Civ 519; [2005] 1 Lloyd's Rep. 688; *Far East Chartering Ltd v Great Eastern Shipping Co Ltd* [2012] EWCA Civ 180; [2012] 2 All E.R. (Comm) 707; *Starlight Shipping Co v Allianz Marine and Aviation Versicherungs AG* [2014] EWHC 3068 (Comm); [2015] 2 All E.R. (Comm) 747 at [88]. See in general *Chitty on Contracts* (33rd edn), paras 15-046–15-047; Treitel, *Law of Contract* (15th edn), para.14-099 onwards; *Privity of Contract: the Impact of the Contract (Rights of Third Parties) Act 1999* (Merkin ed., 2000).

[774] Contract (Rights of Third Parties) Act 1999 s.1(3).

[775] Contract (Rights of Third Parties) Act 1999 s.1(7).

[776] See Comment to Article 90.

[777] See Wade (1991) 107 L.Q.R. 4.

an action could only be brought against the tortfeasor personally. Orders from the Crown, without more, do not justify torts.[778] To this there is one exception, that of Act of State. Where an agent of the Crown, whose act is duly authorised or ratified by the Crown, commits what would otherwise be a tort to an alien not resident in British territory, and the act is committed outside British territory, Act of State will be a defence to any action against the agent.[779] It may also be a defence in respect of an act against an enemy alien within British territory.[780] Whether it can be pleaded as a defence in respect of acts against British subjects outside British territory is not clear.[781] In view of the many changes within the Commonwealth over recent years there is much connected with the doctrine that may require reconsideration.[782]

Illustrations

(1) An agent signed a distress warrant, and after the warrant was issued, but before it was executed, refused a tender of the rent. Held, that the agent was personally liable for the illegal distress.[783]   **9-125**

(2) The manager of a bank signed a letter, as such, falsely and fraudulently representing that the credit of a certain person was good. Held, that the manager was personally liable in an action for deceit.[784]

(3) A solicitor who is employed to conduct the sale of an estate advises trustees to conceal an incumbrance from a mortgagee. He is personally liable with the trustees for the concealment.[785]

(4) A solicitor, on his client's instructions, presents a bankruptcy petition against A, knowing that A has not committed any act of bankruptcy. An action is maintainable against the solicitor for maliciously, and without reasonable and probable cause, presenting such petition, and causing A to be adjudged bankrupt.[786]

(5) A, a printer, is employed to print pictures which are an infringement of copyright. A, though not aware of the infringement of copyright, is liable, as well as his employers, for penalties for the infringement.[787]

(6) A ship is fitted with pumps which are an infringement of a patent. An injunction may be granted[788] against the master, restraining his from using the

---

[778] *Entick v Carrington* (1765) 19 St.Tr. 1029.

[779] *Burton v Denman* (1848) 2 Exch. 167; *Sinclair v Broughton and Government of India* (1882) 47 L.T. 170; *Walker v Baird* [1892] A.C. 491; *Salaman v Secretary of State for India* [1906] 1 K.B. 613; *Johnstone v Pedlar* [1921] 2 A.C. 262; *Commercial & Estates Co of Egypt v Board of Trade* [1925] 1 K.B. 271; *Nissan v Att.-Gen.* [1970] A.C. 179.

[780] *Netz v Ede* [1946] Ch. 224; *R. v Bottrill Ex p. Kuechenmeister* [1947] K.B. 41.

[781] See *Nissan v Att.-Gen.* [1970] A.C. 179.

[782] See Collier [1968] C.L.J. 102; [1969] C.L.J. 166; de Smith (1969) 32 M.L.R. 427.

[783] *Bennett v Bayes* (1860) 5 H. & N. 391.

[784] *Swift v Jewsbury & Goddard* (1874) L.R. 9 Q.B. 301. See Article 91. See also *Standard Chartered Bank v Pakistan International Shipping Corp (No.2)* [2002] UKHL 43; [2003] 1 A.C. 959 (director procured signature of false bill of lading).

[785] *Arnot v Briscoe* (1748) 1 Ves. 95; *Clark v Hoskins* (1867) 36 L.J.Ch. 689.

[786] *Johnson v Emerson & Sparrow* (1871) L.R. 6 Ex. 329. And see *Stevens v Midland Counties Ry Co* (1854) 10 Exch. 352.

[787] *Baschet v London Illustrated Standard Co* [1900] 1 Ch. 73; cf. *Kelly's Directories Ltd v Gavin & Lloyds* [1902] 1 Ch. 631.

[788] 1947 Act s.2; *Lowe v Dorling* [1906] 2 K.B. 772: affirming [1905] 2 K.B. 501, decided under the

pumps, or otherwise infringing the patent.[789] But where a custom-house agent merely passed through the custom-house an article infringing a patent, and obtained permission for landing and storing it in magazines belonging to the principals, who were the importers, it was held that the acts of the agent did not amount to an exercise or user of the patent, and that therefore no action could be maintained against him in respect of the infringement.[790]

(7)   An agent converts goods of a third person to his principal's use. He is liable to the true owner for their value, even if he acted in good faith and in the belief that his principal was the owner.[791] If, in such a case, the owner elects to adopt the transaction and proceed against the agent for an account, the agent is only liable to account for so much of the proceeds of the converted property as still remains in his hands, and not for what he has duly handed over in the course of his agency to the principal.[792]

(8)   An agent of an executor *de son tort* collects assets, and pays them over to his principal. The agent is personally liable to account for the assets to the right executor or administrator, or to the beneficiaries.[793] But an agent who acts by the authority of an executor (even before probate) or of a person who is subsequently granted letters of administration is not liable to account as an executor *de son tort*, because the title of the executor dates from, and that of the administrator relates back to, the time of the death.[794]

(9)   An agent, on behalf of his principal, but without the principal's authority, distrains the goods of a third person. The principal ratifies the distress, which is justifiable at his instance. The agent ceases to be liable, his act being justified by the ratification.[795]

(10)   A solicitor, being retained to sue for a debt, by mistake and without malice takes all the proceedings to judgment and execution against another person of the same name as the debtor; or, having obtained judgment against the debtor, by mistake and without malice issues execution against another person of the same name. The solicitor is not liable, for the tort of wrongful process of law requires malice.[796] But liability in trespass is strict. So where a solicitor directs the seizure of particular goods, so as to make the seizure his act rather than one done as part of a public duty,[797] he is personally liable if the seizure turns out to be wrongful.[798] So, where a solicitor directs or person-

---

Lodgers Goods Protection Act 1871. See also *Interoven Stove Co Ltd v Hibbard, etc.* [1946] 1 All E.R. 263.

[789] *Adair v Young* (1879) 12 Ch.D. 13.

[790] *Nobel's Explosives Co v Jones & Co* (1882) 8 App.Cas. 5.

[791] *Stephens v Elwall* (1815) 4 M. & S. 259; *Hollins v Fowler* (1874) L.R. 7 H.L. 757; *Wilson v New Brighton Panelbeaters* [1989] 1 N.Z.L.R. 74. But see Article 114.

[792] *Re Ely Ex p. Trustee* (1900) 48 W.R. 693. See Article 111.

[793] *Sharland v Mildon* (1846) 5 Hare 468; *Hill v Curtis* (1865) L.R. 1 Eq. 90. See also *Padget v Priest* (1787) 2 T.R. 97; Williams, Mortimer and Sunnucks, *Executors, Administrators and Probate* (20th edn), para.7-12.

[794] *Sykes v Sykes* (1870) L.R. 5 C.P. 113. See Williams, Mortimer and Sunnucks, above.

[795] *Hull v Pickersgill* (1819) 1 B. & B. 282.

[796] *Davies v Jenkins* (1843) 11 M. & W. 745; cf. *Clissold v Cratchley* [1910] 2 K.B. 244.

[797] See *Wilson v Tunman and Fretson* (1843) 6 M. & W. 236; *Smith v Keal* (1882) 9 Q.B.D. 340; *Morris v Salberg* (1889) 22 Q.B.D. 614.

[798] *Rowles v Senior* (1846) 8 Q.B. 677; *Davies v Jenkins* (1843) 11 M. & W. 745; *Clissold v Cratchley* [1910] 2 K.B. 244.

ally takes part in the execution of a warrant for arrest, he is liable in an action for false imprisonment if the warrant is illegal.[799]

(11) Owners of ship's provisions agree with a company to store their goods in a warehouse which is owned by the managing director of the company but leased to the company. The contract is entered into by a director on behalf of the company; but a confirming letter from the managing director and an invoice indicate that the managing director is treating the storage of the goods as his own venture. Because of negligence in supervising the refrigeration the goods are damaged. The managing director is personally liable in negligence, though there is no contract with him and he is not bailee of the goods.[800]

(12) In a matrimonial dispute, solicitors for the husband agree to hold the husband's passport to the order of the court. With the agreement of the wife they allow it to be lodged with the embassy of the husband's country, but negligently fail to inform her of facts creating risks that the husband will obtain it, and they also fail to take practicable steps to prevent this. The husband does obtain it, kidnaps the children and takes them abroad: the wife is injured in the kidnapping. The solicitors are liable to the wife in tort.[801]

(13) Solicitors for a borrower on the security of a yacht certify to the lender that an instrument of security is fully binding on the borrower and that there are no charges on the yacht. In fact the yacht does not belong to the borrower but is being purchased by a company of which he is a shareholder, and the money was not intended to be used to enable the borrower to purchase the yacht. The solicitors knew this. They are liable to the lender.[802]

(14) Solicitors for vendors of an underlease negligently and incorrectly answer questions as to the terms of a superior lease. They are not liable to the purchaser who suffered loss thereby.[803]

(15) Solicitors acting for a borrower on the security of land negligently fail to ensure that the security intended by both parties is valid. They are liable to the lender.[804]

(16) Brokers acting for the seller of a vessel make representations which are not true. They are not parties to the contract and hence cannot be sued under s.2(1) of the Misrepresentation Act 1967, which only applies to a party to a contract.[805]

---

[799] *Green v Elgie* (1843) 5 Q.B. 99; *Codrington v Lloyd* (1838) 8 A. & E. 449.

[800] *Fairline Shipping Corp v Adamson* [1975] Q.B. 180. See also *C. Evans & Sons Ltd v Spritebrand Ltd* [1985] 1 W.L.R. 317 (liability of director for breach of copyright). *Fairline* was doubted in *Mitsui & Co Ltd v Novorossiysk Shipping Co Ltd (The Kilmun)* [1993] 1 Lloyd's Rep. 311 at 328.

[801] *Al-Kandari v J.R. Brown & Co* [1988] Q.B. 665.

[802] *Allied Finance and Investments Ltd v Haddow & Co* [1983] N.Z.L.R. 22.

[803] *Gran Gelato Ltd v Richcliff (Group) Ltd* [1992] Ch. 560; but see Cane (1991) 108 L.Q.R. 539 and discussion of this decision in *McCullagh v Lane Fox & Partners Ltd* [1996] 1 E.G.L.R. 35 at 43–44, per Hobhouse LJ.

[804] *Dean v Allin and Watts* [2001] EWCA Civ 758; [2001] 2 Lloyd's Rep. 249.

[805] *Resolute Maritime Inc v Nippon Kaiji Kyokai (The Skopas)* [1983] 1 W.L.R. 857; followed in *MCI WorldCom International Inc v Primus Telecommunications Inc* [2003] EWHC 2182 (Comm); [2004] 1 All E.R. (Comm) 138 (reversed [2004] EWCA Civ 957; [2004] 2 All E.R. (Comm) 833).

Article 114

CONVERSION BY INNOCENT AGENT

9-126 (1) Where an agent holds possession or control of goods for a principal, and:

    (a) sells and delivers or otherwise deals with the possession of and assumes to deal with the property in the goods without the authority of the true owner[806]; or

    (b) refuses without qualification to deliver possession to the true owner on demand[807]; or

    (c) transfers possession to the principal or any other person except the true owner, with notice of the claim of the true owner,[808]

the agent is liable in conversion to the true owner for the value of the goods, even if the agent obtained possession from the principal, reasonably believing that such principal owned the goods or had the right to dispose of them, and acted in good faith on the authority of such principal.

(2) But an agent is not guilty of conversion who in good faith merely:

    (a) receives or holds goods on behalf of the principal without dealing with them[809];

    (b) refuses to deliver to the true owner goods which the agent holds for the principal in such terms that the refusal does not amount to a repudiation of the title of the true owner[810];

    (c) contracts on behalf of the principal to sell goods of which the agent has neither possession nor control[811];

    (d) by the authority of the principal, and without notice of the claim of the true owner, deals with the possession of, without assuming to deal with the property in, the goods.[812]

Comment

9-127 The tort of conversion raises special problems in connection with agents, in so far as it does not apply where the relevant act is purely ministerial. It therefore requires special treatment.

9-128 **Rule (1)** Conversion may be called:

"an act or complex series of acts of wilful interference, without lawful justification, with any chattel in a manner inconsistent with the right of another, whereby that other is deprived of the use and possession of it."[813]

It is a tort of strict liability, and, as stated in Article 113, the authority of the principal

---

[806] Illustrations 1 to 4.

[807] Illustration 7 and cases cited.

[808] Illustration 5; *Powell v Hoyland* (1851) 6 Exch. 67; *Union Credit Bank v Mersey Docks & Harbour Board* [1899] 2 Q.B. 205. As to agent's right to interplead, see Article 70.

[809] *Caxton Publishing Co v Sutherland Publishing Co* [1939] A.C. 178 at 202.

[810] Illustration 7 and cases cited.

[811] See Comment. And see in general *Clerk and Lindsell on Torts* (22nd edn), paras 17-17 and 17-73 onwards.

[812] Illustration 6.

[813] *Salmond and Heuston on the Law of Torts* (21st edn), pp.97–98 and in general pp.103–105. And see *Restatement, Second*, Appendix, reporter's note to § 349; *18th Report of Law Reform Committee (on Conversion and Detinue)*, Cmnd. 4774 (1971), esp. pp.14–18.

cannot provide immunity from liability for a tort committed by an agent against a third party. Therefore, any act performed by an agent which amounts to a conversion is actionable against the agent, and it is no defence to the agent to prove that another who appeared to be the owner, or to have the authority to perform, or authorise the performance of, such acts authorised the agent to perform the act.[814]

It is not clear whether or not this rule applies to acts done in good faith, and without notice of the claim of the true owner, on the authority of a mercantile agent, or of a buyer or seller, in possession of the goods or of the documents of title thereto with the consent of the true owner within the meaning of the Factors Act. The authorities are conflicting.[815] But the relevant sections refer only to the validity of the disposition made by the mercantile agent personally and do not seem, on their wording, to legalise what would otherwise be conversions by persons assisting in the making of such dispositions.

Rule (2)   Merely to hold goods is however no conversion unless there is refusal   **9-129**
to deliver up, or a dealing with the goods inconsistent with the owner's right.[816] And agents may refuse to deliver goods while making reasonable inquiries, without rendering themselves liable in conversion.[817] Further, there are some cases where, although there is a dealing with the goods to which the agent is a party, the agent is said to have acted as a mere conduit pipe[818] and therefore not to have performed any act amounting to a conversion. Thus an agent who negotiates a sale of goods of which the agent has neither possession nor control between two persons who contract directly does not interfere with the goods and so cannot be held liable for conversion.[819] So also an agent who performs acts with relation to goods, authorised by the principal, which are no more than a bailee or finder of goods could lawfully authorise, does not commit acts of conversion,[820] e.g. where the agent merely stores or carries goods,[821] transfers them to another agent,[822] or, not knowing of any adverse claim, returns them to the principal.[823] It is also probable that an agent does not convert if the agent performs acts in a transaction that actually transfers the title, provided that the agent does not know that such a transaction is involved; and even if the agent does know of it, there is authority that conversion is not committed provided that the agent does not personally participate in the transaction, but acts

[814] See Article 113, Illustration 8; *Consolidated Co v Curtis & Son* [1892] 1 Q.B. 495, Illustration 1.
[815] See *Waddington & Sons v Neale & Sons* (1907) 96 L.T. 786; *Shenstone & Co v Hilton* [1894] 2 Q.B. 452; Article 89.
[816] See *Caxton Publishing Co v Sutherland Publishing Co* [1939] A.C. 178 at 202.
[817] Illustration 7 and cases cited.
[818] *Barker v Furlong* [1891] 2 Ch. 172 at 181, 183; *Consolidated Co v Curtis & Son* [1892] 1 Q.B. 495 at 502; *Greenway v Fisher* (1824) 1 C. & P. 190 at 192.
[819] *Turner v Hockey* (1887) 56 L.J.Q.B. 301; as explained in *Barker v Furlong* [1891] 2 Ch. 172; and *Consolidated Co v Curtis & Son* [1892] 1 Q.B. 495; *Cochrane v Rymill* (1879) 40 L.T. 744 at 746. *Turner v Hockey* was, however, doubted by the Court of Appeal in *R.H. Willis & Son v British Car Auctions Ltd* [1978] 1 W.L.R. 438.
[820] *Hollins v Fowler* (1875) L.R. 7 H.L. 757 at 766–767.
[821] *Union Credit Bank v Mersey Docks & Harbour Board* [1899] 2 Q.B. 205 at 216; *Barker v Furlong* [1891] 2 Ch. 172 at 182 (carriers and packing agents "merely purport to change the position of the goods and not the property in them"). And see *Greenway v Fisher* (1824) 1 C. & P. 190 (packer).
[822] *Re Samuel (No.2)* [1945] Ch. 408, Illustration 8.
[823] *Union Credit Bank v Mersey Docks & Harbour Board* [1899] 2 Q.B. 205; *Marcq v Christie, Manson and Woods* [2004] EWCA Civ 731; [2004] Q.B. 286, Illustration 7. cf. Illustration 5.

only ministerially.[824] The general rule is significant as an analogy in other contexts where it is sought to argue that an agent only acted ministerially.[825]

9-130   **Cheques**   In principle, a bank which collects for a customer a cheque to which the customer has no title commits conversion.[826] But banks have statutory protection. By s.4 of the Cheques Act 1957, where a banker in good faith and without negligence[827] receives payment for a customer of a cheque,[828] or, having credited a customer's account with the amount of a cheque, receives payment thereof for itself, and the customer has no title, or a defective title, to the cheque, the banker does not incur any liability to the true owner of the cheque by reason only of having received payment thereof. This provision extends to uncrossed cheques the protection previously afforded to bankers in respect of crossed cheques.[829] It seems possible that the Law Reform (Contributory Negligence) Act 1945 may apply in this context,[830] though it is not applicable to the tort of conversion.[831]

Illustrations

9-131   (1) An auctioneer was instructed to sell by auction furniture which the possessor and apparent owner had assigned by bill of sale to a third person. The auctioneer, who had no notice of the assignment, sold the furniture at the residence of the assignor, and, in the ordinary course of business, delivered it to the purchaser. Held, that the auctioneer was liable to the assignee for the value of the furniture.[832]

(2) A obtained certain goods by fraud. B, a broker, bought the goods in his own name from A, thinking that they would suit C, a customer of his. B, having sold the goods to C at the same price at which he had bought them from A, merely charging the usual commission, took delivery and conveyed the goods to the railway station, whence they were conveyed to C. The jury found that

---

[824] *National Mercantile Bank v Rymill* (1881) 44 L.T. 767, Illustration 6; queried by *Salmond and Heuston on the Law of Torts* (21st edn), p.109, in view of the opinion of Blackburn J in *Hollins v Fowler* (1875) L.R. 7 H.L. 757 and *Stephens v Elwall* (1815) 4 M. & S. 259. The case was approved in *Consolidated Co v Curtis & Son* [1892] 1 Q.B. 495, where it was pointed out at 501 that the decision is "a long step in the direction which Brett J invited the House of Lords to take in *Hollins v Fowler*" but doubted by the Court of Appeal in *R.H. Willis & Son v British Car Auctions Ltd* [1978] 1 W.L.R. 438. But see *Marcq v Christie, Manson and Woods* [2004] EWCA Civ 731; [2004] Q.B. 286. See also *Wilson v New Brighton Panelbeaters* [1989] 1 N.Z.L.R. 74.

[825] See, e.g. below, para.9-139.

[826] *Arnold v Cheque Bank* (1876) 1 C.P.D. 578.

[827] On good faith, see Bills of Exchange Act 1882 s.90. On negligence, see Cheques Act 1957 s.4(3); *Thackwell v Barclays Bank Plc* [1986] 1 All E.R. 676. See in general *Byles on Bills of Exchange* (30th edn), Ch.22; *Chalmers and Guest on Bills of Exchange* (18th edn), Ch.17; *Paget's Law of Banking* (15th edn), Ch.27.

[828] The protection is not in fact limited to cheques, but applies to certain other instruments: see Cheques Act 1957 s.4(2) as amended.

[829] Bills of Exchange Act 1882 s.82, as amended by Bills of Exchange (Crossed Cheques) Act 1906, both repealed by Cheques Act 1957.

[830] *Lumsden & Co v London Trustee Savings Bank* [1971] 1 Lloyd's Rep. 114.

[831] Torts (Interference with Goods) Act 1977 s.11(1).

[832] *Consolidated Co v Curtis & Son* [1892] 1 Q.B. 405; *Barker v Furlong* [1891] 2 Ch. 172; *Brown v Hickinbotham* (1881) 50 L.J.Q.B. 426.

B bought the goods merely as an agent, in the ordinary course of his business. Held, that B was liable to the true owner for the value of the goods.[833]

(3) A hired cabs from B, and obtained advances on them from an auctioneer. The auctioneer, on A's instructions, and without notice of B's title, in good faith sold the cabs, and after deducting the advances and his expenses, paid the proceeds to A. Held, that the auctioneer was liable to B for the value of the cabs, having had control of them, and having sold them in such a way as to pass the property in them. It would be otherwise, if he had not possession or control of the cabs, and had merely contracted to sell, without delivering them.[834]

(4) An insurance broker effected a policy on behalf of A. A became bankrupt, and after the adjudication instructed the broker to collect money due under the policy and pay it to him. The broker, without notice of the bankruptcy, collected the money and paid it to A. Held, that the broker was liable to the trustee in bankruptcy for the amount.[835]

(5) A husband entrusted goods, which were the property of his wife, to an auctioneer for sale. The auctioneer received notice of the wife's claim, but nevertheless subsequently sold a portion of the goods, and permitted the husband to remove the remainder. Held, that the auctioneer was liable to the wife for the value of the goods removed by the husband, as well as of those which had been sold.[836]

(6) An auctioneer receives goods for sale from one who has not title to them. The goods are offered at public auction but not sold. They are returned to the person who sent them. The auctioneer is not liable in conversion.[837]

(7) A held a bill of sale over horses in the possession of B. B took the horses to C's repository for sale by auction, and they were entered in the catalogue for sale. Before the sale took place, B sold the horses by private contract in C's yard. The price was paid to C, who deducted his commission and charges, and handed the balance to B, and the horses, on B's instructions, were delivered by C to the purchaser. Held, that C, having merely delivered the horses according to B's orders, and not having himself sold or otherwise assumed to deal with the property in them, was not guilty of a conversion.[838]

(8) An agent in possession of goods by the authority of his principal, on demand by the true owner refuses to deliver them up without an order from the principal, or requires a reasonable time to ascertain whether the person demanding the goods is the true owner. Such a qualified refusal is not a conversion. It is otherwise, where the refusal is absolute, or amounts to a setting-up of the principal's title to the goods.[839]

---

[833] *Hollins v Fowler* (1872) L.R. 7 Q.B. 616; affirmed L.R. 7 H.L. 757; *Union Transport Finance Ltd v British Car Auctions Ltd* [1978] 2 All E.R. 385; *R.H. Willis & Son v British Car Auctions Ltd* [1978] 1 W.L.R. 438 (where a "provisional bid" procedure was used).
[834] *Cochrane v Rymill* (1879) 40 L.T. 744.
[835] *McEntire v Potter & Co* (1889) 22 Q.B.D. 438.
[836] *Davis v Artingstall* (1880) 49 L.J.Ch. 609. See also *Winter v Bancks* (1901) 84 L.T. 504.
[837] *Marcq v Christie, Manson and Woods* [2003] EWCA Civ 731; [2004] Q.B. 286.
[838] *National Mercantile Bank v Rymill* (1881) 44 L.T. 767. But this case was doubted by the Court of Appeal in *R.H. Willis & Son v British Car Auctions Ltd* [1978] 1 W.L.R. 438. See *Clerk and Lindsell on Torts* (22nd edn), para.17-74 onwards.
[839] *Alexander v Southey* (1821) 5 B. & A. 247; *Wilson v Anderton* (1830) 1 B. & Ad. 450; *Lee v Bayes and Robinson* (1856) 18 C.B. 599; *Pillott v Wilkinson* (1864) 3 H. & C. 345.

(9) The solicitor of a bankrupt receives after-acquired property on behalf of his client and on his client's instruction transfers it to another agent, knowing that that agent has been instructed to sell it and use the proceeds to educate the bankrupt's son. The solicitor is not liable in conversion.[840]

Article 115

AGENT NOT LIABLE FOR WRONGS OF CO-AGENTS OR SUB-AGENTS WORKING FOR PRINCIPAL

9-132   An agent is not liable as such to any third person for loss or injury caused by the wrongful act or omission of a co-agent not being a partner, or of a sub-agent in privity of contract with the principal, unless the agent authorised or was otherwise party or privy to such wrongful act or omission.[841]

Comment

9-133   The relationship of employer and employee or of principal and agent does not exist between co-agents: therefore an agent is not, as such, liable to third parties for wrongs committed by co-agents acting as such.[842] This applies as much to company directors as others. Equally, senior Crown officials or servants are not normally vicariously liable for the wrongs of more junior servants.[843] Nor is an agent liable for a sub-agent whom the agent appointed to act for the principal, if privity of contract was established between them[844]: indeed such a sub-agent might, but for the fact that the sub-agent often holds a position of lower status than the appointing agent, be called a co-agent. Thus in *Stone v Cartwright*[845] the manager of a colliery was held not liable for the negligence of a colliery employee. But an agent could be liable in accordance with normal principles for the wrongs of a sub-agent whom the agent employs personally, and with whom the agent alone has privity of contract.[846] And the agent is of course liable for personal actionable negligence; delegation to another agent may be evidence of such negligence.[847]

4.   EQUITY

Article 116

ACCESSORY LIABILITY TO BREACH OF TRUST OR FIDUCIARY OBLIGATION AND KNOWING RECEIPT OF PROPERTY SUBJECT TO TRUST OR FIDUCIARY OBLIGATION

9-134   (1)   Where an agent dishonestly procures or assists in a breach of trust or fiduci-

---

[840] *Re Samuel (No.2)* [1945] Ch. 408.
[841] See Comment.
[842] *Cargill v Bower* (1878) 10 Ch.D. 502; *Re Denham & Co* (1883) 25 Ch.D. 752; cf. *Dovey v Cory* [1901] A.C. 477 (cases on directors).
[843] See *Commissioner of Inland Revenue v Chesterfields Preschools Ltd* [2013] NZCA 53; [2013] 2 N.Z.L.R. 679 (misfeasance in public office).
[844] See Ch.5.
[845] *Stone v Cartwright* (1795) 6 T.R. 411. See also *Bear v Stevenson* (1874) 30 L.T. 177; *Weir v Bell* (1878) 3 Ex.D. 238 (directors not liable for torts committed by persons working for the company).
[846] This is the more normal position of a sub-agent: see Article 35.
[847] See *Re City Equitable Fire Insurance Co* [1925] Ch. 407; cf. *Dovey v Cory* [1901] A.C. 477 and Article 35.

ary obligation by the principal the agent is liable to account to the beneficiary or beneficiaries of the trust or fiduciary obligation to restore the assets, the loss of which the agent has caused.

(2) Where an agent receives money or property for personal benefit and (perhaps) with knowledge that it is subject to a trust or fiduciary obligation and that it has been transferred to the agent in breach of such obligation, or discovers this after it has been transferred, the agent is liable to account for that money or property to the person for whom the property is held in trust or to whom the fiduciary obligation is owed.

(3) Where an agent lawfully holds money or property which the agent knows to be subject to a trust or fiduciary obligation, and deals with that money or property in a manner inconsistent with that trust or fiduciary obligation, the agent is liable to the person for whom the property is held in trust or to whom the obligation is owed.

(4) But an agent who has no knowledge that a breach of trust or fiduciary obligation has been or is being committed is not liable merely by acting as agent in a transaction which constitutes or involves such a breach.[848]

Comment

Rule (1): Accessory liability in respect of breach of trust[849] This area of equity, and that of "knowing receipt" which follows, are of general application to parties who become involved in breach of trust and fiduciary duty. But not surprisingly many of the cases involve agents (particularly solicitors, banks, and directors of companies), whose role is to facilitate transactions, and in some cases to handle moneys on behalf of clients. This liability, often referred to as "knowing" or "dishonest assistance", first emerged in connection with trusts, and its components became established during the nineteenth century. Its greater significance at the present time is in relation to funds impressed with a fiduciary obligation. Hence, the action for dishonest assistance is frequently pursued against directors of companies who cause the company to breach fiduciary duties owed by it to the claimant or who involve themselves, through their company, in breaches of fiduciary duty owed by others to the claimant.[850] In such cases, the subject of the litigation may not be money but property (or a "corporate opportunity") that has been wrongly diverted away from the claimant to other parties.[851]

9-135

To be liable under this head the agent must, in addition to possessing the requisite mental element, have contributed in a material way to the commission by the principal or other party in a breach of trust or fiduciary[852] obligations: producing the documentation for the offending transactions, acquiring assets knowing the seller

---

[848] See Comment.

[849] For full discussion see *Lewin on Trusts* (20th edn), Ch. 43; *Snell's Equity* (34th edn), para.30-067; Davies, *Accessory Liability* (2015); Dietrich and Ridge, *Accessories in Private Law* (2015); P. Ridge and J. Dietrich, "Challenging Conceptions of Accessory Liability in Private Law" [2019] C.L.J. 383. As to issues of limitation affecting both the action for dishonest assistance, and that for knowing receipt, see *Williams v Central Bank of Nigeria* [2014] UKSC 10; [2014] A.C. 1189.

[850] See, e.g. *JD Wetherspoon Plc v Van De Berg & Co Ltd* [2009] EWHC 639 (Ch), Illustration 7; *Law Society of England and Wales v Habitable Concepts Ltd* [2010] EWHC 1449 (Ch).

[851] See, e.g. *Satnam Investments Ltd v Dunlop Heywood & Co Ltd* [1999] 3 All E.R. 652.

[852] Where the obligation is a common law one this reasoning would not apply: see *Bristol and West BS v Mothew* [1998] Ch. 1 at 16 onwards.

is acting in breach of trust are examples,[853] but a mere ministerial receipt of assets will not suffice, nor is a mere failure to act (at least unless the agent is a manager who knows that colleagues and subordinates are operating dishonestly).[854] The action is also not available where the principal's or third party's conduct does not involve a breach of fiduciary duty.[855] It is not necessary that there should be a trust in the formal sense: it is sufficient if there is a fiduciary relationship in relation to another's property,[856] but it must have arisen before the acts complained of.[857] In acting, the agent must have appreciated that he or she was assisting in such breach.[858] Generally, however, no appreciation of the full nature of the obligation, nor of the details of the breach is required.[859] It seems also that liability can be incurred without there having been a diversion or illegitimate manipulation of a fund or other distinct item of property subject to a fiduciary obligation.[860] It may even be that acts done which assist in the breach of the equitable wrong of breach of confidence are actionable under this head, though no fiduciary obligation is involved at all.[861] What may in fact be emerging from the cases is a form of accessory liability for assistance in connection with equitable wrongdoing more generally, a liability which would run parallel and analogous to, while not based on, accessory liability to common law wrongs, as in the tort of interference with contract.[862]

The liability was reshaped in the advice of the Privy Council delivered by Lord Nicholls of Birkenhead in *Royal Brunei Airlines Sdn Bhd v Tan*,[863] from which case the phrases "accessory liability" and "dishonest assistance" emanate. Until that time the liability normally went under the name of "knowing assistance" and it was thought that the state of mind of the fiduciary was relevant as well as that of the accessory.[864] But Lord Nicholls indicated that it was only the state of mind of the accessory that was crucial, and it is highly probable that this has been accepted into

---

[853] See *Bilta (UK) Ltd v Natwest Markets Plc* [2020] EWHC 546 (Ch) at [162]–[165], [174].

[854] *Baden Delvaux v Société Générale, etc., SA* (1983) [1993] 1 W.L.R. 509 at 574–575; *Gregson v HAE Trustees Ltd* [2008] EWHC 1006 (Ch); [2008] 2 B.C.L.C. 542; [2009] 1 All E.R. (Comm) 457. cf. *Otkritie International Investment Management Ltd v Urumov* [2014] EWHC 191 (Comm); [2014] 1 W.L.R. 748 at [455].

[855] *Fitzalan-Howard (Norfolk) v Hibbert* [2009] EWHC 2855 (QB); [2010] P.N.L.R. 11(manager not liable for dishonest assistance merely for failing to procure his employing company to repay a simple mistaken payment received by it).

[856] *Baden Delvaux v Société Générale, etc., SA* (1983) [1993] 1 W.L.R. 509 at 573.

[857] *Goose v Wilson Sandford & Co* [2001] Lloyd's Rep. P.N. 189.

[858] See *Bank of America v Arnell* [1999] Lloyd's Rep. Bank 399 at 406–407; *Alpstream AG v PK Airfinance Sarl* [2013] EWHC 2370 (Comm).

[859] *Barlow Clowes International Ltd v Eurotrust International Ltd* [2005] UKPC 37; [2006] 1 W.L.R. 1476: see also *Agip (Africa) Ltd v Jackson* [1990] Ch. 265 at 293–294 (but the defendant did not call evidence); *Att.-Gen. of Zambia v Meer Care & Desai (a firm)* [2007] EWHC 952 (Ch) at [340]; *Group Seven Ltd v Notable Services LLP* [2019] EWCA Civ 614; [2020] Ch. 129 at [100].

[860] See *Banque National de Paris v Credit Agricole Indosuez* [2001] 1 Singapore L.R. 300 at 331–339; in England the matter is certainly arguable: see *Brown v Bennett* [1999] 1 B.C.L.C. 649 at 658–659; *Gencor ACP Ltd v Dalby* [2000] 2 B.C.L.C. 734; *Lewin on Trusts* (20th edn), para.43-027. If the proposition is correct, this reasoning might apply in the context of bribery: see *Petrotrade Inc v Smith* [2000] 1 Lloyd's Rep. 486; Mitchell (2001) 117 L.Q.R. 207; above, para.8-222.

[861] See *Thomas v Pearce* [2000] F.S.R. 718.

[862] See *Royal Brunei Airlines Sdn Bhd v Tan* [1995] 2 A.C. 378 at 386–387; *Markel International Insurance Co Ltd v Surety Guarantee Consultants Ltd* [2008] EWHC 1135 (Comm); affirmed [2009] EWCA Civ 790.

[863] *Royal Brunei Airlines Sdn Bhd v Tan* [1995] 2 A.C. 378. See criticism of the decision by Berg (1996) 59 M.L.R. 443 and Birks [1996] L.M.C.L.Q. 1; cf. Harpum (1995) 111 L.Q.R. 545.

[864] *Royal Brunei Airlines Sdn Bhd v Tan* [1995] 2 A.C. 378 at 384 onwards. Where the defaulting fiduciary is honest, and he is also the only agent of a putative assisting party, then no liability in that party

English law. As to the state of mind required of the accessory (agent), Lord Nicholls indicated that what was required was "objective dishonesty".[865] This has not proved an easy criterion to apply, however, and appeared subsequently to have been interpreted in the House of Lords as prescribing that a defendant was not dishonest unless the defendant appreciated that what was being done would be regarded by an honest person as dishonest,[866] which introduced a subjective element. However, it has since been explained in the Privy Council that the passage in question:

"meant only that his knowledge of the transaction had to be such as to render his participation contrary to normally acceptable standards of honest conduct. It did not require that he should have had reflections about what those normally acceptable standards were."[867]

The person concerned need not have been consciously dishonest: it is likely to be sufficient for liability that he or she had solid grounds for suspicion which were consciously ignored.[868] Nor was it necessary that the assister knew the full details of the wrongdoing:

"someone can know, and can certainly suspect, that he is assisting in a misappropriation without knowing that the money was held on trust or what a trust means."[869]

The application of these dicta make it easier to fix the dishonest with liability, but may create difficulties for professionals who handle money. Such are the problems of formulating objective standards in equity. It is at least clear that defendants who can show that they were duped or merely naïve will escape liability.[870]

The remedy available to a successful claimant, while sometimes said to treat the defendant as a constructive trustee, is in fact an in personam one for compensation

---

can arise since there will be no dishonesty: *Roadchef (Employee Benefits Trustees) Ltd v Hill* [2014] EWHC 109 (Ch).

[865] *Royal Brunei Airlines Sdn Bhd v Tan* [1995] 2 A.C. 378 at 389–390. It is not necessary, it seems, to show that all reasonable people would regard the relevant conduct as dishonest: *Starglade Properties Ltd v Nash* [2010] EWCA Civ 1314 at [32] (it is "irrelevant that there may be a body of opinion which regards the ordinary standard of honest behaviour as being set too high").

[866] See *Twinsectra Ltd v Yardley* [2002] UKHL 12; [2002] 2 A.C. 164 at [35], per Lord Hutton.

[867] *Barlow Clowes International Ltd v Eurotrust Ltd* [2005] UKPC 37; [2006] 1 All E.R. 333 at [15], per Lord Hoffmann; see Yeo (2006) 122 L.Q.R. 171. See also *US International Marketing Ltd v National Bank of New Zealand Ltd* [2004] 1 N.Z.L.R. 589; *Central Bank of Ecuador v Conticorp SA* [2015] UKPC 11; [2016] 1 B.C.L.C. 26 at [9]; *Ivey v Genting Casinos (UK) Ltd* [2017] UKSC 67; [2018] A.C. 391 (noted M. Dyson, "Poison Ivey or herbal tea leaf?" (2018) 134 L.Q.R. 198); *Wingate v Solicitors Regulation Authority* [2018] EWCA Civ 366; [2018] 1 W.L.R. 3969 (want of integrity). Dishonesty is not required for liability for assistance in Australia: *Harstedt Pty Ltd v Tomanek* [2018] VSCA 84.

[868] Lord Hoffmann's views, though expressed in an opinion of the Privy Council, are applied as representing English law in *Abou-Rahmah v Abacha* [2006] EWCA Civ 1492; [2007] 1 All E.R. (Comm) 827; [2007] 1 Lloyd's Rep. 115, where a claimant in an assistance claim was however unable to show that a bank employee had a clear enough suspicion that transactions with which he was engaged were wrongful. See also *City Index Ltd v Gawler* [2007] EWCA Civ 1382; [2008] 3 All E.R. 126; [2008] 2 All E.R. (Comm) 425; [2008] Ch. 213; *Att.-Gen. of Zambia v Meer Care & Desai (a firm)* [2008] EWCA Civ 1007 at [21]; *Group Seven Ltd v Notable Services LLP* [2019] EWCA Civ 614; [2020] Ch. 129 at [60]; *Sandman v McKay* [2019] NZSC 41 at [78].

[869] *Barlow Clowes International Ltd v Eurotrust International Ltd* [2005] UKPC 37; [2006] 1 W.L.R. 1476 at [28], per Lord Hoffmann; see also at [20].

[870] See *Brinks Ltd v Abu-Saleh (No.3)* [1996] C.L.C. 133 (accompanying husband on money laundering trips to Zurich did not create liability); *Autogas (Europe) Ltd v Ochocki* [2018] EWHC 2345 (Ch) at [146]. The onus of proving both breach of trust and dishonesty lies with the claimant: *Attorney General of Zambia v Meer Care & Desai (a firm)* [2008] EWCA Civ 1007 at [147] and [256].

in monetary terms. This category of constructive trusteeship:

> "is nothing more than a formula for equitable relief. The court is saying that the defendant shall be liable in equity as though he were a trustee".[871]

It is calculated by reference to equity's willingness to restore fully funds that can be shown to have suffered a loss by reason of the breach. This could perhaps include profits made by the wrongdoer.[872] Contributory negligence should not be relevant.[873] Where there are several wrongdoers, each is liable for the full loss, subject to the requirements of contribution inter se under the Civil Liability (Contribution) Act 1978,[874] which need not take account of the relative gravity of fault but may be affected by the continuing existence of the profit in the hands of some parties.[875] It seems possible that the reasoning of the leading House of Lords decision on equitable compensation for breach of trust, *Target Holdings Ltd v Redferns*,[876] will provide a guide. Despite this more generous measure than the common law provides, however, it would seem that the liability has totally outgrown its origin in the law of trusts. It bears little or no resemblance to a constructive trust as regards the requirements for liability or the remedy available for breach. Even Lord Nicholls in his judgment in the Privy Council spoke of the liability as involving a "duty of care".[877] The relationship of this liability to the tort of interference with contract remains open to argument and possibly development.[878]

---

[871] *Selangor United Rubber Estates Ltd v Cradock (No.3)* [1968] 1 W.L.R. 1555 at 1582, per Ungoed-Thomas J; see further *Dubai Aluminium Co Ltd v Salaam* [2002] UKHL 48; [2003] 2 A.C. 366 at [140]–[142], per Lord Millett For limitation issues applicable to claims against accessories to a breach of trust or fiduciary obligation, see *Williams v Central Bank of Nigeria* [2014] UKSC 10; [2014] A.C. 1189. See too *Halton International Inc v Guernroy Ltd* [2006] EWCA Civ 801.

[872] See Article 96; *Fyffes Group Ltd v Templeman* [2000] 2 Lloyd's Rep. 643 (bribes: see above, para.8-222); *Ultraframe (UK) Ltd v Fielding* [2005] EWHC 1638 (QB) at [1594]; *Novoship (UK) Ltd v Nikitin* [2014] EWCA Civ 908; [2015] 1 Q.B. 499 at [84] (noted Davies (2015) 131 L.Q.R. 173, Gummow [2015] C.L.J. 405); *Central Bank of Ecuador v Conticorp SA* [2015] UKPC 11; [2016] 1 B.C.L.C. 26 addendum at [9]; *Ancient Order of Foresters in Victoria Friendly Society Ltd v Lifeplan Australia Friendly Society Ltd* [2018] HCA 43. But cf. *Royal Brunei Airlines Sdn Bhd v Tan* [1995] 2 A.C. 378 at 386 (accessory liability not restitution based). See further, para.8-225.

[873] See *Corporacion Nacional del Cobre de Chile v Sogemin Metals Ltd* [1997] 1 W.L.R. 1396; *Standard Chartered Bank v Pakistan National Shipping Corp (No.2)* [2002] UKHL 43; [2003] 1 A.C. 959.

[874] See above, para.8-191.

[875] *Dubai Aluminium Co Ltd v Salaam* [2002] UKHL 48; [2003] 2 A.C. 366. It has been held that there is no necessary inconsistency between a party's being liable in knowing receipt of a claimant's funds and that party having a right of contribution under the Civil Liability (Contribution) Act 1978 against the agents (including directors) of the claimant who caused the misapplication of the funds. The court, however, left open the issue whether the liability would be for the "same damage" within s.1(1): *City Index Ltd v Gawler* [2007] EWCA Civ 1382; [2008] 3 All E.R. 126.

[876] *Target Holdings Ltd v Redferns* [1996] A.C. 421; *Group Seven Ltd v Notable Services LLP* [2019] EWCA Civ 614; [2020] Ch. 129 at [110]. See para.6-043.

[877] *Target Holdings Ltd v Redferns* [1995] 2 A.C. at 391–339.

[878] In *Metall und Rohstoff AG v Donaldson Lufkin & Jenrette Inc* [1990] 1 Q.B. 391 at 481 the Court of Appeal rejected the existence of a tort of procuring a breach of trust. See however the Rt Hon. Lord Hoffmann in *The Frontiers of Liability* (Birks ed., 1994), Vol.1, p.28. A claim under this head was held to lie in "tort, delict or quasi-delict" for the purposes of art.5(3) of the Brussels Convention on Jurisdiction and the Enforcement of Judgments in *Casio Computer Co Ltd v Sayo* [2001] EWCA Civ 661; [2001] I.L.Pr. 43; see also *Grupo Torras SA v Al Sabbah (No.5)* [2001] Lloyd's Rep. Bank 36. cf. *OBG Ltd v Allan* [2007] UKHL 21; [2008] 1 A.C. 1 at [192] and [202].

Rule (2): Receipt of trust property[879]   Traditionally linked with what was   **9-136**
formerly called "knowing assistance" is the liability that can be imposed upon a
person who (on the orthodox formulation) knowingly receives trust property, or
having received it unknowingly becomes aware that it is trust property and that it
has been transferred in breach of duty. This liability is plainly less likely to be applicable to agents as such and it is mentioned here largely for completeness. It is
more likely to be applied to principals, but its historic pairing with dishonest assistance liability makes this a convenient place to offer a brief treatment of the key
issues that arise.

Liability arises from receipt alone and requires no acts of assistance of another
performed by the receiver: but it is confined to beneficial receipt. It, therefore, does
not apply to receipt as a mere conduit.[880] On the other hand, it has been held as a
matter of the application of limitation provisions that receipt by a company which
the fraudulent agent controls can be treated as receipt by the agent.[881]

The basis of such liability has long been and remains controversial. Formerly,
consistent with normal equity terminology, especially as applicable to property
interests, it was often said to be based on notice. The word "knowledge" might more
properly be employed. In *Baden Delvaux v Société Générale, etc., SA*[882] Peter
Gibson J formulated the possible degrees of knowledge for the purposes of the
operation of equity as follows:

> "(i) Actual knowledge; (ii) wilfully shutting one's eyes to the obvious; (iii) wilfully and
> recklessly failing to make such inquiries as an honest and reasonable man would make;
> (iv) knowledge of circumstances which would indicate the facts to an honest and reason-
> able man; (v) knowledge of circumstances which would put an honest and reasonable man
> on inquiry."

The meticulous discriminations of this passage have been criticised,[883] and it is not
always easy to know which part to apply in a particular fact situation. It is also true
that the passage occurs in a judgment on *accessory* liability (formerly knowing assistance), a part of the law that is, as stated above, now separating itself off; and that
in the *Royal Brunei* case Lord Nicholls said that in the context of that liability "the
Baden scale is best forgotten".[884] It remains nevertheless useful, here and
elsewhere[885] as a starting point which draws attention to the problems likely to be
encountered. On this basis it is clear that the constructive notice of conveyancers,
whereby a person is deemed to have notice of property interests in respect of which
inquiry ought to have been made, is not relevant.[886] It has then been said that the
approach should be to ask whether the conscience of the recipient is affected, which
will involve looking for knowledge or appreciation of relevant circumstances—

---

[879]   For full discussion see *Lewin on Trusts* (20th edn), Ch.42.
[880]   See, e.g. *Heperu Pty Ltd v Belle* (2009) 258 A.L.R. 727 (very brief receipt into joint account without
knowledge does not lead to liability). For other cases, see commentary and illustrations to Article
92.
[881]   *Burnden Holdings (UK) Ltd v Fielding* [2018] UKSC 14; [2018] A.C. 857 at [22].
[882]   *Baden Delvaux v Société Générale, etc., SA* [1993] 1 W.L.R. 509 at 575–576.
[883]   *Jacobs' Law of Trusts in Australia* (8th edn, Heydon and Leeming eds), para.1336; *Agip (Africa) Ltd
v Jackson* [1990] Ch. 265 at 293.
[884]   *Royal Brunei* [1995] 2 A.C. at 762.
[885]   See, e.g. Article 73. See too *Farah Constructions Pty Ltd v Say-Dee Pty Ltd* [2007] HCA 22; (2007)
230 C.L.R. 89 at [175]; *Armstrong DLW GmbH v Winnington Networks Ltd* [2012] EWHC 10 (Ch);
[2013] Ch. 156.
[886]   *Re Montagu's ST* [1987] Ch. 264 at 285.

category (iv), running in appropriate contexts into (v) on the *Baden* scale,[887] both of which are addressed to facts rather than adverse property interests (to which the first three are more appropriate). Subsequently, it was said that:

> "It may well be that the underlying broad principle which runs through the authorities regarding commercial transactions is that the court will impute knowledge, on the basis of what a reasonable person would have learnt, to a person who is guilty of commercially unacceptable conduct in the particular context involved."[888]

More recently it has been held in the Court of Appeal that, in contrast to accessory liability, where "dishonest assistance" is required, there is in this context no requirement of dishonesty.[889] In the case in question a more general formulation is adopted, the single test is simply that "the recipient's state of knowledge must be such as to make it unconscionable to retain the benefit of the receipt".[890]

Most of the modern cases have involved breaches of duty by agents, rather than trustees in the strict sense. In such circumstances, if the recipient cannot establish that the agent had apparent authority liability will usually follow.[891] The position is more complex where the breach is merely of an equitable duty; for some breaches, such as where the contract is affected by a mere conflict of interest, it may be necessary for the claimant to be able to rescind the contract with the recipient before any liability arises.[892] The property must be subject to an equitable interest in the claimant's favour at the moment of receipt, and the disposition itself must involve a breach of trust or breach of fiduciary duty.[893] The measure of liability is sometimes described as that of a constructive trustee,[894] but again the action is in effect in personam for the replacement of the value lost, even if the receiver has paid it away. It is therefore not clear whether it should include profits made from the property.

Knowing receipt liability is usually treated as distinct from tracing in equity, where knowledge of the trust interest is not required, profits may be recoverable,[895] but liability ceases when the property is transmitted away, lying against the

---

[887] *Re Montagu's ST* [1987] Ch. 264 at 285.

[888] *Cowan de Groot Properties Ltd v Eagle Trust Plc* [1992] 4 All E.R. 700 at 761, per Knox J, on knowing receipt, but approved also in the *Royal Brunei* case [1995] 2 A.C. at 390.

[889] *BCCI (Overseas) Ltd v Akindele* [2001] Ch. 437; *Uzinterimpex JSC v Standard Bank Plc* [2008] EWCA Civ 819; [2008] 2 Lloyd's Rep. 456; *Despot v Registrar-General of NSW* [2013] NSWCA 313.

[890] *BCCI (Overseas) Ltd v Akindele* [2001] Ch. 437 at 439, per Nourse LJ. On this basis, perhaps not only the awareness issue in dishonest assistance resembles a jury question, as Millett J perceived at first instance in *Agip (Africa) Ltd v Jackson* [1990] Ch. 265, but the receipt issue also. cf. the Rt Hon. Lord Walker (2005) 27 Sydney L.Rev. 187. On the other hand, it is arguable that *Akindele* gave insufficient weight to the test of constructive knowledge favoured in *Belmont Finance Corp v Williams Furniture Ltd (No.2)* [1980] 1 All E.R. 393 at 404 and 412. See too *Credit Agricole Corp and Investment Bank v Papadimitriou* [2015] UKPC 13; [2015] 1 W.L.R. 4265 at [16] and [33] (noted Watts (2015) 131 L.Q.R. 511).

[891] *Thanakharn Kasikorn Thai Chamchat v Akai Holdings Ltd (In Liquidation)* (2010) 13 HKCFAR 479 at [136]; *McFee v Reilly* [2019] NSWCA 322 (benefiting from abuse of lasting power of attorney). See Conaglen and Nolan (2013) 129 L.Q.R. 359.

[892] See further above, paras 8-219–8-221.

[893] See *Courtwood Holdings SA v Woodley Properties Ltd* [2018] EWHC 2163 (Ch) at [61].

[894] See *Thanakharn Kasikorn Thai Chamchat v Akai Holdings Ltd (In Liquidation)* (2010) 13 HKCFAR 479 at [156].

[895] As to recovery of profits against a party receiving money in breach of trust, see *Akita Holdings Ltd v Attorney General of the Turks and Caicos Islands* [2017] UKPC 7; [2017] A.C. 590.

new holder, subject always to the defence of bona fide purchase for value without notice, or in some circumstances, change of position.[896]

The formulations above do no more than escape the old generalised concept of notice in equity and require in this context something which affects the conscience of the receiver.[897] A second possibility is however that the similarity with accessory liability should be abandoned, and the duty analysed as a strict one, based squarely on no more than receipt. If this is correct, receivers are liable unless they can plead the defence of change of position or bona fide purchase[898]; and the burden of proof is reversed.[899] This would involve a development in equity which could be seen as paralleling or assimilating to current developments in restitutionary liability, and be in some ways parallel to the tort of conversion. As such it has authoritative extra-judicial support.[900] There is also some support for it in the *Royal Brunei* case referred to above,[901] and this approach has the advantage of avoiding the difficult questions of proof which arise under any of the tests for knowledge (and indeed notice) so far discussed. But the decision of the English Court of Appeal referred to above casts doubt on the possibility,[902] and it has been rejected by the High Court of Australia.[903]

Rule (3): Inconsistent dealing by agent[904] A further group of cases, much more   **9-137**
relevant to agency, holds an agent who lawfully, but not for personal benefit, holds property which the agent knows to be impressed with a trust or fiduciary interest, liable if without the authority of the trustees the agent deals with it inconsistently with the trust.[905] This is not a "knowing receipt" situation, for the receipt does not generate liability: it is rather the dealing which does so. In such cases the liability is not based on dishonesty (though this may exist), but rather on the inconsistent dealing following the lawful receipt and knowledge of the trust; and since the holder

---

[896] See *Crédit Agricole Corp and Investment Bank v Papadimitriou* [2015] UKPC 13; [2015] 1 W.L.R. 4265; *Heperu Pty Ltd v Belle* (2009) 258 A.L.R. 727.

[897] *Re Montagu's S.T.* [1987] Ch. 264 at 285; *Cowan de Groot Properties Ltd v Eagle Trust Plc* [1992] 4 All E.R. 700; *Eagle Trust Plc v SBC Securities Ltd* [1993] 1 W.L.R. 484; *Eagle Trust Plc v SBC Securities Ltd (No.2)* [1996] 1 B.C.L.C. 121. But cf. the Rt Hon. Lord Millett (1991) 107 L.Q.R. 71 at 78 ("profoundly mistaken").

[898] As established in *Lipkin Gorman v Karpnale Ltd* [1991] 2 A.C. 548: see *Goff and Jones, Law of Unjust Enrichment* (9th edn), Ch.27.

[899] See *Crédit Agricole Corp and Investment Bank v Papadimitriou* [2015] UKPC 13; [2015] 1 W.L.R. 4265; and Harpum in *Frontiers of Liability* (Birks edn, 1994), Vol.1, Ch.1.

[900] See Birks, *Introduction to the Law of Restitution* (1985), p.439 onwards; the Rt Hon. Lord Millett (1991) 107 L.Q.R. 71; the Rt Hon. Lord Nicholls in *Restitution Past, Present and Future* (Cornish ed., 1998), Ch.15; Birks, in *Breach of Trust* (Birks and Pretto eds, 2002), Ch.7.

[901] See esp. [1995] 2 A.C. at 386 ("recipient liability is restitution based"), 387 ("strict liability"); *El Ajou v Dollar Land Holdings Plc* [1994] 2 All E.R. 685.

[902] *BCCI (Overseas) Ltd v Akindele* [2001] Ch. 437 at 455, per Nourse LJ; *DD Growth Premium 2X Fund v RMF Market Neutral Strategies (Master) Ltd* [2017] UKPC 36 at [64]. See also *Citadel General Assurance Co v Lloyd's Bank Canada* [1997] 3 S.C.R. 805; (1997) 152 D.L.R. (4th) 411 (noted L.D. Smith (1998) 114 L.Q.R. 394, "equity's conversion"); L.D. Smith (2000) 116 L.Q.R. 412).

[903] *Farah Constructions Pty Ltd v Say-Dee Pty Ltd* (2007) 236 C.L.R. 89 (noted Ridge and Dietrich (2008) 124 L.Q.R. 26).

[904] See *Lewin on Trusts* (20th edn), para.42-111 onwards.

[905] e.g. *Lee v Sankey* (1873) L.R. 15 Eq. 204; *Purrunsing v A'Court & Co (a firm)* [2016] EWHC 789 (Ch); and see Illustrations below.

received the property lawfully the holder appears to be a genuine constructive trustee rather than one of the sort created by the previous two categories.[906]

9-138 **Trustee de son tort**[907] Similar to, but not the same as, the above, an agent may also incur liability as trustee *de son tort* by assuming to act as trustee when he or she is not. Thus an agent who holds trust money for trustees, and administers and takes decisions as to what is to be done with it without reference to them could become liable to account under this head as if an express trustee. Although technically a constructive trustee, as a trustee *de son tort* the holder is in a very similar position to that of a trustee duly appointed.[908] In general however an agent for trustees holds for and is accountable to the trustees only.[909]

9-139 **Rule (4): Agent performs ministerial functions only** An argument can also be made that, on the analogy of cases on innocent handling in the law of conversion,[910] an agent who acts only ministerially and does no more than carry out instructions cannot be liable at all.[911] Though such a proposition must be correct in principle, the circumstances where it is actually needed to exclude the agent's liability are few. Accessory liability only exists in cases where the agent is dishonest; knowing receipt liability operates only where the defendant holds beneficially and thus not ministerially. In inconsistent dealing cases, where the agent is free of liability the reasoning that this is because the agent acts ministerially is rarely needed: the reasoning simply constitutes a denial of the lack of authority or of the dealing. But it is true that an agent acting on the instructions of trustees or fiduciaries is in general not liable for mere inadvertence, or even (under the heads discussed above) for negligence. For example, an agent is not liable to account for paying over the trust money to the trustee in circumstances in which the agent might suspect (but no more) that the trustee will apply it inconsistently with the trust.[912] The adoption of strict liability for what is now called "knowing receipt" would make a "ministerial function" defence more significant, as it is in conversion.

9-140 **Solicitors**[913] Some of these questions have arisen in connection with solicitors: a solicitor may become a constructive trustee, e.g. by improperly applying trust funds[914] or by paying such funds to one trustee only.[915] On the other hand a solicitor was held not liable when he invested trust funds, on the instructions of the

---

[906] See *Lewin on Trusts*, above.

[907] See *Lewin on Trusts* (20th edn), para.42-101 onwards.

[908] See *Dubai Aluminium Co Ltd v Salaam* [2002] UKHL 48; [2003] 2 A.C. 366 at [132] onwards, per Lord Millett.

[909] *Bath v Standard Land Co Ltd* [1911] 1 Ch. 618; *Gregson v HAE Trustees Ltd* [2008] EWHC 1006 (Ch); [2008] 2 B.C.L.C. 542; [2009] 1 All E.R. (Comm) 457.

[910] See Article 114.

[911] See in general Swadling, in *Laundering and Tracing* (Birks ed., 1995), p.243. See also above, para.8-199.

[912] *Adams v Bank of New South Wales* [1984] 1 N.S.W.L.R. 285 and other cases cited in *Lewin on Trusts* (19th edn), para.42-117.

[913] See Cordery, *Solicitors* (9th (looseleaf) edn), F[409] onwards.

[914] See *Att.-Gen. v Leicester Corp* (1844) 7 Beav. 176 (town clerk); *Morgan v Stephens* (1861) 3 Giff. 226; *Hardy v Caley* (1864) 33 Beav. 365; *Blyth v Fladgate* [1891] 1 Ch. 337; *Soar v Ashwell* [1893] 2 Q.B. 390, Illustration 5; *Cooper v Stoneham* (1893) 68 L.T. 18; *Purrunsing v A'Court & Co (a firm)* [2016] EWHC 789 (Ch). See also Illustration 3.

[915] *Lee v Sankey* (1873) L.R. 15 Eq. 204. As to the liability of the partner of such a solicitor, see *Re Bell's Indenture* [1980] 1 W.L.R. 1217; *Dubai Aluminium Co Ltd v Salaam* [2001] Q.B. 113.

trustee, in unauthorised mortgages: he was acting as agent only.[916] Similar reasoning applies to solicitors acting in connection with fiduciaries. But such cases may require reassessment in the light of the recent developments referred to above.

Banks[917]   The question has also arisen in connection with banks, who may become   **9-141**
constructive trustees, for example by seeking to apply trust money to a fiduciary's personal overdraft,[918] transferring money deposited with them to the personal account of the trustee, honouring cheques drawn on trust accounts for improper purposes, or by facilitating an inadmissible transaction, such as where a company uses its money to purchase its own shares. Unless the account is overdrawn, they are not easily regarded as "receiving" money as agents for their customers; but they can of course be on risk for "accessory" liability.[919] The duties of bankers in such cases are difficult to define. They have an obligation to comply with their customers' instructions in relation to moneys in their customers' accounts.[920] On the other hand they have responsibilities to prevent misuse of trust funds, and evasion of statutory provisions, again such as those that prevent companies from buying their own shares.[921] They are often therefore the subject of conflicting duties.[922] Older dicta can be cited to the effect that a banker was not liable unless the banker was privy to the breach of trust,[923] or where an element of personal benefit was involved.[924] But other authority has placed a stricter duty on banks.[925]

Illustrations

(1)   An agent of an executor applies a fund, which he knows to be part of the estate   **9-142**
      of the testator, in satisfaction of advances made to the executor for his own
      business. He is personally liable to account for the fund to the beneficiaries
      under the will.[926]
(2)   A director is passively involved in transactions arranged by a stranger who

---

[916] *Mara v Browne* [1896] 1 Ch. 199 as explained in *Williams-Ashman v Price and Williams* [1942] Ch.
       219 and *Dubai Aluminium Co Ltd v Salaam* [2002] UKHL 48; [2003] 2 A.C. 366 at [132], per Lord
       Millett; see also Illustration 3; Illustration 4.
[917] See Bryan, in *Restitution and Banking Law* (Rose ed., 1998) at 161; Mitchell, in *Commercial Law:
       Perspectives and Practice* (Lowry and Mistelis eds, 2006), Ch.6.
[918] cf. *Neste Oy v Lloyd's Bank Plc* [1983] 2 Lloyd's Rep. 658 at 666; approved in *Kingscroft Ins. Co
       Ltd v H.S. Weavers (Underwriting Agencies) Ltd* [1993] 1 Lloyd's Rep. 187 at 195.
[919] *Uzinterimpex JSC v Standard Bank Plc* [2008] EWCA Civ 819 (bank ceased to be agent when it had
       entitlement to ring-fence funds for its own benefit).
[920] *Baden Delvaux v Société Générale, etc., SA* (1983) [1993] 1 W.L.R. 509 at 585–586; affirmed [1985]
       B.C.L.C. 258; *US International Marketing Ltd v National Bank of New Zealand Ltd* [2004] 1
       N.Z.L.R. 589 (NZCA) (bank not permitted to decline right of customer to withdraw funds simply
       on basis that a third party had informed the bank that it had claimed the funds and was intending to
       seek a court order freezing the moneys); *Westpac New Zealand Ltd v Map & Associates Ltd* [2011]
       3 N.Z.L.R. 751 (NZSC).
[921] See Companies Act 2006 Pt. 18.
[922] *Gray v Johnston* (1868) L.R. 3 H.L. 1 at 11.
[923] *Gray v Johnston* (1868) L.R. 3 H.L. 1 at 11.
[924] *Foxton v Manchester and Liverpool District Banking Co* (1881) 44 L.T. 406; cf. *Coleman v Bucks
       and Oxon Union Bank* [1897] 2 Ch. 243.
[925] See *Selangor United Rubber Estates Ltd v Cradock (No.3)* [1968] 1 W.L.R. 1555; *Karak Rubber
       Co Ltd v Burden (No.2)* [1972] 1 W.L.R. 602; *Belmont Finance Corp v Williams Furniture Ltd (No.2)*
       [1980] 1 All E.R. 393; (1981) 44 M.L.R. 107; *Baden Delvaux v Société Générale, etc., SA* (1983)
       [1993] 1 W.L.R. 509 (authorities reviewed); and in general cases cited at Illustration 6. See too
       Nicholson v Morgan (No.3) [2013] WASC 110.
[926] *Wilson v Moore* (1834) 1 Myl. & K. 126 and 337.

purchased the majority of the company's shares, whereby the company's money is used to finance the purchase. The director is liable.[927]

(3) A trustee allows his solicitor to retain costs out of the trust estate. The solicitor knows that the trustee has secretly bought for himself part of the trust estate. The solicitor is not a trustee of the sums received out of the estate.[928]

(4) A solicitor receives money from a client in respect of costs and expenses in defending an action under which a third party is claiming that the client is constructive trustee of all the client's assets. The solicitor is not liable as a constructive trustee.[929]

(5) The solicitor to a trust invests trust money mixed with moneys of other trusts, in an equitable mortgage. When the mortgage is redeemed he distributes half the proceeds to beneficiaries who have by that time become absolutely entitled to the same. He retains the other half, to which others are entitled. He holds the retained money on constructive trust.[930]

(6) A bank transfers trust money from a trust account to the personal account of the trustees or otherwise participates in a transfer of trust money in circumstances which would put a reasonable bank on inquiry as to the nature of the transaction being conducted. The bank is liable to the beneficiaries for the amount so transferred, whether it acquired a personal benefit from the transaction or not.[931]

(7) Directors of a company which is an agent to identify suitable public houses for acquisition by the claimant cause the company to breach its fiduciary duties to the claimant, inter alia, by procuring for the claimant leases only of a number of houses and suppressing the availability of freehold interests for them. The directors were held liable for dishonest assistance in their company's breaches of duty.[932]

---

[927] *Selangor United Rubber Estates Ltd v Cradock (No.3)* [1968] 1 W.L.R. 1555; see also *Belmont Finance Corp v Williams (No.2)* [1980] 1 All E.R. 393; (1981) 44 M.L.R. 107.

[928] *Re Blundell, Blundell v Blundell* (1888) 40 Ch.D. 370; *Williams v Williams* (1881) 17 Ch.D. 437; *Competitive Insurance Co Ltd v Davies Investments Ltd* [1975] 1 W.L.R. 1240 (liquidator); cf. *Blyth v Fladgate* [1891] 1 Ch. 337.

[929] *Carl Zeiss Stiftung v Herbert Smith & Co (No.2)* [1969] 2 Ch. 276.

[930] *Soar v Ashwell* [1893] 2 Q.B. 390. See also *Gathergood v Blundell & Brown Ltd* [1992] 3 N.Z.L.R. 643; *Nimmo v Westpac Banking Corp* [1993] 3 N.Z.L.R. 218.

[931] See *Baden Delvaux v Société Générale, etc., SA* [1993] 1 W.L.R. 509; *Selangor United Rubber Estates Ltd v Cradock (No.3)* [1968] 1 W.L.R. 1555; *Karak Rubber Co Ltd v Burden (No.2)* [1972] 1 W.L.R. 602; *Rowlandson v National Westminster Bank Ltd* [1978] 1 W.L.R. 798; *Barclays Bank Plc v Quincecare Ltd* (1988) [1992] 4 All E.R. 363. These cases concern accessory liability. As to knowing receipt, where liability will arise less often, see *Gray v Johnston* (1868) L.R. 3 H.L. 1; *Thomson v Clydesdale Bank* [1893] A.C. 282; *Coleman v Bucks and Oxon Union Bank* [1897] 2 Ch. 243; *Union Bank of Australia v Murray-Aynsley; Shields v Bank of Ireland* [1901] 1 I.R. 222; *Bank of New South Wales v Goulburn Valley Butter Co Pty Ltd* [1902] A.C. 543; *Westpac Banking Corp v Savin* [1985] 2 N.Z.L.R. 41. See in general *Lewin on Trusts* (20th edn), 42-085 onwards and 42-093; Ellinger, Lomnicka and Hare, *Modern Banking Law* (5th edn), p.291 onwards.

[932] *JD Wetherspoon Plc v Van De Berg & Co Ltd* [2009] EWHC 639 (Ch).

CHAPTER 10

TERMINATION OF AUTHORITY

INTRODUCTORY NOTE

The propositions collected in this chapter, like those in Chapter 3, straddle the **10-001** three main aspects of agency, the relations between principal and agent, principal and third party, and agent and third party. Therefore careful attention should be paid to determining which aspects of an agency situation are affected by each rule. Thus the termination of authority between principal and agent may not affect a third party who has no notice of such termination: Article 121 (which deals with apparent authority where actual authority is determined) must be regarded as qualifying some of the earlier Articles in the chapter. And although a termination of authority may as between principal and agent be operative in some respects, e.g. in making further actions by the agent on the principal's behalf ineffective, and terminating the agent's right to remuneration or indemnity, it may also be wrongful as a breach of contract and give rise to a right to damages.[1] Furthermore, the fiduciary obligation and in some cases that as to commission may continue.

Article 117

TERMINATION OF ACTUAL AUTHORITY

(1) The actual authority of an agent is terminated—   **10-002**
 (a) by agreement between principal and agent;
 (b) if given for a particular transaction, by the completion of that transaction[2];
 (c) if given for a limited period, by the expiration of that period, or in any case after the elapsing of a period which is reasonable in all the circumstances[3];
 (d) by the happening of any event upon the happening of which it is agreed between the principal and the agent that the authority shall terminate,[4] or upon the happening of which the agent should reasonably infer that the principal does not or would not wish the authority to continue[5];
 (e) by the destruction of the subject-matter of the agency[6];

---

[1] See Article 120.
[2] Illustrations 1–4.
[3] Illustration 5; *Danby v Coutts & Co* (1885) 29 Ch.D. 550, Illustration 1 to Article 22.
[4] See *Restatement, Third*, § 3.09.
[5] See Comment. Mere cessation of the agent's business does not of itself terminate his authority: *Trif-fit Nurseries v Salads Etcetera Ltd* [1999] 1 All E.R. (Comm) 110; [2000] 1 All E.R. (Comm) 737. cf. *Angove's Pty Ltd v Bailey* [2016] UKSC 47; [2016] 1 W.L.R. 3179.
[6] *Rhodes v Forwood* (1876) 1 App.Cas. 256, Illustration 1 to Article 123; *Northey v Trevillion* (1902) 7 Com.Cas. 201. See Article 123.

> (f) by the happening of any event rendering the agency or its objects unlaw-
> ful, impossible or otherwise frustrating the agency or its objects.[7]
>
> (2) The actual authority of an agent is also terminated, unless it is irrevocable in
> accordance with the provisions of Article 120—
>
> (a) (prima facie) by the death, mental incapacity or (in some situations)
> insolvency of the principal or the agent; or where the principal or agent
> is a body corporate, by its dissolution[8];
>
> (b) by notice of revocation given, whether or not in breach of contract, by the
> principal to the agent[9];
>
> (c) by notice of renunciation given, whether or not in breach of contract, by
> the agent to the principal and accepted by the principal.[10]

Comment

10-003 **Rule (1)** The circumstances stated in Rule (1) above are relevant to the agreement, whether contractual or not, between principal and agent, and relate to implied
(or express) terms of it. They are no more than illustrations of situations in which
the agent is not justified in thinking that authority continues. It should be noted
however that the third party may still be able to rely in some cases on the doctrine
of apparent authority.[11] The propositions contained in (a)–(c) are self-evident. The
second part of (d) is derived from a suggestion in *Restatement, Third*[12] that
circumstances may occur in which at the time the directed act was to be performed
it is no longer reasonable for the agent to believe that the principal would wish the
agent to do so. Where however the agent is in reasonable doubt as to whether
authority persists, the agent's actions are to be treated as authorised if reasonable
in the circumstances.[13] Rule (1)(e) is again self-evident for cases where a subject-
matter can be readily identified, though here the correct analysis of the contractual
position, and hence whether the principal is liable to the agent, is open to much
argument.[14] In both these cases it is a matter of interpretation whether the actual
authority ends on the happening of the event or on the agent's receiving notice of
the happening of the event.

Rule 1(f) involves a more general application of the doctrine of frustration to
agency contracts and agreements. An agent's authority has been held to terminate
when the operation of Military Service Acts made it illegal or impossible for the
agent to perform the given tasks.[15] Where the contract of agency may require
intercourse with the enemy during a war, the agency is normally terminated by the
outbreak of war.[16] Thus when a client becomes an alien enemy the solicitor's

---

[7] See Comment.

[8] Article 119. The dissolution of a partnership may have the same effect: ibid.

[9] Article 120.

[10] Article 120.

[11] See Article 121.

[12] See Comment *b* to § 3.06.

[13] cf. Articles 26 and 38.

[14] See Article 123.

[15] *Marshall v Glanvill* [1917] 2 K.B. 87; and see *Morgan v Manser* [1948] 1 K.B. 184.

[16] *Sovfracht, etc., v Van Udens, etc.* [1943] A.C. 203 at 253–255; *Hugh Stevenson & Sons Ltd v
Aktiengesellschaft für Cartonnagen Industrie* [1918] A.C. 239; *Nordisk Insulin-laboratorium v
Gorgate Products Ltd* [1953] Ch. 430 (in all of which the principal became an enemy); *Kuenigl v
Donnersmarck* [1955] 1 Q.B. 515 (where the agent became an enemy). See also *Daimler Co Ltd v
Continental Tyre & Rubber Co Ltd* [1916] 2 A.C. 307; Webber, *Effect of War on Contracts* (2nd edn);

retainer ceases,[17] though it has been held that while the solicitor remains on the record, service upon the solicitor of an application to strike out the statement of claim is sufficient,[18] It has also been held that a purportedly irrevocable power of attorney to sell land and give a receipt for the purchase money was not avoided by the donor subsequently becoming an alien enemy.[19] This case has however been criticised, and should at least be regarded as turning on special facts: ordinarily the relationship of principal and agent necessitates communication between the parties,[20] which would not be possible in such a situation. But the occurrence of war does not of itself determine the authority of an enemy alien resident in this country who acts for a principal also resident in this country.[21] In general each case of this type must turn on its facts: "the general grounds of abrogation are, broadly speaking, the danger of intercourse and the desire not to enhance, but to cripple, the resources of the enemy".[22] The mere fact that a law change makes it no longer necessary for a principal to employ agents could not justify the termination of a fixed term contract of agency.[23] Authority could always be withdrawn in such circumstances, but the agent would have an action for breach of contract.[24]

Rule (2) The circumstances stated in Rule (2) have a different operation. Those **10-004** in (a) relate to the capacity of the principal to have an agent at all, or of the agent to act as such. The law in this area is still in a state of development. In particular, it is not yet fully settled whether an agent's actual authority is terminated automatically by the principal's mental incapacity, or whether the agent needs to have become aware (or ought to have become aware) of the occurrence of the incapacity. Nor is the position with apparent authority settled.[25] In relation to mental incapacity, there are also certain protections provided by statute.[26] Renunciation by either party, referred to in (b) and (c), terminates authority because as a matter of policy such a rule seems appropriate to the relationship[27]; but there may be repercussions both between principal and agent (where the renunciation may be a breach of contract by one or the other) and as regards third parties (who may be able to rely on the doctrine of apparent authority if they had no notice of the renunciation).[28]

For the *authority* to be terminated, a revocation by the principal does not require to be accepted by the agent. But where there is a contract between them, on general principles a repudiatory breach of it is ineffective unless accepted by the innocent

---

McNair, *Legal Effects of War* (4th edn).
[17] *Sovfracht, etc., v Van Udens, etc.* [1943] A.C. 203.
[18] *Eichengruen v Mond* [1940] Ch. 785 (claim frivolous and vexatious).
[19] *Tingley v Müller* [1917] 2 Ch. 144.
[20] See *Sovfracht, etc., v Van Udens, etc.* [1943] A.C. 203 at 236, 254; *Hangkam Kwingtong Woo v Liu Lan Fong* [1951] A.C. 707 at 720. But cf. *Perpetual Trustee Co Ltd v Aroney* (1944) 44 S.R.(N.S.W.) 313.
[21] *Nordman v Rayner and Sturges* (1916) 33 T.L.R. 87 (where the alien was actually interned for a short period); *Schostall v Johnson* (1919) 36 T.L.R. 75.
[22] *Hangkam Kwingtong Woo v Liu Lan Fong* [1951] A.C. 707 at 720 at 179, per Lord Simonds (a case where the principal was in a country allied to the United Kingdom and the agent in Japanese-occupied Hong Kong). See also *Ottoman Bank v Jebara* [1928] A.C. 269; *Sovfracht, etc., v Van Udens, etc.* [1943] A.C. 203 at 236.
[23] See *W Nagel (A Firm) v Pluczenik Diamond Co NV* [2018] EWCA Civ 2640; [2019] Bus. L.R. 692.
[24] See further, para.10-045.
[25] See below, Articles 119 and 121.
[26] See below, para.10-020; Article 122.
[27] Article 120.
[28] Articles 121 and 122.

party. Thus any *contract* may in some respects be regarded as subsisting, even though the authority is revoked, if the revocation is a breach by the principal and is not accepted by the agent.[29] Even where it is accepted, some contractual duties operating beyond the end of the contract service may continue, as may some fiduciary duties.[30] On the other hand, since the conferring or withdrawal of authority is within the power of the principal, a renunciation by the *agent* does not terminate authority (quite apart from the question of the contractual position between them) unless the principal indicates that it should. It may however be a breach of contract, and may also release the principal from the duty to give notice of the termination of authority.

Illustrations

10-005 (1) A broker is employed to sell goods. As soon as the contract of sale is completed, he is functus officio, and cannot subsequently alter the terms of the contract without fresh authority from the principal.[31]
(2) A solicitor is retained to conduct an action. His authority to act for the client prima facie ceases at the judgment, though it may be renewed by any act showing the client's intention that the solicitor shall continue to act.[32]
(3) An auctioneer is authorised to sell property. He has no authority to sign a memorandum of the sale a week after the sale.[33]
(4) An estate agent was employed to let or sell a house. Having let the house, he negotiated for a sale, and subsequently found a purchaser. Held, that he had no authority to sell after having let the house, and that he was not entitled to commission on the sale.[34]
(5) A broker is authorised to sell goods. It may be shown that by the custom of the particular trade such an authority expires with the expiration of the day on which it is given.[35]

Article 118

WHEN AUTHORITY CANNOT BE TERMINATED (IRREVOCABLE AUTHORITY)

10-006 (1) At common law, where the authority of an agent is given by deed,[36] or for valuable consideration,[37] for the purpose of supporting or effectuating any security, or of protecting or securing an interest of parties other than the principal, it is

---

[29] See *Atlantic Underwriting Agencies Ltd v Cia. di Assicurazione di Milano SpA* [1979] 2 Lloyd's Rep. 240; *Paper Reclaim Ltd v Aotearoa International Ltd* [2007] 3 N.Z.L.R. 169 (N.Z.S.C.) at [22] (see para.7-046, above); *Société Générale, London Branch v Geys* [2012] UKSC 63; [2013] 1 A.C. 523; Treitel, *Law of Contract* (15th edn), para.18-026 onwards.
[30] *Thomas Marshall (Exports) Ltd v Guinle* [1979] Ch. 227; as to fiduciary duties, see Article 43.
[31] *Blackburn v Scholes* (1810) 2 Camp. 341.
[32] *Butler v Knight* (1867) L.R. 2 Ex 109; but cf. *Re Newen, Carruthers v Newen* [1903] 1 Ch. 812. No doubt it covers matters ancillary to the judgment. See in general Cordery, *Solicitors* (8th edn), Ch.4.
[33] *Bell v Balls* [1897] 1 Ch. 663. The situation could not now arise in exactly this form because of the effect of the Law of Property (Miscellaneous Provisions) Act 1989 s.2.
[34] *Gillow & Co v Lord Aberdare* (1892) 9 T.L.R. 12.
[35] *Dickinson v Lilwall* (1815) 4 Camp. 279.
[36] Illustration 1; *Walsh v Whitcomb* (1797) 2 Esp. 565.
[37] Illustrations 2–4.

irrevocable during the subsistence of such security or interest.[38] But authority is not irrevocable merely because an agent would be prejudiced by its revocation, as by loss of commission,[39] or has a special property in, or lien for advances upon, the subject-matter of it,[40] unless the authority was given expressly for the purpose of securing such interest or advances.

(2) By statute, where a power of attorney, whenever created, is expressed to be irrevocable and is given to secure a proprietary interest of the donee of the power, or the performance of an obligation owed to the donee,[41] then, so long as the donee has that interest, or the obligation remains undischarged, the power is irrevocable.[42]

(3) Authority expressed by this Article to be irrevocable is not determined by the death,[43] mental incapacity or insolvency[44] of the principal, nor, where the principal is a body corporate, by its winding-up or dissolution.[45]

(4) A lasting power of attorney as defined in the Mental Capacity Act 2005 is not revoked by the subsequent mental incapacity of the donor, and is exercisable thereafter in accordance with the provisions of that Act.[46]

Comment

Rules (1) and (3): Irrevocability at common law   The dominant assumption in   **10-007**
the cases is that a grant of authority is of its nature revocable.[47] The mere fact that a power is declared in the instrument granting it to be irrevocable does not make it so, even if that instrument is a deed. Authority *can* be irrevocable; but this is only where the notion of agency is employed as a legal device for a different purpose from that of normal agency, to confer a security or other interest on the "agent". In such a case it is intended that the agent use the authority not for the benefit of the principal but for personal benefit, to achieve the objects of the arrangement.

---

[38] See Illustrations. For the wording see *Clerk v Laurie* (1857) 2 H. & N. 199 at 200 ("for the purpose of securing some benefit to the donee of the authority": per Williams J), cited in *Carmichael*'s case, Illustration 4. See also *Slatter v Railway Commissioners (New South Wales)* (1931) 45 C.L.R. 68; *Griffin v Clark* (1940) 40 S.R.(N.S.W.) 409; *Re Hartt Group and Land Securities Ltd* (1984) 7 D.L.R. (4th) 89 (landlord's right to re-enter and take custody as agent of tenant). Revocation may probably be restrained by injunction: see *Knight v Bulkeley* (1859) 5 Jur.(N.S.) 817. See also below, para.12-024.

[39] Illustrations 3 and 5; *Frith v Frith* [1906] A.C. 254; *Angove's Pty Ltd v Bailey* [2016] UKSC 47; [2016] 1 W.L.R. 3179 at [9].

[40] Illustration 5; below, para.10-010.

[41] See Comment.

[42] Powers of Attorney Act 1971 s.4(1). Such a power may be given to the person entitled to the interest and persons deriving title under him to that interest: s.4(2). See in general *Law Com. No.30*, Cmnd. 4473 (1970).

[43] See *Lepard v Vernon* (1813) 2 V. & B. 51; *Spooner v Sandilands* (1842) 1 Y. & C.Ch.Cas. 390; *Carter v White* (1883) 25 Ch.D. 666 (completion of blanks in bill of exchange after death of drawer). But these are not strong cases: see Comment.

[44] *Alley v Hotson* (1815) 4 Camp. 325 (a case on mutual credit under the law of bankruptcy setoff); cf. *Bristow and Porter v Taylor* (1817) 2 Stark. 50 (a case on the then recently changed law on fraudulent releases).

[45] See Powers of Attorney Act 1971 s.4(1). It is normally assumed that the same is true at common law: see Comment. See too *Wellington Steam Ferry Co Ltd (In Liquidation) v Wellington Deposit, Mortgage, and Building Assoc. Ltd* (1915) 34 N.Z.L.R. 913; *Lim Eng Chuan Sdn Bhd v United Malayan Banking Corp* [2011] 1 M.L.J. 486 (Malaysia CA).

[46] See Comment.

[47] See *Angove's Pty Ltd v Bailey* [2016] UKSC 47; [2016] 1 W.L.R. 3179 at [6]; *Jeddi v Sotheby's* [2018] EWHC 1491 (Comm) at [105].

The last two sentences of the immediately preceding paragraph were disapproved in an obiter dictum of Lord Sumption in *Angove's Pty Ltd v Bailey*,[48] as being too narrow a description of the circumstances when authority might be irrevocable. The judge did not provide an alternative formulation but he did make a number of points. First, he rejected the idea that irrevocability must exist solely in order to secure the agent's financial interest. Secondly, he took the view that irrevocability was not incompatible with the agent's being able to promote both personal interests as well as the principal's. Thirdly, it would be possible to infer irrevocability in a clear enough case.[49]

It can be accepted, with respect, that the first of Lord Sumption's points is valid. In cases where a company promoter or an issuer of company shares takes an irrevocable authority to ensure that underwriters or subscribers for shares do not renege on a subscription,[50] it can be readily accepted that the collective interests of the other subscribers are being protected as much as the promoter's or the company's. Similarly, the cases upholding an irrevocable authority given to an auctioneer of land to sign a memorandum in writing on behalf of the successful, but now regretful, bidder are protecting the interests of the vendor as much as the auctioneer.[51] These examples were referred to by Lord Sumption, but, surprisingly, treated as special cases and not relied upon by him for his criticism. More is said about these types of case, below para.10-010. There will be other cases where the interest to be protected is not the agent's; an authority given, for example, to a receiver will usually be given to promote the interests of debentureholders, not the receiver personally.[52]

Lord Sumption's second point is less easy to accept. It seems hard to reconcile with the reasons for the existence of a general principle that authority can always be revoked even when doing so puts the principal in breach of contract with the agent. Those reasons were stated by the judge as follows:

"An agent is empowered to commit his principal within the limits of his authority as if the principal had agreed personally. This is a confidential relationship importing a duty of loyalty, and normally of undivided loyalty, on the part of the agent."[53]

The judge went on to indicate that, while an agent could not have irrevocable authority in order to maintain a right to future commissions, the agent might to secure payment of past commissions. This example, and the judge's broader dicta, cut against the idea that the exercise of authority is indissolubly connected with the principal's autonomy and the article of faith that the principal's confidence in the agent is paramount. This is not to say that agents must place themselves in peril of

---

[48] *Angove's Pty Ltd v Bailey* [2016] UKSC 47 at [9] (noted P. Watts "The insolvency of agents" (2017) 133 L.Q.R. 11; J. Grower, "On the relations between agent and principal: Angove's Pty Ltd v Bailey" (2018) 81 M.L.R. 141; J. Alexander, "Insolvent Agents and Irrevocable Authorities" (2017) 23 N.Z.B.L.Q. 183).

[49] *Angove's Pty Ltd v Bailey* [2016] UKSC 47 at [8] and [16].

[50] See, e.g. *Re Hannan's Empress Gold Mining & Development Co, Carmichael's Case* [1896] 2 Ch. 643, Illustration 5.

[51] See, e.g. *Van Praagh v Everidge* [1902] 2 Ch. 266; reversed on other grounds [1903] 1 Ch. 434.

[52] See *Sowman v David Samuel Trust Ltd* [1978] 1 W.L.R. 22 at 31, per Goulding J: followed in *Re Leslie Homes (Aust.) Pty Ltd* (1984) 8 A.C.L.R. 1020; *Pask v Menon* [2019] EWHC 2611 (Ch); [2020] Ch. 66; and see Millett (1977) 41 Conv. 83. Contra, *Barrows v Chief Land Registrar, The Times* October 18, 1977 Ch.D. See Goode, *Principles of Corporate Insolvency Law* (5th edn), para.10-41.

[53] *Angove's Pty Ltd v Bailey* [2016] UKSC 47; [2016] 1 W.L.R. 3179 at [6].

not being paid by their principal, but if their rights of lien are inadequate they must take a security of some sort, whereby their rights are circumscribed by the property interest they have taken from their principal.[54]

Lord Sumption's third point, as to the possibility of inferring irrevocability must, with respect, be sound. But it will be very rare when it is appropriate to do so, especially given that only damages are available for breach of an express clause.[55] *Angove's case* itself involved an attempt, unsuccessful, to imply irrevocability.

The principle of revocability and its exceptions have a very long history. The wording of Rule 1 remains closely based on that written by Bowstead in the first edition of this work in 1896. He himself derived it from dicta of Lord Kenyon in *Walsh v Whitcomb*[56] in 1797 and the decision in *Smart v Sandars*, in the context of factors, in 1848.[57] These cases date from a time of what one might call experimentation between legal doctrines (not all of which survive),[58] experimentation that also drew on ancient doctrines.[59] By the time Bowstead wrote many of the cases he cited were obsolete by reason of the property, insolvency, commercial and judicature reforms of the nineteenth century. They have not yet been set in order. On any basis, *Angove's* shows that there is still some way to go before the bounds of irrevocability are settled.

Angove's case accepts that cases where an irrevocable authority accompanies a security or proprietary interest and is part of it or a means of achieving it remain central examples of the phenomenon of irrevocability. The fact that the agent subsequently acquires an interest in the property is irrelevant: the authority must be conferred as part of, or as protection of the agent's interest.[60] The authority is referred to as "authority" or "power" "coupled with an interest", a phrase not unconnected with the nineteenth-century notion in a different context of a licence coupled with an interest.[61] The mere right to earn commission is not such an interest[62], nor is an agent's lien, unless the power was conferred specifically to protect it or sums

---

54 See *Smith v Plummer* (1818) 1 B. & A. 575 at 579 (Parke in argument). See too *Jeddi v Sotheby's* [2018] EWHC 1491 (Comm) at [105].
55 See, e.g. *Schindler v Brie* [2003] EWHC 1804 (Ch); [2003] W.T.L.R. 1361 (power of attorney to apply for letters of administration).
56 *Walsh v Whitcomb* (1797) 2 Esp. 565: see McGaw, below, at pp.246–257.
57 *Smart v Sandars* (1848) 5 C.B. 895, Illustration 8.
58 This article draws on the unpublished doctoral thesis of Dr Mark McGaw, "*A History of the Common Law of Agency with Particular Reference to the Concept of Irrevocable Authority Coupled with an Interest*" (2005). Most if not all of the cases cited in the text and Illustrations are there analysed in considerable detail, much more than is possible here. See also on this topic, Reynolds, in *Making Commercial Law* (Cranston ed., 1994), Ch.10 (itself criticised in the above thesis at pp.335–337); F. Reynolds and C.H. Tan, "Agency Reasoning—A Formula or a Tool?" [2018] Sing J.L.S. 43.
59 McGaw (above) mentions the wider pattern of articulation of recognisably modern principles in place of practitioners' rules of pleading and practice and various fictions and estoppels, the recognition of an equitable jurisdiction in the common law courts encouraged by acute delays in Chancery and the experimentation in special pleading associated with the Hilary Rules of 1835 eventually superseded by the judicature reforms of 1852–1875.
60 See *Smart v Sandars* (1848) 5 C.B. 895; *Despot v Registrar-General of NSW* [2013] NSWCA 313.
61 As to which see *Wood v Leadbitter* (1845) 13 M.& W. 838. Aspects of this concept affect the role of receiver in company law—see, in general, Lightman and Moss, *Law of Administrators and Receivers of Companies* (6th edn).
62 *Doward, Dickson & Co v Williams & Co* (1890) 6 T.L.R. 316; *Temple Legal Protection Ltd v QBE Insurance (Europe) Ltd* [2009] EWCA Civ 453; [2009] Lloyd's Rep I.R. 544 at [50].

due under it.[63] Subject to what is said in *Angove's case*, the central cases are different from normal agency, in which the agent must act in the interests of the principal: here the agent acts in his own interests. Agency is here a device for supporting or conferring a property interest (a power of attorney to sue on another's behalf and a power of sale are ways of enforcing a security). Although exposition of this area of law in textbooks on the law of agency is traditional, both in England and the US,[64] it is not really within the bounds of general agency reasoning.

The idea that an irrevocable power survives death and other losses of capacity, stated in Rule 3, is in fact not really supported by the old cases. In particular, it was difficult to see how a power of attorney to be exercised in the donor's name could be exercised after the donor's death.[65] The rule has to be justified on the general basis that what is in issue is a property right, which is (obviously) once granted, unaffected by loss of capacity of the grantor. This justification would not be available for cases of irrevocable authority that do not involve proprietary interests. The general proposition is now confirmed by statute, as appears below: but despite the problems it has been assumed for a considerable time that the same was and is true at common law.[66] Problems of corporate insolvency remain to be worked out.

10-008 **Rules (2) and (3): Statute: powers of attorney**   Special provisions as to the irrevocability of powers of attorney in like situations (for which they might well be used) are laid down in the Powers of Attorney Act 1971 s.4, and the general effect of this provision is reproduced in Rules (2) and (3) of this Article. It may be that the Act aims to declare the common law in this respect, and hence can be cited as an indication of the common law position. But it should be noted that, to be irrevocable, the authority must be contained in a power of attorney, and so witnessed[67]; and it must also be expressed to be irrevocable. Neither is true at common law. On the other hand, by its reference to securing the performance of an obligation owed to the donee, it is drafted, no doubt in accordance with formulations of the law current at the time,[68] to take in more than security interests. By contrast, it has been suggested above that at common law, in the case of a grant of authority coupled with an interest, the interest need not be that of the donee of the

---

[63] See Illustration 4.

[64] *Restatement*, §§ 3.12 and 3.13 (dealing also with irrevocable proxies: below, para.10-013). As to § 3.12, it provides: "A power given as security is a power to affect the legal relations of its creator that is created in the form of a manifestation of actual authority and held for the benefit of the holder or a third person. This power is given to protect a legal or equitable title, or so secure the performance of a duty apart from any duties owed the holder by its creator that are incident to a relationship of agency ...". See too DeMott on irrevocable proxies in American law (2008) 82 A.L.J. 516.

[65] See *Watson v King* (1815) 4 Camp. 272, concerning ship mortgages. Now however a power of attorney can be executed in the attorney's name: Powers of Attorney Act 1971 s.7: see Article 77.

[66] In the US a famous decision of Marshall CJ in *Hunt v Rousmanier's Administrators* 21 U.S. 174 (1823), again in the context of ship mortgages, distinguished between cases where the power accompanied a proprietary security interest and those where it stood alone: in the latter case it was revoked by death. This led to an unsatisfactory distinction, probably not justified from the case itself, between powers coupled with an interest and powers given as security. Only in the first was the power not revoked by death. The distinction was not taken in England and is not accepted in the *Restatement*, in which "power given as security" is the general test for irrevocable authority and is defined as in the previous paragraph. There is discussion in McGaw, above, at p.260 onwards.

[67] Powers of Attorney Act 1971 s.1(1): see above, para.2-039.

[68] See *Law Com. No.30* (1970), para.33, where the provision is stated to "restate the common law position when a power is given by way of security". Introducing his first Bill into the House of Lords, Lord Diplock said "Clause 4 deals with a special case on which I need not linger": 315 HL Debs col.1206 (February 25, 1971).

power: but the statutory wording seems to exclude this possibility.[69] Finally, in the corporate sphere it only applies to winding up or dissolution, which leaves questions not only about these procedures but also about other insolvency procedures. It is sometimes argued that the provision was intended to replace the common law; but there is no indication of this, and it will often be more convenient to rely on the possibly wider common law rules. The Act however contains protection for third parties where the power was expressed to be given by way of security but was in fact not so given,[70] protection which might be difficult to establish at common law.

Rule (4): Lasting Powers of Attorney   From October 1, 2007,[71] the Mental   **10-009**
Capacity Act 2005 has made available a new type of registrable instrument that endures where the donor has lost mental capacity, the Lasting Power of Attorney.[72] Powers of attorney under the Act can be revoked by the donor both before and after registration, but only where the donor retains capacity.[73] Bankruptcy of the donor will revoke the power in relation to the donor's property and affairs.[74] The Act, surprisingly perhaps, does not expressly provide for revocation by the death of the donor, although regulations assume that death does revoke powers of attorney made under the Act, and provide for deregistration accordingly.[75] The Act does provide for termination upon the death of, and other circumstances, relating to the donee.[76] The Act replaces the Enduring Power of Attorney which had been introduced by the Enduring Powers of Attorney Act 1985, now repealed. The Lasting Power is a wider type of power than the Enduring Power, under which the donee, or different donees, can be given authority to act in respect of the donor's personal welfare as well as his or her property and affairs,[77] though limited powers can of course be conferred in either respect. Such powers require two separate documents, one for each power, in prescribed form.[78] The 2005 Act begins with elaborate "principles" regarding what constitutes mental incapacity,[79] and what constitutes the "best interests" of the incapacitated person.[80] Even without such a document, a person may sometimes be justified in acting reasonably in the interests of another in respect of care or treatment,[81] and may in other circumstances be entitled to pledge that

---

[69] But see Millett (1977) 41 Conv. 83 at 86.
[70] See Article 122.
[71] SI 2007/1897. Some parts of the Act had already been brought into effect on April 1 by SI 2007/563. Minor amendments are made by the Mental Health Act 2007. See in general Bartlett, *Blackstone's Guide to the Mental Capacity Act 2005* (2nd edn, 2008); *Cretney and Lush on Lasting and Enduring Powers of Attorney* (8th edn); Aldridge, *Powers of Attorney* (10th edn); Thurston, *Powers of Attorney* (9th edn).
[72] Mental Capacity Act 2005 ss.9–29; stemming from recommendations contained in *Law Com. No.231* (1995), 94. For a discussion of aspects of the legislation, see *Public Guardian v DA* [2018] EWCOP 26; [2018] 3 W.L.R. 2017.
[73] Mental Capacity Act 2005 s.13(1) (2).
[74] Mental Capacity Act 2005 s.13(3), but see s.13(4).
[75] See Lasting Powers of Attorney, Enduring Powers of Attorney and Public Guardian Regulations (SI 2007/1253) reg.22.
[76] Mental Capacity Act 2005 s.13(5)–(11).
[77] Mental Capacity Act 2005 ss.9, 11 and 12. As to property held by the donor on trust for others, see *Godfrey v Marshall* [2017] NZHC 420.
[78] Lasting Powers of Attorney, Enduring Powers of Attorney and Public Guardian Regulations (SI 2007/1253) cl.5 (setting out forms for use).
[79] Mental Capacity Act 2005 ss.1–3.
[80] Mental Capacity Act 2005 s.4 (specifying criteria for establishing reasonable belief).
[81] Mental Capacity Act 2005 ss.5 and 6.

other's credit, use that other's money and obtain reimbursement.[82] These powers are not dissimilar from the more limited authority applicable in cases of agency of necessity and are referred to above under that head.[83] Lasting Powers of Attorney require a "certificate of capacity" that the donor acts voluntarily and understands the purpose of the document.[84] The power is invalid unless registered,[85] but registration can be effected before the onset of incapacity. The court may control the exercise of the power,[86] or appoint a "deputy" to take decisions for the incapacitated person.[87] The Court of Protection is reconstituted by the Act as part of the reforms. There are provisions protecting the donee and bona fide third parties where no power was created or the power has been revoked.[88] Regulations supplement the provisions of Schs 1 and 4 to the Act regarding registration and revocation of powers of the new, and also of the former, types.[89] The Act is supported by a Code of Practice issued by the Lord Chancellor.[90] Enduring Powers of Attorney created under the 1985 Act before the 2005 Act came into operation are still valid (as regards property and affairs),[91] but such powers may no longer be created.[92] An attorney holding a lasting power of attorney may, depending on the principal's intention, continue to exercise powers granted before and outside the power, including drawing on bank accounts for personal benefit where so authorised.[93]

10-010 **Reference to irrevocable authority in other contexts** There are a number of other situations where reference is sometimes made to an agent's authority being irrevocable, but which are better explained on other grounds. These are all situations where the termination of the agent's authority (whether by purported recall by the principal or as a result of the principal's death or insanity) cannot prevent the agent or third party taking steps in relation to each other that are immune to objection by the principal.

(1) Agent's right to reimbursement or indemnity Where in the execution of the agent's authority the agent incurs a personal liability to a third party, such that the agent would be entitled as against the principal to reimbursement or indemnity, the principal cannot, by purporting to revoke the agent's authority to discharge it, destroy that right. Thus where in the pursuance of the agent's authority the agent incurs contractual liability to pay money to a third party, the agent is entitled to discharge the personal liability so incurred over the opposition of the principal, yet

---

[82] Mental Capacity Act 2005 s.8 (the person lacking capacity is liable for necessaries supplied by virtue of s.7).
[83] See above, para.4-012.
[84] Mental Capacity Act 2005 Sch.1 cl.2(1)(e).
[85] Mental Capacity Act 2005 s.9(2)(b).
[86] Mental Capacity Act 2005 ss.22–23.
[87] Mental Capacity Act 2005 s.16.
[88] Mental Capacity Act 2005 s.14, in terms similar to s.9 of the Enduring Powers of Attorney Act 1985 and similarly modifying s.5 of the Powers of Attorney Act 1971.
[89] See Lasting Powers of Attorney, Enduring Powers of Attorney and Public Guardian Regulations (SI 2007/1253).
[90] In accordance with ss.42 and 43 of the Act, and published by TSO.
[91] Mental Capacity Act 2005 s.66(3); they are regulated by Sch.4 to the new Act, which in substance reproduces the 1985 Act. Quaere, whether the "Principles" of ss.1 and 2 of the Act should be applied under Sch.4.
[92] Mental Capacity Act 2005 s.66(1) (2). Nor can they be converted.
[93] See *Day v Harris* [2013] EWCA Civ 191; [2014] Ch. 211 (a case under the 1985 legislation).

retain a right to be reimbursed by the principal.[94] The principle applies also where the agent incurs a liability in respect of an authorised transaction which it is proper for the agent to discharge even though it could not be legally enforced, e.g. a liability to pay wagering debts,[95] or barrister's fees.[96] It is unclear whether this principle extends to the agent's right to take positive action, e.g. initiate proceedings, in respect of matters occurring while the agent had authority, even though, again, the principal forbids such action.[97] The principle would not extend to prevent revocation merely because the agent has incurred other liabilities, for example given a personal undertaking that the agent would have authority at a certain time in the future.

These propositions are sometimes expressed as propositions relating to irrevocable authority.[98] But they do not relate to authority in the sense of the power of an agent to affect the legal position of his principal[99]: their relevance is to authority in the context of the rule that the right to reimbursement and indemnity does not extend to unauthorised acts.[100] The rules as to reimbursement and indemnity, however, are not confined to agents at all, and the common use of the term "authority" in this context can be confusing. Therefore it is submitted that the rule in question is better expressed as in the above paragraph, and without reference to any idea of irrevocable authority.[101] Similar reasoning may apply to cases where the agent is entitled to remuneration: (subject to any contract term) the principal may not, by purporting to revoke authority, deprive the agent of the right to remuneration earned but not yet paid.[102] Such propositions are sometimes also cited in connection with a supposed general rule that authority cannot be revoked once acted on. This is true in the sense that once the act authorised has been done, a purported revocation of authority to do it is ex hypothesi ineffective to prevent the agent carrying it through, and to obtaining reimbursement, indemnity and if appropriate, remuneration in respect of it. As regards authority the proposition can go no further.

---

[94] See, e.g. *Chappell v Bray* (1860) 6 H. & N. 145; *Warlow v Harrison* (1859) 1 E. & E. 309. See in general Article 62. Where the principal indemnifies the agent in advance, the same rule applies: *Yates v Hoppe* (1850) 9 C.B. 541.

[95] *Read v Anderson* (1884) 13 Q.B.D. 779; and see *Seymour v Bridge* (1885) 14 Q.B.D. 460.

[96] *Rhodes v Fielder* (1919) 89 L.J.K.B. 15; *Gwinnutt v George* [2019] EWCA Civ 656 at [26].

[97] See *Daly v Lime Street Underwriting Agencies Ltd* [1987] 2 F.T.L.R. 277, where a former member of a Lloyd's syndicate failed in an action for a declaration that there was no authority to continue an action brought by the managing agents of his syndicate, in respect of matters occurring while he was a member. The power of the agent was described in the agreement conferring it as "irrevocable", but there is no discussion whether there was any proprietary interest, or (more likely in the circumstances) obligation, to protect. There had, however, been no attempt to revoke the authority before it was exercised, and this may be the best explanation. See Reynolds, fn.58 above. See also *Yasuda Fire and Marine Insurance Co Ltd v Orion Marine Insurance Underwriting Agency Ltd* [1995] Q.B. 174 (relationship of principal and agent continued despite termination of contract by repudiatory breach, to entitle principal to see agent's books; *Mortgage Express v Sawali* [2010] EWHC 3054 (Ch); [2010] N.P.C. 114; [2011] 7 E.G. 98; [2011] P.N.L.R. 11 (solicitor common to borrower and lender obliged to hand over client files to lender where borrower's contract with lender irrevocably authorised delivery of such files).

[98] See, e.g. *Chappell v Bray* (1860) 6 H. & N. 145 at 162; and early editions of this book.

[99] See Article 1.

[100] Article 63. See *Pacific and General Insurance Co Ltd v Hazell* [1997] L.R.L.R. 65, per Moore-Bick J; and *Temple Legal Protection Ltd v QBE Insurance (Europe) Ltd* [2009] EWCA Civ 453; [2009] Lloyd's Rep I.R. 544 at [59].

[101] See *Warlow v Harrison* (1859) 1 E. & E. 309, 317; *Read v Anderson* (1884) 13 Q.B.D. 779 (Bowen LJ); Powell, p.395.

[102] See Articles 56–58.

(2)   Agent's exercise of right of lien to sell principal's goods in agent's own name   A further set of old cases the effect of which has been expressed in terms of irrevocability supports the view that where an agent has a lien on the principal's goods over which the agent had a power of sale the agent can proceed to realise that lien by sale in the agent's own name notwithstanding the purported termination of the agent's authority. The agent has the right to sue for the price, and payment to and set-off against him is normally a discharge to the third party to the extent of the lien.[103] In such cases it can be said that the principal to this extent cannot revoke the authority to receive payment.[104] But this is a rule as to performance of contract, relating to payment to or settlement with an agent, whereby the right of the principal to intervene and require payment to himself is inapplicable to the extent to which the agent has a lien. It is accompanied by, and to some extent stems from, the agent's right to sue for the price. A lien, which constitutes the agent a secured creditor, obviously cannot be unilaterally terminated by the principal, even by his bankruptcy,[105] but this is not a rule as to revocation of authority. Irrevocable authority would prevent the revocation of the actual power to sell in the name of the principal.

(3)   Money held to use of third parties   In another group of cases, where an agent holds money for the principal, and the principal directs the agent to pay it to a third party, and the agent notifies the third party of that fact, the agent becomes liable to the third party in restitution, and the principal becomes unable to cancel the instructions: the principal's trustee in bankruptcy is in the same position.[106] Here again it can be said that the authority is irrevocable. But these cases seem really to depend on the idea of attornment of money, the irrevocability being like that of a property disposition: the agent is authorised to participate in such a disposition in favour of a third party, and once that has been done it cannot be recalled.[107]

(4)   Third party's contractual right to serve notices or make payments to named agent   A principal may contract with a third party that during the life of a contract the third party can serve a notice on, or make a payment to, a named "agent". If as a matter of construction that method of performance is a right of the third party then the principal is powerless to object if the third party continues to use the agent notwithstanding a purported withdrawal of the agent's authority.[108] This is not true irrevocable authority; if the clause named a physical address as the place for service, delivery or leaving a payment without reference to any agent, service, delivery or payment to that address would be equally effective.

---

[103] The examples concern factors and auctioneers. See above, paras 8-112 and 9-009.

[104] See *Drinkwater v Goodwin* (1775) 1 Cowp. 251, Illustration 5 to Article 81; *Robson v Kemp* (1802) 4 Esp. 233.

[105] See Article 67. And see above, paras 8-108, 9-009 and 9-023.

[106] See, e.g. *Walker v Rostron* (1842) 9 M. & W. 441; *Griffin v Weatherby* (1868) L.R. 3 Q.B. 753.

[107] The cases are fully discussed under Article 112.

[108] See *DVB Bank SE v Isim Amin Ltd* [2014] EWHC 2156 (Comm) at [5]; *Citicorp Trustee Co Ltd v Al-Sanea* [2017] EWHC 2845 (Comm) at [33]; *Royal Petrol Trading Co UK v Total India Pvt Ltd* [2018] EWHC 1272 (Comm) at [40]; *Bank of New York Mellon, London Branch v Essar Steel India Ltd* [2018] EWHC 3177 (Ch) at [16].

(5) Other cases The idea of irrevocable authority can also be used to explain cases more properly to be considered in connection with the rule in *Milroy v Lord*,[109] which relates to the perfection of gifts and the declaration of trusts through the use of a power of attorney after the death of the donor. Many of the old cases date from a time when no proper method of assignment had been evolved, and powers of attorney and the like were used to effect what would now be an assignment.

Finally, it is arguable that in some situations equity may intervene to restrain a revocation of authority which is in breach of contract. This point is considered under Article 120.

Completion of transactions It might plausibly be thought that there was in some cases an authority to complete transactions commenced before revocation of authority or death or incapacity of the principal.[110] As already stated, an agent can certainly discharge matters in respect of which the agent has incurred a personal liability. There is a relevant provision in the Partnership Act 1890 s.38, which on dissolution gives the remaining partners authority to "complete transactions begun but unfinished at the time of the dissolution".[111] Outside this area, though the *contract* between principal and agent may continue, it is difficult to see that there can be any such continuing *authority* where the mandate has clearly been terminated, even though it might be useful, for example, in connection with practices at Lloyd's.[112] If an interest sufficient to secure irrevocability could be found, it would be under the category of "securing an obligation of the principal", as in the case of underwriting agreements[113]; but this is for most such situations far from certain.

In *Triffit Nurseries v Salads Etcetera Ltd* it was held that, on the appointment by debenture holders of a receiver in respect of an agent for sale, the authority of the agent, and hence the receiver, to call in debts in respect of sales made by the agent was not terminated in a situation where it was intended that the agent should not keep the money received separate but should be free to mix it with the agent's normal cashflow.[114] If the debts are owed to the principal, there seems no reason why the authority to collect them should not, however, be revocable before execution in the normal way if a clear revocation occurs. Robert Walker LJ said that "the debt belonged to [the agent] while it was trading, subject to the charge in favour of the bank".[115] If the case was one of true agency it would seem that the chose in action arose on the sale and belonged to the principal, who could revoke the agent's

10-011

---

[109] *Milroy v Lord* (1862) 4 De G.F. & J. 264. See *Re Williams, Williams v Ball* [1917] 1 Ch. 1; *Ex p. Pye* (1811) 18 Ves. Jur. 140; *Kiddill v Farnell* (1857) 3 Sn. & G. 428; and more generally *Snell's Equity* (34th edn), paras 22-049 and 24-012–24.015.

[110] See Reynolds, in *Making Commercial Law* (Cranston, ed., 1994), Ch.10, at p.266 onwards.

[111] See *Inland Revenue v Graham's Trustees* 1971 S.C.(H.L.) 1 at 21.

[112] See *Daly v Lime Street Underwriting Agencies Ltd* [1987] 2 F.T.L.R. 277; discussed by Reynolds, in *Making Commercial Law* (Cranston, ed., 1994), Ch.10, at p.271 onwards; *Society of Lloyd's v Leighs*, QBD (Colman J), February 20, 1997; decided by CA on other grounds [1997] T.L.R. 449. See also *Temple Legal Protection Ltd v QBE Insurance (Europe) Ltd* [2009] EWCA Civ 453; [2009] Lloyd's Rep I.R. 544.

[113] See above, paras 10-007 and 10-008. PECL art.3:209(3), the UNIDROIT Principles art.2.2.10, and DCFR, II, 6:112(4) all provide for authority to act after termination of (normal) authority, to preserve the principal's interests (of which completion of a transaction or transactions would simply be an example) in such a case: but this can be more easily achieved by (quasi) legislation than by development of general theory. DCFR, II, 6.112 provides for authority to continue where the principal is under an obligation to the third party not to terminate the agency.

[114] *Triffit Nurseries v Salads Etcetera Ltd* [2000] 1 All E.R. (Comm) 737.

[115] *Triffit Nurseries v Salads Etcetera Ltd* [2000] 1 All E.R. (Comm) 737 at 747.

authority to collect the money[116]; and that the permission to merge the proceeds with the agent's funds did not extend to permission to charge the proceeds before the merger. Subsequent authority confirms this.[117] It seems likely that *Triffit*'s case was not one of pure agency, but rather of the equivalent of indirect representation,[118] and this may be the route to an explanation of it.[119]

10-012   **Statute of Frauds** A group of cases holds authority to sign a note or memorandum under the Statute of Frauds irrevocable in the context of auctions.[120] As such they are no longer relevant in England[121]; and they seem in any case best explained as based on considerations of the well-known policy of preventing the Statute being used itself as an instrument of fraud. Before the law was changed, it would certainly have undermined the efficacy of sales by auction were the auctioneer unable to consummate the sale by completing the necessary memorandum. In relation to a buyer, there would be no repose of confidence that an irrevocable authority would intrude upon, but it seems that such an authority also binds the vendor once the property has been knocked down to a successful bidder.[122]

10-013   **Proxies** Special problems can arise in connection with voting proxies in company law. An agent to negotiate for shareholders may acquire proxies from individual members of the group, but the earlier proxies may be revoked before the agent has completed the securing of the number required.[123] In the US statutes deal with this problem in various ways.[124] The agent may well have no personal interest to prevent revocation. In England the only reasoning available to prevent revocation would seem to be the notion of fraud on the other proxy grantors, on the analogy of the law as to compositions with creditors.[125] Less problematic are cases where a bare trustee of shares gives an irrevocable proxy to the beneficial owner. There, the beneficial owner in exercising the proxy is acting solely in its own interests.[126]

Illustrations

10-014   (1) A, being indebted to B, gives him a power of attorney to sell certain land and discharge his debt out of the purchase money. The power is irrevocable.[127]

        (2) Goods are consigned to a factor for sale, and he later makes advances to the

---

[116] Counsel relied on *Re Farrow's Bank Ltd* [1923] 1 Ch. 41, in which it was held that a bank's authority to collect a cheque ceased on the bank's suspending payment.

[117] See *Angove's Pty Ltd v Bailey* [2016] UKSC 47; [2016] 1 W.L.R. 3179.

[118] See above, paras 1-021 and 1-022.

[119] This appears more clearly from the first instance judgment of Longmore J: [1999] 1 All E.R. (Comm) 110 at 115. The argument of counsel appears in general to have been that when authority was revoked even a debt owed to the agent must now be held on trust for the principal, which seems to go too far.

[120] *Van Praagh v Everidge* [1902] 2 Ch. 266; reversed on other grounds [1903] 1 Ch. 434; *Chaney v Maclow* [1929] 1 Ch. 461; *Phillips v Butler* [1945] Ch. 358. See Reynolds, in *Making Commercial Law* (Cranston, ed., 1994), Ch.10, at pp.265–266.

[121] See Law of Property (Miscellaneous Provisions) Act 1989 s.2(5)(b).

[122] See *Nguyen v SM & T Homes Ltd* [2016] NZCA 581.

[123] See Reynolds, in *Making Commercial Law* (Cranston, ed.), at pp.273–275.

[124] Details are given in *Restatement, Third*, § 3-12, Comment and reporter's notes.

[125] See *Cook v Lister* (1863) 13 C.B.(N.S.) 543; *West Yorkshire Darracq Agency Ltd v Coleridge* [1911] 2 K.B. 326; Treitel, *Law of Contract* (15th edn), para.3-111.

[126] See *Coachcraft Ltd v SVP Fruit Co Ltd* (1980) 28 A.L.R. 319 (PC) at 328–329.

[127] *Gaussen v Morton* (1830) 10 B. & C. 731: see McGaw, fn.58 above, at pp.278–283. See also *Re Rose Ex p. Hasluck & Garrard* (1894) 1 Manson 218.

principal on the credit of them. Subsequently, the principal instructs the factor not to sell. The factor's authority is revocable, not being given for valuable consideration.[128]

(3) Goods are consigned to a factor for sale. He makes advances, in consideration of an agreement by the principal that his authority to sell shall be irrevocable. The authority is irrevocable.[129] It is a question of fact whether such an agreement was made, and it may be inferred from the circumstances.[130] In the absence of such an agreement for valuable consideration, the authority of a factor to sell does not become irrevocable by the failure of the principal duly to repay advances made on the security of the goods.[131]

(4) An auctioneer was authorised to sell goods, and after he had incurred expenses in respect of them, the principal revoked his authority. Held, that the authority of the auctioneer was not irrevocable merely by reason of his special property in the goods and his lien on them for advances, and that he was liable to the principal in trespass for going to the premises to sell the goods after notice of the revocation.[132]

(5) A signs and addresses to B an underwriting letter by which he agrees, in consideration of a commission, to subscribe for a certain number of shares in a company, and authorises B to apply for the shares in his name and on his behalf. B, being a vendor to the company, and therefore having an interest in the raising of the capital, by letter accepts the terms of A's agreement. The authority given to B to apply for the shares is irrevocable, and A is bound to take the shares applied for and allotted in pursuance of the underwriting letter, although in the meantime he has given notice to B and to the company repudiating the agreement.[133]

Article 119

TERMINATION OF AUTHORITY BY DEATH, MENTAL INCAPACITY OR INSOLVENCY

The actual authority of an agent, whether or not conferred by deed and whether **10-015** or not expressed to be irrevocable, is determined by the death[134] of either the principal or the agent. The intervention of mental incapacity in the principal or agent

---

[128] *Smart v Sandars* (1848) 5 C.B. 895: see McGaw,fn.58 above, at p.289 onwards; *Raleigh v Atkinson* (1840) 6 M. & W. 670.

[129] See *Smart v Sandars* (1848) 5 C.B. 895; *De Comas v Prost* (1865) 3 Moo.P.C.(N.S.) 158.

[130] *De Comas v Prost* (1865) 3 Moo.P.C.(N.S.) 158.

[131] *Smart v Sandars* (1848) 5 C.B. 895.

[132] *Taplin v Florence* (1851) 10 C.B. 744.

[133] *Re Hannan's Empress Gold Mining & Development Co, Carmichael's Case* [1896] 2 Ch. 643 (see McGaw, fn.58 above, at pp.323–325: the proceedings were for rectification of the register under the Companies Act 1862, which required the court to be "satisfied of the justice of the case". A comment in (1896) 102 L.T.Jo. refers to "a portion of the security for the benefit conferred". One in (1897) 13 L.Q.R.11, presumably by F.P., says the arrangement was "part and parcel of the bargain": "a lawyer's defence—no layman would ever have thought of it"). The case was followed in *Re Olympic Reinsurance Co, Pole's Case* [1920] 2 Ch. 341. cf. *Re Consort Deep Level Gold Mines Ltd, Ex p. Stark* [1897] 1 Ch. 575; *Re Bultfontein Sun Diamond Mine Ltd, Ex p. Cox, Hughes and Norman* (1897) 75 L.T. 669. See also *Schindler v Brie* [2003] EWHC 1804 (Ch); [2003] W.T.L.R. 1361.

[134] Illustrations 1 to 3; *Houstoun v Robertson* (1816) 6 Taunt. 448; *Carr v Levingston* (1865) 35 Beav. 41; *Farrow v Wilson* (1860) L.R. 4 C.P. 744; *Phillips v Jones* (1888) 4 T.L.R. 401; *Lodgepower Ltd v Taylor* [2004] EWCA Civ 1367; [2005] 1 E.G.L.R. 1.

would normally terminate actual authority, but at least in the case of an incapax principal only where the agent is aware or ought to be aware of the fact.

Comment

10-016 **Death** The death of the agent obviously terminates the agent's authority, for the relationship is a personal one.[135] And the death of the principal deprives the agent of anyone for whom the agent can act.[136] Therefore it is normally said that on the principal's death the actual authority terminates unless it comes under the category of irrevocable authority[137]; not only can the agent not sue for remuneration, reimbursement or indemnity in respect of acts committed after the principal dies,[138] but the agent may, in continuing to act, be liable for loss caused to the estate.[139] It may also be that the principal's estate cannot be bound under the doctrine of apparent authority[140]; and that the agent may consequently be liable to the third party for breach of warranty of authority.[141] The question is discussed under Article 121. There is some statutory protection in the case of powers of attorney.[142] It has been suggested that it might be possible for the agent to take a special term in the agency agreement that the agent is to be protected against personal liability arising after the principal's death.[143] In principle, this should be possible, but there is no authority on the validity of such an arrangement. It would in any case only operate inter partes.

Restatement, Third[144] takes the view that actual authority should not terminate until the agent knows of the principal's death. This approach is principally supported by the analogy of existing legislation in the US. Although there is some discussion in connection with revocation of offer by death which might be of assistance,[145] the extremely limited English authority cannot be said to support such a view. It could however be supported on the general basis that actual authority does not terminate until the agent knows, or ought to know, of the termination, by whatever means.[146] It may be that only statutory reform could achieve such a result.

10-017 **Ratification** It is not clear whether the executors or administrators of the deceased can ratify a contract made on behalf of the deceased: it seems that in the case usually cited for the proposition that they can, the contract was made on behalf of the

[135] See *Farrow v Wilson* (1860) L.R. 4 C.P. 744 at 746. As regards joint agents, see *Adams v Buckland* (1705) 2 Vern. 514; *Friend v Young* [1897] 2 Ch. 421 and Article 11. The termination of authority may affect the position of sub-agents: see Chapter 5. Commission may continue payable after the death of the agent: see *Wilson v Harper, Son & Co* [1908] 2 Ch. 370; above, para.7-041.
[136] See *Drew v Nunn* (1874) 4 Q.B.D. 661 at 666.
[137] See Article 118 and Comment.
[138] Illustration 3.
[139] Illustration 2.
[140] See Comment to Article 121.
[141] *Yonge v Toynbee* [1910] 1 K.B. 215; Article 105. But see Article 122 as to powers of attorney. See also *Bank of Scotland v Qutb* [2012] EWCA Civ 1661.
[142] See Article 122. See also Seavey (1930) 44 HarvL.Rev. 265.
[143] Powell, p.389. As to the possibility of deliberately creating authority which does not terminate on the death of the principal, see Wolff (1946) 62 L.Q.R. 272; Fitzgerald (1946) 13 *Solicitor* 224 (which should be read now in the light of the provisions dealt with in Article 122).
[144] § 3.07.
[145] e.g. *Coulthart v Clementson* (1879) 5 Q.B.D. 42.
[146] See para.10-020 and fn.222 below.

administrators.[147] A person who purported to contract with a person who is, unknown to him, already dead, might well not have been willing to contract with the personal representatives, and the permissibility of ratification therefore seems doubtful.[148] That would certainly be the position where the contract was one that contemplated the personal services of the person now deceased. The third party may, of course, make a fresh contract with the executors or administrators.

Companies   The actual dissolution of a company is analogous to the death of a   **10-018** non-corporate principal or agent and arguments similar to those above are applicable. Authorities on the point are surprisingly sparse, and in the case usually cited for automatic termination of actual authority, the point was simply assumed by both counsel and the court.[149] The position is in any event different where a company has simply been placed in liquidation. The company does not cease to exist merely by going into liquidation, and indeed a liquidator generally becomes the agent of the company.[150] However, the authority of its directors to act will in most respects cease, and as a result so will that of those agents who derive their authority from a delegation by the directors.[151] The liquidator might nonetheless ratify action by directors or other agents.[152] The directors would also normally retain authority to challenge the actual appointment of a liquidator or other supplanting authority.[153] It is also possible to restore a dissolved company to the register.[154] Special consequences may follow the appointment of liquidators,[155] receivers and administrators. For instance, an agency for a company which arises on the appointment of administrators to the company does not make the agent the agent of the administrators, nor are the expenses of the agent the expenses of the administration.[156] Reference should be made to specialised works.[157]

Where a company or other corporation has granted a power of attorney that is expressed to be irrevocable and is granted to secure a proprietary interest of the

---

[147] *Foster v Bates* (1843) 12 M. & W. 226. See also Powell, p.388, fn.7.

[148] But see *Alexander Ward & Co Ltd v Samyang Navigation Ltd* [1975] 1 W.L.R. 673 (liquidator: not a contract case, however).

[149] *Salton v New Beeston Cycle Co* [1900] 1 Ch. 43, Illustration 4. See also *Selfe v Colonial Ice Co* (1894) 10 W.N.(N.S.W.) 153; *Wellington Steam Ferry Co Ltd v Wellington Deposit, Mortgage and Building Association Ltd* (1915) 34 N.Z.L.R. 913 at 916–917. As regards partnerships, see Comment. As regards a possible authority to complete transactions, see above, para.10-011.

[150] See, e.g. *Knowles v Scott* [1891] 1 Ch. 717; *Dunphy v Sleepyhead Manufacturing Co Ltd* [2007] 3 N.Z.L.R. 602 at [22]; *DVB Bank SE v Isim Amin Ltd* [2014] EWHC 2156 (Comm) (agency for service not terminated by liquidation). For further discussion, see Tan Cheng Han and Wee Mee Seng, in *Agency Law in Commercial Practice* (Busch, Macgregor and Watts eds, 2016), Ch. 6.

[151] See *Pacific and General Insurance Co Ltd v Hazell* [1997] L.R.L.R. 65. Here the appointment was only of a provisional liquidator but it was still considered that the authority of agents appointed by the directors ceased.

[152] *Re Mawcon Ltd* [1969] 1 W.L.R. 78.

[153] *Re Union Accident Insurance Co Ltd* [1972] 1 W.L.R. 640.

[154] See Companies Act 2006 Pt 31 Ch.3.

[155] See *Pacific and General Insurance Co Ltd v Hazell* [1997] L.R.L.R. 65 (appointment of provisional liquidator revoked authority of agents of company). A liquidator will usually himself act as agent of the relevant company: see, e.g. *Dunphy v Sleepyhead Manufacturing Co Ltd* [2007] 3 N.Z.L.R. 602 (CA) at [22].

[156] *Centre Reinsurance International Co v Freakley* [2006] UKHL 45; [2006] 1 W.L.R. 2863; [2006] 4 All E.R. 1153 (insurers authorised to conduct litigation upon administration in relation to insured claims retained authority, but were not entitled to have expenses treated as administration expenses).

[157] See *Palmer's Corporate Insolvency* (looseleaf); Goode, *Principles of Corporate Insolvency* (5th edn); Lightman and Moss, *Law of Administrators and Receivers of Companies* (6th edn).

donee or the performance of an obligation owed the donee, then neither its winding up nor its dissolution will terminate the power.[158]

Where the company is still fully operational but one or more of the directors who signed a power of attorney given by the company has died, there is no reason for the power to cease to be valid, since the principal is the company not the deceased director.

10-019 Partnerships The rule stated in this Article also applies to cases where the principal[159] or agent[160] is a partnership, and there is by death or retirement a change in the partnership, which thereby technically becomes a new partnership.[161] If the contract is regarded as personal to the particular partners, and an agency contract usually is so regarded,[162] the agency is frustrated. A fortiori the same rule applies where the partnership is dissolved.[163]

10-020 Mental incapacity Mental incapacity in this context means inability to appreciate the nature and quality of the act done,[164] but plainly there can be varying degrees of incapacity. In such circumstances, it is perhaps not surprising that the blunt rule assumed to apply to cases of death, viz. that actual authority automatically ceases, probably does not apply to cases of incapacity. As with the position in respect of mental incapacity in a principal existing at the date of appointment,[165] the law is currently unsettled on the effect on an agent's actual authority of supervening incapacity in the principal. It is submitted that the better view is that supervening mental incapacity does not terminate an agent's actual authority until the agent becomes aware, or at least ought to have become aware, of the incapacity, unless the parties have expressly agreed that incapacity is to terminate the mandate.[166] Recent authority has confirmed that where the agent has a contract of appointment, that contract at least is not automatically determined by supervening incapacity.[167] This paragraph was quoted by the Court with apparent sympathy for the views expressed in it. The Court also indicated that even once an incapax party's solicitor becomes aware of supervening incapacity the solicitor may have a residual authority to take steps to ensure that the interests of the client are properly attended to.[168] In the relatively few other relevant cases, the notion of automatic termination has generally been as-

---

[158] See Powers of Attorney Act 1971 s.4(1).
[159] *Tasker v Shepherd* (1861) 6 H. & N. 575; *Brace v Calder* [1895] 2 Q.B. 253.
[160] *Friend v Young* [1897] 2 Ch. 421.
[161] *Lindley and Banks on Partnership* (20th edn), paras 3-38–3-40.
[162] See *Tasker v Shepherd* (1861) 6 H. & N. 575; *Brace v Calder* [1895] 2 Q.B. 253; *Friend v Young* [1897] 2 Ch. 421.
[163] See *Bovine Ltd v Dent & Wilkinson* (1904) 21 T.L.R. 82. But there may in the case of dissolution or retirement be liability for breach of contract: see *Brace v Calder* [1895] 2 Q.B. 253; *Hurst v Bryk* [2002] 1 A.C. 185; *Lindley and Banks on Partnership* (20th edn), para.3-40.
[164] *Boughton v Knight* (1873) L.R. 3 P. & D. 64 at 72. Elaborate criteria are specified by the Mental Capacity Act 2005 ss.1–4, for matters within its scope: see *Ali v Caton* [2014] EWCA Civ 1313 at [55].
[165] See above, para.2-009. As to the law in Scotland, see Macgregor, para.10-06.
[166] cf. *Restatement, Third*, § 3.08; above, para.10-016.
[167] *Blankley v Central Manchester and Manchester Children's University Hospitals NHS Trust* [2015] EWCA Civ 18; [2015] 1 W.L.R. 4307 at [36]; *Mole v Parkdean Holiday Parks Ltd* [2017] EWHC B10 (Costs). See further, Watts [2015] C.L.J. 140; E. Varney, "Agency Contracts and the Scope of the Incapacity Defence in English Contract Law" [2020] J.B.L. 382
[168] *Blankley v Central Manchester and Manchester Children's University Hospitals NHS Trust* [2015] EWCA Civ 18; [2015] 1 W.L.R. 4307 at [36]; citing *Fore Street Warehouse Co Ltd v Durrant & Co* (1883) 10 Q.B.D. 471. See too *Johnston v Schurr* [2015] NZSC 82; [2016] 1 N.Z.L.R. 403 at [93].

sumed by the parties rather than contested and decided, or it appears that the agent was aware of the incapacity.[169] The agent may also continue to have apparent authority.[170] Statute law has also intervened to some extent. Hence, the agent's authority may continue if the provisions of the Mental Capacity Act 2005 are applicable and complied with.[171] By virtue of the Civil Procedure Rules, compromises of litigation entered into by a party who loses capacity are invalid if that party does not have a litigation friend appointed to assist them and the compromise is not approved by the court.[172]

The position where it is the agent who has become mentally incapable is also not settled. The case for automatic termination of actual authority seems stronger in such a case.[173] The agent is the party who is actively altering the principal's legal position and loss of capacity in the agent could lead to unfortunate consequences, whereas with supervening incapacity in the principal the initial instructions will have been given at a time when the principal was capable and the agent remains sane. Express provision at the time of appointment for termination in such circumstances should also be effective.[174] Where the agent had apparent authority, this might continue so long as the supervening incapacity were not obvious to the third party.[175] In other circumstances, the incapax agent might be liable to the third party on a warranty of authority, again so long as the incapacity had not been apparent to the third party.

Personal insolvency[176] It seems that the formal declaration of bankruptcy would   **10-021** usually terminate the actual authority[177] of any agent of the bankrupt, unless the agent's authority met the criteria for irrevocability.[178] Once a person is adjudicated bankrupt, dispositions from the estate between the date of the presentation of the petition and the taking effect of the appointment of a trustee are void,[179] with exceptions in favour of a bona fide purchaser.[180] When the appointment of the trustee in bankruptcy takes effect the property vests in the trustee[181]: "property" is defined to include things in action and obligations.[182] Therefore an agent of the bankrupt can-

---

[169] *Drew v Nunn* (1874) 4 Q.B.D. 661; *Yonge v Toynbee* [1910] 1 K.B. 215; *Re Coleman* (1929) 24 Tas. L.R. 77 (power of attorney); *Evans v James* [2000] 3 E.G.L.R. 1 (client had stroke, but illness known to agent).

[170] *Drew v Nunn* (1874) 4 Q.B.D. 661.

[171] See above, para.10-009.

[172] See *Dunhill v Burgin* [2014] UKSC 18; [2014] 1 W.L.R. 933. See further above, para.2-009.

[173] But see *Probus Ltd v Treble & Triple Ltd* [2010] HKCU 2485; affirmed on other points CACV270/ 2010, where it was held, largely on pragmatic grounds, that the mental incapacity of an agent did not terminate his actual authority. See further above, Article 5.

[174] See, e.g. Companies (Model Articles) Regulations 2008 (SI 2008/3229) Sch. art.22(d) (incapacity of company directors).

[175] See Article 121.

[176] See *Chitty on Contracts* (33rd edn), Ch.20; *Muir Hunter on Personal Insolvency* (looseleaf).

[177] See Story, *Agency* (9th edn), § 482.

[178] Article 118.

[179] Insolvency Act 1986 s.284(1). See too *Estate of F Jones & Sons v Jones* [1997] Ch. 159.

[180] Insolvency Act 1986 s.284(4).

[181] Insolvency Act 1986 s.306.

[182] Insolvency Act 1986 s.436. If a trustee seeks to ratify an act done on behalf of the bankrupt, it might seem that he cannot, for the same reason as the executors or administrators of a deceased person ratify: above, para.10-017. But the wide wording of s.436 may pass the power to ratify. For an example of ratification, see *Alexander Ward & Co Ltd v Samyang Navigation Co Ltd* [1975] 1 W.L.R. 673.

not in general,[183] unless authorised by the trustee, dispose of the bankrupt's property; and if the agent receives property it is received for the trustee, who may claim[184] or disclaim[185] it. Similar reasoning applies to contracts. The agent can enter into a contract on behalf of the principal in cases where the principal can contract personally: but some contracts may be claimed or disclaimed by the trustee. The bankruptcy does not however of itself frustrate, or constitute a repudiatory breach of any, agency contract, though it sometimes may have this effect; and the bankrupt may retain a solicitor.[186] Likewise the bankruptcy of the agent may or may not frustrate or constitute a repudiation or grounds for termination of any agency contract.[187]

Illustrations

10-022　(1)　A undertakes to pay B £100 if B succeeds in selling a picture at a certain price—"no sale, no pay". B endeavours to sell the picture, and after A's death succeeds in doing so. The representatives of A's estate are not bound by the contract of sale,[188] but they may ratify it if they think fit, at any rate if it purported to be made on their behalf.[189] Even if the representatives ratify the sale, they are not liable to pay B the £100 unless they ratify his contract with A, but they are liable to pay him a reasonable sum for the services performed.[190]

(2)　A stockbroker had a continuation account open with a client. The client died, and the broker, failing to get instructions from his representatives, carried over the transactions instead of closing them on or before settling day, and ultimately sold the shares at a loss. It was held that the representatives were entitled to stand by the carrying-over sale on the first settling day after the death, and that the broker was liable for the subsequent loss.[191]

(3)　A solicitor is retained to conduct a divorce suit. The retainer ceases on the death of the client pending the proceedings, and the solicitor cannot recover costs subsequently incurred, even when he had no knowledge of his client's death.[192]

(4)　While an action against a company was pending, the company was dissolved under the Companies Acts. It was assumed by the parties and the court that the authority of the company's solicitor was determined by the dissolution, though he had no knowledge of it.[193]

---

[183] There are exceptions to what the bankrupt's estate includes: Insolvency Act 1986 s.283.
[184] Insolvency Act 1986 s.307: with exceptions for bona fide purchasers: s.307(4).
[185] Insolvency Act 1986 s.315.
[186] See *Nelson v Nelson* [1997] 1 W.L.R. 233.
[187] See *McCall v Australian Meat Co Ltd* (1870) 19 W.R. 188; *Hudson v Granger* (1821) 5 B. & A. 27. A lasting power of attorney is revoked by the insolvency of the attorney, except so far as the power relates to the donor's personal welfare: Mental Capacity Act 2005 s.13.
[188] *Blades v Free* (1829) 9 B. & C. 167.
[189] *Foster v Bates* (1843) 12 M. & W. 226.
[190] *Campanari v Woodburn* (1854) 15 C.B. 400.
[191] *Re Overweg, Haas v Durant* [1900] 1 Ch. 209, referring of course to former practices.
[192] *Pool v Pool* (1889) 58 L.J.P. 67 (little more than a ruling); *Whitehead v Lord* (1852) 7 Exch. 691.
[193] *Salton v New Beeston Cycle Co* [1900] 1 Ch. 43.

Article 120

TERMINATION OF AUTHORITY BY NOTICE OF REVOCATION OR RENUNCIATION

Subject to the provisions of Articles 118 and 122, the authority of an agent, **10-023**
whether or not conferred by deed, and whether or not expressed to be irrevocable,
is terminated by the principal giving to the agent notice of revocation at any time
before the authority has been completely exercised,[194] or by the agent giving to the
principal notice of renunciation accepted by the principal[195]; but without prejudice
to any remedies that the principal or agent may have against the other for breach
of any contract between them.[196]

Comment

General rule   The general rule, which is perhaps not widely understood, is that   **10-024**
the *authority* of an agent, whether given by power of attorney,[197] or informally, even
if for consideration,[198] and whether or not expressed to be irrevocable,[199] is
revocable, without prejudice to the fact that such revocation may be wrongful as
between principal and agent. It is a very longstanding rule: "a man cannot by his
act make such an authority, power or warrant not countermandable, which is by the
law and of its own nature countermandable".[200] The revocation may be oral whether
or not the authority was conferred in writing.[201] There is a power to revoke: but there
is not necessarily a privilege to exercise the power—there may indeed be a duty not
to do so, with the result that the revocation is a breach of contract. So, the authority given in a liability insurance policy by an insured to an insurer to appoint
lawyers to conduct litigation on the insured's behalf can be revoked by the insured
at any time,[202] but at the risk of jeopardising cover under the policy.[203]

The rule is based on policy. There is little that one ought to be able to retain more
control over than the decision to alter one's legal position. The rule also parallels
that relating to dismissal of persons working under contracts of service: "the proper
conduct of the affairs of life necessitates that this should be so".[204] It is reinforced

---

[194]   See Illustrations.
[195]   See above, para.10-004. For restrictions on the right of a solicitor or barrister to decline to continue
to act, see Cordery, *Solicitors* (looseleaf edn), J2; R. Mahoney, "Mere Mouthpieces, Hopeless Cases,
and a Lawyer's Inability to Terminate a Retainer" (2017) 15 Otago L.R. 101 (New Zealand law);
and *Richard Buxton (Solicitors) v Mills-Owens* [2010] EWCA Civ 122; [2010] 1 W.L.R. 1997.
[196]   See further, Article 123; *Restatement, Third*, § 3.10 (using "manifestation" for what is here described
as notice). See too *Temple Legal Protection Ltd v QBE Insurance (Europe) Ltd* [2009] EWCA Civ
453; [2009] Lloyd's Rep I.R. 544 at [49]; *Gu v Du* [2011] NZCA 577 (real estate agent terminates
agency without giving reasonable notice, liable to damages).
[197]   *Walsh v Whitcomb* (1797) 2 Esp. 565; *Frith v Frith* [1906] A.C. 254; *Sinfra Aktiengesellschaft v
Sinfra Ltd* [1939] 2 All E.R. 675.
[198]   *Doward, Dickson & Co v Williams & Co* (1889) 6 T.L.R. 316.
[199]   See *Vynior's Case* (1609) 8 CoRep. 81b.
[200]   See *Vynior's Case* (1609) 8 CoRep. 81b.
[201]   *The Margaret Mitchell* (1858) Sw. 382; *R. v Wait* (1823) 11 Price 518.
[202]   See *Barrett Bros (Taxis) Ltd v Davies* [1966] 1 W.L.R. 1334 (CA) at 1338–1339.
[203]   See *Groom v Crocker* [1939] 1 K.B. 194 at 227; *Eagle Star Insurance Co Ltd v Cresswell* [2004]
EWCA Civ 602; [2004] 2 All E.R. (Comm) 244 at [17].
[204]   *Frith v Frith* [1906] A.C. 254 at 259, per Lord Atkinson. See also, in the sphere of public law, *Huth
v Clarke* (1890) 25 Q.B.D. 391 at 394 ("delegation does not imply a denudation of power and authority"); followed in *Manton v Brighton Corp* [1951] 2 All E.R. 101. See also below, para.12-009, 12-

by the separate rule that a contract of agency will not usually be enforced by a decree of specific performance.[205]

The application of these general principles to the position of sub-agents has yet to be worked out. In principle, the sub-agent's actual authority terminates with that of the agent. *Restatement, Third* takes the view, however, that a principal who withdraws authority from an agent owes a duty to known sub-agents to communicate that fact to them and that until that occurs their authority continues.[206] The basis given is that, having approved of the appointment of subagents and having ultimate control over chains of command, the principal should bear the risk of the agent's not having communicated with the sub-agents. It is not clear, nonetheless, that English law would take this view. It is one thing to have consented to a delegation, it is another to bear responsibility for the agent's defaults in respect of the agent's delegates (whose contact details the principal may not even possess). Nor, where the agent is not an employee, is there an obvious basis for the imposition of a duty on the principal (direct or vicarious) to indemnify sub-agents in respect of their liability to third parties resulting from the termination of their authority. As between principal and the agent, there may a duty, sounding in damages, to indemnify the agent if, in terminating authority, the principal does not give the agent sufficient time to communicate the fact of termination to any sub-agents. Of course, the foregoing does not affect the position of any apparent authority that the sub-agent may retain following termination of the agent's mandate.

10-025   **Effect of equity**   Equity will sometimes restrain breach of a negative covenant by injunction.[207] A well-known example is revocation of a licence to enter upon land, which would make the licensee a trespasser. Unless the licence is coupled with an interest,[208] the revocation is effective as regards the land even if it involves a breach of contract. But where there is a contract to permit such access covering a fixed period, revocation of the licence may be restrained by injunction, with the result that the licensee cannot be treated as a trespasser.[209] Equity also sometimes restrains termination of employment contracts[210] and distributorship contracts,[211] and in an unreported but well-reasoned decision, the Court of Appeal granted an interim injunction restraining the termination of a company from management of the Dorchester Hotel in London.[212] All of these have some affinity with agency situations. It seems unlikely that a court would grant such a remedy in what may be called a "pure agency" situation, for example one involving no more than the authority of a broker or a person acting as an agent for sale, because of the overriding interest of the principal of such an agent in determining how and by whom

---

023.

[205] See Article 59.

[206] Comment (e) to § 3.15.

[207] *Doherty v Allman* (1878) 3 App.Cas. 709 at 719–720.

[208] cf. above, para.10-007.

[209] See *Hurst v Picture Theatres Ltd* [1915] 1 K.B. 1; *Winter Garden Theatre (London) Ltd v Millennium Productions Ltd* [1948] A.C. 173; Hanbury and Martin, *Modern Equity* (21st edn), Ch.28.

[210] See *Hill v C.A. Parsons & Co Ltd* [1972] 1 Ch 305; Freedland, *The Personal Employment Contract* (2006), p.372 onwards; Article 59.

[211] e.g. *Decro-Wall SA v Practitioners in Marketing Ltd* [1971] 1 W.L.R. 361 (see esp. at 372 and 388); *Evans Marshall v Bertola SA* [1973] 1 W.L.R. 349 (see esp. at 379–380, 382); *Thomas Borthwick & Sons v SOFCO* [1978] N.Z.L.R. 538 per Cooke J; *Dietrichsen v Cabburn* (1846) 2 Ph. 52.

[212] *Re Regent International Hotels (UK) Ltd v Pageguide Ltd* CA, *The Times,* May 13, 1985 (Ackner and Robert Goff LJJ and Sir Roualeyn Cumming-Bruce); referred to with approval in *Lauritzencool AB v Lady Navigation Inc* [2005] EWCA Civ 579; [2005] 2 Lloyd's Rep. 63.

the principal is represented.[213] But many situations brought under the general umbrella of agency in fact bring in other elements, such as employment, distributorship or general management; and when agency functions are undertaken by companies there may be some element of joint venture.[214] Any of these may make the grant of an injunction appropriate.

Reliance   Finally, it may be said that when the agent has foreseeably relied on an assurance that the authority would not be revoked, the principal may be restrained from revoking where revocation would be inequitable or unconscionable. There are certainly dicta which if quoted out of context suggest that there is a rule to this effect.[215] They relate, however, to agents who have done exactly what was authorised and who seek no more than reimbursement or indemnity.[216] The significance of estoppel reasoning such as this in general contract law is undoubtedly increasing. But this reasoning should on principle only operate between the parties: it should not affect the authority of the agent where the only reliance is that of the agent. Where there is reliance by the third party, the doctrine of apparent authority will give such protection as is appropriate.   **10-026**

Notice   As between principal and agent, the agent's authority does not cease until the agent receives notice of the revocation[217]: but there may be implied revocation by an act clearly[218] inconsistent with the continuation of the agency, coming to the notice of the agent,[219] and in some cases the agent may be employed on the basis that no notice of revocation is required.[220] It was suggested in *Restatement, Second*[221] that a repudiatory breach of duties by the agent, as by taking a bribe, would terminate the agent's authority automatically; but in England at any rate it seems that the better view is that this would entitle the principal to terminate the authority and no more. As regards third parties, however, revocation should be effective to remove actual authority even if unknown to the agent; but apparent authority will continue until the third party has notice.[222]   **10-027**

Joint principals and joint agents   Where the authority is conferred by two or more principals jointly, unless the terms of appointment otherwise provide, it is suf-   **10-028**

---

[213] See Mechem, *Outlines of Agency* (1952), § 262. cf. Article 59. See further, above, para.7-045.

[214] See, e.g. *Shell (Petroleum Mining) Co Ltd v Todd Petroleum Mining Co Ltd* [2008] 2 N.Z.L.R. 418 (parties all companies).

[215] e.g. *Read v Anderson* (1884) 13 Q.B.D. 779 at 781.

[216] See above, para.10-010.

[217] See *Re Oriental Bank Corp Ex p. Guillemin* (1884) 28 Ch.D. 634 at 640. This problem should not be confused with the question whether the agent can or cannot be dismissed without notice, under the terms of the agent's contract: see Article 123.

[218] See *Re E (Enduring Power of Attorney)* [2001] Ch. 364 at 373 ("unambiguous"); *Houston v Houston* 2012 BCCA 300; [2012] 12 W.W.R. 215.

[219] See *Smith v Jenning's Case* (1610) Lane 97; *Cousins v International Brick Co Ltd* [1931] 2 Ch. 90; *Heaton's Transport (St Helen's) Ltd v TGWU* [1973] A.C. 15 at 110.

[220] e.g. an estate agent: *E.P. Nelson & Co v Rolfe* [1950] 1 K.B. 139. But in some cases the proper explanation may be that agency never arises, since what is revoked is the offer to appoint an agent. See Comment to Article 123.

[221] Comment to § 112.

[222] In *Robert Simpson Co v Godson* [1937] 1 D.L.R. 454 it was held that notice to a third party, but not to the agent, did not terminate the agent's actual authority. The decision was criticised by Wright (1937) 15 Can.B.R. 196. See also above, para.8-008. See too *Dry Bulk Handy Holding Inc v Fayette International Holdings Ltd* [2013] EWCA Civ 184; [2013] 1 W.L.R. 3440.

ficient if the notice is given by or to any one of the principals,[223] and the same rule presumably applies in respect of notice given to one agent where co-agents are appointed to act jointly.[224] Where authority is conferred as a result of a resolution of a board or committee of a corporation (including a company), authority would not normally terminate unless the resolution were properly rescinded by a further resolution. A board may generally rescind a resolution at any time until it is communicated to a third party by someone with actual or apparent authority to communicate it.[225]

Illustrations

10-029 (1) An indenture of lease provided that an agent named in it should have authority to receive the rent on behalf of the lessor, and that his receipt should be a sufficient discharge, during the term thereby granted. Held, that the lessor might revoke the authority during the term, the agent having no interest in the rent.[226]

(2) An auctioneer is authorised to sell certain goods by auction. His authority may be revoked by the principal at any time before the goods are knocked down to a purchaser, though the auctioneer may be liable to a bidder in consequence of withdrawing the goods.[227]

(3) Money is deposited with A, to be applied for the use of the poor. The authority may be countermanded at any time before the application of the money, and the money recovered by the principal from A.[228]

(4) Money is deposited with a stakeholder, to be paid to the winner of a wager. The authority of the stakeholder may be revoked at any time before he has actually paid over the money to the winner, and if he pays it over after notice of revocation he is personally liable to the depositor for the amount.[229]

(5) A authorised his banker to hold £20 at the disposal of B. The authority of the banker may be countermanded, provided that he has not paid the money to B, nor attorned to him to hold it on his behalf.[230]

(6) An insured is entitled to dismiss a solicitor appointed by the insurer to conduct the insured's defence,[231] but in so doing is likely to forfeit the insurance cover.[232] Similarly, an insurer (whether as principal or agent) may have authority to terminate the retainer for the insured.[233]

---

[223] *Bristow and Porter v Taylor* (1817) 2 Stark. 50.
[224] See Article 11.
[225] See *Powell v Lee* (1908) 99 L.T. 284 (revocation by board of school of resolution appointing headmaster); *Lagunas Nitrate Co Ltd v Schroeder & Co* (1901) 85 L.T. 22 (revocation of dividend); *Potel v IRC* [1971] 2 All E.R. 504 at 511; *Brookton Co-op Society Ltd v FCT* (1981) 147 C.L.R. 441 at 455.
[226] *Venning v Bray* (1862) 2 B. & S. 502; and see *Doward & Co v Williams & Co* (1890) 6 T.L.R. 316; *Frith v Frith* [1906] A.C. 254.
[227] *Warlow v Harrison* (1859) 1 E. & E. 309.
[228] *Taylor v Lendey* (1807) 9 East 49.
[229] *Hampden v Walsh* (1876) 1 Q.B.D. 189; *Diggle v Higgs* (1877) 2 Ex.D. 422; *Trimble v Hill* (1879) 5 App.Cas. 342. These cases were not affected by the Gaming Act 1892, now repealed.
[230] *Gibson v Minet* (1824) 9 Moo.C.P. 31; *Brummell v M'Pherson* (1828) 5 Russ. 263. See Article 112(3).
[231] See *Barrett Bros (Taxis) Ltd v Davies* [1966] 1 W.L.R. 1334 at 1339.
[232] See *Eagle Star Insurance Co Ltd v Cresswell* [2004] EWCA Civ 602 (reinsurer disowns reinsurance).
[233] See *Re Enterprise Insurance Co Plc, White v Ozon Solicitors* [2017] EWHC 1595 (Ch).

Article 121

APPARENT AUTHORITY WHERE ACTUAL AUTHORITY TERMINATED

Where a principal, by words or conduct, represents or permits it to be represented **10-030**
that an agent is authorised to act on the principal's behalf, the principal is bound
by the acts of the agent, notwithstanding the termination of authority (unless
perhaps by the death or insolvency of the principal[234]), to the same extent as would
have been the case if the authority had not been terminated, when it was reasonable for the third party to deal with the agent on the faith of any such representation, without notice of the termination of authority.[235]

Comment

This is an application of the doctrine of apparent authority in the specific context **10-031**
of revocation. It has earlier been pointed out that the doctrine of apparent authority covers two types of case: situations where there is some specific representation, and cases where the representation arises only from the agent's being permitted to assume a position carrying with it a usual authority.[236] Similar ideas operate
where the principal holds the agent out as owner.[237] The question whether apparent authority persists where the principal gives the agent instructions limited to a
particular period, or unexpectedly revokes the agent's instructions, has not yet been
fully worked out, because most apparent authority cases refer to the extent of
authority rather than its duration.[238] It is certainly clear that a third party does not
need to point to fresh evidence of a holding out occurring at or after the time that
the agent's authority was terminated; such an argument has been expressly
rejected.[239] In many circumstances, it will be reasonable for the third party to assume that an express representation as to an agent's authority, or an agent's usual
authority, continues unless and until the principal takes steps to notify the third party
that the authority has been terminated.[240] In earlier editions of this work it was
almost stated as a rule that a holding out would continue to be effective unless and
until the third party had been notified of the termination. There are dicta in *Scarf v
Jardine*[241] which can be read as supporting that view, Lord Blackburn suggesting
that notification was a general requirement of agency law. These dicta, and their

[234] See below, para.10-032.
[235] See Illustrations 1–4; *Pole v Leask* (1862) 33 L.J.Ch. 155 at 162–163; *Ryan v Sams* (1848) 12 Q.B.
460; *Aste v Montague* (1858) 1 F. & F. 264; *Stavely v Uzielli* (1860) 2 F. & F. 30; *Curlewis v Birkbeck*
(1863) 3 F. & F. 894; *Debenham v Mellon* (1880) 6 App.Cas. 24 at 33; *Scarf v Jardine* (1882) 7
App.Cas. 345 at 349; *Willis, Faber & Co Ltd v Joyce* (1911) L.T. 576; *Morgan v Lifetime Building
Supplies Ltd* (1967) 61 D.L.R. (2d) 178. cf. Partnership Act 1890 s.36(1); Factors Act 1889 s.2(2);
Articles 21 and 72.
[236] See Comments to Articles 22 and 72.
[237] *Curlewis v Birkbeck* (1863) 3 F. & F. 894. See Article 84.
[238] Stoljar, pp.166–168.
[239] See *SEB Trygg Liv Holding AB v Manches* [2005] EWCA Civ 1237; [2006] 1 W.L.R. 2276 at [32].
See, generally, Powell, pp.399–402; and Comment to Article 22.
[240] See *SEB Trygg Liv Holding AB v Manches* [2005] EWCA Civ 1237; [2006] 1 W.L.R. 2276; *Rockland
Industries Ltd v Amerada Minerals Corp of Canada* [1980] 2 S.C.R. 2: (1980) 108 D.L.R. (3d) 513,
Illustration 4.
[241] *Scarf v Jardine* (1882) 7 App. Cas. 345 at 349–350, per Lord Selborne LC, and at 356–357, per Lord
Blackburn (principles not confined to partnership). See too *Drew v Nunn* (1879) 4 Q.B.D. 661 at 668;
Willis, Faber & Co Ltd v Joyce (1911) 104 L.T. 576. Movement of a director from one company to
another in a group may not terminate apparent authority to act for the former company unless the

requirement of notification were subsequently incorporated into the Partnership Act 1890.[242] Nonetheless, it is suggested here that a fixed requirement for notification is not a general rule of agency law. It would be contrary to the general principles of apparent authority to permit a third party to rely on an absence of notification that a past representation of authority has been withdrawn when no reasonable person would have assumed its continuance.[243] In *Stavely v Uzielli*,[244] a case brought for payment for services performed, Erle CJ is reported as saying to the jury:

"The lapse of time makes a difference in this case ... there may be notice by other means than by express or actual notice. And here you have the fact, that no accounts were sent, even to the servant (and none to the master), for four years before the servant's death."

Hence, in some cases, the principal's representation may itself indicate the duration for which the authority is to continue,[245] and in others the circumstances may make it inappropriate for the third party to assume that the mandate is continuing. So, if, as in *Stavely*, a long period has elapsed since any earlier dealings with the agent, or there is otherwise something that would alert a reasonable person to the fact that the agent's appointment or authority had ended, it may be unreasonable for the third party to rely on an earlier holding out of authority. The position is put in the following way in the *Restatement, Third*:

"Apparent authority ends when it is no longer reasonable for the third party with whom the agent deals to believe that the agent continues to act with actual authority."[246]

10-032 **Application to cases of death or incapacity** Special problems arise in cases of incapacity. Where the principal dies, it is arguable on a purely theoretical basis that no apparent authority can continue, for "[h]ow can a valid act be done in the name of a dead man?"[247] A similar argument can be put forward on dissolution of a company, or in personal insolvency.[248] It can also be put forward, though less strongly, in cases of mental incapacity, for the principal becomes incapable of continuing consent to the relation, or of making or continuing representations to the third party.

In *Drew v Nunn*,[249] however, a strong Court of Appeal decided that a principal who became mentally incapable could be bound under the doctrine of apparent authority. The decision is clearly based on the desirability of protecting third parties: "insanity is not a privilege, but a misfortune which must not be allowed to injure

---

significance of the move is itself apparent to the third party: see *Benourad v Compass Group Plc* [2010] EWHC 1882 (QB) at [113] (on facts, director himself had made clear to third party termination of actual authority).

[242] Partnership Act 1890 s.36. See *Lindley and Banks on Partnership* (20th edn), para.13-37 onwards.

[243] See above, paras 8-018 and 8-050; and particularly *East Asia Co Ltd v PT Satria Tirtatama Energindo* [2019] UKPC 30. For more detail, see P. Watts, "Does Apparent Authority Wane?" [2018] J.B.L. 663.

[244] *Stavely v Uzielli* (1860) 2 F. & F. 30, Illustration 7. See too *Farrar v Deflinne* (1844) 1 Car. & K. 580 at 581 (reference to surmise that partner has left partnership being sufficient).

[245] See *Pole v Leask* (1862) 33 L.J.Ch.155 at 162.

[246] *Restatement, Third*, § 3.11.

[247] *Watson v King* (1815) 4 Camp. 272 at 274, per Lord Ellenborough (possibly a case on a power coupled with an interest, but no distinction taken).

[248] See above, paras 10-018 and 10-020. See also Partnership Act 1890 s.36(3).

[249] *Drew v Nunn* (1879) 4 Q.B.D. 661. See also *Re Parks* (1956) 8 D.L.R. (2d) 155 (adopting a test of constructive notice).

innocent persons".[250] One of the judgments contains suggestions that the reasoning should be extended also to cases of the principal's death.[251] The decision is said to be inconsistent with *Yonge v Toynbee*,[252] in which a solicitor who took steps in litigation on behalf of a defendant client who had unknown to him become mentally incapable was held liable to pay costs incurred by the claimant: it is argued that if the solicitor had apparent authority there would be no loss to the third party.[253] It is, however, difficult to see how the doctrine of apparent authority could have helped the claimant in that case, who seems to have acted reasonably in discontinuing the action after negotiations regarding the appointment of a guardian ad litem had fallen through.[254] The decision was in any case one on the court's summary jurisdiction over solicitors.[255] There is authority therefore that the doctrine may protect the contracts of the agent of a principal who subsequently becomes mentally incapable; and possibly one who dies.

It is submitted that this is the better view. It might even be argued that there is a stronger case for the continuation of apparent authority in the case of death than in that of mental incapacity, for in the latter case there may be a legitimate interest in protecting the mentally incapable.[256] The policy of protection of innocent third parties appears also in statutes.[257] The authority for cessation of apparent authority is not strong and some of it antedates the development of modern doctrine[258]; such reasoning has also been strongly criticised.[259] It also antedates the strict liability for breach of warranty of authority, which dates from 1857,[260] and which is arguably the real cause of the difficulties in this situation.[261] *Restatement, Third* confines the revocation of authority by incapacity to actual authority and applies the general principles of apparent authority in such situations.[262]

Where the third party knows of the mental incapacity of the principal, it is submitted that the transaction should be void for lack of authority rather than merely voidable.[263] Where the principal's property is, under the Mental Capacity Act 2005, under the control of the court, the analogy seems rather to be with bankruptcy: but

---

[250] *Drew v Nunn* (1879) 4 Q.B.D. 661, per Bramwell LJ at 668; see also Brett LJ at 667–668.

[251] See Brett LJ at 668.

[252] *Yonge v Toynbee* [1910] 1 K.B. 215.

[253] Powell, p.390; Treitel, *Law of Contract* (15th edn), para.16-125.

[254] See Higgins (1961) 1 U.Tas.L.Rev. 569. *Drew v Nunn* was not cited to the court in *Yonge v Toynbee*. It seems in fact to have been an early case on apparent authority as we know it now, and was cited with approval in this connection by the Court of Appeal in *Republic of Chili v London and River Plate Bank* (1894) 10 T.L.R. 658; and by Scrutton J in *Willis, Faber & Co v Joyce* (1911) 104 L.T. 576.

[255] It is difficult to see how an implied contract of warranty of authority could arise in such a case.

[256] See Müller-Frienfels in *Civil Law in the Modern World* (Yiannopoulos ed., 1965), 77 at 111–115 (citing comparative material); (1957) 6 Am.J.Comp.L. 165 at 184–185.

[257] As in the case of powers of attorney: see Article 122. See also Partnership Act 1890 s.14(2). For broader protections found overseas, see Powers of Attorney and Agency Act 1984 (South Australia); and Power of Attorney Act 1996 (British Columbia).

[258] e.g. *Blades v Free* (1829) 9 B. & C. 167, Illustration 5.

[259] See *Restatement, Second*, § 120, Comments *a* and *c* and Appendix, Reporter's Note to § 120; (1933) 11 Proc. Am. Law Inst. p.85 onwards ("shocking result"); Seavey (1921) 29 Yale L.J. 859 at 893–895 ("shockingly inequitable").

[260] See Article 105.

[261] See McGaw, fn.58 above, at pp.331–332. It is noteworthy that statutory protection of persons acting under powers of attorney followed shortly in the Law of Property Amendment Act 1859.

[262] See §§ 3-07, 3-08 and 3-11.

[263] See Powell, pp.390–391; Ashley (1928) 3 Wash.L.Rev. 133; Thomson (1951) 25 Tulane L.Rev. 249; McCormick (1960) 22 Mont.L.Rev. 74.

the matter is too specialised for consideration here. There is again statutory protection in the case of powers of attorney.[264]

Illustrations

10-033 (1) A authorises B to purchase goods on his credit, and holds him out to C as his agent for that purpose. C supplies goods to B, on A's credit, after revocation by A of B's authority to act on his behalf, C having had no notice of such revocation. A is liable to C for the price of the goods, even if B contracted on his own behalf, and did not intend to bind A.[265]

(2) A husband holds out his wife as having authority to pledge his credit, and subsequently becomes mentally incapable. A tradesman, on the faith of such holding out, supplies goods to the orders of the wife, without notice of the husband's incapacity. The husband is liable for the price of the goods.[266]

(3) A policy was effected through the local agent of an insurance company and notice of a loss was given to him after the branch of business concerned had been transferred to another company. The agent in fact reported the loss to the other company. Held, that that was notice to "a known agent of the company" within the meaning of the policy, the assured having no knowledge of the change of company.[267]

(4) A manager has general authority to make sales. He negotiates for a substantial contract. His superior decides that higher approval is needed for a particular transaction into which the manager would previously have been authorised to enter. This new restriction is not communicated to the third party and the manager subsequently ends a telephone conversation "we have a deal". His company is bound.[268]

(5) A woman lived with a man as his wife for some years and ordered necessaries from a tradesman to whom she had been held out by the man as having authority to pledge his credit. The man went abroad and died there, the woman continuing to order necessaries for herself and children, the tradesman having had no notice of the death. Held, that the woman had the same authority as a wife to bind the man, but that his estate was not liable for the price of the goods.[269]

(6) For some years P had A in his employ as a coachman who with actual authority ordered corn from T. A went into business on his own account as a stable keeper leasing premises from P. He (casually) continued to wear the livery of P, and continued to order corn from T. When the corn was not paid for, T sued P. Held, P was liable not having brought the termination of A's employ to T's notice, nor intervened when late in the piece P became aware that T was under the impression that A was still P's employee.[270]

(7) For 12 years P employed A as a groom, who for the first eight of those years regularly engaged T as a farrier and veterinary surgeon. P restricted A's author-

---

[264] Article 122.

[265] *Trueman v Loder* (1840) 11 A. & E. 589; *Summers v Solomon* (1857) 7 E. & B. 879, Illustration 8.

[266] *Drew v Nunn* (1879) 4 Q.B.D. 661. But see Comment; above, para.3-043.

[267] *Marsden v City and County Ass. Co* (1865) L.R. 1 C.P. 232. See also Article 21.

[268] *Rockland Industries Inc v Amerada Minerals Corp of Canada Ltd* [1980] 2 S.C.R. 2; (1980) 108 D.L.R. (3d) 513.

[269] *Blades v Free* (1829) 9 B. & C. 167. But see Comment.

[270] *Aste v Montague* (1858) 1 F. & F. 264.

ity, but some four years' later A purported to engage T again. Held, that T could not rely on A's prior authority continuing after such a gap.[271]

(8) A had for some years managed a shop belonging to B and ordered goods in B's name from C, and B had duly paid for them. A absconded, called on C and bought goods in B's name, and took them away. Held, that B was liable for the price of the goods.[272]

Article 122

STATUTORY PROTECTION OF THIRD PARTIES AND AGENTS IN RESPECT OF ACTS DONE UNDER POWERS OF ATTORNEY

(1) Where a power of attorney has been revoked and a person, without knowledge **10-034** of the revocation, deals with the donee of the power, the transaction between them is, in favour of that person, as valid as if the power had then been in existence.[273]

(2) Where a power of attorney is expressed in the instrument creating it to be irrevocable and to be given by way of security, then, unless the the third party dealing with the donee knows that it was not in fact given by way of security, that party is entitled to assume that the power is incapable of revocation except by the donor acting with the consent of the donee, and will accordingly be treated for the purposes of Rule (1) above as having knowledge of the revocation only if the party knows that it has been revoked in that manner.[274]

(3) Where the interest of a purchaser depends on whether a transaction between the donee of a power of attorney and another person was valid by virtue of Rule (1) above, it will be conclusively presumed in favour of the purchaser that that person did not at the material time know of the revocation of the power if—(a) the transaction between that person and the donee was completed within 12 months of the date on which the power came into operation; or (b) that person makes a statutory declaration, before or within three months after the completion of the purchase, that he or she did not at the material time know of the revocation of the power.[275]

(4) A donee of a power of attorney who acts in pursuance of the power at a time when it has been revoked does not, by reason of the revocation, incur any liability (either to the donor or to any other person) if at that time the donee did not know that the power had been revoked.[276]

---

[271] *Stavely v Uzielli* (1860) 2 F. & F. 30.
[272] *Summers v Solomon* (1857) 7 E. & B. 879. See also *Trueman v Loder* (1840) 11 A. & E. 589. cf. *Knightsbridge Property Development Corp (UK) Ltd v South Chelsea Properties Ltd* [2017] EWHC 2730 (Ch) (third party knew of removal from position of company secretary).
[273] Powers of Attorney Act 1971 s.5(2). Further protection in respect of Stock Exchange transactions is given by s.6.
[274] Powers of Attorney Act 1971 s.5(3).
[275] Powers of Attorney Act 1971 s.5(4).
[276] Powers of Attorney Act 1971 s.5(1).

Comment

10-035   This Article paraphrases the provisions of s.5(1) to (4) of the Powers of Attorney Act 1971,[277] which protect third parties and the donee of the power where the power has, unknown to them, been revoked.[278] The 1971 provisions replace ss.124, 127 and 128 of the Law of Property Act 1925, which were directed towards achieving the same sort of protection, but which were notoriously obscure and unsatisfactory. Rules (1), (2) and (3) therefore represent statutory formulations, in their particular context, of the doctrine of apparent authority. Rule (4) affects the doctrine of warranty of authority.

10-036   **Revocation**   It seems clear that revocation includes not only express or implied revocation but also death, mental incapacity and insolvency: for by s.5(5) it is provided that knowledge of the revocation of the power includes knowledge of the occurrence of any event (such as the death of the donor) which has the effect of revoking the power.[279]

10-037   **Lasting powers of attorney**   These provisions also apply to lasting powers of attorney governed by the Mental Capacity Act 2005, with special variants.[280] That Act also contains provisions protecting the attorney and bona fide third parties in the case of transactions under instruments which did not create valid powers of attorney but have nevertheless been registered[281]; there are presumptions similar to those of the 1971 Act.[282]

Article 123

COMPENSATION AT COMMON LAW ON TERMINATION OF AUTHORITY

10-038   The termination of the authority of an agent, while valid as such—

(1)   may entitle the agent to compensation in accordance with the requirements of statute or delegated legislation; or

(2)   may constitute a breach by the principal of the express terms of any contract of agency or of implied terms or contractual promises, in respect of any of which the principal may be liable in damages or subject to other remedies.[283]

Comment

10-039   The question whether a principal is liable to an agent for terminating the agent's authority turns on the type of contract or other arrangement under which the agent

---

[277]   See in general *Law Com. No.30*, Cmnd. 4473 (1970); (1971) 121 New L.J. 746 at 751, 764, 771, 795; (1971) 115 S.J. 596; (1971) 35 Conv (N.S.) 310; (1971) 68 L.S.Gaz. 434 at 437.

[278]   The section applies whenever the power was created, but only to acts and transactions after the commencement of the Act: s.5(7).

[279]   As to revocation, see in general Article 117.

[280]   Mental Capacity Act 2005 s.14(5).

[281]   Mental Capacity Act 2005 s.14(1).

[282]   Mental Capacity Act 2005 s.14(3). See in general Cretney and Lush, *Enduring Powers of Attorney* (6th edn), Ch.8; Aldridge, *Powers of Attorney* (10th edn); Thurston, *Powers of Attorney* (5th edn).

[283]   See Comment: Powell, pp.380–385. As to continuing commission and repayment of overpaid commission, see above, paras 7-025 and 7-041.

is employed. There will be no right to compensation if the agency contract is unenforceable for being in restraint of trade.[284]

Agent an employee   If the agent is an employee the agent may be entitled to **10-040** compensation for unfair dismissal or redundancy in accordance with the relevant statutory provisions of employment law.[285] Such an agent may also be entitled to damages at common law for wrongful dismissal, viz. dismissal in breach of contract.[286]

Agent a commercial agent   Where the agent is a commercial agent as defined by **10-041** the Commercial Agents (Council Directive) Regulations 1993, the circumstances in which the agent may be dismissed and special compensation payable on dismissal are regulated by statutory instrument. Then provisions are discussed in Chapter 11.[287]

Agent engaged under bilateral contract for services   If the agent is engaged, not **10-042** as an employee but as an independent intermediary, the agent's rights will turn on whether the agency appointment is under a bilateral contract or under a unilateral one. If the agent undertakes duties towards the principal, e.g. to use best endeavours, as seems to be a normal implication of a sole or exclusive agency,[288] the agent's contract is a bilateral one involving reciprocal obligations. Usually such contracts make their own provision for termination[289]; but unless carefully drafted these may not always be as efficacious as might have been hoped.[290] Questions regarding the termination of such a contract depend on whether it has or has not a time limit specified in it.

(1) No time limit[291]   If there is no time limit referred to in the contract, three interpretations are possible as to termination.

A. ***terminable at will***   Decisions[292] and dicta[293] can be found suggesting that the confidential nature of the contract of agency means that where there are no provisions relating to termination such a contract can be terminated at will by the principal. The authority for this approach mostly derives however from unilateral

---

[284] See *Proactive Sports Management Ltd v Rooney* [2011] EWCA Civ 1444; [2012] F.S.R. 16 at [122]; *CJ Motorsport Consulting Ltd v Bird* [2019] EWHC 2330 (QB).

[285] See, e.g. Deakin and Morris, *Labour Law* (6th edn); *Chitty on Contracts* (33rd edn), Ch.40. Special considerations apply when a company alters its articles. See *Southern Foundries Ltd v Shirlaw* [1940] A.C. 701; *Shindler v Northern Raincoat Co Ltd* [1960] 1 W.L.R. 1038; *Russell v Northern Bank Development Corp Ltd* [1992] 1 W.L.R. 588; Davenport (1993) 109 L.Q.R. 553; *Gower's Principles of Modern Company Law* (10th edn), (paras 14-52 and 19-25–19-28). See also *Micklefield v SAC Technology Ltd* [1990] 1 W.L.R. 1002.

[286] See *Chitty on Contracts*, para.40-201 onwards.

[287] See esp. below, para.11-045 onwards.

[288] See above, para.7-036. Contra, Murdoch (1975) 91 L.Q.R. 357 at 373–375, who treats this as involving the offer of a unilateral contract also. See also McConnell (1983) 265 E.G. 547.

[289] e.g. *Christie & Vesey Ltd v Maatschappij, etc., Helvetia NV (The Helvetia-S)* [1960] 1 Lloyd's Rep. 540. See also *Sport International Bussum BV v Inter-Footwear Ltd* [1984] 1 W.L.R. 776.

[290] e.g. *Wickman Machine Tool Sales Ltd v L. Schuler AG* [1974] A.C. 235, where the use of the word "condition" was not sufficient.

[291] See Carnegie (1969) 85 L.Q.R. 392; Lücke (1973) 5 Adelaide L.Rev. 32 at 48 onwards.

[292] e.g. *Alexander v Davis & Son* (1885) 2 T.L.R. 142 (where the contract appears bilateral); followed in *Henry v Lowson* (1885) 2 T.L.R. 199.

[293] e.g. *Martin-Baker Aircraft Co Ltd v Canadian Flight Equipment Ltd* [1955] 2 Q.B. 556 at 582.

contract cases, where it is the *offer* which is terminated[294]; and there is sometimes confusion with the proposition that the termination of authority is *effective* whether a breach of contract or not. It is submitted that such an approach will rarely be appropriate for a binding bilateral contract, which of its nature involves the likely expenditure of time and effort by the agent.

B.   not terminable at all   Conversely, dicta can also be produced for the proposition that such a contract is (in the absence of special provision for termination) not terminable at all (other than on breach or frustration), at least if the express terms provide any support for such a construction.[295] It is submitted however that although there are cases where there is in effect the grant of a perpetual benefit in return for consideration,[296] in the commercial situation of representation such an interpretation would rarely be appropriate.[297] Contracts of indefinite duration do, however, arise from time to time.[298]

C.   terminable on notice   The third and most likely possibility is that the parties are interpreted as having at the time of the contract intended that the contract is terminable on reasonable notice, taking into account the expenditure and time incurred by the agent, the need to meet commitments to customers and conclude transactions under way, the desirability of a period for readjustment of business and so forth.[299] This is so even where the contract itself makes other provision for termination,[300] unless such provision can be treated as exclusive.[301] The matter is sometimes said to turn on whether the contract is similar to an employment contract.[302] That is but one category of case. It is submitted that this interpretation

---

[294] e.g. *Motion v Michaud* (1892) 8 T.L.R. 253; affirmed ibid. at 447: see below.

[295] e.g. *Llanelly Ry and Dock Co v L & NW Ry Co* (1873) L.R. 8 Ch.App. 942 at 949; (1873) L.R. 7 H.L. 550 at 567.

[296] See explanation of the *Llanelly* case by Goff LJ in *Staffordshire Area Health Authority v South Staffordshire Waterworks Co* [1978] 1 W.L.R. 1387 at 1402.

[297] See *Martin-Baker Aircraft Co Ltd v Canadian Flight Equipment Ltd* [1955] 2 Q.B. 556 at 577. See also *Tower Hamlets LBC v British Gas Corp, The Times,* December 14, 1984 (no implication of reasonable duration).

[298] See *W Nagel (A Firm) v Pluczenik Diamond Co NV* [2018] EWCA Civ 2640; [2019] Bus. L.R. 692 (agency to endure so long as principal retained position in market).

[299] There is a useful discussion at both levels of appeal in *Paper Reclaim Ltd v Aotearoa International Ltd* [2006] 3 N.Z.L.R. 188 (CA) at [78]; affirmed on this point in [2007] NZSC 26; [2007] 3 N.Z.L.R. 169 at [6] (12 months). Other illustrative cases include *Bauman v Hulton Press Ltd* [1952] 2 All E.R. 1121 (six months); *Martin-Baker Aircraft Co Ltd v Canadian Flight Equipment Ltd* [1955] 2 Q.B. 556 (12 months: one contract a licence to manufacture); *Decro-Wall International SA v Practitioners in Marketing Ltd* [1971] 1 W.L.R. 361 (distributorship: 12 months); *Crawford Fitting Co v Sydney Valve and Fittings Pty Ltd* (1988) 14 N.S.W.L.R. 438 (stressing in a distributorship contract the notion that "the relationship of the parties should continue long enough to enable the distributor to recoup extraordinary expenditure or effort"; particularly when that was incurred "with the actual or tacit authority of the principal"); *Alpha Lettings Ltd v Neptune Research and Development Inc* [2003] EWCA Civ 704 (distributorship: four months); *Concourse Initiatives Ltd v Maiden Outdoor Advertising Ltd* [2005] EWHC 2995 (advertising); *W Nagel (a firm) v Pluczenik Diamond Co NV* [2017] EWHC 1750 (Comm) at [89] (affirmed on other points, [2018] EWCA Civ 2640). "Reasonableness" is ascertained at the time of the notice given; ibid.; *Ogilvy & Mather (NZ) Ltd v Turner* [1996] 1 N.Z.L.R. 641 at 646; and see in general the *Staffordshire Area Health Authority v South Staffordshire Waterworks Co* [1978] 1 W.L.R. 1387.

[300] As it did in *Martin-Baker Aircraft Co Ltd v Canadian Flight Equipment Ltd* [1955] 2 Q.B. 556 at 573).

[301] As in *Re Barker Sportcraft Ltd's Agreements* (1947) 177 L.T. 420.

[302] e.g. *Lightband v Maine Bros* (1905) 25 N.Z.L.R. 50; *Martin-Baker Aircraft Co Ltd v Canadian Flight*

will often be appropriate in bilateral contract cases. Plainly, misconduct by the agent may still justify summary dismissal.[303]

(2) Time limit If there is a time limit contained in the contract, as where the contract provides for the agent to act for a specified period of years, it might be thought that the agent was by such a term entitled to continue to act for that period unless the contract was discharged by frustration, and that if the agent's authority was terminated before the end of the period there would be an entitlement to damages. There are however many cases which hold that the principal may terminate without breach by simply going out of business[304] or disposing of the subject-matter of the agency.[305] The reasoning is that the promise is only conditional on the business being carried on, which itself is not promised[306]; or that:

"a person is entitled to deal with his property as he chooses, and a person is entitled either to carry on his business or to give up carrying on his business, as he wishes."[307]

Other cases however hold that the principal may not do so and that there is a right to serve for a particular period,[308] sometimes explained as a right to a "continuing benefit".[309] These cases make very fine distinctions.[310] They are often explained as turning on the existence or non-existence of an implied term,[311] which is in general rarely found by the courts unless necessary to give business efficacy to the contract.[312] But in truth the question of implication of a term does not arise until the initial promise has been interpreted as absolute or non-absolute.[313] Thus in one such case[314] one member of a divided Court of Appeal posed the question whether there was any indication that a two-year contract could be ended in less than two years, and another whether there was a term that the business would be continued for two

---

Equipment Ltd [1955] 2 Q.B. 556 at 582; *Paper Sales Corp Ltd v Miller Bros Co Ltd* (1975) 55 D.L.R. (3d) 492; *Knight v Calderlodge Developments* (1978) 238 E.G. 117.
[303] See, e.g. *Gledhill v Bentley Designs (UK) Ltd* [2010] EWHC B8 (dismissal for abusive language).
[304] *Ex p. Maclure* (1870) L.R. 5 Ch.App. 737; *Rhodes v Forwood* (1876) 1 App.Cas. 256, Illustration 1 (even though the contract itself provided for termination); *Hamlyn & Co v Wood & Co* [1891] 2 Q.B. 488 (sale contract); *Northey v Trevillion* (1902) 7 Com.Cas. 201; *Lazarus v Cairn Line Ltd* (1912) 106 L.T. 378; *In Re R.S. Newman Ltd* [1916] 2 Ch. 309; *Leak v Charles & Sons Ltd* (1948) 92 S.J. 154. As to changes in partnerships, see *Tasker v Shepherd* (1861) 6 H. & N. 575; *Cowasjee Nanabhoy v Llallbhoy Vullubhoy* (1876) L.R. 3 Ind.App. 200; *Brace v Calder* [1895] 2 Q.B. 253; *Lindley and Banks on Partnership* (20th edn), para.3-41.
[305] *Lazarus v Cairn Line Ltd* (1912) 106 L.T. 378; *L. French & Co Ltd v Leeston Shipping Co Ltd* [1922] 1 A.C. 451, Illustration 2 to Article 58; *Howard Houlder & Partners Ltd v Manx Islands SS Co* [1923] 1 K.B. 110 (all cases on ships); *Shackleton Aviation Ltd v Maitland Drewery Aviation Ltd* [1964] 1 Lloyd's Rep. 293 (aircraft).
[306] *Warren & Co v Agdeshman* (1922) 38 T.L.R. 588 at 590.
[307] *Alpha Trading Ltd v Dunnshaw-Patten* [1981] Q.B. 290 at 304, per Brandon LJ. See also *Lazarus v Cairn Line Ltd* (1912) 106 L.T. 378 at 380 (Scrutton LJ).
[308] *Re London & Colonial Co Ex p. Clark* (1869) L.R. 7 Eq. 550; *Re Patent Floor Cloth Co Ltd* (1872) 26 L.T. 467; *Turner v Goldsmith* [1891] 1 Q.B. 544, Illustration 2; *Mutzenbecher v La Aseguradora Española SA* [1906] 1 K.B. 254; *Reigate v Union Manufacturing Co (Ramsbottom) Ltd* [1918] 1 K.B. 592; *General Publicity Services Ltd v Best's Brewery Co Ltd* [1951] 2 T.L.R. 875; *Re Premier Products Ltd* [1965] N.Z.L.R. 50 (full analysis of case law: partly distributorship contract).
[309] *Lazarus v Cairn Line Ltd* (1912) 106 L.T. 378 at 380.
[310] *Bauman v Hulton Press Ltd* [1952] 2 All E.R. 1121 at 1124; Burrows (1968) 31 M.L.R. 390 at 399.
[311] e.g. *Mutzenbecher v La Aseguradora Española SA* [1906] 1 Q.B. 254; *Alpha Trading Ltd v Dunnshaw-Patten Ltd* [1981] Q.B. 290.
[312] cf. *The Moorcock* (1889) 14 P.D. 64; above, para.7-001.
[313] See *Re Premier Products Ltd* [1965] N.Z.L.R. 50.
[314] *Brace v Calder* [1895] 2 Q.B. 253; see Burrows (1968) 31 M.L.R. 390.

years.[315] All this emphasises the need for careful drafting of such contracts in order to avoid disputes.

The question may arise whether, if the principal is entitled to cease business, the principal must nevertheless give the agent reasonable notice. On the whole this seems unlikely: a cancellation of authority "from today" has been held valid.[316] The agent will however doubtless be entitled to a reasonable packing-up period before, e.g. becoming a trespasser.[317]

This whole question interlocks very considerably with the question whether the principal is in breach of contract if the principal prevents the agent from earning commission. Such prevention may of course occur during the course of the agency arrangement (as when the principal sells personally or through another agent, or refuses to complete a negotiated transaction[318]) as well as by complete termination of it. Reference should therefore be made also to the discussion of prevention of earning of commission under Article 58.[319]

10-043 **Agent's rights derive only from offer of unilateral contract** In some cases the rights of an agent will be based only on a single or continuing offer by the principal to pay commission, which is best interpreted as an offer of a unilateral contract, under which the agent is not obliged to do anything but simply qualifies for commission if the agent does. It has been submitted elsewhere[320] that this is the best explanation of the estate agent's contractual position where the agent is not a sole or exclusive agent[321] and the same may be true of other canvassing agents.[322] In such a case the question of termination of authority depends on the rules for the revocation of contractual offers[323]; and although the courts have sometimes sought to answer the questions by considering the implication of a *term* it is submitted that the question is here better put as one whether there is an implied *contract* not to revoke the offer.[324] The principal might promise not to withdraw the offer in consideration of the agent commencing or maintaining activities within a reasonable time.[325] Put this way, it is obvious that such a promise will rarely be detected, and that the offer can normally be withdrawn without warning. This seems the true explanation of cases holding that an agent's authority may be withdrawn summarily.[326] This is now the accepted explanation of the position of estate agents who are not sole agents, unless they succeed in securing other terms.[327] Wide dicta

---

[315] See pp.262 and 259.

[316] *Lazarus v Cairn Line Ltd* (1912) 106 L.T. 378.

[317] See *Winter Garden Theatre (London) Ltd v Millenium Productions Ltd* [1948] A.C. 173.

[318] e.g. *Alpha Trading Ltd v Dunnshaw-Patten Ltd* [1981] Q.B. 290, Illustration 3 to Article 58.

[319] See also Article 59 on specific performance.

[320] See Comment to Article 58; *Luxor (Eastbourne) Ltd v Cooper* [1941] A.C. 108, esp. at 124–125; Murdoch (1975) 91 L.Q.R. 357.

[321] Murdoch (1975) 91 L.Q.R. 357 treats sole agencies on the same basis.

[322] As to canvassing agents, see above, para.1-020.

[323] See *Luxor (Eastbourne) Ltd v Cooper* [1941] A.C. 108 at 128–129.

[324] But see Treitel, *Law of Contract* (15th edn), paras 2-052–2-058.

[325] cf. *Errington v Errington* [1952] 1 K.B. 290.

[326] e.g. *Motion v Michaud* (1892) 8 T.L.R. 253; affirmed ibid. at 447; *Joynson v Hunt & Son* (1905) 93 L.T. 470; *Levy v Goldhill* [1917] 2 Ch. 297. See also *Keshen v S. Lipsky Co Ltd* (1956) 3 D.L.R. (2d) 438; *Lowe v Rutherford Thompson McRae Ltd* (1970) 14 D.L.R. (3d) 772.

[327] See above, paras 7-035–7-036.

regarding the irrevocability of offers in such situations should be treated with caution.[328]

Gratuitous agency   An agent who has no contractual relationship, actual or potential, with the principal can be dismissed (in so far as that term is appropriate) without liability on the principal's part, except in so far as the agent has rights under the law of restitution.   **10-044**

Remedies for wrongful termination   In principle a wrongful termination of authority will not terminate the contract also unless the agent accepts the breach as doing so.[329] The usual remedy for wrongful termination will however (apart from the statutory provisions of employment law and the regulations governing commercial agents) be an action for damages; though there may be cases where an injunction or a declaration can be obtained.[330] The damages will normally be calculated by reference to what would have been earned by way of commission if the term of the agency had run its full course,[331] or if reasonable notice had been given,[332] as appropriate in the circumstances, less expenses which would have been incurred, and subject to the duty to mitigate damages.[333]   **10-045**

Illustrations

(1)   A and B agree that for seven years or so long as A shall continue to carry on a business at the town of Liverpool, A shall be sole agent at Liverpool for the sale of B's coals. After four years B sells his colliery. He is not liable to A, for the contract does not bind him to keep the colliery, nor to send coals to Liverpool.[334]   **10-046**

(2)   A shirt manufacturer agreed with the plaintiff to employ him as "agent canvasser and traveller" for five years. After two years the manufacturer's shirt factory burnt down. The business was closed down and he ceased to employ the plaintiff. Held, the plaintiff was entitled to substantial damages, it being

---

[328]   e.g. that of Goff LJ in *Daulia Ltd v Millbank Nominees Ltd* [1978] Ch. 231 at 239.

[329]   *Atlantic Underwriting Agencies Ltd v Cia. di Assicurazione di Milano SpA* [1979] 2 Lloyd's Rep. 240; following *Thomas Marshall (Exports) Ltd v Guinle* [1979] Ch. 227; *Société Générale, London Branch v Geys* [2012] UKSC 63; [2013] 1 A.C. 523; see *Chitty on Contracts* (33rd edn), para.40-193. In any case, ancillary duties survive breach, e.g. a valid exclusive dealing clause (the *Thomas Marshall* case, above) and a clause permitting inspection of books (*Yasuda Fire Ins Co v Orion Marine Insurance Underwriting Agency Ltd* [1995] Q.B. 174).

[330]   Article 59.

[331]   e.g. *Reigate v Union Manufacturing Co (Ramsbottom Ltd)* [1918] 1 K.B. 592; *W Nagel (A Firm) v Pluczenik Diamond Co NV* [2018] EWCA Civ 2640; [2019] Bus. L.R. 692 (affirming [2017] EWHC 1750 (Comm)).

[332]   e.g. *Bauman v Hilton Press Ltd* [1952] 2 All E.R. 1121; *Roberts v Elwells Engineers Ltd* [1972] 2 Q.B. 586 (account not an appropriate remedy); *Paper Reclaim Ltd v Aotearoa International Ltd* [2007] 3 N.Z.L.R. 169 (SC) (compensation for wrongful termination of agency to be calculated on the basis that the repudiation had the same effect as the giving of proper notice). cf. *Berry v CCL Secure Pty Ltd* [2020] HCA 27 (principal misleads agent into terminating agency, and fails to establish that would have terminated contract by lawful means).

[333]   Account must be taken of the probabilities of a sale taking place: *Hampton & Sons Ltd v George* [1939] 3 All E.R. 627; and see also *G. Trollope & Sons v Caplan* [1936] 2 K.B. 382 (overruled on another point in *Luxor (Eastbourne) Ltd v Cooper* [1941] A.C. 108). See in general *McGregor on Damages* (20th edn), Ch. 35.

[334]   *Rhodes v Forwood* (1876) 1 App.Cas. 256. See also Article 58, Illustration 2; *Groves v Stirling Bonding Co* [1935] 3 D.L.R. 481.

an implied term of the particular contract in question that in employing the plaintiff for five years, the manufacturer must be taken to have agreed to continue to send him samples so that he could earn his commission.[335]

---

[335] *Turner v Goldsmith* [1891] 1 Q.B. 544. See also *Comet Group Plc v British Sky Broadcasting Ltd,* QBD, *The Times,* April 26, 1991.

CHAPTER 11

COMMERCIAL AGENTS[1]

1. INTRODUCTION

Background   In continental European countries agents are often placed in named   **11-001**
categories which are the subject of special rules. These may require particular
qualifications in the agent, and sometimes registration as a person authorised to
conduct the commercial activity concerned. It has also been the case that certain
categories of agent have been regarded as requiring protection against their
principals, in a manner not unlike that in which employees are often, and nowadays
in developed countries usually, regarded as requiring protection against their
employers. In particular, it has in some countries been made legally requisite for a
principal who wishes to terminate the services of an agent in certain categories to,
in effect, buy the agent out by the payment of a sum which can be justified on the
basis of the expense he has incurred and/or customer connection which he has
generated—a notion sometimes referred to by the French phrase *indemnité de
cessation*. It is thought that there is a danger that after the agent has built up a market
for his principal the principal may intervene and deal direct with the customers
before the agent has recovered his outlay and legitimate profit. Agents are also
perceived as requiring, and have been given, protection against their principals in
other ways, for example as regards the supply of information as to transactions
entered into by the principal as a result of the agency and (a related question) as to
payment of commission.

   A directive seeking to generalise and harmonise among the EC countries the effect of such legislation, so far as it is applied to commercial agents, a category
generally understood in civil law countries, was in the offing from 1976. The
proposed directive[2] aimed at coordinating national laws on independent commercial agents in order to reduce legal differences that were thought to impede the

---

[1]   Randolph and Davey, *European Law of Commercial Agency* (3rd edn, 2010); Saintier and Scholes,
Commercial Agents and the Law (2005); Christou, *International Agency, Distribution and Licensing Agreements* (6th edn, 2011) (covering other topics also, but containing valuable insights and
drafting examples); Singleton, *Commercial Agency Agreements: Law and Practice* (4th edn, 2015).
Valuable insights appear in Bennett, *Principles of the Law of Agency* (2013). Some insights can also
be obtained from the Draft Common Frame of Reference (2009), IVE 3:101 onwards, and from the
ICC Model Commercial Agency Contract.

[2]   Proposal for a Council Directive to Coordinate the Laws of Member States relating to (Self-
Employed) Commercial Agents [1977] OJ C13/2. On the background, see Commission des Com-
munautés Européennes, *Egalité des droits pour les agents commerciaux: Proposition de directive
relative à la coordination des droits des Etats membres concernant les agents commerciaux
(indépendants)*, Bull.Cté.eur., suppl. 1/77. The proposal was submitted to the Economic and Social
Committee on November 24, 1977 (see [1978] OJ C59/31). The modified proposal was published
in 1979: [1979] OJ C56/5.

functioning of the common market and to affect the conditions of competition in Europe. At the same time the proposal aimed at actually improving the protection of commercial agents throughout the Community. Commercial agents were thought to suffer from the uncertainties of their legal position within the Member States. The scope of the proposed directive was therefore broader than the fundamental freedoms laid down by the EC Treaty because the harmonisation of the laws of the Member States governing commercial agency was advanced irrespective of any cross-border elements.[3]

For some countries such legislation was of a familiar type and the need was only to harmonise details. For the common law countries in the EC, however, the category, and indeed (with some exceptions) the categorisation of agents in general did not exist; and the type of legal control introduced was of a completely new type. The common law rules as to the relationship between any principal and any agent are based on the assumption that freedom of contract prevails. In so far as any protection has been perceived as necessary, it is protection of the principal against misuse of his powers by the agent, as by taking a bribe, making a secret profit and in general assuming a position in which his own interests or those of others for whom he acts are adverse to those of his principal.[4] It was against the context of such perceived dangers that the fiduciary duties of the agent have developed. Their potential breadth is related to the breadth of the common law of agency itself, which does not in general utilise categories, and applies to many types of representative, some of which (e.g. solicitors) would hardly be regarded in some other countries as within the law of agency at all. Where detailed control of types of agent has been introduced, as in the case of estate agents,[5] this has been done in the interest of protecting the principal against the agent, not the reverse; or even (as in the case of financial intermediaries[6]) in the interest of protecting the public.

Thus it was perhaps not surprising that the Law Commission for England and Wales in 1977 reported rather hysterically that the proposed directive "in many respects offend[s] against basic principles of the English law of agency"[7]: but this was not so. It also stated that it was "unable to identify such a social group [as commercial agents] in England"[8]: a claim that was speedily rebutted in the press at the time and, after a gap, by litigation. A more measured report of a committee of the House of Lords assessed the proposal as one to introduce detailed regulation in an area in which it did not exist in the UK,[9] and this was correct. It may also be true that in the UK agents of the type regulated by the Directive are less frequently used as instruments of market penetration than in some other countries.

11-002　**The EC Directive**　The Council Directive on the Co-ordination of the Laws of the Member States Relating to Self-Employed Commercial Agents[10] was adopted in 1986, but the UK and Ireland were given more time to bring it into force, on the

---

3　*Centrosteel srl v Adipol GmbH* (C-456/98) [2000] E.C.R. I-6007, para.13.
4　See Article 43 onwards.
5　See, e.g. above, paras 7-020 and 7-038.
6　See Financial Services and Markets Act 2000.
7　*Law Com. No.84* (1977) (reproduced in Randolph and Davey, fn.1 above, Appendix 4), p.32.
8　*Law Com. No.84* (1977), p.6.
9　*Select Committee on the European Communities*, 51st Report, Session 1976–1977 (reproduced in Randolph and Davey, fn.1 above, Appendix 5).
10　Directive 86/653 [1986] OJ L382/17. Its protective function is stressed in *Bellone v Yokohama SpA* (C-215/97) [1998] E.C.R. I-2191, where it was held that a national law requiring such an agent to register cannot prevent the application of the Directive. See also regarding registration *Centrosteel*

(rather dubious) grounds, stated in the preamble to the Directive, that "a particular effort" had to be made in those countries. In the UK the "particular effort" proved to be confined to copying out the Directive almost verbatim (with two minor errors) and leaving others to interpret it as best they could. In Ireland the Directive was put into effect as it stood, with only a few special provisions at the beginning of the regulation. A second regulation was later promulgated there to make the choice required by the Directive between indemnity and compensation. Time was also granted to Italy, where such protection of the agent existed, but was in fact more elaborate and complex than elsewhere. The Directive has considerable similarities with German law,[11] and reference to German law in particular may therefore sometimes assist in elucidating its likely intention, though it is obviously not to be presumed that the Directive simply intended to generalise the results obtained in any one national system of law. There is no objection to the protection being extended more widely than the Directive requires, i.e. to services, and it should be noted that in some countries (e.g. Germany, France) this has been done.[12]

2. THE COMMERCIAL AGENTS REGULATIONS

The Commercial Agents (Council Directive) Regulations 1993   The Directive   **11-003**
was implemented in Great Britain by the Commercial Agents (Council Directive) Regulations 1993,[13] made under s.2(2) of the European Communities Act 1972. These came into effect on January 1, 1994. They were not confined to contracts made after that date, and hence contracts of agency whenever made were subject to them, save in respect of rights and liabilities accrued before that date.[14]

Interpretation   On general principles of EU law the Regulations must be   **11-004**
interpreted against the background of the Directive itself.[15] Since the wording of the Regulations follows the Directive extremely closely, the Directive is relevant not only as to general purpose but also as to matters of detail. As will be seen, however, the Directive, and hence the Regulations, contain many obscurities and uncertainties. Some of these derive from the structure of the Directive itself: for example, the extent to which particular provisions are *ius cogens*, i.e. cannot be

---

Srl v Adipol GmbH (C-456/98) [2000] E.C.R. I-6007; *Caprini v Conservatore Camera di Commercio, etc.* (C-485/01) [2003] E.C.R. I-2371.

[11] For a brief account of the relevant German law in English, see Reiling, in Randolph and Davey, fn.1 above, Ch.10. As to French law, see Saintier, in Randolph and Davey, fn.1 above, Ch.11; Saintier and Scholes, fn.1 above, esp. Ch.6.

[12] For example, in connection with services: see below para.11-016.

[13] SI 1993/3053, as amended by Commercial Agents (Council: Directive) (Amendment) Regulations 1993 (SI 1993/3173) and Commercial Agents (Council Directive) (Amendment) Regulations 1998 (SI 1998/2868). Effect was given to the Directive in Northern Ireland by the Commercial Agents (Council Directive) Regulations (Northern Ireland) 1993 (SR 1993/483), which was effective on a different date, January 13, 1994. See Schrire (1994) 15 B.L.R. 171; Hodgkinson (1994) 5 E.B.L.Rev 119; Singleton [1994] Tr. L. 26; Bell and O'Toole (1994) 138 S.J. 10; Davis (1994) 144 N.L.J. 388. The Directive applies also to countries in the European Economic Area.

[14] SI 1993/3053 reg.23. The Regulations therefore permitted calculation of indemnity in respect of events occurring before that date, because no right or liability in respect of them accrued at the time of those events but rather, the right to indemnity accrued after that date: *Moore v Piretta PTA Ltd* [1999] 1 All E.R. 174 at 180.

[15] See, e.g. *Von Colson v Land Nordrhein-Westfalen* [1984] E.C.R. 1891; [1986] 2 C.M.L.R. 430; *Litster v Forth Dry Dock & Engineering Co Ltd* [1990] 1 A.C. 546; *Marleasing v La Comercial International de Alimentacion SA* (C-106/89) [1990] 1 E.C.R. 4135; [1992] 1 C.M.L.R. 305; *Moore v Piretta PTA Ltd* [1999] 1 All E.R. 174 at 180.

derogated from, as opposed to *ius dispositivum*, i.e. provisions which only apply in the absence of other agreement, is far from clear.[16] Other problems derive from words selected by translators.[17] It is sometimes appropriate to look at the original proposals for a Directive and the Explanatory Memorandum and see what changes were made in the final form of the Directive.[18] It should be noted that the individual Regulations are preceded by headings. These do not (apart from the chapter headings) appear in the Directive itself. While instructive as to the beliefs of the English drafter, therefore, they provide no certain guide to the intentions of the Directive. The same is true of material issued by the Department of Trade and Industry at the time.[19] Standard English methods of statutory interpretation, or assumptions that common law techniques will fill gaps, will in many cases of dispute, however convenient, be not at all appropriate. The point that what is required is development of "Euro-law" in this context (as in others) is often made.[20] There are certainly areas in which different decisions may be given in different countries; and there are several areas in which the interaction with domestic law is not clear.[21]

The departure of the UK from the EU will however in the end raise considerable problems for decision. On the face of it the Regulations, though they implement an EU Directive, are UK legislation and as such open to be abolished or modified. But the Court of Justice of the European Union has had the power to respond to a request for a preliminary ruling on the meaning of a Directive and the extent to which national law complies with it. Under s.6 of the European Union Withdrawal Act 2018 this will no longer apply. But less directly the Regulations do have considerable EU content. In Pt I, on application, they make reference to an employ the notion of "Member States". This is modified to include states of the European Economic Area, which it is possible that the UK may join. But there is also within the rest of the Regulations a considerable input from EU cases, including in particular one on reference from the Court of Appeal of England and Wales, subsequently followed, which requires that the Regulations be applied whatever the governing law of a commercial agency contract.[22] Since the notion of a commercial agent, and special protection for such agents is, apart from these Regulations, unfamiliar in the UK, it has also been inevitable that guidance be sought from EU and other foreign cases. As stated above, it has also been argued that the Directive, and hence the Regulations, must be given an independent "Euro" interpretation. None of this has always been followed, but arguments based on EU and foreign law certainly appear in this chapter. There are provisions for retention of existing EU law in ss.2–7 of the 2018 Act, which do not bind the Supreme Court of the United Kingdom, and s.26 of the European Union (Withdrawal Agreement) Act 2020 makes further provision for administrative regulation regarding the powers of other courts in respect of retained EU law. All this means that the courts will

---

[16] See, e.g. below, paras 11-033, 11-035 and 11-041.
[17] See, e.g. below, paras 11-024, 11-025, 11-034 and 11-048. A much larger number was listed by the Law Commission, fn.7 above: see Randolph and Davey, fn.1 above, Appendix 4, Annex C (actually omitted).
[18] See Randolph and Davey, fn.1 above, Appendix 4, Annex A.
[19] These are printed in Randolph and Davey, fn.1 above, Appendices 2 and 3.
[20] See, e.g. Tosato (2016) 36 O.J.L.S. 661.
[21] An obvious example is provided by regs 16 and 18, below, paras 11-039 and 11-056.
[22] *Ingmar GB Ltd v Eaton Leonard Technologies Ltd* (C-381/98) [2001] 1 All E.R.(Comm) 329. See below, para.11-006.

in this context (as in many others) require guidance from the Brexit legislation as to dealing with relevant decisions of the CJEU and associated material.

3. APPLICATION OF THE REGULATIONS

Coverage By reg.1(2) the Regulations cover the relations between commercial agents and their principals. They therefore apply only to the internal agency relationship between principal and agent. They do not affect the external authority of the agent, nor the result of transactions entered into by him with third parties. **11-005**

Applicability: conflict of laws[23] Regulation 1(2) states that the Regulations "apply in relation to the activities of commercial agents in Great Britain". It appears therefore that the test for application of the British[24] regulations is principally based on where the activities are conducted, i.e. is geographical. There is no requirement that the agent maintain any place of business in Great Britain. There is no definition of "activities" but the word presumably refers to the typical acts of such an agent, as defined in the Regulations, in soliciting and introducing business and in general acting on the principal's behalf.[25] Since the criterion of application is geographical, many questions of how far this can be done from outside by electronic means remain to be settled. It will be seen from the illustrations below that this basic requirement does not always fit neatly with the choice of law applicable to the internal relationship between principal and agent by virtue of the (later) Rome I Regulation on the Law Applicable to Contractual Obligations ("Rome I").[26] **11-006**

Under the Rome I Regulation, which is discussed in more detail in Chapter 12, the parties may choose a law governing such a contract. If they do not, the Regulation provides that a contract for the provision of services shall be governed by the law of the country in which the service provider (in our context the commercial agent[27]) had his habitual residence[28]; or, if this category is not applicable, by the law of the country in which the person rendering the characteristic performance of the contract (in our context, plainly the agent)[29] had his habitual residence.[30]

The general scheme of the British Commercial Agents Regulations is that their operation is territorial: they govern the relations between commercial agents and their principals and apply in relation to activities of such agents in Great Britain.

---

[23] See Dicey, Morris and Collins, *The Conflict of Laws* (15th edn), Vol.2, para.33-420 onwards. Some of this discussion concerns applicability and does not rank as within the conflict of laws.

[24] Northern Ireland is separately provided for: see SI 1993/483 (NI).

[25] See the description in the opinion of Advocate General Trstenjak referred to in fn.27 below.

[26] Regulation 593/2008 [2008] OJ L177/6, which applies to contracts concluded as from December 17, 2009.

[27] In *Wood Floor Solutions Andreas Domberger GmbH v Silvo Trade SA* (C-19/09) [2010] 1 W.L.R. 1900, the ECJ treated a commercial agency contract as one for the provision of services under Article 5(1)(b) of Council Regulation 44/2001 on jurisdiction and the enforcement of judgments. See the judgment, and in more detail the opinion of Advocate General Trstenjak at [53] onwards. See above, para.1-035.

[28] Rome I Regulation Article 4(1)(b). In so far as the agent is also a franchisee or distributor, the same criterion is applied by Article 4(1)(e) and (f).

[29] Rome I Regulation Articles 3 and 4: see below; *Lawlor v Sandvik Mining and Construction Mobile Crushers and Screens Ltd* [2012] EWHC 1188 (QB); [2012] 2 Lloyd's Rep. 25 (art.4(2) applied: governed by Spanish law). Some agency contracts might rank as consumer contracts (the principal being the consumer) and be governed by Article 6.

[30] "Habitual residence" is defined broadly in Article 19 (see below, para.12-005) and in general in the commercial context denotes something like establishment, which word will be used in the rest of this chapter.

There is no statement specifically directed towards the conflict of laws position, but the starting point has to be the normal one, that the Regulations, being part of English law,[31] should only apply where English law is the governing law. But they may also be superimposed as a matter of public policy on contracts governed by other laws where they involve activities in Great Britain: Articles 9.1 and 2 of the Rome I Regulation allow a court to apply overriding mandatory provisions of the law of the forum to a contract governed by another law,[32] and it seems clear, as is stated below, that the Commercial Agents Regulations, or at any rate their unexcludable part, rank as such. One way of achieving this overriding application in connection with international instruments has been to provide an enacting statute that enables them to have the "force of law". This was done with the Hague-Visby Rules,[33] which contain within them a provision which prevents contracting out in certain circumstances.[34] This has enabled striking out of clauses indirectly inconsistent with the regime of the Rules, for example a jurisdiction clause for a country which would not apply them.[35] The jurisdiction clause in question was embedded in a choice of law clause, and it is possible that the choice of law clause was intended by the court to be void also, which would have necessitated, had a relevant issue arisen, a fresh search for the applicable law. It is submitted that this should not have been so, as the Hague and Hague-Visby Rules do not supersede a whole contract (for example, they have no application to freight) but simply declare invalid certain types of terms within it. There is no such drafting technique used in the Commercial Agents Regulations, but they implement an EU policy directed to the protection of agents so should be regarded as overriding before courts within the EU.[36] They may also justify declaring void particular clauses in the governing law which might indirectly interfere with the operation of the Regulations: for example a jurisdiction or arbitration clause requiring proceedings in a country where the Regulations would, or might, not be applied. To negate a choice of law clause would however be to produce a need for a governing law for the unobjectionable provisions of the contract.

The geographical application of the Regulations has two exceptions. First, if the parties to a contract involving activity of a commercial agent in Great Britain have agreed that the agency contract is to be governed by the law of another Member

---

[31] References to English law are hereafter for the purpose of simplicity of exposition, and cover England and Wales. Where Scots law is relevant parallel reasoning will usually apply.

[32] See Dicey, Morris and Collins, *The Conflict of Laws* (15th edn), Vol.2, para.32-092 onwards. A possibly relevant provision is Article 23, similar to but not identical with Article 20 of the Rome Convention, which provides that the Regulation does not prejudice the application of provisions of Community law which, in relation to particular matters, lay down conflict of laws rules relating to contractual obligations. But it is not clear to what extent reg.1(2) and (3) are to be so regarded, and in any case it is only the operation of the Rome I Regulation which is potentially displaced. There are also provisions permitting the application of overriding law where all other elements relevant to the situation at the time of choice of law are located other than in a country whose law has been chosen, or one or more Member States: Articles 3.3 and 4; as to which see Dicey, Morris and Collins, *The Conflict of Laws* (15th edn), Vol.2, Rule 224.

[33] Carriage of Goods by Sea Act 1971 s.1(2).

[34] Hague-Visby Rules Article III.8.

[35] *The Hollandia* [1983] 1 A.C. 565 (Dutch jurisdiction clause: Dutch law had not at that time adopted the Visby Protocol to the Hague Rules and retained the Hague Rules, which gave less protection to cargo claimants than the Hague-Visby Rules: clause invalid at least in part).

[36] See *Accentuate Ltd v Asigra Inc* [2009] EWHC 2655 (QB); [2009] 2 Lloyd's Rep. 599 (considered below) at [97] onwards.

State,[37] the provisions of the law of that Member State corresponding to the operative part of the Regulations apply.[38] The Regulations stop there, but as regards other matters within the agency contract, the law of that state applies by virtue of the choice of law rules of the Rome I Regulation.

Secondly, they apply to the activities of an English established agent in another Member State where the law of that State enables the parties so to agree that the contract is governed by a foreign law, and they agree that it is governed by English law.[39] Presumably, the Rome I Regulation as applicable in that state, with its acceptance of the principle of choice (and the specific provisions of Article 4), would normally do so. This is in a sense the reciprocal of the previous provision.[40]

If however there is no choice of law, but English law applies by virtue of the Rome I Regulation, the British Regulations, which apply only to activities in England, do not in the above case apply.[41] It might be hoped that the law of the place of acting would do so.

A more controversial matter is whether the overriding mandatory nature of much of the Regulations applies (especially Articles 17 and 18 on indemnity and compensation) where the contract is expressed to be governed by the law of another country (outside the EU), which may know no such protection of agents; or where the law of such a country applies by virtue of the Rome I provisions on the applicable law in the absence of choice because the agent is established[42] in that country. It might be thought not, on the ground that the preamble to the Commercial Agents Directive refers to the mischief potentially occurring "where principal and agent are domiciled in different Member States". The European Court of Justice, on a reference from the Court of Appeal for England and Wales, held however in *Ingmar GB Ltd v Eaton Leonard Technologies Inc*[43] that the provisions apply on two grounds: that the parties should not be able to evade the Directive by "the simple expedient of a choice-of-law clause", and that "the purpose served by the provisions in question requires that they be applied where the situation is closely connected with the Community, in particular where the commercial agent carries on his activity in the territory of a Member State, irrespective of the law by which the parties intended the contract to be governed".[44] This means that the Regulations should certainly be regarded as overriding mandatory rules of the forum and before an English court should (it is submitted) be superimposed on a contract involving activities of a commercial agent in England, by whatever law the agency contract is governed.[45]

This has was confirmed in an English case where the agent's activities were subject to an express choice of the law of Ontario, and furthermore an arbitral tribunal in Canada had rendered an award applying that law and not taking into account the Regulations.[46] On general conflict of laws principles the arbitral tribunal must have been correct: (subject to different considerations within the EU) one country does not apply the public policy of another unless the law of that country is the governing law. But before an English court the result would not be acceptable by reason of EU-based regulations. It was therefore held that the arbitration clause was void before an English court, and this is similar to the refusal, referred to above, to accept a Dutch jurisdiction clause where the Hague-Visby Rules were mandatory for shipments out of the UK, and a Dutch court, applying Dutch law, would have rendered a decision different to that required by those Rules.[47]

The court however went on to grant leave to serve out of the jurisdiction on the basis that the contract was governed by English law, arguing that there was no other candidate to govern the compensation claim under the Regulations than English law. But the requirement is that the contract be governed by English law, not merely a part of it, albeit a discrete part.[48] The Commercial Agents Regulations are not all mandatory, nor do they apply to all parts of a contract involving the activities of a commercial agent, as is shown by the extensive issues in the dispute itself. In the *Ingmar* case referred to above the ECJ simply said that it should not be possible to evade the Regulations by the simple expedient of a choice-of-law clause[49]: but that does not mean that the only way to prevent evasion is to nullify a choice of law altogether. It is submitted that the contract was still governed by the law of Ontario[50] even if parts of it were unenforceable or inoperative and subjected to different terms[51] before an English court by reason of English (EU-originating) public policy.

---

[44] See the judgment at [25].

[45] Where legislation under the Directive is in a particular Member State wider than is required by the Directive, e.g. in applying to services, and the governing law is that of another State which has correctly implemented the minimum protection required by the Directive, the additional protection provided by the first State is only to be applied by a court in the first State if it finds that it is crucial in its legal order to give protection beyond that provided by the Directive: *United Antwerp Maritime Agencies (Unamar) NV v Navigation Maritime Bulgaria* (C-184/12) [2014] 1 Lloyd's Rep. 161 (concerning an arbitration clause in a contract governed by Bulgarian law which a Dutch court had held invalid).

[46] *Accentuate Ltd v Asigra Inc* [2009] EWHC 2655 (QB); [2009] 2 Lloyd's Rep. 599. A German court rendered a very similar decision in 2006: OLG München, May 17, 2006—7 U.1781/06, though perhaps going too far in looking to see only if it was "likely" that the designated tribunal would not apply arts 17 and 18, See Rühl, fn.43 above.

[47] *The Hollandia* [1983] 1 A.C. 565: see above.

[48] CPR r.6.20(5).

[49] See the judgment at [25].

[50] There is some reference to invalidity of the choice of law, however, in [88].

[51] This of course is different from the Hague and Hague-Visby Rules, which simply proscribe certain types of contract clause.

This view, that the overriding provisions of the Regulations do not necessarily affect choice of law clauses themselves, has recently been accepted.[52]

Some illustrations may be of assistance.

1. *Agent established in Great Britain acts in Great Britain*
    (i) The contract contains a choice of English law. English law is the governing law. The acts are performed in England and the Regulations apply as part of the governing law.
    11-007
    (ii) The contract contains no choice of law. In most cases Article 4 of the Rome I Regulation, referred to above, would require to be invoked, leading to the result that the governing law is English because the agent is established in England. The result will therefore be the same as that in (i).
    (iii) The contract contains a choice of the law of a Member State, for example Dutch law, perhaps because the firm acted for is Dutch. By English law, Dutch law is the governing law of the contract of agency. The choice excludes the British regulations by virtue of reg.1(3)(a)above. Dutch law, and its application of the Directive, will apply.
    (iv) The contract contains a choice of the law of a non-Member State, for example that of California, perhaps because the principal operates in California. English law will accept the chosen law as governing the contract unless all its elements are connected with another country, when non-derogable provisions of that country's law may apply, or all the other relevant elements are located in one or more Member States, in which case non-derogable provisions of Community law may apply.[53] Beyond this, the question arises as to whether the British regulations apply. On their (territorial based) wording they clearly do. And it appears that the application of them to commercial agents acting in Great Britain is an overriding mandatory rule of English law which an English court should apply whatever the governing law.[54] The British regulations therefore apply, but in other respects the contract remains governed by the law of California.
2. *Agent established in the Netherlands acts in Great Britain*
    (i) The contract contains a choice of English law. The governing law is English and the Regulations apply both as part of the governing law and because of their territorial application. It might be arguable that this is only so if Dutch law agrees that English law may govern, under
    11-008

---

[52] *Fern Computer Consultancy Ltd v Intergraph Cadworx & Analysis Solutions Inc* [2014] EWHC 2908 (Ch); [2015] 1 Lloyd's Rep. 1 at [34]. The court went on to say (in the context of service out of the jurisdiction) that the cause of action under the Regulations was not in any case to be classified as contractual, but rather, as statutory (see at [38], [39]), and possibly in the nature of a tort (at [55]). The proposition that the cause of action is statutory would still have permitted a claim "in respect of a contract where the contract ... is governed by English law" for the purposes of CPR Pt 6 had the contract been governed by English law, but it was not. On the other hand, jurisdiction "in respect of a breach of contract committed within the jurisdiction" would not be available at all, because the claim was not for breach of a contract (at [47]). See further below, para.11-040, fn.200.
[53] Articles 3.3 and 3.4 of the Rome I Regulation, above, para.11-006.
[54] *Ingmar GB Ltd v Easton Leonard Technologies Ltd* (C-381/98) [2001] 1 All E.R. (Comm) 329; *Accentuate Ltd v Asigra Inc* [2009] EWHC 2655; [2009] 2 Lloyd's Rep. 599, both discussed above, para.11-006.

the wording of reg.1(3)(b), but it is difficult to see any reason why this should be required before an English court.

(ii) The contract contains no choice of law. The governing law will probably be Dutch under art.4 of the Rome I Regulation, as the law of the agent's place of establishment. It might then be argued that the Dutch rules would apply as part of the governing law: but it seems preferable to say that the territorial application of the British regulations means that before an English court they apply to the contract as overriding policy of the forum, and that the parties have not agreed otherwise, which is what reg.1(3)(a) of the Regulations requires. In other respects the contract is governed by Dutch law.

(iii) The contract contains a choice of Dutch law. Dutch law is the governing law. The British regulations do not apply: reg.1(3)(a). The Dutch implementation of the Directive applies.

(iv) The contract contains a choice of German law (perhaps because the principal is German). By the same reasoning as that in (iii) above, German law is the governing law and the German implementation of the Directive applies as part of the governing law under reg.1(3)(a). If the Dutch law would (before a Dutch court) have regarded itself as applicable and is different, the English court would not apply it, as not being part of the governing law nor of that of the forum.

(v) The contract contains a choice of the law of California (perhaps because the principal is from California). The law of California is the governing law. The reasoning of the *Ingmar* case, discussed above, would again lead to the conclusion that the British regulations should be superimposed on the contract.

3. *Agent established in England or Wales acts in the Netherlands*

11-009

(i) The contract contains a choice of English law. English law is the governing law. Under reg.1(3)(b) the English regulations apply if Dutch law allows the choice of law. If not (which is no doubt unlikely), they do not. The English court could, however, apply Dutch law as overriding mandatory provisions of the law of the place of performance, by virtue of Article 9.3 of the Rome I Regulation.[55]

(ii) The contract contains no choice of law. The governing law is likely to be English, as that of the place of establishment of the agent, but the British regulations apply only to activities in Great Britain. An English court could however again apply the Dutch law by virtue of Article 9.3 of the Rome I Regulation.

(iii) The contract contains a choice of German law (the principal may be German). German law is the governing law. With their territorial basis, the British regulations do not apply. The German version may.[56]

(iv) The contract contains a choice of the law of California. The governing law is the law of California. With their territorial basis, the English regulations do not apply. An English court could again

---

[55] See Dicey Morris and Collins, *The Conflict of Laws* (15th edn), Vol.2, para.32-094 onwards.

[56] It is difficult to believe that this can be by virtue of reg.1(3)(a) of the Regulations: despite reg.4(2) being made subject to para.(3), reg.1(3)(a) surely applies only where the activities are conducted in Great Britain.

however apply the Dutch law by virtue of Article 9.3 of the Rome I Regulation.

4. *Agent established in California acts in England*

(i) The contract contains a choice of English law. English law is the governing law and on the territorial basis also the Regulations apply. **11-010**

(ii) The contract contains a choice of the law of California. That law governs. On a territorial basis however the Regulations apply even though there might have been justification for the choice of law. The regulations apply on the basis of the *Ingmar* and *Accentuate* cases, discussed above.

(iii) The contract contains no choice of law. The law of California will probably govern as that of the place of establishment of the agent. It could be argued that the law of California alone should apply, but it seems that the relevant parts of the Regulations should again apply on a territorial basis.

Regulations applicable by agreement of the parties The Regulations largely operate by implying terms into or imposing them upon contracts. There seems no reason why parties should not expressly or impliedly incorporate the Regulations even when they are not compulsorily applicable, though problems of interpretation would arise in respect of the provisions against derogation.[57] Conversely, they do not exclude law applicable overall, except where they are mandatory, and although the common law is not clear on some of the matters covered, a common law claim should often be considered, for example where it is not clear that the claimant ranks within the definition of a commercial agent. **11-011**

Activities This word has already been discussed. It remains to note that since nothing in the Regulations requires the presence of the agent at the place where the activities are conducted, problems will arise as to where the activities of an agent who operates from one country into another by means of telephone, telex, fax or the internet are to be regarded as taking place. Where an agent conducts activities in several jurisdictions, the Regulations presumably apply only in respect of the activities in Great Britain.[58] **11-012**

What is a commercial agent? The term "commercial agent" is, as stated above, unknown to the common law; and the definition in the Regulations is therefore crucial. A designation by the contract itself, or by the parties, cannot be conclusive.[59] Such an agent is defined in reg.2(1) as: **11-013**

---

[57] This is accepted in *Tamarind International Ltd v Eastern Natural Gas (Retail) Ltd* [2000] C.L.C. 1397; [2000] Eu. L.R. 708; and in *McQuillan v McCormick* [2010] EWHC 1112 (QB); [2011] E.C.C. 18.

[58] Beyond the requirement of activities in Great Britain the Regulations do not specify where activities are to take place. It has been held that provided that it does not affect his independence, the fact that the commercial agent's activities were carried out on the principal's premises do not prevent him from being classified as a commercial agent: *Zako SPRL v Sanidel SA (C-452/17)* EU:C:2018:935; [2019] Bus. L.R. 343.

[59] See *Blanc Canet v Europcar France SA* [2005] E.C.C. 34 (French Cour de Cassation).

"a self-employed intermediary who has continuing authority to negotiate the sale or purchase of goods on behalf of another person (the 'principal'), or to negotiate and conclude the sale or purchase of goods on behalf of and in the name of that principal."[60]

There are specific exceptions which are dealt with below. Since "the terms and content of an agent's authority may, change or reduce during the course of an agency as the result of agreement by words or conduct, or sometimes as a result of external events", it has been held that "the relevant time at which to determine the scope of the agent's retainer is...the date on which it is necessary to determine whether it is or is not a commercial agent for the purposes of the relief being claimed".[61]

It is, however, clear that the Directive and Regulations refer to an *agent*. A person who has no function but to transmit the goods in question on predetermined terms and at predetermined prices is not covered.[62] A *distributor* of goods, though often described as an "agent", buys for resale and, unlike an agent, takes a financial risk.[63] Although in some countries distributors and sometimes franchisees may be entitled to protections similar to those afforded to agents, the Directive and regulations are not intended to cover distributors.[64] It is of course possible for a distributor to perform an appropriate agency function also. This would raise a question of whether

---

[60] The Regulations appear to envisage agents acting for multiple principals, and that they do so was held in *Rossetti Marketing Ltd v Diamond Sofa Co Ltd* [2011] EWHC 2482 (QB); [2011] E.C.C. 28, the point being made that the obligation under Article 3 to act "dutifully and in good faith", together with the normal fiduciary duties applicable under English law should protect the principal against abuse by the agent by preferring one customer over another and so forth. On appeal the general possibility was not doubted, but it was held that the normal fiduciary rules and the rules as to implied terms operated to prevent the agent acting without the principal's consent for competitors whose products clashed with those of the principal: see [2012] EWCA Civ 1021; [2013] 1 All E.R. (Comm) 308, esp. at [27] and [42].

[61] *W Nagel (A Firm) v Pluczenik Diamond Co NV* [2017] EWHC 1750 (Comm); [2017] 2 Lloyd's Rep. 215 at [43], per Popplewell J (affirmed on other points, [2018] EWCA Civ 2640; [2019] Bus. L.R. 692). But cf. [44]; also the position as regards secondary activity, below, para.11-022, fn.118.

[62] But the fact that the agent performs other functions for his principal not ranking as secondary within art.2(3) does not affect his status as an independent intermediary: *Zako SPRL v Sanidel SA (C-452/17)* EU:C:2018:935; [2019] Bus. L.R. 343 (agent to negotiate sale of kitchens performed various other functions regarding design and management of staff).

[63] See above, para.1-035.

[64] *AMB Imballaggi Plastici Srl v Pacflex Ltd* [1999] 2 All E.R. (Comm) 249; [1999] C.L.C. 1391; *Mercantile International Group Plc v Chuan Soon Huat Industrial Group Ltd* [2002] EWCA Civ 288; [2002] 1 All E.R. (Comm) 788 (remuneration partly by mark-up to which principal did not object: sale plainly on an agency basis): cf. *Umbro International Ltd v Revenue & Customs Commissioners* [2009] EWHC 438 (Ch); [2009] S.T.C. 1345 (purchase for resale to "principal"); *Crane v Sky In-Home Service Ltd* [2007] EWHC 66 (Ch); [2007] 2 All E.R. (Comm) 599 (agent supplied digital boxes, but acted as agent for digital services: held commercial agent in respect of boxes); *Sagal v Atelier Bunz GmbH* [2009] EWCA Civ 700; [2009] 2 Lloyd's Rep. 303 (agent who acts in own name is not a commercial agent). This appears to exclude cases of indirect representation (above, para.1-021), which seems correct. The actual nature of the contract between the parties is not considered, but it does not appear to have been a sale and resale. (See also the *Mavrona* case regarding indirect agents, fn.101 below, not referred to in the *Sagal* case). Agreements between principal and an agent who does not bear any significant risk in relation to the contracts concluded and/or negotiated on behalf of the principal will normally not be subject to Article 101 TFEU (Treaty on the Functions of the European Union) (formerly Article 81 EC). The relevant principles, in particular in relation to relevant risks, are discussed in paras 12–21 of the European Commission's Guidelines on Vertical Restraints [2010] OJ C 130/1, replacing the Commission's earlier Guidelines on Vertical Restraints [2000] OJ C 291/1.

the activity is secondary or not.[65] A broker acting independently of both parties is not a commercial agent.[66]

Sub-agency The Regulations appear to be drafted on the basis of a contract of **11-014** agency.[67] Thus it has been held that if an agent appoints a sub-agent or sub-agents, and if there is no privity of contract between them and the principal (which is the normal interpretation in English law[68]) the sub-agents are not agents of the principal so as to be entitled to claim compensation under the Regulations even though they negotiate, and/or sell the goods.[69] Nor are they commercial agents of the main agent, since they do not sell on his behalf.[70] It has been suggested that they might be able to "establish a stake" in the compensation due to the main agent,[71] and perhaps this is an indication that the result described above is unlikely to have been intended.[72] The position of sub-agents who have no privity with the principal is in fact controversial in other contexts of agency law as well.[73] A practical solution for the present situation could be to determine on the facts that in such cases they have privity with the principal.[74]

Self-employed This phrase to a common lawyer contains echoes of employ- **11-015** ment law. An employee must be a natural person; hence it might be thought that the reference to self-employment carried the same implication. It seems clear that in this context that is a wrong inference and that the reference is rather to what at common law might be called an independent contractor. Hence a company or partnership can be a commercial agent.[75] In a useful case where an employee agent changed his status to that of an independent commercial agent[76] the court applied English notions of employment law in considering the effect of the change; but it has been argued that primary recourse should have been had to European materials.[77]

Sale or purchase of goods It is convenient next to note that the protection only **11-016** applies to agents who act in connection with sale or purchase of goods, and does not cover agents whose principal activity lies in the provision of services, though similar legislation in other countries (e.g. France and Germany) does so, thus extending the protection. The fact, however, that an agent for sale provides ancillary servicing facilities does not prevent his being a commercial agent. But when

---

[65] See below, para.11-020.
[66] *Ferro v Santoro OJ 2002* (C-323/24); cf. above, para.1-034.
[67] See regs 13, 17(1).
[68] See Article 35.
[69] *Light v Ty Europe Ltd* [2003] EWCA Civ 1238; [2004] 1 Lloyd's Rep. 693.
[70] *Light v Ty Europe Ltd* [2003] EWCA Civ 1238 at [26].
[71] *Light v Ty Europe Ltd* [2003] EWCA Civ 1238 at [26], per Tuckey LJ.
[72] See Tosato [2013] L.M.C.L.Q. 544, arguing in general that insufficient attention has been paid, at any rate in English courts, to the European dimension of the Regulations. cf. above, para.11-004. The relevant discussion of the present point is at 561–565. Such a restriction does not operate in France: Saintier, in Randolph and Davey, fn.1 above, p.161.
[73] See above, paras 5-011 and 5-012.
[74] See above, para.5-010.
[75] The Regulations were applied to a corporate agent in the *Imballaggi* case, fn.64 above. See *Bell Electric Ltd v Aweco Appliances Systems GmbH & Co KG* [2002] EWHC 872 (QB); [2002] Eu.L.R. 443 at [50] (argument to the contrary "wholly unsustainable") (proceedings on appeal [2002] EWCA Civ 1501; [2003] 1 All E.R. 344).
[76] *Smith v Reliance Water Controls Ltd* [2003] EWCA Civ 1153; [2003] Eu.L.R. 874.
[77] See Tosato [2013] L.M.C.L.Q. 544 at 551–553.

it is the selling which is subsidiary, this activity could in Great Britain rank as merely "secondary" under another provision of the Regulations, and they might not then apply.[78] It seems likely that the question whether a contract for work and materials involves a sale of goods will require solution on the basis of asking which element is predominant, as under current English law.[79] There is no definition of "goods".[80] The main problem regularly arising in this connection in the modern context is whether computer software ranks as "goods".[81] Contracts relating to such software are often, however, drafted in other ways, in particular as licences, and this raises special problems.[82]

11-017 **Continuing authority** The authority must be continuing; an agent appointed for a single transaction would not be covered, for if he were, there would be no force in the word "continuing". But it would seem that the phrase "continuing authority" could cover an agent appointed for a number of transactions, definite or indefinite, for a period or for a season (e.g. Christmas),[83] or an agent whose activities are repeatedly accepted by the principal.[84] It has been held, though in the context of legislation applying the provisions to services (chartering), that this covers an agent who negotiates one contract which is then renewed over a period.[85] It has been said that "the question whether an agent has continuing authority to negotiate is a question which is to be determined by the terms of the contract with the principal, not by the extent or frequency of the exercise of that authority".[86]

---

[78] See below, para.11-020 onwards.

[79] The question is discussed in connection with a firm supplying and erecting conservatories in *Marjandi Ltd v Bon Accord Glass Ltd* (Sheriff J.K. Tierney, 2007 WL 4947410). The contract was held to be one for the building of an extension, with the result that the Regulations were not relevant. Tosato [2013] L.M.C.L.Q. 544 at 558–561 suggests the use of a phrase "focal point".

[80] In *Commission of the European Communities v Italy* (7/68) [1968] E.C.R. 423, the ECJ gave a meaning for "goods" for the purposes of art.9 of the Treaty: "By goods, within the meaning of that provision, there must be understood products which can be valued in money and which are capable, as such, of forming the subject of commercial transactions". This gives general guidance, but the differing contexts in which the notion has been considered mean that analysis in a specific context is required. Tosato [2013] L.M.C.L.Q. 544, again argues that European criteria should be employed. In *Tamarind International Ltd v Eastern Natural Gas (Retail) Ltd* [2000] Eur.L.R. 708, gas (and perhaps electricity) were assumed to be "goods"; and this was so held in *Green Deal Marketing Southern Ltd v Economy Energy Trading Ltd* [2019] EWHC 507 (Ch); [2019] 2 All E.R.(Comm) 191.

[81] It has now been held in *Computer Associates UK Ltd v Software Incubator Ltd* [2018] EWCA Civ 518; [2018] 1 Lloyd's Rep. 613 that computer software supplied electronically and not on any tangible medium does not rank as "goods" for this purpose (points referred by UKSC to the CJEU, March 2019). The leading case on the topic has hitherto been *St Albans City and District Council v International Computers Ltd* [1996] 4 All E.R. 481. See further M. Bridge (ed.), *Benjamin's Sale of Goods*, 10th edn (London: Sweet & Maxwell, 2017), para.1-086.

[82] See *London Borough of Southwark v IBM UK Ltd* [2011] EWHC 549 (TCC); 135 Con. L.R. 136. See also *Fern Computer Consultancy Ltd v Intergraph Cadworx & Analysis Solutions Inc* [2014] EWHC 2908 (Ch); [2015] 1 Lloyd's Rep. 1 at [88].

[83] See Saintier and Scholes, fn.1 above, at pp.31–32.

[84] See *Mercantile International Group Plc v Chuan Soon Huat Industrial Group Plc* [2002] EWCA Civ 288; [2002] 1 All E.R. (Comm) 788 at [33]; *W Nagel (A Firm) v Pluczenik Diamond Co NV* [2017] EWHC 1750 (Comm); [2017] 2 Lloyd's Rep. 215 at [55].

[85] See the opinion of Advocate General Geelhoed in *Poseidon Chartering BV v Marianne Zeeschip VOF* (C-3/04) [2007] Bus. L.R. 446; [2006] 2 Lloyd's Rep. 105 (referred to at [25]: but on services—chartering).

[86] *W Nagel (A Firm) v Pluczenik Diamond Co NV* [2017] EWHC 1750 (Comm); [2017] 2 Lloyd's Rep. 215 adding that "An agent may have authority to carry out functions which he never performs or

Negotiate the sale or purchase of goods on behalf of another person: canvass-   **11-018**
ing agents   These words cover agents who are entrusted with negotiation of terms, even though they are not authorised to enter into the final contract itself.[87] It may be questioned whether the wording also covers agents who simply introduce business and leave the principal to negotiate, as in the case (outside the contract of sale of goods and hence outside this context) of estate agents. The category is referred to in this book as one of "canvassing" or "introducing agents".[88] Since in such a case the agent plays a fairly active role on behalf of another it would seem on the wording that the Regulations ought to apply. It seems that actual bargaining is not required[89] and, so long as the agent is not merely passive, he may be regarded as "negotiating".[90] In a recent case an agent was held to rank within these words where what could principally be said was that "the generation and maintenance of [the principal's] goodwill with [the third party] was at the heart of the services which [the agent] was engaged to perform".[91] But some such intermediaries would not be regarded as commercial agents in at least some continental European countries accepting the notion of commercial agent,[92] and of course an estate agent is not likely to be classified as a commercial agent either, quite apart from the fact that he acts in connection with land and not goods. It seems likely that a key lies in the requirement of continuing authority referred to above. A canvassing agent who holds himself out as available to anyone would not be a commercial agent; but one who canvasses on what one could call a "retained" basis could, at least unless he is actually forbidden to solicit contractual offers.[93] Where it can be said that he has no duty to act, problems may arise as to whether he has a *contract* of agency at all.[94]

Negotiate and conclude the sale or purchase of goods on behalf of and in the   **11-019**
name of the principal   This obviously covers agents who are actually authorised to contract on behalf of their principals, including those who acquire repeat orders.[95] The requirement that the agent do so "in the name of", as well as "on behalf of",

---

performs only occasionally": per Popplewell J at [44] (affirmed without reference to this point, [2018] EWCA Civ 2640; [2019] Bus. L.R. 692).

[87]   See *Sagal v Atelier Bunz GmbH* [2009] EWCA Civ 700; [2009] 2 Lloyd's Rep. 303 at [12].
[88]   See above, para.1-020. The term "marketing agent" is also used.
[89]   *Parks v Esso Petroleum Co Ltd* [2000] Eu. L.R. 25 at 32, quoting the Oxford English Dictionary definition "deal with, manage or conduct".
[90]   See the cases cited in fn.91.
[91]   *W Nagel (A Firm) v Pluczenik Diamond Co NV* [2017] EWHC 1750 (Comm); [2017] 2 Lloyd's Rep. 215 at [54] (diamond broking: indicating functions performed) (affirmed without reference to this point, [2018] EWCA Civ 2640; [2019] Bus. L.R. 692).
[92]   Where some intermediaries may be called "courtier", "makler", "mediatore", etc. See *Ferro v Santoro OJ 2002* (C-323/24).
[93]   An agent who effected introductions and played a significant role in persuading third parties to be interested but had no authority to agree terms or prices was held a commercial agent in *PJ Pipe and Valve Co Ltd v Audco India Ltd* [2005] EWHC 1904 (QB); [2006] Eu.L.R. 368; and *Nigel Fryer Joinery Services Ltd v Ian Firth Hardware Ltd* [2008] EWHC 767 (Ch); [2008] 2 Lloyd's Rep. 108; see also *Kenny v Ireland Roc Ltd* 2005 IEHC 241 (Ireland), supporting the argument, but doubting the result in *Parks v Esso Petroleum Co Ltd* [2000] E.C.C. 45; [2000] Eu. L.R. 25 (petrol retailer: as to which see Saintier and Scholes, fn.1 above, at pp.39–40). A useful discussion is to be found in *Invicta UK v International Brands Ltd* [2013] EWHC 1564 (QB); [2013] E.C.C. 30: see at [31]–[32] (sale of wine to supermarkets). An agent whose function was to persuade customers to switch energy supplier but did not negotiate new terms (which were standard) was held a commercial agent in *Green Deal Marketing Southern Ltd v Economy Energy Trading Ltd* [2019] EWHC 507 (Ch); [2019] 2 All E.R.(Comm) 191.
[94]   See above, para.7-016; though this may be a specific common law problem.
[95]   See *Invicta UK v International Brands Ltd* [2013] EWHC 1564 (QB); [2013] E.C.C. 30.

the principal raises problems, as this phrase can be used in civil law but (although it was sometimes used in nineteenth-century cases, usually to differentiate undisclosed principals) has no specific meaning in common law.

Three categories which require consideration in the above context are agents acting for identified principals, agents acting for unidentified principals, and agents acting for undisclosed principals.[96] Clearly, an agent acting for a named principal can be said to act in the principal's name. At common law it is, however, possible that such an agent undertakes personal liability on the contract as well as his principal.[97] Should the agent do this, civil law parallels suggest that he should not be regarded as acting in his own name for the purpose of these regulations in those cases where the agent's liability is upon the same contract; i.e. the words "acts in the name of the principal" should be taken as referring only to an agent who, to use the traditional words, "drops out" of the transaction; but the matter is not at all clear. More difficult is the case of the agent acting for an unidentified principal, for he is more likely (though far from certain) to be regarded at common law as undertaking personal liability.[98] The best view seems to be that here again, if he undertakes no personal liability, but the third party deals solely with the principal, whoever he is, the agent acts in his principal's name: but if the agent undertakes personal liability on the same contract also, it is arguable that he does not do so "in the name of" the principal. The nature of any liability undertaken by the agent may therefore be crucial.[99]

It is, however, difficult to see that an agent acting for an *undisclosed* principal ever acts in the principal's name, for he clearly acts in his own; and indeed the doctrine of the undisclosed principal is a difficult doctrine of common law which those responsible for the Directive are not likely to have had fully in mind. And an agent acting under a contract of *commission*[100] clearly acts in his own name.[101]

11-020 Commercial agency a secondary activity The Regulations do not apply to persons whose activities as commercial agents are to be considered secondary.[102] The meaning of this notion is elaborated for Great Britain[103] by an extensive Schedule to the Regulations which is intended to give further elucidation to the notion of commercial agency and states that where it may reasonably be taken that the primary purpose of the arrangement with the principal is *other than* as set out, the activities of the commercial agent as such are to be considered secondary only. The indications in this schedule are so important to a legal system that has no category

---

[96] For indications of the meaning of these terms, see Article 2.
[97] See Article 98.
[98] See above, para.9-016.
[99] cf. above, para.9-006 onwards. A *del credere* agent (above, para.1-042) only undertakes as such a subsidiary liability and hence should be covered.
[100] Above, para.1-021.
[101] *Mavrona & Sia OE v Delta Etaireia Symmetochon AE* (C-85/03) [2004] E.C.R. I-1573. This is in accord with the later decision taken on other grounds in *Sagal v Atelier Bunz GmbH* [2009] EWCA Civ 700; [2009] 2 Lloyd's Rep. 303. See also *Royal & Sun Alliance Plc v MK Digitial FZE (Cyprus) Ltd* [2006] EWCA Civ 629; [2006] 2 Lloyd's Rep. 110 (interpretation as commissionnaire de transport).
[102] SI 1993/3053 reg.2(4). This exception, and the ways in which it has been utilised in France, Germany and the UK, is convincingly criticised by Saintier [2012] J.B.L. 128. An account of how it operates in France is given by Saintier in Randolph and Davey, fn.1 above, Ch.11.
[103] The application of such a limitation is authorised by art.2(2) of the Directive. This limit was only adopted in some countries. An argument that the implementing provisions were ultra vires was rejected in *Crane v Sky In-Home Service Ltd* [2007] EWHC 66 (Ch); [2007] 2 All E.R. (Comm) 599.

of commercial agent that they require to be set out almost in full. They are stated in para.2 of the Schedule as follows:

"(a)   the business of the principal is the sale, or as the case may be purchase, of goods of a particular kind[104]; and

(b)   the goods concerned are such that—

    (i)   transactions are normally individually negotiated and concluded on a commercial basis, and

    (ii)   procuring a transaction on one occasion is likely to lead to further transactions in those goods with that customer on future occasions, or to transactions in those goods with other customers in the same geographical area or among the same group of customers and

that accordingly it is in the commercial interests of the principal in developing the market in those goods to appoint a representative to such customers with a view to the representative devoting effort, skill and expenditure from his own resources to that end."

There follow in para.3 more specific indications of when an arrangement falls within the above criteria, the absence of any of which is some indication that it does not. They are that:

"(a)   the principal is the manufacturer, importer or distributor of the goods;

(b)   the goods are specifically identified with the principal in the market in question rather than, or to a greater extent than, with any other person;

(c)   the agent devotes substantially the whole of his time to representative activities (whether for one principal or a number of principals whose interests are not conflicting);

(d)   the goods are not normally available in the market in question other than by means of the agent;

(e)   the arrangement is described as one of commercial agency."

Three points may be noted. First, the title or label used by the parties is relevant but not conclusive.[105] Secondly, the method of remuneration used is not one of the features mentioned as relevant,[106] though it plainly is not irrelevant inasmuch as agents are typically remunerated by commission. Thirdly, what is looked at is the initial primary purpose of the arrangement, not an incidental purpose nor its later operation.

Indications that commercial agency is not involved at all or is secondary are stated in para.4, as being that:

"(a)   promotional material is supplied direct to potential customers;

(b)   persons are granted agencies without reference to existing agents in a particular area or in relation to a particular group;

(c)   customers normally select the goods for themselves and merely place their orders through the agent."

This Schedule has been described in the Court of Appeal as "an almost   **11-021**

---

[104] For an example where this was not so see *Crane v Sky In-Home Service Ltd* [2007] EWHC 66 (Ch); [2007] 2 All E.R. (Comm) 599 (sale of digital box: main purpose was to attract subscribers to television services: agency for sale a secondary activity). Further proceedings [2008] EWCA Civ 978.

[105] cf. above, para.1-036.

[106] And indeed, reg.6(3) envisages that a commercial agent need not be remunerated by commission: see below, para.11-027. Some agents are paid by retainer alone, without being employees.

impenetrable piece of drafting".[107] The first difficulty which it creates is that whereas the Directive can be taken to authorise Member States to disapply the Directive where the activities of the agent are secondary *as compared with the rest of the agent's business* (sometimes called the "horizontal approach"), the Schedule itself "seems to contemplate an assessment not of the activities of the agent as a 'commercial agent' as compared with his other business, but an assessment of the agent's arrangement with a principal",[108] which may be called the "vertical approach". Thus it would appear that if the agent has an arrangement with a principal that falls within the wording of the first set of criteria set out above (para.2 of the Schedule), interpreted with the aid of the criteria subsequently mentioned (paras 3 and 4), his activity in that respect is not secondary, however it may appear against the background of his activities generally.[109] Whatever the intention of the Directive, this approach certainly favours protection of the agent.

11-022 The second and principal problem is highlighted by the dictum of Waller LJ in the Court of Appeal referred to above. It being accepted that, whatever the original intention, the investigation must be into whether the particular arrangement between principal and agent is secondary, the drafting largely proceeds on the basis of simply seeking to define the commercial agency arrangement which is presumably primary. Several of the requirements listed above seem fairly obvious, for example that the principal must be the manufacturer, importer or distributor of the goods. Others may be unduly restrictive in this context, for example the reference to goods of a particular kind, and the requirements that transactions are normally individually negotiated and that the agent devotes substantially the whole of his time to representative activities. Further, it seems likely that though the intermediary is a commercial agent, a principal may sometimes supply promotional material direct, and the customers may sometimes select the goods themselves and place their orders through the agent. The current trend of overall interpretation of this unsatisfactory Schedule seems to be to concentrate on the final words of para.2 and use them as a tool for an emphasis on the interest of the principal in developing a market for the goods by means of an agent generating the goodwill which is the basis of the entitlement to indemnity or compensation on the termination of the contract.[110]

If this is so, "secondary" seems to mean "not goodwill-generating", which is unusual, since the word suggests the existence of something else "primary" to which the activity, while still a commercial agency, is secondary. It had however previously been said that "Because there is no easily recognizable way of measuring whether activities are secondary or not, it is ... unnecessary and perhaps misleading to seek to find an antithesis to the word 'secondary'. The contrast is simply between agents who are covered and the agents who are not".[111] The result can be however that a person performing extensive agency functions in marketing the principal's goods and even occupying a dominant market position may find that he

---

[107] *AMB Imballaggi v Pacflex Ltd* [1999] 2 All E.R. (Comm) 249 at 254, per Waller LJ.

[108] *AMB Imballaggi v Pacflex Ltd* [1999] 2 All E.R. (Comm) 249 at 254.

[109] See at 254. The matter was expressly decided by Morison J in *Tamarind International Ltd v Eastern Natural Gas (Retail) Ltd* [2000] Eu.L.R. 708.

[110] See *Gailey v Environmental Waste Controls*, 2004 Scot SC 300 (OH); [2004] Eu. L.R. 708; accepted in *McAdam v Boxpak Ltd* [2006] CSIH 9; 2006 S.L.T. 217.

[111] *Tamarind International Ltd v Eastern Natural Gas (Retail) Ltd* [2000] C.L.C. 1397 at [21], per Morison J.

is not a commercial agent at all because his activity, even if full-time, is found to have been secondary in the sense of not generating goodwill.[112]

The Directive permits States to disapply it in respect of "commercial agents whose activities are considered secondary by the law of that Member State". The law of the UK does not know the notion of a commercial agent, so the only relevant provision of it must be the Schedule itself, which certainly does not reproduce already existing law. The Schedule so interpreted must have the effect of reducing considerably for the UK the number of persons within the basic definition of art.1(2), on the ground that though they are commercial agents their activities can be described as "secondary" without any indication of what they are secondary to.[113] It has even been said that "The concept of activities as a commercial agent which are considered secondary is fundamental to the scheme of the legislation. It distinguishes commercial agents who are affected by the mischief at which the ... Directive is aimed from those who are not".[114] It is difficult to believe that such a result was what the Directive envisaged when it permitted such a limitation on the general wording of art.1(2), in an exception which has only been taken up, and by different means, in some countries.[115] The history of the reservation has however been traced back more than once in judgments, and it has been held in England in a case where this was done that the course taken in the Schedule is consistent with the Directive and so not ultra vires.[116]

At present there are some not very conclusive decisions, many of which are case-specific, and some of which, it has been argued, should be reconsidered.[117] It appears however from the cases decided so far that the matter must be assessed at the time of inception of the contract,[118] with the result that a contract where the activity is secondary cannot from the legal point of view metamorphose by reason of successful operation into a contract where the activity is primary.[119] It has been held that where the main activity, while goodwill-generating, was outside the scope of the Regulations (because it involved the commodity market), a lesser activity in the

---

[112] As in *MacAdam v Boxpak Ltd* [2006] CSIH 9; 2006 S.L.T. 217, where the agent had a dominant position (70–80 per cent of the market for aluminium foil containers: see judgment of the Sheriff at [11], quoted in the judgment of the Extra Division at [7]) but it was held that his activities were secondary.

[113] Two cases where the agent performed functions that were fairly clearly separate are *Crane v Sky In-Home Service Ltd* [2007] EWHC 66 (Ch), where the agent marketed subscriptions to a digital broadcasting services and also sold box packages and dish packages to receive them. Another is *Gailey v Environmental Waste Controls* 2004 Scot SC 300 (OH); [2004] Eu.L.R.423.

[114] See *Gailey v Environmental Waste Controls*, 2004 Scot SC 300 (OH); [2004] Eu.L.R.423 at [40], per Lord Drummond Young (agent for firm selling waste handling equipment and providing administrative facilities). Cf text to fn.111, above.

[115] See Saintier, fn.1 above, stating that in France the option was taken up to deal with the position of car dealers whose main business is selling, and in Germany to protect the insurance sector.

[116] *Crane v Sky In-Home Service Ltd* [2007] EWHC 66 (Ch); [2007] 1 C.L.C. 389, per Briggs J (further proceedings [2008] EWCA Civ 978).

[117] See Randolph and Davey, fn.1 above, para.6.13. There is a discussion of para.2 of the Schedule in *Green Deal Marketing Southern Ltd v Economy Energy Trading Ltd* [2019] EWHC 507 (Ch); [2019] 2 All E.R.(Comm) 191.

[118] *McAdam v Boxpak Ltd* [2006] CSIH 9; 2006 S.L.T. 217; *Crane v Sky In-Home Service Ltd* [2007] EWHC 66 (Ch); [2007] E.C.C. 25 (Ch); *Invicta UK v International Brands Ltd* [2013] EWHC 1564 (QB); [2013] E.C.C. 30 (wine for supermarkets). But cf. in the context of the agent's retainer *W Nagel (A Firm) v Pluczenik Diamond Co NV* [2017] EWHC 1750 (Comm); [2017] 2 Lloyd's Rep. 215, above, para.11-013, fn.61.

[119] A point made by Randolph and Davey, fn.1 above, at para.5.9; and it appears that Mr Randolph QC may have argued it in *Invicta UK v International Brands Ltd* [2013] EWHC 1564 (QB); [2013] E.C.C. 30.

same context that might not be caught by the exclusion is secondary; and that the effect of this is to exclude it altogether rather than create a separate part of the contract governed by the Regulations.[120] Finally, it has been held that the onus of proof is on the agent to prove that his activities were secondary,[121] though this has subsequently been doubted.[122]

11-023 **Specific exceptions** The activities of mail order catalogue agents for consumer goods and consumer credit agents are presumed, unless the contrary is established, not to be within the definition of commercial agency. The term "commercial agent" excludes officers of companies or associations who are authorised to bind the company or organisation, partners authorised to bind their partners and persons acting as insolvency practitioners as defined in the Insolvency Act 1986[123] or its equivalent in other jurisdictions.[124] Nor do the Regulations apply to commercial agents whose activities are unpaid, commercial agents where they operate on commodity exchanges or in the commodity market,[125] or to the Crown Agents.[126]

4. RELATIONS BETWEEN AGENT AND PRINCIPAL

11-024 **Duties of agent to principal** The Regulations then turn to the mutual duties of principal and agent. By reg.3(1) a commercial agent must "in performing his activities look after the interests of his principal and act dutifully[127] and in good faith". In particular he must "(a) make proper efforts to negotiate and where appropriate conclude the transactions he is instructed to take care of; (b) communicate to his principal all the necessary information available to him"[128] and "(c) comply with reasonable instructions given by his principal".[129] These duties are by reg.5(1) non-derogatable, and the consequences of their breach are by reg.5(2) governed by the

---

[120] *W Nagel (A Firm) v Pluczenic Diamond Co NV* [2017] EWHC 1750 (Comm); [2017] 2 Lloyd's Rep. 215 (see at [71]–[74]) (further proof that the Schedule was not well-conceived); affirmed on other points, [2018] EWCA Civ 2640; [2019] Bus. L.R. 692.

[121] *Gailey v Environmental Waste Controls*, 2004 Scot SC 300 (OH); [2004] Eu.L.R.423 at [40]; *Crane v Sky In-Home Service Ltd* [2007] EWHC 66 (Ch) at [51].

[122] *Edwards v International Connection (UK) Ltd* [2006] EWCA Civ 662, per Arden LJ (leave to appeal proceedings, available on BAILII).

[123] Insolvency Act 1986 s.388 (amended).

[124] SI 1993/3053 reg.2(1)(i) (ii) (iii). In respect of (iii) the Directive (art.1.3) uses the words "a receiver, a receiver and manager, a liquidator or a trustee in bankruptcy".

[125] The rationale of this exclusion is considered in *W Nagel (a firm) v Pluczenik Diamond Co NV* [2018] EWCA Civ 2640; [2019] Bus. L.R. 692, where it was held, disagreeing on this point with the court below, that the rationale of the exception is that trading on a commodity exchange is not an activity by which members of the exchange build up goodwill for their clients, the identity of a counterparty in such circumstances being largely irrelevant. It was held that the sale of rough diamonds was not on a commodity exchange or in a commodity market, "commodity" meaning "raw materials". This point, though authoritatively laid down, was not however essential to the actual result of the case, which was decided on the basis of common law.

[126] SI 1993/3053 reg.2(2).

[127] This unusual word for English legal drafting is selected by translators to correspond with the French "loyalement" and German "treu". See *Rossetti Marketing Ltd v Diamond Sofa Co Ltd* [2011] EWHC 2482 (QB); [2011] E.C.C. 28 at [41]; on appeal [2012] EWCA Civ 1021; [2013] 1 All E.R. (Comm) 308. See also the extended discussion by Tosato (2016) 36 O.J.L.S. 661.

[128] A principal was held to have the right to delivery up of documents in order that he could inspect and copy them in *Fairstar Heavy Transport NV v Adkins* [2013] EWCA 886 (order for inspection: not a commercial agency case).

[129] McGee [2013] J.B.L. 534 at 540, draws attention to problems in applying this where the agent prefers to operate on his own but the principal is keen to supervise what he is doing.

normal principles of the law applicable to the contract between principal and agent, which for the purposes of this book is assumed to be English law. Although the terminology of the general duties, with its invocation of the notion of good faith, is different from that which a common lawyer would use, these or similar duties already exist to quite a considerable extent as implied terms at common law or as fiduciary duties in equity.[130] However, dealing in competing products where there is no clause forbidding this would perhaps more easily be caught by reg.3(1) than by the normal rules of equity.[131] The duties will be remediable by actions for damages, sometimes proprietary claims and injunctions; and sometimes a breach will entitle the principal to terminate the contract. They call for no special comment, save that whereas there is controversy as to the extent to which such duties may at common law or in equity be modified or excluded,[132] the duties here laid down for commercial agents in this context plainly may not.

Duties of principal to agent   The common law contains, however, no general law   **11-025** on the implied duties of principal to agent, and here therefore the Regulations break a certain amount of new ground. Regulation 4(1) which, like reg.3, is, by virtue of reg.5(1), non-derogatable, requires that the principal in his relations with the agent in his turn act "dutifully[133] and in good faith". The notion of good faith has been little developed in the common law, and a principal is not normally regarded as owing fiduciary duties to his agent.[134] There is scope here therefore for the development of implied terms of fair treatment, co-operation and disclosure of relevant information; and contract terms in which the principal retains the right to act in a manner contrary to these requirements will not be valid.

As has been stated above,[135] for the purposes of the implication of terms, contracts come into two categories: standardised contracts of a recognisable type, where the implication may be regarded as drawing the purpose out of the contract, and non-standardised contracts, where terms will only be applied to give business efficacy to the contract. It would seem that in common law contracts involving agency powers are too varied to be dealt with under the first category, and the case law, which is parsimonious on implication of terms in favour of the agent, bears this out. However, in the present context it could be said that the effect of the Regulations is to create a new type of standardised contract to which the first technique can apply, thus creating a vessel to carry new law. It is said that in French law the commercial agency contract is regarded as an enterprise of common interest between principal and agent[136]; and it is certainly true that even in common law the relationship is not commercially adverse, and that this is a way of distinguishing agency from distributorship[137] and justifying the rules about secret profits.[138] Parallels providing reasoning may sometimes be drawn from partnership law and from

---

[130] See Articles 36 onwards; *Crane v Sky In-Home Service Ltd* [2007] EWHC 66 (Ch); [2007] 2 All E.R. (Comm) 599 at [82]. But cf. Tosato (2016) 36 O.J.L.S. 661.

[131] See above, para.6-015.

[132] See above, para.6-056 onwards.

[133] See fn.127 above. The duty of good faith is specifically referred to in *Chavassus-Marche v Groupe Danone* (C-19/07) [2008] 2 All E.R. (Comm) 1093 at [22].

[134] See above, para.7-001. But there is recent movement on this notion in common law: see, e.g. Selvaratnam [2020] L.M.C.L.Q. 232.

[135] See above, para.7-001.

[136] Saintier and Scholes, fn.1 above, at pp.80–81 and 84 onwards.

[137] See above, para.1-035.

[138] Article 47.

some modern developments in employment law.[139] Decisions in France[140] and Italy[141] respectively, cited only as providing examples, have concerned a principal who sends another person to solicit offers into the area where the agent is sole representative and one who systematically refuses to conclude the contracts negotiated by the agent; in Germany, inducing the agent's customers to deal with the principal directly.[142] Other examples where such reasoning was deployed have concerned changes in pricing policy or in the list of products entrusted to the agent, the allowing of parallel sales by another agent or distributor of the principal and the unfair exercise of a power to vary the contract.[143] There is certainly considerable potential for advancing arguments under the Regulations which might not be acceptable under the general common law. It has however been held (after most elaborate argument including reference to bona fides[144]) that the Regulations cannot qualify an express right of termination on the principal's part, in respect of which the situation remains as at common law, which is that the right may be an absolute contractual right.[145]

The duty is to some extent filled out with specific indications by reg.4(2) and (3), though it seems unlikely that these are intended to be exhaustive. A principal must "provide [the] agent with the necessary documentation relating to the goods concerned", "obtain for his commercial agent the information necessary for the performance of the agency contract, and in particular notify the commercial agent within a reasonable period once he anticipates that the volume of commercial transactions will be significantly lower than that which the commercial agent could normally have expected" and "inform the commercial agent within a reasonable period of his acceptance or refusal of, and of any non-execution by him of a commercial transaction which the commercial agent has procured for him".[146] The second requirement in particular, in its reference to notification of change of volume of transactions, may involve more than some principals would be in the habit of doing. Again, the consequences of breach of duty are covered by the normal principles of law applicable to the contract, which for the purposes of this book is assumed to be English law.

11-026   **Right to written statement of terms of contract**   By reg.13, which appears in the section entitled "Conclusion and Termination of the Agency Contract", each party is "entitled to receive from the other, on request, a signed written document setting out the terms of the agency contract including any terms subsequently

---

[139] Freedland, *The Personal Employment Contract* (2005), Ch.3; Brodie (2001) 117 L.Q.R. 604.

[140] Cour d'appel de Rennes, December 1, 1993, Dalloz 1994, *informations rapides*, 127.

[141] Corte di cassazione, December 18, 1985, fn.6475, Giur.it. 1986, I, 1, 1649 note di Loreto.

[142] See e.g. BGH, WM 2003, 255; BGH, NJW 2014, 155.

[143] A number of such claims against a principal were however rejected in *Simpson v Grant & Bowman* [2006] Eu. L.R. 933.

[144] Particularly the case of *Mediterranean Shipping Co SA v Cottonex Anstalt* [2015] EWHC 283 (Comm); [2015] 1 Lloyd's Rep. 359.

[145] *Monk v Largo Foods Ltd* [2016] EWHC 1837 (Comm) (where the right arose from a "term of arrangement" under which the operation of the contract was said to be "for a three year period subject to the completion of a successful review", which was held to be at common law an absolute contractual right rather than a contractual discretion: at [64]. It was then held that reg.4(1) did not qualify the operation of the clause. The judgment contains extensive discussion of both issues).

[146] SI 1993/3053 reg.22 makes provision as to how a "notice, statement or other document" is to be given or supplied. It is not clear that it covers merely "informing".

agreed".[147] Any purported waiver of this right is void. It seems that many such arrangements are entered into and varied on an informal basis.[148] In view of the
disputes that can arise it is in the interests of both parties to have such a document.
But it is not clear what the remedy is for failure to comply with the duty to supply
such a document. In principle, there must be a right to damages; but loss arising
from breach of the duty might not be easy to prove, and this is in any case too much
of a common law approach. In labour law in the UK, there are similar requirements to supply a statement of terms of the contract of employment, but breach of
this duty is cognisable in industrial tribunals. A mandatory injunction, an order of
the court or a declaration would seem to be necessary. A party who does not receive
such a document may perhaps refuse to commence performance; but at least on the
side of the agent this may not always be prudent.

5.   REMUNERATION AND COMMISSION

Cases where no agreement on remuneration   Part III of the Regulations deals   **11-027**
with remuneration in some detail. Regulation 6 provides that where no remuneration is agreed, the agent shall be entitled to "the remuneration that commercial
agents appointed for the goods forming the subject of his agency contract are
customarily allowed in the place where he carries on his activities", and in the
absence of such practice to "reasonable remuneration taking into account all the
aspects of the transaction".[149] This seems straightforward, but there is no reason to
think that reasoning such as that already employed at common law[150] will not be
equally valid under the Regulations. The provision is excludable in that specific
remuneration can be agreed and so prevent its application; and if it is agreed that
the activities of the agent shall be unpaid, the person concerned is not a commercial agent at all.[151] However, the Regulations, and the Directive, appear also to
assume that a commercial agent need not be remunerated by commission, for by
reg.6(3), regs 7 to 12 do not apply "where a commercial agent is not remunerated
(wholly or in part) by commission"—an odd way of putting it, which is rendered
in the enactments of some other countries in positive form, i.e. that the following
rules apply where the agent *is* remunerated by commission. Either way, remuneration by commission is not part of the definition of commercial agents, and some
agents may be remunerated by markups, shares of profits and similar
arrangements.[152] There is a danger that a commercial agent remunerated by salary
(as opposed to a retainer) may in some situations and/or countries be regarded as
an employee and not a commercial agent at all.

---

[147] Provisions as to how the giving or supply of such documents is to be effected are to be found in
reg.22. It is likely that in due course an electronic document will be permitted. According to *Bellone v Yokohama SpA* (C-215/97) [1998] E.C.R. I-2191, since writing is the only requirement of form
mentioned by art.13(2) of the Directive and the Community legislature had dealt exhaustively with
the matter, the Member States cannot impose any formal condition for the validity of the contract
other than requiring that a written document be drawn up.

[148] e.g. *AMB Imballaggi v Pacflex Ltd* [1999] 2 All E.R. (Comm) 249; *Mercantile International Group
Plc v Chuan Soon Huat Industrial Group Plc* [2002] EWCA Civ 288; [2002] 1 All E.R. (Comm)
788.

[149] For an example of its application see *PJ Pipe and Valve Co Ltd v Audco India Ltd* [2005] EWHC
1904 (QB); [2006] Eu.L.R. 368, where the fact that the parties had intended a higher commission
than usual was taken into account.

[150] See Article 55.

[151] SI 1993/3053 reg.2(2); above, para.11-023.

[152] An agent remunerated partly by mark-up was held a commercial agent in *Mercantile International
Group Plc v Chuan Soon Huat Industrial Group Plc* [2002] EWCA Civ 288; [2002] 1 All E.R.

11-028 **Commission** The remainder of Pt III deals with the agent's commission, defined in reg.2(1) as "any part of the remuneration of a commercial agent which varies with the number or value of business transactions". It seeks to protect the agent against situations which have been perceived as unfair to him. These particular words prevent the dressing up of commission as, for instance, expenses. As will be seen, the Regulations distinguish between *entitlement* to commission, when commission is *due*, when commission shall be *paid*, and the *right* to commission: though the last phrase may be an oversight of a translator and hence equivalent to "entitlement".[153] There seems no reason why commission agreed should not vary between types of transaction or in particular situations such as where sales targets are exceeded.

11-029 **Entitlement to commission** Under reg.7(1) the agent is "entitled to commission" on "commercial transactions concluded during the period covered by the agency contract—(a) where the transaction has been concluded as a result of his action". In considering this provision it should be borne in mind that the term "commercial agent" covers not only one who concludes transactions, but also one who negotiates them.[154] Where he actually *concludes* them there is no difficulty in seeing that he is entitled to commission. Where he merely *negotiates* them, the reference to the transaction being concluded as the result of his action will give something very like (but not necessarily the same as) the existing "effective cause" rule of English law.[155] There is nothing in the Regulations which would render ineffective an entitlement to commission at an earlier stage, as for example when a customer is introduced: unlike the English estate agent cases, the concern in the Regulations is not about agents providing that they are entitled to commission when there is no sale, but for agents failing to obtain commission despite there having been a sale. Furthermore, it would seem that, subject to the requirement of good faith,[156] the principal can deprive the agent of commission by refusing to conclude a transaction negotiated by the agent. Existing English cases would allow the agent to protect himself against this if the clause is sufficiently clear in making commission due despite the non-conclusion of the contract.[157] Some such clauses may now perhaps be contrary to the good faith requirement; though equally some forms of conduct by the principal may themselves be contrary to good faith.

11-030 **Repeat orders** By reg.7(1)(b) the agent is entitled to commission "where the transaction is concluded with a third party whom he has previously acquired as a customer for transactions of the same kind", i.e. on what is sometimes called a "repeat order" placed without any further intervention of the agent.[158] This is an area

---

(Comm) 788. See also *AMB Imballaggi v Pacflex Ltd* [1999] 2 All E.R. (Comm) 249. As to share in profit, see *Mar-Train Heavy Haulage Ltd v Shipping DK Chartering A/S* [2014] EWHC 355 (Comm) at [38] onwards (context: freight forwarding).

[153] See below, para.11-034.

[154] Above, para.11-018.

[155] Article 57. This rule has largely been developed in connection with estate agents, who are certainly not commercial agents.

[156] Above, para.11-025.

[157] See Article 58.

[158] See *Moore v Piretta Pte Ltd* [1999] 1 All E.R. 174 at 178 ("the first paragraph requires some action on the part of the agent to earn the commission, the second does not").

where the English law is far from clear.[159] In other legal systems the notion of a customer whom the agent has previously acquired for transactions of a similar kind is held to be similar to that emerging from the distinction between new customers and old customers in the context of the provisions concerning the agent's right to indemnity on termination of the agency contract under reg.17(3)(a).[160] There may be dispute as to what is a transaction "of the same kind".

Geographical zone or customer group   Finally, by reg.7(2) the agent is entitled   **11-031**
to commission on transactions concluded during the period of the contract "where he has an exclusive right to a specific geographical area or to a specific group of customers and where the transaction has been entered into with a customer belonging to that area or group", and require no specific activity from the agent. Here there is even less of anything corresponding to a requirement of "effective cause" for the particular transaction; the entitlement is to commission on transactions which do no more than emanate from the agent's area or customer group.[161] However, commission is not due if the transaction not only did not involve action by the agent, but also did not involve action by the principal, direct or indirect, in the conclusion of the transaction. Although art.7(2) might appear to apply, art.10(1) and (2) require or imply execution by the principal.[162] The meaning of "exclusive right" may require determination, in particular on the question whether the principal can himself sell. For this the common law estate agency distinction between "sole" and "exclusive" agency[163] may provide useful argument, though there is no reason whatever to think that the Regulations were drafted with this in mind.

Commission on transactions after agency contract terminated   Regulation 8   **11-032**
deals with this problem, on which English law is again not clear.[164] It provides that the agent is "entitled to commission" in such cases if:

"(a)   the transaction is mainly attributable to his efforts during the period covered by the agency contract and if the transaction was entered into within a reasonable period after that contract terminated; or

(b)   in accordance with the conditions mentioned in regulation 7 above, the order of the third party reached the principal or the commercial agent before the agency contract terminated."

The requirements of (a) are somewhat imprecise and may give rise to difficulties of application. It has been held that "the words 'mainly attributable' impose a heightened causation requirement beyond simply being an effective cause", and this is justified on the basis that anything else would have a detrimental effect on the

---

159   See above, para.7-042.
160   See below, para.11-044.
161   An example is provided by *McQuillan v McCormick* [2010] EWHC 1112 (QB); [2011] E.C.C. 18. See also *Kontogeorgas v Kartonpak AE* (C-104/95) [1996] E.C.R. I-6643; [1997] 1 C.M.L.R. 1093 as to the word "belonging". Quaere whether the principal can exclude named customers.
162   *Chevassus-Marche's Heirs v Groupe Danone* (C-19/07) [2008] 2 All E.R. (Comm) 1093 (where the goods were purchased from other dealers outside the control of the principal). But if the customer is within the area, the fact that delivery is actually made to a party outside the area may be irrelevant: *Edwards v International Connection (UK) Ltd*, Central London County Court, Judge Knight QC, November 25, 2005 (subsequent Court of Appeal proceedings [2006] EWCA Civ 662).
163   See above, para.7-037.
164   See above, para.7-042.

rights of a replacement agent.[165] The following provision, (b), appears to refer to situations where the order has come in at the time the agency contract terminated, but not been accepted. Regulation 9 then deals with situations where an agent claims under reg.7 and commission is payable to his predecessor by virtue of reg.8: the later agent does not qualify for commission "unless it is equitable because of the circumstances for the commission to be shared between the commercial agents"—a provision which could require adjudication if there was a dispute under it.

11-033 **When commission due and date for payment** By reg.10(1) a further refinement is introduced. Commission is actually *due*[166] in one of three situations: when the principal has "executed" the transaction (which presumably means performed it), or according to his agreement with the third party ought to have done so, or the third party has executed the transaction. The first two provisions are facultative only in the sense that other arrangements may be made. But the third provides a final limit which cannot, by para.(4), be derogated from to the detriment of the agent. This provides that commission becomes due *at the latest* when "(2) the third party has executed his part of the transaction or should have done so if the principal had executed his part of the transaction as he should have".[167] Paragraph (3), also non-derogatable, provides that commission shall be *paid* "not later than on the last day of the month following the quarter in which it became due".[168] There follows a provision for determining quarter periods, which may be varied by agreement. Paragraph (2) may raise problems of application when there is no time set for the principal to perform the contract.

11-034 **"Right" to commission** The effect of the above provisions is reinforced by reg.11(1), which provides that:

> "the right to commission can be extinguished only if and to the extent that (a) it is established that the contract between the third party and the principal will not be performed; and (b) that fact is due to a reason for which the principal is *not to blame*."[169]

This provision cannot be derogated from to the detriment of the commercial agent.[170] It seems unlikely that any special significance is to be attached to the word "right" as opposed to "entitlement" in regs 7, 8 and 9, as the same French word ("droit") appears in all these provisions in the French text of the Directive. The word

---

[165] *Monk v Largo Foods Ltd* [2016] EWHC 1837 (Comm); following dicta in *Tigana Ltd v Decoro Ltd* [2003] EWHC 23 (QB); [2003] Eu. L.R. 189, where the reasonable period was set at nine months. See discussion by McGee [2011] J.B.L. 782 at 783, stressing difficulties caused by "attributable" and "reasonable period". It is not clear whether or not reg.8(b) applies to all the situations referred to in reg.7. It is suggested in *Monk v Largo Foods* that it applies neither to repeat orders covered by reg.7(b) nor to orders originating as prescribed in reg.(2): see [109]–[110]. The main reason seems to be inconsistency with the provision for apportioning commission provided by reg.9. But it is not clear that the wording of reg.8(b) permits such a conclusion, and attention should perhaps be directed to the words "order of the third party reached the principal".

[166] French "acquise".

[167] In *Ergo Poist'ovna a.s. v Barlikova* (C-48/16) [2018] Bus.L.R. 41 the agent was paid before this date, and a provision that if the contract was not performed she would refund part on a pro rata basis in the event of partial non-execution of the contract was held not (without more) a derogation to her detriment caught by reg.11(3), because it complied with the scheme of reg.11(a) and (2).

[168] For a similar distinction in common law, see *Explora Group Plc v Hesco Bastion Ltd* [2005] EWCA Civ 646 at [59], [60].

[169] Emphasis supplied. The agent must in such cases refund any commission he has received: reg.11(2).

[170] SI 1993/3053 reg.11(3).

"extinguished" appears to envisage the effect of a specific contract term. The overall result is that the agent only actually earns commission on business entitling him to it where the contract is in fact performed, or not performed for reasons in some way not attributable to the principal—unless of course the contract gives the agent a more generous entitlement, which it may. Although the wording of the provision could be taken to suggest that the right can be extinguished only if it is established that the whole contract will not be performed, it has been held that it covers also partial non-execution of the contract: in the particular case, where the contract provided for the procurement of separate insurance contracts and payment of commission on each.[171]

It should be noted that the reference is actually to non-performance for a reason for which the principal is not to *blame*. At common law a principal can be liable for non-performance even where no blame attaches to him, if the circumstances are such that he is to be regarded as having undertaken responsibility for them. The French text of the Directive uses the word "imputable" and other foreign texts are similar: the variation seems to arise in translation only and it might be thought that it was not intended to convey any effect substantially different from that which would be expected under English law, but to refer to legal reasons which led directly to the termination of the contract between the principal and the third party (for which the word "attributable" would be appropriate). However, it has been held in the same case that such an interpretation is not consistent with the objectives of the Directive in protecting agents, and that the court should make a broad factual assessment as to whether the principal was to blame for the circumstances leading to the termination. In the particular case the principal, an insurer, had treated the clients badly by asking them to reply to numerous questions and sending letters seeking payment of sums already paid, which was said to make the customers lose confidence in the insurer and terminate their contracts, to the disadvantage of the agent who had secured them.[172] This decision introduces an element of uncertainty that is not even linked to the notion of negligence.

If the principal sues the third party for non-performance, the agent should normally be entitled to commission.[173] Problems could arise if the principal refuses or fails to do so. This could lead to the inference that it is not established that the third party will not perform; or perhaps be a breach of the principal's duty of good faith.

Exclusion or modification of commission rules by contract terms   There is   **11-035** certainly nothing in the Regulations preventing an entitlement to commission at an *earlier* stage than they prescribe: the prohibitions on derogation are on derogation to the detriment of the agent. Equally, there is no need for an agent to be allocated a specific geographical area or group of customers. The question whether the provisions as to remuneration may be modified or in some respect altogether excluded, in particular as regards commission on what may loosely be called repeat orders, or in cases where the agent does have a geographical area or group of customers, or where a transaction is concluded after the end of the agency contract, is more difficult.

---

[171] *Ergo Poist'ovna a.s. v Barlikova* (C-48/16) [2018] Bus.L.R. 41. The party in question was not a commercial agent but negotiated and concluded contracts for insurance services. The reasons why the court nevertheless determined the case are to be found at paras 26 to 32 of the judgment.

[172] *Ergo Poist'ovna a.s. v Barlikova* (C-48/16) [2018] Bus.L.R. 41.

[173] See above, para.7-018.

The obvious answer might appear to be that they may, since only some of the provisions of reg.10, those as to the time at which commission is due and must be paid, and of reg.11, as to extinction of the right to commission if the contract will not be executed for reasons not attributable to the principal, are specifically made non-derogatable to the agent's detriment. If this interpretation is correct, it can be argued that as regs 7 and 8 are not, as are other provisions, specifically made unexcludable, the entitlements which they prescribe are merely *ius dispositivum* and only operate if there are no contract terms providing otherwise. On this basis it is possible to exclude the other situations of entitlement to commission and provide that commission only arises on transactions actually concluded as a result of the agent's actions. It would be difficult (but perhaps not impossible) to go further and reduce the right to commission on *concluded* transactions, but an attempt to extinguish the right to commission would be caught by reg.11, and if it is provided that no commission at all is due on such sales, the agency would be gratuitous and not covered by the Regulations at all. On the other hand, as already pointed out, it is also contemplated that the agent may not be remunerated by commission at all, but rather by retainer or salary.

As against this it may be said that it is odd to provide in such firm terms when the entitlement to commission arises, if the rules only operate where there is no provision to the contrary; and that there are other provisions in the Regulations which must be unexcludable, yet where this is not stated.[174] Further, the general wording of reg.11(1), quoted above, which provides that the "right to commission" is extinguished "only if and to the extent that" certain circumstances connected with non-performance of the contract occur, and which cannot be derogated from to the detriment of the agent, could be taken to suggest that where the circumstances indicated in reg.7 apply, commission must be due as there prescribed unless the contract is not carried out in accordance with what is prescribed in reg.11. More generally, it is difficult to see why there should be an unexcludable right to commission in all situations where contracts are not performed bar specific exceptions, while the actual initial entitlement to commission in respect of contracts can itself be modified.

The only English judicial authority is a dictum of Morland J:

> "It should be noted that there is no non-derogation article equivalent to Article 19 applicable to Articles 7 and 8. In my judgment the absence of such a specific nonderogation article means that commercial agents and principals may derogate contractually from Articles 7 and 8 but only in so far as they do not thwart the purpose of the Council Directive."[175]

One English book gives an argued view that the provisions cannot be excluded or modified.[176] A leading German book (significant because the Directive was inspired by German law) took the view that they can, though some support is

---

[174] SI 1993/3053 regs 3, 4, 14, 15(3), 15(5), 20. It should be noted also that when Member States can modify a rule, the Directive says so.

[175] *Ingmar GB Ltd v Eaton Leonard Ltd*, at first instance [2001] EWHC 3 (QB); [2001] Eur. L.R. 755 at [30] (assessment of compensation: for main proceedings see above, para.11-006). There is no reference to Article 9. As to frustrating the purpose of the Directive, see *Bellone v Yokohama Spa* (215/97) [1998] E.C.L.R. I-291. Another example might be a clause providing that the intermediary did not act as a commercial agent, when by the definition given in the Regulations he did.

[176] Christou, fn.1 above, at para.3-227 onwards.

derived from the German law before the Directive.[177] An English book, which contains much discussion on French law, is of the same view for both English and French law,[178] as is the leading English specialised work on the subject.[179] The Italian legislation implementing the Directive actually permits the exclusion of arts 7(1)(b) and 7(2),[180] indicating that the Italian legislator understood the Directive in that way. The dominant view seems to be that the remuneration provisions can be excluded save in so far as the Regulations specifically provide. This does however much reduce the importance of what appear at first sight to be carefully thought-out rules.

It is important to note what this means. It may, as already suggested, be difficult, whatever the scope of the provisions of the Regulations, to exclude completely the right to commission on transactions concluded as a result of the agent's action (reg.7(1)(a)), unless there is remuneration by some other means, as is possible.[181] It is not difficult to accept as a matter of policy that the contract can exclude or restrict commission on (what may loosely be called) "repeat orders" (reg.7(1)(b)), or on orders from particular zone or group of customers (reg.7(2)), orders which may come in without further action by the agent.[182] But if these provisions are excludable, the rules in regs 8 and 9 must be regarded as modifiable also: there is no reason for distinguishing them. This means that it is also permissible to make different provision concluded after the agency contract has terminated, or to modify the rules about apportionment of commission between new and previous agents (reg.9).[183] The only thing that cannot be modified is the rule that the commission, if earned in accordance with what is said above, is due as soon as, or not later than, the contract has been executed,[184] unless it can be established that it will not be executed for a reason not attributable to the principal.[185]

Supply of information   Regulation 12 deals with the supply of information by principal to agent with a view to the calculation of commission earned. The background is plainly, like that of the previous regulation, a perception that the agent is in danger of not getting all the commission to which he is entitled. It provides in paras (1) and (2) that the principal shall supply the agent with a statement of the commission due not later than the last day of the month following the quarter in which the commission has become due, setting out the main components used in calculating it; and that the agent "shall be entitled to demand that he be provided with all the information (and in particular an extract from the books) which is available to his principal and which he needs in order to check the amount   **11-036**

---

[177] Hopt, *Handelsvertreterrecht* (4th edn, München 2009) § 87, No.48, making the point also that such exclusion or modification cannot affect the calculation of the indemnity, which is non-derogatable.

[178] Saintier and Scholes, fn.1 above, pp.115–116; though it is true that the French legislation does not list the relevant provisions as being non-derogatable. A generally helpful discussion in Bennett, fn.1 above, uses the ICC Model Commercial Agency Contract as an example where this is done: see para.8.47.

[179] Randolph and Davey, fn.1 above, at p.80.

[180] Italian CC art.1748, para.2.

[181] See above. The right to commission could of course be formulated more advantageously to the agent than this: see above, para.11-029.

[182] See *Kontogeorgas v Kartonpak AE* (C-104/95) [1997] 1 C.M.L.R. 1093.

[183] See *Explora Group Plc v Hesco Bastion Ltd* [2005] EWCA Civ 646 at [59], per Rix LJ.

[184] As to "execution" see above, para.11-033.

[185] Article 11(1), above, para.11-034.

of the commission due to him".[186] In this case an agreement to derogate from these provisions is by para.(3) stated to be void. This is without prejudice to other enactments or rules of law permitting agents to inspect their principals' books.[187]

It is, however, not clear how the duty is to be enforced. An action for damages, which seems the most obvious remedy at common law, would seem to be of limited utility. Some sort of order of the court, for instance a mandatory injunction, or a declaration, would be required.[188]

6. TERMINATION OF THE AGENCY[189]

11-037 **Fixed period contract which continues to be performed** Where there is an agency contract for a fixed period, and it continues to be performed by both parties after the expiry of the period, reg.14 provides that it "shall be deemed to be converted" into an agency contract for an indefinite period. It then attracts the provisions for the termination of agency contracts concluded for indefinite periods, which follow in reg.15. While this is reasonable, there is obviously here a danger for principals who allow what may be intended to be only a slight run-over, or allow a run-over by inadvertence.

Argument is possible that this provision also is not mandatory, and that the result prescribed can be avoided by an appropriate term in the original contract. As with regs 7–9, it is true that there is no express indication that the regulation cannot be derogated from, whereas non-derogation provisions appear in various forms in respect of regs 13, 15, 17 and 18.[190] On the other hand the wording of the Regulations appears to the English reader firm, and it appears that a provision in the original draft of the Directive allowing derogation was deleted.[191] Perhaps the best solution is that a contract for a fixed period containing a clause providing for what happens if the parties continue performance at the end of the period is not, at any rate at the moment when the clause first comes into operation, for the purposes of the Regulations, a contract for a fixed period.

11-038 **Termination of contract concluded for an indefinite period** The Regulations here provide specific rules for a situation on which English law has, at any rate in the context of agency, not been at all clear.[192] Under reg.15(1) in all such situations either party may terminate the contract by notice: this for English law avoids possible arguments that the contract is not terminable at all.[193] Regulation 15(2) provides that the minimum period of notice is one month for the first year of the contract, two months "for the second year commenced", and three months "for the

---

[186] SI 1993/3053 reg.22 makes provision for how such statements are to be supplied.

[187] SI 1993/3053 reg.12(4). The right to information does not require that it be given where disclosure would be contrary to public policy: reg.21. For an example of a corresponding right in the principal (though not in a commercial agency context), see fn.128 above.

[188] The Access to Medical Reports Act 1988 confers a right to inspect such reports in certain circumstances: but here a special power is given by s.8 to the court to order compliance. In *Yasuda Fire Insurance Co v Orion Marine Insurance Underwriting Agency* [1995] Q.B. 174 a contractual term allowing such inspection was enforced by an order of specific performance, and declarations were also made.

[189] For a very thorough discussion of this topic with strong reference to French law, see Saintier and Scholes, fn.1 above, Ch.5. See also McGee [2011] J.B.L. 782.

[190] See regs 13(2), 15(2), 19.

[191] See Randolph and Davey, fn.1 above, at p.89.

[192] See Article 123.

[193] Provisions as to how the giving of notice is to be effected are to be found in reg.22.

third year commenced and for the subsequent years". Presumably this means that the two-month period becomes necessary as soon as the agent has commenced his second year of operation under the contract. The parties may agree on longer but not on shorter periods. Unless otherwise agreed, "the end of the period of notice must coincide with the end of a calendar month", which may add nearly a further month to the period of notice. Where a fixed period contract is converted into an indefinite period contract under reg.14, discussed above, the fixed period must be taken into account in calculating the period of notice; since this refers back to unexcludable entitlements, it may be assumed that this rule is unexcludable also. No remedies or special time bars are prescribed for noncompliance with these requirements, and it seems that the general law is applicable.[194]

Savings for the domestic law By reg.16 the Regulations do not "affect the application of any enactment or rule of law which provides for immediate[195] termination of the agency contract—(a) because of the failure of one party to carry out all or part of his obligations under that contract; or (b) where exceptional circumstances arise". This provision, which links forward to reg.18,[196] appears intended to preserve the normal rules of domestic[197] law regarding what a common lawyer would call discharge of contract by breach, and frustration, and it may be assumed that the right to damages is unaffected. Paragraph (a) could in fact refer to the operation of both doctrines; paragraph (b) no doubt refers to situations where the contract might be automatically discharged by frustration, though a common lawyer would not express himself in this way. It could cover situations where the principal is by reason of exceptional circumstances unable to continue the contract, for example if his factory is destroyed by an earthquake, or he is affected by unforeseeable personal circumstances. The wording of (a) would presumably cover a wrongful repudiation by the principal accepted by the agent (including repudiation of a fixed term contract): that indemnity or compensation is then due is made clear by reg.18(b)(i). It would also cover wrongful repudiation by the agent accepted by the principal. A force majeure clause would however be a specific contract term and would not come within the words "enactment or rule of law". It is submitted that the common law "rule of law" as to termination for breach takes in that part of it which enables justification of a termination for which an inadequate reason is given where an adequate reason actually existed at the time of termination, a rule usually based on *Boston Deep Sea Fishing and Ice Co v Ansell*.[198]   **11-039**

Entitlement to indemnity or compensation The most significant provision in this part of the Regulations, and indeed, from the common law point of view, in the Regulations as a whole, is reg.17, which together with reg.18 seeks to secure that   **11-040**

---

[194] See *Roy v MR Pearlman Ltd*, 1999 S.C. 459; 2000 S.L.T. 727, rejecting an argument that the Regulations must here be viewed as completely outside the general law. It should however be noted that whereas normal legal remedies are preserved in respect of the mutual duties of principal and agent by reg.5(2), there is no such specific provision here. See further discussion by McGee [2011] J.B.L. 782 at 785.

[195] This word (French "sans délai") appears to be inserted to distinguish the provisions as to notice in the immediately preceding reg.15.

[196] Below, para.11-056.

[197] See the Directive itself, Article 16.

[198] *Boston Deep Sea Fishing & Ice Co v Ansell* (1888) 39 Ch. D. 339. See, e.g. *Crocs Europe BV v Anderson (t/a Spectrum Agencies (A Partnership))* [2012] EWCA Civ 1400; [2013] 1 Lloyd's Rep. 1 (principal terminated agency on insufficient grounds: compensation due).

"after termination of the agency contract"[199] the commercial agent is entitled to be "indemnified ... or compensated for damage" (reg.17(1)). As has been explained above, this idea results from a perception (which takes various forms) that an agent may establish a market and goodwill for a principal, and then be deprived of the benefit of his investment, both in money and in labour, by termination of his authority by a principal who may then seek to deal direct with customers, or perhaps use the services of another agent at a cheaper rate of commission, though the payment of indemnity or compensation is by no means limited to these cases. The agent is in effect to be "bought out", as is sometimes the case in employment law. The sum due in this respect is over and above money contractually due in other respects, for example in respect of unpaid arrears of commission or "repeat orders".[200]

The alternative between compensation and indemnity derives from art.17 of the Directive, and was intended to avoid the clash between the German and the French approaches to the issue, approaches which had developed some time before the harmonisation procedure was set in motion. The choice between the two regimes was to be left open. The indemnity regulated by art.17 of the Directive reproduced almost literally the then para.89b of the German Commercial Code (HGB). The compensation provision was inspired by French law and practice based originally on decree n.58—1345 of December 23, 1958.[201] The Directive did not eliminate these differences, but rather, limited the number of options available on this point to Member States. The divergence is quite great: in the most general terms it seems that compensation under French law can be about double the indemnity paid under German law.[202]

11-041 **Provisions cannot be derogated from** The provisions of regs 17 and 18 cannot, by virtue of reg.19, be derogated from to the detriment of the agent "before the agency contract[203] expires". The provision against derogation is not difficult to understand. A recent example of a clause held to be an inadmissible derogation concerns a clause providing for an indemnity, but for compensation if the amount of it would be less than the amount payable by way of indemnity.[204] It may be asked why derogation may nevertheless be permitted after the expiry of the contract. This

---

[199] In *Scottish Energy Retail Ltd v Taskforce Contracts Ltd* [2008] CSOH 110; [2009] Eu.L.R. 62 it was held that partial termination of the contract (in regard to part of the services required) did not give rise to a right to indemnity or compensation.

[200] See above, para.11-030. In the context of CPR Pt 6 (service out of the jurisdiction) it has been said that this is not a contractual but a statutory action, possibly in the nature of a tort: *Fern Computer Consultancy Ltd v Intergraph Cadworx & Analysis Solutions Inc* [2014] EWHC 2908 (Ch); [2015] 1 Lloyd's Rep. 1 at [38], [39] and [47]. Although the contexts are different, this does not accord with the reasoning adopted concerning jurisdiction under what is now the Brussels I Regulation in *Arcado v Haviland SA* (C-9/87) [1988] E.C.R. 1539, which is clear that the action is contractual, reasoning which, it is submitted, should apply also under the Rome I Regulation on choice of law. It must be questioned whether domestic reasoning should be employed in connection with CPR Pt 6 when the cause of action is of EU origin (the *Arcado* case does not appear have been cited). For an example of a successful claim, see *McQuilllan v McCormick* [2010] EWHC 1112 (QB); [2011] E.C.C. 18 (jewellery). The possibility of amalgamating the two notions is considered by Saintier in *Commercial Contract Law: Transatlantic Perspectives* (Di Matteo and others, eds, 2003), Ch.12.

[201] See in general European Commission, report of July 23, 1996, The Application of the Commercial Agents Directive, COM 96/364 FINAL (reproduced in Randolph and Davey, fn.1 above).

[202] See below, para.11-053.

[203] As to this phrase see regs 16 and 17(1), paras 11-039 and 11-040, above.

[204] *Shearman (t/a Charles Shearman Agencies) v Hunter Boot Ltd* [2014] EWHC 47 (QB); [2014] E.C.C. 12. The invalidity of the clause led to the operation of the basic rule for compensation rather than indemnity. cf. *Brand Studio Ltd v St John Knits Inc* [2015] EWHC 3143 (QB); [2015] Bus. L.R.

seems to be because after such expiry the principal's power to exercise pressure on the agent may be assumed to be no longer operative. However, the surprising opinion of Advocate General Léger in *Ingmar GB Ltd v Eaton Leonard Technologies Ltd*[205] suggests that art.19 of the Directive, which corresponds to reg.19, does not allow derogation of the indemnity and compensation provisions even *after* the contract has expired. This argument, not commented on by the court, is partly based on the notion that the provisions are of a special mandatory nature in so far as they protect competition policy and commercial agents within the community; and partly on the idea that the agent would have no interest in giving up his rights when he is freed of any obligation to the principal, whereas if he was in negotiation to renew the contract the regime would be valueless if derogatable.[206]

When does the entitlement arise? Indefinite period contracts   Assuming that   **11-042**
no breach of contract by principal or agent is involved, the obvious case of entitlement occurs where a contract for an indefinite period is terminated by the principal. An abrupt termination, even though notice is given within the minimum periods specified,[207] may obviously deprive the agent of expected benefits. Although English law has not recognised any rights in the agent in such circumstances, the object of the Directive plainly requires it. Perhaps more surprising, however, is the fact that reg.17(8) provides that the right to indemnity or compensation also arises where the agent dies, and reg.18(b)(ii)[208] assumes that it exists also where he himself terminates the agency contract "on grounds of the age, infirmity or illness of the commercial agent in consequence of which he cannot reasonably be required to continue his activities". This transfers the risk of those events to the principal, but is in accordance with the objects of the Directive as recompensing the agent (or his estate) for connections built up, or more generally his interest in the agency. It has been held that this covers normal retirement of the agent even if his physical condition would permit him to continue.[209] The entitlement may seem on the generous side: one might think that the agent could at the time of contracting have taken into account the fact that he might be prevented from continuing, at any rate if the infirmity was foreseeable or the age at which he might retire was known.

Problems may arise if the agent does a wrongful act which entitles the principal to terminate the contract and then dies. The common law analysis is that the contract is not terminated for breach until the innocent party to the breach elects to exercise the power to do so, and the principal may not have done this. Hence the right to compensation may sometimes be said to have accrued before the innocent party can terminate, though if the parties had agreed for an indemnity it might be possible to say that the payment of it was not (in whole or in part) "equitable" in accordance with reg.17(3)(b). Otherwise, it might sometimes be possible to argue that the agent

1421, where a similar clause was held severable from the choice of an indemnity, which therefore remained valid.
[205] *Ingmar GB Ltd v Eaton Leonard Technologies Inc* (C-381/98) [2000] E.C.R. I-9305; [2001] 1 All E.R. (Comm) 329.
[206] See paras 77–91, with discussion of the legislative history of Article 19 of the Directive.
[207] In *Conseils et mise en relations (CMR) SARL v Demeures terre et tradition SARL* (C-645/16) EU:C:2018:262; [2018] Bus.L.R.1164 the CJEU held that compensation was due where termination occurred during the trial period provided for by the contract.
[208] Below, para.11-057.
[209] *Abbott v Condici Ltd* [2005] 2 Lloyd's Rep. 450 (reaching age of 65).

had by his (wrongful) conduct terminated the contract himself, though this argument is not usually attractive.[210]

11-043 **Fixed period contracts** In the case of agency for a fixed period, or to a certain age, however, it might be thought that (unless the agency is allowed to run on after the period), just as the periods of notice are inapplicable, so also is the requirement of payment of indemnity or compensation, for here the agent has taken on a fixed period contract and in doing so might be expected to have calculated whether or not he would receive adequate recompense for his outlay; though perhaps there should be a provision for termination before the end of the period by death, illness, etc. of the agent. Such an interpretation receives some support from the wording of the UK Regulations, which refer to entitlement on "termination" of the agency contract[211]; though the terminology used in the versions in other languages does not seem to give guidance here. The word "terminate" is used elsewhere in common law of a voluntary act of termination, and one might argue that it does not apply where the contract simply *expires*, or if renewable is not renewed, which is the word used in reg.14 in connection with fixed terms. Further, even if the idea of *indemnity* on expiry of a fixed term contract might be accepted, it is not easy to see why compensable *damage* should follow the (pre-arranged) expiry of a fixed term contract. In this sense, the wording of reg.17(6), which refers to "the damage he suffers as a result of the termination of his relations with his principal" may cause surprise on first reading: if the contract ends by the expiry of time, it might be thought that damage is not suffered thereby, but (if at all) by the agent's wrong estimation of the period of contract needed to recover his outlay or realise his investment. Without further background, therefore, a common lawyer might come to the conclusion that there was nothing due on the regular expiry of a fixed term contract.

It is however clear that not only indemnity, if otherwise available, but also compensation, where there is no indemnity, is available in this case, and that the word "terminates" in reg.17 is used in an intransitive sense meaning no more than "comes to an end".[212] For a start, one might say that although the agent regarded himself as needing a longer period of the contract to recover his outlay, he might not have been able to negotiate this: hence he requires some sort of protection against the results of failure to do so. It could also be said that a fixed term contract can be renewed: when the principal fails to renew such a contract he is doing something very similar to termination, which is only not termination because he has been prudent or commercially strong enough to secure a short term renewable contract.[213] Both these arguments are suggestive of a notion of good faith in the exercise of the power to terminate or not to renew. There are analogies in UK labour

---

[210] See *Geys v Société Générale* [2012] UKSC 63; [2013] 1 A.C. 623 (employment).

[211] SI 1993/3053 reg.17(1).

[212] *Light v Ty Europe Ltd* [2003] EWCA Civ 1238; [2004] 1 Lloyd's Rep. 693 at [32]; *Tigana Ltd v Decoro Ltd* [2003] EWHC 23 (QB); [2003] Eu.L.R. 189; *Frape v Emreco International Ltd* 2002 S.L.T. 371; 2001 S.C.L.R. 997, though the matter was uncertain in the UK before these cases. This applies even to non-renewal where the principal thinks that he has grounds to terminate on the agent's default but does not seek to do so: *Cooper v Pure Fishing (UK) Ltd (formerly Outdoor Technology Group (UK) Ltd)* [2004] EWCA Civ 375; [2004] 2 Lloyd's Rep. 518.

[213] But this argument is rejected, albeit in a slightly different context, in *Cooper v Pure Fishing (UK) Ltd* [2004] EWCA Civ 375; [2004] 2 Lloyd's Rep. 518.

law.[214] Finally, the thinking that entitles the agent to compensation on death or retirement suggests that there should be a right on termination of a fixed term contract.[215] This preferred interpretation requires, however, a special meaning to be attributed to the phrase "compensation for damage", and this is discussed below.

Indemnity[216]   In some countries an indemnity is payable as a matter of course. The   **11-044** directive in its final form, however, allowed countries to choose between indemnity and compensation; and for Great Britain, reg.17(2) provides that "except where the agency contract[217] otherwise provides, the commercial agent shall be entitled to be compensated rather than indemnified". The principal does not have to agree to such an arrangement, therefore, but it has been held that a reference in the contract to "compensation after termination" on the particular facts envisaged an indemnity.[218] Where indemnity is chosen, reg.17(3) provides that:

"the commercial agent shall be entitled to an indemnity if and to the extent that—

(a)   he has brought[219] the principal new customers or has significantly increased the volume of business with existing customers and the principal continues to derive substantial benefits from the business with such customers; and

(b)   the payment of this indemnity is equitable having regard to all the circumstances and, in particular, the commission lost by the commercial agent on the business transactions with such customers." [220]

This indemnity has been described for German law (where it is called "Ausgleich") as "capitalised remuneration for the continued performance". Regulation 17(4) limits it to "a figure equivalent to an indemnity for one year calculated from the

---

[214]   There are also analogies in land law. At common law a tenant for life was entitled to emblements provided that the determination of the tenancy was not caused by his own act.

[215]   The matter had been raised, but not decided, in *Whitehead v Jenks & Caitell Engineering Ltd* [1999] Eu. L.R. 827.

[216]   See in general European Commission, Report of July 23, 1996, COM 96/364 FINAL, where the method of calculation of indemnity is discussed. There is an exhaustive consideration, going up to 2010, of indemnity and compensation in Randolph and Davey, fn.1 above, containing in Ch.9 comparisons with the original proposal for a Directive, the 1996 Report, and in Chs 10 and 11 expositions of German and French law by Reiling and Saintier respectively. Since the UK Regulations created something new for the countries affected, some knowledge of the German and French laws is a help in comprehension. In general, the German law is more valuable, because it is of longer standing and formed the basis of the Directive. The French law developed later, but is essential for the understanding of the notion of compensation. A further chapter by Dr Ruth Bender, Ch.12, addresses business valuation, which is relevant in the context of the right to compensation.

[217]   The original text used the word "contact". This was corrected by SI 1998/2868. Where the parties have a series of agency contracts it can be said that the rights arise at the end of each. It has however been held that the words should normally be taken to apply at the end of the agency in general: *Moore v Piretta PTA Ltd* [1999] 1 All E.R. 173 at 179.

[218]   *Hardie Polymers Ltd v Polymerland Ltd*, 2002 S.C.L.R. 64.

[219]   It has been held that this word simply means that the agent was instrumental in obtaining new customers; specific introduction is not required: *Moore v Piretta PTA Ltd* [1999] 1 All E.R. 173 at 179. In *Marchon Germany GmbH v Karaskiewicz* (C-315/14) [2016] Bus.L.R. 694 the CJEU held that where an agent was responsible for certain of the principal's brands only, the other brands being entrusted to other commercial agents, the principal gave the agent a list of customers for other brands and the agent secured orders from some of those on the list, the agent ranked for the purpose of the indemnity as having brought new customers. See also *Re Sales of Spectacle Frames* [2017] E.C.C.19 (German Bundesgerichtshof).

[220]   See *Honyvem Informazioni Commerciali Srl v De Zotti* (C-465-04) [2006] E.C.R. I-02789 as to the impact (in Italy) of collective indemnity agreements.

commercial agent's average annual remuneration over the preceding five years and if the contract goes back less than five years the indemnity shall be calculated on the average for the period in question". This limit, which is in substantial accord with German law,[221] gives the principal some advantage in use of the indemnity, and it is not necessarily true that principals would be best advised to avoid such an arrangement. The essence of the indemnity arrangement may therefore be regarded as a buy-out on one year's remuneration, but only "if and to the extent that" the agent has brought the business and the principal continues to receive substantial benefits, and the payment is equitable. The burden of proof of these requirements appears to lie on the agent.[222]

Usually, the first step in the calculation is to ascertain the commission earned by the agent in the last year, whether in respect of new customers or additional value of business generated with existing customers. This is however only a starting point. Another feature is the estimated benefit that will accrue to the principal through business relationships with customers originally acquired by the agent or developed by the agent.[223] Of course, after the agency contract terminates a proportion of such relationships will be lost over the years. Therefore, the estimated benefit to the principal must be discounted in this respect. The period considered for this purpose ranges from two to five years. The capital sum due on this basis represents a prospective income which must be discounted at a standard interest rate to reflect the value of the indemnity. The outcome is subject to an equitable adjustment to take into account all the circumstances of the case. This seldom seems necessary, but may take into account matters such as whether the agent worked for several principals; whether he was himself in breach of contract in any respect; and whether he received high commissions in respect of customers whom he might not have introduced. It appears that the "cap" is comparatively seldom reached: it is definitely not a method of calculating the indemnity.

It appears that in Germany equitable considerations may displace the rule denying the right to indemnity where the agent's behaviour would justify immediate dismissal.[224] It is however difficult to extract such possibilities from the UK Regulations, and equally from at least the English version of the Directive itself, with which the Regulations are identical at this point save for a slight difference in punctuation.

---

[221] However, it appears that German courts interpreted the equivalent of reg.17(2)(a) on the basis that the amount of commission lost represented an upper limit for indemnity. This was held wrong by the ECJ in *Semen v Deutsche Tamoil GmbH* (C-348/07) [2009] 1 Lloyd's Rep. 653. Consequent on this, art.89B of the HGB was changed. The case also holds that where the principal is part of a group of companies, benefits accruing to other companies in the group are not to be taken into account.

[222] See the indemnity provision applied in the only English case, *Moore v Piretta PTA Ltd* [1999] 1 All E.R. 174 (fashion clothing): see Segal (1998) 142 S.J. 376 (German law was referred to). The value of the business brought in was taken and deductions were made for the existing customer base, the agent's expenses and accelerated payment. The balance exceeded the cap, and only the cap was therefore awarded (the assessment is questioned by Randolph and Davey, fn.1 above, at pp.105–106). Matters of mitigation of loss (e.g. that the agent could have taken paid employment) were held not relevant. But these, and perhaps the eventual effect of a restraint of trade clause, could perhaps be relevant in some situations. See also discussion by McGee [2011] J.B.L. 782 at 796.

[223] Where there have been several contracts in succession, the period covered by the words "the agency contract" is not confined to the contract operative at the date of termination, but the "agency" can be regarded as operative further back: *Moore v Piretta PTA Ltd* [1999] 1 All E.R. 714.

[224] See brief reference to such considerations in *Volvo Car Germany GmbH v Autohof Weidensdorf GmbH* (C-203/09) [2011] 1 All E.R. (Comm) 906 at [44].

Non-derogation   The indemnity is not compulsory. But the provision against derogation in reg.19[225] seems to mean that if an indemnity is adopted to the exclusion of compensation it must be adopted as specified in the Regulations, or under a scheme more favourable to the agent.[226]   **11-045**

Time limit   By virtue of reg.17(9) the agent loses his entitlement "if within one year following termination of his agency contract he has not notified his principal that he intends pursuing his entitlement".[227] Although informal notice may well be sufficient,[228] a formal notice is a safer procedure.   **11-046**

Damages   But by reg.17(5) "the grant of an indemnity ... shall not prevent the commercial agent from seeking damages". This follows from the nature of the indemnity. Such damages would be over and above the indemnity, and granted on normal principles of domestic law in respect of a breach of contract, where there was one; but it has been held that such an award must not allow double recovery by combining the indemnity with compensation for loss resulting in particular from loss of commission.[229] Unpaid commission could also be recoverable, whether by way of damages or debt.[230]   **11-047**

Compensation[231]   In Great Britain the indemnity is a voluntary arrangement. If, however, there is no indemnity provided for, the agent has, as stated above, a right to be what is called "compensated for damage", a right which again by reg.19 cannot be derogated from to the agent's detriment. The question then arises as to what this "compensation" is and how far it is different from ordinary damages under domestic law for wrongful termination of the contract. It is clear that it is different, for in accordance with what is said in para.11-043 above, it can arise where there is no breach of the contract at all; and further, paras (5) and (6) of reg.17 imply a distinction between "damages" (para.(5)) and "compensation for the damage he suffers as a result of the termination of his relations with his principal" (para.(6)).   **11-048**

---

[225] See above, para.11-041.

[226] cf. *Shearman v Hunter Boot Ltd* [2013] EWHC 47 (QB); [2014] E.C.C. 12, above, para.11-041.

[227] The position when a termination by notice occurs is considered in *Claramoda Ltd v Zoomphase Ltd* [2009] EWHC 2857 (Comm) (primary agency duties had ended but secondary duties continued, with the result that termination occurred at a later date).

[228] A letter from a solicitor was held to be adequate notice in *Hackett v Advanced Medical Computer Systems Ltd* [1999] C.L.Y. 111. But in *Cerascope Ltd v Todagres SA* [2008] EWHC 1502 (Ch); [2010] E.C.C. 1 a letter from lawyers was held to be insufficiently specific under Spanish law (which governed the contract and also the question of interruption of the limitation period).

[229] See *Quenon K SPRL v Beobank SA* (C-338/14) [2016] Bus. L.R. 264. Here Belgian legislation was more specific and provided that where the amount of the indemnity does not fully indemnify the commercial agent for the loss actually incurred, the agent can (in effect) claim damages for proved additional loss. It was held that since the Directive does not give clear guidance as to the circumstances in which damages can be claimed it is for Member States "in the exercise of their discretion, to determine those circumstances and the procedural rules" (at [32]). However, the Directive requires that an initial choice be made between the indemnity and compensation schemes, and "[t]he award of damages may not result in double recovery by combining the indemnity for customers with the compensation for loss resulting, in particular, from the loss of commission following termination of the contract" (at [34]).

[230] The possible overlap is considered by McGee [2011] J.B.L. 782 at 790.

[231] The UK is alone in providing a choice for the parties instead of making the choice itself, and it is not certain that this was a proper implementation of the Directive. All countries chose indemnity except France, Ireland and Iceland, where compensation was chosen; and the UK, which takes in both.

The French text of the Directive uses, indeed, a different word here—"*réparation*"—from that used in art.17(5) (equivalent to reg.17(6))—"*dommages-intérêts*": though the German text uses the same ("*Schadensersatz*"). This notion of compensation under the Directive seems therefore a special one, in effect compensation which is payable even though no breach of contract may have occurred. It may be that, before implementation of the Directive in the Member States, there was no exact parallel to it (as opposed to the indemnity) in the domestic law of any European country.[232]

11-049 **Calculation** Regulation 17(7) provides that:

> "For the purpose of these Regulations such damage shall be deemed to occur *particularly* when the termination takes place in *either or both* of the following circumstances, namely circumstances which—
>
> (a) deprive the commercial agent of the commission which proper performance of the agency contract would have procured for him whilst providing his principal with substantial benefits linked to the activities of the commercial agent; or
>
> (b) have not enabled the commercial agent to amortize the costs and expenses that he had incurred in the performance of the agency contract on the advice of his principal." [233]

11-050 **French law**[234] It has already been said that the compensation method is known to be derived from French law. Under French law it seems that compensation is in principle due to the agent when the contract was wrongfully terminated by the principal, or it expired for other reasons, provided that the agent suffered a loss from the termination of the relationship. The commercial agency is regarded as a matter of common interest of which the agent is (in cases where he does not assign it) deprived: his claim is quasi-proprietary.[235] This seems to be a controlling feature.[236] However, the right to compensation is excluded if the principal terminated the contract because of a serious breach by the agent ("*faute grave de l'agent*"), such as dealing in competing products; or if the agent himself terminated the contract, unless he did so for justifiable reasons such as breach by the principal, or an unjustified reduction of the agent's area of operation; or unless the agent terminated because of age, infirmity, illness and so forth. It should be noted that the French law is drafted to refer to loss ("*indemnité compensatrice en réparation du préjudice subi*" because the relationship between the parties came to an end) and does not

---

[232] Though the similarity is with the French approach, French law before the implementation of the Directive (by law 91-593 of June 25, 1991) did not award compensation in case of expiration of fixed term contracts, nor for termination due to the agent's death. It appears that the new legislation transformed the French approach on these points, thus making clear that the principal's obligation to compensate the agent is not necessarily linked to a wrongful termination of the agency relationship.

[233] Emphasis supplied.

[234] French law has remained unchanged on this point since law 91-593 of June 25, 1991, referred to in McGee [2011] J.B.L. 782, now incorporated into the Code de Commerce as arts L134- to 17. See an authoritative account in Saintier and Scholes, fn.1 above, at p.170 onwards; Christou, fn.1 above, para.3-135 onwards.

[235] See Saintier and Scholes, fn.1 above, at pp.81–82.

[236] Article L134-4(i) of the Code de Commerce states that "Les contrats intervenes entre les agents commerciaux et leurs mandants sont conclus dans l'interêt commun des parties".

refer to the accrual of substantial benefits to the principal mentioned in art.17(3) of the Directive(reg.17(3)).

In contrast with the German law on indemnity the principal owes compensation to the agent even if the agent did not acquire new customers. The emphasis is on whether the agent suffered a loss because the agency contract ended, rather than whether the principal benefited from the agent's activity. The loss is the loss of an asset, his interest in the common enterprise of himself and the principal.[237] There is of course no "cap" as under German law. In France the calculation of the award does not involve the application of a structured formula, though in fact as regards indefinite period contracts, it appears that the agent usually obtains something like the total of two average years' commissions, calculated on the basis of earnings over the last two or three years; and it may be that further sums can be added if the agent's loss is above the average. On the other hand, French courts do have the power to reduce the standard amount of compensation if it exceeds the agent's loss, because reference to that standard is not required by the applicable legislation. It appears that French judges have been reluctant to resort to this power, at least in some contexts, e.g. where the agency was terminated suddenly by reason of the principal's breach, if that breach was completely unjustified in the light of the agent's performance. It appears also that the parties may not determine in advance the amount of compensation to be paid on termination.

British cases　The method of assessment for the UK[238] is now laid down by the　**11-051** House of Lords' decision in *Lonsdale v Howard & Hallam Ltd*,[239] which supersedes all earlier authority, of which a considerable amount (of varied quality) had been accumulating.[240] Such an idea of compensation has so far been unique to French law. The opinion of Lord Hoffmann accepts the French notion that the agent is regarded "as having had a share in the goodwill of the principal's business which he has helped to create".[241] "This means, primarily, the right to future commissions 'which proper performance of the agency contract would have procured

---

[237]　See Saintier and Scholes, fn.1 above, at pp.185–186.

[238]　The Regulations apply in Scotland as well as England and Wales, and there are parallel Regulations in Northern Ireland. The Supreme Court (formerly House of Lords) is the final appellate tribunal for all three jurisdictions. But see Macgregor (2008) 12 Edin.L.Rev 86.

[239]　*Lonsdale (t/a Lonsdale Agencies) v Howard & Hallam Ltd* [2007] UKHL 32; [2007] 1 W.L.R. 2055 (shoes), in substantial accord with the judgment of Moore-Bick LJ in the Court of Appeal: [2006] EWCA 63; [2006] 1 W.L.R. 1281. Noted by Saintier (2008) 124 L.Q.R. 31; Macgregor (2008) 12 Edin.L.Rev 86 (both suggesting that the method laid down makes too much use of criteria relevant to indemnity).

[240]　Principally the decision of the Inner House of the Court of Session in *King v T Tunnock Ltd* 2000 S.C. 424; 2000 S.L.T. 744 (cakes and biscuits), which was not accepted in the House of Lords, though it may remain valid in Scotland. Other cases prior to *Lonsdale* are also considered in the opinion of Lord Hoffmann and in Randolph and Davey, fn.1 above, pp.111–117. Cases decided since the judgment in *Lonsdale*'s case include *McQuillan v McCormick* [2010] EWHC 1112 (QB); [2011] E.C.C. 18 (jewellery) and *Invicta UK Ltd v International Brands Ltd* [2013] EWHC 1564 (QB); [2013] E.C.C. 30 (wine for supermarkets); *Alan Ramsay Sales & Marketing Ltd v Typhoo Tea Ltd* [2016] EWHC 486 (Comm) (food sector, especially cash and carry and wholesale); *Monk v Largo Foods Ltd* [2016] EWHC 1387 (Comm) (agent for marketing of crisps and similar products); *W Nagel (A Firm) v Pluczenik Diamond Co NV* [2017] EWHC 1750 (Comm); [2017] 2 Lloyd's Rep. 215 (diamond dealings; where the discussion is obiter since the judge had decided that the Regulations did not apply). In each of these cases specialist advice was received by the court.

[241]　*Lonsdale (t/a Lonsdale Agencies) v Howard & Hallam Ltd* [2007] UKHL 32; [2007] 1 W.L.R. 2055 at [9].

him'."242 As already stated, in its implementation French courts have regularly awarded, though not by way of applying a rule, a sum equivalent to twice the average annual gross commission over the previous three years. It is clear however that other countries are not under any obligation to follow any one state's method of calculation.243 The French practice appears to be based on the assumption that agencies in France change hands at the sort of valuation mentioned above, whereas there is no such market in the UK.244 The courts of the UK are entitled, therefore, to use their own methods of calculating the loss for which the compensation is payable. "What has to be valued is the income stream which the agency would have generated."245 This should be done "by reference to the value of the agency on the assumption that it continued: the amount which the agent could reasonably expect to receive for the right to stand in his shoes, continue to perform the duties of the agency and receive the commission which he would have received".246 If the agency was unassignable, it must be assumed that a purchaser would have been entitled to take it over, but not that he would thereby acquire an assignable asset.247 The court would require information about "the standard methodology for the valuation of such businesses", though there might be cases where courts could eventually take judicial notice of the "standard case".248 In the case in question the business concerned was declining, and the agency would not be likely to change hands at any considerable value. The court would therefore have been justified in awarding nothing,249 and this is a significant part of the decision. However, a small award made by the judge (much less than the amount claimed) was approved. By the same reasoning, the converse might have been the case had the business been increasing. The earlier judgment of the Court of Appeal in *Lonsdale* had previously been considered in another case250 in which the judge said that he would only have made a nominal award of £2 on a claim unsupported by evidence, and doubted whether the court should simply "make the best estimate it can".

11-052   However, loss of goodwill is not the only damage in respect of which there may be recovery. On this issue, the judgment of Moore-Bick LJ in the Court of Appeal

---

242 *Lonsdale (t/a Lonsdale Agencies) v Howard & Hallam Ltd* [2007] UKHL 32; [2007] 1 W.L.R. 2055 at [10].

243 *Honyvem Informazioni Commerciali SrL v Mariella de Zotti* (C-465/04) [2006] E.C.R. I-02879; and for this reason the House of Lords in Lonsdale declined to make a reference to the ECJ.

244 *Lonsdale (t/a Lonsdale Agencies) v Howard & Hallam Ltd* [2007] UKHL 32; [2007] 1 W.L.R. 2055 at [18]. See also at [26]: "the French practice is of no evidential value whatever". For a critique of the method used, see McGee [2011] J.B.L. 782 at 791 onwards. As to valuation methods, see Randolph and Davey, fn.1 above, Ch.12.

245 *Lonsdale (t/a Lonsdale Agencies) v Howard & Hallam Ltd* [2007] UKHL 32; [2007] 1 W.L.R. 2055 at [12].

246 *Lonsdale (t/a Lonsdale Agencies) v Howard & Hallam Ltd* [2007] UKHL 32; [2007] 1 W.L.R. 2055 at [21]. It may be assumed that where the agency has been covered by more than one contract, its general value rather than that referable to the last contract in time will be taken into account, as has been held in the case of indemnity in *Moore v Piretta PTA Ltd* [1999] 1 All E.R. 174, fn.217 above: see Randolph and Davey, fn.1 above, at p.89.

247 *Lonsdale (t/a Lonsdale Agencies) v Howard & Hallam Ltd* [2007] UKHL 32; [2007] 1 W.L.R. 2055 at [13].

248 *Lonsdale (t/a Lonsdale Agencies) v Howard & Hallam Ltd* [2007] UKHL 32; [2007] 1 W.L.R. 2055 at [35], [36].

249 *Lonsdale (t/a Lonsdale Agencies) v Howard & Hallam Ltd* [2007] UKHL 32; [2007] 1 W.L.R. 2055 at [34]. See also *Warren (t/a On-line Cartons and Print v Drukkeri)* [2014] EWCA Civ 993; [2015] 1 Lloyd's Rep. 111.

250 *Vick v Vogle-Gapes Ltd* [2006] EWHC 1665 (QB); (2006) 150 S.J.L.B. 917 (Richard Seymour QC).

in *Lonsdale* remains significant. When the agency is terminated in circumstances which deprive him of the commission which proper performance of the contract would have enabled him to earn:

"the value of the business at the date of termination ought to reflect the agent's future earnings which are the rewards he was entitled to receive in respect of any benefit that his principal might obtain from his activities. In this type of situation, therefore, the agent should be adequately compensated if he is paid the value at the date of termination of the business he has built up."

But:

"if the agency is terminated in circumstances where the agent has not been able to amortise expenses which he has incurred on the advice of the principal in setting up the agency, the value attaching to the business may or may not provide sufficient compensation ... the agent is entitled to recover whatever loss he can show he has suffered which in a case of this kind might consist in whole or in part of the amount of the unamortised expenses."[251]

This latter point is not adverted to in the opinion of Lord Hoffmann, but there seems no reason why it should not be regarded as correct.

11-053 It remains to ask whether an action in damages for breach of contract might also be available for loss suffered (assuming that double recovery could be avoided) in appropriate circumstances. It would of course not normally apply where the agency determined by death, retirement or expiry of a fixed term; though it might sometimes if appropriate notice is not given. The fact that such an action is expressly preserved by reg.17(5) in respect of the indemnity is some indication that it is not available where the remedy is compensation. It is also possible that in French law some such elements could be taken in under the compensation award, though it would seem likely that a remedy for termination in bad faith might be separate. But there is no indication that the Directive supersedes other remedies, let alone of which remedies would be superseded, and as a matter of principle other remedies for breach of contract should survive if relevant, and if the elements of loss could be separated out.[252] In particular, it is clear that sums due as commission, but payable at a later date, under reg.8(a)[253] would be a separate matter. Overall, though there is undoubtedly overlap in the methods of calculation, that for compensation, which starts by looking to the past, tends the favour the agent more than that for indemnity, which tends to look to future prospects and is subject to a cap of one year's average remuneration.

11-054 **Non-derogation** As has been stated, reg.19 provides that the parties may not derogate from the compensation provisions before the agency contract expires.[254]

---

[251] *Lonsdale v Howard & Hallam Ltd* [2006] EWCA Civ 760; [2006] 1 W.L.R. 1281 at [29].

[252] See Moore-Bick LJ in the *Lonsdale* case, [2006] EWCA Civ 760; [2006] 1 W.L.R. 1281, at [28] (compensation for damage caused by breach of duty could be claimed outside the Regulations); *McQuillan v McCormick* [2010] EWHC 11123 (QB); [2011] E.C.C. 18 (outstanding commission and damages for noncompliance with notice requirements); *Computer Associates UK Ltd v Software Incubator Ltd* [2016] EWHC 1587 (QB); [2017] Bus. L.R. 245; reversed on other grounds [2018] EWCA Civ 518; [2018] 1 Lloyd's Rep. 613. Saintier and Scholes, fn.1 above, at p.160. This point was not discussed in the House of Lords.

[253] See above, para.11-032.

[254] See above, paras 11-041 and 11-045.

11-055 **Time limit**   Like the indemnity, the right to compensation is by virtue of reg.17(9) lost if the agent does not notify his principal within one year that he intends pursuing the entitlement.[255]

11-056 **Cases where no indemnity or compensation due**   Regulation 18 provides that the indemnity or[256] compensation is not payable where:

> "(a)   the principal has terminated the agency contract because of default attributable to the commercial agent which would justify immediate termination of the agency contract pursuant to Regulation 16 above."[257]

This refers straight back to reg.16[258] and is not difficult to understand: the agent loses the right to these benefits if he commits a breach entitling the principal in effect to dismiss him by virtue of general rules of law.[259] It does not however apply where either the principal simply does not renew the agency, even though he may fail to do so because he believes that the agent's conduct justifies termination,[260] or the agent simply refuses a renewal proposal from the principal.[261] Nor, by reason of general common law principles as to discharge by breach, does it apply where the principal does not accept the agent's repudiation.[262] The phrase "attributable to the agent" is preferable for a common lawyer to the reference to "blame" in reg.11(1), which as stated above can be given a rather imprecise meaning.[263] Equally it obviously will not apply if the commercial agent has himself terminated the contract without justification.

---

[255] See above, para.11-046.

[256] These words, which appear in the Directive, seem to have been omitted in error and were added to the Regulations by SI 1993/3173.

[257] As to which see above, para.11-039. For examples see *Vick v Vogle-Gapes Ltd* [2006] EWHC 1665 (TCC) (uncooperative behaviour); *Crane v Sky In-Home Service Ltd* [2007] EWHC 66 (Ch); [2007] 2 All E.R. (Comm) 599 (passing off main supplier's warranty service as agent's own); *Nigel Fryer Joinery Services Ltd v Ian Firth Hardware Ltd* [2008] EWHC 767 (Ch); [2008] 2 Lloyd's Rep. 108 (failure to notify working for other companies, and to make appropriate reports); *Gledhill v Bentley Designs Ltd* [2010] EWHC 1965 (QB); [2011] 1 Lloyd's Rep. 270 (rude behaviour: not stated that the agent was a commercial agent: see above, para.10-042). The question whether this covers termination for an invalid reason when a valid reason operative at the time of the termination is subsequently discovered (which is effective at common law) is briefly considered in *Rossetti Marketing Ltd v Diamond Sofa Co Ltd* [2012] EWCA Civ 1021; [2013] 1 All E.R. (Comm) 308. It was common ground in the *Nigel Fryer* case, above, that this could not be done; but Lord Neuberger in *Rossetti* is doubtful, as was Bean J in *Cureton v Mark Insulations Ltd* [2006] EWHC 2279 (Admin), cited by Lord Neuberger at [59]. Cf above, para.11-039.

[258] Above, para.11-039.

[259] The policy is however questioned, as involving an unjustified forfeiture, by Bennett, fn.1 above, para.11.48.

[260] *Cooper v Pure Fishing (UK) Ltd* [2003] EWCA Civ 375; [2004] 2 Lloyd's Rep. 518. It must be doubtful to what extent the contract can be drafted so as to create such a "default". See *Laboratoires Arkopharma SA v Gravier* [2003] E.C.C. 333, where a contract designated failure to meet targets in such terminology, but the French Cour de Cassation held the question to be subject to the general law. Nor will it apply where the relevant conduct, which would otherwise justify immediate termination, occurs after the giving of notice but before the contract expired: *Volvo Car Germany GmbH v Autohof Weidensdorf GmbH (C-203/09)* [2011] 1 All E.R. (Comm) 906, suggesting however, in the case of an indemnity, that the agent's conduct might sometimes be taken into account in determining what sum was "equitable".

[261] *Elsevier Masson v La Diffusion Sofradif* [2017] E.C.C. 30 (French Cour de Cassation).

[262] *Alan Ramsay Sales & Marketing Ltd v Typhoo Tea Ltd* [2016] EWHC 486 (Comm); [2016] 4 W.L.R. 59. The agent was however held entitled to damages for termination not consistent with the normal notice period.

[263] See above, para.11-034.

Regulation 18(b) thus provides that indemnity or compensation is not payable **11-057** where:

"the commercial agent has himself terminated the agency contract, unless such termination is justified—

(i)   by circumstances attributable to the principal, or

(ii)   on grounds of age, infirmity or illness of the commercial agent in consequence of which he cannot reasonably be required to continue his activities."

Plainly, if it is the agent that terminates the contract without justification he is not entitled to commission. On the face of it (i) is not surprising: if the principal commits a repudiatory breach entitling the agent to terminate the contract, the agent remains entitled to compensation. However, there are differences. The first is that where the "circumstances attributable to the principal" involve a breach of contract by him, the normal common law rules referred to in art.16 would regard the repudiation as requiring acceptance by the agent.[264] This does not appear to be envisaged by the Directive and could cause difficulties if it were argued that the breach had not been accepted, but rather, waived.[265] Secondly, it has been held that *"circumstances attributable to the principal"* include situations where there has been no breach at all, as where the principal ceases to manufacture such goods but no breach of contract by him is involved and there is no frustration.[266] This to some extent fits with the third point, that reg.18(1)(b) makes no reference to "immediate" termination, a word which is obviously more appropriate to termination for breach, nor to "default" as opposed to "circumstances". Although it has been said that reg.18(1)(a) and (b) are "two sides of the same coin"[267] this is not perhaps completely true.

The reference in (ii) to age, infirmity or illness is consistent with the fact that the right to compensation survives the death of the agent, and it has been held that it applies to an agent who simply reaches the retiring age, being still capable of carrying on.[268]

Lastly, under sub-para.(c), the right to indemnity or compensation is excluded where:

"the commercial agent, with the agreement of his principal, assigns his rights and duties under the agency contract to another person."

The assumption seems to be that in such a case the agent has obtained the value

---

[264] See *Roy v MR Pearlman Ltd* 1999 S.C. 459; 2000 S.L.T. 727 at [24]. See also *Bell Electric Ltd v Aweco Appliance Systems Gmbh* [2002] EWHC 872 (QB); [2002] Eu.L.R. 443. In *Alan Ramsay Sales & Marketing Ltd v Typhoo Tea Ltd* [2016] EWHC 486 (Comm) the rule is applied to breach by the *agent*.

[265] There are difficulties in this connection in respect of employment contracts: see *Chitty on Contracts* (33rd edn), Vol.2, para.40-193; *Geys v Société Générale* [2012] UKSC 63; [2013] 1 A.C. 523. The agency context could be considered analogous: but see *Atlantic Underwriting Agencies Ltd v Cia di Assicurazioni di Milano SpA* [1979] 2 Lloyd's Rep. 240; and discussion in *Roy v MR Pearlman Ltd* 1999 S.C. 459; 2000 S.L.T. 727.

[266] *King v T Tunnock Ltd*, 2000 S.C. 424; 2000 S.L.T. 744.

[267] See *Bell Electric Ltd v Aweco Appliance Systems Gmbh* [2002] EWHC 872 (QB); [2002] Eu.L.R. 443 at [48] onwards, per Elias J (non-payment of commission: the case was appealed on a different point [2002] EWCA Civ 1501; [2003] 1 All E.R. 344).

[268] *Abbott v Condici Ltd* [2005] 2 Lloyd's Rep. 450.

of the goodwill and so forth in the purchase price of his business; or has given it to another, for example a son or daughter. If the principal does not consent, the assignment may be ineffective under the general law of assignment, and the attempt to achieve it might be a repudiatory breach of contract by the agent. On the other hand failure to consent might be a breach of the requirement of good faith.[269]

11-058   **Restraint of trade clauses**   A restraint of trade clause is defined as "an agreement restricting the business activities of a commercial agent following termination of the agency contract".[270] Such clauses are dealt with in reg.20, under which a restraint of trade clause is valid:

> "only if and to the extent that—
>
> (a)   it is concluded in writing; and
> (b)   it relates to the geographical area or the group of customers and the geographical area entrusted to the commercial agent and to the kind of goods covered by his agency under the contract."

By para.(2) it shall be valid for not more than two years after termination of the agency contract.

This provision appears to provide a substitute for the normal common law rules in this context. In practice it probably varies little from the common law on contracts in restraint of trade, except for the requirement of writing, and the fact that where a legislative provision uses, as it must, specific wording, the result might not be exactly the same as would be expected in a system only using case law in the area.[271] There is no such requirement at common law, but it does not seem likely that an agreement of this nature, which requires some precision in its drafting, would easily be entered into orally. The restriction to two years is a fixed limit, but it may be that restrictions on agents of this type for longer than two years might not easily be held reasonable at common law. The restrictions to certain types of customers and goods are likewise broadly in accord with the common law rules, though differences of detail could well occur.[272] Paragraph (3) preserves the effect of domestic enactments or rules of law which restrict the enforceability of restraint of trade clauses to a greater extent than the Regulations or enables the court to reduce the obligations on the parties resulting from such clauses. It is in fact conceivable that the common law rules would operate more strictly than this regulation in some instances. The English courts have, however, no specific power to reduce the obligations under such contracts; but the power to sever invalid portions of contracts, which they have, can also come under the words.[273]

---

[269]   See above, para.11-025. On assignment see Saintier and Scholes, fn.1 above, at pp.176–177. In *Rossetti Marketing Ltd v Diamond Sofa Co Ltd* [2012] EWCA Civ 1021; [2013] 1 All E.R. (Comm) 308 it was held that the Regulation envisages the new agent having taken both the principal's rights and duties: see at [55] and [56]. This analysis is accepted in *Invicta UK v International Brands Ltd* [2013] EWHC 1564 (QB); [2013] E.C.C. 30. A possible assignment situation is also analysed (with the conclusion that there was no assignment) in *Barnett Fashion Agency Ltd v Nigel Hall Menswear Ltd* [2011] EWHC 978 (QB).

[270]   SI 1993/3053 reg.2(1).

[271]   See however *BCM Group Ltd v Visualmark Ltd* [2006] EWHC 1831 (QB), where the wording of the Regulations (which covered others than customers "entrusted to" the agent) was applied to make the restriction too wide.

[272]   As to the common law on contracts in restraint of trade see *Chitty on Contracts* (33rd edn), Vol.I, paras 16-106 onwards.

[273]   This seems to be assumed in *BCM Group Ltd v Visualmark Ltd* [2006] EWHC 1831 (QB).

CHAPTER 12

CONFLICT OF LAWS[1]

INTRODUCTION

The first 16 editions of this work did not refer to the conflict of laws at all. The **12-001**
next two contained a "Note on the Conflict of Laws" suggesting that the number
of separate topics deployed within the general law of agency, and within the work,
made considering each separately from the point of view of the conflict of laws
impracticable; and that the central problems of dealing through another, and the
exiguous English case law on the topic, were, like the more specific topics, already
adequately dealt with in books on the conflict of laws in general.

However, English decisions involving points of basic agency law in a foreign
context have become more frequent; also, an early version of the European Commission's proposal for a Regulation on the Law Applicable to Contractual Obligations (Rome I) actually contained a (somewhat unsatisfactory) provision purporting to deal with the topic specifically. This was dropped before adoption of the final
version,[2] which excludes, as did its predecessor the Rome Convention on the Law
Applicable to Contractual Obligations,[3] "the question whether an agent is able to
bind a principal ... in relation to a third party".[4] The scope and significance of this
exclusion are by no means as straightforward as may appear: this will be considered

---

[1]   See Dicey, Morris and Collins, *The Conflict of Laws* (15th edn, 2012), Vol.2, para.33R-407 onwards,
    containing much valuable discussion and material; Verhagen, *Agency in Private International Law*
    (1995), containing text and discussion of the Hague Convention on the Law Applicable to Agency
    of 1978, which was ratified only by Argentina, France, the Netherlands and Portugal, though it has
    had some indirect effect elsewhere; Breslauer, "Agency in Private International Law" (1938) 50
    Jur.Rev 282; Rees and Flesch, "Agency and Vicarious Liability in Conflict of Laws" (1960) 60
    Col.L.Rev 75. For comparative approaches in the English language, see Wolff, *Private International
    Law* (1944), para.424; Rabel, *The Conflict of Laws: a Comparative Study* (2nd edn), Vol.3, Chs 39-
    41; Rigaux, *International Encyclopedia of Comparative Law*, Vol.III, Ch.29; Gebauer, in Leible (ed.),
    General Principles of European Private International Law (Kluwer, 2016), Ch.16; Kleinschmidt,
    in Basedow et al (eds), *Encyclopedia of Private International Law*, Vol.I (Edward Elgar Publish-
    ing, 2017), pp.29–39. The writer of this chapter is much indebted to discussions on this topic with
    Professor Michele Graziadei.
[2]   Regulation 593/2008 [2008] OJ L177/6, taken with Corrigendum [2006] OJL 309/87, which ap-
    plies it to contracts concluded as from December 17, 2009. For an extended discussion see
    McParland, *The Rome I Regulation on the Law Applicable to Contractual Obligations* (OUP, 2015).
    The effect of the Rome I and Rome II Regulations is preserved (with minor changes) by the Law
    Applicable to Contractual Obligations and Non-Contractual Obligations (Amendment, etc)(EU Exit)
    Regulations 2019 (SI 2019/834), effective on IP Completion Day.
[3]   Formerly applicable under the Contracts (Applicable Law) Act 1990.
[4]   Article I.2(g).

below.[5] But while the English case law is scant, it seems worthwhile putting forward what, because of the paucity of authority, are bound to be mostly not much more than suggestions and pointers as to the law which should apply to the salient separate topics within the law of agency in connection with contractual obligations, both under and outside the Rome I Regulation.

Most of the inquiry is directed towards whether an agent can enter into contractual obligations binding and entitling his principal (including corporate principals), though the question can also arise during the performance of contractual obligations by an agent. Questions of the latter type are normally to be solved by the law governing the main obligation.[6] This chapter makes only brief reference to situations where agency reasoning is deployed in the law of tort, property, restitution or unjust enrichment. Questions of statutory representation in cases of incapacity are not considered as part of agency law in common law countries, and situations where agency reasoning is in some limited form found within specific contexts such as succession and insolvency are not discussed here.

12-002   **The internal and external aspects of the law of agency**   It is fundamental to the understanding of the law of agency that it has two aspects, the internal relationship between principal and agent, and the external relationship between principal and third party created by the agent.[7] Any consideration of the law of agency in the conflict of laws must start from this distinction. As in the substantive law of agency, there is in the conflict of laws an ongoing tension between the notion that a principal should not be held for more than what he has authorised and that which seeks to protect a third party who may have had no practicable way of discovering whether or not an agent with whom he dealt was authorised. On the basis of this general distinction, it might seem appropriate then to say that the relationship between principal and agent is governed by the law governing that internal relationship, whereas the relationship between principal and third party is governed by the law governing the external relationship, each of which would under common law involve questions of ascertaining the intentions of the parties to it. There are in fact cases where something like this seems to have been accepted or conceded as regards the agent's actual authority.[8] The general proposition is true for pure contractual issues, but as regards questions of authority it is too simplistic.

12-003   **The internal law: the Rome I Regulation**   If one takes first the law governing the relationship between principal and agent, this relationship normally (but not necessarily) involves some form of contract. As such the law applicable to it is now controlled in the UK by the Rome I Regulation.[9] This starts by providing that the

---

5   See below, para.12-010.
6   See *Lexington Ins Co v Multinacional de Seguros SA* [2008] EWHC 1170 (Comm); [2009] 1 All E.R. (Comm) 35. A case in which a different law was applied may be the *Ruby SS Co* case, discussed below, para.12-016.
7   See above, para.1-019.
8   See *SEB Trygg Holding Aktiebolag v Manches* [2005] EWHC 35 (Comm); [2005] 2 Lloyd's Rep. 129 at [18] onwards. (point not addressed on appeal [2005] EWCA Civ 1237; [2006] 1 Lloyd's Rep. 318); *Emeraldian Ltd v Wellmix Shipping Ltd (The Vine)* [2010] EWHC 1411 (Comm); [2011] 1 Lloyd's Rep.301 at [157], [165]. But see below para.12-017.
9   EC 593/2008, effective December 17, 2009. See in general Dicey Morris and Collins, fn.1 above, Vol.2, Ch.32.

contract is governed by the law chosen by the parties.[10] Failing that, recourse is to be had to a list of rules concerning specific types of contract laid down in Article 4. Under these, if the agency contract is to be regarded as one for the provision of services, the contract is governed by the law of the country where the service provider has his habitual residence[11]; a distribution contract, which may sometimes involve lesser agency functions,[12] is governed by the law of the distributor's habitual residence.[13] An agent's contract would often be one for the provision of services. If that classification is inapplicable, or if the elements of the contract would be covered by more than one of these rules, the contract is governed by the law of the country where the party required to effect the characteristic performance of the contract has his habitual residence. In general it may be assumed that it is normally the agent's performance which ranks as characteristic.[14] However, if it is clear from the circumstances of the case that the contract is manifestly more closely connected with another country, the law of that country applies[15]; and if the law applicable cannot be determined by the criteria laid down, a contract is governed by the law of the country with which it is most closely connected.[16]

Some persons exercising agency powers may be employees. For individual employment contracts, a separate article is relevant, Article 8, the purpose of which is to preserve the protection conferred on the employee by the law that would have been applicable in the absence of choice.[17] In the absence of choice of law, the law of the country in or from which the employee habitually caries out his work in performance of the contract applies; if that cannot be determined, the law of the country where the place of business in which the employee was engaged is situated; and there is a similar provision to that above for situations where it appears that a contract is more closely connected with another country.

It should be noted that the Rome I Regulation may apply where the relationship **12-004** between principal and agent is not, or may not be, contractual in common law terms. This might occur, for example, where a non-professional agent simply acts without remuneration under a power of attorney. From a common law point of view there

---

[10] Article 3.1.

[11] Article 4.1(b). In *Wood Floor Solutions Andreas Domberger GmbH v Silvo Trade SA* (C-19/09) [2010] 1 W.L.R. 1900 the ECJ treated a *commercial agency* contract (a specialised institution: see Ch.11 above) as one for the provision of services under Article 5(1)(b) of Council Regulation 44/2001 on jurisdiction and the enforcement of judgments. See the judgment, and in more detail the opinion of Advocate General Trstenjak at [53] onwards, where the nature of the contract is considered.

[12] See above, para.1-035.

[13] Article 4(1)(f). Likewise a franchise contract is governed by the law of the place of habitual residence of the franchisee: Article 4.1(e). A contract for the sale of goods by auction is governed by the law of the country where the auction takes place, if such a place can be determined: Article 4(1)(g).

[14] In *Hogg Insurance Brokers Ltd v Guardian Insurance Co Inc* [1997] 1 Lloyd's Rep. 412 it was held under the original Rome Convention that the employment of an English insurance broker evidenced an intention that the broker should perform his professional services and if possible obtain reinsurance in England. See also (under the original Convention) *Bank of Baroda v Vysya Bank Ltd* [1994] 2 Lloyd's Rep. 87 (confirming bank); *Albon v Naza Motor Trading Sdn Bhd* [2007] EWHC 9 (Ch); [2007] 1 W.L.R. 2489 at [30]; *Lawlor v Sandvik Mining and Construction Mobile Crushers and Screens Ltd* [2012] EWHC 1188 (QB); [2012] 2 Lloyd's Rep. 25 (commercial agency: governed by Spanish law).

[15] Article 4.3. See *Intercontainer Interfrigo (ICF) SC v Balkenende Oosthuizen BV* (C-133/080) [2010] Q.B. 411; noted by Dickinson [2010] L.M.C.L.Q. 27.

[16] Article 4.4.

[17] See Dicey, Morris and Collins, fn 1 above, Rule 238.

may be no supporting contractual relationship between principal and agent, or at best an exiguous one.[18] It is submitted that the idea of contract referred in the Regulation must be an autonomous and (to a common lawyer) loose one[19] which takes in mandate, a civil law notion under which one person is mandated to act on behalf of another, an arrangement which has been classified as a consensual contract from Roman times. On this basis the Regulation should at any rate usually be applied to the internal relationship arising under a power of attorney or otherwise, whether or not a common lawyer would recognise it as contractual.[20] Although the word "mandate" is sometimes used at common law in an agency context, there is no direct common law parallel with the contract of mandate, and indeed the phrase "contract of agency" itself has little meaning, though it could accurately be applied to a contract with a broker who simply brings two parties together, such as a stockbroker. As to *how* the Regulation applies in such cases, the relevant categories seem to be those of a service provider or more simply an agent rendering characteristic performance as such.

12-005 **Concepts used by the Rome I Regulation: habitual residence**   The notion of habitual residence, used in several of the specific rules referred to above, is developed in Article 19 of the Rome I Regulation. The habitual residence of companies and other bodies, corporate or unincorporated, is their place of central administration; of an individual, it is his or her principal place of business. Where a contract is concluded in the course of operations of an agency, branch or any other establishment, the place where it is located[21] is the place of habitual residence. The relevant time is that of conclusion of the contract.

12-006 **Consumer contracts**   The Rome I Regulation contains special provisions for consumer contracts, directed to protection of the consumer, in Article 6, and these also may affect the law applicable to the internal relationship. Under these provisions it is likely to be the principal who is the consumer. These will be relevant, for example, to contracts between clients and auctioneers, real estate agents, lawyers, or stockbrokers who do not operate solely in the client's country, and they may entitle the consumer to the protection of the law of the country of his own residence.[22] Real estate agents, however, though they may attract the provisions of Rome I in some respects, normally act as canvassing agents only: as such they are considered below.[23] Lawyers perform various different functions, of which agency is only one.

---

[18]   cf. below, para.12-008.
[19]   What is required can be said to be an "obligation freely assumed by one party towards another"; *Jakob Handte & Co GmbH v Traitments Mecano-Chimniques des Surfaces SA* (C-26/91) [1992] E.C.R. I-3967; Dicey, Morris and Collins, fn.1 above, Vol.2, para.32-016.
[20]   There is recent discussion of such issues in *Pan Oceanic Chartering Inc v UNIPEC UK Co Ltd* [2016] EWHC 2774 (Comm); [2017] 2 All E.R. (Comm) 196 at [151] onwards (shipbroker deprived of commission by act of charterer); see also *Kent v Paterson-Brown* [2018] EWHC 2008 (Ch) (no consideration in relationship between principal and agent: governed as a contract by Swiss law).
[21]   In *Etablissements Somafer SA v Saar-Ferngas AG* (C-33/78) [1979] 1 C.M.L.R. 490 the ECJ held that the place of business "must have the appearance of permanency": at [12].
[22]   See Dicey, Morris and Collins, fn.1 above, Vol.2, Rule 235.
[23]   See below, para.12-029.

The internal relationship: conferral of authority separate from accompany- **12-007**
ing contract   It must be noted next that if there is an internal contract between
principal and contemplate the exercise of agency powers by one of the parties to
it, it is still not easy nor by modern standards appropriate to consider that contract
as of itself constituting the source of the agent's authority. As is stated earlier in this
work, the conferral of authority is and must be, at least from an analytical point of
view, a separate unilateral manifestation of will.[24] This is demonstrated by at least
three features. First, it is generally accepted that the authority may in most cases
be withdrawn notwithstanding that doing so may create a breach of any internal
contract between principal and agent.[25] Secondly, the relationship between principal
and agent may vary: it may be a contract for the hire of services, or it may be the
equivalent of a mandate but, as is said above, it may, at least at common law, not
be contractual at all—the agent may act gratuitously, and/or may have no duty to
act. Thirdly, in civilian jurisdictions it is often pointed out that the capacity to act
as agent may be different from that required of principal or agent for the contract
made to be effective.[26] The conferral of authority is therefore analytically best
regarded as something separate, whether prior to, simultaneous with or (by ratification) subsequent to any accompanying contract. Although it appears that in some
legal systems the mandate, though a contract, can be or has been itself thought of
as a source of authority, this is not easy to justify analytically.[27] The correct approach is reflected in substance in a distinction taken by civil lawyers between
mandate and representation. The mandate is the internal element between principal
and agent, representation the agent's power to create relations with others. Where
it is not intended that the agent have such power, some expositions may speak of
mandate without representation. When representation is intended, the question
arises: what law should govern such conferral?

Powers of attorney   The separate nature of conferral of authority is in fact   **12-008**
demonstrated for common law by the institution of a power of attorney. In the
important case of *Chatenay v Brazilian Submarine Telegraph Co*[28] a power of attorney was said to be a "one-sided instrument ... not in any sense a contract".[29] It
is simply evidence of a grant of authority as described above; but its separate and
tangible nature certainly makes it easier to look for a separate law governing it, and
hence, pursuant to what is said above, for a law governing the grant of authority in
general. Internally, in some cases the attorney will operate under a mutual contract,
whether mandate or some other, entitling him to remuneration and indemnification, but in others there may be no obligation to act at all nor entitlement to any
remuneration against his principal (though there could be a right to
indemnification[30]). The absence of a contract of mandate in common law means that
the nature of the internal arrangements supporting a power of attorney may require
careful analysis before a governing law or laws are determined.

---

[24]   See above, para.1-006; and especially Müller-Freienfels, "Legal Relations in the Law of Agency"
(1964) 13 Am.J. Comp. Law 193 at 203.
[25]   See above, Articles 117 and 120.
[26]   See above, Articles 4 and 5.
[27]   See Graziadei, Mattei and Smith, *Commercial Trusts in European Private Law* (2005), pp.48-52:
"A Note on Terminology".
[28]   *Chatenay v Brazilian Submarine Telegraph Co* [1891] 1 Q.B. 79.
[29]   *Chatenay v Brazilian Submarine Telegraph Co* [1891] 1 Q.B. 79 at 85, per Lindley LJ.
[30]   See above, Article 62.

12-009 **The external relationship**   When one comes to the external contractual relationship between principal and third party, this, as a separate contract, is also governed by the Rome I Regulation and hence by the law chosen by the parties to that contract in question, or failing that the law indicated under the various additional criteria indicated in the Regulation.[31] But here a different agency phenomenon may arise: even if the contract is not authorised by the authority actually conferred on the agent, there may be a question of whether the principal is liable under the doctrine of apparent authority, because it reasonably appears to the third party that the agent has such authority. English law, and the laws of most common law countries,[32] base this liability on estoppel, which means that it only operates against the principal, who can sue on the contract only if he ratifies.

12-010 **The exclusion of authority questions from the Rome I Regulation**   Article 1(2)(g) of the Rome I Regulation excludes altogether from its scope "the question whether an agent is able to bind a principal, or an organ to bind a company or other body corporate, in relation to a third party". This plainly covers apparent as well as actual authority. The *Giuliano/Lagarde Report* attached to the original Rome Convention on the Law Applicable to Contractual Obligations,[33] which initiated the exclusion, says that the reason for this is that "it is difficult to accept the principle of freedom of contract on this point". What is intended to be excluded by this provision is simply the rules for determining the law governing the conferring of authority (as opposed to any contract accompanying or resulting from the conferral) referred to above. This approach therefore regards the granting of authority, including ratification and the principal's manifestation leading to apparent authority, as a separate notion, entitled to its own choice of law rule, and seeks an indication for what that rule is. A rule actually utilising the notion of choice of the parties is said to be unacceptable for this purpose, perhaps because it may be thought to create a danger of one party in effect choosing himself into a law that suits his purposes.[34] To separate off authority of all types from the contractual arrangements associated with it in this way fits with the distinction made in the nineteenth century by Laband between the internal and external aspects of agency: the authority goes to the external element.[35] But for the purposes of the conflict of laws it gives rise to

---

[31]   See Dicey, Morris and Collins, fn.1 above, Vol.2, Ch.32.

[32]   In the US, a different approach is taken by *Restatement, Third, Agency*, para 2.03, comment b, p.136.

[33]   Rome Convention on the Law Applicable to Contractual Obligations [1980] OJ C282, comment to Article 1 at para.7.

[34]   See Dicey, Morris and Collins, fn.1 above, Vol.2, para.33-447. But see Kleinschmidt, fn.1 above, pp.36–37. Article 14 of the Hague Convention on the Law Applicable to Agency of 1978 applies a chosen law in specific circumstances.

[35]   See above, para.1-025; Rabel, fn.1 above, Ch.40, esp. at pp.123–127: "The German, and to a certain degree the English, courts have recognised that the power of an agent to affect the rights and duties of the principal constitutes an independent institution and ought to have its own proper law, not necessarily coincident with those governing either of the two other relationships". The Hague Convention on the Law Applicable to Agency of 1978 states that among matters governed by the internal law are "the existence and extent of the authority of the agent" (Article 8(a)), and that a different law governs "the existence and extent of the agent's authority and the effect of the agent's exercise or purported exercise of his authority" as regards third parties (Article 11). The internal rule presumably governs, for example, the question whether the agent is liable to the principal for exceeding his authority, the external, whether the principal is liable to the third party where the agent was unauthorised but had apparent authority: see Verhagen, fn.1 above, paras 5.2.2, 5.2.3 and 5.2.18. On this point, see also McParland, *The Rome I Regulation on the Law Applicable to Contractual Obligations*, fn.2 above, paras 7.150 et seq.

problems as to exactly which elements within the phenomena of agency reasoning are excluded, and as to what connecting factor or factors should be used for such questions of authority.

Problems with such an exclusion It may be presumed that what is isolated as related to the conferring of authority is at least its creation, scope and termination, and questions of apparent authority. Some would take it further than this, for example into the question of liability to a third party for lack of authority.[36] But it may be suggested that, however correct in theory, the isolating of the conferring of authority for the purposes of choice of law encounters practical problems in duly differentiating between questions relating to the authority itself and questions arising out of its exercise, the latter of which would be dealt with by the law governing the contract entered into.[37] And from a common lawyer's point of view the connecting factors that may be invoked create difficulties in themselves. Reference to the place where the authority is to be or is exercised, which on the whole appears to be the dominant approach among civil lawyers, introduces an undesirable geographical criterion open to the same objections in days of rapid communication in commerce as the old reliance on *lex loci contractus*. Further, where the authority may be exercised in more than one jurisdiction, a problem arises as to whether there can be different applicable laws.[38] On the other hand, if criteria relating to the residence or place of residence or business of the agent are to be used, as they often are in international instruments,[39] the selection of the applicable law, while no doubt intended to give fair and predictable results in as many cases as possible, is likely to create potentially arbitrary consequences of a sort to which common lawyers are again not usually sympathetic. Therefore, while separating off questions of authority may indeed be acceptable in principle, and assist in the perception of agency phenomena, the special choice of law rule or rules which doing so is likely to entail makes it less easy to accept fully for the purposes of the conflict of laws.[40]

12-011

Where there is a power of attorney it is often easier easy to seek to fix this with its own governing law, which may be that of the place where exercise is contemplated or takes place. The two English cases usually cited for this proposition, however, can also be explained on the basis, not of the place of exercise, but that the power was regulated by the law of the transaction in connection with which it was to be exercised.[41] So even here precise solutions are not easy.

As has already been mentioned, proposals were at one time unsuccessfully put

---

[36] See below, para.12-024.
[37] See Rabel, fn.1 above, at pp.140–142; Verhagen, fn.1 above, Ch.6.
[38] This seems unlikely. See for example *Intercontainer Interfrigo (ICF) SC v Balkenende Oosthuizen BV* (C-133/08) [2010] Q.B. 411; noted by Dickinson [2010] L.M.C.L.Q. 27, on this point at 31.
[39] As in the Hague Convention, above, Articles 5–8, and in the unsuccessful proposal made in connection with Rome I.
[40] See below, para.12-012; Rabel, fn.1 above, at 161–162.
[41] *Chatenay v Brazilian Submarine Telegraph Co* [1891] 1 Q.B. 79; and *Sinfra Aktiengesellschaft v Sinfra AG* [1939] 2 All E.R. 675. *Chatenay*'s case is often approved by those advocating the place of exercise or similar as the general choice of law rule. Thus Rabel (fn.1 above, Vol.3, p.153) said: "While numerous other English decisions are elusive or confusing, this Court of Appeal decision is outstanding." See also *Bendigo and Adelaide Bank Ld v DY Logistics Pty Ltd* [2018] VSC 558 at [27], where it is said that the creation of a power of attorney is governed by the law of the jurisdiction in which it was made, but its construction and operation is governed by the law of the jurisdiction where it operates or is intended to operate.

forward for dealing with this matter in the Rome I Regulation[42]; and in 2017 provisions dealing with the matter were adopted in Germany in a new Article 8 of the Introductory Law to the German Civil Code (EGBGB) which utilises notions of choice, habitual residence and the country in which the agent exercises his powers.[43] For the present, however, subject to the problems of interpretation, certain questions of agency are simply excluded from the scope of the Rome I Regulation and where this is so a common law court, at any rate, is entitled to proceed in the excluded area on the basis of what it regards as the existing law, as indicated below.

12-012   **The common law approach to the exclusion**   With the possible exception of situations involving a power of attorney mentioned above, common law commentaries tend to assume that the exclusion from the scope of the Regulation leaves the court free to apply the law which it would normally apply to this question—in so far as the issue excluded can be isolated. To apply a special common law rule, whatever it might be, to this highly restricted question would be difficult and probably sometimes inappropriate in result. At the other extreme, the view can be taken that the exclusion leaves the court free to apply to the entire contract between principal and third party the rules for choice of law that it would otherwise have applied. On this interpretation, simply because of the intervention of an agency element, the law applicable to the whole relationship between principal and third party is determined by existing principles of the common law conflict of laws, unaffected by the Regulation. Although the English books do not always make completely clear what they envisage, this could have a very wide effect and hence seems an unlikely approach.[44] The better, and certainly more convenient, approach would seem to be that the court should take the view that, the question excluded not being a separate one under common law, the court should apply to it the law which it would otherwise apply. This would normally be the law governing the external contract, but as determined by the Rome I Regulation, as indicated below. There may also be some role for the internal law between principal and agent: this also is dealt with below.[45] Overall, this is undoubtedly somewhat paradoxical, in that the Regulation specifically and for good reason excludes the questions identified from its scope. But it is submitted that where the Regulation makes an exclusion of something that a particular system of conflict of laws does not necessarily recognise as a discrete topic, it is not impermissible to allow that system of law to bring the Regulation back in where appropriate, as it were, by incorporation and without its exclusions.[46] This in fact already links easily with the common law view as to the law governing questions of apparent authority explained below.[47]

---

[42]   For a detailed exposition see McParland, fn.2 above, paras 7-153 onwards.
[43]   The background to this approach is usefully considered (in English) by Gebauer, in Leible (ed), *Principles of European Private International Law*, (2016) Ch.16. See also Kleinschmidt in Basedow et al (eds), *Encyclopedia of Private International Law*, pp.33-39.
[44]   See Dicey, Morris and Collins, fn.1 above, para.33-434.
[45]   See below, para.12-015.
[46]   For a slightly different view, see Dicey, Morris and Collins, fn.1 above, Vol.2, para.33-434.
[47]   See paras 12-014 and 12-015.

Which law governs the main contract between principal and third party?   This should be the law designated in the various provisions of the Rome I Regulation referred to above.[48] If there is doubt as to whether a contract has been formed, the putative governing law will determine whether or not a contractual relationship exists.[49]

12-013

Questions of apparent authority arising in connection with the main contract   It is well established at common law, and independently of the approach which seeks a special choice of law rule for authority, that questions of *apparent* authority are governed by the law governing the main contract entered into.[50] This entails that the apparent authority of an agent extends in appropriate cases to subjecting the contract, whether directly or indirectly,[51] to a particular system of law.[52] It can be argued, however, that when the applicable law for the main contract under the Rome I Regulation is based on an express choice of law, rather than on a test of substantial connection, such a rule should not apply, on the ground that it enables an agent who has not been authorised, or has even been forbidden to do so, to choose a law for the contract. In such a case, it has been suggested that the choice should only be valid if it coincides with the law applicable in the absence of choice.[53] This view is similar to, and partly based on, one sometimes put forward

12-014

---

[48]   See para.12-003.

[49]   See Article 10, which deals with formation of contract; Dicey, Morris and Collins, fn.1 above, Vol.2, Rule 225. But as to agreement on choice of law, see below, fn.56. See also Rome II Article 12, dealing with *culpa in contrahendo*, considered by Dickinson, *The Rome II Regulation* (2008), Ch.12; Dicey, Morris and Collins, fn.1 above, Vol.2, Rule 255. Questions of capacity are specifically excluded: see below, para.12-019.

[50]   The point is specifically decided by David Steel J in *Rimpacific Navigation Inc v Daehan Shipbuilding Co Ltd* [2009] EWHC 2941 (Comm); [2010] 2 Lloyd's Rep. 236 and cases there cited (further proceedings before Teare J [2011] EWHC 2618 (Comm)), rejecting an argument, previously rejected elsewhere, that Regulations modifying s.36 of the Companies Act 1985 excluded the rules of apparent authority as applicable to companies. See also *Britannia SS Ins Assn v Ausonia Assecurazioni SpA* [1984] 2 Lloyd's Rep. 98; *Azov Shipping Co v Baltic Shipping Co* [1999] 2 Lloyd's Rep. 159; *Sea Emerald SA v Prominvestbank* [2008] EWHC 1979 (Comm) at [106]; *Donegal International Ltd v Zambia* [2007] EWHC 197 (Comm); [2007] 1 Lloyd's Rep. 397 (applying English law's reluctance to find apparent authority in a governmental agent: see at [844]–[845] and distinguishing on this point *Marubeni Hong Kong and South China Ltd v Mongolia* [2004] EWHC 472 (Comm); [2004] 2 Lloyd's Rep. 198); *Standard Chartered Bank v Ceylon Petroleum Corp* [2011] EWHC 1785 (Comm); affirmed without reference to this point [2012] EWCA Civ 1049; *Spar Shipping AS v Grand China Logistics Holding (Group) Co Ltd* [2015] EWHC 718 (Comm); [2015] 2 Lloyd's Rep. 407 (reversed without reference to this point [2016] EWCA Civ 982; [2016] 2 Lloyd's Rep. 447); *Wallis Trading Inc v Air Tanzania Co Ltd* [2020] EWHC 339 (Comm) at [102].

[51]   An example of "indirectly" would be agreeing to an arbitration clause which is held to be relevant to the choice of law issue. See *Habas Sinai Ve Tibbi Gaziar Isthisal Endustrisi AS v VSC Steel Co Ltd* [2013] EWHC 4071 (Comm); [2014] 1 Lloyd's Rep. 479.

[52]   This statement, in a slightly different form, was approved by Hamblen J in *Habas Sinai Ve Tibbi Gaziar Isthisal Endustrisi AS v VSC Steel Co Ltd* [2013] EWHC 4071 (Comm); [2014] 1 Lloyd's Rep. 479 at [113].

[53]   See Dicey, Morris and Collins, fn.1 above, Vol.2, para.33-447. In *Habas Sinai Ve Tibbi Gaziar Isthisal Endustrisi AS v VSC Steel Co Ltd* [2013] EWHC 4071 (Comm); [2014] 1 Lloyd's Rep. 479, such an argument was put forward in connection with an arbitration clause alleged not to be authorised, for which there is an even weaker case. These are not subject to Rome I, so the question had to be resolved at common law. The matter is discussed in some detail. It was argued that the matter would have triggered off Article 8(2) of the Rome Convention, now Article 10(2) of the Rome I Regulation (concerning situations where it is not reasonable to hold a party bound in accordance with the main principles of the Convention) and that such a rule should apply at common

in connection with capacity.[54] Whatever its value there (which is open to doubt) it is a negation of the principles of choice and of the putative proper law as now understood[55] to apply it here.[56]

The law governing the contract with the third party will determine questions of how such authority can be established, its extent, when the third party is put on inquiry and the degree of inquiry required[57] and so forth. This is despite the fact that on one account, accepted elsewhere in this work,[58] apparent authority is based on estoppel, and the possibility of arguing that estoppel is, at least in some contexts, a matter of evidence or procedure.[59] It seems clear that apparent authority is one of the areas in which it must be regarded as having a substantive character.[60]

12-015   **The problem of actual authority**   Even if it is accepted that questions of apparent authority arising under the main contract with the third party are governed by the law governing that contract, it is obviously tempting to think that questions of actual authority are governed by the law applying between principal and agent. This is normally, though not always, a contract. It has already been suggested that the law governing any contract between principal and agent is not appropriate to the question of conferring of authority. However, it could be argued that there should be a special choice of law rule for actual conferral of authority, as opposed to the notion of apparent authority arising in the context of an external transaction. As already stated, there is some English case law which can be taken to assume, sometimes by simple concession of counsel, that the law applicable to the question of the actual (as opposed to the apparent) authority of an agent is still that governing the internal relationship between principal and agent.[61] The difficulty with such a view is to find a law other than that governing any internal contract

---

law. This was rejected. The main text of Dicey, Morris and Collins is accordingly modified in the subsequent Supplement. A similar argument was rejected by Andrew Smith J in *PEC Ltd v Asia Golden Rice Co Ltd* [2014] EWHC 1583 (Comm) at [73]–[74]. This is a case where the adoption of a special rule for the law governing conferral of authority might have made a difference.

54   See Dicey, Morris and Collins, fn.1 above, Vol.2, para.32-176, cited in *Habas Sinai Ve Tibbi Gaziar Isthisal Endustrisi AS v VSC Steel Co Ltd* [2013] EWHC 4071 (Comm); [2014] 1 Lloyd's Rep. 479 at [105].

55   As to which see Dicey, Morris and Collins, fn.1 above, Vol.2, Rule 225.

56   That the putative proper law governing the contract in question covers the existence of apparent authority to conclude such a contract is expressly decided in *Habas Sinai Ve Tibbi Gaziar Isthisal Endustrisi AS v VSC Steel Co Ltd* [2013] EWHC 4071 (Comm); [2014] 1 Lloyd's Rep. 479, rejecting a contrary view expressed in Dicey, Morris and Collins, fn.1 above, Vol.1, para.33-447 and citing, in addition to several of the cases in fn.8 above, *The Parouth* [1982] 2 Lloyd's Rep 351; and *The Atlantic Emperor* [1989] 1 Lloyd's Rep 548. It is however arguable that the actual question of consent to a choice of law, express or implied, should be dealt with by the *lex fori* as a connecting factor, rather than by the putative proper law. See Dicey, Morris and Collins, fn.1 above, Vol.2, para.32-066. This would not have made a difference in the present case. (I am grateful to Professor Andrew Dickinson for this point.)

57   See (for powers of attorney) *Jacobs v Morris* [1902] 1 Ch. 816, above, para.8-052; and for the general rules above, Article 73.

58   See above, para.8-028.

59   See Yeo, *Choice of Law for Equitable Doctrines* (2004), para.7.118 onwards.

60   See Handley, *Estoppel by Conduct and Election* (2nd edn, 2016) para.1-015; *The Amazonia* [1990] 1 Lloyd's Rep. 236 at 247; *First Laser Ltd v Fujian Enterprises (Holdings) Co Ltd* [2012] HKEC 946 (HKCFA, judgment delivered by Lord Collins). It would seem that cases of true estoppel in a contractual agency situation, as in *Spiro v Lintern* [1973] 1 W.L.R. 1002 (see above, Article 21) should also be governed by the same law as the relevant contract.

61   See above, para.12-002.

between the two—a solution of which, it is submitted, the exclusion of agency matters from the Rome I Regulation involved rejection. However, the great majority of these cases refer to situations where the agent's authority to act for a corporate body is at least partly controlled by the constitution of that body and hence governed by the law governing the body.[62] This is justifiable on the ground that the corporation only exists under the system of law that governs it. Granted the relevance of the law governing a corporation to its agents, it is possible to argue that where questions of corporate procedures are not involved the other available law, the law governing the main contract, should apply to this question, and that the reach of the law governing the internal relationship should not extend to questions of the authority conferred. This would have considerable advantages. If, as at present, the third party is entitled to rely on the main putative contract that he has with the principal where the question is (as it very frequently is) one of appearance of authority (apparent authority), then where apparent authority under that law cannot be established, the third party may reasonably seek to rely on actual authority. Indeed alternative defences of actual authority, apparent authority and ratification are common. It is surely unsatisfactory to require the third party to transfer to a law which he may have had no means of knowing and may find it difficult to prove—bearing in mind that it is the principal who, by giving authority to the agent, can usually be regarded as having taken the risk of his activities.[63] There are certainly

---

[62] See *Merrill Lynch Capital Services Inc v Municipality of Piraeus (No.2)* [1997] C.L.C. 1214; *Marubeni Hong Kong and South China Ltd v Government of Mongolia* [2004] EWHC 472 (Comm); [2004] 2 Lloyd's Rep. 198; *Donegal International Ltd v Zambia* [2007] EWHC 197 (Comm); [2007] 1 Lloyd's Rep. 397; *Sea Emerald SA v Prominvestbank* [2008] EWHC 1979 (Comm); *Novus Aviation Ltd v Onur Air Tasimacilik AS* [2009] EWCA Civ 122; [2009] 1 Lloyd's Rep. 576; *Calyon v Wytwornia Sprxetu Komunikacynego Pzl AS* [2009] EWHC 1914 (Comm); [2009] 2 All E.R. (Comm) 603; *Rimpacific Navigation Inc v Daehan Shipbuilding Ltd* [2009] EWHC 2941 (Comm); [2010] 2 Lloyd's Rep. 236; *Emeraldian Ltd v Wellmix Shipping Ltd (The Vine)* [2010] EWHC 1411 (Comm); [2011] 1 Lloyd's Rep. 301 at [165]; *Standard Chartered Bank v Ceylon Petroleum Corp* [2011] EWHC 1785 (Comm); affd without reference to this point [2012] EWCA Civ 1049; *Haugesund Kommune v Depfa ACS Bank* [2010] EWCA Civ 579; [2012] Q.B. 549 at [7], fn.3 and [47]; *Spar Shipping AS v Grand China Logistics Holding (Group) Co Ltd* [2015] EWHC 718 (Comm); [2015] 2 Lloyd's Rep. 407. This fits with the policy of the Companies Act 2006 s.43(1)(b) (as substituted by Overseas Companies (Execution of Documents and Registration of Charges) Regulations 2009 (SI 2009/1917)): see below, para.12-019.

[63] "There is no sense in differentiating in conflicts of law powers conferred by the principal on the agent directly, or by declaration or conduct on which the third party relies": Rabel, fn.1 above, Vol.3, pp.139–140. See also at p.145: "Where a principal constitutes authorisation by an ordinary, private, voluntary act, intending its use in a foreign state, the law of this state is justifiedly considered competent to construe the validity and effects of the authorisation". In *Habas Sinai Ve Tibbi Gaziar Isthisal Endustrisi AS v VSC Steel Co Ltd* [2013] EWHC 4071 (Comm); [2014] 1 Lloyd's Rep. 479 the unsuccessful argument entailed an assumption that in some contexts lack of actual authority could have a function of "trumping" apparent authority. The context was of agreement to an arbitration clause relevant to the ascertainment of the putative governing law: see above. The general view advanced above receives some support from the judgment of Hamblen J at [110]: "As between the principal and the third party there is no difference between actual and ostensible authority"; and in *PEC Ltd v Asia Golden Rice Co Ltd* [2014] EWHC 1583 (Comm) at [4], Andrew Smith J said that he saw some force in it; see also *Credit Suisse International v Stichting Vestia Group* [2014] EWHC 3103 (Comm); [2015] Bus.L.R. D5 at [280]. Briggs, *Private International Law in English Courts* (2014), paras 7.279-7.280 can be read as taking a similar view. But for a different view, see Dicey, Morris and Collins, fn.1 above, Vol.2, para.33-439-440; adopted in *National Bank of Kazakhstan v Bank of New York Mellon SA/NV London Branch* [2020] EWHC 916 (Comm) at [55]. In fact English courts tend to fall back quite easily on applying English rules of interpretation for ascertaining actual authority: for recent examples in the cases cited in fn.8 above, see the *Sea Emerald* case, the *Ceylon*

some points at which the internal contract comes near to the realm of authority. Thus the agent may be liable to his principal under any internal contract for exceeding his authority: this could occur where the principal ratified an unauthorised contract for commercial reasons, but without exonerating the agent.[64] Equally, there may be contractual questions as to the degree of care with which any authority is to be exercised. But whether the agent has exceeded that authority should arguably be a question for the main contract (in the absence of problems of formality, capacity or corporate procedures, or a situation where there had never been any authority granted at all). A problem then arises, that to expose the principal to the law of the main contract is still to expose him to matters of choice, this time under the contract between principal and third party. It can also be said that until the contract is made its governing law cannot be determined, leading to earlier uncertainty as to authority.[65] But in view of the present common law solution that that law governs questions of apparent authority, it can be said that the drawback should be accepted.

12-016   **Possible reservations**   To the above point about actual authority there are two possible reservations. First, in interpreting the actual authority, the court should take account of the understandings which might attach to the conferral of authority according to the internal law. Thus in the *Chatenay* case, referred to above,[66] English law governed the effect of a power of attorney executed in Brazil in the Portuguese language, intended to be executed by a London stockbroker, but subject to taking into consideration the sense likely to have been intended for the document in Brazil. The same technique could be applied to persons exercising a usual authority: it can be asked what the understandings as to their authority would be in the place where they operate.[67]

A second possible reservation is that where the law governing the internal relationship confers authority but the law governing the main contract does not because it finds no apparent authority (obviously the principal situation in which actual authority may be significant), the contract is in any case to be regarded as authorised: that is to say that the internal law should have a validating but not an invalidating effect and can be relied on by the third party as such. This is a possible interpretation of a notorious (because difficult to interpret) decision of a not undistinguished tribunal in 1933, *Ruby SS Corp v Commercial Union Assurance Ltd*,[68] in which actual authority under the law operative between principal and agent was held effective despite the fact that under the law governing the contract between third party and principal it would seem that by reason of the usages of the London insurance market the agent had no such authority. It was held that an agent had power to cancel an insurance policy under New York law, which governed the agent's contractual relationship with its principal, because the principal had not paid

---

Petroleum case (though in the latter it appears that some evidence was given that the law of Sri Lanka was similar to English law in relevant respects), and *Golden Ocean Group Ltd v Salgaocar Mining Industries PVT Ltd* [2011] EWHC 56 (Comm); [2011] 1 W.L.R. 2575 at [161]; affd on other grounds [2012] EWCA Civ 265; [2012] 1 W.L.R. 3674.
[64]   See above, para.2-096.
[65]   See Kleinschmidt, fn 1 above, p.35.
[66]   Para.12-008.
[67]   See *Sea Emerald SA v Prominvestbank* [2008] EWHC 1979 (Comm) (Ukrainian bank employee). As to usual authority see above, para.3-005.
[68]   *Ruby SS Corp v Commercial Union Assurance Ltd* (1933) 39 Com.Cas. 48 (Scrutton, Greer and Romer LJJ).

the premiums; though the law governing the policies, English law, would regard the premiums as paid by virtue of its own special rule regarding the payment of the premium by broker to insurer. The reasoning in the case is however far from clear[69] and its significance seems largely to be due to the fact that there are so few other cases.[70] A simple rule that questions of actual authority as well as those of apparent authority are governed by the law governing the main contract seems the best solution.[71]

Ratification   It seems to be generally accepted that ratification is likewise   **12-017**
governed by the law governing the relationship between principal and third party.[72] It is in fact important in common law as understood in England that this should be so, as it is only by ratifying that a principal can sue in situations where he would be liable under the doctrine of apparent authority.[73] If it is accepted that questions of actual authority are also so governed, this creates no problems, being explicable on the basis that ratification is equivalent to antecedent authority. If however, contrary to what is argued above,[74] a view is accepted that *actual* authority is regulated by the law governing the internal relationship, the ratification would require to be isolated from the authority, as a separate event occurring after the formation of the contract, and related specifically to the contract ratified. Questions of estoppel from proving that one has not ratified[75] would probably come under the same law as that governing the putative ratification itself. Ratification seems to be an almost universal concept, but it should be noted that it may have slightly different applications in different legal systems. Thus, under the American *Restatement, Third, Agency*,[76] an undisclosed principal may ratify, which is not so in English law. It also seems that in some legal systems the notion can apply where the third party actually knows the agent to be unauthorised but anticipates ratification. This latter is a situation to which the common law (at any rate outside the US) might apply a completely different analysis.[77]

Capacity of natural persons   By Article I.2(a) the Rome I Regulation does not   **12-018**
apply to "Questions involving the status or legal capacity of natural persons, without prejudice to Article 13". This exclusion applies to any contract accompanying the

---

[69]   Rabel, fn.1 above, describes it as "scantily equipped": p.154.
[70]   For another explanation of this case see Dicey, Morris and Collins, fn.1 above, Vol.2, paras 33-441–33-445.
[71]   This is called the "accessory approach" by Kleinschmidt, fn 1 above, p.35, stating that few proponents of it remain.
[72]   See *Britannia SS Ins Assn v Ausonia Assecurazioni SpA* [1984] 2 Lloyd's Rep. 98; *Merrill Lynch Capital Services Inc v Municipality of Piraeus* [1997] C.L.C. 1214; *Sea Emerald SA v Prominvestbank* [2008] EWHC 1979 (Comm) at [100]; *Law Debenture Trust Corp Plc v Ukraine* [2018] EWCA Civ 2026; [2019] Q.B.1121. The matter is raised in *Presentaciones Musicales SA v Secunda* [1994] Ch. 271, but only in connection with ratification of English proceedings commenced by an English solicitor whose retainer was governed by English law; in this context see also *Grupo Torras SA v Al-Sabah (No.5)* [1999] C.L.C. 1469 at 1505–1506 (reversed on other grounds [2001] C.L.C. 221); *Bao Xiang International Garment Centre v British Airways Plc* [2015] EWHC 3071 (Ch); [2016] C.P. Rep. 8 (ratification of English proceedings, as opposed to of solicitor's retainer, governed by English law).
[73]   See above, para.8-029.
[74]   See above, para.12-015.
[75]   Above, para.2-080.
[76]   See above, para.2-063, fn.376.
[77]   See above, para.2-051.

conferral of authority between principal and agent, and also to the main contract entered into between principal and third party. Such questions are therefore a matter for the conflict of laws rules of the forum,[78] but subject to Article 13, which provides certain restrictions on a plea of incapacity.[79] As regards English law, the special questions relevant to this chapter concern capacity to act as principal and capacity to act as agent, i.e. capacity to confer authority and capacity to act on it. As to principals, it is stated above in this work,[80] that "Capacity to contract or do any other act by means of an agent is co-extensive with the capacity of the principal himself to make the contract or do the act which the agent is authorised to make or do". For the purposes of the conflict of laws, this refers the question of the law governing the principal's capacity to act as such to the law governing the main, external contract, and the normally accepted rules on capacity add the possibility that the principal's personal law may enlarge but not diminish the capacity.[81] As to the agent's capacity to act as such, the rules simply require soundness of mind and ability to understand what the person concerned is doing.[82] The rather limited requirements for capacity to act as agent operative in most legal systems mean that the matter will not often arise except in the context of public law controls on the operation of certain types of agent, e.g. stockbrokers, freight forwarders, which would raise questions of interpretation of scope. But in general it is submitted that, like formalities,[83] such controls need not affect capacity under the main contract. The question of corporate capacity is separate and is dealt with below.

12-019   **Corporations**   The Rome I Regulation likewise excludes in Article 1.2(f) various matters governed by the law governing corporations, and in Article 1.2(g) excludes the question whether "an organ" can "bind a company or other body corporate or unincorporated, in relation to a third party". In general, the normal principles of agency apply in connection with corporations, which many of the cases concern, and the notion of "organ" is not normally deployed in common law. Any proposition that capacity is regulated by the law governing the contract entered into must however be modified in relation to corporations, which only exist under a particular system of law. Obviously, though the law governing the contract is still applicable, the law governing the incorporation must have considerable say in what bodies incorporated (or otherwise associated) under it can do and how they can do it. This will necessarily raise questions of the limits of the notion of capacity, for it is in this context primarily to matters of capacity that the law governing the corporation (the law of the place of incorporation) should apply.[84] In English law, the initial starting point has been that companies can only do what is authorised by their memorandum of association and articles. Anything outside this would be void as

---

[78]   Dicey, Morris and Collins, fn.1 above, Vol.2, Rule 228(1) (objective proper law of main contract plus personal law as an additional validating factor). The view that the relevant law should be the governing law of the contract objectively ascertained is to avoid the possibility that a choice of law might enable a person to confer capacity on himself: see para.32-176. Such a rule is however not immune from question.

[79]   See Dicey, Morris and Collins, fn.1 above, Vol.2, Rule 228(2) (situations where both parties in same country and one unaware of incapacity of the other under an applicable law).

[80]   Article 4.

[81]   Dicey, Morris and Collins, fn.1 above, Vol.2, Rule 228(1)(b).

[82]   See Article 5.

[83]   See below, para.12-020.

[84]   See above, para.12-015; Dicey, Morris and Collins, fn.1 above, Vol.2, Rule 175.

ultra vires. The rule was established as one of capacity: a result was that if an act within the company's capacity was done for improper motives it was not invalid under the ultra vires doctrine.[85] Such constitutional limits have long been circumvented by wide objects clauses; and the ultra vires doctrine has for most purposes been abolished in the UK by statute.[86] There are related provisions dealing with agency arguments directed to the authority of company directors, whereby a third party may be entitled to assume that internal procedural rules have been complied with.[87] But this statutory modification and protection only applies to UK registered companies.

When one comes to consideration of the position of *foreign* companies under a contract governed by English law, it must be arguable that something like an ultra vires analysis is to be applied where the foreign company can be said to have no power to act.[88] Rule 175 of *Dicey, Morris & Collins on the Conflict of Laws* provides that the capacity of a corporation to enter into any legal transaction is governed both by the constitution of the corporation and by the law of the country which governs the transaction in question, but that all matters concerning the constitution of a corporation are governed by the law of the place of incorporation. To the latter extent the law governing the contract entered into must yield to the law governing the incorporation.

This matter is considered in a leading case concerning the power of a Norwegian municipality to enter into a "swap" agreement, in which it was clear that the analysis of the position adopted by Norwegian law would be quite different from that which a common lawyer would apply.[89] By English law such a question would be regarded as one of the capacity of the corporation; and this question being one of characterisation it was therefore before an English court governed by English law.[90] It was said that the notion of capacity should not be interpreted in the normal domestic sense, but in a broad internationalist way that accommodates different notions as to capacity and also as to what constitutes the constitution of the corporation; though both of these led to the conclusion that a question of capacity was involved and the transaction void.[91] More recently it has been held that such reason-

---

[85] *Rolled Steel Products (Holdings) Ltd v British Steel Corp* [1986] Ch. 246.
[86] For the present day, see Companies Act 2006 s.39. See above, para.8-035.
[87] For the present day, see Companies Act 2006 ss.40 and 41. See above, paras 8-037 to 8-039.
[88] See Dicey, Morris and Collins, fn.1 above, Vol.2, Rule 175 and para.33-451. The Giuliano/Lagarde Report, the official commentary on the Rome Convention and the Rome I Regulation, mentions ultra vires in connection with the scope of Article 1(f), which excludes most corporate matters from the scope of the Regulation. This reasoning is not to be applied to foreign states even where an inability to act in certain ways can be represented as arising from its constitution, for a state has unlimited capacity in public international law: *Law Debenture Trust Corp Plc v Ukraine* [2018] EWCA Civ 2026; [2019] Q.B. 1121 (where it was held that the Minister of Finance had apparent authority to sign).
[89] *Haugesund Kommune v Depfa ACS Bank* [2010] EWCA Civ 579; [2012] Q.B. 549. The question of capacity of an EU entity is discussed in *Canary Wharf (BP4) T1 Ltd v European Medicines Agency* [2019] EWHC 335 (Ch); (2019) 183 Con. L.R. 167 at [178] onwards, where the point is made that the law of the country governing the transaction cannot add to the capacity conferred by the law governing the incorporation. The case rejects frustration of a lease of English land to a European entity on account of "Brexit".
[90] See at [40]. Article 1(g) of the Rome I Regulation, referred to above, also excludes "capacity", thus leaving this to national laws.
[91] See at [47] and [48]. See also *Credit Suisse International v Stichting Vestia Groep* [2014] EWHC 3103 (Comm); [2015] Bus.L.R. D5 at [254]; *Law Debenture Trust Plc v Ukraine* [2019] EWCA Civ 2026; [2019] Q.B.1121.

ing also applies to provisions of the foreign law as to the procedures by which the corporation can act: these may be regarded as relating to the corporation itself rather than the contract into which it enters.[92] But where there is no question of lack of power, the matter is likely to be one of authority only and governed by the law applicable to that topic.[93] A general provision, applicable both to corporations and to individuals, requiring certain formalities for all contracts (or documents) of a certain type (e.g. relating to land) would however attach to the contract and hence to the law governing formalities for it.[94]

English law also has special rules for *how* contracts are made *by* companies and *for* companies, and for the execution of documents *by* companies[95]: these again only apply to UK registered companies. But it also has corresponding provisions for the making of contracts and the execution of documents by overseas companies where business is done "under the law of England and Wales",[96] i.e. the contract is governed by English law.[97] These contain provisions permitting in some cases that the signatory have authority under the laws of the territory in which the company is incorporated.[98] It has been held however that these provisions relate to formal validity, where they are not exclusive,[99] and that they do not exclude the English law rules of apparent authority, which will apply where the contract is governed by English law.[100]

If the governing law of the transaction is foreign, it will be appropriate to ask, over and above the law governing the incorporation, what the foreign law would do on the question of corporate capacity; but though the provisions as to the execu-

---

[92] *Integral Petroleum SA v SCU-Finanz AG* [2015] EWCA Civ 144; [2015] Bus.L.R. 640 (Swiss law required signature by two *prokurists* for validity of transaction by corporation: transaction void). See also *Janred Properties Ltd v ENIT* [1989] 2 All E.R. 444 (purchase of land in London requiring assent of Italian Ministry of Tourism); *Rimpacific Navigation Inc v Daehan Shipbuilding Ltd* [2009] EWHC 2941 (Comm); [2010] 2 Lloyd's Rep. 236 at [36] (further proceedings [2011] EWHC 2618).

[93] See above paras 12-013 to 12-015 and *Law Debenture Trust Corp Plc v Ukraine* [2018] EWCA Civ 2026; [2019] Q.B. 1121.

[94] See Rome I Regulation Article 11.

[95] Companies Act 2006 ss.43 and 44 (for Scotland, s.48. Not all provisions apply in Scotland). See above, paras 8-040 and 8-041.

[96] Overseas Companies (Execution of Documents and Registration of Charges) Regulations 2009 (SI 2009/1917), amending ss.43, 44 and 46 of the Companies Act 2006 for overseas companies. Equivalent provisions apply to limited liability partnerships by virtue of the Limited Liability Partnerships (Application of Companies Act 2006) Regulations 2009 (SI 2009/1804).

[97] Difficulty is raised by the wording of s.44(4) of the original Act and its amended version s.44(5) which is applicable to overseas companies. Both provide that a document which "purports to be signed" in accordance with provisions earlier in the section are valid in favour of a good faith purchaser. But s.44(4) is drafted in such a way that might apply even to forged documents, and this is even more so of s.44(5), part of the modification of the rules in respect of overseas companies, the wording of which is not identical. See above, para.8-040.

[98] Companies Act s.43(1)(b) and s.44(2)(a). As to authority to affix a corporate seal, see above, para.8-040.

[99] *Integral Petroleum SA v SCU-Finanz AG* [2015] EWCA Civ 144; [2015] Bus.L.R. 640.

[100] See *Habas Sinai Ve Tibbi Gaziar Isthisal Endustrisi v VSC Steel Co Ltd* [2013] EWHC 4071 (Comm); [2014] 1 Lloyd's Rep. 479 at [125]; *Rimpacific Navigation Inc v Daehan Shipbuilding Ltd* [2009] EWHC 2941 (Comm); [2010] 2 Lloyd's Rep. 236 at [30]–[31]: further proceedings [2011] EWHC 2618. See also *Azov v Baltic Shipping Co (No.3)* [1999] 2 Lloyd's Rep. 159 at 170; *Golden Ocean Group v Salgaocar Mining Industries PVT Ltd* [2011] EWHC 56 (Comm); [2011] 1 W.L.R. 2575 at [160], [161] (further proceedings [2012] EWCA Civ 265; [2012] 1 W.L.R. 3674). In the *Rimpacific* case there was no actual authority because board approval was required for such a transaction: see at [36]. This would in fact acceptably bring in the rules of the law of the place of incorporation, as to which see above, text to fn.98.

tion of documents only apply to business done under the law of England and Wales it seems that the rules of English law as to what constitutes the capacity to which the law of the place of incorporation is relevant should prevail, *renvoi* reasoning being normally irrelevant in contract.[101]

Formalities   The law governing the relationship between principal and agent may   **12-020**
sometimes require formalities for the validity or efficacy of an agency relationship. In so far as the relationship is a contract, Article 11 of the Rome I Regulation (which contains detailed provisions on the topic) applies. But the Regulation excludes, as stated above, from its scope, the question of whether an agent is able to bind a principal. For example, in England an agent authorised to contract by deed must be authorised by deed,[102] but this need not be so everywhere. It is submitted that lack of formalities for conferring of authority by any law operating internally need not affect the external contract between principal and third party, though such lack under the law governing the main contract will (subject to interpretation of the scope of Article 11, and any relevant statute or similar provision) be relevant.

Public law   There can be little doubt that if there are public law restrictions on an   **12-021**
agent's authority, as in the case of public officials, these should be effective as against the law governing the main transaction. As regards public officials, it seems to be accepted that constitutional and other public restrictions of a disabling nature on their actual authority should be effective, and the interpretation of such restrictions is a matter for the law imposing them[103]; though in the absence of clear evidence the court falls back fairly easily on English interpretation techniques, at least where the governing law of the main transaction is English,[104] and similarly estoppel, apparently under English law, has been applied to later conduct relevant to earlier authorisation.[105] The reluctance of English law to find apparent authority in public officials has recently been applied in the context of foreign officials,[106]

Revocation of authority   It is submitted that authority is of its nature revocable   **12-022**
in the absence of relevant rules making it irrevocable. This follows from the law's recognition of the dangers of conferring on another a power to bind oneself.[107] The question whether authority has actually been revoked as between principal and

---

[101] See Dicey, Morris and Collins, fn.1 above, Vol.2, para.32-029.

[102] See above, Article 10.

[103] See *Janred Properties Ltd v ENIT* [1989] 2 All E.R. 444 (consent of Minister of Tourism required for taking lease); *Merrill Lynch Capital Services Inc v Municipality of Piraeus* [1997] C.L.C. 214 (authority of Mayor to raise loans); *Marubeni Hong Kong and South China Ltd v Mongolia* [2004] EWHC 472 (Comm); [2004] 2 Lloyd's Rep. 198 (authority of Minister of Finance, rejecting a distinction between public and private entities); cf. *Donegal International Ltd v Zambia* [2007] EWHC 197 (Comm); [2007] 1 Lloyd's Rep. 397 (authority of Minister of Finance: constitutional provisions).

[104] See *Donegal International Ltd v Zambia* [2007] EWHC 197 (Comm); [2007] 1 Lloyd's Rep. 397 at [436]–[437].

[105] See *Janred Properties Ltd v Ente Nazionale Italiano per il Turismo (ENIT) (No.2)* [1989] 2 All E.R. 444.

[106] Above, para.8-042; *Donegal International Ltd v Zambia* [2007] EWHC 197 (Comm); [2007] 1 Lloyd's Rep. 397. But cf. *Law Debenture Trust Corp Plc v Ukraine* [2018] EWCA Civ 655; [2019] Q.B.1121 (Minister of Finance had apparent authority (in the sense of usual authority: above, para.3-005), to enter into a transaction involving borrowing under Eurobonds.) But cf above, para.12-019, fn.88.

[107] See above, para.10-024.

agent must depend on the law governing the grant of authority, unaffected by any contract between them: this would on the view adopted in this chapter be the law governing the external contract. This is an example of the help afforded by the recognition of the independence of the grant of authority from the accompanying contract.[108] The revocation may or may not be a breach of such a contract.[109] However, that need not affect third parties. Thus apparent authority under the law governing the external transaction may persist despite internal revocation of authority as between principal and agent (unless the third party has notice of it), and the existence of apparent authority comes under the normal rules applicable to such authority in a case between principal and third party.[110] Under English law at any rate it is arguable that if the authority is revoked by death, it cannot survive even within a doctrine of apparent authority, for the principal has simply been removed.[111] It is submitted elsewhere in this work[112] that this reasoning should in any case no longer be permitted to affect the normal operation of the doctrine of apparent authority. In any case it is a rule of English law, applicable where English law applies.

Termination of authority by lack of mental capacity, insolvency or bankruptcy is apt to be dealt with specifically by statute, though questions of the conflict of laws application of such statutes could undoubtedly arise. In England and Wales the law applicable to certain aspects of a lasting power of attorney[113] is now governed by the Hague Convention of 2000 on the International Protection of Adults,[114] which attributes jurisdiction primarily to the authorities of the adult's habitual residence,[115] but Article 15 of which permits the designation of an applicable law in certain circumstances.

12-023 **Irrevocable authority**   There can be cases where authority is, under some relevant system of law, not revocable, either at all or for a particular period. At common law this occurs where a power is given as security or (perhaps) to protect some other interest of the agent.[116] Obviously other legal systems could provide differently, though there seems some unanimity in the use in this context of the idea of protecting an interest of the agent. For common law at least, such an arrangement is not really agency at all, because the agent, as the holder of a security, is entitled and indeed expected to act in his own interest, which is not true of agents in general. It could also be said that it is contrary to the nature of authority that it should be irrevocable. The problem is (again) easier to deal with if the conferral of authority is regarded as governed by its own law, for it can be said that the governing law may make the authority revocable or irrevocable. But again[117] it is possible

---

[108] See above, para.12-007.
[109] The remedy for which may in some jurisdictions include an order for performance.
[110] See above, Article 121; e.g. *AMB Generali Holding AG v SEB Trygg Liv, etc.* [2005] EWCA Civ 1237; [2006] 1 Lloyd's Rep. 318.
[111] See above, Article 119.
[112] See above, para.10-032.
[113] See above, para.10-009.
[114] This Convention was apparently enacted into law for England and Wales by s.63 of and Sch.3 to the Mental Capacity Act 2005, which took effect on October 1, 2007 by virtue of the Mental Capacity Act 2005 (Commencement No.2) Order (SI 2007/1897), though the Convention itself (to which the UK had only acceded on behalf of Scotland) did not take effect until January 1, 2009.
[115] Article 5: but see also Articles 7–10.
[116] See above, Article 118.
[117] See above, paras 12-012, 12-015, 12-022.

alternatively to say that the (internal) actual authority is in fact regulated by the law governing the main external transaction, and that will determine the question of revocability. Consistently with what is suggested, the effect of such irrevocability was in *Sinfra Aktiengesellschaft v Sinfra AG*[118] held to be governed by the law governing the document used, a power of attorney, which was said to be the law of the country where the power was to operate. In the case in question this was English law, though the document had been prepared under German law.[119] It was held that whatever the position under German law, the power under English law was not such as to create the type of authority that would be irrevocable.[120] It is submitted however that the law governing the *transaction* in which it is used or to be used, i.e. the main contract, might be more appropriate. Where security is created by such arrangements, it is possible that some forms of such authority might be classified as assignments or the creation of a specific security interest or as part of a multiparty transaction, to which other choice of law rules might be appropriate.[121]

The unauthorised agent (falsus procurator): warranty of authority   The com-   **12-024**
mon law approach to the problem of a person who purports to act as agent without having any authority to do so, either at all or in the particular respect, is to say that he has made a collateral contract with the third party under which he promises absolutely that he has authority and will be liable to the third party for the consequences of the lack of authority if this proves not to be so.[122] The liability covers the positive or expectation interest, i.e. it seeks to put the claimant in the position in which he would have been had there been authority.[123] On this interpretation there is a contract freestanding from that between principal and third party. Such a contract does not seem to come within the "agency" exception in the Rome I Regulation referred to above, because the question whether the agent can bind the principal to a third party would not appear to cover the (secondary) consequences of not doing so. Hence Rome I applies. Such a result has recently been reached in a case applying the Rome Convention, applicable under the Contracts (Applicable Law) Act 1990 but now superseded by the Rome I Regulation, the relevant wording of which is not however quite the same.[124] In this case the contract usually arises by implication, and it is not likely to contain a choice of law. It has been suggested that the characteristic performance is not the provision of the warranty but, rather, the seeing to it that the agent has authority.[125] In the Court of Appeal however it was said in the same case that there was in such a case no characteristic performance.[126] Such a contract will presumably often come within the residual provisions of Articles 4.3 or 4.4 and as it is clearly a contract ancillary to the proposed contract between principal and third party, albeit such a contract did not come into force, it

---

[118] *Sinfra Aktiengesellschaft v Sinfra AG* [1939] 2 All E.R. 675. See also above, para.12-008.
[119] Under which it was in fact probably not irrevocable: but the matter did not require decision.
[120] Apparent authority was not arguable, as the third party was aware of the purported revocation.
[121] See Dicey, Morris and Collins, fn.1 above, Vol.2, Ch.24.
[122] See above, Article 105.
[123] See above, Article 106.
[124] *Golden Ocean Group Ltd v Salgaocar Mining Industries PVT Ltd* [2012] EWCA Civ 265; [2012] 1 W.L.R. 3674.
[125] See *Golden Ocean Group Ltd v Salgaocar Mining Industries PVT Ltd* [2011] EWHC 56 (Comm); [2011] 1 W.L.R. 2575 at [133].
[126] *Golden Ocean Group Ltd v Salgaocar Mining Industries PVT Ltd* [2012] EWCA Civ 265; [2012] 1 W.L.R. 3674 at [52].

is arguable that it should be governed by that law, or what it would have been, by attraction. It should however be noted that civil law opinion is apt to see this as not being a voluntary arrangement at all, so not involving Rome I and for that reason simply governed by the law governing the agent's authority. This approach is taken in the Hague Convention.[127]

12-025 Other classifications of the above situation The above assumes that the agent's liability is contractual and for the expectation interest, which seems to be the majority view.[128] However, the situations involved certainly could be classified as giving rise to an action in tort, which would almost certainly require negligence and would limit recovery to the reliance, or negative, interest. This seems to be true in some countries[129] and would, where it operated, bring the Rome II Regulation[130] into operation. Other analyses are possible, for example that the liability arises as a matter of law.

12-026 Undisclosed principal The doctrine of the undisclosed principal applies in its typical form only in common law countries and may contain differences of detail between even them. It is submitted that it is best to regard it as starting from the proposition that the undisclosed principal intervenes on, or is the subject of intervention in respect of, a contract between agent and third party.[131] This means that trying to formulate general, internationally understood rules for the law of agency which take in the common law doctrine of the undisclosed principal is unlikely to be helpful. On this basis, it is necessary to look first at the contract between agent and third party, which is crucial to this inquiry in a way which is not so for identified and unidentified principal situations. There must in fact as a starting point be such a contract, and its governing law and existence will be ascertained in the same way as is applicable to contracts in general (i.e. applying the Rome I Regulation in countries where this applies). Such a contract being established, it will be necessary to know whether its governing law permits intervention by an undisclosed principal. If it does not, that is probably the end of the matter.[132] It may be assumed that such is not permitted (at any rate in such a simple form) for any contract not governed by the law of a common law country. If a common law regime governs, intervention probably will be permitted, but there may be differences between jurisdictions as to situations where the undisclosed principal cannot intervene to sue, or be sued.[133] Assuming these are not significant, the doctrine is normally taken as requiring that there was actual authority to enter into a contract

---

[127] Article 15.

[128] Rabel, fn.1 above, Vol.3, p.142 says that "common law has led the way in this construction", though it is not clear what he thought the construction was. See *The Unauthorised Agent* (Busch and Macgregor eds, 2008), considering the law of eight countries, the Principles of European Contract Law and the UNIDROIT Principles of International Commercial Contracts: most appear to give the expectation interest and hence to adopt the contractual basis. The Draft Common Frame of Reference, para.II.6-107 appears to make the same assumption.

[129] See Dickinson, *The Rome II Regulation* (2008), para.12.10; Dicey, Morris and Collins, fn 1 above, Rule 249. Hartley, (2008) 57 I.C.L.Q.899 at 907 suggests analysis on the basis of *culpa in contrahendo*.

[130] Below, para.12-033.

[131] See above, para.8-069.

[132] As to the possibility of deploying the notion of indirect representation, see below, para.12-027.

[133] For the English position see above, para.8-079.

binding the principal.[134] It is tempting to suggest that the application of this rule and the establishment of such internal authority must come outside the law governing the contract itself by reason of the "agency" exception of Article 1(2)(g) of the Rome I Regulation. This would lead to an unnecessary complication, and it is submitted that the question should be governed by the law governing the relevant contract.[135] In effect this requires that that contract be governed by the law of a common law jurisdiction.

Indirect representation   As has been already explained elsewhere in this work,[136]   **12-027**
indirect representation is a civil law notion, the facts constituting which can perfectly well occur in respect of a dispute regulated by common law, but which are not normally analysed under that system on the basis that a special type of agency or representation is involved. The arrangement is sometimes referred to as operation under a contract of *commission*. The notion represents a way of dealing whereby an agent (frequently pursuing a known occupation such as freight forwarder) deals on his own account with the third party: but internally accounts to his principal on an agency basis, e.g. (in common law terms) promising reasonable endeavours, not guaranteeing a result, typically remunerated on commission, owing fiduciary duties, and (a more controversial element) subject to the principal's control.[137] The few common law cases dealing with such situations have often assumed that either the relationship is one of normal agency, or that there are two back-to-back contracts, such as a purchase for resale.[138] In England, only Lord Blackburn paid articulate attention to such a method of commercial operation.[139]

This has similarities with the undisclosed principal situation of which an analysis has been given above, and indeed some civil law commentators have seen a connection. But it is in fact not the same because the English undisclosed principal doctrine requires that the agent be actually authorised to contract so as to bind the principal,[140] but does not disclose the principal's existence or connection with the transaction. The principal under a contract of *commission* does not grant authority for the creation of privity of contract with himself at all; conversely, the third party may be well aware that the agent, who may specialise in acting in this way, has a principal.

Apart from the incidence of fiduciary duties, this has no connection with the rules for agency considered above.[141] Though it may in civil law commentaries be treated together with direct representation, to a common lawyer they have analytical

---

[134] See above, paras 8-071 and 8-072.
[135] cf. above, para.12-016. *Mildred Goyeneche & Co v Maspons y Hermano* (1882) 9 Q.B.D. 530 CA can be taken as authority for this: but the case went to the House of Lords, which decided it on other grounds. The judgments of the Court of Appeal, are considered below, para.12-028.
[136] See above, paras 1-021 and 1-022.
[137] See above, para.1-018.
[138] e.g. *Anglo-African Shipping Co of New York Inc v J.Mortner Ltd* [1962] 1 Lloyd's Rep. 610.
[139] See *Ireland v Livingston* (1871-72) L.R. 5 H.L. 395; *Armstrong v Stokes* (1871-72) L.R. 7 Q.B. 598; *Die Elbinger Actien Gesellschaft für Fabricatien von Eisenbahn Materiel v Claye* (1872-73) L.R. 8 Q.B. 313; *Hutton v Bulloch* (1873) L.R. 8 Q.B. 312; affirmed (1874) L.R. 9 Q.B. 572; and *Mildred Goyeneche & Co v Maspons y Hermano* (1882) 9 Q.B.D. 530 CA; (1883) 8 App.Cas. 874 HL. There is discussion of this interpretation in relation to freight forwarders above, para.9-024.
[140] Above, para.8-071.
[141] But see Kortmann and Kortmann, "Undisclosed indirect representation—protecting the principal, the third party or both?", Ch.6 in Busch, Macgregor and Watts (eds), *Agency Law in Commercial Practice* (2016).

disparities. If such an arrangement is entered into, there is no grant of authority and the relationship between principal and agent is presumably governed by the transaction between them, and that between agent and third party by the law governing that contract (for example, a sale), in both cases subject to the Rome I Regulation. Undisclosed principal reasoning is excluded by the lack of actual authority, and assuming no apparent authority, the principal is not affected.[142] In some civil law countries the principal may, especially in insolvency situations, in fact sometimes intervene to sue, and may less commonly even be sued.[143] Which law should govern the exercise of such special rights and the incidence of such special liabilities is beyond the scope of this chapter.[144]

However, as discussed both above[145] and below, it appears that English courts have sometimes tended to override this difference and simply classified an indirect principal as coming under the undisclosed principal rules; though perhaps this should not happen if the court is adequately briefed as to the relevant law. A leading case now discussed bears this out.

12-028   **A leading case: Mildred v Maspons**   The above context requires specific discussion of another of the few, and hence celebrated, English cases specifically dealing with agency in the conflict of laws, *Mildred, Goyeneche & Co v Maspons y Hermano*.[146] This deserves attention because in it the Court of Appeal at least addresses agency issues specifically. In that case agents in Cuba, Demestre Chia, consigned tobacco to Messrs Mildred & Co in London, who were to sell it and account for the proceeds as agents. Demestre chartered a vessel, took out a bill of lading in their own name, and arranged for Mildred to insure the goods. The vessel was lost. Demestre became insolvent and Maspons, the actual exporter, intervened to claim the insurance money from Mildred as having still been the owner of the goods insured. During the dealings between Mildred and Demestre there had been frequent references to the "*interesado*", i.e. the person interested, and it must have been clear to Mildred that Demestre was only some sort of agent. To the question "did [Mildred] know or have reason to believe that Demestre & Co were acting as agents for some other person or persons not named?" the jury answered "yes; they knew or had reason to believe it".[147] On the insolvency of Demestre, Mildred claimed a lien (or right of set-off[148]) over the policy money in respect of the general balance of account between themselves and Demestre under a contract between them, itself one of agency and presumably governed by English law. It was held that this did not attach because at the time the insurance was effected Mildred knew that another party was involved.

If Mildred knew this, the contract with Demestre would appear in common law terms to have been made for unidentified principals; but the court treated the case as one of undisclosed principal (a confusion not unknown at the time and subsequently[149]). The result must have been much the same in either case, as

---

[142] cf. above, para.12-007.
[143] See above, para.8-071.
[144] See Verhagen, fn.1 above, p.380 onwards, esp. p.386.
[145] See above paras 1-021, 1-022.
[146] *Mildred, Goyeneche & Co v Maspons y Hermano* (1882) 9 Q.B.D. 530 CA; (1883) 8 App.Cas. 874 HL.
[147] See (1883) 8 App.Cas. at 883.
[148] See above, para.7-077.
[149] See above, para.8-105.

Maspons intervened to sue on a marine policy in favour of "every other person or persons to whom the same doth may or shall appertain", and the general lien or right of set-off of Mildred against Demestre in respect of the policy money, presumably governed by English law, would not have applied against an identified or unidentified principal, nor against an undisclosed principal who intervened before a sum had attached to the lien.[150]

If however Demestre was an agent acting as an indirect agent (as seems not unlikely) the dealing was by virtue of the internal arrangements between Demestre and Maspons entirely between Demestre and Mildred, and the fact that Mildred was aware that there was an *interesado* should have been irrelevant. The Spanish law quoted appears to create a *commission* situation: such appears likely to have been the explanation given by an expert witness from the Spanish bar.[151] The Court of Appeal however said that the Spanish law was to be taken into account in considering the nature and extent of the authority given by Maspons to Demestre, but that the overall question was to be determined by English law, not the law of Spain. The contract conferring the lien or right of set-off was between Demestre and Mildred: and the law governing that contract determined whether an undisclosed principal could intervene. He could do so since Mildred already knew of him when the lien attached.[152]

The case is therefore one where the Court of Appeal imposed its own domestic analysis on the situation, and this fits with the proposition that the law governing the main contract between agent and third party determines whether an undisclosed principal can intervene.[153] However, the English law of undisclosed principal requires that the principal has authorised the agent to create privity of contract with the third party.[154] In so far as that requirement is disregarded, and the Spanish law on indirect representation not taken into account at all, the statements of doctrine in the case seem doubtful.[155] The court said that it would do no more than take the Spanish law into account, and this is consistent with other cases[156]: but it is surely going too far to override an intention not to authorise a contract at all under the internal law, especially when the law applicable to the main transaction actually requires such an intention.[157]

The House of Lords affirmed the decision without reliance on the agency point, Lord Blackburn saying that the provisions cited went so far as to show that the Spanish law differed from the English, but that the matter did not turn on privity of contract: the goods had belonged to Maspons and he had the same right to

---

[150] See above, Article 81.

[151] See reference to this evidence at p.539.

[152] See above, Article 81. An attempt to apply the foreign principal rule (above, para.9-020) was rejected.

[153] See the judgment of the Court of Appeal at 541–543, where it was said by Lindley LJ that the English law as to undisclosed principals is known to differ from that of other countries, whose law is similar to the law of Spain, but that it was now too late to reconsider the matter.

[154] See above, para.8-071.

[155] But that the doctrine of undisclosed principal was correctly applied is argued by Busch, *Indirect Representation in European Contract Law* (2005), pp.171-172.

[156] Especially the later case of *Chatenay*, para.12-008.

[157] It is however worth noting that the Court of Appeal was in one of its strongest constitutions even for the present day: Jessel MR and Lindley and Bowen LJJ.

demand the insurance money as the goods.[158] He refused to follow Lindley LJ in discussing matters which did not arise.[159]

12-029 **Canvassing agents** A canvassing agent[160] normally has no power, or very limited power, to create a contract between principal and third party: he simply introduces business. As such his only relationship is internal, and if this is, as is likely, contractual, whether in common law terms unilateral or bilateral (either of which is possible) it is governed by the law governing that contract, as regulated by the Rome I Regulation. As with indirect representation, the grant of authority does not (normally) arise. Such agents may owe fiduciary duties, which may, as is said above of fiduciary duties in general,[161] in principle come within the scope of the Rome I or II Regulations but would probably usually be regarded under the latter Regulation as governed by the same law as the contract anyway.[162] Some such agents, for example estate agents acting for private clients, will be affected by the consumer provisions of Article 7 of Rome I.[163] Such agents come within the Hague Convention.

12-030 **Agency of necessity** It is submitted elsewhere in this work that the clearest agency applications of this doctrine, under which an agent may in certain situations of emergency make contracts binding his principal, ought now to be assimilated into ordinary notions of actual and apparent authority,[164] in which case as a separate category it would disappear. The traditional formulation of the rules in common law, however, regards them as a separate matter of law.[165] In their best-known form they confer authority on shipmasters to act for ship and/or cargo, for example when a salvage agreement is entered into; and a traditional argument, apparently accepted in many countries, is in fact that the matter, being related to a maritime venture, is generally known as being subject to the law of the flag of the vessel.[166] It is not clear that such an analysis is still required.[167] In so far as it involves the law of property (where ship or cargo are mortgaged or sold) the situation would be controlled by the *lex situs* of the property at the relevant time.[168] There is however another aspect of the doctrine operating only internally between principal and agent, which may justify the agent's intervention and sometimes

---

[158] See Lord Blackburn at 887. He also based his judgment (with some acerbity) on the Factors Acts.
[159] *Mildred, Goyeneche & Co v Maspons y Hermano* (1882) 9 Q.B.D. 530 CA; (1883) 8 App.Cas. 874 HL at 888.
[160] See above, para.1-020.
[161] See below, para.12-032.
[162] See Dicey, Morris and Collins, fn.1 above, Vol.2, para.34-087; Dickinson, *The Rome II Regulation* (2008), paras 3.141-142. An agency relationship considered in *Kent v Paterson-Brown* [2018] EWHC 2008 (Ch) and held governed by Swiss law seems to have been of this type, but no fiduciary or other relationship was held to arise under Swiss or English law.
[163] See Dicey, Morris and Collins, fn.1 above, Vol.2, Rule 235.
[164] See above, para.4-008.
[165] See *Industrie Chimiche Italia Centrale and Cerealfin SA v Alexander G Tsavliris & Sons Maritime Co (The Choko Star) (1990)* [1990] 1 Lloyd's Rep. 516.
[166] See Rabel, fn.1 above, Vol.3, pp.146–148.
[167] See Dicey, Morris and Collins, fn.1 above, Vol.2, para.33-108.
[168] As in the leading case of *Cammell v Sewell* (1860) 5 H. & N. 728. See Dicey, Morris and Collins, fn.1 above, Vol.2, Ch.24.

entitling him to compensation or indemnity.[169] These latter entitlements seem restitutionary in character and, at least unless there is already an agency relationship in operation, may be linked to the Roman and civil law concept of *negotiorum gestio* and the choice of law rules applicable for such cases under the Rome II Regulation.[170] Some of the powers conferred by the Mental Capacity Act 2005 enabling persons to act on behalf of others in certain circumstances are similar to one or the other of the two categories of agency of necessity,[171] and their conflict of laws aspects may be governed by the Hague Convention on the Protection of Adults.[172]

Commercial agents   The category of commercial agent was unknown to the common law. Regulations on such agents implementing an EC Directive were introduced in 1993. The Regulations contain indications of their own application and certain choice of law provisions, which are discussed in Chapter 11.[173]   **12-031**

Agent's fiduciary duties to principal   In so far as general fiduciary duties apply between principal and agent, it could be said that these are non-contractual. There are certainly dicta that fiduciary duties are separate from any related contract. There are also indications that the duty is or can be contractual.[174] In the UK, if the duty is regarded as contractual, the Rome I Regulation would apply. In so far as the duty is characterised as non-contractual this might bring such duties under the (Rome II) Regulation on the Law Applicable to Non-Contractual Obligations.[175] However, the effect of that Regulation seems to be that such duties should often be regarded as arising in connection with the contract between principal and agent for the purposes of that Regulation and hence governed by the law governing that contract.[176] So by one means or another (but more probably by virtue of Rome I) the law governing any contract between principal and agent seems likely normally to apply to such duties.[177]   **12-032**

Torts   Where it is claimed that an agent is in any respect personally liable in tort, or that his principal is liable in tort for the agent's acts, as is perfectly possible,[178]   **12-033**

---

[169] A leading case is *China-Pacific SA v Food Corp of India (The Winson)* [1982] A.C. 939: above, Illustration 2 to Article 33.

[170] As to restitutionary liability, see below. As to *negotiorum gestio*, dealt with in Article 11 of the Rome II Regulation, see below; Dickinson, *The Rome II Regulation* (2008), paras 11.13-11.14; Dicey, Morris and Collins, fn 1 above, Rule 258.

[171] Above, para.4-012.

[172] This Convention was enacted into law for England and Wales by s.63 of and Sch.3 to the Mental Capacity Act 2005, which took effect on October 1, 2007 by virtue of the Mental Capacity Act 2005 (Commencement No.2) Order (SI 2007/1897).

[173] Above, paras 11-006 to 11-010.

[174] See discussion above, para.6-035.

[175] Regulation 864/2007 [2007] OJ L199/40, effective January 11, 2009: see below, paras 12-033 and 12-035.

[176] Article 4.3.

[177] See Dickinson, *The Rome II Regulation* (2008), paras 3.141-3.142; Dicey, Morris and Collins, fn 1 above, para.34-087. Directors' fiduciary duties would seem to be outside the scope of the Rome I and Rome II Regulations by virtue of Article 1.2(f) and 1.2(d) respectively, and governed by the law of the place of incorporation (*Base Metal Trading Ltd v Shamurin* [2004] EWCA Civ 1316; [2005] 1 W.L.R. 1157). See also *Kent v Paterson-Brown* [2018] EWHC 2008 (Ch), where no fiduciary responsibility was found under any relevant law.

[178] The main instances occur in Articles 42, 48, 90, 91 and 113–115 above.

the normal rules for torts in the conflict of laws, now laid down by the Rome II Regulation on the Law Applicable to Non-Contractual Obligations, will apply.[179] Within those rules, the connection with a contract may sometimes be a reason for adopting the law governing that contract. The equitable wrongs (often applicable to persons who can be called agents) of accessory liability to breach of trust or fiduciary obligation and knowing receipt of property subject to such obligation,[180] or at least the first of them, may require treating on the analogy of torts and hence brought within Rome II under that head.[181]

12-034   **Property**   Where a question of property arises,[182] as with an agent for sale or purchase of goods, the normal rules for property in the conflict of laws, viz. usually the *lex situs* of the property at the time of the disposition, will apply.[183]

12-035   **Restitution and unjust enrichment**   The question whether an issue should be classified as restitutionary or related to the principle of unjust enrichment is of itself difficult,[184] and the allocation of appropriate laws to the issues so identified is also controversial. Such problems certainly arise in the context of agency.[185] Both problems continue after the Rome II Regulation, which (in so far as they are seen to fall within the category of non-contractual obligations) deals with them in Articles 10 and 11.[186] Questions of the law applicable where the common law uses trust reasoning in an agency context may also arise.[187] Article 1.2(e) excludes from the scope of the Regulation "non-contractual obligations arising out of the relations between the settlors, trustees and beneficiaries of a trust created voluntarily". This refers to (what may be called) express trusts, which are the subject of the Hague Convention on the Law Applicable to Trusts, which was implemented in the UK by the Recognition of Trusts Act 1987; but the exception may go further. Beyond this, situations where trust reasoning is used, especially in a remedial context, may be capable of giving rise to non-contractual obligations within the scope of Rome II. The impact of that Regulation on such cases is a matter of some complexity outside the scope of this chapter.[188]

---

[179] Regulation 864/2007, effective January 11, 2009. See Dicey, Morris and Collins, fn.1 above, Vol.2, Ch.35; Dickinson, *The Rome II Regulation* (2008), Ch.4. For an example of the rules applied to bribery (of an agent), treated as a tort, see *Fiona Trust & Holding Corp v Skarga* [2013] EWCA Civ 275, where the law governing the relevant contracts was not applied.

[180] Above, Article 116.

[181] As to this topic, see above, Article 116. See Dicey, Morris and Collins, fn.1 above, Vol.2, paras.34-089, 34-090, 36-057 onwards; Dickinson, *The Rome II Regulation* (2008); 4.101, 102 (accessory liability), 103–105 (knowing receipt); Yeo, *Choice of Law for Equitable Doctrines* (2004), p.272 onwards.

[182] See esp. Articles 33, 69 and Ch.8.2.

[183] See Dicey, Morris and Collins, fn.1 above, Vol.2, Ch.24.

[184] See in general Goff and Jones, *Law of Unjust Enrichment* (9th edn).

[185] Issues which are arguably of this type arise in Articles 46, 48, 50, 51, 62, 88, 92, 92, 96 and 111–112.

[186] See Dicey, Morris and Collins, fn.1 above, Vol.2, Ch.36; Dickinson, *The Rome II Regulation* (2008), Chs 10 (Restitution), 11 (Negotiorum Gestio); Yeo, *Choice of Law for Equitable Doctrines* (2004).

[187] Questions involving trust reasoning of one sort and another appear in Articles 45–49, 50 and 53.

[188] On the application of the Regulation to such issues, see Dicey, Morris and Collins, fn.1 above, Vol.2, para.36-075 onwards; Dickinson, *The Rome II Regulation* (2008), paras 3.173-3.207 (saying, at para.3.174, that at least from an English law perspective, Article 1.2(e) is probably the most complex in the Rome II Regulation).

THE COMMERCIAL AGENTS (COUNCIL DIRECTIVE) REGULATIONS 1993[1]

(SI 1993/3053)

Made 7 December 1993.
Laid before Parliament 8 December 1993.
Coming into Force 1 January 1994.

---

[1] This S.I. is printed as amended by the Commercial Agents (Council Directive) (Amendment) Regulations 1993 (S.I. 1993 No. 3173) and 1998 (S.I. 1998 No. 2868).

23   Transitional provisions

The Secretary of State, being a Minister designated[2] for the purposes of section 2(2)of the European Communities Act 1972[3] in relation to measures relating to relations between commercial agents and their principals, in the exercise of the powers conferred by him by that section, hereby makes the following Regulations:

PART I

GENERAL

Citation, commencement and applicable law

1.—(1)   These Regulations may be cited as the Commercial Agents (Council Directive) Regulations 1993 and shall come into force on 1st January 1994.

(2)   These Regulations govern the relations between commercial agents and their principals and, subject to paragraph (3), apply in relation to the activities of commercial agents in Great Britain.

(3)   A court or tribunal shall:
- (a)   apply the law of the other member State concerned in place of regulations 3 to 22 where the parties have agreed that the agency contract is to be governed by the law of that member State;
- (b)   (whether or not it would otherwise be required to do so) apply these regulations where the law of another member State corresponding to these regulations enables the parties to agree that the agency contract is to be governed by the law of a different member State and the parties have agreed that it is to be governed by the law of England and Wales or Scotland.

Interpretation, application and extent

2.—(1)   In these Regulations—

"commercial agent" means a self-employed intermediary who has continuing authority to negotiate the sale or purchase of goods on behalf of another person (the "principal"), or to negotiate and conclude the sale or purchase of goods on behalf of and in the name of that principal; but shall be understood as not including in particular:
- (i)   a person who, in his capacity as an officer of a company or association, is empowered to enter into commitments binding on that company or association;
- (ii)   a partner who is lawfully authorised to enter into commitments binding on his partners;
- (iii)   a person who acts as an insolvency practitioner (as that expression is defined in section 388 of the Insolvency Act 1986[4]) or the equivalent in any other jurisdiction;

"commission" means any part of the remuneration of a commercial agent which varies with the number or value of business transactions;

"EEA Agreement" means the Agreement on the European Economic Area signed at Oporto on 2nd May 1992 as adjusted by the Protocol signed at

---

2   S.I. 1989/1327.
3   1972 c.68.
4   1986 c.45.

1

Brussels on 17th March 1993;

"member State" includes a State which is a contracting party to the EEA Agreement;

"restraint of trade clause" means an agreement restricting the business activities of a commercial agent following termination of the agency contract.

(2) These Regulations do not apply to—

    (a) commercial agents whose activities are unpaid;

    (b) commercial agents when they operate on commodity exchanges or in the commodity market;

    (c) the Crown Agents for Overseas Governments and Administrations, as set up under the Crown Agents Act 1979[5], or its subsidiaries.

(3) The provisions of the Schedule to these Regulations have effect for the purpose of determining the persons whose activities as commercial agents are to be considered secondary.

(4) These Regulations shall not apply to the persons referred to in paragraph (3) above.

(5) These Regulations do not extend to Northern Ireland.[6]

PART II

RIGHTS AND OBLIGATIONS

Duties of a commercial agent to his principal

3.—(1) In performing his activities a commercial agent must look after the interests of his principal and act dutifully and in good faith.

(2) In particular, a commercial agent must—

    (a) make proper efforts to negotiate and, where appropriate, conclude the transactions he is instructed to take care of;

    (b) communicate to his principal all the necessary information available to him;

    (c) comply with reasonable instructions given by his principal.

Duties of a principal to his commercial agent

4.—(1) In his relations with his commercial agent a principal must act dutifully and in good faith.

(2) In particular, a principal must—

    (a) provide his commercial agent with the necessary documentation relating to the goods concerned;

    (b) obtain for his commercial agent the information necessary for the performance of the agency contract, and in particular notify his commercial agent within a reasonable period once he anticipates that the volume of commercial transactions will be significantly lower than that which the commercial agent could normally have expected.

(3) A principal shall, in addition, inform his commercial agent within a reasonable period of his acceptance or refusal of, and of any non-execution by him of, a commercial transaction which the commercial agent has procured for him.

---

[5]   1979 c.43.

[6]   But similar regulations apply there; above, para. 11-003.

Prohibition on derogation from regulations 3 and 4 and consequence of Breach

5.—(1)   The parties may not derogate from regulations 3 and 4 above.

(2)   The law applicable to the contract shall govern the consequence of breach of the rights and obligations under regulations 3 and 4 above.

PART III

REMUNERATION

Form and amount of remuneration in absence of agreement

6.—(1)   In the absence of any agreement as to remuneration between the parties, a commercial agent shall be entitled to the remuneration that commercial agents appointed for the goods forming the subject of his agency contract are customarily allowed in the place where he carries on his activities and, if there is no such customary practice, a commercial agent shall be entitled to reasonable remuneration taking into account all the aspects of the transaction.

(2)   This regulation is without prejudice to the application of any enactment or rule of law concerning the level of remuneration.

(3)   Where a commercial agent is not remunerated (wholly or in part) by commission, regulations 7 to 12 below shall not apply.

Entitlement to commission on transactions concluded during agency contract

7.—(1)   A commercial agent shall be entitled to commission on commercial transactions concluded during the period covered by the agency contract—
- (a)   where the transaction has been concluded as a result of his action; or
- (b)   where the transaction is concluded with a third party whom he has previously acquired as a customer for transactions of the same kind.

(2)   A commercial agent shall also be entitled to commission on transactions concluded during the period covered by the agency contract where he has an exclusive right to a specific geographical area or to a specific group of customers and where the transaction has been entered into with a customer belonging to that area or group.

Entitlement to commission on transactions concluded after agency contract has terminated

8.   Subject to regulation 9 below, a commercial agent shall be entitled to commission on commercial transactions concluded after the agency contract has terminated if—
- (a)   the transaction is mainly attributable to his efforts during the period covered by the agency contract and if the transaction was entered into within a reasonable period after that contract terminated; or
- (b)   in accordance with the conditions mentioned in regulation 7 above, the order of the third party reached the principal or the commercial agent before the agency contract terminated.

Apportionment of commission between new and previous commercial agents

9.—(1)   A commercial agent shall not be entitled to the commission referred to in regulation 7 above if that commission is payable, by virtue of regulation 8 above, to the previous commercial agent, unless it is equitable because of the circumstances for the commission to be shared between the commercial agents.

(2)   The principal shall be liable for any sum due under paragraph (1) above to the person entitled to it in accordance with that paragraph, and any sum which the other commercial agent receives to which he is not entitled shall be refunded to the principal.

When commission due and date for payment

10.—(1)   Commission shall become due as soon as, and to the extent that, one of the following circumstances occurs:

    (a)   the principal has executed the transaction; or

    (b)   the principal should, according to his agreement with the third party, have executed the transaction; or

    (c)   the third party has executed the transaction.

(2)   Commission shall become due at the latest when the third party has executed his part of the transaction or should have done so if the principal had executed his part of the transaction, as he should have.

(3)   The commission shall be paid not later than on the last day of the month following the quarter in which it became due, and, for the purposes of these Regulations, unless otherwise agreed between the parties, the first quarter period shall run from the date the agency contract takes effect, and subsequent periods shall run from that date in the third month thereafter or the beginning of the fourth month, whichever is the sooner.

(4)   Any agreement to derogate from paragraphs (2) and (3) above to the detriment of the commercial agent shall be void.

Extinction of right to commission

11.—(1)   The right to commission can be extinguished only if and to the extent that—

    (a)   it is established that the contract between the third party and the principal will not be executed; and

    (b)   that fact is due to a reason for which the principal is not to blame.

(2)   Any commission which the commercial agent has already received shall be refunded if the right to it is extinguished.

(3)   Any agreement to derogate from paragraph (1) above to the detriment of the commercial agent shall be void.

Periodic supply of information as to commission due and right of inspection of principal's books

12.—(1)   The principal shall supply his commercial agent with a statement of the commission due, not later than the last day of the month following the quarter in which the commission has become due, and such statement shall set out the main components used in calculating the amount of the commission.

(2)   A commercial agent shall be entitled to demand that he be provided with all the information (and in particular an extract from the books) which is available

to his principal and which he needs in order to check the amount of the commission due to him.

(3) Any agreement to derogate from paragraphs (1) and (2) above shall be void.

(4) Nothing in this regulation shall remove or restrict the effect of, or prevent reliance upon, any enactment or rule of law which recognises the right of an agent to inspect the books of a principal.

PART IV

CONCLUSION AND TERMINATION OF THE AGENCY CONTRACT

Right to signed written statement of terms of agency contract

13.—(1) The commercial agent and principal shall each be entitled to receive from the other, on request, a signed written document setting out the terms of the agency contract including any terms subsequently agreed.

(2) Any purported waiver of the right referred to in paragraph (1) above shall be void.

Conversion of agency contract after expiry of fixed period

14. An agency contract for a fixed period which continues to be performed by both parties after that period has expired shall be deemed to be converted into an agency contract for an indefinite period.

Minimum periods of notice for termination of agency contract

15.—(1) Where an agency contract is concluded for an indefinite period either party may terminate it by notice.

(2) The period of notice shall be—
    (a) 1 month for the first year of the contract;
    (b) 2 months for the second year commenced;
    (c) 3 months for the third year commenced and for the subsequent years;
and the parties may not agree on any shorter periods of notice.

(3) If the parties agree on longer periods than those laid down in paragraph (2) above, the period of notice to be observed by the principal must not be shorter than that to be observed by the commercial agent.

(4) Unless otherwise agreed by the parties, the end of the period of notice must coincide with the end of a calendar month.

(5) The provisions of this regulation shall also apply to an agency contract for a fixed period where it is converted under regulation 14 above into an agency contract for an indefinite period subject to the proviso that the earlier fixed period must be taken into account in the calculation of the period of notice.

Savings with regard to immediate termination

16. These Regulations shall not affect the application of any enactment or rule of law which provides for the immediate termination of the agency contract—
    (a) because of the failure of one party to carry out all or part of his obligations under that contract; or
    (b) where exceptional circumstances arise.

Entitlement of commercial agent to indemnity or compensation on termination of agency contract

17.—(1)   This regulation has effect for the purpose of ensuring that the commercial agent is, after termination of the agency contract, indemnified in accordance with paragraphs (3) to (5) below or compensated for damage in accordance with paragraphs (6) and (7) below.

(2)   Except where the agency contract otherwise provides, the commercial agent shall be entitled to be compensated rather than indemnified.

(3)   Subject to paragraph (9) and to regulation 18 below, the commercial agent shall be entitled to an indemnity if and to the extent that—

    (a) he has brought the principal new customers or has significantly increased the volume of business with existing customers and the principal continues to derive substantial benefits from the business with such customers; and

    (b) the payment of this indemnity is equitable having regard to all the circumstances and, in particular, the commission lost by the commercial agent on the business transacted with such customers.

(4)   The amount of the indemnity shall not exceed a figure equivalent to an indemnity for one year calculated from the commercial agent's average annual remuneration over the preceding five years and if the contract goes back less than five years the indemnity shall be calculated on the average for the period in question.

(5)   The grant of an indemnity as mentioned above shall not prevent the commercial agent from seeking damages.

(6)   Subject to paragraph (9) and to regulation 18 below, the commercial agent shall be entitled to compensation for the damage he suffers as a result of the termination of his relations with his principal.

(7)   For the purpose of these Regulations such damage shall be deemed to occur particularly when the termination takes place in either or both of the following circumstances, namely circumstances which—

    (a) deprive the commercial agent of the commission which proper performance of the agency contract would have procured for him whilst providing his principal with substantial benefits linked to the activities of the commercial agent; or

    (b) have not enabled the commercial agent to amortize the costs and expenses that he had incurred in the performance of the agency contract on the advice of his principal.

(8)   Entitlement to the indemnity or compensation for damage as provided for under paragraphs (2) to (7) above shall also arise where the agency contract is terminated as a result of the death of the commercial agent.

(9)   The commercial agent shall lose his entitlement to the indemnity or compensation for damage in the instances provided for in paragraphs (2) to (8) above if within one year following termination of his agency contract he has not notified his principal that he intends pursuing his entitlement.

Grounds for excluding payment of indemnity or compensation under regulation 17

18.   The indemnity or compensation referred to in regulation 17 above shall not be payable to the commercial agent where—

[817]

    (a)   the principal has terminated the agency contract because of default attributable to the commercial agent which would justify immediate termination of the agency contract pursuant to regulation 16 above; or

    (b)   the commercial agent has himself terminated the agency contract, unless such termination is justified—

        (i)   by circumstances attributable to the principal, or

        (ii)   on grounds of the age, infirmity or illness of the commercial agent in consequence of which he cannot reasonably be required to continue his activities; or

    (c)   the commercial agent, with the agreement of his principal, assigns his rights and duties under the agency contract to another person.

Prohibition on derogation from regulations 17 and 18

19.   The parties may not derogate from regulations 17 and 18 to the detriment of the commercial agent before the agency contract expires.

Restraint of trade clauses

20.—(1)   A restraint of trade clause shall be valid only if and to the extent that—

    (a)   it is concluded in writing; and

    (b)   it relates to the geographical area or the group of customers and the geographical area entrusted to the commercial agent and to the kind of goods covered by his agency under the contract.

(2)   A restraint of trade clause shall be valid for not more than two years after termination of the agency contract.

(3)   Nothing in this regulation shall affect any enactment or rule of law which imposes other restrictions on the validity or enforceability of restraint of trade clauses or which enables a court to reduce the obligations on the parties resulting from such clauses.

PART V

MISCELLANEOUS AND SUPPLEMENTAL

Disclosure of information

21.   Nothing in these Regulations shall require information to be given where such disclosure would be contrary to public policy.

Service of notice etc

22.—(1)   Any notice, statement or other document to be given or supplied to a commercial agent or to be given or supplied to the principal under these Regulations may be so given or supplied:

    (a)   by delivering it to him;

    (b)   by leaving it at his proper address addressed to him by name;

    (c)   by sending it by post to him addressed either to his registered address or to the address to his registered or principal office;

or by any other means provided for in the agency contract.

(2)   Any such notice, statement or document may—

    (a)   in the case of a body corporate, be given or served on the secretary or clerk of that body;

(b)　in the case of a partnership, be given to or served on any partner or on any person having the control or management of the partnership business.

Transitional provisions

23.—(1)　Notwithstanding any provision in an agency contract made before 1st January 1994, these Regulations shall apply to that contract after that date and, accordingly any provision which is inconsistent with these Regulations shall have effect subject to them.

(2)　Nothing in these Regulations shall affect the rights and liabilities of a commercial agent or a principal which have accrued before 1st January 1994.

THE SCHEDULE

Regulation 2(3)

1.　The activities of a person as a commercial agent are to be considered secondary where it may reasonably be taken that the primary purpose of the arrangement with his principal is other than as set out in paragraph 2 below.

2.　An arrangement falls within this paragraph if—
(a)　the business of the principal is the sale, or as the case may be purchase, of goods of a particular kind; and
(b)　the goods concerned are such that—
(i)　transactions are normally individually negotiated and concluded on a commercial basis, and
(ii)　procuring a transaction on one occasion is likely to lead to further transactions in those goods with that customer on future occasions, or to transactions in those goods with other customers in the same geographical area or among the same group of customers and

that accordingly it is in the commercial interests of the principal in developing the market in those goods to appoint a representative to such customers with a view to the representative devoting effort, skill and expenditure from his own resources to that end.

3.　The following are indications that an arrangement falls within paragraph 2 above, and the absence of any of them is an indication to the contrary—
(a)　the principal is the manufacturer, importer or distributor of the goods;
(b)　the goods are specifically identified with the principal in the market in question rather than, or to a greater extent than, with any other person;
(c)　the agent devotes substantially the whole of his time to representative activities (whether for one principal or for a number of principals whose interests are not conflicting);
(d)　the goods are not normally available in the market in question other than by means of the agent;
(e)　the arrangement is described as one of commercial agency.

4.　The following are indications that an arrangement does not fall within paragraph 2 above—
(a)　promotional material is supplied direct to potential customers;
(b)　persons are granted agencies without reference to existing agents in a particular area or in relation to a particular group;
(c)　customers normally select the goods for themselves and merely place their orders through the agent.

5.　The activities of the following categories of persons are presumed, unless the contrary is established, not to fall within paragraph 2 above—
Mail order catalogue agents for consumer goods
Consumer credit agents.

[819]

INDEX

LEGAL TAXONOMY
FROM SWEET & MAXWELL

This index has been prepared using Sweet & Maxwell's Legal Taxonomy. Main index entries conform to keywords provided by the Legal Taxonomy except where references to specific documents or non-standard terms (denoted by quotation marks) have been included. These keywords provide a means of identifying similar concepts in other Sweet & Maxwell publications and online services to which keywords from the Legal Taxonomy have been applied. Readers may find some minor differences between terms used in the text and those which appear in the index. Suggestions to *sweetandmaxwell.taxonomy@tr.com*.

Sentencing Principles, Procedure and Practice 2021

Lyndon Harris, 6KBW College Hill, Lecturer, King's College, University of London and Sebastian Walker, University of Cambridge

This new annual title is an essential introduction and companion to the new Sentencing Code. The book is split into two parts: Part A contains everything you need to know about sentencing procedure, courts' sentencing powers and the sentencing principles, including the Sentencing Code; Part B provides guidance on determining the appropriate sentence for almost all criminal offences.

Lyndon Harris and Sebastian Walker were the lead lawyers at the Law Commission working on the drafting of the Sentencing Code. This new work guides practitioners though the various stages of a sentencing hearing and clearly indicates the considerations applicable to a sentencing decision. The title includes extensive expert commentary and summaries of all the relevant case law. For use in sentencing hearings and appeals, in court and for research.

- Written and structured to follow the Sentencing Code indicating the extent to which previous case law remains relevant and applicable
- Includes explanatory commentary from the authors who were closely involved in drafting the Code at the Law Commission
- Important case summaries with expert commentary
- Analysis of sentencing guidelines, identifying particular issues and providing commentary
- Includes all relevant legislation such as Magistrates' Courts Act 1980, Proceeds of Crime Act 2002 and Criminal Justice Act 2003
- All in just one volume and designed for ease of reference
- Updated annually
- Coverage extends to both the Crown and the Magistrates' Courts

Publication date: December 2020

Hardback | 9780414080591
Proview | 9780414082854
Hardback & Proview | 9780414082847

Crown Court Index 2021

HH Judge Mark Lucraft QC, Chief Coroner of England & Wales and Tom Payne, Barrister, Red Lion Chambers

The **Crown Court Index 2021** provides a guide to common penalties and formalities in cases tried on indictment or committed for sentence to the Crown Court, as well as appeals in criminal proceedings.

This edition includes coverage of:
- The newly consolidated Criminal Procedure Rules with all amendments made up to October 2020;
- The Criminal Practice Directions 2015 with all the amendments made in the period up to 2020. The Criminal Practice Directions along with the Criminal Procedure
- Rules provide a comprehensive set of rules and directions on all aspects of the criminal process;
- The latest sentencing guidelines issued by the Sentencing Council;
- All statutory developments from the last twelve months; and
- Notable recent authorities from the Supreme Court and Court of Appeal.

Publication date: December 2020

Hardback | 9780414080089
Proview | 9780414080119
Hardback & Proview | 9780414080102